Encyclopedia of Race and Racism

Encyclopedia of Race and Racism

VOLUME 1
a–f

John Hartwell Moore
EDITOR IN CHIEF

MACMILLAN REFERENCE USA
An imprint of Thomson Gale, a part of The Thomson Corporation

Detroit • New York • San Francisco • New Haven, Conn. • Waterville, Maine • London

Encyclopedia of Race and Racism
John Hartwell Moore, Editor in Chief

For more information, contact
Macmillan Reference USA
An imprint of The Gale Group
27500 Drake Rd.
Farmington Hills, MI 48331-3535
Or you can visit our Internet site at
http://www.gale.com

LIBRARY OF CONGRESS CATALOGING-IN-PUBLICATION DATA

Encyclopedia of race and racism / John H. Moore, editor in chief.
p. cm.
Includes bibliographical references and index.
ISBN 978-0-02-866020-2 (set : alk. paper) — ISBN 978-0-02-866021-9 (vol 1 : alk. paper) — ISBN 978-0-02-866022-6 (vol 2 : alk. paper) — ISBN 978-0-02-866023-3 (vol 3 : alk. paper) — ISBN 978-0-02-866116-2 (ebook)
1. Racism—United States—Encyclopedias. 2. United States—Race relations—Encyclopedias. 3. United States—Ethnic relations—Encyclopedias. 4. Minorities—United States—Social conditions—Encyclopedias. 5. Race relations—Encyclopedias. 6. Racism—Encyclopedias. I. Moore, John H., 1939– II. Title.

E184.A1E584 2008
305.800973—dc22

2007024359

ISBN-13: 978-0-02-866020-2 (set);
ISBN-10: 0-02-866020-X (set);
0-02-866021-8 (vol. 1);
0-02-866022-6 (vol. 2);
0-02-866023-4 (vol. 3)

This title is also available as an e-book.
ISBN-13: 978-0-02-866116-2; ISBN-10: 0-02-866116-8
Contact your Gale representative for ordering information.
Printed in the United States of America

10 9 8 7 6 5 4 3 2 1

Editorial Board

Editorial and Production Staff

PROJECT EDITORS

Rachel Kain
Mark Mikula
Nicole Watkins

CONTRIBUTING EDITORS

Deirdre Blanchfield
Jason M. Everett
Dawn M. Sobraski
Andrew Specht

EDITORIAL TECHNICAL SUPPORT

Mark Drouillard
Mike Weaver

MANUSCRIPT EDITORS

Judith Clinebell
Jessica Hornik Evans
Peter Jaskowiak
Christine Kelley
John Krol
Michael J. O'Neal
Dave Salamie

PROOFREADERS

Stacey Chamberlin
Pamela S. Dear
Melodie Monahan
Kathy Wilson

INDEXER

Laurie Andriot

PRODUCT DESIGN

Pamela A. E. Galbreath

IMAGING

Leitha Etheridge-Sims
Lezlie Light

GRAPHIC ART

Pre-PressPMG

RIGHTS ACQUISITION MANAGEMENT

Sue Rudolph

Mardell Glinski-Schultz

Tracie Richardson

COMPOSITION

Evi Abou-El-Seoud

MANUFACTURING

Wendy Blurton

DIRECTOR, NEW PRODUCT DEVELOPMENT

Hélène Potter

PUBLISHER

Jay Flynn

Contents

Introduction

Race and racism are two distinct concepts which have separate histories. The term *race* was borrowed by human biologists from general biology, and simply means a local kind or variety within a *species*, especially applied to those common plants and animals which were of interest to early naturalists and philosophers such as Herodotus (484–425 BCE), Aristotle (384–322 BCE), Lucretius (99–55 CE) and Albertus Magnus (1193–1280). With the discovery of genes in the early twentieth century, a species was defined more precisely as a group which shares an inventory of genes, freely exchanging genetic material among themselves, but not with other species. A race, then, might represent a minor adaptation to local conditions within the species. A species of butterflies, for example, might include "races" which present different patterns of camouflage on their wings in different parts of their range where the vegetation and assortment of predators and other butterflies are different. Arctic races of mammals tend to be whiter than southern varieties, while races of forest mammals tend to be more emphatically striped or spotted than races of the same species living on the plains. A single species, then, might consist of several component local races, all of which are mutually fertile with one another.

Members of the human species are highly variable in appearance, which should be expected in a species with a wide—in this case world-wide—distribution. For reasons explained in this encyclopedia, regional populations of humans have adapted themselves to local conditions of climate, nutrition, and diseases, so that some human groups are darker in color than others, some taller, some shorter, some with curly hair, and some with straight hair.

These variations in appearance among human populations, seemingly trivial in the eyes of early observers, were suddenly seized upon in the eighteenth and nineteenth centuries by biologists, anthropologists, historians and even philosophers, who alleged that these superficial traits were far from trivial, but signified deep and profound differences among human populations in their psychology, temperament, and even moral structure. And thus the ideology of *racism* was invented, the belief that human races were not just different from one another, but that some were superior to others. Not surprisingly, the persons who invented racism were themselves members of the race that they alleged was superior—the white race—Nordic and European. Carolus Linnaeus (1707–1778), Johann Blumenbach (1752–1840), and Arthur de Gobineau (1816–1882) are usually "credited" with inventing racism, if we can use that word, and they alleged further that their taxonomy of racism was not based on mere opinion but was "scientific," based on careful methods of observation and analysis.

And thus the phrase "scientific racism" has survived to describe a field of study which is not truly scientific, but pretends to be. As the reader will see in example after example in this encyclopedia, the use of numbers and statistics does not automatically mean that an assertion is logical or correct by scientific standards.

It is not mere coincidence that racism was invented during the time that tens of thousands of Africans were being captured, enslaved, and transported in chains to the Americas to work as field hands and manual workers for European owners. And it is interesting and important to note that the institution of chattel slavery, in which human beings were considered as mere property, was put into place before scientific racism was invented. Chattel slavery in North America was put into law in Virginia in 1640, but Linnaeus's *Systema Naturae* was not published until 1735, Blumenbach's *Natural Varieties of Mankind* in 1775, and Gobineau's *The Inequality of Human Races* not until 1853. Thus racism was practiced for about one hundred years in North America before scientific racism was put into print to justify what was already a highly developed institution.

Although racism is a recent invention, with its assertions about inherent human inequality, slavery was a very old institution in the Mediterranean region of the Old World. Sumeria, Egypt, Greece, and Rome all maintained vast numbers of slaves, which they had acquired by various means. The Spartans, for example, subdued neighboring Laconians and forced them into slavery. The Romans captured slaves from Britain to Carthage, and likewise created a slave-based economy. But these slaves were not marked by their outward physical appearance—in fact, their physiognomy was very much like that of their owners. Greek and Roman slaves had to wear collars or distinctive dress to differentiate themselves from other members of society.

Blackness in ancient times was not equated with the status of slave. In Rome there were prominent black men, like Emperor Septimius Severus, Consul Lusius Quietus, and a Roman general who became Saint Maurice, the patron saint of medieval chivalry. But according to Plato, there were invisible, inherent differences among men which led some to be kings and others to be slaves. Plato tried to capture the essence of the supposed inequalities among men (leaving aside his allegations about female inferiority) in a supposed dialogue between his teacher Socrates and Socrates's student Glaucon, included in Plato's *Republic*. Author Stephen Chorover has called this fragment of philosophy "the most frightening document in European history."

The dialogue consists in part of an analogy between human character and metallurgy. According to Plato, although all Greeks might look alike on the surface, they were different inside. Some were essentially "golden" in their intelligence and character, while others were silver, brass, iron, wood, or lead. Those with golden spirits, the children of golden parents, were destined to be monarchs or "philosopher-kings." Those who were brass or iron would become soldiers, craftsmen and tradesmen, while those who were wood or lead, would be slaves. The frightening part of this idea is the notion of an invisible inner self, an early forerunner of the notion of intelligence, and hence of "intelligence quotient" (IQ), which emerged as the foremost rationale for racism in the twentieth century. Plato is clearly a forerunner of the idea that human character and intelligence are innate, are inherited from parents to children, and can be measured by specialists such as philosophers, or in modern times, by psychologists.

The study of race, and of racism, presently requires at least two general and somewhat different approaches, one from science and the other from the humanities. It is up to scientists to test the biological assertions of racist theory—that human groups, regional populations, "races," are significantly different from one another in their mental, artistic, and physical abilities. The struggle between racist and antiracist biologists has been continuous since the invention of racism. But it seems that as soon as one racist allegation is refuted, others spring forward. Much of this encyclopedia is devoted to examinations of particular propositions and how they have been criticized in the last three hundred years.

Even if all racist assertions about human inequality are refuted, it remains to explain how and why these assertions were generated in the first place, and what functions these beliefs served in human society. As the reader will see in this encyclopedia, the perspective loosely called "post-modernism" has provided a critical vocabulary for explaining how opinions and ideologies are "socially constructed" or "culturally constructed" in a particular time or place. It is not enough simply to refute the supposedly scientific biological assertions of racist individuals; it is also necessary to explain how and why people came to believe these propositions, and who was promoting them.

Racism is not merely a psychological disorder, then, curable by hearing the biological facts. Racism not only poisons minds, it also lines the pockets of certain well-placed elites. American farmers, contractors, store owners, and manufacturers, for example, reap enormous profits from the difference between what they pay workers of color and what they would have to pay white workers to do the same jobs. In the past, some of the greatest advances in human rights have been on those occasions when racism, by various means, was made to be unprofitable. When industrial capital expanded into the South after World War II, for example, industrialists did not want to build factories with dual facilities for whites and blacks, and so they joined the struggle for integration.

The nearly four hundred articles in this encyclopedia are roughly of two kinds—biological and historical. But many articles are both historical and biological, and overlap with one another in the coverage of a particular geographical region, historical figure, or topic. For example, "civil rights," "migration," and "people of color" are mentioned in several places, in different contexts. To help the reader navigate among overlapping articles, we have listed "Related Topics" at the end of each article. Each article also contains a list of suggested readings where the reader can find more information and more references to the topic under discussion. All articles are signed by authors who are prominent in their fields. All of them are well published, and their other books and articles can be found in local libraries.

This project began in 2004 with a discussion among Macmillan editors concerning the need for a new reference source which would "fit a wide range of the social sciences, from history to multicultural studies to sociology and psychology," but would also be "appropriate for the high school curriculum." That is, the publisher wanted a kind of "one-stop" reference for students in high school and college to lead them to other inter-related sources in the subjects of race and racism.

There followed a telephone call from editorial director Hélène Potter to me, asking me to serve as editor in chief of the proposed volumes on the basis of my research in both the scientific and humanist sides of race and racism and based on the distribution of topics I had included in the on-line course syllabus which had guided my teaching of a college class called "Race and Racism" for more than twenty years.

The next step was the selection of a board of editors, who would solicit articles for particular fields of scholarship, their own specialties, and edit the manuscripts they solicited. Our first meeting was at Macmillan offices in New York City on September 2–4, 2004. The editors are as follows, along with their institutional affiliations, and primary responsibilities as editors.

Russell Adams, Department of Afro-American Studies, Howard University, history of American slavery, anti-slavery, and civil rights.

J. Keith Akins, Sociology Department, New Mexico State University, racist organizations, criminology.

Karen Brodkin, Anthropology Department, University of California—Los Angeles, ethnicity, social theory, feminism.

Gregory R. Campbell, Department of Anthropology, University of Montana, Missoula, Native Americans, national minorities.

Kevin Cokley, Department of Educational Psychology and Center for African and African American Studies, University of Texas, Austin.

Patricia Hill Collins, Emeritus African American Studies, University of Cincinnati, Sociology, University of Maryland – College Park, feminism, sociology, history of racism.

Alan Goodman, Department of Natural Science, Hampshire College, biological anthropology, sports.

Faye Harrison, Department of Anthropology, University of Florida, politics, feminism, ethnicity.

Antoinette T. Jackson, Anthropology Department, University of South Florida, slavery, plantation communities, socio-economic structures; heritage studies.

Leonard Lieberman, Department of Sociology and Anthropology, Central Michigan University, human variation, history of scientific racism.

Kenneth B. Nunn, Levin College of Law, University of Florida, race and law, constitutional law, civil rights.

Denise Segura, Sociology Department, University of California—Santa Barbara, Hispanic topics, feminism.

We must note here the passing of our dear friend, Len Lieberman, during the course of editing this encyclopedia. Len was a notable figure in the struggle against racism, among other things serving as editor of the memorial volume for Ashley Montagu, entitled *Race and Other Misadventures* (1996, with Larry Reynolds).

Our project editors at Macmillan have been Nicole Watkins, Rachel Kain, and Mark Mikula. Hélène Potter has not only served as our editorial director, but also as our intellectual guide, when we needed one.

John Hartwell Moore
Department of Anthropology, University of Florida
August 15, 2007

SUGGESTED READING

Barkan, Elazar. 1992. *The Retreat of Scientific Racism*, Cambridge University Press.

Chorover, Stephen. 1979. *From Genesis to Genocide*. Cambridge, MA: MIT Press.

Finley, Moses. 1980. *Ancient Slavery and Modern Ideology*. New York: Penguin.

Frederickson, George M. 2002, *Racism, A Short History*. Princeton, NJ: Princeton University Press.

Lucretius. 1977. *The Nature of Things*. New York: Norton.

Meltzer, Milton. 1993. *Slavery: A World History*. Chicago: De Capo.

Plato. 1952. "The Republic, Book II," pp. 310–323 in *Plato*, "Great Books of the Western World" series, vol. 7, edited by Mortimer J. Adler, Chicago: Benton.

Snowdon, Frank M. 1971. *Blacks in Antiquity*, Cambridge, MA: Belknap Press.

List of Articles

Contributors

Richard J. Abanes
Journalist
Religious Information Center
Irvine, California
CHRISTIAN IDENTITY

Russell L. Adams
Professor Emeritus
Department of Afro-American Studies
Howard University
SLAVE TRADE IDEOLOGY

Delia D. Aguilar
Adjunct Professor
Women's Studies Program
University of Connecticut
ASIAN-AMERICAN FEMINISM

J. Keith Akins
Assistant Professor
Department of Criminal Justice
New Mexico State University
DUKE, DAVID
ENGLISH SKINHEADS
KU KLUX KLAN

Gerardo V. Aldana
Associate Professor
Department of Chicana and Chicano Studies
University of California, Santa Barbara
VIOLENCE AGAINST INDIGENOUS PEOPLE, LATIN AMERICA

Leslie D. Alldritt
Associate Professor
Department of Religion and Philosophy
Northland College
BURAKUMIN

Garland E. Allen
Professor
Department of Biology
Washington University (St. Louis, Missouri)
GENETICS, HISTORY OF

Kevin S. Amidon
Assistant Professor of German Studies
Iowa State University
CHAMBERLAIN, HOUSTON STEWART

Julius Amin
Professor and Chair
Department of History
The University of Dayton
GARNET, HENRY HIGHLAND

Keith Aoki
Professor
School of Law
University of California at Davis
ALIEN LAND LAWS

Bettina Aptheker
Professor
Department of Feminist Studies
University of California, Santa Cruz
DAVIS, ANGELA

Shelley Arlen
University of Florida
LANGUAGE, INCENDIARY

Ralph Armbruster-Sandoval
Assistant Professor
Department of Chicana and Chicano Studies
University of California, Santa Barbara
LATINO SOCIAL MOVEMENTS

Joshua Aronson
Professor
Department of Applied Psychology
New York University
STEREOTYPE THREAT AND RACIAL STIGMA

John Asimakopoulos
Professor
Department of Social Sciences
Bronx Community College, City University of New York
TRANSNATIONAL LABOR ORGANIZING

Dustin Avent-Holt
University of Massachusetts
PAY EQUITY

Ronald Bailey
Professor
Department of African-American Studies
Northeastern Illinois University
RACIAL SLAVE LABOR IN THE AMERICAS

Lee D. Baker
Associate Professor

Department of Cultural
Antrhropology
Duke University
ANTHROPOLOGY, HISTORY OF

Lawrie Balfour
University of Virginia
DU BOIS, W. E. B.

Elazar Barkan
Professor of International and Public Affairs
Columbia University
GENOCIDE
UNESCO STATEMENTS ON RACE

Susan M. Barnett
Wolfson College
Cambridge University
IQ AND TESTING: CRITIQUES

Juan Battle
Professor
Department of Sociology
Hunter College and The Graduate Center, City University of New York
GAY MEN

Mia Bay
Associate Professor
Department of History
Rutgers, The State University of New Jersey
ANTEBELLUM BLACK ETHNOLOGY

Heidi L. Beirich
Deputy Director
Intelligence Project
Southern Poverty Law Center
INTELLIGENCE PROJECT
NATIONAL ALLIANCE
SOUTHERN POVERTY LAW CENTER

David H. Bennett
Professor
Department of History
Maxwell School, Syracuse University
NATIVISM

Amos J. Beyan
Professor
Department of History
Western Michigan University
AMERICAN COLONIZATION SOCIETY AND THE FOUNDING OF LIBERIA
CUFFE, PAUL
DEW, THOMAS RODERICK

Christopher Bickel
Associate Instructor
Department of Sociology
University of California, Santa Barbara
TRIRACIAL ISOLATES

Brad M. Biglow
Visiting Assistant Professor of Anthropology
University of North Florida
INDIGENISMO IN MEXICO

Bob Blauner
Professor
Department of Sociology
University of California, Berkeley
COLONIALISM, INTERNAL

Barry Bogin
Reader
Department of Human Sciences
Loughborough University
ANTHROPOMETRY

Eduardo Bonilla-Silva
Professor
Sociology Department
Duke University
COLOR-BLIND RACISM

Denise Ileana Bossy
Assistant Professor
Department of History
University of North Florida
INDIAN SLAVERY

C. Loring Brace
Professor of Anthropology and Curator of Biological Anthropology
Museum of Anthropology,
University of Michigan
CLINES
CLUSTERS
FACIAL ANGLE
RACIAL HIERARCHY: RACES RANKED BY EARLY SCIENTISTS
RACIAL HIERARCHY: DISPROVEN

Glenn E. Bracey II
Texas A&M University
HOAXING

Bryan McKinley Jones Brayboy
Borderlands Associate Professor
Educational Leadership and Policy Studies
Arizona State University
EDUCATION, DISCRIMINATION IN HIGHER

John D. Brewer
Professor
Department of Sociology
University of Aberdeen
MANDELA, NELSON
SOUTH AFRICAN RACIAL FORMATIONS

Rose M. Brewer
Professor and Morse Alumni Distinguished Teaching Professor
University of Minnesota
BLACK FEMINISM IN THE UNITED STATES

Roy L. Brooks
Warren Distinguished Professor of Law
University of San Diego
JAPANESE AMERICAN REDRESS MOVEMENT
REPARATIONS FOR RACIAL ATROCITIES

B. Ricardo Brown
Associate Professor of Cultural Studies
Department of Social Science and Cultural Studies
Pratt Institute
NOTT, JOSIAH

W. Fitzhugh Brundage
Professor
Department of History
University of North Carolina at Chapel Hill
WASHINGTON, BOOKER T.

Pem Davidson Buck
Professor of Anthropology
Division of Social and Behavioral Sciences
Elizabethtown Community and Technical College
RURAL WHITE STEREOTYPING

Michelle J. Budig
Associate Professor
Department of Sociology
University of Massachusetts
PAY EQUITY

Louise Cainkar
Assistant Professor
Department of Social and Cultural Sciences
Marquette University
ARABS AND ARAB AMERICANS

John O. Calmore
Professor
School of Law
University of North Carolina at Chapel Hill
VOTING RIGHTS ACT OF 1965

Gregory R. Campbell
Professor
Department of Anthropology
University of Montana
BLOOD QUANTUM
SUBSTANCE ABUSE

Mariana P. Candido
Assistant Professor
Department of History
University of Wisconsin-La Crosse
RACIAL DEMOGRAPHICS IN THE WESTERN HEMISPHERE
SLAVERY AND RACE

Nergis Canefe
Associate Professor
Department of Political Science
York University (Canada)
FOURTH WORLD

Christina M. Capodilupo
Department of Clinical and Counseling Psychology
Teachers College, Columbia University
MENTAL HEALTH AND RACISM

Devon W. Carbado
Professor
School of Law
University of California, Los Angeles
RUSTIN, BAYARD

Allison Carter
Professor
Department of Sociology
Rowan University
TOURISM AND NATIONAL HERITAGE (U.S.)

Rachel Caspari
Associate Professor of Anthropology, Department of Sociology, Anthropology, and Social Work
Central Michigan University
"OUT OF AFRICA" HYPOTHESIS

Raphael Cassimere Jr.
Seraphia D. Leyda Professor
Department of History
University of New Orleans
NIAGARA MOVEMENT

Angelina E. Castagno
Assistant Professor
Educational Leadership and Foundations
Northern Arizona University
EDUCATION, DISCRIMINATION IN HIGHER

Josef Castañeda-Liles
Department of Sociology
University of California, Santa Barbara
MULTIRACIAL IDENTITIES

Ingrid E. Castro
Assistant Professor
Department of Sociology
Northeastern Illinois University
IMPLICIT RACISM

A. Scott Catey
Department of Anthropology and Levin College of Law
University of Florida
RESERVATION SYSTEM

Jorge Chapa
Professor of Sociology
Director, Center for Democracy in a Multiracial Society
University of Illinois at Urbana-Champaign
LATINOS

James C. Chatters
Founder
Applied Paleoscience
KENNEWICK MAN

Ernesto Chávez
Associate Professor
Department of History
University of Texas at El Paso
CHICANO MOVEMENT

Leo Chavez
Professor
Department of Anthropology
University of California, Irvine
LATINA GENDER, REPRODUCTION, AND RACE

Lisa Chavez
Department of Women's Studies
San Diego State University
LESBIANS

Erwin Chemerinsky
Alston and Bird Professor of Law and Political Science, School of Law
Duke University
AFFIRMATIVE ACTION

Erica Chito Childs
Assistant Professor
Department of Sociology
Hunter College, City University of New York
BLACK-WHITE INTERMARRIAGE

Johnna Christian
Assistant Professor
School of Criminal Justice
Rutgers, The State University of New Jersey
CRIMINAL JUSTICE SYSTEM

Mark Christian
Associate Professor
Department of Sociology and Black World Studies
Miami University (Ohio)
UNITED KINGDOM RACIAL FORMATIONS

Michelle Christian
Duke University
COLOR-BLIND RACISM

Peter Chua
Assistant Professor
Department of Sociology
San Jose State University
CULTURAL RACISM

Colin Clark
Senior Lecturer
Department of Geography and Sociology
University of Strathclyde
ROMA

Todd Clear
Distinguished Professor of Criminal Justice
John Jay College of Criminal Justice
City University of New York
CRIMINAL JUSTICE SYSTEM

Mark Nathan Cohen
University Distinguished Professor of Anthropology
State University of New York, Plattsburgh
IQ AND TESTING: CULTURE, EDUCATION, AND IQ SCORES
MONTAGU, ASHLEY
SICKLE CELL ANEMIA

Kevin O. Cokley
Associate Professor of Counseling Psychology and Black Studies
University of Missouri
INTERNALIZED RACIALISM

James E. Crisp
Associate Professor
Department of History
North Carolina State University
ALAMO

Yacine Daddi Addoun
History Department
York University (Canada)
SLAVERY AND RACE

G. Reginald Daniel
Associate Professor
Department of Sociology
University of California, Santa Barbara
MULTIRACIAL IDENTITIES
TRIRACIAL ISOLATES

Brianne A. Davila
Department of Sociology
University of California, Santa Barbara
HUERTA, DOLORES

Thomas J. Davis
Professor
Department of History and College of Law
Arizona State University
BAKER, ELLA
DOUGLASS, FREDERICK
POWELL, ADAM CLAYTON, JR.

Roberto M. De Anda
Professor
Chicano/Latino Studies
Portland State University
GALARZA, ERNESTO

Thomas F. DeFrantz
Associate Professor
Theater Department
Massachusetts Institute of Technology
DANCE

Nicholas De Genova
Assistant Professor
Anthropology and Latina/o Studies
Columbia University
IMMIGRATION TO THE UNITED STATES

Adelaida R. Del Castillo
Associate Professor
Department of Chicana and Chicano Studies
San Diego State University
LA MALINCHE

Héctor L. Delgado
Associate Professor
Department of Sociology and Anthropology
University of La Verne
LABOR MARKET

Vanaja Dhruvarajan
Adjunct Professor
Sociology and Women's Studies
Carleton University (Canada)
FORCED STERILIZATION

Heather A. Diamond
Lecturer
Department of American Studies
University of Hawai'i at Mānoa
ORIENTALISM

Gail Dines
Professor
Department of American Studies
Wheelock College
PORNOGRAPHY

Rod Dixon
Senior Attorney
U.S. Department of Education
Silver Springs, Maryland
NAACP: LEGAL ACTIONS, 1935–1955

Roxanne Lynn Doty
Associate Professor
Department of Political Science
Arizona State University
CITIZENSHIP AND "THE BORDER"

John F. Dovidio
Professor
Department of Psychology
University of Connecticut
AVERSIVE RACISM

Brian M. du Toit
Professor Emeritus
Department of Anthropology
University of Florida
AFRIKANER BROEDERBOND
APARTHEID

Dawn Duke
Assistant Professor
Department of Modern Foreign Languages and Literatures
University of Tennessee
BLACK FEMINISM IN BRAZIL

Ira Dworkin
Visiting Assistant Professor
English Department
Gettysburg College
SHEPPARD, WILLIAM

Walter R. Echo-Hawk
Senior Staff Attorney
Native American Rights Fund
Boulder, Colorado
GENOCIDE AND ETHNOCIDE
NATIVE AMERICAN GRAVES PROTECTION AND REPATRIATION ACT (NAGPRA)

Douglas R. Egerton
Professor
Department of History
Le Moyne College
ALLEN, RICHARD
VESEY, DENMARK

Clyde Ellis
Professor
Department of History and Geography
Elon University
INDIAN BOARDING SCHOOLS

Paul A. Erickson
Professor
Department of Anthropology
Saint Mary's University (Canada)
BOAS, FRANZ

Philomena Essed
Antioch University
EVERYDAY RACISM

Tanya A. Faberson
Cultural Resource Analysts, Inc.
RACIAL PURITY (U.S.), 1900–1910
SEXUALITY

Elisa Facio
Associate Professor
Ethnic Studies
University of Colorado at Boulder
CUBAN RACIAL FORMATIONS

Sylvanna M. Falcón
Assistant Professor
Department of Sociology
Connecticut College
BORDER CROSSINGS AND HUMAN RIGHTS

Mary Farmer-Kaiser
Department of History and Geography
University of Louisiana at Lafayette
FREEDMEN'S BUREAU

Joe R. Feagin
Professor
Department of Sociology
Texas A&M University
HOAXING
INSTITUTIONAL RACISM

Stephen C. Feinstein
Director, Center for Holocaust and Genocide Studies

University of Minnesota
HOLOCAUST

Alexander M. Feldman
Research Analyst, Civil Rights Division
Anti-Defamation League, New York
JEWISH DEFENSE LEAGUE

James V. Fenelon
Professor of Sociology
California State University
CRIME AND AMERICAN INDIANS

Edward Fergus
Director
Research and Evaluation, Metropolitan Center for Urban Education
New York University
CULTURAL DEFICIENCY

Paul Finkelman
President, William McKinley Distinguished Professor of Law and Public Policy
Albany Law School
BLACK CODES
DRED SCOTT V. SANDFORD
RACIAL DESEGREGATION (U.S.)
SLAVE CODES

Nadia Y. Flores
Assistant Professor
Department of Sociology
Texas A&M University
UNDOCUMENTED WORKERS

Carolyn Fluehr-Lobban
Professor
Department of Anthropology
Rhode Island College
FIRMIN, ANTÉNOR
GALTON, FRANCIS

James R. Flynn
Professor
Department of Political Studies
University of Otago (New Zealand)
JENSEN, ARTHUR

James W. Fox Jr.
Professor
College of Law
Stetson University
BLACK RECONSTRUCTION

A. Roberto Frisancho
Arthur F. Thurnau Professor of Anthropology and Research Professor of the Center for Human Growth and Development
University of Michigan
HUMAN BIOLOGICAL VARIATION

Samuel L. Gaertner
Professor
Department of Psychology
University of Delaware
AVERSIVE RACISM
SOCIAL PSYCHOLOGY OF RACISM

Rajmohan Gandhi
Visiting Professor
International Programs and Studies
University of Illinois at Urbana-Champaign
GANDHI, MOHANDAS KARAMCHAND

Alma M. Garcia
Professor of Sociology
Santa Clara University
CHICANA FEMINISM

Juan R. García
Associate Professor
Department of History
University of Arizona
OPERATION WETBACK

Mario T. Garcia
Professor
Department of History and Chicana and Chicano Studies
University of California, Santa Barbara
CORONA, BERT

Gladys García-López
University of California, Santa Barbara
ANZALDÚA, GLORIA

John D. Garrigus
Associate Professor
Department of History
University of Texas at Arlington
HAITIAN RACIAL FORMATIONS

Paula J. Giddings
Professor
Afro-American Studies
Smith College
WELLS-BARNETT, IDA B.

Dorie J. Gilbert
Associate Professor
School of Social Work
University of Texas at Austin
HIV AND AIDS

Cheryl Townsend Gilkes
Professor of African American Studies and Sociology and Director of African American Studies Program
Colby College
WOMANISM

Zvi Gitelman
Professor
Department of Political Science
University of Michigan
ANTI-SEMITISM IN RUSSIA

Tanya Golash-Boza
Assistant Professor
Departments of Sociology and American Studies
University of Kansas
EDUCATION, RACIAL DISPARITIES

Ellen J. Goldner
Associate Professor
College of Staten Island, City University of New York
STOWE, HARRIET BEECHER

Andrew Goliszek
Department of Biology
North Carolina A&T State University
MEDICAL EXPERIMENTATION

Vernadette V. Gonzalez
Assistant Professor
Department of American Studies
University of Hawai'i at Mānoa
TRANSNATIONALISM

Gloria González-López
Assistant Professor
Department of Sociology
University of Texas at Austin
IMMIGRATION, RACE, AND WOMEN

Alan Goodman
Professor
Department of Natural Science
Hampshire College
NONCONCORDANT VARIATION

Michele Goodwin
College of Law
DePaul University
CITIZENSHIP AND RACE

Roderick Graham
Department of Sociology
Graduate Center, City University of New York
CALHOUN, JOHN C.

Joseph L. Graves Jr.
Dean, University Studies, and Professor of Biological Sciences
North Carolina A&T State University
BASKETBALL
BOXING
CIVIL WAR POLITICS AND RACISM
EYSENCK, HANS JURGEN
TRACK AND FIELD

Clarence C. Gravlee
Assistant Professor
Department of Anthropology
University of Florida
LIFE EXPECTANCY

Andrew R. Graybill
Assistant Professor
Department of History
University of Nebraska–Lincoln
TEXAS RANGERS

Stanton W. Green
Dean, McMurray School of Humanities and Social Sciences, Professor of Anthropology
Monmouth University
BASEBALL

Colleen Greer
Associate Professor
Department of Sociology
Bemidji State University
MOTHERHOOD, DEFICIENCY IN

Richard Griswold del Castillo
Professor
Department of Chicana and Chicano Studies
San Diego State University
BARRIO
TREATY OF GUADALUPE HIDALGO

Zoltan Grossman
Member of the Faculty
Geography and Native American & World Indigenous Peoples Studies
The Evergreen State College
ANTI-INDIAN MOVEMENT

Allen Carl Guelzo
Director of Civil War Era Studies
Gettysburg College
EMANCIPATION PROCLAMATION

Shobha Hamal Gurung
Assistant Professor
Department of Sociology, Anthropology, and Social Work
Eastern Connecticut State University
HUMAN TRAFFICKING

José Angel Gutiérrez
Professor
Department of Political Science
University of Texas at Arlington
LA RAZA

Mel Gutterman
Professor of Law
Emory University School of Law
CHAIN GANGS

Euan Hague
Assistant Professor
Department of Geography
DePaul University
WHITE CITIZENS' COUNCIL AND THE COUNCIL OF CONSERVATIVE CITIZENS

Janice E. Hale
Professor of Early Childhood Education and Director of the Institute for the Study of the African American Child (ISAAC)
Wayne State University
CHILDREN, RACIAL DISPARITIES AND STATUS OF

Joan Wylie Hall
Instructor
Department of English
University of Mississippi
LORDE, AUDRE

Darrell Y. Hamamoto
Professor
Asian American Studies Program
University of California, Davis
FILM AND ASIAN AMERICANS

Melissa D. Hargrove
Department of Anthropology
University of Tennessee
SEX WORK

Scott R. Harris
Assistant Professor
Department of Sociology and Criminal Justice
Saint Louis University
SOCIAL PROBLEMS

Tina M. Harris
Associate Professor
Department of Speech Communication
University of Georgia
TELEVISION

John Hawks
Assistant Professor
Department of Anthropology
University of Wisconsin–Madison
CRANIAL INDEX
HUMAN AND PRIMATE EVOLUTION
MORTON, SAMUEL GEORGE

Morris G. Henderson
Assistant Professor
Department of African-American Studies
Virginia Commonwealth University
TURNER, HENRY MCNEAL

P. J. Henry
Assistant Professor
Psychology
DePaul University
SYMBOLIC AND MODERN RACISM

David Manuel Hernández
Assistant Professor
Chicana and Chicano Studies
University of California, Los Angeles
ILLEGAL ALIEN

Kevin Hicks
Assistant Professor
University College/English & Humanities
Alabama State University
DIXON, THOMAS, JR.

Janell Hobson
Assistant Professor
Department of Women's Studies
University at Albany, State University of New York
HOTTENTOT VENUS

Marianne Hoyd
University of Sydney
AUSTRALIAN ABORIGINE PEOPLES

Janis Faye Hutchinson
Professor
Department of Anthropology
University of Houston
MEDICAL RACISM

Anthony A. Iaccarino
Assistant Professor
Department of History
Reed College
GARRISON, WILLIAM LLOYD

Noel Ignatiev
Professor
Department of Critical Studies
Massachusetts College of Arts
IRISH AMERICANS AND WHITENESS
PHILLIPS, WENDELL
WATSON, THOMAS E.
ZIONISM

Lisa C. Ikemoto
Professor
Davis School of Law, University of California
REPRODUCTIVE TECHNOLOGIES

Joseph E. Inikori
Professor
Department of History
University of Rochester
AFRICAN ENSLAVEMENT, PRECOLONIAL

Yasmiyn Irizarry
Department of Sociology
University of Indiana
INFANT MORTALITY AND BIRTH WEIGHT

Nina G. Jablonski
Professor and Head of the Department of Anthropology
Pennsylvania State University
SKIN COLOR

Antoinette T. Jackson
Assistant Professor
Department of Anthropology
University of South Florida
FILMOGRAPHY *IN THE APPENDIX*
PLANTATIONS

Pamela Braboy Jackson
Professor
Department of Sociology
Indiana University
INFANT MORTALITY AND BIRTH WEIGHT

Steven Leonard Jacobs
Department of Religious Studies
University of Alabama
ANTI-SEMITISM
ANTI-SEMITISM IN THE ARAB WORLD

M. A. Jaimes-Guerrero
Professor
Department of Womens Studies
San Francisco State University
FORCED STERILIZATION OF NATIVE AMERICANS

Angelene Jamison-Hall
Department of African and African American Studies
University of Cincinnati
BALDWIN, JAMES

J. Craig Jenkins
Professor
Department of Sociology
Ohio State University
CHÁVEZ, CÉSAR ESTRADA

Catherine A. John
Assistant Professor
African Diaspora Studies
University of Oklahoma
BLACK CONSCIOUSNESS

Greg Johnson
Feature Writer
Philadelphia Tribune
BATES, DAISY

Troy R. Johnson
Professor
Department of History
California State University, Long Beach
INDIAN RIGHTS ASSOCIATION

William Johnson
Co-Editor, Labor Notes
Brooklyn, New York
LABOR, CHEAP
LEAGUE OF REVOLUTIONARY BLACK WORKERS

Christopher Jones
Independent Scholar
France
CAGOTS

D. Marvin Jones
Professor of Law
University of Miami (Ohio)
CIVIL RIGHTS ACTS

David S. Jones
Assistant Professor
Program in Science, Technology, and Society
Massachusetts Institute of Technology
INFECTIOUS DISEASE, SUSCEPTIBILITY, AND RACE

James M. Jones
Professor
Department of Psychology
University of Delaware
SOCIAL PSYCHOLOGY OF RACISM

Joseph Jones
Department of Anthropology
University of Massachusetts Amherst
NONCONCORDANT VARIATION

Ngozi Caleb Kamalu
Professor
Department of Government and History
Fayetteville State University, North Carolina
SOUTHERN POLITICS, 1883–1915

Leon J. Kamin
Professor
Department of Psychology
University of Cape Town
IQ AND TESTING: ORIGIN AND DEVELOPMENT

David Kamper
Assistant Professor
Department of American Indian Studies
San Diego State University
"PLAYING INDIAN"

Stephen Kantrowitz
Associate Professor
Department of History
University of Wisconsin–Madison
TILLMAN, BENJAMIN "PITCHFORK"

J. Kehaulani Kauanui
Associate Professor
Wesleyan University
INDIGENOUS

Jay S. Kaufman
Professor
Department of Epidemiology, School of Public Health
University of North Carolina at Chapel Hill
HYPERTENSION AND CORONARY HEART DISEASE

Mary E. Kelly
Department of Sociology and Social Work
University of Central Missouri
SYMBOLIC ETHNICITY

Deseriee A. Kennedy
College of Law
University of Tennessee
HOUSTON, CHARLES HAMILTON
MARSHALL, THURGOOD

Kenneth A. R. Kennedy
Department of Ecology and Evolutionary Biology
Cornell University
FORENSIC ANTHROPOLOGY AND RACE

Carool Kersten
Lecturer
Islamic Studies
King's College, London
MUSLIMS

Ann Kingsolver
Associate Professor
Department of Anthropology
University of South Carolina
CAPITALISM

Edward Kissam
Aguirre Division, JBS International
Burlingame, California
FARMWORKERS

Julie A. Kmec
Assistant Professor
Department of Sociology
Washington State University
OCCUPATIONAL SEGREGATION

Peter H. Knapp
Professor
Department of Sociology
Villanova University
IQ AND TESTING: OVERVIEW

Allen Kohlhepp
Anti-Defamation League
NATIONAL STATES RIGHTS PARTY

Kathleen Korgen
Professor
Department of Sociology
William Paterson University
BIRACIALISM

Arnd Krüger
Institut fur Sportswissenschaften der George-August-Universitat
OLYMPIC GAMES OF 1936

Michel S. Laguerre
Professor and Director
Center for Globalization and Information Technology
University of California, Berkeley
CARIBBEAN IMMIGRATION

Jayati Lal
Assistant Professor
Departments of Sociology and Women's Studies
University of Michigan
SWEATSHOPS

Stephanie M. Laudone
Fordham University
BLACK-WHITE INTERMARRIAGE

Kristen M. Lavelle
Department of Sociology
Texas A&M University
INSTITUTIONAL RACISM

Novotny Lawrence
Assistant Professor
Radio-Television Department
Southern Illinois University-Carbondale
BUFFALO SOLDIERS

Angelica Lawson
Assistant Professor
Native American Studies
University of Montana
NATIVE AMERICAN POPULAR CULTURE AND RACE

Shawn Lay
Department of History
Coker College, South Carolina
SECOND KLAN

Mark M. Leach
Associate Professor
Department of Psychology
University of Southern Mississippi
WHITE RACIAL IDENTITY

Byoungha Lee
Department of Political Science
Rutgers, The State University of New Jersey
IMMIGRATION REFORM AND CONTROL ACT OF 1986 (IRCA)

Robert G. Lee
Associate Professor
Department of American Civilization
Brown University
MODEL MINORITIES

Joselyn Leimbach
Department of Women's Studies
San Diego State University
LESBIANS

LaVonne Jackson Leslie
Associate Professor
Department of Afro-American Studies
Howard University
REMOND, CHARLES LENOX

Daniel Levitas
Author, *The Terrorist Next Door: The Militia Movement and The Radical Right*
SWIFT, WESLEY

Cecil M. Lewis Jr.
Department of Human Genetics
University of Michigan
HUMAN GENETICS

R. C. Lewontin
Agassiz Research Professor
Department of Organismic and Evolutionary Biology
Harvard University
GENE POOL
HERITABILITY

Peter S. Li
Professor
Department of Sociology
University of Saskatchewan, Canada
CANADIAN RACIAL FORMATIONS

Leonard Lieberman
Professor Emeritus
Department of Sociology and Anthropology
Central Michigan University
CLINES AND CONTINUOUS VARIATION

Alice Littlefield
Professor
Department of Anthropology
Central Michigan University
EXPLOITATION

Donald E. Lively
Vice President for Program Development
InfiLaw
UNITED STATES CONSTITUTION

Richard A. Lobban Jr.
Department of Anthropology
Rhode Island College
GENOCIDE IN SUDAN
SLAVERY, RACIAL

Mamie E. Locke
Dean
School of Liberal Arts and Professor of Political Science
Hampton University
HAMER, FANNIE LOU
NAACP
REPRODUCTIVE RIGHTS
WILKINS, ROY

Francisco A. Lomelí
Professor
Department of Chicana and Chicano Studies
University of California, Santa Barbara
AZTLÁN

Jeffrey C. Long
Professor
Department of Human Genetics
University of Michigan
HUMAN GENETICS

Mary Alice Long
Department of Women's Studies
University of California, San Diego
MOTHERHOOD

Felipe H. Lopez
Department of Urban Planning
University of California, Los Angeles
MEXICANS

Judith Lorber
Professor Emerita
Graduate Center and Brooklyn College
City University of New York
GENDER IDEOLOGY

Paul E. Lovejoy
Professor
Department of History
York University (Canada)
RACIAL DEMOGRAPHICS IN THE WESTERN HEMISPHERE
SLAVERY AND RACE
TRIANGULAR SLAVE TRADE

Kelly Lytle Hernandez
Department of History
University of California, Los Angeles
BORDER PATROL

Gaynor Macdonald
Senior Lecturer
Department of Anthropology
University of Sydney, Australia
AUSTRALIAN ABORIGINE PEOPLES

Robin K. Magee
Associate Professor
School of Law
Hamline University, Minnesota
FELONY DISENFRANCHISEMENT

Bill Mallon, M.D.
Past President
International Society of Olympic Historians (ISOH)
OLYMPIC GAMES OF 1904

Mahmood Mamdani
Herbert Lehman Professor of Government and Professor of Anthropology
Columbia University
GENOCIDE IN RWANDA

Xolela Mangcu
Visiting Public Scholar and Director of the Centre for Public Engagement
University of the Witwatersrand
BIKO, STEPHEN BANTU

Eric W. Mania
Professor
Department of Psychology
University of Delaware
SOCIAL PSYCHOLOGY OF RACISM

Maxine L. Margolis
Professor
Department of Anthropology
University of Florida
BRAZILIAN RACIAL FORMATIONS

Jonathan Marks
Professor
Department of Anthropology
University of North Carolina at Charlotte
GENETIC DISTANCE
GENETIC MARKER
GREAT CHAIN OF BEING
SCIENTIFIC RACISM, HISTORY OF
SUBSPECIES

Perry Mars
Professor
Department of Africana Studies
Wayne State University
AFRICAN DIASPORA
CARIBBEAN RACIAL FORMATIONS

Tony Martin
Professor
Department of Africana Studies
Wellesley College
GARVEY, MARCUS

Carolyn Martin Shaw
Professor
Department of Anthropology
University of California, Santa Cruz
BODY POLITICS

Oscar J. Martínez
Regents' Professor
Department of History
University of Arizona
BRACEROS, REPATRIATION, AND SEASONAL WORKERS

Nancy A. Matthews
Associate Professor
Northeast Illinois University
NEO-NAZIS

Wendy Patrick Mazzarella
Deputy District Attorney
San Diego County, California
HATE CRIMES

Cecilia Menjívar
Associate Professor
Department of Sociology
Arizona State University
CENTRAL AMERICANS

Ann V. Millard
Associate Professor
School of Rural Public Health and South Texas Center
Texas A&M University
LATINOS

Gilbert Felipe Mireles Jr.
Assistant Professor
Department of Sociology
Whitman College
UNITED FARM WORKERS UNION

Heidi Safia Mirza
Professor of Racial Equality Studies
Middlesex University
BLACK FEMINISM IN THE UNITED KINGDOM

Michael J. Montoya
Professor
Anthropology and Chicano/Latino Studies
University of California, Irvine
DIABETES

John H. Moore
Professor
Department of Anthropology
University of Florida
BLACK INDIANS
ETHNOCENTRISM
FEDERAL RECOGNITION: WHAT IS AN INDIAN?
GENES AND GENEALOGIES
GENESIS AND POLYGENESIS

Russell Mootry Jr.
Dean/Professor of Social Sciences
Bethune-Cookman University
BETHUNE, MARY McLEOD
FORTUNE, TIMOTHY THOMAS
WHITE, WALTER FRANCIS

Anthony Moran
Lecturer
School of Social Sciences
La Trobe University
WHITE SETTLER SOCIETY

Wilson J. Moses
Professor
Department of History
Pennsylvania State University
MAGIC FLUTE, THE
WAGNERIAN MUSIC

Alfred A. Moss Jr.
Department of History

University of Maryland, College Park
AMERICAN NEGRO ACADEMY

Barbara A. Moss
Professor
Department of History
Clark Atlanta University
CHISHOLM, SHIRLEY

Joia S. Mukherjee
Medical Director
Partners in Health (PIH)
HEALTH CARE GAP

Carol C. Mukhopadhyay
Department of Anthropology
San Jose State University
CULTURAL RACISM

Joane Nagel
University Distinguished Professor
Department of Sociology
University of Kansas
AMERICAN INDIAN MOVEMENT (AIM)
SYMBOLIC ETHNICITY

Diane Brook Napier
Program Head
Social Foundations of Education
University of Georgia
PAN-AFRICANISM

George O. Ndege
Associate Professor
Department of History
St Louis University
AFRICA: GERMAN COLONIES

Angela M. Nelson
Associate Professor
Department of Popular Culture
Bowling Green State University
BLACK POPULAR CULTURE

Francis Njubi Nesbitt
Associate Professor
Department of Africana Studies
San Diego State University
ANTI-APARTHEID MOVEMENT

Caryn E. Neumann
Visiting Assistant Professor
Wesleyan University
AFRICA: PORTUGUESE COLONIES

Joseph Nevins
Assistant Professor
Department of Geology and Geography
Vassar College, New York
OPERATION GATEKEEPER

Obioma Nnaemeka
Professor
Department of World Languages and Cultures
Indiana University
AFRICAN FEMINISMS

Donald M. Nonini
Professor
Department of Anthropology
University of North Carolina at Chapel Hill
CHINESE DIASPORA

Molly Townes O'Brien
Senior Lecturer
Faculty of Law
University of Wollongong
PLESSY V. FERGUSON

Tamika Corinne Odum
Program Manager, Outreach, Promotion and Education
Women's Center
University of Cincinnati
FAMILIES

Mojúbàolú Olúfunké Okome
Associate Professor
Department of Political Science
Brooklyn College, City University of New York
AFRICAN ECONOMIC DEVELOPMENT

Michael J. O'Neal
Independent Researcher
AMERICAN ANTI-SLAVERY SOCIETY
MALCOLM X
URBAN LEAGUE

Carlos Salvador Ordóñez
Postdoctoral Fellow
National Autonomous University of Mexico
MAYAN GENOCIDE IN GUATEMALA
ZAPATISTA REBELLION

Paul Ortiz
Associate Professor
Department of Community Studies
University of California, Santa Cruz
RACE RIOTS (U.S.), 1917–1923

Michael Alan Park
Professor
Department of Anthropology
Central Connecticut State University
DEME

Isaac F. Parr
Phoenix Indian Medical Center
HEALTH DISPARITIES BETWEEN INDIANS AND NON-INDIANS

Rhacel Salazar Parreñas
Associate Professor
Asian American Studies
University of California, Davis
IMMIGRANT DOMESTIC WORKERS

Antonio Pastrana Jr.
The Graduate Center
City University of New York
GAY MEN

Abha Sood Patel
Lecturer
Department of English
Monmouth University
RACE RIOTS (U.S.), 1900–1910

Diane B. Paul
Professor
Department of Political Science
University of Massachusetts at Boston
EUGENICS, HISTORY OF

Peter N. Peregrine
Professor
Department of Anthropology
Lawrence University
RACIAL HIERARCHY: OVERVIEW

James Peterson
Assistant Professor
Department of English
Penn State
HIP-HOP CULTURE
RAP MUSIC

Layli Phillips
Associate Professor
Department of Women's Studies
Georgia State University
HETEROSEXISM AND HOMOPHOBIA

Fritz G. Polite
Assistant Professor
Sport Management
University of Tennessee
GENETICS AND ATHLETIC PERFORMANCE

Mark Potok
Director, Intelligence Project
Editor, Intelligence Report
Southern Poverty Law Center
INTELLIGENCE PROJECT
NATIONAL ALLIANCE
SOUTHERN POVERTY LAW CENTER

Ralph R. Premdas
Professor
Department of Behavioral Sciences
University of the West Indies,
Trinidad and Tobago
ETHNIC CLEANSING

Michael Pretes
Assistant Professor
Department of Geography
University of North Alabama
AFRICA: ITALIAN COLONIES

Patrick Rael
Associate Professor
Department of History
Bowdoin College
SMITH, JAMES MCCUNE
WALKER, DAVID

Shirley Ann Rainey
Fisk University
GLOBAL ENVIRONMENT MOVEMENT

Catherine S. Ramírez
Assistant Professor of American Studies
University of California, Santa Cruz
ZOOT SUIT RIOTS

Barbara Reed
Associate Professor
Journalism and Media Studies
Rutgers, The State University of New Jersey
TROTTER, WILLIAM MONROE

John H. Relethford
Distinguished Teaching Professor
Department of Anthropology
State University of New York, Oneonta
GENETIC VARIATION AMONG POPULATIONS

Shelley Z. Reuter
Assistant Professor
Department of Sociology and Anthropology
Concordia University (Canada)
TAY-SACHS AND "JEWISH" DISEASES

David S. Reynolds
Distinguished Professor
Baruch College
City University of New York
BROWN, JOHN

Norma M. Riccucci
Professor
School of Public Affairs and Administration
Rutgers, The State University of New Jersey
TOKENISM

Beth E. Richie
Professor and Head of Department of African-American Studies
University of Illinois at Chicago
VIOLENCE AGAINST WOMEN AND GIRLS

Lynn Roberts
Assistant Professor
Urban Public Health
Hunter College, City University of New York
ADOLESCENT FEMALE SEXUALITY

Dean E. Robinson
Associate Professor
Political Science
University of Massachusetts Amherst
SOCIAL CLASS AND MORTALITY

Cheryl R. Rodriguez
Associate Professor
Africana Studies
University of South Florida
RAPE
SOCIAL WELFARE STATES

Donald Roe
Assistant Professor of History
Howard University
BIRTH OF A NATION, THE

Michelle Ronda
Assistant Professor
Department of Sociology
Marymount Manhattan College
PUERTO RICANS

F. Arturo Rosales
Professor
Department of History
Arizona State University
EL PLAN DE SANTA BARBARA

Charles K. Ross
Director, African American Studies, and Associate Professor of History and African American Studies
University of Mississippi
FOOTBALL (U.S.)

Rosetta E. Ross
Associate Professor
Department of Religion
Spelman College
TRUTH, SOJOURNER

Esther Rothblum
Professor
Department of Women's Studies
San Diego State University
LESBIANS

Paula Rothenberg
Senior Fellow
Murphy Institute, City University of New York
SEXISM

Ananya Roy
Associate Professor and Chair
Urban Studies Department of City and Regional Planning
University of California, Berkeley
POVERTY

John Ruedy
Emeritus Professor
Georgetown University, Washington, D.C.
ORGANISATION ARMÉE SECRÈTE (SECRET ARMY ORGANIZATION)

Kristi Ryujin
Director of Utah Opportunity Scholarship and Grants Programs
University of Utah
EDUCATION, DISCRIMINATION IN HIGHER

Elizabeth Salas
Associate Professor
Department of American Ethnic Studies
University of Washington
SOLDIERS OF COLOR

Xuan Santos
Department of Sociology
University of California, Santa Barbara
LABOR MARKET, INFORMAL

Gretchen E. Schafft
Applied Anthropologist in Residence
American University
RASSENHYGIENE

Nicole Scott
Medical School
University of Michigan
HUMAN GENETICS

David O. Sears
Professor
Psychology and Political Science
University of California, Los Angeles
SYMBOLIC AND MODERN RACISM

Oren Segal
Director
Center for the Study of Left-Wing and Islamic Extremism
Anti-Defamation League, New York
NATION OF ISLAM AND NEW BLACK PANTHER PARTY

Donald R. Shaffer
Professor
Division of Liberal Arts
Upper Iowa University
BLACK CIVIL WAR SOLDIERS
SCOTTSBORO BOYS

Eugenia Shanklin
Author, *Anthropology and Race: The Explanation of Differences*
FOLK CLASSIFICATION

Chuan-kang Shih
Assistant Professor
Departments of Anthropology and Asian Studies
University of Florida
RACISM, CHINA

Frederick J. Simonelli
Associate Professor
Department of History and Political Science
Mount St. Mary's College
ROCKWELL, GEORGE LINCOLN

Manisha Sinha
Associate Professor
Departments of Afro-American Studies and History
University of Massachusetts
ABOLITION MOVEMENT

Lanny Smith
Doctors for Global Health/People's Health Movement, Residency Programs in Primary Care and Social Medicine
Montefiore Medical Center, New York
HEALTH CARE GAP

Robert Samuel Smith
Assistant Professor
Department of Africana Studies
University of North Carolina at Charlotte
CIVIL RIGHTS MOVEMENT

C. Matthew Snipp
Professor
Department of Sociology
Stanford University
DEMOGRAPHICS AND RACE

Ilya Somin
Assistant Professor of Law
George Mason University
PEONAGE CASES

Cassia Spohn
Professor
School of Criminology and Criminal Justice
Arizona State University
CRIMINALITY, RACE AND SOCIAL FACTORS

Brett C. Stockdill
Associate Professor of Sociology, Latin and Latin American Studies, and Women's Studies
Northeastern Illinois University
ANTIRACIST SOCIAL MOVEMENTS

Darin B. Stockdill
School of Education
Eastern Michigan University
NEW DEAL AND OLD RACISM

Derald Wing Sue
Professor
Department of Counseling and Clinical Psychology
Teachers College, Columbia University
MENTAL HEALTH AND RACISM

Harold D. Tallant
Professor
Department of History
Georgetown College (Kentucky)
BIRNEY, JAMES GILLESPIE

George Tamblyn
Department of History
University of Washington
JOHNSON, MORDECAI WYATT

Clarence Taylor
Professor
Department of History
Baruch College, City University of New York
MAYS, BENJAMIN E.

Anderson Thompson
Associate Professor
Jacob Carruthers Center for Inner-City Studies
Northeastern Illinois University
ASSOCIATION FOR THE STUDY OF NEGRO LIFE AND HISTORY

Daniel J. Tichenor
Associate Professor of Political Science and Research Professor at the Eagleton Institute of Politics
Rutgers, The State University of New Jersey
IMMIGRATION REFORM AND CONTROL ACT OF 1986 (IRCA)

Mark C. Tilden
Native American Rights Fund
Boulder, Colorado
NATIVE AMERICAN RIGHTS FUND (NARF)

Gerald Torres
Bryant Smith Chair
Law
University of Texas at Austin
CRITICAL RACE THEORY

George R. Trumbull IV
Assistant Professor and Faculty Fellow Institute of French Studies
New York University
AFRICA: FRENCH COLONIES

William H. Tucker
Professor
Department of Psychology
Rutgers, The State University of New Jersey
HERRNSTEIN, RICHARD J.
STODDARD, T. LOTHROP

France Winddance Twine
Professor of Sociology
University of California, Santa Barbara
RACIAL FORMATIONS

John Obioma Ukawuilulu
Associate Professor of Sociology/Gerontology and Head of Department of Gerontology
Bethune-Cookman University
AFRICA: BELGIAN COLONIES
AFRICA: BRITISH COLONIES

Avelardo Valdez
Professor
Graduate College of Social Work
University of Houston
MACHISMO

Zulema Valdez
Assistant Professor
Department of Sociology
Texas A&M University
UNDEREMPLOYMENT

Abel Valenzuela Jr.
Department of Chicano Studies and Center for the Study of Urban Poverty
University of California, Los Angeles
DAY LABORERS, LATINO

Jeffrey M. Valla
Department of Human Development
Cornell University
IQ AND TESTING: CRITIQUES

Michelle VanNatta
Director of Criminology
Dominican University (Illinois)
SINGLETON, BENJAMIN "PAP"

Olga A. Vásquez
Associate Professor
Department of Communication
University of California, San Diego
LANGUAGE

James Diego Vigil
Professor
University of California, Irvine
GANGS AND YOUTH VIOLENCE
MEXICANS

L. Marie Wallace
Pima College
HEALTH DISPARITIES BETWEEN INDIANS AND NON-INDIANS
MISSIONARIES AMONG AMERICAN INDIANS

Hanes Walton Jr.
Professor
Department of Political Science
University of Michigan
KING, MARTIN LUTHER, JR.

L. Ling-chi Wang
Professor
Department of Ethnic Studies
University of California, Berkeley
CHINA-U.S. RELATIONS AND CHINESE AMERICANS
CHINESE AMERICANS AFTER WORLD WAR II
CHINESE IMMIGRATION AND EXCLUSION (U.S.), NINETEENTH CENTURY

Leland Ware
Louis L. Redding Professor of Law and Public Policy
University of Delaware
BROWN V. BOARD OF EDUCATION

Rachel J. Watkins
Assistant Professor
Department of Anthropology
American University
DISEASES, RACIAL

Bruce Webb
Independent Researcher
Atlanta, Georgia
STANDARDIZED TESTS

Norman E. Whitten Jr.
Professor Emeritus, Anthropology and Latin American Studies, and Curator Emeritus, Spurlock Museum
University of Illinois at Urbana-Champaign
BLACKNESS IN LATIN AMERICA
EL MESTIZAJE
LATIN AMERICAN RACIAL TRANSFORMATIONS

Harold L. Wilensky
Professor Emeritus of Political Science
University of California, Berkeley
WORKFARE AND WELFARE

Amy Fischer Williams
University of Wisconsin–Oshkosh
MISSIONARIES AMONG AMERICAN INDIANS

Wendy M. Williams
Department of Human Development
Cornell University
IQ AND TESTING: CRITIQUES

Julie Winch
Professor
Department of History
University of Massachusetts, Boston
FORTEN, JAMES

Peter H. Wood
Professor
Department of History
Duke University
TURNER, NAT

Handel Kashope Wright
Canada Research Chair–Cultural Studies and Director Centre for Culture, Identity, and Education
University of British Columbia
MULTICULTURALISM

Naomi Zack
Professor
Department of Philosophy
University of Oregon
FEMINISM AND RACE

Eleanor Zelliot
Professor Emerita
History Department
Carleton College
DALITS

John J. Zokovitch III
Pax Christi USA
Gainesville, Florida
PORRES, MARTIN DE, ST.

Thematic Outline

The following classification of articles arranged thematically gives an overview of the variety of entries and the breadth of subjects treated in the encyclopedia. Along with the index and the alphabetic arrangement of the encyclopedia, the thematic outline should aid in the location of topics. It is our hope that it will do more, that it will direct the reader to articles that may not have been the object of a search, that it will facilitate a kind of browsing that invites the reader to discover new articles, new topics, related, perhaps tangentially, to those originally sought.

1. African American Culture
2. Associations and Organizations
3. Business, Labor, and Economics
4. Children and Youth
5. China
6. Citizenship
7. Civil Rights and Social Activism
8. Colonialism
9. Concepts and Constructs
10. Controversial Organizations and Individuals
11. Cultural Groups
12. Education
13. Film
14. Gender and Sexuality
15. Genetic and Biological Concepts
16. Genocide
17. Health
18. History
19. Immigration
20. Latino/Hispanic Culture
21. Legal Cases, Individuals, and Issues
22. Literature
23. Native American Culture
24. Performing Arts
25. Popular Culture
26. Religion and Spirituality
27. Slavery and Freedom
28. Sports

1. AFRICAN AMERICAN CULTURE

Abolition Movement
Affirmative Action
African Diaspora
American Anti-Slavery Society
American Colonization Society and the Founding of Liberia
American Negro Academy
Antiracist Social Movements
Association for the Study of Negro Life and History
Birth of a Nation, The
Baseball
Basketball
Black Civil War Soldiers
Black Codes
Black Consciousness
Black Feminism in the United States
Black Popular Culture
Black Reconstruction
Black-White Intermarriage
Boxing
Brown v. Board of Education
Civil Rights Acts
Civil Rights Movement
Civil War Politics and Racism
Colonialism, Internal
Dance
Emancipation Proclamation
Felony Disenfranchisement
Freedmen's Bureau
Hip-Hop Culture
Hoaxing
League of Revolutionary Black Workers
NAACP
NAACP: Legal Actions, 1935–1955
New Deal and Old Racism
Niagara Movement
Occupational Segregation
Olympic Games of 1904
Olympic Games of 1936
Pan-Africanism
Plantations
Plessy v. Ferguson
Racial Purity (U.S.), 1900–1910
Race Riots (U.S.), 1900–1910
Race Riots (U.S.), 1917–1923
Racial Desegregation (U.S.)
Racial Slave Labor in the Americas
Rap Music
Scottsboro Boys
Sickle Cell Anemia
Slave Codes
Slave Trade Ideology
Slavery and Race
Slavery, Racial
Soldiers of Color
Southern Politics, 1883–1915
Southern Poverty Law Center
Tourism and National Heritage (U.S.)
Track and Field
Triangular Slave Trade

Urban League
Voting Rights Act of 1965
Biographies
Allen, Richard
Baker, Ella
Baldwin, James
Bates, Daisy
Bethune, Mary McLeod
Chisholm, Shirley
Davis, Angela
Douglass, Frederick
Du Bois, W. E. B.
Forten, James
Fortune, Timothy Thomas
Garnet, Henry Highland
Garvey, Marcus
Hamer, Fannie Lou
Houston, Charles Hamilton
Johnson, Mordecai Wyatt
King, Martin Luther, Jr.
Lorde, Audre
Malcolm X
Marshall, Thurgood
Mays, Benjamin E.
Powell, Adam Clayton, Jr.
Remond, Charles Lenox
Rustin, Bayard
Sheppard, William
Singleton, Benjamin "Pap"
Smith, James McCune
Stowe, Harriet Beecher
Trotter, William Monroe
Truth, Sojourner
Turner, Henry McNeal
Turner, Nat
Vesey, Denmark
Walker, David
Washington, Booker T.
Wells-Barnett, Ida B.
White, Walter Francis
Wilkins, Roy

2. ASSOCIATIONS AND ORGANIZATIONS

Afrikaner Broederbond
American Anti-Slavery Society
American Colonization Society and the Founding of Liberia
American Negro Academy
Association for the Study of Negro Life and History
Freedmen's Bureau
Jewish Defense League
League of Revolutionary Black Workers
NAACP
NAACP: Legal Actions, 1935–1955
Southern Poverty Law Center
Texas Rangers
Urban League

3. BUSINESS, LABOR, AND ECONOMICS

African Economic Development
Braceros, Repatriation, and Seasonal Workers
Chain Gangs
Day Laborers, Latino
Farmworkers
Labor Market
Labor Market, Informal
Labor, Cheap
League of Revolutionary Black Workers
Occupational Segregation
Pay Equity
Sweatshops
Transnational Labor Organizing
Underemployment
Undocumented Workers
United Farm Workers Union
Workfare and Welfare
Biographies
Chávez, César Estrada
Corona, Bert
Galarza, Ernesto
Huerta, Dolores
Singleton, Benjamin "Pap"

4. CHILDREN AND YOUTH

Children, Racial Disparities and Status of
El Plan de Santa Barbara
Gangs and Youth Violence

5. CHINA

China-U.S. Relations and Chinese Americans
Chinese Americans after World War II
Chinese Diaspora
Chinese Immigration and Exclusion (U.S.), Nineteenth Century
Racism, China

6. CITIZENSHIP

Citizenship and Race
Citizenship and "The Border"
Illegal Alien

7. CIVIL RIGHTS AND SOCIAL ACTIVISM

Affirmative Action
American Indian Movement (AIM)
Anti-Apartheid Movement
Anti-Indian Social Movements
Antiracist Social Movements
Apartheid
Civil Rights Acts
Civil Rights Movement
Global Environment Movement
Intelligence Project
Latino Social Movements
Niagara Movement
Pan-Africanism
Southern Poverty Law Center
Voting Rights Act of 1965
Zapatista Rebellion
Biographies
Baker, Ella
Baldwin, James
Bates, Daisy
Bethune, Mary McLeod
Biko, Stephen Bantu
Chisholm, Shirley
Davis, Angela
Douglass, Frederick
Du Bois, W. E. B.
Forten, James
Fortune, Timothy Thomas
Galarza, Ernesto
Gandhi, Mohandas Karamchand
Garvey, Marcus
Hamer, Fannie Lou
Johnson, Mordecai Wyatt
King, Martin Luther, Jr.
Lorde, Audre
Malcolm X
Mandela, Nelson
Mays, Benjamin E.
Powell, Adam Clayton, Jr.
Rustin, Bayard
Trotter, William Monroe
Washington, Booker T.
Wells-Barnett, Ida B.
White, Walter Francis
Wilkins, Roy

8. COLONIALISM

Africa: Belgian Colonies
Africa: British Colonies
Africa: French Colonies
Africa: German Colonies
Africa: Italian Colonies
Africa: Portuguese Colonies
Colonialism, Internal
Pan-Africanism
White Settler Society
Biographies
Cuffe, Paul
Dew, Thomas Roderick
Garvey, Marcus
Sheppard, William
Turner, Henry McNeal

9. CONCEPTS AND CONSTRUCTS

Anthropology, History of
Aversive Racism
Biracialism
Black Consciousness
Black-White Intermarriage
Blood Quantum
Body Politics
Capitalism

Color-Blind Racism
Critical Race Theory
Cultural Deficiency
Cultural Racism
Demographics and Race
El Mestizaje
Ethnocentrism
Everyday Racism
Exploitation
Families
Fourth World
Great Chain of Being
Hoaxing
Illegal Alien
Implicit Racism
Indigenous
Institutional Racism
Internalized Racialism
IQ and Testing: Overview
IQ and Testing: Origin and Development
IQ and Testing: Culture, Education, and IQ Scores
IQ and Testing: Critiques
Language
Language, Incendiary
Machismo
Model Minorities
Multiculturalism
Multiracial Identities
Nativism
Orientalism
"Out of Africa" Hypothesis
Poverty
Racial Demographics in the Western Hemisphere
Racial Desegregation
Racial Formations
Racial Hierarchy: Overview
Racial Hierarchy: Races Ranked by Early Scientists
Racial Hierarchy: Disproven
Rural White Stereotyping
Scientific Racism, History of
Skin Color
Social Class and Mortality
Social Problems
Social Psychology of Racism
Social Welfare States
Standardized Tests
Stereotype Threat and Racial Stigma
Symbolic and Modern Racism
Symbolic Ethnicity
Tokenism
Tourism and National Heritage (U.S.)
Transnationalism
White Racial Identity

10. CONTROVERSIAL ORGANIZATIONS AND INDIVIDUALS

Christian Identity
English Skinheads
Ku Klux Klan
Nation of Islam and New Black Panther Party
National Alliance
National States Rights Party
Neo-Nazis
Organisation Armée Secrète (Secret Army Organization)
Second Klan
Texas Rangers
White Citizens' Councils and the Council of Conservative Citizens

Biographies

Chamberlain, Houston Stewart
Dixon, Thomas, Jr.
Duke, David
Herrnstein, Richard J.
Jensen, Arthur
Nott, Josiah
Rockwell, George Lincoln
Stoddard, T. Lothrop
Swift, Wesley
Tillman, Benjamin "Pitchfork"
Watson, Thomas E.

11. CULTURAL GROUPS

Arabs and Arab Americans
Australian Aborigine Peoples
Black Indians
Brazilian Racial Formations
Burakumin
Cagots
Canadian Racial Formations
Caribbean Racial Formations
Central Americans
Cuban Racial Formations
Dalits
Haitian Racial Formations
Indigenismo in Mexico
Irish Americans and Whiteness
Latin American Racial Transformations
Latinos
Mexicans
Puerto Ricans
Roma
South African Racial Formations
Triracial Isolates
United Kingdom Racial Formations
White Racial Identity

12. EDUCATION

Education, Discrimination in Higher
Education, Racial Disparities
IQ and Testing: Overview
IQ and Testing: Origin and Development
IQ and Testing: Culture, Education, and IQ Scores
IQ and Testing: Critiques
Standardized Tests

Biographies

Bethune, Mary McLeod
Johnson, Mordecai Wyatt
Mays, Benjamin E.
Montagu, Ashley

13. FILM

Birth of a Nation, The
Film
Film and Asian Americans

14. GENDER AND SEXUALITY

Adolescent Female Sexuality
African Feminisms
Asian-American Feminism
Black Feminism in Brazil
Black Feminism in the United Kingdom
Black Feminism in the United States
Chicana Feminism
Feminism and Race
Gay Men
Gender Ideology
Heterosexism and Homophobia
Hottentot Venus
Latina Gender, Reproduction, and Race
Lesbians
Machismo
Motherhood
Motherhood, Deficiency in
Pornography
Reproductive Rights
Reproductive Technologies
Sex Work
Sexism
Sexuality
Violence against Women and Girls
Womanism

Biographies

Anzaldúa, Gloria

15. GENETIC AND BIOLOGICAL CONCEPTS

Antebellum Black Ethnology
Anthropometry
Clines
Clines and Continuous Variation
Clusters
Cranial Index
Deme
Eugenics, History of
Facial Angle
Folk Classification
Forensic Anthropology and Race
Gene Pool
Genes and Genealogies
Genetic Distance
Genetic Marker
Genetic Variation among Populations
Genetics, History of

25. POPULAR CULTURE

Black Popular Culture
Hip-Hop Culture
Rap Music
Television

26. RELIGION AND SPIRITUALITY

Anti-Semitism
Anti-Semitism in Russia
Anti-Semitism in the Arab World
Genesis and Polygenesis
Jewish Defense League
Missionaries among American Indians
Muslims
Zionism
Biographies
- Allen, Richard
- Mays, Benjamin E.
- Porres, Martin de, St.
- Powell, Adam Clayton, Jr.
- Sheppard, William
- Turner, Henry McNeal

27. SLAVERY AND FREEDOM

Abolition Movement
African Enslavement, Precolonial
Emancipation Proclamation
Indian Slavery
Plantations
Racial Slave Labor in the Americas
Slave Codes
Slave Trade Ideology
Slavery and Race
Slavery, Racial
Triangular Slave Trade
Biographies
- Allen, Richard
- Birney, James Gillespie
- Brown, John
- Calhoun, John C.
- Dew, Thomas Roderick
- Douglass, Frederick
- Forten, James
- Fortune, Timothy Thomas
- Garnet, Henry Highland
- Garrison, William Lloyd
- Phillips, Wendell
- Remond, Charles Lenox
- Singleton, Benjamin "Pap"
- Smith, James McCune
- Stowe, Harriet Beecher
- Truth, Sojourner
- Turner, Nat
- Vesey, Denmark
- Walker, David

28. SPORTS

Baseball
Basketball
Boxing
Football (U.S.)
Genetics and Athletic Performance
Olympic Games of 1904
Olympic Games of 1936
Track and Field

A

ABOLITION MOVEMENT

The history of the movement to abolish slavery is virtually coeval with the establishment of racial slavery in the New World. In the Western Hemisphere, millions of enslaved Africans were embedded in the workforces of all of the Americas and the Caribbean Islands from 1502 to 1888. Unlike slavery elsewhere in the modern world, these societies had economies dependent on chattel slavery or the labor of individuals who could be bought, sold, bequeathed, rented, or pawned as if they were inanimate property. Consequently, abolition caused tremendous dislocation in western slave societies. Between the first Quaker disavowal of slavery in Pennsylvania in 1688 and the formal abolition of bondage in Brazil in 1888, the process of abolition covered two centuries, occasioned civil war in Haiti and the United States, and led to bartering for the liberation of slave soldiers in Central America.

EARLY ANTISLAVERY EFFORTS

The first European protests against certain types of racial slavery occurred in the early colonial era. A few individuals, mostly Dominican and Jesuit priests, were sickened by the Spanish destruction and enslavement of Indian populations, and they recorded their objections to slavery. Among these clerics was Bartolomé de Las Casas, who in 1518 started his long crusade against Indian slavery. These efforts culminated in the famous Valladolid debate of 1550–1551, in which he was opposed by the learned Juan Ginés de Sepúlveda. At bottom, the debate was about which was the morally superior choice of slave workers in Spanish America: Native Americans or enslaved Africans. Ironically, while Las Casas argued against the enslavement of the Native population, he suggested that Africans, whom he considered hardier workers, replace Indian slaves in the Spanish colonies. Sepúlveda supported the continued use of Native Americans, but as serfs (*encomienderos*) responsible for providing goods and services to their Spanish masters. Spain subsequently employed both arrangements, using Africans as individual slaves and Native Americans as community slaves. Many European colonists used white indentured workers, as well as Native Americans, but eventually enslaved Africans became their primary source of labor. The Atlantic slave trade and establishment of African slavery in the New World, especially in plantation economies that produced staple cash crops for the world market, were an important part of European commercial and geographical expansion in the early modern world. Racial slavery existed in all the American colonies by the end of the seventeenth century, and white settlers developed elaborate slave codes and racist ideas to justify and legitimize it.

With the expansion of Europe and the economic exploitation of overseas settlements, racialist thought became a powerful bulwark of slavery. Montesquieu criticized racial slavery but made an exception for warmer climes. John Locke, who wrote the fundamental constitutions of the colony of South Carolina that established slavery, characterized the state of slavery as outside the social contract but justified the enslavement of Africans as prisoners taken in a "just war." American slaveholders would use his notion of the right to property to defend chattel slavery. Similarly, while Adam Smith criticized all forms of servitude in favor of free labor, his notion of individual economic self-interest could justify modern racial slavery. Enlightenment thinkers such as David Hume, Voltaire, Immanuel Kant, and, later, Thomas Jefferson made racially derogatory remarks against Africans. Some Christians, Jews, and Arab Muslims twisted the biblical story of "Ham's Curse" by claiming that Africans were the descendants of Ham, who had been cursed by God for disrespecting Noah, and that this justified their enslavement. Enlightenment thought about "universal nature," "natural rights," and Western religious traditions of sin and punishment bequeathed a mixed heritage to the Americas: It fostered a critical attitude toward slavery but also gave birth to an intellectual racism that saw Africans as less than fully human, thus legitimizing their enslavement by Europeans. Abolitionism was to emerge from this mixture of traditions, with the abolitionists eventually arguing that the slave owners, and not the slaves, were sinners in danger of God's wrath.

In colonial British North America, a few extraordinary Quakers and Puritans started criticizing slavery and, at times, its racist justifications. One of the first protests against the enslavement of Africans came from four Dutch Quakers in Germantown, Pennsylvania, who sent an antislavery petition to the Monthly Meeting of Quakers in 1688. No action was taken on this petition, at least in part because the Quakers were deeply involved in European commercial expansion. In 1693 the Philadelphia Quaker George Keith published *An Exhortation and Caution to Friends Concerning Buying and Keeping of Negroes,* in which he argued against the abuses of slavery and for the humanity of Africans. Following Keith, other Quakers—such as Robert Piles, John Hepburn of New Jersey, Ralph Sandiford of Philadelphia, and Elihu Coleman of Nantucket, Massachusetts—wrote against slavery and slaveholders. The Puritan Judge Samuel Sewall, in his 1700 pamphlet *The Selling of Joseph*, also condemned slavery as "man stealing," and hence contrary to the word of the Bible. He concluded, however, that free black people could never be incorporated into "our Body Politick" and must exist "as a kind of extravasat Blood [involuntary resident]."

In 1735 the British philanthropist James Oglethorpe founded the convict colony of Georgia as an alternative to the slavery-based plantation colonies of the South. However, with England's subsequent permission, white settlers, mainly from South Carolina, successfully introduced slaves and plantation agriculture to Georgia, leading to the first southern antislavery petition, which came from eighteen Scotsmen in Darien, Georgia, in 1739. By 1755, Georgia's experiment in free labor had come to an end, and like the other southern colonies, it instituted a slave code.

From the 1730s to the 1760s, three Quaker abolitionists, Benjamin Lay, John Woolman, and Anthony Benezet, devoted their lives to the abolitionist effort. Lay, who had been a West Indian slaveholder, came to abhor slavery, and he became known for his dramatic antislavery tactics, such as kidnapping the child of a slaveholder to acquaint him with the grief of slaves. Woolman wrote a pamphlet, *Some Considerations on the Keeping of Negroes* (1754), in which he presented a strong critique of the racist justifications of slavery. He argued that "Negroes are our fellow creatures" and that justice should take precedence over profit. Benezet, who stayed mainly in Philadelphia, wrote a number of pamphlets against the slave trade, collected antislavery writings and documents on slavery, and corresponded with early British abolitionists such as Granville Sharp. He taught slave children from his home, and in 1770 he set up the Negro School, which eventually served more than 250 pupils, both slave and free. Under Woolman's and Benezet's leadership, Quaker meetings passed resolutions against the slave trade and excluded slaveholders from positions of leadership.

Following the American Revolution, a Quaker-led Anglo-American antislavery movement burgeoned during the last quarter of the eighteenth century. This movement led to the abolition of slavery in the northern states of the new American Republic. The British and American prohibition of the Atlantic slave trade occurred in 1807–1808. Revolutionary ideology, with its emphasis on natural rights and a criticism of "political slavery," furnished the first theoretical challenge to the existence of slavery in the Western world, according to historian David Brion Davis. A few American revolutionaries such as James Otis and Benjamin Rush, who wrote *An Address to the Inhabitants of the British Settlements in America upon Slave Keeping* (1773), wrote and spoke out against racial slavery.

The First Great Awakening (1730–1770) of evangelical Protestant sects (e.g., the Methodists, whose founder John Wesley opposed slavery, and the Baptists) and the rise of religious egalitarianism also led to a questioning of slavery. Many of these sects preached spiritual equality regardless of race. They appealed to the common man and woman in mass revival meetings, leading to what one historian has called "the democratization of American Christianity." While the famous evangelical preacher George Whitfield defended slavery even as he pleaded for the Christianization of slaves, other ministers—such as the Calvinists Nathaniel Niles and Thomas Cooper and the Methodists Francis Asbury and Thomas Coke—spoke out against slavery. Deacon Benjamin Coleman, of Newbury, Massachusetts, fought against his slave-owning minister on the slavery issue. Among the Congregationalists, New Divinity theologians such as Jonathan Edwards Jr. and Samuel Hopkins became strong abolitionists. Hopkins not only wrote one of the most effective abolitionist tracts of the period, *A Dialogue Concerning the Slavery of Africans* (1776), he also tried to educate black men to send them back to Africa as missionaries. Another aggressive opponent of slavery and proponent of revolutionary republicanism was the black clergyman Lemuel Haynes of Vermont.

EARLY EFFORTS OF BLACKS

The role of Africans and African Americans in the abolition movement stood unappreciated for a long time. Africans had obviously opposed slavery from the first moments of enslavement. There were rebellions and runaway slave communities on the African coast, shipboard rebellions during the Atlantic slave trade (known as the "Middle Passage"), and colonial slave revolts and conspiracies in New York (1712 and 1741) and South Carolina (1739). During the American Revolution, blacks brought freedom suits against their masters, ran away in massive numbers, and fought on both sides in often successful efforts to win their freedom.

As early as the 1765 Stamp Act crisis, slaves in Charleston, South Carolina, marched in protest, crying "Liberty!" and alarming their masters. African-American writers such as the slave preacher Jupiter Hammon of Long Island, New York, the poet Phillis Wheatley of Boston, and, more explicitly, the former slave essayist Caesar Sarter of Newburyport, Massachusetts, critiqued the existence of slavery and defied racist pronouncements that claimed Africans were incapable of learning and suited only for hard, physical labor. In the 1770s, groups of slaves in New England petitioned their colonial governments, demanding an end to slavery and the rights of citizenship or transportation back to Africa.

In Massachusetts, early black abolitionists such as Prince Hall, founder of the African Masonic Lodge, and Paul Cuffe, the black Quaker sea captain who inaugurated the first Back-to-Africa movement, headed petition drives. Cuffe, in his petition, applied the slogan "no taxation without representation" in asking for relief from taxation because he did not have the right to vote. The black freedom petitions pointed to the shortcomings of the revolutionary statements of white leaders that did not include African Americans, thus laying the foundations of black abolitionism. Thousands of black loyalists—runaway slaves freed by British proclamations in 1779 and by Virginia governor Lord Dunmore in 1775 for joining the British—left the American colonies to be resettled in Nova Scotia, Canada, and then Africa in their search for freedom.

REVOLUTIONARY ERA ABOLITIONISM

Antislavery sentiment among African Americans and whites during the Revolutionary era gave birth to the American abolition movement. In 1775 the first abolition organization, the Society for the Relief of Free Negroes Unlawfully Held in Bondage, was founded in Philadelphia. The organization was reorganized as the Pennsylvania Abolition Society in 1787. In 1785, the Society for Promoting the Manumission of Slaves was founded in New York. Prominent revolutionary leaders such as Alexander Hamilton and John Jay were members of the society, and Benjamin Franklin would assume the presidency of the Pennsylvania Abolition Society before his death. By the end of the Revolution, all the states had antislavery societies, except for Georgia and South Carolina, the two states most committed to slavery and the slave trade. Whites dominated the organized antislavery movement, and they saw African Americans as the objects of their benevolence. Nonetheless, these societies provided valuable legal and political services to the slaves and free blacks who fought against enslavement, kidnapping, and attempts to bypass emancipation laws. In 1794 all the antislavery societies met in Philadelphia and formed a national antislavery convention. Yet while the Founding Fathers of the new American republic expressed their abhorrence of slavery, many were slave owners themselves, and only those in the North joined antislavery societies. Men such as Thomas Jefferson undermined their antislavery pronouncements with their intense racism, though others, such as Thomas Paine, George Mason of Virginia, Luther Martin of Maryland, and Gouverneur Morris of Pennsylvania, were unequivocal in their condemnation of slavery.

NORTHERN ABOLITIONISM

In the North, where slavery was not the mainstay of the economy and society, antislavery sentiment made greater headway. In 1777, Vermont became the first state to abolish slavery in its constitution. In 1780, Pennsylvania passed a gradual emancipation law, which served as a model for similar laws passed in other northern states. Rhode Island and Connecticut, for example, adopted similar laws in 1784. In New Hampshire and Massachusetts, judicial interpretation of the states' constitutions led to the abolition of slavery in 1783.

In Massachusetts, slaves themselves initiated the emancipation process by suing their masters for freedom. In 1765 Jenny Slew of Ipswich successfully brought her master to court. In 1781, Elizabeth "Mumbet" Freeman won her freedom by suing her master for abuse and appealing to the notion of universal natural rights. A similar case,

Commonwealth v. Jennison, brought by Quock Walker, outlawed slavery in Massachusetts.

The battle for abolition was more protracted in New York and New Jersey, where slavery was widespread. New York passed its gradual emancipation law in 1799, and New Jersey in 1804. In New York, additional laws had to be passed to prevent masters from selling their slaves in the South and to prevent the kidnapping of free blacks into southern slavery. In 1827 a law freed all remaining slaves in the state. In New Jersey, despite emancipation, a handful of slaves survived to the very eve of the Civil War (fifteen slaves were counted in the 1860 census). However, the Revolution did abolish northern slavery, creating a nation that was half slave and half free.

Abolitionist efforts did not make any headway in the South, however, though Virginia passed a manumission law in 1782 that eased restrictions on individual slaveholders who wanted to emancipate their slaves. In the Upper South, some slaveholders were so influenced by Revolutionary ideas and the decline of the tobacco economy that they freed their slaves, creating a large free black population in Virginia, Maryland, and Delaware. In 1787, the Northwest Ordinance prohibited the expansion of slavery north of the Ohio River. Jefferson's original version of this ordinance would have banned slavery in the Southwest, but it lost by one vote in Congress, thus ensuring the expansion of slavery into Alabama, Mississippi, and the trans-Mississippi West. The continued expansion of slavery in the southern states ensured that there were more slaves in the United States after the Revolution than in the thirteen American colonies before it.

Immediate Emancipation in the West Indies, August 1, 1838. *The British Parliament passed the Slavery Abolition Act in 1833. In most British colonies, however, slaves underwent a period of enforced "apprenticeship," which ended in 1838. Alexander Rippingille's painting, seen here in an engraving by S. H. Gimber, shows slaves in the West Indies celebrating their freedom.* **THE LIBRARY OF CONGRESS.**

ABOLITION OUTSIDE THE UNITED STATES

More thoroughly than the American Revolution, the Haitian Revolution (1791–1804) sounded the death knell of racial slavery in the New World. What began as a slave rebellion and a fight for the rights of citizenship by Haiti's mixed-race population, who were inspired by the 1789 French Revolution, ended with the abolition of slavery and the founding of the first modern black republic and the second independent nation in the Americas. Led by the remarkable former slave Toussaint Louverture, the Haitian Revolution is the only instance of a successful slave rebellion in world history. It thus inspired generations of black and white abolitionists throughout the nineteenth century.

As early as 1770, Guillaume Thomas François (Abbé) Raynal had published his searing indictment of slavery and the African slave trade in his multivolume history of European colonization. He also predicted a black revolution that would drench the New World in blood. In 1788, revolutionaries such as Jean-Pierre Brissot and Honoré Mirabeau founded the French abolition society, Société des Amis des Noirs (Society of the Friends of the Blacks), which included among its ranks Julien Raimond and Vincent Ogé, men of mixed-race origins, who led the mulatto revolt in Haiti, and other luminaries such as the French thinker and mathematician Marquis de Condorcet, the Marquis de Lafayette, and Bishop Henri Grégoire, a champion of black equality. In 1794, under the Jacobins, France abolished slavery, though this decree was later revoked by Napoleon.

The Haitians, some of whom had fought in the American Revolution with Lafayette, defeated the French, including Napoleon's army that had conquered so much of Europe, the British, and the Spanish. Despite Toussaint's capture and death, the Haitian Republic declared its independence in 1804 under the leadership of Jean-Jacques Dessalines. It would not be until the 1848 revolutions in Europe that France and Denmark would abolish slavery in their colonies. By the 1820s the Latin American Wars of Independence had abolished slavery in most Latin American countries, including Mexico. At the end of the Age of Revolution only Brazil, the Spanish colonies of Cuba and Puerto Rico, and the United States South had not abolished racial slavery. The Constitution of the United States not only recognized slavery as a legal institution, it also postponed the abolition of the Atlantic slave trade until 1808.

THE ABOLITION MOVEMENT IN GREAT BRITAIN

After American independence, a mainly British movement to abolish the slave trade picked up in the 1780s. In 1787 the Society for Effecting the Abolition of the Slave Trade was founded. English Quakers such as John Fothergill and the indefatigable Granville Sharp, a champion of slaves and free blacks, led the movement to abolish the slave trade. Earlier, in the landmark 1772 *Somerset v. Steuart* case, Sharp had defended a runaway Virginian slave, James Somerset. The Somerset decision was widely interpreted as having abolished slavery in Britain. Sharp also publicized the famous *Zong* slave ship case in which the ship's captain, in order to collect insurance, threw 133 Africans overboard after the outbreak of disease. The anti-slave trade effort was led by Thomas Clarkson, who had published *An Essay on the Slavery and Commerce of the Human Species* in 1786. Black abolitionists such as Quobna Ottobah Cugoano and Olaudah Equiano (both former slaves) contributed to the cause, first by bringing Sharp's attention to the *Zong* incident, and then by writing popular narratives of their capture and enslavement. Cugoano published *Thoughts and Sentiments on the Evil and Wicked Traffic of the Commerce of the Human Species*, the first black abolitionist tract, in 1787, and Equiano published *The Interesting Narrative of the Life of Olaudah Equiano, or Gustavus Vassa* in 1789.

In 1788 the British government regulated the number of slaves that could be carried in a ship and in 1789 William Wilberforce headed the fight against the slave trade in Parliament. At his behest, Parliament formed a select committee, whose hearings on the slave trade still provide the best evidence historians have on the conduct of the trade. Throughout the 1790s Wilberforce and abolitionists such as James Stephens led the fight to end the slave trade. After successive defeats, they were finally successful in 1807, when the law that abolished the British slave trade passed Parliament. Britain would go on to negotiate treaties with France, Spain, and Portugal to end the slave trade, and it used its navy to enforce the law and the treaties.

BLACK ABOLITIONISM IN THE UNITED STATES

Across the ocean, African Americans emerged as strong critics of slavery in the early republic, writing most of the abolitionist pamphlets of the time. In 1794, addressing "those who keep slaves and uphold the practice," Reverend Richard Allen and Absalom Jones, founders of the African Methodist Episcopal (AME) Church, stated, "you … have been and are our great oppressors." They implied that America, like Egypt, would be destroyed for its "oppression of the poor slaves" by God, "the protector and avenger of slaves." Daniel Coker, another AME clergyman, wrote in a fictional 1810 dialogue between a slaveholder and a black minister that the slave's right to liberty outweighed the slaveholder's right to property. In his 1813 *Series of Letters by a Man of Colour*, James Forten, a black sail maker and Revolutionary War hero, strongly criticized racial discrimination against free blacks (he was writing in response to a Pennsylvania law that limited the migration of blacks to that state) by appealing to the principles of republicanism.

In the South, where any sort of writing by enslaved blacks was illegal, there were at least four abortive slave rebellions and conspiracies against the tightening and expansion of the slave regime in the United States. In 1800 Gabriel Prosser, inspired by French and American revolutionary ideals, headed a conspiracy of a thousand slaves in Henrico County, Virginia. In 1811 Charles Deslandes, inspired by the Haitian Revolution, sparked a rebellion of 500 slaves about forty miles northwest of New Orleans. In the fighting, federal troops killed sixty blacks in battle, and they executed twenty-one others, including Deslandes. The former slave Denmark Vesey led a failed slave conspiracy in Charleston, South Carolina, in 1822. In 1831 Nat Turner headed a slave rebellion in Southampton County, Virginia, that left nearly sixty whites dead before he and his comrades were captured. An intense white backlash of paranoia and violence followed Turner's rebellion.

BLACK ABOLITIONISM

Black abolitionism arose more strongly in the 1820s as a response to the 1817 founding of the American Colonization Society (ACS). The colonization movement, which included prominent national politicians from the North and South, proposed to remove all free blacks to Africa, a plan first conceived by Thomas Jefferson. An overwhelming majority of African Americans opposed the colonization movement, believing it to be a racist scheme to strengthen slavery and deny blacks equal citizenship in the United States. Black abolitionists thus developed the "immediatist" program of anticolonization and the immediate abolition of slavery and racial discrimination. In

Punishment Aboard a British Slave Ship. *George Cruikshank's 1792 engraving, titled* The Abolition of the Slave Trade, *shows Captain John Kimber preparing to whip a female slave for refusing to dance naked on the ship. The abolitionist William Wilberforce brought the matter to Parliament and Kimber was arrested and tried for causing the girl's death. The High Court of Admiralty acquitted him, however, ascribing the girl's death to disease.* THE LIBRARY OF CONGRESS.

1827, the first black abolitionist newspaper, *Freedom's Journal,* founded by Reverend Samuel Cornish and John Russwurm (who would later change his mind and emigrate to Liberia), espoused this program, as did the Massachusetts General Colored Association (MGCA), a Boston black abolitionist organization founded in 1826.

The famous black abolitionist pamphleteer, David Walker, who was an agent for *Freedom's Journal* and a member of the MGCA, published his *Appeal to the Colored Citizens of the World* in 1829 in Boston. Walker roundly critiqued colonization and American pretensions to being a republican and Christian country. He demanded an immediate end to slavery and vowed to alert the world of "black sufferings" in this "Republican land of liberty!" Walker died suddenly a year later, but his *Appeal* would be reprinted several times and remained the founding document of black abolitionism. The pioneer black feminist Maria Stewart of Boston, a follower of Walker's, became the first American woman to speak in public on abolition and black rights.

Though not an African American, William Lloyd Garrison, an intrepid political journalist, became an effective spokesman for black freedom and equality. A convert to the agenda and uncompromising rhetorical style of the new black abolitionists, Garrison had earlier met black leaders such as William Watkins, Hezekiah Grice, and James Forten. Through them, Garrison was converted from colonization to immediatism. In 1831, financed mainly by blacks in Boston and Philadelphia, he started publishing an extraordinary newspaper, *The Liberator,* in which he wrote his famous words, "I will not equivocate—I will not excuse—I will not retreat a single inch—and I will be heard." Garrison's newspaper, which remained the premier voice of abolitionism until the end of the Civil War, was bankrolled by Forten, and African Americans made up 400 of its first 450 subscribers. Garrison also founded the New

England Anti-Slavery Society in 1832, into which the MGCA merged, in the basement of the African Meeting House in Boston, and he formed close personal and professional ties with black abolitionists.

ABOLITIONISM MATURES

The founding of the American Anti-Slavery Society (AASS) in Philadelphia in 1833 marked the start of the interracial antebellum abolitionist movement and the coming together of three important antislavery groups: African Americans, Quakers, and a handful of radical whites such as Garrison. The Declaration of Sentiments of the AASS, written by Garrison while he was staying in the Philadelphia home of Dr. James McCrummill, a black dentist, committed the new movement to immediatism, anticolonization, blacks rights, and the tactic of "moral suasion." White evangelical Christians such as Theodore Dwight Weld and the wealthy brothers Arthur and Lewis Tappan of New York City would be important converts to Garrisonian abolitionism. The Tappan brothers, along with prominent black abolitionists such as Samuel Cornish, Theodore Wright, and William Hamilton, led the movement in New York. African Americans participated as members of the board of the AASS, and as its agents, but they also retained their separate independent organizations, such as the American Society of Free People of Color, the antislavery Bethel Church Free Produce Society and American Moral Reform Society. The all-black Female Anti-Slavery Society of Salem was founded in 1832, followed by two important interracial female abolitionist organizations, the Boston Female Anti-Slavery Society and the Philadelphia Female Anti-Slavery Society. Members of these and other groups collectively supported the National Black Conventions that met periodically from 1830 to 1864. The black press was represented by the *Colored American, Frederick Douglass' Paper* and the *Anglo-African Magazine*. In Canada, the runaway slave Henry Bibb published *Voice of the Fugitive*, that nation's first black-owned newspaper, from 1851 until 1853 and Mary Ann Shadd Cary published the *Provincial Freeman*.

—VOL. I. NO. 5.—

THE AMERICAN ANTI-SLAVERY ALMANAC, FOR 1840,

BEING BISSEXTILE OR LEAP-YEAR, AND THE 64TH OF AMERICAN INDEPENDENCE. CALCULATED FOR BOSTON; ADAPTED TO THE NEW ENGLAND STATES.

NORTHERN HOSPITALITY—NEW YORK NINE MONTHS' LAW.
The slave steps out of the slave-state, and his chains fall. A free state, with another chain, stands ready to re-enslave him.

Thus saith the Lord, Deliver him that is spoiled out of the hands of the oppressor.

NEW YORK & BOSTON:
PUBLISHED BY THE AMERICAN ANTI-SLAVERY SOCIETY,
NO. 143 NASSAU STREET, NEW YORK;
AND BY J. A. COLLINS, 29 CORNHILL, BOSTON.

The American Anti-Slavery Almanac for 1840. *The American Anti-Slavery Society was founded in 1833; it began publishing its almanac in 1837. The cover of this 1840 edition takes a jab at Northern hypocrisy by depicting a slave being unchained by a "Slave State" while a "Free State" prepares to rechain him.* **MANUSCRIPTS, ARCHIVES, AND RARE BOOKS DIVISION, SCHOMBURG CENTER FOR RESEARCH IN BLACK CULTURE, THE NEW YORK PUBLIC LIBRARY, ASTOR, LENOX AND TILDEN FOUNDATIONS.**

Women also formed an important part of the new abolition movement. Starting with Lucretia Mott, Lydia Maria Child, and the Grimké sisters, Angelina and Sarah, some women joined the antislavery lecture circuit and societies. Others organized antislavery fairs, picnics, and bazaars, raising hundreds of dollars for the movement. In the 1840s and 1850s, many charismatic white female abolitionists, such as Lucy Stone and Abby Kelley Foster, as well as black female activists, such as Sojourner Truth, Sarah Parker Remond, and Francis Ellen Watkins Harper, lectured for the antislavery societies. However, many clergymen and evangelical Christians were strongly opposed to abolitionist women who spoke in public or sought leadership positions within the movement. Women were expected to remain silent but active in raising monies and circulating antislavery petitions.

In the 1830s the interracial and radical nature of immediate abolitionism aroused intense opposition in both the North and South. Abolitionist mail was confiscated and burned by proslavery vigilantes in the South, and prominent politicians and merchants—"gentlemen of property and standing"—led mobs against abolitionist meetings, which were seen as "promiscuous" because they included women and blacks. In 1834 anti-abolition sentiments led to a riot in New York City that resulted in the torching of black churches and the Tappans' home. In 1837 the abolitionist editor Elijah Lovejoy was killed defending his press in Alton, Illinois. Garrison himself barely escaped the anger of an anti-abolition mob in Boston. Finally, the United States Congress instituted a "Gag Rule," temporarily silencing Congressional discussion of abolitionist petitions from 1836 to 1844.

Nevertheless by 1838, the AASS, with its large numbers of paid antislavery agents and more than a million pieces of abolitionist literature, comprised 1,346 local antislavery societies with around 100,000 members. A new cadre of black abolitionists, most of them former slaves, became prominent in the movement and the country at large. The most famous of these was Frederick Douglass, whose slave narrative and oratory established him as one of the foremost leaders of the movement. Douglass began his abolitionist career as a Garrisonian, but he split with Garrison over the issue of politics by the early 1850s. While Garrison denounced the Constitution as a "compact with the devil and covenant with hell" and advocated "No Union with Slaveholders," Douglass supported antislavery parties and saw the constitution as antislavery. Other black abolitionists included the black doctor James McCune Smith, William Cooper Nell, William Wells Brown, James W. C. Pennington, Samuel Ringgold Ward, and Henry Highland Garnet. Pennington and Brown wrote narratives describing their experiences as slaves, while Ward and Garnet became famous orators. Garnet is best remembered for his 1843 *Address to the Slaves*, in which he urged slave resistance.

Most abolitionists in the 1840s and 1850s justified the use of violence in self-defense in controversies over the rendition of fugitive slaves and the kidnapping of free blacks. David Ruggles, the black abolitionist who in 1835 had founded the New York Vigilance Committee to defend fugitive slaves and protect free blacks from kidnappers, stated that self-defense was the first law of nature. The Fugitive Slave Law of 1850 mandated citizen participation in chasing and apprehending alleged fugitive slaves anywhere in the nation. Hundreds of fugitives fled to Canada in fear, and this sweeping law gave birth to active opposition among free blacks and abolitionists. In 1851 in Christiana, Pennsylvania, a group of free blacks defended four runaway slaves who were being pursued by their owner, who was from Maryland. The slave owner and a federal marshal were killed in the altercation. In Boston the abolitionist Thomas Wentworth Higginson and others managed to prevent the rendition of a number of runaway slaves. In Syracuse, New York, abolitionists succeeded in rescuing the slave Jerry McHenry, and in Ohio's Western Reserve district abolitionist "riots" made the law a dead letter in parts of the North that were strongholds of abolitionists and antislavery politics.

THE PRELUDE TO CIVIL WAR

Along with physical resistance, political resistance to slavery expanded. The annexation of Texas in 1845 and the Mexican-American War of 1846–1848 made slavery into a national political issue. Many northerners in Congress supported Pennsylvania Representative David Wilmot's attempt to restrict the expansion of slavery into the newly acquired Mexican territories. In the 1848 presidential elections, the newly formed Free Soil Party made antislavery a potent force in northern politics. Thus, thousands of readers were primed for the 1852 publication of Harriet Beecher Stowe's antislavery novel, *Uncle Tom's Cabin*. The novel was America's first runaway bestseller, with some 300,000 copies being sold in twelve months.

The passage of the Kansas-Nebraska Act of 1854 reignited the issue of slavery expansion into the west and led to a fierce and violent contest over the fate of Kansas between free state migrants and southern slaveholders. The antislavery and nonextensionist Republican Party was founded as a result of a new coalition between Free Soilers, Antislavery Whigs and Democrats, and political abolitionists. In the *Dred Scott* v. *Sandford* case of 1857, the U.S. Supreme Court essentially held that the Constitution did not curtail the rights of slaveholders to move their human property anyplace within the United States. The Court also declared that the rights enunciated in the Constitution did not apply to blacks because they were not American citizens. John Brown's failed 1859 raid on the federal armory at Harper's Ferry made him into an abolitionist martyr. The question of slavery became a part of the famous 1858 debates between the antislavery Republican congressman Abraham Lincoln and the Democrat Stephen A. Douglas, who were running against each other for one of the Senate seats from Illinois. The debates made Lincoln a national figure and paved the way for his successful presidential campaign in 1860.

Lincoln's election led to the secession of the states of the Deep South (South Carolina, Georgia, Mississippi, Alabama, Texas, Florida, and Louisiana), and the formation of the Confederacy would spell the doom of slavery. After the Confederates fired the first shot at Fort Sumter, inaugurating the American Civil War, four states from the Upper South (Virginia, North Carolina, Tennessee, and Arkansas) seceded. Abolitionists such as Wendell Phillips and Frederick Douglass, as well as Radical Republicans in Congress, pressured President Lincoln to make the war for the Union a war against slavery. In 1863 Lincoln not only issued the Emancipation

Proclamation, he also enlisted black men—some 130,000 of them former slaves—into the Union Army. In 1865 the Thirteenth Amendment to the Constitution finally ended racial slavery in the United States. The war, which cost around 600,000 American lives, resulted in the emancipation of four million enslaved Americans of color. Millions more were peacefully freed when slavery was abolished in Puerto Rico in 1873, in Cuba in 1886, and in Brazil in 1888.

By the end of the nineteenth century, racial slavery had ended in the New World. Among the causes of its demise was a general belief that chattel slavery was both an outmoded and morally unacceptable labor system. The efforts of countless abolitionists and slaves also helped governments to end one of the worst instances of human bondage in world history.

Throughout the Western Hemisphere, even though slavery had ended, the problem of race continued to bedevil former slave societies. Only in the United States did the legacy of abolitionism live on beyond the end of slavery. Following the Civil War, the United States became the only slave society to adopt a policy of systemic reconstruction based on interracial democracy. Unfortunately, the U.S. Reconstruction era, which lasted from 1865 until 1875, was overthrown, and, just as in other former slave societies, freed persons were subjected to new coercions and relegated to second-class citizenship. With the start of the U.S. civil rights movement in the twentieth century, and similar struggles elsewhere, the abolitionist dream of creating a society based on racial justice re-emerged. In the 1960s, civil rights workers, recalling the long history of the struggle for black equality, called themselves "the new abolitionists." Thus, while the abolitionists succeeded in ending slavery, if not racism, the legacy of their fight for racial justice lived on.

SEE ALSO *American Anti-Slavery Society; Cuffe, Paul; Douglass, Frederick; Dred Scott v. Sandford; Emancipation Proclamation; Forten, James; Garnet, Henry Highland; Garrison, William Lloyd; Indian Slavery; Phillips, Wendell; Slave Codes; Stowe, Harriet Beecher.*

BIBLIOGRAPHY

Abzug, Robert H. 1994. *Cosmos Crumbling: American Reform and the Religious Imagination.* New York: Oxford University Press.

Baronov, David. 2000. *The Abolition of Slavery in Brazil: The "Liberation" of Africans through the Emancipation of Capital.* Westport, CT: Greenwood Press.

Bender, Thomas. 1992. *The Antislavery Debate: Capitalism and Abolitionism as a Problem in Historical Interpretation.* Berkeley: University of California Press.

Bethell, Leslie. 1970. *The Abolition of the Brazilian Slave Trade: Britain, Brazil, and the Slave Trade Question, 1807–1869.* Cambridge, U.K.: Cambridge University Press.

Blackburn, Robin. 1988. *The Overthrow of Colonial Slavery, 1776–1848.* London: Verso.

Blight, David W. 1989. *Frederick Douglass' Civil War: Keeping Faith in Jubilee.* Baton Rouge: Louisiana State University Press.

Brown, Christopher Leslie. 2006. *Moral Capital: Foundations of British Abolitionism.* Chapel Hill: University of North Carolina Press.

Corwin, Arthur F. 1967. *Spain and the Abolition of Slavery in Cuba, 1817–1869.* Austin: University of Texas Press.

Craton, Michael. 1982. *Testing the Chains: Resistance to Slavery in the British West Indies.* Ithaca, NY: Cornell University Press.

Da Costa, Emilia Viotti. 1994. *Crowns of Glory, Tears of Blood: The Demerara Slave Rebellion of 1823.* New York: Oxford University Press.

Davis, David Brion. 2006. *Inhuman Bondage: The Rise and Fall of Slavery in the New World.* New York: Oxford University Press.

Drescher, Seymour. 2002. *The Mighty Experiment: Free Labor versus Slavery in British Emancipation.* New York: Oxford University Press.

Dubois, Laurent. 2004. *Avengers of the New World: The Story of the Haitian Revolution.* Cambridge, MA: Harvard University Press.

Foner, Eric. 1970. *Free Soil, Free Labor, Free Men: The Ideology of the Republican Party before the Civil War.* New York: Oxford University Press.

Hatch, Nathan O. 1989. *The Democratization of American Christianity.* New Haven, CT: Yale University Press.

Holt, Thomas C. 1992. *The Problem of Freedom: Race, Labor, and Politics in Jamaica and Britain, 1832–1938.* Baltimore, MD: Johns Hopkins University Press.

Jeffrey, Julie Roy. 1998. *The Great Silent Army of Abolitionism: Ordinary Women in the Antislavery Movement.* Chapel Hill: University of North Carolina Press.

Jennings, Lawrence C. 2000. *French Anti-Slavery: The Movement for the Abolition of Slavery in France, 1802–1848.* Cambridge, U.K.: Cambridge University Press.

Kraditor, Aileen S. 1969. *Means and Ends in American Abolitionism: Garrison and His Critics on Strategy and Tactics, 1834–1850.* New York: Pantheon.

McCarthy, Timothy Patrick, and John Stauffer, eds. 2006. *Prophets of Protest: Reconsidering the History of American Abolitionism.* New York: New Press.

Midgley, Clare. 1992. *Women against Slavery: The British Campaigns, 1780–1870.* London: Routledge.

Newman, Richard S. 2002. *The Transformation of American Abolitionism: Fighting Slavery in the Early Republic.* Chapel Hill: University of North Carolina Press.

Oostindie, Gert, ed. 1995. *Fifty Years Later: Antislavery, Capitalism, and Modernity in the Dutch Orbit.* Leiden, the Netherlands: KITLV Press.

Perry, Lewis. 1973. *Radical Abolitionism: Anarchy and the Government of God in Antislavery Thought.* Ithaca, NY: Cornell University Press.

Rael, Patrick. 2002. *Black Identity and Black Protest in the Antebellum North.* Chapel Hill: University of North Carolina Press.

Scott, Rebecca J. 1985. *Slave Emancipation in Cuba: The Transition to Free Labor, 1860–1899.* Princeton, NJ: Princeton University Press.

———, et al., eds. 1988. *Abolition of Slavery and the Aftermath of Emancipation in Brazil.* Durham, NC: Duke University Press.

Stauffer, John. 2002. *The Black Hearts of Men: Radical Abolitionists and the Transformation of Race.* Cambridge, MA: Harvard University Press.

Toplin, Robert Brent. 1971. *The Abolition of Slavery in Brazil.* New York: Atheneum.

Manisha Sinha

ADAPTATION

SEE *Human Biological Variation.*

ADOLESCENT FEMALE SEXUALITY

Public opinion of adolescent female sexuality in American society remains limited by the emphasis on adolescent sexual behaviors and the perceived negative outcomes of these behaviors (namely pregnancy). This understanding is also mired in racial stereotypes and myths about poor and working-class African-American, European-American, Latina, Native-American, and Asian-American girls. Although teen pregnancy and birth rates have steadily declined since 1990, the teen birth rate is two to ten times higher in the United States than in other industrialized nations (United Nations 2005). This appears to justify the U.S. government's spending of millions of dollars on programs to prevent adolescent pregnancy, particularly by promoting abstinence-only programs through the Adolescent Family Life Act passed in 1981 and amendments to the 1996 Welfare Reform Act. On the other hand, in 1994 the National Commission on Adolescent Sexual Health concluded that "society can enhance adolescent sexual health if it provides access to comprehensive sexuality education and affordable, sensitive, and confidential reproductive health care services, as well as education and employment opportunities" (p. 4). While this call for a broader framework than "just say no" was endorsed by forty-eight organizations across a wide spectrum of ideological and religious beliefs, it neglects the complexity of the sexuality of young women of different racial and class backgrounds, as well as the ways in which their ability to act in self-protective ways may be constrained by certain aspects of their culture; by historical, social, political, and economic forces; and by racist stereotypes.

AFRICAN-AMERICAN ADOLESCENT FEMALES

Explorations of adolescent sexuality are inextricably linked with the constructions of race, gender, and class that permeate the larger society and become embodied in the sexualized image of the black girl. As Joyce Ladner pointed out in her 1971 landmark study of African-American girls in St. Louis, "the total misrepresentation of the black community and the various myths which surround it can be seen in microcosm in the black female adolescent" (p. xxxiii).

The ubiquitous image of the promiscuous black teen mother has always belied the reality. The black girl in the United States is held accountable for the politically convenient crisis of teen pregnancy, even though more babies are born to white adolescent mothers (Roberts 2000). In addition, teen birth rates for African-American females fell by 41 percent, from 116.2 to 68.3, between 1990 and 2002, more than for any other ethnic group (see Table 1). It is true that more African-American high school girls report being sexually active (60.9 %) than do their Latina (46%) and European-American counterparts (43%) (CDC 2003). As a result, the black girl may be considered sexually irresponsible, though in 2000 the National Family Growth Survey found that African-American females aged fifteen to nineteen were also more likely (32%) than Latinas (23%) or European-American females (20%) to have a partner who used a condom. Moreover, the impact of the historical sexual oppression and violence visited upon enslaved African women, and later projected on and internalized within their daughters, has never been presented in the popular media or in government reports as a basis for the disproportionate rate of cumulative AIDS cases among young African-American and Latina females (83% in 2000). While further research in this area is still needed, there is evidence that some African-American female rape survivors recall stories of the rape of their ancestors during slavery, which may contribute to their sense that they do not deserve and cannot expect to be protected from sexual assault (Wyatt 1992). Popular media also does not acknowledge the fact that homicide, often at the hands of an intimate partner, was the second leading cause of death among African-American females aged fifteen to twenty-four in 2002 (CDC 2002). Sexual violence and coercion may also contribute to the fact that the percentage of African-American females having sexual intercourse before age thirteen (6.9%) is more than double the percentage of European-American females (3.4%) (CDC 2003).

EUROPEAN-AMERICAN ADOLESCENT FEMALES

In contrast to young African-American women, the middle-class European-American adolescent female has been

Teen Births and Birth Rates by Race and Hispanic Origin of Mother in the United States, 1990 and 2002

	Total	Non-Hispanic		
		White	Black	Hispanic
Number				
2002	425,493	179,511	101,494	127,900
1990	521,826	249,954	147,521	97,685
% Change	−18	−18	−31	+31
Birth Rate				
2002	43.0	28.5	68.3	83.4
1990	59.9	42.5	116.2	100.3
% Change	−28	−33	−41	−17

SOURCE: Adapted from Ventura, Stephanie J., Abma, J.C., Mosher, W.D., Henshaw, S.K. Recent trends in teenage pregnancy in the United States, 1990–2002. *Health E-stats.* Hyattsville, MD: National Center for Health Statistics. Released December 13, 2006.

Table 1.

portrayed as a paragon of asexual virtue, a parallel myth that originated during slavery. As the historian Nell Painter points out, "the sexually promiscuous black girl … represents the mirror image of the white woman on the pedestal. Together, white and black woman stand for woman as Madonna and as whore" (Rose 1998, p. 177). Unlike the African-American female who must counter the myth with representations of herself as chaste and superhuman to counteract her mythology, the liberated European-American adolescent female affirms her sexuality by daring to admit she enjoys sex. If the European adolescent female appears too sexual, she too may be marginalized, but the pejorative myth more commonly associated with the urban black girl does not pertain to all white girls, only those designated as "sluts" among them (White 2002).

Beginning in 1997, anecdotal newspaper headlines proclaiming that suburban middle-school girls were having oral sex provoked the anxiety of many European-American parents (Lewin 1997). In 2002, 12 percent of European-American females, 9.9 percent of Latinas, and 5.8 percent of African-American females aged fifteen through nineteen had had oral sex but not vaginal sex (Mosher 2005). These data signaled an alarm that young middle-class European-American women might be choosing oral sex to prevent pregnancy but not protecting themselves from sexually transmitted diseases (Remez 2000). In contrast, in the early 1990s African-American females were targeted for the distribution of Norplant, a long-term hormonal contraceptive that was taken off the market amid controversy in 2002 because it prevented pregnancy without protecting women from HIV infection (Roberts 2000). Thus, when middle class white girls have sex, there is concern for their health, but when poor and young women of color have sex, there is fear that they will get pregnant.

Socioeconomic class and level of education may be better predictors of early sexual debut and pregnancy for both African-American and European-American young women (Singh 2002). Middle-class European-American girls may have resources, such as access to abortion and adoption, available to them that minimize the consequences of their sexual activity, compared to poor and working-class young women of all races.

LATINA ADOLESCENT FEMALES

Despite the diversity in racial-identity and national origin that exists among Latinas, data on adolescent sexuality are typically reported for all Latinas as a group. Thus, differences in experiences that might be attributed to skin color or national origin cannot be assessed. In 1996 Deborah Tolman proclaimed that the black girl has been replaced by the more euphemistic "urban girl," who might also be Latina and is undoubtedly poor, but whose sexuality is still perceived as a singular threat to American values and the economy.

In 2000, Latina adolescents had a lower pregnancy rate than African-American teens (133 vs. 154 per 1,000 women), but they had the highest teen birth rate of all ethnic groups (94 per 1,000 women). The high Latina teen birth rate has been attributed to changing and conflicting cultural norms associated with assimilation, with discrimination in education and employment that contributes to poverty and reduces access to health care, with religious prohibitions on contraceptive use and abortion, and with the lack of culturally and linguistically competent health services, but it can also be traced to a history of class and race-based social policies.

Soon after the Hyde Amendment (passed by the U.S. Congress in 1976) severely restricted public funding for abortion, Rosie Jiménez, who could not afford an abortion from a licensed provider, became the first young woman to die from a back alley abortion since the *Roe v. Wade* decision of 1973. Her face soon adorned posters to repeal the Hyde Amendment, making her a martyr for the Latina reproductive rights movement. This was not the first time the government sought to control the reproductive choice of Latinas, however. It is estimated that one-third of Puerto Rican women of child-bearing age living in the mainland United States and Puerto Rico underwent government authorized forced sterilizations between the 1930s and 1970s (Lopez 1993).

NATIVE AMERICAN ADOLESCENT FEMALES

Native Americans represent the smallest racial/ethnic group in the United States, though there are more than 554 federally recognized tribal groups. Despite 1997 guidelines requiring all federally funded research to collect and disseminate data on all racial/ethnic categories, most national studies report data only for whites, blacks, and Hispanics/Latinos (Burrhansstipanov 2000). When data are available, Native Americans are not identified by their tribe and many are counted in other categories due to their mixed heritage. An 1837 Presidential Order calling for the violent removal of the Cherokee Nation to Oklahoma (commonly known as the Trail of Tears) has been compounded through a paper trail that removes the possibility of their descendants being properly acknowledged and counted.

The wholesale removal of Indian children from their families to boarding schools, which was initiated by the Bureau of Indian Affairs with the purpose of eradicating indigenous cultures, resulted in many young people being physically and sexually abused up until the 1970s.

Young Native women who must rely on the federal Indian Health Service have also been subjected to mass sterilizations without informed consent, and to extreme restrictions on their access to safe reproductive health care, according to a General Accounting Office report spearheaded by Senator James Abourezk of South Dakota. A former Northern Cheyenne chief tribal judge heard the case of two fifteen-year-old Native girls who were sterilized during what they were told were tonsillectomy operations (Smith 2000), and thirty-six Native women under age twenty-one were sterilized in an Indian Health Service hospital between 1972 and 1974 (Akwesasne 1974).

New Futures School for Teen Mothers. *The New Futures School, in Albuquerque, New Mexico, provides an education to pregnant teens and teenage mothers in a supportive environment, preparing them to participate economically in society.* STEPHEN FERRY/GETTY IMAGES.

ASIAN-AMERICAN AND PACIFIC ISLANDER ADOLESCENT FEMALES

Like their Native American counterparts, young Asian-American women are underrepresented in research reports on adolescent sexuality and reproductive health. Based on the available national data, Asian-American adolescent women have lower pregnancy and birth rates compared to other young women, though the variation across specific Asian ethnic groups frequently goes underreported. For example, despite the popular image of young Asian women as the "model minority," according to the National Asian Pacific American Women's Forum (2005), Laotian young women are reported to have the highest teen birth rate (19%) of any racial or ethnic minority group in the state of California in 2000.

Reminiscent of the African women and girls who experienced sexual abuse during the trans-Atlantic slave trade, many young immigrant women in the United States are the victims of modern-day sexual trafficking. The image of women of Asian descent as passive and servile geisha girls, mail-order brides, or sexual exotics is reflected in the high rates of sexual trafficking of young women from some of the poorest Southeast Asian countries (Hynes 2000).

LESBIAN, BISEXUAL, AND TRANSGENDER ADOLESCENT FEMALES OF COLOR

Adolescence is a time for young people to explore and establish their sexual identities. Societal and cultural homophobia and heterosexism—and the related discrimination that ensues—can place young people who show signs of, or are perceived as showing signs of, same-sex attraction at increased risk for violence, mental illness, and substance abuse. Young lesbians of color may be at particular risk for rape, pregnancy, and sexually transmitted diseases such as HIV. Lesbian, gay, bisexual, and transgender (LGBT) youth of color also risk family rejection and violence, as indicated by a survey in which 61 percent of LGBT youth reported they had been victims of violence from family members (Transitions 2002). LGBT youth of color may also experience bullying and harassment in school and in the community because of both racism and their sexual orientation.

Adolescent sexuality has been framed by the intersection of race, class, gender, and sexual orientation in the public media, in social policies, and in program interventions. A full understanding of adolescent sexuality requires more complete and specific data within and across ethnic groups to correct the myths and stereotypes that continue to demonize, erase or censor adolescent female sexuality. Also necessary is an analysis of how the mechanisms of oppression based on race, gender, class and sexual orientation undermine adolescent sexual and reproductive health. Only through these types of efforts can all adolescents living in America have the opportunity to reconstruct their own sexual identities and exercise their reproductive choice in safe and loving ways.

SEE ALSO *Forced Sterilization; Forced Sterilization of Native Americans; HIV and AIDS; Latina Gender, Reproduction, and Race; Motherhood; Reproductive Rights; Sexuality.*

BIBLIOGRAPHY

Burrhansstipanov, Linda, and Delight E. Satter. 2000. "Office of Management and Budget Racial Categories and Implications for American Indians and Alaska Natives." *American Journal of Public Health* 90 (11): 1720–1723.

Centers for Disease Control and Prevention. 2002. "10 Leading Causes of Death, United States, 2002–2003." Hyattsville, MD: National Center for Injury Prevention and Control. Available from http://webapp.cdc.gov/cgi-bin/broker.exe.

Centers for Disease Control and Prevention. 2004. "Youth Risk Behavior Surveillance—United States, 2003." *Morbidity and Mortality Weekly Report* 53 (SS-2): 1–96. Available from http://www.cdc.gov/mmwr/preview/mmwrhtml/ss5302a1.htm.

Coles, Robert, and Geoffrey Stokes. 1985. *Sex and the American Teenager*. New York: Harper and Row.

Hynes, H. Patricia, and Janice G. Raymond. 2002. "Put in Harm's Way: The Neglected Health Consequences of Sex Trafficking in the United States." In *Policing the National Body: Race, Gender, and Criminalization*, edited by Jael Silliman and Anannya Bhattacharjee, 197–229. Cambridge, MA: South End Press.

Kaplan, Elaine Bell. 1997. *Not Our Kind of Girl: Unraveling the Myths of Black Teenage Motherhood*. Berkeley: University of California Press.

Ladner, Joyce A. 1971. *Tomorrow's Tomorrow: The Black Woman*. Garden City, NY: Doubleday.

Lewin, Tamar. 1997. "Teen-Agers Alter Sexual Practices, Thinking Risks Will Be Avoided." *New York Times*, April 5.

Lopez, Iris Ofelia. 1993. "Agency and Constraint: Sterilization and Reproductive Freedom among Puerto Rican Women in New York City." *Urban Anthropology and Studies of Cultural Systems* 22 (3/4): 299.

Mosher, William D., Anjani Chandra, and Jo Jones. 2005. "Sexual Behavior and Selected Measures: Men and Women 15–44 Years of Age, United States, 2002." Hyattsville, MD: National Center for Health Statistics. Available from http://www.cdc.gov/nchs/products/pubs/pubd/ad/361-370/ad362.htm.

National Asian Pacific American Women's Forum. 2005. "Expanding Reproductive Choice for Young APA Women: A Fact Sheet." Washington, DC: NAPAWF. Available from http://www.napawf.org.

National Commission on Adolescent and Sexual Health. 1995. "Facing Facts: Sexual Health for America's Adolescents." New York: Sexuality Information and Education Council of the United States. Available from http://www.seicus.org.

Papillo, Angela, Kerry Franzatta, Jennifer Manlove, et al. 2002. *Facts-at-a-Glance*. Washington, DC: Child Trends.

Remez, Lisa. 2000. "Oral Sex among Adolescents: Is It Sex or Is It Abstinence?" *Family Planning Perspectives* 32 (6): 298–304.

Roberts, Dorothy. 1997. *Killing the Black Body: Race, Reproduction, and the Meaning of Liberty*. New York: Vintage Books.

Rose, Tricia. 1998. "Race, Class, and the Pleasure/Danger Dialectic: Rewriting Black Female Teenage Sexuality in the Popular Imagination." *Renaissance Noire* 1 (3): 173–190.

Singh, Susheela, Jacqueline E. Darroch, and Jennifer J. Frost. 2001. "Socioeconomic Disadvantage and Adolescent Women's Sexual and Reproductive Behavior: The Case of Five Developed Countries." *Family Planning Perspectives*, 33 (6): 251–259.

Smith, Andrea. 2002. "Better Dead Than Pregnant: The Colonization of Native Women's Reproductive Health." In *Policing the National Body: Race, Gender, and Criminalization*, edited by Jael Silliman and Anannya Bhattacharjee, 123–146. Cambridge, MA: South End Press.

"Sterilization of Young Native Women Alleged at Indian Hospital." 1974. *Akwasasne Notes*, July.

Tolman, Deborah. 1996. "Adolescent Girls' Sexuality: Debunking the Myth of the Urban Girl." In *Urban Girls: Resisting Stereotypes, Creating Identities*, edited by Bonnie J. Ross Leadbeater and Niobe Way, 255–271. New York: New York University Press.

Transitions. "Stressors in the Lives of GLBTQ Youth." 2002. *Transitions* 14 (4). Available from www.advocatesforyouth.org/publications/transitions/transitions1404.htm.

United Nations. 2005. *Demographic Yearbook*, 2002. New York: United Nations.

U.S. General Accounting Office. 1976. *Investigation of Allegations Concerning the American Indian Health Service*. B-164031(5); HRD-77-3. Washington, DC: USGAO.

Ventura, Stephanie J., J.C. Abma, W.D. Mosher, and S.K. Henshaw. "Recent trends in teenage pregnancy in the United States, 1990-2002". *Health E-stats*. Hyattsville, MD: National Center for Health Statistics. Released December 13, 2006.

Ventura, Stephanie J., T. J. Matthews, and Brady E. Hamilton. 2001. "Births to Teenagers in the United States: 1940–2000." *National Vital Statistics Reports* 49 (10). Available from http://www.cdc.gov/nchs/data/nvsr/nvsr49/nvsr49_10.pdf.

White, Emily. 2002. *Fast Girls: Teenage Tribes and the Myth of the Slut*. New York: Scribner.

Wyatt, Gail E. 1992. 'The Sociocultural Context of African American and White American Women's Rape." *Journal of Social Issues* 48 (1): 77–91.

Lynn Roberts

AFFIRMATIVE ACTION

Affirmative action means taking positive steps to improve the material status of the less advantaged in society, usually through the provision of educational or economic benefits. In the United States, affirmative action usually takes place through the provision of government or private benefits in education, employment, or contracting. Affirmative action is controversial, particularly when the beneficiaries are women or people of color.

Affirmative action can take many forms—ranging from rigid quotas to targeted outreach meant to encourage minorities to apply—but all have in common the effort to increase the number of minorities in educational institutions, in the workplace, or in receiving contracts. Affirmative action programs differ in terms of how much weight they give to race as a factor in decision making and the extent to which they require results. For example, rigid quotas or set-asides that mandate that a certain percentage of beneficiaries be members of designated racial groups are very different from programs that use race as one factor among many in decision making. Likewise, there is a significant difference between the government's setting targets or goals and the government's mandating that there be specific results.

PROS AND CONS

Several justifications can be offered for affirmative action. Because, by definition, affirmative action involves working to assist society's less-advantaged members, one reason to promote affirmative action policies is to remedy the effects of past discrimination. This remedial justification of affirmative action recognizes that wrongs have been committed in the past and acknowledges a moral obligation to set things right. Opponents of affirmative action do not contest the moral obligation to remediate past harm. Their objection to remedial policies is frequently centered on the claim that specific affirmative action policies will not help those who have in fact been harmed, but will sweep too broadly and provide benefits to those who do not deserve them. Sometimes opponents of affirmative action argue that the harm to be remediated did not occur, or if it did occur—as in the case of racial discrimination in the United States—the harm has dissipated so that remedial measures are no longer necessary.

Another important justification for affirmative action is the so-called diversity rationale. Advocates for the diversity rationale argue that society as a whole benefits when affirmative action is used to maintain diverse schools, workplaces, and businesses. According to this argument, people from different backgrounds, cultures, and genders bring complementary skills that collectively enrich the places where they work and learn. Some affirmative action opponents reject the diversity argument outright. They claim there is no inherent social benefit to diverse workplaces or schools. Others accept the assertion that diversity is a social benefit, but express doubt over whether racial or gender characteristics provide a meaningful basis on which to assess diversity's social benefit.

This latter claim is related to what is arguably the most important objection to affirmative action. Opponents of affirmative action argue that it is wrong to allocate social benefits on the basis of immutable characteristics, such as race or gender. They claim that affirmative action is itself a form of racial/gender discrimination that discriminates against white males, contrary to historic forms of discrimination that were targeted against women and people of color. Thus the charge is often made that affirmative action is in fact "reverse discrimination." Supporters of affirmative action argue that the claim that affirmative action is discriminatory is overly formalistic. Although admitting that affirmative action does discriminate in a technical sense, supporters claim affirmative action is morally justified because its goal is not to harm the white majority, but to provide social justice for those who have been deprived of opportunity in the past.

THE ORIGINS OF AFFIRMATIVE ACTION

The concept of affirmative action can be traced to efforts after the Civil War to remedy the devastating effects of slavery. Government efforts, such as the creation of the Freeman's Bureau, unquestionably were forms of affirmative action in that they provided benefits to racial minorities. The term *affirmative action* apparently was first used in the National Labor Relations Act (29 U.S.C. §§151–169), adopted in 1935. The context was not race, but rather the affirmative duty of employers to remedy discrimination against union members and union organizers. Employers found to have engaged in such discrimination were required to remedy this by taking steps to ensure that the employers were in the same position in which they would have been had there been no discrimination.

The term apparently was first used in the race context by President John F. Kennedy. In 1961, three years prior to the enactment of the first major post-Reconstruction civil rights law, President Kennedy issued an executive order preventing race discrimination by federal agencies. Executive Order 10,925, promulgated in 1961, mandated "affirmative action to ensure that the applicants are employed, and that employees are treated during employment without regard to race, color, creed, or national origin." President Lyndon Johnson extended this policy, though without using the phase affirmative action, when he issued

Executive Order 11,246, demanding that all executive departments and agencies "shall establish and maintain a positive program of equal employment opportunity."

The 1964 Civil Rights Act (42 U.S.C. §2000[e]) implemented this prohibition of race discrimination by statute. Title II of the 1964 act prohibited places of public accommodation, such as restaurants or hotels, from discriminating based on race. Title VII prohibited employers from discriminating on the basis of race, gender, or religion. The act did not speak directly to affirmative action, but it did prohibit discrimination and open the door to claims that affirmative action was essential to meet the statutory prohibition against discrimination. It was quickly realized that prohibiting discrimination is not enough to achieve equality. Positive steps toward remedying the legacy of discrimination and enhancing diversity are essential. Thus affirmative action programs of all sorts began to proliferate and flourish in the 1970s.

LEGAL TREATMENT OF AFFIRMATIVE ACTION

U.S. courts have addressed the question of whether the use of affirmative action to help a disadvantaged group is as objectionable as the use of race or gender to harm or subjugate socially disfavored groups. Dominated since the 1980s by conservative judges appointed by Presidents Ronald Reagan and, later, George H. W. Bush, the courts have concluded that "any" use of affirmative action is a form of racial discrimination. In the courts, invidious racial discrimination must meet *strict scrutiny*; that is, it must be necessary to achieve a compelling government purpose. Strict scrutiny is a very rigorous level of judicial review that is rarely met. Indeed, Stanford law professor Gerald Gunther once famously claimed that strict scrutiny was "strict in theory, but fatal in fact." In *Adarand Constructors, Inc. v. Pena*, in 1995, the Supreme Court said: "All racial classifications, imposed by whatever federal, state, or local governmental actor, must be analyzed by a reviewing court under strict scrutiny."

Those who are opposed to affirmative action argue that the Constitution requires that the government treat each person as an individual without regard to his or her race; strict scrutiny is used to ensure that this occurs. Justice Clarence Thomas, in *Adarand*, espoused this view: "In my mind, government-sponsored racial discrimination based on benign prejudice is just as noxious as discrimination inspired by malicious prejudice. In each instance, it is racial discrimination, plain and simple." Moreover, supporters of strict scrutiny for affirmative action argue that all racial classifications stigmatize and breed racial hostility, and therefore all should be subjected to strict scrutiny. Justice Sandra Day O'Connor stated: "Classifications based in race carry a danger of stigmatic harm. Unless they are strictly reserved for remedial settings, they may in fact promote notions of racial inferiority and lead to politics of racial hostility."

On the other side of the debate, supporters of affirmative action argue that there is a significant difference between the government's use of racial classifications to benefit minorities and the government's use of racial classifications to disadvantage minorities. There is a long history of racism and discrimination against minorities, but no similar history of persecution of whites. Those in favor of affirmative action point to the tremendous continuing disparities between blacks and whites in areas such as education, employment, and public contracting as necessitating remedial action.

Supporters also argue that there is a major difference between a majority discriminating against a minority and the majority discriminating against itself. John Hart Ely explains in a 1974 article:

> When the group that controls the decision making process classifies so as to advantage a minority and disadvantage itself, the reasons for being unusually suspicious, and consequently, employing a stringent brand of review are lacking. A White majority is unlikely to disadvantage itself for reasons of racial prejudice; nor is it likely to be tempted either to underestimate the needs and deserts of Whites relative to those of others, or to overestimate the cost of devising an alternative classification that would extend to certain Whites the disadvantages generally extended to Blacks.

In the Rehnquist court of the 1990s the Supreme Court was split, five to four, between these two views. The majority—Chief Justice William Rehnquist, and Justices O'Connor, Antonin Scalia, Anthony Kennedy, and Thomas—adopted strict scrutiny in evaluating racial classifications benefiting minorities. The dissenters—Justices John Paul Stevens, David Souter, Stephen Breyer, and Ruth Bader Ginsburg—would use intermediate scrutiny, a less stringent standard of review.

THE SUPREME COURT'S TREATMENT OF AFFIRMATIVE ACTION

The Court first considered the issue of affirmative action in *Regents of the University of California v. Bakke*. Bakke involved a challenge to the University of California at Davis Medical School's set-aside of sixteen slots in the entering class of one hundred for minority students. There was no majority opinion for the Supreme Court. Four justices—William Brennan, Byron White, Thurgood Marshall, and Harry Blackmun—said that intermediate scrutiny was the appropriate test for racial classifications benefiting minorities, and voted to uphold the University of California at Davis Medical School's affirmative action program.

Four justices—Stevens, Warren Burger, Potter Stewart, and Rehnquist—concluded that the affirmative action program violated Title VI of the 1964 Civil Rights Act, which prohibited discrimination by institutions receiving federal funds. They did not reach the constitutional issue or discuss the level of scrutiny.

Finally, Justice Powell, writing only for himself, said that strict scrutiny should be used for affirmative action. He said that "racial and ethnic distinctions of any sort are inherently suspect and thus call for the most exacting judicial examination." Powell concluded that the set-aside was unconstitutional, but that it *was* permissible for race to be used as *one* factor in admissions decisions to enhance diversity. Thus, the vote was 5 to 4 invalidating the set-aside—Powell, Stevens, Burger, Rehnquist, and Stewart voting for this conclusion—but 5 to 4 that it is permissible for universities to use race as a factor in admissions to increase diversity—Powell, Brennan, Marshall, White, and Blackmun coming to this conclusion.

Two years later, in *Fullilove v. Klutznick*, the Supreme Court again considered an affirmative action program but did not produce a majority opinion. The Court upheld a federal law that required that 10 percent of federal public works monies given to local governments be set aside for minority-owned businesses. Chief Justice Burger, in an opinion joined by Justices White and Powell, concluded that the affirmative action program was justified to remedy past discrimination, but said that the "opinion does not adopt, either expressly or implicitly, the formulas of analysis articulated in cases such as *University of California Regents v. Bakke*."

Three Justices Marshall, Brennan, and Blackmun concurred in the judgment to uphold the affirmative action program, but argued again that intermediate scrutiny should be used for racial classifications serving a remedial purpose. Finally, on the other hand, three Justices Stewart, Rehnquist, and Stevens dissented and said that strict scrutiny was the appropriate test. It was not until 1989, in *Richmond v. J. A. Croson Company*, that the Supreme Court expressly held that strict scrutiny should be used in evaluating state and local affirmative action programs. The Court invalidated a Richmond, Virginia, plan to set aside 30 percent of public works monies for minority-owned businesses. Five Justices O'Connor, Rehnquist, White, Kennedy, and Scalia wrote or joined in opinions declaring that strict scrutiny was the appropriate test in evaluating such affirmative action plans. As Justice Marshall lamented in his dissenting opinion: "Today, for the first time, a majority of the Court has adopted strict scrutiny as its standard of Equal Protection Clause review of race-conscious remedial measures."

But a year later, in *Metro Broadcasting, Inc. v. Federal Communications Commission*, the Supreme Court held that congressionally approved affirmative action programs only need to meet intermediate scrutiny. The Supreme Court, in a 5 to 4 decision, upheld FCC policies that gave a preference to minority-owned businesses in broadcast licensing. The majority expressly said: "We hold that benign race-conscious measures mandated by Congress, even if those measures are not 'remedial' in the sense of being designed to compensate victims of past governmental or society discrimination, are constitutionally permissible to the extent that they serve important governmental objectives within the power of Congress and are substantially related to the achievement of those objectives."

Justice Brennan wrote the majority opinion in *Metro Broadcasting*, joined by Justices White, Marshall, Blackmun, and Stevens. Justices O'Connor, Kennedy, Scalia, and Rehnquist dissented. Between *Metro Broadcasting*, in 1990, and *Adarand Constructors, Inc. v. Pena*, in 1995, four of the Justices in the majority, but none of the Justices in the dissent, resigned from the Court. In *Adarand*, the four dissenters from *Metro Broadcasting* were joined by Justice Thomas to create a majority to overrule it. The Court thus concluded that "federal racial classifications, like those of a State, must serve a compelling governmental interest, and must be narrowly tailored to further that interest."

In its affirmative action decisions in the first decade of the 2000s, the Supreme Court reaffirmed that strict scrutiny is the test for affirmative action but held that colleges and universities may use race as a factor in admissions decisions to benefit minorities and enhance diversity. In *Grutter v. Bollinger*, in a 5-4 decision, with Justice O'Connor writing for the majority, the Court upheld the University of Michigan Law School's affirmative action program. The Court ruled that colleges and universities have a compelling interest in creating a diverse student body and that they may use race as one factor, among many, to benefit minorities and enhance diversity. In a companion case, *Gratz v. Bollinger*, the Court, 6-3, invalidated an affirmative action program for undergraduate admissions that added twenty points to the applications for minority students. In an opinion by Chief Justice Rehnquist, the Court ruled that the undergraduate program was not sufficiently "narrowly tailored" to meet the strict scrutiny used for government racial classifications. In essence, the Court adhered to the position articulated by Justice Lewis Powell in *Regents of the University of California v. Bakke* a quarter century earlier: Diversity is a compelling interest in education

Rallying for Affirmative Action. *A Bridgeport University student carries a sign as part of a demonstration outside the U.S. Supreme Court on April 1, 2003, when the Court was hearing arguments on the University of Michigan's admission policy. The Court would later rule that the university can consider race when considering applicants for admission.* ALEX WONG/GETTY IMAGES.

and universities may use race as a factor to ensure diversity, but quotas or numerical quantification of benefits is impermissible.

Is this a distinction that makes a difference? Practically speaking, can colleges and universities effectively add points so long as it is not done explicitly and officially? Is there really a difference between a college having a set-aside and a college using race as a factor in admissions decisions and keeping track of the number of minority students to ensure "critical mass"? Colleges and universities long have valued diversity in education; it always has been easier for a person from Wyoming or Montana to get into Harvard or Yale than an applicant with the same qualifications from Boston or New York. Individuals with special skills, like making downfield tackles or shooting jump shots, long have been admitted to college with lower grades and test scores. These variables generally are not quantified. The Court's affirmative action cases stand for the proposition that racial diversity matters, too, and that it should be treated like other factors considered in ensuring a diverse class. Any quantification, in terms of adding points or using a set-aside, seems arbitrary and inflexible.

The bottom line from the Supreme Court's affirmative action decisions over a quarter of a century is that any use of racial classifications, whether to benefit or disadvantage minorities, must meet strict scrutiny and be shown to be necessary to achieve a compelling government interest. The Court regards remedying past discrimination and enhancing diversity in education as compelling goals. The Court has been clear that it rarely will allow quotas or set-asides, but it will allow educational institutions to use race as one factor in admissions decisions to benefit minorities.

POLITICAL AND SOCIAL DEBATES

Affirmative action has been tremendously divisive. Opponents of affirmative action embrace the noble-sounding rhetoric of color-blindness and maintain that it is wrong for a person to lose out on something valuable solely because of his or her race. Supporters of affirmative action point out that it is designed to remedy a long history of discrimination and ensure racial equality in the long term.

One manifestation of the political and social debate is the initiatives that have been adopted across the country limiting affirmative action. In 1996 California voters passed Proposition 209, the so-called California Civil Rights Initiative. The initiative amended the state constitution to bar discrimination or preferences on the basis of race in government contracting, education, or employment. A similar initiative was adopted almost simultaneously in Washington state. In November 2006, Michigan voters passed Proposition 2, which was almost identical to California Proposition 209 in banning discrimination or preference based on race.

These initiatives reflect the public's disapproval of affirmative action. The rhetoric that the government should be color-blind is appealing and allows for people to limit (or eliminate) affirmative action while feeling noble. On the other hand, those who believe that affirmative action is essential to remedy past discrimination and achieve diversity have had a hard time overcoming the impression that such programs are reverse discrimination.

THE FUTURE

Affirmative action remains enormously controversial, and political and legal battles over the issue are sure to continue. In the courts, challenges to affirmative action programs may gain additional momentum with a change in the composition of the Supreme Court. With the departure of Justice O'Connor from the High Court, opponents of affirmative action are sure to look for test cases to bring the issue back for reconsideration. The Supreme Court has limited, but not ended, affirmative action as reflected in the *Grutter* decision. The survival of government affirmative action programs is a topic likely to be considered again in the years ahead.

SEE ALSO *Color-Blind Racism; Labor Market; Symbolic and Modern Racism.*

BIBLIOGRAPHY

CASES

Adarand Constructors, Inc. v. Pena, 515 U.S. 200 (1995).

Fullilove v. Klutznick, 448 U.S. 448 (1980).

Gratz v. Bollinger, 539 U.S. 244 (2003).

Grutter v. Bollinger, 539 U.S. 306 (2003).

J. A. Croson v. City of Richmond, 488 U.S. 469 (1989).

Metro Broadcasting, Inc. v. Federal Communications Commission, 497 U.S. 547 (1990).

Regents of the University of California v. Bakke, 438 U.S. 265 (1978).

ARTICLES

Bergmann, Barbara R. 1996. *In Defense of Affirmative Action*. New York: Basic Books.

Ely, John Hart. 1974. "The Constitutionality of Reverse Racial Discrimination." *University of Chicago Law Review* 41 (4): 723–741.

Lempert, Richard. 1984. "The Force of Irony: On the Morality of Affirmative Action and *United Steelworkers v. Weber*." *Ethics* 95 (1): 86–89.

Rosenfeld, Michel. 1989. "Decoding Richmond: Affirmative Action and the Elusive Meaning of Constitutional Equality." *Michigan Law Review* 87 (7): 1729–1794.

Erwin Chemerinsky

AFRICA: BELGIAN COLONIES

Belgium created two colonies in Africa: the entities now known as the Democratic Republic of the Congo (formerly the Republic of Zaire) and the Republic of Rwanda, previously Ruanda-Urundi, a former German African colony that was given to Belgium to administer after the defeat of Germany in World War I. The scramble for colonies was the brainchild of Leopold II, king of Belgium.

HISTORY OF BELGIAN COLONIZATION

Belgium itself had gained independence in 1831 when it broke away from the Netherlands and became a new nation. The second king of Belgium, Leopold II, was a very ambitious man who wanted to personally enrich himself and enhance his country's prestige by annexing and colonizing lands in Africa. In 1865 he succeeded his father, Leopold I, to the Belgian throne. In 1876 he commissioned Sir Henry Morton Stanley's expedition to explore the Congo region. This exploration led initially to the establishment of the Congo Free State. The new colony comprised a land bigger than western Europe and seventy-four times larger than Belgium, and belonged to Leopold II as a personal possession. He proclaimed himself king-sovereign of Congo Free State at a time when France, Britain, Portugal, and Germany also had colonies in the area. In 1885 Leopold II secured U.S. recognition of his personal sovereignty over the Congo Free State.

Leopold II was absolute ruler of Congo. His rule was brutal and millions of Congolese died as a result. By 1895 the British press started to expose Leopold II's atrocities in Congo. In 1897 a Swedish missionary told a London meeting how Leopold's soldiers were rewarded by the number of Congolese hands they amputated as punishment to native workers for failure to work hard enough. By 1899 the British vice consul confirmed and further reported the brutality of Leopold's misrule in Congo. Finally in 1908, Leopold was forced to hand over the Congo Free State, his personal fiefdom, to the Belgian state.

THE ADMINISTRATION OF CONGO BY THE BELGIANS (1908–1960)

The takeover of the administration by the Belgian government brought some improvements in the lives of the Congolese peoples, who had suffered untold hardships under Leopold II and his private militia. There were slight improvements in the everyday economic and social life of the Congolese that were comparable to conditions in other European colonies in Africa. The Belgian colonial administration built some schools, railways, roads, plantations, mines, industrial areas, and airports. Despite the modest improvements in the lives of the Congolese, the Belgians created two separate societies in the Congo: the whites and the natives. The whites had all the luxuries, and the native Africans lacked everything. It was an apartheid type of social and political system. All the major decisions concerning the Congo were made in Brussels, and the Congolese were not allowed to participate in the running of their own country.

In 1955 some of the few Congolese educated-elites organized a resistance to the lack of democracy and the apartheid policies of the Belgian colonial masters. The main aim of these so-called *évolués* in resisting the Belgian colonial administration was to redress the gross inequality

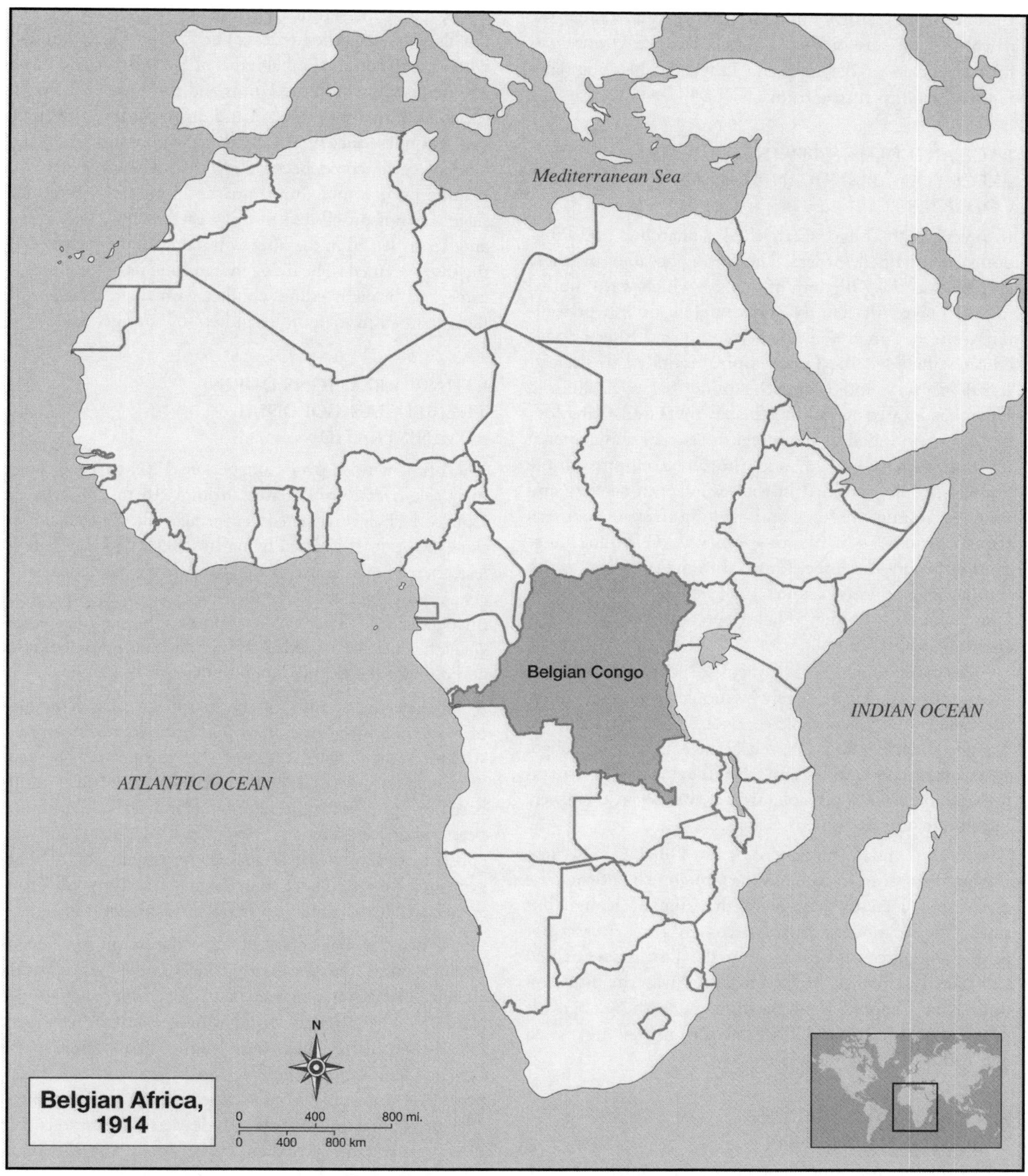

Belgian Africa, 1914. MAP BY XNR PRODUCTIONS. GALE.

that existed between the Europeans and the Africans. They used civil disobedience, strikes, and civil unrest against the Belgian colonialists. This uprising led to the disintegration of the Belgian colonial administration and helped in winning independence for the Congo in 1960.

HISTORY OF BELGIUM COLONIZATION OF RWANDA

Belgium's other colony, Rwanda, was an independent monarchy until the Germans annexed it in 1899 and made it part of German East Africa. Belgium seized Rwanda and

Burundi from Germany in 1916; two years later, after the defeat of Germany in World War I, Ruanda-Urundi was formally given to Belgium as a League of Nations (later United Nations) trust territory.

RACE AND ETHNICITY IN PRECOLONIAL AFRICAN BELGIAN COLONIES

In precolonial Congo, established monarchies and kingdoms maintained order. The most notable of these empires was the Kingdom of Kongo, which was founded in the fourteenth century and centered around present-day western Congo and northern Angola. Other notable empires included the Luba empire, founded in the sixteenth century and centered around Lakes Kisale and Upemba, located in central Shaba; the Lunda kingdom of Mwata, founded in the fifteenth century and centered in southwestern Congo; and the Kuba empire of the Shonga people, founded in the seventeenth century and centered around the Kasai and Sankura rivers in southern Congo. Another notable kingdom was the Lunda kingdom of Nwata Kazembe, founded in the early eighteenth century and centered around the Luapula River near the Congo-Zambia border. There were other small Luba-Lunda states in Congo.

Relations among the Congolese peoples during the precolonial period were largely harmonious. Through intermarriage and socioeconomic contacts, interethnic strife was benign. These kingdoms, especially the Kingdom of Kongo, were comparably wealthy, and when the standard of living is high, people tend to get along well. Nevertheless, there were interethnic wars on some occasions.

In 1482 the Portuguese navigator Diogo Cão became the first European to come to the Congo. The Portuguese established a relationship with the king of Kongo but stayed in the modern Angolan coastal areas. It was not until the eighteenth century that the Portuguese gained substantial influence in Congo. This was the situation until King Leopold II of Belgium made the Congo his personal possession, and it became the only colony owned and run by a single individual.

RACE AND ETHNICITY IN PRECOLONIAL RWANDA

Before the European incursion into Rwanda and the Belgian colonization, Rwanda was united under the central leadership of an absolute Tutsi monarchy. The people, although classified as Hutu, Tutsi, and Twa, essentially spoke the same language. They also shared the same culture, ate the same or similar foods, and practiced the same religion.

Precolonial Rwanda under the monarchy was highly stratified. The aristocracy, who were essentially the Tutsi, owned all the land and earned tributes from the farmers, who were mainly Hutu. Whereas the Hutus were farmers, the Tutsis were cattle herders. The Twa or the "pygmies," who were the original inhabitants of Rwanda, were outcasts and despised by both the Hutus and the Tutsis. There was social mobility (both upward and downward) in this stratified Rwandese society. A rich Hutu who purchased a large herd of cattle could become a Tutsi, while a Tutsi who became poor would drop into the Hutu caste. Intermarriage was not prohibited in this caste system. Both Hutus and Tutsis served in the king's military. All the members of the castes seemed to be living in harmony until the Belgians came and brought ethnic conflict with them. These conflicts resulted in many wars and episodes of genocide.

ETHNIC RELATIONS DURING THE BELGIAN COLONIAL ADMINISTRATION

The Belgians ruled over Congo from 1909 to 1960, while their rule over Rwanda lasted from 1918 to 1962. In the Congo, the Belgians created an apartheid-like system between the Europeans (Belgians) living in Congo and the Congolese, thereby marginalizing the Congolese in their own society. Among the Congolese, the Belgians used the strategy of divide and rule. They favored certain ethnic groups, especially the ones that would allow them to continue to colonize and plunder the rich natural resources of the Congo.

Before the coming of the Europeans, the Kingdom of Kongo had well-organized political and administrative structures that rivaled those of the Europeans. The economic system of the kingdom was organized into guilds based on agriculture and handicraft industries. The European incursion into the west coast of Africa and the consequent slave raids increased the migrations of refugees into Kongo. These migrations created myriad problems both at the time and in subsequent periods.

When the Belgians took over the administration of Rwanda from the Germans in 1918, they significantly changed the Rwandese system of government and social relations. The Belgians found willing elites to help them rule Rwanda. The Tutsis were willing collaborators to the Belgian colonization. The Belgians, in turn, gave the Tutsis privileged positions in politics, education, and business. The Belgians even took the few leadership positions that the Hutus had and gave them to the Tutsis. Specifically, in 1929, they eliminated all the non-Tutsi chiefs, and as a result the Hutus lost all their representation in the colonial government. A further blow came in 1933, when the Belgians issued identity cards to all Rwandans. These mandatory identity cards removed the fluidity from the Rwandan stratification (caste) system, thereby confining people permanently as Hutus, Tutsis, and "pygmies." The Belgians empowered the Tutsis so much that their exploitation of the Hutu majority reached new heights. As the independence of Rwanda became inevitable in the 1950s, however, the Belgians changed course and started to empower the Hutus by increasing their political and economic muscle and providing them access to modern education.

These conflicting measures brought anarchy and led to the creation of extreme groups—from both the majority Hutus and the minority Tutsis—wanting to protect the interests of their respective peoples. It was the activities of these extreme groups that led to the various episodes of genocide that reached appalling heights in 1994 with the killing of nearly one million people, mostly Tutsis and moderate Hutus, by extreme Hutus.

The first wave of genocide by the Hutus against the Tutsis took place earlier, however, under the administration of the Belgians in 1959. Like the 1994 genocide, it started when extremist Tutsis attacked a Hutu leader, and the Hutus retaliated by killing hundreds of Tutsis. In the Western press, this conflict was portrayed as a racial and cultural one, between the tall, aristocratic, pastoral Tutsis, and Hutus who were uneducated peasant farmers. That the Tutsi and Hutu were originally two castes of the same people, speaking a common language, and that the antagonism had been created by Belgian colonial forces for their own purposes, were facts somehow lost in the international dialogue.

To summarize, the ethnic rivalries and tensions in the former Belgian colonies of Congo and Rwanda that escalated following independence and continued into the twenty-first century had their roots in the Belgian colonial administration. It was during the Belgian colonial administration that the foundations for the postcolonial and present-day ethnic tensions and political instability were laid.

ETHNIC AND POLITICAL CONFLICTS IN POSTCOLONIAL BELGIAN COLONIES IN AFRICA

In the Congo, political instability started as soon as the Congolese gained their independence from the Belgians in 1960. Congo is a multiethnic country with about two hundred ethnic groups. Most of the ethnic groups speak languages of the widespread Bantu family: Kongo, Mongo, Luba, Bwaka, Kwango, Lulua, Luanda, and Kasai. There are also Nilotic-speaking peoples near Sudan and some "pygmies" in northeastern Congo. Although there were several political parties, the two most prominent were Joseph Kasavubu's ABAKO, a party based among the Kongo people, and Patrice Lumumba's Congolese National Movement. After the June 1960 elections, Lumumba became prime minister and Kasavubu the ceremonial president.

Immediately after independence on June 30, 1960, ethnic and personal rivalries—influenced by Belgium, other European nations, and the United States—sent the newly independent country into political crisis. On July 4, the army rebelled. Seven days later, Moise Tshombe, the provisional president of Katanga, in a move instigated by the Belgians, declared the mineral-rich Katanga province an independent country. Subsequent political problems led to military intervention by the Belgians, who claimed that they intervened to protect Belgian citizens from attack. On July 14, the United Nations Security Council authorized a force to help to establish order in the Congo, but this force was unable to bring the seceded Katanga province to order. As a result, Lumumba asked the Soviet Union to help him bring Katanga back to Congo. On September 5, President Kasavubu dismissed Lumumba as prime minister. Lumumba in turn dismissed the president, creating a political stalemate.

Joseph Mobutu, who later changed his name to Mobutu Sese Seko, was appointed army chief of staff by Lumumba. Taking advantage of the political conflict between the president and the prime minister, Mobutu encouraged the military to revolt. The United States and Belgium provided the money that Mobutu used to bribe the Congolese army to commit treason against their properly elected government. The United States, Belgium, and other Western governments aided Mobutu in overthrowing the government of Lumumba as part of their cold war rivalry with the communist bloc countries led by the Soviet Union. Mobutu was used as a Western stooge to stop an alleged communist incursion into Africa.

On January 17, 1961, the government of Moise Tshombe in Katanga, with the full support of the U.S. Central Intelligence Agency (CIA), murdered Lumumba and two of his associates in cold blood. Besides the cold war rivalry, the other main reason for killing Lumumba and supporting the secession in the provinces of Katanga and Kasai was for Belgians to secure controlling interests in the rich mineral resources of the Congo.

After the assassination of Lumumba, many governments ruled Congo in rapid succession: Évariste Kimba, Joseph Ileo, Cyrille Adoula, and Moise Tshombe. But in 1965, after ruling from behind the scenes for four years, Mobutu finally overthrew Kasavubu in a coup widely believed to be sponsored by the CIA. Mobutu ruled for thirty-one years and pauperized the Congo. Mobutu and his supporters were so corrupt and stole so much money from the Congolese people that his government was described as a kleptocracy, or government by thieves. When Laurent Kabila drove him from power in 1997, Mobutu's wealth deposited in foreign banks was in excess of $4 billion.

Despite Mobutu's dictatorship, relative peace reigned during most of his regime. In 1966 he renamed the Congolese cities of Léopoldville (Kinshasa), Stanleyville (Kisangani), and Elisabethville (Lubumbashi). In 1971, in a continuation of his Africanization policy, the

Congo River was renamed the Zaire River and consequently, Congo was renamed the Republic of Zaire.

In Rwanda, independence brought increased ethnic tensions because of the policies of the Belgian colonial administration. There had been vicious cycles of violence beginning in December 1963 when Hutus killed more than 10,000 Tutsis and sent about 150,000 into exile. The worst of the genocide took place in 1994 when nearly a million Rwandan citizens (mostly Tutsis and some moderate Hutus) were massacred. This well-planned genocide started when the Hutu presidents of Rwanda and Burundi were shot down, allegedly by Tutsi rebel soldiers. Hutus went on a rampage, killing Tutsis in their midst with the aim of exterminating them. The killing stopped only when Paul Kagame, with the help of Uganda, led a Tutsi army that drove the Hutu-led military into exile in neighboring Congo.

The Rwanda genocide of 1994 helped exacerbate ethnic and political tensions in the Congo. As the strategic importance of Mobutu disappeared with the end of the cold war, little or no attention was paid to the Congo. Mobutu in his bid to stay in power for life did not build a strong army. His inability to disarm the ex-Rwandan soldiers and perpetuators of the 1994 genocide who were now living in Congo led to the invasion of the Congo by a combined army of Tutsi-led governments of Rwanda, Burundi, and Uganda and the Congolese rebel leader Laurent Kabila. It was relatively easy for this army to overrun Congo. Mobutu first escaped to Togo and then to Morocco, where he died a few months later from cancer. On reaching Kinshasa in May 1997, Kabila declared himself president and changed the name of Zaire back to the Democratic Republic of the Congo.

Kabila's inability to disarm the Hutu militia and to share power with his former Tutsi allies led to war with his allies. In 1998 Rwanda, Burundi, and Uganda jointly invaded Congo, and Angola, Zimbabwe, Namibia, Chad, and the Sudan fought on the side of Kabila's Congo. This conflict has been labeled "Africa's war." Although fighting stopped in 1999, rebel groups continued their attacks on defenseless civilians and the Congolese central government. In 2001, when Kabila was assassinated by one of his bodyguards, he was succeeded by General Joseph Kabila, his son. The new leader signed a peace treaty with the rebel groups and appointed four vice presidents hailing from former rebel groups. In 2006 a new constitution was written and approved for the Third Republic, and elections were conducted with Joseph Kabila emerging as victorious. Rwanda also has a new constitution, and amnesty was granted for most of the Hutu genocide perpetrators. Since the 1994 genocide, Rwanda has successfully conducted both local and national elections.

Several Belgian colonial policies sowed the seeds of racial and ethnic rivalries that led to the killings of millions of Africans and also sent millions more into exile from the former Belgian colonies. First, the post-colonial political leaders of Congo and Rwanda continued the Belgian colonial policies. Second, these leaders exacerbated ethnic rivalries and tensions to stay in power. Third, most of the ethnic tensions in these countries are caused by rapid population growth and the fight for scarce resources by the leaders of the various ethnic groups. Fourth, European and American governments and the multinational business and interests have fueled ethnic conflicts in Africa's former Belgian colonies for their own purposes. For example, Belgian and other foreign interests engineer these conflicts so they can continue to loot the resources of Africa. Finally, the constant interventions of the Belgians in the affairs of their former colonies of Congo and Rwanda have made ethnic and political rivalries worse. In spite of this legacy of the colonial period, political developments in the Congo and Rwanda (peace agreements, new constitutions, and new elections) show that there is a new hope for the former African colonies of Belgium.

BIBLIOGRAPHY

Cawthorne, Nigel. 2004. *Tyrants: History's 100 Most Evil Despots and Dictators*. New York: Barnes and Nobles.

Davidson, Basil. 1972. *Africa: History of a Continent*, rev. ed. New York: Macmillan.

———. 1992. *The Black Man's Burden: Africa and the Curse of the Nation-State*. New York: Times Books.

Ekwe-Ekwe, Herbert. 2006. *Biafra Revisited*. Dakar, Senegal: African Renaissance.

Forrest, Joshua B. 2004. *Subnationalism in Africa: Ethnicity, Alliances, and Politics*. Boulder, CO: Lynne Rienner.

Handelman, Howard. 2006. *The Challenge of Third World Development*, 4th ed. Upper Saddle River, NJ: Pearson/Prentice Hall.

Harris, Joseph E. 1998. *Africans and Their History*, 2nd ed. New York: Penguin.

Kanyandago, Peter, ed. 2002. *Marginalized Africa: An International Perspective*. Nairobi, Kenya: Paulines Publications Africa.

Sadowski, Yahya. 1998. "Ethnic Conflict." *Foreign Policy* No. 111: 12–23.

John Obioma Ukawuilulu

AFRICA: BRITISH COLONIES

Colonialism by its very nature has racist connotations. British colonialism in particular was structured as a dictatorship, using violence to pacify the colonial subjects and to maintain order. There was no input from the colonized in the way that they were governed: The British Colonial Office in London made all the decisions concerning the colonies. The British also tended to choose a preferred ethnic group over all the others in the countries that they colonized. These preferred groups, usually a conservative minority within the country, were supported to the extent that they worked against the interests of their fellow Africans. For example, the British chose the Arab minority to lord it over the majority Africans in the Sudan and favored the Fulani in Nigeria. The British preferred ethnic societies with dictatorial and hierarchical systems like their own, and they recruited members of these ethnicities in disproportionate numbers into the colonial military. At independence, these soldiers often staged coups and removed the democratically elected civilian governments of their countries.

HISTORY OF BRITISH COLONIAL RULE IN AFRICA

It is important to note that the advent of British colonization of Africa coincided with the era of scientific racism as represented by social Darwinism (survival of the fittest). The British believed that because they had superior weaponry and were therefore more technologically advanced than the Africans, that they had a right to colonize and exploit the resources of the Africans in the name of promoting civilization. But it is inherently contradictory for an invading force to usher in "civilization."

Britain had many colonies in Africa: in British West Africa there was Gambia, Ghana, Nigeria, Southern Cameroon, and Sierra Leone; in British East Africa there was Kenya, Uganda, and Tanzania (formerly Tanganyika and Zanzibar); and in British South Africa there was South Africa, Northern Rhodesia (Zambia), Southern Rhodesia (Zimbabwe), Nyasaland (Malawi), Lesotho, Botswana, and Swaziland. Britain had a strange and unique colonial history with Egypt. The Sudan, formerly known as the Anglo-Egyptian Sudan, was jointly ruled by Egypt and Britain, because they had jointly colonized the area. The joint colonial administration of the Sudan by Egypt and Britain was known as the condominium government. The British system of government affected the type of racial or ethnic problems that all of Britain's African colonies had during the colonial period, the immediate postcolonial period, and from the 1980s into the twenty-first century.

PRECOLONIAL RACIAL AND ETHNIC RELATIONS IN BRITISH COLONIAL AFRICA

Ethnic rivalries were not serious in precolonial Africa. The majority of ethnic nations lived in their independent small polities. There were, however, some large conquering empires: the Bugandan Empire in Uganda; the Zulus in South Africa; the Mwene Mutapa Empire of the Shona people in Zambia, or Great Zimbabwe; the Benin Empire; the kingdoms of the Yoruba (Ife, Oyo, and Ibadan); the Ashanti in Ghana; the Fulani Empire in northern Nigeria, which even tried to extend into regions of Sierra Leone; the Kanem-Bornu Empire around the Lake Chad area of northern Nigeria; and the Igbo of southeastern Nigeria, who lived in small democratic states with the few exceptions of some representative monarchies. But things changed with the British Empire's entrance into Africa.

TYPES OF BRITISH COLONIAL RULE IN AFRICA

The British employed various systems of governance in their African colonies. These were through the agency of (1) trading companies, (2) indirect rule, (3) the settler rule, and then the unique joint rule of the Sudan with the Egyptians known as the (4) condominium government.

Trading Companies. In the early years of colonialism, Britain granted private companies large territories to administer in Africa. Companies such as the United African Company and United Trading Company in West Africa, the Imperial British East Africa Company, and the British South Africa Company were formed by businesspersons who were interested only in exploiting and plundering the rich natural resources of the territories of Africa that they were allowed to govern. Illiterate African leaders were conned into signing over their sovereignty to the British. The British government provided charters for these companies, but the companies themselves paid for the expenses incurred in establishing and administering the colonies. To support their administrations, the companies set up their own systems of taxation and labor recruitment.

The Imperial British East Africa Company, founded in 1888, colonized Kenya for Britain, ruling there until 1893. The British South Africa Company, established in 1889 under the control of Cecil John Rhodes, used excessive force and coercion to colonize and rule Nyasaland (present-day Malawi), Northern Rhodesia (present-day Zambia), and Southern Rhodesia (present-day Zimbabwe); the company reigned over these colonies until 1923. None of these private companies were very profitable, so the British government eventually took them over.

Company rule on behalf of Britain was very harsh on the Africans as the companies practiced an apartheid-like system during their rule. In spite of the numerous blunders of these companies in running colonies in Africa, the British government allowed most of them to rule for a very long time. Interested only in making profits, the companies were ill suited to administer territories or colonies, and they found that doing so was neither easy nor profitable. To increase their profit margins, they employed racist and draconian policies. Unfortunately, the adverse policies they enacted were continued when the British government took over administration of the colonies. These policies had far-reaching effects that lasted into the postcolonial period.

Indirect Rule. Indirect rule, the brainchild of the British colonial administrator Frederick Lugard, became the main system the British used to administer their African colonies. The British used African traditional rulers to work on their behalf and help subjugate their fellow Africans. Although these Africans were nominally "ruling," the actual decisions rested with the British colonial officers. Lugard first experimented with indirect rule in northern Nigeria where the Fulani had established the Sokoto caliphate and emirship. As the system seemed to have worked in northern Nigeria, Lugard exported the system to southern Nigeria where it failed woefully in the Igbo areas of eastern Nigeria. Still Lugard took the system to East Africa where it again failed. Lugard wrongly believed that all the African societies were monarchies and that those that were not could become so with the establishment of chiefdoms.

In West Africa, the British had no pretensions about their attitude toward their colonies and colonial subjects. Britain did not want to be paternalistic like the French colonialists, and it did not practice the assimilation policies of the French. Thus, Britain did not attempt to make English persons out of the Africans. Although the British claimed that they used the indirect rule system because they wanted to preserve their colonies' indigenous cultures, the main reason was to minimize the cost of running the colonies while at the same time maximizing the exploitation of the resources. Britain ended up inventing new cultures for its colonies, thereby destroying the indigenous cultures. The British created new leaders (chiefs) who were invariably corrupt and who did not have the mandate of the Africans and were consequently not respected by the people they governed. Thus, this strategy more often than not failed woefully, as in Igboland in Nigeria.

In northern Nigeria, where the indirect system seemed to have worked, the ethnic relations were horrible. The Fulani emirs were very autocratic and corrupt. Non-Fulani and non-Muslims rioted many times to protest the misrule of the Fulani over them. Another aspect of misrule was the creation of synthetic political groupings by forcing the amalgamation of ethnic groups and native nations that had previously been independent, forming a polity dominated by British interests. Such a situation and the struggle for scarce resources helped to exacerbate ethnic tensions. During British colonialism in Nigeria, there were numerous massacres of minorities. These episodes of genocide have continued into the early twenty-first century.

The British policies in West Africa and East Africa led to the ethnic consciousness or subnationalism of most of the ethnic groups in these colonies. Ethnic rivalries between the major groups in Nigeria—the Igbo, Hausa-Fulani, and Yoruba, who constitute about 65 percent of the population of Nigeria—started during the British colonial period. Some of the ethnic groups, such as the Yoruba, the Igbo, and the Hausa, did not have pan-ethnic consciousness, and they resisted the British colonial structure. In Nigeria, the main political parties formed around ethnic affiliations: The National Convention of Nigerian Citizens, founded by Herbert Macaulay and championed by Nnamdi Azikiwe, was primarily centered in the Igbo-dominated Eastern Region; the Action Group, led by Obafemi Awolowo, was based in the traditional Yoruba area of the Western Region; and the Northern Peoples Congress, led by Ahmadu Bello and Abubakar Tafawa Balewa, was dominated by the Hausa-Fulani and based in the Northern Region. It was in the interest of the British to promote ethnic tensions in their colonies. The creation of antagonistic political parties helped to delay independence agitations within the colonies, and enabled the British to continue their uninterrupted plundering of resources in Africa. The case of Nigeria was similar to the situations of other British colonies in West Africa—Gambia, Sierra Leone, and Ghana.

Under the leadership of Kwame Nkrumah, Ghana may have been spared ethnic rivalries to a considerable extent. In Sierra Leone, the British fomented tensions between the colony of Freetown, which was dominated by former slaves, the Creoles; and the rest of the indigenous population, the Protectorate of Sierra Leone.

Settler Rule. Another system of British colonial administration was the settler rule system that occurred where Britain had large populations of European immigrants. These immigrants settled and established direct rule over the colonies in Africa especially in southern and eastern Africa. They planned to make Africa their permanent home. British settler colonies were founded primarily in South Africa, Southern and Northern Rhodesia (Zimbabwe and Zambia), and South-West Africa (Namibia). Settlers from Holland, Britain, Germany, and Portugal colonized these areas. In addition, settler rule was practiced in Kenya, a British colony in East Africa. These settlers, who came to Africa to exploit the natural resources, made sure that laws were enacted or forces created that enabled them to dominate the numerically larger African populations, economically, socially, and politically. In colonies with settler rule, there was harsher treatment of native Africans than in the colonies with the indirect rule system or where there were no sizable white settler populations. West Africa was spared settler rule because of the harsh hot climate and because of malaria. Malaria

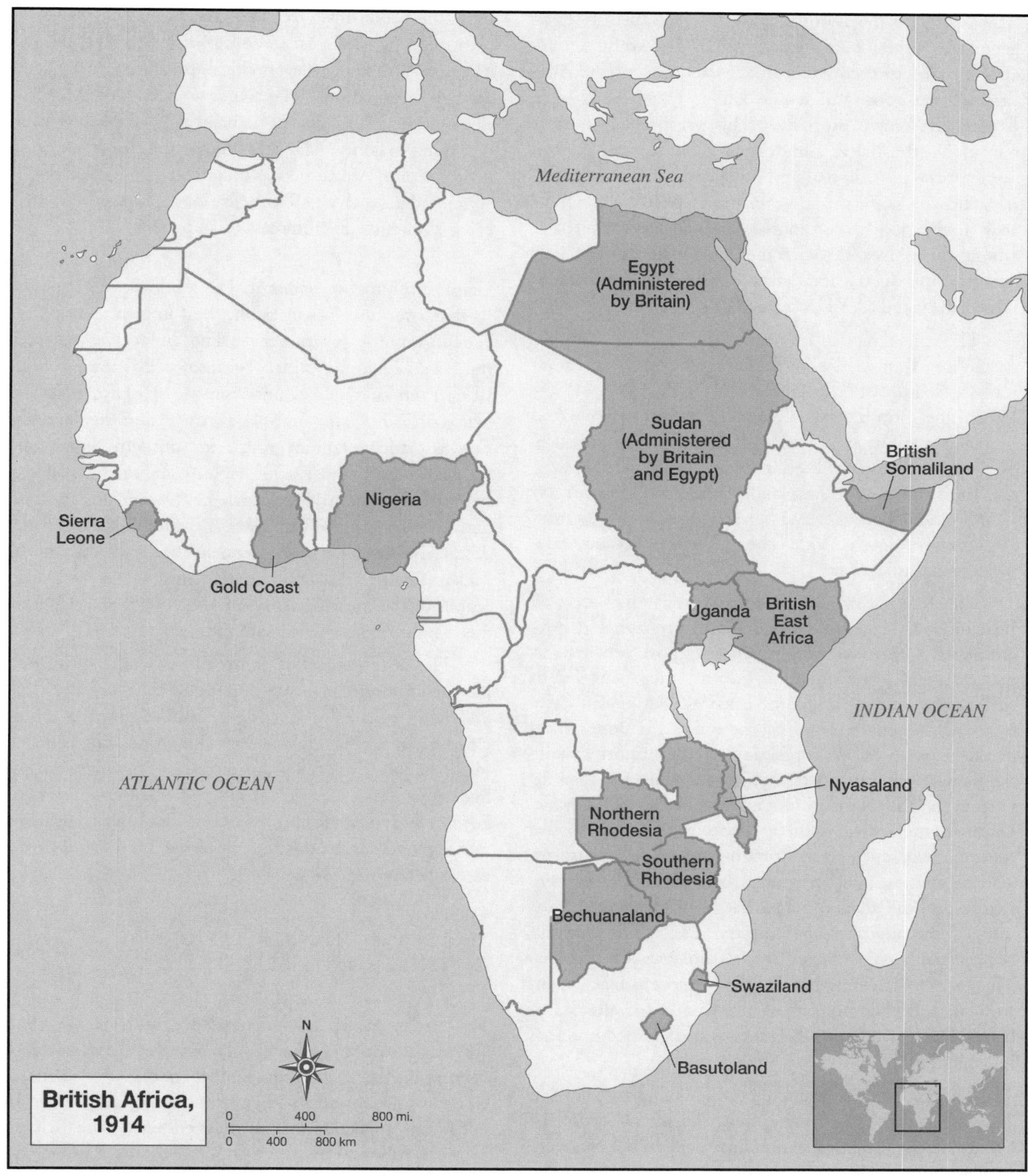

British Africa, 1914. MAP BY XNR PRODUCTIONS. GALE.

killed so many early European adventurers and colonial agents in West Africa that Europeans nicknamed it the "white person's grave."

Settlers regarded themselves to be naturally superior to the "natives," as the British called their African colonial subjects. They saw the Africans as people who must be subjected and who were good only for being domestics to the white settlers. The methods of oppression and repression by the European settler populations were not known in precolonial Africa. At least the internal conquerors in

Africa prior to the Europeans did not see themselves as genetically superior to the conquered. The white settlers appropriated to themselves to the exclusion of the Africans all the good and arable lands. These lands were designated "crown property." This practice was notorious in South Africa, Zimbabwe, Zambia, and Kenya. Some of the postcolonial and independent African countries did the same thing; government officials nationalized huge tracts of communal lands and distributed it among themselves, their families, and their cronies. This occurred in Nigeria, for example, when the government passed the Land Use Decree of 1977.

The settler colonies later unilaterally declared independence from Britain. The first British colony in Africa to do this was South Africa. In 1910, after the Boer War (1899–1902), the British gave all administrative and political powers to the European settler population in the provinces of Natal, Cape, Orange Free State, and Transvaal. However, the British removed Swaziland, Basutoland (present-day Lesotho), and Bechuanaland (present-day Botswana) from the Union of South Africa. These provinces became independent countries later.

The settler British colonies in Africa that declared their independence from Britain instituted minority governments. The worst case of minority governments was the apartheid government of South Africa. The South African government under the Boer-led Nationalist Party legalized the separation of the races and the domination of the majority black population by the minority white population. In South Africa whites made up less than 20 percent of the population and the blacks 80 percent. Under the apartheid system, blacks were forced to live on nonarable lands and in urban ghettoes or townships. "Miscegenation" and marriages between the races were legally prohibited, and blacks had no rights in the running of the affairs of the country. The white minority government used violence and terrorism against blacks. They arrested, tortured, and killed innocent black men, women, and children. Later the barren lands allotted to blacks were divided into Bantustans and granted nominal independence.

The African National Congress (ANC) was formed in 1912 to fight the racial segregation and the racism of the black majority. Later, other anti-apartheid groups emerged, such as the Pan-African Congress and the black consciousness movement started by Stephen Biko. These groups were banned by the South African minority government. In 1964 Nelson Mandela and his fellow ANC members were arrested and tried for treason because of their fight for racial equality and for the end of the oppressive apartheid system. Mandela and his associates were sentenced to life imprisonment with hard labor at the notorious penal colony of Robben Island. In 1990, after he took office as president, F. W. de Klerk finally removed the ban on all previously proscribed political parties and associations, and released Mandela and the other political prisoners. After some detailed negotiations following the release of Mandela, elections were held in 1994, and the ANC won an overwhelming majority. Mandela became the first black president of South Africa; he was magnanimous in victory. He appointed a Truth and Reconciliation Commission to help bring closure to the bitterness of all parties.

Condominium Government. The joint rule of Egypt and Britain over the Sudan is the best-known example of "condominium government." The Sudan was renamed the Anglo-Egyptian Sudan because of this joint rule by Britain and Egypt. The Sudan is made up of the Arabs and black Africans. The Arabs are in the minority and the various African ethnic groups in southern Sudan and western Sudan (the Darfur region) are in the majority numerically. The Arab minority has historically discriminated against the majority black Africans. These racial and ethnic rivalries have led to genocide and civil wars in the Sudan (first in the southern Sudan and now in the Darfur region of the Sudan) where hundreds of thousands have died and millions turned into refugees.

The British governor, James Robertson, originally left the Arab minority in power to dominate the majority black Sudanese, essentially creating a climate for the ethnic cleansing and genocide that has been an ongoing problem in the Sudan. Even the peace accord of 2004 between the Sudan People's Liberation Army and the Arab-dominated government in Khartoum has failed. The latter continually marginalized black Sudanese citizens from 1956 into the early twenty-first century.

RACIAL AND ETHNIC RELATIONS IN POSTCOLONIAL BRITISH AFRICA

The Sudan gained its independence in 1956. In 1957 Ghana (formerly Gold Coast) became the first black country in Africa to regain its independence from Britain. Ghana was followed by Nigeria and Somalia in 1960. In 1961 Tanganyika gained its independence from Britain. This was followed by Kenya in 1963 and by Zambia and Malawi in 1964. Gambia secured its independence in 1965. It took the countries with settler communities longer to secure their independence and establish majority rule. Zimbabwe got its independence and majority rule in 1980, and South Africa was the last to gain majority rule in 1994. The independence of the former British colonies actually exacerbated the ethnic rivalries because of the inimical policies of the British colonial administration. The British reluctantly relinquished their control of the colonies and tried to set up their African colonies for failure when they had regained their independence.

As soon as British colonies were free of British control, the ethnic rivalries that had been kept in check because of the nationalistic struggles for independence came out in the open. In Nigeria for instance, ethnic tensions escalated immediately after independence and culminated in the civil war that lasted from 1967 to 1970. This war can be understood only as the conclusion of a series of events that began with accusations of electoral fraud six years earlier. In 1962 and 1963, Nigeria had attempted a census of the population. The census was rigged, as were the federal elections of 1964. The governments of Nigeria's Western and Eastern Regions, which were dominated by the Yoruba and the Igbo, respectively, protested vigorously against the Hausa-Fulani, who were the major beneficiaries of the census and election malpractices. The Western Region was ungovernable because the leader of the Yoruba and the Action Group, Chief Obafemi Awolowo, had been imprisoned along with his close associates in 1962 on the treasonable charges of trying to overthrow the Hausa-Fulani-led federal government.

The corruption of the politicians, ethnic tensions, and the uprising in Western Nigeria led to the first military coup in Nigeria on January 15, 1966. Led by Majors Emmanuel Ifeajuna, Chukwuma Nzeogwu, and Adewale Ademoyega, and therefore known as the "majors' coup," this overthrow led to the deaths of the prime minister and the premiers of the Northern and Western Regions. The premiers of the Eastern Region, Michael Okpara, and of the newly created Mid-Western Region, Dennis Osadebe, escaped death. Some senior military officers of the Nigerian army also lost their lives. The coup was partially successful. General Johnson Aguiyi-Ironsi, the highest-ranking Nigerian military officer, was asked by the remaining members of the overthrown civilian government to take over the government. He established the National Military Government, suspended some parts of the constitution, and ruled by decree. He banned the ethnic and tribal associations. He also abolished the regions and instead installed a unitary government with a group of provinces. At first, students and members of the media hailed his policies. With British connivance, however, the Ironsi government was quickly overthrown by a Hausa-Fulani-engineered coup. On July 29, 1966, Yakubu Gowon, who secretly worked for British intelligence, assumed the office of head of state. The immediate repercussion of this coup was the ethnic cleansing of the Igbos living in northern Nigeria. It was estimated that about three million Igbos died in the subsequent Biafran war.

The purpose of the coup plotters, led by Murtala Mohammed and Theophilus Danjuma, was for the North to secede from Nigeria, but it was the British who advised them against seceding from Nigeria. Gowon divided Nigeria into twelve states but could not stop the genocide of the Igbo. The military governor of the eastern group of provinces, Chukwuemeka Odumegwu Ojukwu, refused to accept Gowon's coup and the subsequent lack of protection for the Igbo in Nigeria. He was persuaded to secede from Nigeria. In May 1967 he declared the independence of the Republic of Biafra, and Gowon declared war on Biafra. This war lasted until 1970, when Biafra was reincorporated into Nigeria. By the early twenty-first century, the ethnic rivalries in Nigeria had actually increased, with many ethnic and national groups calling for secession.

The case of Nigeria is similar to what happened in the other postcolonial British colonies in Africa. For example, in Sierra Leone in the 1990s, a civil war caused by ethnic rivalries resulted in the deaths of hundreds of thousands of citizens.

There have been ethnic and racial tensions in former British colonies in East Africa as well. In Kenya, where there was a settler population, the British took the Kikuyu lands in the Kenyan highlands and forced the Africans to work for them in a sharecropper type of arrangement. The Africans were levied high taxes, and the only way they could afford to pay the taxes was to work for the European settlers. The Kikuyu organized themselves and resisted the confiscation of their lands in what is known as the Mau Mau rebellion. The British colonial administrators used excessive force in suppressing the rebellion. The Kenyan African Union, a political party led by Jomo Kenyatta, was nonetheless able to force the British to grant Kenya its independence in 1963. He became the first prime minister and later ruled as president until his death in 1978. He was succeeded by his vice president, Arap Moi, who ruled until 2002, when he was forced to organize a multiparty election that was won by the opposition.

In Uganda, the military dictatorship of Idi Amin expelled the Asians (Indians), who were Ugandan citizens. During Amin's regime (1971–1979), there were many ethnically motivated killings. About 300,000 Ugandans lost their lives, with the Bugandans suffering the heaviest toll.

In the southern African subregion where there were settler populations, racial and ethnic relations have largely improved in the postcolonial period. The one notable exception is Zimbabwe, where Robert Mugabe since the late 1990s has promoted racial and ethnic tensions as a means of staying in power. South Africa, meanwhile, has become a model country where racial and ethnic tensions have decreased significantly since the gaining of majority rule in 1994. This achievement was largely accomplished through the legendary leadership of

Mandela and his ANC government, who dismantled the notorious apartheid system and reconciled racial and ethnic difficulties. Mandela promoted a South Africa where all the races and ethnic groups would enjoy equal benefits of their country.

The British colonial policies planted the seeds of the racial and ethnic rivalries that led to the killings of millions of Africans in the former British colonies. Unfortunately, the custodians of political power have not yet divorced themselves from British colonial policies. First of all, the leaders of these nations continue to exploit ethnic rivalries and tensions to stay in power. Second, most of the ethnic tensions in these countries stem from the struggle for the limited resources that are not but must be shared among these groups. Third, there are hidden hands in the ethnic conflicts in Africa's former British colonies. It is interesting that most of the ethnic conflicts are in the African countries with the most natural resources. It is in these countries that British and other foreign interests engineer civil wars so that they can continue to loot the resources of Africa. Finally, the constant interventions of the British in the affairs of their former colonies have not helped matters. They continue to covertly and overtly support their preferred ethnic groups and thereby continue to dominate and marginalize all the other groups.

SEE ALSO *Mandela, Nelson.*

BIBLIOGRAPHY

Cawthorne, Nigel. 2004. *Tyrants: History's 100 Most Evil Despots and Dictators.* New York: Barnes and Noble.

Davidson, Basil. 1972. *Africa: History of a Continent*, rev. ed. New York: Macmillan.

———. 1992. *The Black Man's Burden: Africa and the Curse of the Nation-State.* New York: Times Books.

Ekwe-Ekwe, Herbert. 2006. *Biafra Revisited.* Dakar, Senegal: African Renaissance.

Forrest, Joshua B. 2004. *Subnationalism in Africa: Ethnicity, Alliances, and Politics.* Boulder, CO: Lynne Rienner.

Handelman, Howard. 2006. *The Challenge of Third World Development*, 4th ed. Upper Saddle River, NJ: Pearson/Prentice Hall.

Harris, Joseph E. 1998. *Africans and Their History*, 2nd ed. New York: Penguin.

Kanyandago, Peter, ed. 2002. *Marginalized Africa: An International Perspective.* Nairobi, Kenya: Paulines Publications Africa.

Nnoli, Okwudiba. 1978. *Ethnic Politics in Nigeria.* Enugu, Nigeria: Fourth Dimension Publishers.

Sadowski, Yahya. 1998. "Ethnic Conflict." *Foreign Policy* No. 111: 12–23.

John Obioma Ukawuilulu

AFRICA: FRENCH COLONIES

The construction of race in France's African colonies arose out of the turbulent political, intellectual, and cultural contexts of nineteenth- and twentieth-century France, as well as the specific dynamics of each colony itself. An understanding of race and racism as operative conceptual categories in French political culture must pay particular attention to the specific colonial contexts in which these concepts arose. There are broad themes that emerge out of the French colonial experience in Africa. Empire itself represented a profoundly racialized extension of state power outside of the boundaries of the incipient French nation-state, while at the same time it fundamentally reconfigured the French nation through the internalization of colonial policies of racist exclusion. The colonization of Africa profoundly altered both France and the various African nations that were colonized.

POLITICAL ORGANIZATION OF FRENCH COLONIES IN AFRICA

Administratively, politically, and practically, Africa never functioned as a unified object in French colonialism. Indeed, even at the height of its African empire, France never governed Africa under a single colonial apparatus. Rather, numerous forms of political control arose in geographically discrete portions of the continent, all of which were, to varying degrees, authoritarian and aggressively imperialist. Long-term French colonization of Africa began in earnest in 1830 with the French invasion of Algeria. The long duration of French occupation, its intense violence, and the large numbers of European colonial settlers made Algeria—in law, in political cultural, and in administrative fact— an entirely unique case in the French colonial world. Indeed, an administrative decree in 1878 ended the status of Algeria as a colony, ostensibly integrating it as part of metropolitan France. This decree merely served to reinforce the two-tiered political system that accorded rights to European settlers while denying them to Algerians, and Algeria largely remained, in fact if not in law, a colony.

Tunisia, despite its geographic proximity and linguistic affinities with Algeria, became a French "protectorate" rather than a colony. The establishment of the protectorate in 1881 ushered in a fundamentally different form of French imperialism on the north coast of Africa. Although Tunisia retained its cosmopolitan, Mediterranean atmosphere, the imposition of French rule represented yet another form of empire in Africa. Similarly, in 1912, France established a protectorate in Morocco, nominally maintaining the role of the Sultan while effectively controlling economic and political life in the kingdom. Though the structures of governance in Tunisia and Morocco differed both from each other and from those in Algeria, the protectorate system insured French control over the remainder of North Africa.

In sharp contrast, other forms of political control arose in other parts of French-controlled Africa. The creation in 1895 of *Afrique Occidentale Française* (French West Africa, or AOF) unified a vast, culturally and linguistically diverse region under one administrative body. Comprising the area of the modern nations of Benin, Burkina Faso, Côte d'Ivoire (Ivory Coast), Guinea, Mali, Mauritania, Niger, and Senegal, French West Africa attracted very few European settlers. As a result, the administrative policies that French governors implemented here differed substantively from those of the Maghrib (Morocco, Algeria, Tunisia, and at times Libya and Mauritania). Similarly, *Afrique Équatoriale Française* (French Equatorial Africa, or AEF) contained only a tiny number of European settlers in an area of tremendous diversity. The colony, covering what later became the nations of the Central African Republic, Chad, the Republic of Congo (Congo-Brazzaville), and Gabon, combined under one central administrative body a large number of disparate ethnic and linguistic groups. Both French West Africa and French Equatorial Africa functioned primarily as administrative and political bodies, and in no way did they respect preexisting boundaries or groupings. France governed its other African colonies—Madagascar, the Indian Ocean territories, the Territory of the Afars and Issas (French Somaliland; later Djibouti)—through separate administrative structures. Finally, following the dismantling of Germany's colonial empire after World War I, France acquired two so-called mandate territories, Togoland and Cameroun (later called Togo and Cameroon).

Thus, the political organization of French colonial Africa did not correspond to clearly defined ethnic, linguistic, or other boundaries. Not only did French colonial boundaries embrace a tremendous diversity of peoples and places, it also comprised a wide variety of divergent and often incommensurable internal political systems.

INTELLECTUAL CONTEXT OF FRENCH COLONIALISM IN AFRICA

Despite this wide variety of colonial political systems in French colonial Africa, and without regard to the diversity of colonized populations, Africa itself at times functioned as a discursive unity in French culture. Particularly in the twentieth century, primitivism (whether in art or literature) represented Africa as a unified space, juxtaposing artwork and cultural objects and attributes from vastly different places, contexts, and even chronological periods and combining them under the rubric of "African art." Indeed, at times both popular images and scholarly treatises conceived of Africa as an indeterminate, yet somehow ultimately cohesive and coherent, signifier. The diversity of the continent—whether ecological, linguistic, ethnic, geographic, religious, or political—at times disappeared, subsumed under the generalizing and homogenizing impulse of imperial political culture into an irreducible African Other.

This coalescing of cultural diversity into such overly generalized representations arose in part out of the larger intellectual climate of the emergence of social scientific thought in France. In the nineteenth century in particular, physical anthropology emerged as the dominant intellectual paradigm to describe human differences. Racial pseudoscience drew conclusions about cultural attributes, "civilization," intellectual abilities, and social characteristics from wholly spurious cranial measurements, meaningless descriptions of facial and other physical "characteristics," and a wide variety of racialized assumptions about individual potential. Utilizing such "data," early human scientists (largely physical anthropologists) elaborated collective portraits of racial "types," including Africans. Despite their complete lack of foundation, these "portraits" functioned as broad-based, intellectually unfounded stereotypes with the force of scientific authority behind them.

At the same time, this impulse towards the creation of simplified, unitary discursive representations of Africa were by no means totalizing within France. Scholars and popular figures could and did recognize a cultural multiplicity and diversity within the African colonies that both undermined the conception of irreducible difference and failed to correspond to the political boundaries of the French colonies on the continent. Most notably, many French writers (whether in academic journals, in popular newspapers, or at the colonial expositions) distinguished between the Maghrib and sub-Saharan Africa, frequently labeled *Afrique noire* (Black Africa). Despite the longstanding economic, cultural, and political links between the Maghrib and sub-Saharan Africa, many in France and Europe more broadly preferred to conceive of the Sahara not as the highway and meeting place it was, but rather as a racialized boundary dividing black Africa from the Mediterranean world. In particular, representations of Algeria were an attempt to sever France's largest and most important colony from Africa and bind it to France through the racialization of colonial boundaries. Algeria was, according to such thinking, not "black" but Mediterranean, a kind of lesser-white region more closely tied to Europe than to Africa. In many ways, this exercise succeeded in effecting the intellectual separation of North Africa from Africa in French thinking. Colonial scholars largely dismissed the continued connections across the Sahara, and across Africa, and administrators encouraged

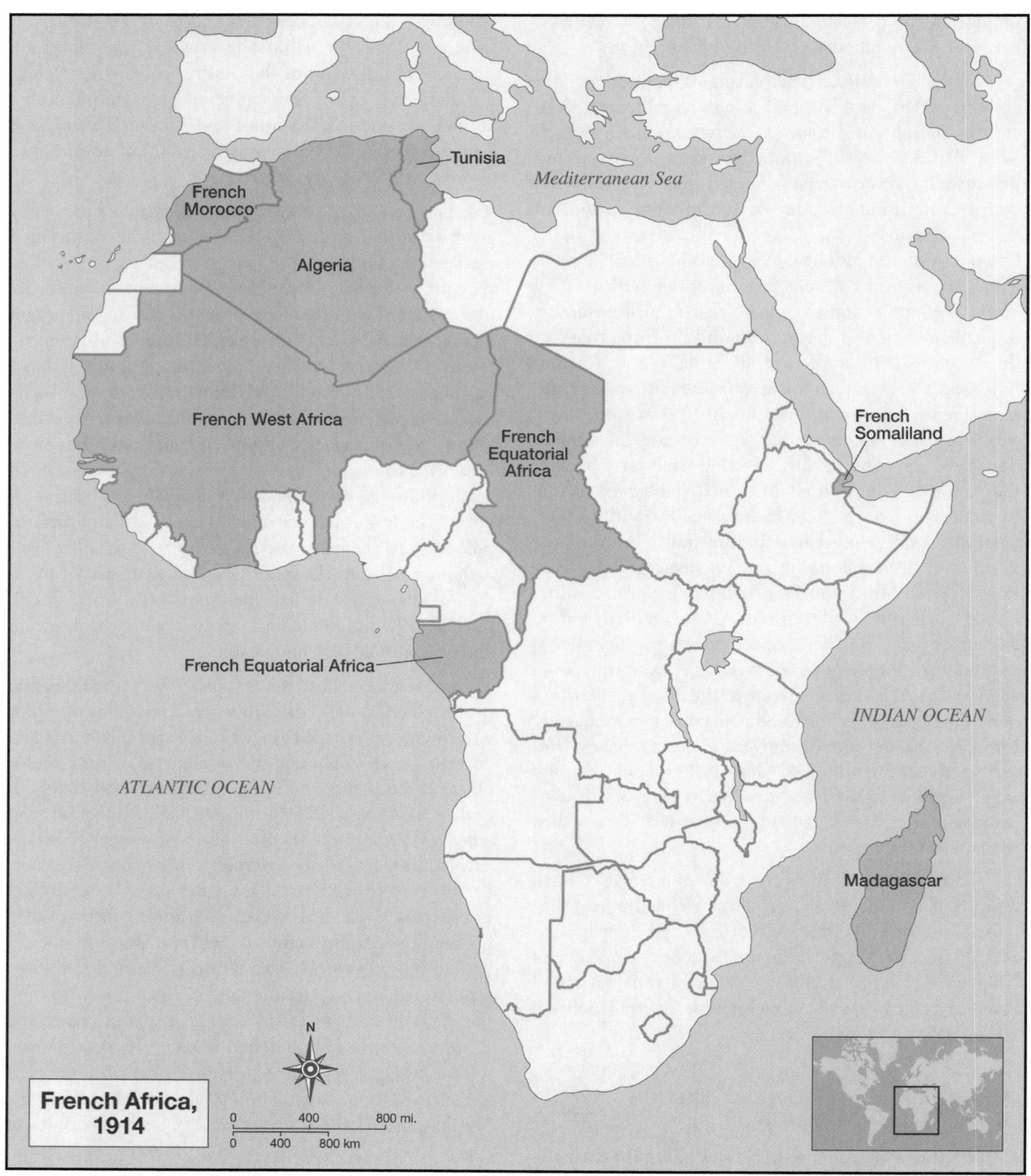

French Africa, 1914. MAP BY XNR PRODUCTIONS. GALE.

attempts to hermetically seal North (meaning "white") Africa from *l'Afrique noire.*

Thus, there arose a fundamental paradox in French colonial thought. Although the colonial project predicated its political organization on the recognition of two basic categories of political rights (those of the colonizer and those of the colonized, whose rights were often nonexistent), colonial states, including France, at times admitted the diversity of peoples included under the rubric of "colonized." French recognition of cultural plurality among Africans was in no way constant, however. Instead, administrators strategically deployed their limited understandings of differences for politically useful purposes that varied from colony to colony. The forms and articulations of French colonial racism differed dramatically, and they require elucidation in the context of individual situations in order to emphasize the responses and resistance of Algerians, Togolese, Senegalese, and countless others.

Nevertheless, certain patterns in colonial politics emerge across the French colonial empire in Africa. As Alice L. Conklin has demonstrated in *A Mission to Civilize* (1997), colonial bureaucrats in French West Africa (and, by analogy, throughout the empire) conceived of their role as part of a civilizing mission. The French civilizing mission maintained the necessity of European tutelage for the peoples of Africa, Asia, the Pacific Islands, and the Americas. Portraying non-Europeans as fundamentally less civilized, colonial apologists drew upon a long tradition of evolutionary racial pseudoscience that categorized the world's peoples according to hierarchies that implicitly valorized European civilizations. As a result, French colonial bureaucrats interpreted their role as one of education, of tutelage, and of bringing advancement and enlightenment to colonial children. As the essays in Julia Clancy-Smith and Frances Gouda's edited volume *Domesticating the Empire* (1998) demonstrate, the logic of the civilizing mission, and of colonialism more broadly, concealed a profoundly racist and gendered configuration of the relationship between colonizer and colonized, with the colonizing nation providing education, protection, and chastisement to wayward colonial children. The civilizing mission functioned as both an ostensible rationale for empire and as a convenient cloak for colonial violence, casting the oppressive apparatus of colonial statecraft as tutelage and guidance for the benefit of the very victims of that oppression.

ASSOCIATION AND ASSIMILATION

At least two major intellectual strands emerged out of the cultural politics of French colonialism. Indeed, French colonial administrators rarely pursued one to the exclusion of the other, instead vacillating between the two as the exigencies of colonial domination demanded. Both strands shared the fundamental assumption that the cultural identity of Africans should rightly become a site for the political intervention of France. Drawing upon the racist conceptions of cultural evolutionary thought implicit in the civilizing mission, the ideas of "association" and "assimilation" imagined African cultures and identities solely in terms of comparison with normative French political and social values. Association reached its apex in French West Africa in the early twentieth century, according to Conklin. Politically speaking, association promoted the coexistence of preexisting political structures with the superstructure of empire, allowing, for example, continued roles for chiefs and other African elites alongside new colonial elites, such as African bureaucrats educated in colonial schools. Associationist policies imagined a colonial governance in which older elites joined with new African leaders in reinforcing the colonial order through nominally consultative assemblies and other such superficially participatory institutions. Association rested on a profoundly racist conception of cultural identity. The doctrine of association held that the differences between colonizer and colonized prevented the establishment of political systems in Africa divorced from preexisting institutions. In other words, association, as an intellectual concept, viewed Africans as inextricably wedded to the past and incapable of attaining the level of French political and social forms. Association took root in twin assumptions: (1) that French social and political organization represented the pinnacle of cultural achievement, and (2) that Africans could never quite achieve that pinnacle.

As a political program, assimilation required the eventual adoption of French culture, politics, social mores, and beliefs by Africans. Assimilation followed directly upon the conception, incorrect though it was, of empire as a project of tutelage. As the civilizing mission maintained that colonialism aimed at raising Africans to the level of European colonizers, at its core it implied the ultimate abandonment of colonial cultures in favor of assimilation to the French model. Assimilation was, in its essence, an ideology of cultural annihilation. Assimilationists held that colonial cultures, whether in Madagascar or Africa or Djibouti, would inevitably die out as people abandoned their previous, backward practices in favor of the civilized, French model. Assimilation was, of course, in no way less racist than associationist thought—the first implied a teleology that valorized French norms and denigrated any non-European ways of life, while the later reinforced a belief in the definitive inability of non-Europeans to accommodate change. Assimilation, with its implied cultural annihilation, and association, with its ideology of irreducible difference and inferiority, articulated diametrically opposed political programs for the colonies, yet both refused to grant Africans the ability to participate, as equals, in political and intellectual life in the French colonies.

RELIGION AND RACIALIZATION IN FRENCH COLONIAL AFRICA

In addition to its intellectual ramifications, French colonial racism manifested itself in specific policies implemented in the colonies. These policies arose out of, and in dialog with, other forms of colonial racism, such as representational, academic, and political racisms. Nineteenth-century and early twentieth-century conceptions of religion interpreted African Islam as essentially racialized. Reaffirming the largely artificial division of North Africa and sub-Saharan Africa, colonial administrators and academics conceived of Islam south of the Sahara as *Islam noir* (Black Islam). Islam, however, emphasizes the total equality of all Muslims, regardless of ethnic origin, in the eyes of God and the faith. Thus, the term *Islam noir* reflected a division unrecognizable to African Muslims of the time. In sharp contrast, as Christopher Harrison demonstrates in *France and Islam in West Africa* (1988), French policy clearly distinguished Muslim practices and beliefs in Algeria, Morocco, and Tunisia from those of French West Africa and, to a lesser extent, French Equatorial Africa.

According to the hypothesis positing an *Islam noir*, sub-Saharan Islam differed from Islam in the Middle East and North Africa because of racial difference. Racial pseudoscience (the legacy of early, evolutionist physical anthropology) had created clearly articulated and rigidly defined hierarchies of race. As a result, colonial scholars and the administrators they influenced could not conceive of religious practice outside of a highly racialized schema that ranked civilizations and races, attaching collective and spurious cultural and intellectual traits to entire groups of people. This categorization placed Europeans (and especially French) at the pinnacle of civilizational achievement, evaluating Arabs as a distinctly less advanced society, though largely still interpreted as "white." Racial pseudoscience placed Africans dwelling south of the Sahara towards the bottom of this scale.

These artificial categorizations not only reinforced colonial racism, they drew on other, broader, popular representations. Such images often portrayed Africans as primitive, as existing at a previous stage in human development. Thus, scholars of religion in the colonial period ascribed to "Islam noir" traits deemed primitive. Following their lead, administrators denigrated the beliefs of pious African Muslims as superstitious, primitive, and base, discounting the numerous centers of Islamic learning scattered throughout the Sahel and Sahara. Islam in sub-Saharan Africa was in no way more "primitive" than Islam anywhere else, and it resembled rather closely Islam in the part of Africa deemed "white" by scholars, the Maghrib, whose denizens had initiated the conversion to Islam centuries earlier.

However, the interpretation of "Islam noir" bore no stable relationship to colonial primitivism. Whereas many viewed ostensibly primitivist elements of religion as signs of an insufficiently advanced civilization, others viewed that same ostensible primitivism as rejuvenating. French writers who were invested in reaffirming hierarchies of civilization often demeaned Arab societies as ossified and decadent, having lost the vestiges of their greatness in the medieval and early modern eras. As a result, they depicted purported African primitivism as rejuvenating a frozen and backward Islam. Moreover, administrators maintained, Arab Muslims that shared a cultural predisposition towards fanaticism and anti-European hostility, a predisposition that sub-Saharan Africans could mitigate.

Even within North Africa, colonial administrators created largely artificial, racialized distinctions within Islam. Algeria (like much of the rest of North Africa) had two major population groups speaking the languages of two distinct groups, Arabic and the various Berber languages. Berbers, the original inhabitants of North Africa, and Arabs, who were later arrivals, had coexisted largely without conflict for centuries. They could be found trading, intermarrying, and often cooperating despite differences in language, customs, and culture. The advent of empire in Algeria substantially altered such previous relationships. Colonial scholarship on Algeria depicted Arabs as invaders, as usurpers who brought Islam to the region and imposed it, by force, on Berbers. As a result, administrators and scholars contended, Berbers maintained a collective cultural affinity for France and for European civilization. Vestiges of a pre-Islamic (Christian) past, Berbers appeared in colonial texts as more akin to Europeans, as amenable to the civilizing mission, as noble and ultimately less refractory to French colonialism. Patricia Lorcin calls this the "Kabyle Myth," and it completely diminished both manifest and frequent demonstrations of Berber opposition to the extension of French colonial rule *and* the similarities and connections between Arabs and Berbers.

Nevertheless, the Kabyle Myth had very real consequences for both colonial statecraft and postcolonial Algeria. To some extent, French policy did in fact favor Berbers, but the greatest legacy of the Kabyle Myth was discursive, as Lorcin notes. Colonial representations reinforced notions of difference between Arabs and Berbers. These myths set the two up in opposition to each other, imagining Algerian Arabs as fanatical, intractable, unruly, and inclined to violence and disruption. In contrast, representations of Berbers offered images of nobility, honor, and hospitality. Even Berber opposition to colonial rule fed into myths about Algerian cultural identities. Arab resistance loomed in texts as a violent menace, whereas uprisings deemed "Berber" appeared as a more romanticized and somehow heroic, if doomed, struggles. Moreover, colonial administrators and scholars consistently portrayed Berbers as less Islamic and more civilized. Just as many writers distinguished a wholly illusory "Islam noir," so too did they create an artificial separation between Arab and Berber Muslims in Algeria. In contemporary Algeria and among Algerian populations in France, Arab and Berber have become operative categories of social, cultural, and political difference. French colonial mythmaking and racialization of identity exacerbated, and, indeed, largely instigated, tensions between ethnic communities in Algeria.

These strategies of racialization took place throughout French colonial Africa. In Madagascar, the presence of a mixture of African and Austronesian populations resulted in the extension of racialized anthropological discourse to colonial practice in the island. Indeed, Françoise Raison-Jourde (2002) sees in the colonial literature on Madagascar the infusion of racist hierarchies of civilization. Colonial writers and administrators distinguished among three races, hierarchically arranged, on the island: whites (French colonists); *jaune* (yellow), used to refer to the highland Merina who speak an Austronesian language; and *noir*, for speakers of African languages. These illusory categories conflated linguistic and ethnic identity, racializing population groups and individuals' affiliations without regard to culture contact and internal class divisions. Chantal Valensky, in *La nation malgache*, describes such racialized depictions of ethnic groups operating not just in colonial manuals and anthropological texts, but also in popular images such as postcards, the dissemination of which contributed to the popularization of racial imagery of nearly all colonial populations. Racialized categories of difference not only determined the political, economic, and social roles of peoples in colonial Madagascar and complicated the internal political dynamics of interethnic relations; they also proliferated throughout the nineteenth- and twentieth-century French-speaking world through photography and colonial postcards. French manipulation of communal relations during the colonial period may have exacerbated tensions that came to the forefront during the political crisis of the 2002 presidential elections in Madagascar.

SOLDIERS AND SUBJECTS: COLONIAL VETERANS AND THE CONTESTATION OF RIGHTS

Even participation in colonial bureaucracy and administration provided no insulation against French colonial racism. In particular, African soldiers (known as *tirailleurs*) serving in French armies found little recompense or recognition, and almost no compensation for their sacrifices for the French colonial state. In some colonies, although service in the armed services seemed like an opportunity for social advancement (and at times provided an advantage for future administrative employment), serving as a colonial soldier to some extent alienated such troops from communal social structures, particularly after independence. They were, in the words of one scholar, "caught between two worlds and uncomfortable in either" (Echenberg 1991, p. 140). At the same time, Gregory Mann contends, in *Native Sons* (2006), that the preexisting social and political structures, conceptions of responsibility, and communal ties inflected Malian soldiers' conceptions of their relationship with the colonial state (and, by implication, those of colonial soldiers more broadly). In particular, the legacy of slavery and the transition to a postslavery social system in Mali fundamentally reordered social relations, a reordering whose consequences were felt in the ties between soldier and state.

As Myron Echenberg explains in *Colonial Conscripts* (1991), of the European colonial powers, only France utilized colonial soldiers throughout its empire, including in France itself. Germany and Britain used colonial soldiers extensively in the actual colonies but refused to use them on the home front. World War I had taken as great a toll on African soldiers as it did on Europeans, as battle deaths, climate, and epidemics decimated the soldiers. By World War II, French colonial soldiers loomed in the imagination of the German Nazis as an indication of the decadence and depravity of the French "race." Echenberg notes that both Adolf Hitler and Erwin Rommel singled out African soldiers in the French army for particular disdain.

Even before the massive battles of World War II, African veterans (of both World War I and various colonial clashes) organized into political pressure groups. Collectively organized with roots in prior political actions, veterans played a major role in the politics of postwar French colonies and newly independent African nations. As both Mann and Echenberg describe, the 1944 mutiny of African colonial troops at Thiaroye in Senegal demonstrated the insistence of veterans upon fair treatment and equitable recompense. French colonial administrators quashed the rebellion with the use of other colonial units.

Despite such activism, the *tirailleurs* rarely received a fair response. Not until 2001 did the French state admit to the injustice of the unequal pensions allotted to French and African soldiers, by which point most veterans had died. France utilized colonial soldiers not only to police the boundaries of its empire, but also to protect France itself. However, the racist logic of empire could not acknowledge the equality of the sacrifice of African and French soldiers. In the allocation of unequal pensions, the state quite literally attached a different value to the lives of former colonial subjects and French citizens.

COLONIAL RACISM AFTER (OTHER) EMPIRES: GENOCIDE AND FOREIGN POLICY

The legacy of colonialism in French Africa has extended, after independence, to other French-speaking colonies in the region. Broadly speaking, France has pursued active connections with Francophone Africa, with varying intents and consequences. Such foreign policy has, at times, veered toward the interventionist, with various French governments of all political stripes providing support or even arms to client states and friendly regimes.

Perhaps the most infamous of such interventions occurred, not in a former French colony, but in the former German and later Belgian colony of Rwanda. French President François Mitterand's government considered Rwanda to be part of Francophone Africa, and as such a region of special interest for France. As Andrew Wallis notes,

> French intervention in Rwanda in the last 1980s and early 1990s was first and foremost an attempt to keep its beloved *francophonie* intact. It was symptomatic of 30 years of military intervention by Paris on the continent. Despite appalling human rights abuses by its 'client' African governments, France has continued to support dictators and regimes whose murderous policies towards their own people have been well documented. The continuity of this policy is as striking as its longevity through Presidents de Gaulle, Pompidou, Giscard d'Estaing and Mitterand, and has survived changing times, values and world politics." (2006, p. 11)

International scholars, human rights activists, and others have levied against the French government charges of complicity with the Hutu regime responsible for Rwanda's 1995 genocide. Within France as well, academics, activists, and, to a lesser extent, elements of the media (most notably Patrick Saint-Exupéry in the French newspaper *Le Figaro*) have called for further investigation into the Mitterand government's alliance with the genocidal Rwandan government, and into the French army's intervention on their behalf, a decision undertaken with no parliamentary debate in France. Jean-Paul Gouteux's *Un génocide secret d'État* draws a direct link between European colonial racism, both French and Belgian, and the Rwandan genocide. Indeed, many French writers have pointed to the French response to the Rwandan genocide as indicative of the need for a larger engagement with the ethical responsibilities of empires to their former colonies (despite the fact that France had, in fact, never colonized Rwanda). However, in an indication of the still-fraught relationship between postgenocide Rwanda and France, the Rwandan president severed ties with Paris in 2006.

The legacy of colonial racism and the political constructions of race in French colonial Africa reverberate throughout both the former colonies and France itself. Divisive policies enacted in the name of empire, the creation of racialized differentiations among peoples, and their rearticulation in the present complicate the postcolonial inheritance of France and the independent nations of Africa. The profound and intrinsic racism of the colonial project, expressed in manifold ways, continues to haunt the present.

BIBLIOGRAPHY

Cole, Jennifer. 2001. *Forget Colonialism? Sacrifice and the Art of Memory in Madagascar*. Berkeley: University of California Press.

Conklin, Alice L. 1997. *A Mission to Civilize: The Republican Idea of Empire in France and West Africa, 1895–1930*. Stanford, CA: Stanford University Press.

Echenberg, Myron. 1991. *Colonial Conscripts: The Tirailleurs Sénégalais in French West Africa, 1857–1960*. Portsmouth, NH: Heinemann.

Gouda, Frances, and Julia Clancy-Smith, eds. 1998. *Domesticating the Empire: Race, Gender, and Family Life in French and Dutch Colonialism*. Charlottesville: University Press of Virginia.

Gouteux, Jean-Paul. 1998. *Un génocide secret d'État: La France et le Rwanda 1990-1997*. Paris: Éditions Sociales.

Harrison, Christopher. 1988. *France and Islam in West Africa, 1860–1960*. New York: Cambridge University Press.

Lorcin, Patricia M.E. 1995. *Imperial Identities: Stereotyping, Prejudice and Race in Colonial Algeria*. London: I.B. Tauris.

Mann, Gregory. 2006. *Native Sons: West African Veterans and France in the Twentieth Century*. Durham, NC: Duke University Press.

Mas, Monique. 1999. *Paris-Kigali 1990–1994: Lunettes coloniales, politique du sabre et onction humanitaire pour un génocide en Afrique*. Paris: L'Harmattan.

McDougall, James. 2006. *History and the Culture of Nationalism in Algeria*. Cambridge, U.K.: Cambridge University Press.

Raison-Jourde, Françoise, and Solofo Randrianja, eds. 2002. *La nation malgache au défie de l'ethnie*. Paris: Éditions Karthala.

Silverstein, Paul A. 2004. *Algeria in France: Transpolitics, Race, and Nation*. Bloomington: Indiana University Press.

Valensky, Chantal. "Le sortilège des images." In *La nation malgache au défie de l'ethnie*, edited by Françoise Raison-Jourde and Solofo Randrianja Paris, 77–79. Paris: Éditions Karthala.

Wallis, Andrew, 2006. *Silent Accomplice: The Untold Story of France's Role in the Rwandan Genocide*. London: I.B. Tauris.

George R. Trumbull IV

AFRICA: GERMAN COLONIES

Germany was a late entrant into the race for colonies in Africa. Chancellor Otto von Bismarck was initially not a colonial expansionist. His preoccupation was the unification of Germany and its attaining a preeminent role in European politics. However, following the unification of Germany in 1871, the issue of colonies began to preoccupy German society and leadership, and various lobbying groups exerted pressure on the government to be proactive in the acquisition of colonies in Africa, arguing that Germany needed colonies to maintain its economic preeminence. The leading lobbying groups, formed after the unification, included the West German Society for Colonization and Export (1881) and the Central Association for Commercial Geography and the Promotion of German Interests Abroad (1878). The government reluctantly agreed with their view and embraced the idea of colonization, primarily to further the nation's economic interests.

Bismarck came to envision colonies as a stabilizing force in domestic politics by emphasizing nationalism and the greatness of Germany internationally. Bismarck was a pragmatist, however, and his drive to acquire colonies in Africa was largely a function of economic considerations in the emerging imperial world order, European diplomacy, and domestic politics. It is against this backdrop that Germany hosted the international Berlin Conference of 1884–1885. The conference constituted a watershed in African history, for it sanctioned European claims in Africa, though with the caveat that those powers that claimed possessions in Africa had to manifest a physical occupation of their areas for their claims to be legitimate.

This caveat was instrumental in the subsequent partition and physical occupation of Africa. Germany acquired South West Africa (present-day Namibia), German East Africa (present-day mainland Tanzania, Rwanda, and Burundi), Togo, and Cameroon. In establishing formal institutions and structures in support of colonial governance in these newly acquired territories, Germany's policy was characterized by ruthlessness, a policy of racial supremacy, and economic dispossession of the indigenous populations. These features became more pronounced in colonies to which Germans emigrated and sought to establish a homeland. German South West Africa best exemplifies a colonial situation in which race constituted a group identity that had certain predetermined advantages.

COLONIAL ADMINISTRATION

The most vital link between metropolitan Germany and the colonies was the colonial governor, who had enormous powers in steering the colony according to the official policy emanating from Berlin. Under the governor were European civilian officials and the commanders of the armed forces in the colony. Although the commanders were answerable to the governor, they retained considerable power because they were subject to the High Command in Berlin. The military performed the vital function of maintaining a superiority of arms in the colony. A number of the officers also doubled as regional administrators. It was the responsibility of the governor to mediate the various competing interests within the colony. This was far from easy, especially because the interests of the settlers were sometimes in conflict with the official colonial policy or the rights of Africans. The Germans established a colonial administration that embraced both direct and indirect rule in proportions that varied from one colony to another, and even at times within the same colonial territory, depending on the local situation.

Below the European colonial administrators were African chiefs. These were local leaders who were appointed and made subject to the authority of the local German officials, who were invariably few in number. Their loyalty was primarily to the appointing colonial authority. They served at the pleasure of the colonial government and were responsible for functions ranging from collecting taxes and conscripting labor for colonial projects to being the public face of the government at the lowest local level. Yet their ability to rise up in the ranks of the colonial administration was restricted because Africans were disqualified from holding senior positions at the district level. Thus, race was a critical determinant of one's status and level in the service of German colonial state.

The German policy was to construct an image of "Deutschtum" among the colonists. In other words, the colonies were to comprise a hardworking, parsimonious, Protestant agrarian class filled with staunch nationalist values and devotion to the Kaiser. In the settler colony of South West Africa, the intended result was the establishment of a new Germany with a culture, language, institutions, and structures that mirrored the homeland. Suffice it to note that this envisioned "new Germany" was incompatible with the interests of Africans. Its creation could only succeed at the expense of the indigenous populations. A corollary to this development was the promotion of German interests by sacrificing African political, economic, and sociocultural interests on the altar of racial prejudice.

German colonists were projected as members of a superior and enlightened race, while the native Herero and Nama communities were depicted as inferior, indolent, and destined to be permanent subjects of the Kaiser. The native people were treated as members of a collective group, and individual personality and capability were less significant than the community to which a person belonged. The rationale was to legitimize the supremacy of the colonists. The indigenous populations, meanwhile, were forced to conform to the new power hierarchy brought on by colonialism. This coerced conformity manifested itself in several ways that ranged from newly introduced colonial taxation and land alienation to forced labor and outright brutality.

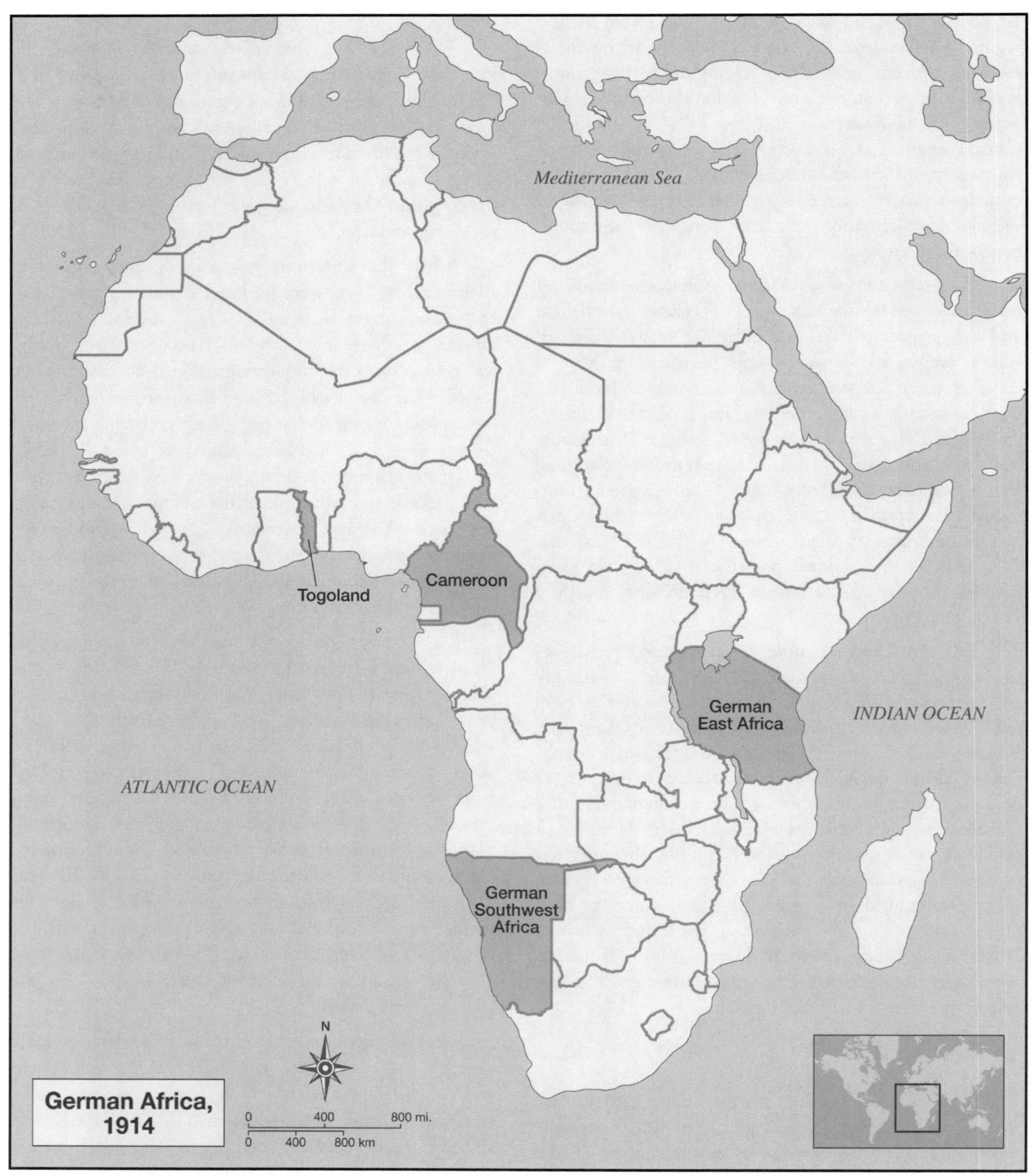

German Africa, 1914. MAP BY XNR PRODUCTIONS. GALE.

AFRICA REVOLTS

Distaste for the new German colonial order provoked a sharp reaction from the Herero in 1904. The German response was extreme to the extent that it sought to exterminate the Herero. The Herero uprising of 1904 was ruthlessly suppressed, resulting in the deaths of nearly 60,000 out of a population of 80,000. The Germans not only shot the victims, they also poisoned their water holes, resulting in the deaths of thousands more. Those who survived were forced into work camps and became the subject of various medical experiments and examinations.

The Nama faced the similar fate, and such atrocities were visited upon communities in other German colonies. During the Maji Maji uprising (1905–1907), the communities in southern German East Africa were defeated when the Germans resorted to a scorched earth policy that caused a massive destruction of crops and killings on a large scale. The African deaths from this war are estimated at between 75,000 and 100,000. The Duala (1914) and Dagomba (1896) uprisings—in Cameroon and Togo, respectively—were similarly crushed.

The German use of brute force was based on the notion that might is right, and on the belief that the interests of German colonists reigned supreme. They claimed that their skin color entitled them to subjugate the Africans. In maintaining an ideology of order and racial superiority, their methods of choice varied from overt military and scorched earth campaigns to economic coercion and land seizure.

RACIAL PURITY

At the sociocultural level, the Germans strove to maintain racial purity by reining in the behavior of some of their own. The official positions of whiteness and right were not only intertwined, they were also forced on Africans to accept as the norm of colonial society. However, whites who cohabited with or married African women posed a major threat to maintaining racial superiority. It was argued that miscegenation undermined the perceived order of white superiority by creating a class of mulattoes who defied the established categorization of colonial citizenry as black or white. Cohabitation also lowered the status of whites in the colonies. Cohabiting with the Africans who were perceived to be their inferiors, and those whites who did so were perceived by the colonial authorities to be undermining their own race and all it stood for and represented among the colonized. Yet there were more European men than women in all of Germany's colonies at any given time, and this situation encouraged cohabitation and miscegenation. The actualities of cohabitation and miscegenation debunked the myth of the German "gentleman" who shouldered the moral burden of maintaining the purity and superiority of the white race.

The case for racial purity was defended on the grounds of preserving class status and disallowing degeneracy. In order to guarantee class status, officials discouraged transgressions against the color divide by enacting legislation that forbade interracial marriages. Good Germans were supposed to behave well by marrying within their racial group. German colonialism espoused ideals of German manhood and womanhood in order to discourage interracial marriages. The result was that such marriages were stigmatized, and those involved were viewed as social deviants. Officials sought to ensure conformity to the norms of segregated society because it was seen as desirable in the maintaining of a status quo that was anchored in economic elitism, political hegemony, and a racially divided society.

The administration of justice in the German colonies was anything but impartial. The Germans nurtured and constantly reinforced a legal system that served the interests of the Europeans. The African was considered to be inferior before the law. As a result, race determined the way justice was dispensed. Punishment was meted out based on the color of one's skin. German colonialism was replete with racism and was not based on equality before the law. In addition, Africans were subjected to degrading corporal punishments as well as arbitrary executions.

VOICES OF CONCERN

The policies in place in the colonies, especially the use of brute force, coerced labor, and the resultant loss of African lives, led to intense criticism of German colonial policy from within, especially as the first decade of the twentieth century drew to a close. The debate on policy focused on how to manage the colonies for the benefit of Germany while protecting African rights to some extent. The colonial office desired to position itself as the mediator of conflicts in the colonies. This meant reducing the role of local governors who had hitherto wielded enormous powers in determining the outcome of the conflicts in areas under their jurisdiction. But even within the colonial office there were two viewpoints that were in play.

While some officials felt that a strong settler voice had to be encouraged for the purpose of promoting economic colonialism, others were of the view that humanitarian concern for African protection ought to be the paramount consideration. The latter group opined that if European settler colonialism was to succeed, colonial authorities had to avoid provoking unnecessary African resistance and ought to bring them into the orbit of the colonial economy as a plantation proletariat. It was felt that the establishment of a plantation proletariat would regularize and stabilize the working class by ensuring that it was well paid and its interests taken into account, albeit in the context of a polarized society in which Africans knew their role and place.

The intent to humanize colonialism and exploitation through paternalism was viewed as a shift from the previous blatant and overt brutality to a more considerate one in which the colonists would have their interests protected while the pecking order in the society would remain intact. Yet even under this emerging paternalistic policy, the African was still viewed as an inferior being that exhibited a "big child" mentality. It is somewhat surprising, therefore, that Africans were described as capable of becoming reasonable facsimiles of Europeans, though it was believed they had to be guided for the foreseeable future by the colonial authorities to attain that desired level. Such preconceived ideas, based on racial prejudice, informed the evolution and development of German colonial policy.

ECONOMIC AND SOCIAL DEVELOPMENT

The Germans soon embarked on the construction of railroads in their African colonial possessions. The railroads would link the coast with areas of high economic potential in the hinterland, an economic agenda aimed at boosting the economy of the colonies for the benefit of the metropolitan country. This physical infrastructure, however, was supposed to benefit Africans only indirectly, through their participation in the colonial economy as workers and not investors. The focus was on opening up the colonies for European settlement as well as economic investment. The development of physical infrastructure emphasized the polarized nature of colonial society, with both the colonizer and the colonized having a distinct role to play in the making of the colonial economy.

The development of social services was equally important in the planning and marketing of German colonialism as a benevolent and humane undertaking aimed at benefiting the Africans. The Germans developed public hospitals as well as educational institutions. But even in these two areas, the facilities were inadequate to cope with the large number of Africans who were gradually and consistently being drawn to Western educational and public health institutions. The German colonial government encouraged the participation of missionary societies as partners in providing health care and educational services. Through the development of such services, the government hoped that Africans would cherish the fruits of the German civilizing mission.

WORLD WAR I AND ITS AFTERMATH

The redefining of German colonial policy in 1914 was relegated to the periphery of the mainstream events of World War I, although race continued to determine the position of Africans in political, economic, and social spheres during the entire war period. Africans aligned and identified themselves with their respective colonial powers during the war. In this regard, the war revealed the divide among the major Europeans, thereby forcing Africans to enlist in support of their European colonial power. Africans were relegated to the lower ranks and served under the command of German officers, a development that reasserted their position in colonial society. Nevertheless, Africans fought gallantly in support of the German cause. In German East Africa, under the command of General Paul von Lettow-Vorbeck, Africans and Germans put up determined resistance in confronting British and South African forces. Despite the fact that they were outnumbered, German and African troops in the region remained undefeated throughout the war.

World War I constituted a turning point in the history of German colonialism in Africa. One of the provisions of the Versailles Treaty that ended the war was that Germany had to surrender all its colonies. With the surrender of the colonies, German colonial policy, and its attendant negative connotations of race, came under review. German colonies were taken over by the League of Nations, as Trust Mandates, and by other competing powers.

In South West Africa, the Germans demanded political equality and the recognition of German as the third administrative language next to English and Afrikaans. The interests of the South African Afrikaners were not incompatible with those of the South West African Germans, as both groups wanted the establishment of a white-dominated society in this former German colony. A conflict pitting the two groups against one another, therefore, would be detrimental to the primary goal of establishing a white settler society in South West Africa. It was in this political context that Jan Smuts, the South African prime minister, entered into a direct negotiation with the German government, resulting in the signing of the 1923 London Agreement. This accord granted Germans concessions in a wide range of areas, including politics, language, education, immigration, culture, and economics. The importance of this development was that German privileges were still protected under the South African special mandate. The interests of whites, both German and Afrikaners, were privileged over those of the Africans.

In the other former colonies, however, the interests of Germans were not accorded special privileges. In German East Africa, for example, the British ruled the country as if it were any other British colony. South West Africa was thus a unique case, primarily because it was initially managed as a settler colony. In addition, the white-dominated society of South Africa, where Afrikaner interests were being promoted at the expense of those of the Africans, necessitated a more considerate and sympathetic policy that favored the German interests even after their defeat in the war. In sum, World War I marked the formal end of German colonialism in Africa.

SEE ALSO *Apartheid; South African Racial Formations.*

BIBLIOGRAPHY

Dedering, Tilman. 1993. "The German-Herero War of 1904: Revisionism of Genocide or Imaginary Historiography." *Journal of Southern African Studies* 19 (1): 80–88.

Smith, Woodruff D. 1974. "The Ideology of German Colonialism, 1840-1906." *Journal of Modern History* 46 (4): 641–662.

———. 1978. *The German Colonial Empire.* Chapel Hill: University of North Carolina Press.

Stoler, Ann L. 1989. "Making Empire Respectable: The Politics of Race and Sexual Morality in Twentieth-century Colonial Cultures." *American Ethnologist* 16: 634–660.

Walther, Daniel Joseph. 2002. *Creating Germans Abroad: Cultural Politics and National Identity in Namibia.* Athens: Ohio University Press.

George O. Ndege

AFRICA: ITALIAN COLONIES

Italy was one of the European countries with colonies in Africa during the modern period. Lasting from 1890 to 1941, Italian colonialism in Africa included the present-day countries of Libya, Ethiopia, Eritrea, and Somalia. Italian colonialism in Africa came to an end with the death of the Italian leader Benito Mussolini, the collapse of the Fascist regime, and the defeat of Italy in World War II. Half a century of Italian colonialism had long-term effects on attitudes towards race and racism in both Italy and its colonies.

Italian colonization of Africa took place during the same period as other European colonization in the region. In many respects, Italian colonial policy was similar to that of other colonizing powers. Italian colonial policy differed, however, in that it was premised more on enhancing the glory and overall international prestige of Italy, rather than on the economic benefits that could be gained from colonies. Italian colonialism was also not guided by religious motives of converting native populations to Christianity. Italian imperialism was later shaped by Fascist doctrines of governance and social policy, which affected methods of administration and treatment of the indigenous African population.

Italy's colonial experience forced Italians to confront the presence of non-Europeans within the Italian Empire. The presence of black Africans, especially, led some Italians to construct racial hierarchies in which Italians and other Europeans stood at the top, Arabs and North Africans somewhere in the middle, and black Africans at the bottom in terms of rights and privileges. Such racialist thinking led some Italians to consider the position of Jews within Italy in a parallel manner, and to place them on this racial hierarchy. Italian attitudes toward Jews, which had previously been generally benign, began to change as a result of African colonization.

Italian colonization can be divided into two periods. The first begins in 1890, with the Italian colonization of Eritrea, and continues with the acquisition of Libya and Somalia, and the invasion and occupation of Ethiopia. The second period begins around 1937, when the occupation of Ethiopia was complete and when Fascist racial policy became more explicit and extreme. This article will examine racial policies in the Italian colonies during both periods and will conclude by noting the impact of the colonial experience on post-imperial Italy.

COLONIAL RACISM BEFORE AND DURING THE RISE OF FASCISM

By European standards, Italy is a young country, having become unified as one nation only in 1861. Before that time, what is twenty-first-century Italy consisted of several independent kingdoms. Unification brought Italians together as one people and created a sense of shared national identity—as Italians rather than as Florentines or Neapolitans—including a feeling of common national destiny. Part of this feeling, among some Italians, included a desire to acquire overseas colonies—as other European countries were doing—and to relive the glories of the Roman Empire.

Italy, as a relative latecomer to the colonial project, acquired what many Europeans considered to be the less desirable territories in Africa, including Eritrea, where Italian colonization was established in 1890; Somalia, where Italian rule began in 1905; and Libya, where Italian rule commenced in 1912. Italy had also attempted to invade Ethiopia in 1895, but was repulsed by Ethiopian forces in the Battle of Adwa, a sharp blow to many Italians in that a European army was defeated by an African one. The memory of this defeat would later inspire a second invasion of Ethiopia.

Late-nineteenth-century and early-twentieth-century anthropology was concerned with racial classification. With new colonies in Africa, Italian scholars became interested in how colonial subjects fit into racial classifications. Such classifications grew from work done in the early nineteenth century, and were based on the traditional Biblical division of peoples into the Caucasians, Semites, and Hamites, who were the descendants respectively of Japheth, Shem, and Ham, the sons of Noah. In the Bible, the descendents of Ham are cursed and destined to become slaves. An alternative interpretation argued that the descendants of Canaan, one of Ham's sons, and not the other children of Ham, were cursed. This interpretation allowed for a separate, fourth race, which was associated with black Africans and was used by Europeans to justify African slavery. It was also used by Europeans to explain how the pyramids and other monuments of Egypt were created—not by black Africans, the descendants of Canaan, but by the Hamites, the descendants of Ham's other children. Such an interpretation helped form racial attitudes toward black Africans, who were considered inferior and incapable of civilization.

Early twentieth-century anthropologists such as Aldobrandino Mochi and Vincenzo Giuffrida Ruggeri modified such traditional European views using what they considered "scientific" methods, such as skull measurements. They nevertheless perpetuated the argument that black Africans were an inferior people, but that the peoples of Libya, Eritrea, Ethiopia, and Somalia, being of Semitic background (with some Hamitic or African admixture), were capable of civilization. From this racist perspective, Italy could congratulate itself on acquiring colonies in those parts of Africa where the potential for civilization was greatest. Other anthropologists, such as Giuseppe Sergi, argued that Europeans actually originated in Africa. Thus Italy's racialist views of its colonial subjects differed in some respects from that of other colonial powers.

Using such arguments, Italy could justify its conquest and subjugation of Africans, with the hope that Italian civilization would spread to the colonized regions. There was general support among the Italian population for imperialism, as it was seen as the "mandate of history" and a continuation of the conquests of the Roman Empire. At the same time, the Roman Catholic Church wanted recognition of its primacy over the Orthodox churches in Egypt and Ethiopia, furthering the attitudes of Italian destiny.

Despite the theoretical respect for peoples of Semitic and Hamitic origin, actual Italian conquest was brutal. For example, the conquest of Libya—sometimes called the "Fourth Shore" of Italy—was lengthy and oppressive. Italy began its invasion of Libya in 1911, and succeeded in driving out the Turks, who controlled the territory, in 1912. But the Arab Libyans did not see the Italians as liberators; they resisted the Italians until 1932. The resistance movement, the Sanussi, was repressed, and its mosques closed and its leaders, such as Omar Mukhtar, imprisoned and executed. More than 100,000 Libyans were imprisoned in concentration camps, and from 1928 on cities were bombed with poison gas (despite Italy being a signatory of the Geneva Convention in 1925), which one Fascist commentator described as a "cleansing." Separate communities were established for Italians, keeping them apart from Arabs and Jews.

Similar actions took place during the Italian colonization of Somalia and Eritrea. Official Italian rule began in Somalia in 1905. Slavery, which existed in the country, was abolished by the Italians and the slave trade was outlawed, leading to opposition from some Somali tribes. The Italians looked upon the Somalis as children needing paternal guidance, but they permitted local chiefs to rule, and the Italians were also generally unconcerned about race, permitting some marriages between Italians and Somalis, and tolerating informal sexual relations between the two groups. In Eritrea, three residential districts were established in the capital, Asmara: one for whites, one for blacks, and one for people of mixed race (indicating that intermarriage was a common practice).

In Italy itself, racism was largely absent. People of mixed Italian-Jewish background who did not practice Judaism as a religion were considered to be Italian, and not in a separate category of "Jewish." Religion was more important than race or national origin. Italians saw themselves as a spiritual community to which Jews could also belong. This was to change, however, with the rise of Benito Mussolini and the Fascist Party, which came to power in 1922.

COLONIAL RACISM UNDER FASCISM

In general, there was not much change in Italian attitudes towards colonialism and imperialism during the transition from pre-Fascist to Fascist Italy. Most Italians supported the idea of empire with moderate enthusiasm, but did not hold particularly racist attitudes towards non-Italians. The Fascist Party, however, began implementing new racial policies in Africa, which began to change perceptions of race in Italy itself.

Fascist policy emphasized war and conquest, the revitalization of the state, the rejection of tradition and the past, and the forging ahead to a new future that was to be achieved through force. Fascist policy in the colonies introduced legal racism. Laws banning mixed marriages were introduced in Eritrea in 1933 and in Ethiopia in 1937 (one year after the conquest of that country by Italy in 1936). Fascists thought that mingling Italians with Africans weakened the Italian people. Fascists also considered as a problem the children born from mixed marriages, resulting in persons who did not completely fit within either Italian or African culture. As Fascist Party secretary Achille Starace noted, "With the creation of the Empire, the Italian race came into contact with other races. Hence it had to guard itself against hybridity and contamination."

In its colonies, Italy began to impose racial separation. Blacks and whites were not allowed to live together, and children of mixed marriages were not considered legitimate. Colonial administrations created separate facilities for Italians and Africans, including separate buses, restaurants, and movie theaters. Some professions

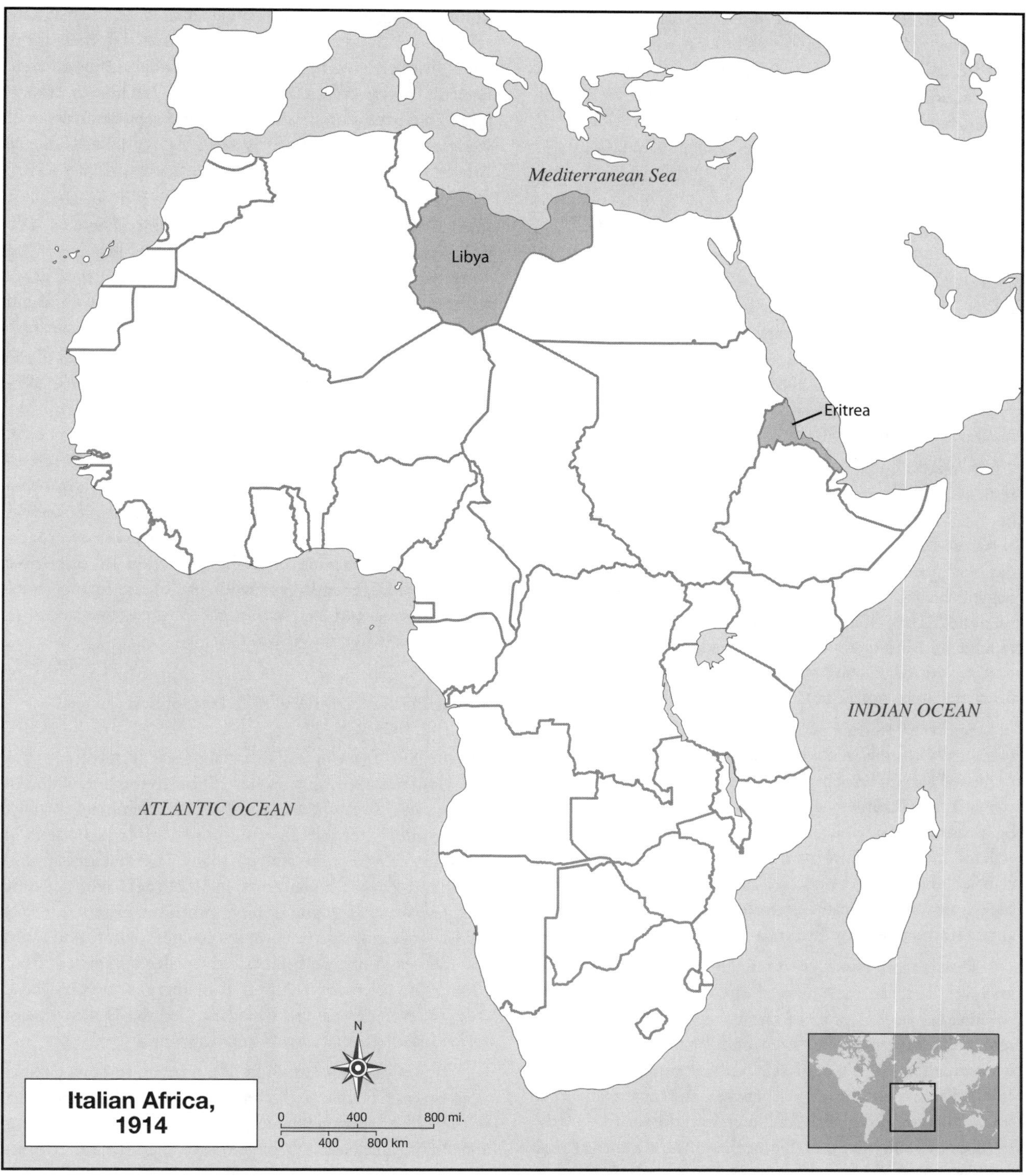

Italian Africa, 1914. MAP BY XNR PRODUCTIONS. GALE.

were limited to blacks or whites only. Italian and African workers could not work on the same site at the same time. Italians could not serve Africans in shops. Italian taxis could not accept Africans as passengers. Films shown to Africans were censored, lest any sign of weakness be perceived among Italians. Italian Fascists justified this "apartheid" on the basis that too much concern for native populations smacked of nineteenth-century liberalism, rather than of the New Order created by Fascism. As one colonial engineer stated, "We must ban natives from any access to our cities unless we can force them to pass through a sort of station of human reclamation. In a perfect colonial city, the destruction of bugs and the disinfection of clothing must be carried out in a totalitarian fashion" (Bosworth 2006).

Fascist leaders determined that the party had to take the lead in explaining racism to the public. These policies would not be copied from the Nazis in Germany but would spring from three thousand years of Italian history. In 1938 Mussolini had little interest in the persecution of Jews; he did not have the racial fanaticism of Hitler. Even hardcore Fascists such as Roberto Farinacci disliked Nazi doctrines, especially Alfred Rosenberg's racist ideas, because he believed that ideas about German racial superiority could be used against Mediterranean people as well as Jews. Farinacci and other Italian Fascists disliked Nazi talk of blond, blue-eyed people as superior.

Mussolini's policy on race in Ethiopia and other Italian colonies was that the native peoples were not to be held in contempt, but there was to be separation between the races. Italians, including Fascists, generally did not approve of Nazi doctrines, thinking them crude, pagan, brutal, and unprincipled. The Nazis had even suggested that Italians had African blood (Mussolini replied by hinting that Germans had Jewish blood)! The Fascist journal *Critica Fascista* noted in 1934 that racial doctrines were not fascist, but rather a threat to fascism.

But by 1938 the Fascists established a racial policy that specifically emphasized white superiority. Africans could be punished for not respecting Italians. If an Italian was caught committing a crime by an African policeman, he could not be arrested because that would undermine the prestige of Italians and the white race generally. Indeed, Mussolini claimed that Italy conquered Ethiopia because of Italian superiority and African inferiority (he conveniently forgot about Italy's defeat by Ethiopia in 1895).

Fascist racial laws were often ignored and not enforced, however, because they seemed alien to both Italians and colonial subjects. A practice known as *madamismo*—sexual relations between Italian men and African women—was widespread in Italy's East African colonies. Madamismo resulted from the imbalance between the large number of Italian men working in the colonies, and the relatively small number of Italian women living there (most men left their families home in Italy). Many children with Italian fathers and African mothers were born, and were accepted as legitimate until the race laws of 1938 criminalized madamismo and delegitimated children of mixed race. Nevertheless, the practice continued and laws against it were rarely enforced: Around 10,000 children of mixed race were born during the period 1936–1941 in Ethiopia alone.

Laws mandating racial separation were hardly effective. Whites and blacks continued to live side by side, despite segregation orders. Italians and Africans did share taxis, dined together in cafes, and walked together in the street, though laws forbade this. Ethiopian notables were deferred to by Italians and served by Italians in restaurants and bars. Racist laws mandating separation by race were alien to most Italians, and most Italians in the colonies therefore ignored them with impunity.

Many Italians remembered the brutality of the conquest of Ethiopia in 1935, and were sympathetic with its inhabitants and critical of racist laws and policies. One working-class Italian was quoted as saying that the Fascist regime "would have been better off first to think about civilizing the Italians" before trying to civilize Africans.

The ability of Italians and the colonized to get along meant that Italians, after the defeat of Italy in World War II, were treated well by the people they colonized, especially in Ethiopia and Eritrea. The Ethiopian emperor, Haile Selassie, when restored to his throne, granted clemency to Italians in Ethiopia. Many Ethiopians even thought that Italy had brought many benefits to the country, including the abolition of slavery, new roads, the control of famine, and the reduction of intertribal warfare. This generally positive view of the former colonizing power can be attributed to the good relations between Italians and Africans.

THE LEGACY OF FASCIST COLONIAL RACIAL POLICY

The greatest legacy of Italian racial policy in its colonies was the rise of anti-Semitism in Italy. Prior to the imposition of Fascist racial policy, there was little anti-Semitism in Italy, and certainly nothing like the hatred of Jews present in Germany. There were indeed many Jewish Fascists, and many anti-Zionist Italian Jews. In 1911 the mayor of Rome was Jewish, and many Italian prime ministers were of Jewish ancestry, as were many senators, professors, and war heroes. Italy gave sanctuary to Jews expelled from Russia and Germany. Alfred Rosenberg, the Nazi racial theorist, even denounced what he called the "Judeo-Fascist regime" located in "world-polluting Rome."

Yet Italy's colonization in Africa began to draw distinctions between people of different races. Italians began to think of themselves as somehow different from colonized Africans and Arabs, and Fascist doctrine urged them to think themselves superior to the people they had colonized. Allying racism with nationalism and national identity, the Fascist Party motivated Italians to also think of ethnicity, rather than religion or culture, as what separated them from others, thus leading to increasing anti-Semitism in Italy. Though never urgently proactive in attacking Jews as Germans had been, Italians began to see Jews as foreign and alien.

Italy has not yet confronted its colonial past, and issues of racism and anti-Semitism are not commonly discussed and analyzed in the country. Italian colonialism in Africa, motivated largely by the desire to enhance the historic glory of Italy and to help Italy find its "place in the sun" along with other colonial powers, forced Italians to think about racial difference, and many Italians came to accept racial difference to some degree, even though they may have treated their colonial subjects well.

BIBLIOGRAPHY

Bosworth, Richard J. B. 2006. *Mussolini's Italy: Life under the Dictatorship 1915–1945*. New York: Penguin.

Gillette, Aaron. 2003. *Racial Theories in Fascist Italy*. London: Routledge.

Hess, Robert L. 1966. *Italian Colonialism in Somalia*. Chicago: University of Chicago Press.

Morgan, Philip. 1995. *Italian Fascism, 1919–1945*. New York: St. Martin's Press.

Palumbo, Patrizia, ed. 2003. *A Place in the Sun: Africa in Italian Colonial Culture from Post-Unification to the Present*. Berkeley: University of California Press.

Sbacchi, Alberto. 1985. *Ethiopia under Mussolini: Fascism and the Colonial Experience*. London: Zed Books.

Smith, Denis Mack. 1976. *Mussolini's Roman Empire*. New York: Viking.

Michael Pretes

AFRICA: PORTUGUESE COLONIES

Portugal is noted as the first modern European country to have large numbers of black slaves. As one of the major sea powers of the fifteenth, sixteenth, and seventeenth centuries, Portugal also shipped and sold large numbers of African slaves to other parts of the world. Not surprisingly, the issue of slavery has shaped racial tensions between Portugal and Africa. It dominated Portuguese colonialist practices and prompted Africans to hold hostile attitudes toward the Portuguese. Other offensive colonialist practices also complicated race relations between blacks and whites in the Portuguese colonies of Angola, Mozambique, Guinea-Bissau, São Tomé and Príncipe, and Cape Verde.

SLAVERY

Southern Europe had a tradition of slavery that dated to ancient times. In the twelfth and thirteenth centuries, Portugal enslaved captured Muslims as Christians engaged in the Reconquista (the recapturing of the Iberian Peninsula from the Muslims). Beginning in the 1440s, voyages sponsored by Prince Henry the Navigator and his successors brought black slaves from Africa to Portugal. The 1455 papal bull *Romanus Pontifex* issued by Pope Nicholas V justified these activities by authorizing the Portuguese monarch to subdue all "enemies of Christ" wherever they were and to keep them in perpetual slavery. The Portuguese African trade evolved from raids along the African coast that began in 1441 to more peaceful exchanges with African chieftains and merchants by the 1450s.

The trade in African slaves soon extended from Mauritania to the area along the upper Guinea coast. In the sixteenth and seventeenth centuries, the trade extended to the Congo and Angola. Most of the slaves gathered from the African mainland were transported back to Portugal and then sent to Spain or South America. Slaves were also imported from Guinea and sent to Cape Verde. The island of São Tiago (Santiago) in the Cape Verde archipelago became a distribution center for slaves on their way to the Americas. São Tomé later assumed this role. In the upper Guinea area, Portuguese traders, entrepreneurs, and *degredados* (exiles) penetrated into the interior. Called *lançados* (outcasts), they often settled in African villages. The *lançados* served as intermediaries in the slave trade and frequently left Euro-African descendants who acted in the same capacities.

The Portuguese slave trade is divided into four periods. In the Guinea wave of the sixteenth century most of the slaves came from both upper Guinea (Senegal River to Cape Palmas) and lower Guinea (Volta River to Cape Catarina). In the seventeenth century, the Portuguese pulled slaves from equatorial and central Africa, particularly Angola and the Congo, as well as Guinea. By the eighteenth century, the Portuguese slave trade expanded to the Gold Coast (Ghana) and the Bight of Benin. In the nineteenth century, Portuguese slaves came predominantly from Angola and Mozambique.

In the eighteenth century, the slave trade came under attack from within Portugal. The Marquis of Pombal pushed through legislation that eliminated the slave trade. On September 19, 1761, legislation halted the transportation of slaves from Africa to Portugal. On January 16, 1773, legislation passed to emancipate black slaves living in Portugal. Existing slaves, however, remained in bondage for the remainder of their lives. Slavery continued in Portugal, although slave traders were often prosecuted.

In the nineteenth century, changing European opinion gradually eliminated Portugal's involvement in the international slave trade. In 1854 all slaves that were the property of the Portuguese government were freed. Two years later, all slaves owned by Portuguese town councils, religious organizations, and churches were freed as were all children born of slave mothers. Finally, the Portuguese government, headed by the Marquis of Sá da Bandeira, enacted a law on February 25, 1869, to abolish slavery in Portugal and all of its colonies.

The end of the slave trade removed the most obvious purpose for Portugal's presence in Africa. These colonies lacked effective Portuguese administration for other purposes. In Guinea, the Portuguese had comparatively little presence. In Angola, Portuguese control existed little beyond the ports of Luanda and Lobito. In Mozambique, apart from the virtually autonomous *prazos* (agricultural estates) that were developed starting in the seventeenth century along the basin of the Zambezi River, Lisbon's authority could be found only on Mozambique Island, at a few points on the Indian Ocean coastline, and in isolated riverine strongholds.

These Portuguese administrative and commercial outposts were chiefly supervised by a heterogeneous Creole population. In Cape Verde as well as São Tomé and Príncipe, the majority of the population was Creole. In Mozambique, the Creole elite engaged in trade with India and eventually succeeded in taking control of the Zambezi *prazos*. The concept of a Portuguese empire in Africa in the late nineteenth century was problematic because of this dominant Creole presence. Portuguese merchants and adventurers continued to view the remnants of Portugal's South American empire as their natural source of operations and accordingly devoted their energies and resources to Brazil.

AFRICAN COLONIES IN THE AGE OF IMPERIALISM

Meanwhile, Portugal had lost most of its territory in Asia, but the decline of Portugal's East Asian empire increased interest in its African colonies. The increasing push by other European countries to engage in African imperialism also pulled the Portuguese to Africa. During this phase, Portugal focused on expanding its outposts in Africa into nation-sized territories to compete with other European powers on the continent. It had mixed success. Portugal lost its claim to the Congo in the 1880s to Belgium, largely as a result of diplomatic maneuvering. Yet it won arbitration in the 1870s when the French president ruled for Portugal against British complaints over its control of Delagoa Bay in Mozambique. The bay formed a major outlet for the rapidly developing Transvaal and constituted a very useful piece on the political chessboard upon which the partition of Africa was played out. Portugal lost an attempt in 1890 to establish a single colony across the breadth of Africa by connecting Mozambique and Angola when Britain politically blocked the effort. The Anglo-Portuguese Treaty of 1891 formalized Portugal's imperial borders in Africa with a fairly relaxed definition of "effective occupation." The treaty, however, also required Portugal to exercise systematic control of its African colonies and to expand the Portuguese presence in Africa.

The African colonies played a critical role in the Portuguese economy. They provided a protected market, supplying raw materials at prices cheaper than the world market rates and buying Portuguese products that had a low world demand. Foreign exchange earnings from exports and services also reduced the chronic deficit on Portugal's balance of trade. To safeguard the advantages brought by the colonies, the Portuguese had to protect the white population in Lusophone (Portuguese-speaking) Africa against possible African competition by the policy of economic segregation. Numbers of impoverished whites had emigrated to the colonies. The immigration relieved population pressure in Portugal, one of the most crowded and poorest countries in Europe. Of equal importance to Portugal, the white settlers provided a bulwark against rebellious Africans and covetous Europeans in neighboring African countries. Accordingly, whites were congregated in the cities or other places of critical economic importance. They pressured Portugal to defend their interests with edicts that favored whites over Africans and Creoles.

RISE OF AFRICAN RESISTANCE

In the 1950s and 1960s, three factors helped to bring about a change in traditional Portuguese colonialism. A general anticolonialist sentiment bubbled up as the result of economic and political developments in Europe in the wake of World War II. France and Great Britain granted independence to almost all of their African colonies. Portugal, forced to defend its presence in Africa, introduced some nominal reforms. In 1951 it also recategorized its African colonies as Portuguese provinces to block any intervention efforts by the United Nations. Meanwhile, armed revolts led by Africans offered blacks an alternative to the acceptance of Portuguese domination. Portugal introduced more reforms in response to the revolts. And finally, in the 1960s, industrial interests began to compete for the dominant political role that agrarians in Portugal had long held. The need for a less restricted economy, new labor techniques, and increased productivity demanded changes both at home and in the formerly inflexible economic and social structures of the colonies.

Rather than paying wages to free black workers, as the other colonial countries did, Portugal forced compulsory labor from blacks. Portugal first responded to the anticolonist movement by passing legislation in 1955 that regulated the use of compulsory labor for public works. The use of compulsory labor by private concerns had been formally abolished by law in 1928. Nevertheless, the practice remained widespread, and Portugal instituted

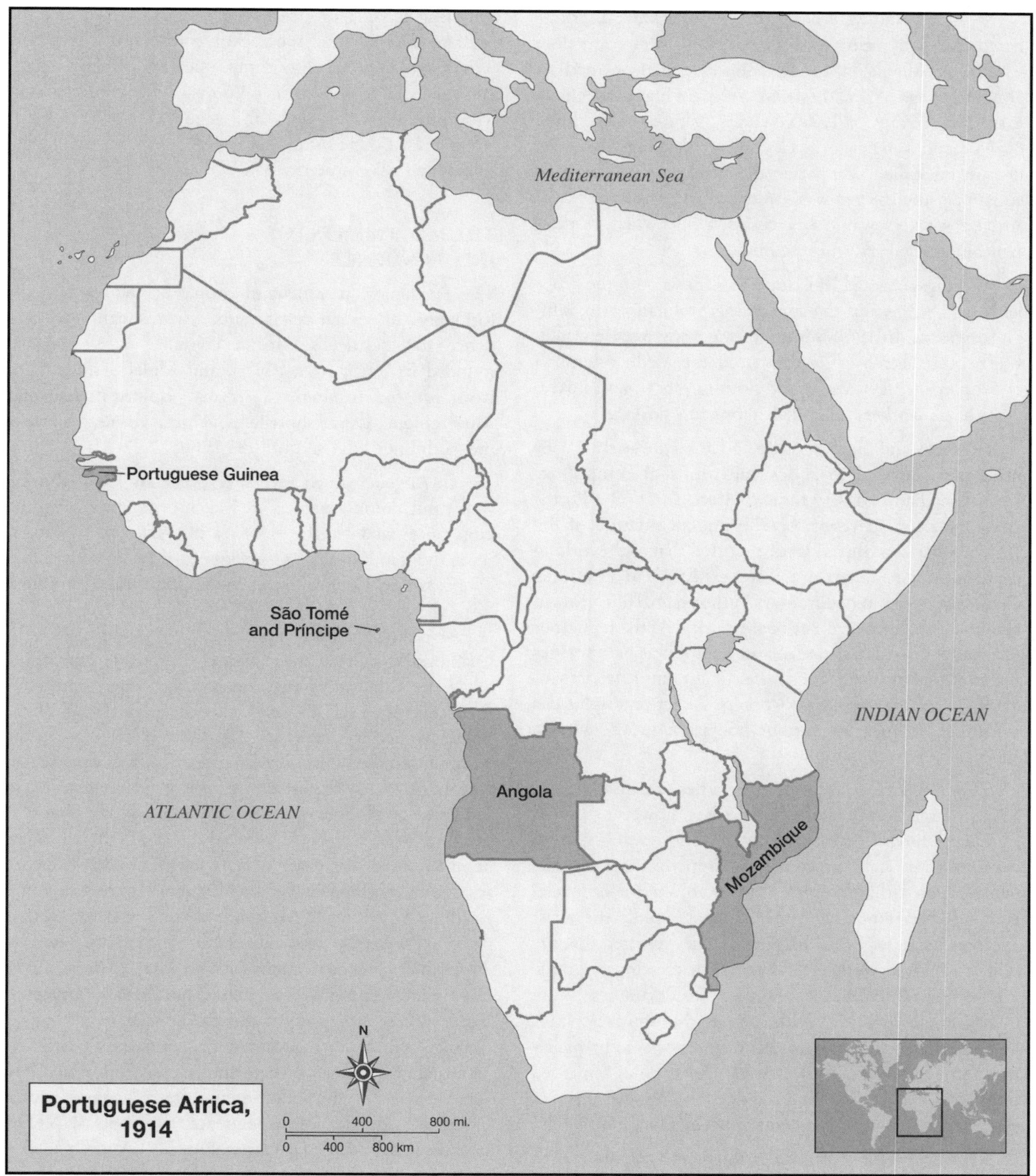

Portuguese Africa, 1914. MAP BY XNR PRODUCTIONS. GALE.

heavier penalties on those using such labor in an effort to give the ban bigger teeth. These two responses were designed to improve Portugal's standing in world opinion. Unfortunately, as the United Nations subsequently reported, in 1956, 500,000 Africans in Mozambique were forced to work on cotton farms. Each head of household received an average of $11.17 as a year's payment for the labor of an entire family. In 1958 an estimated 120,000 Africans were still conscripted in Angola, and about 95,000 worked for private employers.

Africans who were not forced to work were discriminated against by being paid considerably lower wages than whites. In Angola in 1958, white carpenters earned an annual average of 3,120 escudos, whereas black carpenters earned an average of 1,690 escudos. White cooks earned 3,334 escudos, whereas black cooks took home 500 escudos. In no skilled occupation did blacks and whites earn equal pay, and the gap was substantial. The average pay of African workers was 600 escudos, while white workers typically earned six times as much.

Portugal enacted legislation to address both the problems with wages and the continuing problems with compulsory labor. In 1960 minimum wage laws were enacted. But because employers were permitted to deduct as much as 50 percent from wages for clothing, food, and board, most black workers remained trapped in poverty.

Rioting and fighting in Angola in the early 1960s prompted Portugal to abolish all forms of compulsory labor. The ban had very limited effect. In 1969 a Portuguese government report on the implementation of the 1957 abolition of forced labor reported that such working conditions continued and were expected to continue. Civil, military, and paramilitary authorities defined forced labor on the grounds of national security. At the request of individual employers, police and paramilitary authorities used various means of repression, including extreme violence, to control rebellious workers. Anger among blacks continued to fuel the various liberation movements in Portugal's African colonies.

The liberation movements gained recruits in the 1960s. Large numbers of white settlers, however, wanted to remain under Portuguese control. They even helped to develop a rationale for continued imperial control: The whites argued that Portugal had established a nonracial form of cooperation with the Africans, unlike the racist apartheid regimes in British Africa. They asserted that the races socialized, worked, and married, creating a unique Luso-tropical civilization. While the Portuguese were clearly not as obsessed with race as the South Africans and Rhodesians, Portuguese Africa did not exactly qualify as a color-blind paradise. Africans and Creoles remained trapped in poverty and at the mercy of a repressive police state designed to crush any attempts at rebellion.

Portugal took several steps to try and maintain control over its colonies in this era. In 1961 it abolished the legal distinction between "civilized" and "noncivilized." The latter group, consisting of almost all blacks, had no civil rights, with all of the economic and social consequences resulting from this status. The *assimilados*, or Africans who had fully adopted Portuguese customs and language, did have rights, but there were only 30,089 *assimilados* among Angola's four million blacks in 1950. The *assimilado* category was ended. Nevertheless, these changes did not bring equality to Africa. The electoral laws limited the right to vote to only those people who could read and write Portuguese. In 1965 only 5 percent of black Angolans qualified to vote; in 1969 only 1 percent of blacks in Mozambique voted. Only an insignificant percentage of Africans had the educational qualifications to participate in colonial government.

THE MOVEMENTS FOR INDEPENDENCE

The Portuguese treatment of people of color led to the formation of several organizations that sought independence for Portugal's African colonies. Liga Africana, founded in 1919, joined black and Mulatto students to work for the freedom of Angola, Guinea-Bissau, and Mozambique. It was short-lived. African liberation movements did not flourish until the 1960s.

In Angola, armed resistance began in 1960. Rioting broke out among farmers in Malanje province over low crop prices that had been set by the government. About seven thousand protesters were killed in clashes with police. The Bakongo, along with the Ovimbundu and Kimbundu, form the major indigenous ethnic groups in Angola. The Bakongo took the lead in pushing for autonomy, with the Ovimbundu more closely aligned with white employers, while the Kimbundu were resented by other groups for their control of the job market in the ports. In 1960 the police arrested an *assimilado*, Agostinho Neto, who led the Kimbundu-based Popular Movement for the Liberation of Angola (MPLA). His arrest set off riots in Luanda. In an unrelated development, the Bakongo, led by the Union of the Peoples of Northern Angola (later the National Liberation Front in Angola or FNLA) under Holden Roberto, rose up in rebellion in 1960 with almost twenty thousand Bakongo killed. In 1961 hundreds of blacks in Luanda protested police brutality by storming the prisons and freeing political prisoners along with ordinary criminals. The city's whites responded by killing hundreds of unarmed blacks. This last event marks the official beginning of Angola's war of liberation. Subsequently, ethnic conflicts damaged the cause of Angolan independence. In 1966 Jonas Savimbi, an Ovimbundu, created the National Union for the Total Independence of Angola (UNITA) to counter the ethnic exclusiveness of FNLA.

In Mozambique, armed resistance began in 1964. However, there were several wildcat strikes by African workers in Mozambican ports in the 1950s followed in 1960 by a massive protest by farmers angry about low prices set by government-controlled marketing boards. The *assimilados* led the rebellion. In 1962 they formed the Liberation Front of Mozambique (Frelimo) under Eduardo Mondlane. Frelimo relied upon guerilla tactics. In response, the Portuguese moved many Africans and

Creoles into resettlement camps where they could not assist Frelimo.

In São Tomé and Príncipe, the Batepá Massacre of 1953 led to the death of several hundred African workers in fighting with Portuguese authorities. In the late 1950s, a small group of São Tomeans formed the Movement for the Liberation of São Tomé and Príncipe (MLSTP). Meanwhile, in Guinea-Bissau, the pan-Africanist Amilcar Cabral joined several others in 1956 to form the African Party for the Independence of Guinea and Cape Verde (PAIGC). Guerilla fighting began in earnest in 1962.

The efforts to suppress rebellions in its African colonies put too much stress on the government of Portugal and its dictator, Marcelo Caetano. With the government nearly bankrupt, he was overthrown in April 1974. Among the first decisions made by the leftist coup leaders was to rid Portugal of its overseas possessions as quickly as possible. The decolonization process in the aftermath of the April 1974 revolution in Portugal produced dramatic results, particularly in Angola and Mozambique. Most of the Portuguese population suddenly fled from these countries. The movement happened more rapidly and dramatically in the case of Angola because of the armed clashes among liberation movements with the support of foreign armies. Both the MPLA in Angola and the Frelimo in Mozambique (and, to a lesser extent, the PAIGC in Guinea-Bissau and Cape Verde and the MLSTP in São Tomé and Príncipe) encouraged this exodus, under the assumption that most of the settler communities would react against further moves toward the creation of a socialist state, redistribution of wealth, or a centrally planned economy. These radical policies only strengthened the settler communities' feelings against the installation of a black government. In Mozambique, when about 180,000 of the 200,000 Portuguese in the country fled, they spitefully destroyed much of the country's infrastructure before they left.

The PAIGC declared the independence of Guinea-Bissau on September 24, 1973. Guinea-Bissau would be wracked by civil war until the end of the century. On June 25, 1975, Portugal formally surrendered power in Mozambique. While the country had fewer internal ethnic conflicts than Angola, it also faced danger in the form of white-dominated neighboring Rhodesia. Many former Portuguese colonists from Mozambique now living in Rhodesia supported the terrorist Mozambique National Resistance (Renamo). Fighting between Frelimo and Renamo shook Mozambique until a 1992 peace settlement. São Tomé and Príncipe achieved independence on July 12, 1975. The country subsequently enjoyed peace, democracy, and multiparty elections. Angola achieved formal independence on November 11, 1975. The FNLA had largely collapsed with the MPLA in control of most of the country. UNITA retreated to rural areas in southern and central Angola. Ethnic conflicts continued to ravage the country into the next century.

BIBLIOGRAPHY

Boxer, Charles Ralph. 1963. *Race Relations in the Portuguese Colonial Empire, 1415–1825.* Oxford: Clarendon Press.

Brüne, Stefan, Joachim Betz, and Winrich Kühne, eds. 1994. *Africa and Europe: Relations of Two Continents in Transition.* Münster, Germany: Lit.

Duffy, James. 1968. *Portuguese Africa.* Cambridge, MA: Harvard University Press.

Ferreira, Eduardo de Sousa. 1974. *Portuguese Colonialism in Africa: The End of an Era.* Paris: Unesco Press.

Macqueen, Norrie. 1997. *The Decolonization of Portuguese Africa: Metropolitan Revolution and the Dissolution of Empire.* London: Longman.

Newitt, Malyn. 1981. *Portugal in Africa: The Last Hundred Years.* London: Longman.

Caryn E. Neumann

AFRICAN DIASPORA

The concept of "diaspora" suggests the spread or scattering of a specific population or race of people to different and far-flung places throughout the world. Without alluding to the earliest development of humans in Africa as the foundation of all human diasporas, the African continent, beginning in the fifteenth century at least, was the original source of a significant black diaspora, which in the early twenty-first century embraces the entire globe. The European slave trade to the New World started a massive wave of forced migration of the cream of African populations, particularly from West and Central Africa, to the Caribbean and thence to South and North America, the objective being to provide cheap labor on white-owned plantations. This was the known post-Columbian beginning of the African diaspora. A second wave of out-migration from the Caribbean to North America and Europe—virtually completing a circle in the spread of black populations around the world—took place during the latter part of the twentieth century.

THE SLAVE TRADE

The question is whether the European-initiated slave trade from Africa to the New World starting in the late fifteenth and early sixteenth centuries was motivated by economic factors or by racial considerations. Eric Williams, who became the first prime minister of Trinidad and Tobago in 1956, believed that the main motivation of the plantation owners was cheap labor, which also fueled the financial greed of the slave traders and helped to catapult a backward feudal-dominated Europe to the age of industrial capitalism beginning in the eighteenth century.

The race question would thus seem to be a secondary phenomenon with regard to the motivation behind the African slave trade. Much has already been written about the racist preoccupations of Europeans during the slavery period, particularly their belief in the myth about "the white man's burden," which held that they had to control the world in order to civilize or Christianize it. Europeans also adhered to so-called scientific theories of race, which relegated the darker-skinned peoples of the world to the bottom of a supposed hierarchical human order, and to false biblical (Old Testament) notions about blacks being fallen angels condemned to eternal servitude by God. But while these ideas helped justify the African slave trade, Williams thought that the bottom line had always been an economic one. The search for gold and the profitability in trade in slaves, raw material, and commodities that the Indies made possible were necessary inputs in the development of the Industrial Revolution in Europe.

However, the race question in this New World quest for gold and riches cannot be dismissed out of hand. The level of brutality, repressiveness, and what could be called a cultural genocide suffered by African slaves at the hands of the white planter classes and colonial authorities alike far surpassed the conditions under which the native Indians and indentured European laborers operated on New World plantations before the arrival of the Africans. But if racism was not the principal determining factor responsible for the genesis of the African slave trade to the Caribbean, it certainly developed as a consequence of this inhuman trade, for racism characterized and influenced the very unequal hierarchical structure and fabric of plantation and social life in the region as a whole.

The African slaves resisted their lot frequently. Such resistance ranged from runaway slaves to open rebellion and, ultimately, revolution. Colonies of runaway slaves (Maroons) were established in locations such as Jamaica, Surinam, and Brazil, and the historical legacy of resistance and rebellion persisted up to the twentieth century in the forms of the defiant creation of black villages following emancipation and the political struggles for democracy and independence between the 1940s and 1960s. The success of the Haitian Revolution of 1791–1804 influenced a generation of similar rebellious and revolutionary struggles throughout the hemisphere, including the slave rebellions between 1800 and 1831 in the Americas and the Latin American revolution for independence from Spain in the 1920s.

Emancipation came first in the British West Indies in 1934, when, in addition to the slaves being freed, the white plantation owners were financially compensated by the British authorities for their loss of slave labor. The former slaves proceeded to build independent farming villages for themselves, while the planters imported fresh labor from as far away as China and India. The African villages then became the centers of Africanist cultures, which by the time of emancipation were significantly influenced by European values, thereby creating a hybrid, or "creole," cultural frame of existence. This hybrid creolization of Africanist culture in the New World is seen in Caribbean musical expressions such as reggae and calypso, as well as in Caribbean religious lifestyles such as Vodou and Rastafarianism. Both Vodou and Rastafarianism marry African traditions and beliefs with Western Christian influences. Some of the richness of this Caribbean hybrid experience, particularly reggae and Rastafarianism, has become internationalized, and their influences can be seen on all continents of the globe.

REVERSE MIGRATION

From the Caribbean, many African slaves (after having been "seasoned" for some time) were transshipped to both North and South America to serve on similar plantations in these other parts of the world. Thus the migration of Africans in the New World continued both during slavery when slaves from the Caribbean were further relocated and sold to South American and North American plantations, and after slavery when voluntary migration to metropolitan centers in Europe and North America became widespread. However, the essential aspect of this latter reverse flow of Caribbean migration to Europe and North America took place essentially in the twentieth century, several decades after African slavery had been abolished from these shores in the nineteenth century.

There are several push factors responsible for the increasing waves of out-migration away from Africa, the Caribbean, and Latin America, which in the early 2000s constitute the bulk of the African diaspora. Most significant among these push factors are political instability, repressive or oppressive state policies, economic hardships, and lack of personal advancement. Migrants also desire to settle in the more advanced metropoles of Europe and North America because of better economic opportunities and higher educational attainments. But what is mostly fueling out-migration from the New World region is the phenomenon of economic and technological globalization, which tends to concentrate wealth and more lucrative economic and job opportunities in the metropolitan centers of the world, particularly in North America and Europe. Metropolitan cities such as New York, London, Toronto, Paris, and Amsterdam take up the bulk of immigrant populations from Africa and the Caribbean. Meanwhile, the major concentrations

UNITED STATES SLAVE TRADE.
1830.

Slave Traders at Work. *An abolitionist print found in the ruins of Philadelphia's Anti-Slavery Hall, which was burned by a mob in 1838. The scene depicts a mother and her children being sold with the U.S. Capitol building looming in the background.* THE LIBRARY OF CONGRESS.

of people of African descent, outside the African continent, are in the United States and Brazil.

CONTRIBUTIONS OF THE AFRICAN DIASPORA

African diaspora communities in North America and Europe have made important economic, political, cultural and intellectual contributions to the development of their homeland territories and the world. In particular, it is their economic contributions to their homeland territories that distinguish members of the African diaspora from other international aid donors. In many instances these economic contributions from the diaspora, principally in the form of what are called "remittances," account for the greatest proportion of financial contributions to the domestic economies of African and Caribbean nations. According to a 2003 World Bank working paper, remittances from the African diaspora in the United States to African countries amount to $12 billion annually, with about $4 billion of that going to sub-Saharan Africa alone. Similarly, the contributions of Caribbean diaspora represent a significant proportion of the gross domestic product (GDP) of their respective homelands. For example, according to the International Monetary Fund (IMF), remittances to the Dominican Republic represented 9.3 percent of GDP in 2002, while for Jamaica and Haiti the figures were 13.6 percent and 24.2 percent, respectively.

Political contributions of members of the African diaspora abroad range from organizing historical mass movements for black and minority civil and political rights to direct involvement in the decision-making processes in metropolitan states. The decolonization struggles in Africa, the Caribbean, and around the world, and the black civil rights movement in the United States are the most prominent examples of African diaspora political contributions, while the prominent roles played by black representatives in the U.S. Congress (such as Shirley Chisholm) and government (such as Colin Powell as secretary of state), are examples of African diaspora political capabilities at the very highest levels of government. Similar contributions of African diaspora individuals apply to the British government, in which the Guyanese nationals Baroness Valerie Amos (in the House of Lords) and David Lammy (in the British Cabinet) are prominent examples.

Cultural contributions of members of the African diaspora are numerous. These include, most prominently, artistic and musical creations, intellectual outputs, and specific religious practices. Major musical contributions include the creation of jazz in the United States, reggae and calypso music in the Caribbean, and samba in Brazil, each of which has made a significant international impact. Similarly, the colorful and dazzling creativity of Carnival parades in Trinidad and Tobago rivals that of Mardi Gras in both Brazil and New Orleans, with all three vying for coveted international acclaim as "the greatest show on earth."

Intellectual contributions are seen in the tremendous literary attainment of African, African American, Caribbean, and Afro Latin-American writers such as Richard Wright, Wole Soyinka, and Derek Walcott, while the academic contributions of Arthur Lewis, Walter Rodney, and Ali Mazrui are also noteworthy. African diaspora contributions to political thought and practices are found in the consciousness raising works of Marcus Garvey, members of the African Blood Brotherhood (ABB) of Harlem during the 1920s, and C.L.R. James, Frantz Fanon, and Walter Rodney, among others, during more recent times.

AFRICAN DIASPORA COMMUNITIES BEYOND THE WEST

The fact that the African diaspora has been made almost synonymous with what has been termed "the Black Atlantic" can hardly be disputed (Gilroy 1993). However, there are also significant African diaspora communities beyond the Atlantic region. Within the Pacific region in Asia, for example, there are long-established communities that trace their historical and racial roots to Africa. The Sidis of the Western Indian state of Gugarat constitute "tens of thousands" of African-derived peoples who were brought to India beginning in the twelfth century as slave-soldiers for the Indian princely states. The Sidis distinguished themselves as powerful military fighters who sometimes usurped power from the princely rulers they served. In the early twenty-first century, the Sidis have lost much contact with and knowledge of Africa, but they have retained many remnants of their African past, particularly in music and dance, such as in the use of certain African-derived musical instruments.

Africans in Russia and China have a significant presence mainly as students. This presence has grown significantly since the 1960s, after African and Caribbean states obtained political independence from European colonial control. Many African and Caribbean students were sent to Russia (the then Soviet Union) and China to study at universities there, mainly in keeping with non-alignment and Afro-Asian solidarity principles (as expressed at the Bandung Conference in 1955) of the cold war age. However, serious controversies emerged about the reception of African students in these far-flung countries. In Russia, for instance, African students complained about racial discrimination and neglect by state authorities. In China, African students rioted in the 1980s in Nanjing and Hangzhou over what they regarded as officially sanctioned discrimination against them.

Then there are the Afroid Melanesian peoples of the Indian Ocean-South Pacific region, who are said to have predated even the Chinese and Indians in the prehistory of the region. They possess distinctively African physical characteristics, and they have also suffered the fate of colonial exploitation, dispossession, and economic disadvantage. Countries such as Papua New Guinea, Fiji, and Vanuatu are the most prominent examples of the South Pacific homelands of these peoples of the older African diaspora.

FUTURE OF THE AFRICAN DIASPORA

The African diaspora is a very dynamic universe of creativity, but it faces a series of challenges to ensure its continued development. First, there is the issue of clearly defining African identity, particularly in the context of the controversy surrounding the self-definition of mixed offspring of African descendants within this universe. Thus, the famous golfer Tiger Woods would prefer to be identified as "mixed" rather than as African American, and the mixed Garifuna people of the Caribbean are very much concerned with recapturing the traditions of their Carib ancestry alongside their interest in their African roots. Many Mulattoes in the Caribbean area prefer to distance themselves from their African ancestry and culture.

A second issue affecting the future of African diaspora development is the consistent disadvantaged position of African-descended people in the hierarchy of political and economic relationships throughout the globe. The persistent subordination of the black race is witnessed at the global level in terms of the history of colonial and capitalist exploitation of Africa, while within the diaspora blacks have often been at the disadvantaged end of the increasing economic and political inequalities that attend the processes of economic and technological globalization.

A third issue is the persistent need for continuous struggle to redress the difficulties posed by economic and political disadvantages, and again to overcome the further difficulties posed by the struggles themselves. While, for example, affirmative action policies are identified as necessary to overcome economic disadvantages, there is still the need to struggle against a growing number of opponents to these policies, particularly among conservative whites in the United States. The issue of "reparations" for the wrongs of slavery represents another frontier in this struggle, with the same implications of countering significant opposition, mainly from white conservatives. In the British Caribbean, the emancipation of slaves in 1834 brought monetary reparations, but it was paid to the white plantation owners to compensate for their "lost" slaves, not to the ex-slaves who lost so much more in the centuries of their forced labor on Caribbean plantations.

A fourth issue has to do with the persistence of deadly violent political and military conflicts (including genocide) among the peoples of Africa and the African diaspora. Political (including militarized) conflicts involving ethnic or communal divisiveness and narcotics trafficking are endemic in the Caribbean, and in such countries as Guyana, Trinidad and Tobago, Jamaica, and Surinam. In Africa, political and military violence have affected the lives of millions of continental Africans, particularly in such countries as Nigeria, Sierra Leone, Liberia, the Congo, and the Sudan. Genocide of major proportions, involving hundreds of thousands of peoples, has occurred in Rwanda and Burundi, and is still ongoing in Darfur in Northern Sudan.

The African diaspora, which has produced so many gifted, inspired, and inspiring internationally recognized leaders—such as of Marcus Garvey of Jamaica, Aimé Césaire of Martinique, W. E. B. Du Bois of the United States, Nelson Mandela of South Africa, Martin Luther King Jr. of the United States, and Kofi Annan of Ghana—has indeed come to an impasse on many issues. A new generation of capable leadership is needed to deal with the significant problems facing this diverse worldwide community.

SEE ALSO *African Economic Development; Black Consciousness; Brazilian Racial Formations; Caribbean Racial Formations; Cuban Racial Formations; United Kingdom Racial Formations; White Settler Society.*

BIBLIOGRAPHY

Centers for Disease Control and Prevention (CDC), National Center for HIV/AIDS. 2000. "Race/Ethnicity in the US and HIV/AIDS." *The Body: Prevention News Update.* Atlanta, GA., January 14.

D'Monte, Darryl. 2005. "Africans in India: Interview with Helene Basu, Associate Professor, Free University, Berlin." *Frontline* 22 (18)L August 27–September 9.

Gilroy, Paul. 1993. *The Black Atlantic: Modernity and Double Consciousness.* Cambridge, MA: Harvard University Press.

International Monetary Fund (IMF). 2002. *Balance of Payments Statistics Yearbook.* Washington, DC: IMF.

James, C.L.R. 1938. *The Black Jacobins.* New York: Vintage.

Mars, Perry. 1998. *Ideology and Change: The Transformation of the Caribbean Left.* Detroit, MI: Wayne State University Press.

Price, Richard, ed. 1979. *Maroon Societies: Rebel Slave Communities in the Americas,* 2nd ed. Baltimore, MD: Johns Hopkins University Press.

Rapley, John. 2004. *Globalization and Inequality: Neoliberalism's Downward Spiral.* Boulder, CO: Lynn Rienner.

Rodney, Walter. 1972. *How Europe Underdeveloped Africa.* London: Bogle-L'Ouverture.

Sander, Cerstin, and Samuel M. Maimbo. 2003. "Migrant Labor Remittances in Africa: Reducing Obstacles to Development Contributions." *Africa Region Working Paper Series (ARWPS),* no. 64. Washington, DC: World Bank Group.

Whitehead, Andrew. 2000. "The Lost Africans of India." *BBC News,* November 27. Available from http://news.bbc.co.uk.

Williams, Eric. 1994 (1944). *Capitalism and Slavery.* Chapel Hill: University of North Carolina Press.

———. 1970. *From Columbus to Castro: The History of the Caribbean 1492–1969.* London: Andre Deutsch.

Young, Allan. 1958. *The Approaches to Local Self-Government in British Guiana.* London: Longmans.

Perry Mars

AFRICAN ECONOMIC DEVELOPMENT

Globalization, race, and African economic development intersect in deep, intricate, complicated ways that can only be understood if a long view is taken on the nature of globalization. Further, the connections are best contextualized as an inquiry into Africa's place in the world system. As Filomina Steady points out, many factors are involved, including the institutionalization of "economic domination through corporate globalization," which has generated a reproduction of colonization and, consequently, impoverishment. Other factors include "protracted recession, the debt burden, Structural Adjustment Programmes, externally controlled privatization, ... an emphasis on exports, ... a cultural crisis of major proportions, ... the destruction of many African economies, social dislocations and civil strife," all "compounded by the erosion of the life-supporting capacities of many African ecosystems. Authoritarian regimes and gender-based discrimination complete the picture" (Steady 2002).

THE ROOTS OF GLOBALIZATION

Most analysis on globalization focuses on the contemporary era. A few scholars take the long view, however, dating globalization back into the distant past. This perspective considers it an imperialistic process, inclusive of "the age of exploration," the period of the transatlantic slave trade, the "legitimate trade," so named to signal its purveyors' noninvolvement in the slave trade, in spite of the use of slave labor to plant, harvest, and/or gather commodities that were used in the factories during Europe's industrial revolution. The trade was undertaken in the period immediately following the end of the transatlantic slave trade, and lasted from the late eighteenth to the nineteenth century colonization, and the postcolonial era. This immediately puts "race" front and center in discussions of the connections between globalization, race, and African economic development. European imperialism created a paradoxical relationship between Africa and Europe that included both a centralized and marginalized position for Africa in global political and economic systems. Africa was central to the extent that it was plundered, raped, and exploited for its human and material resources. It was marginal because it did not have any power in the emerging global system, where Western dominance was built upon Africa's plundered resources. It was also marginal because the West's dominance was predicated upon Africans' presumed racial, cultural, and physiological inferiority to Europeans, a belief that was proclaimed by many of the most distinguished Western intellectuals.

From the fifteenth century to the 1930s, samples of "exotic" peoples, including Africans, were acquired and displayed—for "education" and entertainment—in the homes of the wealthiest Europeans and in public exhibits at zoos and regional and world fairs. Upon this foundation was built racist and essentialist consensus of the early twenty-first century: that Africa is a basket case of impoverished, diseased, and crisis-ridden countries led by inept and kleptocratic leaders, and that its marginality to global political, social, and economic affairs is therefore well earned.

THE ROLE OF GLOBAL FINANCIAL FORCES

A better way to understand Africa's predicament is to focus on how the conjunctures between structural inequities and failing markets generate underdevelopment. The consequences of these conjunctures in the black community in the United States include being underserved in education, health care, and housing security, while also being overcharged and offered less credit than others. White monopolies are also entrenched in the job market and many career ladders. Blacks bear the spillover costs when whites flee to the suburbs, which leads to smaller tax rolls to maintain public services and provide requisite infrastructure in cities. The cycle continues when black neighborhoods are replaced and appropriated through gentrification and white return to urban centers.

This is similar to conditions in Africa, whose people and land were enslaved, underdeveloped, and overexploited to guarantee capitalist development in Europe. As Walter Rodney observes, "Racism, violence and brutality were the concomitants of the capitalist system when it extended itself abroad in the early centuries of international trade" (Rodney 1973). Consider, as Timothy Shaw has done, the relationship between the political-existential condition of the continent and the analytical-epistemological inquiry of its historical and contemporary experiences. Existentially and politically, Africa stands in the gap between nominal or flag independence and the legacy of underdevelopment bestowed on it by its encounters with imperialism and globalization (which dates as far back as the fifteenth century). Epistemologically, scholars have tried to explain why Africa is so embattled. As Shaw notes, those who do more successful analysis take a historical and critical perspective.

ASPECTS OF GLOBALIZATION

Globalization is best conceived as a process of inexorable worldwide integration that applies to all spheres of life. Historically, it is a process that encompasses the internationalization of trade, manufacturing, and business enterprises. As it relates to Africa, the transatlantic slave trade, "legitimate trade," and the activities of the Royally Chartered Companies from various European countries were part of the early markers of globalization and the precursors of current foreign direct investment. Race, racism, and gender affect social conditions and economic development initiatives in Africa in a myriad of ways. Globalization cannot be understood outside the context of how neoliberal economic ideology has saturated the scholarly and popular imagination worldwide.

Historically, the idea that Africans belong to an inferior race has been pervasive in European and American thought. The concept of "race"—the socially constructed categorization of humans based on external appearance, stereotypes, and myths about physical, mental and psychological capacity; cultural difference; and the capacity to be civilized or uncivilized—has been deployed to support a hierarchy in which Europeans are categorized as superior and Africans the most debased. From the earliest Christian exegesis to Shakespeare and his heirs in Western literature and on to theories of scientific racism, black has been predominantly characterized as evil, while white has been seen as good and pure. Consequently, social discrimination, economic exclusion, and racial segregation have marginalized peoples of African descent from global political, social, and economic systems. Moving from the margins to the center in these systems has proved to be challenging and, in some cases, elusive. A historical scholarly analysis, meanwhile, takes African marginalization as a timeless reality generated by characteristics that are argued to be essential to Africans.

The presumption of an intrinsic and immutable African racial inferiority has generated a self-fulfilling prophecy in Africa's marginality. This has led to a conflation of presumed racial inferiority, economic impoverishment, and lack of political power. This "reality" is so disheartening, and African educational systems are so mired in the reproduction of colonial ideological "Otherizing" of Africans, that many Africans embrace a marginalized social, political, and economic characterization as emerging out of something deep in their nature.

There is overwhelming evidence of the depth of social privations in the African continent. The debate on the future is defined as being between Afro-pessimistic and Afro-optimistic perspectives. The Afro-pessimists, observing that anomie, disillusionment, and alienation have become pervasive among the impoverished majority (a condition made even more difficult by the flamboyant gestures of the noveau riche), see no hope for positive, autonomous development. In particular, they see the problems faced by the continent as driven by domestic stimuli, including the failure of leadership exemplified by a kleptocratic "politics of the belly," through which criminalized states sponsor "economies of plunder."

The Afro-optimists do not dispute that the age of globalization has also coincided with the rending of the social fabric in the African continent, but they are hopeful that an African renaissance will emerge out of the detritus of the continent's historical experiences. For them, the sources of Africa's marginalization are external, derived from the exploitation of the age of exploration and colonization. Even independence and postcolonial relations have brought new kinds of economic dependency and the persistence of colonization in other forms. Yet while the imposition of changes that have benefited external forces has rendered African communities weaker in many respects, it has also made them stronger in others, because a few people have become extremely wealthy, and new forms of communal organization for self help have been instituted to provide services that the state is no longer willing or able to offer. It is out of the stronger elements of African resilience that its renaissance is expected to spring. Pervasive and enduring social inequalities will only be defeated with dogged and relentless planning and an optimistic belief in African agency.

RACISM AND ECONOMIC DEVELOPMENT

Race and racism have profound effects on economic development initiatives. What constitutes good investment, where those investments should be directed, and who should be consulted in the process are all influenced by prior beliefs on who is considered an expert, and on established agendas. Elmer E. Schattschneider has identified a "mobilization of bias," a very essential element of power that legitimizes some issues as worthwhile and some agents as best able to tackle the issues, thus ignoring alternative issues, methods, and ideas because they are considered important by those who are marginal to the decision-making process, or considered incapable of participating because they have no expertise. The hegemonic dominance of European and North American ideas has given them priority in the consideration of alternatives. Thus, most of the investments made tend to be concentrated in sectors located in the extractive industries such as mining and logging, or in labor-intensive industries such as plantation agriculture or global sweatshop production. Yet even these options are only available to a few select countries that compete with countries in Asia and other regions believed to be more investor-friendly in a race to the bottom. Thus, while one cannot necessarily make a causative argument on the linkage between racial discrimination and inadequate, inappropriate, and irrelevant investment in Africa, there is a definite correlation between these investment patterns and Africa's lack of economic development.

Most foreign direct investment (FDI) by multinational and transnational corporations is made in Europe and the United States, and Africa lags woefully behind. This is in part because of the infrastructural, bureaucratic, and labor difficulties that confront potential investors, and largely because Africa's historical marginalization virtually ensures such difficulties. Thus, a self-fulfilling prophecy is created, where Africa is not considered a worthwhile arena for FDI because of its marginalization, while its not being considered for FDI ensures further marginalization. The economic development initiatives made available to Africa are, by and large, not those likely to yield either tremendous growth or appreciable increases in social well-being. Instead, the opportunities that exist in the contemporary global economy steer Africa toward a concentration on the production of raw materials.

Gender is socially constructed, and thus takes differing forms in different locales and historical eras. Gender is also embedded in social relations and permeates all social structures, relations, norms, values, and processes. Labor markets, households, political systems, and economic institutions and processes are also gendered in a manner that privileges males over females. Most analysts rightly observe that there is a great deal of gender-based discrimination in Africa. Yet most of them inaccurately attribute the sources of such discrimination solely to African traditions and culture. A historically sound analysis would emphasize the extent to which the conceptualization and deployment of tradition is affected by relations of power, and by the jockeying to maintain and extend power in society. Race plays a part in this political process, not only for the obvious cases of countries where there are divisions between whites and blacks (e.g., Zimbabwe, Kenya, South Africa), or even for the countries where these divisions are along the lines of Arab-black struggles for resources and power (e.g., Mauritania, Sudan), but also for the rest of the continent, where the experience of colonialism led to the insertion of white supremacist ideology into the social and political consciousness and the economic sphere.

In the process of colonization, old, fluid relations that may well have privileged men but also allowed for the complementarity of men and women in society, and the institutionalized inclusion of women in public positions of power as formal office holders in certain locales, got solidified and concretized ideologically into the ubiquitous invention of African women as powerless, and politically into the absence of African women in positions of power. Whereas there is historical evidence of African women's participation in the precolonial economy as producers, the refusal to acknowledge such contributions presents a distorted picture of the economy and marginalizes women. Colonization congealed and rigidified these relations such that rules and laws that had previously been subject to negotiation and multiple interpretation were

Italian Oil Pipes in Nigeria, 2006. *Oil exploration and development has been growing in West Africa, which has proven oil reserves. Both the United States and China buy large amounts of oil from this region. These pipes in Obrikom, Nigeria, are owned by an Italian oil company.* AP IMAGES.

presented as uncompromising, fixed, and often written documents that could not be challenged.

Given these antecedents, it is no wonder that gender politics affects social conditions in a manner that denigrates women and discriminates against them. Decisions are made within the confines of male-dominant structures that privilege males over females in policymaking and the allocation of resources. This reinforces the structural inequalities that are intrinsic to the construction and exercise of power. In most African countries, women are treated as jural minors, and they are kept away from the commanding heights of political and social affairs. Although vestiges of the old social and political powers of women exist in languages, social practices, and customs in much of Africa, there is a need to excavate the fundamental bases of women's power that have been buried by the combined forces of imperialism, colonialism and postcoloniality. Some success is observable in the rise to prominent political positions of women such as Ellen Johnson-Sirleaf, who was elected president of Liberia in 2005. In Rwanda, women currently make up 49 percent of the national parliament, while in Mozambique and South Africa this figure is 30 percent. In many other African countries, women average 15 percent representation in national parliaments. This is, surprisingly, much better than the accomplishment of women in the Northern Hemisphere (Mutume 2004).

DEVELOPMENT ISSUES

There is a North-South divide in development, with the countries of the Northern Hemisphere more economically buoyant and stable than the countries of the South. However, Africa lags behind other regions in the Southern Hemisphere in assessments of economic development. This is obvious in comparisons of social and economic indicators, which reveal that—in contrast with the rest of the world, which grew at a rate of approximately 2 percent from the 1960s to 2000—Africa experienced negative growth rates from 1974 to the 1990s. From 1990 to 1994, the growth rates dropped as low as

–1.5 percent. Africa experienced an 11 percent decline in gross domestic product (GDP) between the 1970s and 2004. While one in every ten poor persons in the world was African in 1970, one in every two poor persons was African in 2000. This represented 140 million people in 1975 and 360 million in 2000, according to the National Bureau of Economic Research. Compared with the rest of the world, Africa has also experienced a profound lack of investment. While investment in East Asia has grown an average of 30 percent since 1975, African countries experienced a decline of 8.5 percent, despite World Bank and International Monetary Fund (IMF) directed economic reforms, with most of the minuscule investment directed toward the public sector.

Education and health are generally regarded as the two critical variables that shape human capital, and Africa also performs worse in these areas than East Asia. Compared with East Asian countries, where primary school enrollment rate was almost 100 percent in the 1960s, Africa averaged only 42 percent enrollment, according to the National Bureau of Economic Research. This grew to 60 percent between 1996 and 2004 in sub-Saharan Africa, compared with 74 percent in the Middle East and North Africa, 79 percent in South Asia, 93 percent in Latin America and the Caribbean, and 96 percent in East Asia. Life expectancy is also low in Africa. It stood at a little more than forty years in 1960, compared with sixty-two in East Asia. From 2002 to 2004, sub-Saharan Africa experienced an increase in life expectancy, but only to forty-six years, while East Asia and the Pacific region experienced an increase to seventy years. Latin America, meanwhile, had a life expectancy of seventy-one in 2004, while in the Middle East and North Africa it was a little more than sixty-nine years.

According to the IMF, the World Bank, and renowned economists such as Alassane D. Ouattara and Joseph Stiglitz, there is nothing intrinsically positive or negative about globalization. This is similar to the contention that the phenomenon produces antinomies that generate economic growth, improvements in health, and advances in telecommunications technology in some countries, regions, and sectors, while also producing the opposite phenomena in other places. Ouattara claims that African countries do not benefit from globalization because they refuse to open up their economies, persist in the implementation of flawed policies, have weak institutions, and lack transparency, thus causing external investors to mistrust and avoid them. Stiglitz, in contrast, places the blame squarely on the IMF and the World Bank, due to their erroneous ideological commitment to the market-driven policies that they recommend to jump-start economic development in countries where poor institutions, incomplete markets, and imperfect information coexist, as is the case in Africa.

Critics of globalization believe that trade liberalization creates an environment that destroys domestic industries. They hold that the liberalization of capital markets favors wealthier and more efficient foreign financial interests and banks, and that privatization of state-owned enterprises favors the emergence of a small, predatory, capital-owning class that dominates an economy, particularly where there are few legal restraints on their activities. Compounding the problem, the IMF's commitment to market fundamentalism and the interests of lenders and the rich ensures the implementation of policies endorsed by the neoliberal Washington Consensus. The destructive consequences of such policies are exemplified by the economic collapse of the "East Asian Tigers" (South Korea, Taiwan, Hong Kong, and Singapore) in the 1990s. Many argue for more democracy and increased transparency in multilateral institutions, which will help give voice to the developing countries that are being impacted by these policies.

Because it rewards market-oriented policies to the exclusion of all else, contemporary globalization is often held responsible for the dismal state of African economies. A pro-market bias generates the antinomies observed, where some sectors, countries, and world regions thrive and others deteriorate. The debacle faced by African countries must also be blamed on the decision makers who ignore the general good in favor of sectional, and sometimes personal, interests.

SEE ALSO *Capitalism; Pan-Africanism; South African Racial Formations; Transnationalism.*

BIBLIOGRAPHY

Ayittey, George. 1992. *Africa Betrayed.* New York: St. Martin's Press.

Bayart, Jean-François, Stephen Ellis, and Béatrice Hibou. 1999. *The Criminalization of the State in Africa.* London: James Currey.

Chabal, Patrick, and Jean-Paul Daloz. 1998. *Africa Works: Disorder as Political Instrument.* London: James Currey.

Cotton, Jeremiah. 1992. "Towards a Theory and Strategy for Black Economic Development." In *Race, Politics and Economic Development: Community Perspectives,* edited by James Jennings, 11–32. New York: Verso.

Held, David, and Anthony McGrew, eds. 2003. *The Global Transformations Reader: An Introduction to the Globalization Debate,* 2nd ed. Cambridge, U.K.: Polity Press.

Kisiang'ani, Edward Namisiko. 2002. "Decolonizing Gender Studies in Africa." Paper delivered at CODESRIA Conference on African Gender in the New Millennium, Cairo, April 7–10. Available from http://www.codesria.org/Links/conferences/gender/KISIANGANI.pdf.

Mbembe, Achille. 2001. *On the Postcolony.* Berkeley: University of California Press.

Mutume, Gumisai. 2004. "Women Break into African Politics." *Africa Recovery* 18 (1): 4. Available from http://www.un.org/ecosocdev/geninfo/afrec/vol18no1/181women.htm.

Onwudiwe, Ebere, and Minabere Ibelema, eds. 2003. *Afro-Optimism: Perspectives on Africa's Advances*. Westport, CT: Praeger.

Ouattara, Alassane D. 1997. "The Challenges of Globalization for Africa." Address at the Southern Africa Economic Summit sponsored by the World Economic Forum, Harare, May 21. Available from http://www.imf.org/external/np/speeches/1997/052197.htm.

Picker, Les. "The Economic Decline in Africa." National Bureau of Economic Research. Available from http://www.nber.org/digest/jan04/W9865.html.

Rodney, Walter. 1972. *How Europe Underdeveloped Africa*. London: Bogle-L'Ouverture.

Shaw, Timothy M. 1980. "Foreign Policy, Political Economy and the Future: Reflections on Africa in the World System." *African Affairs* 79 (315): 260–268.

Steady, Filomina Chioma. 2002. "An Investigative Framework for Gender Research in Africa in the New Millennium." Paper delivered at the Conference on African Gender Research in the New Millennium, Cairo, Egypt, April 8–10. Available from http://www.codesria.org/Links/conferences/gender/STEADY.pdf.

Stiglitz, Joseph. 2002. *Globalization and Its Discontents*. New York: W.W. Norton.

UNICEF. 2006. "State of the World's Children 2006." Available from http://www.unicef.org/sowc06/.

Williamson, John. 1990. "What Washington Means by Policy Reform." In *Latin American Adjustment: How Much Has Happened?*, edited by John Williamson. Washington, DC: Institute for International Economics.

World Bank Group. 2006. "Africa Development Indicators 2006." Available from http://web.worldbank.org.

Worth, Owen, and Carmen Kuhling. 2004. "Counter-Hegemony, Anti-Globalisation and Culture in International Political Economy." *Capital* & *Class*, 84 (Winter): 31–42.

Mojúbàolú Olúfunké Okome

AFRICAN ENSLAVEMENT, PRECOLONIAL

Between the 1440s and the 1860s, European traders and colonists shipped millions of people from sub-Saharan Africa to the Americas. The total number of Africans sent across the Atlantic is variously estimated to be no less than 12 million and no more than 20 million, making it by far the greatest forced migration of people the world has ever seen. Indeed, the long-term global impact of this massive transfer of people against their will is just beginning to be fully understood.

The role of diasporic Africans in the socioeconomic history of the Atlantic world has become recognized as a central issue in global history. As researchers have documented the violent process of procuring millions of people for export overseas, it has become clear that the impact of the long-term socioeconomic damage to Africa was immense, no matter what figures scholars prefer to accept. The debate has therefore shifted to the counterfactual question of whether inadequate agricultural resources and the disease environment in Africa would not have produced a similar outcome in the absence of transatlantic slaving. This and related issues continue to be examined by scholars. This entry focuses on the factors that facilitated the supply of the massive numbers of captives for export to the Americas.

Modern historians have struggled with this puzzle for several decades. Some have argued that widespread slavery in Africa prior to the arrival of Europeans in the fifteenth century was the main factor. This argument was first made by the European slave traders in response to the onslaught mounted against their business by the abolitionist movement in the late eighteenth century. In the late nineteenth century, the alleged widespread existence of slavery in Africa also became a popular theme for the agents of European colonialism, who tried to mobilize popular support in Europe behind the imperial enterprise, which was presented as a "civilizing mission in a dark continent." Thus, they argued that the abolition of slavery and its evils in Africa would be one of the benefits of European colonial rule.

In the hands of modern historians, the argument has undergone much refinement. Social anthropology has provided a conceptual framework that perceives precolonial African societies as operating a uniquely African economic system, in which land laws precluded the development of private ownership of land; consequently, wealth accumulation took the form of the enlargement of the number of dependents (people with limit rights who depend on others) instead of the accumulation of land and capital that is said to characterize the history of Europe. Proponents of this view proceed to argue that the Atlantic slave trade grew out of this indigenous process of accumulating dependents as wealth and that the expanded supply of captives for export was sustained by the same process for the entire duration of the trade. As several of them claim, the Atlantic slave trade presented opportunities for African political and economic entrepreneurs to accumulate dependents. In contrast to European capitalists, who reinvested their profits in order to accumulate more capital, the argument goes, African political and economic entrepreneurs employed the surplus imported goods they received (in exchange for the captives they supplied) to accumulate more dependents.

Is this explanation consistent with what is known now of precolonial Africa? Or are there other factors that better explain what happened? Given prevailing conditions, precolonial societies in Africa responded to market opportunities much like their precapitalist counterparts in the rest of the world. The limited development of market economies in nineteenth-century sub-Saharan Africa, relative to the economies of other major regions at the time, was in fact the long-term effect of the transatlantic slave trade, and not the cause of it. This view is consistent with the historical reality, embedded in the intersection of the political and economic processes. The economic process involved the actions of individuals and groups of individuals responding to market opportunities as they struggled to meet the material needs of life. The political process, entailed the collective efforts of organized societies to resolve conflicts arising from the actions of individuals and groups of individuals, and to protect the lives and property of members. Conceptually, different market opportunities pose different problems, and societies at different levels of politico-military development possess differing capabilities in dealing with crises. It is therefore important to examine the structure of socioeconomic and political organization in sub-Saharan African societies on the eve of their contact with the Europeans, and to follow the historical process as it unfolded for the next four hundred years. This historical process can be organized into four broad periods: (1) the pre-European contact period; (2) the first two hundred years or so of the European coastal presence (c. 1441–1650), during which trade in African products generally dominated commercial intercourse between Europeans and Africans; (3) the main period of the transatlantic slave trade (c. 1650–1850); and (4) the last decades of the nineteenth century, after the effective abolition of the trade in captives across the Atlantic to the Americas.

It is also pertinent to examine briefly the export trade in European captives to the Middle East, which preceded the trade in African captives. A discussion of the factors that promoted and ended that trade can shed light on the main factors in the African case. This discussion also offers the opportunity to examine a related issue: Why the demand for slave labor in the Americas was focused exclusively on sub-Saharan Africa. Why were captives from Europe not exported to meet the demand? Was widespread anti-African racism in fifteenth-century Europe the explanation or, again, was it a result of the intersection of political and economic processes in Europe and Africa?

THE RISE AND DEMISE OF THE TRADE IN EUROPEAN CAPTIVES

One of the most elaborate slave systems in Europe developed in the Roman Empire (44 BCE–476 CE). The wars that established the empire generated captives from the conquered territories in Europe and the Mediterranean region resulting in the establishment of a large slave system. However, once incorporated into the empire, the general populations in the conquered territories became Roman citizens and were protected by the imperial government against

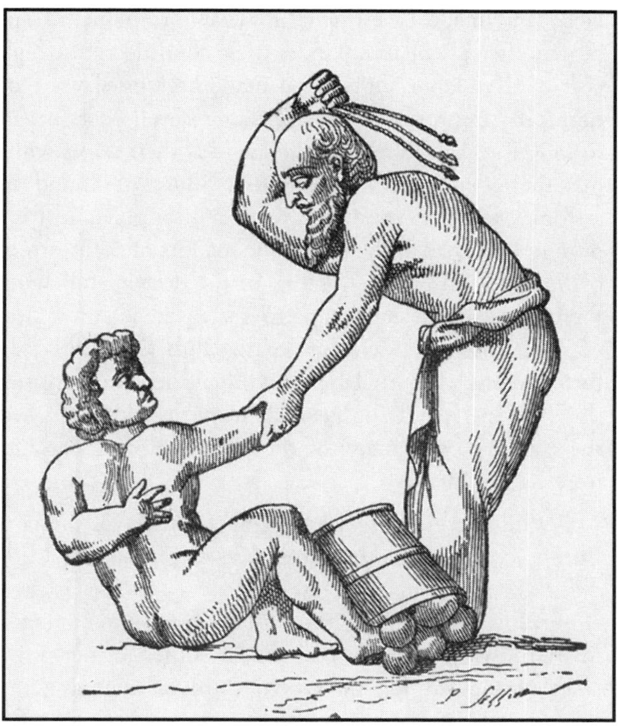

A Roman Slave Being Whipped. *The Roman Empire captured slaves from the territories it conquered, including parts of Europe, the Middle East, and Africa. In ancient Rome itself, there were at times more slaves than citizens.* **PICTURE COLLECTION, THE BRANCH LIBRARIES, THE NEW YORK PUBLIC LIBRARY, ASTOR, LENOX, AND TILDEN FOUNDATIONS.**

capture and enslavement. Thereafter, the Roman slave system was sustained by imports from territories outside the borders of the empire. While the imperial government in Rome remained strong and the provinces were effectively administered, *pax romana* (Roman peace) ensured that people in all parts of the empire—from the British Isles to the Balkans and beyond—were protected against capture and enslavement.

But with the collapse of the empire and the disappearance of its strong centralized state, the provinces descended into political fragmentation. Effective imperial protection in Britain ended with the withdrawal of the Roman legions in 407 CE; Roman authority in the Balkans collapsed in the late sixth century; and from the fifth to the eighth century, German political entrepreneurs broke up western Europe into several small Germanic kingdoms. This proliferation of small political units presented a fertile ground for sociopolitical conflict that would expose many people to capture and slavery.

Nevertheless, political fragmentation by itself did not immediately lead to capture and enslavement. For one thing, many of the large urban centers in the Roman Empire, which provided markets for the products of slave labor and made investment in slaves profitable, disappeared after its collapse. Under these conditions, the high cost of slave labor supervision made holding slaves economically unprofitable. Hence, large slaveholders began to look for ways to exploit the labor of their slaves without the high cost of supervision. This was found in serfdom, which gave former slaves more rights and freedom in exchange for labor (on the manors of their former owners) and other dues. Thus, in the decades following the collapse of the empire, there was a general conversion of slaves into serfs, who settled in lands they cultivated for themselves, paying labor and other dues to the former slaveholders. Amid the general insecurity that followed the collapse, even many of the previously free peasants were reduced to serfs.

While serfdom was emerging in parts of western Europe, a large slave market was developing in the Middle East, following the establishment of the Islamic empire in the seventh century. This market encouraged many individuals in the Balkans and other former provinces of the empire in western Europe (including the British Isles) to raid politically fragmented regions for captives in order to satisfy the growing demand from the Middle East. Without relatively strong centralized states to prevent internal breakdown of law and order and hold external raiders in check, internal man-hunting generated internal sociopolitical conflict, and raiding across political boundaries provoked wars among neighbors, both of which produced captives sold for export and for local use.

The cycle of conflict, wars, and enslavement induced by export demand for captives continued in the former Roman provinces for centuries until the general emergence of relatively strong centralized states—first, the Frankish kingdom (786–814) and its successor states in continental Europe; then, the Norman state in Britain after 1066. These states were more or less politico-militarily equally matched. They were strong enough to stop destabilizing internal man-hunt by their own people and maintain law and order internally, while general politico-military parity among them restrained them from exporting each other's subjects, even in wartimes. For the rest of the Middle Ages and early modern times, trade in European captives became limited to the Balkans and the Black Sea region, where political fragmentation lasted much longer. But with the Ottoman conquest and incorporation of the small autonomous political units in the Balkans into the Ottoman empire in the fourteenth and fifteenth centuries, and a similar incorporation of the small political units in the Black Sea region into the expanding Russian empire in the fifteenth century, the export of white captives from both regions also came to an end.

About the same time that political developments in Europe were ending the export of European slaves to the Middle East, western European explorers and traders were establishing seaborne contacts with the coastal societies of Atlantic Africa in the fifteenth and sixteenth centuries. The drying up of supply from Europe had long been shifting Middle East demand for captives to sub-Saharan Africa, leading to the growth of the trans-Saharan slave trade.

SOCIOECONOMIC AND POLITICAL PROCESSES IN PRECONTACT SUB-SAHARAN AFRICA

The massive export of people from Africa to the Americas occurred largely in western Africa—that part of sub-Saharan Africa bordering on the Atlantic, together with the immediate and distant hinterland. In order to correctly identify the main factors at play, two broad regions in western Africa must be distinguished—Atlantic Africa (the societies of the Atlantic coast and their immediate hinterlands, which were directly affected by the European presence) and the Savanna territories in the interior that had been the center of major precolonial socioeconomic and political developments before the establishment of regular seaborne contact with the Europeans.

From the ninth to the third millennium BCE, when climatic and ecological conditions were conducive to extensive human settlement in the Sahara region, African societies—from the Sahara to the Nile valley, and from Ethiopia to Egypt—were major players in the political and economic processes of the Afro-Asian world. However, long-term climatic changes turned the Sahara into a desert and severely limited interactions between western Africa and the Mediterranean and Afro-Asian regions. The use of the camel reestablished regular commercial and other links between western Africa and the evolving commercial centers in the Mediterranean and the Middle East. But the huge Sahara desert, with its unforgiving climate and terrain, dispersed populations southward and limited trans-Saharan trade to goods with high value-to-weight ratio, such as gold. Historians have yet to study in detail the impact of these developments on socioeconomic and political processes in sub-Saharan Africa, particularly in a comparative global context.

From the latter half of the first millennium CE to the middle of the second, the first large state systems in western Africa—Ancient Ghana, Mali, Songhay, and Kanem-Borno—were established. From the mid-thirteenth century to 1591, a large part of western Africa's total population was located in the territories that formed the Mali and Songhay empires. In the Songhay Empire, the three Niger-bend towns of Jenne, Timbuktu, and Gao had total populations of 30,000–40,000, 80,000, and 100,000, respectively, during the late sixteenth century.

Arab Slave Trader. *The Arab slave trade from East Africa predated the European transatlantic slave trade by many centuries. The trader in this illustration, published in France in 1891, accompanies five captured slaves.* GENERAL RESEARCH & REFERENCE DIVISION, SCHOMBURG CENTER FOR RESEARCH IN BLACK CULTURE, THE NEW YORK PUBLIC LIBRARY, ASTOR, LENOX AND TILDEN FOUNDATIONS.

The combination of population concentration, the openness of the savanna, the ease of river transportation over long stretches of the Niger, and the security provided by the governments of Ancient Ghana, Mali, and Songhay made the interior savanna the center of manufacturing and trade in West Africa (western Africa from Mauritania to southeastern Nigeria) before seaborne contact with the Europeans in the fifteenth century. Differing population densities and natural resource endowment encouraged the growth and development of interregional trade between the interior savanna and Atlantic Africa. Gold and kola nuts, the main products of Atlantic Africa, were exchanged for the manufactures of the interior savanna, mostly cotton textiles and leather goods. Internal factors making for the growth of interregional trade in West Africa were reinforced by trade with the southern Sahara, North Africa, and the Middle East, particularly the trade in West African gold to meet growing European demand intermediated by Mediterranean merchants, who shipped the gold out of West Africa.

All of West Africa, from Mauritania to southeastern Nigeria, was involved in the precontact interregional long-distance trade between the interior savanna and Atlantic Africa that was centered in the Niger bend. But because of its extensive involvement in the production of the two main products in the trade, gold and kola nuts, the Gold Coast (southern modern Ghana) occupied a special place in the trade. The trade in kola nuts grew in volume as Islam spread in the savanna states (kola nuts being the only stimulant Muslims are allowed to consume). At the same time, the demand for gold in the trans-Saharan trade expanded with growing demand from Europe.

These developments created trade networks and a commercial culture that would facilitate the establishment of trade relations with the Europeans from the fifteenth century onward. But the sociopolitical organization of the societies in western Africa in the mid-fifteenth century would play a role in the procurement of the massive supply of captives for export to the Americas. In contrast to the relatively large centralized states in the interior savanna, in what geographers call the West African Middle Belt, there were a large number of small, kin-based autonomous political units. Further south, all along the Atlantic coast from Senegambia (modern-day Senegal and Gambia) to modern Namibia, political fragmentation was also the norm in the mid-fifteenth century. This was evident as late as the seventeenth century, for a Dutch map drawn in 1629 shows thirty-eight autonomous political units in the area of modern southern Ghana. In the sixteenth century, there were five independent political units in the small area of modern Republic of Benin; in modern Yorubaland, in southwest Nigeria, there were more than a dozen autonomous political units, even though the Yoruba kingdom of Ife was a relatively complex state system at the time. East of Yorubaland the political scene was much the same, apart from the kingdoms of Benin (in mid-western Nigeria) and Kongo (in West-Central Africa), which were already undergoing a process of expansion and the consolidation of state authority in the fifteenth century.

In terms of social structure, there was very little social stratification and class differentiation in the small kin-based societies of Atlantic Africa. Unlike the areas of the interior, there were no accumulated dependents (whether serfs or slaves). In West-Central Africa, where the Portuguese started exporting captives early in the sixteenth century, even the king of Kongo had no accumulated dependents for sale. The political economy of the kingdom was based on redistribution by the king: The provincial governors sent the staple products of their provinces to the king, and the king redistributed these products to the governors according to what each province lacked. This system made the accumulation of slaves or serfs by state elites unnecessary, given the relatively low level of commercial development.

The main authorities on the history of precontact West-Central Africa (Jan Vansina, Anne Hilton, Robert Harms) confirm that there were no slaves, and no slave trade, in the region when the Portuguese arrived in the late fifteenth century. Nor were there words for slaves or purchased people. When, in the early sixteenth century, the king of Portugal sent a trade mission to negotiate with the king of Kongo a switch from copper to captive export, the Kongo king had no slaves to give in return for the gifts sent by the Portuguese king. Instead, he had to raid weakly organized neighboring communities for the needed captives. Subsequently, following the growth of transatlantic slaving in the region, "loanwords" were applied to describe the new social phenomena that developed along the slave trade routes, spreading from the Atlantic coast to the interior.

In West Africa, evidence shows that in the interior savanna, where class differentiation developed, state rulers, Muslim clerics, and merchants used dependent cultivators (approximating serfs rather than slaves), in basically the same way that their counterparts in medieval Europe did. They were settled in villages, where they produced for themselves and paid dues in kind to their lords, who were generally resident in the cities. Large numbers of such villages existed in Mali, Songhay, Kanem-Borno, and the small city-states of the savanna from the fourteenth to the sixteenth century. Some writers loosely apply the terms *slave* and *slavery* to describe these populations. Consistent with the scientific precision in the use of terms that characterizes the writing of medieval European history, there can be no doubt that the more appropriate terms to apply are *serfs* and *serfdom*. The populations were built up over time by conquest, with captives that had been taken from the fragmented societies of the West African Middle Belt mentioned earlier. Some of these societies fed the trans-Saharan trade, which took a few thousand captives per year from the fragmented communities in the interior savanna. When historians make the point that African societies were involved in selling and buying people before the arrival of the Europeans in the fifteenth century, the point is valid largely for the interior savanna. But for most of Atlantic Africa that came into direct contact with Europeans in the fifteenth century, this was not the case.

It is particularly important to note that the elites in socially stratified societies in fifteenth-century western Africa were not involved in the accumulation of dependents as an end in itself. Contrary to the belief of some social anthropologists, economic rationality was involved. The growth of elaborate state systems—with a large number of specialized state functionaries (administrators and military men), religious leaders, scholars, and merchants—occurred at a time when the geographical spread of the market economy was limited, land was abundant and accessible to all cultivators, and, therefore, free wage labor was unavailable. Hence, the provisioning of the specialized elites on a regular basis required dependent producers whose labor could be exploited under conditions that did not involve high supervision costs.

EARLY EUROPEAN TRADE IN AFRICAN PRODUCTS, 1450–1650

In the first two hundred years of European trade in western Africa, products from Africa's natural endowment overwhelmingly dominated the trade. The flamboyant display of West Africa's gold wealth by Mali's Mansa Musa, during his pilgrimage to Mecca in the 1320s, inspired the Portuguese to search for a direct seaborne route to the source of the precious metal in West Africa. Thus, trade in West African gold was the main concern of the Portuguese in the fifteenth and sixteenth centuries. That trade centered on the Gold Coast, so called because of the large amount of gold sold in the region. Another important product for the Portuguese in the fifteenth and sixteenth centuries was red pepper from the Benin trading area of southwest Nigeria, which also supplied them with cotton cloth. In West-Central Africa, copper was the main product for several decades. All across western Africa, other products, such as ivory, supplemented the trade in gold, pepper, and copper.

Right from the beginning, a few captives were also shipped by the Portuguese. These were initially the victims of direct raids by the Portuguese on the small coastal communities. But in the first two hundred years of European trade in western Africa, the trade in captives paled in comparison with the trade in gold and other African products. Like the preexisting trans-Saharan trade in captives, the numbers involved were small and, with some exceptions (including the Kongo-Angola area of West-Central Africa), the socioeconomic and political disruption caused was limited.

As long as European trade concentrated on African products, political fragmentation posed no serious problem to the societies in Atlantic Africa. These societies responded positively to the market opportunities, as all societies across the globe have done. The case of the Gold Coast, where the early product trade was particularly large, may be taken to illustrate.

The European demand for gold considerably expanded the market for the Akan gold producers and traders. This stimulated the growth of specialization in gold production and trade, which created a domestic market for other producers in agriculture and manufacturing. The opportunities for productive investment in agriculture were seized by people who had accumulated wealth from the gold trade.

Beginning in the sixteenth century, these wealthy merchants invested their profits from commerce in clearing forests to develop farmlands. Given the early stages of development of the market economy in the region—and hence the nonexistence of a virile market for free wage labor—the Akan agricultural entrepreneurs had to rely on purchased imported labor. Some of these laborers were supplied from the north by the gold and kola nuts traders operating along the Jenne-Begho trade route, while others were brought by the Portuguese from other parts of western Africa (including the Benin and Kongo kingdoms). Again, economic rationality underpinned the investment decisions of the Akan merchants who invested their profits from trade in agriculture. They were not motivated by the desire to accumulate dependents as a form of wealth. On the contrary, they took care to avoid the creation of a slave class. What is more, no Akan land laws hindered the investment of profits from commerce in agriculture by wealthy traders when the market conditions were conducive for the investment. Indeed, in response to the general developments of the fifteenth and sixteenth centuries, a land market had begun to evolve in the region. The site on which Kumasi was later built was purchased at this time for the equivalent of £270 (sterling) in gold. Similar developments were more or less associated with the early product trade in the other regions of western Africa.

The Beginning of Slavery in America. *The first Africans arrived in Jamestown, Virginia, in August 1619, when "20 and Odd" blacks were brought there aboard a Dutch ship. In the early years of the colony, Africans worked as "servants," often alongside whites, and they could gain their freedom after a period of servitude.* KEAN COLLECTION/GETTY IMAGES.

THE MASSIVE SHIFT TO CAPTIVE EXPORT

Beginning in the mid-seventeenth century, the growth in demand for slave labor in the Americas, associated with the rapid expansion of large-scale mining and plantation agriculture (at a time when the pre-Columbian indigenous population of the Americas had been largely destroyed), shifted European traders' demand decisively from African products to African captives. Whereas the demand for products created conditions that favored individuals with the talent and aptitude to organize the production and distribution of goods and services, the demand for captives favored individuals with violent dispositions. As these individuals engaged in rampant kidnapping within their own communities and organized raids across political boundaries to obtain captives, the politically fragmented societies were unable to prevent an internal breakdown of law and order and keep external raiders at bay. Thus, indiscriminate kidnapping created prolonged internal social conflicts, while raids across political borders provoked political conflicts between neighbors, which led to protracted wars. All of this made captives available for sale to the European exporters.

Some people in the fragmented societies adopted various defensive measures, the most successful of which was migration to sites with natural defenses (hilltops in particular). But their success was limited, and the bulk of the captives exported ultimately came from politically fragmented societies. Only when political and economic entrepreneurs succeeded in establishing relatively strong centralized states and incorporated the weakly organized societies were the people adequately protected against capture and sale for export. When this occurred, the frontier of capture and sale was pushed outward to other weakly organized societies. Yet while the newly constituted and relatively strong centralized states protected their citizens from capture and export, they continued to export captives from outside their political boundaries as a way of securing the resources needed to maintain stability at home and protect their territorial integrity.

It is clear from the evidence that political fragmentation in Atlantic Africa was the permissive factor that allowed a sustained response to the growing demand for slave labor in the Americas. What western Africa shared with the European societies that supplied captives exported to the Middle East was not some peculiar economy in which dependents were accumulated as a form of wealth. Nor was it some special cultural element that permitted the massive export of people. Instead, the common condition was political fragmentation. Both in Europe and in western Africa, the eventual incorporation of fragmented societies into relatively strong centralized states protected the citizens against capture and sale. The main difference, however, was the much greater magnitude of the transatlantic demand, which fed a slave system aimed at the production of commodities for an evolving capitalist world market. The magnitude of the demand created conditions that slowed the generalized development of strong states in all of sub-Saharan Africa, which would likely have ended the trade as it did in Europe.

A comparative discussion of the rise and demise of captive export from Europe and the rise of transatlantic slaving from western Africa also helps to explain why the demand for slave labor in the Americas focused on western Africa instead of Europe. Some historians have offered an ideological explanation for this. By the sixteenth century, they say, Europeans in Europe and the Americas were unwilling to enslave other Europeans, but they had no racial constraint enslaving Africans (Eltis 2000). This explanation is unsatisfactory, however. There was no pan-European identity in the sixteenth century that could ideologically prevent the enslavement of Europeans by other Europeans, just as there was no pan-African identity to ideologically prevent rulers in Africa from exporting people outside their polities. These identities were nineteenth- and twentieth-century developments. As has been seen, it was not the collective action of Europeans that ended the export of captives from Europe. Individual states in Europe ended the export of their citizens for domestic political reasons, the same way that individual states in western Africa ended the export of their citizens. Anti-African European racism grew out of the racialization of slavery in the Americas; it was not the cause of the transatlantic slave trade.

THE GROWTH OF DEPENDENT POPULATIONS DURING AND AFTER ABOLITION

A major long-term consequence of the transatlantic slave trade—arising from its adverse impact on population growth, its disruption of the development of export trade in products, and the widespread conflict and insecurity associated with the violent procurement of millions of people for export—was a retardation of market development and the spread of the market economy in western Africa between 1650 and 1850. Given this condition, merchants, rulers and their officials, religious leaders, and warlords had to rely on dependent populations to produce their subsistence—what has been called "subsistence servitude." The fact that few of the dependent populations were employed by their lords in large-scale production of commodities for the market at the time was due to the limited market for the products of bonded labor, not because of laws that discouraged investment in large-scale commercial agriculture. As the case of sixteenth-century Ghana discussed earlier shows, there were no such legal barriers. Developments following abolition make this point even clearer.

A number of developments preceding and following the abolition of the slave trade led to a rapid growth of servile populations in western Africa. The conditions for sociopolitical conflicts created by the export demand for captives continued to generate conflicts after abolition.

But without the export market in the Americas to absorb the captives produced by the conflicts, prices tumbled. At the same time, European demand for African products (vegetable oil and woods in particular) began to grow once again, stimulating the growth of the "legitimate commerce" of the nineteenth century. The domestic market for foodstuffs also began to develop, stimulated by the expansion of commodity production for export and population growth. African entrepreneurs responded to these market opportunities against the backdrop of falling captive prices and the nonexistence of wage labor. It was under these conditions that the population of servile producers grew rapidly in western Africa in the nineteenth century. There was economic rationality for the growth, and dependents were not just accumulated as a form of wealth.

SEE ALSO *African Diaspora; Racial Slave Labor in the Americas; Slave Trade Ideology; Slavery and Race.*

BIBLIOGRAPHY

Austen, Ralph. 1977. "Slavery among Coastal Middlemen: The Duala of Cameroon." In *Slavery in Africa: Historical and Anthropological Perspectives*, edited by Suzanne Miers and Igor Kopytoff, 303–333. Madison: University of Wisconsin Press.

Braude, Benjamin. 1997. "The Sons of Noah and the Construction of Ethnic and Geographical Identities in the Medieval and Early Modern Periods." *William and Mary Quarterly* 54 (1): 103–142.

Ehret, Christopher. 2003. *Sudanic Civilization*. Washington, DC: American Historical Association.

Eltis, David. 2000. *The Rise of African Slavery in the Americas*. Cambridge, U.K.: Cambridge University Press.

Evans, William McKee. 1980. "From the Land of Canaan to the Land of Guinea: The Strange Odyssey of the 'Sons of Ham.'" *American Historical Review* 85 (1): 15–43.

Hilton, Anne. 1985. *The Kingdom of Kongo*. Oxford: Clarendon Press.

Inikori, Joseph E. 1996. "Slavery in Africa and the Transatlantic Slave Trade." In *The African Diaspora*, edited by Alusine Jalloh and Stephen Maizlish, 39–72. College Station: Texas A&M University Press.

———. 2002. "The Development of Entrepreneurship in Africa: Southeastern Nigeria during the Era of the Transatlantic Slave Trade." In *Black Business and Economic Power*, edited by Alusine Jalloh and Toyin Falola, 41–79. Rochester, NY: University of Rochester Press.

———. 2003. "The Struggle against the Transatlantic Slave Trade: The Role of the State." In *Fighting the Slave Trade: West African Strategies*, edited by Sylviane A. Diouf, 170–198. Athens: Ohio University Press.

Kea, Ray A. 1982. *Settlements, Trade, and Polities in the Seventeenth-Century Gold Coast*. Baltimore, MD: Johns Hopkins University Press.

Miller, Joseph C. 1988. *Way of Death: Merchant Capitalism and the Angolan Slave Trade, 1730–1830*. Madison: University of Wisconsin Press.

Thornton, John. 1992. *Africa and Africans in the Making of the Atlantic World, 1400–1680*. Cambridge, U.K.: Cambridge University Press.

Vansina, Jan. 1989. "Deep-Down Time: Political Tradition in Central Africa." *History in Africa* 16: 341–362.

Wilks, Ivor. 1977. "Land, Labour, Capital and the Forest Kingdom of Asante: A Model of Early Change." In *The Evolution of Social Systems*, edited by Jonathan Friedman and M. J. Rowlands. London: Duckworth.

Joseph E. Inikori

AFRICAN FEMINISMS

Documentation of women's social activism and collective action in Africa dates as far back as the eighteenth century. In the nineteenth century, women in North Africa and the Arab world owned and published feminist journals in which discussions of gender, as well as religious and nationalist struggles, were featured prominently. These feminist writings were projected and intensified in the twentieth century by Arab women scholars and writers such as Nawal El Saadawi, Leila Ahmed, and Fatima Mernissi. Women's insurgencies for social change have been encouraged and sustained by the capacity of many African cultures (the patriarchal contexts notwithstanding) to create spaces of female power in social and religious spheres. Colonial interventions and other forms of foreign intrusions and imperial hegemonies forced shifts in power distribution and gender relations that to a large extent placed women at a disadvantage. As internally induced inequities became complicated and intensified by externally generated structures of domination, African women's fight against multiple colonialisms took different forms, with the refashioning of culturally defined strategies to meet new realities and challenges.

The women who engaged in these struggles for social change and survival neither forced a theory/practice oppositional paradigm nor imposed a particular label on their struggles. Attempts by scholars to understand, contextualize, frame, and name these struggles provoked heated debates and controversies in the last two decades of the twentieth century. At issue is the appropriateness and adequacy of the "feminist" label for African women's struggles. Some reject the imposition of a foreign label on an African phenomenon. Others reject the ascription of the feminist label on African women's insurgencies because they were not driven by gender-specific issues. It may be difficult to sustain the latter position, particularly in an environment in which gender-specific considerations are occluded by larger contexts of struggle. African women's dissatisfaction with colonialism's exacerbation of gender inequalities and marginalization of women could well have been the subtext of women's participation in anticolonial struggles. The rationale, strategies, modalities, and contexts governing women's social action in Africa are as heterogeneous and complex as the continent itself and cannot be adequately captured by a monolithic idea such as feminism; hence the use of the plural, feminisms, in the title of this entry.

The contextualization and theorizing of African feminisms emerged in the 1990s in response to the exclusions and inadequacies of second-wave Western feminism. If the 1980s was the decade of the women of color feminisms, the 1990s constituted the decade of African feminisms. Just as the women of color movement compelled Western feminist thinking and theorizing to liberate itself from the myopia of gender-specificity to broaden and intensify its context and texture by allowing other categories such as race and class to intersect with gender, African feminisms made further demands on feminism to expand its analytical horizon by incorporating other considerations such as culture, colonialism, ethnicity, and imperialism and, in particular, examining the ways in which these considerations intersect to construct and (re)produce "gender."

The disagreement between two schools of thought—on the one hand those insisting that feminism is foreign to the African environment and on the other hand those affirming that feminism is indigenous to Africa—is primarily due to perceptions of Western feminism, particularly its packaging and what it has come to represent. Feminist ideals of equity and resistance to all forms of domination are indigenous to Africa and have propelled women's social action for centuries.

African feminisms share certain features that mark their differences from Western feminisms. African feminism is not as exclusionary, in terms of articulation and gender participation, as Western feminism appears to be. In its articulation, African feminism is suffused with the language of compromise, collaboration, and negotiation; in its practice, it invites men as partners in social change. Motherhood and maternal politics are not peripheralized in African feminism; on the contrary, they have fueled feminist activism in many African contexts. African feminism is proactive, marks its specificities, and maps priorities that often go beyond the intersection of gender, race, and class to include the consequences of colonialism and its aftermath as well as the new order imposed by global capitalism. By locating African feminism solely as an oppositional moment in the scheme of things, one risks undercutting its scope, import, and significance. African feminism's reason for being is not determined by its resistance to Western feminism. Rather, African feminism derives its impetus and meaning from its cultural and historical contexts. The attempts to theorize African feminisms that began in the 1980s are mindful of these contexts.

The 1990s saw the emergence of serious and concerted efforts by women writers and scholars from sub-Saharan Africa to conceptualize, contextualize, and theorize African feminisms. Included among these figures were Catherine Acholonu, Simi Afonja, Ama Ata Aidoo, Olabisi Aina, Omofolabo Ajayi-Soyinka, Tuzyline Jita Allan, Ifi Amadiume, Bolanle Awe, Ada Azodo, Calixthe Beyala, Gloria Chukukere, Helen Chukwuma, M. J. Daymond, Florence Abena Dolphyne, Akachi Ezeigbo, Aisha Imam, Mary E. Modupe Kolawole, Amina Mama, Patricia McFadden, Micere Mugo, Juliana Nfah-Abbenyi, Obioma Nnaemeka, Molara Ogundipe-Leslie, Chikwenye Okonjo Ogunyemi, Chioma Opara, Oyeronke Oyewumi, Mansah Prah, Zulu Sofola, Filomina Chioma Steady, Marie Umeh, and Zoë Wicomb. Resisting the maternalistic tendencies and imperialistic modus operandi of Western feminists, and interrogating the limitations of Western feminisms, African women scholars sought to name and theorize the feminisms unfolding in their environment in ways that would capture their specificity and uniqueness as well as their diverse meanings and dimensions—including womanism, African womanism, motherism, stiwanism, and negofeminism—although there are some who believe that the feminist label is adequate, and so new labels are not needed.

In the 1980s Chikwenye Okonjo Ogunyemi came up with a concept/terminology, womanism, that she argued was more appropriate than feminism to describe African women's engagement in social transformation. Ogunyemi claims that she came up with the terminology independently of the African-American writer Alice Walker who popularized the term in a publication that first appeared in 1983. Ogunyemi's womanism, which morphed into African womanism in later writings, claims affinity with feminism but asserts its difference by expanding the boundaries of feminism to "incorporate racial, cultural, national, economic, and political considerations." African womanism insists that the gender question must be reimagined in light of other issues that are peculiar relevant to African women in local, national, and global contexts, which, unfortunately, are not prioritized in Western feminism and African-American womanism. Mary Kolawole also argues for a womanism that is rooted in African values and is not concerned with some of the sexuality questions that are central to Western feminist theorizing. Indeed, lesbianism has no place in Ogunyemi's African womanism or Kolawole's womanism.

In the early 1990s Catherine Acholonu proposed motherism as an Afrocentric alternative to feminism. Acholonu's motherism places motherhood, nature, nurture, and respect for the environment at the center of its theorizing. In 1994 Molara Ogundipe-Leslie introduced a new terminology, stiwanism (from STIWA—an acronym for Social Transformation Including Women in Africa), that is designed to discuss African women's needs and agendas in the context of strategies fashioned in the environment created by indigenous cultures. Stiwanism insists on the participation of women as equal partners in the social transformation in Africa. At the end of the decade, Obioma Nnaemeka proposed another alternative, negofeminism (feminism of negotiation and "no ego" feminism), which captures central concerns in many African cultures—including negotiation, complementarity, give-and-take, and collaboration.

Attempts by African scholars and writers to name, contextualize, and theorize African feminism are colored and determined by the need to ensure its grounding in African cultural imperatives. Gender inclusion, not alienation, takes center stage in these theoretical frameworks that create the possibilities for women and men to become (African) womanists, motherists, stiwanists, and negofeminists. African women's affirmation of the feminist ideals of gender equity and social justice and their interrogation of different aspects of feminist theory and practice has contributed significantly to expanding the boundaries of feminism and compelling numerous disciplines in the humanities, social sciences, and applied sciences—from literature and human rights to health and peace/conflict resolution—to revisit their assumptions and interrogate their methods.

SEE ALSO *African Economic Development; Black Feminism in Brazil; Black Feminism in the United Kingdom; Black Feminism in the United States; Feminism and Race.*

BIBLIOGRAPHY

Arndt, Susan. 2002. *The Dynamics of African Feminism: Defining and Classifying African-Feminist Literatures.* Translated by Isabel Cole. Trenton, NJ: Africa World Press.

Cornwall, Andrea, ed. 2005. *Readings in Gender in Africa.* Bloomington: Indiana University Press.

Daymond, M. J., ed. 1996. *South African Feminisms: Writing, Theory, and Criticism, 1990–1994.* New York: Garland Publishing.

Mikell, Gwendolyn, ed. 1997. *African Feminism: The Politics of Survival in Sub-Saharan Africa.* Philadelphia: University of Pennsylvania Press.

Nnaemeka, Obioma, ed. 1998. *Sisterhood, Feminisms, and Power: From Africa to the Diaspora.* Trenton, NJ: Africa World Press.

Ogunyemi, Chikwenye Okonjo. "Womanism: The Dynamics of the Contemporary Black Female Novel in English." *Signs: Journal of Woman in Culture and Society,* 11 (1985/86): 63–80.

Obioma Nnaemeka

AFRIKANER BROEDERBOND

In the wake of the Anglo-Boer War (1899–1902), the impoverished and largely rural Afrikaners of present-day South Africa experienced an ethnic awakening, particularly regarding aspects of language, religion, and education. It was also, at first, largely an anti-English movement. In May 1918 a group of fourteen white men in Johannesburg formed an organization they called "Jong Suid-Afrika." On June 5 this loose organization was recast as the Afrikaner Broederbond (AB), which aimed to bring together Afrikaners and to serve their interests. The constitution of the AB made it clear that only Afrikaners—in fact only "super-Afrikaners"—would be invited to join the group. In time, membership implied religious conservatism, linguistic priority, and racial prejudice. Young persons, especially students, were brought into the fold through a junior secret society, the Ruiterwag.

To better achieve their aims, the AB became a secret society in 1924, and henceforth membership was by invitation only. As a front the secret society employed the FAK (Federation of Afrikaner Cultural Organizations), established in 1929. The AB leadership had clearly conceptualized their role in South Africa. At the Bond Congress in August 1932 the chairman of the Executive Council, stated: "After the cultural and economic needs, the AB will have to dedicate its attention to the political needs of our people ... the aim must be a completely independent real Afrikaans Government for South Africa" (du Toit 1976, p. 116). To this end, the AB surreptitiously supported the HNP (United National Party) under Daniel Francois Malan, who led the party to victory in the 1948 general elections. Meanwhile, AB leaders within the church justified the political policy of apartheid through the selective use of Biblical texts.

In 1965, Brian M. du Toit published *Beperkte lidmaatskap* (Restricted Membership), the first exposé of the AB. He pointed out that early members occupied prominent positions in the Afrikaans churches, educational institutions, and in the increasingly important industrial and business world. AB members looked and sounded like their neighbors, but their hidden agenda and prejudice was always uppermost in their values and decisions. Jan Hendrik Philippus Serfontein, in his study *Brotherhood of Power* (1978), explains that "for an Afrikaner who defects, or opposes the Broederbond, the price is terrible—total excommunication. He will be ostracized from Afrikaner society, and a man in business faces economic destruction" (p. 11). All persons in leadership positions, especially those in politics, were AB members.

The greatest challenge for South Africa's leaders involved the multiethnic population. Beginning in 1948, D. F. Malan was able to prevent Indian representation in

Parliament. In 1958 the new prime minister, Hendrik F. Verwoerd, introduced increasingly severe policies concerning geographical separation of "tribal" homelands (referred to as "Bantustans"), while a policy of residential separation (for blacks working in white areas) was used to prevent social contact. Laws on population registration, miscegenation, mixed marriages, and other issues were clearly based on skin color. As a political residue of more enlightened and liberal days, "colored" people remained on the voting roles in the Cape Province. When all vestiges of colored representation in Parliament were removed under Prime Minister John Vorster, however, the AB was ecstatic.

One of the best-kept secrets, and one of the most powerful instruments for the pursuit of the AB's ideals, was a system of secret watchdog committees. Each committee included specialists in a particular field or profession, and the AB thus had its fingers on the very pulse of South Africa. The AB, through the government, directed an increasingly isolationist national policy. What started out as an anti-English cultural organization gradually became more exclusionist as a secret society that was instrumental in gradually ushering in total apartheid in South Africa. Blacks were only tolerated in "white areas" as workers, and coloreds and Indians had their own residential areas. The rest of South Africa was supposed to belong to whites, especially the Afrikaners guided by the AB.

As the race-based policies flowing from apartheid in South Africa reached fruition, they were increasingly challenged by those with more democratic sentiments. This included organizations representing the four "racial" groups, including the African National Congress, which represented black Africans. Some Afrikaners in leadership positions were covertly meeting with ANC members outside South Africa. In response, a number of organizations on the far right emerged, all aimed at maintaining a white society in a separate geographical region. Among these were the Afrikaner Weerstandsbeweging (AWB, founded in 1973); Vereniging van Oranjewerkers (Organization of Orange Workers, 1980); Afrikanervolkswag (Afrikaner People's Guard, 1984); Blanke Bevrydingsbeweging (White Liberation Movement, 1985); Boere-Vryheidsbeweging (Boer Freedom Movement, 1989); and the Boerestaat (Boer State) Party (1990). Each of these movements had grandiose ideas about perpetuating a white South Africa, or at least retaining white ethnic enclaves in a future South Africa under majority rule. Some proclaimed themselves willing to take up arms to defend their claims.

THE AFRIKANER WEERSTANDSBEWEGING

The Afrikaner Weerstandsbeweging (AWB) was formed in 1973 as a secret society in Heidelberg (Transvaal) by Eugene Terre Blanche and a few friends. In 1979 they abandoned the secrecy component to gain greater impact. This semi-militant, ultraconservative extremist group formed the Blanke Volkstaat Party (White People's State Party) in 1980 and started working toward the ideal of a white homeland. Some members, finding that they had no political clout, disbanded the party in 1982, joining two rightist political parties, the Herstigte Nasionale Party (HNP) and the Conservative Party (CP). But the AWB movement continued.

One wing of the movement, the Stormvalke (Storm Falcons) served as a military group, and in time they were replaced by the khaki-clad Wenkommando. The AWB operated through small vigilante cells, called Boere-Brandwag, consisting of seven to ten members. In 1990 the movement claimed approximately 150,000 active supporters, but only 15,000 registered members.

Other rightist spokesmen characterized the AWB as an emotional group structured around the personality of Eugene Terre Blanche, who was the most emotional and dynamic orator on the political scene. Carl Boshoff (a onetime chairman of the Afrikaner Broederbond and the leader of the Vereniging van Oranjewerkers) told this writer in August 1990: "It is a glorious experience to hear him speak ... but his plan is infeasible." Most spokesmen for other groups agreed that his plans, namely to establish a volkstaat (nation state) that included the Transvaal, the Orange Free State, and the Republic of Vryheid (this refers to the so-called Nieuwe Republiek formed in 1884 in northern Natal) was a complete illusion.

The AWB flag resembles a swastika. Terre Blanche denied its link to Nazism or to an anti-Christ symbolism of three sixes, insisting it is a pro-Christ configuration of three sevens. The flag and the movement, Terre Blanche claimed, served to galvanize conservative Afrikaners. In fact, he maintained, the CP would not have been the official opposition party if it were not for AWB support. In any case, Terre Blanche claimed, the CP parliamentarians were all members of the AWB. They opposed President de Klerk's "giving away" the country to Nelson Mandela and the ANC.

Terre Blanche's racist proclamations and treatment of blacks working on his and other farms in the Ventersdorp (western Transvaal) region frequently led to police confrontation and intervention. Eventually, he was sentenced to five years in jail for the attempted murder of a black security guard. He gained his freedom in June 2005.

Like all other political parties and movements, the AWB gradually dissolved. Ultra-conservative sentiments linger in the new South Africa and find expression in opposition organizations.

SEE ALSO *Apartheid.*

BIBLIOGRAPHY

Booysen, Hercules. 1985. *Dinamiese Konserwatisme.* Pretoria: Oranjewerkers Promosies.

du Toit, Brian M. 1965. *Beperkte Lidmaatskap.* Cape Town: John Malherbe.

———. 1976. *Configurations of Cultural Continuity.* Rotterdam: A.A. Balkema.

———. 1991. "The Far Right in Current South African Politics." *Journal of Modern African Studies* 29 (4): 627–667.

Lubbe, W. J. G., ed. 1983. *Witman, Waar is jou Tuisland?* Pretoria: Oranjewerkers Promosies.

Serfontein, J. H. P. 1978. *Brotherhood of Power.* Bloomington: Indiana University Press.

Wilkins, Ivor, and Hans Strydom. 1978. *The Super-Afrikaners: Inside the Afrikaner Broederbond.* Johannesburg: Jonathan Ball.

Zille, Helen. 1988. "The Right Wing in South African Politics." In *A Future South Africa: Visions, Strategies, and Realities,* edited by Peter L. Berger and Bobby Godsell. Cape Town: Human & Rousseau.

Brian M. du Toit

AGOTES

SEE *Cagots.*

ALAMO

The Alamo, located in the heart of the city of San Antonio, Texas, is one of the most recognized symbols and most visited historic sites in the world. Between four and five million people per year pass through the partially restored ruins of the mission of San Antonio de Valero, which was founded by Spanish Franciscans in 1718. Labeled by the Daughters of the Republic of Texas—legal caretakers of the Alamo since 1905—as the "Shrine and Cradle of Texas Liberty" (Brear, p. 1), the Alamo has also been branded as "America's premier white identity shrine" (Gable 1995, p. 1061). Each of these descriptions derives from the complex history of the site and its relation to the evolving society in which it is embedded.

Abandoned by the Franciscans in the 1790s, the old mission acquired its current name early in the nineteenth century, after it became the headquarters of a company of Spanish soldiers from the Mexican city of Álamo de Parras. Some historians claim, however, that the name came from nearby stands of cottonwood—*álamo* in Spanish.

Though not designed as a fortress, the Alamo achieved lasting fame due to a thirteen-day siege, which culminated in the total annihilation of its defenders on March 6, 1836, during a Texan revolt against the government of Mexico, which had itself won independence from Spain in 1821. Among the dead was the celebrated American frontiersman David Crockett.

Although often portrayed as a stark racial and cultural clash between Mexicans and Anglo-Americans, the Texas Revolution of 1835-1836 and the Battle of the Alamo occurred amid considerably more complex circumstances. The conflict began as part of a larger Mexican civil war between the increasingly authoritarian Centralist regime of President Antonio López de Santa Anna and his Federalist opponents, who favored local autonomy and states' rights in such matters as taxes, trade, and immigration. Prior to sending troops to Texas in 1835, Santa Anna had already dismissed state legislatures throughout Mexico and violently crushed Federalist opposition in the north Mexican state of Zacatecas.

Texas presented a special case, however. Santa Anna suspected that unrest there could lead to a secessionist movement, and even to the seizure of the province by the United States. Under Mexican rule, thousands of immigrants from the United States had come to Texas, attracted by the winning combination of generous land grants and the lax enforcement of Mexican laws against slavery and smuggling. It appeared to some concerned Mexican observers that the Anglo-Texans were already transforming Texas into an extension of the United States.

Slavery had been banned in most of Mexico, and it was theoretically under tight legal restrictions in Texas, but slaves were imported, bought, worked, and sold in the Anglo-Texan settlements with little regard for the law. By 1835 there were more than 30,000 American immigrants, including their slaves, and together they outnumbered the Spanish-speaking Texans (Tejanos) by a factor of almost ten to one. The American settlements were concentrated in eastern Texas, however, and when the revolt began Tejanos still dominated the southwestern borderlands of Texas.

Despite their residential separation and cultural differences, the Tejanos and Anglo-Texans were in general agreement with respect to both their Federalist politics (including the encouragement of further American immigration and the toleration of slavery) and their determination to resist the imposition of Santa Anna's dictatorship. Juan N. Seguín of San Antonio, the first Texan official to call for armed resistance to the Centralists, is emblematic of Tejano participation in the revolt. Seguín led a large cavalry force and cooperated with an "Army of the People" raised by the Anglo-Texan leader Stephen F. Austin. The rebels defeated the Centralists at San Antonio, and in December 1835 they expelled all of the Mexican troops that Santa Anna had ordered to Texas.

Santa Anna, leading a large Mexican army, responded with a surprise counterstrike in February 1836. He

Battle of the Alamo. *One of the most famous and mythologized battles in American history, the defeat of the Texan rebels on March 6, 1836, became a rallying cry in the struggle for the independence of Texas.* KEAN COLLECTION/GETTY IMAGES.

reoccupied San Antonio and trapped approximately two hundred rebels in the Alamo. Seguín escaped almost certain death when he was dispatched by the Alamo's commander, William Barret Travis, to seek reinforcements. But the disorganized Texan revolutionary government could not relieve the doomed defenders. Centralist armies overwhelmed the Texan forces at the Alamo; they also captured and executed more than four hundred Texan troops who had manned a stronger fortress at Goliad, ninety miles downriver from San Antonio.

In the meantime, rebel leaders declared the independence of the Republic of Texas on March 2. The Texans also decided to place all of their remaining military forces under the command of General Sam Houston, a former governor of Tennessee. Seguín gathered a company of Tejano horsemen and joined Houston's army, which retreated eastward across Texas for six weeks before surprising and overwhelming an incautious Santa Anna on April 21. Hundreds of Mexican soldiers were slaughtered at the Battle of San Jacinto by rebels shouting "Remember the Alamo!" and "Remember Goliad!" Santa Anna was captured, and the remaining Centralist forces withdrew from Texas.

However, not all Mexican Texans followed Seguín and the Tejano political leadership as far as endorsing separation from Mexico; some supported the Centralists, and many tried to avoid the fighting altogether. But the Anglo-Tejano alliance that prevailed was cemented when Houston, who was elected president of the new Texas Republic, appointed Seguín as commandant of the Texan army post at San Antonio. In 1841 the first monument to the fall of the Alamo was constructed—a traveling exhibit made of stones from the walls of the mission. It bore an inscription that compared the battle at San Antonio to the Spartans' heroic stand against the Persians at Thermopylae (480 BCE). It would be several more decades, however, before the Alamo would become a stark symbol of Anglo-Saxon civilization standing against so-called Mexican depravity.

Relations between Tejanos and Anglo-Texans worsened as a result of a renewed border war with Mexico in 1842. Seguín, who had become the mayor of San

Antonio, was forced into exile in Mexico by unruly Anglo-American volunteer soldiers who falsely accused him of treason. Upon reaching the Río Grande, Seguín was given the choice of life in prison or service with the Mexican army; his appearance with his former enemies in a raid on San Antonio in September 1842 confirmed the opinion of those who thought him a traitor to Texas.

But neither Seguín's apparent apostasy nor the bitter war between Mexico and the United States (1846–1848) that followed the American annexation of Texas was sufficient to turn the Alamo into an anti-Mexican "white identity shrine." Significantly, Seguín returned to Texas after the Treaty of Guadalupe Hidalgo ended the conflict. Welcomed back into citizenship by many of his old comrades (including Sam Houston), Seguín wrote his memoirs of the Texas Revolution, became a Democratic Party leader in San Antonio, and was elected a county judge before retiring to Mexico in the 1870s.

The Alamo itself was essentially neglected for more than a generation following the famous battle. Most of the walls and buildings were gobbled up by the growing city of San Antonio, until all that remained was the mission's chapel and a portion of the barracks known as the *convento*. The Catholic Church had leased the property to the American forces during the Mexican War, and it was the U.S. Army that put a roof on the chapel, and thus gave it its famous "hump." The State of Texas purchased the chapel in 1883, but even in 1886, the year of the battle's fiftieth anniversary, there was no memorial service at the site, and in that same year the *convento* passed into the ownership of a grocer who used it to store onions and potatoes.

Only in the 1890s, with the organization of the Daughters of the Republic of Texas (DRT), did a serious effort to create an Alamo shrine begin. This campaign was led by two women—the ranching heiress Clara Driscoll and Adina De Zavala, the granddaughter of Lorenzo de Zavala, a Mexican Federalist who had signed the Texan Declaration of Independence and become the Texas Republic's first vice president. Their efforts resulted in a state law purchasing the *convento* and transferring control of the entire Alamo property to the DRT in 1905.

A prolonged dispute, much ballyhooed as the "second battle of the Alamo," ensued within the DRT between Driscoll, De Zavala, and their respective followers over the technical and aesthetic details of historic preservation of the site, but all factions of the DRT were in essential agreement that the preserved Alamo should serve as a sacred monument to the heroism of its Texan defenders.

The labors of the DRT coincided with national trends of historic preservation and ancestor worship that exalted the Anglo-Saxon heritage of the United States, but deeper and more troubling developments were afoot in Texas. This was a time when the arrival of railroads and commercial agriculture created a great demand for cheap, transient, and docile Mexican labor in South Texas. The Jim Crow laws of segregation and disfranchisement were being applied to Mexicans as well as African-Americans in Texas between 1890 and 1920, and the historian David Montejano has argued that a simplified and mythicized version of the Texan past was employed to rationalize and to justify the degraded social position of Mexicans.

In the early twentieth century, Tejanos such as Seguín were purged from the collective Texan memory of the Revolution. In the blatantly racist 1915 film *Birth of Texas, or Martyrs of the Alamo* (made in the same D. W. Griffith studio that produced *Birth of a Nation* that same year), the revolt is portrayed as one of outraged whites rising up against a drunken and lecherous Mexican soldiery. The literary critic Don Graham has shown that an emphasis on Mexican racial depravity suffused the early twentieth-century novels about the Texas Revolution, in contrast to earlier works by Texan authors who blamed Mexico's backwardness on the benighted heritage of Spanish Catholicism. At the same time, Texan painters Robert Jenkins Onderdonk (*The Fall of the Alamo,* 1903) and Henry Arthur McArdle (*Dawn at the Alamo,* 1905), whose iconic works have been enormously influential in Texas, depicted a Manichean struggle at the Alamo between the forces of light and dark—of civilization and savagery—in a clear departure from earlier Texan artists who portrayed Santa Anna's Mexican troops as a classic, European-style Napoleonic army. Thus, in print and picture, the Alamo story was rewritten as a war between two hostile races.

In their late twentieth-century San Antonio fieldwork, the anthropologists Richard R. Flores and Holly Beachley Brear found the same binary logic still at work at the Alamo shrine itself, where the tacit erasure of the Tejanos and the juxtaposition of noble Anglo defenders against debased servants of Mexican tyranny continued. During the 1990s, however, the caretakers of the Alamo took several conscientious steps to remove the implicit denigration of Mexicans that had once permeated the shrine's narrative, symbols, and rituals. The Mexican flag was introduced into the "Hall of Honor" to represent the Tejano defenders of the Alamo; an illustrated "Wall of History" was created by a professional historical staff to contextualize both the Spanish mission and the Alamo battle in the broader history of the city and the state; and the Alamo Defenders' Descendants Association—with many Tejanos among the membership—began holding yearly memorial services for their ancestors in the Alamo chapel. Even as the racist aspects of the Alamo's symbolism were being diminished, however, many Mexicans, and some Mexican-Americans, still saw the Alamo as a symbol not of courage and sacrifice, but of greedy North American land pirates determined to rob Mexico of its patrimony.

SEE ALSO *La Raza; Mexicans; Social Psychology of Racism; Treaty of Guadalupe Hidalgo; Zoot Suit Riots.*

BIBLIOGRAPHY

Brear, Holly Beachley. 1995. *Inherit the Alamo: Myth and Ritual at an American Shrine.* Austin: University of Texas Press.

Crisp, James E. 2005. *Sleuthing the Alamo: Davy Crockett's Last Stand and Other Mysteries of the Texas Revolution.* New York: Oxford University Press.

Flores, Richard R. 2002. *Remembering the Alamo: Memory, Modernity, and the Master Symbol.* Austin: University of Texas Press.

Gable, Eric. 1995. "Review of *Inherit the Alamo: Myth and Ritual at an American Shrine* by Holly Beachley Brear." *American Ethnologist* 22 (4): 1061–1062.

Graham, Don. 1985. "Remembering the Alamo: The Story of the Texas Revolution in Popular Culture." *Southwestern Historical Quarterly* 89 (1): 35–66.

Montejano, David. 1987. *Anglos and Mexicans in the Making of Texas, 1836–1986.* Austin: University of Texas Press.

Seguín, Juan Nepomuceno. 2002. *A Revolution Remembered: The Memoirs and Selected Correspondence of Juan N. Seguín.* Edited by Jesús F. de la Teja. Fred H. and Ella Mae Moore Texas History Reprint Series. Austin: Texas State Historical Association.

James E. Crisp

ALIEN LAND LAWS

Private ownership of land occupies a central position in American law. In the nineteenth century a link emerged in West Coast states between property ownership and race, exemplified by the 1859 Oregon Constitution, which declared that no "Chinaman" could ever own land in Oregon. During this period, "race" was legally constructed along a white-nonwhite binary, with Chinese immigrants categorized as "nonwhites." For the Chinese in the United States, this subordinate racial status entailed strict labor and residential segregation from whites, as well as a vulnerability to mob violence. Their inability to become citizens only compounded their subordinate racial status.

White antipathy to foreign laborers from China culminated in the federal Chinese Exclusion Act of 1882, which barred Chinese immigration for a ten-year period (it was later extended a number of times). This anti-Chinese racism was easily transferred to Japanese agricultural workers, who began entering the country in increasing numbers after 1890. Like the Chinese before them, Japanese agricultural laborers were classified as "nonwhite," and they were therefore barred from becoming U.S. citizens. Yet despite the racialized disabilities imposed upon them, Japanese immigrants thrived in the first decade of the twentieth century. Their success in agriculture was held against them, however: White farmers viewed them as unfair competitors because entire Japanese families would work their farms and save labor costs.

This racial animosity congealed into efforts to prevent the Japanese from owning or acquiring agricultural land. An "Alien Land Law" was passed by the California legislature in 1913. The law granted aliens eligible for U.S. citizenship plenary property ownership rights but limited "aliens ineligible to citizenship" to those rights explicitly granted by treaties. The relevant 1911 U.S.-Japan treaty, however, did not mention protecting the property rights of Japanese persons residing on agricultural land in the United States. While facially neutral, this law relied on the federal racial prerequisite to naturalization—one had to be a "free white person" to become naturalized—to bar Japanese farmers from land ownership. This legal sanction was a response to the economic success of Japanese truck farmers in California in the early twentieth century.

Despite the 1913 law, Japanese land holdings increased. Japanese farmers used various strategies to circumvent the law, such as assigning title in the name of citizen children, with land held in trusts or guardianships, or forming title-holding agricultural corporations with noncitizen farmers as shareholders. By 1920 anti-Japanese activists—including members of the California Grange, which was supported by the Hearst newspapers—placed an initiative on the ballot outlawing the methods used to circumvent the 1913 law. The 1920 initiative passed with a majority in every California county and resulted in a decline in acreage under Japanese ownership throughout the decade.

Other western states soon followed. Arizona had enacted an Alien Land Law in 1917, and between 1921 and 1925 Washington, Louisiana, Oregon, Idaho, Montana, and Kansas passed similar laws. During World War II Wyoming, Utah, and Arkansas also passed Alien Land Laws.

In 1923 the U.S. Supreme Court ruled on the constitutionality of these laws. In *Terrace v. Thompson* (1923), the Court upheld the Washington Alien Land Law on the ground that a state could rightly restrict property ownership to U.S. citizens, and that doing so did not amount to impermissible racial discrimination. *Porterfield v. Webb* (1923) upheld California's 1920 initiative amending the 1913 Alien Land Law. In *Webb v. O'Brien* (1923), *Frick v. Webb* (1923), and *Cockrill v. California* (1925), the Court upheld the 1920 initiative's various restrictions on circumventions of the law.

After World War II the California law was challenged in *Oyama v. California* (1948). The U.S. Supreme Court overturned, on equal protection grounds, a provision of the 1920 initiative that forbade an "alien ineligible to citizenship" from being a guardian to a minor U.S.-born child. The California Supreme Court finally overturned the entire 1920 law in *Fujii v. State of California* (1952), and the Oregon and Montana supreme courts also set aside their Alien Land Laws in *Namba v. McCourt* (1949) and *State of Montana v. Oakland* (1955), respectively.

Washington's Alien Land Law was repealed in 1966 by ballot initiative. The Wyoming legislature was successfully lobbied by the Alien Land Law Project of the University of Cincinnati Law School in 2001 to repeal its Alien Land Law.

SEE ALSO *Immigration to the United States.*

BIBLIOGRAPHY

Aoki, Keith. 1998. "No Right to Own?: The Early Twentieth-Century 'Alien Land Laws' as a Prelude to Internment." *Boston College Law Review* 40: 37–72.

Lazarus, Mark L., III. 1989. "An Historical Analysis of Alien Land Law: Washington, Territory and State, 1853–1889." *University of Puget Sound Law Review* 12: 197–246.

Yamamoto, Eric K., et al. 2001. *Race, Rights, and Reparation: Law and the Japanese American Internment.* Gaithersburg, MD: Aspen Law and Business.

Keith Aoki

ALLEN, RICHARD
1760–1831

Richard Allen was an abolitionist and the first bishop of the African Methodist Episcopal (AME) Church. Allen was born a slave on February 14, 1760, in Philadelphia to parents owned by Benjamin Chew, the colony's attorney general and chief justice of the High Court of Appeals. Allen later remembered Chew as a kind master, but the attorney's practice faltered when Allen was seventeen, and Allen, his parents, and his three siblings were sold to Stokely Sturgis, a wealthy farmer who lived near Dover, Delaware. Sturgis was far less benevolent than Chew, and after a short time he sold Allen's parents and two of his siblings. He did allow Allen to attend local Methodist services, and Allen learned to read and write and soon began to preach at the meetings.

With the help of Freeborn Garretson, an itinerant Methodist minister, Allen was able to persuade Sturgis that the ownership of another was morally wrong. At length, Sturgis agreed to manumit Allen and his brother, provided that they were able to purchase themselves by raising either $2,000 in Continental paper or £60 in gold or silver currency. Both were able to do so by 1780, and at the age of twenty, Allen began a new life as a free day laborer, bricklayer, and wagon driver.

While working as a teamster during the last days of the Revolutionary War, Allen began to preach at regular stops around Delaware, New Jersey, and Pennsylvania. His sermons attracted the attention of Bishop Francis Asbury, the leader of American Methodism. Asbury invited Allen to become his traveling companion, and for the next several years Allen traveled by foot from New York to North Carolina, often preaching to interracial groups up to five times each day. His labors earned him an invitation to return to Philadelphia to preach to black congregants at Saint George's Methodist Church, a rustic, dirt-floored building. Allen would spend the rest of his days in the city.

During his years in Philadelphia, Allen married twice. His first wife, Flora, died shortly after their 1791 marriage, and in 1805 he wed Sarah, who bore him six children. (The surname of neither woman is known.) He also grew close with fellow Methodist Absalom Jones, who shared his interest in building a separate place of worship for blacks, free of white control. Their determination to reach out more effectively to their "African brethren," few of whom attended public worship, only grew stronger in 1792, when white church elders yanked Jones to his feet during prayer and instructed him to retreat to the segregated pews upstairs. Allen and Jones then led a mass exodus from the church. Together, they formed the Independent Free African Society, the first mutual aid group for blacks in the United States, and then issued a plan for "The African Church." Founded upon the belief that African Americans needed "to worship God under our own vine and fig tree," Allen and several patrons (most notably Benjamin Rush) bought an abandoned blacksmith shop and had it moved to Sixth Street. In July 1794 the renovated building opened as the Bethel Church.

Despite the fact that a majority of his congregation opposed continued affiliation with the Methodist hierarchy due to their treatment of blacks, Allen believed that no "denomination" suited "the capacity of colored people as well as the Methodist." But white churchmen stubbornly tried to maintain control over the popular Allen, even insisting that the Bethel structure belonged to the larger church. In response, Allen formed the first African Methodist Episcopal congregation, and in 1799 Bishop Francis Asbury ordained him as deacon. Friction with the Methodists continued until 1816, however, when the Pennsylvania Supreme Court upheld the economic independence of Bethel, and official contact between the two groups finally ended.

Allen was one of the two leading freedmen in Philadelphia, and his charitable and political contributions spread far beyond theology. As a result, Bethel quickly became the focal point of the city's emerging free black society. In the fall of 1796, Allen opened the First Day School at Bethel, and a night school for adults soon followed. Allen and Jones publicly assisted the sick and dying during the yellow fever epidemic of 1793, at a time when most white politicians fled the nation's capital. Despite a public commendation from the mayor for the charitable labors of Allen's congregants, he later had to fight off charges that black nurses and undertakers had used the crisis to rob their patients. His 1794 *Narrative of the Proceedings of the Black People, During the Late Awful Calamity* not only defended his churchmen but also attacked the white racism that lay beneath such charges.

As a prosperous businessman, Allen was particularly sensitive to the idea that black Philadelphians were dependent on white charity, and much of the success of Bethel was due to his adroit ability to appeal to the city's business elite while assisting former slaves relocating into Pennsylvania from Delaware, Virginia, and Maryland. His antislavery essays and pamphlets brought him into contact with white and black abolitionists in other northern states and in Britain. Late in life, in November 1830, Allen helped to organize the American Society of Free Persons of Colour, a group dedicated to purchasing lands in the North or in Canada so that black agriculturalists might become self-sufficient. During that same year, he also cosigned the call for the First Annual Convention of the People of Colour. The conventions, which met sporadically through the Civil War, met to discuss antislavery and the possibility of emigration (although Allen generally regarded mass colonization as a mistake).

As independent black congregations emerged in urban areas along the Atlantic coast, most chose to attach themselves to the Bethel Church. Aware of the continuing friction between white and black Methodists in other cities, Allen sent an invitation for black delegates to meet in Philadelphia for the purpose of confederation, and on April 9, 1816, sixty delegates from five predominantly black churches did so. The next day, the group ordained Allen as elder, and shortly thereafter he was consecrated a bishop. Three years later, in July 1820, Bishop Allen hosted the first General Conference in Philadelphia. Allen even dispatched six ministers to Charleston to bring South Carolina's leading black congregation into the fold. City authorities arrested the six men, however, and they finally razed the building in late 1822 after the discovery that AME member Denmark Vesey had used the church in organizing a conspiracy against slave owners, which had been revealed by an informant. But by the early 1830s, Bethel's reach included eighty-six churches, four conferences, two bishops, and 7,594 members.

Allen died in Philadelphia on March 26, 1831. (Sarah lived another eighteen years, until 1849.) His funeral proved to be one of the largest gatherings of blacks and whites the city had yet witnessed.

SEE ALSO *Antebellum Black Ethnology; Vesey, Denmark.*

BIBLIOGRAPHY

George, Carol V.R. 1972. *Segregated Sabbaths: Richard Allen and the Rise of Independent Black Churches.* New York: Oxford University Press.

Nash, Gary B. 1988. *Forging Freedom: The Formation of Philadelphia's Black Community, 1720–1840.* Cambridge, MA: Harvard University Press.

Newman, Richard S. 2006. *Black Founder: Richard Allen, African Americans and the Early American Republic.* Rochester, New York: Rochester Institute of Technology.

Sernett, Milton C. 1975. *Black Religion and American Evangelicalism: White Protestants, Plantation Missions, and the Flowering of Negro Christianity, 1787–1865.* Metuchen, NJ: Scarecrow Press.

Douglas R. Egerton

AMERICAN ANTI-SLAVERY SOCIETY

The American Anti-Slavery Society played a significant role in furthering the cause of abolition during the decades leading up to the Civil War. The society was founded in 1833 in Philadelphia by the white abolitionists Theodore Dwight Weld, Arthur Tappan, and Arthur's brother Lewis. Its most prominent member was William Lloyd Garrison, who served until 1840 as the society's first president. Noteworthy members included Frederick Douglass and William Wells Brown, two former slaves who, as "agents" for the society, spoke eloquently about the brutality of slavery. Other well-known members included James Gillespie Birney, Maria Weston Chapman, Lydia Child, Samuel Eli Cornish, James Forten, Henry Highland Garnet, Wendell Phillips, Robert Purvis, and Charles Lenox Remond.

The organization grew rapidly throughout the North, with 400 chapters by 1835; 1,350 by 1838; and 2,000 by 1840. Individual membership estimates vary but generally fall in the range of 150,000 to 250,000. The American Anti-Slavery Society was noteworthy because it was the first such organization with a national reach to call for the immediate (rather than gradual) abolition of slavery.

BACKGROUND

The decade preceding the formation of the American Anti-Slavery Society was one of widespread unrest over the issue of slavery. In 1820, after rancorous debate, the U.S. Congress passed the Missouri Compromise to regulate slavery in the expanding nation's western territories. The debate between antislavery and proslavery factions in Congress and elsewhere intensified the parallel debate over the issue of federalism and the relative powers of the federal and state governments. This debate eventually led to the formation of the Democratic Party, which supported slavery, and the Republican Party of Abraham Lincoln, which opposed it.

Slavery was squarely on the national agenda: The Virginia legislature conducted intense debates on the issue in 1829 and 1831; David Walker published his famous "Appeal to the Coloured Citizens of the World" in 1829; and the state of South Carolina, in an act that presaged its leading role in secession and the Civil War, resisted federal efforts to collect tariffs in the state in 1831. The tension between the federal and state governments led to Southern fears that it was only a matter of time before the federal government would intervene in the issue of slavery.

Also in 1831, Garrison launched *The Liberator*, a newspaper that called for racial equality and demanded immediate abolition. That same year, Nat Turner launched a slave rebellion in Southampton County, Virginia. Turner's rebellion left sixty white people dead before it was put down by the state militia, adding to a climate of fear throughout the South and a tightening of laws pertaining to slave behavior. In the North, however, these events contributed to a growing abolitionist sentiment, much of it led by the Quakers and other religious groups.

At its founding meeting, the American Anti-Slavery Society issued a "Declaration of Sentiments," written by Garrison. In addition to arguing that plantation owners were not entitled to compensation for the freeing of slaves, the declaration argued that slavery was a violation of natural law, the U.S. Constitution, and—reflecting the sentiments of the religious revival of the 1830s called the Second Great Awakening—the will of God. The declaration read, in part:

> That all those laws which are now in force, admitting the right of slavery, are therefore, before God, utterly null and void; being an audacious usurpation of the Divine prerogative, a daring infringement on the law of nature, a base overthrow of the very foundations of the social compact, a complete extinction of all the relations, endearments and obligations of mankind, and a presumptuous transgression of all the holy commandments; and that therefore they ought instantly to be abrogated.
>
> We further believe and affirm—that all persons of color, who possess the qualifications which are demanded of others, ought to be admitted forthwith to the enjoyment of the same privileges, and the exercise of the same prerogatives, as others; and that the paths of preferment, of wealth and of intelligence, should be opened as widely to them as to persons of a white complexion. (Quoted in Ruchames 1963, p. 78)

The goal of the American Anti-Slavery Society was to reach the public through speeches and public lectures, petitions, and mass publications. Frederick Douglass and William Wells Brown frequently lectured in the name of the society, often in the face of mob violence. Garrison recruited Maria Weston Chapman to write for *The Liberator* and *The National Anti-Slavery Standard* (*NASS*), both official publications of the society, and Lydia Marie Child edited *NASS* for two years. Garrison, however, was the society's guiding hand, and in that capacity he urged Northerners to refuse to vote as a means of expressing their disapproval of slavery. He and the society bombarded Congress with petitions, prompting Congress to institute a gag rule under which it refused to accept any petitions having to do with slavery.

GENDER POLITICS

Women were initially barred from membership in the society. This ban even included such women as Maria Weston Chapman and Lydia Marie Child, who supported the society with their labor. Most male members, many of them churchmen, regarded female involvement in the rough-and-tumble of the debate as unseemly. They raised their eyebrows in sharp disapproval when the sisters Angelina and Sarah Grimké were among the first to lecture publicly on behalf of the society. Nevertheless, numerous prominent women supported the society's goals and worked in its behalf, including Lucretia Mott, Susan B. Anthony, Elizabeth Cady Stanton, Lucy Stone, and Amelia Bloomer, but they found themselves the targets of condescension from male members.

The Congregationalist Church, in a pastoral letter of 1837, condemned women for speaking out against slavery, characterizing female involvement in such public matters as "unnatural." Although many men agreed with this position, they believed that the goal of ending slavery took precedence over issues involving women's rights. In their view, too many churches supported slavery, or at least acquiesced in it, and were therefore corrupt. These men were often said to have "come out" of their church membership, and they became known as "come-outers."

In response to the society's gender bias, women took their own route. Lucretia Mott organized the Philadelphia Female Anti-Slavery Society (PFASS) in 1833, and similar organizations were formed in other cities. In the years that followed, the society and its members gained

CAUTION!!

COLORED PEOPLE

OF BOSTON, ONE & ALL,

You are hereby respectfully CAUTIONED and advised, to avoid conversing with the

Watchmen and Police Officers of Boston,

For since the recent ORDER OF THE MAYOR & ALDERMEN, they are empowered to act as

KIDNAPPERS

AND

Slave Catchers,

And they have already been actually employed in KIDNAPPING, CATCHING, AND KEEPING SLAVES. Therefore, if you value your LIBERTY, and the *Welfare of the Fugitives* among you, *Shun* them in every possible manner, as so many *HOUNDS* on the track of the most unfortunate of your race.

Keep a Sharp Look Out for KIDNAPPERS, and have TOP EYE open.

APRIL 24, 1851.

An Abolitionist Poster. *This 1851 handbill warned the "Colored People of Boston" to avoid talking to watchmen and police officers, who had been empowered by the Fugitive Slave Act of 1850 to kidnap escaped slaves.* THE LIBRARY OF CONGRESS.

valuable experience in fund-raising and organization, and this experience would serve women well in the later battle for the right to vote. Meanwhile, antislavery sewing circles allowed women to use their skills in the domestic arts to make craft items, which they sold at fairs and bazaars to raise funds to support their efforts. There is little exaggeration in saying that sexism in some quarters of the antislavery movement galvanized women to fight for equal rights. The Grimkés, for instance, shifted their focus from the slavery issue to that of women's rights and became important pioneers in the nineteenth-century women's suffrage movement.

ORGANIZATIONAL SPLIT

The American Anti-Slavery Society split in 1839. At issue was the belief by some members that Garrison's ideas were too radical. To Garrison, the U.S. Constitution (a "document from hell") was illegal because it allowed the existence of slavery. Thus, he believed that the very foundations of the nation were illegitimate, and he called for the North to secede from the Union and form its own nation. Garrison's opponents within the society argued that the Constitution, and therefore the U.S. government, was legitimate, for it allowed people the right to redress their grievances and end forms of oppression such as slavery. For this faction, the society's principal goal was to elect antislavery candidates to public office, where they would be able to enact laws outlawing slavery.

Meanwhile, the gender issue led to sharp disagreements. Garrison, along with Wells, Phillips, and Douglass, strongly supported equal rights for women. The controversy came to a head when Child, Mott, Chapman, and Abby Kelly were elected to the society's executive committee. In response, Lewis Tappan remarked, "to put a woman on the committee with men is contrary to the usages of civilized society." Accordingly, in 1840, Tappan and several other prominent members of the society broke away to form a rival organization, the American and Foreign Anti-Slavery Society. Concentrating entirely on slavery, the rival organization refused to lend support to women's rights. In the decade that followed, the new organization formed the Liberty Party (1840–1848), which evolved into the Free-Soil Party (1848–1854), and then into the Republican Party. The split weakened the American Anti-Slavery Society, however, as it shifted its focus from national to state and local efforts.

The American Anti-Slavery Society was formally dissolved in 1870. The society is not to be confused with a modern organization by the same name that fights slavery and racial oppression throughout the world, nor with the British Anti-Slavery Society, formed in 1823.

SEE ALSO *Abolition Movement; Birney, James Gillespie; Douglass, Frederick; Forten, James; Garnet, Henry Highland; Garrison, William Lloyd; Remond, Charles Lenox; Turner, Henry McNeal.*

BIBLIOGRAPHY

Duberman, Martin, ed. 1965. *The Antislavery Vanguard: New Essays on the Abolitionists*. Princeton, NJ: Princeton University Press.

Filler, Louis. 1986. *The Crusade Against Slavery: Friends, Foes, and Reforms, 1820–1860*. Algonac, MI: Reference Publications.

Kraditor, Aileen S. 1969. *Means and Ends in American Abolitionism: Garrison and his Critics on Strategy and Tactics, 1834–1850*. New York: Pantheon Books.

Nye, Russell B. 1955. *William Lloyd Garrison and the Humanitarian Reformers*. Boston: Little, Brown.

Ruchames, Louis, ed. 1963. *The Abolitionists: A Collection of Their Writing*. New York: Putnam.

Michael J. O'Neal

AMERICAN COLONIZATION SOCIETY AND THE FOUNDING OF LIBERIA

The American Society for Colonizing the Free People of Color of the United States was organized on December 21, 1816, in the Davis Hotel in Washington, D.C. The stated purposes of the organization, which was commonly known as the American Colonization Society (ACS), were threefold: (1) to create an unfettered haven for free blacks whose continued presence in the United States was seen as posing insoluble problems of civic and social integration; (2) to promote "civilization" and Christianity in Africa through their presence there; and (3) to develop receiving stations for enslaved Africans taken from vessels illegally transporting them on the high seas. England had already established Sierra Leone in 1787 as a catchall colonization destination of blacks from Britain. Talk of removing free persons of color from American soil antedated the adoption of the U.S. Constitution in 1787 and rested on the following premises: (1) their presence was a social nuisance; (2) their presence was inimical to the institution of slavery; and (3) the new social system had no place for them. Thus they should be colonized in distant locales such as the Pacific Coast, South America, the Far West, or Africa itself. As early as 1773, Thomas Jefferson advocated establishing colonies for free blacks, but he never stated this view publicly. Along with George Washington, Jefferson believed black colonies should be a precondition for emancipation. In 1790, three years after the U.S. Constitution was adopted, the census counted a free black population of about 59,557 individuals and an enslaved population of 697,624. In the 1810 census, the new nation had 108,435 free blacks and 1,191,446 enslaved blacks.

BLACK COLONIZATION: FROM TALK TO ACTION

After blacks, slave and free, had fought in the American Revolution and the War of 1812 and with the advent of peace, discussions of colonizing free blacks became public. In December 1816, two key colonization events took place: The Virginia Assembly adopted resolutions calling on the U.S. government to settle emancipated blacks outside the boundaries of the United States, and a meeting on black colonization was held in the hall of the U.S. House of Representatives to form the ACS. Seven days later the founding members of this group ratified a constitution for the ACS, the sole object being "to promote and execute a plan for colonizing (with their consent) the Free People of Color residing in our Country, in Africa, or such other place as Congress shall deem most expedient." Membership was open to any citizen of the United States upon payment of one dollar. Lifetime memberships were available for thirty dollars. Further informal discussion prompted the group to hold the first of its annual meetings on January 1, 1817, at the Davis Hotel in Washington. As he had done at the earlier meeting, U.S. Congressman Henry Clay of Kentucky presided, for Kentucky had already organized its State Colonization Society. The sixty-odd high-profile, self-selected delegates were not as distinguished as the fifty-five men who had drafted the Constitution some thirty years earlier, but they were indeed "gentlemen of property and standing."

Among the founders of the ACS were Robert Finley, a New Jersey Presbyterian minister and in 1817 president of the University of Georgia; Bushrod Washington, associate justice of the U.S. Supreme Court; Elias B. Caldwell, clerk of the Supreme Court; Richard Rush, attorney general of the United States; Daniel Webster, then a congressman from New Hampshire; Congressman John Randolph of Roanoke, Virginia, owner of 363 slaves and 160 horses; William Phillips, lieutenant governor of Massachusetts; wealthy international trader Robert Ralston of New York; William Thornton, architect of the U.S. Capitol; Henry Carroll, secretary of the American legation to Ghent, Belgium, where the War of 1812 was declared officially over; John E. Howard, former governor of Maryland; General Andrew Jackson, much the military hero of the Battle of New Orleans (1815); and Francis Scott Key, the Washington lawyer and poet, newly famous for writing "The Star-Spangled Banner." These men hailed from different parts of the nation, which had varying proportions of slaves and free blacks.

COLONIZATION SOCIETIES: NATIONAL, STATE, AND LOCAL

Between 1817 and 1825, the so-called Era of Good Feelings among the regions of the new nation, there arose a generalized belief that free blacks in the United States would soon pollute the expanding community of transplanted Europeans. In the years from 1816 to 1836, the colonization idea was so popular that even without a national staff, more than a dozen states, from Vermont to Mississippi, formed their own colonization societies. Two of the most powerful were founded in New York City and Philadelphia, the latter the informal "capital" of free black America. Whatever may have been a given region's level of

ACS Officers: Directors, Managers, and Vice Presidents, 1833–1841

STATE	OFFICERS	**FREE BLACKS (%)	**ENSLAVED (%)
(Washington, D.C.)	20	6,499 (*29.1%*)	3,320 (*9.8%*)
Virginia	18	49,342 (*4.7%*)	448,987 (*42.1%*)
New York	13	50,027 (*2.2%*)	4 (–%)
Connecticut	9	8,105 (*2.8%*)	17 (–%)
Kentucky	8	7,317 (*0.9%*)	182,258 (*23.4%*)
Georgia	6	2,753 (*0.4%*)	280,944 (*40.6%*)
New Jersey	6	21,044 (*5.6%*)	674 (*0.2%*)
Maryland	4	62,078 (*13.2%*)	89,737 (*19.1%*)
Ohio	4	17,242 (*1.1%*)	3 (–%)
Pennsylvania	3	47,354 (*2.8%*)	64 (–%)
Louisiana	3	25,502 (*7.2%*)	168,452 (*47.8%*)
Mississippi	2	1,366 (*0.4%*)	195,211 (*52%*)
Delaware	2	16,919 (*21.7%*)	2,605 (*3.3%*)
North Carolina	1	22,732 (*3%*)	245,817 (*32.6%*)
Rhode Island	1	3,238 (*3%*)	0 (–%)
Vermont	1	738 (*3%*)	0 (–%)

** All of the percentage references identify the ratio of each category of blacks to the total white population of each state ranked by number of national officers it supplied during the period covered by the 1840 census. Four ACS officers from abroad were not counted in the above table: Two represented England and two represented France.

SOURCE: Adapted from the Maryland State Colonization Papers (1835–1861); *Historical Statistics of the United States, From Colonial Times to 1857.* Washington DC: United States Department of Commerce, Bureau of Census, 1961.

Table 1.

involvement with the ACS, the number of national officers from a given state was essentially an index of local support for the national ACS goals. As seen in Table 1, not unexpectedly the headquarters site of the ACS, Washington, D.C., supplied the organization with twenty officers. Supplying the next two largest numbers of officers were Virginia, with eighteen officers and nearly a half million enslaved Africans within its borders, and New York, with thirteen officers, 50,000 free blacks, and no slaves in 1840. Distant from Washington was the Mississippi State Colonization Society based in Greenville, so active in Liberia that a section of it is called Greenville. In the case of the state of Maryland, ACS leader John H. B. Latrobe and associates were so active and independent that the national ACS lost control of them in 1829. The Maryland society, extraordinarily determined to reduce the number of free blacks in the city, basically set up an independent operation in Liberia. Very active also was the Ohio State Colonization Society, which had four officers at the national level of the ACS, representing a free black population of 17,000 individuals and no slaves. In an ACS annual report, the officers of the ACS praised the industry of its Ohio representatives, and declared that the ACS should seek agents similar to those in Ohio "to do a good service in vitalizing State Societies now in a condition of suspended animation."

Rhode Island and Vermont, with no slaves and only a handful of blacks, ideologically supported the objectives of the ACS. Representing the state with the largest proportion of ships formerly importing slaves, Rhode Islanders stood to profit as freedpeople exporters in the event the colonization movement went truly national. Pennsylvania's large representation, with no slavery, might be attributed to the exceptional promotional work of its Quaker Young Men's Colonization Society. The same was true of the New York City Colonization Society and its larger companion group, the New York State Colonization Society. Vermont, whose population included only 3 percent free blacks and no slaves in 1820, nevertheless had one of the most active local colonization societies in the country. Its members at a meeting in 1826 in Montpelier heard a Middlebury College professor complain that "the state of the free colored population of the United States is one of extreme and remediless degradation, of gross irreligion, of revolting profligacy, and of course, deplorable wretchedness." His words echoed those of other speakers throughout the country. Membership on the national board of the ACS, then, was very much a reward for state and local support of its objectives.

CONTRADICTORY CONCEPTIONS OF BLACK CAPABILITIES

As well-placed and informed as ACS leaders may have been, they appeared to be unaware of the glaring contradictions in their program and promotional materials. In print and in person, they used the language of humanitarian solicitude and benevolent Christianity. In the pages of their *African Repository and Colonial Journal*, they argued that colonization was an act of social justice.

The ACS was defined by its constitution in ways that made it appealing to some extent to antislavery and proslavery groups, humanitarians, racists, religious leaders, and, they thought, free blacks. To win the support of free blacks, humanitarians, and clergymen, ACS officials maintained that among the main goals of their colonization organization was to afford free blacks a place of unfettered freedom and to promote Christianity and American civilization.

Shortly after the ACS adopted its constitution, information regarding its membership and motives had the effect of organizing free blacks in different parts of the country to resist its plans. In January 1817 some 3,000 anticolonization blacks from Pennsylvania, Massachusetts, New York, New Jersey, and Connecticut met in Philadelphia. This was the first time blacks had reacted on an interstate basis to a public issue. They traveled to Philadelphia in the dead of winter on the outside of stagecoaches or next to animals on coastal vessels.

Meeting in the de facto capital of black America, these free persons of color expressed themselves in the following resolutions: "that we never will separate ourselves voluntarily from the slave population of this country" and "that we view with deep abhorrence the unmerited stigma attempted to be cast upon the reputation of the free people of color, by the promoters of this measure, 'that they are a dangerous and useless part of the community.'" Led by James Forten, a major dry-dock owner in Philadelphia and one of the wealthiest blacks in the country, the ad hoc group formed a committee to convey their views to Congressman John Hopkinson. Among the eleven members of the committee was Richard Allen, the most esteemed black leader of the era.

Taken aback by the scope and intensity of the black rejection of the colonization scheme, the ACS dispatched its general agent, Robert Finley, to Philadelphia to explain to blacks the purposes and intended operations of the association. He stressed the essentially voluntary nature of the national colonization society, saying that its members were private volunteers and its funding was likewise. His visit, however, did not satisfy or silence blacks. Hundreds of free blacks met again in Philadelphia in August 1817. They declared that the ACS plan was "not asked for by us nor will it be requested by any circumstances of our present or future condition." A few free blacks elsewhere supported the idea of colonization. For example, several free persons of color met in Richmond, Virginia, and said that while they opposed transporting blacks across the Atlantic, they asked that the nation "grant to free blacks a small portion of territory, either on the Missouri River, or any place that may seem to them most conducive to the public good and our future welfare." In 1810 Virginia had 30,000 free blacks and 392,000 slaves. However, Baltimore's most prominent leader, Reverend William Watkins, a self-educated schoolteacher of great erudition and command of oral and written English (and a reading knowledge of Greek and Latin), vigorously opposed both the ACS philosophy and program. He said that contrary to some of the assertions made in the ACS monthly publication, the *African Repository*, that it was God's will that blacks go to Africa to uplift it, within the ACS "they know that we are not begging them to send us to Liberia." He said further: "if we are begging them to do anything, it is to let us alone." Indeed it was Watkins who, in the 1820s, persuaded a young newspaper editor, William Lloyd Garrison, to convert from pro- to anti-colonizationism. The *Repository* itself had a split personality: Half of its columns attacked free blacks in America as inferior and undesirable creatures. The other half argued that a "backward pagan" Africa was a place where blacks would have opportunities to demonstrate their talents without interference from whites.

COLONIZATION PROGRAM BACKFIRES

In 1831, with the help of major funding from Forten and black churches, Garrison launched an anticolonization, immediate-emancipation newspaper, *The Liberator*, which printed the objections of black and white abolitionists to the ACS program. In 1832 Garrison collected statements from blacks throughout the North and published them in a thick volume titled *Thoughts on African Colonization; or, An Impartial Exhibition of the Doctrines, Principles, and Purposes of the American Colonization Society, Together with the Resolutions, Addresses, and Remonstrance's of the Free People of Color*. Through the agency of Garrison's newspaper and book, the views of free blacks on a public issue received a national hearing for the first time. It was in the context and vortex of anticolonization, antislavery, and pro-black citizenship rights that Garrison had placed himself in danger of life and limb. But he and his black supporters held unwaveringly that America was the natural home of blacks, with Watkins writing that if poor blacks were to be sent to their ancestral homes, then America should do the same for poor whites.

The ACS, then, not only made free blacks conscious of a national enemy but had also encouraged further hostility between whites and free blacks. The election of ACS member Andrew Jackson as president emboldened working-class whites to physically attack blacks, the most infamous incident being the routing toward Canada of some 800 black workers from Cincinnati in the depression of 1829. Unemployed whites desired their jobs. These and similar events led blacks to begin in 1830 what is now known as the Colored Convention Movement, an annual gathering of black leaders to explore collective response options to their declining civic situation. Usually held in New York or Philadelphia, these conventions, for thirty years, became the one semi-national organ for addressing white America. Most of them had a common theme of opposition to the ACS. The first two conventions, in 1830 and 1831, set up a committee to explore the possibility of migrating to Canada if things got worse for free blacks in the United States. At the 1833 convention, a "Report on Colonization" was issued that contained the following: "The Committee consisting of one delegate from each State, for the purpose of reporting the views and sentiments of the people of color in their respective States, relative to the principles and operations of the American Colonization Society, respectfully beg leave to say 'That all the people of the States they represent, feel themselves aggrieved by its very existence.'"

The report further stated that regardless of what the *African Repository* or spokespersons of the ACS might say, "the inevitable tendency of the ACS doctrine is to strengthen the cruel prejudices of our opponents, to steel the heart of sympathy to the appeals of suffering humanity, to retard our advancement in morals, literature and science, in short, to extinguish the last glimmer of hope, and throw an impenetrable gloom over our fairest and most reasonable prospects" (p. 27). Out of these conventions emerged black spokespersons such as Charles L. Remond, Henry Highland Garnet, and Frederick Douglass.

Despite its mixed motives and contradictory utterances, the ACS managed to settle approximately 15,000 freeborn, emancipated, and recaptured blacks in West Africa between 1822 and 1861. Of this number, an estimated 8,000 were a mixture of domestic and field-hand slaves manumitted and transported to Liberia as a reward for having informed their masters of insurrectionary plans and plots of their fellow bondsmen. This practice was necessary, because if informers remained in the neighborhood and were discovered, they ran the risk of being destroyed by the insurgents or their companions who faced torture, whippings, mutilation, sale out of the region, and/or execution. Liberia thus served as a safety valve not only for free blacks in the North but also for Southern emancipated blacks who rendered "meritorious" service to their masters and communities.

HOLDING FAST TO COLONIZATION RATIONALES

Despite the clear and vocal rejection of colonization by most blacks in the North, the leaders of the ACS continued to stress that the colonization scheme was the best solution to the problems they associated with them. Beginning in 1817, ACS's board of managers began to argue that whites were not responsible for the barriers retarding and separating blacks from mainstream society; they held that these barriers were a product of nature and the will of God. The leaders of the ACS also declared that the free blacks in urban centers were responsible as well for their own status problems.

Bushrod Washington, the first president of the ACS and a white man, expressed the view that among the main goals of the ACS was to "purify" the American social and political systems by colonizing free blacks in Africa or other places outside white America. Robert G. Harper of Maryland, another early strong supporter of the ACS, maintained that black colonization would boost the interests of the United States, because the main objective of the ACS was to get rid of free blacks that he considered to be troublemakers. Henry Clay, one of the vice presidents of the ACS, noted that free blacks were the most "ferocious" people in America, a condition resulting from oppression and their own bad habits. He added that free blacks were a bad influence on enslaved blacks, as well as on whites. For Clay, settling blacks in West Africa would comprise moral, religious, and humanitarian blessings for the indigenous Africans, the colonized blacks, and the whites, especially the whites that supported the ACS effort.

Bishop William Meade of the Episcopal Church in Virginia, who once declared that well-behaved black people in the secular world would become white people in heaven, and who also translated the Bible for the African-American settlers in Liberia, noted that while blacks would not be good Christians in the United States they would be in Liberia. He therefore recommended to the ACS that the emancipation of blacks should be followed by their colonization in Liberia. The Reverend Robert Finley had expressed views regarding black colonization that were similar to those of Bishop Meade and Clay. His early ministry was in Baskerville, New Jersey, which had a free but socially shunned, impoverished black population of fifteen hundred. He had noted that everything associated with blacks, including the pigment of their skin, was against them. He therefore declared that there was no prospect for blacks in America, and added that as such, they should be colonized in West Africa. He concluded that the colonization of blacks in West Africa would accomplish the following objectives: America would be purged of unwanted people; the colonized blacks would promote American civilization in Africa, because they were in some measure Christians and civilized people; and besides they would be in a better position to improve their material, social, and political well-being in West Africa. Not all officers of the ACS saw Africa as the proper destination for free blacks. When James Madison, the former U.S. president, became president of the ACS in 1833, he saw the new American Southwest as a possible home for emancipated blacks.

The position of free blacks notwithstanding, after much political maneuvering, the ACS persuaded Congress to appropriate $100,000 to help underwrite indirectly the colonization scheme, even though it had high hope that the state units of the ACS would continue to raise funds. The thirty-dollar lifetime fees and the one-dollar annual dues did not begin to cover the expense of trying to establish a distant colony reachable only by a sea voyage. The ACS was well aware of the work of a British private association, the African Institution, in establishing Sierra Leone in 1797 as a colony for blacks from England. Thus, the Reverend Samuel J. Mills and Ebenezer Burgess consulted with representatives of the African Institution in Sierra Leone. These two white Americans were sent to Africa by the ACS in 1818 to locate a

Joseph Jenkin Roberts, circa 1851. *Roberts was born free in Virginia in 1809 and moved to Liberia in 1829. In 1842 he became the first black governor of the Commonwealth of Liberia, and in 1848 he became the first (and later the seventh) president of the independent Republic of Liberia.* **THE LIBRARY OF CONGRESS.**

suitable place for the colonization of blacks. The leader, Mills, had made his reputation as a missionary explorer of the American Southwest. Despite their condescension to the local African authorities, Mills and Burgess worked out a deal with them permitting the ACS to settle emancipated blacks on specific portions of African territory. This land usage agreement was the very last act of these two men, as both died of malaria while en route back to the United States.

ON THE GROUND IN LIBERIA

Greatly encouraged by the prospect of actually sending blacks to Africa, the ACS gathered some eighty-four free persons of color, mostly from Maryland and Virginia, and commissioned the ship *Elizabeth* based in New York Harbor as their carrier to go to Africa. The voyage began on January 31, 1820. Only three of the passengers were whites: Samuel Crozer, an ACS representative, the Reverend Samuel Bacon, who represented the U.S. government, and John Bankson, Bacon's assistant. Among the blacks were men of superior ability, such as the Reverend Lott Carey and the Reverend Daniel Coker, both of whom were destined to hold high positions once Liberia was founded. The whites on the *Elizabeth* continued to treat the African-American emigrants paternalistically throughout the voyage from the United States to the West African coast. Blacks deeply resented this, their rage almost provoking a racial conflict at sea, had they not been calmed down by Rev. Coker.

Once on the ground in Africa, the ACS Liberian agent, now Governor Eli Ayres of Liberia, like all the white governors who succeeded him, led the black settlers paternalistically. Ayres's autocratic leadership style was shown when he unilaterally drew up the layout plan of Monrovia, the chief town of the African-American settlers, which was named after James Monroe, then U.S. president. The settlers, especially those who had already constructed their own homes, resented the imposed town plan, because it required them to relocate. This action and related behaviors on the part of Ayres reinforced settlers' resentment toward him, finally forcing his departure from Liberia. In 1823 the equally autocratic Jehudi Ashmun replaced Ayres.

Although he was a competent governor, Ashmun was among the most racist and paternalistic governors in colonial Liberia. He held the view that nearly all the black settlers behaved like children. Ashmun not only continued Ayres's arbitrary food and land distribution policies, he also arrogantly demanded that all adult male settlers perform two days of free service on public land. He warned them that food and other necessities, usually provided by the ACS, would be withheld from those who refused to carry out the required tasks.

Ashmun's behavior led to settlers' strong antipathy toward him. Reinforcing such resentment was his reduction of the food ration by half on March 19, 1823. These actions together with no attempt at conciliation led the settlers to attack and ransack the colonial store. The black settlers also wrote to the officials of the ACS in Washington, accusing Ashmun of dishonesty, discrimination, and partiality.

Ashmun told the male colonists that the contracts they had with the ACS obligated them to his leadership, which included his responsibility for the safety of their wives, children, relatives, belongings, and community. He asserted that the problems they faced were caused by their failure to accept his governorship and their unwillingness to cultivate local foodstuffs.

As in the antebellum South, Ashmun tried to use religion as a means of control in Liberia. He told the settlers he expected them to recommit themselves to God and to the very vows or agreements that already obligated them to the ACS and that body's representatives, including himself, in Liberia.

Liberian Coat of Arms. *The American Colonization Society established Liberia as a haven for freed slaves in 1822. The Republic of Liberia came into existence in 1847, and its coat of arms pictures a ship, symbolizing the voyage of the settlers.* **THE GRANGER COLLECTION, NEW YORK.**

Although he had hoped to bring harmony in the Liberian settlement, Ashmun did not succeed. In fact opposition to his leadership continued to intensify, because he and the ACS were unwilling to make the changes that were needed to satisfy the black colonists. Ashmun was forced to leave Liberia in 1824 for Cape Verde Islands. The ACS and the U.S. Navy, however, reinstated him a few months after his expulsion. Ashmun's declining health coupled with the aforementioned problems forced him to leave Liberia in 1828 for the United States. He died in New Haven, Connecticut, on August 25, 1828.

Ashmun's successors through 1847 continued the outlined racist and paternalistic governing system. Among these governors were Richard Randall, Joseph Mechlin, John Pinney, Ezekiel Skinner, Anthony Williams, Thomas Buchanan, and Joseph J. Roberts, the latter of whom was a descendant of African Americans. Although the Colonial Assembly of the Liberian colony was an elected body, the governor of the colony had final say over who would be elected to that body. In common with prevailing beliefs, the top officials of the ACS were of the opinion that mental ability among nonwhites was a function of the degrees of their kinship to Caucasians. Accordingly, these governors were more receptive to light-skinned blacks than dark-skinned settlers in Liberia. When Liberia technically became an independent country rather than an ACS colony in 1847, its once exclusively Caucasian presidential leadership was replaced for the remainder of the century by a near-white leadership consisting of the following men: Presidents Joseph J. Roberts (1848–1856 and 1872–1876), Stephen A. Benson (1856–1864), Daniel B. Warner (1864–1868), James S. Payne (1868–1870 and 1876–1878), Anthony Gardner (1878–1883), Alfred H. Russell (1883–1884), Hilary R. W. Johnson (1884–1892), Joseph Chesseman (1892–1896), and William D. Coleman (1896–1900). Edward J. Roye (1870–1871) and James S. Smith (1871–1872) were dark-skinned. This group, later called Americo-Liberians, was almost as color-conscious as the white leadership it replaced.

Below the light-skinned African Americans in status were the dark-skinned settlers descended from African-American field hands, and the assimilated recaptives—Africans who had been enslaved but never experienced plantation slavery. Beneath these categories were the traditional ethnic groups such as the Bassa, Dei, Gbandi, Gio, Gola, Grebo, Kissi, Kpelle, Krahn, Kru, Loma, Mano, and Vai, whose members did not become Liberian citizens until the early 1900s, and could not vote until 1946. Such was the political reality created by the ACS in its first fifty years.

Begun by some of America's leading lights, and given the private assignment of ridding America of the free blacks making up an average of 17 percent of the nation's total antebellum black population, the ACS never became politically or financially strong enough to nullify its own internal contradictions or to persuade technically free people of color to leave the only country they had ever known. On the contrary, its program jolted black Americans into a defense of their presence here, making them more determined than ever to become simply Americans. The ACS itself slowly became a letterhead association, operated by a virtually unknown leadership until 1964, when it declared itself dead.

BIBLIOGRAPHY

Barnes, Kenneth C. 2004. *Journey of Hope: The Back-to-Africa Movement in Arkansas in the Late 1800s.* Chapel Hill: University of North Carolina Press.

Beyan, Amos J. 1989. "The American Colonization Society and the Origin of Undemocratic Institutions in Liberia." *Liberian Studies Journal* 14 (2): 140–151.

———. 1991. *The American Colonization Society and the Creation of the Liberian State: A Historical Perspective, 1822–1900.* Lanham, MD: University Press of America.

———. 1994. "The American Background of Recurrent Themes in the Political History of Liberia." *Liberian Studies Journal* 20 (1): 20–40.

———. 1995. "The Transatlantic Trade and the Coastal Area of Pre-Liberia." *Historian* 57 (4): 757–768.

———. 2005. *African American Settlements in West Africa: John Brown Russwurm and the American Civilizing Efforts*. New York: Palgrave Macmillan.

Blyden, Nemata Amelia. 2004. "'Back to Africa': The Migration of New World Blacks to Sierra Leone and Liberia." *OAH Magazine of History* 18 (3): 23–25.

Clegg, Claude A., III. 2004. *The Price of Liberty: African Americans and the Making of Liberia*. Chapel Hill: University of North Carolina Press.

Fox, Early Lee. 1919. *The American Colonization Society, 1817–1840*. Baltimore, MD: Johns Hopkins Press; New York: AMS Press, 1971.

Fredrickson, George M. 1971. *Black Image in the White Mind: The Debate on Afro-American Character and Destiny, 1817–1914*. New York: Harper and Row.

Freeman, Frederick. 1838. *A Plea for Africa, Being Familiar Conversations on the Subjects of Slavery Colonization*. Philadelphia: William Stavely.

Freeman, George Washington. 1836. *The Rights and Duties of Slaveholders: Two Discourses Delivered on Sunday, November 27, 1836. In Christ Church, Raleigh, North Carolina*. Raleigh, NC: J. Gales and Sons.

Friedman, Lawrence J. 1970. "Purifying the White Man's Country: The American Colonization Society Reconsidered, 1816–1840." *Societas* 6 (3): 1–24.

Garrison, William Lloyd. 1832. *Thoughts on African Colonization; or, An Impartial Exhibition of the Doctrines, Principles, and Purposes of the American Colonization Society, Together with the Resolutions, Addresses, and Remonstrance's of the Free People of Color*. Boston: Garrison and Knapp.

Harris, Katherine. 1985. *African and American Values: Liberia and West Africa*. Lanham, MD: University Press of America.

Horsman, Reginald. 1981. *Race and Manifest Destiny: The Origins of American Racial Anglo-Saxonism*. Cambridge, MA: Harvard University Press.

Liebenow, J. Gus. 1987. *Liberia: The Quest for Democracy*. Bloomington: Indiana University Press.

Litwack, Leon F. 1961. *North of Slavery: The Negro in the Free States, 1790–1860*. Chicago: University of Chicago Press.

Lynch, Hollis R. 1967. *Edward Wilmot Blyden: Pan-Negro Patriot, 1832–1912*. London: Oxford University Press.

Maugham, Reginald C. F. 1920. *The Republic of Liberia, Being a General Description of the Negro Republic, with Its History, Commerce, Agriculture, Flora, Fauna, and Present Methods of Administration*. London: Allen & Unwin; New York: C. Scribner's Sons; New York: Negro Universities Press, 1969.

McColley, Robert. 1973. *Slavery and Jeffersonian Virginia*. 2nd ed. Urbana: University of Illinois Press.

McPherson, John T. 1891. *History of Liberia*. Baltimore, MD: Johns Hopkins University Press. New York: Johnson Reprint, 1973.

Meade, William. 1834. *Pastoral Letter of the Reverend William Meade, Assistant Bishop of Virginia to the Ministers, Members, Friends of the Protestant Episcopal Church in the Diocese of Virginia, on the Duty of Affording Religious Instruction to Those in Bondage*. Printed at the Gazette Office in Alexandria, VA.

Mellow, Matthew T. 1934. *Early American Views on Negro Slavery, from the Letters and Papers of the Founders of the Republic*. Boston: Meador Publishing.

Moses, Wilson Jeremiah. 1989. *Alexander Crummell: A Study of Civilization and Discontent*. New York: Oxford University Press.

Ruchames, Louis, ed. 1969. *Racial Thought in America: A Documentary History*, Vol. 1: *From the Puritans to Abraham Lincoln*. Amherst: University of Massachusetts Press.

Sanneh, Lamin. 1999. *Abolitionists Abroad: American Blacks and the Making of Modern West Africa*. Cambridge, MA: Harvard University Press.

Shick, Tom W. 1980. *Behold the Promised Land: A History of Afro-American Settler Society in Nineteenth-Century Liberia*. Baltimore, MD: Johns Hopkins University Press.

Staudenraus, P. J. 1961. *The African Colonization Movement, 1816–1865*. New York: Columbia University Press.

Takaki, Ronald T. 2000. *Iron Cages: Race and Culture in Nineteenth-Century America*, rev. ed. New York: Oxford University Press.

Tise, Larry E. 1987. *Proslavery: A History of the Defense of Slavery in America, 1701–1840*. Athens: University of Georgia Press.

Van Deburg, William L. 1984. *Slavery and Race in American Popular Culture*. Madison: University of Wisconsin Press.

West, Richard. 1970. *Back to Africa: A History of Sierra Leone and Liberia*. New York: Holt, Rinehart and Winston.

Wood, Forrest G. 1990. *The Arrogance of Faith: Christianity and Race in America from the Colonial Era to the Twentieth Century*. New York: Knopf.

Amos J. Beyan

AMERICAN INDIAN MOVEMENT (AIM)

The American Indian Movement (AIM) is an activist organization dedicated to protecting indigenous peoples' rights around the world. AIM's founders and continuing leadership have been American Indians, however, and its agenda and protests have focused primarily on issues of concern to Native North Americans. AIM was founded in Minneapolis, Minnesota, in 1968 as an Indian rights organization that monitored law enforcement treatment of Native people in American cities. AIM chapters quickly became established in several U.S. cities, including Cleveland, Denver, and Milwaukee, and AIM's initial membership was drawn from the ranks of the urban Indian population. AIM's early, and perhaps best-known leaders, included Clyde and Vernon Bellecourt, Dennis Banks, and Russell Means.

AIM'S BACKGROUND

American Indian resistance movements have existed throughout U.S. history, although early Indian collective actions often were officially defined by the U.S. government as "wars," and they were thus responded to by the U.S. military. During the nineteenth century there were numerous Native American "revitalization" movements, such as the Ghost Dance in the West and the Handsome Lake revival among the Iroquois in the East. Such movements had an important spiritual dimension and emphasized the elimination of European influence and the return of native traditions and communities. In the twentieth century, American Indian rights organizations emerged to represent Indian interests locally and nationally; these included the Society of American Indians (1911), the Indian Defense League of America (1926), the National Congress of American Indians (1944), the National Indian Youth Council (1961), and Women of All Red Nations (1974). The 1960s ushered in an era of Indian protest activism, beginning with a series of "fish-ins" protesting legal restrictions of traditional tribal fishing rights in the Pacific Northwest and the nineteen-month occupation of Alcatraz Island in San Francisco Bay by "Indians of All Tribes" protesting the living conditions and rights violations of urban Indians. Although AIM did not organize the fish-ins or the Alcatraz occupation, the intertribal, nationally publicized native-rights focus of both protests served as a template for much of AIM's activism, and many who had been involved in 1960s protests became associated with AIM in the 1970s.

AIM emerged not only from a rich history of American Indian protest activism. The organization was formed during a period of U.S. history marked by the African American civil rights movement and anti–Vietnam War activism. Although there were few formal links between AIM and civil rights organizations, the ethnic pride, racial grievances, and political demands of civil rights leaders and activists resonated with the dissatisfactions, needs, and resentments of many urban and reservation Indians. AIM blended civil rights and antiwar protest strategies—such as marches, demonstrations, occupations, and sit-ins—with Indian symbolic targets and repertoires of resistance, such as the "capture" of the *Mayflower II* on Thanksgiving in 1970, a brief occupation of Mount Rushmore in 1971, the "Longest Walk" from San Francisco to Washington, D.C., in 1978, and the encampment at Camp Yellow Thunder in South Dakota's Black Hills in the 1980s. The following description of a 1976 protest against a commemoration of the Battle of Little Bighorn illustrates the rich and confrontational dramaturgy associated with much AIM activism:

> Today on a wind-buffeted hill covered with buffalo grass, yellow clover and sage, in southeastern Montana where George Armstrong Custer made his last stand, about 150 Indians from various tribes danced joyously around the monument to the Seventh Cavalry dead. Meanwhile at an official National Parks Service ceremony about 100 yards away, an Army band played. . . . Just as the ceremony got underway a caravan of Sioux, Cheyenne and other Indians led by Russell Means, the American Indian Movement leader, strode to the platform to the pounding of a drum. (Lichtenstein 1976)

EARLY AIM ACTIVISM

The "Trail of Broken Treaties" was AIM's first national protest event of the 1970s, and the event was crucial to publicizing AIM's central role in organizing American Indian activism, raising Indian rights consciousness in both urban and reservation Indian communities, and recruiting new members in support of the organization and its actions. The "Trail" took place in 1972 as a cross-country caravan that began in California and ended in Washington, D.C., culminating in a weeklong occupation of the Bureau of Indian Affairs. As AIM activists traveled across the country, they stopped at reservations along the way, where many reservation youth joined the caravan. Mary Crow Dog describes the response by young people on the Rosebud Sioux Reservation in South Dakota as AIM passed through:

> The American Indian Movement hit our reservation like a tornado, like a new wind blowing out of nowhere, a drumbeat from far off getting louder and louder. It was almost like the Ghost Dance fever that had hit the tribes in 1890. . . . I could feel this new thing, almost hear it, smell it, touch it. Meeting up with AIM for the first time loosened a sort of earthquake inside me. (Crow Dog and Erdoes 1990, p. 73–74)

AIM's best-known and most controversial protest action began in February 1973 in Wounded Knee, South Dakota, a small town on the Pine Ridge Reservation. The conflict began as a dispute within Pine Ridge's Oglala Lakota (Sioux) tribe over the controversial tribal chairman, Richard Wilson. Wilson was viewed as a corrupt puppet of the U.S. Bureau of Indian Affairs (BIA) by some segments of the tribe, including those associated with AIM. An effort to impeach Wilson resulted in a division of the tribe into opposing camps, which eventually armed themselves and entered into a seventy-one-day siege of surrounded AIM supporters that involved tribal police; reservation residents; federal law enforcement officials; the BIA; local citizens; nationally prominent entertainment figures; national philanthropic, religious, and legal organizations; and the national news media. When the siege ended on May 9, 1973, two Indians were dead and an unknown number were wounded on both sides, including casualties among federal government forces. Dick Wilson remained in office, though he was challenged at the next election. Many AIM members spent the next years in litigation, in exile, and in prison, and several armed conflicts occurred in the wake of the siege as a result of U.S. government counterintelligence programs and vigorous prosecutions that targeted AIM members. The most well known of these cases is that

Armed Indian Protesters at Wounded Knee. *On February 27, 1973, members of AIM took over the town of Wounded Knee, South Dakota, to protest the actions of the tribal government of the Oglala Sioux. The 71-day siege brought the plight and concerns of Native Americans to the attention of the American people.* © BETTMANN/CORBIS.

of Leonard Peltier, who in 2007 remains in prison for a conviction for murder on the Pine Ridge Reservation in 1975.

Less well known is the 1976 death on the Pine Ridge Reservation of Anna Mae Aquash, a Native woman involved with AIM. The controversy surrounding her death centered on whether she died from exposure, as was originally reported, or was shot, and on whether her shooting was politically motivated and carried out by AIM members or by U.S. agents. The Aquash case illustrates the problems faced by Indian women associated with AIM, which (like many native and nonnative protest and political organizations) was run primarily by men, with women often relegated to service and support roles. Despite the limits faced by women in AIM, many Native American women from the generation of AIM activism have risen to prominent positions in tribal government and as leaders of native rights organizations, including Winona LaDuke, the program director of the Honor the Earth Fund; Gail Small, the director of Northern Cheyenne's Native Action; and LaDonna Harris, the founder and president of Americans for Indian Opportunity. Some of these native women leaders recognize the importance of Indian activism in shaping their lives. Wilma Mankiller, a former Principal Chief of the Cherokee Nation, describes the personal impact of the Alcatraz occupation as an awakening that ultimately changed the course of her life:

> I'd never heard anyone actually tell the world that we needed somebody to pay attention to our treaty rights, that our people had given up an entire continent, and many lives, in return for basic services like health care and education, but nobody was honoring these agreements. For the first time, people were saying things I felt but hadn't known how to articulate. It was very liberating. (Johnson 1996, p. 128)

AIM AND ATHLETIC MASCOTS

The use of Indian mascots by athletic teams, schools, and universities has been an issue for AIM activists since the organization's early days, when Russell Means sued the

Cleveland Indians sports franchise over the use of "Chief Wahoo," its Native American cartoon caricature mascot. AIM's efforts to retire native sports mascots have met with a good deal of success especially in schools and on college campuses, but Indian mascots remain an ongoing protest issue. In the 1990s, for instance, Charlene Teters, a Spokane graduate student at the University of Illinois, launched a campaign to expose and eliminate the "fighting Illini's" mascot, "Chief Illiniwek." Her efforts are documented in an award-winning film, *In Whose Honor*. Despite her efforts, and those of other Indian women and men, opposing the use of sports mascots remains an ongoing struggle for AIM: Chief Illiniwek continues to dance at University of Illinois games, and Chief Wahoo continues to smile on Cleveland Indians fans. In 2005 the National College Athletic Association informed Florida State University (FSU) that it could not compete in national championships if it continued to use the "Seminoles" as its team name and "Chief Osceola" as its mascot. The team was granted a waiver and allowed to continue the use of both the Indian name and the mascot, however, after Max Osceola, member of the Tribal Council of the Seminole Tribe of Florida, testified that it was an "honor" to be associated with FSU. The Seminole Nation of Oklahoma dissented, however, and continued to oppose the use of its name and the Indian mascot. This disagreement among native nations and between a particular tribe and AIM reflects both the diversity in Indian country and the ongoing tensions between AIM and some tribal communities that emerged during and after the Wounded Knee occupation.

EXPANDING THE AIM MISSION

In the nearly forty years since its founding, AIM's major focus has been on American Indian rights in the United States. Since the 1970s, however, AIM leadership has identified many common interests of indigenous people inside and outside the United States. The International Indian Treaty Council, for example, is an AIM-linked organization of indigenous peoples from the Americas and the Pacific focused on issues of sovereignty, self-determination, and the protection of cultural, legal, and land rights.

SEE ALSO *Genocide; Native American Graves Protection and Repatriation Act (NAGPRA).*

BIBLIOGRAPHY

Crow Dog, Mary, and Richard Erdoes. 1990. *Lakota Woman.* New York: Grove Weidenfeld.

Johnson, Troy. 1976. *The Occupation of Alcatraz Island: Indian Self-Determination and the Rise of Indian Activism.* Urbana: University of Illinois Press, 1996.

Lichtenstein, Grace. 1976. "Custer's Defeat Commemorated by Entreaties on Peace." *New York Times*, June 25.

Joane Nagel

AMERICAN NEGRO ACADEMY

The American Negro Academy (ANA), founded on March 5, 1897, in Washington, D.C., was the first national African-American learned society. Although American blacks had established numerous local literary and scholarly societies beginning in the late 1820s, the goals and membership of the American Negro Academy made it a distinct and original endeavor. The academy's constitution defined it as "an organization of authors, scholars, artists, and those distinguished in other walks of life, men of African descent, for the promotion of Letters, Science, and Art." The decision to exclude women was based on the belief that "literary . . . and social matters do not mix."

Although the chief concerns of the ANA's founders were to strengthen the intellectual life of their racial community, improve the quality of black leadership, and ensure that arguments advanced by "cultured despisers" of their race would henceforth be refuted, it was equally significant that the organization was established at a time when European Americans were creating hundreds of learned, professional, and ethnic historical societies. The academy's birth was an expression of this general movement among educated members of the American middle class.

EARLY MEMBERSHIP

From its establishment until its demise in 1928, the academy claimed as members some of the most important male leaders in the African American community. Alexander Crummell, its first president, was an Episcopal clergyman who held an A.B. from Queen's College, Cambridge University. Other founders included Francis J. Grimké, a Presbyterian clergyman trained at Lincoln University and Princeton Theological Seminary; W.E.B. Du Bois, a professor of economics and history at Atlanta University and later a founder of the National Association for the Advancement of Colored People (NAACP); William H. Crogman, a professor of classics at Clark University in Atlanta; William S. Scarborough, a scholarly classicist who was on the faculty of Wilberforce University; and John W. Cromwell, a lawyer, politician, and former editor of the *People's Advocate*, a black newspaper published in Washington, D.C., from 1878 to 1884.

Throughout its existence, the academy continued to attract some of the most intellectually creative black men in the United States. Some of those associated with the organization who achieved their greatest prominence after the turn of the century were John Hope, the president of Morehouse College and later of Atlanta University; Alain Locke, a writer, critic, and key figure in the Harlem Renaissance; Carter G. Woodson, a historian; and James Weldon Johnson, a poet, writer, and civil rights leader.

Relatively speaking, only a handful of educated black men were ever members of the academy. There were several reasons for this. First, the ANA was a selective organization, and entrance was controlled by the membership. Second, its activities and goals appealed mainly to a small group of black men who sought to function as intellectuals and who believed that the results of their efforts were crucial to the development and defense of their racial group. Third, it experienced continuous difficulties in realizing its goals. Finally, the organization never enjoyed the support of Booker T. Washington, the powerful principal of Tuskegee Institute, who for more than half the organization's life was the dominant figure in the African-American community. Washington was invited to become a founding member of the ANA and attend the inaugural meeting in 1897, but he declined, pleading a busy schedule and prior commitments. The real reason for his absence and lack of involvement, however, was his recognition that the major founders and early leaders of the academy (especially Crummell) were sharply critical of his educational theories, particularly his stress on industrial training as the best education for the majority of blacks. They were also at odds with his willingness to compromise with prominent white racists in both the South and the North.

OCCASIONAL PAPERS

Between 1897 and 1924, the ANA published twenty-two "Occasional Papers" on subjects related to the culture, history, religion, civil and social rights, and social institutions of African Americans. The process of choosing who would be invited to present papers at academy meetings, and the selection of which of the talks would be printed as Occasional Papers, was managed by the Executive Committee, a body composed of the president, first vice president, corresponding secretary, recording secretary, and treasurer. Although the quality of the papers varied, all of them illuminate the many ways in which, during the first quarter of the twentieth century, an important segment of the small community of educated American blacks attempted intellectually to defend their people, justify their own existence, and challenge the ideas, habits, attitudes, and legal proscriptions that seemed to be locking their race permanently into an "inferior caste."

The Occasional Papers represent the ANA's strongest efforts to refute white supremacist ideology and actions on a scholarly level. Kelly Miller's review of a white statistician's published arguments that Negroes were degenerate and on the verge of extinction (Occasional Paper Number 1, 1897) presented a forceful counterargument. *The Attitude of the American Mind toward the Negro Intellect* (Number 3, 1898), by Alexander Crummell, identified European Americans' hostility to black intellectual achievement as an expression of white racism that had appeared simultaneously with the arrival of the first Africans in the English colonies. Published in 1899, Theophilus G. Steward's *How the Black St. Domingo Legion Saved the Patriot Army in the Siege of Savannah, 1779* (Number 5) was a reminder of the contribution of black soldiers to the creation of the United States and their valor. In various ways all of the subsequent Occasional Papers challenged racism and its intellectual and practical justifications. Among the most forthright, cogent, and incisive were John L. Love's *Disfranchisement of the Negro* (1899) and *The Potentiality of the Negro Vote, North and West* (1905); Lafayette M. Hershaw's *Peonage* (1915); John W. Cromwell's *The Challenge of the Disfranchised: A Plea for the Enforcement of the 15th Amendment* (1924); and the numerous published papers by Archibald H. Grimké, especially *Right on the Scaffold, or the Martyrs of 1822* (1901), *The Meaning and Need to Reduce Southern Representation* (1905), *The Ballotless Victims of One-Party Government* (1915), *The Sex Question and Race Segregation* (1916), and *The Shame of America or the Negro's Case against the Republic* (1924).

Grimké's *The Sex Question and Race Segregation* demonstrates the willingness of ANA members to engage a controversial topic and offer a forceful analysis. His central argument was that as long as whites ruled Negroes, both the oppressors and the oppressed would experience "moral deterioration." For southern blacks and whites, Grimké noted, this process had begun in 1619, when the first cargo of African slaves arrived, and it had led, inevitably, to a "double moral standard" for white men and black women in the South. The consequences of this moral breakdown were reflected in the region's inability to fairly or effectively regulate sexual conduct between males of the dominant race and females of the subordinate race. This moral paralysis stemmed from southern white society's unwillingness to place restraints on white males by providing protection for black women, or to demand that white males accept responsibility for the consequences of their sexual relations with black women. Grimké used blunt language to make absolutely clear his certainty that sexual contacts between black women and white men were shaped and dominated by the predatory and exploitative tendencies of white men.

This situation, Grimké pointed out, was offensive and disturbing to black men, for it was a constant reminder of

Francis James Grimké. *Born a slave, Grimké (1850–1937) eventually became pastor of the Fifteenth Street Presbyterian Church in Washington D.C. With the help of his brother Archibald, and others, he helped found the American Negro Academy.* **GENERAL RESEARCH – REFERENCE DIVISION, SCHOMBURG CENTER FOR RESEARCH IN BLACK CULTURE, THE NEW YORK PUBLIC LIBRARY, ASTOR, LENOX AND TILDEN FOUNDATIONS.**

their powerlessness. They could not protect black women from the aggressions of white males, nor did they have similar access to white women. It also stimulated black men to imitate, within their own racial community, the worst sexual behavior of their white counterparts. Grimké also attacked southern white women for their efforts to reform the men of their race through activities that had the effect of further degrading the legal and social standing of their black sisters.

The ANA's publication of occasional papers reflected the organization's determination to challenge white supremacist ideology and actions by including black intellectuals in scholarly and public discourse about matters of consequence at a time when most European Americans refused to give serious attention to the ideas and opinions of educated African Americans. In these papers, the ANA made available to the American public thoughtful, perceptive, provocative essays on important subjects relating to history, politics, and race relations written by selected members of the organization.

INTERNAL PROBLEMS

Throughout its existence, the ANA was preoccupied with survival. As a result, its officers and members were forced to put as much energy into keeping the organization alive as they did into conducting its programs. There was continual concern over issues such as poor member participation, the high rate of dues delinquency, and the lack of public interest in the association's yearly meetings. At annual meetings, officers and members searched for solutions to these problems. The failure of such efforts increased the frustrations of committed members. In addition, there was the discouraging reality of how few of the academy's goals were being realized. The projected full membership of fifty was never attained; hopes that the society would become a strong influence on educated blacks—especially those in education and politics—were not realized; efforts by the ANA to combat racist ideas propagated by whites received little attention from either the white or black community; and when the organization entered the twentieth year of its existence, in 1917, it still lacked a journal. The irregular publication of the Occasional Papers remained its only printed offering.

From 1919 to 1928, the fortunes of the American Negro Academy declined further. Officers and members sought to strengthen the association by attempting to enrich the programs at annual meetings, expand membership, and rewrite the group's constitution. Some efforts were more successful than others, but none succeeded in transforming the academy into a major intellectual force in the African-American community or the American community at large. By 1921 the leading members of the black intellectual community had lost interest in the organization, most judging it to be either in unstoppable decline or a failure. With the exception of Alaine Locke, who accepted ANA membership as a courtesy to older black friends trying to keep the society alive, the few willing to be inducted into the organization during the 1920s were neither intellectuals nor scholars, nor were they involved directly in such important developments in the black community as the Marcus Garvey movement or the New Negro movement. Locke's position as a distinguished academic, and his role as one of the major spokespersons and interpreters of the "New Negro's" artistic and cultural "awakening" made him unique among those who remained active in the ANA.

Between 1920 and 1928 the academy experienced a steady loss of nominal members—many of whom were inactive anyway—through attrition and death. A considerable number joined "mainstream" learned societies that had a predominantly white membership. This was especially true of those who were academics. Others, including some who had been among the ANA's most active members, accelerated their involvement in the work of the NAACP and the National Urban League. It did not help ensure a future for the ANA so that Carter G. Woodson, the founder of the Association for the Study of Negro Life and History (ASNLH) and for a time a member of the ANA, concluded that the society had outlived its usefulness. With great success, he encouraged educated blacks to invest in his organization and ignore the ANA.

Many of the ANA's problems, and some of its failures, were related to the unresolved tension between two of its goals: a commitment to honor men of intellectual achievement and promote their writings, and a commitment to honor and affirm men whose careers were deemed to be positive models of racial leadership. Because Crummell and the ANA's other founding members had combined both functions in their careers, they built this double commitment into the organization's criteria for membership. In his inaugural address, Crummell spoke for most of the persons present, as well as many who would later become members of the academy, when he stressed the inseparable link between scholarly work and public service, declaring that true scholars were also "reformers" and "philanthropists."

In 1897 this was a widely held perspective in the black community, where many educated blacks viewed themselves (just as they were viewed by the majority of their race) as being under a moral obligation not only to make a contribution in the fields for which they were trained, but also to serve their race in the broadest way possible. The fact that many white Americans had a similar conception of the responsibilities of intellectuals served to reinforce black commitment to this understanding. However, at the very time the academy was launched, this understanding was being challenged in both the black and white communities by societal and attitudinal changes that were steadily producing more sharply delimited definitions of occupational roles, particularly in the professions. After 1897, these forces would become even stronger, eventually displacing older conceptions of the intellectual's role. This development, which strongly influenced the self-concept of many black intellectuals, especially those educated after 1900, accentuated the problems created for the academy by tensions that existed between its stated goals.

The ANA's failure to clarify the relationship between these two goals had a major impact in the area of membership, both in regard to the type of men who were elected and to what they were able and willing to do to support the organization. As a result, from the time it was founded, the academy had a built-in problem in regard to its criteria for membership, one that would become all the more troublesome because the nature of the problem would be unclear for some time. Indeed, during the first eighteen to twenty years of the group's existence, no one analyzed the problem carefully enough to get at the heart of the difficulty.

THE NATURE OF THE MEMBERSHIP

Although on paper it was a society of scholars, the academy elected a large number of members who were only marginally intellectual. These men respected scholarship and the life of the mind, but their work and interests were neither scholarly nor intellectual. At the same time, the organization included other members who were engaged personally in the production of ideas and research, either because they valued such activities per se or as a means of furthering the goals of the ANA. The continuous disappointments the organization experienced as it sought unsuccessfully to secure the regular payment of dues, to increase member attendance at annual meetings, and to persuade certain members to prepare and deliver papers at annual meetings were—not solely, but to a large extent—related to this unresolved tension between differing goals that led to the election of many persons who were unable, unwilling, and uninterested in being working members of a learned society.

Throughout its existence, to some of its members the ANA was an honorary society rather than a working group. Many of those elected as members treated their induction, and that of others, as if it were similar to being elected to Phi Beta Kappa or the Royal Geographic Society, rather than as being admitted to a working group such as the American Academy of Political and Social Science or the Society of American Historians. Although this problem affected the society negatively from its earliest days, no member identified it or offered a solution until Carter G. Woodson did in 1921. When the members of the organization rejected the reforms proposed by Woodson and chose to continue to function as before, Woodson decided he was through with the ANA. This refusal to endorse Woodson's reforms had a direct bearing on the ANA's growing difficulties thereafter, and on its subsequent collapse. Intellectually productive members continued to become inactive, and those who had already done so found their decision reinforced. To black intellectuals who were not members, especially younger ones, the rejection of Woodson's reforms was a clear indication that the majority of the society's members were unwilling to permit changes that would transform the ANA into an organization whose central activity was to generate and publicize scholarship that challenged white supremacist ideology and actions.

The failure to resolve the tension between intellectual activity and racial leadership had another negative consequence. With the membership criteria unchanged, marginal intellectuals continued to be drawn into the ANA, and eventually they constituted the majority of members. After 1921, as older members who were productive scholars and intellectuals withdrew, died, or became more involved in other organizations and activities, marginal intellectuals were elected to positions of leadership. These officers were detached from the scholarly and intellectual tradition embodied by the ANA's founders, and they were out of touch with the most creative black intellectuals and scholars of the middle and late 1920s. In their choice of programs and selection of new members, they were influenced strongly by the society's honorific tradition. However, because the ANA was essentially unknown in the larger black community, there was no legitimate basis for considering membership in it to be an honor.

THE FINAL YEARS

The 1920s, the decade of the "New Negro," was a time of crisis for the ANA. During this decade, the organization was forced to come to terms with the ineffectiveness of its efforts to function as the intellectual voice of the "Talented Tenth." The fundamental reasons for this ineffectiveness were the society's poverty, its lack of a broadly based and supportive audience in either the black or white community, and an unresolved tension in its criteria for membership that undercut its efforts to be a learned society and confused its public image. These were difficulties with a history as long as the existence of the society.

In the 1920s the ANA was confronted by a new problem that proved to be as insoluble and as destructive as any of the earlier ones. The "civilizationist" goals espoused by the academy were based on the belief of its founders that blacks, in order to progress as a race, had to gain the respect of whites. These leaders wanted to appropriate for themselves the most positive aspects of "the more advanced cultures" of Europe and the United States in order to become a political, economic, and cultural force in the world. But this view was at odds with the new mood of blacks, as expressed by their enthusiastic endorsement of the leadership and ideas of Marcus Garvey and embodied in Garvey's Universal Negro Improvement Association. The tension between these two views, combined with its internal failures, would bring the existence of the ANA to an end.

Despite all the difficulties that led to the demise of the American Negro Academy in 1928, it survived for thirty-one years, functioning for much of its existence as a setting in which a significant number of its members and supporters shared their intellectual and scholarly work with each other and engaged in critical reflection on it. Through annual meetings, the Occasional Papers, exhibits, and the public interest these activities generated, the ANA was able to initiate dialogues in both the black and white communities that were important contributions to a growing discussion in the United States, Africa, and Europe about race and the relationship between blacks and whites. The ANA introduced the concerns and opinions of educated blacks into a few places where they had previously been ignored or gone unnoticed, and it encouraged the growing pride among a small but influential group of educated African Americans, young and old, in their culture and history.

The ANA both sustained and perpetuated the black protest tradition in an age of accommodation and proscription. By functioning as a source of affirmation and encouragement for an important segment of the black intelligentsia and as a setting in which they could seek to understand the meaning of the African American experience, the ANA was a model for other (and sometimes more successful) black organizations founded after 1897 that engaged in similar work or attempted to realize goals the ANA found unattainable. Perhaps most important, for its active members, the academy's various programs and activities and the interactions they promoted formed a dynamic process in which participants began to free themselves from the entanglements and confusions of ideas and theories that made them feel insecure about their own worth, ashamed of the history and condition of blacks, and doubtful of their race's future possibilities. By strengthening and adding to the intellectual autonomy and insight of its members, the academy helped to prepare them and their supporters for more informed, honest dialogue with each other, with blacks in the United States and other parts of the world, and, when they would listen, with whites.

SEE ALSO *Du Bois, W. E. B.; Washington, Booker T.*

BIBLIOGRAPHY

Meier, August. 1988 (1963). *Negro Thought in America, 1880–1915.* Ann Arbor: University of Michigan Press.

Moses, Wilson Jeremiah. 1989. *Alexander Crummell: A Study of Civilization and Discontent.* New York: Oxford University Press.

Moss, Alfred A., Jr. 1981. *The American Negro Academy: Voice of the Talented Tenth.* Baton Rouge: Louisiana State University Press.

Alfred A. Moss Jr.

ANTEBELLUM BLACK ETHNOLOGY

Antebellum black ethnology arose as a challenge to mainstream ethnology, the nineteenth-century "science of the races." Most prevalent in the United States, the field of ethnology emerged in the 1830s and 1840s as white American scientists first began to study anatomy, craniology, and human development. At the time, human development was still understood in a religious framework, and these scientists sought to reconcile racial difference with biblical history in a way that led to new questions about the unity of the human family, and about the place of people of color within it. Now often known as "scientific racism," this work focused on racial differences, and it invariably classified blacks and other people of color as inferior and innately distinct from white people. Accordingly, American ethnology, as put forth by white authors, lent support to proslavery apologists such as Josiah Nott (1804–1873), who drew on its arguments for black inferiority to support the perpetuation of slavery. Black Americans, however, countered with ethnological arguments of their own.

Antebellum black ethnology defended the status of black people in the human family and the scriptures, stressing that all the races of humanity descended from a shared ancestry. Among the nineteenth-century blacks who wrote and spoke about ethnology were a number of well-known figures such as Frederick Douglass (1817–1895) and Martin Delany (1812–1885), as well as scores of more obscure black thinkers.

THE ORIGINS OF BLACK ETHNOLOGY

In addressing ethnology in the 1850s, Delany and Douglass joined an already well-established tradition of black racial self-defense. Published African-American defenses of the capacities of the black race date back to the eighteenth-century, when African-Americans first confronted published arguments for black inferiority. Among the earliest arguments they encountered came from Thomas Jefferson. Writing in *Notes on the State of Virginia* (1789), Jefferson "advanced, as a suspicion only, that blacks whether originally a distinct race, or made distinct by time, are inferior to whites in the endowments of body and mind" (p. 262). Jefferson's speculations were soon answered by an African-American contemporary named Benjamin Banneker (1731–1806), a self-educated former slave who achieved considerable renown as a mathematician, astronomer, and surveyor. In a public letter to Jefferson written in 1792, Banneker stressed that "we are all of the same human family" and implored the founding father to "embrace every opportunity to eradicate that train of absurd and false opinions and ideas, which so generally prevails with respect to us" (Nash 1990, p. 178). Jefferson's response to Banneker was cordial, but his views seem to have remained the same. In a private letter to a friend, Jefferson wrote "I have a long letter from Banneker, which shows him to have a mind of a very common stature indeed" (Bay 2000, p. 17).

Jefferson's negative assessment of the capacities of the black race would be increasingly widely supported in the nineteenth century. Antiblack thought proliferated in both the North and South in the early decades of the nineteenth century, as the egalitarian spirit of the Revolutionary era ebbed and slavery became ever more entrenched in the South. Among southerners, theories of black inferiority were used to defend slavery from the small but active group of northern abolitionists who began to challenge the morality of slavery. Meanwhile, in the North, blacks achieved the freedom mandated under the Revolutionary-era gradual emancipation laws, only to find themselves despised by many northern whites. As the North's free black population burgeoned, whites there expressed little enduring support for African-American emancipation and quickly came to view the poverty and lack of education common among free blacks as evidence of the limitations of their race. Black ethnology thus had its beginning as African Americans mobilized to defend themselves from critics in both the North and South.

Such self-defenses became ever more necessary as the nineteenth century progressed. By the 1820s, the traditional environmentalist understanding of racial differences as the product of the distinctive climates and environments that nurtured the world's different peoples had begun to give way to new questions about human unity—and about whether all humans really descended from the same ancestors. In an era when the transmission of physical traits from generation to generation was still something of a mystery, and when the time span covered by the scriptures was still thought to record the entire human history, environmentalism posed a number of scientific conundrums when it came to explaining racial difference. The most mysterious had to do with the brevity of human history: How had human beings developed such divergent physical characteristics over the few thousand years covered in the scriptures? Human physical characteristics did not change all that rapidly from one generation to the next, no matter what the influence of climate was. In the 1830s and 1840s these issues were taken up by the American School of Ethnology, a group of prominent American scientists led by Samuel Morton (1799–1851) of Philadelphia, who would ultimately argue that the races of humanity were the product of polygenesis, or separate creations.

POLYGENESIS VERSUS MONOGENESIS IN BLACK AND WHITE

In polygenesis, African Americans encountered a galling new and scientifically authoritative theory of black inferiority, which literally wrote them out of traditional accounts of human history. Morton and other members of the American School rejected the time-honored monogenetic understanding of human development favored by earlier American thinkers such as Samuel Stanhope Smith (1751–1819). Whereas Smith held that men and women of all races descended from Adam and Eve, and attributed the diversity of human populations to environmental influences, Morton questioned whether the different human races had common ancestors. A craniologist, Morton researched the skull as a measure of human capacity and assumed that, studied across time, skull measurements could be used to trace the history of human development and racial differences. Accordingly, Morton's research was based on a collection of 900 skulls, both ancient and modern and from all over the world. The measurements from his collection, he said, showed a pattern of racial differences across time in which whites had the largest skulls and blacks the smallest, and other people of color ranged in between. These persistent differences between the races led him to conclude that racial distinctions were far too ancient and enduring to be the product of environmental forces. Instead, he maintained, the racially distinct cranial measurements seen in the populations of ancient Egypt, early America, and the modern United States provided irrefutable evidence that the races did not share the same ancestors. There must have been more than one genesis: Only a polygenesis could explain human diversity.

Twenty-first-century scientists have rejected creationism in favor of evolution, and they have also proved that Morton's measurements were riddled with errors. Moreover, even in his own day, the theory of polygenesis was by no means universally accepted among whites, many of whom greeted the notion of multiple creations as rank heresy. Still, polygenesis horrified African-Americans, especially as they saw it achieving increasing scientific prominence over time. Black intellectuals mobilized to reject this new theory with an ethnology of their own, which enlarged upon previous African-American defenses of the African race with increasingly detailed discussions of the origins and character of the races of humans. Benjamin Robert Lewis (1802–1859), a Maine resident, wrote the first book-length work on ethnology by a black author—a work called *Light and Truth: Collected from the Bible and the Ancient and Modern History Containing the Universal History of the Colored and Indian Races; from the Creation of the World to the Present Time* (1844). Lewis stressed that Adam and Eve were people of color, as were the Egyptians and many of the heroes of the ancient world—including Plato and Julius Caesar. Lewis's enthusiastic account of the history of the colored race was overblown enough to make the black nationalist Martin Delany worry that *Light and Truth* did little more than reverse the errors of white ethnologists such as George Glidden, "who makes all ancient black men *white*... this colored man makes all ancient great white men *black*" (Bay 2000, p. 45). But in the years to come, other black writers, including well-known figures such as Delany, would produce more measured critiques of white ethnology.

The African-American ministers Hosea Easton (1779–1837) and James Pennington (1807–1870), for example, both drew on their knowledge of the scriptures to underscore the unity of the human race. Born free in 1779, Easton led the African Methodist Episcopal Church in Hartford, Connecticut, until his early death in 1837—just six weeks after he published *A Treatise on the Intellectual Character, and Civil and Political Condition of the Colored People of the United States* (1837). Easton's *Treatise* defended the history and origins of the black race with a detailed reading of the history of the races as recorded in the scriptures. Like Lewis, he underscored that the African race descended from Adam and Eve, and he traced the race's ancestry down from Noah's son Ham, who settled Africa and Egypt. It was Ham's children, he maintained, rather than the "savage" European descendents of Ham's brother Japhet, who carried "the blessings of civilization to Greece" (p. 10). Despite this unfavorable comparison, Easton rejected any notion of innate distinctions between the races. Variations in complexion and hair texture among different groups, he argued, were "casual or incidental," and any racial deficiencies seen in African-Americans were caused by slavery, which, he believed, created physical and mental deformities that could pass from mother to child. In addition to defending the lineage and innate capacities of the black race, Easton also presented a searing critique of white theories about black inferiority, which he described as "the production of European philosophy, bearing date [originating] with European slavery" (p. 42). White American complaints about blacks were little more than a "plea of justification" for slavery, he contended. "What could better accord with the object of this nation with reference to blacks than to teach their little ones that the Negro is part monkey?" (p. 42).

Writing in 1841, James Pennington, who had escaped from slavery to become a Congregationalist minister, made a similar case for the common origins of the human family and the illustrious history of the African race. "The arts and sciences had origins in our ancestors," he wrote of the Egyptians and Ethiopians, and "from them have flown forth to the world." Pennington took on not only polygenesis, but also some older theories of black inferiority that

Dr. James McCune Smith. *After becoming the first African American to earn a medical degree and practice medicine in the United States, Smith (1813–1865) used his scientific knowledge to refute racist stereotypes. He was also a leader in the fight for black voting rights.* **MANUSCRIPTS, ARCHIVES AND RARE BOOKS DIVISION, SCHOMBURG CENTER FOR RESEARCH IN BLACK CULTURE, THE NEW YORK PUBLIC LIBRARY, ASTOR, LENOX AND TILDEN FOUNDATIONS.**

located its causes within the Bible. "We are not the seed of Cain as the stupid say," he wrote, making short work of one such theory (p. 7). Cain's offspring perished in the deluge. However, he devoted more time to debunking the notion that black people labored under the Curse of Ham, a theory that held considerable currency in the white South, and complicated African-American claims to Hamitic ancestry. The idea of a curse originated in a confusing biblical story (Genesis 9:20–25) in which Noah condemns Ham's son Canaan to be "a servant of servants" after Ham comes across Noah lying naked and drunk in his tent. Long associated with slavery in Western culture, the story of the Curse of Ham was widely applied to blacks after the development of racial slavery in the Americas. However, as Pennington points out, such interpretations of Ham's curse do not mesh with the scriptural record. The curse was on Canaan rather than his brother Cush, who settled Ethiopia. Moreover, the story seemed dubious as a justification for the slavery of any group, as it required God to empower the ill-tempered curses of a drunken patriarch: "Is the spirit of wine the spirit of God?" (p. 18)

African Americans also tried to challenge white ethnology on more scientific ground. The most scientifically accomplished African-American to do so was James McCune Smith (1813–1865), America's first black M.D. Rejected by American medical schools on account of his race, Smith received his M.D. in Glasgow, Scotland, in 1837. An abolitionist and physician, Smith was a prolific essayist, and he used his medical training to challenge the ethnological arguments made by the white scientists of his day. In a series of essays published during the 1830s and 1840s, Smith mobilized data drawn from his medical practice to reject the idea that blacks and whites were anatomically distinct, and to refute the popular belief that African Americans were more short-lived than white Americans. An environmentalist, like most blacks who wrote on ethnology, Smith believed that racial differences were neither ancient nor immutable. Rather, he saw them as the result of the diverse climates that nurtured different human groups. He also contended that, under the influence of their nation's temperate climate, black Americans would eventually become indistinguishable from whites, that "the Ethiopian can change his skin."

Likewise, Martin Delany also approached ethnology with scientific training. Raised in Pennsylvania, Delany apprenticed with a doctor there and was subsequently admitted to Harvard Medical School. However, he was forced out of Harvard after only one semester by white medical students who opposed the enrollment of African Americans in their program. Nonetheless, during his subsequent career as a political activist and writer, Delany returned to the study of science, presenting several discussions of ethnology in his written works. In *The Condition, Elevation, Emigration, and Destiny of the Colored People of the United States* (1852), Delany rejected the idea of polygenesis, but he did not rule out important racial differences. He contended, in fact, that the African race was "physically superior to any living race of men" (p. 36). Further expanding on these distinctions in the postbellum era, he published *Principia of Ethnology: The Origin of Races and Color* (1879). A detailed ethnological monograph, *Principia* underscored the different historical records of blacks and whites—whom Delany saw as a naturally aggressive people. Delany attributed both physical and temperamental distinctions among human races to the varying amounts of concentrated rouge, or "pigmentum nigrum," in the skin that distinguished the descendants of Ham, Japhet, and Shem (p. 23).

The careers of Smith and Delany illustrate the immense difficulties African-Americans faced in gaining access to the kind of scientific training and credentials that might have allowed nineteenth-century African-American writings on ethnology to be taken seriously by mainstream scientists. By and large unschooled in science, African Americans could offer little concrete evidence to counter the data offered by white scientists such as Morton. Most of the African Americans who wrote on ethnology had to rely on the scriptures for evidence that all people were "of one blood." Still, from the early twenty-first century vantage point, nineteenth-century black ethnology was only a little less scientific than the findings of the American School of Ethnology. Both were products of an era in which science and religion were not yet distinct. The theories of polygenesis and monogenesis alike mixed biblical and scientific thought in ways that made scriptural exegesis a scientific activity. Moreover, in the long run, the environmentalism theories of human development defended by African-American authors have proven far less preposterous in the light of modern understandings of human evolution than the American School's arguments against the common ancestry of the human species.

In the nineteenth century, however, black authors could bring little scientific or cultural authority to their arguments, and they therefore made little headway in challenging the findings of the American School. Morton's racial rankings, by contrast, "outlived the theory of separate creations, and were reprinted widely during the nineteenth century as irrefutable 'hard' data on the mental worth of the races" (Gould 1981, p. 53). As the abolitionist and fugitive slave Frederick Douglass observed in reference to mainstream antebellum ethnology, "the wish is the father of the thought," by which he meant that white scientists who lived in a nation that tolerated racial slavery needed to see black people as inferior, and they thus found data to support their presumptions (p. 500).

Douglass addressed the subject of ethnology in a popular lecture titled "The Races of Man," which he delivered frequently during the 1840s and 1850s, and also in a more learned discourse, "The Claims of the Negro Ethnologically Concerned" (1854). In the latter volume, he marshaled the full range of scientific and scriptural arguments presented by previous black authors to affirm "the oneness of the human family," defend the historical record of the African race, and reject the American School's "profound discoveries of ethnological science." These "Southern pretenders to science" were little more than spokesmen for slavery, he wrote. "When men oppress their fellow men: the oppressor ever finds in the characterization of the oppressed, their justification" (p. 510).

The antebellum black ethnology produced by Frederick Douglass and others is perhaps more impressive for its prescient critique of mainstream white science than it is for its defense of monogenesis, environmentalism, and black accomplishments in Africa and Egypt—which sound a little quaint to the modern reader. But black ethnology's staunch defense of the origins and accomplishments of the African race was considered crucial by antebellum black authors, who worried that theories such as polygenesis would perpetuate slavery and foster a belief in black inferiority among blacks and whites alike. Accordingly, antebellum black ethnology should be appreciated not only within the context of early African-American scholarship on science, the scriptures, and human history—all of which it engages—but also as a chapter in black resistance to racism. By rejecting and refuting the mainstream white-authored ethnology that branded black people as a race distinct in origin and inferior by nature, the African Americans who wrote on ethnology helped provide an intellectual foundation for the African-American emancipation struggles of the era.

SEE ALSO *Allen, Richard; Black Reconstruction; Christian Identity; Douglass, Frederick; Genesis and Polygenesis; Morton, Samuel George; Scientific Racism, History of; Smith, James McCune.*

BIBLIOGRAPHY

Bay, Mia. 2000. *The White Image in the Black Mind: African-American Ideas about White People, 1830–1925*. New York: Oxford University Press.

Browne, Stephen Howard. 2000. "Counter-Science: African-American Historians and the Critique of Ethnology in Nineteenth-Century America." *Western Journal of Communication* 64 (3): 268–284.

Delany, Martin R. 1968 (1852). *The Condition, Elevation, Emigration, and Destiny of the Colored People of the United States*. New York: Arno Press.

———. 1879. *Principia of Ethnology: The Origin of Races and Color, with an Archeological Compendium of Ethiopian and Egyptian Civilization from Years of Careful Examination and Enquiry*. Philadelphia: Harper and Brother.

Douglass, Frederick. 1982. "The Claims of the Negro Ethnologically Considered: A Speech Delivered to the Prestigious Philozetian and Phi Delta Societies of Western Reserve College in Hudson, Ohio, 12, July, 1854." In *The Frederick Douglass Papers*, Series One: *Speeches, Debates, and Interviews*. Vol. 2, *1847–54*, edited by John W. Blassingame. New Haven, CT: Yale University Press.

Easton, Hosea. 1837. *A Treatise on the Intellectual Character, and Civil and Political Condition of the Colored People of the United States*. Boston: Isaac Knapp.

Fredrickson, George M. 1971. *The Black Image in the White Mind: The Debate over Afro-American Character and Destiny 1817–1914*. New York: Harper & Row.

Gossett, Thomas F. 1963. *Race: The History of an Idea in America*. Dallas: Southern Methodist University Press.

Gould, Stephen J. 1981. *The Mismeasure of Man*. New York: W. W. Norton.

Jefferson, Thomas. 1944. "Notes on the State of Virginia." In *The Life and Selected Writings of Thomas Jefferson,* edited by Adrienne Koch and William Peden. New York: Modern American Library.

Lewis, R. B. 1844. *Light and Truth: Collected from the Bible and Ancient and Modern History Containing the Universal History of the Colored and Indian Race; from the Creation of the World to the Present Time.* Boston: Committee of Colored Gentlemen.

Morton, Samuel. 1844. *Crania Aegyptiaca: Or, Observations on Egyptian Ethnography Derived from Anatomy, History, and the Monuments.* Philadelphia: J. Penington.

Nash, Gary. 1990. *Race and Revolution.* Madison, WI: Madison House.

Pennington, James, W. C. 1969 (1841). *A Text Book of the Origins and History of the Colored People.* Detroit, MI: Negro History Press.

Mia Bay

ANTHROPOLOGY, HISTORY OF

Anthropology is the discipline that studies races, cultures, languages, and the evolution of the human species. It is broad in scope, incorporating the archeologist surveying Inca ruins, the cultural anthropologist collecting folklore in Appalachia, and the biological anthropologist mapping the gene sequences of lemurs. Yet the science of anthropology has long been steeped in debates, discussions, and controversies concerning race, racism, and the very meaning of human differences.

Anthropology has also been concerned with the so-called psychic unity of humankind, and with the fact that races and peoples the world over are essentially the same, both in terms of evolutionary biology and the acquisition and manipulation of culture. Tensions between investigating the universalism or particularism of the human condition, and between calibrating difference in relative terms or in terms of a hierarchy have been responsible for shaping much of this science that politicians, journalists, philanthropists, and even Supreme Court justices have routinely used in the rather messy and contradictory processes of race making in America. Perhaps more than any other social science, the development of anthropology has been instrumental in shaping racial constructs, while the development of racial constructs has also been instrumental in shaping anthropology.

COLONIAL ERA AND SLAVERY

The concept of "race" is a modern one, and the sustained study of it in the United States emerged when proponents of the institution of slavery needed scientists to defend that institution from religious abolitionists, who called for the unity of God's children, and from Enlightenment critics, who called for liberty, fraternity, and equality of man. During the early colonial experience in North America, "race" was not a term that was widely employed. Notions of difference were often couched in religious terms, and comparisons between "heathen" and "Christian," "saved" and "unsaved," and "savage" and "civilized" were used to distinguish African and indigenous peoples from Europeans. Beginning in 1661 and continuing through the early eighteenth century, ideas about race began to circulate after Virginia and other colonies started passing legislation that made it legal to enslave African servants and their children.

In 1735 the Swedish naturalist Carl Linnaeus completed his first edition of *Systema Naturae,* in which he attempted to differentiate various types of people scientifically. He identified humans as a single species within the primate family and did not explicitly rank types of people within a hierarchy. However, his value-laden judgments that Europeans were "governed by laws" while Africans were "governed by caprice" reinforced ideas that European society was the apex of Christian civilization (Linnaeus 1997 [1735], p.13).

The same year that Thomas Jefferson penned the *Declaration of Independence* and claimed, as self-evident, "that all men are created equal" Johann Blumenbach published *On the Natural Varieties of Mankind,* in which he divided the human race into separate and unequal varieties. It was Blumenbach who provided the four basic racial categories that people still grapple with in the early twenty-first century: Caucasian, Mongolian, Ethiopian, and American (he later added a fifth category, Malayan). Despite his claims about the unity of humanity, Blumenbach viewed Europeans as the most advanced, and he argued that all other varieties degenerated from Caucasians, which he believed was "the most handsome and becoming" type (Blumenbach 1997 [1776], p. 84).

Enlightenment scientists helped to shift the discussion of human difference from the ecclesiastical to the natural world, but this did little to reduce institutional racism. In fact, scientific racism flourished in the wake of the French and American revolutions. In North America, the lofty ideals of equality, freedom, and liberty could not be reconciled with the institution of slavery and the acquisition of indigenous land. In Europe, meanwhile, these ideals did not square with colonialism and anti-Semitism. Indeed, the fraternity of those who were equal and free was exclusive: women, children, and the insane were always excluded from the rights and privileges of citizenship and equality under the law, and many began to turn to the science of ethnology to exclude nonwhite men as well (Fredrickson 2002, p. 68). People who had a stake in maintaining the idea that all people had inalienable rights and a stake in maintaining racial inequality found scientific categories of race useful because those who were deemed racially inferior were also deemed incapable of shouldering the responsibilities of citizenship and thus did not qualify for rights and privileges—rights and privileges were contingent upon the responsibilities of citizenship.

Stated differently, only men of the "superior" white race were considered fully capable, while members of inferior races and all women were not equal, not free, did not have liberty, and could not be citizens. For example, Thomas Jefferson, in *Notes on the State of Virginia*, turned to the language of ethnology to advance the notion "that the blacks, whether originally a distinct race, or made distinct by time and circumstances, are inferior to the whites in the endowments both of body and mind." Jefferson was clear that one should and could clearly rank the races and keep them "as distinct as nature has formed them" (1996 [1781], p.143).

Despite using race to justify inequality, most enlightenment thinkers still believed in the doctrine of "monogenetic origins," of a single creation of all humanity. Although beliefs in monogenism were neither coherent nor consistent, ideas of human unity did not of themselves imply equality, and consequently monogenism did not necessarily support arguments for the abolition of slavery and the sovereignty of indigenous nations.

Several Enlightenment scholars, however, used the language of ethnology and scientific methods in an attempt to prove that racial differences were inconsequential and that it was a fool's errand to rank the races and view racial differences in terms of inferior and superior. For example, Samuel Stanhope Smith (1751–1819), a Presbyterian minister and the president of Princeton University, passionately argued that blacks and whites shared innate characteristics. He persuasively documented how "it is impossible to draw the line precisely between the various races," explaining that it would be "a useless labor to attempt it" (1810 [1787], p. 240). Benjamin Rush, a prominent Philadelphia physician who signed the *Declaration of Independence*, was certain that science and Christianity both demonstrated the "original and natural equality of all mankind" (1987 [1798], p. 686).

JACKSONIAN AMERICA AND POLYGENISM

Late eighteenth-century ethnology established the scientific foundation for the field, which began to mature during Andrew Jackson's term as president of the United States (1829-1837). Jackson was responsible for implementing the Indian Removal Act of 1830, which resulted in the coerced and forced removal of an estimated 100,000 persons racially identified as American Indians. In addition, Jackson's policies insured that the franchise was extended to all white men, irrespective of financial means while virtually all black men were denied the right to vote. He also suppressed abolitionists' efforts to end slavery while vigorously defending that institution. Finally, Jackson was responsible for appointing Roger B. Taney as Chief Justice of the U.S. Supreme Court. It was Taney who would decide, in *Scott v. Sandford* (1857), that Negroes were "beings of an inferior order, and altogether unfit to associate with the white race . . . and so far inferior that they had no rights which the white man was bound to respect." As a result of this decision, black people, whether free or enslaved, were denied citizenship in the United States.

It was in this context that the so-called American school of anthropology thrived as the champion of polygenism (the doctrine of multiple origins), sparking a debate between those who believed in the unity of humanity and those who argued for the plurality of origins and the antiquity of distinct types. Like the monogenists, the polygenists were not united in their views, and they often used words such as *race*, *species*, *hybrid*, and *mongrel* interchangeably. A scientific consensus began to emerge during this period that there was a genus *Homo* made up of several different primordial types of species. Charles Caldwell, Samuel George Morton, Samuel A. Cartwright, George Gliddon, Josiah C. Nott, Louis Agassiz, and even South Carolina Governor James Henry Hammond were all influential proponents of polygenetic origins. While some were apparently disinterested scientists, others were passionate advocates who used science to promote slavery in a period of increasing sectional strife. All were complicit in establishing the putative science that justified slavery, informed the Dred Scott decision, underpinned miscegenation laws, and eventually fueled the establishment of Jim Crow laws. Samuel G. Morton, for example, claimed to be just a scientist, but he did not hesitate to provide evidence of Negro "inferiority" to John C. Calhoun, the prominent proslavery secretary of state, to help him negotiate the annexation of Texas as a slave state.

TYPES OF MANKIND, 1854

The high-point of polygenetic theories was Josiah Nott and George Gliddon's voluminous 800-page book entitled *Types of Mankind,* published in 1854. Reprinting selected works by Louis Agassiz and Samuel Morton, the authors spread vituperative and explicitly racist views to a wider, more popular audience. The first edition quickly sold out, and by century's end the book had undergone nine editions. Although many proponents of slavery felt that the Bible provided enough justification, others used the new science to defend slavery and the repression of American Indians, and abolitionists felt compelled to take on this science on its own terms. In the immediate

John Wesley Powell with Paiute Indian. *Powell headed the U.S. Geological Survey from 1881 until 1894. He created a Bureau of Ethnology to collect information on Indian societies, believing this knowledge would help the government "civilize" the Native population. He is seen here on a survey of Arizona in 1873.* AUTHENTICATED NEWS/GETTY IMAGES.

wake of *Types of Mankind*, African American intellectuals jointed the effort and waded into to the contemptuous debate. For example, during the pitched political battles that led to the Civil War, the statesman and persuasive abolitionist Frederick Douglass (1818–1895) directly attacked the leading theorists of the American school. In an 1854 address, entitled "The Claims of the Negro, Ethnologically Considered," Douglass underscored the peculiar logic in these arguments:

> By making the enslaved a character fit only for slavery, [slave owners] excuse themselves for refusing to make the slave a freeman. ... For let it be once granted that the human race are of multitudinous origin, naturally different in their moral, physical, and intellectual capacities ... a chance is left for slavery, as a necessary institution. ... There is no doubt that Messrs. Nott, Glidden, Morton, Smith and Agassiz were duly consulted by our slavery propagating statesmen. (p. 287)

Critiquing the same science in the service of racism, Haitian anthropologist Joseph-Anténor Firmin published *De l'egalité des races humaines* (*On the Equality of Human Races*) in 1885. This painstakingly researched tome was a direct rebuttal to Count Arthur de Gobineau's politically motivated four-volume work *Essai sur l'inégalité des races humaines* (*Essay on the Inequality of Human Races*, 1853–1855). Gobineau had asserted flatly that the Aryan race was superior and that Negroes and other people of color were simply inferior. Firmin argued the opposite, that "all men are endowed with the same qualities and the same faults, without distinction of color or anatomical form. The races are equal" (2000 [1854], p. 450). Firmin grew up in Haiti, but served as a diplomat in Paris where he was admitted to the Societé d' Anthropologie de Paris in 1884. His persuasive arguments and penchant critique of many of that society's leading members made him one of the first to engage in the so-called vindicationist struggle in anthropology. Many scholars also associate his work with early ideas of Pan-Africanism.

THE BUREAU OF ETHNOLOGY

Although the American Civil War and Charles Darwin's theories of natural selection brought about the eventual demise of theories of polygenism, the close relationship between scientific racism and ethnology continued. After the Civil War, anthropology in the United States became professionalized, associated with museums, and focused almost exclusively on the "Indian problem." The institution that led the way was the Smithsonian Institution's Bureau of American Ethnology. In the spring of 1879 the Civil War hero John Wesley Powell (1834-1902) convinced Congress to consolidate various geographical surveys into the U.S. Geological Survey and establish a special bureau of ethnology. Powell emphasized the application of knowledge to justify the bureau's inception. Ethnology, he argued, could help to solve the Indian problem. In a prospectus for the bureau, he demonstrated the utility of having a stand-alone agency that could use science in this regard:

> The rapid spread of civilization since 1849 had placed the white man and the Indian in direct conflict throughout the whole area, and the "Indian Problem" is thus thrust upon us and it *must* be solved, wisely or unwisely. Many of the difficulties are inherent and cannot be avoided, but an equal number are unnecessary and are caused by the lack of our knowledge relating to the Indians themselves. (Powell 1878, p.15)

Powell indicated that ethnology could provide intelligence about Indians, and that this was important because their practices "must necessarily be overthrown before new institutions, customs, philosophy, and religion can be introduced" (1878, p. 15). His blueprint for the bureau was twofold: it would serve Indian agencies by providing information to help manage and control dissimilar tribes, and it would serve Smithsonian science by providing research about disappearing societies. The bureau produced research under the rubric of natural history. The discovery, description, and cataloguing of Indian languages, customs, and kinship terminologies soon filled the elaborate annual reports, which highlighted the collective work of the bureau as well as individual staff members. Although most of the Bureau's scientists respected American Indian culture, all were clear in their belief that whites were racially superior. James Mooney (1861–1921), however, was a strident force within the bureau. He carefully analyzed American Indian religious practices and argued that "the difference is only relative," explaining that there was not a hierarchical or vast difference between so-called savage Indians and civilized whites. He also wrote, under the auspices of the bureau, *The Ghost Dance Religion and the Sioux Outbreak of 1890*, which was a devastating critique of the U.S. Army's massacre at Wounded Knee and an eloquent explanation of the Ghost Dance religion.

FRANZ BOAS

Anthropology soon began to move from museums to universities and liberal arts colleges, beginning with Harvard University and the University of Pennsylvania. Anthropology was slowly institutionalized at Columbia University, and by 1904 Columbia's program was under the leadership of Franz Boas (1858-1942). A German-born Jew, Boas came to Columbia by way of the American Museum of Natural History, where he pursued research on American Indians of the Pacific Northwest. He was skeptical of theories of culture or civilization that ranked and ordered objects and races from low to high and from simple to complex. Drawing on German philosophy, he argued that people around the world created distinct and particular cultures, and that these should be viewed holistically and relative to other cultures, not within a hierarchy. He was a critic of the comparative method, which compared different groups and races within the rubrics of savage, barbarian, and civilized. Boas believed that the objects people make, the languages they speak, and the gods they worship contribute to unique cultures that have a specific history and view of the world.

This was an important paradigm shift in an era when restrictive immigration, Jim Crow segregation, and forced sterilization were justified by racialist science and eugenics, which entailed the use of selective breeding and sterilization to improve society. Boas, who is widely perceived as the father of American anthropology, worked closely with such notable African-American intellectuals as William E. B. Du Bois, Carter G. Woodson, Alain Locke, Arthur Fauset, and Zora Neale Hurston, and anthropology emerged as an important tool to challenge ideas of Negro inferiority during the Harlem Renaissance and the New Negro movement.

Boas also trained many students who became leading professors and instructors around the country. In the United States during the nineteenth century, anthropology was used to defend slavery, Jim Crow segregation, Indian removal and assimilation schemes, restrictive immigration, and forced sterilization. However, it was also used by activists and intellectuals to combat these policies and fight for religious freedom, equality under the law, and human and civil rights.

SEE ALSO *Boas, Franz; Eugenics, History of; Forensic Anthropology and Race; Genetics, History of; Human and Primate Evolution; Human Genetics.*

BIBLIOGRAPHY

Blumenbach, Johann. 1997 (1776). "*The Degeneration of Races.*" In *Race and the Enlightenment: A Reader,* edited by Emmanuel Eze, 79–91. Oxford: Blackwell.

Douglass, Frederick. 1999 (1854). "The Claims of the Negro, Ethnologically Considered." In *Frederick Douglass: Selected Speeches and Writings,* edited by Philip S. Foner and Taylor Yuval, 282–297. Chicago: Lawrence Hill Books.

Firmin, Joseph-Anténor. 2000 (1854). *De l'egalité des races humaines* (The Equality of the Human Races). Translated by Charles Asselin, with an introduction by Carolyn Fluehr-Lobban. New York: Garland.

Fredrickson, George M. 2002. *Racism: A Short History.* Princeton, NJ: Princeton University Press.

Jefferson, Thomas. 1996 (1781). *Notes on the State of Virginia.* Chapel Hill: University of North Carolina Press.

Linneaus, Carl (Carl von Linne). 1997 (1735). "*'Hommo' in the System of Nature.*" In *Race and the Enlightenment: A Reader,* edited by Emmanuel Eze, 10–14. Oxford: Blackwell Publishers.

Mooney, James. 1891. "Sacred Formulas of the Cherokee." In *Seventh Annual Report of the Bureau of Ethnology, 1885-86,* edited by John W. Powell, 307–397. Washington, DC: U.S. Government Printing Office.

———. 1965 (1896). *The Ghost Dance Religion and the Sioux Outbreak of 1890.* Chicago: University of Chicago Press.

Powell, John W. 1878. *Report on the Methods of Surveying the Public Domain.* Washington, DC: U.S. Government Printing Office.

Rush, Benjamin. 1987 (1798). "Of the Mode of Education Proper in a Republic." In *The Founders' Constitution,* edited by Philip B. Kurland and Ralph Lerner. Vol. 1, Chap. 18, Document 30. Chicago: University of Chicago Press. Available from http://press-pubs.uchicago.edu/founders/documents/v1ch18s30.html.

Smith, Samuel S. 1810 (1787). *An Essay on the Causes of the Variety of Complexion and Figure in the Human Species.* New Brunswick, NJ: J. Simpson & Co.

Lee D. Baker

ANTHROPOMETRY

Anthropometry is the scientific study of variation in the size and shape of the human body. Anthropometric data have been used both to justify the belief in human biological "races" and to discredit this erroneous belief. This entry provides an overview of anthropometry and its relationship with "race" and racism.

EARLY ANTHROPOMETRIC BELIEFS

The earliest written records about human size date from about 3500 BCE in Sumeria. Several texts from this period mention a positive relationship between health, social status, and stature. The Sumerians were thus surprisingly astute, for this essentially echoes the current biocultural view of the causes of variation in human body size and shape. Groups of people growing and developing under social, economic, and cultural conditions that foster better nutrition and health tend to be, on average, taller and have longer arms and legs than groups of people growing up under less favorable sociocultural conditions. After more than a century of scientific research, this view may seem commonsensical, but it has not always been so.

The philosophers of the ancient Greeks, such as Plato and Aristotle (c. 350 BCE), considered living people and their cultures to be imperfect copies of an ideal type of physical human being and sociocultural system. The variation in body size and shape among various cultures was seen to be a consequence of the degree of imperfection within different societies. The Greeks of ancient Athens believed that they were closest to the ideal, and that the people of other societies were less perfect. However, the Greeks did not believe in the concept of "race," of fundamental biological divisions of humankind. Rather, they accepted the unity of all humankind.

MODERN ANTHROPOMETRY

The term "anthropometry" was coined by Johann Sigismund Elsholtz (1623-1688), who also invented an anthropometer, a device for measuring stature and the length of body parts such as arms and legs. Elsholtz was interested in testing the notion of the Greek physician Hippocrates (460?–357 BCE) that differences in body proportion were related to various diseases. In 1881, the French anthropologist Paul Topinard (1830–1911) applied anthropometry to the study of human "races, so as to distinguish them and establish their relations to each other" (Topinard 1881, p. 212).

Another line of racial investigation was craniology, the study of the skull. The Dutch physician Petrus Camper (1722–1789) and his followers measured various angles of the facial bones to determine the race and sex of skulls. Johann Friedrich Blumenbach (1752–1840), a German naturalist and anthropologist, identified five "races," based on a visual inspection of skull shape and size. One of these was named the "Caucasian race," based on skulls from the Caucasus Mountains region of Georgia. Blumenbach believed that the living people of Georgia were the closest to the original form of the primordial Caucasian type, with European Caucasians being the next closest to the original.

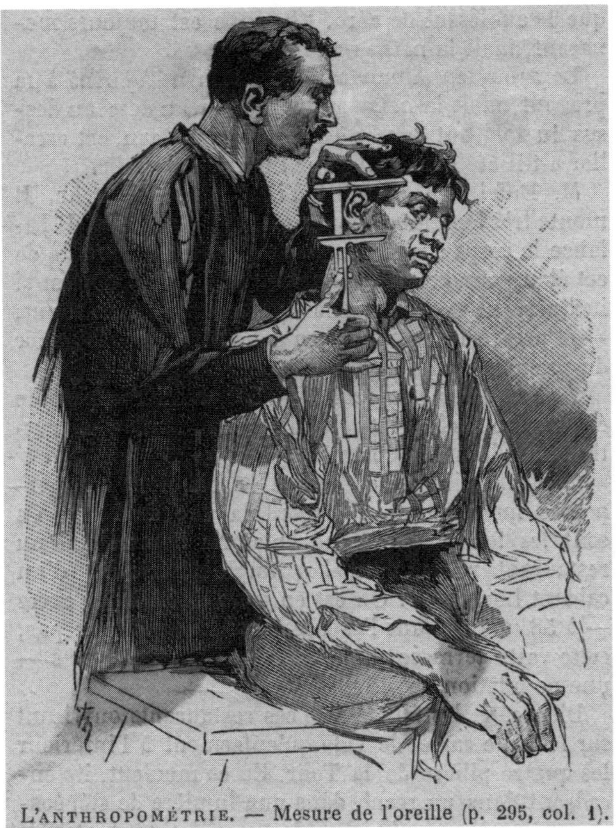

Anthropometrical Measurements. *An engraving from around 1900 shows a man taking the measurements of a criminal's ear. An anthropometrical system for criminal identification was developed in France by Alphonse Bertillon in the early 1880s.* © BETTMANN/CORBIS.

In the United States, Samuel George Morton (1799–1851) refined the methods and equipment of craniometry. Believing that exacting measurement is more scientific than Blumenbach's visual method, Morton invented devices to compute a dozen skull measurements. In contrast, the Swedish anthropologist Anders Adolf Retzius (1796–1860) reduced Morton's assortment of skull measurements to only two (length and breadth), and he applied these to the heads of living people as well. A simple ratio—head length divided by breadth, or the cephalic index—could then be calculated. One school of craniometrists proposed that "inferior" races were characterized by people with round heads, or by a ratio greater than 0.80. Northern Europeans, the alleged "superior" race, had relatively longer, narrower heads, or a ratio below 0.75. Other craniometrists, such as Paul Broca (1824–1880) disproved this fantasy by showing that all human groups, living and dead, had all types of cranial indices. In place of the cephalic index, Broca proposed that the size of the brain, and its shape, varied between the "races," the sexes, and between individuals of higher and lower intelligence. In time, this notion was also proven false, but the belief in head shape or brain size as a determinant of "race" and intelligence persisted well into the twentieth century.

ANTHROPOMETRY AND RACIAL POLITICS IN THE UNITED STATES

By the late nineteenth century, "race scientists" and politicians in the United States were using anthropometry for all sorts of pernicious purposes. American slavery had long been justified based on the "inferior" racial biology of Africans. Segregation in post–Civil War America was similarly justified by race science. In addition, the influx of immigrants from southern and eastern Europe and from China was seen as a new threat to privileged white Americans. Racists used the measurement of stature, body shape, head shape, and brain size as a means to prevent these undesirable "races" entry into the United States.

Some researchers, however, challenged the use of anthropometry for immigration policy. Starting in 1875, Henry Pickering Bowditch (1840–1911) gathered measurements of height and weight of 24,500 school children from around Boston, Massachusetts. In a series of reports published in 1877, 1879, and 1891, Bowditch applied modern statistical methods to describe differences in growth associated with sex, nationality, and socioeconomic level. Bowditch was the first person to construct percentile growth charts, which show the range of normal body growth by sex and age. His findings, published in 1885, showed that the "races" overlapped considerably in their range of body sizes, but that children from the laboring classes were smaller than children from the nonlaboring classes. To account for this fact, Bowditch offered an environmental explanation. He said the nonlaboring classes were taller because of the "greater average comfort in which [they] live and grow up" (Boyd 1980, p. 469).

This conclusion ran counter to that of English savant Francis Galton (1822–1911). In his book *Natural Inheritance* (1889) Galton suggested that stature and other physical traits were highly heritable. Galton's work led some to believe that heredity was the all-powerful determinant of human form and functional capabilities. Galton's work was used to support the eugenics movement, a pseudoscientific political movement that claimed to be able to improve the human species through controlled breeding. Eugenicists held that the laboring classes were genetically inferior to the nonlaboring classes. One supposed proof of this inferiority was their short stature. Eugenicists also believed that the race, or ethnic origin, of American-born children could easily be determined on the basis of physical measurements, and that racial admixture, especially between Anglo-Saxons and people from southern and eastern Europe, would bring about a physical degeneration of Americans.

Franz Boas (1858–1942), a German-born anthropologist working in the United States, demolished the position of the eugenicists using the data of Bowditch and his own studies of migrants to the United States. Boas found that the children of recent immigrants grew up to look much like the "good old Americans" (older generations of immigrants from northern Europe) due to modifications in the process of growth and development as a response to environmental change. Accordingly, Boas concluded that human physical plasticity is what is real, while the belief in the permanence of "races" is false. The changes in growth discovered by Boas applied to both the laboring and nonlaboring classes. Boas ascribed these changes in physical form to the better health care, nutrition, and child-rearing practices in the United States.

Despite this work, many eugenicists and politicians still called for quotas on the immigration of so-called inferior peoples into the United States. In 1911, Boas presented to the U.S. Congress a report titled *Changes in the Bodily Form of Descendants of Immigrants*, which explained his research and probably helped delay the imposition of limitations on immigration. Nevertheless, the American Congress eventually passed the "Immigration Restriction Acts" of 1921 and 1924, which specifically placed immigration quotas on southern and eastern Europeans and Asians.

Yet while Boas and the environmentalists may have lost that political battle, their work influenced future generations of anthropologists, public health workers, epidemiologists, and others. A full appreciation of Boas' work waited until after the Nazi holocaust of World War II (committed in the name of "racial purification") and new discoveries in genetics after 1950. Anthropologists then began to reject the typological approach and the concept of "race" in favor of a population approach to the study of human variation and adaptation.

THE MODERN POPULATION PERSPECTIVE

The population approach employs an understanding of human anthropometry, genetics, demography, and sociocultural behavior to show that there are no scientifically definable boundaries between human groups—meaning that there are no biological "races." It is known in the early twenty-first century that there is more genetic and anthropometric variation among individuals within any of the "races" than there is between people of different "races." Africa and Europe, for example, include populations that are both tall (Tutsi men of Rwanda average 5'8", while Dutch men average 6') and short (Efe Pygmy men average 4'8", while Portuguese men average 5'6").

It is also understood in the early 2000s that there are an unlimited number of social races, or groups of people who are defined on the basis of shared social, economic, political, and religious characteristics, as well as other cultural values such as child-rearing practices. These sociocultural traits can influence the development of biological traits. For example, racism can lead to poverty for some groups, which decreases stature and other body measurements (Komlos 1994). Some social races place infants on their backs to sleep, which tends to produce rounder heads. Social races change over time, and the anthropometric traits of these groups also change. None of these changes in body size or shape are genetic. Rather they are evidence of biological plasticity in body form during the years of growth and development (Lasker 1969). A change in the environment, such as alleviation of poverty or a change in infant sleeping position from stomach to back, will alter the body shape of the affected generation in new ways.

Body proportions, such as leg length relative to total stature, have been widely used to define "races." In this view, Africans have the relatively longest legs, Asians (including Native Americans) have the shortest legs, and Europeans are intermediate in leg length. These proportions were believed to be immutable, but research has shown that the body proportions of a group can change significantly. Since 1960, the relative leg length of Japanese has increased to the point where it is indistinguishable from that of the British. The Maya of Guatemala are very short-legged, but Mayan children born in the United States have relative leg length that falls within the normal range of both white and black American children. The change among the Maya-Americans occurred in less than a generation, meaning that it cannot be due to genetics. Instead, it seems to be due to improvements in the total quality of their life in the United States.

Thus, at the start of the twenty-first century, a biocultural understanding of human development is replacing outdated applications of anthropometry. The new anthropometry is used to assess the social, economic, and political history of human groups, the health of individuals, and the well-being of the human population.

SEE ALSO *Boas, Franz; Cranial Index; Cultural Racism; Eugenics, History of; Galton, Francis; Genetics, History of; Human and Primate Evolution; Human Genetics; Immigration to the United States; Racial Hierarchy; Racial Purity (U.S.), 1900-1910.*

BIBLIOGRAPHY

Boas, Franz. 1940. *Race, Language, and Culture*. New York: Free Press.

Bogin, Barry. 1999. *Patterns of Human Growth*, 2nd ed. Cambridge, U.K.: Cambridge University Press.

Bogin, Barry, et al. 2002. "Rapid Change in Height and Body Proportions of Maya American Children." *American Journal of Human Biology* 14: 753–761.

Boyd, Edith. 1980. *Origins of the Study of Human Growth*. Edited by Bhim S. Savara and John F. Schilke. Eugene: University of Oregon Press.

Gould, Stephen J. 1996. *The Mismeasure of Man*, 2nd ed. New York: Norton.

Komlos, John, ed. 1994. *Stature, Living Standards, and Economic Development: Essays in Anthropometric History*. Chicago: Chicago University Press.

Lasker, Gabriel W. 1969. "Human Biological Adaptability." *Science* 166: 1480–1486.

Marks, Jonathan. 1995. *Human Biodiversity: Genes, Race, and History*. New York: Aldine de Gruyter.

Spencer, Frank, ed. 1997. *History of Physical Anthropology: An Encyclopedia*. New York: Garland.

Tanner, James M. 1981. *A History of the Study of Human Growth*. Cambridge, U.K.: Cambridge University Press.

Topinard, Paul. 1881. "Observations upon the Methods and Process of Anthropometry." *Journal of Anthropological Institute* 10: 212.

Barry Bogin

ANTI-APARTHEID MOVEMENT

The anti-apartheid movement was the first successful transnational social movement in the era of globalization. The movement began after a massive turnout by rural Afrikaners gave Rev. Daniel Malan's Nationalist Party a majority of five seats in the whites-only Parliament of the Union of South Africa on May 26, 1948. The Nationalists won on a racist platform that played on white fears of the "black threat" and promised to establish strict "apartheid" or separate development policies to counter it.

In its transnational scope and eventual success, the anti-apartheid movement can be compared to the abolitionist movement of the nineteenth century. What is unique about the anti-apartheid movement is the extent of support it received from individuals, governments and organizations on all continents. Few social movements in history have garnered anywhere near the international support that was mobilized against the racist apartheid regime in South Africa. Although national liberation and Marxism might both be considered as successful, transnational social movements, neither of these had the global support that the anti-apartheid movement garnered.

There were two main aspects of the anti-apartheid movement: the internal campaign to destabilize the racist apartheid regime in South Africa, and the external campaign for political, economic, and cultural sanctions. At the heart of the movement was the struggle of black Africans to end white supremacy in South Africa. This internal movement was both a catalyst for actions at the international level and the critical link that gave coherence to the movement as a whole. The external effort can be divided into two fronts: (1) regional efforts to provide military bases, material, and diplomatic support for liberation movements; and (2) the diaspora movement, which focused on seeking international sanctions against the regime and providing direct aid to the liberation movements.

The internal struggle within South Africa was the core of the movement, and it served as a catalyst for regional and international support movements. This effort emerged to oppose apartheid legislation imposed after the all-white election of 1948 brought Rev. Daniel Malan's Nationalist Party to power. The regime quickly passed segregationist legislation, including:

1. The Prohibition of Mixed-Marriages Act (1950), which made interracial marriage a criminal act;
2. The Population Registration Act (1949), which required registration and racial classification of all persons above sixteen years of age;
3. The Suppression of Communism Act (1950), which associated anti-apartheid activities with communism;
4. The Group Areas Act (1950), which allowed the government to determine the areas in which people of different races and nationalities could reside and own property;
5. The Bantu Education Act (1953), which brought mission schools under government control and circumscribed the education of Africans.

The resistance movement responded at first with nonviolent direct-action tactics under the leadership of organizations such as the African National Congress (ANC), the South African Communist Party (SACP), the Indian National Congress (INC) and the Pan Africanist Congress (PAC). On May 1, 1950, this coalition organized a national strike to oppose the Suppression of Communism Act. When thousands of workers boycotted their jobs, the government responded by sending troops to the townships, and eighteen workers were killed. Nevertheless, the coalition called another strike for June 26, and workers again responded in good numbers.

These strikes were a prelude to the mass civil-disobedience campaigns of 1952-1953 known collectively as the "Campaign of Defiance of Unjust Laws." Between June and December 1952, thousands of activists were arrested for defying petty apartheid laws, such as "whites only" drinking fountains, train compartments, and waiting rooms. The ANC's volunteer-in-chief Nelson Mandela made hundreds of speeches across the country urging black people to defy apartheid laws, and the government responded by shooting demonstrators and arresting movement leaders, including Mandela; Yusuf

Dadoo, president of the INC; and J. B. Marks of the Mineworkers Union.

These internal struggles against apartheid, and the violent response they engendered, galvanized the international movement. The Defiance Campaign, for instance, inspired supporters in India, Africa, and the United States. On September 12, 1952, thirteen African and Asian countries brought the issue of racial discrimination before the Secretary General of the United Nations (UN), calling on the organization to establish a commission to study the issue and report its finding at the next General Assembly. The United States vetoed the resolution, however, beginning a forty-year history of U.S. diplomatic support for apartheid. Yet while this specific campaign failed, the effort to raise the world's consciousness of the plight of black people in South Africa would eventually result in a comprehensive sanctions resolution.

On March 23, 1960, South African police gunned down seventy-two men, women, and children in Sharpeville Township. The demonstrators were protesting against the Natives Act of 1952 (collectively known as the Pass Laws) that required black people to carry identification with them at all times. The laws were designed to restrict the movement of black people into urban areas. The massacre sparked outrage around the world, and photographs of the victims became iconic images of apartheid. Although the original call for international sanctions had come from the ANC in 1959, it was the Sharpeville Massacre that made South Africa a pariah state and precipitated international action. South Africa was expelled from sports, cultural, and academic institutions, and on November 6, 1962, the UN General Assembly voted to sever diplomatic, transportation, and economic relations with South Africa. Although the resolution was voluntary, it was a major victory for the anti-apartheid movement. International organizations such as the International Labor Organization and the United Nations Educational, Scientific and Cultural Organization (UNESCO) also voted to expel South Africa.

The apartheid regime responded to this pressure by declaring a state of emergency, banning anti-apartheid organizations such as the SACP, ANC, and PAC. In response, the liberation movements went underground and into exile, where they launched the second phase of the movement: the armed struggle. This phase was characterized by the internationalization of the struggle, with regional and broader African support organized by the Organization of African Unity (OAU). The exiles acquired bases of operation, military training, and political education through both the OAU and a coalition of South Africa's neighbors known as the "frontline states." The apartheid regime responded by attacking its neighbors and sponsoring terrorist organizations such as Renamo and UNITA to disrupt, discredit, and overthrow hostile governments. By the 1970s the southern African region had become a Cold War theater, with the United States and South Africa sponsoring terrorist insurgencies and Cuba and the Soviet Union supporting the governments of Mozambique and Angola. South African forces invaded Angola and attacked Lesotho, Mozambique, Zimbabwe, and Zambia. Meanwhile, hundreds of youth were killed in police crackdowns in South African townships such as Soweto.

In the 1980s, the movement entered a third stage: massive resistance. The movement reached its climax in this stage, which was characterized by the determination of anti-apartheid activists within South Africa to make the country ungovernable through strikes, boycotts, demonstrations, and acts of sabotage. In 1983 a coalition of the internal organizations and church groups formed the United Democratic Front to lead the new phase of the movement. In an attempt to split the opposition, the regime offered Indians and Coloreds (people of mixed race background) limited franchise in the elections of 1984. The strategy failed, however, and instead galvanized further acts of civil disobedience and sabotage. Moreover, the international anti-apartheid movement had matured, and most countries in the world had imposed military and economic sanctions against South Africa. The exceptions were Britain and the United States, but the movement overcame this hurdle in 1986 when the United States Congress passed the Comprehensive Anti-Apartheid Act (CAAA). The bill was written and proposed by Rep. Ron Dellums (D-Calif.), a veteran anti-apartheid activist and member of the Congressional Black Caucus. The CAAA delivered a crippling blow to a South African economy that was already reeling from the withdrawal of U.S. banks the year before. In 1987, 250,000 African mineworkers went on strike, further undermining the economy and the legitimacy of the apartheid state.

Thus, it was the combined pressures of international sanctions and internal strife that led to the demise of the apartheid state. The retreat began with the repealing of the pillars of apartheid legislation, beginning with the repeal of the pass laws in 1986. By 1990 the government had lifted the ban on the SACP, ANC, and PAC and repealed the 1913 and 1936 Land Acts, the Population Registration Act, and the Separate Amenities Act. Nelson Mandela was released in 1991, having spent twenty-seven years in prison. Four years later, on May 10, 1994, Mandela was sworn in as president of South Africa. Mandela and his African National Congress won an overwhelming victory in the elections of 1994, defeating both black and white opposition parties to become the undisputed leader of the new South Africa.

Nelson Mandela Voting, April 27, 1994. *After spending 27 years in prison, Mandela's anti-apartheid struggle finally succeeded. He is seen here voting in South Africa's first democratic election, which made him the nation's first black president.* © REUTERS/CORBIS.

Despite the political defeat, the effects of apartheid are still evident in the early twenty-first century, particularly in the economic sphere. More than ten years after apartheid, the white minority still owns more than 80 percent of agricultural land and is in control of the economy. Further, reports indicate that racial inequality has grown since 1994. The ANC's neoliberal policies have not succeeded in redistributing resources or reducing poverty to any significant degree. Instead, these policies benefit the rich and the new black professional class. In August 2005, religious, civic groups, and the country's largest trade union body (Cosatu) formed a coalition to challenge the ANC government's economic policies. Although a part of the ANC's ruling coalition, Cosatu has opposed the ANC's focus on building a black professional and business class. This federation has campaigned for a broad-based redistribution of resources and for black economic empowerment. As of 2005, however, the ANC has managed to hold together the three-way coalition with Cosatu and the South African Communist Party.

SEE ALSO *Apartheid; Mandela, Nelson; South African Racial Formations.*

BIBLIOGRAPHY

Barber, James. 1999. *South Africa in the 20th Century: A Political History–In Search of a Nation State.* Oxford: Blackwell.

Guelke, Adrian. 2005. *Rethinking the Rise and Fall of Apartheid.* New York: Palgrave Macmillan.

Harvey, Robert. 2001. *The Fall of Apartheid: The Inside Story from Smuts to Mbeki.* Basingstroke, U.K.: Palgrave.

Hostetter, David. 2006. *Movement Matters: American Antiapartheid Activism and the Rise of Multicultural Politics.* New York: Routledge.

Lodge, Tom. 2002. *Politics in South Africa; From Mandela to Mbeki.* Cape Town: David Philip.

Mandela, Nelson. 1994. *Long Walk to Freedom.* Randburg, South Africa: Macdonald Purnell.

Meli, Francis. 1989. *A History of the ANC: South Africa Belongs to Us.* Bloomington: Indiana University Press.

Mermelsein, David, ed. 1987. *The Anti-Apartheid Reader: The Struggle against White Racist Rule in South Africa.* New York: Grove Press.

Nesbitt, Francis N. 2004. *Race for Sanctions; African Americans against Apartheid, 1946-1994.* Bloomington: Indiana University Press.

O'Meara, Dan. 1996. *Forty Lost Years: The Apartheid State and the Politics of the National Party 1948-1994.* Randburg, South Africa: Ravan Press.

Waldemeir, Patti. 1997. *Anatomy of a Miracle: The End of Apartheid and the Birth of the New South Africa.* London: Viking.

Francis Njubi Nesbitt

ANTI-INDIAN MOVEMENT

The U.S. anti-Indian movement was created out of a white backlash against gains made by Native American nations since the 1960s. The modern movement is the heir to the historic hostility exhibited toward Native sovereignty, treaty rights, and cultural and economic autonomy. It originally brought together white reservation residents challenging tribal jurisdiction, white sportsmen opposing Native treaty rights, and resource interests viewing tribal sovereignty as an obstacle to profit and development. In the decades around the turn of the twenty-first century, it has incorporated gaming interests and anti-gambling groups fearing tribal casinos, animal rights groups opposing tribal hunting, and New Age groups demanding unhindered access to exploit tribal spiritual practices.

MOTIVATING FACTORS

At least five major factors motivate anti-Indian groups. The first is the call for "equal rights for whites"—the argument that the increased legal powers and jurisdiction of tribes infringes on the liberties or private property rights of non-Indian residents on and off the reservations. The use of civil rights imagery can reach such lengths that whites are described as oppressed individuals victimized by "Red Apartheid," and the legacy of Dr. Martin Luther King Jr. is invoked in support of an agenda to roll back Native rights.

The second factor is access to natural resources, such as fish, game, land, and water. Treaty rights guarantee some tribes access to resources on their ceded lands outside their reservations. Anti-treaty activists assert that no citizens should have "special rights" to use natural resources (even though non-Indians also can retain property use rights over land that they sell). Natural resource interests oppose sovereignty when it enables tribes to block projects—such as mines or dams—that may harm treaty resources.

The third factor is cultural superiority, which can be exhibited in sports team logos and mascots, the excavation of mounds and burial sites, disrespect of sacred objects, or efforts to restrict Native languages. Native objections to these practices often provoke strong accusations of "political correctness." The very existence of an enduring non-Western belief system, rooted in the middle of the most powerful Western country, is seen as a fundamental problem.

The fourth factor is outright racism, including not only slurs and violent harassment, but also the belief that Indians are unfit to govern themselves, and are merely recipients of government hand-outs (or passive pawns in government conspiracies). Anti-Indian groups accuse Native people who appear white or African American of using their "blood quantum" only to obtain financial benefits. Most anti-Indian activists deny any trace of racism; their more subtle approach is to romanticize past Indian cultures and compare them to modern Natives who have adapted to Western technologies, presenting Native peoples as "authentic" only if they are frozen in the past, rather than living, dynamic cultures that incorporate outside cultural elements.

The fifth factor is economic dependency. In a rural reflection of the "Welfare Cadillac" myth, reservation Indians are said to wallow in food stamps, free housing and medical care, and huge federal cash payments—all tax-free. (No one has to pay state sales tax on reservations, but otherwise Indians have had virtually identical tax obligations as non-Indians.) The anti-Indian groups condemn tribes if they are poor, but also if they try to pull out of poverty through economic self-reliance, such as gaming.

REGIONAL ORGANIZING

The modern white backlash was first seen in the late 1960s in the Pacific Northwest, where tribal fish and shellfish harvests form the basis of traditional tribal economies. The backlash portrayed tribal harvests as a threat to the commercial and sport fishing industries (ignoring the threats posed by dams, pollution, and huge trawlers). State of Washington anti-Indian groups mushroomed after the 1974 Boldt Decision ruled that tribal members were entitled to up to 50 percent of the salmon harvest. The leading group, Steelhead/Salmon Protective Association and Wildlife Network (S/SPAWN), was joined by groups such as the United Property Owners of Washington, made up of white reservation residents. They won support among politicians and local communities, as police and vigilantes regularly assaulted tribal harvesters. They lost much support after the State and tribes reached a 1989 co-management agreement, in which tribal and state governments negotiate not only over the allocation of the fish harvest, but over practices (such as logging) that can damage fish habitat.

The Center for World Indigenous Studies stated in 1992 that "individuals associated with the anti-Indian movement now appear to have occasional, if not frequent association with right-wing extremist groups." The late Washington State U.S. Representative Jack Metcalf provided a bridge between these right-wing networks and groups against tribal fishing and Makah whaling. Anti-Indian activism continued on Washington reservations into the 2000s, most notably by the Citizens Stand-Up Committee, which strongly opposed a Yakama tribal alcohol ban and other tribal regulations. Idaho local and county governments joined in the North-Central Idaho Jurisdictional Alliance to challenge Nez Perce tribal programs to reclaim allotted lands, assert tribal authority, and protect salmon habitat.

In the Upper Midwest, the 1983 Voigt Decision affirmed Wisconsin Ojibwe (Chippewa) treaty rights to harvest off-reservation natural resources, particularly through the traditional practice of spearfishing. Some sportsmen decried what they saw as the tribal "rape" of the fish resource, vital to the local tourist economy, even though the tribes never took more than 3 percent of the walleye. Protect Americans' Rights and Resources (PARR) and Stop Treaty Abuse (which marketed "Treaty Beer") organized protests at northern lakes during spring spearfishing seasons. Protesters chanted taunts such as "timber niggers," carried signs reading "Save a Spawning Walleye, Spear a Pregnant Squaw," and threw rocks, bottles, and full beer cans, documented by media coverage and Midwest Treaty Network reports. Spearers' vehicles were assaulted, pipe bombs were exploded, boats were blocked or swamped, and snipers fired rifles and high-powered slingshots. Hundreds of Witnesses for Nonviolence monitored the harassment and violence, which slowed after a 1991 federal court injunction.

At the same time as the fishing rights conflict, mining companies began moving into Ojibwe ceded territory, potentially endangering the fish. After Wisconsin's anti-treaty movement collapsed in 1992, the Midwest Treaty Network initiated a dialogue between the tribes and sport-fishers, forming an environmental alliance that in 2003 stopped the proposed Crandon mine at Mole Lake. Similar unlikely alliances growing out of treaty conflicts have also defeated harmful projects in other states.

Opposition to Ojibwe fishing in Michigan has developed since the 1979 Fox decision upheld treaty rights on the Great Lakes. In Minnesota, Proper Economic Resource Management (PERM), Mille Lacs Tea Party, and the White Earth Equal Rights Committee have challenged Ojibwe jurisdictional rights in federal court. In Illinois, the white backlash centers on cultural/religious issues, such as Native efforts to change demeaning team mascots and to preserve burial sites.

In the Great Plains, land and water disputes erupted between the tribes and white reservation residents in the 1970s. The result was the formation of Montana groups such as All Citizens Equal and the Citizens Rights Organization; other groups organized in the Dakotas and Nebraska. Whites live on the parts of the reservations that were heavily allotted (privatized and divided) from the 1880s through the 1920s. Majority-white counties within some reservations have voted to secede, and thereby diminish the tribal land base. One Nation United (in Oklahoma) has become a leading anti-Indian group in the 2000s by bringing together oil, agricultural, and other business interests to oppose tribal jurisdiction and taxation, gaming, and contributions to political candidates.

NATIONAL ORGANIZING

Anti-Indian groups tried to coordinate their efforts as early as the 1970s, through the Interstate Congress for Equal Rights and Responsibilities, succeeding in the 1990s with the formation of the Citizens Equal Rights Alliance (CERA). CERA's advisory board reflects participation from groups in at least twelve states, with leadership rotating among the states. It meets annually to lobby Congress to modify or abrogate treaties, limit tribal regulations affecting non-Indians on the reservations, and roll back tribal gaming rights.

The 1988 Indian Gaming Regulatory Act permits tribes within states that practice Class III gaming (such as a lottery) to develop casinos. Some antigambling groups and white gambling interests (including Donald Trump) have targeted Indian casinos without opposing the state gaming that make them possible. The success of a handful of tribal casinos (close to cities or tourist centers) has fed a myth of "rich Indians," though other tribes with and without casinos have not prospered. This myth of tribes "taking over" local economies threatens government aid to all tribes. Like European Jews of the medieval era, who had agriculture virtually closed to them, Native nations have been denied control over their land-based economies. Left with few other development options, both groups have been scapegoated for engaging in unpopular financial practices such as moneylending or gambling.

Anti-Indian advocacy has been carried out by other national issue-based organizations. County governments have lobbied against tribes taking trust land off of local tax rolls. "Wise Use" (or anti-environmental) groups such as the Alliance for America claim that tribal jurisdiction threatens private property rights. A few environmental and conservation organizations have opposed tribal land claims over parklands or recreational areas, or opposed tribal governments pressured into accepting toxic projects. Some archaeologists and anthropologists also strongly defend their professional "right" to dig up and display Native people's ancestors and sacred objects.

Anti-Indian movements have been countered, sometimes successfully, by pro-Indian movements of Native Americans and their supporters, who educate non-Indians about tribal histories, cultures, and legal rights, expose the racial double standards behind anti-Indian groups' agendas, and reveal how these groups may be fronting for corporate interests. Supporters assert that Native sovereignty not only benefits the tribes, but through protecting the environment and local economies, it can also be good for America.

SEE ALSO *Native American Popular Culture and Race.*

BIBLIOGRAPHY

"Centennial Accord between the Federally Recognized Indian Tribes in Washington State and the State of Washington." 1989. Available from http://www1.dshs.wa.gov/ipss/centaccord.htm.

Cohen, Fay G. 1986. *Treaties on Trial: The Continuing Controversy over Northwest Indian Fishing Rights.* Seattle: University of Washington Press.

Cook-Lynn, Elizabeth. 2001. *Anti-Indianism in Modern America: A Voice from Tatekeya's Earth.* Urbana: University of Illinois Press.

Dudas, Jeffrey. 2005. "In the Name of Equal Rights: 'Special' Rights and the Politics of Resentment in Post-Civil Rights America." *Law and Society Review* 39: 723.

Gedicks, Al, and Zoltan Grossman. 2004. "Defending a Common Home: Native/Non-Native Alliances Against Mining Companies in Wisconsin." In *In the Way of Development: Indigenous Peoples, Life Projects, and Globalization,* edited by Mario Blaser, Harvey A. Feit, and Glenn MacRae. London: Zed Books. Available from http://www.idrc.ca.

Grossman, Zoltan. 1992. "Treaty Rights and Responding to Anti-Indian Activity." In *When Hate Groups Come to Town: A Handbook of Effective Community Responses,* 2nd ed. Atlanta, GA: Center for Democratic Renewal.

———. 2005. "Unlikely Alliances: Treaty Conflicts and Environmental Cooperation between Native American and

Rural White Communities." *American Indian Culture and Research Journal* 29 (4): 21–43. Also title of University of Wisconsin doctoral dissertation, 2002. Available from http://academic.evergreen.edu.

Henry-Tanner, Leah, and Charles Tanner. 2005. *Living like Neighbors*. Poulsbo, WA: Northwest Communities Alliance. Available from http://westernstatescenter.org/resource/Living Like Neighbors.pdf.

Honor Our Neighbors' Origins and Rights (HONOR). 2000. "The Anti-Indian Network: A Profile." *HONOR Digest* 11 (2).

Johansen, Bruce E. 2000. *The New Terminators: A Guide to the Anti-Sovereignty Movement*. Olympia, WA: Center for World Indigenous Studies.

Kallen, Stuart A., ed. 2006. *Indian Gaming*. Farmington, MI: Greenhaven Press.

Lowman, Bill. 1978. *220 Million Custers*. Anacortes, WA: Anacortes Printing & Publishing.

Midwest Treaty Network. 1990–91. *Witness for Nonviolence Reports: Chippewa Spearfishing Season*. Available from http://www.uwec.edu/ais/Spearfishing%20Reports/1990_Spearfishing_Report.pdf and http://www.uwec.edu/ais/Spearfishing%20Reports/1991_Spearfishing_Report.pdf

Midwest Treaty Network Web site. 2007. Available from http://www.alphacdc.com/treaty/content.html.

Montana Human Rights Network. 2000. *Drumming Up Resentment: The Anti-Indian Movement in Montana*. Helena, MT: Montana Human Rights Network.

Rÿser, Rudolph C. 1995. *Anti-Indian Movement on the Tribal Frontier*. Olympia, WA: DayKeeper Press. Available from http://www.cwis.org.

Smith, Andrea. 1991. "For All Those Who Were Indian in a Former Life." *Ms.* 2 (3): 44–45.

Whaley, Rick, and Walter Bresette. 1999. *Walleye Warriors*, 3rd ed. Enfield, NH: Essential Books.

Wilkinson, Charles F. 2000. *Messages from Frank's Landing: A Story of Salmon, Treaties, and the Indian Way*. Seattle: University of Washington Press.

Willman, Elaine D. 2006. *Going to Pieces: The Dismantling of the United States of America*. Toppenish, WA: Equilocus LLC.

Williams, C. Herb, and Walt Neubrech. 1976. *Indian Treaties—American Nightmare*. Seattle: Outdoor Empire Publishing, Inc.

Zoltan Grossman

ANTIRACIST SOCIAL MOVEMENTS

Vibrant social movements have defied myriad forms of racial oppression across the globe. Strategies, tactics, and ideologies have varied widely, with challenging economic domination as a common theme. Antiracism has encompassed challenges to genocide, the seizure and/or control of land and other resources, slavery, and the exploitation of human labor. Antiracist social movements have also targeted cultural degradation, political exclusion, and many other patterns of racial prejudice and discrimination.

Racism became intertwined with colonialism throughout the period of European conquest of Africa, the Americas, Asia, Australia, and Oceania. In response, subjugated peoples around the globe forged collective struggles against European imperialism. Anticolonial movements in many areas of the world initially were explicitly framed in terms not of race but of resisting outside colonial powers. Across time, many of these struggles became increasingly racialized, reflecting the racism embodied in global capitalism. Racist European powers have been joined by other industrialized nations, particularly the United States, in subjugating people of color over the past two centuries.

FORMS OF ANTIRACISM

Antiracist resistance is shaped by the particular manifestations of race and racism in any given system of racial oppression. The forms that antiracist activism has taken are not linear and often occurred simultaneously. Because of the distinctive development of racism in different countries around the world, no one example can accurately represent all antiracist social movements. However, the examples below reflect central, overlapping dynamics of antiracist activism in different historical periods and countries. These movements have been local, national, and transnational in character.

The survival of racially oppressed groups has birthed cultures of resistance and antiracist collective consciousnesses. These two intertwined phenomena typically emerge simultaneously and have forged the foundation of formal political movements.

The continued use of traditions, language, and religion has sustained racially oppressed groups and defied racism. Cultures of resistance do not merely replicate preconquest cultural forms, but are dynamic. They often unite previously diverse groups and result in the synthesis of more than one culture. For instance, the Garifuna culture arose from the intermarriage of shipwrecked Africans (en route to be slaves) and Arawak "Indians" on the Caribbean island of San Vicente. This group resisted military conquest by the English, Spanish, and French for centuries before they were forcibly relocated to coastal areas in Guatemala, Honduras, and Belize, where they continue to fight against racial discrimination today.

Throughout the Americas, slave communities developed rich cultures of resistance. Slaves fought racism on both individual and collective levels. Slaves engaged in work slow-downs, played dumb, and stole property. Across generations, they passed on survival strategies that took the form of music, art, dance, and religion/spirituality.

Slaves also defied racist oppression by escaping. In Brazil, thousands of escaped slaves formed the *quilombo* of Palmares in the 1600s. Palmares was a self-sustaining agricultural kingdom that withstood Dutch and Portuguese military attacks for nearly 100 years. In the United States, runaway slaves formed Maroon communities and sometimes joined indigenous communities/nations such as the Seminole in Florida. In the United States, a vast network of conductors, stations, and pathways formed the Underground Railroad that led thousands of slaves to freedom. This collective action threatened the institution of slavery and provided powerful symbols of resistance for future generations.

STRATEGIES

Antiracist collective consciousness—a shared identity of belonging to a group that faces and defies systemic racial oppression—has often developed within cultures of resistance. Compelling examples of antiracist collective consciousness are seen in the history of indigenous, slave (and former slave), and immigrant populations. In the early years of the twenty-first century, Middle Eastern immigrants have had to overcome their own national, religious, and ethnic divisions to create collective identities that foster resistance to xenophobic, racist practices and policies in France and other industrialized nations. Antiracist activists have worked to raise awareness among members of racially oppressed groups to demonstrate that poverty, low wages, inadequate housing, and the like are not the result of individual successes and/or failures but stem from institutionalized racism that benefits whites and marginalizes people of color. For example, in the 1960s, the *Alianza de Mercedes Federales* (the Landgrant Movement), led by Reies Lopez Tijerina, documented the roots of Chicano/a poverty in the illegal seizure of family- and community-held land grants by Anglo settlers in the southwestern United States during the second half of the nineteenth century. While galvanizing collective consciousness has been a constant strategy in antiracist activism, it is an ever-changing process as diverse, intersecting communities of color—indigenous, slave/former slave, immigrant—build coalitions. For example, indigenous people and people of African descent in countries such as Colombia, Ecuador, and Peru have found common cause in challenging their respective governments to recognize political autonomy, land ownership, and human rights. Antiracist consciousness, often intertwined with anticolonialist consciousness, has been articulated in cogent political analyses by antiracist activist-scholars around the world.

Another key strategy among antiracist activists is to raise awareness about racial injustices, not only within the specific group targeted but also among external groups—domestic whites, other communities of color, and people living in other countries. Black and white abolitionists publicly exposed the atrocities of U.S. slavery in speaking engagements and written tracts across the United States and in Europe. In the late 1800s and early 1900s, African American activists such as journalist Ida B. Wells published books and articles and spoke internationally to bring to light the horrors of lynching—a practice that terrorized black communities and played a key role in maintaining white supremacy in the United States. Quiche-Maya advocate Rigoberta Menchú (1984) detailed the ruthless torture and violence used by the Guatemalan government to enforce inhumane work conditions for indigenous people. In the early years of the twenty-first century, sweatshop workers in countries such as Indonesia and El Salvador have risked death to educate others about the inhumane employment practices of multinational corporations operating within the web of global racist capitalism.

Antiracist activists have relied on the mass media to educate and mobilize people to take action. They have written novels (*One Day of Life* [1983] by Manuel Argueta); written letters to and articles in newspapers (the abolitionist *Northstar*) and magazines (the NAACP's *Crisis*); and produced art (Chicano/a mural art in the United States), films/videos (*Rabbit-proof Fence* [2002], which illustrates aboriginal defiance in Australia), and music (Bob Marley's antiracist reggae lyrics). For more than a decade, the *Ejército Zapatista de Liberación Nacional* (Zapatista Army of National Liberation, the Zapatistas) has garnered national and international support for the rights of indigenous people in Chiapas, Mexico, by skillfully using the Internet to disseminate their communiqués. Antiracist solidarity that grows out of these and other antiracist campaigns plays a key role in pressuring elites to concede to antiracist demands.

Having documented the particular forms of racial injustice in their community or nation, activists often apply pressure to different social institutions to bring about social change. After years of negotiation between Inuit leaders and the Canadian government, the Land Claims Agreement Act was passed in 1993, creating the newest Canadian province of Nunavut in 1999. This historic event also illustrates a sovereignty movement in which an indigenous group successfully regained much of its land and natural resources as well as a level of political autonomy.

Antiracist activists employ letters and petitions to government officials, companies, and the mass media to push for racial equality. Frequently this has been done to challenge racist legislation and political policies such as the Fugitive Slave Act and Jim Crow laws in the United States and the Pass Laws in South Africa. In turn, political pressure is applied to promote antiracist laws such as antilynching legislation in the United States and immigrant-rights legislation in Britain. Decades of antiracist legal work by the National Association for the Advancement of Colored People (NAACP) led to the pivotal U.S. Supreme Court decision in *Brown v. Board of Education*, outlawing racial segregation in public schools in 1954.

Direct appeals have also been made to international organizations. In 1919, Japan submitted a proposal for racial equality to be included in the articles of the League of Nations; facing opposition from delegates from Britain, Australia, and the United States, it was overturned by the chairperson, U.S. president Woodrow Wilson. In the 1950s, W. E. B. Du Bois pushed the United Nations to recognize the denial of civil and other rights to black Americans as a violation of basic human rights outlined in the Geneva Convention.

Around the globe, antiracist activists have developed a vast repertoire of protest strategies to expose racial injustice and apply pressure on racist governments and other entities. Abolitionists organized boycotts of goods produced by slave labor. Civil rights activists in the United States implemented bus boycotts in their struggles against racial segregation in public transportation. Marches and rallies against racism have been organized to gain media coverage. The 1963 March on Washington, where Dr. Martin Luther King Jr. delivered his captivating "I Have a Dream" speech, received widespread media coverage that publicized the mass base of the civil rights movement.

A key strategy in many antiracist social movements has been civil disobedience. Indians utilized innovative and disruptive acts of nonviolent civil disobedience to force the British colonizers out of India. Mahatma Gandhi's philosophical and strategic model of nonviolent civil disobedience had a profound impact on antiracist movement participants around the world, including the Student Nonviolent Coordinating Committee's sit-in tactic challenging white-only public accommodations in the U.S. South in the 1960s. Since then, variations of the sit-ins have been employed by various antiracist groups, including students of color, AIDS activists, and prison-rights activists.

Labor unions have sometimes acted collectively against racism, and strikes have played a central role in antiracist collective action. For example, the black miners' strike for higher wages in 1946 galvanized the anti-apartheid movement in South Africa. In the United States in the 1990s, striking was one of the key tactics used by Justice for Janitors to win higher wages and benefits for many janitors, disproportionately people of color.

Antiracist movements have also occupied land seized by white settlers and white-dominated governments and corporations. In the 1970s and 1980s, the Maori land-rights movement occupied land held by the government and real estate developers as part of broader campaigns to challenge racism in New Zealand. Members of the American Indian Movement took over Alcatraz Island in 1970 to dramatize the plight of Native Americans. Antiracist protest has also taken the form of graffiti, guerrilla theater, student walk-outs, and the disruption of government and corporate meetings. Antiracist slogans and demands have been publicized in fliers, broadsides, T-shirts, buttons, and bumper stickers.

Antiracist protest has also included activities that are technically legal but are threatening to local, national, or international power structures. For example, civil rights activists in the U.S. South tested federal laws prohibiting segregation on interstate buses, mounted massive voter registration drives for blacks, and established Freedom Schools to educate both children and adults. With the interconnected goals of providing for the basic needs of urban blacks and catalyzing antiracist political consciousness, Black Panther Party chapters across the United States created extensive grass-roots programs (free breakfast and after-school programs for children, adult literacy and political education classes, street cleaning, free health clinics, busing family members to visit loved ones in prison, and the like).

Many Black Panthers also became experts in local, state, and federal law to monitor, document, and challenge police abuse. Citing the constitutional right to bear arms, the Black Panther Party and other groups such as the American Indian Movement defended themselves against racist law enforcement officers who routinely brutalized antiracist activists, assassinating movement participants in the 1960s and 1970s.

Faced with centuries of systemic violence and exploitation, antiracist movements have sometimes utilized armed struggle. Slaves burned crops, sabotaged machinery, and orchestrated slave revolts. Slave rebellions were a regular occurrence in the Caribbean and South America. While less common in the United States, many revolts were planned and some implemented, including the raids on white slave plantations led by escaped slave Nat Turner in Virginia that left over fifty people dead in 1831.

The use of armed struggle by antiracist activists in the twentieth century typically occurred only after decades, often centuries, of European/white-orchestrated violence and arduous efforts to negotiate peacefully with European/white elites. For example, the African National Congress engaged in nonviolent political organizing for half a century before deciding to use armed struggle (bombings of military buildings, assassinations of apartheid leaders) in the wake of the 1960 Sharpesville Massacre in which South African police murdered nonviolent protestors. In the 1970s and 1980s, the Southwest Africa People's Organization used armed self-defense against the South African military after decades of apartheid rule in what is now Namibia.

Antiracist social movements have typically utilized a range of strategies that vary over time, depending on level of popular support, resources, elite responses, and other factors. Antiracist movements have historically faced elite cooptation (governments giving token positions to people of color, foundations providing funding for individualistic educational and social service programs) and repression (intimidation, surveillance, misinformation campaigns, infiltration, prosecution and imprisonment, destruction of property, and physical assaults and assassinations). Both cooptation and repression have contributed to divisions within movements themselves. Social movement organizations have often experienced conflict around strategies (nonviolence versus armed struggle, separatism versus integration). Many antiracist organizations have marginalized poor and working-class people, female, and LGBT (lesbian, gay, bisexual, and transgender) activists, a dynamic that in turn has led to internal tensions. Such tensions have sometimes catalyzed the development of other movements. The women's suffrage movement in the mid-1800s emerged within the context of sexism in the abolitionist movement. Over a century later, sexism in both the civil rights movement and the antiwar movement catalyzed the growth of the "second wave" feminist movement.

Antiracist social movements have profoundly changed the political, economic, and social landscape in many parts of the world. Slavery was abolished in the Americas, and de jure racism was outlawed. Antiracist social movements, particularly the U.S. civil rights movement and the anti-apartheid movement in South Africa, have provided ideological and strategic models that have been utilized by other movements, including women's movements, antiwar movements, LGBT movements, disability rights movements, and the AIDS movement.

While living conditions, educational and job opportunities, and political power for many people of color have improved, racism persists, often in new and more complicated forms. Antiracist activism in the twenty-first century targets a plethora of crisscrossing issues such as war, environmental injustice, farmworker rights, immigrant rights, violence against women of color, welfare policy, health care, HIV/AIDS, the criminal justice system, homophobia, and the dismantling of affirmative action. Antiracist activism has increasingly taken aim at the racist practices of multinational corporations, international financial institutions (International Monetary Fund, World Bank), and the foreign policies of the most powerful industrialized nations. This has increasingly involved the development of coalitions and alliances between different organizations, communities of color, and antiracist whites, often at the transnational level. The continuing transformation of racism and its modern manifestations—from genocide in Darfur to the mass incarceration of African Americans in the United States to anti-immigrant violence in Europe—will necessitate evolving strategies and alliances among those who challenge racism in all its forms to create more just societies.

SEE ALSO *Abolition Movement; American Indian Movement (AIM); Anti-Apartheid Movement; Civil Rights Movement; Feminism and Race; Global Environment Movement; Indian Rights Association; Latino Social Movements; Reproductive Rights; Turner, Nat.*

BIBLIOGRAPHY

Carson, Clayborne. 1981. *In Struggle: SNCC and the Black Awakening of the 1960s*. Cambridge, MA: Harvard University Press.

Davis, Angela. 1983. *Women, Race and Class*. New York: Vintage Books.

Fanon, Frantz. 1963. *The Wretched of the Earth*. Translated by Constance Farrington. New York: Grove Press.

Galeano, Eduardo. 1973. *Open Veins of Latin America: Five Centuries of the Pillage of a Continent*. Translated by Cedric Belfrage. New York and London: Monthly Review Press.

Gedicks, Al. 2001. *Resource Rebels: Native Challenges to Mining and Oil Corporations*. Cambridge, MA: South End Press.

Menchú, Rigoberta. 1984. *I Rigoberta Menchú: An Indian Woman in Guatemala*. Edited by Elisabeth Burgos-Debray. Translated by Ann Wright. London: Verso.

Mermelstein, David, ed. 1987. *The Anti-Apartheid Reader: The Struggle Against White Racist Rule in South Africa*. New York: Grove Press.

Zinn, Howard. 1980. *A People's History of the United States*. New York: Harper & Row.

Brett C. Stockdill

ANTI-SEMITISM

Anti-Semitism is most easily defined as "hatred of Judaism and the Jewish people." It is possibly the world's oldest hatred, having inspired aberrant behaviors ranging from simple social distancing to outright murder and mass exterminations for thousands of years.

The term anti-Semitism itself is a misnomer that originally came out of the German world of nineteenth century pseudo-scholarship. *Antisemitismus* replaced the word *Judenhaas* (hated of the Jews), and it is usually associated with the writing of the failed journalist Wilhelm Marr (1819–1904) in his book *The Way to Victory of Germanicism over Judaism*, published in 1879. Marr was attempting to coin a term with a certain "scientific" or rational quality, and he borrowed the word *Semitic* from the field of language study, where it refers to those languages spoken in the Middle or Near East (i.e., Hebrew, Arabic, Aramaic). The term was translated into English as "anti-Semitism," though some scholars now prefer to spell it "antisemitism, without the hyphen and capital "S," to highlight that this phenomenon of hatred and prejudice has no opposite equivalent whatsoever.

Early on, in the books of the Torah, or Hebrew Bible, the enemy of the Jews is given voice on numerous occasions, echoing concerns that still exist in the twenty-first century. In the book of Exodus, for example, the Pharaoh of Egypt remarks to his courtiers, "the Israelites have become much too numerous for us. Come, we must deal shrewdly with them or they will become even more numerous and, if war breaks out, will join our enemies, fight against us and leave the country" (Exodus 1:9–10 [New International Version]). In the book of Esther, the prime minister of Persia, Haman, says to King Ahashuerus, "There is a certain people dispersed and scattered among the peoples in all the provinces of your kingdom whose customs are different from those of all other people and who do not obey the king's laws; it is not in the king's best interest to tolerate them. If it pleases the king, let a decree be issued to destroy them, and I will put ten thousand talents of silver into the royal treasury for the men who carry out this business" (Esther 3:8–9). In both instances, such characterizations may be termed forms of *xenophobic*, or *social, anti-Semitism*; that is, they reflect a collective uncomfortability of these peoples with Israelites or Jews in their midst, as well as the governmental power to do something about it (either enslavement or annihilation). Such views were the norm not only in Egypt and Persia prior to the Christian period, but in Greece and Rome as well. Indeed, this view was held in all locations where Jews resided in larger numbers outside of ancient Palestine.

With the appearance of Christianity approximately 2,000 years ago, and commensurate with the destruction of the Second Temple in Jerusalem by the Romans in the year 90 CE, a shift towards *religious*, or *theological, anti-Semitism* presented itself. Here, both Jews and devotees of this new religion attempted to make sense of what, most assuredly, must have been a holocaust-like tragedy. For normative Judaism, self-reflection and introspection saw the destruction of their sacred Temple as a Judaic failure to observe the condition of the *b'rith*, their covenant with their God. For adherents of Christianity, who were becoming increasingly "gentilized," this horrific destruction of God's central sanctuary was seen as the result of Jewish perfidy, particularly in the collective failure of Jews to accept Jesus as their own messiah. This failure was highlighted by the complicity of the Jewish religious leadership and for some, Jewish manipulation of the Romans to accomplish a Judaic agenda regarding Jesus.

As Christianity became increasingly successful, it allied itself with the power of the state. By the time of Emperor Constantine (280–337) in the third century, the negative view of Jews as "the enemies of God" became normative, with Judaism perceived as an inferior and rejected path to God. The Jews were subjected to miserable living conditions, ongoing economic deprivations, unsuccessful attempts at mass conversions, and increasing ghettoizations. However, they were allowed to survive as a reminder to others of the consequences of the failure to embrace the Christ, as determined by the highest levels of the Roman Catholic Church, its cardinals, its archbishops, its bishops, and its Pope. This remained the prevailing understanding of Western (Christian) civilization until the period of the Enlightenment in the eighteenth century.

With the French Revolution at the end of the eighteenth century, the walls of the various European ghettos were breached, and Jews began their slow, uneven, and often painful integration into Western society. While religious anti-Semitism was no longer dominant, it was still very much present in eastern Europe and places where the Roman Catholic Church held sway. Further, Jews experienced a renewed form of social anti-Semitism, despite their successes in business, government, university education, and even the military.

Building upon a historic foundation of 2,000 years of animus, the Nazi leader Adolf Hitler (1889-1945) saw "the Jew" as a different and powerful creature (though still inferior), one that was mercilessly intent on either destroying Western civilization or subjugating it for his own exploitation. Hitler viewed the Jewish people as the cause of all of civilization's problems and difficulties over the generations. This view was also held by those who allied themselves with him and shared his vision, as presented in his autobiographical and political testament *Mein Kampf* ("My Fight" or "My Struggle"). These individuals also adopted a reinterpretation of Charles Darwin's thinking on evolution, particularly the concept of "survival of the fittest," and injected this "social Darwinism" onto the plain of history, whereby the physical conflict between Germans and others and Jews was now understood akin to the battle amongst various species within the animal kingdom itself. Such an understanding may, therefore, be termed either *biological anti-Semitism* or *racial anti-Semitism,* the poisoned fruit of which was the Holocaust, or Shoah, of World War II (1939–1945), which saw the murders of approximately six million Jewish men, women, and children throughout Europe and Russia.

Manifestations of all of these understandings of anti-Semitism remain present in the twenty-first century, even in places where Jewish populations are notoriously small (e.g., Poland) or essentially nonexistent (e.g., Japan). In the latter half of the twentieth century, a new form of anti-Semitism made its appearance in the Middle East, both prompted and encouraged by a renewal of anti-Semitic expressions throughout several European countries (e.g., Britain, France) and associated with the State of Israel and its ongoing conflicts with other nation-states in that region.

SEE ALSO *Holocaust; Language.*

Kristallnacht. *Men walk by damaged businesses and properties in Berlin. On the night of November 9, 1938, the "Night of Broken Glass," mobs of Nazi stormtroopers and civilians unleashed a wave of vandalism and violence against the Jewish population of Germany. Jewish properties and synagogues were destroyed, many Jews were killed or wounded, and as many as 30,000 were arrested.*

BIBLIOGRAPHY

Carmichael, Joel. 1992. *The Satanizing of the Jews: Origin and Development of Mystical Anti-Semitism.* New York: Fromm International.

Harrison, Bernard. 2006. *The Resurgence of Anti-Semitism: Jews, Israel, and Liberal Opinion.* Lanham: Rowman & Littlefield.

Jacobs, Steven Leonard, and Mark Weitzman. 2003 *Dismantling the Big Lie: The Protocols of the Elders of Zion.* Los Angeles: Simon Wiesenthal Center in association with KTAV Pub. House, Jersey City, NJ.

Lerner, Michael. 1992. *The Socialism of Fools: Anti-Semitism on the Left.* New York: Institute for Labor and Mental Health.

Mamet, David. 2006. *The Wicked Son: Anti-Semitism, Self-hated, and the Jews.* New York: Schocken Books.

Schoenfeld, Gabriel. 2004. *Turn of Anti-Semitism.* New York: Encounter Books.

Steven Leonard Jacobs

ANTI-SEMITISM IN RUSSIA

The term *anti-Semitism* was coined in the nineteenth century in central Europe and is generally understood as dislike or hatred of Jews. Popular and state anti-Semitism have long histories in the territories of the former Soviet Union. Until the late eighteenth century, Jews were legally barred from living in the Russian Empire. Much of the animus against Jews was rationalized by the Christian belief that the Jews had killed Jesus Christ. Czarina Elizabeth (1741–1762) responded to merchants pleading with her to allow Jews to trade in Russia by writing, "From the enemies of Christ I wish neither gain nor profit." Only the annexation of eastern Poland, with its large Jewish population, in the late eighteenth century forced the Russian tsars to admit Jews to the empire. However, they were confined to those territories where they already lived and that were declared a "Pale of

Settlement." This area was a kind of huge ghetto to which Jews were restricted, and, with few exceptions, they could not live in Russia itself, but only on its western borderlands. In the nineteenth century, the basis of anti-Semitism shifted from Christian theology to a more racial one, as the assumption spread throughout Europe that Jews were a race. Many believed this race was united in a sinister conspiracy to control the world and undermine Christian civilization.

ANTI-SEMITISM IN CZARIST RUSSIA

For most of the nineteenth century, and even up to the Russian Revolutions of 1917, Czarist governments imposed restrictions and disabilities on Jews, such as a *numerus clauses* in education and the professions, a quota system that restricted the number of Jews. There was also the "cantonist" episode beginning in 1827, when Jewish communities had to deliver a government-determined number of Jewish boys to the military, where they would serve twenty-five years, sometimes being taken for "pre-military" training for some years before their service would start. Jews were also barred from the civil service and officer rank in the military. Jews were generally barred from owning land in a country in which four of five people derived their livelihoods from agriculture.

The Russian Empire became notorious as the site of pogroms, which were attacks on Jews by mobs of local people. Especially in 1881–1882, following the assassination of Czar Alexander II, a wave of pogroms washed over Ukraine and dashed Jewish dreams of acceptance and integration into the larger society. Mobs of peasants and city dwellers roamed through the streets, attacking Jews, looting their homes and stores, and destroying property, with policemen generally doing nothing. Only after a few days would troops be called out to restore order. A few hundred lives were lost, and there was great material damage, but the psychological impact was greater than the physical one. Jews who had hoped that acculturation into Russian culture would bring social acceptance, and who had preached the idea of Haskalah or "enlightenment" as the path to political, economic, and social improvement, were shocked by the behavior of the mobs and the passivity of the authorities. In 1903, at Easter, always a time of religious fervor and anti-Jewish feelings, forty-five Jews were killed in a pogrom in the city of Kishinev, arousing protests against Russian anti-Semitism in western Europe and the United States. Two years later, in the turbulent year of 1905, pogroms broke out again while Russia was engaged in a war against the Japanese, and while the government was putting down a revolution.

It used to be thought that pogroms were planned by the government, but recent scholarship sees them as spontaneous outbursts, often fanned by the Russian Orthodox Church. The government did little to prevent the pogroms, and it interceded when matters threatened to "get out of hand" and spill over into demonstrations against the regime itself. Russian anti-Semitism became an issue in that country's relations with England, France, and the United States, and it is also thought to have propelled much of the massive Jewish emigration from the 1880s to the eve of World War I.

THE SOVIET ERA

After the fall of czarism in 1917, the Provisional Government, and then the Bolsheviks who seized power in October-November, abolished legislation and policies that discriminated against Jews. However, in the course of the Russian civil war, another wave of pogroms engulfed the western parts of the country. The pogroms of 1917–1921 were much larger in scale and more horrific than the earlier pogroms. It is estimated that nearly sixty thousand Jews were killed, mostly by the White Army opponents of Bolshevism and by Ukrainian nationalists.

The Bolsheviks who ruled Russia after 1918, while militantly opposing Judaism, Zionism, and traditional Jewish culture including Hebrew, opened the doors to individual Jewish advancement wider than probably any other European country. For the first time in history, Russian (and Ukrainian, Belorussian, and other) Jews enjoyed complete legal and social equality. The Soviet government financially supported Jewish cultural institutions such as schools, theaters, magazines, research institutes and book publishing—as long as that culture was Soviet, socialist, secular, and expressed in Yiddish (but not Hebrew). For about fifteen years, Jews had free access to all forms of higher education and to all areas of the state-run economy. Whereas Jews could not even be policemen under the czarist regime, under the Soviets some Jews served as heads of the secret police, as officers in high military and government posts, as editors of important newspapers and journals, and as high-ranking administrators of research institutes and other academic institutions. A Jew served as foreign minister as late as 1939, another as chief political commissar of the Soviet army. There were Jews on the Politburo, the Communist Party's highest organ, as well as Jewish ministers of the Soviet government, ambassadors, and occupants of leading positions in many fields of endeavor, most of which had been completely closed to Jews before 1917.

This openness was narrowed in the late 1930s, eventually giving way completely to a policy of discriminating against Jews by the late 1940s, for reasons not altogether clear. Some have speculated about Joseph Stalin's increasing paranoia and fear of internal enemies and the West, which he identified with Jews. Others point to a rising

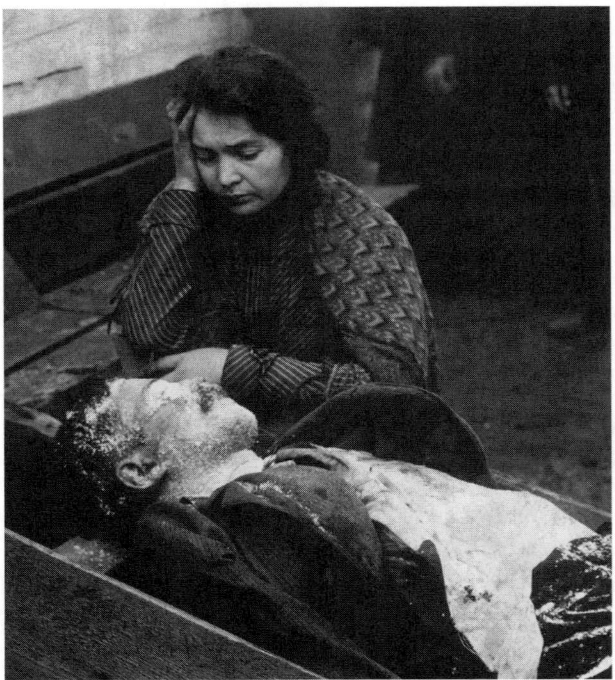

A Woman Mourns for a Pogrom Victim, circa 1919. *Jews were the victims of pogroms in Russia throughout the nineteenth century, but a devastating wave of violence against Jews occurred in the years following the 1917 Russian Revolution.* © HULTON-DEUTSCH COLLECTION/CORBIS.

Russian nationalism, spurred by the same world war that saw large parts of the Soviet Union flooded with Nazi anti-Semitic propaganda. The turn to anti-Semitic policies was visible to all. Whereas in the early years after the revolution there were relatively few Russians who were sufficiently educated to run the government and the economy, the enormous drive to make the country literate and expand Soviet education made literate Jews far less crucial to the system than they had been earlier.

Between 1948 and Stalin's death in 1953, often referred to as the "black years of Soviet Jewry," the remnants of Soviet Yiddish culture were done away with. Yiddish theaters and publishing houses were closed, not a single Jewish school remained open, and an "anti-cosmopolitan" campaign led to the removal of thousands of Jews from responsible positions in the arts, science, government, and the economy. About twenty leading Jewish cultural figures, along with a few who still occupied important governmental positions, were shot as "enemies of the people" on August 20, 1952. The "doctors' plot" in the same year saw a group of Jewish doctors in the Kremlin (derisively called "murderers in white coats") accused of plotting on behalf of foreign governments and Jewish organizations to poison Soviet officials. This seemed to be the harbinger of a collective punishment of Soviet Jews—perhaps the deportation of large numbers to labor camps. A general atmosphere of terror prevailed among the Jewish population when Stalin died in March 1953. A month later it was announced that the "doctors' plot" had been fabricated. The surviving physicians were released, deportation plans were cancelled, but the idea that Jews were not trustworthy Soviet citizens and should be restricted in their access to higher education and to responsible positions continued to guide Soviet policy until the late 1980s.

In the 1960s and thereafter, a series of "campaigns" were mounted against the Jews. The campaign against "speculation" resulted in a greatly disproportionate number of Jews executed for "economic crimes." When the "universal" religions, Islam and Christianity, were attacked, no particular ethnic group was targeted. But because Judaism was considered an "ethnic" religion, practiced by one people only, attacks on Judaism were construed as attacks on Jews. Thus, the campaigns against Judaism took on an anti-Semitic cast. Following the June 1967 war in the Middle East, when the Soviet Union was embarrassed by the defeat of its Arab clients by Israel, a sustained anti-Zionist campaign was mounted and lasted two decades. Jews were equated with Zionists, and hostility toward the State of Israel was easily transferred to Soviet Jews.

For forty years, from the end of the 1967 war until the advent of glasnost and perestroika, Soviet Jews lived in a state of tension. They had been forced to abandon their traditional culture, including their Soviet Yiddish culture, and acculturate (mostly to Russian culture), without being able to assimilate and become fully Russian. Most welcomed the opportunity to "trade in" Jewish culture for the "higher" Russian culture, yet they were not allowed to lose their Jewish identities and become officially Russian. Their internal passports made that clear. Thus, they were culturally Russian but socially and officially Jewish, and being Jewish was to be a pariah or, at least, a second-class citizen.

In *Like a Song, Like a Dream* (1973) Alla Rusinek describes dread she faced each year on the first day of school, when each child had to announce his or her name, nationality, and father's occupation: "She asks my nationality and then it begins. The whole class suddenly becomes very quiet. Some look at me steadily. Others avoid my eyes. I have to say this word . . . which sounds so unpleasant. Why? There is really nothing wrong with its sound, *Yev-rei-ka* [Jewish girl]. But I never heard the word except when people are cursing somebody" (p. 20). The feeling of being marginal and despised is why the fierce loyalty that many Soviet Jews had to their state, and some to its ideology, was gradually replaced by a sense of alienation and rejection, leading over a million people to emigrate.

THE POST-SOVIET ERA

No successor state to the Soviet Union has pursued anti-Semitic policies, though many have not curbed anti-Semitic agitation. When Boris Yeltsin became Russia's first post-Soviet president in 1991, there were said to be forty anti-Semitic journals published there, but eight years later the number of such publications had risen to more than three hundred. Perhaps afraid of arousing a reaction, Yeltsin did not combat anti-Semitism and other manifestations of ethnic intolerance. His successor, Vladimir Putin, has condemned anti-Semitism but has not moved aggressively against its purveyors. A young woman was injured in 2002 when an anti-Semitic road sign she attempted to take down blew up. President Putin met with her in the Kremlin to award her the Order of Courage. While not mentioning anti-Semitism specifically, the president condemned the "bacillus of chauvinism." In July 2002 he signed a law granting courts and other government agencies the authority to curb "extremism," including the incitement to ethnic hostility. Yet several prominent politicians have used blatantly anti-Semitic rhetoric in political campaigns. It would be naïve to suppose that popular anti-Semitism has disappeared or even necessarily waned, but there is disagreement among scholars on the level of anti-Semitic sentiments within the Russian population.

Russian scholars conducted surveys in 1990 in four regions where Russian Orthodoxy was traditionally dominant. They found that those who identified as Orthodox believers had the least favorable attitude toward Jews, while Baptists—who generally rank very low in the eyes of other Christians—had the most favorable views. Even nonbelievers ranked Judaism very low, with only Islam ranking lower. There seems to be a pronounced animus against Judaism, certainly compared to Christianity and, to a lesser extent, Islam and even "eastern cults," though there may be stronger negative feelings toward Caucasian and Central Asian peoples than toward Jews. Other research has found that those who attend church services frequently are twice as likely to be xenophobic and hostile toward Jews than those who do not, though it is mainly older and poorly educated people who attend services regularly.

Unlike the Catholic and many Protestant churches, the Russian Orthodox Church has not changed its traditionally anti-Jewish attitudes. To the extent that this church is identified with the state and with Russian ethnicity, anti-Semitic attitudes are conveyed by it far beyond the realm of religion.

National surveys conducted in 1990, 1992, and 1997 by the All-Russian Center for Research on Public Opinion (VTsIOM) concluded that "the general mass attitude toward Jews can be characterized as the predominance of positive, or at least tolerant, views ... not substantially different from attitudes toward any other ethnic group in Russia" (Gudkov 1998). However, the data show an increase in anti-Jewish sentiments in 1997 (especially after the financial crisis of 1998 and the rising ethnic tensions of the late 1990s) and during the first years of the twenty-first century. The people most likely to view Jews negatively are older, less-educated men who live in small- and medium-sized cities, and who have mid-level incomes and no Jews among their close relatives, acquaintances, coworkers, or neighbors.

There are significant minorities in Russia who have strong feelings about Jews, and these are evenly divided between those who like and dislike them. The largest number of people, however, have no strong feelings one way or another. As the number of Jews living in the country has declined, and as Chechens and other nationalities of the Caucasus have become the objects of widespread fear and animosity, the traditional Jewish bogeyman has receded from the consciousness of Russians. Still, the fact that so many of the economic "oligarchs" are of Jewish origin, and that they are the objects of widespread hatred, is likely to have kept alive stereotypes of Jews as economic speculators and exploiters. Anti-Semitism is an age-old sentiment that rarely disappears, though its visibility varies with the times and the context.

BIBLIOGRAPHY

Aronson, Michael. 1990. *Troubled Waters: The Origins of the 1881 Anti-Jewish Pogroms in Russia.* Pittsburgh, PA: University of Pittsburgh Press.

Baron, Salo. 1964. *The Russian Jew under Tsars and Soviets.* New York: Macmillan.

Dubnow, Simon. 1920. *History of the Jews in Russia and Poland,* Vol. III. Philadelphia: Jewish Publication Society.

Gitelman, Zvi. 2001. *A Century of Ambivalence: The Jews of Russia and the Soviet Union, 1881 to the Present,* 2nd ed. Bloomington: Indiana University Press.

Gudkov, Lev. 1998. "Parameters of Antisemitism in Russia, 1990–1997." *Economic and Social Change: The Monitoring of Public Opinion* 2: 41.

Klier, John Doyle. 1986. *Russia Gathers Her Jews.* Dekalb: Northern Illinois University Press.

———.1995. *Imperial Russia's Jewish Question, 1855–1881.* New York: Cambridge University Press.

———, and Shlomo Lambrozo, eds. 1992. *Pogroms: Anti-Jewish Violence in Modern Russian History.* New York: Cambridge University Press.

Pinkus, Benjamin. 1984. *The Soviet Government and the Jews, 1948–1967.* New York: Cambridge University Press.

Rogger, Hans. 1986. *Jewish Policies and Right-Wing Politics in Imperial Russia.* Berkeley: University of California Press.

Rubenstein, Joshua, and Vladimir Naumov. 2001. *Stalin's Secret Pogrom: The Postwar Inquisition of the Jewish Anti-Fascist Committee.* New Haven, CT: Yale University Press.

Rusinek, Alla. 1973. *Like a Song, Like a Dream: The True Story of a Soviet Girl's Quest for Freedom.* New York: Charles Scribner's Sons.

Vaksberg, Arkady. 1994. *Stalin against the Jews*. New York: Alfred A. Knopf.

Zvi Gitelman

ANTI-SEMITISM IN THE ARAB WORLD

Manifestations of anti-Semitism erupted in the Arab world during the late twentieth century. However, discrimination against Jews has relegated them to second-class status under Arab hegemony ("dhimmitude") since the successful uniting of the tribes in the Arabian peninsula by Muhammad (570–632) in the sixth century. Jews were initially supportive of Muhammad's agenda, for he labeled both Jews and Christians as the "peoples of the Book." However, some Jewish tribes in the region fought against him and his army, while others refused to embrace his Qur'anic revelations, surrender their Judaism, and accept Islam (the new religious interpretation of the Divine-human encounter, which Muhammad defined as total submission to the "will of Allah"). At this point, animus against the Jews set in. This animus continues in the early twenty-first century throughout the Middle East, and even in those Middle Eastern countries where a small and vulnerable Jewish population remains (e.g., Syria, Iraq, Iran). The vast majority of Jews fled from these nations during the twentieth century, especially after the re-creation of the Third Jewish Commonwealth (in the form of the State of Israel) on May 14, 1948. However, to label these earlier various forms of discrimination against Jews in Arab lands as anti-Semitic would be to elevate them to a status not commensurate with historical realities.

As is the case with both the Hebrew Bible and the New Testament, the Qur'an contains passages that alienate "the Other" (in this case the Jews) as "unbelievers" and "infidels," and that address the responsibilities of Muslims to pursue unto death these "enemies of God." For example, the following statement occurs in Sura 4:155, "Then because of their breaking of their covenant, and their disbelieving in the revelations of Allah, and their slaying of the prophets wrongfully, and their saying: Our hearts are hardened—Nay, but Allah set a seal upon them for their disbelief, so that they believe not save a few." Sections 155 through 161 paint a further portrait of the Jews as engaged in wrongdoing, practicing usury, speaking against Mary, and slaying the Messiah (the Christ). Sura 82 posits "the Jews and the polytheists" as the groups most fundamentally against Muslims, while Sura 120 says that both Jews and Christians will "never be pleased with Muslims." Far worse is Sura 5:64, which says, "Among them (the Jews) Allah has placed enmity and hatred till the Day of Judgment," though this is rivaled somewhat, perhaps, by Sura 7:166, which says, "When in their insolence they transgressed prohibitions, we said to them: 'Be you apes, despised and rejected.' "

Whereas such passages are counterbalanced somewhat by positive assessments of Jews in the Qur'an (e.g., 2:47, 2:122, 5:20, 44:32), they do enable those who, like their European Christian counterparts, continue to draw upon a scriptural-textual tradition of sacred words to evoke a religious, or theological, form of anti-Semitism. In the early years of the new millennium, such Qur'anic passages continue to be a mainstay of radical fundamentalist Muslims in their hatred of Israel and Israelis.

According to Meir Litvak of the Dayan Center for Middle Eastern and African Studies at Tel Aviv University, "In 1894, before the creation of the Zionist movement, a book entitled *The Talmud Jew* by the German anti-Semite Eugen Duhring [1833–1921], was translated into Arabic. The publication of this book—which popularized the concept of the 'Jewish threat'—can be considered the beginning of modern Arab anti-Semitism" (Jerusalem Center for Public Affairs 2003). World War II and the Nazi collaborationist efforts of the virulently anti-Zionist Mufti of Jerusalem, Mohammed Amin al-Husayni (1895–1974), brought about a further deterioration of relations with Jews, not only in pre-state Palestine but throughout the Arab world. In addition to continuing and strengthening discriminatory practices against Jews, violent clashes would become the norm in Palestine. Throughout the war period, al-Husayni worked in Germany as an Arab propagandist for the Nazi cause, all the while urging Hitler and the Nazis to implement their annihilatory policies against the Jews in the Middle East. One such example is a comment he made on Berlin radio on March 1, 1944: "Arabs, rise as one man and fight for your sacred rights. Kill the Jews wherever you find them. This pleases God, history and religion. This saves your honor. God is with you" (Pearlman 1947, p. 51).

Since the founding of the State of Israel in 1948, it has fought wars against its neighbors in 1948, 1956, 1967, 1973, 1981, and 2006. It has thus remained a source of bitterness and frustration throughout the Arab world, a situation exacerbated by the ongoing political crises occasioned by the plight of the Palestinian refugees, whose own leadership, primarily Yasser Arafat (1929–2004), has refused to still the violent attacks against Jews in Israel and enter into a realizable peace. His successor as president of the Palestinian Authority, Mahmoud Abbas (also known as Abu Mazen) is the author of *The Other Side: The Secret Relationship between Nazism and the*

Zionist Movement, in which he claims that German-Jewish Zionists colluded with the Nazis in the deaths of European Jews to further their own aims. With the exception of Egypt under Anwar al-Sadat (1918–1981), whose historic 1977 visit to Israel marked a true turning point in Egyptian-Israeli relations, and King Hussein of Jordan (1935–1999), whose own peaceful relations with Israel were continually marred by the presence of large numbers of refugee Palestinians in Jordan, the Arab nations continue to view Israel as a blight or cancer within *Dar al-Islam* (the world of Islam) that needs to be excised.

Throughout the Arab world, including Egypt and Jordan, copies of the notorious antisemitic conspiracy forgery *The Protocols of the Learned Elders of Zion* remain easily available in bookshops. This text was a product of the Russian secret Police, the *Okrana,* at the beginning of the nineteenth century, and it was long a favorite of the late King Faisal of Saudi Arabia (c. 1906–1975) It tells of a supposed secret meeting of rabbinic elders at which they planned to subjugate the world. Long-running television series based upon this text have been shown in both Egypt ("The Horseless Rider," 2002) and Syria. In addition, anti-Semitic cartoons, many depicting Israelis in Nazi uniforms with bloodied and dead Arabs, appear regularly in newspapers throughout the Arab world. Books, pamphlets, and articles, including some by seemingly reputable scholars, depicting Jews, Judaism, Israel, and Israelis as the world's quintessential evil continue to be published. For example, *The Matzah of Zion* by the former Syrian Defense Minister Mustafa Tlas, repeats the Western anti-Semitic canard that Jews require the blood of innocent children in the preparation of the unleavened bread used in the celebration of the Festival of Passover.

Even the terrorist attacks of September 11, 2001, was given an anti-Semitic spin when it was suggested that the events themselves were orchestrated by Israeli and American Zionists, and that Jewish individuals who worked in the World Trade Center were told not to show up to work that day (Gorowitz 2003). Thus, in the Arab world, no distinction appears to be drawn between anti-Semitism (hatred of the Jews and Judaism) and anti-Zionism (hatred of Israelis, the State of Israel, and those who support them).

As to solutions to the seemingly intractable problem of anti-Semitism in the Arab world, the first must be a resolution of the ongoing Palestinian-Israeli conflict. This would remove a long-standing source of anti-Semitism and anti-Zionism among Arab and Islamic extremists and force those in the region to confront the possibility of peaceful, nonmilitary coexistence. Even if this resolution brought about only a "cold peace" of mutual toleration rather than a "warm peace" of mutual cooperation, a justification of Israel as an enemy would be weakened.

A second possible solution, with quite far-reaching implications, would be the more public exposure within the Arab world of a nonliteral and more metaphoric reading of the Qur'an by scholars. Such a *midrashic* reinterpretation of scriptural texts might potentially involve dialogues among both Jewish and Christian scriptural scholars, as has occurred among Jews and Christians in the aftermath of the Holocaust.

A vital part of any peace process would be a commitment within the Arab world, in the aftermath of an eventual peace between Israel and her neighbors, of new educational endeavors at all levels of education, including the universities and Islamic midrasas of higher learning, that would present Jews and Judaism in a positive light. This might include Jewish specialists of Judaic studies teaching about Jewish history (including the history of Israel itself), Jewish religious and philosophical thought, and Jewish holy day and life-cycle celebrations. This would be a sharp break from the situation that has existed for decades, in which many Arab and Muslim students are fed a steady diet of myths, negative characterizations, and false information about Jews, Judaism, Israel, and Zionism, which only continues to foster anti-Semitism.

BIBLIOGRAPHY

Jacobs, Steven Leonard, and Mark Weitzman. 2003. *Dismantling the Big Lie: The Protocols of the Elders of Zion.* Los Angeles: Simon Wiesenthal Center in association with KTAV Pub. House, Jersey City, NJ.

Jerusalem Center for Public Affairs. 2003. "The Development of Arab Anti-Semitism: An Interview with Meir Litvak." *Post-Holocaust and Anti-Semitism* 5. Available from http://www.jcpa.org/phas/phas-5.htm.

Middle East Media Research Institute (MEMRI). Available from http://www.memri.org.

Nirenstein, Fiamma. 2005. *Terror: The New Anti-Semitism and the War against the West.* New York: Smith & Kraus.

Pearlman, Moshe. 1947. *Mufti of Jerusalem: The Story of Haj Amin el Husseini.* London: V. Gollancz.

Poliakov, Leon. 1961. *From Mohammed to the Marranos (The History of Anti-Semitism).* Philadelphia: University of Pennsylvania Press.

Tolchin, Martin, and Susan Tolchin. 2006. *A World Ignited: How Apostles of Ethnic, Religious and Racial Hatred Torch the Globe.* Lanham: Rowman and Littlefield.

William and Naomi Gorowitz Institute on Terrorism and Extremism. 2003. *Unraveling Anti-Semitic 9/11 Conspiracy Theories.* New York: Anti-Defamation League.

Steven Leonard Jacobs

ANZALDÚA, GLORIA
1942–2004

Gloria Anzaldúa was an internationally renowned Chicana lesbian feminist scholar-poet and gay rights activist. She was born in Jesus Maria Ranch, Texas, on September 26, 1942, to a family of Mexican migrant farmworkers and grew up to become one of the most highly celebrated Chicana theorists in the United States. She is best known for her path-breaking work on the intersections of race, class, gender, and sexuality in her highly acclaimed, award-winning book *Borderlands/La Frontera: The New Mestiza* (1987) and her co-edited volume (with Cherrie Moraga) *This Bridge Called My Back: Writings by Radical Women of Color* (1981). She also edited *Making Face, Making Soul/Haciendo Caras: Creative and Critical Perspectives of Women of Color* (1990) and authored numerous essays and poems.

In *Borderlands,* Anzaldúa used standpoint theory as a point of departure to demonstrate the complex realities of people of color in general, and Mexican women in particular, who live "betwixt and between" multiple worlds. Using poetry and an unconventional style of writing, Anzaldúa offered a snapshot of the dilemmas of life in the United States for people traditionally viewed as "Other" to mainstream society, with a major emphasis on the working class, Chicanas, and lesbians.

Anzaldúa described the borderlands as "an open wound," a "vague and undetermined place created by the emotional residue of an unnatural boundary" (1999, pp. 24–25). The borderlands represent both a metaphorical and a geographical space, where the cultural influx of opposing nations creates an unstable, shifting ideological re-creation of those caught in the middle. The result of this constant interaction and renegotiation of power relations is the formation of a new culture informed by the Mexican, indigenous, and Anglo worlds—in short, a "borderlands culture."

In her writings, Anzaldúa challenges conventional models of oral tradition and history. She explores how various cultures have curtailed the opportunities for women, and for those who do not abide by the heterosexual norm. Anzaldúa argues that cultural beliefs are formed by and for men, but that it is primarily women who instill these norms in younger generations. The ultimate form of rebellion within Mexican culture is thus to eschew these norms. One potent form of rebellion is to reclaim one's sexuality. Anzaldua's account of her assertion of her own lesbian identity reveals the contradictions latent within ethnic and heteronormative cultures.

For Anzaldúa, the borderlands is a space to reclaim human rights and reconstitute those Mexican cultural components that have stripped women of their rights, their potential, and their life chances. However, it is not only Mexican culture that stifles women's existence. White privilege, upheld by U.S. national policies, also drives women of color toward marginality. As she writes in *Borderlands*:

> Woman does not feel safe when her own culture, and white culture, are critical of her, when males of all races hunt her as prey. Alienated from her mother culture, 'alien' in the dominant culture, the woman of color does not feel safe within the inner life of her Self. Petrified, she can't respond, her face caught between *los intersticios,* the spaces between the different worlds she inhabits. (p. 42)

Integral to the process of asserting agency and claiming one's identity is the recognition of *mestizaje,* the hybrid nature of ethnic identity among Mexicans in the United States. Anzaldúa argues that a recognition of one's *mestiza* identity is the key to empowerment and forms the heart of a new borderlands culture. She thus seeks to adopt or retain elements that foster strength. But these elements come not only from Mexican culture, but from the Anglo and indigenous cultures as well. One of Anzaldúa's greatest contributions to Chicana feminist theory is the concept of *la conciencia mestiza.* This consciousness is in a constant state of transformation, for it straddles three cultures that at times send contradictory messages. *La mestiza* must therefore be flexible as she develops:

> a tolerance for contradictions, a tolerance for ambiguity. She learns to be an Indian in a Mexican culture, to be Mexican from an Anglo point of view. She learns to juggle cultures. She has a plural personality, she operates in a pluralistic mode—nothing is thrust out, the good the bad and the ugly, nothing rejected, nothing abandoned. Not only does she sustain contradictions, she turns ambivalence into something else. (1999, p. 101)

The objective of this emerging consciousness is to come to terms with all of the inconsistencies and oppositional messages of these cultures. Anzaldúa made it clear that "the answer between the white race and the colored, between males and females, lies in healing the split that originates in the very foundation of our lives, our culture, our languages, our thoughts" (1999, p. 102). When the capabilities of *la concienica mestiza* are duplicated in other individuals and enter into the collective consciousness, change and social equality are made possible. Anzaldúa will always be remembered for her contributions to Chicana/o theory, queer studies, and her activism. She died on May 15, 2004, from complications due to diabetes.

SEE ALSO *Chicana Feminism; Chicano Movement; Mexicans.*

BIBLIOGRAPHY

Anzaldúa, Gloria. 1999. *Borderlands/La Frontera*, 2nd ed. San Francisco, CA: Aunt Lute Foundation Books.

———, ed. 1990. *Making Face, Making Soul/Haciendo Caras: Creative and Critical Perspectives by Feminists of Color*. San Francisco, CA: Aunt Lute Foundation Books.

Anzaldúa, Gloria, and Cherrie Moraga, eds. 1981. *This Bridge Called My Back: Writings by Radical Women of Color*. Watertown, MA: Persephone Press.

Gladys García-López

APARTHEID

In Afrikaans, the language of Afrikaners, the word *apartheid* implies things set apart or separated. The concept and practice of apartheid grew from the history of human interaction in southern Africa. As Brian du Toit explains, "This relationship was born on the frontiers of the seventeenth and eighteenth centuries, given legal recognition in the republican constitutions in the nineteenth century, and justified by church and state in the twentieth century. Essentially, it is a philosophy that assumes the superiority of whites and their responsibility of guardianship over blacks" (1982, p. 157).

By the end of the eighteenth century a variety of slaves (African and Malay) and Khoikhoi (non-Bantu speaking native Africans, or the so-called "Hottentots,") were associated with European communities in South Africa. Settlers, and especially frontier communities, contrasted themselves with the indigenous peoples, who at the time were decidedly different in thought and action (e.g., practicing animism and ancestor worship, making sacrifices, and expressing values that contrasted with those of Europeans). They were also differentiated by color. Whites saw "Christian" and "European" (and "white") as nearly equivalent concepts.

A number of preachers, including H. R. van Lier (in 1786) and M. C. Vos (in 1794), and religious societies, such as the London Missionary Society (in 1799), accepted the duty of serving "slaves and Hottentots." In the early years of the nineteenth century, the Dutch Reformed Church (DRC) considered itself as having a monopoly on religious practice. Thus, the interest and involvement in mission work grew, marked by the establishment of separate churches drawn along lines of color. During the early years of the nineteenth century, following the freeing of slaves and the granting of rights to Khoikhoi in the Cape, frontiersmen trekked north to establish a number of independent republics. They saw this as essential for the preservation of their language (following permanent British Administration starting in 1806 and the arrival of the British settlers in 1820), religion (in contrast to Islam and indigenous religions), culture (civilization as they saw it), lifestyle, and especially color. In *Colour and Culture in South Africa,* Sheila Patterson notes, "Then as now, in the interest of self-preservation, the Boers closed their community.... Racial, cultural and religious criteria were by now completely linked.... The colour-line was to be drawn once and for all, and thereafter the blood was to be kept pure. There was to be one marriage law for the whites and another for the non-whites, and no provision for intermarriage" (1953, p. 173). Due to a labor shortage in the rapidly growing sugar industry in Natal Province, East Indians were imported as indentured laborers. They were mostly Hindus and Muslims, and few of them returned to India following the completion of their contracts. In time, they spread throughout South Africa, establishing themselves in various businesses. During the late nineteenth and early twentieth centuries, colored peoples (the offspring of interracial unions) were on the common voters role in the Cape Province, although segregation was practiced widely. They were removed from these roles in 1955.

Following the establishment of the Union of South Africa in 1910, the separation of the population along lines of culture and color was increasingly glossed under the somewhat benign designation of "segregation." This already meant that whites received favorable opportunities, choice residential locations, job opportunities, and security, as well as unobstructed chances for schooling and higher education. In 1913, General Louis Botha, the first prime minister after establishment of the Union of South Africa, passed the Natives' Land Act, which prohibited Africans from purchasing land outside of the reserves (and a few other special areas). These reserves constituted about 13 percent of the area of the Union.

Following its establishment in 1918, the Afrikaner Broederbond, a secret nationalistic and Calvinistic society, started to give direction to Afrikaner aims and policies. Most historians recognize June 4, 1918, as the date of origin of this secret society. This was when a group of young Afrikaner males met in Johannesburg dedicating themselves to work for "the good right of the Afrikaner cause." Their commitment was non-political, supporting Afrikaner economic conditions as well as Afrikaner art and culture. On December 9, 1919, they decided to become a secret society requiring of each member to take an oath of secrecy and a declaration "affirming his willingness to subject himself to the aim."

Their power grew through their work in the Reunited National Party (Herstigte Nasionale Party, or HNP). The general election of 1948 pitted General Smuts and the United Party (with a strong majority in Parliament) against Daniel Francois Malan (an ex-DRC minister) and the HNP. During the election, the slogan "Keep South Africa White" was prominently used by the National Party. This is the first clear use of "apartheid" as concept and policy. (In the 1982 general elections and after political changes in neighboring Rhodesia—now Zimbabwe—the HNP employed billboards with a beautiful white girl and the words "for her sake don't repeat Rhodesia—vote HNP.") The spokesmen of the Afrikaner Broederbond and HNP proclaimed the importance of this policy everywhere, from church pulpits to academic publications. In 1942, Gerhardus Eloff had published his *Rasse en rassevermeging* (*Races and Racial Mixing*), in which he proclaimed that "the pure-race tradition of the Boer nation must be assured at all costs ... the natives and coloureds—according to our Christian convictions as practiced by our forbears—must be treated as less endowed. ... The guardianship must be one which can stand the strongest test" (p. 104). This philosophy was given shape by studies such as Geoffrey Cronje's *Voogdyskap en apartheid* (*Guardianship and Apartheid,* 1948), which laid out the white government's philosophy and policy with reference to "the coloureds, the natives, and the Indians." The official government policy in 1948 was that the Indians should be repatriated, coloreds should be segregated, and blacks should be returned to their homelands. Thus, Afrikaner nationalism and white supremacy, which brought the National Party to power, ultimately culminated in the establishment of the Republic of South Africa in 1961. What Malan started in his term as prime minister (1948–1954) was carried to its extreme conclusion by Hendrik Verwoerd, first as minister of native affairs (1950–1958) and then as prime minister (1958–1966).

Segregation Sign. *This sign on a South African beach designates a "White Area." Such signs were all too common during the apartheid era.* HULTON ARCHIVE/GETTY IMAGES.

Almost immediately upon assuming the reins of government, the Nationalists started implementing apartheid. In the national elections of 1948 the National Party under Dr. Malan barely won, entering parliament having a majority of only five seats. In the provincial elections the following year the United Party recaptured the seats in Paarl and Bredasdorp and the National Party was convinced that this was the result of the Colored vote. This population category were the only "non-whites" who had full voting privileges. Thus the Nationalists decided to remove the Coloreds from the common voting role. These same considerations resulted in the abolition of African representation in 1959. In time this divided society consisted of the core dominant whites, racially and residentially separated Coloreds (served by the Department of Colored Affairs and the Colored Representative Council), Indians (served by the Department of Indians Affairs and the South African Indian Council), and finally Africans (supposed to be residents of different Bantustans or homelands and living in South Africa with temporary work permits).

Laws, acts, and amendments followed in quick succession. In 1949 they passed the Prohibition of Mixed Marriages Act. The following year the Group Areas Act made sure that white and nonwhite persons were residentially separated, which led to the creation of slums. In cases where whites had maids who lived on the premises, their quarters had to be physically separate from the employer's residence. It is logical that the government, which was guided by the absurd notion of a pure white race, next passed the Immorality Act (1950), which made physical contact across racial lines a punishable offense. Next came the Population Registration Act No. 30 of 1950, which created a register of the total population of the Union. Every person on the register was to be classified as being white (a white person is described as being "a person who in appearance obviously is, or who is generally accepted as a white person"), Colored (which included "Cape Coloured, Malay, Griqua, Chinese, Indian, other Asiatic, and other Coloured") or native, according to the ethnic group to which a person belonged or with which the person identified and associated. An identity number was assigned to every person on the register, and that number was retired only when a person died or permanently left South Africa.

The Constitution of the Union of South Africa established English and Dutch (replaced by Afrikaans in 1925) as official languages of the country. These languages were employed as media of instruction throughout the country. In 1953 the government passed the Bantu Education Act, which enforced separate school facilities and mother-tongue instruction (in the lower grades). It should be kept in mind that especially in rural areas there was a traditional distribution of Africans, including the Nguni languages (Zulu, Swazi, Xhosa and Ndebele) the Sotho languages (Sotho, Rswana, Pedi) as well as Tsonga and Venda. In higher grades English and Afrikaans were employed both as medium of instruction and as course subjects. It is this latter enforcement that resulted in the Soweto student uprising of 1976. The Bantu Education Act also gave direct control of education by the minister of Bantu affairs. Church and mission schools were curtailed and centralized under the government, along with farm schools, secondary schools, and industrial and training institutions. Under the Separate Universities Act (1959) the government closed down a number of black educational and training institutions, including the century-old Adams College—which counted Sir Seretse Khama (Botswana), Joshua Nkomo (Zimbabwe), and Gasha Buthelezi (KwaZulu) among its alumni. It also forced all nonwhite students to attend black (at Fort Hare, Ngoya and Turfloop), colored (in Bellville), or Indian (Westville in Durban) universities. This assured that there would be all-white schools and institutions of higher learning. It also assured that opportunities for friendship, association, better understanding, and intimate relationships could be restricted and avoided where possible.

With separation envisioned in all aspects of living (except, of course, labor and the economy), Verwoerd quickly appointed a commission to look into total geographical apartheid. In 1964 he stated, "One either follows the course of separation, when one must accept the logical consequences right up to the final point of separate states, or else one believes in the course of assimilating the various races in one state and then one must also accept the eventual consequences. These are, domination by the majority, that is black domination." The 13 percent of land surface that had been set aside for nonwhites was soon being designated "reserves," "home-lands," and finally "Bantustans." Under separate development, blacks were supposed to become "citizens" of their black states. As Joel Mervis points out, "It could be described as a kind of bargain—full rights for Africans in the homelands in exchange for no rights for Africans in the White areas. The fact that this bargain is dictated by the Whites and thrust upon the Non-Whites, whether they like it or not is, again, another matter" (1972, p. 73).

The Group Areas Act (1950) assured residential separation and this included Coloreds and Indians. Blacks (through the hated Pass Laws) were assigned to certain "tribal homelands". The pass was a document that every African had to carry and produce for identification. It contained a personal history and work history of the bearer. It was a term that referred to the pass but also involved curfew laws, location regulations, and mobility. When there was an outcry against the "dom pas" (glossed as "stupid pass") government spokesmen excused them as "just like a passport that you and I carry." All persons who were considered redundant, or not central to the industrial and labor needs of the white economy, were expected to return to their homelands. This included persons who had been born in, and spent half their lives in, (white) urban areas. Males who lived in black satellite cities and worked for whites were allowed to remain living either in bachelor quarters or homes, as long as they were employed. Section 58 Act 42 of 1964 (the Urban Areas Act) applied a countrywide system of influx control to women and men alike. They were prohibited (according to Article (10) 1 of this law) from remaining in any town for more than seventy-two hours. Authorities declared that a wife should be allowed into town only if she was needed on the labor market. Under the law a woman could qualify for permanent residence in town only if she was born there or had lived there lawfully and continuously for the last fifteen years.

Women who qualified under Section Ten of the Native (Urban Area) Consolidation Act could also remain. All other women needed work permits. Thus, all black women in urban areas needed to possess documentary proof of their right to be in a town or city. The wife or unmarried daughter of a man who was legally admitted and employed in the town or city had a fair measure of security on condition that she was lawfully admitted, satisfied the conditions of carrying an updated pass, and ordinarily resided with that African male in such an area. An "unqualified" woman who did not satisfy these requirements could take up employment in urban areas but she must receive prior consent from her guardian (if she was under twenty-one years of age), have a certificate of approval from the commissioner of her home district, possess a permit from the urban labor officer, and a certificate stating that housing was available issued by the municipality where she was to be employed. The employment was to be entered in her pass book. The hope of the government was that women in rural areas would draw men back to the reserves.

In the early twenty-first century, a decade after majority rule established a black government, many poor blacks are still stuck in hovels without light and water, and unemployment among urban blacks is higher than ever. The old reserves, which became Bantustans, are still cesspools of poverty and underdevelopment. In short, the legacy of apartheid lives on.

SEE ALSO *Afrikaner Broederbond; Anti-Apartheid Movement; South African Racial Formations.*

BIBLIOGRAPHY

Brooks, Edgar H. 1968. *Apartheid: A Documentary Study of Modern South Africa*. London: Routledge & Kegan Paul.

du Toit, Brian M. 1970. "Afrikaners, Nationalists, and Apartheid." *Journal of Modern African Studies* 8 (4): 531–551.

———. 1982. "Dynamic Factors in the Emergence of the Afrikaner." In *Beliefs and Self-Help: Cross-Cultural Perspectives and Approaches*, edited by George H. Weber and Lucy M. Cohen. New York: Human Sciences Press.

Mervis, Joel. 1972. "A Critique of Separate Development." In *South African Dialogue: Contrasts in South African Thinking on Basic Race Issues*, edited by Nic J. Rhoodie. Johannesburg: McGraw Hill.

Patterson, Sheila. 1953. *Colour and Culture in South Africa*. London: Routledge & Kegan Paul.

Rhoodie, Nic J., and H. J. Venter. 1960. *Apartheid: A Socio-Historical Exposition of the Origin and Development of the Apartheid Idea*. Cape Town: HAUM.

Stultz, Newell M. 1974. *Afrikaner Politics in South Africa, 1934–1948*. Berkeley: University of California Press.

Brian M. du Toit

ARABS AND ARAB AMERICANS

Within one week of the September 11, 2001, terrorist attacks on New York City and Washington, D.C., law enforcement authorities in the United States received 96,000 tips about the allegedly suspicious behavior of persons who fit a racial phenotype associated with Arabs. For at least the next three years, Arab Americans experienced collective revenge for the attacks from the U.S. government and public alike in the form of assaults, harassments, mass arrests and deportations, denials of civil and political rights, media vilification, employment discrimination, and invasions of privacy. Public opinion polls taken after 9/11 revealed wide support for restricting the civil rights of Arab Americans, requiring Arab Americans to carry special identity cards, and subjecting them to special security checks before boarding planes. These suspicions and punishments were related to the Arabic origin of the 9/11 hijackers, but they would not have been imposed on Arab Americans if Arabs had not been previously racialized as a monolithic group with an alleged predisposition to violence and hatred.

Prejudicial attitudes and discriminatory behaviors toward human groups based on their alleged racial traits are certainly not new in American society. Indeed, they lie at the foundation of American society and characterize the historic experiences of Native Americans, African Americans, Asian Americans, and Latinos. Receiving such treatment, however, was relatively new for Arab Americans, who had spent more than half a century in the United States as a comparatively advantaged group. When one compares the Arab American experience in the first half of the twentieth century to that of the second half, one finds that Arab Americans have been racialized in a process similar in form but different in pretext and timing from that of other historically racialized groups. Arab Americans have historically been afforded some of the benefits and protections of whiteness, and their exclusion from the social and political perquisites of whiteness postdates the historic experiences of other negatively racialized groups. It is therefore not perfectly tied in its genesis to ideas about race and the superiority of whiteness that have existed since the founding of the United States. Instead, the racialization of Arabs emerged from the rise of the United States as a global superpower, and particularly from its perceived foreign policy interests.

EARLY ARAB AMERICAN IMMIGRANTS

Arabs who migrated to the United States in the first decades of the twentieth century held structural positions and faced barriers of prejudice and discrimination largely similar to those of white ethnics. Using legal rights concerning property ownership, voting, immigration, naturalization, residential and marital patterns, and employment experiences as primary indicators of their social status at the time, early Arab immigrants and their American-born children—numbering some 100,000 persons by 1924, according to Philip Hitti (1924)—largely fit into a marginal white category, a position similar to that of Italians, Poles, Slavs, Jews, and Greeks in America. Although Arabs were barred from a broad range of institutions run by mainstream whites, they settled without documented restrictions in urban and rural areas, ran businesses, traveled freely about the country as traders, worked as unionized laborers in manufacturing, built community institutions, flourished as writers, and held offices in state and local governments. They achieved a degree of economic success, experienced upward social mobility, and led social lives that were intertwined with members of white ethnic groups, often resulting in intermarriage.

Of course, there are meaningful exceptions to this broadly simplified history, and there were specific localities where the right of Arabs to become naturalized was challenged. During the era of widespread nativism that characterized the United States between 1910 and 1924, Arab whiteness was contested by specific local court clerks and judges seeking to block their naturalization. Such incidents occurred in places like Detroit, Buffalo, Cincinnati, St. Louis, and parts of Georgia and South Carolina. In the words of the historian Helen Hatab Samhan, in some places Arabs were "not quite white" (Samhan 1999). These disparate experiences around racial location underline the notion that race is socially constructed, and that Arabs sat at a disputed margin of whiteness. This marginality is graphically illustrated in the boundaries of the Asia

Barred Zone, a map attached to 1917 legislation passed by the U.S. Congress that erected geographic barriers to immigration and included small sections of the Arab world. The inclusion of parts of Yemen provided ammunition for those who opposed Yemeni naturalization.

These contested racial experiences were neither universal nor representative of the early Arab American experience, and they were counterposed by the widely documented and largely unfettered freedom of movement experienced by Arabs engaged in commerce, which was as true of Christian Arabs as it was of Muslim and Druze Arabs. The existence of variations around race in the early Arab American experience highlights the notion that racial projects are given meaning as they are embedded in local social relationships. Overall, in the early part of the twentieth century, Arab Americans experienced levels of social and political inclusion and economic mobility largely reserved for whites and denied to negatively racialized groups, such as African Americans, Asian Americans, Native Americans, and Latinos. Their experiences were also vastly better than what Arab Americans have faced since the late 1960s. Since that time, substantial evidence indicates a widening social distance between Arab Americans and all other Americans. This social distance is measurable, and it is manifested in government policies, mainstream cultural representations, public perceptions and attitudes, discriminatory behaviors, physical insecurity, and social and political exclusion.

THE SHIFT TOWARD RACIALIZATION

The differences in experience between past and present Arab American generations are due in part to religious factors. The earliest Arab immigrants were more likely to be Christian than Muslim, while the reverse has been the case since the 1980s. But reducing historical changes in the Arab American experience to a Muslim-Christian dichotomy is not as analytically useful as it may appear to be. Anti-Arab sentiments were common in the United States decades before Muslim Arabs outnumbered Christian Arab immigrants. Additionally, since their formation, beginning in 1968, all major pan-American Arab organizations have been staffed by members of both religious groups and share the same objectives: reducing discrimination, stereotyping, political exclusion, and ethnic vilification. Persons with Arabic-sounding names, whether Christian or Muslim, report experiencing job discrimination and anti-Arab comments, and persons with the "Arab-Middle Eastern" phenotype have been physically attacked regardless of religion. It is not clear that the American public has a differentiated view of the Christian versus the Muslim Arab, for the utter simplicity of monolithic, anti-Arab messages has succeeded in precluding thoughtful distinctions. The negative experiences around which Arab American organizations have mobilized preceded by decades the 9/11 attacks, but they laid the groundwork for the collective backlash that followed.

The deterioration in Arab American experiences over time also cannot be explained by economic factors. The earliest Arab immigrants were predominantly uneducated Lebanese, Syrian, and Palestinian farmers and workers, while Arab immigrants since the 1950s have included highly educated Egyptians and Iraqis, predominantly entrepreneurial Jordanians and Yemenis, and better-educated Lebanese, Syrians, and Palestinians. In 2000, According to the U.S. Census, the proportion of Arabs in the United States with high school diplomas and bachelor's degrees was higher than that of the total U.S. population, and this applied to every Arab nationality group. Arab men and women working full-time had higher median incomes in 1999 than did the total U.S. population, a characteristic that applied to all Arab nationality groups except Moroccans and Iraqi and "Arabic" men. ("Arabic" corresponds here to persons who described their ethnicity on the Census form as Arab, Arabian, or Arabic. It differs, therefore, from the collective Arab category. Analysis of census data for metropolitan Chicago showed that, among Arabs, Palestinians were the most likely group to use this term.) At the same time, Arabs had higher poverty rates than did the total U.S. population (17% versus 12%), although this difference is largely explained by recently arrived Iraqi refugees and, to a lesser extent, Palestinian immigrants fleeing continuing deteriorating conditions. While many newer Arab immigrants have low levels of education and job skills, the overall social class background and human capital of Arab immigrants has certainly not lowered over time.

The theoretical construction that best captures the Arab American experience over time is racial formation, as elaborated by Michael Omi and Howard Winant in *Racial Formation in the United States* (1994). The structural exclusion of Arab Americans from a wide range of social institutions has evolved from a plethora of "racial projects" (e.g., in the media, arts, news, pedagogy, academia, civil society, political organizations, public policy, and popular culture) in which social constructions of the essential differences of Arabs (and later Muslims) were put forth so extensively as to be widely accepted as common sense, as evidenced in public opinion polls.

Arab Americans have been racialized using dominant discourses about their inherent violence, which are propped up with confirming images (such as angry mobs) in a process tied to the rise of the United States as a superpower and its *foreign* (not domestic) policy interests. This stigmatization threw Arab American communities off their previous course in American society, for it re-created them as "Others," as people who stand in opposition to Americanness because of their alleged inherent values and dispositions. Palestinian opposition to the Israeli military occupation of their homeland was thus constructed as illegitimate, and Arabs were cast as not only violent but also racist and anti-Semitic, in opposition to core "American values." The Palestinian case exposed the racialized nature of these discourses: Whereas the Soviet, Cuban, and Sandinista enemies were governments and political ideologies, the Arab enemy was the Arab people, men and women supposedly imbued with innate cultural dispositions to violence and hatred. Media fascinations with questions such as "Can Arabs be democratic?" followed, again positing that Arabs, by nature, hold values that clash with the essential values of the United States.

Thus, in their history in the United States, stretching over more than 100 years, the social status of Arabs changed from marginal white to a more subordinate status that shares many features common to the experiences of people of color. Just as one can document and measure the process of becoming white (see Roedigger 1991; Ignatiev 1995), a downgrading of the social status of Arabs in America through processes identified as "racial formation" is also measurable and can be seen in public policies; mainstream representations; social patterns of discrimination, separation, and exclusion; and even self-identification. By the late 1970s, pollsters found that American attitudes toward Arabs were "close to racist" (Lipset and Schneider 1977) and that "Arabs remain one of the few ethnic groups that can still be slandered with impunity in America" (Slade 1981). M. Cherif Bassiouni, a law professor at DePaul University, documented systematic efforts to deny Arab Americans their civil rights in a 1974 monograph titled *The Civil Rights of Arab-Americans: The Special Measures.* Jack Shaheen's 1984 examination of portrayals of Arabs in American television found pervasive and persistent negative stereotypes, including in children's educational programming. In his 1991 study of Arab portrayals in comic books, Shaheen found that out of 218 Arab characters, 149 characters were portrayed as evil. Ronald Stockton's 1994 analysis of anti-Arab images and themes appearing in newsprint caricatures pointed out their similarity to earlier images that showed blacks as inferior and subjectable, Japanese as savage and subhuman, and Jews as socially hostile with "thought processes alien to normal humans." Laurence Michalak, the author of *Cruel and Unusual: Negative Images of Arabs in American Popular Culture,* found that negative representations of Arabs could be located across a broad spectrum of American popular culture, including songs, jokes, television, cartoons, and comics. In his research he found "overwhelming and undeniable evidence that there exists a harshly pejorative stereotype of Arabs in American cinema" (Michalak 1983, p. 30). These and other scholarly studies offer substantial evidence of measurable levels of negative structural discrimination and a dramatic widening of the social distance between Arab Americans and all other Americans.

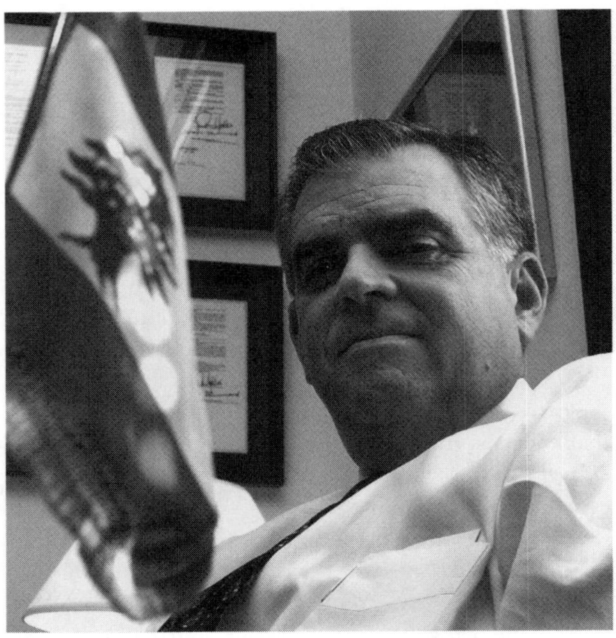

Representative Ray LaHood, 2001. *LaHood, a Republican from Illinois, is only one of a handful of Arab Americans to have served in the U.S. Congress. He is of Lebanese descent. First elected in 1994, he was re-elected to his seventh term in 2006.* AP IMAGES.

Indeed, the most important pan–Arab American organizations founded since the 1960s—the Association of Arab-American University Graduates (AAUG), the American-Arab Anti-Discrimination Committee (ADC), the Arab American Institute (AAI), and the National Association of Arab Americans (NAAA)—have had as their primary organizational objectives the reversal of these conditions of inequality and the dismantling of the propositions of innate cultural difference that lay at their root. One of the first historic studies of Arab American communities commissioned by an Arab American organization (the ADC) noted:

> At a time when the United States is more receptive to cultural pluralism, and ethnicity is no longer socially unacceptable, Arab Americans remain primary targets of defamatory attacks on their cultural and personal character. Thus, much of the activity of the Arab-American community has been directed at correcting the stereotypes that threaten to produce a new wave of anti-Arab

racism in the United States and endanger the civil and human rights of the Arab-American community. (Zogby 1984, p. 21)

SOCIAL AND POLITICAL FORCES IN RACIAL FORMATION

The racial-formation processes experienced by Arab Americans cannot be perfectly tied, in their genesis, to ideas about race and the superiority of whiteness that have existed since the founding of the United States. Rather, the fall of Arabs from the graces of marginal whiteness is traceable to the emergence of the United States as a global superpower. This sociopolitical relationship, although not framed in racial terms, is acknowledged in some of the earlier scholarship on Arab Americans. For example, Baha Abu-Laban and Michael Suleiman note in *Arab Americans: Continuity and Change* that the source of bias against Arabs in the United States relates "more to the original homeland and peoples than to the Arab-American community" (Abu-Laban and Suleiman 1984, p. 5). In the same 1984 ADC report, domestic "images of greedy oil sheiks and bloodthirsty terrorists" are tied to political and economic events in the Middle East (Zogby 1984, p. 21). More to the point, Fay notes that "the source of today's defamation of Arab-Americans might be described as the domestic counterpart of the Arab-Israeli conflict" (Fay 1984, p. 22).

The domestic transformation of Arabs from marginal white to structurally subordinate status was facilitated by the flexibility of whiteness and the historic and "observable" racial liminality of Arabs (a concept that can be extended to South Asians and Latinos). But, at its core, the social and political exclusion of Arabs in the United States has been a racial formation process. Arab inferiority has been constructed and sold to the American public using essentialist constructions of human difference, resulting in specific forms of structural isolation. The seemingly race-neutral lens of essentialized cultural differences became useful after blatant racism had lost its power as an effective hegemonic tool. Nonetheless, the components of racialization were there, including the assertion of innate characteristics held by all members of a group and the use of power to reward, control, and punish based on these determinations.

Because race remains one of the fundamental tools for claiming rewards and organizing discipline in American society (and because this is something Americans know and understand), these notions of essential human difference have been corporealized, as if they were about color. The corporealization is evident in the actionable but sloppy phenotypic category of "Arabs, Muslims, and persons assumed to be Arabs and Muslims." Without these terms and this categorization, analysts could not accurately describe the victims of hate crimes and verbal assault in the United States after the 9/11 attacks. In August 2005, for example, some New York legislators called for baggage checks of persons entering New York subways who fit the "Middle Eastern" profile. But "Middle Eastern" is an artificial construct created in the West, and it has varying definitions. For some, the Middle East ranges from North Africa through Muslim South Asia; for others, it is the Arab countries in Asia; and sometimes its geographic area is left undefined. Very few persons from "Middle Eastern" countries identify with the term. In Census 2000, only 2.4 percent of Arab respondents gave their ethnicity as "Middle Eastern."

Because the racialization of Arabs is tied to larger American global policies, the domestic aspect of this project differs in some ways from that of historically racialized groups in its focus on the manufacture of public consent needed to support, finance, and defend these policies. For this reason, the most noted features of Arab exclusion in the United States are tactical. They thus include persistent, negative media representations; denial of political voice; governmental and nongovernmental policies targeting Arab American activism; and distortions of Arab and Muslim values, ways of life, and homelands. All of these actions are tied to the delegitimation of Arab claims and the disenfranchisement of dissenting voices in order to assert an informational hegemony. Arab Americans have maintained their economic successes despite the context of political and social exclusion, in part because they tend to work as professionals and entrepreneurs, occupations that are largely peripheral to power and the corporate mainstream.

Since the "darkening" of Arabs began in earnest after the beneficiaries of the U.S. civil rights movement had been determined and the categories of "nonwhite" and "minority" had been set, Arabs have experienced the double burden of being excluded from the full scope of whiteness and from mainstream recognition as people of color. They are therefore still officially white and ineligible for affirmative action programs. Therese Saliba notes that while Arab Americans have been victims of racist policies, their experiences are rendered invisible by dominant discourses about race. The political exclusion of Arab voices in mainstream civil society has been reinforced by issue control, through which organizational leadership silences any discussion of issues that challenge U.S. policies in the Arab world (e.g., Palestine, Iraq) if asserting them may frustrate other organizational objectives. In pedagogy, prior to 9/11, Arabs were generally excluded from race and ethnic studies textbooks, and when they were mentioned they were often treated differently than other groups by being held responsible for their own stereotyping (see Cainkar 2002).

The exclusion of Arab Americans and their organizations from mainstream vehicles of dissent left them with few powerful allies after the 1960s, despite efforts to establish ties with other ethnic and racial groups in order to forge antiracist alliances (although they have had some measurable local successes). This allowed their challenges to hostile media representations, textbook biases, and selective policy enforcement to be ignored without repercussions (see Fay 1984). Because they stood virtually alone, discrimination and the production of negative images flourished, pointing to the importance of strategies that ensured Arab American exclusion from civil society groups. The perpetuation and reinforcement of stigmatized views, as well as political isolation, allowed Arab Americans to be open targets for collective punishment after the 9/11 attacks on the United States.

SEE ALSO *Aversive Racism; Cultural Racism; Hate Crimes; Institutional Racism; Racial Formations; White Racial Identity.*

BIBLIOGRAPHY

Abu-Laban, Baha, and Michael W. Suleiman, eds. 1989. *Arab Americans: Continuity and Change*. Belmont, MA: Association of Arab-American University Graduates.

Bassiouni, M. Cherif. 1974. "The Civil Rights of Arab-Americans: The Special Measure." Information Paper No. 10. Belmont, MA: Association of Arab-American University Graduates.

Cainkar, Louise. 2002. "The Treatment of Arabs and Muslims in Race and Ethnic Studies Textbooks." Paper presented at the Annual Meeting of the American Sociological Association, Atlanta, Georgia.

Fay, Mary Ann. 1984. "Old Roots, New Soil." In *Taking Root, Bearing Fruit: The Arab American Experience*, edited by James Zogby. Washington, DC: American-Arab Anti-Discrimination Committee.

Hitti, Philip. 1924. *The Syrians in America*. New York: George H. Doran.

Ignatiev, Noel. 1995. *How the Irish Became White*. New York: Routledge.

Lipset, Seymour M., and William Schneider. 1977. "Carter vs. Israel: What the Polls Reveal." *Commentary* 64 (5): 21-29.

Michalak, Laurence O. 1983. *Cruel and Unusual: Negative Images of Arabs in American Popular Culture*. Washington, DC: ADC Research Institute.

Omi, Michael, and Howard Winant. 1994. *Racial Formation in the United States: From the 1960s to the 1990s*, 2nd ed. New York: Routledge.

Roediger, David. 1991. *The Wages of Whiteness: Race and the Making of the American Working Class*. New York: Verso.

Saliba, Therese. 1999. "Resisting Invisibility: Arab Americans in Academia and Activism." In *Arabs in America: Building a New Future*, edited by Michael Suleiman, 304–319. Philadelphia, PA: Temple University Press.

Samhan, Helen Hatab. 1999. "Not Quite White: Racial Classification and the Arab-American Experience." In *Arabs in America: Building a New Future*, edited by Michael Suleiman, 209–226. Philadelphia, PA: Temple University Press.

Shaheen, Jack G. 1984. *The TV Arab*. Bowling Green, OH: Bowling Green State University Popular Press.

———. 1991. "The Comic Book Arab." *The Link* 24 (5). Available from http://www.ameu.org/thelink.asp.

Slade, Shelley. 1981. "Image of the Arab in America: Analysis of a Poll on American Attitudes." *Middle East Journal* 35 (2): 143–162.

Smith, Mirian L. 2002. "Race, Nationality, and Reality: INS Administration of Racial Provisions in U.S. Immigration and Nationality Law Since 1898." Parts 1, 2, and 3. *Prologue* 34 (2). U.S. National Archives and Records Administration. Available from http://www.archives.gov.

Stockton, Ronald. "Ethnic Archetypes and the Arab Image." In *The Development of Arab-American Identity*, edited by Ernest McCarus, 119–153.

U.S. Census Bureau. 2003. *The Arab Population: 2003*. Washington DC: U.S. Government Printing Office. Available from http://www.census.gov.

Zogby, James, ed. 1984. *Taking Root, Bearing Fruit: The Arab-American Experience*. Washington, DC: American-Arab Anti-Discrimination Committee.

Louise Cainkar

ASIAN-AMERICAN FEMINISM

Women were indispensable to the Asian-American movement from its inception in the late 1960s. Following its black and Latino counterparts, the Asian-American movement evolved out of the antiwar and student movements and, somewhat more distantly, the civil rights movement. As with other racial/ethnic groups that have sought cultural and political rights, the Asian-American movement laid the ground for forging its own distinct feminism.

Activists in the people's movements of the 1960s and 1970s saw clear parallels between their racialized class oppression in the United States and the national liberation struggles in the Third World. But identification with the independence struggles of Vietnam (and the extraordinary valor of its women), then under relentless bombardment by vastly superior United States forces, was particularly strong among Asian Americans (at the time this meant Chinese and Japanese, who were later joined by Filipinos and Koreans). Imbued with an anti-imperialist outlook, Asian-American women did not project men as the adversary when they started questioning their support roles within the movement. The feminism that developed continued to be informed by the perspective that capitalism was the main obstacle to social justice, a view shared by many black and Latino women, but not necessarily by the mainstream women's liberation movement.

The arrival of Asian-American women at a feminist consciousness came after Latino and black women did so. In many Asian countries, families are heavily patriarchal, with women expected to dutifully perform familial responsibilities and, in return, to receive protection by their men. This traditional arrangement, combined with the history of United States exclusionary immigration policies, antimiscegenation, and other repressive actions (such as the internment of Japanese Americans during World War II), magnified the importance of family formation and stability. Moreover, the portrayal of Asian Americans as the "model minority" effectively dissociated them from ethnic groups engaged in street protests, resulting in their invisibility. It similarly rendered Asian-American women invisible to the white, middle-class women's movement. For the latter, "women of color" meant black and Latina women, not Asian-American women.

FIRST FEMINIST STIRRINGS

Because Asian Americans sought alliances with other racialized groups that saw themselves as constituting "internal colonies," or as a "Third World" within the United States, the first feminist stirrings among Asian-American women were anchored to ethnic/racial and class identity. Despite their experience of marginalization by men in the movement, they neither pressed for autonomy nor reached out to white women's organizations for much-needed resources. They held "rap sessions" and study groups to exchange individual stories and analyze their specific predicament as Asian-American women. Two elders committed to overall social change, not mainly to gender, emerged as their role models—the Japanese-American Yuri Kochiyama in New York, and the Chinese-American Grace Lee Boggs in Detroit.

Believing in collective action, women organized to change conditions in their own communities, prompted by the slogan "Serve the People" from the 1960s Chinese Cultural Revolution. They maintained a profound interest in, and connection to, international politics. A landmark event that proved singularly inspiring to Asian-American feminists was the 1971 Vancouver Indochinese Women's conference, at which they expressed solidarity with delegates from that war-ravaged region.

The early Asian-American feminist movement was composed of grassroots, middle-class, and student activists who mobilized around local issues. In Los Angeles, among their first projects were Asian Sisters, a drug-abuse center for women set up in 1971, and the Little Friends Playgroup, a child-care center established in 1972 (Ling 1989). When this women's collective received a Department of Health, Education, and Welfare fund award designated for drug abuse in 1972, its members decided to establish an Asian Women's Center that would encompass drug abuse and child care as well as provide a variety of new services. These included health and pregnancy counseling, birth control, and abortion referrals. Beyond its provision of services, however, the Los Angeles Asian Women's Center acquired enormous significance as a crucial meeting place for the Asian-American movement until its closure in 1976.

Colleges also supplied a hospitable climate for the articulation of feminism. The Third World student strikes of 1968 paved the way for the offering of ethnic studies courses in several California colleges in 1969. The first course on Asian-American women was offered at the University of California at Berkeley in 1970. At the University of California at Los Angeles, the first team-taught course, titled "Asian Women in America," was presented in the Experimental College in 1972. Faced with a paucity of literature dealing directly with Asian-American women, the team of instructors, themselves learning as they taught, assembled readings on women in social movements in Vietnam, China, and Japan. They also called on grassroots women to share their life stories, conducted class meetings at sites such as the Asian Women's Center and the Pilipino Community Center, and solicited community members' attendance. Only in the area of racist stereotypes of Asian women in the media was there an abundance of materials to examine.

Although these courses were designed to address women's issues, race and racism retained primacy. The matter of class cleavages, furthermore, created tensions and exacerbated the problem of focus. To resolve these tensions, a conference held in 1974 presented the concept of the "triple oppression" of "sexism, racism, and capitalism." This formulation, while remote from the thinking of the main current, solidly aligned Asian-American women with Latino and black women. Needless to say, the anticapitalist thrust of the course did not elicit approval from the curriculum committee.

The mid-1970s witnessed a government infiltration of social movements, principally the Black Panthers and the Brown Berets, contributing to their eventual demise. Such a situation could not but reverberate among Asian-American activists. The 1976 closing of the Asian Women's Center has been identified with the end of the Asian-American movement, which was a profound testimony to women's mobilizing. A neoconservative tide swept in that would soon change the character of progressive thinking in general. "Minority" funding once aimed for grassroots organizations was soon funneled to middle-class, professional associations.

In colleges, team-teaching was replaced by specialists trained in ethnic studies and women's studies who now had the benefit of a burgeoning body of literature. The 1989 publication of *Making Waves: An Anthology of Writings by and about Asian American Women*, edited by Asian Women

United of San Francisco, is said to mark the professionalization of Asian-American feminism (Kim 2000). Asian Women United, founded in 1979, departs from earlier associations in its middle-class composition and purpose, which is the production of educational materials.

THE PROFESSIONALIZATION OF FEMINISM

The collapse of the women's movement and its consignment to the academy in the 1980s professionalized feminism and blunted its radical edge. Still, new approaches underpinned by postmodernism have emphasized specificities and the notion of "difference," allowing women of color the space previously denied them. This in turn has led to the recognition of differences, if not hierarchies, inside the pan-ethnic "Asian American" category, which has been considerably expanded by the influx of new immigrants—Southeast Asia (e.g., Vietnamese, Cambodian, Lao, Hmong, Indonesian, Malaysian, Thai, and Singaporean) and South Asia (e.g., Indian, Pakistani, Sri Lankan, Nepalese, and Bangladeshi). These new approaches have also permitted the invention of separate racial/ethnic feminisms, such as "Pinayism" or "Pinay Power," a Filipina feminist response to the once hegemonic (and presumably male) "Yellow Power" (de Jesús 2005).

The flurry of publications by and on Asian-American women reflects these new feminist trends, which are succinctly encapsulated by the "intersectionality" paradigm (involving gender, race, and class, among a multiplicity of identities) that have come to dominate women's studies scholarship. Intersectionality recounts, yet also reverses and undercuts, the "triple oppression" theory of the past by foregrounding individual identity at the expense of systemic analyses.

Whether or not contemporary feminism retains a transformative project, or in what ways and to what extent it does so, is subject to debate. That the focus has shifted from the economic and material to the cultural and discursive is readily apparent, however. Feminist vocabulary, furthermore, has become specialized and accessible only to the initiate. The revised 1997 edition of *Making Waves*, titled *Making More Waves*, illustrates this change. While the first edition took up issues of class and work, war, and activism, the more recent version captures wholly new themes—such as multiple identities, biculturalism, and decolonization—that are patently individualist and discursive in nature, closely hewing to the "cultural turn" privileged by the academy.

If Asian-American feminism has had to make accommodations to the mainstream trend, globalization has also forced it to confront poverty-induced practices such as sex trafficking, mail-order brides, and migrant and sweatshop labor, each of which holds the potential for contesting hegemonic frameworks. But research on these topics, in order to gain legitimacy in the academy, must sidestep global capitalist exploitation and center instead on the everyday "agency" and empowerment exhibited by their subjects. The basic premise is that a socioeconomic elaboration would depict women as victims. Consequently, while able to say more about individual women's daily lives, Asian-American feminism's confinement to the academy has limited its ability to address systemic ills (if, indeed, that is still its aim). It might take another social upheaval to shake the foundations of this conjunctural worldview.

SEE ALSO *Antiracist Social Movements; Feminism and Race.*

BIBLIOGRAPHY

Asian Women United, eds. 1989. *Making Waves: An Anthology of Writings by and about Asian American Women.* Boston: Beacon Press.

Chow, Esther Ngan-Ling. 1987. "The Development of Feminist Consciousness among Asian American Women." *Gender and Society* 1 (3): 284–299.

Chu, Judy. 1986. "Asian American Women's Studies Courses: A Look Back at Our Beginnings." *Frontiers: A Journal of Women Studies* 8 (3): 96–101.

De Jesús, Melinda, ed. 2005. *Pinay Power: Peminist Critical Theory—Theorizing the Filipina/American Experience.* New York: Routledge.

Epstein, Barbara. 2001. "What Happened to the Women's Movement?" *Monthly Review* 53 (1): 1–13.

Espiritu, Yen Le. 1997. *Asian American Women and Men: Labor, Laws, and Love.* Thousand Oaks, CA: Sage.

Kim, Elaine H., Lilia V. Villanueva, and Asian Women United, eds. 1997. *Making More Waves: New Writing by Asian American Women.* Boston: Beacon Press.

Kim, Nancy I. 2000. "The General Survey Course on Asian American Women: Transformative Education and Asian American Feminist Pedagogy." *Journal of Asian American Studies* 3 (1): 37–65.

Ling, Susie. 1989. "The Mountain Movers: Asian American Women's Movement in Los Angeles." *Amerasia* 15:1: 51–67.

Ng, Franklin, ed. 1998. *Asian American Women and Gender: A Reader.* New York: Garland.

Shah, Sonia, ed. 1997. *Dragon Ladies: Asian American Feminists Breathe Fire.* Boston: South End Press.

Wei, William. 1993. *The Asian American Movement.* Philadelphia, PA: Temple University Press.

Delia D. Aguilar

ASSOCIATION FOR THE STUDY OF NEGRO LIFE AND HISTORY

In 1940 Carter G. Woodson wrote to his fellow Americans: "Do not let the role which you have played be obscured while others write themselves into the foreground of your story" (*Negro History Bulletin*, February 1940). Woodson and the members of the organization that he founded played a very important role in fighting the negative stereotypes of African Americans that were created during slavery. In the fight against racism in America, history itself has always been an important battleground. Woodson and his colleagues tackled this huge task by researching, writing, and promoting a truthful history of African Americans. They made it their mission to spread the word of the many positive contributions that blacks made to the building of America and the world.

The Association for the Study of Negro Life and History (ASNLH) was organized in Chicago, Illinois, on September 15, 1915. The next month, on October 9, the association was incorporated in Washington, D.C., and it has operated there ever since. In 1972 the name was changed to the Association for the Study of African American Life and History, or ASALH. In 2007, the association had thousands of members and operated fifty-three branches in twenty-one states, as well as an additional branch in Nigeria, West Africa.

The ASALH collects historical and sociological materials and data about African Americans, as well as about black people throughout the world. This research material is used to publish pamphlets, monographs, and books on the African diaspora throughout history. The association has sought to "promote the study of Negroes through churches, clubs, schools, colleges, and fraternal organizations, and to bring about harmony between the races by interpreting the one to the other" (ASALH).

In January 1916 the organization published the first issue of its quarterly, *The Journal of Negro History*. The *Journal* has long been considered one of the best historical publications in the world. It is an influential outlet for pioneering works of African-American history and a major proponent for the development of the field of African-American studies.

The Association for the Study of Negro Life and History and the *Journal of Negro History* were the brainchildren of Carter Godwin Woodson, who was born on December 19, 1875 and died on April 3, 1950. During his lifetime he became known as the "father of the black history movement," and he was the founder of Negro History Week (later expanded to Black History Month). Woodson devoted his life to documenting the accomplishments of Africans and African-Americans and getting black history accepted as a serious field of scholarship. In addition to being a prolific writer, he was a tireless researcher, an obsessive collector, a gifted orator, and a very accomplished educator.

For more than thirty-five years, Woodson waged an unrelenting, multifront war against intellectual racism in America. He battled antiblack American social thought and misguided educational polices and programs in many segregated black schools and colleges. Through his establishment of the ASNLH, Woodson popularized black history among the black masses. He almost single-handedly opened the long suppressed and neglected field of black history to students, writers, scholars, and researchers seeking the truth about the black presence in the world.

WOODSON'S EARLY LIFE

The son of James Henry Woodson and Anne Eliza (Riddle), both former slaves, Carter Woodson was born in New Canton, Buckingham County, Virginia. He was the oldest of nine children. Woodson and his family experienced extreme poverty compounded by the trauma of widespread racism in one of the poorest counties in Virginia. However, Woodson belonged to a close-knit family in which the chores of farming were shared, and his parents related many stories about slavery.

The late 1800s were a very difficult period for African Americans. It was the end of the Reconstruction period, and federal troops had been withdrawn from the South, leaving the recently freed slaves to survive on their own, unprotected from the wrath of their former masters. Many white Southerners blamed blacks for the Civil War, and many sought them out for revenge. Black public officials were frequently murdered, run out of town, or removed from their positions through violent means, and Jim Crow laws were being instituted throughout the South. The white-hooded members of the Ku Klux Klan, as well as similar vigilante groups, were riding in the night spreading terror and committing countless murders. Lynchings were a part of everyday life in the South. In some towns, lynching "holidays" were held so that whites could picnic and watch a black person being beaten, hanged, mutilated or burned, and finally killed.

Many African Americans began to leave the South during this period. As news of these horrific events reached Woodson's family, they were deeply saddened and more than a little nervous about their well-being. Woodson's father had escaped from slavery and joined the Union Army during the Civil War. He settled in Buckingham County in 1872, and Carter Godwin Woodson was born three years later.

At an early age, Woodson developed a deep hunger for learning. Jacqueline Goggins, a Woodson biographer, wrote of him, "Even as a small boy, Carter G. Woodson was passionate about history. When he founded the Association for the Study of Negro Life and History, it seemed as if he was destined to do so and it became his life work" (Papers of Carter G. Woodson and the Association for the Study of Negro Life and History, 1915–1950, University Publications of America, Introduction by Goggin, 1999).

Carter Godwin Woodson. *Dedicated to correcting the biased view of blacks in America's history books, Woodson was a cofounder of the ASNLH and the founder of Negro History Week, which later expanded into Black History Month.* GENERAL RESEARCH & REFERENCE DIVISION, SCHOMBURG CENTER FOR RESEARCH IN BLACK CULTURE, THE NEW YORK PUBLIC LIBRARY, ASTOR, LENOX AND TILDEN FOUNDATIONS.

As the world would learn, Woodson possessed a rare combination of genius and intellect coupled with unstoppable determination and almost boundless energy.

The young Woodson was not able to attend the local district school during the customary five-month period because he was needed to work on the small farm of his parents. Woodson's father was a carpenter and a farmer who was unable to read or write. His mother and an uncle had somehow learned to read and write however, and taught him the rudiments of reading. He attended a one-room grammar school that was open only four months per year, but he was largely self-taught until he entered high school at the age of twenty. Like other literate blacks of the era, Woodson was often paid to read to groups of illiterate men and women in his spare time, a situation that enlightened both him and his listeners.

In 1892, Woodson left Buckingham County and joined his brother Robert Henry in Huntington, West Virginia. At first he worked on the railroad laying railroad ties, and later he worked in the dangerous mines of the Fayette County coalfields. Woodson became the black community "reader" for many illiterate coal miners, including one Oliver Jones, who despite his inability to read had built up a surprisingly good collection of black historical works. Using Jones's books, Woodson became the literate attraction of the area.

WOODSON'S EDUCATION

In 1895 Carter G. Woodson entered Douglass High School in Huntington, West Virginia. He earned his diploma in less than two years. In the fall of 1897 and the winter of 1898, Woodson attended Berea College in Kentucky, one of the few white schools of that day that had a liberal policy of opening its doors to black students.

Woodson taught in Winona in Fayette County, West Virginia, from 1898 to 1900. Just four years after his graduation from Douglass High School, young Woodson returned to the school first as a teacher then as its principal and remained there from 1900-1903. After several interruptions he received his degree of Bachelor of Literature from Berea College in 1903.

Woodson took a position as supervisor of schools in the Philippines until 1907. He completed correspondence courses in Spanish and French at the University of Chicago while overseas, and in 1907 he traveled to Europe and Asia and took classes at the Sorbonne in Paris, where he learned to speak French. In 1908 he went to the University of Chicago, where he simultaneously took undergraduate and graduate classes. In March 1908 he received his second bachelor of arts degree and in August received his master's degree. Late in 1908, he began work on his doctorate in history from Harvard University.

In 1909 Woodson returned to Washington D.C. to make full use of the Library of Congress. He continued work on his doctoral thesis while teaching French, English, and History at the fabled M Street (Paul Laurence Dunbar) High School. Later he became principal at the nearby Armstrong Manual Training High School, while still managing to do research on his thesis. While Woodson worked on getting his degree, Edward Channing, one of his Harvard professors, argued that Negroes had no history. Channing later challenged Woodson to undertake research to prove that Negroes had a history. He discovered that Albert Bushnell Hart, another of his professors, believed blacks to be an inferior race.

Woodson satisfied his dissertation committee in 1912 and received his Ph.D. from Harvard University. He was the second African American to receive this degree from Harvard; William Edward Burghardt (W. E. B.) DuBois, the only son of freeborn parents, had been awarded the same degree from the same department in 1895.

Sometime in 1913 or 1914, Woodson became a member of the American Negro Academy, a scholarly organization founded in 1897 by Alexander Crummell, an erudite black Episcopalian minister. Modeled on the Académe Français and limited to forty members, the academy had the following objectives: to defend African Americans against vicious racist attacks, to publish scholarly works on racial issues, and to encourage higher education and an appreciation for literature, science, and art within the black community. It was the first organization to bring together black scholars and artists from all over the world, and it had a strong influence on Woodson.

THE FOUNDING OF THE ASNLH

In the summer of 1915 Woodson journeyed to Chicago to attend the Exposition of Negro Progress, which was being held to mark fifty years of black freedom. While living at Chicago's downtown YMCA during the exposition, Woodson met a number of other black history enthusiasts and became convinced that the time was ripe to organize them. Thus on September 9, before returning to Washington, Dr. Woodson organized the Association for the Study of Negro Life and History (ASNLH). According to Dr. Charles Wesley, one of Woodson's biographers, "he was convinced by this date that the Negro would become a negligible factor in the thought of the world and would stand in danger of being exterminated unless something was done to rescue him from history's neglect at that time" (Wesley 1965, p. 173).

Four people helped Woodson form the ASNLH: George Cleveland Hall, Booker T. Washington's personal physician; W. B. Hartgrove, a teacher in the Washington D.C. public schools; Alexander L. Jackson, the executive secretary of the Wabash YMCA in Chicago; and James Stamps, a Yale University graduate student in economics. In October Woodson returned to Washington and incorporated the ASNLH as a not-for-profit historical and educational organization. The board of directors included its founding members. He bought a house at 1538 Ninth Street, Northwest. In addition to living here, the house served as the association's national headquarters for the remainder of his life. Also in 1915, Woodson published his first book, *The Education of the Negro Prior to 1861*, which is often referred to as his most scholarly book.

On January 1, 1916, Woodson published the first issue of his quarterly *Journal of Negro Life and History*. To finance the printing of the first issue, Woodson borrowed four hundred dollars against his $2,000 life insurance policy. He mailed copies of the first *Journal* to the ASNLH membership and to white foundations, and each copy was accompanied by a request for donations and subscription orders. He raised enough money in this way to pay for the printing of the second issue.

While Woodson served as executive director of the association, George Cleveland Hall became its first president in 1916. A renowned surgeon, social activist, and community leader, Hall was a vice president of the Urban League, an early member of the NAACP, and a tireless leader for black rights. He was also instrumental in the operation of Chicago's now extant Provident Hospital. (For many years Provident was the only private hospital in Chicago that would treat blacks.) The Dr. Cleveland Hall Library, located on the south side of Chicago, is a monument to his memory.

Robert E Park, a white sociologist with nine years experience as public relations director for Booker T. Washington and the Tuskegee Institute, became the only white president of the association in 1917. He served in this position until 1921. Park had been a professor at the University of Chicago, and he was to become a teacher and mentor of the pioneering black sociologists Charles S. Johnson and E. Franklin Frazier.

In 1917 the first national meeting of the ASNLH was held in Washington, D.C. Since then the annual meeting of the association has attracted members and observers from all over the country. Held in different cities each year, the event attracts upward of a thousand participants who attend educational and historical workshops, meetings, and a variety of other events. Current leaders in the fields of history, education, sociology, and other relevant professions are invited to speak and make presentations. Representatives of other scholarly associations and book publishers usually are present.

Whereas the association is now housed at Howard University and has a small staff, during its early years it barely survived. The publicity engendered by his Harvard degree helped Woodson create an Executive Council, which once included luminaries such as Julius Rosenwald, the millionaire retailer; George Foster Peabody; J.G. Phelps Stokes, of the Phelps Stokes Fund; and Jesse Moorland, the national secretary of the YMCA.

Woodson worked like a one-man band, lecturing, teaching, researching, writing, and publishing. He used part of his salary from his regular teaching jobs to help keep the ASNLH afloat. To save money he often cleaned the association's office himself. In 1918 he was appointed principal of the Armstrong School in Washington, D.C. He also published another scholarly work, *A Century of Negro Migration,* in which he documented some of the most pressing issues facing African Americans.

Howard University appointed Woodson to the position of Dean of the School of Liberal Arts in 1919. However, a conflict with Howard's white president, J. Stanley Durkee, over the issue of academic freedom led to his being fired just one year after he joined the staff. His friend John Davis, who had just become president of West

Virginia State College (then known as West Virginia Collegiate Institute), offered Woodson a position at his school. After two years at this institution, Woodson found that academic administration was not to his liking, and he left the college.

In 1921, while he was still living in Virginia, he published *The History of the Negro Church*, a pioneering work on the subject. In 1922 he published *The Negro in Our History*, one of his best-selling works. By 1972 twelve editions of the book had been printed. In 1922 he also established Associated Publishers, an independent book publishing organization that he created after having trouble with biased white publishers.

NEGRO HISTORY WEEK

In 1926 Woodson and the association began the celebration of Negro History Week, which was to be used to shed light on and celebrate the contributions blacks had made to America. Woodson stated "What we need is not a history of selected races or nations, but the history of the world void of national bias, hate and religious prejudice. There should be no indulgence in undue eulogy of the Negro. The case of the Negro is well taken care of when it shown how he has influenced the development of civilization" (Woodson 1940). The month of February was selected for Negro History Week in honor of the birthdays of Frederick Douglass and Abraham Lincoln. In explaining the need for Negro History Week, Woodson said:

> The fact is that so-called history teaching in our schools and colleges is downright propaganda, an effort to praise one race and to decry the other to justify social repression and exploitation. The world is still in darkness as to the actual progress of mankind. Each corner of the universe has tended to concern itself merely with the exploits of its own particular heroes. Students and teachers of our time, therefore, are the victims of this selfish propaganda. (Woodson 1940)

WOODSON'S LATER LIFE AND WORKS

In the 1920s and 1930s Woodson donated many of the materials that he had collected to the Library of Congress. In 1926 the National Association for the Advancement of Colored People (NAACP) awarded Woodson the Springarn Medal for his contributions in promoting a more accurate view of blacks in America. From the 1920s through the late 1940s Woodson spent a great deal of time traveling throughout the country, speaking about black history at schools, churches, colleges and universities, fraternities, social and cultural groups, and wherever else there was an audience. *The Mis-Education of the Negro*, Woodson's best-known book, was first published

The Mis-Education of the Negro. *Carter Godwin Woodson's book, published in 1933, criticized the Eurocentric approach to education in the United States.* GENERAL RESEARCH DIVISION, THE NEW YORK PUBLIC LIBRARY, ASTOR, LENOX AND TILDEN FOUNDATIONS.

in 1933 and remains in print in the early twenty-first century. In 1937 he published the first issue of the *Negro History Bulletin,* a history magazine designed for school children and the general public. Woodson's great ambition, beyond isolated books and articles, was to create a massive coherent historical document, which he entitled *Encyclopedia of the Negro*. Other black scholars (DuBois in particular) dreamed of creating a similar work, each hopeful of receiving philanthropic financing. Some seventy-odd years were to pass before such a volume appeared under the title of *Africana: the Encyclopedia of the African and African American Experience* (1999), edited by Kwame Anthony Appiah and Henry Louis Gates.

Woodson had much greater success in popularizing the idea that black history was intrinsically and socially important. Black History Week highlighted this importance, as did the publication of the *Negro History Bulletin*. From his Washington office Woodson promoted the establishment of state and local chapters of the ASALH. Throughout the nation, in the various state and local chapters, thousands of African Americans read his publications and were stimulated to share their ideas with other blacks. Black History Week was a natural outgrowth of these chapters. In 1927 Woodson established a division within the association that contained units he dubbed

"Lecture Bureau" and "Home Study Department." The purpose of this division was to coordinate the work of local ASNLH chapters (Goggin, 1993, pp. 86–87).

For years, Carter G. Woodson was the only African-American historian working independently of any formal educational institution, an unusual situation that attracted the attention of the U.S. government. In 1938 the FBI, the Military Intelligence Division of the War Department, and the House Un-American Activities Committee (HUAC) began monitoring Woodson's activities, thinking it odd that a black Harvard Ph.D. recipient was devoting his professional life to promoting a different version of the nation's past than that presented by mainstream educators. HUAC subjected Woodson to heightened surveillance after he spoke to nontraditional white organizations such as the Samuel Adams School for Social Studies in Massachusetts and the Rackham Educational Memorial School in Detroit. In addition, several of his publications critical of the state of race relations were favorably reviewed by the Communist Party newspaper, the *Daily Worker*.

Woodson received an honorary doctorate degree in Laws from West Virginia State College in 1941. On April 3, 1950, he died abruptly of a heart attack at his home in Washington D.C. He was seventy-five years old. Over the course of his life, Woodson wrote a total of eighteen books, published dozens of articles, and was a regular columnist in several magazines and newspapers. Among the books Woodson wrote and edited are *Negro Orators and Their Orations* (1926), *The Mind of the Negro as Reflected in Letters Written During the Crisis, 1800–1860* (1926), *Negro Makers of History* (1928), *The History of the Negro Church* (1927), *The Negro Wage Earner* (1930, with Lorenzo Greene), *The Rural Negro* (1930), *The Negro Professional Man and the Community* (1934), *The Story of the Negro Retold* (1935), *The African Background Outlined* (1936), and *The Works of Francis J. Grimké* (1942, 4 volumes).

FUNDING THE ASSOCIATION

From the outset, Woodson had trouble raising substantial funds from white foundations and philanthropic organizations. In 1916 he received his first donations from white foundations; a commitment of an annual $200 donation from the Phelps-Stokes Fund, a pledge of $800 a year from the Julius Rosenwald Foundation, and other small donations.

Beginning in 1916 Woodson submitted proposals to the Rockefeller Foundation, the Carnegie Foundation, and others. His proposals were rejected for many years, however. Finally, in 1922 the Carnegie Institute awarded Woodson his first grant in the amount of $25,000. The money from this grant was to be spread over a five-year period, and it was used to secure additional funding from the Laura Spelman Memorial Fund. With these funding commitments in place, he was able to retire from teaching and devote all of his time to the association and his research and writing. Until this time, Woodson's main challenge was finding enough money to support himself, the association, and the *Journal*. He often told people that he was married to the association, and that that was the reason he never married. Beginning in 1922, the ASNLH was finally able to pay Woodson a salary of $3,000 a year.

In 1922, however, Woodson clashed with the transplanted Welshman Thomas Jesse Jones, the educational director of the Phelps-Stokes Funds, over educational policy, and the association lost most of its foundation support. Woodson supported liberal education, while Jones favored low-level vocational education, which he felt better suited the "realities" of black life. By the height of the Great Depression in the 1930s, Jones had succeeded in blocking almost all support for the ASNLH from other white philanthropic organizations and foundations. Despite this loss, as well as pressure to make the association a unit of an existing college, Woodson remained defiantly independent, relying on African Americans for the bulk of the group's revenue.

GREAT LEADERSHIP

In addition to Woodson's tireless efforts on behalf of the organization, the ASALH has been led by some of the most brilliant and influential scholars that the United States has ever produced. The directors of the association have played a large role in making black history a part of the fabric of American life. Presidents of the ASNLH have come from the fields of education, sociology, black studies, and history and more. Among those who have served as president were John Hope, a Morehouse College president; Mary McLeod Bethune, founder/president of Bethune Cookman College; Andrew Brimmer, an economist and member of the Federal Reserve Board; Lorenzo Greene, professor at Lincoln University; and historians Edgar Toppin, Earl E. Thorpe, and William Harris.

After Woodson's death, Rayford Logan, who was chairman of the History Department at Howard University, became executive director of the association for a year. While the association searched for an executive director to replace Woodson, Charles Wesley filled the positions of president and executive director. Wesley ended up working for the association until 1964, when he left to become president of Central State College in Ohio.

Wesley was a historian, minister, and educator. Born in Louisville, Kentucky, he received his master's degree in art from Yale University. He then attended Harvard University, where, in 1925, he received the third doctorate degree ever awarded to an African American. He served on the faculty of Howard University from 1913 to 1942. Wesley first joined the ASNLH in 1916, and he served as president from 1950 to 1965. In 1965 Wesley returned to Washington, D.C., and he was again elected executive director, a position he held until 1972. Later Wesley became president of Wilberforce University in Ohio, one of the oldest historically black colleges or universities in the United States. He served as the first director of the Afro-American Historical and Cultural Museum in Philadelphia in 1976.

For more than twenty years Wesley also served as a minister in the African Methodist Episcopal (AME) church. For several years he served as president of Alpha Phi Alpha, a black fraternity about which he wrote a book. He wrote several other books including: *Collapse of the Confederacy* (1937); *Negro Labor in the United States, 1850–1925* (1967); and *The History of the National Association of Colored Women's Clubs: A Legacy of Service* (1984). Charles Wesley died in 1987.

THE ASSOCIATION CHANGES ITS NAME

By 1970 the word *Negro* had become offensive to many people. In keeping with the changing times, in 1972 the association changed its name to the Association for the Study of Afro-American Life and History. The name was then changed to the Association for the Study of African American Life and History. The association expanded Negro History Week to Black History Month in 1976. That same year Woodson's home was designated a National Historic Landmark by the National Trust for Historic Preservation. In 2003, after years of effort, the U.S. Congress authorized the National Park Service to acquire the house and operate it as a museum, an office for the association, and as a National Historic Site. Renovation on the house began in 2004. During the renovation the association's headquarters was temporarily moved to Howard University.

A library in Chicago was named in honor of Dr. Carter G. Woodson in 1975. In 2003 a ceremony was held for the installation of a historical marker in his honor in West Virginia. In 2004 the state of Virginia's Archives and History Department honored Woodson with a historical marker near his birthplace. Also in 2004, Emory University in Atlanta, Georgia, finally opened to the public the collection of papers, books, and other materials that Woodson and the association had donated to the university's library. Lorenzo Johnson Green, a former president of the association, once said, "The Association is indelibly stamped upon me. It is my cause and shall transcend everything else, even my allegiance to Woodson" (1989, p. 424).

In the first decade of the new millennium the ASALH is a membership organization that has more than twenty branches in many U.S. cities and college campuses. Every year its members choose a new African-American history theme on which to focus for the year. In 2007, for instance, the focus was from slavery to freedom. The association hosts an annual conference—a tradition that began in 1915—where researchers, historians, and scholars present the newest research on African-American history and related topics. Throughout the year they offer teacher training, book signings by new and noted authors and scholars, student activities, and cultural and historical programs. Their annual awards luncheon honors historians, scholars and researchers who have made significant contributions to African-American history. In 2000 the association partnered with the Library of Congress to create an oral history project to collect the stories of U.S. veterans. The *Black History Bulletin*, a publication targeted to primary and secondary teachers, continues to be published semi-annually.

SEE ALSO *Bethune, Mary McLeod.*

BIBLIOGRAPHY

Association for the Study of African American Life and History. "About ASALH: Mission, Vision, Structure, Activities." Available from http://www.asalh.org/aboutasalhmain.html.

Douglass, Frederick. 1863. "The, Past, Present and Future of the Colored Race." *Douglass Monthly* January (final issue).

Goggin, Jacqueline. 1993. *Carter G. Woodson: A Life in Black History.* Baton Rouge: Louisiana State University Press.

Greene, Lorenzo. 1989. *Working with Carter G. Woodson, the Father of Black History: A Diary, 1928–1930.* Baton Rouge: Louisiana State University Press.

———. 1996. *Selling Black History for Carter G. Woodson: A Diary, 1930–1933.* Columbia: University of Missouri Press.

Hine, Darlene Clark, ed. 1986. *The State of Afro-American History: Past, Present, and Future.* Baton Rouge: Louisiana State University Press.

Meier, August, and Elliot Rudwick. 1986. *Black History and the Historical Profession 1915–1980.* Urbana: University of Illinois Press.

Thorpe, Earl E. 1971. *Black Historians: A Critique.* New York: William Morrow.

Wesley, Charles H. 1965. "Our Fiftieth Year: The Golden Anniversary." *Negro History Bulletin* 28 (Special Summer Issue).

Woodson, Carter G. 1940. "Editorial." *The Negro History Bulletin* 25 (October): 422–431.

———. 1970. *A Century of Negro Migration.* New York: AMS Press.

Anderson Thompson

ATHLETICS AND SOCIAL MOBILITY

SEE *Basketball, Boxing, Football (U.S.).*

AUSTRALIAN ABORIGINE PEOPLES

What it means to be "Australian" cannot be understood without appreciation of how race, as a marker of difference, has permeated the colonial and national psyche. In Australia, "race" once implied a difference of appearance perceived as inferior, unworthy, polluting, or threatening, but it has increasingly come to simply mean "different." Two parallel histories interweave to ensure the hegemony of whiteness: one of the exploitation of indigenous peoples, and the other of the vulnerability of a settler colony and nation distant from its founding metropolis.

INDIGENOUS MULTIETHNICITIES

Although imaginings of Australia held throughout the world are predominantly of a "white" nation, it has been and remains one of the most multiethnic nations in the world. The appropriation of an entire continental land mass—with its hundreds of distinct peoples, languages, and cultural expressions—by the British in the late 1700s meant the colony, and later the nation, would always be multiethnic. Military force ensured the suppression of resistance from peoples indigenous to the continent. In homogenizing hundreds of thousands of people as a single "Aboriginal" Other, the diversity of cultural practice was camouflaged, as were the distinctive experiences of colonialism's violent displacements, including the genocide of whole societies.

Different cultural traditions are subsumed under the notion of "indigenous," including the hundreds of societies on the mainland and in Tasmania glossed as Aboriginal peoples, as well as the maritime Torres Strait Island societies that lie between Cape York and Papua New Guinea. It is impossible to do justice to cultural and historical differences here, but they should be borne in mind, for pan-continental generalizations do not serve them well. None of Australia's indigenous peoples developed theories of human social difference based on race. They distinguished "us" from the "other" on the basis of cultural or religious difference. The "us" were linked through relations to kin and country, which established rights and legitimacy. To have neither kin nor country—which might happen to someone fleeing because of serious transgressions—left a person without rights and at the mercy of the society that took in him or her. The first infants of mixed white-indigenous ancestry (generally from white fathers and Aboriginal mothers) were often killed as evidence of abnormality, as were deformed or twinned infants. In time, these children began to be accepted by their stepfathers into the wider Aboriginal social world. It was rare for white fathers to acknowledge their children, preventing acceptance of such children in white Australia.

COLONIAL RELATIONS

The British colonists brought labor to Australia in the form of convicts. They had little need of Aboriginal workers, therefore, but they did need knowledge. The Dharug people of the Sydney area were unimpressed by the new arrivals and kept their distance, so much so that Captain Arthur Phillip arranged for adult men to be kidnapped so he could learn more about them and the harsh country in which he had arrived. Although Aboriginal people found new foods and artifacts attractive, they evidenced little desire to enter into social relations with the colonists or change their own ways of life and belief. Within five years, Phillip gave up trying, commencing a century of government indifference. By the twentieth century, if Aboriginal people appeared at all in Australian history books, it was as an ethereal presence drifting into the mists of time. It was not until the 1970s that historians started to address the silence about the high price Aboriginal peoples had been paying for the building of the Australian nation.

The appropriation of land and the exploitation of women led to hostile retaliation by Aboriginal men, although this was remarkable for its targeting of the actual people who had done them harm. This was not the case for the British, however, whose responses were indiscriminate and often included women and children. The British had the firepower to subdue armed resistance, and one society after another found itself repeating the pattern of resistance, casualties, and eventual accommodation as British pastoralists took over Aboriginal lands.

Labor shortages were common in the rural sector, for heat, loneliness, and a life without luxuries were not attractive to British colonists. As hostilities ceased, Aboriginal people found opportunities to stay on their own land by developing relations with pastoralists. Those pastoralists prepared to accept an Aboriginal presence found themselves with valued workers, and these relations were often reproduced over generations. Aboriginal workers came into their own in the 1850s with the beginning of a half century of gold rushes, the announcement of which would deplete a sheep station of its non-indigenous workers in an hour. Aboriginal labor kept the vital wool industry healthy on one station after another.

The gold rushes also attracted migrants, a large number of whom were nonwhite (particularly Chinese), and this intensified concerns that nonwhite labor would erode working conditions. Racism in the workforce became entrenched and was upheld by trade unions for the next century. Aboriginal workers had better conditions in the Southeast because they were a nonthreatening, and Australian, minority. Equal wages were legislated in New South Wales in the late 1920s. The North, dependent on Aboriginal labor, was very different. Conditions ranged from tough to slave-like, and workers were kept in line by a harsh regime. Equal wages came to the Northern Territory in the mid-1960s, but not without much protest from property owners. This decade also saw mechanization replace many rural workers, including a high percentage of Aboriginal people. Aboriginal employment opportunities have been in decline ever since, statistically camouflaged by a "work for the dole" scheme (the Community Development Employment Program) that records participants as employed.

As the colonies of Australia were being established, liberal democratic and humanist ideas that stressed the equality of all people were developing in Europe. Slavery became anathema, as did repressive regimes. The appropriation of land and exploitation of labor in the colonies clearly contradicted these values, but a concurrent idea, that of progress, sustained the contradiction. "Progress" was a search for purity that encouraged an obsession with social diversity and origins. When Lewis Henry Morgan categorized human societies in 1877 as being in states of savagery, barbarism or civilization, he placed Australian Aborigines into the "middle status of savagery," thus feeding Australia's version of "social Darwinism." On the basis of this retrospective confirmation of the legitimacy of British rule, Britain affirmed the rightness of its appropriation of Aboriginal lands on the grounds that savages didn't have systems of law, governance, property, or religion. Aboriginal people were depicted as the evolutionary forebears of the civilized English, from whom one could learn one's origins, but who were inevitably doomed by their encounter with the modern.

ABORIGINAL PEOPLES UNDER THE NEW COMMONWEALTH

The racializing of Aboriginal peoples' differences constituted them as "less than human" and thus justified excluding them from a modern state. When Australia decolonized from Britain in 1901, Federation further entrenched Aboriginal peoples as Other. Although the Australian Constitution accorded the rights of citizens to all, it explicitly restricted Aboriginal people from certain of those rights by excluding them from the Commonwealth census. The Constitution's "race clauses" protected the colonial hegemony, for citizenship implied judicial equality and the right to vote, an alarming prospect for states with large Aboriginal populations. Aboriginal people who, according to the state in which they lived, had been able to work, vote, buy land, develop small farms and businesses, marry as they chose, and choose their own lifestyle were now denied such rights throughout Australia. Because Commonwealth legislation did not apply to them, individual states had a *carte blanche* to treat Aboriginal peoples as they wished. Subsequently, they became some of the most legislatively restricted people in history, ensuring their segregation from the developmental prospects of the nation.

One of best known of Australia's racist laws is the Immigration Restriction Act of 1901, known colloquially as the "White Australia policy." It symbolizes Australia's preoccupation with racial purity and was designed to exclude nonwhite migrants. So, while the Constitution targeted the racialized Other within, this act targeted the racialized external Other. Both reinforced a nationalist discourse about white superiority, which was now assured by institutions of the state. Even the fiercely egalitarian Australian Labor Party committed itself to cultivating an Australian ethos "based upon the maintenance of racial purity." In the half century to follow, Australia strove to remain the most monoethnic nation in the world. Excluding indigenous peoples, less than 2 percent of the population was nonwhite by the time of World War II.

PEOPLE OF MIXED ANCESTRY

Miscegenation (both voluntary and forced) was common but not discussed, except to condemn its frequency. Manne (2006) has written of this "discomforting new racial type" emerging at the frontier, noting Western Australian Chief Protector, Henry Prinsep's concern that half-castes were "a menace to the future moral safety of the community" and lamented that the law did not allow the removal of Aboriginal children from native camps without parental consent. Western Australian traveling protector, James Isdell, agreed, writing in 1908, "I consider it a great scandal to allow any of these half-caste girls to remain with the natives." He thought sentimental protests detailing the "cruelty and harrowing grief of the mothers" was nonsense as he didn't believe the Aboriginal mother felt the forcible removal of her child any more deeply than did a bitch the loss of a pup. "I would not hesitate," he wrote, "to separate any half-caste from its aboriginal mother, no matter how frantic momentary grief might be. They soon forget their offspring" (cf. Manne 2006). The Chief Protector in North Queensland, Walter Roth, likewise described "half-caste waifs and strays" in 1904 as a "menace to society and a moral disgrace." He pushed for, and received, the legislation to remove children at will (Haebich 2000, p. 215), as did all other states during that same decade.

Racializing discourses argued that the white blood in the "half-caste" meant they had capacities of value and could be civilized into menial work. Decades of legalized abductions of children, even at gunpoint, followed. Most of those taken were children sufficiently fair-skinned to be raised in institutions or foster homes and trained for domestic or farm labor. They have become known as the "stolen generations," and there are many thousands of them throughout Australia.

It took until the 1930s for Australian governments to accept that Aboriginal peoples were not "dying out," and that the "problem" of their presence had to be tackled. A 1937 Commonwealth-wide conference led to policies of assimilation, which were ostensibly moral and material programs of civilizing. Their rationale stemmed from the characteristic belief of liberal democracies that social engineering is a means to shape and manage the good society. But the policy was supported by little public or political will. White Australia was not prepared to assimilate the risks they had been taught to believe indigenous people posed. Aboriginal people had been labeled as biologically inferior, innately hostile and lazy, a health hazard, a moral pollutant, criminal, or simply disorderly and unsightly. Assimilation simply continued a harsh regime of segregation, with some training but more surveillance, legitimated within liberalist philosophy because it was "for their own good." The New South Wales representative, Harkness, reported: "We have 1,000 full-bloods, and the number is diminishing, and about 10,000 half-castes, and the number is rapidly increasing." He added, "It is awful to think that the white race in the Northern Territory is liable to be submerged, notwithstanding that on this continent 98 per cent of the population is of British nationality. It is not for this generation that we must work, it is for the next generation" (Commonwealth of Australia 1937). Assimilation was to particularly target the half-castes. The fear of submergence was real and legitimized the violent dismembering of families.

Aboriginal protest and suffering was intense but ignored. Jack Patten and Bill Ferguson, both of mixed ancestry, were campaigning for Aboriginal rights in New South Wales in the same year, 1937, and wrote a manifesto on behalf of the Aborigines Progressive Association submitted in January 1983 when Australia celebrated its sesquicentenary. It includes the following assertions (see also http://www.reasoninrevolt.net.au/biogs/E000261b.htm):

> You came here only recently, and you took our land away from us by force. You have almost exterminated our people, but there are enough of us remaining to expose the humbug of your claim, as white Australians, to be a civilised, progressive, kindly and humane nation. By your cruelty and callousness towards the Aborigines you stand condemned in the eyes of the civilised world. … You hypocritically claim that you are trying to 'protect' us; but your modern 'policy of protection' (so-called) is killing us off just as surely as the pioneer policy of giving us poisoned damper and shooting us down like dingoes! … We do not wish to be "studied" as scientific or anthropological curiosities. All such efforts on our behalf are wasted. We have no desire to go back to primitive conditions of the Stone Age. … Why do you deliberately keep us backward? Is it merely to give yourselves the pleasure of feeling superior? … We ask for equal education, equal opportunity, equal wages, equal rights to possess property or to be our own masters–in two words: *equal citizenship*! How can you honestly refuse this? In New South Wales you give us the vote, and treat us as equals at the ballot box. Then why do you impose the other unfair restriction of rights upon us? Do you really think that the 9,884 half-castes of New South Wales are in need of your special 'protection'? Do you really believe that these half-castes are 'naturally backward' and lacking in natural intelligence? If so, you are completely mistaken. When our people are backward, it is because your treatment has made them so. Give us the same chances as yourselves, and we will prove ourselves to be just as good, if not better, Australians, than you! … We ask you to be proud of the Australian Aborigines, and not to be misled any longer by the superstition that we are a naturally backward and low race. This is a scientific lie, which has helped to push our people down and down into the mire. At worst, we are no more dirty, lazy, stupid, criminal, or immoral than yourselves. Also, your slanders against our race are a moral lie, told to throw all the blame for our troubles on to us. You, who originally conquered us by guns against our spears, now rely on superiority of numbers to support your false claims of moral and intellectual superiority.

Unable to be white, those of mixed descent were not regarded as legitimately Aboriginal either. Considered neither genetically nor culturally pure, they were evidence of the moral danger these liaisons posed, and they carried white Australia's moral outrage within their persons. "Mixed bloods" became a political problem for governments simply because they existed in a category too hard to confront. Even a person with only one Aboriginal great-grandparent in eight (officially designated an "octaroon") was tainted by this "bit of color." The "half-caste" or "part-Aborigine" (never part-white) often aspired to become acceptable to the Australian "us," but these individuals were consistently denied the right to do so. Their presence confronted the nation not only with its race hypocrisy, but also with its fragile hold on race-based sovereignty.

MOVING TOWARD INDIGENOUS RIGHTS

The civil rights movement in the United States of America turned an embarrassing spotlight on Australia and propelled change. In 1967 the Australian public overwhelming voted in favor of a referendum to change the Constitution to acknowledge indigenous peoples. Some civil rights had been restored by state governments during this decade, and indigenous rights in the form of land rights were also put on the agenda. New freedoms of speech and movement opened up opportunities for political movements aimed at changing decades of deprivation. Attitudes towards Aboriginal people prior to the protest movements of the 1960s and 1970s are best characterized as apathetic. Although the "race" concept was becoming associated with cultural rather than genetic difference, the same inequalities were reproduced. Lorna Lippmann, a social historian and advocate for Aboriginal rights, introduced a new dimension into debates about racism by examining its impacts on Aboriginal peoples themselves. She observed that they expected to be despised, rejected, or ignored, resulting not only in their distrust of whites but also in a low self-image, with long-term negative consequences for social, psychic, and physical well-being. Attitudes and policies started to change in favor of enabling Aboriginal people to take their place within the nation. Land rights and special programs to combat disadvantage were taken seriously by governments.

At the same time, Australia's population was changing dramatically. The White Australia policy was abandoned to accommodate the nation's need for labor in the post–World War II boom. Within a few decades, Australia became one of the most ethnically diverse nations in the world, though this extraordinary shift was not always a smooth one. Labor and refugee migration, and the move from Pax Britannica to Pax Americana precipitated a crisis of national identity during which the distinctiveness of being Australian was often at the forefront of public discussion. In the early 1980s Australia looked forward to the 1988 bicentenary of the arrival of the First Fleet from Britain, but it was not clear what kind of Australia was to be celebrated. Nor was it clear how indigenous Australians would respond to this festival of invasion. A federal government campaign highlighted and celebrated Australia's cultural diversity, and Australianness was redefined as the ability of many ethnicities to live together. Multicultural television, arts, and festivals were supported, and the education curriculum changed its emphasis on foreign languages (German and French) to "community languages," meaning those spoken by Australians (such as Vietnamese, Spanish, Arabic), and languages of trade such as Japanese. Multicultural and Aboriginal studies were introduced in schools, and overt racism became socially unacceptable. However, multiculturalism was conceptualized as an add-on rather than a threat to the hegemony of whiteness. Rather than destroy the myths of purity and whiteness, multiculturalism served to fix differences in the categorization of "Other Australians." Aborigines were incensed at being lumped into a migrant category and fought vigorously and successfully for independent representation in government portfolios.

Unlike colonies with a majority indigenous population, Aboriginal people have rarely called for the decolonization of Australia, but in *Coe v. Commonwealth* (1979), a Wiradjuri man, Paul Coe, challenged the basis of the British claim to sovereignty and the legitimacy of Aboriginal dispossession. The case was dismissed on a technicality, namely that Coe had no right to represent the Aboriginal peoples of Australia. Until 1994, courts continued to uphold the notion that Aboriginal peoples had possessed no property rights in 1788, thus upholding Britain's right to declare sovereignty over the continent under the legal fiction of *terra nullius* (unoccupied or unowned land). In 1992 a High Court ruling in a case brought by Torres Strait Islander, Eddie Mabo, a decade earlier recognized for the first time the prior ownership of Australia by Aboriginal peoples, enabling the recognition of "native title" where these rights had not been extinguished. This led to almost hysterical debate over many months, with erroneous but influential threats that Aboriginal people could now "take over your backyard." The federal government passed the native title act in 1994 to reassure landowners and provide a mechanism through which native title, where it did still exist, could be claimed. It was a major step in the recognition of Aboriginal rights but one vigorously contested by many Australians. In response, the act has been amended twice, reducing Aboriginal rights on each occasion.

There is currently no consensus as to whether the Mabo decision did reverse the apparently disproved notion of *terra nullius*. Isabel Coe, sister to Paul Coe and now with the support of the Wiradjuri people, took a further challenge to the high court in 1993 claiming there had been no act of state on the part of the crown that dispossessed Wiradjuri people of their lands. This case was also dismissed on technical grounds, with the suggestion that it be re-submitted as a native title claim.

Native title claims have been effectively limited by the racist demand that Aboriginal claimants prove their cultural traditions of land inheritance have remained in place, unchanged, over the entire period of their colonization. Now the designation of those with "a bit of color" became a new problem: Did these people have rights as "Aborigines"? When the mixed-ancestry Yorta Yorta people lost their native title case in 2002 it was on the dehumanizing grounds that any entitlement they had to claim Aboriginal traditions had been "washed away by the tide of history." Defined as Aboriginal when exclusion suited the nation, they were denied it when that same nation saw itself as having something to lose. It is a racist legal system that can reinvent peoples' histories at will and deny people the right to change in a society in which change is the hallmark of humanity's success.

ENTERING THE TWENTY-FIRST CENTURY

Two contemporary movements in the early twenty-first century threaten boundaries that have maintained Aboriginal people as Australia's Other. One is migration into urban areas, which is collapsing two centuries of spatial segregation. The second is the recognition of the rights of those maligned as part-Aborigines to call themselves Aboriginal. The Human Rights and Equal Opportunity Commission (1997) held an inquiry into the practices of forcibly taking thousands of Aboriginal children from their families for "a better life," highlighting the personal and social trauma this caused, as well as the denial of cultural inheritance. Although acknowledging the pain of this history, the federal government refused the opportunity for an apology, seen by Aboriginal peoples as a fundamental requirement for reconciliation.

This inquiry did open up greater understanding within Australia to the colonial and recent histories of those of mixed blood. Many who had wanted to pass as white to avoid discrimination, or who had not known they had "Aboriginal blood," were able to identify as Aboriginal. This would have been hard to imagine in an earlier Australia, so intense was the stigma. Now even well-known white Australians refer to their Aboriginal ancestry. However, this "whitening" of Aboriginality is cultural as well as genetic, and it is becoming an issue for "grass roots" Aboriginal people, who now have to deal with people claiming Aboriginality (sometimes through having lately discovered an Aboriginal great-great-grandparent), even though they have no cultural knowledge of what this means. Aboriginal cultural practice, focused primarily on the qualities of social relatedness, is not necessarily visually or materially different. Thus, the assumption that mixed-ancestry people are not different because they are lighter-skinned, wear clothes, or live in houses, which has been commonly but erroneously made by politicians and social workers, is now often made by newly identifying people who are eligible for influential Aboriginal-designated jobs.

A small, educated, and well-known Aboriginal elite is emerging. They do not constitute a single voice and rarely gain widespread pan-Aboriginal support but they do have positions of influence. These are people who understand themselves not as challengers to the state but as legitimate leaders of moves to modernize indigenous lives and reduce poverty and marginalization. Indigenous initiatives are still, however, tightly controlled by governments that hold the reins through funding. A nationally elected Aboriginal political voice, through the Aboriginal and Torres Strait Islander Commission (ATSIC), was silenced when it was disbanded by the federal government in 2004. With no economic autonomy, political autonomy is vulnerable. Federal and state governments have been successful in turning around movements for political autonomy by focusing on the deplorable social and health conditions that persist throughout the nation.

Reconciliation March in Sydney, Australia. *On May 28, 2000, a quarter of a million people marched across Sydney Harbor Bridge to promote reconciliation between Aborigines and the majority white population. The term "Stolen Generation" refers to the Aboriginal children taken from their parents and placed in orphanages and other institutions between 1915 and 1969.* © JOHN VAN HASSELT/CORBIS SYGMA.

The act of racializing is thus being reconceptualized through the pathologizing of the marginal Other. Accusations of substance abuse, violence, hopelessness, and laziness are common—and not without cause, as conditions in Aboriginal communities are becoming worse than they have ever been. Increasingly marginalised by conditions not of their own making, they are accorded little respect by Australians being encouraged to greater individualism and consumerism as hallmarks of success. Otherness is reinforced by an apparently concerned but nevertheless pathologizing discourse that represents "rights" as unimportant, or even as being causal (as in the "failure" of self-management programs), in the face of these escalating social and health crises. The modernist discourse that stressed the inevitability of the demise of different other remains influential. It is an approach that legitimates further state intervention but does not deliver long-term economic viability.

DEFINING AUSTRALIA

An irony of Australian history making was the choice of January 26 as Australia Day, celebrating the landing of the First Fleet from Britain in 1788. In the 1980s Australia Day was reconceptualized in response to Aboriginal activism, bringing greater recognition of the act of injustice it also represented. By the early 1980s, Aboriginal peoples were sufficiently outspoken to fuel fears about how they would respond to the bicentennial celebrations in 1988. In the end, the largest ever pan-Aboriginal protest, when it culminated in a march through the streets of Sydney, was sufficiently peaceful, noisy and colorful that it was co-opted into the overall festivities and reported as just another event in an eventful day. In the mid-1990s federal politicians started to refocus the nation toward the commemoration of Anzac Day, thus de-emphasizing the contradictions of Australia Day and the multicultural ethos. Anzac Day recalls the first major loss of life of the Australian army at Gallipoli during World War I. It has allowed for a more conventional "blood and soil" form of nationalism, with the soil conveniently overseas in Turkey. Yet Aboriginal peoples who have served in the defense forces have struggled to gain recognition and even receive their medals.

The struggle for an inclusive Australianness that admits a painful past and ongoing diversity has led to the recent "history wars." How Australia tells its national story is at stake. On the one hand are those who discredit reports of Aboriginal land appropriation on the basis of state-sanctioned, often genocidal, violence, while others argue that only by looking honestly at one's history does one come to terms with the present and enable a shared future. The history wars have emerged in the context of the 9/11 catastrophe in the United States. Since then, Australian politicians have been faced with waves of refugees from the Middle East. Many have successfully played the "race card" in response, demonstrating the ease and rapidity with which a nation's sentiments can be turned around. Support for Aboriginal people has significantly declined over the same period, as ongoing Aboriginal demands for justice are defused by the simple strategy of pathologizing. Poor housing, inadequate health care and schooling, and the lack of employment opportunities are creating an unprecedented social malaise, and it is not difficult to point to people in dire circumstances and render them a problem of their own making. The media is full of concerned stories about child sexual abuse, domestic violence, organizational failures, and corruption, with Aboriginal people angry at this homogenization and the suggestion that these are uniquely "Aboriginal problems." The late 1990s and the early 2000s were a reminder in Australia that racializing is still an effective political tool, and one that continues to speak loudly to the hip pocket.

The fear of being subsumed by the Other (internal or external) in the Australian psyche is legitimate. As a settler nation, Australians know only too well the violence, denial, and destruction involved in the colonization process. White Australians certainly do not want to become the Other. Ideas of "race" as a means of legitimizing difference change over time, but this history is so little known that the concept is able to be naturalized, as are the injustices and inequalities that "race" theories sustain. The mystification of the origins of the race concept—as an arbitrary categorization of human beings who can be exploited and excluded—works to convince Aboriginal people that if they improve their social and material conditions, the racism will cease. But racism is not the problem, it is the strategy and the symptom. By focusing on it as a problem, one risks believing in it and denying what it serves to conceal; namely the structures of power and privilege that are the reason for selective denigration and exclusion. Race and racism will not be eliminated while they serve the interests of those in power and while those in power control history.

BIBLIOGRAPHY

Aberdeen, Lucinda. 2000. "Australian Scientific Research: 'Aboriginal Blood' and the Racial Imaginary." In *'A Race for a Place': Eugenics, Darwinism and Social Thought and Practice in Australia*, edited by Martin Crotty, John Germov and Grant Rodwell, 101–112. Newcastle, NSW: University of Newcastle Press.

Anderson, Kay. 2007. *Race and the Crisis of Humanism*. London: Routledge.

Anderson, Warwick. 2002. *The Cultivation of Whiteness: Science, Health and Racial Destiny in Australia*. Melbourne: Melbourne University Press.

Attwood, Bain, ed. 1996. *In the Age of Mabo: History, Aborigines and Australia*. Sydney: Allen and Unwin.

Augoustinos, Martha, and Amanda LeCouteur. 2004. "On Whether to Apologize to Indigenous Australians: The Denial of White Guilt." In *Collective Guilt: International Perspectives*, edited by Nyla Branscombe and Bertjan Doosje, 236–261. Melbourne: Cambridge University Press.

Beresford, Quentin, and Paul Omaji. 1998. *Our State of Mind: Racial Planning and the Stolen Generations*. Fremantle: Fremantle Arts Centre Press.

Betts, Katherine. 1999. *The Great Divide: Immigration Politics in Australia*. Sydney: Duffy and Snellgrove.

Bird, Greta. 1987. *The 'Civilising Mission': Race and the Construction of Crime*. Layton: Monash University.

Butcher, Barry, 1999. "Darwin Down Under: Science, Religion and Evolution in Australia." In *Disseminating Darwin*, edited by Ronald Numbers and John Stenhouse, 39–59. Melbourne: Cambridge University Press.

Chesterman, John, and Brian Galligan, 1997. *Citizens without Rights: Aborigines and Australian Citizenship.* Melbourne: Cambridge University Press.

Commonwealth of Australia. 1937. *Aboriginal Welfare: Initial Conference of Commonwealth and State Aboriginal Authorities.* Canberra: Government Printer.

Cowlishaw, Gillian. 1988. *Black, White or Brindle: Race in Rural Australia.* Melbourne: Cambridge University Press.

———. 2004. *Blackfellas, Whitefellas, and the Hidden Injuries of Race.* Oxford: Blackwell Publishing.

———, and Barry Morris, eds. 1997. *Race Matters.* Canberra: Aboriginal Studies Press.

Cunneen, Chris, David Fraser, and Stephen Thomsen, eds. 1997. *Faces of Hate: Hate Crime in Australia.* Sydney: Hawkins Press.

Curthoys, Ann. 2002. *Freedom Ride: A Freedom Rider Remembers.* Sydney: Allen and Unwin.

———, and Andrew Markus, eds. 1978. *Who Are Our Enemies? Racism and the Australian Working Class.* Sydney: Hale and Iremonger.

Dodson, Mick. 1994. "The End of the Beginning: Re(de)fining Aboriginality." *Australian Aboriginal Studies.* 1994/1: 2–13.

Dunn, Kevin. 2003. *Racism in Australia: Findings of a Survey on Racist Attitudes and Experiences of Racism.* National Europe Centre Paper No. 77, University of Sydney.

Evans, Raymond, Kay Saunders, and Kathryn Cronin. 1993 [1975]. *Race Relations in Colonial Queensland: A History of Exclusion, Exploitation and Extermination,* 3rd edition. Queensland: University of Queensland Press.

Francis, Mark. 1996. "'Social Darwinism' and the Construction of Institutionalised Racism in Australia." *Journal of Australian Studies* 50/51: 90–105.

Gardiner-Garden, John. 1994. "The Mabo Debate—A Chronology." In *Parliamentary Research Service: Mabo Papers,* 141–193. Australian Government Publishing Service.

Gascoigne, John. 2002. *The Enlightenment and the Origins of European Australia.* Melbourne: Cambridge University Press.

Gilbert, Kevin. 1973. *Because a White Man'll Never Do It.* Sydney: Angus and Robertson.

Haebich, Anna. 2000. *Broken Circles: Fragmenting Indigenous Families 1800-2000.* Fremantle: Fremantle Arts Centre Press.

Hage, Ghassan. 1998. *White Nation: Fantasies of White Supremacy in a Multicultural Society.* Sydney: Pluto Press.

———. 2003. *Against Paranoid Nationalism: Searching for Hope in a Shrinking Society.* Sydney: Pluto Press.

Hall, Richard. 1998. *Black Armband Days.* Vintage: Random House Australia.

Hartwig, Mervyn. 1972. "Aborigines and Racism." In *Racism: The Australian Experience,* Vol. 2, edited by Frank Stevens, 9–24. Sydney: ANZ Book Company.

Hiatt, Lester Richard. 1996. *Arguments about Aborigines.* Cambridge: Cambridge University Press.

Horton, David, ed. 1994. *The Encyclopedia of Aboriginal Australia.* Canberra: Aboriginal Studies Press.

Human Rights and Equal Opportunities Commission (HREOC). 1997. "Bringing Them Home: Report of the Inquiry into the Forcible Removal of Aboriginal and Torres Strait Islander Children from their Families Sydney." Australian Government Publishing Service.

Human Rights and Equal Opportunities Commission (HREOC). 2002. "Aboriginal and Torres Strait Islander Social Justice Commissioner Report 2002." Australian Government Publishing Service.

Jackman, Simon. 1998. "Pauline Hanson, the Mainstream, and Political Elites: The Place of Race in Australian Political Ideology." *Australian Journal of Political Science* 33: 167–186.

Jayasuriya, Laksiri, David Walker, and Jan Gothard, eds. 2003. *Legacies of White Australia: Race, Culture and Nation.* Nedlands, WA: University of Western Australian Press.

Kevin, Tony. 2004. *A Certain Maritime Incident.* Melbourne: Scribe.

Libby, Ronald. 1992. *Hawke's Law: The Politics of Mining and Aboriginal Land Rights in Australia.* Nedlands: University of Western Australian Press.

Lippman, Lorna. 1972. "Aboriginal-White Attitudes: A Syndrome of Race Prejudice." In *Racism: The Australian Experience.* Vol. 2, *Black versus White,* edited by Frank S. Stevens, 25–34. Sydney: Australia and New Zealand Book Company.

Manne, Robert. 2001. *In Denial: The Stolen Generations and the Right.* Australian Quarterly Essay. Issue 1.

———. 2003. "A Long Trek to the Truth." *The Washington Post* February 2: B01.

Marcus, Andrew. 1990. *Governing Savages.* Sydney: Allen & Unwin.

———. 2001. *Race: John Howard and the Politics of Race.* Sydney: Allen and Unwin.

McGregor, Russell. 1997. *Imagined Destinies: Aboriginal Australians and the Doomed Race Theory, 1880–1939.* Melbourne: Melbourne University Press.

Gaynor Macdonald, with Marianne Hoyd

AVERSIVE RACISM

Aversive racism is a form of contemporary racism that manifests at the individual level. Compared to the traditional form of racism, aversive racism operates, often unconsciously, in subtle and indirect ways. People whose behavior is characterized by aversive racism (aversive racists) sympathize with victims of past injustice, support the principle of racial equality, and regard themselves as nonprejudiced, but at the same time they possess negative feelings and beliefs about blacks or other groups. It is hypothesized that aversive racism characterizes the racial attitudes of many well-educated and liberal whites in the United States, as well the attitudes of members of dominant groups toward minority groups in other countries with strong contemporary egalitarian values but discriminatory histories or policies. Despite its subtle expression, the consequences of aversive racism are as significant and pernicious as those of the traditional, overt form (e.g., the restriction of economic opportunity).

NATURE OF THE ATTITUDES

A critical aspect of the aversive racism framework is the conflict between aversive racists' denial of personal prejudice and the underlying unconscious negative attitudes and beliefs about particular minority groups. Because of current cultural values in the United States, most whites have strong convictions concerning fairness, justice, and racial equality. However, because of a range of normal cognitive, motivational, and sociocultural processes that promote intergroup biases, most whites also develop some negative feelings toward or beliefs about blacks. They are often unaware of these feelings, however, or they try to dissociate such attitudes from their nonprejudiced self-images. The negative feelings that aversive racists have toward blacks do not reflect open hostility or hatred. Instead, aversive racists' reactions may involve discomfort, uneasiness, disgust, and sometimes fear. That is, they find blacks "aversive," while at the same time they find any suggestion that they might be prejudiced "aversive" as well. Thus, aversive racism may often involve more positive reactions to whites than to blacks, reflecting a pro-in-group rather than an anti-out-group orientation, thereby avoiding the stigma of overt bigotry and protecting a nonprejudiced self-image. Recent research in social cognition has yielded new techniques for assessing both unconscious (implicit) and conscious (explicit), attitudes and stereotypes, and these methods provide direct evidence of the dissociated, often ambivalent, attitudes that characterize aversive racism.

In contrast to traditional approaches that emphasize the psychopathology of prejudice, the feelings and beliefs that underlie aversive racism are rooted in normal, often adaptive, psychological processes. These processes include both individual and intergroup factors. Individual-level factors involve cognitive biases associated with social categorization. For instance, when people categorize others as members of specific groups, which often occurs automatically, people evaluate in-group members more favorably than out-group members, remember positive information better about in-group than about out-group members, and discount negative actions by in-group members more than those by out-group members. In terms of motivation, people have needs for power and status, not only for themselves but also for their groups, and bias can help foster a sense of status and esteem, both individually and collectively. Sociocultural influences also contribute to aversive racists' negative feelings and beliefs. For example, upon categorization, cultural stereotypes are spontaneously activated. Intergroup processes, such as system-justifying ideologies, perceived competition over material resources, or conflict between cultural values, can also form a basis for the negative component of aversive racists' attitudes.

Other forms of contemporary racial biases, such as symbolic racism and modern racism, also recognize the complex nature of whites' racial attitudes. Like aversive racism, Modern Racism Theory posits that whites' attitudes toward blacks have both positive and negative components, but the role of ideology is different. Aversive racism is presumed to reflect the racial biases of political liberals, whereas modern racism is hypothesized to represent the subtle bias of conservatives. Although both aversive racists and modern racists strongly endorse egalitarian values, what they mean by "equality" differs. Whereas aversive racists are concerned about equality of outcomes, modern racists, because of their conservatively based ideologies, emphasize equality of opportunity. Thus, beliefs associated with conservative ideologies, such as the perception that blacks' lack of motivation accounts for racial disparities, can justify discriminatory behaviors.

What distinguishes the aversive racism framework from Symbolic Racism Theory is the nature of the relationship between the components. The aversive racism position proposes that the attitudes of aversive racists involve separate, dissociated positive and negative components, which are in conflict and thus may, at times, be experienced as ambivalence. The concept of symbolic racism, which has evolved over time, emphasizes the blending of the different components into a single orientation. Specifically, symbolic racism reflects the unique assimilation of individualistic values and negative racial affect. It involves both the denial of contemporary discrimination and negative beliefs about blacks' work ethic, which produces resentment of blacks' demands for special benefits because of their race. Thus, although aversive racism and symbolic racism perspectives often predict similar behaviors, such as resistance to policies designed to benefit blacks, they are the result of different underlying processes.

SUBTLE BIAS

The aversive racism framework also helps to identify when discrimination against blacks and other minority groups will or will not occur. Whereas old-fashioned racists exhibit a direct and overt pattern of discrimination, aversive racists' actions may appear more variable and inconsistent. Sometimes they discriminate (manifesting their negative feelings), and sometimes they do not (reflecting their egalitarian beliefs).

Because aversive racists consciously recognize and endorse egalitarian values and because they truly aspire to be nonprejudiced, they will not discriminate in situations in which strong social norms would make discrimination obvious to others and to themselves. Specifically, when people are presented with a situation in which the normatively appropriate response is clear (i.e., in which right and wrong is clearly defined), aversive racists will not discriminate against blacks. In these contexts, aversive racists will

Aversive Racism and Police Violence. *A cartoon by the sometimes controversial Kirk Anderson highlights the circular thinking that can lie behind race-based prejudice and violence.* KIRK ANDERSON.

be especially motivated to avoid feelings, beliefs, and behaviors that could be associated with racist intent. To avoid the attribution of racist intent, aversive racists will either treat blacks and whites equally or they will respond even more favorably to blacks than to whites. In such a situation, wrongdoing, which would directly threaten their nonprejudiced self-image, would be too costly. However, because aversive racists still possess feelings of uneasiness, these feelings will eventually be expressed, but they will be expressed in subtle, indirect, and rationalizable ways. For instance, discrimination will occur in situations in which normative structure is weak, when the guidelines for appropriate behavior are vague, or when the basis for social judgment is ambiguous. In addition, discrimination will occur when an aversive racist can justify or rationalize a negative response on the basis of some factor other than race. Under these circumstances, aversive racists may engage in behaviors that ultimately harm blacks, but they will do so in ways that allow them to maintain their self-image as nonprejudiced and that insulate them from recognizing that their behavior is not color-blind.

Evidence in support of the aversive racism framework comes from a range of paradigms. For instance, white bystanders who are the only witness to an emergency (and thus are fully responsible for helping) are just as likely to help a black victim as a white victim. However, when white bystanders believe that others also witness the emergency (distributing the responsibility for helping), they are less likely to help a black victim than a white victim. In personnel or college-admission selection decisions, whites do not discriminate on the basis of race when candidates have very strong or weak qualifications. Nevertheless, they do discriminate against blacks when the candidates have moderate qualifications and the appropriate decision is therefore more ambiguous. In these circumstances, aversive racists weigh the positive qualities of white applicants and the negative qualities of black applicants more heavily in their evaluations. Analogously, aversive racists have more difficulty discounting incriminating evidence that is declared inadmissible when evaluating the guilt or innocence of black defendants relative to white defendants in studies of juridic decisions. In interracial interactions, whites' overt behaviors (e.g., verbal behavior) primarily reflect their expressed, explicit racial attitudes, whereas their more spontaneous and less controllable behaviors (e.g., their nonverbal behaviors) are related to their implicit, generally unconscious attitudes.

Aversive racism also contributes to opposition to policies designed to benefit blacks, such as affirmative action, but also primarily in rationalizable ways. Whites generally support the principle of affirmative action more than specific policy implementations, which contain elements that allow them to rationalize opposition on the basis of factors other than race (e.g., unfairness). Thus, aversive racists' responses to public policies are substantially influenced by how these policies are framed. They express general support for affirmative action when addressing historical and contemporary discrimination, but they tend to oppose a policy when it is portrayed as benefiting blacks in particular, or when the description implies it involves quotas or reverse discrimination.

Generally, then, aversive racists may be identified by a constellation of characteristic responses to racial issues and interracial situations. First, aversive racists, in contrast to old-fashioned racists, endorse fair and just treatment of all groups. Second, despite their conscious good intentions, aversive racists unconsciously harbor feelings of uneasiness towards blacks, and thus they try to avoid interracial interaction. Third, when interracial interaction is unavoidable, aversive racists experience anxiety and discomfort, and consequently they try to disengage from the interaction as quickly as possible. Fourth, because part of the discomfort that aversive racists experience is due to a concern about acting inappropriately and appearing prejudiced, aversive racists strictly adhere to established rules and codes of behavior in interracial situations that they cannot avoid. Fifth, their feelings will get expressed, but in subtle, unintentional, rationalizable ways that disadvantage minorities or unfairly benefit the majority group. Nevertheless, in terms of conscious intent, aversive racists do not intend to discriminate against people of color—and they behave accordingly when it is possible for them to monitor the appropriateness of their behavior.

COMBATING AVERSIVE RACISM

Traditional prejudice-reduction techniques have been concerned with changing conscious attitudes ("old-fashioned racism") and blatant expressions of bias. Attempts to reduce this direct, traditional form of racial prejudice have typically involved educational strategies to enhance knowledge and appreciation of other groups (e.g., multicultural education programs), emphasize norms that prejudice is wrong, and involve direct (e.g., mass media appeals) or indirect (dissonance reduction) attitude-change techniques. However, because of its pervasiveness, subtlety, and complexity, the traditional techniques for eliminating bias that emphasized the immorality of prejudice and illegality of discrimination are not effective for combating aversive racism. Aversive racists recognize that prejudice is bad, but they do not recognize that *they* are prejudiced.

Nevertheless, aversive racism can be addressed with techniques aimed at its roots at both the individual and collective levels. At the individual level, strategies to combat aversive racism can be directed at unconscious attitudes. For example, extensive training to create new, counter-stereotypic associations with social categories (e.g., blacks) can inhibit the unconscious activation of stereotypes, an element of aversive racists' negative attitudes. In addition, aversive racists' conscious attitudes, which are already egalitarian, can be instrumental in motivating change. Allowing aversive racists to become aware, in a nonthreatening way, of their unconscious negative attitudes, feelings, and beliefs can stimulate self-regulatory processes that not only elicit immediate deliberative responses that reaffirm conscious nonprejudiced orientations (such as increased support for policies that benefit minority groups), but that also produce, with sufficient time and experience, reductions in implicit negative beliefs and attitudes.

At the intergroup level, interventions may be targeted at processes that support aversive racism, such as in-group favoritism. One such approach, the Common In-group Identity Model, proposes that if members of different groups are induced to conceive of themselves more as a single, superordinate group, or as subgroups within a more inclusive social entity, rather than as two completely separate groups, attitudes toward former out-group members will become more positive through processes involving pro-in-group bias. Thus, changing the basis of categorization from race to an alternative dimension can alter perceptions of "we" and "they," thus undermining a contributing force to contemporary forms of racism, including aversive racism. For example, black interviewers are even more likely to obtain the cooperation of white respondents than are white interviewers when they emphasize their common group membership (e.g., shared university identity, as indicated by insignia on their clothes) than when they do not. Intergroup interaction within the guidelines of the Contact Hypothesis and anti-bias interventions with elementary school children that emphasize increasing their social inclusiveness can also reduce bias through the processes outlined in the Common In-group Identity Model.

Despite apparent and consistent improvements in expressed racial attitudes over time, aversive racism continues to exert a subtle but pervasive influence on the lives of black Americans and members of other disadvantaged groups. Although the expression of this form of bias is more subtle than are manifestations of old-fashioned racism, aversive racism has consequences as significant as blatant bias. Even though it is expressed in indirect and rationalizable ways, aversive racism operates to systematically restrict opportunities for blacks and members of other traditionally underrepresented groups.

In addition, because aversive racists may not be aware of their implicit negative attitudes and only discriminate against blacks when they can justify their behavior on the basis of some factor other than race, they will commonly deny any intentional wrongdoing when confronted with evidence of their bias. To the extent that minority-group members detect expressions of aversive racists' negative attitudes in subtle interaction behaviors (e.g., nonverbal behavior) and attribute the consequences of aversive racism to blatant racism, aversive racism also contributes substantially to interracial distrust, miscommunication, and conflict. Nevertheless, aversive racism can be addressed by encouraging increased awareness of unconscious negative feelings and beliefs, emphasizing alternative forms of social categorization around common group membership, and providing appropriate intergroup experiences to support the development of alternative implicit attitudes and stereotypes and to reinforce common identities.

SEE ALSO *Affirmative Action; Social Psychology of Racism; Symbolic and Modern Racism.*

BIBLIOGRAPHY

Dovidio, John F., and Samuel L. Gaertner. 2004. "Aversive Racism." In *Advances in Experimental Social Psychology*, Vol. 36, edited by Mark P. Zanna, 1–51. San Diego, CA: Academic Press.

Dovidio, John F., Samuel L. Gaertner, Kerry Kawakami, and Gordon Hodson. 2002. "Why Can't We Just Get Along? Interpersonal Biases and Interracial Distrust." *Cultural Diversity & Ethnic Minority Psychology* 8 (2): 88–102.

Gaertner, Samuel L., and John F. Dovidio. 1986. "The Aversive Form of Racism." In *Prejudice, Discrimination, and Racism*, edited by John F. Dovidio and Samuel L. Gaertner, 61–89. Orlando, FL: Academic Press.

———. 2000. *Reducing Intergroup Bias: The Common Ingroup Identity Model.* Philadelphia, PA: Psychology Press.

Kovel, Joel. 1970. *White Racism: A Psychohistory.* New York: Pantheon.

Nail, Paul R., Helen C. Harton, and Brian P. Decker. 2003. "Political Orientation and Modern versus Aversive Racism: Tests of Dovidio and Gaertner's (1998) Integrated Model." *Journal of Personality and Social Psychology* 84 (4): 754–770.

Pettigrew, Thomas F., and Roel W. Meertens. 1995. "Subtle and Blatant Prejudice in Western Europe." *European Journal of Social Psychology* 25 (1): 57–76.

Saucier, Donald A., Carol T. Miller, and Nicole Doucet. 2005. "Differences in Helping Whites and Blacks: A Meta-Analysis." *Personality and Social Psychology Review* 9 (1): 2–16.

John F. Dovidio
Samuel L. Gaertner

AZTLÁN

The concept of Aztlán has had a long life in the realms of myth, symbolism, and archetype in both Mexican and Chicano cultures. While the common denominator can be found in the two cultures' perception of themselves with respect to origins and identity, the application and associations are measurably different. Mexican culture, for example, tends to view Aztlán as an abstract historical past that vaguely defines the mother lode in which the nomadic tribe known as Mexicas or Aztecs originated in an imprecise northern region of Mexico. On the other hand, when Chicanos allude to such a mythological past they are inclined to emphasize, in real geographical terms, the contours of the region known as the Southwestern borderlands of the United States (including California, Arizona, Nevada, New Mexico, Texas, and parts of Colorado, Oregon, and Utah). While Mexicans characterize their connection with Aztlán as an integral part of cultural anthropology, Chicanos tend to couch it more in terms of cultural politics for the sake of ethnic reaffirmation.

Aztlán invokes an indigenous past, a point of reference shared by a common foundation in culture. Archaic myth dictates that the Aztecs, a kind of chosen people, set out on a legendary pilgrimage or migration in a southerly direction to duplicate, or recreate, the promised land of Aztlán, which was to be identified by a series of specific conditions: an eagle, perched on a cactus plant on an island or patch of land in the middle of a lake, devouring a serpent. Archival documentation prior to Hernán Cortés's incursion into the Aztec capital in 1519 claims that the Aztecs made such an encounter in 1325, thus creating the beginnings of the Aztec civilization and empire. Having met their destiny, they nostalgically recalled Aztlán—meaning "place near/of the white herons"—as a kind of earthly paradise, a hill dotted with caves and grottoes, for which they forever longed. Here, people did not age, starve, suffer or experience evil. This worldly utopia, according to the colonial historian Fray Diego Durán in his *Historia de las Indias de Nueva España e Islas de Tierra Firme* (*History of the Indies of New Spain,* 1588), was a lush setting teeming with flora and fauna capable of sustaining a culture: "Our ancestors went about in canoes and made floating gardens upon which they sowed maize, chili, tomatoes, amaranth, beans and all kinds of

The Founding of Tenochtitlan. *A Painting in the Museo de la Ciudad de México depicts a vision of an eagle swallowing a snake. This was the divine prophecy that told the Aztecs where to build the city of Tenochtitlan in 1325.* THE ART ARCHIVE/MUSEO CIUDAD MEXICO/DAGLI ORTI (A).

seeds which we now eat and which were brought here from there" (p. 134). Abandonment of the mythical Aztlán by these indigenous peoples, much like leaving the biblical Garden of Eden, had its consequences: It brought on hardship and their inevitable downfall as prescribed by some aspects of their myth. Such conditions paved the way for the Aztecs to believe that Cortés might be their forsaken deity/cultural hero Quetzalcóatl ("plumed serpent") who had promised to return from the East. Aztlán, therefore, conveyed a sense of cosmic tragedy of what could have been.

Since pre-Columbian times, Mexicans have desired to locate Aztlán as the point where history and myth merge to create a cultural narrative of a primordial nature, but the quest has been heightened by Chicanos in the United States in their pursuit of reconnecting with their indigenous ancestors to recover a sense of the past. Much like an elusive Atlantis, Ponce de León's fountain of youth, or the golden cities of Quivira in New Mexico, Aztlán does not readily adhere to a single point in geography. Some cultural anthropologists and historians assert that it can be found just north of Mexico City, or near the coastal state of Nayarit, or even possibly north of the Gulf of Mexico and as far north as Washington state and southwestern Canada. Others believe it could be in Wisconsin, Florida, Southern California, New Mexico, or China. Clearly, the power of myth, legend, and symbolism provokes multiple interpretations—most of them exercises in fantasy. The earliest allusion to Aztlán in the United States appeared in a 1885 work by William G. Ritch, then Secretary of the Territory of New Mexico. This book, titled *Aztlán: The History, Resources, and Attractions of New Mexico,* served as a promotion ploy to attract easterners to the Hispanic state.

Despite varying notions about Aztlán, it still carries considerable cultural weight as a concept. In his 1987 study *In Search of Aztlán*, Luis Leal asserts that Chicanos tend to render it two meanings: First, it identifies the American Southwest as the original source of their past; secondly, "Aztlán symbolized the spiritual unity of the Chicanos, something that is carried within the heart, no matter where they may live or where they may find themselves" (p. 8). One fundamental difference between Mexicans and Chicanos is noteworthy here: The former couch it within a mythic framework of fate, while the latter emphasize its regenerative qualities. For Chicanos, Aztlán completes the full circle of existence by returning to and "claiming" their mythic and spiritual homeland. It conveys a sense of roots and background, myth, and history, partly justifying the trajectory of immigration into the Southwestern United States. They do not perceive themselves as intruders, but rather, as a people coming back home.

Aztlán acquired a new sense of significance and relevance with the Chicano Movement of the 1960s, a decade that fostered a critical inward examination into the nature of ethnicity and its role in American history. Among U.S. minorities, one result was the emergence of new labels of self-identification ("black" instead of "Negro" or "colored," and "Chicano" instead of "Mexican American" or "Spanish"). Chicanos sought to reconnect with the remote past of Mexico while romanticizing what they knew of Mexican culture (i.e., its music, traditional dress, historical figures, events such as the Mexican Revolution, and so on). Pride in anything Mexican overflowed, thus helping to compensate for the pressures of assimilation through the processes of Americanization experienced in schools, work, and other institutions. Chicanos sought to reshape their identity, and possibly their essence.

The backdrop of social unrest led persons of Mexican descent in the United States to seek and construct a new identity. The term "Chicano" conjured up echoes of the ancient Mexicas ("Me-shica" evolved into "Mejicano," so "Chicano" would appear to resemble the original pronunciation). Suddenly, Chicanos felt they had pinpointed a name that had deep cultural roots, connoted political defiance, and crystallized an ethnic label, thus providing the four basic ingredients of social legitimacy as a people: 1) a unique *cultural identity*; 2) the beginnings of accepting their hybrid *language*—code-switching or Spanglish (the use of Spanish and English in the same sentence)—as a viable form of artistic expression; 3) a sense of community; and 4) a place to which they belonged that fulfilled the yearning for nationhood—that is, Aztlán. Rudolfo A. Anaya shares a slightly different perspective in *Aztlán: Essays on the Chicano Homeland* (1989): "[T]hrough Aztlán we come to better understand psychological time (identity), regional makeup (place), and evolution (historical time). Aztlán allows us . . . to maintain ourselves as fully integrated individuals" (p. iv).

It is Alurista, the renowned poet of code-switching, however, who is credited with the re-emergence of Aztlán as applied to Chicanos. While reading an article in 1968 by the anthropologist John Disturnell in *Life* magazine, he came across this concept, thus changing the course of Chicano history. It became a key rallying point for the Chicano Movement, a centerpiece and foundation for promoting a given social agenda. In addition, it defined a geographical, cultural, psychological, political, and symbolic entity modeled in myth and archetype, except that he considered it a living, decolonized entity. Aztlán became the instrument for proposing a new consciousness about the condition of his people, while alluding to a long history of suffering and quiet oppression. Alurista also explicitly associates the term with the Mexican territory ceded to the United States in 1848. In the First National Chicano Youth Liberation Conference in Denver in 1969, he officially introduced Aztlán in a spiritually charged manifesto referred to as *El Plan Espiritual de Aztlán*. As Michael Pina observes: "*El Plan* weaves both strands of the Chicano nationalism's mythic horizon into a comprehensive program that calls for the geographical and spiritual resurrection of Aztlán" (Pina 1989, p. 39). Alurista declared that "before all our brothers in the bronze continent, we are a nation, we are a union of free pueblos, we are *Aztlán*" (Alurista 1989, p. 1). As a plan of liberation, he claimed that nationalism was the key for mass mobilization and organization, defining the Cause ("La Causa") as a united front: "Our struggle then must be for the control of our barrios, campos [fields], pueblos [towns], lands, our economy, our culture, and our political life" (Alurista 1989, p. 2). One of the results of the conference was the creation of a militant student organization called MECHA (Movimiento Estudiantil de Chicanos de Aztlán [Chicano Student Movement of Aztlán]).

As a result, Aztlán became an inexorable symbol that spurred a new sense of creativity. In the spring of 1970 the first issue of the UCLA journal *Aztlán: Chicano Journal of the Social Sciences and the Arts* appeared, with a prologue by Alurista called "Poem in Lieu of Preface" in which he reasserted the practicality of Aztlán to his era. Shortly thereafter, in 1972, Alurista co-edited with Jorge González an anthology titled *Ombligo de Aztlán*, which propagated an artistic agenda of tapping into an indigenous sensibility. In the same year he published *Nationchild plumaroja*, a deeply philosophical, and sometimes obscure, rendition of an indigenous worldview in which he imagines what Aztlán has to offer. "Nationchild" here refers to the offspring from that mythic homeland.

A proliferation of titles either using or suggesting the concept of Aztlán appeared in quick succession. For example, Miguel Méndez cast his novel *Peregrinos de Aztlán* (1974) within the framework of migrants returning to their homeland. However, their apparent movement is actually a form of stagnation and inertia, and the characters encounter alienation and exploitation. Consequently, Aztlán here becomes even more elusive (but it must be stated that the novel traces a pilgrimage in reverse, that is, from south to north instead of the typical construct conceptualized by the Aztecs as north to south), a place of self-realization or entrapment, or somewhere in between.

The work that perhaps provides the definitive critical assessments is *Aztlán: Essays on the Chicano Homeland* (1989) by Rudolfo A. Anaya and Francisco A. Lomelí. The twelve essays in this volume offer critical opinions, scientific data, historical documentation, anthropological criteria, philosophical angles, political applications, and examples of specific literary analyses. While considerable overlapping is evident among the essays, they succeed in outlining virtually every perspective extant up to 1989—including Gloria Anzaldúas' refashioning from a gender, border dweller, and gay person's vantage point.

The term has also been borrowed for a number of social-science projects, such as *Return to Aztlán: The Social Process of International Migration from Western Mexico* (1987), by Douglas S. Massey et al., which examines the complex nature of migration as an international process. On the other hand, Rafael Pérez-Torres, in an essay titled "Refiguring Aztlán" (1997), proves the durability of the term by reconsidering its significance in postcolonial times: "To call Aztlán an empty signifier is not to say the term is vacuous or meaningless. On the contrary, if anything, Aztlán is overly 'meaningful' " (p. 16). He problematizes how Aztlán embodies a rich network of discussion regarding its fundamental meaning as a form of hybridity, and he demonstrates the contradictions of its usage due to its political and ideological vagueness. In sum, he claims that its richness is its multiple meanings, particularly if the vague idea of "homeland" is replaced by the more specific "borderlands." Pérez-Torres concludes by pointing out how the term has played a key role in Chicano critical thought, in that it refers more to "an absence, an unfulfilled reality in response to various forms of oppression" (p. 37). He shows that Aztlán continues to haunt those involved in attempting to define a space of liberation in the present instead of focusing on the past.

Aztlán is many things to many people, but it appears to function as an apex of measuring Chicanos' progress in their respective social, historical, political, and mythic spheres. Therefore, it is something highly personal, even psychological, though its application to social reality is useful through the various facets it represents for both Mexican and Chicano culture.

SEE ALSO *Anzaldúa, Gloria; Chávez, César Estrada; Chicana Feminism; Chicano Movement; Mexicans.*

BIBLIOGRAPHY

Alurista. 1971. *Floricanto en Aztlán.* Los Angeles: UCLA Chicano Cultural Center.

———. 1989. "El Plan Espiritual de Aztlán." In *Aztlán: Essays on the Chicano Homeland,* edited by Rudolfo A. Anaya and Francisco A. Lomelí, 1–5. Albuquerque, NM: Academia/El Norte Publications.

———. 1982. *Return: Poems Collected and New.* Ypsilanti, MI: Bilingual Press/Editorial Bilingüe.

Anaya, Rudolfo A. *Heart of Aztlán.* Berkeley: Editorial Justa, 1976.

———, and Francisco A. Lomelí. 1989. *Aztlán: Essays on the Chicano Homeland.* Albuquerque, NM: Academia/El Norte Publications.

Anzaldúa, Gloria. 1989. "The Homeland, Aztlán/El Otro México." In *Aztlán: Essays on the Chicano Homeland,* edited by Rudolfo A. Anaya and Francisco A. Lomelí, 191–204. Albuquerque, NM: Academia/El Norte Publications.

Arias, Ron. 1978. *The Road to Tamazunchale.* Albuquerque, NM: Pajarito Publications.

Casas, Celso de. 1979. *Pelón Drops Out.* Berkeley, CA: Tonatiuh Internacional.

Durán, Diego. 1964. *The Aztecs: The History of the Indies of New Spain.* Translated by Doris Heyden and Fernando Horcasitas. New York: Orion Press.

González, Ray. 1992. *After Aztlán: Latino Poets of the Nineties.* Boston: David R. Godine.

Grandjeat, Yves-Charles. 1989. *Aztlán: terre volée, terre promise; les peregrinations du peuple chicano.* Paris: Presses de l'Ecole Normale Supérieure.

Leal, Luis. 1985. *Aztlán y México: Perfiles literarios e históricos.* Binghamton, NY: Bilingual Press/Editorial Bilingüe.

———. 1989. "In Search of Aztlán." In *Aztlán: Essays on the Chicano Homeland,* edited by Rudolfo A. Anaya and Francisco A. Lomelí, 6–13. Albuquerque, NM: Academia/El Norte Publications.

Massey, Douglas S., Rafael Alarcón, Jorge Durand, and Humberto González, eds. 1987. *Return to Aztlán: The Social Process of International Migration from Western Mexico.* Berkeley: University of California Press.

Méndez, Miguel. 1974. *Peregrinos de Aztlán.* Tucson: Editorial Peregrinos.

Pérez-Torres, Rafael. 1997. "Refiguring Aztlán." *Aztlán: A Journal of Chicano Studies* 22 (2): 15–41.

Pina, Michael. 1989. "The Archaic, Historical, and Mythicized Dimensions of Aztlán." In *Aztlán: Essays on the Chicano Homeland,* edited by Rudolfo A. Anaya and Francisco A. Lomelí, 14–48. Albuquerque, NM: Academia/El Norte Publications.

Ritch, William G. 1885. *Aztlán: The History, Resources, and Attractions of New Mexico.* Boston: D. Lothrop.

Francisco A. Lomelí

B

BAKER, ELLA
1903–1986

Ella Josephine Baker was a leading radical democracy crusader, adviser, organizer for social justice, and a key figure in U.S. civil rights activism. As a civil rights activist from the 1930s onward, she fought racism and oppression in its many forms, both in America and around the world, particularly in Africa. She was a central figure in the National Association for the Advancement of Colored People (NAACP), the Southern Christian Leadership Conference (SCLC), and the Student Nonviolent Coordinating Committee (SNCC).

Born in Norfolk, Virginia, on December 13, 1903, Ella Jo was the second of three surviving children of Georgianna (Anna) Ross Baker and Blake Baker. She repeatedly credited her mother as her guiding influence, particularly in the black Baptist tradition of directing women, no less than men, to take personal responsibility for doing good works. After the 1910 Norfolk race riot, the seven-year-old Ella—along with her mother, her older brother Blake Curtis, and her younger sister Maggie—moved to Littleton, North Carolina, where her parents had grown up.

The church was the center of this rural black community. Her mother and grandmother were active in the church, and her grandfather, Ross Baker, a black Baptist preacher, had been a church leader until his death in 1909. Thus, early in her life, Ella Jo learned lessons of a hard-working leadership of service in a respectful community of equals.

Education was a key tenet of Baker's family belief in cooperative Christian uplift. In 1918, after attending grammar school in Littleton, the fourteen-year-old Ella was sent to Raleigh, North Carolina, to attend Shaw University, a historically black college affiliated with the Baptist Church. Here, she attended both the institution's normal school and the college. She graduated in 1927 with a bachelor of arts, and as the class valedictorian she exhorted her classmates to "accept this noble challenge of salvaging the strong ship of civilization by the anchors of right, justice and love."

Baker considered doing graduate work in sociology, and she also harbored hopes of becoming a medical missionary, which she viewed as an ideal means of productive personal service in what she called "the uplift of the fallen humanity." Money was an issue, however, as the late 1920s economic downturn collapsed into the Great Depression, putting further schooling out of her reach. Rather than heading for the University of Chicago, as she once hoped, Baker went to stay with her cousin Martha Grinage in New York City's Harlem. She waited tables, took factory jobs, and learned about the new mix of people she encountered. The need for fundamental social reform became ever more palpable to her, and she put her considerable talents to work espousing wrongs and advocating rights. She was determined for people to see things as they were, so information and insight were ever important to her. In 1928 she organized a Negro History Club at Harlem's 135th Street YMCA. She served on the editorial staff of the *American West Indian News* from 1929 to 1930 before joining the *Negro National News*, where she worked until 1932.

Understanding the value of collective economic power, Baker joined the Young Negroes Cooperative League, where she urged collective and selective buying. She continued advocating this approach as an employee of the federal Works Progress Administration, which she joined after its creation in May 1935. Then, in 1938, she became a field organizer for the NAACP. Traveling around the South, she raised money and recruited members. She eventually became a field secretary and in 1943 national director of branches. She had a hand also in the 1940 founding of the NAACP Legal Defense and Education Fund. Everywhere she went, Ella connected with the people—she knew everyone, and everyone knew her. But she was a woman, and the male-dominated national NAACP hierarchy bristled at her brashness. In 1946 she left the NAACP national office to work for school desegregation in New York City. She became the local NAACP branch president there in 1952, and she ran unsuccessfully as a Liberal Party candidate for New York City Council in 1953.

Campaigning against racism and segregation, Baker spent time in the South after the 1955–1956 Montgomery Bus Boycott success in Alabama. She worked with Bayard Rustin, Martin Luther King Jr., and others in 1957 to form the SCLC and develop its voter registration drive, "Crusade for Citizenship." She served as SCLC interim executive director until April 1960. But she again bumped heads with a male hierarchy. The SCLC dropped "interim" from the job title of Reverend Wyatt Tee Walker, the man who replaced her.

Before leaving the SCLC, Baker convinced its other leaders to allow youth independence in the civil rights movement. She organized a Youth Leadership Conference at her alma mater, Shaw University, on Easter weekend 1960. The immediate result was SNCC, where Baker went to work helping to arrange the 1960 sit-ins and the 1961 freedom rides. She worked also with the Young Women's Christian Association (YWCA) and the interracial Southern Conference Educational Fund to further integration in southern higher education.

Working with SNCC, Baker helped organize the Mississippi Freedom Democratic Party (MFDP), and she delivered the keynote address at its 1964 state convention in Jackson. Again confronting the political mainstream with its hierarchical and segregated local and national parties, Baker orchestrated the interracial MFDP delegation's challenge to Mississippi's old-line, lily-white delegation at the National Democratic Party's 1964 Atlantic City convention. In the credentialing battle, Baker helped secure new party rules to insure seating blacks and women as future delegates.

Bucking the established hierarchy seldom made Baker politically popular or put her in good stead with national leaders, whether it was President John F. Kennedy or Martin Luther King Jr. Her backing of the anti-Vietnam War movement and the feminist movement in the 1960s and 1970s similarly distanced her from broad popular acceptance. But she was never interested in the limelight. She was interested in helping people solve problems.

Baker's group-centered, direct-action approach to social change through participatory democracy infused a broad range of organizations, from SNCC to the radical Students for a Democratic Society (SDS). Her work endeared her to many, particularly SNCC veterans, as the "godmother of civil rights." Preaching and teaching people empowerment, she insisted on the value of grassroots development and action as the truest solutions to social problems. She dismissed "great leader" schemes, believing effective change arose from what she described as "group-centered leadership, rather than a leadership-centered group." Her mantra was "give light and people will find a way."

While unsung on the national stage, Baker stood as a heroic model of selfless service for racial and social justice. She lived her credo that "a life that is important is a life of service." In her later years she spread her aid and assistance ever more broadly, working with groups ranging from the Harlem Youth Council to the Puerto Rican Solidarity Committee and the Third World Women's Coordinating Committee. But her activities were increasingly limited by Alzheimer's disease. She died in New York City on December 13, 1986, her eighty-third birthday. The Ella Baker Center for Human Rights, founded in 1996 in Oakland, California, carries forward her name in a mission of direct-action grassroots organizing and mobilizing against human rights abuses.

SEE ALSO *NAACP.*

BIBLIOGRAPHY

Barker-Benfield, G. J., and Catherine Clinton. 1991. *Portraits of American Women: From Settlement to the Present.* New York: St. Martin's Press.

Cantarow, Ellen, Susan Gushee O'Malley, and Sharon Hartman Strom. 1980. *Moving the Mountain: Women Working for Social Change.* New York: McGraw-Hill.

Grant, Joanne. 1998. *Ella Baker: Freedom Bound.* New York: Wiley.

Morris, Aldon. 1984. *The Origins of the Civil Rights Movement: Black Communities Organizing for Change.* New York: Free Press.

Ransby, Barbara. 2003. *Ella Baker and the Black Freedom Movement: A Radical Democratic Vision.* Chapel Hill: University of North Carolina Press.

Thomas J. Davis

BALDWIN, JAMES
1924–1987

James Baldwin was a novelist, essayist, playwright, poet, scriptwriter, and filmmaker. Born in Harlem, New York, on August 2, 1924, he understood poverty, injustice, and the parasitic nature of city streets. Some of his teenage experiences with bigoted police and sexual predators are recounted in the well-known volume, *The Fire Next Time* (1963). Also in that volume, in the section titled "Letter to My Nephew on the One Hundredth Anniversary of the Emancipation," Baldwin articulates his position on race: "You must accept them [whites] ... accept them and accept them with love." He considered racism a matter of morality and human dignity, and it was blacks' responsibility to save whites from their own ignorance, fear, and loss of identity. His ideas about racism were not the most popular, but they clearly distinguished him as an eloquent visionary.

The oldest of nine children, Baldwin was the son of a domestic worker mother and a hostile and hateful stepfather, who thought his son was ugly and disavowed his intelligence. Baldwin was raised in a Pentecostal church, dominated by the theology of "sinners in the hand of an angry God." He followed his preacher-father to the pulpit, and by the age of fourteen he was preaching the fundamentalist doctrine of his parents. For three years, he bellowed out Old Testament scriptures, while also realizing that the church provided no sanctuary from social, economic, and political injustices.

Baldwin found his refuge in reading and writing when he attended DeWitt Clinton High School. Realizing he was black and smart, and that his mind belonged solely to him, he declared he would take advantage of his intelligence. He wrote for the school paper and published several short stories that often reflected his religious background. This beginning led to an international reputation as one of the world's most gifted writers.

When Baldwin finished high school in 1942, he did freelance writing and worked for the railroad in New Jersey. After a succession of jobs, he moved to Greenwich Village. It was there that he met the writer Richard Wright, who helped him secure a fellowship, after which Baldwin expatriated himself to Paris in 1948. Some of his essays indicate that he left America to escape racial discrimination only to discover that his adopted country, France, was no panacea for social justice and equality.

Baldwin's treatment of racism, though engaging and thoughtful, is comparatively restrained in much of his work. While the scope of his most critically acclaimed novel, *Go Tell It on the Mountain* (1953), covers religion and personal identity, the second part of the three-part story, "The Prayers of the Saints," reveals the racial hostility and violence of the Jim Crow South, as well as the social and economic inequality of the urban North. Some of his other work, notably the 1964 play, *Blues for Mister Charlie,* and the short story collection, *Going to Meet the Man* (1965), explore racial conflict, with the title story, "Going to Meet the Man," from the point of view of the racist.

Baldwin's essays are more fervent in the exploration of race. *Notes of a Native Son* (1955), offers a view of expatriation that contradicts the notion of Paris as the promised land, while *Nobody Knows My Name* (1961) deals, in part, with race relations in the United States. Some of his fiction, including *Another Country* (1962), *If Beale Street Could Talk* (1974), and *Just Above My Head* (1979), present characters who suffer deliberate racism as they negotiate other problems in their lives. With graceful eloquence, James Baldwin stirred the moral consciousness of a nation bogged down in matters of race.

SEE ALSO *Gay Men.*

BIBLIOGRAPHY

PRIMARY WORKS

Go Tell It on the Mountain. 1953. New York: Knopf.

Notes of a Native Son. 1955. New York: Dial Press.

Nobody Knows My Name: More Notes of A Native Son. 1961. New York: Dial Press.

Another Country. 1962. New York: Dial Press.

The Fire Next Time. 1963. New York: Dial Press.

Going to Meet the Man. 1965. New York: Dial Press.

The Amen Corner; A Play. 1968. New York: Dial Press.

A Dialogue (with Nikki Giovanni). 1973. Philadelphia: Lippincott.

If Beale Street Could Talk. 1974. New York: Dial Press.

SECONDARY WORKS

Campbell, James. 1991. *Talking at the Gates: A Life of James Baldwin.* New York: Viking.

Harris, Trudier. 1997. "James Baldwin." In *The Oxford Companion to African American Literature,* edited by William Andrews, Frances Smith Foster, and Trudier Harris. New York: Oxford University Press.

Jarret, Hobart. 1977. "From a Region in My Mind: The Essays of James Baldwin." In *James Baldwin: A Critical Evaluation,* edited by Therman B. O'Daniel. Washington, DC: Howard University Press.

Olson, Barbara K. 1997. "'Come-to-Jesus Stuff' in James Baldwin's *Go Tell It on the Mountain* and *The Amen Corner.*" *African American Review* 31 (2).

Public Broadcasting Service. "James Baldwin." *American Masters Series.* Available from http://www.pbs.org/wnet/americanmasters/database/baldwinj.html.

Reilly, John M. 1977. "'Sonny's Blues': James Baldwin's Image of Black Community." In *James Baldwin: A Critical Evaluation,* edited by Therman B. O'Daniel. Washington, DC: Howard University Press.

Whitlow, Roger. 1973. *Black American Literature: A Critical History.* Chicago: Nelson Hall.

Angelene Jamison-Hall

BARRIO

Barrios are urban neighborhoods within the United States that have a high concentration of Hispanics, variably identified as Latinos, Hispanos, Mexicans, Chicanos, Puerto

Ricans, or other nationalities from Central and Latin American. These neighborhoods often have deep emotional and cultural meanings for those who live there, for they are places where families and friends share both the positive and negative experiences of growing up Latino in the United States. Individuals often have a strong identification with their barrio, a pride in being from this place and of knowing other people from the barrio. It is a place where the inhabitants can be themselves, speak Spanish, conduct business, and generally feel accepted by others. It also serves at times as a refuge for poor and marginalized people who have been affected by the consequences of poverty, segregation, and discrimination. The barrio, then, is a both a place of familial and cultural identification and a place where there is often an experience of crime, poverty, and racism. Many barrios are characterized as having poor housing, bad schools, gangs, police harassment, and illicit drugs. Nevertheless, the Latinos who live there often feel a pride in being "from the barrio."

BIRTH OF THE BARRIO

Perhaps the first barrio within the United States was the Tlasclalan barrio of Analaco, located in Santa Fe, New Mexico. This barrio was inhabited by the Mexican Indian servants and slaves who accompanied the Spanish settlers to New Mexico in 1598. After 1848 many barrios grew up within Southwestern cities as the result of the Anglo-American military conquest. Sometimes, as in the case of Los Angeles, San Antonio, and Tucson, the Mexican barrio grew out of the historic pueblo or town where the Mexicans had always lived. As Anglo-Americans came to predominate in these areas, they surrounded and isolated the barrios, which became segregated areas where Mexican workers and their families were expected to live.

Before World War II, the mining towns of New Mexico, Arizona, and Colorado were strictly segregated, with the Mexican miners being restricted to the less favorable part of town, where they were forced to live by the mining company who owned the dwellings. By custom, and sometimes by regulation, Mexican residents were expected to stay on their side of the town. In the agricultural towns of California and Texas, Mexican farm workers and their families were often segregated by having to live "on the other side of the tracks" in dilapidated housing. In the late nineteenth century, white Americans developed a culture of segregation with respect to African Americans, and they often applied this to dark-skinned Mexicans, who were also segregated to prevent mixing with whites in public places such as movie halls, schools, parks, "plunges" (swimming pools), barber shops, churches, and the like. Almost everywhere in the Southwest before World War II, ethnic Mexicans were segregated in public schools, public facilities, and housing.

As a result of this segregation, Latinos developed their own ways of surviving, fashioning a culture that relied on family and cultural relationships within the barrio. They formed social, political, and cultural groups, and mutual aid societies sprang up in the barrios to provide emergency relief for those who were unemployed or to pay for funeral expenses of loved ones. The barrio was also the place where Mexican musicians, singers, dancers, and performers could find an eager audience. Local restaurants, owned and operated by barrio residents, catered to Mexican and local tastes. In southern Texas, especially before World War II, the barrio was the political base of many aspiring Tejano leaders who managed to achieve modest electoral successes because of the voter concentrations in the barrio.

POST–WORLD WAR II GROWTH

Barrios emerged outside of the traditional Southwest as different groups from Latin America immigrated to the United States. Puerto Rican immigrants established urban barrios in New York City, and especially in Brooklyn, following World War II. Over the years their barrios have grown in size, mixing with other urban poor, particularly African-American and Afro-Caribbean immigrants in central Brooklyn. Puerto Rican immigrants also found their way to south Chicago, where they lived in barrios along with Mexican immigrant working-class families. The Puerto Rican barrios, whether in New York or Chicago, remain vital communities in the early twenty-first century, and new immigrants from Puerto Rico still go there to find jobs, housing, and a familiar culture. As the numbers of poor urban residents increase, however, so do the accompanying problems of family stress, illicit drugs, underemployment, and school dropout rates.

Cuban immigrants to the United States came in great numbers after the end of the Cuban Revolution in 1959. Encouraged by the U.S. government and given special assistance, the Cuban enclave established itself primarily in Miami, Florida, living in several barrios. Because of the large number of educated, middle-class Cuban immigrants who were assisted by the U.S. government because they were anticommunist, the barrios developed into a launching pad for economic success and political achievement. Within their barrios, the Cubans have an extremely high sense of cohesion and unity. Spanish is spoken by rich and poor alike, and family solidarity and assistance is high. Involvement in local, state, and national politics is the norm, and Cubans have a high rate of graduation from secondary schools and colleges. There are also poor Cuban and other Caribbean immigrants in the barrios, and they provide the low-wage laborers for Cuban-controlled businesses.

Mural in Los Angeles, California. *A 1993 mural by Ernesto de la Loza and others adorns the Estada Courts Housing Project in East L.A. Depicted are Emiliano Zapata, Pancho Villa, and the Spanish comic actor Cantinflas.* © STEVE CRISE/CORBIS.

THE BARRIOS OF LOS ANGELES AND SAN ANTONIO

The most important Hispanic barrios, in terms of numbers and visibility, are those in Los Angeles and San Antonio, where the majority are of Mexican descent. According to the 2000 census, Los Angeles had a Latino population of 1.7 million. Not all of these individuals live in barrios, however. A large number live in suburban enclaves mixed with other groups and nationalities. The historic Mexican barrios of Los Angeles, located in East Los Angeles, have been followed by newer ones emerging further east. Immigration from Mexico and Latin America has been a major factor in changing barrio life, renewing language and culture even as older barrio residents move out. As noted by Joan Moore and Raquel Pinderhughes (1993), the trend has been toward increased political participation and a decline of community-based organizations. Family ties and loyalties are still important for linking barrio residents to those who have moved out. The barrio merchants, schools, churches, theaters, and restaurants reflect a revitalization of a metropolis. At the same time, gang violence and crime remain a constant reality of life in the barrios.

During the civil wars in Central American republics in the 1980s, hundreds of thousands of refugees and immigrants came to Los Angeles. At the beginning of the twenty-first century, it was estimated that more than 500,000 of these individuals lived in barrios located in the central and south central part of the city. Of necessity, the Central American communities are mixed with other nationalities and groups. Whites, Mexicanos, Salvadorians, Guatemalans, Nicaraguans, African Americans, Chinese, Vietnamese, and other immigrant groups vie for inexpensive housing and jobs within the regions of heavy Central American residence, such as Pico Union, the Westlake District, and Watts. Despite a high crime rate, gangs, and drug dealing, the Central Americans have revitalized the decaying inner-city neighborhoods that have become their barrio. Churches, social action agencies, schools, and political organizations are working to meet the community's special needs.

According to the 2000 census, 60 percent of San Antonio's population is Latino, mostly of Mexican descent. This means that these barrios, some historic and some relatively new, predominate in city life. San Antonio's urban problems are the problems of the barrios: Poverty, crime, inadequate housing, and bad schooling are all on the agendas of the local politicians and numerous community agencies. City life remains vibrant in places, attracting tourists who enjoy the Mexican flavor and ambiance. San Antonio's older barrios, particularly the Westside, have a long history going back to the nineteenth century. The economic, cultural, and political elite of the city have come from its barrios. While Mexican immigration to San Antonio's barrios continues, it is not a major cause of the city's growing Latino population. The rising birth rate is. The barrios have experienced a general population growth, and they have a strong tradition of family and community leadership. The barrios are responsible for a growing Tejano music industry as well as a thriving Spanish-language media industry.

The diversity of the Hispanic condition in the United States must be considered when thinking about the word *barrio*. There are barrios with histories going back 300 years (Albuquerque); there are barrios where Latinos live with African-American, Central-American, and Asian neighbors. Some Cuban barrios reflect an affluence that one would not encounter in Spanish Harlem in New York. In most barrios, a degree of urban decay and lawlessness is mixed with a vibrant, hopeful, and confident rebirth of cosmopolitan life. Ancient traditions from Mexico, Central America, and the Caribbean mix with modern technology and behavior. The barrio in the United States has become a metaphor for the future of urban life: a fast paced, multilingual and cultural experiment that offers creativity mixed with challenges.

SEE ALSO *Caribbean Immigration; Central Americans; Latinos; Mexicans; Puerto Ricans.*

BIBLIOGRAPHY

De León, Arnoldo. 1989. *Ethnicity in the Sun Belt: A History of Mexican Americans in Houston*. Houston: Mexican American Studies Program, University of Houston.

Moore, Joan. 1991. *Going Down to the Barrio: Homeboys and Homegirls in Change*. Philadelphia: Temple University Press.

———, and Raquel Pinderhughes. 1993. *In the Barrios: Latinos and the Underclass Debate*. New York: Russell Sage Foundation.

Morales, Julio. 1986. *Puerto Rican Poverty and Migration: We Just Had to Try Elsewhere*. New York: Praeger.

Orfield, Gary. 1988. *Latinos in Metropolitan Chicago: A Study of Housing and Employment*. Monograph No. 6. Chicago: Latino Institute.

Portes, Alejandro, and Alan Stepick. 1993. *City on the Edge: The Transformation of Miami*. Berkeley: University of California Press.

Romo, Ricardo. 1983. *East Los Angeles: History of a Barrio*. Austin: University of Texas Press.

Richard Griswold del Castillo

BASEBALL

As "America's pastime," baseball is inextricably bound to the history of U.S. race relations and racism. At its 1867 convention, baseball's first national organization, the National Association of Base Ball Players (NABBP), called for the banning "of any club which be comprised of one or more colored persons" (Peterson 1970, pp. 16–17). It did so based on the patronizing rationale that "if colored clubs were admitted there would in all probability be some division of feeling, whereas excluding them no injury would result to anyone." (Tygiel, quoted in Hogan 2006, p. vii).

The development of professional major league baseball through the 1880s, however, saw the signing of about twenty black players. Segregation was reintroduced in the late 1880s, and by 1890 no integrated teams remained. This was consistent with the 1896 Supreme Court decision in *Plessy v. Ferguson*, which affirmed separation of white and black social institutions. As a result, the number of African-American teams grew, and in 1920 the Negro Leagues were formed. The segregation of professional baseball lasted until 1947.

Baseball was central to the civil rights movement of the mid-twentieth century. Martin Luther King Jr. called the breaking of the color line by Jackie Robinson and his fellow black ballplayers fundamental to the desegregation of American society (Aaron and Wheeler 1992). At the same time, the abuse Robinson endured reflected the resistance of white Americans to racial integration.

Whereas the primary story line of baseball and racism pertains to African Americans, Latin Americans and Native Americans have played important roles in the history and evolution of baseball. Baseball's globalization, beginning in the late twentieth century, continued to intertwine issues of race and ethnicity, especially with regard to players from Latin America and Japan.

EARLY BASEBALL

American baseball, which was probably derived from a form of English baseball, has been documented since colonial times. George Washington played "base ball" with his troops, while the earliest black baseball was played by slaves. The game became increasingly popular during the Civil War, when it was played in army camps and military prisons. By the late 1860s, baseball was becoming organized through the formation of more than 100 professional teams. African-American players were on the rosters of many of these minor league teams, although racist attitudes and Jim Crow laws made it difficult for black ballplayers to play and travel with their teams. Black players often had to eat and sleep on their team busses or stay in the private homes of black families in towns where they played.

One response to this discrimination was the formation of Negro teams and leagues. The Philadelphia Pythians, formed in 1869, was one the first Negro teams. When they were not allowed to join the NABBP, they joined the National Colored Base Ball League, which was the first professional Negro league. Unfortunately, the league ran out of money after two weeks and disbanded.

During the 1860s, black baseball teams formed in northern cities. The first intercity games were played in 1866 between Albany and Philadelphia teams. The Washington Mutuals' third baseman was Charles Douglass, the son of Frederick Douglass. The first baseball game between black and white teams occurred on September 3, 1869, when the Pythians played the Olympics. The final score favored the Olympics 44-23, but as Hogan notes, "the Pythians were ... the real winners of the day, having had recognition from the white sporting community finally bestowed upon them" (Hogan 2006, p. 16).

The first nationally recognized black team was the Cuban Giants. This team evolved from the Keystone Athletics, formed in 1885 as a team of barnstorming all-stars comprising the best players from the Philadelphia Orions and Washington, D.C., Manhattans. They won many games against white teams, but perhaps their greatest accomplishment was playing (although losing to) two major league teams, the Philadelphia Athletics and the New York Metropolitans. The team was renamed the "Cuban Giants" to attract white fans. Team members also pretended to speak Spanish in order to pass as Latino.

EARLY BLACK PROFESSIONAL PLAYERS

John W. Jackson, who subsequently took the name Bud Fowler, was the first African-American professional baseball player. Born in Fort Plain, New York, in 1858, Fowler grew up in Cooperstown, New York, the subsequent home of the National Baseball Hall of Fame and the mythological place of origin of baseball. He joined a white team from New Castle, Pennsylvania, around 1872. He was a gifted second baseman and played for nearly twenty-five years. He was the first of about sixty black players to play on white teams before 1890.

Moses Fleetwood Walker is considered the first black major league ballplayer. Born in 1857—the year of the Dred Scott decision and the formation of the NABBP—"Fleet" Walker's career and life reflect the history of baseball and race in the late nineteenth century. The son of a medical doctor, he played baseball at Oberlin College, one of the first integrated colleges in the United States, and at the University of Michigan. In 1883, he played for the Toledo Blue Stockings in the Northwestern League (part of the NABBP) and became the first black major league ballplayer when his team joined the American Association in 1884. He was an accomplished bare-handed catcher (catchers did not start wearing gloves until the 1890s). He played only on integrated teams, and his experiences of racial abuse led him to become a part of the Back-to-Africa movement, on which he wrote a major treatise, *Our Home Colony* (1908). In 1883, Cap Anson, the manager and star of the Chicago White Stockings, threatened to cancel his game against Toledo if Walker played. The Toledo team called Anson's bluff, however, and the game was played. Unfortunately, this event was the start of Anson's campaign to get the team owners to ban black ballplayers.

George Stovey, the first great African-American pitcher, played for several white clubs. In 1886 he was the top pitcher for the Jersey City team. He played for the Newark Eagles in 1887, the year the team set an International League record for wins. Frank Grant was probably the most accomplished black baseball player of the nineteenth century. Grant joined the Buffalo Bisons team in 1886 and became the first black to play on the same team in organized baseball for three consecutive seasons. By 1887, approximately twenty black ballplayers were on the rosters of major league teams. Even more significantly, the League of Colored Ball Players, formed in 1887 and sometimes referred to as the National Colored Baseball League Clubs, was considered a legitimate minor league.

In 1887, the baseball owners resumed discussing a "color line" in baseball. Some players were refusing to sit beside black ballplayers, and others balked at playing integrated teams. The owners ultimately bent to these racist attitudes by assenting to a "gentleman's agreement" not to sign any black ballplayers. Cap Anson again announced that his team would not play any team that had black players on its roster. Because his team drew the league's largest attendance, the other owners yielded to his economic blackmail. By 1890 there were no longer any black players on major league or minor league teams.

The story of the great Penobscot ballplayer Louis Sockalexis is another episode in nineteenth-century American race relations. Sockalexis, the first Native American to play major league baseball, was signed by the Cleveland

Spiders in 1897. Although he played only parts of three years, his prowess as a ballplayer is legendary. Indeed, his accomplishments led to the team being renamed the Cleveland Indians. At the time, team nicknames were sometimes given to celebrate great players. This use of laudatory nicknames contrasts sharply with the practice of using racial caricatures as mascots—such as Chief Wahoo of the Cleveland Indians—who was adopted in 1933. The tension between celebrating ethnicity and dehumanizing ethnic groups through the use of sports mascots came to the fore in 2005 when the National Collegiate Association banned the use of Native American mascots for all schools. Subsequently, Florida State University's use of Seminoles as its nickname was exempted because the Seminole tribe agreed to this sponsorship.

THE NEGRO LEAGUES

The Negro National League was established on February 13, 1920, at a YMCA in Kansas City, Missouri. It was founded by Andrew "Rube" Foster, a star pitcher who served as the league's first president. He undertook the challenge to create a league that would ultimately merge with the white major leagues. The Negro Leagues had great success, with the teams playing before big crowds in major league parks. Negro League teams also played against white teams in barnstorming tours and developed some of the greatest players in baseball history.

The Negro League World Series and All Star "East-West" Game were national events that attracted tens of thousands of fans and national press coverage. In 1924 the first Negro League World Series was played between the Kansas City Monarchs (Negro National League Champions) and the Hilldale Club (Eastern Colored League Champions). Kansas City won the series championship, five games to four. The first East-West Colored All-Star Game was played at Chicago's Comiskey Park before more than 20,000 fans.

SOME GREAT NEGRO LEAGUE TEAMS

Most major cities east of the Mississippi River had great Negro League teams. The Newark Dodgers merged with the Brooklyn Eagles to form the Newark Eagles in 1936. The Eagles were owned by Abe and Effa Manley. Effa Manley, who was raised by a white mother and an African-American father, was the first woman to operate a professional baseball team. Though her biological father was white, she portrayed herself as black and was an important member of the black community. The Eagles rented Ruppert Stadium from the Newark Bears (a New York Yankees affiliate) for 20 percent of the gate receipts, providing an economic incentive to maintain the segregation of the leagues. The team also produced four Hall of Famers: Larry Doby, Leon Day, Monte Irvin, and Roy Dandridge. Both Doby and Irvin eventually played in the major leagues.

In the 1930s and 1940s, Pittsburgh was the home of two of the Negro League's most talented teams. In 1935, Gus Greenlee's Pittsburgh Crawfords' lineup showcased five future Hall-of-Famers: Satchel Paige, Josh Gibson, Cool Papa Bell, Judy Johnson, and Oscar Charleston. Cumberland Posey's Homestead Grays won nine consecutive Negro National League titles from the late 1930s through the mid-1940s. They featured former Crawfords stars Gibson and Bell and Hall-of-Fame first baseman Buck Leonard.

From 1936 to 1948, the New York Black Yankees heralded such great players as Clint Thomas, Fats Jenkins, DeWitt "Woody" Smallwood, Barney Brown, "Crush" Holloway, and the powerful George "Mule" Suttles. In 1937, the Negro American League was formed from the best western and southern teams. The league featured some of the greatest players in baseball history, including Jackie Robinson, Willie Mays, and Hank Aaron.

TWO GREAT NEGRO LEAGUE PLAYERS

Leroy "Satchel" Paige (1906–1982) is considered by some to be the greatest right-handed pitcher in baseball history. He was certainly the most durable, winning most of more than 2,000 games. He pitched almost daily, and claimed to have won 104 or 105 games in 1934. That same year, he refused a salary offer from Gus Greenlee and the Pittsburgh Crawfords and was banned from the Negro National League. He subsequently joined several Negro League stars to play in the Dominican Republic for the team owned by the country's president, Rafael Trujillo. Determined to have his professional team win the Dominican championship, Trujillo recruited Paige, Josh Gibson, and Cool Papa Bell. The Negro Leaguers played for one year and then returned to the United States. When Paige was sold to the Newark Eagles in 1938, he left again, this time to play in Mexico. He was again banned from Negro League Baseball, this time for life. In 1948, Paige was signed by the Cleveland Indians and became major league baseball's all-time oldest rookie at the age of forty-two. Joe DiMaggio called Satchel Paige "the best and fastest pitcher I've ever faced."

Josh Gibson (1911–1947), is considered by some to be baseball's greatest hitting catcher. He is often referred to as "the black Babe Ruth," though some baseball historians have commented that Ruth should be considered the white Josh Gibson. Gibson, who is reputed to have hit more than 800 home runs, desperately wanted to be the first black ballplayer in Major League Baseball. Tragically, he died at the age of thirty-five in 1947, the

Newark Eagles, 1936. *The Eagles were part of the Negro League from 1936 until 1948. One of the team's players, Larry Doby, became the first black player in the American League (with the Cleveland Indians), and Don Newcombe went on to be a star for the Brooklyn Dodgers.* © LUCIEN AIGNER/CORBIS.

year baseball was integrated. He was elected to the Hall of Fame by the Negro Leagues Committee in 1972.

JACKIE ROBINSON AND THE INTEGRATION OF BASEBALL

The signing of Jackie Robinson in 1945 by Branch Rickey of the Brooklyn Dodgers marked a new era of integration in baseball, as well as the beginning of the demise of the Negro Leagues. Significantly, Robinson's signing occurred one year after the death of baseball commissioner Kennesaw Mountain Landis. A staunch segregationist, Landis had presided over the 1913 trial that convicted Jack Johnson, the black heavyweight boxing champion of violating the Mann Act. He asserted that the integration of baseball was not necessary, because "colored" ballplayers had their own league (Burns 1994).

Jackie Robinson, a stellar college athlete, lettered in baseball, football, basketball, and track and field at the University of California, Los Angeles (UCLA). Just as important as his athletic talent, however, was Robinson's strength of character. While serving in the U.S. Army, Robinson was court-martialed for not going to the back of a public bus while in uniform. He stood his ground and was acquitted.

Robinson first played professional baseball in 1945 with the Kansas City Monarchs of the Negro American League. When he signed with the Brooklyn Dodgers on October 23, 1945, he became the first African American to join a major league organization in almost fifty years. Knowing that this was going to provoke racist reactions by many fans and players, the Dodgers assigned Robinson to their Canadian farm club, the Montreal Royals, and they moved the Dodgers' spring training to Havana, Cuba. Robinson made his major league debut on April 15, 1947. He excelled immediately, stealing two bases in his first game. He won the 1947 National League Rookie of the Year Award, despite the verbal and physical abuse he took all year from fans, players, and managers. Robinson retired in 1957 and was inducted into the Hall of Fame in 1962.

Jackie Robinson's debut was followed shortly by the Cleveland Indians' signing of Larry Doby, who integrated the American League and won that league's Rookie of the Year Award. But the breaking of the color line in Major League Baseball also meant the end of the Negro Leagues. The last Negro League World Series was played in 1949 between the Birmingham Black Barons and the Homestead Grays. The Negro National League folded in 1950 after the last East West All-Star game was played, although some Negro League teams played into the 1950s.

The integration of baseball continued very slowly. The final two teams to integrate were the New York Yankees in 1955 and the Boston Red Sox in 1959. Spring training facilities in Florida were not fully integrated until 1962. Wendell Smith, a journalist for the African-American newspaper *The Pittsburgh Courier,* was a leader in the fight to integrate baseball. His stories on spring training facilities in Florida, where African-American ballplayers had to stay in private residences and could not bring their families with them, brought the story of segregation to the public.

Many African-American ballplayers followed Robinson into the major leagues, some of whom became the game's greatest stars. Hank Aaron started his professional play with the Negro League's Indianapolis Clowns at the age of nineteen. He signed with the Milwaukee Braves in 1950 and eventually became Major League Baseball's all-time home run leader. As Aaron approached Babe Ruth's record of 714 home runs, he received numerous death threats from racist white fans who feared a black ballplayer bypassing their white hero. When he retired in 1976, Aaron was the last Negro Leaguer playing in the integrated major leagues.

Because his high school had no baseball team, Willie Mays began playing semi-pro ball on his father's team at age fourteen. He joined the Birmingham Black Barons at sixteen. He was paid the significant sum of $250 per month for just playing home games during the school year. He began his professional career by hitting a double against Satchel Paige in his first at bat. Mays was signed by the New York Giants organization in 1950 and was sent to play for their Trenton, New Jersey, team when one of their southern minor league teams would not accept a Negro ballplayer. He soon joined the Giants, leading them to the 1951 World Series. His total career statistics are among baseball's best, despite giving up two of his prime athletic years to the U.S. Army.

THE HALL OF FAME

The movement to induct black ballplayers who played before racial integration into the Hall of Fame began seriously in the 1960s. Baseball researchers began compiling information and statistics on early black baseball in the 1960s, and Robert Peterson's seminal book *Only the Ball Was White (*1970) spurred additional research. John Holway's *Voices from the Great Black Baseball Leagues* (1975) included interviews with ballplayers and Effa Manley. When the great Boston Red Sox player Ted Williams was inducted into the Hall of fame in 1966, he called for Negro Leaguers to be included in the Hall of Fame balloting process. The Society for American Baseball Research formed a Negro League research group in 1971 (Hogan 2006).

Beginning in 1971, Negro League ballplayers began being admitted to the Hall of Fame. The first group to be inducted included Satchel Paige, Rube Foster, Josh Gibson, Ray Dandridge, Buck Leonard, Leon Day, Monte Irvin, Willie Foster, Cool Papa Bell, Willie Wells, Judy Johnson, Bullet Rogan, Oscar Charleston, Smokey Joe Williams, John Henry "Pop" Lloyd, Turkey Stearnes, Martin Dihigo, and Hilton Smith.

From 1995 through 2001, Hall of Fame electors were given supplemental lists of Jim Crow era players, and several of them were elected. In 2003, Major League Baseball funded a project to research the statistics of pre-integration black ballplayers. This has resulted in a comprehensive compilation of baseball statistics, as well as Larry Hogan's *Shades of Glory* (2006) companion narrative. In 2005 the National Baseball Hall of Fame determined that there was sufficient knowledge to nominate more than seventy players and administrators from the Negro League and pre-Negro League eras for a special Hall of Fame election. In February 2006, seventeen players and administrators were elected to the Hall of Fame from this list. Among these were Effa Manley, the first woman voted into the hall of fame, and J. L. Wilkinson, the white owner of the Kansas City Monarchs.

LATIN AMERICAN BASEBALL

The first organized baseball game in Cuba occurred in 1868, only twenty-two years after the invention of the modern game of baseball on the diamond at Elysian Fields in Hoboken, New Jersey, in 1846. In 1878 the first Cuban baseball league was formed. By 1871 Esteban Enrique Bellán, a Cuban who had studied at Fordham University, was playing for the Troy Haymakers, part of the National Association of Professional Baseball Players. Between 1890 and 1911, U.S. teams regularly visited the Caribbean. Racism intervened in 1911, when Ban Johnson, the president of the American League, banned these visits. Several white Cuban players were signed by U.S. teams around the turn of the twentieth century.

The corporate expansion of the Boston-based United Fruit Company into the Caribbean in the early twentieth century and the 1916 U.S. military occupation of the Dominican Republic helped spread the game throughout the Caribbean. Cuba built baseball into a national game, especially after the Revolution of 1959.

Prior to the integration of U.S. baseball, only light-skinned Latinos, primarily Cubans, could play professional baseball in the United States. Players who could not pass as white played in the Negro Leagues. Three Negro League Latino players from this time were

Ichiro Suzuki, 2002. *Suzuki won the American League MVP and the Rookie of the Year Award in 2002. The growing popularity of baseball around the world has brought players from other nations, particularly Japan and Latin American countries, to teams in the United States.* AP IMAGES.

eventually elected to the Hall of Fame: José Méndez (The Black Diamond), Cristóbal Torrienti, and Martin Dihigo. After integration, Latino players increasingly succeeded in U.S. professional baseball. In 1947, only three Latin Americans were playing in Major League Baseball. By 1854, this number had increased to fifty-four, and by 2006, almost 30 percent of the 750 major league players were Latino. The 2005 All-Star game had representatives from eight Latin American countries.

The proper recognition of Latin American ballplayers has been called into question by the omission of Roberto Clemente, a Hall of Fame Player for the Pittsburgh Pirates, from Major League Baseball's All-Century Team. Clemente, who was of Puerto Rican descent, died in an airline crash while delivering supplies to Nicaragua after the 1972 earthquake in that country. In 2005, partly in response to this controversy, Major League Baseball launched a campaign to recognize great Latin American ballplayers, including those who played in the Negro Leagues. The result was the Latino Legends Team.

JAPANESE BASEBALL

The history of baseball in Japan goes back to the late 1800s, when Japanese plantation workers formed company teams. In 1903 a Japanese baseball team came to the United States for the first time, and this was followed by the formation of many Japanese teams in the United States. Kenso Nushida played in the Pacific Coast league as the first Japanese minor league player. Babe Ruth's tours of Japan with other major league all-stars in the 1930s also spurred an increased interest in baseball.

The popularity of the game among the Japanese is illustrated by the fact that baseball was played in all of the World War II Japanese internment camps. After this unfortunate episode in U.S. history, Japanese Americans played widely on college teams and in Japan. The first Japanese player to play in the major leagues was Masonori Murakami, a pitcher who played for the San Francisco Giants from 1963 to 1965. It took thirty years for the next Japanese player, the pitcher Hideo Nomo of the Los Angeles Dodgers, to play Major League Baseball. Despite notions that Japanese players were not good enough to play positions other than pitcher, the first Japanese position players, signed in the 1990s, had great success. Ichiro Suzuki and Hideki Matsui, have indeed become all stars, while Kenji Johjima was signed in 2006 as the first Japanese catcher. There have only been a few Japanese-American players, however. Ryan Kurosaki signed in 1975, while in 1977 Lenn Sakata became the first Japanese-American position player in the major leagues.

BASEBALL AND RACE

Baseball has always reflected U.S. race relations. At times it has reinforced racial division, as in the "gentleman's agreement" that kept owners from signing black baseball players to professional contracts. At other times, it has led the way toward social justice, as the signing of Jackie Robinson demonstrates. The biographies of black ballplayers reveal the injustices of racism. Henry Aaron's recounting of his Negro League team eating in a restaurant in Washington D.C., and hearing the wait staff break the plates that the players had used reveals the virulent, personal nature of racism (Aaron and Wheeler 1992). Throughout the history of the sport, baseball and American culture have remained intertwined.

SEE ALSO *Basketball; Boxing; Football (U.S.); Genetics and Athletic Performance; Track and Field.*

BIBLIOGRAPHY

Aaron, Henry, with Lonnie Wheeler. 1992. *I Had a Hammer: The Hank Aaron Story.* New York: HarperCollins.

Bjarkman, Peter C. 1994. *Baseball with a Latin Beat: A History of the Latin American Game*. Jefferson, NC: McFarland Press.

Block, David. 2005. *Baseball before We Knew It: A Search for the Roots of the Game*. Lincoln: University of Nebraska Press.

Burns, Ken. 2005. *Unforgivable Blackness: The Rise and Fall of Jack Johnson*. DVD. Florentine Films and WETA, Washington, D.C.

Einstein, Charles. 1979, *Willie's Time: A Memoir*. New York: Lippincott.

Erskine, Carl, with Burton Rocks. 2005. *What I Learned from Jackie Robinson: A Teammate's Reflection on and off the Field*. New York: McGraw Hill.

Gould, Stephen Jay. 2004. "The Creation Myths of Cooperstown." In *Triumph and Tragedy in Mudville: Lifelong Passion for Baseball*, 190–204. London: Jonathan Cape.

Hogan, Lawrence. 2006. *Shades of Glory: The Negro Leagues and the Story of African-American Baseball*. Washington, D.C.: National Geographic Press.

Lanctot, Neil. 2004. *Negro League Baseball: The Rise and Ruin of a Black Institution*. Philadelphia: University of Pennsylvania Press.

McKissack, Patricia C., and Fred McKissack, Jr. 1994. *Black Diamond: The Story of the Negro Baseball Leagues*. New York: Scholastic.

Naakagawa, Kerry Jo. 2001. *Through a Diamond: 100 years of Japanese Baseball*. Iowa City, IA: Rudi Publishing.

Nisei Baseball Research Project. Available from http://www.niseibaseball.com.

Peterson, Robert. 1970. *Only the Ball Was White: A History of Legendary Black Players and All-Black Professional Teams*. Englewood Cliffs, NJ: Prentice-Hall.

Regaldo, Samuel. 1998. *Viva Baseball: Latin Major Leaguers and their Special Hunger*. Urbana: University of Illinois Press.

Ruck, Rob. 1999. *Tropic of Baseball: Baseball in the Dominican Republic*. Lincoln: University of Nebraska Press.

Simon, Scott. 2002. *Jackie Robinson and the Integration of Baseball*. New York: John Wiley.

Vignola, Patricia. 2005. "The Enemies at the Gate: An Economic Debate about the Denouement of Negro League Baseball." *NINE: A Journal of Baseball History and Culture* 13 (2): 71–81.

Villegas, Jose Luis, and Marcos Bretón. 2003. *Home Is Everything: The Latino Baseball Story: From Barrio to the Major Leagues*. El Paso, TX: Cinco Punto Press.

Ward, Geoffrey C., and Ken Burns. 1994. *Baseball: A Film by Ken Burns*. Produced by Ken Burns and Lynn Novick. DVD. Florentine Films and WETA, Washington, D.C.

White, Sol. 1995. *Sol White's History of Colored Baseball, with Other Documents on the Early Black Game, 1886–1936*. Compiled and introduced by Jerry Malloy. Lincoln: University of Nebraska Press.

Stanton W. Green

BASKETBALL

The perceived dominance of African Americans in basketball has been taken as proof of the natural athleticism of blacks (defined as any people of African origin). However, the history of sport quickly dismisses this notion.

Basketball was invented by the Canadian-born James Naismith in December 1891. Naismith, a physical education teacher at the School for Christian Workers (now Springfield College) in Springfield, Massachusetts, was charged with inventing a game to entertain the school's athletes during the winter. The original game used a soccer ball, two peach baskets attached to the railing of gym balcony, two nine-player teams, and thirteen rules. Between 1906 and 1916 a series of rules changes were implemented, including opening the net to allow the ball to fall through after a goal. Players fouled out after committing five fouls, and foul shots were awarded depending on the severity of the infraction. In 1916 dribbling followed by a shot was allowed. (Prior to this players could not move after the ball was passed to them.)

Many of the early basketball games were played in gymnasiums with floor to ceiling netting separating the crowd from the players. This is where the term "cager" originated, though the practice was discontinued in 1929.

In 1892, Senda Berenson Abbot, a Lithuanian-born physical education teacher at Smith College in Northampton, Massachusetts, twenty miles north of Springfield, developed a modified game for women because it was believed that the men's game was too physically demanding for the "fairer" sex. The court was divided into three equal sections, with players required to stay in an assigned area; players were prohibited from snatching or batting the ball from the hands of another player; and they were prohibited from holding the ball for longer than three seconds and from dribbling the ball more than three times.

The spread of basketball in the United States and abroad was facilitated by the Young Men's Christian Associations (YMCAs), the armed forces, and colleges. Factors that helped it grow in popularity were the simple equipment requirements, indoor play, competitiveness, and easily understood rules. These were also the same attributes that would make it well-suited for the urban African-American neighborhoods that would spring up across America after World War II.

The first intercollegiate league, the New England Intercollegiate Basketball League, was formed in May 1901. It included teams from Yale and Harvard Universities and Trinity, Holy Cross, Amherst, and Williams Colleges. It is highly unlikely that any African Americans played in this first league. Indeed only eight African Americans are recorded as having played for European American collegiate teams from 1904 to 1919 (see Table 1).

African-American athletes were not allowed to play basketball for predominantly European American institutions in the Jim Crow South until after the 1950s. Colored YMCAs and YWCAs throughout the nation formed the first African-American teams. This effort

African Americans Who Starred for European American Colleges Prior to 1920

Player	Years	University or College	State
Samuel Ransom	1904–08	Beloit College	Wisconsin
Wilbur Wood	1907–10	University of Nebraska	Nebraska
Fenwich Watkins	1909	University of Vermont	Vermont
Cumberland Posey	1909, 1916	Pennsylvania State University, Duquesne University	Pennsylvania
Sol Butler	1910	Dubuque College	Iowa
William Kindle	1911	Springfield College	Massachusetts
Cleve Abbot	1913	South Dakota State	South Dakota
Paul Robeson	1915–18	Rutgers University	New Jersey

SOURCE: Adapted from Ashe, Arthur. (1988). *A Hard Road to Glory: A History of the African-American Athlete 1619–1918.* Warner Books: New York, p. 175.

Table 1.

was hampered in the South however, due to poor gymnasiums, a lack of equipment, few coaches, and year-round warm weather. YMCA college student associations played a major role in introducing African-Americans' colleges to basketball.

PROFESSIONAL BASKETBALL IN THE GOLDEN AGE

Professional basketball began in 1896 at a YMCA in Trenton, New Jersey, and in 1898 the National Basketball League (NBL) was founded. The NBL consisted of six franchises from Pennsylvania and New Jersey. At the same time, club teams were being formed. The Smart Set Athletic Club, from Brooklyn, New York, was the first African-American club team, and it was soon joined by the St. Christopher Athletic Club and the Marathone Athletic Club. These clubs formed the Olympic Athletic League. Similar clubs were formed in Washington, D.C., Baltimore, Philadelphia, St. Louis, Wilmington, Delaware, and northern New Jersey. The Buffalo Germans, a team with players of German descent that won 111 straight games between 1908 and 1911, and the Original Celtics (who were started by Irish players from New York's Hell's Kitchen), were extraordinarily successful professional teams in the early twentieth century. The Original Celtics pioneered many of the tactics still used in modern basketball, including zone defense and post play. The first successful national professional league was the American Basketball League (ABL), which lasted from 1925 to 1931 and resumed play again from 1933 to 1934. The ABL was formed without any African-American players; teams and league rules disallowed games against African-American teams. For this reason, the Original Celtics refused to join.

The racially segregated character of American society meant that most sports clubs were composed of a single ethnic group, or of groups that were considered socially equivalent (such as poor Irish and Jews). The 1920s through 1930s saw three prominent ethnically based professional teams dominate basketball: the Original Celtics, the South Philadelphia Hebrew Association team (the SPHAs), and the New York Renaissance (the Rens), an all-African American team. The Original Celtics compiled an amazing record as a barnstorming team, with more than 700 victories and only 60 losses in the 1920s. (*Barnstorming* refers to the practice of touring a region playing local club teams). They were eventually forced into the ABL when the league disallowed its members to play nonmembers, thus reducing the number of competitors. In 1926 and 1927 the Original Celtics won the first two league championships. The league owners responded by breaking up the team and dispersing their players throughout the league. In 1928 the New York Rens won the championship, defeating the Original Celtics, who featured the future Hall of Famers Joe Lapchick and Nat Holman. A year later, the Original Celtics again won the title. The contests between the Celtics and the Rens were some of the hottest tickets in town, and at least five race riots were sparked by their games.

The SPHAs won seven ABL titles between 1933 and 1945, and they lost in the championship series twice. The team's uniform tops featured the Hebrew letters spelling SPHAs and a Jewish star. The back of the team's road uniforms said "Hebrews"! In 1926 during a break in ABL play, the SPHAs defeated both the Original Celtics and the New York Renaissance in best-of-three game series, showing that, though a minor league team, they were able to compete against the best professional teams of the period.

The early success of Jewish athletes in basketball spawned biologically based racial theories to explain this phenomenon. Paul Gallico, a sports editor for the *New York Daily News* wrote in his 1938 *Farewell to Sports*: "The reason, I suspect, that basketball appeals to the Hebrew with his Oriental background is that the game places a premium on an alert, scheming mind, flashy trickiness, artful dodging and general smart aleckness." Other writers suggested that Jews had an advantage in basketball because short men have better balance and more foot speed. They also suggested that they had sharper eyes, which was in contradiction to the stereotype that Jewish men were nearsighted.

In 1923, the New York Rens became the first full-salaried African-American professional basketball team. Like the Original Celtics and the SPHAs, the Rens were a barnstorming squad that had to take on all levels of competition to earn a living. The Rens were not allowed to join the ABL or the National Basketball League (NBL), which was formed in 1937. Yet in their nearly three-decade existence, starting in 1922, the Rens compiled a 2,588–529 record. They took their name from Harlem's

World Basketball Champions, Chicago Herald Tournaments, 1939–1948

Winning Team/Runner Up	Race/Ethnicity	Year
New York Rens/Oshkosh All-Stars	African Am./European Am.	1939
Harlem Globetrotters/ Chicago Bruins	African Am./European Am.	1940
Detroit Eagles/Oshkosh All-Stars	European Am./European Am.	1941
Oshkosh All-Stars/Detroit Eagles	European Am./European Am.	1942
Washington Bears*/ Oshkosh All-Stars	African Am./European Am.	1943
Fort Wayne Zollner Pistons/ Brooklyn Eagles	European Am./European Am.	1944
Fort Wayne Zollner Pistons/ Dayton Acmes	European Am./European Am.	1945
Fort Wayne Zollner Pistons/ Oshkosh All-Stars	European Am./European Am.	1946
Indianapolis Kautskys/ Toledo Jeeps	European Am./European Am.	1947
Minneapolis Lakers/ New York Rens	European Am./African Am.	1948

Note: The Washington Bears featured many of the New York Rens in this year.

SOURCE: Adapted from statistics compiled by William F. Himmelman in Peterson, Robert W. (1990). *Cages to Jump Shots: Pro Basketball's Early Years.* New York: Oxford University Press.

Table 2.

Renaissance Casino, which opened in 1922. Bob Douglas, called the "father of black basketball" organized the team, which practiced and played home games at the casino's dance hall. The Rens games were part of combined social-athletic events, with dances usually beginning right after the games.

During the Depression era, professional basketball leagues were not financially lucrative enough to allow players to make a living or team owners to make sufficient profits. Thus many teams survived by barnstorming. These teams were often ethnically based, such as the Terrible Swedes, the Harlem Globetrotters (African Americans out of Chicago, not New York), the House of David (Jewish), an even the Hong Wah Q'ues (a Chinese-American team.) During the 1940s many cities hosted basketball tournaments for professional teams, including the World Professional Basketball Tournament, played in Chicago Stadium each year from 1939 to 1948. At this time, professional teams were either owned by individuals or by corporations. On the corporate teams, the players had year-round jobs with the company, though they owed these jobs to the fact that they could play basketball. The records of the World Professional Basketball Tournament show no evidence of "African-American superiority" in basketball (see Table 2).

THE RACIALIZATION OF MODERN BASKETBALL

The history of early basketball does not support any theory of biologically based racial participation in the sport. Beginning in the 1960s, however, there was an increased participation of African Americans in the sport at all levels, including some of the greatest superstars of American sport. This pattern has spawned biologically based racial theories of African-American participation, including ideas of biologically superior athletic ability—particularly leaping ability—as explanations for the predominance of African-American stars. One CBS sports commentator, Jimmy "the Greek" Snyder, pronounced that the superior athletic ability of blacks was due to the fact that "blacks had been bred like race horses" during slavery. Another prominent racially based athletic theory is the supposedly greater innate jumping ability of African Americans. (Conversely, European Americans are supposed to suffer from the "white man's disease," or the inability to jump.) The supporters of this theory cite the results of slam-dunk competitions, which have been overwhelmingly dominated by athletes of African descent.

As convenient as these theories are, they all suffer from lack of genetic or physiological evidence to support their claims. In fact, the dominance of African Americans in American basketball is more easily explained by social and cultural changes that occurred in the United States between the 1940s and 1970s. In this period, governmental policies allowed persons of European descent to escape the inner cities while African Americans were denied access to the means to live elsewhere. Between 1934 and 1962, Federal Housing Authority (FHA) programs provided $120 billion in loans, but less than 2 percent of these went to nonwhites. The loans made cheap housing available to European Americans outside the cities and created the American suburbs. This occurred just as new waves of African Americans migrated to the northern cities in search of greater economic opportunity and freedom from racial discrimination. New Deal projects, such as government-owned buildings designed to save the poor from the dilapidated tenements, began to concentrate poor African Americans. These buildings were appropriately called "the projects." The youths living within their confines were encouraged to pursue athletic activities that could be played on the blacktop surfaces of this urban landscape, and basketball was a natural candidate for this environment.

Sports culture, like music and the arts, was influenced by this new form of segregation. In the 1950s, many African-American educators and community leaders were still touting sports as a way to get ahead in a racist society. Holcomb Rucker was an example of someone who held these notions. Rucker was a New York City Department of Public Works employee who developed teen-oriented summer basketball leagues in Harlem. By 1955 his summer tournaments were heavily attended by scouts from major universities. The Rucker tournaments included such future basketball greats as Wilt Chamberlain, Walt Hazzard, Willis Reed, and Julius Erving, who played against equally talented individuals, many of whom later died of drug overdoses or went to prison. The emphasis on sports as a way to overcome racism meant that some of the brightest and most talented African Americans in this era pursued careers in sports.

While a student at Oakland's McClymonds High, the future Boston Celtic great Bill Russell imagined new ways of playing defense in basketball. He devised the idea that defensive players could leave their feet to block a shot and keep the ball in play so that it could be recovered by a teammate. At playgrounds all over the inner cities of America, basketball skills that had been pioneered by earlier professionals of European descent, such as the jump shot and behind-the-back dribbling, were being improved on by African-American youth. In 1962, John McLendon, a former student of James Naismith and a successful college coach, published *Fast Break Basketball: Fine Points and Fundamentals*. Thus, during the 1950s and 1960s a distinctive African-American style of basketball developed and became as integral a part of African-American culture as "the blues" and "rhythm and blues" music.

Concomitant with the demographic shifts in the cities, a series of rules changes made basketball a faster and more athletic sport. Prior to these rule changes, basketball had essentially become football played on hardwood floors. On the inner-city playgrounds of America, African-American athletes had already begun to redefine how the game was played. Soon, college basketball could not ignore the lure of these talented individuals. The 1949-1950 NCAA champions, City College of New York (CCNY), were integrated and coached by basketball legend Nat Holman (of the Original Celtics). Conversely, the 1951 NCAA champions, the University of Kentucky, were all European Americans and coached by segregationist Adolph Rupp (a college basketball coaching legend). Despite their athletic greatness, both schools were shown to be involved with point-shaving gambling scandals, but at the time more was made of the CCNY problem due to the participation of African-American athletes.

The late 1950s would see four stellar African Americans open the doors to integrating basketball at the college level. These were Bill Russell at the University of San Francisco, Wilt Chamberlain at the University of Kansas, Elgin Baylor at Seattle University, and Oscar Robertson at the University of Cincinnati. In 1966, Texas Western would be the first team to win a NCAA basketball title with an all-black starting five. They defeated a heavily favored—and segregated—Kentucky squad.

Texas Western, 1966. *Texas Western was the first team to win a NCAA basketball title with an all-black starting five. The team defeated a heavily favored—and segregated—Kentucky squad 72-65.* © BETTMANN/CORBIS.

INTEGRATION AND THE BIRTH OF THE NATIONAL BASKETBALL ASSOCIATION

In 1950, Chuck Cooper became the first African-American player drafted by the fledgling National Basketball Association (NBA). By the 1960s, African-American participation at both the college and professional level had drastically increased, so much so that the Boston Celtics had an all–African-American starting line-up in 1964. The percentage of African Americans playing in the collegiate and professional ranks continued to increase in the 1970s.

The increase in African-American dominance of professional basketball during the latter decades of the twentieth century was such that a survey of NBA all-franchise players in 1994, covering the league from its beginnings, showed that out of 124 players, 86 were African Americans, 35 were European Americans, 1 was African, 1 was European, and 1 was an Iranian American. The NBA named its fifty greatest players from its first fifty years in 1996. Of these, thirty-one were African Americans and eighteen were European American. In 2001, the Basketball Hall of Fame included 34 African Americans and 77 European Americans. James Naismith and the Nigerian-born Hakeem Olajuwon were the only non–American-born inductees.

However, this increase in African-American participation coincided with a decline in the popularity of the professional game. By the end of the 1970s, the NBA (which had merged with the American Basketball Association, or ABA, in 1977) was the only one of the three major spectator sports without a national television contract. In 1981, sixteen of the twenty-three teams were losing money, and there was serious talk of folding the small-city franchises and downsizing to a twelve-team league. Earvin Magic Johnson (an African American from East Lansing, Michigan) and Larry Bird (a European American from French Lick, Indiana) helped to change all of that. Their rivalry began in the 1979 NCAA tournament and continued on into the NBA. Magic Johnson was one of the most versatile players the game had ever known, while Larry Bird was one of the game's greatest pure shooters and competitors. Johnson's Lakers and Bird's Celtics faced each other in the NBA finals three times in the 1980s, and one of their teams captured the title eight out of ten years in that decade. This stimulated the rebirth of the NBA and set the stage for the emergence of the one of the greatest athletes the world has ever known, Michael Jordan of the Chicago Bulls.

Jordan is of African-American descent, and he played his college basketball under NCAA legend Dean Smith at North Carolina. Smith's coaching style did not allow Jordan to showcase his formidable talents, and few expected him to be the superstar he became in the NBA. Jordan's Bulls won six titles in the 1990s and he became the center of one of the greatest sports merchandising franchises of all time. Before signing Michael Jordan in 1987, annual sales of the athletic-shoe company Nike were only $900 million. Ten years later, based on the impact of their "Air Jordan" line, Nike annual sales were $9.19 billion, an increase of more than 1,000 percent. The popularity of basketball had changed so much in fifty years that Michael Jordan was still earning $33 million per year in endorsements two years after his retirement.

RACIAL GENETICS OF BASKETBALL

In a period of fifty years, professional basketball in America went from 100 percent to 16 percent European American. In the 2000-2001 season, African Americans dominated NBA rosters. European Americans, or "whites," are persons whose genetic ancestry can be traced to some area in Europe and who have no detectable African ancestry. African Americans, or "blacks," have genes that originated among Western Africans, Europeans, and American Indians. The average percentage of non-African genes in African Americans has been estimated to vary from as low as 6 percent to as high as 40 percent. Many of the early twenty-first century's successful black athletes are the children of men who were athletically or socially successful in the last generation and who married European-American wives. Racial theories of basketball performance rely on the idea that there is something genetically "African" that predisposes an individual to be a better basketball player.

To test this assertion, however, it would be best to compare the number of Africans versus the number of Europeans in the NBA. African Americans are, in fact, not appropriate in this regard because a substantial fraction of their genes originated in Europeans and American Indians. In 2000, there were three Western Africans, nine Europeans, and one Australian in the NBA. An examination of the NBA 2002 rosters showed twenty-one Europeans, one East Asian, and nine Africans in the league. In that same season, Yao Ming, formerly of the Shanghai Sharks, made a particularly dramatic entry into the NBA, finishing second in Rookie of the Year voting. Thus, in a direct comparison of individuals who have "purely" African or European genes, there are more of those with European genes than African. This is directly opposite to the racial theory of basketball participation.

THE INTERNATIONALIZATION OF BASKETBALL

Basketball was introduced to the Summer Olympic Games in 1936. Since then, the United States has pretty much dominated the competition. The 1972 victory of the Soviet Union has always been attributed to dubious officiating. In 1988, however, the Soviet Union won the gold, Yugoslavia the silver, and the United States settled for the bronze medal. Americans criticized this defeat as due to the essentially "professional" character of the European basketball programs. This criticism led to a changing of International Olympic Committee rules, and by 1992 professional athletes could compete in the Olympic Games. The 1992 Barcelona Olympics featured the U.S. "Dream Team," consisting of eight players of African-American ancestry and four players of European-American descent. The Dream Team easily won the gold medal, but their victory also helped to spread the popularity of basketball to such an extent that the dominance of the United States, and of African Americans, in basketball may soon be a thing of the past.

Indeed, the 2002 U.S. men's international basketball team, which was predominantly African American, was eliminated by Yugoslavia in the quarterfinals and lost to Spain in the consolation game of the World Championships. The USA finished seventh, while the only African nation in the competition finished in an abysmal eleventh place. At the men's competition in the 2004 Olympic Games, Argentina won the gold, Italy the Silver, and the United States the bronze. In the women's competition, the United States won the Gold, Australia the Silver, and Russia the Bronze. No African nations qualified for the medal rounds at these Olympics. Of the 177 players drafted by the NBA from 2003 to 2005, 28 were

Michael Jordan in the NBA Finals, 1998. *Considered by many to be the best basketball player in history, Jordan led the Chicago Bulls to six NBA championships.* AP IMAGES.

Europeans, 2 were East Asians, 1 was from East Africa, 22 from West Africa, and 4 were from Latin America. Finally, the 2005 NBA championship was won by the San Antonio Spurs, who featured five international players on their twelve-man roster. Two of their three most important players, Tim Duncan and Tony Parker, have some detectable African ancestry. These results indicate that the "black" dominance of professional and international basketball is fading.

Basketball ability, just like any other human behavior, is determined by a complex interplay between individual genetic ability, personality, culture, and society. African Americans, who currently dominate the game, represent a genetically and culturally unique population, one that is not equivalent to any particular Western African population, either in genes or in culture. Success at the modern game of basketball is facilitated by speed, endurance, agility, strength, height, hand-eye coordination, and leaping ability, among other athletic traits. There is no reason to suppose that these traits are found disproportionately among people of African descent in the United States, nor is there any scientific way of separating the genetic, environmental, or cultural effects that determine athletic predisposition. Thus, any claims of African genes providing superior athletic performance are at best speculation, and at worse racist ideology. The difference between the ethnic composition of the participants of American basketball and volleyball illustrates the social construction of sports performance. Both games require similar athletic skills, yet basketball is currently dominated by African-American athletes, while volleyball is dominated by European-American athletes.

When Michael Jordan retired from professional basketball, he was asked once again by reporters why he thought black players dominated the sport. "Okay, I'll tell you," he said. As reporters leaned forward, pencils poised, he whispered into the microphone, "We practice."

SEE ALSO *Baseball; Football (U.S.); Genetics and Athletic Performance; Track and Field.*

BIBLIOGRAPHY

Ashe, Arthur. 1993. *A Hard Road to Glory—Basketball: The African American Athlete in Basketball.* New York: Amistad Press.

Basketball Hall of Fame. "The Original Celtics." Available from http://www.hoophall.com/halloffamers/Celtics%20Original.htm.

Bjarkman, Peter. 1992. *The History of the NBA.* New York: Crescent Books.

———. 1994. *The Encyclopedia of Pro Basketball Team Histories.* New York: Caroll and Graf.

Deutsch, Robin Jonathan, and Wayne Patterson. 2001. "Basketball." In *Microsoft® Encarta® Online Encyclopedia.* Available from http://encarta.msn.com/encyclopedia_761571883/Basketball.html.

Entine, Jon. 2001. *Taboo: Why Black Athletes Dominate Sports and Why We Are Afraid to Talk about It.* New York: Public Affairs.

George, Nelson. 1992. *Elevating the Game: Black Men and Basketball.* New York: Harper-Collins.

Gutman, Bill. 1993. *The History of NCAA Basketball.* New York: Crescent Publishers.

International Jewish Sports Hall of Fame. "Philadelphia SPHAs." Available from http://www.jewishsports.net/BioPages/PhiladelphiaSPHAs.htm.

McCallum, John Dennis. 1978. *College Basketball, U.S.A., since 1892: The History of the Game since Its Beginnings, Storied Players, Teams, and Coaches.* New York: Stein and Day.

National Basketball Association. "The Original Dream Team." Available from http://www.nba.com/history/dreamT_moments.html.

———. "Remembering the Rens." Available from http://www.nba.com/history/encyclopedia_rens_001214.html.

Peterson, Robert W. 1990. *Cages to Jump Shots: Pro Basketball's Early Years.* New York: Oxford University Press.

Sands, Robert R., ed. 1999. *Anthropology, Sport, and Culture.* Westport, CT: Bergin & Garvey.

Wetzel, Dan, and Don Yaeger. 2000. *Sole Influence: Basketball, Corporate Greed, and the Corruption of America's Youth*. New York: Warner Books.

Wolff, Alexander. 1991. *100 Years of Hoops: A Fond Look Back at the Sport of Basketball*. New York: Crescent Publishers.

Joseph L. Graves Jr.

BATES, DAISY
1912–1999

Daisy Bates was born Daisy Lee Gatson in Huttig, Arkansas, on or around November 12, 1912. In her autobiography, *The Long Shadow of Little Rock*, she described Huttig, located at the very bottom of the state, as a "sawmill plantation," where "everyone worked for the mill, lived in houses owned by the mill, and traded at the general store run by the mill."

Tragedy struck the Bates family when Daisy was only a child. Her birth mother was raped and murdered by three white men, and her father, fearing for his safety, fled town. Orlee and Susie Smith, two family friends, adopted Daisy. It was not until she was older that she would learn the truth about her mother and father.

Growing up in Huttig, a town of less than 1,000 persons, Bates said she did not really understand what being black meant until she was seven. She went to the store to buy some meat for her mother and was told by the butcher, "Niggers have to wait 'til I wait on the white people" (1987 [1962], in chapter "What It Means to Be Negro"). Bates developed a deep-seated hatred of the white race living in the Jim Crow South. Her adoptive father, bothered by his daughter's rage, counseled her not to hate white people just because they are white. "Hate can destroy you," he told her. "If you hate, make it count for something. Hate the humiliations we are living under in the South. Hate the discrimination that eats away at the soul of every black man and woman. Hate the insults hurled at us by white scum—and then try to do something about it, or your hate won't spell at thing" (http://ut.essortment.com/whoisdaisybat_ogp.htm).

When Bates was a teenager, her father's friend, Lucius Christopher (L.C.) Bates, an insurance salesman and former journalist, came calling. He pursued her for several years before they finally tied the knot in 1942. Bates and L.C. moved north to Little Rock. L.C. dreamed of returning to his journalistic roots so he and Daisy leased a printing plant and started the *Arkansas State Press*.

The *State Press*'s circulation reached 10,000 in its first few months of publication. It soon grew into the largest, most influential black newspaper in the state. It publicized violations of the Supreme Court's 1954 *Brown v. Board of Education* desegregation ruling, as well as gruesome instances of police brutality, and it fought to free blacks from slum housing, menial jobs, and injustice in the courtrooms.

In 1952 Daisy was elected president of the Arkansas NAACP. As state president, she participated in litigation to pressure the Little Rock School Board to abide by the *Brown* decision and integrate. "To the nation's Negroes," she wrote in *The Long Shadow*, "the Supreme Court decision meant that the time for delay, evasion, or procrastination was over."

Facing increasing pressure from black parents, the NAACP, and a Supreme Court ruling, Virgil Blossom, superintendent of the Little Rock Public School District, announced a plan to begin the desegregation process with Little Rock Central High School in September 1957.

Seventy-five black students initially registered for admission into Central High, but school officials chose the nine whom they thought were the most emotionally mature. The Little Rock Nine, as they came to be known, were Ernest Green, Elizabeth Eckford, Jefferson Thomas, Terrence Roberts, Carlotta Walls Lanier, Minnijean Brown Trickey, Gloria Ray Karlmark, Thelma Mothershed-Wair, and Melba Pattillo Beals. Bates served as an adviser and mentor to these students. She provided protective custody for them and was their leading advocate. She had no children of her own, and the Little Rock Nine were affectionately referred to as "Daisy Bates's children."

The Little Rock Nine were initially slated to enter Central High on Tuesday, September 3, 1957. The night before, Governor Orval Faubus called up the state's National Guard to surround Central High and prevent the students from entering. He did this, he claimed, in order to protect citizens and property from white supremacists that were headed in caravans toward Little Rock. If the Little Rock Nine attempted to enter Central High, Faubus said, "blood would run in the streets." The Nine did not, in fact, attend Central High on September 3, the first day of school. On September 4, Bates phoned them and instructed them to meet a few blocks from Central and walk to school as a group. Elizabeth Eckford did not have a phone in her home, however, and never received the message. She attempted to enter Central High by herself, through the front door. As the Arkansas National Guard looked on, she was met by an angry white mob who berated her and threatened to lynch her. Ironically, it was two whites who stepped forward to assist her. They helped her get on a city bus and away from the school without injury. The rest of the Little Rock Nine were denied entry by the National Guardsmen.

The National Guard troops finally left Central High on September 20, after a federal judge had granted an injunction against Faubus's use of National Guard troops to prevent integration. On Monday, September 23, school resumed. There were no troops, but Central High was surrounded by policemen. A white mob, numbering close to 1,000, gathered in front of the school, waiting to spew more hatred at the black students. But instead of entering through the front door, the police escorted the Nine through a side entrance. When the mob learned that the Nine had made it inside, they began to attack the police and charge towards the building. For their own safety, the Nine were removed from school before noon.

With a crisis on their hands, Congressman Brooks Hays and Mayor Woodrow Mann asked the Eisenhower administration to intervene. "Hysteria in all of its madness enveloped the city," Bates later wrote, and "racial feelings were at a fever pitch." On September 24, Mann sent a telegram to Eisenhower requesting federal troops. Eisenhower obliged, and federal troops were dispatched that day. He also federalized the Arkansas National Guard, which removed Faubus's power over them. On September 25, the Little Rock Nine entered Central High School under the protection of 1,000 members of the 101st Airborne Division of the United States Army.

The Little Rock Nine were not the only ones who were tormented during the Central High Crisis. In August 1957, a rock was thrown through the picture window of the Bates home. A note attached to the rock read, "Stone this time. Dynamite next." Two days later, an eight-foot cross was burned on the Bates's lawn, accompanied by the message, "Go back to Africa. KKK." On July 7, 1958, a bomb was set off in front of the Bates home, but no one was injured. Bates said it took many weeks for her to become accustomed to seeing "revolvers lying on tables in my own home" and "shotguns loaded with buckshot, standing ready near the doors."

The Bates family was also forced to shut down the *State Press*. After Daisy became involved in the civil rights struggle, white businesses stopped advertising in the paper, and it had to stop publishing because of lost revenue. L.C. Bates joined the paid staff of the NAACP in 1960.

Only three of the Little Rock Nine eventually graduated from Central High. Ernest Green became the school's first black graduate in 1958. Jefferson Thomas and Carlotta Walls Lanier graduated in 1960. Minnijean Brown Trickey was expelled from the school in February 1958, after several incidents, including one in which she dumped a bowl of chili on one of her tormentors. Throughout their time at Central High, Bates remained deeply concerned about their welfare, often intervening with school officials during conflicts.

Daisy Bates in the Little Rock Municipal Court, 1958. *Bates's involvement with the Arkansas NAACP and the Little Rock Nine led to her arrest for violating the "Bennett Ordinance," which required that various organizations submit membership and other information. She was convicted and paid a $25 fine.* © BETTMANN/CORBIS.

After the success at Central High, Bates worked in voter registration campaigns for the Democratic National Committee, and President Lyndon Johnson appointed her to help administer his antipoverty programs. She revived the *State Press* in 1984, only to sell it three years later.

After Daisy Bates passed away on November 4, 1999, the state of Arkansas permitted her body to lay in state in the rotunda of the capitol. The third Monday in February has been established as an official state holiday in her honor, the Daisy Gatson Bates Holiday, making Arkansas the first state to honor an African American woman with a named holiday.

SEE ALSO *Civil Rights Movement.*

BIBLIOGRAPHY

Bates, Daisy. 1987 (1962). *The Long Shadow of Little Rock: A Memoir.* Fayetteville: University of Arkansas Press.

Drew, Keith. 2004. "Eckford: Central High in 1957 'Was Not … a Normal Environment.'" CNN.com, May 17. Available from http://www.cnn.com/2004/LAW/05/17/eckford.transcript/index.html.

Encyclopedia of Arkansas History and Culture. Available from http://www.encyclopediaofarkansas.net.

Fradin, Dennis Brindell, and Judith Bloom Fradin. 2004. *The Power of One: Daisy Bates and the Little Rock Nine*. New York: Clarion.

King, Martin Luther, Jr. 2001. *The Autobiography of Martin Luther King, Jr.* Edited by Clayborne Carson. New York: IPM/Warner Books.

Library of Congress. 2004. "'With an Even Hand': Brown v. Board at Fifty." Available from http://www.loc.gov/exhibits/brown.

Little Rock Central High School. "The Little Rock Nine." Available from http://www.centralhigh57.org.

Ordorica, Daniel. "Women and Jim Crow: A Geographic Perspective." Available from http://www.jimcrowhistory.org/history/history.htm.

Philadelphia Tribune. 2006. "Bates, an integration forerunner: Daisy Bates is often-forgotten hero of the 'Little Rock Nine.'" Jan. 16: 1H–2H.

National Park Service. "We Shall Overcome: Historic Places of the Civil Rights Movement—Daisy Bates House." Available from http://www.cr.nps.gov/nr/travel/civilrights/.

National Park Service. "We Shall Overcome: Historic Places of the Civil Rights Movement—Little Rock Central High School National Historic Site." Available from http://www.cr.nps.gov/nr/travel/civilrights/.

University of Arkansas Libraries, Special Collections. *Daisy Bates Papers*. Available from http://libinfo.uark.edu/SpecialCollections.

Greg Johnson

BETHUNE, MARY McLEOD
1875–1955

Mary McLeod Bethune dedicated her life to promoting education and combating the debilitating effects of racism in America. Two of her major accomplishments—the founding of a school for young black girls, which in the early twenty-first century is one of the major historically black colleges and universities, and organizing the Council for Negro Women, now housed in its own building on Pennsylvania Avenue in the nation's capital—have insured her place as one of the great leaders in black American history.

Born near Mayesville, South Carolina, on July 10, 1875, Mary Jane McLeod was the fifteenth of seventeen children born to Samuel and Patsy McLeod. Her parents were former slaves, and they wanted their children to receive an education. They also desired to be independent, so they worked hard and sacrificed to buy a farm for the family. As a child, Mary Mcleod was eager to learn as much as she could. When the Mission Board of the Presbyterian Church opened a school for blacks four miles from her home, her parents registered her. Mary had to walk the eight miles each day, but she understood at an early age that education was the key to a better life for blacks. Her love of learning may also have had roots in an incident that occurred when she was a child. When the young white children at the home where her mother worked saw her pick up a book, they reproached her and told her books were not for blacks. Indeed, they believed blacks did not have the ability to read. This accusation made Mary even more determined to excel in school.

Mary McLeod did indeed stand out at the mission school, and she was given a scholarship to attend Scotia Seminary in North Carolina. She was then awarded a second scholarship to attend Moody Bible Institute in Chicago, where she also performed exceptionally well and completed the school's two-year missionary training program. She was told, however, that there were no positions available for black missionaries in Africa. Though deeply disappointed, she returned to Mayesville and taught for one year in the mission school she had once attended. She then taught at Haines Institute in Augusta, Georgia, for one year, after which she went to Kendall Institute in Sumter, South Carolina, where she taught for two years.

CALLED TO FLORIDA

In 1898, while still at Kendall, she married Albertus Bethune. The couple left South Carolina and moved to Savannah, Georgia, where her husband had a new job. Their only son, Albert, was born in Savannah in 1899, the same year she got a teaching job at a mission school in Palatka, Florida. After settling in Florida with her family, Mary taught school and visited local prisons, where she read to the mostly illiterate inmates.

Feeling more could be done to help African-American girls, she resolved to start a school of her own. A minister in Palatka suggested that she considered going to Daytona Beach to found a school for the children of black railway workers, who were extending the Atlantic Coast Line into Florida. Though she knew nothing about Daytona Beach, she decided to give it a try. She arrived there in 1904, virtually penniless, and found a vacant house for her school. She used old boxes and crates for desks and chairs, and the Daytona Educational and Industrial Training School opened for business in October 1904 with five young girls, a budget of one dollar and fifty cents, and a lot of prayers. In addition to teaching the domestic arts, such as cooking and sewing, the girls were taught the "three R's" (reading, writing, and arthmetic).

Because of her tireless efforts, and the great educational needs among the blacks in Daytona Beach, within three years Bethune was able to relocate the school to a permanent facility, literally transforming what was a garbage dump into an institution of learning. In 1923 her school became coeducational when it merged with the then all-male Cookman Institute of Jacksonville, Florida. At the time of Bethune's death in 1955, Bethune-Cookman College had a faculty of 100 and an enrollment in excess of 1,000 young African-American men and women. In the first decade of the twenty-first century, it served some 3,000 students.

Following the passage of the Nineteenth Amendment in 1920, which gave women the right to vote, Bethune joined the Equal Suffrage League and taught at a night school, helping blacks learn how to read and write well enough to pass the literacy tests necessary to vote. This activity drew threats from the local Ku Klux Klan, but she stood her ground, and more than one hundred blacks voted in the next election. Her school's library was, for a time, the only free library open to blacks in the state of Florida.

A NATIONAL FIGURE

As Mary Bethune's school grew in reputation and influence, she was called on to lend her support to several causes. She was elected to the National Urban League's executive board in 1920, becoming its first female board member as well as its first black member. In 1935 she founded the National Council of Negro Women, an umbrella group of different black female organizations throughout the nation. She also served as the council's first president. Because of the scope of her work, presidents of the United States, from Calvin Coolidge to Franklin D. Roosevelt, appointed her to several governmental positions, including Special Advisor on Minority Affairs, director of the Division of Negro Affairs of the National Youth Administration, and chair of the Federal Council on Negro Affairs. This last organization was known to many as the "Black Cabinet." Bethune was one of the three black consultants to the United States delegation involved in crafting the United Nations Charter. She was a friend of President Roosevelt's mother in the 1920s, and she later formed a close friendship with the president's wife, Eleanor Roosevelt.

Mary McLeod Bethune became a revered figure in America and throughout the world. In 1935 she was the recipient of the NAACP's highest honor, the Spingarn Award. She died of a heart attack on May 18, 1955. In 1974 a statue was erected in her honor in Lincoln Park, in Washington, D.C., making her the first African American to be honored with a statue in a public park. Bethune's portrait hangs in the State Capitol in Columbia, South Carolina, and a U.S. postage stamp bearing her likeness was issued in 1986.

BIBLIOGRAPHY

Holt, Rackham. 1964. *Mary McLeod Bethune: A Biography.* Garden City, NY: Doubleday.

Long, Nancy Ann Zrinyi. 2004. *The Life and Legacy of Mary McLeod Bethune.* Cocoa Beach: Florida Historical Press.

Love, Carroll, ed. "Mary Jane McLeod Bethune." 1984. In *Salute to Historic Black Women.* Chicago: Empak Publishing.

Reagon, Berinice. 1980. "Bethune, Mary Jane McLeod." In *Dictionary of American Negro Biography,* 41–43. New York: Norton.

Sterne, Emma Gelders. 1957. *Mary McLeod Bethune.* Illustrated by Raymond Lufkin. New York: Alfred A. Knopf.

Russell Mootry Jr.

BIBLICAL JUSTIFICATION

SEE *Genesis and Polygenesis.*

BIKO, STEPHEN BANTU

1946–1977

Stephen Bantu Biko was born to Alice Duna Biko and Mzingaye Biko, Stephen was the third of four children. His eldest sister Bukelwa and elder brother Khaya were born in Queenstown in 1942 and 1944 respectively. His youngest sister Nobandile was born in 1949. Biko's birthplace is uncertain because his parents frequently moved around. As a policeman, his father was transferred to different locations in the Eastern Cape province of South Africa. At the time of Stephen's birth his father was stationed in the small town of Tilden just outside of Queenstown, and his mother was staying at her home in the nearby town of Tarkastad. Home births were common among black people because of lack of other health facility options.

Mzingaye Biko had resigned from the police force by 1948 and took a position as a government clerk in King William's Town. Because of apartheid laws, the family moved into the nearby black township of Ginsberg. Alice took various jobs as a cook at the local hospital and a domestic worker for the township's superintendent. She devoted her weekends to the Anglican Church in Ginsberg. However, Mzingaye died from a mysterious illness soon after their arrival in Ginsberg, and Alice was left to fend for the children from her meager wages. Young Stephen attended primary and secondary school in Ginsberg, where by all accounts he was a gifted student, always at the top of his class. In 1963 he obtained a scholarship to attend the prestigious Lovedale College in Cape Province, South Africa, just outside of the small town of Alice also in the Eastern Cape, where his older brother Khaya was enrolled. However, the two Biko brothers were expelled in March 1963, mainly because of Khaya's political activities. They were also barred from attending government schools. The unfairness of it all had a radicalizing impact on Stephen. In Khaya, according to Biko, "the giant was awakened" (said in frequent conversations with the author).

In 1964 Biko was admitted to the equally prestigious missionary school at St. Francis in Marianhill, just outside Durban in Kwazulu-Natal. He excelled academically at St. Francis and was admitted to the University of Natal Medical School in Durban. It was while at St. Francis that Steve started writing letters to his mother questioning the church's support of apartheid. His mother's friends were progressive white priests, David Russell and Aelred Stubbs (who had been sent to South Africa by the U.K.-based Community of the Resurrection). They took to writing back, and from there on began to develop lifelong friendships.

The political seed had already been planted when Biko arrived at the University of Natal. There he found a group of older students who often got together to discuss the place of black students in a predominantly white university and their specific political role in the predominantly white National Union of South African Students (NUSAS). They tried to get Biko to leave NUSAS, but he remained steadfast in his belief that black students needed to be part of the multiracial student movement. A wakeup call for Biko took place during a NUSAS conference at Rhodes University in 1967. The university authorities went along with the government's position that black students had to leave the university campus every evening to sleep in the townships. Biko asked the white students to join them in the township. He also proposed a motion that the conference be cancelled until a venue where they could all be accommodated in one place could be found. He lost both arguments.

Biko then left the conference to join another conference organized by the newly established University Christian Movement (UCM). Led by two white radical clerics—Colin Collins and Basil Moore—UCM was far more radical than NUSAS. The group invited him to attend a subsequent UCM conference in 1968 in the small town of Stutterheim. One of apartheid's stipulations was that black people could not be in a white area for longer than seventy-two hours, so black students were forced to leave the boundaries of the town, then reenter it. Biko stood up at one of the plenary sessions and suggested that black students needed to have a separate meeting to discuss their continued participation in white-led organizations. The students left the meeting, having decided to explore the formation of an all-black organization. The South Africa Student Organization (SASO) was thus launched in 1968 at the University of the North (Turfloop), and Biko was elected the first president. However, SASO immediately recognized its limitations as a student body trying to organize a community that had been demoralized when the African National Congress and the Pan Africanist Congress had been in 1960.

SASO set on a course of building community-based organizations in the arts, education, health, the economy, and politics. It established community-based research institutes and newspapers and journals. These programs were later incorporated into the activities of the Black Community Programmes. In 1972 Biko announced the formation of the Black People's Convention as the home of black political opinion in the country, thereby formally filling the political hole left by the banning of the ANC and the PAC. The apartheid government first welcomed the birth of black consciousness and thought these were harmless activities. Little was the government aware of the potential for revolution being awakened in communities and students through the movement's cultural, theological, and political consciousness raising. This changed with the explosion of the student uprisings on June 16, 1976.

For a very long time Biko wanted to unite South Africa's various liberation movements—the African National Congress, the Pan Africanist Congress and the Unity Movement. On August 17, 1977, he undertook a dangerous journey from King William's Town—where he was restricted from leaving—to meet for unity talks with veteran activist Neville Alexander of the Unity Movement. The meeting however did not materialize and Biko had to return to King William's Town immediately. He was arrested on 18 August 1977 together with his colleague Peter Jones at a roadblock near the small town of Grahamstown, only an hour from his home, and taken to the notoriously violent police headquarters in Port Elizabeth. After severe beatings he was transported naked and manacled at the back of a van for 800 miles to Pretoria. Stephen Bantu Biko died from brain damage on September 12, 1977.

The apartheid government covered up for his murderers, and they all died before they could face a court of law. But as Biko had prophesied in one of his writings, his death became "a politicizing thing." The international outcry and mass mobilization following his death would in less than a decade lead to the first tentative steps toward a negotiated settlement in South Africa. The unique contribution of the black consciousness movement lay in its political approach to black identity.

Stephen Biko's Funeral, 1977. *A man holds a poster of Stephen Biko, with a large group of anti-apartheid militants in the background, at Biko's funeral in King William's Town, South Africa.* STF/AFP/GETTY IMAGES.

Instead of defining blackness as a matter of skin pigmentation, the movement defined blackness in terms of identification with the black liberation struggle. Blacks were defined, according to the generally prevalent description from black consciousness activists, as all those who are by law and tradition discriminated against and identify themselves as a unit towards their liberation. Instead of seeing themselves as distinct groups, the so-called coloureds, Indians, and Africans now saw themselves as part of one black political identity. Inspired by people such as Aimé Cesaire, Paolo Freire, Malcolm X, and Frantz Fanon, they gave the black community a new sense of pride, dignity, and political agency, leading ultimately to the reclamation of political space and the birth of democracy in 1994.

BIBLIOGRAPHY

Biko, Stephen Bantu. 1978. *Black Consciousness in South Africa.* New York: Random House.

———. *I Write What I Like.* London: Bowerdean Press, 1978; reprint. London: Pacador Press, 2006.

Woods, Donald. 1991. *Biko,* 3rd ed. New York: Holt.

Xolela Mangcu

BIRACIALISM

The term *biracial* refers to a person with parents of two different "races." However, the more inclusive term *multiracial* is increasingly being used instead. Biracial and multiracial Americans can come from any combination of racial backgrounds. While all multiracial Americans have faced, and continue to deal with, some degree of discrimination, those with both black and white parentage have encountered the most bias and negative treatment in the United States. Although interracial sexual relationships have existed throughout the history of the nation, the number, acceptance of, and recognition of these unions and the multiracial offspring they produce have changed dramatically over the years. The fluctuating attitudes towards interracial relationships, and the changing notions of how to define racial groups, are evident in the way multiracial Americans have been counted as part of the U.S. population. Few Americans who lived in the 1800s would recognize the racial demarcations taken for granted in the twenty-first century.

INCONSISTENT RACIAL CATEGORIES ON THE U.S. CENSUS

The racial categories used by the U.S. Census Bureau are based on socially determined ideas of race, underscoring the fact that race is a social construction rather than a biologically based reality. Moreover, not all respondents share the same definitions of race assumed by the Census Bureau. Different societies have different understandings of race. Many Latino Americans, for example, do not identify themselves in racial terms in the manner that Census officials assume they will. The fact that race is a social creation is made evident by the way the definitions and uses of racial groupings have changed throughout the history of the U.S. Census. For example, the Censuses of 1790 through 1820 the categories "Free white males and females," "Slaves," and "All other free persons, except Indians, not taxed." The 1820 Census added "foreigners not naturalized" and the 1830 census dropped "all other free persons, except Indians not taxed." The 1850 Census, the first to include options for black-white multiracial Americans, had the following racial categories: "White," "Free Black," "Free Mulatto," "Slave Black," and "Slave Mulatto." With the 1870 Census (after the end of slavery), "Slave Black" and "Slave Mulatto" were removed and "Indian" and "Chinese" were added. "Japanese" became a category in 1880. The term "Mulatto" was used by the Census Bureau to enumerate all persons having any trace of black heritage. Black-white race mixing was tallied in even more detail in the Census of 1890, when "Quadroon" (one-quarter black) and "Octoroon" (from any trace to one-eighth black) were added. However, this level of detail proved too complicated, and these designations were not included on the 1900 Census.

An "other" category was added in 1910. By 1930, black-white multiracial categories were dropped, but other Asian groups were added, along with a "Mexican" category. The "Mexican" category was deleted in 1940, and different Asian groups were added through the 2000 Census. On the 2000 Census, respondents were asked to answer whether they were "Hispanic or Latino" or "Not Hispanic or Latino," and to then choose one or more of the following racial categories:

- White
- Black, African American, or Negro
- American Indian or Alaska Native
- Asian Indian
- Chinese
- Filipino
- Japanese
- Korean
- Vietnamese
- Other Asian
- Native Hawaiian
- Guamanian or Chamorro
- Samoan
- Other Pacific Islander
- Some other race

Clearly, understandings of race and the racial choices deemed necessary on the U.S. Census have changed in relation to the political power of the different racial groups in the U.S., the discrimination they face, and the changing demographic characteristics of the nation's population.

THE RISE AND FALL OF THE "ONE-DROP RULE"

The deletion of the "Mulatto" category after the 1920 Census was directly related to the increased separation of whites and blacks after the end of Reconstruction in 1877. Discrimination against black Americans gained legal support with the 1896 *Plessy v. Ferguson* Supreme Court decision, which established the legality of "separate but equal" public facilities for blacks and whites. As the distinctions among races became accepted social and legal practice, the need to distinguish clearly between black and white Americans resulted in the "one-drop rule," by which any American with any trace of black ancestry was deemed black. Therefore, the U.S. Census no longer carried any terms connoting mixed black-white races. All those who had a "drop" of black "blood" were considered black.

The civil rights movement and the abolishment of Jim Crow legislation that accompanied civil rights legislation in the 1960s did not lead to the immediate demise of the one-drop rule. However, it did create conditions in U.S. society that began to challenge and undermine the rule in the decades to follow. Civil rights legislation and affirmative action policies enabled black Americans to gain more social and economic power, as well as leading to increased interaction among racial groups. The identity movements that followed the civil rights movement (e.g., the black liberation movement, the women's movement, the lesbian and gay movements) led, in turn, to the formation of a multicultural movement. Starting in the 1970s, Americans began to seek out, embrace, and celebrate their various racial and ethnic roots.

IMPACT OF CHANGING DEMOGRAPHICS

The Immigration Act of 1965 was passed at the height of the civil rights movement, amid pressure to overturn legalized racial discrimination in the United States. It abolished national quotas (replacing them with quotas for the Eastern and Western Hemispheres) and did much to increase immigration and alter the racial makeup of the United States. According to the U.S. Census Bureau, the foreign-born population rose from 4.7 percent in 1970 to 11.7 percent in 2003. Among those U.S. residents who were born outside the United States in 2003, 53.3 percent were from Latin America, 25 percent were from Asia, 13.7 percent were from Europe, and 8 percent were from other areas of the globe. These different racial groups were an important impetus for the rise and success of the multicultural movement in the United States. While intergroup tensions have grown as more immigrants enter the United States, the influx of diverse groups has also led to larger numbers of interracial marriages and multiracial offspring.

IMPACT OF LEGALIZATION OF INTERRACIAL MARRIAGE

Before racial intermarriage was legalized throughout the United States with the *Loving v. Virginia* Supreme Court decision, it was very rare and, in fact, was still against the law in sixteen states as of 2007. Since the *Loving* decision in 1967, the number of interracial relationships and marriages has increased dramatically, and there has been a growing acceptance and appreciation of all racial backgrounds, leading to a strong multiracial community. A "biracial baby boom" has taken place over the decades since the Supreme Court struck down laws against interracial marriage. Between 1970 and 2000, the racial intermarriage rate grew from less than 1 percent to 5 percent of all marriages. According to the Population Reference Bureau, in 1970, only 0.4 percent of married whites were in interracial marriages. In 2000, 3 percent of married whites were married to a person of color. Similarly, the percentage of blacks married to nonblacks moved from 1 percent to 7 percent. In 2006, 16 percent of married Asian Americans in the United States were married to non-Asians and approximately one in four Hispanics/Latinos marry a non-Hispanic/Latino (usually a white person).

In 2000, when people were allowed to choose more than one race on the U.S. Census for the first time, 2.4 percent of the population did so. Moreover, 4 percent of Americans under the age of eighteen indicated a biracial identity. An additional 5.5 percent said they were some "other" race than those listed on the Census form. As American culture has embraced multiculturalism and experienced the biracial baby boom, support groups for interracial couples and their offspring have been formed. In addition, an increasing social acceptance has enabled biracial persons to proclaim both sides of their racial background.

DEBATE OVER MULTIRACIAL CATEGORY

Multiracial organizations have led large-scale efforts for the establishment of a multiracial category on official forms of racial demarcation. Many members of interracial unions, and many of the offspring of such unions, have organized effectively to advocate for a "Multiracial" category on the U.S. Census form. Organizations such as Project RACE (Reclassify All Children Equally) maintain that a multiracial designation will make people of mixed racial heritage visible, allow them to acknowledge all parts of their racial heritage, and give them the rights and benefits that other racial minority groups enjoy. For example, groups can only be protected from racial discrimination if the government tracks people by racial category. It is very difficult, if not impossible, to determine the levels of discrimination facing multiracial Americans because of their racial background if there is not an officially designated multiracial category. Members of these organizations have proposed the addition of a multiracial category, with subheadings consisting of all the monoracial categories included on the U.S. Census. Respondents of more than one race would check off "Multiracial" and then check off the racial subcategories that apply to them. This method of racial demarcation allows mixed-racial persons to have a universal racial label—multiracial—while recognizing their unique racial backgrounds.

On the other hand, racial/ethnic advocacy groups such as the Asian American Justice Center (formerly the National Asian Pacific American Legal Consortium) and the National Association for the Advancement of Colored People (NAACP) have worked to prevent the establishment of a multiracial category. They note that legislative districting and the allocation of federal education and health-care dollars are based on population numbers. They fear that the establishment of a multiracial category will result in their losing members of their own racial/ethnic groupings to the new category, thereby reducing their own political power and allocation of resources.

THE COMPROMISE ON CENSUS 2000

The decision to allow people to choose more than one racial box on the 2000 Census was a compromise that enabled respondents to check off as many boxes as they wished, while also allowing officials to group the statistics in ways that satisfy the racial/ethnic advocacy groups that fear a multiracial category will siphon their power. The decision to forego a separate multiracial box but allow people to check off more than one race allows statisticians to count all those who check off two racial groups in the group with the lowest number of respondents. For example, someone who checked off both Black/African American and White would be counted as Black/African American when population figures are determined.

On the other hand, allowing people to check off more than one box also makes it possible to track how many people identify with more than one racial grouping. On the 2000 Census, when people were given the opportunity to identify with more than one race for the first time, 2.4 percent of all Americans did so. Among those who checked off Black/African American, 4.5 percent also checked off another race. While this figure is not necessarily an accurate picture of how many Americans with both a black and a nonblack parent identify as multiracial, it does indicate that the "one drop rule" is beginning to lose its power. The relative youth of the biracial population provides further evidence of this trend. In 2000, the median age of all U.S. residents was thirty-five but the median age of those who checked off both White and Black/African American was just ten.

A DEMOGRAPHIC OVERVIEW OF THE BIRACIAL POPULATION

While the word *multiracial* is replacing the term *biracial*, 93 percent of people who checked off more than one race on the 2000 Census checked off only two races. It is also important to remember that the U.S. Census considers Hispanic/Latino an ethnic, rather than a racial, category. Therefore, those Latino Americans categorized as being from "more than one race" checked off "Hispanic or Latino" plus two or more racial groups. The Native Hawaiian and other Pacific Islander population was the racial group with the highest number of respondents (54.4 percent) checking off two or more races on the 2000 U.S. Census. They were followed by American Indian and Alaska Native (39.9 percent), Asian (13.9 percent), black or African American (4.8 percent) and White (2.5 percent). However, because two-thirds of Americans are white, most interracial unions consist of a white person and a person of color. Thus, even though white people are least likely to marry outside of their racial group, most biracial Americans have a white parent.

Most biracial Americans live in states with relatively high levels of diversity and metropolitan centers. According to the 2000 Census, 40 percent of biracial persons reside in the West, 27 percent in the South, 18 percent in the Northeast, and 15 percent in the Midwest. The state with the highest percentage of multiracial persons is Hawaii, with 21 percent. In descending order, the other states with above-average biracial populations are Alaska, California, Oklahoma, Arizona, Colorado, Nevada, New Mexico, Oregon, Washington, New Jersey, New York, Rhode Island, and Texas. Each of these states has a biracial population greater than the 2.4 percent national average.

BIRACIAL AMERICANS IN THE SOCIAL SCIENTIFIC LITERATURE AND POPULAR MEDIA

The literature on biracial Americans before the biracial baby boom that followed the civil rights era was primarily negative, focusing on the problems that biracial Americans might have fitting into a monoracial society. The sociologist Robert Park notes that in this era the biracial individual was often referred to as "marginal," condemned to live as a "stranger" in "two worlds." Interracial couples who announced plans to marry were automatically asked "But what about the children?" This question is indicative of the difficulty biracial children faced in a racist society with a one-drop rule.

Since then, however, social science research and popular writing on the topic of biracial Americans has been much more positive. Since the 1990s, most published work on biracial Americans has stressed their ability to bridge racial divides and see both sides of racial issues, indicating an increasing acceptance of multiracial identity in the United States. The question "But what about the children?" has a very positive answer in the early twenty-first century.

The popularity of biracial artistic stars such as the singer Mariah Carey and the mixed-race golfer Tiger Woods has also done much to publicize the benefits of a multiracial background. As their numbers and presence grow, more and more biracial Americans are questioning the traditional racial hierarchy in the United States and embracing all sides of their racial heritage. This transformation from the one-drop rule to a society in which all aspects of racial heritage are acknowledged and appreciated reveals how definitions of race are continually constructed and reconstructed. Future U.S. Census racial categories will certainly change as the understanding of race continues to evolve and U.S. society becomes more multiracial.

SEE ALSO *Affirmative Action; Families.*

BIBLIOGRAPHY

Jones, Nicholas A., and Amy Symens Smith. 2001. "The Two or More Races Population: 2000." In *Census 2000 Brief.* Available from http://www.census.gov.

Korgen, Kathleen Odell. 1998. *From Black to Biracial: Transforming Racial Identity among Americans.* Westport, CT: Praeger Publishers.

Lee, Sharon M., and Barry Edmonston. 2005. "New Marriages, New Families: U.S. Racial and Hispanic Intermarriage." *Population Bulletin* 60 (2). Available from http://www.cs.princeton.edu/chazelle/politics/bib/newmarriages05.pdf.

Rockquemore, Kerry Ann, and David L. Brunsma. 2002. *Beyond Black: Biracial Identity in America.* Thousand Oaks, CA: Sage.

Rockquemore, Kerry Ann, and Tracey Laszloffy. 2005. *Raising Biracial Children.* Lanham, MD: AltaMira Press.

Rodriguez, Clara E. 2000. *Changing Race: Latinos, the Census, and the History of Ethnicity in the United States.* New York: New York University Press.

U.S. Census Bureau. 2001. "Population by Race and Hispanic or Latino Origin for the United States: 1990 and 2000." Available from http://www.census.gov.

Kathleen Korgen

BIRNEY, JAMES GILLESPIE
1792–1857

James Gillespie Birney was born in Danville, Kentucky, on February 4, 1792. A politician and reformer, Birney was one of the leading abolitionists in the United States, serving as corresponding secretary of the American Anti-Slavery Society (AAS) and twice as the presidential candidate of the abolitionist Liberty Party.

The son of a southern slaveholder, Birney graduated from the College of New Jersey (now Princeton University) in 1810, and later he privately studied law. Upon returning home to Kentucky in 1814, he was elected to the town council of Danville, and then to the state legislature in 1816. In that same year, Birney acquired his first slaves. In 1818 Birney moved to Alabama

Territory, where by 1821 he had a total of 43 slaves. Although not a delegate, he played an important behind-the-scenes role in the writing of Alabama's first state constitution, and served in Alabama's first state legislature in 1819.

However, Birney soon experienced a crisis that changed his life. Business reverses, crop failures, gambling debts, and extravagant spending brought him to financial ruin. These problems and the death of a daughter led to alcohol abuse. After selling most of his slaves, he moved to Huntsville, Alabama, to practice law and serve as a state attorney from 1823 to 1827. Birney ultimately found solace in religion. He joined the Presbyterian Church in 1826 and quickly became a zealous convert and moral reformer. He was elected to Huntsville's Board of Aldermen in 1828, and he became mayor of the city in 1829. Birney served in both positions until 1830, pursuing a controversial reformist agenda of securing free public education and a municipal temperance ordinance.

Increasingly, however, Birney focused on the problem of slavery. He had long held mildly antislavery views, claiming that slavery was a great economic, social, and moral evil that did much harm to the nation. He saw slavery as a necessary evil, however, one that would have to be borne with patience until some practical plan of emancipation could be found. As a politician, Birney tried to soften the laws of slavery in Kentucky and Alabama. After his religious conversion, Birney increasingly supported African colonization, the plan to resettle American blacks in Africa. Birney hoped this plan would encourage slaveholders to free their slaves, while also removing African Americans to a place where—freed from the limitations imposed by racism—they could achieve success. In 1832 and 1833, Birney served as a full-time agent for the American Colonization Society, promoting the cause in several southern states.

After returning to Kentucky in 1833 to be near his aged father, Birney initially continued his work of promoting gradual abolition and colonization. Yet he had increasing doubts about colonization, a logistically complex and expensive plan that had so far stirred little genuine support from slaveholders, except from those who believed colonization might actually strengthen, rather than weaken, slavery. Colonization or any other plan of gradual emancipation now seemed fundamentally flawed to Birney, who saw that gradualism failed to condemn slavery—and the selfishness and prejudice that undergirded it—as immoral.

Encouraged by his antislavery friend Theodore Dwight Weld, the now well-known and highly regarded Birney shocked the South in 1834 by publicly denouncing slavery as sin and calling for its immediate abolition. He underscored the sincerity of his conversion by freeing his own slaves and paying them back wages. Birney went even further in 1835, when he announced his intention of publishing an abolitionist newspaper, the *Philanthropist*, in his hometown of Danville. Threats of mob violence against him soon forced Birney to move to Cincinnati, Ohio, for his physical safety. There he finally established the *Philanthropist* in January 1836, under the sponsorship of the Ohio Anti-Slavery Society. In July 1836, a mob attacked the publication's offices as well as Cincinnati's African American community. Birney, however, persevered and quickly resumed publishing the *Philanthropist.*

By 1836, Birney's nationally publicized conversion from slaveholder to abolitionist and his heroic defense of freedom of the press made him arguably the most universally respected and admired figure among the abolitionists. For this reason, as well as for his legal training and long experience as a professional reformer, Birney was appointed corresponding secretary of the American Anti-Slavery Society in 1837.

At a time of growing factionalism among the abolitionists, it was hoped that this widely admired figure could be a peacemaker and unifier. Instead, Birney became entangled in growing controversies regarding the role of women and political action in the abolitionist movement. A born and bred southern gentleman, Birney was too cautious to breech the gender line by supporting leadership roles for women, and he feared that radical positions on side issues like women's rights and nonresistance might alienate potential supporters. Birney, therefore, sided with Lewis Tappan and others who fought against the radical followers of William Lloyd Garrison, trying unsuccessfully to limit the role of women in the AAS. After the Garrisonians gained control of the AAS in 1840, Birney withdrew from the organization and increasingly concentrated on abolitionist political activity.

Although he initially opposed the formation of an abolitionist third party, believing that it would be more practical to convert one of the two major parties to antislavery, Birney allowed himself to be nominated for the presidency by the newly formed Liberty Party in 1840. Birney's candidacy in 1840 was largely symbolic; he did not bother to set up a campaign organization and was in England attending the World Antislavery Convention for virtually the entire period between his nomination and the election. Not surprisingly, he won only about 7,000 votes. Upon returning to the United States, Birney moved to the Michigan frontier, hoping to find opportunities to improve his family's financial circumstances.

In 1844, Birney ran as the Liberty Party candidate for a second time and waged a much more vigorous campaign, speaking throughout the northeastern states in opposition to the candidates of the two major parties, the Democratic expansionist candidate, James K. Polk, and the Whig candidate, Henry Clay. In a campaign dominated by the issue of Texas annexation, thousands of abolitionist Whigs shifted their votes to Birney when Clay softened his earlier opposition to annexation. Although observers at the time believed this defection cost Clay the election, many modern historians have cast doubt on this idea.

Birney anticipated running again in 1848, but a stroke in August 1845 virtually ended his political career. He continued to write antislavery articles and pamphlets, and he also tried to influence Liberty Party politics. He opposed, unsuccessfully, the merger of the party with the Conscience Whigs and Democratic Barnburners to create the Free-Soil Party in 1848. In 1853 Birney retired to a utopian community, the Raritan Bay Union, in Eagleswood, New Jersey, where he died on November 25, 1857.

SEE ALSO *Abolition Movement; American Colonization Society and the Founding of Liberia; Garrison, William Lloyd.*

BIBLIOGRAPHY

Birney, William. 1890. *James G. Birney and His Times: The Genesis of the Republican Party with Some Account of Abolition Movements in the South before 1828*. New York: D. Appleton.

Dumond, Dwight L., ed. 1938. *Letters of James Gillespie Birney, 1831-1857*. 2 vols. New York: D. Appleton-Century.

Fladeland, Betty. 1955. *James Gillespie Birney: Slaveholder to Abolitionist*. Ithaca, NY: Cornell University Press.

Lamb, Robert Paul. 1994. "James G. Birney and the Road to Abolitionism." *Alabama Review* 47 (2): 83–134.

Harold D. Tallant

BIRTH OF A NATION, THE

African Americans were concerned about race and racism in the motion picture industry from its inception. The negative portraits of blacks on film resulted from popularly held, romantic beliefs in the white community about blacks and black lifestyles as depicted in historical and contemporary literature and personal accounts about the old plantation and happy, faithful slaves. Film is a powerful medium, and any study of race and racism must examine the impact of negative motion picture images of blacks on the larger community, because images carry ideas, and in the social construction of race, ideas are of supreme importance.

THE HISTORICAL BACKDROP

The Progressive Era, which spawned the motion picture industry toward the beginning of the twentieth century, coincided with a period of great technological advancement that resulted in more leisure time for many urban people. The opportunity to provide recreation and entertainment for Americans became a significant endeavor. Late in the nineteenth century baseball had become a national pastime; vaudeville and blackface minstrelsy were popular forms of entertainment, as was ragtime music after the black pianist and composer Scott Joplin appeared in concert at the Chicago World's Fair in 1893; and the old and the young, black and white, working and middle classes enjoyed such leisurely activities as attending amusement parks and circuses. Eventually, however, going to the movies would be one of the most fascinating and popular forms of entertainment, and the images one saw created a lasting impression.

From the time that new technology made possible the creation of moving pictures and their projection on a screen, the images of African Americans on film were pejorative caricatures that presented them as lazy, stupid, happy-go-lucky, watermelon-eating, thieving "darkies." For example, a few seconds of footage from an early Thomas Edison film (c. 1896) simply presented blacks as chicken thieves. Many of these early films had suggestive and derogatory titles such as *The Wooing and Wedding of a Coon* (1905) and *A Nigger in a Woodpile* (1904). Nevertheless, none had the same political or social impact as a single, racist, entertainment film that David Wark Griffith (known as D. W. Griffith) would make.

Filmmaker Griffith was born in Floydsfork (now Crestwood), Kentucky, in 1875. His father was a Confederate officer during the Civil War and was among the many politically disaffected whites who blamed Radical Reconstruction for their plight. Griffith grew up in an environment where white carpetbaggers (white Northerners who sided with blacks during Reconstruction) and scalawags (white Southerners who cooperated with both) were viewed with contempt and distrust. African Americans, especially in the South, were seen as inferior people who required the guiding hand of the civilized white man to prevent their further degeneration into uncontrollable savagery.

The historical and other literature of the time confirmed these racist beliefs for Griffith. As early as 1873, James S. Pike published *The Prostrate State* in which he denigrates black legislators elected during Reconstruction. Pike contends that they were ignorant and incompetent and were in power only through a conspiracy with President Ulysses S. Grant to punish white Southerners. Respected historians such as James Ford Rhodes and William Archibald Dunning accepted the view that blacks were inferior. In 1907 Dunning published a critical study on Radical Republicanism in the South titled *Reconstruction* in which he accuses blacks in state legislatures of being corrupt, irresponsible, and incapable of governing. Dunning, a professor at Columbia University, taught and mentored many white students from the South, who in turn

***Poster for* The Birth of a Nation.** *A hooded member of the Ku Klux Klan strikes a heroic pose in this American poster of Griffith's film. Also highlighted is the source material, Thomas Dixon's novel* The Clansman. THE GRANGER COLLECTION, NEW YORK.

published a variety of historical monographs that castigated the North for forcing Radical Reconstruction on the South and placing despicable, uneducated, and corrupt blacks in control of the political system. These studies formed what was called the Dunning school of Reconstruction interpretation, which became the standard and accepted view of Reconstruction for nearly half a century.

While this historical literature would provide Griffith with what he believed was a factual background for his views on blacks, his film was an adaptation of Thomas Dixon's racist novel *The Clansman* (1905). This novel, along with *The Leopard's Spots* (1902) and *The Traitor* (1907), comprised a trilogy that Dixon wrote romanticizing the Ku Klux Klan as the savior of whites in the South from bestial blacks who, unchecked, would eventually destroy white civilization through miscegenation. Dixon, a fervent racist and ordained minister, asserted that his novels were based on the truth, and they were advertised as such. These novels were very popular and had a significant impact in many white communities. White Americans in general believed that these powerful antiblack images were true, particularly that oversexed black men lusted for white women and that it was the duty of the Klan to protect their women. Ignored was the fact that at this time it was expected that white men would have sexual relations with their black domestics as a teenage rite of passage.

Indeed, from the 1880s forward black sexuality and white female virtue were at the center of the ghastly and barbaric practice of lynching. For white males, cross-racial sex was a mark of "manhood"; for black males, the same action mandated as gruesome a death as possible. Any cross-racial sexual encounter by black males was interpreted as "assault" or rape requiring vigilante vengeance, the intention of either party being irrelevant. The infamous Atlanta Race Riot of 1906 provides an example.

In September 1906 the *Atlanta News* published several editions detailing alleged violent sexual attacks against white women committed by blacks. Immediately, white mobs gathered and began to roam the streets beating and assaulting random blacks. A full-scale riot ensued that left twenty-five blacks and two whites dead. An investigation by a Northern journalist showed that a play based on Dixon's novel, *The Clansman*, had been presented in Atlanta just prior to the riot and that it helped to exacerbate antiblack feeling among white Atlantans.

THE FILM'S PORTRAYALS AND PLOTLINES

In 1915, eight years after the Atlanta riot, Griffith made and released perhaps the most controversial film of the twentieth century, *The Birth of a Nation*. Griffith used innovative cinematic techniques including fade-outs, close-ups, parallel action shots, elaborate costuming, high-angle panoramic shots, and realistic battlefield scenes to tell an emotional and compelling story in an epic and spectacular manner. In deference to Southern sensibilities, he used white actors in blackface to portray black characters that came into close contact with or touched white actors and actresses. Real blacks had only small roles in the film. *Birth* was a message film designed to stigmatize blacks in the most offensive way. It was clear that images in motion pictures could be used for more than just entertainment and that their potential use as propaganda was unlimited.

Thematically, *Birth* was a relentless attack against Radical Reconstruction and a glorification of the pre–Civil War South. In Griffith's South, Northern carpetbaggers and Southern blacks were the villains, and those whites who upheld traditional Southern values, including keeping black people in their place, were the heroes. The film glorified racial vigilantism, lynching, Jim Crow segregation, and the Ku Klux Klan. It helped to revive the Klan; it rationalized lynching in the interest of protecting the virtue of white women; it incited rioting and prompted protests; it helped to launch the race movie industry; it gave credence to a school of historiography that claimed that Radical Reconstruction was a failure; and it received an official stamp of approval from the president of the United States. Dixon, who knew President Woodrow Wilson from their college days at Columbia University, persuaded the president to have a special showing of *Birth* at the White House. After the screening in the company of his daughters, Wilson described the film as akin to seeing history "written with lightning" and claimed it was a true account of Reconstruction.

Griffith's epic film traces the impact of the Civil War, Radical Reconstruction, and Redemption on the citizens of Piedmont, South Carolina, through the eyes of two families, the Camerons, who live in Piedmont, and the Stonemans of Pennsylvania. Austin Stoneman is the powerful leader of the Radical Republicans, but his sons have known the Camerons since the romantic days of the idyllic antebellum South. Prior to the Civil War, Dr. Cameron and his family are depicted as being kind and caring toward their slaves. The slaves in turn, are portrayed as happy-go-lucky Negroes who just love picking cotton for the master. In fact, everyone on the Cameron plantation is happy because all understand and are satisfied with the social order. Griffith creates an environment where benevolent paternalism assures that conflicts are minimized. As the Civil War begins, the Stonemans and the Camerons find themselves on the opposite sides of abolitionism.

To show that many Northerners supported the Southern view of blacks, Griffith has the Stonemans arriving in Piedmont as carpetbaggers. However, they soon come to sympathize with the plight of the Camerons and Southerners whose lives had been disrupted and whose society had been thrown into turmoil under the leadership of Radical Republicans and incompetent, ignorant, and bestial blacks and Mulattoes who came to control state legislatures in the South. Griffith shows the idyllic Piedmont under siege by carpetbaggers and newly freed, sex-crazed, and uppity blacks. Disorder and chaos reign in Piedmont as disobedient ex-slaves roam the streets mistreating, disenfranchising, and disrespecting whites while the fields lay fallow because the ex-slaves refuse to work. They are more interested in dancing, singing, and mocking the good white citizens of Piedmont. The blacks who are elected to the state legislature are shown as incompetent and arrogant. In addition, they show no respect for the legislative process and are more interested in eating fried chicken, drinking, and resting their tired feet on their statehouse desks.

Birth addresses the theme of interracial sexual contact in a manner consistent with the view that miscegenation would destroy white civilization. The film's characters Gus, an uppity black, and Silas Lynch, a Mulatto, are depicted as aggressive, oversexed, and savage in their lust for white women. Lynch's status as a Mulatto suggests that any amount of black blood, no matter how small, would be enough to pollute the bloodline of whites. Lynch's greatest desire is to force Elsie Stoneman, the daughter of Republican Austin Stoneman, to marry him. Lynch and Gus symbolize and conjure up a once deeply held and persistent fear in white America—that every black man wants a sexual relationship with a white woman. Thus, Gus, in a lustful rage, chases the young Flora Cameron through a wood trying to convince her to marry him, but rather than submitting to his sexual advances, she hurls herself over a cliff. This unites the Camerons and the Stonemans, and even the great abolitionist Austin Stoneman comes into the Southern fold when he learns that his appointee, the Mulatto Lynch, wants to marry his daughter Elsie, who is in love with Colonel Ben Cameron, the last of the Cameron sons.

The film ends with members of the Cameron and Stoneman families having survived a siege in a local cabin where they were hiding from black renegades. Ben forms the local Klan into a fighting force, and they confront and defeat blacks in what is, essentially, a race war. They rescue Piedmont and its white citizens from the control of blacks and carpetbaggers and reestablish social order under white leadership. The triumphant Klan and the Camerons and Stonemans ride into Piedmont as heroes and prepare for the marriage of Phil Stoneman to Margaret Cameron, and the marriage of Elsie Stoneman to Ben Cameron. Griffith uses the last scene to show that Southern and Northern whites must unite to keep blacks in their place. It is only when the Stonemans see firsthand the depraved nature of black males that they come to understand that they have been misguided in their belief that blacks could ever be the equal of whites.

IMPACT AND RESPONSES

Most historians believe that *Birth* played a role in the reemergence of an even more powerful Klan after the film was released in 1915. William J. Simmons, a flamboyant white supremacist, chose the opening of the film in Atlanta, Georgia, to announce the rebirth of the new Klan. Simmons proclaimed himself the Imperial Wizard of the Invisible Empire of the Knights of the Ku Klux Klan. He cloaked the organization in the fabric of 100 percent Americanism and laid down the gauntlet to Jews, Catholics, *niggers*, and foreigners, saying that the Klan would do whatever was necessary to protect the American way of life. This meant, of course, that only white Anglo-Saxon Protestants would receive protection. Simmons would often parade around with several weapons to showcase his readiness to confront America's enemies.

The Birth of a Nation. *Actors costumed in the full regalia of the Ku Klux Klan hold down a white character in blackface in a still from director D.W. Griffith's 1915 movie. The film, while praised for its use of pioneering film techniques, presents a racist, white-supremacist view of American history, particularly the period of Reconstruction. It caused riots in many cities when it was released.* HULTON ARCHIVE/GETTY IMAGES.

The release of the film occurred as thousands of blacks were migrating to the North, and it was easy to transfer the antiblack message in the film to Jews and Catholics and the hundreds of thousands of eastern and southern European immigrants who were coming to the United States. In fact, in Atlanta during the late summer of 1915, two weeks before *Birth* was shown, a mob of armed men lynched and mutilated the body of Leo Frank, a Jewish American, who had been tried and convicted, on specious evidence, of killing Mary Phagan, a thirteen-year-old white girl. *Birth* served to encourage this kind of mob mentality.

Insofar as blacks were concerned, *Birth*'s impact was pervasive. Threats of rioting were associated with its release, but some of the most destructive race riots in the nation's history occurred in Northern cities only a few years later, in 1919. The film echoed America's violent racial history, the roots of the Ku Klux Klan dating back to the late 1860s. From the beginning of the twentieth century to the 1920s, the Klan had grown from a few thousand members to well over 100,000, and continued to grow throughout the country, virtually controlling the state of Indiana in the 1930s. Ironically, the white terrorist organizations that emerged during Reconstruction after the Civil War were concerned only about the political restoration of the Old South. Organizations such as the Klan, the Knights of the White Camellia, the White Brotherhood, the Pale Faces, and others wanted to disrupt radical rule and redeem the South from the clutches of what they contended were incompetent blacks, Northern carpetbaggers, and traitorous scalawags. During the period from 1867 to 1871, terrorists in secret societies flogged, lynched, shot, and murdered Republicans and their black and white supporters. Finally, the escalating violence and near anarchy in the South compelled the U.S. Congress to pass the Ku Klux Klan Act of 1871, which imposed heavy fines and jail sentences on those convicted in federal courts of terrorist acts. When President Rutherford B. Hayes withdrew the last of the federal troops from the South in 1877, and the Southern Democrats gained control, participation in secret organizations began to decline. The Klan and other secret societies were never a major problem in the North until the Progressive Era.

The nascent National Association for the Advancement of Colored People (NAACP), which black and white progressives had created in 1909, organized one of its first biracial protests as a result of *Birth*. It published a pamphlet titled *Fighting a Vicious Film: Protest against The Birth of a Nation*, calling the film filth. The NAACP moved quickly to prevent the film from being shown in cities across the nation. Their protests resulted in the banning of the film in Chicago, Denver, Pittsburgh, and St. Louis and the editing out of some of the most offensive sequences, specifically, the attempted sexual assault scene and also scenes recommending that all blacks be shipped to Africa, when the film premiered in Boston. Much to the organization's dismay, however, the NAACP's response raised the issue of censorship, and this alienated the support of some progressives and liberals. In addition, the more the NAACP protested, the more publicity the film received and the more popular it became. In New York City, moviegoers bought more than three million tickets over several months to see the film. In Atlanta, thousands of Klansmen paraded through the streets to celebrate the opening of the film in 1915. By 1920, *Birth* had grossed more than $60 million. It was the first film treated as a major cultural event, with theaters charging an unprecedented two dollars per ticket.

Changing its tactics, the NAACP decided to make a film relating to the positive contributions of African Americans to American society. In 1915 Mary White Ovington, one of the founding members of the NAACP, approached Universal Studios about making the film. Universal was wary about undertaking such a controversial project, and because financial backing was minimal, the idea died. However, Booker T. Washington and his assistant Emmett J. Scott were also interested in making a film similar to what the NAACP had proposed. They wanted to make a film that would portray African Americans in a more positive manner from the Civil War through World War I. Scott organized and developed the project and John W. Noble and Rudolph De Cordova wrote and directed a film initially titled *Lincoln's Dream* but eventually released as *Birth of a Race* (1918). What was to have been a short film turned into a much longer one that took more than three years to complete at a cost of approximately $500,000. The film was shot in Chicago, Illinois, New York, and Florida but inclement weather, inexperienced production crews, poorly designed sets, and financial problems hampered its completion. The final film was about three hours long but was reedited after an initial screening to sixty minutes. *Race* was neither a financial nor an artistic success when Scott released the film in 1919. Many blacks liked the film, but critics questioned the historical accuracy of the film and complained about *its* sexual content and violence. Scott had attempted, unsuccessfully, to replicate what Griffith had accomplished, but in a manner more favorable to blacks. It appears that a nonfiction film would have been more appropriate for what Scott wanted to achieve, but, unfortunately, the documentary format had not yet become a film genre.

While *Race* was not a successful film venture, it did encourage other African Americans to make their own films that would present blacks as normal human beings unlike the black caricatures so pervasive in *Birth*. In 1916 the Johnson brothers, George and Noble, founded the Lincoln Motion Picture Company, one of the first black film companies, and produced and released two films, *The Realization of a Negro's Ambition* (1916) and *Trooper of Troop K* (1916). The Lincoln Company was short-lived and produced only a few films, but black film companies such as Ebony Pictures, The Birth of a Race Company, and others quickly joined the filmmaking fray.

In retrospect, the Johnson brothers may well have been more successful had they agreed to work on an Oscar Micheaux film project. Micheaux was an enterprising black entrepreneur and writer who started the Western Book Supply Company as an outlet to publish his books. George Johnson read one of his novels, *The Homesteader* (1917), which was about the difficulties of a black farmer and wanted to make a film based on the book. Micheaux agreed, but only if he could direct the film. In addition, he disagreed with Johnson about the location and length of the film, and the deal was never consummated. Micheaux returned to his home in Sioux City, South Dakota, and reorganized his company into the Micheaux Film and Book Company and, in time, would become the most important of the independent black filmmakers who made what became known as "race" films. Two of Micheaux's best-known films, *Within Our Gates* (1920) and *The Symbol of the Unconquered* (1920), as well as several of his other films, concern interracial marriage and sexual contact, lynching, and the Ku Klux Klan, but from a black perspective. These films directly challenge many of the views on blacks set forth in *Birth*.

One need not accept a single premise or theme in *The Birth of a Nation* to understand why it is one of the most important films in the history of cinema. It literally changed the way films were made. For good or bad, feature films with a message attempted to persuade the audience to accept a specific point of view, and *Birth* was the first film in this genre to have such a pervasive impact on American society. Unfortunately, it created black phenotypes and genotypes in film consisting of coons, toms, Mulattoes, mammies, and bucks that have persisted and that refuse to die easily. Even in the early twenty-first century, *Birth* generates heated discussion, much of it involving the balance between artistic creative freedom and social responsibility. The film gave the movies its technical vocabulary, but it also gave comfort to the racism that continues to besmirch America's social life. In the meantime, Griffith died in 1948, having made and lost a fortune trying and failing to replicate the financial success of *Birth*. Two years earlier, Dixon had died a wealthy man from monies he made and kept as a result of his one-fourth financial interest in *Birth*.

SEE ALSO *Black Reconstruction; Ku Klux Klan; NAACP; NAACP: Legal Actions, 1935-1955.*

BIBLIOGRAPHY

Bogle, Donald. 2001. *Toms, Coons, Mulattoes, Mammies, and Bucks: An Interpretive History of Blacks in American Films*, 4th ed. New York: Continuum.

Cripps, Thomas. 1977. *Slow Fade to Black: The Negro in American Film, 1900–1942*. New York: Oxford University Press.

———. 1978. *Black Film as Genre*. Bloomington: Indiana University Press.

Diakité, Madubuko. 1980. *Film, Culture, and the Black Filmmaker: A Study of Functional Relationships and Parallel Developments*. New York: Arno Press.

Dixon, Thomas. 1905. *The Clansman: An Historical Romance of the Ku Klux Klan*. New York: Doubleday, Page.

Dunning, William Archibald. 1962 (1907). *Reconstruction: Political and Economic, 1865–1877*. New York: Harper.

Gaines, Jane M. 2001. *Fire and Desire: Mixed-Race Movies in the Silent Era*. Chicago: University of Chicago Press.

Green, J. Ronald. 2000. *Straight Lick: The Cinema of Oscar Micheaux*. Bloomington: Indiana University Press.

Hale, Grace Elizabeth. 1998. *Making Whiteness: The Culture of Segregation in the South, 1890–1940*. New York: Pantheon Books.

Harlan, Louis R. 1983. *Booker T. Washington: The Wizard of Tuskegee, 1901–1915*. New York: Oxford University Press.

Henri, Florette. 1975. *Black Migration: Movement North, 1900–1920*. Garden City, NY: Anchor Press.

Jones, G. William. 1991. *Black Cinema Treasures: Lost and Found*. Denton: University of North Texas Press.

Leab, Daniel J. 1975. *From Sambo to Superspade: The Black Experience in Motion Pictures*. Boston: Houghton Mifflin.

Lewis, David Levering. 1993. *W. E. B. Du Bois*, Vol. 1: *Biography of a Race, 1868–1919*. New York: Henry Holt.

Mapp, Edward. 1972. *Blacks in American Films: Today and Yesterday*. Metuchen, NJ: Scarecrow Press.

Perman, Michael. 2001. *Struggle for Mastery: Disenfranchisement in the South, 1888–1908*. Chapel Hill: University of North Carolina Press.

Reid, Mark A. 1993. *Redefining Black Film*. Berkeley: University of California Press.

Rhines, Jesse Algeron. 1996. *Black Film/White Money*. New Brunswick, NJ: Rutgers University Press.

Rocchio, Vincent F. 2000. *Reel Racism: Confronting Hollywood's Construction of Afro-American Culture*. Boulder, CO: Westview Press.

Staiger, Janet. 1994. "*The Birth of a Nation*: Reconsidering Its Reception." In *The Birth of a Nation*, edited by Robert Lang, 195–213. New Brunswick, NJ: Rutgers University Press.

Wells, Ida B. 1970. *Crusade for Justice: The Autobiography of Ida B. Wells*. Edited by Alfreda M. Duster. Chicago: University of Chicago Press.

Donald Roe

BLACK CIVIL WAR SOLDIERS

The service of black soldiers in the Union army during the American Civil War (1861–1865) represents one of the most dramatic episodes in African-American history. Over a short time period, black men went from being powerless chattel to being part of a liberating army, helping to free nearly four million slaves from bondage. Yet their experience was not entirely positive. Their services as soldiers were initially refused, and they had to fight for the right to fight. Even when the Union army did accept them, black men had to serve in segregated units under the command of white officers. The federal government also tried to pay African Americans less than white soldiers, and it subjected them to other humiliating forms of discrimination and ill treatment. Nonetheless, black soldiers served loyally and proved their worth in battle, winning the grudging admiration of even their Confederate enemies and a permanent place in the postwar U.S. Army.

The service of black soldiers seemed unlikely at the beginning of the Civil War. White Northerners and Southerners alike were of the opinion that the conflict would be a war for white men only. In part, the resistance to black soldiers was the result of racist beliefs that African Americans were mentally and temperamentally unsuited for military service. Whites accepted this myth in spite of the participation of black men in the Revolutionary War and the War of 1812, and African Americans were turned away in both the Union and the Confederate ranks. However, resistance to black military service also stemmed from conceptions of citizenship in the nineteenth-century. At the time, Americans tended to see citizenship as not only bestowing rights, but also entailing duties—the foremost of which was military service. If black men were allowed to serve, they would have a strong argument for claiming citizenship rights, having borne the most onerous obligation of citizenship.

Black leaders were keenly aware of this connection between citizenship and military service. Frederick Douglass famously told an audience in July 1863, "Once let the black man get upon his person the brass letters U.S.; let him get an eagle on his button, and a musket on his shoulder, and bullets in his pocket, and there is no power on earth or under the earth which can deny that he has earned the right of citizenship in the United States" (Foner 1999, p. 536). This belief helps explain the later presence of Frederick Douglass and other African-American leaders at the forefront of Union recruitment efforts in free black communities. In addition to Douglass, prominent leaders such as Henry Highland Garnet, William Wells Brown, Martin R. Delany, and George T. Downing recruited literally thousands of young blacks for the Union army in the hope that their service would help transform the struggle into one that would free the slaves and bring African Americans equal rights in a transformed and redeemed republic.

Some white persons shared the aspirations of black Americans. Army officers and politicians with abolitionist sentiments, dissenting from racism and the apathy toward slavery in the North, saw black enlistment as a way to undermine slavery and bolster postwar claims of African Americans for citizenship, and so they sought to organize black military units without the blessing of the federal government. James H. Lane, a Kansas abolitionist turned U.S. senator, organized the first all-black unit in the Union army, the Kansas Colored Regiment, in July 1862. General John W. Phelps, in the Department of the Gulf in Louisiana, and General David Hunter, in the Sea Islands region of South Carolina and Georgia, also recruited African Americans for military service shortly thereafter. None of these men had the authority to recruit black soldiers, however, but they hoped to force the hand of President Abraham Lincoln and the War Department to accept black soldiers by presenting their presence as a fait accompli.

The Lincoln administration disavowed the activities of Lane, Phelps, and Hunter as unauthorized and premature. Until September 1862, Lincoln was reluctant to take any action that might alienate slaveholders in the loyal border states and in areas of the Confederacy under Union occupation. During the fall of 1862, however, Lincoln was reaching the conclusion that black soldiers in the Union army were a military necessity. Congress pushed the President in this direction by passing the Militia Act of July 1862. This law authorized the recruitment of "persons of African descent" for "any military or naval service for which they may be found competent."

With the legal obstacles and executive resistance to black recruitment melting away, other Northern leaders began organizing black regiments in the fall of 1862. Governor John A. Andrew of Massachusetts had long favored black enlistment in the Union army, and that autumn he organized the 54th Massachusetts Infantry, recruiting African Americans not only in Massachusetts but throughout the North. In the wake of the Battle of Baton Rouge, Louisiana, where Confederate forces had seriously called into question Union control of the state, General Benjamin F. Butler began recruiting three "Native Guards" regiments to bolster his forces. The Native Guards, drawn from New Orleans' free elite, were especially notable because initially many of their officers were of African descent. Both the 54th Massachusetts and the Louisiana Native Guards would achieve lasting fame by becoming the first African-American units to see combat in the Civil War. The 54th would bravely assault Fort Wagner, South Carolina, outside of Charleston in July 1863; and the Native Guards would go into battle even earlier, at Port Hudson (May 1863) and Milliken's Bend (June 1863) in Louisiana.

The success of black soldiers at Fort Wagner, Port Hudson, and Milliken's Bend, and the insatiable need of the Union army for fresh soldiers, encouraged the large-scale enlistment of African Americans. President Lincoln gave his blessing to the effort in his final Emancipation Proclamation on January 1, 1863. Union recruiters fanned out across the North, the border states, and the Union-occupied South. They found thousands of willing black men, eager to enlist to help liberate their race from bondage. Some recruiters, however, were not above using trickery or coercion when African-American recruits were not immediately forthcoming. With tens of thousands of black men pouring into Union ranks, it became necessary to regularize the administrative supervision of black troops. In May 1863, the War Department organized the Bureau of Colored Troops. It also reorganized existing black regiments as federalized units (except for the Massachusetts and Connecticut black regiments). By war's end, the United States Colored Troops (USCT) consisted of 163 regiments (mostly infantry, but there were also cavalry and artillery units), and federal statistics indicate that 178,975 black men served in the Union army during the Civil War. In addition, some 18,000 black men joined the U.S. Navy.

With few exceptions, soldiers in the USCT served under white officers. The War Department was extremely reluctant to commission African Americans as officers, and few if any white soldiers or officers were willing to place themselves in a position where they would be required to take orders from a black man. During the war, qualified African Americans sometimes received commissions as chaplain or surgeon, which left them outside of the chain of command.

Of course, the Louisiana Native Guards were a significant exception, because they were organized with African-American officers. General Butler, a former Democratic congressman from Massachusetts, was in charge of Union-occupied New Orleans. He was impressed with the intelligence and refinement of the city's free colored elite, and he shrewdly recognized that the promise of commissions would make leading men in that community energetic recruiters. Consequently, the Native Guards regiments were

Civil War "Contrabands." *Throughout the war, fugitive slaves sought protection behind Union lines. Those that stayed under U.S. protection were termed "contrabands of war." The seven former slaves shown here are dressed in old Union uniforms.* THE LIBRARY OF CONGRESS.

quickly filled, and Butler came through with the promised commissions. These black officers led the Native Guard regiments into their initial battles, assaulting Port Hudson some thirty miles above Baton Rouge and blocking Confederate movement from the west at Milliken's Bend. Black troops performed heroically at each location.

Yet despite their success as combat leaders, Butler's successor, Nathaniel Banks, made a determined, and ultimately successful, effort to purge African-American officers from the Native Guards. Banks encouraged white soldiers to defy African-American officers. He also ordered black officers to appear before qualifying boards, a humiliating requirement for men who had already proven themselves as leaders. A Native Guard officer who resigned as a result said he did so "because daily events demonstrate that prejudices are so strong against Colored Officers that no matter what be their patriotism and their anxiety to fight for the flag of their native Land, they cannot do it with honor to themselves" (Berlin et al 1982, p. 327).

Outside of Louisiana, the struggle for black men was not to keep commissions, but rather to obtain them in the first place. Leading noncommissioned officers in the Massachusetts 54th and 55th Infantry, drawn from the cream of the prewar African-American community in the North, were eager to join the ranks of commissioned officers. They had a powerful ally in Governor Andrew. In March 1864, he commissioned Stephen A. Swails, a light-skinned sergeant in the 54th Massachusetts, as a lieutenant. However, neither Swails nor any of the other six other men commissioned by Andrew were able to exercise their promotions because the War Department refused to discharge them as enlisted men, a necessary preliminary step to taking up an officer's commission. It was not until early 1865 that the War Department reversed this position, and only Swails received his commission before the war's end. During the war itself, most black commissioned officers were recruiters, physicians, or chaplains, activities that did not involve commanding anyone.

A small number of African Americans received commissions in the aftermath of the war. For example, O.S.B. Wall was commissioned as a captain, and Martin Delaney was made a major. Both men served with the Freedmen's Bureau after a short stint with the 104th U.S. Colored Infantry. All told, including the Native Guard regiments, non-line officers, and men commissioned near the end of the war, about 100 African Americans served as officers during the Civil War.

Far more troubling to black soldiers than the lack of officers' commissions for African Americans was the matter of unequal pay. Black men recruited in 1862 and early 1863 had often enlisted with the promise that they would receive the same pay and allowances as white Union soldiers ($13 per month, with an additional $3.50 allowance per month for clothing). In June 1863, however, the War Department decided that the pay of black soldiers was covered under the 1862 Militia Act, which fixed the pay of African Americans working for the government at $10 per month, regardless of their type of employment. Then, adding insult to injury, the War Department determined $3 per month would be deducted for clothing, leaving black soldiers with only $7 per month, regardless of rank. (Normally, higher enlisted ranks above corporal received more pay.)

African-American troops were outraged by this decision. Not only did it make it harder for black soldiers to support their families, it was also an insult to their manhood. In the 54th Massachusetts Infantry, black soldiers refused to accept their pay until they were paid the same as white soldiers. They even declined an offer from Governor Andrew to use state funds to make up the difference in pay. Clearly, the men of the 54th were concerned about the black soldiers outside of Massachusetts who would not have their pay differential covered by a sympathetic state government. In addition, accepting Andrew's offer would compromise the principle of equal pay for all Union soldiers. Seeing the racist intent of the War Department in offering unequal pay, they made a resolute and principled stand, at considerable hardship to themselves and their families.

Yet the reaction of the men of the 54th Massachusetts was restrained compared to black soldiers in South Carolina. In November 1863, a company of the 3rd South Carolina Volunteers (later the 21st U.S. Colored Infantry), led by Sergeant William Walker, stacked their arms and refused to continue serving until their pay was equalized with those of white men. This action constituted mutiny in the eyes of federal authorities, and Colonel Augustus G. Bennett, despite being sympathetic to his men's plight, had Walker arrested when he refused to lead his men back to duty. Walker was convicted of mutiny, and he was executed by firing squad in front of the regiment on February 29, 1864. Upon hearing of Walker's death, Governor Andrew declared that "the Government which found no law to pay him except as a non-descript or a contraband, nevertheless found law enough to shoot him as a soldier" (Trudeau 1998, p.254).

The actions of the 54th Massachusetts and the 3rd South Carolina brought the unequal pay controversy to the attention of the Northern public. Nowhere else was racial discrimination so blatant, quantifiable, and demonstrably unfair. Finally, in June 1864, Congress passed legislation equalizing pay retroactively to Jan. 1, 1864. Later, Congress equalized pay for free blacks back to the time of their enlistment, and subsequent administrative action by Attorney General Edward Bates effectively did the same for African-American soldiers who had enlisted in the Union army straight out of slavery.

The unequal pay issue politicized black troops to a degree neither they nor anyone else could have anticipated before the war. In protesting the pay inequity, they learned political skills such as organizing, formulating arguments, wooing allies, and petitioning higher authority for redress of grievances. They thus came to realize their political power, which they would continue to exercise in the postwar period.

These soldiers would also discover their power in the execution of their military duties. As previously indicated, African-African soldiers saw their baptism in blood in the late spring and summer of 1863. Their contributions in battle disproved the racist ideas that African Americans were cowardly by nature and lacked either the discipline or intelligence to succeed in combat. Yet such notions died hard, and the use of black soldiers in battle was largely limited to units from states that pressed for them to be used in combat, or in places where military commanders were willing to employ them or could not dispense with their services. Nevertheless, as a practical matter, the significant use of black soldiers in battle during the Civil War is indicated by the fact that these soldiers took part in 39 significant battles and 419 skirmishes, even though they did indeed have disproportionate fatigue, picket, and garrison duties.

Casualty statistics bear out the reality that racism played a role in the use of black troops. Of the 300,000 Union dead of all causes, 90,638 whites were killed in battle or as a result of wounds, compared to 7,189 blacks killed in battle or as a result of wounds. Figures compiled by Frederick H. Dyer (in *A Compendium of the War of the Rebellion*, Vol. 1) show that a total of 36,847 black men died in Union service, or about one in five of the 178,975 that enlisted in the USCT. Yet 29,658 of these men died of disease rather than from combat-related causes, constituting more than 80 percent of all black deaths in the Union army. While the majority of white soldiers also died of disease, only about 60 percent did so.

Although black troops fought in many engagements in Grant's yearlong effort to crush Robert E. Lee's Army of Northern Virginia, their most prominent moment arguably came in July 1864 at the Battle of the Crater. This engagement occurred early in Grant's siege of Petersburg, Virginia. Union troops dug a mine below the Confederate trenches, hoping to literally blast a hole in the Southern defense. Black troops were initially supposed to lead the charge once Union engineers exploded four tons of gunpowder charges in the mine, but General Grant decided he could not use them for this purpose because he feared he would be criticized for using African Americans as cannon fodder.

As it turned out, casualties were high anyway among African-American troops at the Crater, because both they and the white troops leading the assault plunged into the crater caused by the explosion, rather than following its edges through to the Confederate rear. Many found themselves unable to climb out of the crater and exposed to deadly Confederate fire. Like many other battles involving black troops in the Civil War, black troops fought bravely but were poorly used by white commanders who put them into essentially impossible tactical situations.

That African-American soldiers fought bravely nonetheless speaks to their recognition that even when they fought in a failing effort, they were showing manly fortitude and could win a moral victory. This courage and determination won them the admiration of their white officers and soldiers, and of members of the Northern public who read about their exploits in the paper. By the end of the war, the army had recognized their valor by awarding black soldiers many decorations, including sixteen Congressional Medals of Honor.

Yet the reality was that most black troops in the Union Army saw little or no combat. Many Union commanders could not overcome their own racism sufficiently to trust African Americans in combat, and they chose to utilize them only for labor or garrison duty, thus freeing up white soldiers for battle. For example, William Tecumseh Sherman refused to use black troops directly in his 1864-1865 campaign in Georgia and Carolinas, except for "Pioneer" units that were used to build roads. He detailed most black units under his command to labor and garrison duty guarding his rear, or to units of General George H. Thomas's Army of the Cumberland (with whom black troops did see combat at Franklin and Nashville).

Yet despite this racism, black soldiers in the Union army had lower desertion rates than their white counterparts. More than 14 percent of white Union soldiers deserted during the Civil War, compared to fewer than 5 percent of African-American troops. In part, the lower desertion rate was a reflection of the fact that whether they were free-born volunteers or confiscated slaves, many black soldiers realized they had no place else to go. Certainly the fate of former slaves was tied up with Union victory and the end of slavery. These men understood they were fighting for the freedom of their race and for legal equality and civil rights.

The value of black troops to the Union cause received recognition near the end of the war from the most unlikely of sources: the Confederate government. In March 1865, on the eve of the fall of Richmond, the Confederate Congress authorized the recruitment of black soldiers, reversing a long-standing policy of only using them in noncombatant support roles. In 1861, free southern blacks had formed quasi-military units in Savannah, Georgia; Richmond, Virginia. Nashville, Tennessee; Fort Smith, Arkansas; and in New Orleans, Louisiana. Confederate authorities declined their services, however, including those of the Louisiana Native Guards. But when faced with a possible defeat, the Confederates were willing to have African Americans, enslaved or free, work digging trenches, hauling supplies, cooking food, tending to the wounded, and providing personal service. They would not permit them to serve formally as soldiers, however. While most Confederate leaders denied throughout the war that the preservation of slavery was a war aim for the South, it is unlikely that Southern grievances would have ever caused secession had many white Southerners not feared for the survival of the "peculiar institution." For most of the war, Jefferson Davis and other Southern leaders energetically squashed proposals to arm the slaves, most notably from Confederate Gen. Patrick R. Cleburne on January 2, 1864. It was not until last desperate hours of the Confederate government that its leaders were willing to risk slavery's survival in order to recruit black troops.

Yet their action was not just a sign of how hopeless the Confederate cause had become. It also was an implicit recognition of the value of black troops. In its desperation, the Confederate Congress was acknowledging that black men had made a significant enough contribution to the Union cause, and that it would be worthwhile for the Confederacy to take the same measure. Yet their decision came too late for significant recruitment to get underway prior to the final Southern collapse, let alone the organization and deployment of black Confederate troops.

Hence, it can be said with great certainty that the tens or hundreds of thousands of black Confederate soldiers claimed by modern neo-Confederates did not and could not have existed. Certainly many thousands of African Americans worked for and moved with the Confederate army during the course of the war, but they acted in support roles only. Persons of African descent may have worked as spies and scouts, and a few might even have been formally enlisted or served by virtue of being able to pass as whites. Yet their existence is poorly documented at best, and their numbers pale in comparison to the hundreds of thousands of black men who can be documented to have joined the Union cause. A small minority of African Americans in the South may have harbored Confederate sympathies, but their existence is an obscure and insignificant phenomenon.

One governmental organization that needed no education on the value of African Americans, and recruited them from the earliest days of the war, was the U.S. Navy. Always more desperate than the army for personnel because of its rougher conditions of service, the navy had never barred African Americans from enlisting (although prior to the Civil War service was limited to free persons of color). Likewise, the realities of shipboard service meant it was impossible to segregate crews by race, although African Americans generally were limited to the lowest "ratings" or enlisted naval ranks of boys, landsmen, or ordinary sailors. The great need for new personnel to expand the navy during the Civil War led Navy Secretary Gideon Wells to authorize the enlistment of slaves in September 1861 (an entire year prior to the Emancipation Proclamation).

The integration of crews makes it difficult to determine exactly how many black men served in the Union navy. Figures vary from as high as 29,511, a figure provided by the U.S. Navy and promoted by the historian Herbert Aptheker, to as low as 10,000, a sum arrived at by David L. Valuska, who studied enlistment records for the Union navy. Perhaps the most accurate estimate comes from Joseph Reidy and his Howard University team, which made a more thorough survey of Civil War navy records than Valuska and arrived at the figure of 18,000 black enlistments. The actual number of black Union sailors is probably immaterial, for whatever the number, they played an important role in keeping the Union navy in operation, both in its blockade against the Southern coastline and in its activities on inland waterways, which were just as essential in defeating the Confederacy.

The U.S. Army did seek to make a permanent place for black men its ranks after the war. Congress authorized six regiments in the postwar U.S. Army (four infantry, two cavalry), based on the Civil War pattern of black enlisted men led by white officers (with occasional black officers, such as Henry O. Flipper). This organization was later scaled back to four regiments: the 24th and 25th Infantry and the 9th and 10th Cavalry. These black regiments, especially the 10th Cavalry, became renowned for their prowess fighting Native Americans on the frontier. They got their nickname, "Buffalo Soldiers," from Plains Indians who thought the curly hair of many black soldiers reminded them of the buffalo. These units would also serve with distinction in the Spanish-American War (1898) and the Philippine War (1899-1902). They would win twenty Congressional Medals of Honor and countless lesser decorations, but they would continue to be beset by the racism and doubts about their ability that had plagued African-American troops during the Civil War. They would last see service in the Korean War, when the U.S. Army implemented President Harry S. Truman's 1947 order to desegregate the U.S. Army. The 24th U.S. Infantry was dissolved, and black soldiers thereafter served with white troops in integrated units.

Black Civil War veterans played a critical role in the early history of the postwar black regiments in the U.S. Army, providing a cadre of experienced soldiers to teach military ways to new raw recruits. A small number of these men would remain in the army for some decades, but the actual number of African-American veterans who served in the postwar army was quite small. Most black soldiers were eager to leave the army after the Civil War. Particularly for black troops who had joined as slaves, their discharge was the first moment they could truly enjoy their own freedom. Black Civil War veterans, whatever their status before the war, were eager to participate in the possibilities that the postwar period promised.

Former black soldiers would play a prominent role during Reconstruction and in the leadership of the postwar African-American community. Although veterans would actually be slightly underrepresented among black officeholders from 1867 to 1877, many of the most prominent African-American politicians of this period had served in the Civil War. Six of the sixteen black members of the U.S. House of Representatives during Reconstruction, for instance, claimed Civil War service. More importantly, as black leaders had hoped, African-American military service in the Civil War provided an important argument in favor of voting rights, culminating with the ratification of the 15th Amendment to the U.S. Constitution in 1870. Veterans would be at the forefront of leadership in the late nineteenth and early twentieth centuries resisting efforts to disenfranchise black voters and segregate the races. Even though they failed in this effort, they remained an honored group in the postwar black community until the death of the last black Civil War veteran, Joseph Clovese, in July 1951. Their memory as stalwart warriors against slavery and racism remains strong to the present day.

SEE ALSO *Buffalo Soldiers; Emancipation Proclamation; Soldiers of Color.*

BIBLIOGRAPHY

Berlin, Ira, Joseph P. Reidy, and Leslie S. Rowland, eds. 1982. *Freedom: A Documentary History of Emancipation. 1861-1867.* Cambridge, UK: Cambridge University Press.

Cornish, Dudley Taylor. 1956. *The Sable Arm: Negro Troops in the Union Army.* New York: Longmans, Green.

Foner, Philip S., ed. 1999. *Frederick Douglass: Selected Speeches and Writings*. Chicago: Lawrence Hill Books.

Glatthaar, Joseph T. 1990. *Forged in Battle: The Civil War Alliance of Black Soldiers and White Officers*. New York: Free Press.

Greenberg, Martin H., and Charles G. Waugh, eds. 2000. *The Price of Glory: Slavery and the Civil War*. Nashville, TN: Cumberland House.

Levine, Bruce. 2005. *Confederate Emancipation: Southern Plans to Free and Arm Slaves during the Civil War*. New York: Oxford University Press.

Ramold, Steven J. 2002. *Slaves, Sailors, Citizens: African Americans in the Union Navy*. Dekalb: Northern Illinois University Press.

Shaffer, Donald R. 2004. *After the Glory: The Struggles of Black Civil War Veterans*. Lawrence: The University Press of Kansas.

Trudeau, Noah Andre. 1998. *Like Men of War: Black Troops in the Civil War, 1862-1865*. Edison, NJ: Castle Books.

Donald R. Shaffer

BLACK CODES

In the United States, the term *black codes* usually refers to statutes designed to regulate and define the status of free blacks. Black codes were found in some antebellum northern states, all the antebellum slave states, and, immediately after the Civil War, in most of the former slave states. In some antebellum slave states, black codes were incorporated into the laws regulating slaves, which were known as *slave codes*. Louisiana inherited the French *Code Noir*, which regulated both slaves and free blacks. After the Civil War, most of the former slave states adopted new black codes, which were designed, as much as possible, to re-establish slavery. The purpose of these codes differed significantly from antebellum codes, however. The antebellum codes discouraged or even prohibited African Americans from moving to particular states, and they provided disincentives for blacks to remain in the states where the codes existed. They were, in other words, designed to oppress blacks and to either diminish or eliminate the small free black population in the South and in the few Northern states that passed such laws. In contrast, the South's postwar black codes were designed to rigidly structure the lives of former slaves and prevent them from leaving the South.

The reasons for this difference are economic. Antebellum Southern lawmakers believed that free blacks undermined the stability of their society and threatened the institution of slavery. There were about a quarter of a million free blacks in the antebellum South, and most whites believed that they were not necessary to the economy. Thomas Jefferson expressed the common view of antebellum southern whites when he told a correspondent that free blacks were "as incapable as children of taking care of themselves" and that they were "pests in society by their idleness, and the depredations to which this leads them." After the war, however, Southern whites needed the labor of millions of recently emancipated African Americans, and the postwar black codes were therefore designed to prevent free blacks in the South from moving elsewhere or having any economic independence.

The postwar black codes disappeared after the adoption of the federal Civil Rights Act of 1866 and the ratification of the Fourteenth Amendment in 1868. However, after Reconstruction all of the former slave states as well as West Virginia and, after it gained statehood, Oklahoma, would adopt elaborate systems of segregation, which had some of the elements of the older black codes, but were different in significant ways.

ANTEBELLUM NORTHERN BLACK CODES

In 1804, Ohio passed an act "to regulate black and mulatto persons." This law became the prototype for subsequent laws passed in Ohio, Indiana, Illinois, and the Michigan Territory. A few other states adopted scattered provisions from these laws, but they never had full-fledged black codes. The 1804 Ohio law required blacks migrating to the state to provide proof that they were free, and not fugitive slaves. Any white hiring a black who did not have such proof would be fined up to fifty dollars. On its face, this law could be seen as a good faith effort to help masters from Kentucky and Virginia, whose slaves might try to escape to Ohio. In fact, this law and others that followed were designed to discourage or even prevent black migration into the new state. An 1807 law raised the fine for hiring an undocumented free black to one hundred dollars. This law also required migrating blacks to find two sureties to guarantee their "good behavior" by signing a surety bond for five hundred dollars. This bond did not require that any cash change hands—bond sureties merely promised to pay the county up to five hundred dollars if the free black migrant ever needed public assistance or did not maintain "good behavior." There were several ways to avoid actually having to pay on the bond, but the law still presented a severe limitation on blacks coming to the state. Subsequent amendments to these laws prevented blacks from serving on juries and testifying against whites, as well as severely limiting their access to public schools. Although discriminatory, these laws did not prevent blacks from owning real estate, entering professions (including law and medicine), or exercising the freedoms of speech, press, assembly, and worship. Moreover, once legally present in a state, the black codes of the North did not inhibit their geographic mobility.

By Jacob Radcliff Mayor, and Richard Riker
Recorder. of the City of New-York,

It is hereby Certified, That pursuant to the statute in such case made and provided, we have this day examined one certain male Negro Slave named George the property of John Delancy

which slave is about to be manumitted, and he appearing to us to be under forty-five years of age, and of sufficient ability to provide for himself we have granted this Certificate, this twenty four day of April in the year of our Lord, one thousand eight hundred and seventeen

Jacob Radcliff

R Riker

Register's Office Lib No. 2 of Manumissions page 62 —
Wm T Slocum Register

Manumission Certificate. *This certificate of manumission signed by New York mayor Jacob Radcliffe and city recorder Richard Riker freed a slave named George in 1817. Southern whites considered free blacks to be a dangerous class that threatened social stability.* MANUSCRIPTS, ARCHIVES AND RARE BOOKS DIVISION, SCHOMBURG CENTER FOR RESEARCH IN BLACK CULTURE, THE NEW YORK PUBLIC LIBRARY, ASTOR, LENOX AND TILDEN FOUNDATIONS.

These laws were generally ineffective in inhibiting the growth of the free black population. From 1803 to 1860, Ohio's black population actually grew at a slightly faster rate than did its white population. Between 1830 and 1860, Indiana, Illinois, and Ohio all saw growth in their black populations of over 300 percent. There is little evidence that migrating blacks were usually asked to prove their freedom, or that anyone enforced the requirement that migrating blacks find sureties to sign bonds for them. There are no recorded cases of any whites being fined for hiring blacks who failed to provide proof of their freedom. Iowa, California, and Oregon also adopted some aspects of the Northern black codes, although Iowa and California abandoned virtually all of these rules before or during the Civil War.

Michigan repealed its black laws almost immediately after its admission to the Union, and Ohio did the same in 1849. The Ohio black law repeal was part of an elaborate legislative compromise that also sent the abolitionist Salmon P. Chase to the U.S. Senate. Only Indiana and Illinois retained their discriminatory laws until after the Civil War.

Legal discrimination against African Americans in the North had subsided by the end of the Civil War with the exception that blacks could not vote or serve on juries in most states. These legal disabilities disappeared after the ratification of the Fourteenth and Fifteenth Amendments, in 1868 and 1870, respectively. After 1870, some Northern states still prohibited marriages between blacks and whites, and schools were segregated in some states, but otherwise most remnants of the black codes were no longer on the books. In the 1880s and 1890s almost every Northern state passed civil rights acts that prohibited discrimination in public accommodations. Michigan banned segregated education and specifically allowed for interracial marriages. Widespread social discrimination remained, but except for education and marriage regulations in a few states, this discrimination was not openly enforced, and it often took place in violation of the law.

ANTEBELLUM SOUTHERN BLACK CODES

In 1860 there were nearly four million slaves and just over 250,000 free blacks in the South. Southern whites considered free blacks to be a dangerous class that threatened social stability, for they believed that free blacks, by their very presence, fostered discontent among those blacks who remained enslaved. Whites also believed free blacks were likely to start rebellions. Thus, the purpose of Southern black codes (as opposed to slave codes) was to suppress free blacks, prevent them from moving into the state, and make them so uncomfortable that they would leave.

Almost every slave state made it illegal for a free black to move into the state, and all of the slave states with ocean ports passed laws requiring the incarceration of any free black sailor who entered the state while serving on a ship. South Carolina set the standard for such laws in 1822 by requiring that ship captains bring their black sailors to the local jail, where they would be held for a fee until the ship was ready to set sail. If the fees were not paid, the black sailor would be auctioned off for temporary service and then expelled from the state. Similar rules applied to emancipated slaves. By 1860 most of the eleven states that formed the Confederacy prohibited the emancipation of slaves within their jurisdiction. Thus, if a master wanted to free his slaves he had to remove them from the state, either before emancipating them or immediately afterwards.

Southern states also prohibited free blacks from engaging in professions that might enable them to foster or aid slave revolts. Thus free blacks could not be pharmacists, gunsmiths, printers or publishers, or operate taverns or places of entertainment. Mississippi made it a crime for blacks to even work for printing offices. Georgia prohibited free blacks from being masons or mechanics, or from contracting to build or repair houses. Most of the slave states prohibited free blacks from learning to read or write. They could also be severely punished for owning antislavery literature. Under a Mississippi law of 1830, whites who circulated "seditious pamphlets," which would have included antislavery pamphlets, could be jailed, but free blacks were to be executed for the same offense. In 1842, Virginia made it a felony for free blacks to receive abolitionist material in the mail.

Free blacks faced other criminal penalties that free whites did not face. Alabama made attempted rape a capital offense for free blacks but not for whites. A number of states followed Virginia's rule of whipping free blacks for minor offenses, rather than giving them jail terms or fining them as they would with whites. A Georgia law prohibited anyone from selling goods to slaves who did not have written permission from their masters to purchase such goods. Whites might be fined for this, but free blacks who sold goods to slaves would be whipped. While most states prohibited private gambling, the crime carried a greater punishment if a white gambled with a free black.

Such rules were not limited to the Deep South. In the 1840s, Missouri prohibited free blacks from entering the state, made it a crime to "keep or teach any school for the instruction of Negroes or mulattoes in reading or writing," and prohibited free blacks from holding religious services without a law enforcement or judicial officer being present. In 1859, Arkansas passed a law "to remove the free Negroes and mulattoes from the state." However, secession and the Civil War prevented the implementation of this law.

POST–CIVIL WAR SOUTHERN BLACK LAWS

The most important outcome of the war was the emancipation of four million formerly enslaved African Americans. The loss of the war and the abolition of slavery immediately and dramatically affected Southern society. Emancipation upset the system of racial control that had kept blacks subordinate to whites since the seventeenth century, and it also destroyed the economic relationship that allowed planters to count on a pliable and ever-present source of labor. With slavery gone, the legal status of the freed men and their role in the postwar South was uncertain. Immediately after the war, Southern legislatures began to adopt "black codes" to define the status of former slaves, to insure that the former slaves would continue to provide labor in the South, and to cope with the emerging problems resulting from emancipation.

The new black codes did give former slaves some rights. For example, the laws not only allowed African Americans to marry each other (but not whites), they also declared that all slaves who had lived as married couples would be considered legally married. The black codes also gave the former slaves some other rights. The end result, however, was to give former slaves most of the responsibilities of freedom, but few of the benefits. Mississippi's laws of 1865—the first adopted in the postwar South—illustrate the nature of these new black codes.

An 1865 Mississippi law, misleadingly titled "An Act to confer Civil Rights on Freedmen," declared that blacks could "sue and be sued" in all state courts. This law gave the freedmen rights they did not have as slaves, but it did not give them equal rights. For example, the law allowed them to testify only in cases involving blacks, and it prohibited them from serving on juries. It allowed the freedmen to acquire and dispose of property "to the same extent that white persons may," but at the same time, it prohibited freedmen from renting any land, except in "towns or cities." In other words, free blacks could not rent farm land. In the overwhelmingly rural Mississippi, this meant freedmen would become a peasant class, forced to work for white landowners and unable to acquire land on their own.

Another provision of this law required that all labor contracts made with freedmen lasting longer than a month had to be in writing, even though most freedmen could not read and write. They were therefore at the mercy of unscrupulous whites, who could put almost anything into a written contract, with the black who signed the contract not knowing what it really said. This law also provided that any freedman who quit before the end of the term of a contract would "forfeit his wages for the year," including those earned up to the time he quit. In a provision similar to the antebellum slave codes, this law obligated "every civil officer" to "arrest and carry back to his or her legal employer any freedman, free negro or mulatto, who shall have quit the service of his or her employer before the expiration of his or her term of service." This effectively made the free blacks of Mississippi slaves to their employers, at least for the term of their employment. Anyone attempting to hire a black under contract to someone else was subject to a fine, jail term, and civil damages.

Another Mississippi statute allowed counties to apprentice African-American children if their parents appeared too poor to support them. To many, this appeared to be an attempt to re-enslave the children of the freedmen. Still another statute, also enacted in 1865, declared that any blacks who did not have a labor contract would be declared vagrants and subject to fines or imprisonment. This law provided punishments for free blacks who were "found unlawfully assembling themselves together either in the day or night time," whites who assembled with such blacks, or whites and blacks who married or cohabitated.

Other states adopted laws with similar intent but different provisions. Rather than prohibiting blacks from renting land, South Carolina prohibited them from working in nonagricultural jobs unless they paid special taxes that ranged from $10 to $100. South Carolina also enacted harsh criminal laws that were aimed at blacks. The stealing of a hog could lead to a $1,000 fine and ten years in jail. Other crimes had punishments of whipping, the stocks, or the treadmill, as well as fines and long prison terms. Hired farm workers in South Carolina could not even sell farm produce without written authorization from their employers. Other provisions of the law created special taxes and fines for blacks, as well as imprisonment or forced labor for those who lacked the money to pay them. Like Mississippi, South Carolina also provided for the apprenticing of black children. These, and similar laws, created something close to a reimposition of slavery in South Carolina. In 1865, Louisiana and Alabama adopted laws similar to those of South Carolina and Mississippi.

The black codes of 1865 shocked the North. In South Carolina, General Daniel E. Sickles, who was serving as the military governor of the state, suspended the law, and even some white governors, including William L. Sharkey of Mississippi and Robert Patton of Alabama, opposed some of the more blatantly discriminatory laws. In Congress, Republicans responded by introducing legislation that led to the Civil Rights Act of 1866, and eventually to the Fourteenth Amendment.

In 1866 the rest of the former Confederacy adopted black codes. Florida's code was as harsh as those of Mississippi and South Carolina. The Florida code provided whipping, the pillory, and forced labor for various offenses. Florida prohibited any blacks from moving into the state, prohibited African Americans from owning firearms, and allowed the creation of schools for blacks, while prohibiting the use of state money to pay for them.

Other states were more discreet in their legislation, trying to avoid giving ammunition to Republicans in Congress who were growing increasingly impatient with the South's attempts to reimpose bondage and oppression on the freedmen. Virginia's vagrancy law carefully avoided any reference to race, but still allowed forced labor and was clearly directed at the freedmen. Not surprisingly, General Alfred H. Terry, one of the military commanders in Virginia after the Civil War, suspended its operation because he saw that the law was subterfuge for an attempt to reenslave blacks. During the war Terry had pushed for the enlistment of blacks, and was deeply sympathetic to black equality. Two other generals, in other parts of Virginia, however, allowed it to go into force. Tennessee's new criminal code provided the death penalty for breaking and entering with the intent to rob, for robbery itself, and for horse stealing. This law did not use any racial terms, but was clearly aimed at blacks. Similarly, Georgia and North Carolina tried to avoid the use of racial terms that might have jeopardized their chances of readmission to the Union. Nevertheless, none of the former Confederate states were ready to have racially blind statutes, much less racially blind justice. North Carolina's law, arguably the least offensive, nevertheless provided a death penalty for blacks who raped whites, but not for whites who raped whites or whites or blacks who raped blacks.

Like the 1865 laws, those passed in 1866 regulated the movement of blacks, their ability to live where they wished, and their ability to sell their labor on an open market. All of the 1866 laws also tried to create racial controls to keep African Americans in a subordinate role, even as they tried to avoid the appearance of racial discrimination.

These laws were the subject of investigation by Congress's Joint Committee on Reconstruction. Congressional responses to these laws (coming out of the Joint Committee's report) included the passage (over President Johnson's veto) of the Civil Rights Act of 1866 and the drafting of the Fourteenth Amendment, which Congress sent to the states in 1866. By 1867, Southern legislatures had repealed most of the provisions that designated specific punishments by race. But even without racial designations, courts were able to enforce the codes to keep blacks subordinate. Even without racially specific language, courts continued to apply solely to African Americans provisions of the black codes regulating vagrancy, contracts, and children. In 1868 the states ratified the Fourteenth Amendment, and in 1870 the Fifteenth Amendment led to the enfranchisement of black adult males. In the next few years, what remained of the black codes disappeared. After 1877 the South gradually reimposed those provisions of the black codes that segregated blacks and regulated labor contracts. Such laws led to peonage and a second-class status for Southern blacks in the late nineteenth and early twentieth centuries.

SEE ALSO *Slave Codes; United States Constitution.*

BIBLIOGRAPHY

Benedict, Michael Les, and John F. Winkler, eds. 2004. *The History of Ohio Law.* Athens: Ohio University Press.

Finkelman, Paul. 1986. "Prelude to the Fourteenth Amendment: Black Legal Rights in the Antebellum North." *Rutgers Law Journal* 17: 415–482.

———, ed. 1992. *Race, Law, and American History, 1700-1990.* Volume 3, *Emancipation and Reconstruction.* New York: Garland.

Finkelman, Paul, and Martin J. Hershock, eds. 2006. *The History of Michigan Law.* Athens: Ohio University Press.

Middleton, Stephen. 2005. *The Black Laws: Race and the Legal Process in Early Ohio.* Athens: Ohio University Press.

Nieman, Donald. 1979. *To Set the Law in Motion: The Freedman's Bureau and the Legal Rights of Blacks, 1865–1868.* Millwood, NY: KTO Press.

U.S. Congress. 1868. *Report of the Joint Committee on Reconstruction.* Washington, DC: Government Printing Office.

Wilson, Theodore B. 1965. *The Black Codes of the South.* University, AL: University of Alabama Press.

Paul Finkelman

BLACK CONSCIOUSNESS

Black consciousness is a broad category that encompasses things as varied as race consciousness, race relations, black pride, black power, and even rebellion and revolutionary consciousness as it relates to a historically oppressed community, nation, or group acting and reacting against its oppression. The scholar, Dorscine Spigner-Littles, an elder from Oklahoma who lived through the civil rights era, defined black consciousness as "being aware of the history of your people and understanding your place within it; maintaining the same level of commitment that your ancestors brought but realizing also that you are not blazing new trails but are simply carrying on a tradition with a long past." Changa Masamakali, a young male hip-hop generation activist, described it as "a framework of thoughts that pushes you to action which is defined in a black nationalist or Pan-African way." Although it began in all instances as a reaction to forces such as white supremacy, slavery, colonization, and/or social and economic oppression, in the process of developing black consciousness became a force in itself that compelled the group or community to look deeply within itself and seek out a self-definition rooted within its own history and culture and not simply its oppression.

A group or community's development of black consciousness is frequently characterized by several specific realizations and actions. The prerequisite is recognition on the part of a downtrodden people that they are trapped in an oppressive system that depends for its own survival on their racial, economic, political, social, and often cultural exploitation. Coming to consciousness within such a system involves an awareness that strategies of survival must come from within the oppressed community. At such a point, the group has to remember the long tradition of survival and resistance that has been a part of the life of both Africans on the continent and their descendants all over the world for several hundred years. A deep understanding of the particular history of struggle that the people or group has gone through is also crucial to the evolution of its consciousness at this stage. How deeply it takes root and how long-lasting this consciousness becomes depends on the group or nation's self-love and belief in the power of its culture to renew itself. The life span of this consciousness also depends on the group's ability to internalize and transmit this new sense of itself to its descendants and the community at large. The evolution of black consciousness has taken different forms in the United States, South Africa, and Brazil.

ORIGINS AND DEVELOPMENT

Within the United States, black consciousness on the most basic level originated in the resistance to slavery. *Appeal to the Coloured Citizens of the World* (1829), by David Walker (1785–1830), functioned as a black nationalist counterpoint, written by a free black, to the more integration-oriented rhetoric of Frederick Douglass. Reacting to the brutality and violence of the transatlantic slave trade and the institution of New World slavery, he writes, "The whites have always been an unjust, jealous, unmerciful, avaricious and blood-thirsty set of beings, always seeking after power and authority" (p. 16). The scholar Sterling Stuckey states that for Walker, "the essence of European character was . . . a desire for power linked to an insatiable love of gain. . . . Walker's cry was at bottom one of hatred of the spirit of capitalism as well as of slavery and racism" (1987, p. 121). Walker went to an early grave, dying of a suspected poisoning, but his rhetoric laid the foundation for a radical tradition of resistance within the United States.

Following Walker, Martin Robinson Delany (1812–1885), abolitionist, doctor, and soldier, could be seen making the notion of black consciousness more of a reality than it was in Walker's lifetime. He wrote *The Condition, Elevation, Emigration, and Destiny of the Colored People of the United States, Politically Considered*, after he and several black students were dismissed from Harvard medical school due to the protests of white students who objected to integrated education. His book argued that there was no future for black people in the United States, and emigration to Africa was a more desirable alternative. His novel, *Blake: Or the Huts of America*, imagined as part of its plot, resistance and rebellion to the system of slavery. The novel was also conceived of as a response to Harriet Beecher Stowe's *Uncle Tom's Cabin*, which Delany thought depicted blacks too passively.

Delany traveled to West Africa in 1859 and apparently negotiated with several African chiefs, garnering permission for a new settlement of formerly enslaved Africans to occur in exchange for their contributing to the community's overall development. Although this venture never came to fruition, for twenty years on and off Delany remained interested in making emigration to Liberia a reality. In the meantime, he was instrumental in recruiting black men to fight on the side of the North in the Civil War, assisting black cotton farmers in improving their business, working for the Freedman's Bureau, and running for political office. In 1877 the Liberia Exodus Joint Stock Steamship Company was formed and Martin Delany was chairman of the finance committee. This particular venture was a precursor to, and may have laid the foundation for Marcus Garvey's *Black Star Line* ships and his widespread Pan-African movement to follow. Delany died of consumption in 1885.

Following in David Walker and Martin Delany's footsteps, Marcus Garvey (1887–1940), born in Jamaica two years after Delany's death, is probably the most significant single individual in terms of the promotion of black consciousness on a worldwide scale. His organization, the Universal Negro Improvement Association (UNIA), began and flowered in the United States but had chapters throughout the black world. The scholar Horace Campbell states:

> Garveyism brought together diverse working people, independent trade unionists, pacifists, cultural nationalists, women liberation fighters, militant self-help groups, socialists, members of church organizations and a whole host of unorganized black folk. . . . Garveyism used the propaganda . . . available at that time to give meaning to the claim that the UNIA spoke for the liberation of all blacks and for the liberation of the African continent. . . . On the specific question of the liberation of Africa . . . it was instilled in the minds of the Africans in the West that their freedom was inextricably bound up with the freedom of the African continent. (1988, p. 173)

More than any movement before it, the Garvey movement made black consciousness more of a concrete reality for black folks dispersed throughout the West. It laid the foundation for the Rastafari movement in Jamaica, and, as Campbell further states, "South Africa at this time was an area of intense capitalist penetration . . . It is therefore not accidental that the UNIA took deeper roots in that society than elsewhere on the continent [of Africa]" (1988, p. 173).

In South Africa nineteenth-century Ethiopianism, which was a fusion of spirituality and black consciousness, had spawned several independent black churches throughout southern Africa and helped to lay a foundation that was receptive to Garvey's message. What seemed to have particularly struck the consciousness of the South African masses was the slogan, "Africa for Africans," and the idea of the UNIA's *Black Star Line* fleet of ships as a naval battalion transporting black Americans ready to fight

Europeans and liberate oppressed Africans. Robert Hill and Gregory Pirio describe this period:

> The recurrent myth of imminent black liberation from America was clearly an active feature in the South African arena of struggle, on the eve of the black mine-workers' strike of 1920. A native identified only as "Mgoja of Johannesburg" took the floor at a meeting of the Transvaal Native Congress, at Boksburg, on 8 February, a few days before the strike began, stat[ing] that... "the Congress members who were sent to Europe are on their way to America and that they will get satisfaction there, America said they will free all natives, and they will help. *That America had a black fleet and it is coming.*" (1987, p. 211)

Apparently, many rural native South Africans at the time held the view that "all Americans were Negroes—who would drive the whites of South Africa into the sea" (Hill and Pirio 1987, p. 227). However, at that time the South African state "viewed all Afro-Americans as agents of racial consciousness who were bent on contaminating the African natives with visionary and disruptive ideas" (Hill and Pirio 1987, p. 225). Rural native South Africans—for whom this mode of independent resistance to the state, unconnected to any spiritual directive, was new—apparently viewed even the local leaders of the Industrial and Commercial Workers' Union of South Africa (ICU) (a black, nationally founded organization) as "ambassadors of Marcus Garvey...and American Negroes who had come to deliver them from slavery... The image of the 'American Negro' ha[d] come to symbolize a radical black consciousness... [This was reinforced by the] multitude of organizational and political linkages between the ICU and UNIA and their respective leaders in Cape Town" (Hill and Pirio 1987, pp. 215–216).

Garvey's influence in South Africa provoked a backlash on a variety of levels. On March 12, 1921, the *Umteteli wa Bantu*, the newspaper of the Chamber mines, stated that "the American Negro is a force to reckon with—a force which may well affect the destiny of South Africa through its effect upon South Africa's black population" (Hill and Pirio 1987, p. 214). Further, heads of state who had previously claimed to dismiss the power of Garveyism expressed great national anxiety when Garvey announced that he intended to visit Africa. Despite conflicting views and reactions to the influence of Garveyism in South Africa, the movement is still credited with shifting popular black focus away from the belief that benevolent British rule was better than Dutch rule and toward the concept of black self-rule. Garveyism set off a chain reaction in the United States, and research shows that figures such as Malcolm X and former Black Panther Geronimo Ji Jaga Pratt, among others, were the product of parents who were members of the UNIA.

CIVIL RIGHTS MOVEMENT

In the United States in the 1950s and early 1960s, the lynching of Emmett Till (1955) and the struggles faced by activists within the Civil Rights movement created the conditions for the ideological shift toward black power, black consciousness, and black nationalism. Between 1963 and 1966 several events turned the tide of consciousness. Severe confrontations arose involving civil rights marchers, police dogs, and white mobs; Malcolm X was assassinated; the racism of white activists within the movement created tension over the formation of a new nonracial society; and the Johnson administration made it clear that racial progress would be slow at best and nonexistent at worst when, at the 1964 Democratic Convention, the delegates from the all-white Mississippi Democratic Party were treated by and large as the representatives of the citizens of Mississippi as opposed to those people who were members of the movement-inspired Mississippi Freedom Democratic Party.

This series of events, among other events, spawned recognition within the Civil Rights movement that America was not a democracy and that, despite rhetoric to the contrary, corporate values superceded human rights. Writing about Martin Luther King Jr., Malcolm X, and the movement as a whole, the scholar Grace Lee Boggs sharply summarizes and quantifies the implications of these transformations:

> King's great contribution to the movement was the clarity with which he stated his goal and the consistency with which he pursued his strategy. His goal was *integration* but his strategy was *confrontation*, and in the actual struggle the first was turned into its opposite by the second. The strategy of confrontation, or disciplined demonstrations in search of reform, systematically exposed both the pitiful inadequacy of the reforms and the bestiality of the whites with whom the demonstrators were seeking to integrate. Thus, while King's professed *aim* was civil rights legislation and integration, the *means* of confrontation taught black people that all the civil rights legislation in the world could not solve their real grievances and led them to question whether, after all, whites were good enough to integrate with. As the saying goes, "Why fight to get into a burning house?" or "Why integrate with cancer?"... King did not draw the dialectical conclusion of his movement. This was the historical contribution of young blacks in SNCC [the Student Nonviolent Coordinating Committee] who pursued his strategy in every state of the South. Thus in 1966 the movement arrived in

> practice, before the eyes of the whole nation, at the concept of *the struggle for black Power* which Malcolm had been developing before black audiences in the North since his break with the Muslims. (1970, p. 213)

As Stokely Carmichael (Kwame Toure, or Ture) stated in the documentary *Eyes on the Prize*, SNCC workers were made to realize that the issue of morality on which the civil rights movement was based was in reality an issue of power. The SNCC workers had seen raw terror, and they realized that the political, social, and economic system of governance in the United States might in fact have no moral center; but it would not hesitate to continue to exert its raw power against the demonstrators, while allowing whites with implicitly more social and economic power to continue to oppress blacks without consequence. These events provoked a collective turn inward—a reassessment of the nature of the black self within American society. This was the moment when the U.S. black population began to seek a definition that was not simply based on fitting into mainstream society or reacting against it. This consciousness fueled the concrete development of black nationalist organizations as well as an inner transformation within the population resulting in a rebirth of black pride and an interest in African culture and style. Out of this era of black consciousness emerged iconic and internationally known black figures such as James Brown and Muhammad Ali.

RAMIFICATIONS FOR SOUTH AFRICA AND BRAZIL

In South Africa between 1970 and 1972, Steve Biko, influenced by his exposure to the speeches and writings of Malcolm X, Eldridge Cleaver, Stokely Carmichael, Martin Luther King Jr., and James Cone, wrote a column titled "I Write What I Like" for the newsletter of the South African Student Organization (SASO), in which he described the tenets of black consciousness and its relationship to South Africa as he saw it. SASO represented black university students who had split off from the National Union of South African Students, an integrated group with a philosophy of "liberal nonracialism." The split can be explained in part by black students' recognition that certain contradictions existed; these were best expressed when Biko claimed that working with whites during apartheid was like "expecting the slave to work with the slavemaster's son to remove all the conditions leading to the former's enslavement." He further stated that until "blacks gained self-confidence, integration would be artificial ... with whites doing all the talking and blacks doing all the listening" (as quoted in Sanders 2002, pp. 166–167). Despite influences from the Black Power movement in the United States, it was the specific homegrown conditions of oppression faced by blacks in South Africa that shaped and molded resistance in that context. Although Biko did not live to see the world change its official position on South African apartheid, years later an emancipated Nelson Mandela thanked Fidel Castro for sending troops to support the Angolan resistance, as shown in Estela Bravo's documentary *Fidel*. Cuban backing of the MPLA (Popular Movement for the Liberation of Angola) made the training of Angolan guerrilla fighters possible and provided essential medical support to those troops. This created the conditions for the MPLA to resist South African troops in 1975, while also weakening the geopolitical position of South Africa in the region. Some scholars claim that it was this regional pressure that forced the South African government to make the concession of freeing Mandela.

In Brazil, with the largest black population in the Western Hemisphere, the development of black consciousness had yet another incarnation. Brazilian society is organized not by a system of apartheid but by the existence of a so-called "racial democracy" in which race is not an institutionalized part of the bureaucratic daily affairs and "black" as a category does not carry the legal weight that it does in either the United States or South Africa. However, these ambiguities apparently coexist with the vast majority of the black Brazilian population having proportionately less social and political access to institutional power than does the colored elite in South Africa or the African-American middle class in the United States. *Frente Negra Brasileira* was founded in 1930 as a black civil rights organization, but its societal influence was relatively small, considering the size of the Brazilian population and the impact that the civil rights movement and student demonstrations had in both the United States and South Africa.

However, African culture appears to have its strongest continuities in Brazil, of all the countries affected by the African diaspora. Here, the Angola-originating martial art of capoeira, the Yoruba-influenced spiritual practice of Candomble, and the rich heritage of Maroon settlements such as Palmares (one of the largest Maroon communities in the Americas) laid the foundation for a culture in which music and dance were inextricably connected to the fabric of everyday life. Although black consciousness appears to have split off from indigenous African spirituality in the case of South Africa, and functions in relation to Christianity and Islam in the United States, transplanted African spiritual practices are inextricably and directly linked to music and dance and a cultural sense of self in black Brazil. It is no surprise therefore that James Brown, as the godfather of soul in the United States; Bob Marley, as the father of reggae in Jamaica; and the contemporary music phenomenon hip-hop have made some of the most significant inroads within this Brazilian culture. Since the one-hundredth anniversary of the official end of slavery in Brazil and the election of Benedita da Silva as the country's first black female senator in 1994, a rebirth in Brazilian black consciousness has been taking shape.

Black consciousness continues to be a transformative part of the life of oppressed populations in the Americas, the Caribbean, and continental Africa. Its form changes and expands with the times. Although it officially took shape in response to racism and oppression, in the processes of these struggles, Africans and their overseas diasporic descendants discovered that their music, their dance, and the spiritual ethos at the core of these forms of expression had the power to transform both their own communities and influence the larger societies in which they exist.

SEE ALSO *African Diaspora; Antiracist Social Movements; Apartheid; Biko, Stephen Bantu; Malcolm X; Walker, David.*

BIBLIOGRAPHY

Boggs, Grace Lee. 1970. "The Black Revolution in America." In *The Black Woman*, edited by Toni Cade Bambara, 211–223. New York: New American Library. (Repr., New York: Washington Square Books, 2005.)

Bravo, Estela. 2001. *Fidel: The Untold Story*. Bravo Films, Four Point Entertainment.

Campbell, Horace. 1988. "Garveyism, Pan-Africanism, and African Liberation in the Twentieth Century." In *Garvey: His Work and Impact*, edited by Rupert Lewis and Patrick Bryan, 167–188. Mona, Jamaica: Institute of Social and Economic Research, University of the West Indies.

Clisby, Suzanne. 2000. "Ethnic Minorities and Indigenous Peoples in Latin America: An Exploration of Contemporary Commonalities of Experience." In *Papers in International Development*. Centre for Development Studies, University of Wales, Swansea. Available from http://www.swan.ac.uk/cds/devres/pubs/pids.htm.

Hampton, Henry. 1987. "The Time Has Come." One-hour segment from *Eyes on the Prize: America's Civil Rights Years (1954–1965)*. Public Broadcasting Service.

Hill, Robert A., and Gregory A. Pirio. 1987. "'Africa for the Africans': The Garvey Movement in South Africa, 1920–1940." In *The Politics of Race, Class and Nationalism in Twentieth Century South Africa*, edited by Shula Marks and Stanley Trapido, 209–253. New York and London: Longman.

John, Catherine. 2003. *Clear Word and Third Sight: Folk Groundings and Diasporic Consciousness in African Caribbean Writing*. Durham, NC: Duke University Press.

Masamakali, Changa. 2007. Interview by author, March 12.

Mochary, Matt, and Jeff Zimbalist. *Favela Rising*. Documentary, 2005.

Sanders, Mark. 2002. *Complicities: The Intellectual and Apartheid*. Durham, NC: Duke University Press.

Scott, Anna. 1998. "It's All in the Timing: The Latest Moves, James Brown's Grooves, and the Seventies Race-Consciousness Movement in Salvador, Bahia-Brazil." In *Soul: Black Power, Politics and Pleasure*, edited by Monique Guillory and Richard Green, 9–22. New York: New York University Press.

Spigner-Littles, Dorscine. 2007. Interview by author, March 12.

Stuckey, Sterling. 1987. *Slave Culture: Nationalist Theory and the Foundations of Black America*. New York: Oxford University Press.

T'Shaka, Oba. 2005. *The Integration Trap the Generation Gap*. Oakland, CA: Pan African Publishers.

Wiltse, Charles, ed. 1965 [1829]. *David Walker's Appeal*. New York: Hill and Wang.

Catherine A. John

BLACK FEMINISM IN BRAZIL

Among women of African descent in Brazil, feminist consciousness is positioned at the intersection of racism and women's concerns. It is generally approached in two ways. First, women activists place the roots of their consolidation in the post-slavery era, when former slaves started to organize themselves. The early twentieth century witnessed important achievements in this regard, including the formation of the first association of Brazilian female domestic workers in 1936 in Santos, São Paulo, and the 1950 inaugural convention of the National Council of Black Women in São Paulo. The 1970s represented a moment of considerable expansion, and the establishment of links with international feminism had a great impact on women in Brazil. At the 1975 Brazilian Women's Congress held in Rio de Janeiro, delegations of Afro-Brazilian women denounced racial and sexual discrimination. In the early twenty-first century, there are various nongovernmental Afro-Brazilian women's organizations, with the important ones located in the cities of São Paulo, Rio de Janeiro, and Bahia.

The second approach is historical in nature and important to Afro-Brazilian writers and activists. In their quest to revert the legacy of invisibility, militants and researchers have emphasized that there is substantive evidence of female initiative and leadership in Brazil's historical past. Their approach adds another dimension to the idea of "feminism" by indicating that long before slavery's end women of African descent in Brazil participated in struggles to defend their communities and families and to ensure their basic human rights. What has been elusive is a recognition of their achievements.

THE ROLE OF RELIGION

Over time, women of African descent in Brazil have established their own arenas in which they have been able to assume positions of leadership and control. Political and social spheres continue to provide increasing opportunities for debating with the state, political parties, the legal system, and institutions of education. But it is in the sphere of religion that Afro-Brazilian women have achieved unquestioned respect, power, and dignity. As *mães de santo* (mothers-of-saints) of the Candomblé religion, they are the unquestioned authorities on all matters that pertain to the spiritual, physical, and mental well-being of their religious followers. These stately older women are associated with a legacy of spiritual understanding inherited from their African forbears and a wisdom that cannot be merely learned. They collaborate with organizations at all levels, and their influence among black activists and women's groups is due to the fact that many militants are Candomblé followers.

In Bahia, Rio de Janeiro, and São Paulo, there are many revered mothers of saints and priestesses. Born in 1923 in Bahia, Mãe Hilda Jitolu exemplifies this legacy. She is the director and founder of Ilê Aiyê, one of the important Afro-Brazilian cultural entities in Salvador, Bahia. A Guardian of the Faith and the African Tradition, she has spent more than sixty-five years as a Candomblé priestess and has earned the respect and admiration of politicians, followers, and the community. In 2004, Ilê Aiyê paid homage to her during their Carnival celebrations marking their thirtieth anniversary.

Benedita da Silva. *Born in a favela (shanty town) in Rio de Janeiro, da Silva went on to become the first black woman in Brazil's National Congress. A member of the Worker's Party, she also served as governor of the state of Rio de Janeiro. She is seen here in November 2002 addressing a meeting of the Organization of American States.* AP IMAGES.

AFRO-BRAZILIAN FEMINISM

The Brazilian black women's movement has succeeded in empowering women and their communities far beyond expectations. It is a movement that is not homogeneous, but rather diverse and widespread. It comprises associations and groups whose specific agendas serve the needs of the communities in which they are located. During the late 1970s and early 1980s these movements did not separate from the Brazilian black movement, and many did organize within its parameters. Increased autonomy arose due to the black movement's insufficient attention to the race, gender, and class specificities of black women. Feminist consciousness is also associated with distinguished Brazilian icons, including Benedita da Silva, a former governor of the state of Rio de Janeiro, and Lélia González (1935–1994), an anthropologist, feminist, researcher, and black militant. González is revered as one of the Afro-Brazilian women whose untiring efforts transformed the lives of many.

While there are women's organizations all over the country, the most well-known are Geledés (São Paulo), Fala Preta (São Paulo), Criola (Rio de Janeiro), and Casa de Cultura da Mulher Negra (Santos). These groups share some characteristics in terms of infrastructure and organization, and each one owes its establishment to a woman activist who was initially involved in black movement militancy. They all operate in the early twenty-first century with boards of directors, subcommittees, and teams working on long-term and short-term projects. They collaborate fully with men and women in all walks of life, government agencies, feminists, and black activists. These organizations also express a reverence for African cultural symbols, a strategy that reinforces diasporic connections and serves as reminders of their origins. Their inspirational figures are famous Afro-Brazilian women who have been leaders of rebellions and resistance movements or advocates against injustice, such as the African princesses Anastácia and Aqualtune, Maroon leader Dandara, insurrection leader Luiza Mahin, prominent slave leader Xica da Silva, first Afro-Brazilian woman writer Maria Firmina dos Reis, and slum dweller and writer Carolina Maria de Jesus.

TWO NONGOVERNMENTAL ORGANIZATIONS

Geledés, Instituto da Mulher Negra (Geledés, The Black Woman's Institute) is an organization located in São Paulo that has attained recognition in the arenas of politics, race, and women's rights. The name is originally derived from Geledé, a secret society of women found in traditional Yoruba societies. It refers to female power over the land, fertility, procreation, and the community's well-being. The organization was founded in 1988, with Sueli Carneiro as founding director. It is a politicized entity dedicated to combating racism and sexism and to promoting black women and the black community. It emphasizes the need for changes in public policy in order to guarantee the principles of inclusion, equality, and opportunity for all. With its primary fields of activity centered around human rights, racism, education, and health, Geledés stands as the example of a successful nongovernmental organization (NGO) in Latin America. The organization has also received numerous awards, including the Human Rights Award granted by the Ministry of Justice on the Human Rights International Day in 1996 and the Human Rights Award granted by the government of France in 1998 on the fiftieth anniversary of the Human Rights Declaration.

Located in Santos, the Casa de Cultura da Mulher Negra (Black Women's Cultural Center) confirms how feminism has influenced women to take control, become political, and effect transformations in their community. One of the earliest of these groups to be formed, it was the brainchild of Alzira Rufino, one of the leading advocates of women's rights, a founding member of the Partido dos Trabalhadores (the Workers' Party) and a serious black movement activist. A feminist, author, poet, essayist, and *ialorixá* (or priestess of Candomblé), Rufino is known for her studies and publications on the biographies and historical experiences of Afro-Brazilian woman.

When it was first established under Rufino's guidance in 1984 the group represented a community effort among women, bearing the name Coletivo de Mulheres Negras da Baixada Santista (the Baixada Santista Black Women's Collective). In the early 2000s, as Casa de Cultura da Mulher Negra, it is an NGO with its own headquarters located in the city of Santos. Since its inception Rufino has been its first and only director, and it is acknowledged as one of the success stories of the women's movement in Brazil. It has a very community-oriented agenda and is dedicated to combating racial, domestic, and sexual violence. Through a professional staff of lawyers and psychologists it provides legal aid, counseling, and psychological assistance; and courses, work studies, seminars, workshops, and campaigns are part of an ongoing program of community outreach in the areas of health, education, and development. Other projects include an archive and an Afro-Brazilian restaurant, and the center hosts many cultural events.

CONNECTING WITH INTERNATIONAL FEMINISM

Afro-Brazilian feminists promote contact with women's organizations in the Caribbean and Latin America primarily through conference networking. International caucuses and gatherings provide a number of forums for women of the region to exchange ideas, share experiences, and discuss strategies for dealing with issues such as globalization, poverty, labor, health, and political representation. Important examples of international encounters include the first meeting of the Afro-Caribbean and Afro-Latin American Women's Network (in the Dominican Republic, 1992), the Women's Caucus to the World Conference against Racism (South Africa, 2001), the meeting of the Black Women's Network (Costa Rica, 2002), the Fifth International Women's Conference (Cuba, 2003), and the Tenth Latin American and Caribbean Feminist Encounter (Brazil, 2005).

Sonia Alvarez , a professor in Latin American Politics and Studies at the University of Massachusetts, Amherst, believes that Brazilian black women's movement is more ideologically diverse than ever, following many paths that are largely determined by the issues black women seek to prioritize. Feminism, a close alliance with black men to fight racism, and a rejection of the "feminist" label represent the three major directions that shape current groups and are determining the kinds of relationships they maintain with black men and white women.

SEE ALSO *African Feminisms; Black Feminism in the United Kingdom; Black Feminism in the United States; Feminism and Race.*

BIBLIOGRAPHY

Alvarez, Sonia. 1990. *Engendering Democracy in Brazil: Women's Movements in Transition Politics*. Princeton, New Jersey: Princeton University Press.

———. 1994. "The (Trans)formation of Feminism(s) and Gender Politics in Democratizing Brazil." In *The Women's Movement in Latin America: Participation and Democracy*, 2nd ed., edited by Jane Jaquette, 13–65. Boulder, CO: Westview Press.

Carneiro, Sueli. 1999. "Black Women's Identity in Brazil." In *Race in Contemporary Brazil: From Indifference to Inequality*, edited by Rebecca Reichmann, 217–228. University Park: Pennsylvania State University Press.

Lovell, Peggy. 2000. "Gender, Race, and the Struggle for Social Justice in Brazil." *Latin American Perspectives* 27 (6): 85–103.

Rufino, Alzira. 1996. "The Black Women's Movement in Brazil." *Women in Action* 2: 79–80.

Dawn Duke

BLACK FEMINISM IN THE UNITED KINGDOM

Black feminism in the United Kingdom (UK) has it roots in the postcolonial activism and struggles of black women migrants from the Caribbean, Africa, and the Indian subcontinent. These women came to Great Britain during the post–World War II recruitment drive for cheap labor. Official statistics as well as historical and social texts documenting this period often overlook the female contribution to this major wave of migration during the 1940s and 1950s. However, stories of black women's participation have been kept alive by black women writers whose accounts disrupt the official historical narratives of those times. Among these women are Una Marson (1905–1965) who campaigned for the League of Coloured Peoples in the 1940s; the political activist Claudia Jones (1915–1964) in the 1950s; and the grassroots activist Olive Morris (1953–1979) and the trade unionist Jayaben Desai (*d.* 2003) in the 1970s.

As a theoretical and intellectual movement, black British feminism emerged in the 1970s. A fundamental premise of this movement is that to be black and female in Scotland, England, or Wales is to disrupt all the safe closed categories of what it means to be white and British and living in the United Kingdom. With its questioning of the racial and gendered subtext of Britishness, black British feminism profoundly challenges the meaning of British national identity and its unspoken assumption of whiteness. In this sense, black British feminism as a body of scholarship occupies a unique and destabilizing position, often referred to as a "third space." From this position, black women reveal "other ways of knowing" that challenge the way white privilege and patriarchal power is constructed and pervades everyday interactions. In her seminal essay, "Difference, Diversity and Differentiation," Avtar Brah explains this unique positioning, asserting that black feminism pried open previously closed ways of thinking that had asserted the importance of class or gender over all other axes of differentiation, such as race. Black feminism thus questioned the primacy of simplistic unified constructions such as gender or class in mainstream explanations for inequality and oppression.

Though there are many different voices among black feminists, they all speak of black feminism, not black feminisms, as if the political project has one single purpose. This purpose is to reveal the normative absence (i.e., everyday invisibility of black women from mainstream analysis) and the pathological presence (i.e., negative descriptions of black women when they are visible) of a group of women collectively assigned as the "black other." Black women are largely invisible in the separate narrative constructions of race, gender, and class. Situated at the intersection of these ideological blind spots, black women are seen to occupy a critical place in racial discourse, where the subject is black and male; in gendered discourse, where the subject is white and female; and in class discourse, where "race" and gender have no place.

The concept of "black" as an umbrella term to signify multiracial difference emerged in Britain in 1960s. It was seen as a strategic political term embracing African, Caribbean, and South Asian peoples living in postcolonial Britain. Colonial and former colonial subjects, who were perceived as mainly male (not female) "colored commonwealth citizens," found themselves occupying a broadly similar structural position as migrant workers facing racist discrimination in arenas such as employment, education, housing, media, the criminal justice system, immigration, and the health services. Though divided by language, religion, nationality, and culture, a new politics of solidarity became possible for postcolonial migrants under these new, shared economic and social relations of equivalence.

However, the concept of "black" has not been without its tensions, as the call to Afro-Asian unity by the Organisation of Women of African and Asian Descent (OWAAD) demonstrates. In the 1960s and 1970s, black British feminism evolved as a political project. In *The Heart of the Race: Black Women's Lives in Britain* (1985) Beverely Bryan, Stella Dadzie, and Suzanne Scafe show how in 1978 the grassroots black women's movement became important to an emerging black British feminist consciousness. Their struggles reveal the political agency of black women of different languages, religions, cultures, and classes who consciously constructed a politically based identity in response to the exclusion of women's experiences of racism within the antiracist movement. While Afro-Asian unity appeared to be a strategic political articulation at the time, OWAAD folded under pressure from internal tensions within the organization as it became increasingly difficult to subsume women's diverse ethnic and political identities within a single movement. Other black women's coalitions, such as Southall Black Sisters and Women Against Fundamentalism, that have campaigned for African and Asian women's rights over many years still survive, demonstrating the value of difference and diversity and the conflict it engenders as a dynamic for expanding democratic practices within feminist organizations.

Black British feminism, in the context of the globalization of capital, places gender at the center of the new radicalized working class. In the 1970s and 1980s the insidious erosion of rights in the workplace emphasized Asian, African, and Caribbean women's shared social and material conditions in a highly-structured, gendered, and radicalized labor market. Amina Mama's article "Black Women: The State and Economic Crisis" (1984) maps the clear-sighted, lucid project of a restructuring postcolonial capitalist state, rationalizing its logic through the active production of a disenfranchised—and thus contingent and disposable—workforce. Black women, in large numbers (compared to the white female population), were (and are) disproportionately employed in low-paid, low-status work. The pervasive image of the invisible or passive black woman was interrupted by the labor struggles that exploded in the 1970s and exposed the world of British sweatshops. Amrit Wilson, in *Finding a Voice: Asian Women in Britain* (1978), gives a first-person account of the conditions and struggles for social and economic justice among Asian women workers on the picket line in the Grunwick (photo processing) dispute.

In the 1980s and 1990s, black British feminism—as a critical theoretical project—was concerned with a micro, or localized, analysis revealing the mechanisms that promote, contest, and resist racist logics and practices in the everyday lives of the collectively constituted "black woman." One such critique was the struggle of black women to claim a space within the modernist Western feminist discourse. The effort to raise the racial consciousness of white feminists through engendering critical self-reflection consumed the black feminist project in 1980s. Hazel Carby's seminal article "White Woman Listen! Black Feminism and the Boundaries of Sisterhood" (1982) embodies the classic black British feminist response to white feminist exclusion and authority. Centering her argument around the key areas of feminist discourse (e.g., the family, patriarchy, and reproduction), Carby explores the contradiction of the white feminist theoretical claim to universal womanhood, on the one hand, and the practice of excluding women who are different on the other.

While black feminists called for the recognition of racism in white feminist theorizing in the 1980s, white feminists were reluctant to relinquish their authority to define the social reality of the gendered subject. They strategically responded with liberal recognition of their ethnocentrism (the assumed authority of the white cultural perspective). In a heated debate in the pages of the journal *Feminist Review* (1984–1986), British white socialist feminists suggested that the solution to the problem of black female invisibility was to simply insert an appreciation of black cultural difference into the analysis of the family, work, and reproduction. Black feminists responded by arguing that racism had to be acknowledged if a truly critical position in relation to the discourse on whiteness was to take place.

By the end of the 1980s, the black feminist theoretical legitimacy began to be questioned by black women themselves, as the tensions of incorporating different ethnic, religious, political, and class differences among women under the banner of "black" remained unresolved. Sensitive to the limitations of such racial reductionism, and to the desire of many to explore emerging theories on postmodern difference, black feminist theorists have since turned to locating black female identity at the center of their analysis. In the space opened up by the discourse on postmodern identity and difference, black women continue the critical task of excavating new forms of cultural racism legitimated by dominant regimes of representation.

Key writings in collections such as *Black British Feminism: A Reader,* edited by Heidi Safia Mirza (1997), are orientated around issues of identity and difference, exemplifying new directions within critical black British feminist theory. Black feminist scholars explore issues as diverse as mixed-race identity, lone motherhood, popular culture, literature, art and media representations. They challenge theories of racism and nationalism through their writings on citizenship and belonging, hybridity, diaspora, religion, culture, and sexuality. By placing the "self" and the body at the center of their theorizing on power and patriarchy, black British feminists are challenging fixed ideas of racial difference (i.e., essentialism) by rethinking "black" and Asian identity as fluid, complex and fragmented in nature. Through a variety of methodologies—such as the oral traditions of storytelling, life histories, and autobiography, and reworking sociological and psychological theory—black British feminists have demonstrated the critical creativity engendered by the "marginal" or "third" space they occupy.

As a critical social force, black British feminism is an intellectual and activist movement that is contingent in nature, shifting, confronting, and deconstructing the intersectionality of class, gender, and racial exclusion wherever it appears, not only in Eurocentric and Western feminist academic discourse, but also in regions and nations historically associated with Great Britain.

SEE ALSO *African Feminisms; Black Feminism in Brazil; Black Feminism in the United States; Feminism and Race; Womanism.*

BIBLIOGRAPHY

Ahmed, Sara. 2004. *The Cultural Politics of Emotion.* Edinburgh: University of Edinburgh Press.

Amos, Valerie, and Pratibha Parmar. 1984. "Challenging Imperial Feminism." *Feminist Review* 17: 3–19.

Brah, Avtah. 1996. *Cartographies of Diaspora: Contesting Identities.* London: Routledge.

Bryan, Beverely, Stella Dadzie, and Suzanne Scafe. 1985. *The Heart of the Race: Black Women's Lives in Britain.* London: Virago.

Carby, Hazel. 1982. "White Woman Listen! Black Feminism and The Boundaries of Sisterhood." In *The Empire Strikes Back: Race and Racism in 70s Britain,* edited by the Centre for Contemporary Cultural Studies (CCCS). London: Hutchinson.

Grewal, Shabnam, et al., eds. 1988. *Charting the Journey: Writings by Black and Third World Women.* London: Sheba.

Gupta, Rahila, ed. 2003. *From Homebreakers to Jailbreakers: Southall Black Sisters.* London: Zed Books.

Jarrett-Macauley, Delia, ed. 1996. *Reconstructing Womanhood, Reconstructing Feminism: Writings on Black Women.* London: Routledge.

Mama, Amina. 1984. "Black Women, the Economic Crisis, and the British State." *Feminist Review* 17: 21–35.

Mirza, Heidi S., ed. 1997. *Black British Feminism: A Reader.* London: Routledge.

Puwar, Nirmal, and Parvati Raghuram, eds. 2003. *South Asian Women in the Diaspora.* Oxford: Berg.

Samantrai, Ranu. 2002. *AlterNatives: Black Feminism in the Postimperial Nation.* Stanford, CA: Stanford University Press.

Sudbury, Julia. 1998. *Other Kinds of Dreams: Black Women's Organisations and the Politics of Transformation.* London: Routledge.

Wilson, Amrit. 1978. *Finding a Voice: Asian Women in Britain.* London: Virago.

Heidi Safia Mirza

BLACK FEMINISM IN THE UNITED STATES

A major sociological issue in any analysis of race and racism is the absence of a gender lens in race studies. This may seem surprising in the early twenty-first century in the wake of the growth and development of the feminisms of women of color in general and black feminist theorizing in particular. Nonetheless, the attempt to fully integrate gender and class into studies of race and racism remains incomplete. Yet the effort to transform studies of race and racism to reflect a complex matrix of inequalities continues. For at least two decades the absence of embedding race and racism relationally and interrelationally with gender, class, and sexuality has been challenged by black feminist thinkers and activists in the United States. Thus, black feminist thinkers have played a major role in recentering our understanding of race through an intersectional analysis: gender, sexuality, race, and class. Indeed, capitalist patriarchy profoundly shapes male/female relations generally, but it operates in the context of racism and white supremacy. This fundamental idea is at the core of black feminist thinking. Black feminist E. Frances White (2001) points out that in the race-centered political stances found in black nationalism, a gender-centered analysis is often not visible. This erasure of gender among black men is matched by the erasure of race in white feminism. As White asserts, neither of these approaches is analytically sound and both need to be rethought. In short, black women are rendered invisible in such either/or approaches.

Another signature move in the theory and practice of black feminism is placing black women at the center of analyses of race and racism. By theorizing from the bottom up, that is, through the everyday lives of African-American women and from the top down by analyzing social structure and political economy, the explication of the interplay between agency and social structure is central to black feminist theory and practice. Moreover, running through black feminist analyses is the principle of what Gloria Hull, Patricia Bell-Scott, and Barbara Smith, in their 1982 book, call "the simultaneity of oppression." These systems of inequality are in play at the same time but must be viewed in historical context. Race, for example, operates as a master signifier in a white supremacist society such as the United States, but not without being deeply shaped by class and gender. This is the conceptual underpinning of much of black feminist conceptualizations of African-American life.

The black feminist sociologist Deborah King (1988) calls attention to the multiplicative effects of race, class, and gender. These are not simply in additive relationship to one another (race + class + gender); these systems forcefully shape one another. Her work critiques additive thinking, parallelist tendencies, and oppositional dualistic thinking found in Western European intellectual thought. Gender must be articulated and theorized in the context of race and racism. This is a point largely absent from the "race alone" analyses of racism.

Black feminism is also rooted in a relational framework. This idea of relationality can be thought about in the context of the gendered, racialized, and class histories of peoples of color. These interrelated histories cannot be written strictly as comparative narratives. The issue is how deeply dependent and interconnected these legacies are. Indeed, the decisions and actions regarding the history of Asians, for example, is connected and informed by the decisions and actions regarding Africans, Native Americans, Europeans, and Latinos/Chicanos. Race, for example, is called into being simultaneously around the making of whiteness and the othering of so-called "non-whites." This fundamental ideological rationalization for exploitation takes on a number of dimensions. Certainly the centrality of blackness and "absolute inferiority" of Africans, as was argued by racist scientists, conditions the way other groups are thought about in relationship to "whites." Whiteness is made as are these other identities. Race is called into being in deep relationality to the expropriation of labor, enslavement, land theft, and the making of empire.

The gender dynamic must be considered in these histories. If white maleness represented the height of the "Great Chain of Being," as Anne McClintock contends (1995), women of all groups were inferiorized and black, brown, and yellow men were feminized. Black women were masculinized and sexualized; and Asian women were sexualized and exploited. Latinas were sexualized as well as exploited as workhorses. Native women were sexualized and killed. These stories have to be thought about in relationship to the issues of labor and land as well as the deep intersectionality of race, class, and gender in these interconnected histories.

Most critically, black feminist theoretical moves are grounded explicitly in the black cultural experience in the United States and go beyond the simple inclusion of black feminist thought in white feminist sociology. This is the thanks that black feminists give to black nationalism, even in the wake of its gender problem. The power of representation and self-definition is a key theme in black nationalism, and these important ideas have certainly influenced black feminist thinkers. Analysts like White (2001) understand that race is deeply embedded in gender and class in the United States. Oyuranke Oyewumi (2005) contends that a feminist framework, rooted in white privilege and power, too often imposes a conceptual logic on black women that distorts or misrepresents that experience.

In sum, what is central about black feminism in the United States is its rootedness in the articulation of multiplicity, intersectionalities, relationality, and the simultaneity of oppressions. This intellectual frame not only challenges traditional studies of race and racism but a range of existing frameworks in sociology, women's studies, ethnic studies, and other disciplines that treat these inequalities in analytical isolation. Patricia Hill Collins (1986), for example, defines the disciplinary liability of dichotomous oppositional thinking. Upon this epistemological assumption is built the categories "white" over "black," "male" over "female," and all other hierarchies of oppression. An intellectual agenda that draws on the both/and cultural traditions of African-American women represents a healthy transformation of Eurocentric epistemologies.

Nonetheless, conflict around the meaning of black feminism is evident. The philosophical splintering on meaning runs the gamut from a mild form of feminism that weakly chastises men for sexism, placing a strong emphasis on the significance of complementarity in African life, to womanism in its various expressions. Complementarity and Africana womanist articulations of the gender dynamic in black life are rooted in more conventional black nationalist notions of womanhood. Some versions of womanism, such as that of Clenora Hudson-Weems (1998), locate it deeply in African principles rather than white European women's so-called culturally saturated feminism. This Afrocentric feminist perspective places itself squarely in a framework articulating the centrality of African culture, especially the principles of complementarity, self-determination, self-definition, and race first. These ideas coincide, of course, with the basic tenets of cultural nationalism.

Whatever the philosophical bent, black women's feminist or proto-feminist organizations have defined themselves broadly. Organizations such as Combahee River Collective stressed the simultaneity of oppressions: race, class, gender, sexism, and hetereosexism. Black feminists have called to task and criticized analyses that miss the powerful interplay of gender, race, and class. Their inventions have implications for the way the social sciences conceive of race. Most important, black feminist interventions have influenced the way black life in the United States is conceptualized.

At the center of black feminist thinking in the academy are the following questions: Where are the black women in scholarly analyses? How might one shift the center of much of the disciplinary scholarship locating the nexus of race, class, and gender as organizing frames in the production of knowledge? How do we render visible the history of lived experiences of black men and women in Africa and the African diaspora? African feminist centered knowledge(s) underpin a good deal of the current critique of black feminist thought in the United States. Oyewumi (2005) locates African thought and culture in knowledge reconstitution. She challenges through her cultural lenses the body logic of Western gender frames. Finally, a queer color critique has developed in the innovative work of scholars such as Roderick Ferguson (2004). Ferguson draws deeply on black feminist thinking while simultaneously challenging the embrace of the hetereonormative in sociological theorizing.

The influence of black feminist thinking appears to be shaping the scholarship of those analysts who do not explicitly define themselves as black feminists. They seem to be somewhat more attuned to gender and race as interlocking realities in studies of race (for example, see the 2000 work of Joe Feagin, *Racist America*). Also worth noting is the recognition that black feminists in the academy, such as Angela Davis (1981), give to black women's activism and everyday lived experiences in the development of black feminist thought. As evidenced by Beverly Guy-Sheftall's 1995 anthology, this knowledge has begun to be systematically incorporated into the social sciences and humanities. Black feminist scholarship has affected the arts, humanities, history, social sciences, black studies, and health sciences, among other fields.

Yet some questions still remain: Whose interests are served by black women's scholarship within the academy? How might these scholars balance social responsibility with career imperatives? Studies in established university and research settings are centered in issues of power and inequality. Even so, the case can be made that African-American women have forged a resistive, self-defined, even sometimes feminist identity in the academy. Even before black feminism's visibility in the halls of academe, there was a long history of black women acting along both gender and race lines. Racially conscious women such as Anna J. Cooper and Ida B. Wells-Barnett were active in race and gender struggles at the turn of the twentieth century and into its early years.

Angela Davis. *In the 1960s, Davis was associated with the Communist Party USA and the Black Panthers. She has also been outspoken on many women's issues and is a professor at the University of California, Santa Cruz.* AP IMAGES.

The power of representation and self-definition is a key theme in black feminism, and these important ideas have certainly influenced the way social scientists have begun to rethink African-American agency. Yet the difficulties of understanding multiplicity within black communities, cross-cut by age, region, ethnicity, and class, are not resolved. Nevertheless, black feminists have placed gender at the center of race and class analyses. This intervention is changing the way race is being conceptualized and the way black life and thought are being imagined through the intersectional frames of black feminism.

SEE ALSO *African Feminisms; Black Feminism in Brazil; Black Feminism in the United Kingdom; Feminism and Race; Sexism; Sexuality; Womanism.*

BIBLIOGRAPHY

Brewer, Rose M. 1993. "Theorizing Race, Class and Gender: The New Scholarship of Black Feminist Intellectuals and Black Women's Labor." In *Theorizing Black Feminism: The Visionary Pragmatism of Black Women*, edited by Stanlie M. James and Abena P.A. Busia, 13–30. London and New York: Routledge.

Cole, Johnnetta Betsch, and Beverly Guy-Sheftall. 2003. *Gender Talk*. New York: Ballantine Books.

Collins, Patricia Hill. 1986. "Learning from the Outsider Within: The Sociological Significance of Black Feminist Thought." *Social Problems* 33 (6, Special Theory Issue): S14–S32.

Davis, Angela Y. 1981. *Women, Race, and Class*. New York: Random House.

Feagin, Joe R. 2000. *Racist America: Roots, Current Realities, and Future Reparations*. New York: Routledge.

Ferguson, Roderick A. 2004. *Aberrations in Black: Toward a Queer of Color Critique*. Minneapolis: University of Minnesota Press.

Guy-Sheftall, Beverly. 1995. *Words of Fire: An Anthology of African-American Feminist Thought*. New York: New Press.

hooks, bell. 1981. *Ain't I a Woman: Black Women and Feminism*. Boston: South End Press.

———. 1984. *Feminist Theory: From Margin to Center*. Boston: South End Press.

Hudson-Weems, Clenora. 1998. "Africana Womanism." In *Sisterhood, Feminisms, and Power: From Africa to the Diaspora*, edited by Obioma Nnaemeka, 170–182. Trenton, NJ: Africa World Press.

Hull, Gloria T., Patricia Bell-Scott, and Barbara Smith. 1982. *All the Women Are White, All the Blacks Are Men, But Some of Us Are Brave: Black Women's Studies*. Old Westbury, NY: Feminist Press.

King, Deborah K. 1988. "Multiple Jeopardy, Multiple Consciousness: The Context of a Black Feminist Ideology." *Signs* 14 (1): 42–72.

McClintock, Anne. 1995. *Imperial Leather: Race, Gender, and Sexuality in the Colonial Context*. New York: Routledge.

Oyewumi, Oyeronke. 2005. *African Gender Studies*. New York: Palgrave Macmillan.

White, E. Frances. 1983. "Listening to the Voices of Black Feminism." *Radical America* 18 (2–3): 7–25.

Rose M. Brewer

BLACK INDIANS

The term *Black Indian* is used to describe a broad range of roles and identities that are very different from one another. At one end of the spectrum are people of African ancestry who also have Native Americans in their genealogies but generally have not participated in native society or culture. These include such prominent Americans as Crispus Attucks (a victim of the Boston Massacre in 1770), Frederick Douglass, Langston Hughes, Martin Luther King Jr., Oprah Winfrey, and Tiger Woods. At the other end of the spectrum are people of African ancestry who "went native" by joining an Indian nation and staying there as adopted citizens. These include such interesting and significant persons as Joseph "Black Joe" Hodge, a trapper and trader who joined the Seneca Nation of upstate New York about 1771 and served as interpreter and mediator between them and the English colonists. Perhaps the most celebrated of black people who joined the Indians was Jim Beckwourth. Born in Virginia in 1798, Beckwourth became a "Mountain

Man" in the Rocky Mountain area, married a Crow Indian woman, and became a chief of the Crow Nation. His testimony was crucial in exposing the atrocities of the Sand Creek Massacre in 1864. He narrated his biography to one T. D. Bonner, and it was published in 1856.

MAROON COMMUNITIES

Such personages as these, however, constitute only a tiny fraction of those who combined African ancestry in some manner with Native American culture. Among the earliest were the "Maroon" populations that developed in the Atlantic coastal areas from Brazil to Virginia, and in the Caribbean, during the time of the slave trade. Some of them had an "Amistad" experience, having seized their slave ships and gone ashore as fugitives. They were soon joined by thousands of escaped slaves, and some took spouses from local Indian tribes. In this manner, they soon came to constitute a hybrid society. Because they spoke different African languages, some of them developed a European Pidgin language. In other cases, they learned a local Indian language that they developed to suit their own purposes, with the addition of some African vocabulary. The northernmost remaining representatives of these Maroon communities are the "Gullah" people of the Georgia Sea Islands, and the most numerous South American group comprises the "Bush Negroes" of Suriname (formerly Dutch Guiana). In between, geographically, the most numerous group is the Garifuna, or "Black Caribs," of Central America and the Caribbean. Altogether, the Garifuna number several hundred thousand people.

As southern slave society expanded along the Atlantic coast of North America in the eighteenth century, the Maroon communities along the coast increasingly came under attack from slave raiders who sold them to southern planters. The Maroons were forced to gradually move south to seek refuge. Some joined with Indian nations, notably the Seminoles of Florida and the Creeks of Georgia and Alabama, who had a history of accepting foreign allies into their Confederacy. Previously, the Creeks had accepted hundreds of escaped white indentured servants, as well as thousands of refugees from devastated eastern tribes, such as the Hitchitis and Shawnees. Individuals or families could be absorbed by the existing towns of the Confederacy, but larger groups of Maroons could negotiate some kind of "client" status. As clients, they paid an annual "tribute" in products or services to their Indian patrons, but were not under their direct control.

The "elite" ranks of southeastern Indian tribes, or those who owned land and livestock, also took on black people, but as chattel slaves rather than clients. These slaves lived under the same conditions that existed under the institution of slavery elsewhere in the United States. Both groups of blacks—slaves and clients—became somewhat "Indianized" in this situation, but the extent varied depending on local circumstances. At the extreme, Seminole blacks, who became known as Freedmen, spoke the Seminole language and participated fully in tribal politics. The man known to history as "Negro Abraham" was the chief negotiator for Seminole treaties with the U.S. government. Fully half the Seminole warriors who defeated the United States in a succession of three wars in the early nineteenth century were black. At the cessation of warfare, some black Seminoles joined the U.S. Army in the Southwest, where four of them earned the Congressional Medal of Honor.

After the Emancipation Proclamation, some confusion developed concerning the meaning of the word *freedmen*. The term *free black* was in use during slave times to designate a black who was not a slave. The newly freed slaves tended to use the term *freedman* to indicate their new status, though the term was already in use among Black Indians. But the Black Indians among the southeastern tribes, who were largely descended from Maroons, resented the implication that they were former slaves, and their descendents are still adamant in reserving the designation for themselves, stating that their ancestors "never were slaves."

The last major incident of organized Maroon resistance to slavery in North America occurred in 1815, when the British abandoned their fort near Pensacola, Florida, leaving it and its armaments under control of 330 of their Maroon and Indian allies. Eight hundred black warriors from surrounding tribes soon joined them. The fort became known as "Negro Fort" and was attacked by the U.S. Army in March of 1816. After a lucky shot to the powder magazine by the Americans nearly destroyed the fort, the survivors who did not escape were killed or sold as slaves.

Some of the surviving Maroons joined major southeastern Indian tribes, while others fled to one of the small communities in isolated areas of the eastern United States, which became known as "triracial" communities. The people in these communities had ancestry among whites, blacks, and Indians, and they tried to remain inconspicuous to avoid persecution as blacks or removal to Indian Territory as Indians. Some are only now emerging from obscurity, hoping to be recognized as Indians by the Bureau of Indian Affairs. There are more than a hundred such communities, some of the more visible being the Brass Ankles and Turks of South Carolina, the Haliwas of North Carolina, the Melungeons of Tennessee, and the Red Bones of Louisiana. Some of them have Web sites supporting their historical claims.

BLACK INDIANS IN INDIAN TERRITORY

Most Black Indians attached to the five "Civilized Tribes" of the Southeast (the Seminoles, Creeks, Choctaws, Chickasaws, and Cherokees) ultimately moved with these tribes when they were moved onto reservations in what is now Oklahoma in the 1830s. Their role in tribal government varied, however, from direct participation to a more marginal status, but they were all regarded legally as Indians, for example, when land was distributed to individuals under the Dawes Act in the early 1900s. As tribal claims have arisen since then concerning land and other settlements, Black Indians, or freedmen, have always demanded and received their share.

Ever since Indian Territory became part of the state of Oklahoma in 1907, there has been a steady tendency of Black Indians to melt into the general African-American population, unless there was some issue in the tribe that maintained their attention. In the city of Tulsa, Oklahoma, for example, there are a large number of African Americans descended from Black Indians on the Dawes enrollment rosters. Periodically, there have been attempts by racist elements in the Indian tribes to expel their black citizens. One such incident occurred in March 2006, when Cherokee Principal Chief Chad Smith proposed the removal of 2,800 Black Cherokees from the tribal roster.

BLACK INDIANS IN CENTRAL AND SOUTH AMERICA

The experiences of Black Indians south of the United States has been rather different, for both economic and geographic reasons. In Dutch Guiana, which the Dutch received as a colony from England in 1667 in exchange for Manhattan Island, the original inhabitants were Arawak and Carib Indians. The Dutch imported West African slaves for agriculture and treated them very brutally, perhaps not understanding that the slaves understood quite well how to live in the tropical forest and could escape and live successfully in the interior, which was not occupied by the colonists. Hundreds of slaves escaped in the first few decades of slavery and intermarried with the two tribes of Indians. Over the next three centuries, Indians and Africans created a mosaic of hybrid societies in the interior, which evolved through time to become the Djuka, Saramaccaner, Matuwari, Paramaccaner, and Quinti tribes, with a present population of about 30,000 persons. Collectively, they became known as "Bush Negroes."

From the first, the Bush Negroes aggressively attacked the Dutch plantations, raiding them for goods and to free other slaves, so that a "no man's land" was created between what is now known as the district of Sipaliwini, in the interior, and the coastal area that the Dutch were developing for agriculture and mineral extraction. Dutch Guiana was renamed Suriname when it became self-governing in 1954, and political tensions became exacerbated among all the ethnic groups, resulting in an outright Bush Negro insurgency in 1986. The revolt, which became known as the "Maroon Insurgency," was led by a former soldier named Ronnie Brunswijk, who began attacking economic targets in the interior. The army retaliated brutally, forcing many Bush Negroes to flee to neighboring French Guiana. A peace treaty, called the Kourou Accord, was negotiated in 1989, but it was not implemented. The political situation has remained tense and complex since then, but the Bush Negroes have emerged as a significant and independent political force in the national arena.

The Black Indians called Garifuna have a past that may be, in part, mythological, beginning with a pre-Columbian incident in which the Arawaks of St. Vincent Island were attacked by Kalipuna from mainland South America, who killed the Arawak men and married their women. A more reliable story concerns the arrival of Africans aboard two Spanish ships carrying slaves for the Americas in 1675, which were wrecked on the same island. The Spanish-Kalipuna-Arawak-Nigerian admixture is supposed to be the origin of the Garifuna, or Black Caribs.

More historical documents come into play with the struggle between British and French forces for control of the island. The British won in 1763 and promptly expelled the Garifuna, killing many of them out of fear that a population of free blacks would be troublesome on an island where they wanted to establish slave plantations. The expelled Garifuna were then settled around the Caribbean in appropriate places, providing the seeds for a pan-Caribbean population that now numbers about 200,000 people. The Spanish helped in the dispersion of Black Caribs, transporting them to Spanish colonies to become independent farmers, craftsmen, and even soldiers. Because of their presence in the Spanish army, the Black Caribs were made to feel unwelcome when the former Spanish colonies became independent in the nineteenth century. Consequently, many Black Caribs migrated to Belize, then under British control and called British Honduras. The date of their arrival, November 19, 1832, is referred to as Garifuna Settlement Day among Garifuna communities, and it has become a major holiday.

Because of their participation in maritime trade, the Garifuna have established colonies in major cities around the world, especially New Orleans, Los Angeles, and New York City. Present population estimates for nearly 200,000 people from various sources are as follows: Honduras, 120,000; Belize, 17,000; Guatemala, 3,000;

New York City, 30,000; Los Angeles, 25,000; and New Orleans, 4,000.

The historical experience of the Garifunas has been quite different from that of other Black Indians. Instead of being forced to defend their territories from an encroaching colonial frontier, they found themselves transported around the Caribbean by various colonial powers for political and economic purposes. Spread among many countries, they have not constituted a unified political threat to established governments. But their proficiencies in the arts and crafts are widely celebrated, and they are currently the focus of efforts to increase tourism in the countries where they live. The experiences of other groups of Maroons around the Caribbean are included in the collection *Maroon Societies*, edited by Richard Price and originally published in 1973.

SEE ALSO *Triracial Isolates.*

BIBLIOGRAPHY

Bonner, T. D. 1965 (1865). *The Life and Adventures of James P. Beckwourth: Mountaineer, Scout, Pioneer and Chief of the Crow Nation.* Hudson, WI: Ross and Haines.

Forbes, Jack D. 1993. *Africans and Native Americans: The Language of Race and the Evolution of Red-Black Peoples.* Urbana: University of Illinois Press.

Gonzalez, Nancie L. 1988. *The Sojourners of the Caribbean: Ethnogenesis and Ethnohistory of the Garifuna.* Urbana: University of Illinois Press.

Herskovits, Melville Jean, and Frances S. Herskovits. 1934. *Rebel Destiny: Among the Bush Negroes of Dutch Guiana.* New York: McGraw-Hill.

Katz, William L. 1986. *Black Indians: A Hidden Heritage.* New York: Atheneum.

Mulroy, Kevin. 1993. *Freedom on the Border: The Seminole Maroons in Florida, the Indian Territory, Coahuila, and Texas.* Lubbock: Texas Tech University Press.

Price, Richard. 1996. *Maroon Societies: Rebel Slave Communities in the Americas*, 3rd ed. Baltimore, MD: Johns Hopkins University Press.

John H. Moore

BLACK POPULAR CULTURE

Although black popular culture involves all people of African descent internationally, U.S. black popular culture is often highlighted because it is within U.S. culture and U.S. culture is increasingly exported to the entire world. Black popular culture is the part of all black cultures that is concerned with pleasure, enjoyment, and amusement; that represents the identity and politics of black cultures according to each culture's beliefs, values, experiences, and social institutions; and that is expressed through aesthetic codes and genres. British cultural studies pioneer Stuart Hall in *Black Popular Culture* (1992) describes the "black repertoire" of which black popular culture originates as involving style, music, and the use of the body as a canvas of representation. He further qualifies "good" and authentic black popular culture as the kind that refers to black experiences, black expressivity, and black counternarratives. Eight distinguishing features characteristic of popular culture are also applicable to black popular culture:

1. Its components of people, objects, activities, events, and the arts.
2. Theological aspects, including ultimate concern, faith, religious symbols, and revelation and ecstasy.
3. Cultural struggle, resistance, contestation, and opposition.
4. Production, circulation, consumption, reproduction, and distribution.
5. Its socially constructed nature.
6. System of signs and symbols.
7. Mode of communication.
8. Commodification, commercialization, and stereotyping.

In general, black cultural expression has always been a way of resisting racial oppression, articulating experiences of resistance and struggle, and articulating oppositional identities. Historian Kevern Verney in *African Americans and U.S. Popular Culture* (2003) notes several key issues that exist between black popular culture and the concepts of race and racism. These include:

1. The persistent negative stereotyping of African Americans in popular culture, and the impact this had on the racial perceptions of both black and white Americans.
2. The role of popular culture in holding back or facilitating change in U.S. race relations, particularly between blacks and whites (but with far-reaching impact on race relations of all groups in the United States).
3. The recurring historical paradox that whereas white Americans have frequently recognized black cultural achievement, African Americans themselves continued to be perceived as socially and racially inferior.
4. The enormous, and continuing, contribution made by African Americans to U.S. popular culture.
5. How Hollywood and the entertainment industry in particular have encouraged racism through misrepresentations and caricatured images of African Americans.

INTELLECTUAL GENEALOGY OF STUDY OF BLACK POPULAR CULTURE

The intellectual genealogy of the study of black popular culture begins with the first collection of Negro spirituals (or black spirituals), *Slave Songs of the United States* (1867), edited by William Allen, Charles Ware, and Lucy Garrison, and the work of several African American intellectuals, professors, and composers. Ethnomusicologist Portia Maultsby explains in her essay "Music in African American Culture" (1996) that the introduction to *Slave Songs of the United States* and research by scholars such as Maud Cuney-Hare (1874–1936), R. Nathaniel Dett (1882–1943), W. E. B. Du Bois (1868–1963), Zora Neale Hurston (1891–1960), Alain Locke (1886–1954), Eva Jessye (1895–1992), James Weldon Johnson (1871–1938), James M. Trotter (1842–1892), and John Work (1901–1967) were the first scholarly studies on African American music, focusing particularly on black spirituals. They represent early attempts to provide a sociocultural context for understanding the complexities of this black American religious musical tradition.

In all, these studies not only initiated the scholarly study of black music but also initiated the study of black popular culture. The connection between the study of black music and the study of black popular culture is important to note because music has been often characterized as *the* central element of all black cultures. In his book *Black Talk* (1981), sociologist Ben Sidran states that black music is both conspicuous and "crucial" to black culture. In addition, he contended that music was "not only a reflection of the values of black culture but, to some extent, the basis upon which it is built" (p. xxi). Stuart Hall concurred when he described black music as the "deep form, the deep structure" of black popular culture (1992, p. 27). Sociologist Ellis Cashmore, in *The Black Culture Industry* (1997), describes black music as being "virtually synonymous with black culture" (p. 3). Furthermore, when describing an African American aesthetic in her book *Signifyin(g), Sanctifyin', and Slam Dunking* (1999), Gena Degal Caponi asserts that music is the "key" to the aesthetic she is discussing and the "fulcrum of African culture and the expression that sustained African aesthetic principles in the Americas" (p. 10). Scholarship on black music provides cues for locating and discovering other forms of black popular culture.

Little Black Sambo, *1933.* *The character of Little Black Sambo first appeared in a children's book in 1899. Set in India, it did not have the racist overtones that later depictions would highlight. The poster shown here is a vivid example of such versions.* IMAGE COURTESY OF THE ADVERTISING ARCHIVES.

DU BOIS AND THE STUDY OF BLACK POPULAR CULTURE

The leading black intellectual who bridged the gap between the study of black music and black popular culture was sociologist William Edward Burghardt Du Bois. Du Bois, a preeminent scholar-intellectual, wrote extensively on the sociology and history of African Americans and pioneered the editing of numerous journals of opinion devoted to racial issues. Not only did Du Bois analyze black slave songs in his *Souls of Black Folk* (1903) and *The Gift of Black Folk* (1924), he also wrote about the sociological implications of popular culture and blacks in a little-known article in 1897 titled "The Problem of Amusement." Du Bois did not label the phenomenon he was describing and pondering as "black popular culture" but rather "the question of the amusements of Negroes" (2000 [1897]). However, it was an inquiry into black popular culture because he referred to dancing, playing cards, drinking, smoking, and playing football, all of which are activities considered to be popular culture.

In "The Problem of Amusement," Du Bois described late-nineteenth-century black urban attitudes toward popular culture, what institutions among them conducted popular culture, and what the "tendency of indulgence" was toward particular types of popular culture. Whereas Du Bois maintained that the pursuit of popular culture in the city by young black men and women from rural communities was "disastrous," he believed amusement was a necessary and legitimate pursuit. Du Bois reveals an interesting problematic that had to do with conditions that were peculiar to urban black Americans and their pursuit of popular culture at that time. The first condition was that African Americans were excluded from mainstream public amusements in the cities to which they migrated and, second, that the chief purveyor of popular culture to black people was the black church, which in theory was opposed to modern popular culture. Du Bois concludes that the activities of the black church should become differentiated and that it must surrender its default function of providing "amusement" for its members to the school, home, and other social organizations. This was because he surmised that it was difficult for the black church to deny the need for popular culture while at the same time dissipating its spiritual purpose by furnishing popular culture activities for its members.

Largely a sociological analysis of the role of popular culture in the lives of late-nineteenth-century urban black Americans, Du Bois's essay revealed the need to study black popular culture in American culture, connected the production and experience of black popular culture to American culture and society, articulated the importance and relationship of the black church to popular culture and its members, and formulated questions about the issues of pleasure, race, racism, and the African presence in America.

CRITICAL ISSUES IN BLACK POPULAR CULTURE

Scholars of black popular culture generally examine it from two broad theoretical approaches: popular culture as object and popular culture as practice. This is to say that one type of scholarly work about black popular culture isolates its forms and discovers and interrogates its components. The other approach regards popular culture as a practice that facilitates an understanding of how political, social, and economic conditions and contexts affect the everyday lives of people. Therefore, for example, the first approach might examine rap music and describe its aesthetic and its relationship to African traditions, while the other approach would seek to explain how the rap aesthetic or its relationship to African traditions could empowers its creators.

The first two edited volumes of essays on black popular culture are aligned with the "popular culture as object (or text)" approach. Essays in Marshall Fishwick's *Remus, Rastus, Revolution* (1971) and Harry B. Shaw's *Perspectives of Black Popular Culture* (1990) investigated and introduced (as was the case with *Remus, Rastus, Revolution*) relatively unknown forms of black folk and popular expression to American scholarship on culture. Many of the contributors in both volumes incorporated semiology, or the system of signification, to explore such black cultural forms as the Sambo stereotype, the calypso tradition in the West Indies, and the black tavern. Interestingly, both volumes included essays on the Sambo stereotype, which demonstrates the enduring importance of representation and image in U.S. black popular culture. Also aligning with the "popular culture as text" approach, Gena Dagel Caponi's *Signifyin(g), Sanctifyin', and Slam Dunking: A Reader in African American Expressive Culture* (1999) focuses on building an aesthetic of black expressive culture (which is essentially black popular culture) in the areas of music, dance, orature, sports, and the display of the body.

Edited volumes of the 1990s were informed by the "popular culture as practice" theoretical paradigm. These include Gina Dent's *Black Popular Culture* (1992) and Joseph K. Adjaye and Adrianne R. Andrews's *Language, Rhythm, and Sound: Black Popular Cultures into the Twenty-First Century* (1997). Both volumes are informed by cultural theories of the British tradition of ideology, hegemony, and counterhegemony; the French tradition of semiology; and the construction of reality and black feminism and postmodernism. Essays examine such questions as production and consumption; youth, gender, and sexuality; technology, capital, and labor; the relationship between mainstream and the marginal; and popular culture as a site of resistance. In the British tradition of cultural studies, Ellis Cashmore's *The Black Culture Industry* (1997) examines how black culture has been converted into a commodity (usually in the interests of white-owned corporations); how blacks have been permitted to excel in entertainment only on the condition that they conform to whites' images of blacks; and how blacks themselves, when they rise to the top of the corporate entertainment ladder, have tended to act precisely as whites have in similar circumstances.

Harry J. Elam Jr. and Kennell Jackson's 2005 collection of essays on popular culture and global performance, *Black Cultural Traffic,* is significant for its stress on the actual movements of black cultural material from place to place geographically. Elam and Kennell describe Paul Gilroy's *The Black Atlantic* (1993) as the seminal work promoting black cultural traffic. Contributors analyzed various forms of black popular culture and "tracked" them in travel, observing what happened to the materials as they crossed local, regional, national, racial, and ethnic boundaries. They also extended or challenged the meaning of such concepts in cultural studies as authenticity (the capacity for cultural

Richard Pryor. *The comedian and actor Richard Pryor became famous for his brilliant stand-up comedy routines in the 1970s and 80s. Pryor transformed African American culture into humorous performance art.* AP IMAGES.

productions to be true to their roots and origins), appropriation (the borrowing, or theft, of an element of cultural expression of one group by another group), hybridity (the idea that traces of other cultures exist in every culture), globalization (the increasing global connectivity, integration, and interdependence in the economic, social, technological, cultural, political, and ecological spheres of everyday life), commodity (the reference to such cultural expressions as music and style as standardized for consumption by the masses), and cultural tradition.

Apart from these approaches is Kevern Verney's *African Americans and U.S. Popular Culture* (2003), which analyzes the role and significance of race in several major forms of popular culture, including sport, film, television, radio, and music. Verney's study is useful because it is an introduction to the history of African Americans in U.S. popular culture, examining its development from the early nineteenth century to the present. In addition, books and essays by black scholar-intellectuals Michele Wallace (*Dark Designs and Visual Culture,* 2004), Michael Eric Dyson (*Reflecting Black: African-American Cultural Criticism,* 1993), Todd Boyd (*Am I Black Enough for You?: Popular Culture from the 'Hood and Beyond,* 1997), and Mark Anthony Neal (*Soul Babies: Black Popular Culture and the Post-Soul Aesthetic,* 2002) should be noted because of their specific intent to explore black popular culture for insights into contemporary black American culture.

HIP-HOP, RACE, AND BLACK POPULAR CULTURE

The popular and academic interest in hip-hop culture and its expressive domains, rapping, graffiti writing, break dancing, emceeing, and deejaying (through mass media coverage in newspapers and magazines and in the presentation of conferences, publication of books, and college course offerings) has grown exponentially since the early 1990s. Murray Forman and Mark Anthony Neal's edited volume, *That's the Joint!: The Hip-Hop Studies Reader* (2004), attests to the depth and breadth of hip-hop cultural productions. This increase in popular and academic attention to hip-hop culture is the result in part of the fact that hip-hop culture and rap music, through globalization and the transnationalization of U.S. popular culture, is circulated internationally, giving birth to other hip-hop forms and genres in such disparate regions as Colombia, France, Poland, Bosnia and Croatia, Japan, Brazil, South Africa, Jamaica, Cuba, and Native Hawaii.

Hip-hop culture is decidedly global, urban, and connected to youth culture, according to Halifu Osumare in *Black Cultural Traffic* (Elam and Jackson 2005). Hip-hop culture, particularly rap music, brings together some of the most complex social, cultural, and political issues in contemporary American society. According to cultural studies scholar Tricia Rose in her seminal work on rap music, *Black Noise: Rap Music and Black Culture in Contemporary America* (1994), rap music is a black cultural expression that prioritizes black voices from the margins of urban America. These voices articulate the pleasures and problems of black urban life in contemporary America and the shifting terms of black marginality in contemporary American culture. Rap music's multidimensional nature builds from its primary context of development in hip-hop culture, the Afro-diasporic traditions it extends and revises, and the New York urban terrain in the 1970s.

As publications by Michael Eric Dyson (*Holler If You Hear Me: Searching for Tupac Shakur,* 2001) and Jon Michael Spencer (*The Emergency of Black and the Emergence of Rap,* 1991) demonstrate, race, racism, religion, and spirituality are connected to hip-hop culture, just as they are connected to black popular culture in general. For example, negative stereotyping persists in the entertainment industry especially through rap videos that disseminate misrepresentations and caricatured images of African Americans and that portray black females as sexual objects. Stereotyping is also seen in such television programs as MTV's *Pimp My Ride* and VH-1's *Flavor of Love* that subtly exalt the "gangsta" lifestyle. While hip-hop culture, particularly through the lyrics and videos of rap music, illustrate the culture's valuing of sexism, consumerism, and violence, it also reflects ultimate concerns about life and death, hopes and fears, self-affirmation, social and political liberation, and the ethic of truth telling. Hip-hop culture is a microcosm of and is the epitome of contemporary U.S. black popular culture because it encompasses the meanings, values, complexities, pleasures, and experiences of being black in the United States.

SEE ALSO *Hip-Hop Culture; Rap Music.*

BIBLIOGRAPHY

Adjaye, Joseph K., and Adrianne R. Andrews, eds. 1997. *Language, Rhythm, and Sound: Black Popular Cultures into the Twenty-First Century.* Pittsburgh, PA: University of Pittsburgh Press.

Boyd, Todd. 1997. *Am I Black Enough for You?: Popular Culture from the 'Hood and Beyond.* Bloomington: Indiana University Press.

———. 2002. *The New H.N.I.C. (Head Niggas In Charge): The Death of Civil Rights and the Reign of Hip Hop.* New York: New York University Press.

———. 2003. *Young, Black, Rich, and Famous: The Rise of the NBA, the Hip Hop Invasion, and the Transformation of American Culture.* New York: Doubleday.

Caponi, Gena Dagel, ed. 1999. *Signifyin(g), Sanctifyin', and Slam Dunking: A Reader in African American Expressive Culture.* Amherst: University of Massachusetts Press.

Cashmore, Ellis. 1997. *The Black Culture Industry.* London and New York: Routledge.

Dent, Gina, ed. 1992. *Black Popular Culture: A Project by Michele Wallace.* Seattle, WA: Bay Press.

Du Bois, W. E. B. 1903. *The Souls of Black Folk: Essays and Sketches.* Chicago: A. C. Mcclurg.

———. 1924. *The Gift of Black Folk: The Negroes in the Making of America.* Boston: Stratford Co.

———. 2000. "The Problem of Amusement." In *Du Bois on Religion,* edited by Phil Zuckerman, 19–28. Walnut Creek, CA: AltaMira Press.

Dyson, Michael Eric. 1993. *Reflecting Black: African-American Cultural Criticism.* Minneapolis: University of Minnesota Press.

———. 1995. *Making Malcolm: The Myth and Meaning of Malcolm X.* New York: Oxford University Press.

———. 1996. *Between God and Gangsta Rap: Bearing Witness to Black Culture.* New York: Oxford University Press.

———. 2001. *Holler If You Hear Me: Searching for Tupac Shakur.* New York: Basic Civitas.

———. 2004. *Mercy, Mercy Me: The Art, Loves, and Demons of Marvin Gaye.* New York: Basic Civitas, 2004.

Elam, Harry J., Jr., and Kennell Jackson, eds. 2005. *Black Cultural Traffic: Crossroads in Global Performance and Popular Culture.* Ann Arbor: University of Michigan Press.

Fishwick, Marshall, ed. 1971. *Remus, Rastus, Revolution.* Bowling Green, OH: Bowling Green University Popular Press.

Forman, Murray, and Mark Anthony Neal, eds. 2004. *That's the Joint: The Hip-Hop Studies Reader.* New York: Routledge.

Gates, Henry Louis, Jr. 1988. *The Signifying Monkey: A Theory of Afro-American Literary Criticism.* New York: Oxford University Press.

Gilroy, Paul. 1993. *The Black Atlantic: Modernity and Double Consciousness.* Cambridge, MA: Harvard University Press.

Hall, Stuart. 1992. "What Is This 'Black' in Black Popular Culture?" In *Black Popular Culture: A Project by Michele Wallace,* edited by Gina Dent, 21–33. Seattle, WA: Bay Press.

Kellner, Douglas. 1995. *Media Culture: Cultural Studies, Identity and Politics between the Modern and the Postmodern.* New York: Routledge.

Maultsby, Portia. 1996. "Music in African American Culture." In *Mediated Messages and African-American Culture: Contemporary Issues,* edited by Venise T. Berry and Carmen L. Manning-Miller, 241–262. Thousand Oaks, CA: Sage.

Neal, Mark Anthony. 1999. *What the Music Said: Black Popular Music and Black Public Culture.* New York: Routledge.

———. 2002. *Soul Babies: Black Popular Culture and the Post-Soul Aesthetic.* New York: Routledge.

Osumare, Halifu. 2005. "Global Hip-Hop and the African Diaspora." In *Black Cultural Traffic: Crossroads in Global Perspective and Popular Culture,* edited by Harry J. Elam, Jr. and Kennell Jackson, 266–288. Ann Arbor: University of Michigan Press.

Rose, Tricia. 1994. *Black Noise: Rap Music and Black Culture in Contemporary America.* Hanover, NH: University Press of New England.

Shaw, Harry B., ed. 1990. *Perspectives of Black Popular Culture.* Bowling Green, OH: Bowling Green University Popular Press.

Sidran, Ben. 1981. *Black Talk.* New York: Da Capo Press.

Spencer, Jon Michael. 1991. *The Emergency of Black and the Emergence of Rap.* Durham, NC: Duke University Press.

Verney, Kevern. 2003. *African Americans and U.S. Popular Culture.* London and New York: Routledge.

Wallace, Michele. 2004. *Dark Designs and Visual Culture.* Durham, NC: Duke University Press.

Angela M. Nelson

BLACK RECONSTRUCTION

The term *Black Reconstruction* refers to the actions and activities of both black and white Americans in the period immediately after the Civil War. It involved the transformation of Southern political, economic, and social institutions in a manner consistent with the Thirteenth, Fourteenth, and Fifteenth Amendments, which collectively established black freedom and equality. Many historians define Black Reconstruction as spanning the years from 1863 (the year of the Emancipation Proclamation, which made possible widespread black military participation in the Civil War) through 1877 (the year of the national political agreement to remove federal troops from the South). However, significant political and other Reconstruction activity by African Americans continued at the local and state levels beyond 1877.

The rebuilding of Southern society and the political reintegration of the South into the nation after the Civil War is referred to more generally simply as Reconstruction. Unfortunately, for the first half of the twentieth century, scholarly and historical attention focused almost exclusively on the actions of whites, both in the South and in the North, and ignored the immense contributions of African Americans. Moreover, to the extent that white historians considered the activities of African Americans at all, for much of the twentieth century they adopted the white supremacist views that Columbia University professor William Dunning and his followers held at the turn of the nineteenth century. These historians denigrated Reconstruction as a "mistake" precisely because black Americans briefly attained some political power in the regions of their former bondage. This view was reproduced in popular form by the film *The Birth of a Nation* (1915) and the book on which it was based, *The Clansman* (1902), both of which stigmatized African Americans and lauded white terrorist groups such as the Ku Klux Klan. The history of Reconstruction became a principal means by which whites, in both the South and the North, manipulated historical memories in order to reify a post-slavery racialism.

A dissenting view of Reconstruction that recognized African-American achievements was preserved and developed by some scholars, most notably W. E. B. Du Bois, whose magisterial 1935 work on the period was titled *Black Reconstruction,* and John Hope Franklin, whose *From Slavery to Freedom* was first published in 1947 and is still widely read some four million copies later. Thus, the term *Black Reconstruction* operates at two levels: (1) it focuses on the overlooked contributions of black Americans to this period in American history; and (2) it presents a corrective to the racism of first decades of the twentieth century by more fairly analyzing the achievements and failures of both black and white actors during Reconstruction.

THE INITIAL STAGES

One can trace the beginnings of Black Reconstruction to the service of some 160,000 former slaves and 40,000 free African Americans who served as soldiers in the Union during the Civil War. These soldiers not only provided the manpower essential to the North's victory, they also staked an undeniable claim to be transformed from a state of slavery into full citizenship after the war. Many of these former soldiers became integral to the black and interracial civic and political organizations in the South. This story is evident, for example, in the experience of Abraham Galloway, who had been born a slave near Wilmington, North Carolina, and who may have been inspired by the writings and ideas of David Walker, a free black who was also from Wilmington. Saving money as a brick mason beyond that demanded by his owner, Galloway escaped to an African-American abolitionist community in Ontario, Canada. When the Civil War began, he returned to the United States and served as a spy in the intelligence service of the Union army in eastern North Carolina. In recruiting other blacks for the Union army, Galloway was seen as a natural leader and was made a member of a delegation of blacks who met with President Abraham Lincoln in 1863 on the issue of black suffrage. Galloway attended the massive National Convention of Colored Citizens held in Syracuse, New York, in 1864 to consider the postwar situation of African Americans. He also started state and local chapters of the Equal Rights League. These leagues served as political and civic associations throughout the country, fighting for equal civil, political, and social rights for black citizens. They also represented, along with black churches, schools, and other organizations, the framework of a burgeoning African-American civic life.

Galloway and other leaders, such as Tunis Campbell in Georgia, soon discovered that the resistance of most white Southerners to citizenship claims by blacks was swift and violent. First, in 1865 and 1866, the white South passed the "Black Codes," separate laws modeled in part on the antebellum laws restricting free blacks in both the North and South. These laws restricted basic contract and property rights for African Americans, imposed particularly severe criminal and vagrancy punishments, and otherwise established a legal basis for second-class citizenship. In turn, these reactionary laws radicalized the Republican Party in Congress, which passed the Civil Rights Act of 1866 to outlaw the Black Codes. Then, in 1867, the Congress passed Reconstruction legislation that required black suffrage as a condition of readmission of the former Confederate states to the Union.

What former Confederates could not achieve through law, however, they sought to gain by violence. Thus began, in earnest, the white terrorist or vigilante organizations such as Red Shirts, the Regulators, the Knights of the White Camelia, and, above all, the Ku Klux Klan. The Klan engaged in extreme violence, often against blacks who, in the words of one former Confederate, had attained some "status in society" through property holdings, labor or political activism, or general social standing. In the face of such violence, both Galloway and Campbell helped form black militias that provided some level of protection against white terrorism. For a time, the freedpeople depended on the federal government as a means of protection against white Southern violence and legal manipulation. The Bureau of Freedmen, Refugees, and Abandoned Lands, or the Freedmen's Bureau, had been established on March 3, 1865, to provide basic necessities to freed slaves and refugees in the South. At first there had been some hope that congressmen committed to black rights, including Thaddeus Stevens and Charles Sumner, would be able to implement land reform through the bureau and realize the goal of the then common phrase, "forty acres and a mule." President Andrew Johnson and his conservative allies in Congress, however, eliminated this essential reform, and the bureau thereafter concentrated on labor, education, public welfare, and access to justice. Although the Freedmen's Bureau often supported white Southern landowners in attempts to secure black labor, it also provided basic food, medical aid, education, and legal protection to many African Americans in the South. In addition, the bureau presented African Americans with opportunities for leadership as officers and agents. John Mercer Langston, for example, served as a national officer in the bureau after the war. Langston went on to establish the law department at Howard University (the school was named after the head of the bureau, General O. O. Howard), serve as the school's acting president, become a member of Congress from Virginia, and represent the United States as minister to Haiti.

Tunis Campbell had also served in the Freedmen's Bureau, where he was in charge of the initial land redistribution in the Sea Island region of Georgia. When President Johnson pardoned former Confederates in 1865 and allowed former slaveholders to reclaim their land, Campbell organized the black community and purchased land to better secure the rights, property, and safety of his community. Like many other black leaders from both the North and the South, Campbell then became a leader in Southern state and local Republican politics. With the support of congressional legislation and federal troops, many Southern states were required to implement African-American suffrage in their reconstructed legislatures and state constitutional conventions. People such as Campbell and the Reverend Henry McNeal Turner served prominently in the Reconstruction state constitutional conventions, and many black veterans and officers of the Freedmen's Bureau served in the conventions and the Reconstruction legislatures.

Through these interracial political bodies, many Southern states ratified the Fourteenth and Fifteenth Amendments, which would likely not have been ratified without black political participation, both as voters and as convention delegates. Several Southern states also passed broad legislative reform programs that included laws desegregating public accommodations, founding and supporting public schooling, and reforming criminal laws and punishments. Moreover, the composition of these legislatures reflected the broad civil society that had formed so quickly in Southern black communities. Of the African-American members of these reconstructed state legislatures, over one hundred were ministers and seventy were teachers, attesting to the importance of religious organizations and education in the civil and political life of the black South. This is evident, for instance, in the career of Reverend Turner, a South Carolina free man. Turner was trained as a minister and appointed by President Lincoln as the Union army's first black chaplain. Like Tunis Campbell, Turner worked for the Freedmen's Bureau in Georgia after the war. He later founded the African Methodist Episcopal (AME) Church in Georgia and served in the state legislature until he was expelled without cause.

BLACK POLITICAL POWER

Federal assistance also occasionally helped blacks combat white violence. Extensive Klan violence forced the hand of congressional Republicans, who, under the authority of the Fourteenth and Fifteenth Amendments, enacted federal legislation to enable federal prosecution of the perpetrators. Black members of Congress, including the first African-American U.S. senator, Hiram Revels of Mississippi, and the first African-American member of the House of Representatives, Joseph Rainey of South Carolina, together praised this legislation as essential to protecting freedom and citizenship. In South Carolina, federal prosecution of the Klan under this law helped curb Klan violence and made it safer for the black majority in the state to hold and exercise political power. Indeed, this combination of federal enforcement of the laws and the initiative of black citizens—in politics, self-protection, and community organization—briefly appeared to be a viable counterweight to Southern white efforts to reimpose the slave system. In South Carolina, for instance, African-American politicians such as Rainey, Robert Smalls, and Robert B. Elliot were able to win election to the U.S. House of Representatives, African Americans held a majority in the state house of representatives for several years, and African Americans served as Speakers of the House for four years (including Elliot, from 1874–1876).

Blacks also saw significant political success in Louisiana, where Oscar J. Dunn, P. B. S. Pinchback, and Caesar Antoine served as lieutenant governors for most of the Reconstruction era. Pinchback even served as America's first black governor for a brief period. In Mississippi, African Americans held positions as lieutenant governor, secretary of state, and superintendent of education, and John R. Lynch served as Speaker of the House and was subsequently elected to Congress. All told, twenty-two African Americans served in Congress as a result of Reconstruction, and more than 600 African Americans served in state legislatures throughout the South, mostly from 1868 through 1877.

Black political power was also felt on the local level, where African Americans held numerous positions, such as sheriffs, justices of the peace, city aldermen, and county commissioners. Indeed, it was perhaps at this everyday level that the immediacy of racial equality had the greatest impact on whites and blacks alike. For black Southerners, the prospect of having black local officials available for dispensing government assistance or everyday justice made real the hope of equal citizenship. For many white Southerners, on the other hand, the same situation seemed to turn reality upside-down. Many whites viewed this period not as an experiment in racial equality but as an era of "Negro domination" in which blacks seemed to exercise power at all levels of government. For these whites of the postwar South, there could be no racial equality; any and all exercises of power by African Americans amounted to "domination."

On the other hand, as long as the Republicans saw black suffrage as clearly aligned with their own political interests, federal support for suffrage was possible. Indeed, even after the Compromise of 1877, national Republicans continued for about fifteen years to support, albeit in vain, federal actions and legislation to protect black suffrage.

As part of this battle for black equality and power during Reconstruction, African Americans throughout the South developed newer strategies for claiming rights through demonstrations and protests. In New Orleans, for instance, African Americans and white supporters marched in July 1866 in favor of suffrage in what has been described as the first American civil rights march. The New Orleans Race Riot of 1866 erupted when the marchers were met by an angry, violent white mob. Other forms of protest included successful sit-ins on streetcars in Richmond, Charleston, and New Orleans in 1867. The passage of the Civil Rights Act of 1875, which gave private persons a right of action against owners of segregated public accommodations, also inspired protest actions and litigation. Black workers also engaged in strikes for better working conditions, both in the early years of Reconstruction and in the waning days of the late 1870s into the 1880s when a national union, the Knights of Labor, supported black workers in the South.

THE END OF RECONSTRUCTION

Still, despite these early achievements and the tireless work of people such as Campbell, Elliot, and Rainey, conservative whites were often able to defeat or overturn Republican reform programs. Indeed, such a coalition of whites in Georgia denied the right of black legislators who had been elected in 1868 to take their seats (Georgia legislators also refused to ratify the Fifteenth Amendment). White democrats used election fraud and violence to recapture political power. The most notorious of these events occurred in Colfax, Louisiana, where, on Easter Sunday, April 13, 1873, armed whites attacked blacks in an effort to unseat local black officeholders after a disputed local election. Over 105 blacks were killed in the violence.

The growing unwillingness of the federal government and the national Republican Party to support African Americans in the South in the 1870s culminated in the election of 1876. The presidential contest between the Republican candidate, Rutherford B. Hayes, and the Democrat Samuel J. Tilden remained undecided after election day, with the electors from three southern states—South Carolina, Louisiana, and Florida—in dispute. As part of a political compromise, Hayes was awarded the electors and the presidency, but Republicans agreed to remove all troops from the South. Blacks in the South were left without even minimal federal protection, and white Democrats were able to regain and secure full political power in the ensuing decade.

While the Compromise of 1877 marked the sharpest sign that Reconstruction was over, its full demise took several more years. In 1883, the U.S. Supreme Court extinguished the embers of Reconstruction when it ruled, in the *Civil Rights Cases*, that the federal Civil Rights Act of 1875, the last of the federal Reconstruction Acts that sought to protect civil rights in public accommodations, was unconstitutional. In this and related cases, the Supreme Court ensured that the Constitution would be transformed from a document creating equal citizenship to a roadblock to freedom. Still, for a period of about fifteen years, African Americans in certain areas of the South maintained some level of political power, particularly where they were able to join with populist white politicians, and where the law had not yet reverted to the Jim Crow regime of legally compelled segregation that had been implemented before Reconstruction under the Black Codes. The achievements of Reconstruction thus lingered for several years, finally falling away near the turn of the century with the federal acceptance of legal segregation in *Plessey v. Ferguson* and the complete implementation of disenfranchisement by the start of the twentieth century.

LAYING THE FOUNDATION FOR FUTURE RESISTANCE

This defeat of Reconstruction and its promise of racial equality and equal citizenship has led many people to see that era as a tragic failure. W. E. B. Du Bois famously wrote in 1935: "the slave went free; stood a brief moment in the sun; then moved back again toward slavery." While such a conclusion is correct in terms of the fundamental access of African Americans to political and economic power, one should not forget that some of the structures built by blacks, and some of the hopes fostered by the experiences of Black Reconstruction, lived on. Even as federal and moderate white support for Reconstruction waned in the 1870s, and as African Americans lost many of the political and economic gains they had achieved during Reconstruction, many blacks continued to build communities and maintain some political power. With the resistance of whites to interracial politics and society plainly evident, many African Americans, including Turner and Campbell, emphasized black-centered communities and organizations. Some even formed African American towns—such as Nicodemus, Kansas, and Langston, Oklahoma—which were started by African Americans after the end of Reconstruction in 1877 as part of a black emigration known as the Exoduster movement.

In response to white efforts to impose racialism on the southern polity, and thus extend the race ideas of slavery into the postslavery world, black Southerners sought to redefine an identity for themselves. While some did this by moving out of the South, for most African Americans it was the continued building of strong black communities, rather than mass emigration, that kept alive the hopes and possibilities of Reconstruction. The foundations built during Reconstruction—foundations in black education, black churches, and black political and community organizations—would continue to provide support to African Americans in the South throughout the long years of Jim Crow.

The ways in which the Reconstruction era allowed for the building of foundations in black communities can be seen in the development of a parallel civil society within black communities, a process that began during Reconstruction and continued throughout the Jim Crow era. For example, in Reconstruction-era Richmond, Virginia, mass meetings held at local black churches to celebrate the end of slavery in 1865 quickly transformed into the political, educational, and public-assistance organizations that acted and advocated on behalf of African Americans throughout Reconstruction. Particularly important to this struggle was the contribution of black women, who were fully engaged in the activities and ideas of these organizations. Women even formed or took part in militias and carried arms in an effort to support and protect black communities and the exercise of freedom, including the protection of black men attempting to vote in the face of white violence and threats. Ultimately, despite the overwhelming failure of Reconstruction to realize equal citizenship, it was the creation of these frameworks for the development of black communities that maintained the promise of Reconstruction. Through these efforts, African Americans would attain the education, begin the economic development, and build the supportive communities that would be necessary to eventually challenge Jim Crow.

SEE ALSO *Black Codes; Civil Rights Acts; Freedmen's Bureau; Ku Klux Klan; Plessy v. Ferguson; Turner, Henry McNeal; United States Constitution; Walker, David.*

BIBLIOGRAPHY

Brown, Elsa Barkley. 2000. "Negotiating and Transforming the Public Sphere: African American Political Life in the Transition from Slavery to Freedom." In *Jumpin' Jim Crow: Southern Politics from Civil War to Civil Rights*, edited by Jane Dailey, Glenda Elizabeth Gilmore, and Bryant Simon, 28–66. Princeton, NJ: Princeton University Press.

Cecelski, David S. 1998. "Abraham H. Galloway: Wilmington's Lost Prophet and the Rise of Black Radicalism in the American South." In *Democracy Betrayed: The Wilmington Race Riot of 1898 and Its Legacy*, edited by David S. Cecelski and Timothy B. Tyson. Chapel Hill: University Press of North Carolina.

Du Bois, W. E. B. 1935. *Black Reconstruction in America*. New York: Harcourt, Brace.

Duncan, Russell. 1986. *Freedom's Shore: Tunis Campbell and the Georgia Freedmen*. Athens: University of Georgia Press.

Foner, Eric. 1988. *Reconstruction: America's Unfinished Revolution, 1863–1877*. New York: Harper & Row.

Franklin, John Hope, and Alfred A. Moss Jr. 2000. *From Slavery to Freedom: A History of African Americans*, 8th ed. New York: Knopf.

Hollandsworth, James G. 2003. " 'Damned Sons of Bitches': The First Demonstrations for Black Civil Rights in the Gulf South." In *Sunbelt Revolution: The Historical Progression of the Civil Rights Struggle in the Gulf South, 1866–2000*, edited by Samuel C. Hyde Jr. Gainesville: University Press of Florida.

McFeely, William S. 1968. *Yankee Stepfather: General O. O. Howard and the Freedmen*. New Haven, CT: Yale University Press.

Painter, Nell Irvin. 1977. *Exodusters: Black Migration to Kansas after Reconstruction*. New York: Knopf.

Rabinowitz, Howard N., ed. 1982. *Southern Black Leaders of the Reconstruction Era*. Urbana: University of Illinois Press.

James W. Fox Jr.

BLACK-WHITE INTERMARRIAGE

The term *intermarriage* typically refers to marriages between individuals of different socially constructed racial and ethnic groups. In the United States, however, these unions are usually defined as *interracial*. Such unions are often depicted as being between white and nonwhite persons, with an emphasis on white-black unions. Historically, interracial sexuality, especially between white women and nonwhite men, was forbidden in both public discourse and laws; it was legally and socially stigmatized. For white men, having sex with women of any race was acceptable as long as it was not public. Legal, political, and social restrictions against these relationships have existed at various times, and even in the early twenty-first century interracial marriage rates remain low, accounting for only 5.4 percent of all marriages in the country, according to the 2000 Census.

THE EARLY HISTORY OF MISCEGENATION IN AMERICA

Maintaining racial purity within the white race has been the dominant discourse in marriage laws and intermarriage prohibitions. Historically, legal restrictions placed on intermarriage and miscegenation have varied by state. In some states intermarriage was legal, while in others it was illegal. Miscegenation had been discouraged and treated as socially deviant since the arrival of African slaves in the American colonies, but it was not until 1691 that interracial sex was made illegal. Virginia passed the first statute against miscegenation between blacks and whites. The goal was to prevent "that abominable mixture and spurious issue which hereafter may increase in this dominion, as well by negroes, mulattoes, and Indians intermarrying with English, or other white women, as by their unlawful accompanying with one another" (Wadlington 1966, p. 1192).

Since the beginning of the sixteenth century, people involved in interracial sex have faced informal sanctions, punishment, and social exclusion. White women romantically or sexually involved with black men were punished, often by being banished from the colony or by being beaten and arrested. The political and social ideology centered on protecting white womanhood and demonizing black men, and free access to black women was largely held by white men in positions of power. These beliefs and social norms were never formally legalized, but the ideology penetrated the legal system. Interracial sex was constructed as deviant within the institution of slavery, and from the beginning this view was primarily aimed at preventing black male slaves from engaging in sexual relations with white women. The frequent abuse and lynching of black men for allegedly raping or desiring sexual relations with white women, as well as the widespread rape and sexual abuse of black women by white men, played an integral part in the socio-historical construction of race and the rules of race relations.

Legal sanctions, as opposed to social ones, were more often focused on interracial unions than on interracial sex. Indeed, interracial sex reified the racial divide and hierarchy through the sexual mistreatment of black women by white men, and through the severe punishment of black men who were sexually involved with a white woman. By 1940, thirty-one states had laws against interracial marriage, but only six had laws prohibiting interracial sex. But both laws and social sanctions against interracial sex and marriage were racist social constructions, formulated largely by white men to protect the "purity" of the white race and prevent racial mixture.

Interracial sex was also used as a symbol of white male privilege. Sex between black men and white women was punished, for these relations posed a threat to the power and privilege of white men. But sex between white men and black women did not threaten the white power structure, but instead reinforced the domination of white men up through the 1800s. White men had free access to black women, and these relations often involved rape or other forms of violence. Black women were oversexualized in the minds of white men, especially in contrast to white women. White men used this depiction to justify the idealization of the white woman, the degradation of black women, and the privilege awarded to white men, especially in terms of unlimited sexual access. Interracial sex did not challenge the purity of the white race because children born of white fathers and black mothers were demoted to slave status.

DEFINING RACIAL CATEGORIES

Throughout the seventeenth and eighteenth centuries, the social construction of racial categories and the increasing desire to quantify race, particularly blackness, led to frequent modifications in the legal and social status of interracial marriage and children born of interracial relations. Children born to a black parent and a white parent were forced to assume the mothers' status: children of slave mothers assumed the slave status, while children of white mothers were sold as indentured servants until the age of thirty. White mothers of mixed-race children had to serve five years and were then banished from the colony. These sentences of servitude and banishment often varied over time and place. The first legal efforts to classify race came in a Virginia law of 1787, which stipulated that any person having one-fourth black blood, or having any grandparent who was black, was considered black. The legal quantification of blackness and of people of color was revised until it eventually came to include any person who is not white, so that "white" legally meant any person with no trace of any other blood besides Caucasian, and having even "one drop" of "black blood" defined a person as black.

DEMONIZING ASIAN IMMIGRANTS

At the same time, while the definition of racial categories became legal, so did the legal protection of white womanhood. In 1819 a code was passed in the southern United States that included the punishment of any attempted sexual relations or expressed desire for a white woman by a slave. While African Americans were the central focus of miscegenation laws, other men of color, notably Asians, were also targeted for racial exclusion. Chinese men, for example, were represented as threats to white womanhood. Congress passed laws restricting Chinese immigration even as the popular press presented them as sexually deviant and dangerous. Chinese women were also excluded, based on perceptions of them as prostitutes and sexually immoral. In 1875, Congress passed the Page Law, which forbade the entry of Chinese and other "Mongolian" prostitutes. Immigration restriction laws passed in 1903, 1907, and 1917 allowed for the deportation of Chinese women suspected of prostitution and defined Asian women as sexual objects.

Given that prostitution was widespread at this time, singling out Chinese women for "exclusion," and portraying them as transmitters of diseases, drug addiction, and temptation of sin, was more about controlling the reproduction and sexuality of Asian women. Given the lack of available Asian women for Asian men to marry, Asian men were also constructed as a potential threat to white women. Therefore, antimiscegenation laws were enacted against interracial marriage in general, and specific laws forbade Asian-white intermarriage. Immigration laws concerning Chinese and Japanese immigration were also enacted to control and limit intermarriages. For example, the 1882 Chinese Exclusion Act prohibited Chinese from immigrating to the United States for ten years, thus eliminating most Chinese-white intermarrying. Similarly, the "Gentleman's Agreement" with Japan was used to eliminate Japanese immigration to the United States by prohibiting Japanese laborers from obtaining passports.

INTERMARRIAGE IN THE CIVIL RIGHTS ERA

The legal landscape of intermarriage and interracial relations remained divided and inconsistent until the 1960s. Support of the one-drop rule persisted, and laws regarding intermarriage were changed, revised, revoked, and reestablished until 1967. In 1960, when every southern state had a law against interracial marriage, the U.S. Census documented 51,409 black-white couples in the United States. And while the U.S Congress never outlawed miscegenation, forty-one out of fifty states had laws against interracial unions at some time in their history.

Changes in the racial landscape during the 1960s and 1970s were reflected in the legal support for interracial unions. The civil rights movement, grassroots political and social movements, and similar changing ideologies were the driving force behind the changing legal system. Legal support for interracial unions produced a significant increase in the number of black-white marriages between 1960 and 1970, when the total number of interracial marriages increased by 26 percent. Interracial couples remained mostly in the northern and western regions of the country, while the rate of interracial marriages in the South declined by 34 percent between 1960 and 1970.

The discrepancy among interracial marriages in the North and in the South may be due, in part, to the fact that most of the southern states had laws against interracial marriages until 1967. Most of the interracial marriages were between black men and white women. These marriages increased 61 percent from 1960 to 1970, while marriages between black women and white men decreased by 9 percent during this period. The issue of interracial sex and marriage is an integral part of the construction of race and racial groups, and the fear of interracial sexuality has often been used to justify racist ideologies and practices. The case of Emmett Till, a young black teenager who allegedly whistled at a white woman and was brutally murdered in 1955, attests to the enduring strength of the ideology of protecting white womanhood.

LOVING V. VIRGINIA

The historic 1967 Supreme Court ruling in the case of *Loving v. Virginia* changed the legal landscape of intermarriage permanently. Richard Loving, a white man, and Mildred Jeter, a black woman, left their home state of Virginia, where intermarriage was illegal, to get married in Washington, D.C. When they returned to Virginia they were arrested and sentenced to one year in prison. However, the judge suspended the sentence on the condition that the couple leave Virginia and not return for twenty-five years. The Lovings appealed the decision in a state court, but the ruling was upheld based on a previous case, in order for the state to "preserve the racial integrity of its citizens" and prevent "the obliteration of racial pride." Previous essentialist thinking that interracial marriages were unnatural and deviant was heavily reliant upon "scientific" assertions about the genetic and biological hierarchy of the "races."

Finally, the decision was appealed to the U.S. Supreme Court, and the ruling was overturned. Whereas Chief Justice Warren's decision remained free of any controversial sociological or anthropological evidence or studies, the *Loving* case signaled the beginning of a change in interracial ideology within U.S. society. Racist ideologies that pervaded the legal system for more than three centuries were retracted. While these ideologies remained dominant in the larger society, they were no longer to be used to justify legal decisions. Although a majority of whites supported laws against interracial marriage, the decision to make laws forbidding interracial marriages unconstitutional legalized a relationship that had been criminalized in the United States since the seventeenth century (Romano 2003).

While the *Loving v. Virginia* case granted legal support to interracial marriages and initiated an increase in the number of interracial couples, antimiscegenation ideology persisted and adapted to the continuously changing racial landscape. In *Race Mixing* (2003), Renee Romano reports that in 1970, 56 percent of southern whites and 30 percent of nonsouthern whites supported laws against interracial relationships. Though support for antimiscegenation laws had decreased

Richard and Mildred Loving, 1965. *The* Loving *case signaled the beginning of a change in interracial ideology within U.S. society.* AP IMAGES.

by 1990, social tolerance for interracial marriage was still reminiscent of antimiscegenation ideology. Robin Goodwin and Duncan Cramer report in *Inappropriate Relationships* (2002) that 61 percent of white Americans polled in 1991 said they would oppose a union between a close family member and a black person. At the same time, two-thirds of black Americans said they would neither support nor oppose an interracial marriage between a family member and a white person.

RESEARCH FINDINGS ABOUT INTERMARRIAGE

Researchers have looked in great depth at interracial marriage and various aspects of interracial couples or families. This research has tended to use either psychological or sociological theories to explain how or why the couples came together. In addition, the characteristics of the couples, including their demographic similarities and differences, have been examined.

The Assimilationist Approach. Much of the research relies on an assimilationist framework, using intermarriage as an indicator of assimilation of the minority group or a site of comparison with same-race couples. The noted race scholars Michael Omi and Howard Winant argue that this assimilationist framework arose as an "ethnicity-based theory" in the early twentieth century as a response to biologically based theories of race. This ethnicity-based paradigm includes the debate between an assimilationist perspective, beginning with Robert Park's race relations cycle in 1964, and the concept of cultural pluralism, which was introduced by Horace Kallen in 1924 and focuses on the acceptance of different cultures. Omi and Winant note that this framework has a number of shortcomings, especially when discussing black-white interracial marriage. In particular, it tends to use an immigrant analogy for racial groups, it reduces race to ethnicity, and it does not take into consideration the different ways racial groups are constructed and conceptualized within society.

These various studies on interracial couples all express or imply that interracial couples are inherently different from same-race couples, therefore making it necessary to explain, account for, or describe their relationships. Studies that use an assimilationist framework are problematic because they "uncritically take race as a given reality (and) contribute to the reification of race as a foundation beyond cultural interrogation" (Ferber 1998, p. 11). Underlying this work is the assumption that distinct racial groups exist in the first place, and can thus engage in "interracial" marriage. By comparing interracial couples to same-race couples, same-race couples are established as the "standard" or the "norm." It is only within a society such as America, which places such an emphasis on race and racial groups, that the idea of an interracial couple has meaning.

Within an assimilationist framework that focuses on the couple, interracial marriage is seen as the final stage of assimilation, a sign of improving race relations that can mask any opposition that may exist towards the couple. As Stanford Lyman argues, the assimilation model of race relations "was ideology too, for Park believed that once the racial cycle was completed, the social arena would be cleared of those racial impediments interfering with the inevitable class struggle" (Lyman 1997, p. 27).

Psychological Measures. Interracial sexuality and marriage have also been explained using psychological approaches and theories. Different "racial motivation" theories state that interracial marriages occur because of racial differences, rather than in spite of them (see Kouri and Laswell 1993, p. 242). Among interracial couples; the white partner is usually argued to be involved in the relationship as a result of some neurotic conflictor pathology, or as an act of rebellion and punishment against his or her family. One example of this type of racial motivation theory is classic Freudian theory, which explains black-white intermarriage as a function of the inadequate "repression" of attraction to the opposite-sex parent.

It is suggested that a black man and white woman, by marrying, can manage their Oedipal/incest fantasies, satisfy beliefs of sexual and sensual superiority, and provide themselves the opportunity to act out racial hostility through sexual behavior. Low self-esteem and guilt theories have also been offered to explain the motives of blacks and whites who intermarry. Interracial marriage has sometimes been viewed as a "deviant" behavior, and those who intermarry are labeled deviant, psychologically disturbed, or maladjusted individuals whose behaviors require explanation. The "motives" for engaging in the act of intermarrying are seen as a product of something distinctive to the individual and his or her psychological history, usually a result of a certain instinctive drive. Yet it is important to consider how deviance is a consequence of the application of rules and sanctions by others to an "offender." Howard Becker, in his book *Outsiders* (1963), notes that the crucial dimension is the societal reaction to an act, not any quality of the act itself.

Socioeconomic Factors. There have also been many studies about the individual traits and characteristics of blacks and whites who intermarry, examining similarities or differences in education, employment, involvement in social activities, recreation, residential area, and socioeconomic status. One study done in 2000 sought to examine factors that might influence interracial marriage such as immigration, age, college attendance, socioeconomic status, region and military service (Heaton and Jacobson 2000). In a 1997 study, Richard Lewis and colleagues looked at the role that nonracial and racial factors play in spouse selection among those who are interracially married. The goal was to determine whether nonracial factors, such as socioeconomic status, common social and entertainment interests, and personal evaluation of attractiveness, are more or less important than racial factors, such as the excitement and novelty of being interracially married and the sexual attractiveness of someone of the "opposite" race (Lewis et al. 1997). Based on surveys of 292 respondents, they concluded that nonracial factors are more important in the spouse selection process than racial factors.

Interracial couples come together for varied reasons, just as same-race couples do, and race or racial factors do not necessarily play a primary role in the couples coming together. When looking at interracial marriage, it is important to consider the socially constructed nature of racial categories, and at how interracial marriage remains an issue because "race" still matters. In a race-conscious society such as America, even when whites and blacks are similar in terms of education, employment, recreation, socioeconomic status, and other factors, the perceived and ascribed racial differences remain a deterrent to intermarriage. Furthermore, because most blacks and whites do not inhabit the same areas, acquire similar education and employment levels, and are involved in different social activities, the focus of these studies should be on the structural constraints that prevent or discourage black-white proximity and intermarriage—such as segregation in residential areas and segregation and racial discrimination in schools, the workplace, and other institutions—rather than focusing on those individuals who do engage in interracial relationships.

One major concept that has been used to explain interracial marriage is "hypergamy." Defined as the marriage of a female to a male of a higher caste or class standing, hypergamy has been a major theoretical thread in the study of interracial marriage. Using this type of theory to understand interracial relationships emphasizes that these couples come together primarily because black men who have a higher socioeconomic status can marry a white woman of lower socioeconomic status, and thereby exchange his class standing for her socially defined superior racial status. Recent studies have also used the hypergamy argument to explain intermarriage. In a 1993 article titled "Trends in Black/White Intermarriage," Matthijs Kalmijn found that racial caste prestige and socioeconomic prestige still function as substitutes in the selection process of mates for interracial marriages.

These studies, however, have been faulted because they do not address cultural factors when considering the low rates of intermarriage for black women. These factors include the disturbing history of sexual relations between black women and white men; the lack of power of black women in society relative to whites, and even to black men; the white standard of beauty that devalues black women; and the opposition to intermarriage reported by black women in attitudinal studies.

CONTEMPORARY TRENDS

Studies that address the issue of interracial families or couples from a personal perspective offer insight into the difficulties that interracial couples and families can still face. Research on interracial couples also includes in-depth interviews with black-white couples, which provides information about the couples' relationships, their parenting experiences, what the partners learn from each other, the role of race in the relationships, and the "special blessings" of being an interracial couple. Other works have documented the contemporary experiences of interracial couples and changing societal attitudes and behaviors, which reveal that while interracial couples are more acceptable in the twenty-first century, significant opposition remains.

Nearly forty years after the ban on interracial marriages was considered unconstitutional, interracial marriages have increased. The 2000 U.S. Census found there were 287,576 interracial marriages in the United States, making up about .53 percent of the total number of marriages. Marriages between black men and white women are still far more common than those between white men and black women, of which there were about 78,778 in 2000. These numbers are reflective of the remaining racial ideologies that inform societal

Legalizing Interracial Marriage. *When this couple married in early 2000, the section of the 1901 Alabama Constitution prohibiting interracial marriage was still on the books. On November 7, 2000, the voters of Alabama repealed the prohibition, making it the last state to repeal such a law.* AP IMAGES.

understandings of interracial relationships and, more specifically, individuals involved in interracial relationships.

The U.S. Census documents all interracial couples and marriages, including marriages between Asian, Hispanic, Native American, Pacific Islander, and multiracial individuals. Socially constructed perceptions of interracial dating also include white-Hispanic, and white-Asian marriages as interracial couples. The 2000 U.S. Census documented 504,119 white-Asian marriages. Marriage between a white person and a person of Hispanic origin are difficult to document. The socially constructed nature of racial categories in America leaves the definition of race and interracial couples ambiguous. On the 2000 Census, individuals could identify themselves racially as one or more of the following: Black or African American, White, Asian, Native Hawaiian or Other Pacific Islander, American Indian or Alaska Native, or Some Other Race. People of Hispanic origin, however, could identify themselves as belonging to one or more of these racial categories as well as indicating their Hispanic origin, which is classified as an ethnic category, not a racial one, by the Census Bureau. Yet couples with one Hispanic partner and one non-Hispanic partner are often thought of as interracial, reinforcing the idea that any white-nonwhite couple is an interracial couple. (The 2000 Census counted 924,352 Hispanic-white marriages, a higher number than any "interracial" pairing.) Though Hispanic is not a race, it is often socially considered a racial group. Hispanic-white intermarriage is the highest amount of all intergroup marriage, due to the ambiguity of race and the definitions of race.

Interracial relationships have long been viewed as a sign of improving race relations and assimilation, yet these unions have also been met with opposition from whites and other racial groups. While the number of interracial couples continues to rise, this does not signify a complete transformation of societal ideologies and ideas. While significant changes have occurred in the realm of race relations, U.S. society still has racial borders. Most citizens live and socialize with others of the same race, even though there are no longer such legal barriers as laws against intermarriage. The relatively low numbers of interracial couples in the United States attests to the continual reproduction and construction of dominant racial ideologies. While the ability of two individuals of different races to love each other cannot change the social structure of race, the societal responses to these relationships (e.g., the images produced, the discourses used, the meanings attached) provides insight into the social and political hierarchy of race. Issues concerning the children of interracial marriages, the racism the couple will encounter from the larger society, the disapproval of the family, and traditional ideas of race mixing are all used to challenge the formation of interracial relationships. Interracial couples are continuously being constructed not only through the couples' experiences, but through larger society, including the family, neighborhood, community, church, school, workplace, and other social institutions.

SEE ALSO *Biracialism; Multiracial Identities; Racial Formations.*

BIBLIOGRAPHY

Becker, Howard S. 1963. *Outsiders: Studies in the Sociology of Deviance*. New York: Free Press.

Bennett, Lerone, Jr. 1962. *Before the Mayflower: A History of Black America*. Chicago: Johnson Publishing Co.

Collins, Patricia Hill. 2000. *Black Feminist Thought*. 10th anniversary ed. New York: Routledge.

Crester, Gary A., and Joseph J. Leon. 1982. "Intermarriage in the U.S.: An Overview of Theory and Research." *Marriage and Family Review* 5: (3–15).

Davis, F. James. 1991. *Who is Black? One Nation's Definition*. University Park: Pennsylvania State University Press.

Ferber, Abby. 1998. *White Man Falling: Race, Gender, and White Supremacy*. Lanham, MD: Rowman & Littlefield.

Frankenberg, Ruth. 1993. *White Women, Race Matters: The Social Construction of Whiteness*. Minneapolis: University of Minnesota.

Gaspar, David Barry, and Darlene Clark Hine. 1996. *More Than Chattel: Black Women and Slavery in the Americas.* Bloomington: Indiana University Press.

Goffman, Erving. 1963. *Stigma: Notes on the Management of Spoiled Identity.* Englewood Cliffs, NJ: Prentice-Hall.

Goodwin, Robin, and Duncan Cramer, eds. 2002. *Inappropriate Relationships: The Unconventional, the Disapproved, and the Forbidden.* Mahwah, NJ: Lawrence Erlbaum.

Heaton, Tim B., and Cardell K. Jacobson. 2000. "Intergroup Marriage: An Analysis of Opportunity Structures." *Sociological Inquiry* 70: 30-41.

hooks, bell. 1981. *Ain't I a Woman: Black Women and Feminism.* Boston: South End Press.

———. 2000. *Feminist Theory: From Margin to Center*, 2nd ed. Boston: South End Press.

Kallen, Horace. 1924. *Culture and Democracy in the United States.* New York: Boni and Liveright.

Kalmijn, Matthijs. 1993. "Trends in Black/White Intermarriage." *Social Forces* 72: 119–176.

———. 1998. "Intermarriage and Homogamy: Causes, Patterns, Trends." *Annual Review of Sociology* 24 (395–421).

Kouri, Kristyan M., and Marcia Lasswell. 1993. "Black-White Marriages: Social Change and Intergenerational Mobility." *Marriage and Family Review* 19 (3–4): 241–255.

Lewis, Richard, Jr., George Yancey, and Siri S. Bletzer. 1997. "Racial and Nonracial Factors That Influence Spouse Choice in Black-White Marriages." *Journal of Black Studies* 28 (1): 60–78.

Lyman, Stanford M. 1997. *Postmodernism and a Sociology of the Absurd, and Other Essays on the "Nouvelle Vague" in American Social Science.* Fayetteville: University of Arkansas Press.

Omi, Michael, and Winant Howard. 1994. *Racial Formation in the United States From the 1960s to the 1980s*, 2nd ed. New York: Routledge.

Park, Robert E. 1950. *Race and Culture.* Glencoe, IL: Free Press.

Romano, Renee Christine. 2003. *Race Mixing: Black-White Marriage in Postwar America.* Cambridge, MA: Harvard University Press.

Takaki, Ronald. 1993. *A Different Mirror: A History of Multicultural America.* Boston: Little, Brown.

Wadlington, Walter. 1966. "The Loving Case: Virginia's Anti-miscegenation Statue in Historical Perspective." *Virginia Law Review* 52: 1189–1223.

Weber, Max. 1977. "Membership of a Race." In *Max Weber: Selections in Translation*, edited by Walter G. Runciman. Cambridge, U.K.: Cambridge University Press.

Stephanie M. Laudone
Erica Chito Childs

BLACKNESS IN LATIN AMERICA

In Latin America, the Spanish Crown created two republics: the Republic of Spaniards and the Republic of Indians. Although excluded from both of these republics, African and African-descended people grew and diversified throughout Latin America. In Spanish, the quality of blackness is called *lo negro.* The racialized ethnic category *negro* (black) emerged as a representation of human chattel between 1450 and 1480, when the Portuguese entrepreneur known as Prince Henry the Navigator sent more and more ships down the coast of West Africa, where they captured native peoples to be sold in Lisbon and throughout Europe. Ironically, perhaps, as the concept of blackness expanded in Portugal and Spain to include diverse African peoples such as Wolof, Mandingo, Ibo, and Biafara, concepts of racial mixture (European-African) together with African conversion to Christianity became important in the European-dominated West African slave markets.

A concept of blackness subsuming all African and African-descended people entered the Americas with, or soon after, the first voyage of Christopher Columbus in 1492. By 1500 the concept of *raza* (race) emerged and was applied to people of indigenous American, African, and African-descended Spaniards and Portuguese, as well as to people of "mixture." African-descended people who spoke Spanish were called *ladinos* in Spain, where they occupied positions of modest prestige and, sometimes, middle-range power. Their status contrasted with that of the enslaved Africans, who were called *bozal* (plural: *bozales*), a name derived from the horse halter used prior to the invention of the iron bit in Iberia. In the Americas, once-free *ladinos* became enslaved because of their blackness. Soon after the Europeans arrived, the categories of Spaniards and Indians were set in opposition to one another as immutable categories of people: the Spaniards to profit, the Indians to labor. The third category of humans—originally *ladinos* and *bozales*—that constituted the images of Africa and of blackness, was without a cultural place in the dominant scheme of people and profit. What blackness was to become in the New World depended on how black people (African- and dark-complexioned European-descended people, and now people of the Americas) were to represent themselves. Such representations are probably the least understood and the most ignored of all such cultural constructions in the New World.

PERSPECTIVES ON BLACKNESS IN THE AMERICAS

African-American systems of life and thought are profoundly cultural. They are clearly African descended and African diasporic. Any study of Afro-American cultural systems must comprehend commonalities of experience as well as local interpretations of experiences at specific places in given periods in time. African-descended cultural constructions of meaningful historical pasts are ubiquitous, but they may be obliterated or highly distorted by written literature. In *Silencing the Past* (1995), Michel-Rolph Trouillot discusses two dimensions of history that must always be considered. The first is what actually happened. This could be an event such as a forced passage from an African location across the Atlantic Ocean to a specific slave market in the Americas, or one or more of the myriad revolts, rebellions, and movements of self-liberation of Africans in the Americas. The second dimension of history is that of the stories told about the events. When stories are not told, not remembered, or hidden, history is silenced. The stories themselves must be opened up and studied to be reasonably sure that they reflect events critical to the real cultural histories of people, not bent and distorted to the canons of a rigid dominant cultural system with many biases in written presentations.

Unfortunately, the stories told about black suffering and black liberation often come from those who are dominant in a given situation, from those whose popular and academic writings become hegemonic. Hegemonic writing, backed by those who hold political and economic power, is that which is taken as "truth" by the reader. Perspective enters here: What is often lacking in narratives of the past are the myriad of black perspectives that have been neglected or silenced. These perspectives come from real people who are able and willing to tell others what is significant in their past, their present, and their view of a future. In Latin America, what comes through strongly is not a remembrance of slavery, but rather a stress on self-liberation, an emphasis on freedom. As the Saramaka of Suriname repeatedly told the ethnographer Richard Price, people are either free or they are enslaved; there is no middle ground. Across the continent, in the Chocó of Colombia, black people refer to themselves as *libres*, or free (self-liberated) people. But anthropology and history have all too often obscured these assertions of the close association of blackness and freedom in favor of a "search for survivals" or a "legacy of slavery" that render existing black and African-descended people as hollow vessels of past cultural knowledge.

HEGEMONIC DIFFUSIONISM

The hegemonic perspective on cultural survivals is connected most strongly with Melville J. Herskovits (1895–1963), one of the students of Franz Boas (1858–1942), who established the Americanist school of cultural anthropology—sometimes called the cultural diffusionist, or cultural historical, school. Some Boasians countered racist thought in anthropology specifically by attacking it in society generally. Herskovits shifted the emphasis of blackness from what were often taken to be deculturated Americans of color to a timeless and seemingly unchanging "Africa", out of which peoples from distinct "tribes" were mixed in American slave marts following the infamous Middle Passage across the Atlantic Ocean. People in the Americas, from this hegemonic diffusionist position, were considered to be people burdened by the vestiges of retentions, reinterpretations, syncretisms, and cultural complexes.

Herskovits went so far as to rank "Africanisms" in the Americas in terms of their retained African accumulations, using A, B, C, D, and E, to denote "very African" (A grade) to "little or no African" (E grade). Those at the bottom of the "scale of intensity of Africanisms" were found in the United States and the northwest coast of South America. Such people were effectively deemed cultureless, people who had lost their basis in Africanity. They were taken to be darker people of color within mainstream lower-class life. Their histories and historicities were of no further interest to the scholarly world or to readers of popular literature. It is said that students returning from research with African-descended peoples to Northwestern University, where Herskovits founded the Department of Anthropology and long served as its chair, were themselves ranked on how many Africanisms they could find and present in their theses.

At the top of Herskovits' scale of Africanism were the people of the interior of Suriname, once called Dutch Guiana. He and his wife spent several weeks there over two summers "studying" the Saramaka people and "mining" their African heritage. Herskovits came away with a psychological model for the study of all of Afro-America, regarded as a great, partially filled cultural vessel from which Africanisms were disappearing. Hence, "salvage" research was needed to turn up data and objects to be placed in books and museums. The actual techniques of ethnography, however, those for understanding the viewpoint and perspectives of real people (the native's point of view), were subverted by Herskovits as he endeavored to teach the Saramaka about their Africanisms so as to record them more effectively. After a search of Herskovits's notes at the Schomburg Center for Black Culture in New York City, Richard and Sally Price commented: "That he [Melville J. Herskovits] never quite got the Saramaka ethnography right seems in the end not to have mattered much, to him or to anyone else. Go figure" (2003, p. 87).

The anthropologist Jean Muteba Rahier, who has extensive field research experience in Northwest Ecuador, notes that "black resistances in the diaspora, just like Black identities, cannot be essentialized [e.g. Africanized], . . . African diaspora communities develop different strategies for struggles against particular forms of racism, exclusion, and exploitation" (1999, p. xxv).

African traditions, as taken from the perspectives of black people in the Americas, constitute intertwined, or braided, traditions that continue to span Africa, Europe, and the Americas. One thing found everywhere is an African-American stress on freedom and self-liberation, rather than on slavery and repression. The historian Gwendolyn Midlo

A Maroon in Central Suriname, 1998. *A Saramaka Maroon woman carries water in her village near the Suriname River. Maroons, the descendants of escaped slaves, make up about 15 percent of the Suriname population.* ROBERT CAPUTO/AURORA/GETTY IMAGES

Hall, in her book *Slavery and African Ethnicities in the Americas* (2005), demonstrates clearly that rich data on changing Africanity in the Americas is buried in archives, and how much of this can be revealed by serious research.

CIMARRONAJE/MARRONAGE: THE MAKING OF MAROON SOCIETIES

According to Richard Price, the first recorded (written) instance of an African escaping slavery took place on Hispañola Island in 1502 when "an anonymous slave . . . 'escaped to the Indians'" (1996, Introduction). The indigenous people who received this unknown escapee (and subsequent escapees from enslavement) were the Taíno people, who called the mountainous and forested interior of their island *haití*. They spoke a language known as Arawak. Here, early in the sixteenth century, indigenous people and African people forged a new life of freedom on the fringes of the largest profit-oriented slave-owning system the world had ever known. With sugar and slavery at the center, subsistence agriculture, fishing, and hunting were on the periphery. Although blackness was defined as a condition of slavery by the Spanish and Portuguese, self-liberation—called *cimarronaje* in Spanish and *marronage* in French—characterized much of the region. Michel S. Laguerre writes, in *Voodoo and Politics in Haiti:*

> Marronage was a central fact in the life of the colony [Hispañola-Haiti], not only because of maroon military power and the number of slaves who constantly joined them, but also because of the danger inherent in expeditions to destroy revolutionary centers of these fugitive slaves . . . [W]herever there were slaves, there were also maroons . . . Living in free camps or on the fringes of port cities, they were a model for the slaves to imitate, embodying the desires of most of the slaves. What the slaves used to say in *sotto voce* on the plantations, they were able to say aloud in the maroon settlements. (1989, p. 41)

Indeed, from varied indigenous perspectives and cosmologies, freedom and self-liberation actually characterized the very nature of "blackness." Chiefdoms, or even small states, sprang up within colonial territories throughout the vast area that ranges from the Caribbean and Mexico, through Central America, down the spine of the Andes to Argentina, and into the huge tract of territory of today's Guianas, Venezuela, Brazil, Uruguay, Paraguay, and the Amazonian regions of Bolivia, Peru, Ecuador, and Colombia. The two most famous of these were Palmares, in Brazil, and the Zambo Republic, in Ecuador.

CONCEPTS OF BLACKNESS IN LATIN AMERICA

Blackness is a fluid category throughout Latin America, but it is nonetheless salient in its varied dimensions that range from a pejorative term such as black (*negroide*) to specific references to black admixture, such as *mulato* and *zambo*, connoting white-black mixture and black-indigenous mixture, respectively. The primary meaning of *lo negro* stands in opposition to whiteness, and all of the terminology denoting admixture must be seen with this fundamental contrast in mind. Unlike North America, however, whiteness and blackness grade into one another in Latin American nations; there is usually no sharp color line, and phenotype, or outward appearance, often reflects social status or cultural orientation as well as supposed biology or genetic makeup. In the French Antilles, the Martiniquan writer Aimé Césaire, coined the word *négritude* to connote the positive qualities of blackness, in contradistinction and in political opposition to concepts developed by dominant white power wielders of Europe and the United States. This has more recently caught on in Spanish as *negritud*, and in Brazilian Portuguese as *negritude*. The variety of terms, concepts, identity referents, and representations that crowd into the overarching concept of blackness is striking. But the category *lo negro* nonetheless continues to exist.

ZAMBAJE

One concept that stands out in some regions—such as Lower Central America, the Spanish-speaking Caribbean, Venezuela, Colombia, and Ecuador—is *zambo*, which refers to a mixture of indigenous and African-descended peoples. Some of these mixed populations comprise African descendants of those who fled slavery and established free communities (called *palenques* in Spanish and *quilombos* in Portuguese) and of those indigenous descendants who also escaped slavery and received their African congeners. Historically, such people are well-known in various parts of Brazil; the *yungas* of Bolivia; the northwest coast of Ecuador; the Pacific and Atlantic coasts and Cauca Valley of Colombia; the Venezuelan *llanos* (eastern plains) and northern coastal crescent; the interior of the Guianas; the Darién, coasts, and interior of Panama; the Mosquitia of Honduras and Nicaragua; the west coast of Guatemala, Belize, Honduras, and Nicaragua; the mountains of Haiti and the Dominican Republic; the Jamaican Blue Mountains and Red Hills regions; and the Cuban Oriente region. A few named people include the Miskitu of Nicaragua and Honduras, the Garífuna of Central America, the black lowlanders of northwest Ecuador, and the *pardos* of the eastern plains of Venezuela. In colonial times such people were sometimes said to be "the Devil's mix."

The concept of *Zambaje* as an American-indigenous–African-descended fusion implying power, creativity, and adaptability has re-emerged in some Latin American nations. It illustrates an interest among many intellectuals and emergent cultural leaders in re-examining the roots of "naming." An example is that of *llaneros* (plainsmen of color) of eastern Venezuela. These are people known as *pardos*, once allies of black Haitians in revolt. The liberator Simón Bolívar called on them in his first march into the interior of South America. In the twenty-first century, the President of Venezuela, Hugo Chávez, has sought to refurbish the positive image of *pardo* ethnicity and cultural heritage, of indigeneity and Africanity and their fusions. This assertion of *pardo* power is part of a sociopolitical movement called Boliviarian, which is directed against the elite of Venezuela and is in strong opposition to perceived United States dominance in Latin American countries.

Because of the prevalence of African-descended people and indigenous American people in historical conjuncture over a very long period of time, Norman Whitten and Rachel Corr undertook a study to see how indigenous people conceptualized blackness in selected areas of Venezuela, Lower Central America, Colombia, Ecuador, and Bolivia. What they found was that indigenous people *reject* "slavery" as the embodiment of blackness. Such a rejection clearly contradicts the dominant white perspective on slavery and its legacies as the defining features of blackness in the Americas. *Lo negro*, Whitten and Corr found, is full of images and representations of *self-liberation*, including power, cultural creativity, adaptability in the realms of the known and the unknown, knowledge of real history and historicity, and constantly emerging and transforming cultural systems.

AN ENDURING CONTRADICTION OF BLACKNESS AND DIVERSITY

In the late twentieth and early twenty-first centuries, there seems to be an ideological movement in Europe and Latin America to both emphasize differences within the broad category of *lo negro* and simultaneously to crowd out those very differences by subsuming them into an immutable category of blackness, often in pejorative dimensions. There is ample historical precedent for such contradiction. In 1599, three Zambo Lords from the Zambo Republic of Esmeraldas (northwest Ecuador) trekked up the Andes to Quito to pay homage to the Spanish crown. Their portrait was painted by an indigenous artist using European techniques. This magnificent painting was eventually hung in the Museo de Américas, in Madrid, Spain; the two most common English designations of its title are "Esmeraldas Embassadors" and "Zambo Chiefdoms." It clearly portrayed the three princes as indigenous-African descended in complexion. The crown rejected this portrayal, however, and relabeled the Zambo Lords "*mulatos*" to stress a false European admixture. Over a four-hundred-year period, what was unacceptable to the intellectuals of Spain was an indigenous-descended–African-descended admixture, the very admixture that emerged in the bursts of self-liberation that characterized the silenced part of America's history. Then, in 1992, the Spanish museum curators decided to "restore" the painting, so they reblackened the princes to make them correspond to a more stereotypic African appearance, thereby redividing the races of the Americas into white, black, and Indian (or red).

In Spanish, it could be said that the diversity represented in the original painting was doubly *negreado*, or blackened: first by infusing European admixture sometime in the seventeenth century, and then by removing all admixture in the late twentieth century. *Negreado* is a pejorative word, which in vernacular Spanish means "blackened" or "demeaned." It epitomizes Trouillot's extended argument about the silencing of African-American pasts, particularly the accomplishments of black people who resisted colonial repression and, in the case of Haiti, enacted the first successful revolutionary movement against colonial rule in the Americas outside of the United States. The Haitian revolution was, in every conceivable manner, a *black* revolution. It was composed of self-liberated *bozales*, dark-complected creoles, and newly

Esmeraldas Embassadors. *This painting by Andrés Sanchéz Gallque has been the subject of much controversy for over four hundred years.* THE ART ARCHIVE/AMERICAN MUSEUM MADRID.

arrived and self-liberated Congo warriors. At the time, and perhaps in the early 2000s, such a revolution was culturally inconceivable to whites; but it did happen, and it was and is very real.

Such is the ongoing paradox presented by the varied and diverse phenomena of blackness in the Americas, a category that emerged in the sixteenth century in the fires of black liberation, continued through the colonial era as forces of dark resistance to white rule and emerging *mestizaje*, played a strong hand in the wars of liberation, and in the early twenty-first century constitutes a significant, if paradoxical, congeries of peoples within modern republics. The Spaniards left no room for blackness in their colonial placement of peoples. What emerged were many black-created and black-defined cultural and value systems and systems of social relations, often in conjunction with indigenous movements and collaboration against oppression. In the twenty-first century these cultural systems of alternative modernity have yet to be explored adequately in their own right through the voices and actions of the people themselves.

SEE ALSO *African Diaspora; Boas, Franz; Brazilian Racial Formations; Caribbean Racial Formations; Cuban Racial Formations; El Mestizaje; Haitian Racial Formations; Latin American Racial Transformations; Latinos; Slavery and Race.*

BIBLIOGRAPHY

Andrews, George Reid. 2004. *Afro-Latin America, 1800–2000.* New York: Oxford University Press.

Estupiñán Bass, Nelson. 1954. "Canción del niño negro y del incendio." In *Canto Negro por la Luz: Poemas para Negros y Blancos.* Esmeraldas, Ecuador: Casa de la Cultura Ecuatoriana.

Hall, Gwendolyn Midlo. 2005. *Slavery and African Ethnicities in the Americas.* Chapel Hill: University of North Carolina Press.

Herskovits, Melville J. 1958 (1941). *The Myth of the Negro Past.* Boston: Beacon Press.

Laguerre, Michel. 1989. *Voodoo and Politics in Haiti.* New York: St. Martin's Press.

Lane, Kris. 2002. *Quito, 1599: City and Colony in Transition.* Albuquerque: University of New Mexico Press.

Price, Richard. 1983. *First-Time: The Historical Vision of an Afro-American People.* Baltimore, MD: Johns Hopkins University Press.

———, ed. 1996. *Maroon Societies: Rebel Slave Communities in the Americas*, 3rd ed. Baltimore, MD: Johns Hopkins University Press.

———, and Sally Price. 2003. *The Root of Roots, or How Afro-American Anthropology Got Its Start.* Chicago: Prickly Paradigm Press.

Rahier, Jean Muteba, ed. 1999. *Representations of Blackness and the Performance of Identities.* Westport, CT: Bergin & Garvey.

Rout, Leslie B., Jr. 1976. *The African Experience in Spanish America: 1502 to the Present Day.* New York: Cambridge University Press.

Trouillot, Michel-Rolph. 1995. *Silencing the Past: Power and the Production of History*. Boston: Beacon Press.

Whitten, Norman E., Jr., and Rachel Corr. 1999. "Imagery of 'Blackness' in Indigenous Myth, Discourse, and Ritual." In *Representations of Blackness and the Performance of Identities*, edited by Jean Muteba Rahier. Westport, CT: Bergin & Garvey.

Whitten, Norman E., Jr., and Arlene Torres, eds. 1998. *Blackness in Latin America and the Caribbean: Social Dynamics and Cultural Transformations*. Volume 1, *Central America and Northern and Western South America*. Bloomington: Indiana University Press.

Norman E. Whitten Jr.

BLOOD QUANTUM

Among Native peoples, blood quantum is an ingrained fact of everyday existence. Since its origin and institutional interjection into numerous federal policies concerning peoples of indigenous descent, it remains one of the most controversial and divisive issues afflicting contemporary Native North America. The origins of blood quantum are directly linked to the development of chattel slavery. By 1661 the institution of slavery had been formally recognized by Virginia. Over the next four decades other colonies formalized slavery as a legal economic and social institution. The development of slavery encouraged the construction and separation of races in America on the basis of phenotype.

Octoroon Performers. *A poster from around 1879 advertises a performance by a musical ensemble made up of "Colored" and "Octoroon" performers. Once blood quantum became established as a mechanism for assessing inferiority, its use continued unabated into the nineteenth century.* THE LIBRARY OF CONGRESS.

DEFINING "RACE"

Color, as a demarcation of race (along with other phenotypic characteristics used to define racial and social inferiority) was supported by a growing body of philosophical and scientific literature holding that Africans, Native Americans, and Mulattos possessed inferior intellectual, moral, and social qualities, which stood in direct opposition to "whiteness" and its inherent qualities.

The notion of "blood quantum" was created to track racial ancestry and define legal rights. In 1705 the Commonwealth of Virginia enacted a series of laws that denied certain civil liberties to any Negro, Mulatto, or American Indian. The laws also applied to generations, defining children, grandchildren and great grandchildren as inferior members of society, based on their ancestry. Consequently, the descendants of "full blood" members of a race were defined as half-blood ("maroon"), quarter-blood ("quadroon") or eighth-blood ("octoroon"). Following Virginia's example, other colonies adopted similar laws, using blood quantum as a mechanism to determine the status, privilege, and rights of a free person or slave. The growing body of laws, although originally rooted in the institution of chattel slavery, evolved into a legal and social system that measured the extent of participation and privileges associated with full citizenship under the banner of "whiteness."

Once blood quantum became established as a mechanism for assessing inferiority, its use continued unabated into the nineteenth century. Increasingly, the development and progress of American society was guided by the belief in the nation's racial destiny. In his 1839 publication *Crania Americana*, Dr. Samuel Morton stated that his studies of skulls showed that Native Americans had a "deficiency of higher mental powers" and an "inaptitude for civilization," making it impossible for Natives and Europeans to interact as equals. Thus, the building of an American civilization, including its future social and moral development, would be determined by its racial composition.

The construction of an Anglo-Saxon nation that extended from one coast to another under the banner of Manifest Destiny required the further separation of the races. The removal of indigenous populations, authorized by the Indian Removal Act of 1830, provided one solution for physically separating the races. Another solution was the passage of laws prohibiting marriages between European-Americans and "inferior" races. North Carolina, early on, passed a code that forbade marriages between a white and an "Indian, Negro, Mustee, or Mulatto" or any other mixed person to the third generation. Over time, such blood quantum laws concerning race-mixing became not only widespread, but also more intensive.

Legal identity also became closely attached to blood quantum. An 1866 Virginia decree specified that every person with one-fourth or more Negro blood would be considered a colored person, whereas every person not colored having one-fourth or more Native American blood would be deemed an "Indian."

RACE AND EVOLUTIONARY THEORY

After the Civil War, new racial questions arose. Foremost was whether "inferior racial stocks" could be assimilated into the national fold, and whether these "races" would be a benefit to national progress. These questions coincided with the acceptance of Darwinian evolutionary principles that predicted a unity of humankind. The application of Darwinian evolution also was extended to the development of social complexity, not just biology. Therefore all societies must follow similar but separate trajectories in biosocial development, further limiting the possibilities for the incorporation of "inferior" races.

By the 1880s, most surviving Native American societies had been placed on reservations. For some policymakers, reservations were considered a refuge for a declining race that could be salvaged by forcing them out of their "inferior" state. This was to be done by breaking up the habits of savagery and replacing them with the accoutrements of civilization. From 1880 until 1934, using evolutionary theory and scientific racism as guiding principles, ethnocide became officially instituted toward solving the "Indian Problem."

BLOOD QUANTUM AND GOVERNMENT POLICY

Blood quantum, an insidious expression of scientific racism, became the centerpiece in many federal policies of forced assimilation. The premise that biophysical characteristics, mental attributes, and cultural capabilities were imparted through a "race's" blood found a home in the management of Indian affairs though the passage of the 1887 General Allotment Act, or "Dawes Act."

The degree of a person's Indian blood was used to determine land inheritance among the descendants of original allottees. Blood quantum linked forced assimilation with scientific racism by legally defining a Native American.

The allotment process required the compilation of formal tribal rolls, which listed individuals belonging to each recognized reservation tribe. While the Dawes Act posited no specific criteria by which this would be accomplished, Indian Agents used blood quantum "standards," as an already established mechanism for delineating racial status.

Once established, blood quantum was used by the Indian Office to not only track "civilized progress," but also to assign entitlements as an enrolled tribal member and to define the extent of wardship restrictions. In the racialist configuration to construct and regulate Indian identity, "full-bloods" were deemed racially incapable of managing their own affairs and were issued trust patents for their allotments. "Mixed-bloods," by virtue of their "white" racial ancestry, were deemed more competent, often receiving patents in simple fee, with fewer restrictions. Section six of the Dawes Act specified that an Indian who had "adopted the habits of civilized life, is hereby declared to be a citizen of the United States," with all the entitled rights. Competency or the adoption of civilization equated with being biologically and socially "White" enough, meaning that they were no longer defined as being Indian. The blatant preferential treatment bestowed upon those of mixed ancestry would eventually drive societal wedges based on the false assumptions of racism that did not exist among Native people prior to the reservation period.

BLOOD QUANTUM AMONG NATIVE TRIBES

Advanced research undertaken in the late twentieth century has shown that there is little genetic distinction to demarcate among America's indigenous peoples, despite the pre-Contact cultural diversity across Native North America. Tribal boundaries and ethnic distinctiveness did not inhibit a high degree of reproductive exchange and gene flow between distinct societies. Thus, prior to establishing blood quantum to define racial identity, social kinship rather than biology was the core component of both societal composition and individual ethnic affiliation. Every aboriginal society employed a number of sociological mechanisms—such as adoption, marriage, capture, and naturalization—for the incorporation of individuals and groups from foreign societies. After colonization, numerous Europeans and Africans were adopted and fully integrated into Native American societies. Escaped African slaves, for example, typically were accepted among Native peoples. Whether African or European their host societies incorporated them without any phenotypic or cultural stigma.

By the turn of the century, most Native American societies replaced these social mechanisms for defining their communities with the borrowed notion of blood quantum. The substitution insured that Native Americans would evaluate each other, phenotypically and culturally, through the prism of racialist criteria.

As Indian policy evolved, the legal significance of blood quantum expanded to determine eligibility for federal resources and services, determine tribal membership, and delineate economic and political benefits. Blood quantum criteria became internalized among Indian communities with the passage of the 1934 Indian Reorganization Act (IRA). Most IRA constitutions adopted blood quantum as a criterion for defining ethnic identity, tribal enrollment, and tribal citizenship. By advancing the prevailing quantum standard, a living vestige of nineteenth-century scientific racism, many Native Americans began to use it as the litmus test for defining "Indianness."

Most Native Americans have become indoctrinated into assessing each other in terms of blood quantum. This has led to a continual reevaluation of cultural competence and social acceptance, based largely on phenotypic characteristics. At a conference of Native American scholars held in February 1993, under the auspices of the Center for Indian Education at Arizona State University, the issue of "ethnic fraud" arose. Native American scholars in attendance were disturbed by the extent of academics in American universities falsely claiming to have Indian ancestry in order to receive educational and hiring benefits. The discussion led to six recommendations. The number one recommendation was to require documentation of enrollment in a state or federally recognized tribe, giving hiring preference to those who met this criterion. Allegations of "ethnic fraud" have continued to surface, not only on college campuses but all across Indian Country.

Three years earlier, the 1990 passage of the Act for the Protection of American Indian Arts and Crafts made it a criminal offense for anyone not enrolled in a federally recognized tribe to identify themselves as Indian while selling art. Critics claim that after its passage, "identity monitors" scoured Native American art venues demanding to see the documentation of anyone suspected of committing ethnic fraud. The evaluation of ethnic identity using blood quantum has resulted in a rise in infighting, and on occasion outright race-baiting, between and among indigenous people.

BLOOD QUANTUM IN THE TWENTY-FIRST CENTURY

On many reservations and within indigenous communities, blood quantum is a contentious issue, one often distorted by the blind acceptance of the concept. Native American demographic data reveal that during the twentieth century there was an increasing level of mixing between tribal members and non-Indian peoples. This trend has not only continued but accelerated, raising concerns among some about preserving tribal biological and cultural purity. Some reservation tribal leaders are arguing that tribal constitutions should be amended, this time to purge enrolled members who married non-Indians, or to raise blood quantum levels on the premise that such measures are vital to protect the "purity" of their Native American blood.

The implications of using blood quantum are evident in every aspect of contemporary Native American life. A Certificate of Degree of Indian Blood (CDIB) or a Certificate of Degree of Alaska Native Blood is issued to determine citizenship in a specific federally recognized tribe or indigenous community. An enrolled member with a CDIB is entitled to certain rights, and to the allocation of resources. In 1985, Congress passed the Quarter Blood Amendment Act, which mandated that Native students must have one-quarter Indian blood to be eligible for Indian education programs and tuition-free assistance at Bureau of Indian Affairs or contract schools. The act requires that the quarter-blood requirement be met with a CDIB.

In the 1990s, a proposal was put forth to significantly alter the manner by which the Bureau of Indian Affairs calculates and invalidates CDIBs. The proposed change in the law that received the most criticism across Indian Country was limiting the calculation of "Indian blood" to only federally recognized tribes, effectively eliminating any ancestry from terminated tribes, state-recognized tribal entities, or Native ancestry from other sources. It was, critics maintained, a mechanism to quicken the pace of self-termination.

The internalization by Native peoples of Euro-America's conception of race through the adoption of blood quantum, along with the virulence with which it is being manifested in indigenous communities, represents a culmination of federal colonial policies originating nearly three hundred years ago. Native North America, some critical scholars claim, has been rendered self-colonizing, if not self-liquidating. Over the centuries, blood quantum has divorced thousands of people from their Native American ethnic heritage by arbitrarily defining who is or is not a person of Native American descent. For some individuals, blood quantum is a eugenics policy designed to "statistically exterminate" the remaining Native American people. For others, it is a mechanism to legitimately define who may claim to be Native American. Blood quantum, as a concept, will thus remain a contested arena on the cultural and political landscape of Native North America for the foreseeable future.

SEE ALSO *Scientific Racisim, History of.*

BIBLIOGRAPHY

Campbell, Gregory R. 1994. "The Politics of Counting: Critical Reflections about the Depopulation Question of Native North America." In *The Unheard Voices: American Indian*

Responses to The Columbian Quincentenary, 1492–1992, edited by Carole M. Gentry and Donald A. Grinde Jr., 67–131. Los Angeles: American Indian Studies Center, University of California, Los Angeles.

———. 1998. "Many Americas: The Intersection of Class, Race, and Ethnic Identity." In *Many Americas: Critical Perspectives on Race, Racism, and Ethnicity,* edited by Gregory R. Campbell, 3–38. Dubuque, IA: Kendall Hunt.

Churchill, Ward. 1999. "The Crucible of American Indian Identity: Native Traditions versus Colonial Imposition in Post-Conquest North America." *American Indian Culture and Research Journal* 23 (1): 39–68.

Cook-Lynn, Elizabeth. 1993. "Meeting of Indian Professors Takes Up Issues of 'Ethnic Fraud,' Sovereignty, and Research Needs." *Wicazo Sa Review* 9 (1): 57–59.

Crawford, Michael H. 2001. *The Origins of Native Americans: Evidence from Anthropological Genetics.* New York: Cambridge University Press.

Gould, Stephen J. 1981. *The Mismeasure of Man.* New York: W.W. Norton.

Jaimes, M. Annette. 1989-1991. "Federal Indian Identification Policy." In *Critical Issues in Native North America,* edited by Ward Churchill, document 62, 15–36. Copenhagen: International Work Group for Indigenous Affairs.

———. 1992. "Federal Identification Policy: An Usurption of Indigenous Sovereignty in North America." In *The State of Native America: Genocide, Colonization, and Resistance,* edited by M. Annette Jaimes, 123–138. Boston: South End Press.

Jones, Nicholas A. 2005. *We the People of More than One Race in the United States.* Washington, DC: U.S. Department of Commerce.

Moore, John H. 1992. "Blood Quantum and How Not to Count Indians." Unpublished lecture. Missoula: Department of Anthropology, The University of Montana, Missoula.

Ogunwole, Stella U. 2006. *We the People: American Indians and Alaska Natives in the United States.* Washington DC: U.S. Department of Commerce.

Stanton, William. 1960. *The Leopard's Spots: Scientific Attitudes toward Race in America, 1815–59.* Chicago: University of Chicago Press.

Thornton, Russell. 1987. *American Indian Holocaust and Survival: A Population History since 1492.* Norman: University of Oklahoma Press.

Gregory R. Campbell

BOAS, FRANZ
1858–1942

Franz Boas was the pre-eminent early-twentieth-century American anthropologist who oriented anthropology toward the view that knowledge about race is a product of culture rather than biology. Known as "the father of American anthropology," Boas trained a whole generation of influential anthropologists who spread this view both academically and publicly. As a result, his impact was widespread.

THE FORMATIVE YEARS

Boas was born in German Westphalia and attended the universities of Heidelberg, Bonn, and Kiel, where in 1879 he earned a doctorate in physics and geography. The subject of his doctoral dissertation was the human perception of the color of water, launching his lifelong interest in the relationship between human science and natural science. Boas, a Jew, had another formative experience in Kiel, for it was there that he first encountered anti-Semitism, sustaining facial injuries in a scuffle with anti-Semitic students. Later, Boas made anthropology into a science that combated racism and other forms of cultural intolerance.

Boas continued his studies at the University of Berlin, where he came under the influence of the historical geographer Adolf Bastian (1826–1905) and the biological anthropologist Rudolph Virchow (1821–1902). From Bastian he learned about the "psychic unity of mankind," the precept that all human populations have the same mental capacity, with their differing cultural achievements caused by local history and geography. From Virchow, a rigorous empiricist, he learned to anchor biological generalizations with facts while mastering techniques for measuring differences in human body form.

In 1883, Boas undertook a year-long expedition to Baffin Island in the Canadian Arctic to study the Eskimo perception of sea water. The historian of anthropology George W. Stocking Jr. has shown how this experience converted Boas from physics and geography to anthropology, and particularly to ethnography, or anthropological fieldwork. Boas returned to Germany briefly to work for Adolf Bastian at the Berlin Museum für Völkerkunde (Ethnology). He then returned to Canada on the first of many trips to the Pacific Northwest to study the Bella Coola and the Kwakiutl Indians of Vancouver Island, British Columbia. Upon completing the first phase of this fieldwork, he decided to settle in the United States.

After working briefly in New York City, Boas joined the faculty of Clark University in Worcester, Massachusetts. G. Stanley Hall (1844–1924), the president of Clark, envisioned the university as a major center for graduate research, but his vision failed to take hold, and in 1892 Boas joined other faculty members in relocating elsewhere. Along with several of these individuals, Boas relocated to Chicago, where he ended up helping the anthropologist Frederic Ward Putnam (1839–1915) prepare exhibits for the 1893 Chicago World's Columbian Exposition. After the Exposition, Boas supervised the transfer of the exhibits to the new Field Columbian Museum, where he expected to become head of the anthropology division. A clash of personalities, however, led to his resignation. He then returned to New York, where in 1895 he became curator of anthropology at the American Museum of Natural History. He also continued his fieldwork in the Pacific Northwest, spearheading an ambitious project of the museum's president, Morris K. Jesup (1830–1908), called the Jesup North Pacific Expedition. At the same time, he began nurturing a relationship between the museum and Columbia University, but administrative conflict thwarted his efforts, and in 1905 he resigned and moved to Columbia full-time. Columbia became his base of operations for almost four decades, during which time it was the major center for academic anthropology in the United States.

BOAS ON RACE

When Boas moved to Columbia, American anthropology was operating within a nineteenth-century theoretical legacy that, in retrospect, appears conspicuously racist. In cultural anthropology, the reigning paradigm was cultural evolutionism, a scheme that ranked human populations along a continuum from primitive to civilized and regarded less-than-civilized populations as stunted. In the United States, the foremost cultural evolutionist was Lewis Henry Morgan (1818–1881), whose tripartite (or three-part) scheme of savagery/barbarism/civilization implied that the civilized state was superior. Using this scheme to reconstruct prehistory, with archaeological evidence being so limited, anthropologists relied on ethnographic descriptions of living primitive populations to represent past primitive populations. Boas objected strenuously to this logic, known as the comparative method, and in 1896 he published an influential critique of it, showing it to be excessively speculative and blind to the effects of cultural borrowing (or diffusion) rather than parallel evolution in explaining cultural similarities. Every culture with the bow and arrow, for example, need not have evolved it in parallel. One culture might have borrowed it from another culture. These efforts helped overturn the concept that contemporary primitive people were essentially living in the Stone Age. The counter argument was that primitive people, while still primitive, had nonetheless changed over time.

In biological anthropology, the nineteenth-century legacy appears even more racist. At midcentury, biological anthropologists were arguing about the origin of races. The two major camps were monogenists and polygenists. Monogenists argued that human races shared an ancient common origin and then diversified, but that they remained a single biological species. Polygenists countered by arguing that human races had recent separate origins, remained unchanged, and constituted separate biological species. The polygenists were ascendant at this time, especially in the United States, where the anthropologist Samuel George Morton (1799–1851) and his followers measured skulls of different races, concluding that the skulls and (in life) the enclosed brains of different races varied in size, and that therefore the races varied in mental capacity. In the period leading up to the American Civil War, Morton's views found favor among supporters of the institution of racial slavery. After the War, however, hard-nosed polygenism abated because of Charles Darwin's (1809–1882) theory of biological evolution, published in *Origin of Species* (1859), which showed that all biological populations are interrelated and changing. Still, many anthropologists failed to accept or fully understand Darwin's theory, and hereditarian views about race persisted. In 1896, the year Boas critiqued the comparative method, the anthropologist Daniel G. Brinton (1837–1899), in his presidential address to the American Association for the Advancement of Science, pronounced, "The black, the brown and the red races differ anatomically so much from the white, especially in their splanchnic [visceral] organs, that even with equal cerebral capacity, they could never rival its results by equal efforts" (Harris 1968, p. 256).

Boas recognized that the scientific fallacy of pronouncements such as Brinton's lay in the confusion of race, language, and culture. He had spent the equivalent of a number of years living among Pacific Coast Indians, learning their language and culture, and while working for the Chicago World's Columbian Exposition he had begun a comprehensive study of the racial, or physical, characteristics of aboriginal North Americans. He knew from these experiences that correlation does not necessarily imply cause; that is, just because a population with particular racial characteristics speaks a particular language and practices a particular culture, the language and culture are not necessarily caused by the racial characteristics. In fact, race, language, and culture are independent, each capable of changing without changing the others. Proof of this assertion was Boas himself, who remained racially white while learning how to speak the Kwakiutl language and participate in Kwakiutl culture. To right the scientific wrong of racial determinism, Boas wrote *The Mind of Primitive Man* (1911), a watershed book that helped pave the way for the modern understanding of race as a cultural construct. A similar understanding characterized his later book, *Race, Language, and Culture* (1940).

Boas's early years at Columbia coincided with great public debate in the United States about the alleged deleterious (or subtle harmful) effects of an influx of eastern and southern European immigrants. Between 1908 and 1910, he conducted a massive study for the United States Immigration Commission, in which he measured the heads of more than 17,000 European immigrants and their American-born children. For decades, going back to the heyday of polygenism, anthropologists had treated the ratio of head length and breath, called the cephalic index, as a fixed mark of racial ancestry. Boas's statistical study, published in 1911 as *Changes*

Franz Boas, 1941. *Known as the "father of American anthropology," Boas was dedicated to empiricism, field research, cultural determinism, and cultural relativism. His work continues to be influential in many fields.* © BETTMANN/CORBIS.

in the Bodily Form of Descendants of Immigrants, proved otherwise. In just one generation, the cephalic index of immigrants had changed in response to the American environment, presumably to better diet and health. Since then, however, some anthropologists have statistically re-evaluated Boas's study and questioned the magnitude of its reported change. Nevertheless, the study remains a landmark demonstration of how racial characteristics can change rapidly in response to the environment.

SPREADING THE WORD

Boas's influence on American anthropology has been far-reaching. He was a founding member and president of the American Anthropological Association, as well as president of the New York Academy of Science, the American Folklore Society, and the American Association for the Advancement of Science. He supervised the journal *American Anthropologist*, wrote several books, and published more than seven hundred scholarly articles. He exerted his greatest influence, however, through the students he trained at Columbia University.

At Columbia, Boas was a powerful professor who attracted students with his message that, in the words of the anthropologist Ruth Benedict, "anthropology mattered." It mattered because it demonstrated the twin principles of cultural determinism and cultural relativism. Cultural determinism taught that nurture, not nature, was responsible for the overwhelming array of ethnographically observed cultural similarities and differences. Cultural relativism, meanwhile, taught that one culture should not be judged by the standards of another culture. Together, these two principles showed that racism and ethnocentrism were wrong.

Between 1901 and 1928, twenty students earned their doctoral degrees under Boas. Among them were Ruth Benedict (1887–1948), Alexander Goldenweiser (1880–1940), Melville Herskovits (1895–1963), Alfred Kroeber (1876–1960), Robert Lowie (1883–1957), Margaret Mead (1901–1978), Paul Radin (1883–1959), and Edward Sapir (1884–1939). Kroeber and Lowie helped establish anthropology at the University of California at Berkeley; Sapir, at the University of Chicago; and Herskovits, at Northwestern University. As a result, the Boasian view became academically entrenched in the American Midwest, and on its East and West Coasts.

Boasian anthropologists explored and promoted the importance of culture in a variety of ways. Goldenweiser, Herskovits, Lowie, and Radin wrote insightful ethnographies with African-American and Native American settings. Radin pioneered the life history approach with *Crashing Thunder: The Autobiography of a Winnebago Indian* (1926), and Herskovits wrote the first biography of Boas, *Franz Boas: The Science of Man in the Making* (1953). On a more theoretical level, Sapir, in collaboration with his student Benjamin Lee Whorf (1897–1941), demonstrated the power of language to shape categories of thought, including, in principle, thoughts about race. Kroeber and Benedict developed the idea of cultural configuration, or ethos, which they used to characterize cultures and urge respect for behavior that might otherwise appear inexplicable or odd. In *Patterns of Culture* (1934), an all-time anthropology best-seller, Benedict vividly portrayed three cultures with different standards of normalcy and deviance.

Boas also influenced his most famous student, Margaret Mead. At the time, he thought that much of psychology, especially the psychology of Sigmund Freud (1856–1939), overemphasized biology as a contributor to personality development. In particular, he objected to Freud's assertion that adolescence is necessarily a period of psychological turmoil. Boas urged Mead to conduct her doctoral dissertation research in American Samoa, where she might find that adolescence unfolded differently than it did in the United States. After spending time in Samoa, Mead found just that. In the book based on her research, *Coming of Age in Samoa* (1928), she argued that a sexually permissive upbringing allowed Samoan girls to experience adolescence smoothly. Mead followed up this book with others in which she described cultural variation in the behavior of women and men. She went on to become widely known in the United

States as an advocate of cultural understanding and tolerance. In 1983, however, the anthropologist Derek Freeman (1916–2001) published a critical account of Mead's Samoan fieldwork in his book *Margaret Mead and Samoa: The Making and Unmaking of an Anthropological Myth*. He argued that Mead was overly zealous in trying to prove Boas's claim for the power of culture over biology. Freeman's account touched off a major debate within anthropology about whether Boas's cultural determinism was ideological as well as scientific.

During World War II, some of Boas's students worked actively in Washington, D.C. to help the United States defeat Germany and the racist ideology of Nazism. On December 21, 1942, Boas was having lunch at Columbia University with the anthropologist Claude Lévi-Strauss (b. 1908) when suddenly he slumped over and died. Lévi-Strauss observed later that he had witnessed the death of an intellectual giant and the end of an anthropological era.

SEE ALSO *Anthropology, History of; Anti-Semitism; Cranial Index; Genesis and Polygenesis.*

BIBLIOGRAPHY

Boas, Franz. 1911. *The Mind of Primitive Man*. New York: Macmillan.

———. 1945. *Race, Language, and Culture*. New York: Macmillan.

Cole, Douglas. 1999. *Franz Boas: The Early Years, 1858–1906*. Vancouver: Douglas & McIntyre.

Erickson, Paul A., and Liam D. Murphy. 2003. *A History of Anthropological Theory*, 2nd ed. Peterborough, ON: Broadview Press.

Freeman, Derek. 1983. *Margaret Mead and Samoa: The Making and Unmaking of an Anthropological Myth*. Ann Arbor, MI: Books on Demand.

Harris, Marvin. 1968. *The Rise of Anthropological Theory: A History of Theories of Culture*. New York: Thomas Y. Crowell.

Herskovits, Melville J. 1953. *Franz Boas: The Science of Man in the Making*. New York: Charles Scribner's Sons.

Public Broadcasting System. 1981. *Odyssey: Franz Boas (1858–1942)*. UMBC # VC-83. VHS videotape, 58 minutes.

Spencer, Frank, ed. 1997. *History of Physical Anthropology*, 2 vols. New York: Garland.

Stocking, George W., Jr., ed. 1974. *The Shaping of American Anthropology 1883–1911: A Franz Boas Reader*. New York: Basic Books.

U.S. Immigration Commission. 1911. *Changes in the Bodily Form of Descendants of Immigrants*. Washington, DC: U.S. Government Printing Office.

Paul A. Erickson

BODY POLITICS

The term *body politics* refers to the practices and policies through which powers of society regulate the human body, as well as the struggle over the degree of individual and social control of the body. The powers at play in body politics include institutional power expressed in government and laws, disciplinary power exacted in economic production, discretionary power exercised in consumption, and personal power negotiated in intimate relations. Individuals and movements engage in body politics when they seek to alleviate the oppressive effects of institutional and interpersonal power on those whose bodies are marked as inferior or who are denied rights to control their own bodies.

FEMINISM AND BODY POLITICS

Body politics was first used in this sense in the 1970s, during the "second wave" of the feminist movement in the United States. It arose out of feminist politics and the abortion debates. Body politics originally involved the fight against objectification of the female body, and violence against women and girls, and the campaign for reproductive rights for women. "The personal is the political" became a slogan that captured the sense that domestic contests for equal rights in the home and within sexual relationships are crucial to the struggle for equal rights in the public. This form of body politics emphasized a woman's power and authority over her own body. Many feminists rejected practices that draw attention to differences between male and female bodies, refusing to shave their legs and underarms and rejecting cosmetics and revealing, form-fitting clothing. The book *Our Bodies, Our Selves,* published in 1973, aimed to widen and deepen women's knowledge of the workings of the female body, thus allowing women to be more active in pursuit of their sexual pleasure and reproductive health.

Second-wave feminist body politics promoted breaking the silence about rape, sexual abuse, and violence against women and girls, which many interpreted as extreme examples of socially sanctioned male power. The feminists who followed at the end of the twentieth century accepted this stance on rape and violence against women and girls, but they found the gender ideals of second-wave feminists too confining. Members of this generation, sometimes called third-wave feminists or post-feminists, endorse a range of body modification and gender practices that include butch-fem gender roles, gender-blending, transgender lifestyles, transsexual surgeries, body piercing, and tattoos.

Women's bodies were the political battleground of the abortion debates. A protracted struggle to establish a woman's right to terminate her pregnancy was won when the U.S. Supreme Court upheld the right to abortion in the case of *Roe v. Wade* in 1974. Almost immediately after that decision, anti-abortion (also called pro-life) activists began protesting against this extension of women's reproductive rights. Anti-abortion advocates likened aborting a fetus to murder, while pro-abortion advocates (also called pro-choice) pointed to the legion of women who had died in illegal abortions, and to the many more who would doubtlessly follow them if abortion were to become illegal again. In that adversaries square off over the issue of individual versus social control of a woman's pregnancy, the abortion debates are prime examples of body politics.

Debates about laws and women's bodies sparked the interests other groups of women who felt that government or institutional power had unfairly exercised control over their bodies or that society should take greater responsibility for the care and protection of women and children. Noting that the abortion debates were about whether or not to have a child, activists pointed to policies and practices that denied reproduction to women in minority communities, especially the forced sterilization of Native Americans. Activists from both sides of the abortion debates joined in to press for employment rights for pregnant women and for maternity and paternity leave for new parents. Arguing that the laws and ethics governing commercial sex transactions were outdated, organizations of prostitutes argued for decriminalization of their work.

RACIAL BODY POLITICS

The attribution of ethical, moral, temperamental, and social characteristics to individuals or populations based on skin color, facial features, body types, and sexual anatomy figure prominently in racial body politics. This practice is most pronounced in the United States in racism against African Americans. As African people were turned into commodities in the Atlantic slave trade, western countries used bodily differences to justify African subjugation. According to racist logic, dark skin was at the negative pole in the dichotomy of white and good versus black and evil, broad facial features denote licentiousness and lack of intelligence, and the brawny bodies of black men and women cry out for hard labor. The fabled sexual organs of black men and women were credited to be the seat of excessive sexuality, a belief used to blame the bodies of black women and men for their being victims of rape, lynching, and castration. Other populations have also been subject to negative characterizations. For example, the bodies of Mexicans are supposedly built low for farm labor, while the "delicate, nimble" fingers of Asian women supposedly suit them for fine work such as computer-chip manufacture.

Because body politics covers the power to control bodies on the one hand, and resistance and protest against such powers on the other hand, body politics can both uphold and challenge racism. In the United States, the civil rights movement unseated the predominant racial body politics in abolishing Jim Crow laws and abating racial segregation. The slogan "Black is Beautiful" heralded a moment in the 1960s when African Americans pointedly attributed positive values to black physical features. Body politics during that time included wearing hair in a natural, unprocessed "Afro" and donning African-inspired clothing. Remnants of this politics remain in those who attribute positive social and psychological qualities to melanin, the pigment that causes dark skin.

CROSS-CULTURAL REACTIONS TO AND STUDIES OF BODY POLITICS

A major challenge to racial body politics came from within the feminist movement. In the 1970s, Black, Latina, Native American, and Asian feminists insisted that an inclusive feminism examine and redress the historic evaluations of bodily difference that structured oppression of women according to race. Women of color objected to the narrow construction of gender politics by white feminists, and they moved to include the differences that race, class, and sexuality make in women's position in society. The welfare mothers' movement, radical lesbians of color, and black feminist theorists were among those to call attention to the ways in which race inflected feminism. The 1981 anthology *This Bridge Called My Back* captured the physical nature of the social and cultural experience of women of color who tried to bridge the gap between nationalist movements where sexism flourished and the feminist movement's singular concentration on gender. The editors, Cherie Moraga and Gloria Anzaldúa (1942–2004) are celebrated writers, theorists, and activists, who in this influential, transformative volume brought together poetry, critical and reflective essays, and photographs of artwork by noted women of color. *This Bridge Called My Back* contained the first publication of Audre Lorde's (1934–1992) essay, "The Master's Tools Will Never Dismantle the Master's House," which along with her essays on breaking silence and the erotic as power were crucial in forging a language of body politics for women of color and lesbian feminists. This push within the feminist movement contributed to the inclusive politics of diversity and multiculturalism in the United States.

Scholarly research on body politics was greatly influenced by French philosopher Michel Foucault (*Discipline and Punish*, 1977), who used the terms "bio-power" and "anatomo-politics" to refer to the insinuation of governmental and institutional power into people's everyday activities. He argued that such power shapes people's subjectivity—their sense of themselves as persons. From Foucault's point of view, disciplinary mechanisms such as prisons, as well as medical knowledge and the education system, provide the discourse, ideas, resources, and procedures through which individuals come to know who they are and through which they learn to conform to the social and political order. What begins as externally imposed discipline becomes internalized, such that individuals become their own disciplinarians. Even though Foucault's work represents human subjectivity as caught in the thrall of discourses that impose meaning and shape action, inherent in body politics is the optimistic possibility that by changing the body's relationship to power, one might change the expression of power in society. Using the concept of body politics, scholars have studied the status of women and racial minorities, and somatic or body norms generated in particular cultures (and individuals' appropriation or rejection of them), as well the regulation of the body through hygiene, medicine, law, and sports. The study of European colonial policies and practices has been a particularly prolific area of scholarship on body politics.

Colonialism produced body politics intended to create acquiescent subjects, and it was, in part, successful. But colonialism also inspired resistance and revolution. The bodies of colonial subjects built the colonial infrastructure, fueled its economy, and bought its products. Clothing, in specified styles and patterns, and soaps and oils advertised and sold by colonizers pulled colonized bodies into the moral and aesthetic spheres of the colonizers. Colonized people were often treated as disease vectors, necessitating residential segregation and public health programs to ensure the health and well-being of the colonizers. Colonial administrations grouped colonized people according to race and tribe and used these distinctions to control their access to rights and resources. In some cultures, body politics took a supernatural turn, as the spirits of colonizers were believed to take over the bodies of former colonial subjects. This spirit possession highlights cultural memory and the embodiment of political power. Anticolonial movements rejected colonial rules of deference, fought for political sovereignty, revived older demonstrations of respect, and instituted new policies and practices to regulate the human body.

SEE ALSO *Feminism and Race; Forced Sterilization; Forced Sterilization of Native Americans; Rape; Reproductive Rights; Reproductive Technologies; Violence against Women and Girls.*

BIBLIOGRAPHY

Boston Women's Health Collective. 1973. *Our Bodies, Ourselves.* New York: Simon & Schuster.

Foucault, Michel. 1977. *Discipline and Punish: The Birth of the Prison.* Translated by Alan Sheridan. New York: Vintage Books.

Ginsburg, Faye. 1998. *Contested Lives: The Abortion Debate in an American Community.* Berkeley: University of California Press.

Lock, Margaret. 1993. "Cultivating the Body: Anthropology and Epistemologies of Bodily Practice and Knowledge." *Annual Review of Anthropology* 22: 133–155.

Lourde, Audre. 1984. *Sister Outsider: Essays and Speeches by Audre Lourde.* New York: The Crossing Press.

Moraga, Cherrie, and Gloria Anzaldúa. 1983. *This Bridge Called My Back: Writings by Radical Women of Color.* Watertown, MA: Persephone Press, 1981.

Riggs, Marlon. 1987. *Ethnic Notions.* Director and Producer, Marlon Riggs. DVD, VHS. Distributed by California Newsreel.

Stoller, Paul. 1995. *Embodying Colonial Memories: Spirit Possession, Power, and the Hauka in West Africa.* New York: Routledge.

Carolyn Martin Shaw

BORDER CROSSINGS AND HUMAN RIGHTS

Migration is a global phenomenon, a consequence of corporate globalization, neoliberal economic policies, political instability, ethnic conflicts, war, and domestic violence. The United Nations (UN) estimates that "one out of every 35 persons worldwide is an international migrant," a figure inclusive of migrant workers, families, refugees, and other immigrants. Countries typically receiving an influx of migrants are better positioned economically than the migrants' countries of origin. Migration has human rights implications because the migrating population, though often undocumented, maintains inalienable human rights. The human rights of migrants are recognized by the UN and the international community as a result of the Universal Declaration of Human Rights and the International Convention on the Protection of the Rights of All Migrant Workers and Members of Their Families.

The UN and human rights groups, such as Human Rights Watch and Amnesty International (AI), monitor border crossings around the world and report that common problems occur along the world's national borders, which include a lack of legal representation or due process and lengthy detentions. Illiteracy, language barriers, racism, and xenophobia exacerbate human rights violations. Undocumented migrants can suffer indignities and human rights abuses due to their uncertain legal status because they are often treated as if they have no legal rights. The U.S.–Mexico border and Spain's borders have distinct entry points for border crossers; yet patterns of human rights abuses and the racial dimensions of those abuses are evident.

U.S.–MEXICO BORDER

In March 2002, the UN Special Rapporteur of the Commission on Human Rights on the human rights of migrants, Ms. Gabriela Rodríguez Pizarro, visited parts of the 2,000-mile U.S.–Mexico border at the invitation from the U.S. and Mexican governments. Through her own investigation and interviews with migrants, she identified the following risks when crossing the border from Mexico to the United States:

> Lack of protection against smugglers in the irregular crossing of the border; the problem of trafficking in persons; excessive use of force against migrants; crossing of the border through dangerous areas; vulnerability of children on the border; racist, xenophobic and discriminatory attitudes; and the conditions in which undocumented migrants are detained, especially when they are in the custody of private security agencies. (United Nations 2002, p. 2)

Entire families migrate to the United States from Mexico, despite the tremendous risk and insecurity involved, because of prospective better-paying job opportunities in the United States as compared to Mexico. Migrants face human rights abuses by the U.S. Border Patrol, other border patrolling units, smugglers, U.S. civilians, and private security agencies. The Special Rapporteur reviewed many allegations of abuse by Border Patrol agents, including severe beatings and shootings of unarmed migrants (Dunn 1996). Other abuses along the U.S.–Mexico border include rape and sexual assault of women (Falcón, forthcoming). Moreover, the judicial and legal rights of undocumented migrants have become severely restricted due to various immigration laws adopted in the United States since the mid-1990s (United Nations 2002, pp. 7–8). Smugglers exploit the vulnerability of migrants and have been known to leave them in the desert where many become severely dehydrated, suffer heat strokes, and die (Marosi 2005). Smugglers are also known to engage in the trafficking of persons, including for prostitution. Private security agencies are not under the authority of the U.S. government, raising questions about their obligation and accountability to human rights standards and international law. The Special Rapporteur revealed that migrants detained in private detention centers were less aware of their rights and the status of their cases when compared to U.S. government-operated detention centers (United Nations 2002, p. 14). She recommended that the United States ratify the International Convention on the Protection of the Rights of All Migrant Workers and Members of Their Families to affirm the human rights of migrants along this international border (United Nations 2002, p. 7).

Redress in abuse cases has occurred in a few court cases, but it is far from common. Fearful of reprisals, migrants may forego filing a formal complaint, making it extremely difficult to investigate alleged abuse. Many of these alleged abuse cases happen in remote areas of the U.S.–Mexico border, with no additional witnesses beyond the U.S. official and the undocumented migrant(s). The undocumented migrant can file a complaint, but the prospect of challenging a very powerful state is intimidating for many. At the international level, the UN has established an individual complaints system available on its Web site for reporting human rights violations experienced by migrants, which is reviewed by the Special Rapporteur. But this international process can be complicated if there is lack of access to the Internet.

SPAIN'S BORDERS

Spain shares borders with Portugal and France and has a unique entry point for migrants in its southern region due to its coastline. Migrants entering Spain are from other European countries, Latin America, and Africa (in particular Morocco). Many of these migrants qualify for refugee consideration and they enter Spain via Madrid's international airport and by using boats to cross the strait of Gibraltar. Rodríguez Pizarro and AI conducted investigations regarding the treatment of migrants by the Spanish government during the period 2003–2005.

AI's investigation specifically focused on the plight of refugees fleeing human rights violations. In its 2005 report, AI stated that the public discourse concerning migrants in Spain and other European countries is focused "almost exclusively on immigration control," which has "undermined the protection of refugees." In some cases, asylum-seekers throughout Europe "are returned to third, supposedly 'safe,' countries" until their case is reviewed, a practice that AI condemned (Amnesty International 2005, p. 3). The number of refugee applicants in Spain, including those granted refugee status, fell between 2000 and 2005 as a result of restrictive state immigration policies. In 2001, only 278 out of 9,490 applicants were granted asylum, whereas 166 out of 5,544 applicants were granted asylum in 2004 (Amnesty International 2005, p. 4). According to the AI report, "Spain has one of the lowest per capita rates in the European Union [of refugee applicants]: one application for every 10,000 residents," which it cited as a grave concern (p. 3).

Both AI and Rodríguez Pizarro have documented similar kinds of human rights abuses and both expressed concern over the treatment of minors, women and girls, members of ethnic minorities (i.e., Roma), and foreign nationals. They documented an "excessive use of force when expelling foreign nationals" and an "increase in complaints of racist or xenophobic behaviour" (Amnesty International 2005, p. 4). Examples of human rights issues identified by AI for migrants entering through Cueta, Spain, include:

- Clandestine expulsion of foreign nationals.
- Illegal expulsion of asylum-seekers.
- Illegal expulsion of minors.
- Inadequate reception facilities for asylum seekers and foreign nationals.
- Inadequate information provided to foreign nationals on arrival.
- Insufficient legal and interpreting/translation assistance.
- Problems and irregularities in the asylum process (pp. 16–29).

Many of these issues were also outlined in Rodríguez Pizarro's report on Spain. Following her visit in September 2003, the Special Rapporteur, also troubled by the inadequate legal guarantees (guarantees that should be afforded to all migrants), stated "migrants are frequently confronted with the risk of defencelessness in the face of possible abuses and violations due to the absence or insufficiency of legal assistance" (United Nations 2004, p. 2). Concerned about incidents of racism and xenophobia, the Special Rapporteur encouraged the Spanish media and government to "avoid statements and remarks which tend to foster fear of foreigners" (p. 21). She also recommended that Spain ratify the migrant workers convention.

The human rights concerns along the world's borders are strikingly parallel and show a clear pattern. Rodríguez Pizarro also found similar human rights abuses and a resistance to reporting abuses during her investigation of the treatment of Peruvian migrants crossing the borders of Ecuador, Colombia, Chile, and Brazil (United Nations 2005). The Peruvian economy is noticeably divergent from that of its neighbors, with more than half of Peru's population living below the poverty line. Dependent on jobs outside of Peru for survival, these undocumented migrants prefer not to file complaints "in order to be able to continue going… to work" (United Nations 2005, p. 8). Filing a formal complaint could result in reprisals for undocumented migrants. The Special Rapporteur's report on Peruvian migrants, the majority of whom are poor, indigenous, and female, cited additional problems with human trafficking, exploitative working conditions, and violence.

Human rights abuses range from not informing migrants of their legal rights to violent and degrading treatment by border patrol units. Minors, women, and the undocumented are particularly vulnerable. Migrants experience racism and xenophobia by border patrol groups, whose actions are supported by state immigration policies that jeopardize the rights of migrants. Domestic and international redress are difficult to process due to the lack of documentation regarding abuses and migrants' fears of reprisals. Migration is a direct consequence of the domestic, global, and geopolitical context in which everyone lives. International law and human rights groups are not opposed to governments controlling immigration, however; they argue that all people—including undocumented migrants—are entitled to dignified, humane treatment and legal rights. As of 2005, thirty-four countries have ratified the human rights convention on migrants and their families, but the United States and Spain have yet to ratify it.

BIBLIOGRAPHY

Amnesty International. 2005. "Spain: the Southern Border." Amnesty International (AI Index: EUR 41/008/2005).

Dunn, Timothy. 1996. *The Militarization of the U.S-Mexico Border 1978–1992: Low-Intensity Conflict Doctrine Comes Home*. Austin: University of Texas, Austin: Center for Mexican American Studies.

Falcón, Sylvanna M. Forthcoming. "Rape as a Weapon of War: Advancing Human Rights for Women at the U.S.-Mexico Border Region." In *Women in the U.S.-Mexico Borderlands: Structural Violence and Agency in Everyday Life*, edited by Denise A. Segura and Patricia Za Vella. Durham: Duke University Press.

Marosi, Richard. 2005. "Border Crossing Deaths Set a 12-Month Record. " *Los Angeles Times*, October 1, p. 1A.

United Nations. 2002. "Mission to the Border between Mexico and the United States of America." Report submitted by Ms. Gabriela Rodríguez Pizarro, Special Rapporteur on the human rights of migrants. Document No. E/CN.4/2003/85/Add.3. New York: United Nations, Office of the High Commissioner for Human Rights.

———. 2004 (14 January). "Specific Groups and Individuals: Migrant Workers and Visit to Spain." Report submitted by Ms. Gabriela Rodríguez Pizarro, Special Rapporteur on the human rights of migrants. Document No. E/CN.4/2004/76/Add.2. New York: United Nations, Office of the High Commissioner for Human Rights.

———. 2005 (13 January). "Specific Groups and Individuals: Migrant Workers and Visit to Peru." Report submitted by Ms. Gabriela Rodríguez Pizarro, Special Rapporteur on the human rights of migrants. Document No. E/CN.4/2005/85/Add.4. New York: United Nations, Office of the High Commissioner for Human Rights.

Sylvanna M. Falcón

BORDER PATROL

The National Origins Act of 1924 placed strict limitations upon legal immigration to the United States. Persons prohibited from entering the United States included, but were not limited to, Chinese and Japanese laborers, epileptics, beggars, prostitutes, lunatics, convicts, and those likely to become public charges. Further, the National Origins Act established a national quota system that promoted immigration from western Europe while limiting the number of legal immigrants from other regions of the world, particularly Asia, Africa, and eastern Europe. Congress understood, however, that prohibited persons would seek illegal entry into the United States by crossing U.S. borders without official inspection and sanction, and it established the U.S. Border Patrol to enforce U.S. immigration restrictions.

THE EARLY YEARS

In addition to preventing persons from crossing into the United States without official sanction, the Border Patrol was assigned the job of policing borderland regions to detect and arrest those who had successfully effected illegal entry. The Border Patrol's jurisdiction stretched along the 5,525-mile Canadian border, spanned the 2,000-mile U.S.-Mexico border, and, in time, extended to include the Florida Gulf Coast region and various coastlines. In the early days and months of its existence, the new Border Patrol officers were confused about how to translate their broad mandate and jurisdiction into a practical course of law enforcement. But as the years wore on, Border Patrol officers along the U.S.-Mexico border began to focus almost exclusively upon apprehending and deporting undocumented Mexican nationals. During the early 1940s, the entire national emphasis of the U.S. Border Patrol shifted to the southern border, where officers continued to target unsanctioned Mexican border crossers. Since the end of World War II, this national police force, which had been established to broadly enforce U.S. immigration restrictions, has been almost entirely dedicated to policing the problem of unsanctioned Mexican immigration in the U.S.-Mexico borderlands. The rise of the U.S. Border Patrol in this region reshaped the story of race in twentieth-century America by racializing the crime of illegal immigration.

Illegal immigration is a crime that is inscribed upon the lives of those who enter the national territory of the United States without sanction. Denied official recognition and living under the constant threat of detection and deportation, those who commit the crime of illegal immigration live in zones of social, political, and economic marginalization. For them, every breath and every movement is illegitimate. Illegal immigration, therefore, is a living crime that transforms persons guilty of the act of illegal entry into persons living within the condition of being illegal. The condition of being illegal is articulated through an overall unequal distribution of political rights, social protections, and economic defenses. As the historian Mae Ngai describes it, illegal immigrants are "a caste, unambiguously situated outside the boundaries of formal membership and social legitimacy." (2004, p. 2)

Despite the deep marginalization of being illegal, the caste of "illegals" is highly abstract in everyday life. There are countless ways of becoming illegal. In addition to entering without inspection, one can enter with false documents or fail to maintain the conditions of legal residency. Without any precise indicators of the crime of illegal immigration, it is difficult to detect the illegals among the population. However, with a mandate to detect, detain, interrogate, and apprehend persons for the crime and condition of being illegal, officers of the U.S. Border Patrol spend their working hours personifying the abstract political caste of illegality. Border Patrol officers, therefore, have played a critical role in shaping this site of political disenfranchisement, economic inequity, and social suspicion within the United States. Despite the many peoples and groups that have fallen into the category of illegal immigrants, Border Patrol officers have mostly targeted Mexican nationals for the crime of illegal immigration. This focus on policing unsanctioned Mexican immigration has assigned the inequities, disenfranchisements, suspicions, and violence of being illegal to persons of Mexican-origin, thereby effectively "Mexicanizing" the set of inherently and lawfully unequal social relations that emerge from the crime of illegal immigration.

While there is no question that the racialization of U.S. Border Patrol practice took shape in response to the large number of Mexican nationals who illegally crossed the U.S.-Mexico border during the twentieth century, police practices and priorities are socially and politically negotiated processes rather than a system of unmitigated responses to criminal activity. Police officers do not police every crime or criminal so much as rationalize and prioritize their mandate for law enforcement in response to the social anxieties, political tensions, and economic interests invested in the overall police project of using state violence to establish and maintain social control. The U.S. Border Patrol's racialization of the caste of illegals, therefore, must be understood within the sociohistorical context of the politics of policing the crime of illegal immigration.

RACE AND THE POLITICS OF MIGRATION CONTROL

In the years following the passage of the National Origins Act, Border Patrol officers were uncertain as to how to create a practical course of law enforcement. They could have patrolled the border to prevent unsanctioned crossings; they could have enforced the spirit of the law by focusing on apprehending the law's main racial and ethnic targets, particularly Asian and eastern European immigrants; or they could have policed prostitutes and clinics, searching out immigrants whose alleged moral depravity or poor health rendered them illegal. Despite the broad field of possible subjects of Border Patrol work, the officers received little guidance from supervisors within the Immigration Service. The men hired as Patrol Officers, therefore, were able to exert significant control over the everyday development of U.S. Border Patrol priorities and practice.

In the U.S.-Mexico borderlands, a region where the deeply rooted divisions between Mexican migrant laborers and white landowners dominated social organization and interactions, Border Patrol officers—who were often landless, working-class white men—gained unique entry into the region's principal system of social and economic relations by directing the violence of immigration law enforcement against the region's primary labor force, Mexican migrant laborers. Mexican immigration was the foundation of the region's primary economy, agribusiness. During the 1920s and 1930s, an "army" of migrant laborers moved northward from field to field, beginning with 25,000 laborers in the Lower Rio Grande Valley and growing to 300,000 migrants at the height of the cotton-picking season between July and September. In California, 35,000 laborers were required for the cotton crop alone. In 1940, the Texas State Employment Service estimated that 85 percent of full-time migrant laborers were Mexicanos. Until the arrival of white dustbowl immigrants in California in the mid-1930s, Mexicans comprised between 80 and 95 percent of the migrant workforce. Mexican labor, therefore, played a pivotal role in making the Southwest the nation's most productive and profitable agricultural region. Some estimated that up to 85 percent of the Mexicans in the mobile "army" of migrant laborers lived and worked in the United States illegally. Border Patrol officers, therefore, with the power to police the crime of illegal immigration, held considerable authority over the region's primary labor force.

Although disputes with agribusinessmen were not uncommon, Border Patrol officers during the 1920s and 1930s typically enforced federal immigration law according to locally defined interests in maintaining an accessible, temporary, and disciplined labor force. Most important, officers did not interrupt the flow of Mexican workers during peak seasons, but rather focused on apprehending and deporting workers at the end of the harvest. Working in an intensely local context of labor control, these early Border Patrolmen did not imagine the impact of their work beyond their local communities. Yet while they were busy enforcing federal U.S. immigration laws according to the seasonal labor needs of local ranchers and farmers, U.S. Border Patrol officers during the 1920s and 1930s transformed the story of race in twentieth-century America.

THE CROSS-BORDER POLITICS OF U.S. MIGRATION CONTROL

World War II ripped the Border Patrol from its local roots and transformed the politics of migration control. Within the context of international military conflict, U.S. national borders assumed new significance as the first lines of defense against invasion and sabotage. During 1940 and 1941, wartime worries about saboteurs illegally entering the United States across the southern border threatened to undo the long history of targeting Mexican nationals. At this time, the U.S. Immigration and Naturalization Services (INS) supervisors assigned U.S. Border Patrol officers to guard Japanese internment camps and warned officers to be on the lookout for European saboteurs. The new demands placed upon Border Patrol officers promised a transformation in U.S. Border Patrol practice along the U.S.-Mexico border by shifting the officers' focus away from Mexicans and toward racially and socially ambiguous saboteurs. The establishment of the Bracero Program in 1942, however, placed migration control in a binational context that refocused Border Patrol attention upon policing the unsanctioned border crossings of Mexican nationals.

The Bracero Program (1942–1964) was a series of agreements between the U.S. and Mexican governments that facilitated the migration of short-term Mexican contract laborers into (and out of) the United States. Known as braceros, these laborers generally worked on southwestern farms, and U.S. and Mexican officials closely managed their movement between the United States and Mexico. At a time when the Mexican government was sponsoring an ambitious project of rapid industrialization, Mexican politicians, in part, agreed to participate in the Bracero Program as a strategy to limit the loss of Mexican laborers to higher-paying jobs in the United States. In exchange for legal bracero workers, Mexican officials demanded that the United States prevent Mexican laborers from surreptitiously crossing into the United States and, when unsuccessful in this, aggressively detect and deport those who had effected illegal entry.

In response to Mexican demands within the context of the Bracero Program, INS officials shifted the entire national organization of the U.S. Border Patrol. Prior to 1943, more U.S. Border Patrol officers worked along the northern border than along the southern border. Beginning in 1943, the INS doubled the number of Border Patrol inspectors working in the U.S.-Mexico borderlands and established the U.S.-Mexico border as the national center of operations for the Border Patrol. With additional officers and new strategies, the number of Mexicans, as a percentage of the national total number of apprehensions, increased from a roving average of 17 percent to 56 percent between 1924 and 1940 to a steady

Patrolling the U.S.–Mexican Border. *A U.S. Border Patrol agent looks out over the desert south of Sunland Park, New Mexico, on May 15, 2006. Concerns over both illegal immigration and terrorism have made border security an important political issue in the United States.* **AP IMAGES.**

average of more than 90 percent between 1943 and 1954. Therefore, at a time when detecting, detaining, and deporting enemy aliens and saboteurs could have emerged as a priority of migration control within the United States, the bilateral promises of the Bracero Program directed the U.S. Border Patrol's attention to policing the southern border and deporting undocumented Mexican nationals (see Lytle-Hernández 2006)

Further, the rise of the U.S. Border Patrol in the U.S.-Mexico borderlands developed in partnership with the Bracero program as a cross-border system of migration control during the 1940s and early 1950s. During the Bracero years, U.S. and Mexican officers participated in joint raids upon border settlements, cooperatively patrolled the border, and coordinated collaborative deportation schemes that removed undocumented Mexicans from the U.S.-Mexico border to the interior of Mexico. Mexican participation in creating, shaping, and collaborating with U.S. migration control practices added a binational dimension to the problem of race that emerged from the U.S. Border Patrol's uneven enforcement of U.S. immigration restrictions. What had first begun as a local interpretation of federal immigration laws evolved upon the cross-border foundation of U.S. and Mexican collaboration during the Bracero era.

When the Bracero Program ended in 1964, the U.S. Border Patrol entered its third generation of U.S. immigration law enforcement. In these years, INS and Border Patrol officials reframed the Border Patrol's mission away from controlling unsanctioned labor migration and toward preventing a broad range of cross-border criminal activities, such as prostitution and drug trafficking. This shift allowed the Border Patrol to maintain its institutional relevance despite the low apprehension rates between the mid-1950s and late 1960s. Further, the switch from migration control to crime control linked immigration law enforcement to border enforcement and drug interdiction, each of which were core elements of the rising U.S. war on crime in the late twentieth century. In these years, the policing of the unsanctioned migrations of poor Mexican-born workers increasingly intersected with the policing of the cross-border trafficking of marijuana and narcotics, such as Mexican-grown heroin. The impact was an implosion of race, crime, and immigration at a moment when the United States embraced crime control as a primary system of governance and social organization. Border Patrol officers and INS officials, therefore, played a critical role in linking the racialized problem of illegal immigration to the problems of crime that have dominated American politics and social organization since the late 1960s.

RACIALIZATION AND LEGITIMIZATION

The United States Supreme Court legitimated the U.S. Border Patrol's racialized policing of the crime of illegal immigration in a case that had begun on the evening of June 11, 1973. That evening, two Border Patrol officers sat in a parked car on the northbound side of Highway 5 in southern California. Sometime after dark, the officers looked into their headlights and saw a car carrying Felix Humberto Brignoni-Ponce and two of his friends. According to the officers, the three men appeared to be of "Mexican descent," which was sufficient evidence to suspect the men of the crime of illegal immigration. The officers launched a short pursuit, pulled the men over, and questioned them about their citizenship status. Brignoni-Ponce was a U.S. citizen, but his two passengers both admitted that they had entered the country illegally. The officers arrested all three men: the two passengers for illegal entry and Brignoni-Ponce for "knowingly transporting illegal immigrants," a felony punishable by a fine of $5,000 and up to five years in prison for each violation.

Brignoni-Ponce appealed his conviction in a legal battle that ended in the Supreme Court in June 1975. According to Brignoni-Ponce and his lawyers, "Mexican descent" was insufficient evidence of the crime of illegal entry and the Border Patrol officers had therefore violated Brignoni-Ponce's Fourth Amendment protections against unreasonable search and seizure. The Supreme Court, however, decided that decades of Border Patrol statistics revealed a close relationship between the problem of illegal immigration and persons of Mexican origin. While acknowledging Brignoni-Ponce's Fourth Amendment concerns regarding the uneven distribution of state surveillance and violence toward persons of Mexican origin through U.S. Border Patrol practice, the Supreme Court legitimated the Border Patrol's use of "Mexican appearance" as an indicator for the crime of illegal immigration. The Border Patrol's practice of linking persons of Mexican origin to the caste of illegals, therefore, entered the late twentieth century as a legitimate practice of racialization.

In the years following the *Brignoni-Ponce* decision, war and poverty pushed increasingly large numbers of Salvadorans and Guatemalans to seek both sanctuary and work in the United States. Many entered the United States by crossing the U.S.-Mexico border without sanction. Although the U.S. Border Patrol remained focused upon policing unsanctioned Mexican immigration, the intensive regional focus of U.S. Border Patrol practices entangled Salvadoran and Guatemalan immigrants in the racial projects of U.S. immigration law enforcement.

SEE ALSO *Immigrant Domestic Workers; Immigration Reform and Control Act of 1986 (IRCA); Immigration to the United States.*

BIBLIOGRAPHY

Calavita, Kitty. 1992. *Inside the State: The Bracero Program, Immigration, and the I.N.S.* New York: Routledge.

Foley, Neil. 1997. *The White Scourge: Mexicans, Blacks, and Poor Whites in Texas Cotton Culture.* Berkeley: University of California Press.

Galarza, Ernesto. 1964. *Merchants of Labor: The Mexican Bracero Story.* Charlotte: McNally & Loftin Publishers.

Garland, David. 2001. *The Culture of Control: Crime and Social Order in Contemporary Society.* Chicago: University of Chicago Press.

———, ed. 2001. *Mass Imprisonment: Social Causes and Consequences.* Thousand Oaks, CA: Sage.

Hall, Stuart et al. 1978. *Policing the Crisis: Mugging, the State, and Law and Order.* London: Macmillan.

Lytle-Hernández, Kelly. 2006. "The Crimes and Consequences of Illegal Immigration: A Cross Border Examination of Operation Wetback, 1943–1954." *Western Historical Quarterly* 37 (4): 421–444.

Montejano, David. 1987. *Anglos and Mexicans in the Making of Texas, 1836–1986.* Austin: University of Texas Press.

Ngai, Mae. 2004. *Impossible Subjects: Illegal Aliens and the Making of Modern America.* Princeton, NJ: Princeton University Press.

Niblo, Stephen. 1995. *War, Diplomacy, and Development: The United States and Mexico, 1938–1954.* Wilmington, DE: Scholarly Resources.

Reiner, Robert. 1985. *The Politics of the Police.* New York: St. Martin's Press.

Reisler, Mark. 1976. *By the Sweat of their Brow: Mexican Immigrant Labor in the United States, 1900–1940.* Westport, CT: Greenwood Press.

Simon, Jonathan. 2007. *Governing through Crime: How the War on Crime Transformed American Democracy and Created a Culture of Fear.* Oxford: Oxford University Press.

Smith, Peter H., ed. 1992. *Drug Policy in the Americas.* Boulder, CO: Westview Press.

Taylor, Paul Schuster. 1928–1934. *Mexican Labor in the United States.* 3 vols. Berkeley: University of California Press.

Weber, Devra. 1994. *Dark Sweat, White Gold: California Farm Workers, Cotton and the New Deal.* Berkeley: University of California Press.

Kelly Lytle Hernandez

BOXING

Today the sport of boxing is associated with a variety of racial stereotypes. In the late twentieth century these included the belief that no white man would be able to contend for the world heavyweight championship. This idea results from the general racial stereotype circulating in the Western world that persons of African descent are simply better athletes compared to persons of European descent. In addition, stereotypes concerning the innate violence of the African American male support the notion that Africans or African Americans should dominate boxing, which is by nature a violent sport.

In the early 1990s both the in-ring and out-of-ring behavior of then heavyweight champion Mike Tyson contributed to bringing these disturbing images to the forefront of European American consciousness. Tyson was convicted of raping Desiree Washington, then Miss Black Rhode Island, as well as being in possession of twenty-nine pounds of marijuana and cocaine. Tyson served three years of a six-year sentence. In 1997, in his match with Evander Holyfield, Mike Tyson's ring behavior sank to a new low. In the third round, Tyson clinched Holyfield, biting off a piece of his ear. This display feeds into the modern idea that violence and blackness are associated. For example, in 1995 President Bill Clinton stated that "violence for white people too often comes with a black face" (Hutchinson 1995).

The history of boxing does not indicate that Africans or African Americans per se dominate it. Rather, this history shows that participation in professional boxing is multiethnic and mostly associated with poverty rather than socially defined race. This becomes more apparent as one examines boxing participation across weight classes as opposed to just the heavyweight category. Also, virtually every cultural group has some form of boxing, including the Eastern martial arts and Latin American forms such as Brazilian capoeira.

ORIGINS OF WESTERN BOXING

The sport we know today as boxing probably began in ancient Greece and was included in the first Olympic Games. In ancient Rome, the sport was part of gladiatorial contests, and the boxers often wore a metal-studded leather hand covering called the *cestus*. Serious injury or death often resulted from these contests. The sport came to England with the arrival of the Roman Empire (Fleisher and Andre 1993). Modern boxing began there in the eighteenth century. In 1719, James Figg was recognized as the first heavyweight champion, and he is now recognized as the father of boxing. Figg openly advertised exhibitions of his skill and taught the sport. He was also a master swordsman, and thus he attracted the patronage of the English "bloods," the socially well-to-do sportsmen of the country. His boxing exhibitions were held on a stage with wooden rails; the referee called the bouts while standing outside the ring. In 1734, another English champion, John Broughton, formulated the first set of rules and invented the boxing glove, though boxing gloves were used only at sparring exhibitions. Boughton's rules governed boxing until 1838 and eliminated the practice of hitting opponents when they were down or grabbing opponents by the hair.

In 1838, the Original London Prize Ring rules were devised. Soon after, these were modified to form the Revised London Prize Ring rules (1853), and finally, at the turn of the century, the Queensberry rules were adopted. John Graham Chambers authored these rules under the patronage of John Sholto Douglas, eighth marquis of Queensberry.

Boxing in eighteenth-century England was dominated by contests of brute strength. Champions tended to be men who both could inflict great bodily harm on their opponents and withstand such harm themselves. Daniel Mendoza, a man of Spanish-Jewish descent, is credited as being the first boxer to change this model. After sustaining significant injuries in his first victorious bout, he spent three years developing a system of guarding, sidestepping, and effective use of the straight left (today called the left jab). Mendoza utilized these tactics to be crowned English champion in 1794. However, this victory was not without a price. Many boxing critics of the day characterized his tactics as "cowardly," as opposed to standing up in the true "British bulldog" style (Fleisher and Andre 1993). Yet it was fighting in this style, as well as the adoption of the Queensberry rules, that would establish boxing as a legitimate sport as opposed to its prior image as a barbaric spectacle.

PERSONS OF AFRICAN DESCENT IN EARLY BOXING

Bill Richmond was the first person of African descent to make a mark in English boxing. During the occupation of New York by the British in 1777, Richmond was noticed by General Earl Percy after he routed three English soldiers who accosted him in a tavern. Percy took Richmond into his household as a servant, and later that year sent him to England to apprentice as a carpenter. There he developed a style of fighting similar to that of Mendoza. Richmond stood 5 feet 6 inches and weighed 170 pounds. He listed among his most important victories those over George Moore, Paddy Green, and Frank Mayers. His prowess in the ring earned him the nickname "The Black Terror." In his later years, Richmond ran a boxing academy in London, dying in that city on December 28, 1829, at the age of sixty-six.

Tom Mollineaux was born in Virginia on March 23, 1784. He arrived in England in 1809 and was trained by Bill Richmond. A year later, Mollineaux fought in the first international title involving a person of African descent. His opponent was Tom Cribb. The bout, which took place in December, lasted thirty-nine rounds, after which Mollineaux collapsed from exhaustion. English boxing correspondent Pierce Egan described Mollineux as "the tremendous man of colour" and wrote that he had "proved himself as courageous a man as ever an adversary contended with" (Fleisher and Andre 1993). Egan was also impressed with both Mollineaux's strength and knowledge of the science of boxing. Cribb and Mollineaux fought a rematch in September 1811 before a crowd that swelled to more than 25,000 spectators. Once again Cribb was the victor.

Molllineux would defeat William Fuller in 1814. These fights made Mollineaux a celebrity in England. He lived there for the rest of life, engaging in periodic sparring bouts. He died in Dublin, Ireland, in 1818.

At this point in history there seemed to be no specialized racial theory of boxing, apart from the general racial theories of the time. The ability of non-Europeans in any sector of social endeavor was always viewed through the prism of the existing racial ideologies, which uniformly viewed such persons as inferior. Successful non-European individuals were exceptions to the general racial norms of day.

BOXING COMES TO AMERICA

In 1816, Jacob Hyer and Tom Beasley fought the first publicly acknowledged boxing match in the United States, in New York City. In 1849, the first heavyweight championship fight was held, pitting Jacob Hyer's son Tom against "Yankee" Sullivan at Still Pond Creek, Maryland. Yet, it is important to understand that prize fighting was still considered illegal throughout the United States. In 1849, most states had enacted "prize fight statutes." In 1876, the Massachusetts Supreme Court held that "Prize fighting, boxing matches, and encounters of that kind serve no useful purpose, tend to breaches of the peace, and are unlawful even when entered into by agreement and without anger or ill will" (Sammons 1988). That same year, organizers of the reputed world heavyweight championship fight between Englishman Joe Goss and American Paddy Ryan chose Colliers, West Virginia, so that if the fight was raided by hostile police officers, the participants would be able to flee quickly across state lines to Ohio or Pennsylvania.

The illegality of the sport meant that it stayed popular with the urban masses, many of whom were immigrants who saw it as a way to work themselves out of poverty. This is also a characteristic of modern-day boxing and to some degree accounts for the racial stereotyping associated with it. The Social Darwinists of the period supported boxing as consistent with Darwinian laws. William Graham Sumner declared that a society with "no-holds" business competition was in consonance with Darwinian law and that boxing was the reduction of "survival of the fittest" to its simplest and most tangible terms (Altschuler and LaForse 1983). These views explain why many early boxing contests revolved around the theme of "native-born" Americans pitted against Irish immigrants. Animosity against the Irish, both in America and England, was great in this period. For example, Professor Edward Freeman of Oxford, a devotee of the Count de Gobineau, carried out a successful lecture tour in the United States between 1881 and 1882. His lectures decried the corruption of the Anglo-Saxon and Teutonic bloodlines by the Irish, Jews, and Negroes. The solution Freeman offered the Americans was that every Irishman would kill a Negro and be hanged for it (Chase 1977).

The final sixty years of boxing in the nineteenth century was dominated by Irish Americans. The most notable was John L. Sullivan, who first began to garner national attention in 1879 with impressive victories over Joe Goss, John Donaldson, and John Flood. In February 1882, Sullivan fought for the U.S. heavyweight crown at Mississippi City against Paddy Ryan. The public's interest in the fight attracted major media attention, with newspapers hiring famous journalists and authors to record their impressions of the fight. Henry Ward Beecher, Reverend Thomas De Witt Tallmage, Nat Goodwin, and Oscar Wilde were among those who covered the fight (Fleisher and Andre 1993). Sullivan dispatched Ryan in nine rounds.

Sullivan, now dubbed "the Boston Strong Boy," took on all comers in the heavyweight ranks for the next ten years. Sullivan fought and won the last sanctioned bare-knuckle fight in 1889, against Jake Kilrain. The fight was held in Richburg, Mississippi, and lasted seventy-five rounds.

Sullivan's willingness to fight all candidates did not extend to persons of African descent. Sullivan consistently refused to fight Peter Jackson, an Australian boxer of African descent, even though most considered Jackson a serious contender for the heavyweight title (Ward 2004). Jackson was born in the West Indies in 1861 and began his boxing career in Australia in 1882. In May 1891, Jackson fought a sixty-one-round draw with Jim Corbett in San Francisco. It was Corbett's success against Jackson that led to calls for a championship match with Sullivan. That match was held on September 7, 1892, in New Orleans, which had become the capital of American boxing. This fight was conducted with gloves under the Queensberry rules and Sullivan lost. This event also featured, in the featherweight division, George "Little Chocolate" Dixon against Jack Skelly. Dixon's victory against Skelly, and the violently negative European American reaction to that victory, led to "interracial" fights being banned in that city (Sammons 1988).

THE GREAT WHITE HOPE

Sullivan's decision not to entertain bouts with persons of African descent can be linked to his manager, William Muldoon. Muldoon wished to spare his champion the humiliation of being defeated by a Negro. Given the symbolic role that the heavyweight boxing champion had taken on as the "emperor" of manhood, it was inconceivable for them that this mantle would be held by a Negro (Ward 2004). However, within sixteen years of Sullivan surrendering the belt, Jack Johnson, an African American born in Galveston, Texas, would be declared heavyweight champion of the world. Johnson began his boxing career in contests called "battle royals," which pitted several African American men in the ring until the last man standing was declared the winner. European Americans would then throw coins into the ring as payment for the bout. Johnson turned professional in 1897 and amassed a string of impressive victories, until finally he forced then world champion Tommy Burns into a bout in Rushcutters Bay, Sydney, Australia. The fight promoter, Snowy Baker, had to guarantee Burns $30,000 for him to agree to the match. Johnson greatly outclassed Burns, and the police stepped in to end the bout in the fourteenth round. The new heavyweight champion won a string of impressive victories within the year, and the search for "a great white hope" began, with fight promoters all over Europe and the Americas hunting for a "Caucasian" challenger to win the title back for the "white" race.

Johnson's victories dispelled a variety of racist theories in boxing that had developed over the nineteenth century. It is argued that Johnson pursued the Burns fight in a way to expose the fallacies that black fighters

Jack Johnson Defeats Jim Jeffries, 1910. *Johnson defied every racist convention of the early twentieth century. Most significantly it was his relationships with white women that turned the public against him.* © BETTMANN/CORBIS.

were weak in the stomach, that they betray a yellow streak under pressure, and that they were unable to think on their feet like white fighters (Ward 2004). All of these stereotypes were consistent with the general nineteenth-century racial views of the Negro. However, it was not Johnson's behavior inside the ring that aggravated European Americans; it was his personal life. Johnson defied every racist convention of the early twentieth century. Most significantly, it was his romantic affairs with a series of European American women that turned both the African and European American public against him. For example, on March 12, 1909, Texas authorities threatened to arrest Johnson if he brought his white wife with him to that state. He was going to Galveston to attend a parade in his honor. D. A. Hart, the African American editor of the *Nashville Globe*, chastised Johnson for not marrying a member of his own race, thus insulting Negro women and placing others of his race in mortal danger (Ward 2004).

Shortly after the Burns defeat, Anglo-Saxonist author Jack London implored Jim Jeffries to come out of retirement to take the crown back from Johnson. The Jeffries–Johnson match, fought in Reno, Nevada, on July 4, 1910, had all of America's attention. Twelve hundred African Americans prayed for a Johnson victory in Hutchinson, Kansas, and a special telegraph line was installed at Tuskegee Institute to receive round-by-round reports of the fight. Booker T. Washington disapproved of Johnson and prize fighting, but he allowed the fight to be broadcast to Tuskegee. In the ring, the band began with "Just Before the Battle Mother," "America," and "Dixie." Johnson demolished Jeffries in fifteen rounds, so much so that Jack London could not bear watching the finish. African Americans in Chicago swept Johnson's mother on their shoulders and carried her around the south side. At every stop on the return train ride to Chicago, Johnson was greeted by cheering crowds, including 1,000 members of the all-African American 9th Calvary (Buffalo Soldiers) in Cheyenne, Wyoming.

Not everyone was happy; race riots broke out over the Johnson victory in Chattanooga, Tennessee; Clarksburg, West Virginia; Columbus, Ohio; Los Angeles; Manhattan; New Orleans; Norfolk, Virginia; Pueblo, New Mexico; Philadelphia; Roanoke, Virginia; Uvalda, Georgia; and Washington, D.C. It is estimated that from eleven to twenty-six people died, and hundreds were wounded, the vast majority African Americans.

Johnson maintained the heavyweight championship until April 5, 1915. The pressure of being the champion as well as the disorders of his personal life combined to defeat him at the age of thirty-seven. He lost the championship to the last of the great white hopes, Jess Willard, in Havana, Cuba. In 1920 he would surrender to federal authorities for violation of the Mann Act (which prevented the transportation of white women across state lines for "immoral" purposes) and spent eight months in prison. After he was killed in a car accident in 1946, he was buried in Graceland Cemetery next to Etta Duryea Johnson, the European American woman who had been the love of his life. For his courage against insurmountable odds, many rank Johnson as the most significant African American athlete of the twentieth century (Ward 2004).

FIGHTING FOR DEMOCRACY

The next notable heavyweight champion was Jack Dempsey ("the Manassa Mauler"), who took the title from Jess Willard on July 4, 1919, in Toledo, Ohio. Dempsey was a European American born in Colorado, one of eleven children, and started fighting as a matter of survival. He rode the rails looking for work in assorted mining towns. Dempsey amassed sixty wins, fifty by knockout, over his career. Dempsey lost the title to Gene Tunney on September 23, 1926. Tunney, also European American, grew up the son of a longshoreman. He also learned how to fight to survive on the brutal streets of New York City. He won the armed forces title while a member of the expeditionary force in France during World War I. Tunney's lifetime record was sixty wins, forty-five by knockout. Dempsey's and Tunney's championships occurred at a time when America had locked the African-American athlete out from competition for the world heavyweight title. This reaction was a direct response to the success of Jack Johnson.

With Tunney's retirement, the heavyweight championship passed over to Europe. A series of contenders vied for the belt, but on June 30, 1931, German Max Schmeling was declared world champion after a bout with Jack Sharkey. Schmeling's victory came at a time when boxing had completely moved out of its former criminal/sideshow atmosphere into the mainstream of respectable public entertainment (Bathrick 1990). Indeed, boxing in general and Schmeling in particular took on tremendous importance in the cultural transformation of German society during the Weimar period (1918–1933). This transformation involved the glorification of the human body. In the 1920s, Germany, which had labored in the corset and stiff collar, moved to embody a new cult of nakedness in cultural venues from vaudeville to sport (Bathrick 1990). This was also the period in which racial hygiene ideas were gathering strength throughout German society. The eugenics (racial hygiene) of the Weimar Republic was mainly concerned with preventing the decline of the German "volk," or "rasse" (Weiss 1990).

In this way, achievement in sport represented the antithesis of racial degeneration. The one-time European heavyweight champion Georges Carpentier (a Frenchman) stated that boxing had done more to improve the moral and physical character of the younger generation than had previous centuries of physical and moral teaching. He also stated that there was reason to hope that France's military prowess would increase because of boxing (Carpentier 1926). Carpentier's claims about the value of boxing seem to be at odds with modern science. A 2005 study of 477 boys in Norway found that participation in boxing was associated with a significantly greater probability of being involved in violent or antisocial behavior outside the ring (Endresen and Olweus 2005).

Bertolt Brecht, considered by many the most important German playwright of the twentieth century, also became enamored with boxing in the Weimar period (Bathrick 1990). In the same years, Adolf Hitler wrote of the importance of boxing in *Mein Kampf*: "There is no sport that cultivates a spirit of aggressiveness, that demands lighting-quick decisiveness, that develops the body to such steely smoothness." Further, Hitler argued that had Germans studied boxing instead of etiquette, then the deserters, pimps, and rabble responsible for the Weimar Republic could have never taken power (Margolick 2005).

Schmeling became the world heavyweight champion on June 11, 1930, defeating Jack Sharkey before 79,222 fans in Yankee Stadium. Schmeling met Sharkey again for a second defense of his title in June 1932, losing by decision in fifteen rounds. Four years later Schmeling would be matched against Joe Louis (nicknamed "the Brown Bomber") in Yankee Stadium before 39,878 fans. The term "Brown Bomber" had been developed by the American press to stir up racial animosity in preparation for the Louis-Carnera fight of 1935. Louis was portrayed as symbolic of Ethiopia, fighting off the Italian fascist invasion, symbolized by Primo Carnera (Sammons 1988). The cultural significance of the Louis–Schmeling bouts will always be intertwined in the context of American and German racism and the international political situation culminating in World War II. This is ironic, since neither fighter was particularly racist or anti-Semitic; for example, Schmeling's manager, Max Jacobs, was of Jewish descent. Schmeling, however, would become the darling of Nazi sports culture, especially after he defeated Louis in the first fight. He would support the Nazi Party throughout his career, although there is no conclusive evidence that he agreed with its anti-Semitic and genocidal policies. Schmeling was a man of the period, and before Louis–Schmeling I, American newspapers were still portraying Louis using racist Sambo stereotypes. One newspaper showed Louis trembling with fear of Schmeling, after the Mantan Moreland character "feets don't fail me now," while another represented him as a chicken-stealing thief in farmer Max's henhouse (Wiggins 1988). German caricatures of Louis were just as bad. A cartoon that appeared in *Der Kicker* on June 23, 1936, portrays Schmeling spanking a Sambo caricature of Louis (Margolick 2005). Response to the Schmeling victory followed racial and ethnic lines: Jews, African Americans, Africans, and other colonized populations were plunged into immediate depression, while southern whites, Germans, South Africans, and other European populations in racially stratified societies jumped for joy. Films of the first Schmeling–Louis fight were rapidly made available throughout the United States. This was in contrast to the ongoing ban of films from the fights that Joe Louis had won against white opponents (Margolick 2005).

LOUIS KOs THE FASCISTS

Louis–Schmeling II was undoubtedly the greatest professional fight of the twentieth century. This was not because of the technical mastery that either fighter showed in the ring but rather the social significance of the fight. No one was neutral. Aryanists, German Bundists in the United States, South African colonialists, and

American white supremacists were all pulling for Max Schmeling to win again. American Jews, as well as the Communist Party, had originally opposed the fight to protest treatment of Jews in Germany. However, both groups realized that a Joe Louis victory would be a crushing blow to the theory of Aryan supremacy. African Americans were divided. Many were worried that Louis would lose again, but all of them were praying for the Brown Bomber. W. E. B. Du Bois sat listening to the fight with a group of academicians in Atlanta, Eleanor Roosevelt sat by the radio, and the owner of the Hope diamond, Evalyn Walsh McLean, had a ringside seat. The fight was carried live over German radio from New York. No one had to wait long; Louis defeated Schmeling by technical knockout (TKO) at 2:04 in the first round. Schmeling was knocked down three times, the last ending the fight. After the fight, to save face, Schmeling claimed he was fouled, but no one believed him.

Despite the abuses that occurred during some of the celebrations following, some argued that the Louis victory did more to improve race relations in America than any event since the Civil War. One writer wrote that the decline of Nazi prestige began with a left hook delivered by a former unskilled autoworker who had never read Neville Chamberlain's policies (Margolick 2005, p. 322). Nazi propaganda minister Paul Joseph Goebbels distanced himself from the Schmeling loss immediately, as did Nazi Germany as a whole. The United States entered the war against the Nazis with a segregated army. Louis served the war effort more as an icon than as a soldier, although he later served in the U.S. Army.

BOXING AND SOCIAL MOBILITY

The Johnson–Jeffries and Louis–Schmeling fights illustrate all of the racial themes associated with boxing. When fighters from socially subordinated groups win, their victories are attributed to natural athleticism or innate animal-like savagery. Conversely, if the victory goes to fighters from socially dominant groups, it supposedly resulted from their greater courage and intellect. Try as it may, professional boxing has always had an unsavory reputation. Its appeal has always been to the poor and disenfranchised, who often barter their physical health and sometimes their lives as a way out of their social situation. In addition, this peddling of human flesh was consistently connected with various kinds of greed and crime (organized and individual). Yet boxing has seen its fair share of great athletes, and these individuals have originated from all portions of the formal racial spectrum.

Boxing and sports in general have given the public the idea that it is possible for individuals to better their condition by exemplary achievement in the professional ranks. This idea has been particularly popular among African Americans in the latter twentieth century. Sport has been one of the few industries where African Americans seemed highly mobile, visible, and their accomplishments consistent with the general racial theories of the twentieth century (all brawn, but no brain). Role models such as Joe Louis and Jackie Robinson through to Michael Jordan in the modern era are taken as a sign of physical superiority and increased social acceptance of all African Americans.

However, it is difficult to make a case that athletic excellence has had an overall positive effect on race relations in the United States or that it has played a significant role in the social mobility of African Americans. First off, achievement at the highest ranks in professional sports is statistically very rare. For example, in 1972 a high school athlete of any color had the following chances of making it into each of the following professional sports: 1 in 4,000 for baseball, 1 in 3,750 for the National Football League, and 1 in 10,000 for the National Basketball Association. The situation in boxing was not any better. Between the 1930s and 1950s, of 127 active professional boxers, only 7.1% received national recognition, 8.7% achieved local headlines, and the vast majority (84.2%) never achieved anything beyond warm-up bouts (Reiss 1990). Today it is still true that only boxers who are major contenders have a chance to make the "big money." Also, even those who make a high salary may not keep their money for long. Most of these athletes, black or white, don't have the background in money management or the support system required to handle their fortunes. In boxing, as in other sports, this combined with the lavish lifestyle that is expected of professional athletes, as well as the unscrupulous character of many of the fight promoters and managers associated with sport has led many top champions to squander their fortunes or retire bankrupt (Joe Louis, Ike Williams, Mike Tyson).

If professional sports has historically had any positive impact on the social mobility of oppressed groups, it must have occurred indirectly. There is some evidence that the Irish and Jewish communities may have been positively impacted by their period of dominance in professional boxing—in part, because several individuals used the sport to launch business ventures associated with their prominence in prize fighting. Athletes might also contribute to the social mobility of others by donating their wealth to help charitable ventures, such as the Muhammad Ali Institute at the University of Louisville or The Tiger Woods Foundation. The NBA Cares Foundation was launched in 2005, and since that time has raised over 50 million dollars for various charity initiatives. But all these laudable efforts must also be viewed in the light of the false ideology of guaranteed riches for poor youth who excel at sport. Statistics show that the

Joe Louis Defeats Max Schmeling, 1938. *Due to its social significance, many judge the rematch of Louis and Schmeling as the greatest professional fight of the twentieth century.* AP IMAGES.

vast majority of such youth would stand a better chance of achieving social mobility (what little is actually possible in the United States) by focusing their time on their education, as opposed to athletic activity.

SEE ALSO *Baseball; Basketball; Football (U.S.); Rassenhygiene.*

BIBLIOGRAPHY

Altschuler, Glenn C., and Martin W. LaForse. 1983. "From Brawn to Brains: Football and Evolutionary Thought." *Journal of Popular Culture* 16 (4): 75–88.

Bathrick, David. 1990. "Max Schmeling on the Canvas: Boxing as an Icon of Weimar Culture." *New German Critique* 51: 113–136.

Carpentier, Georges. 1926. "Die Psychologie des Boxens." *Querschnitt* 6: 384.

Cashmore, Ernest. 2005. *Tyson: Nurture of the Beast.* Cambridge, U.K., and Malden, MA: Polity.

Chase, Allan. 1977. *The Legacy of Malthus: The Social Costs of the New Scientific Racism.* New York: Knopf.

Endresen, I., and D. Olweus. "Participation in Power Sports and Antisocial Involvement in Preadolescent and Adolescent Boys." *Journal of Child Psychology and Psychiatry* 46 (5): 468–478.

Fleisher, Nat, and Sam Andre. 1993. *A Pictorial History of Boxing.* New York: Carol Publishing Group.

Hutchinson, E. 1995. "Racial Myths Reinforce White Fears." *Los Angeles Times*, October 22: M5.

International Boxing Hall of Fame. http://www.ibhof.com/ibhfhome.htm.

Margolick, David. 2005. *Beyond Glory: Joe Louis vs. Max Schmelin, and a World on the Brink.* New York: Knopf.

Reiss, Steven, A. 1990. "Professional Sports as an Avenue of Social Mobility in America: Some Myths and Realities." In *Essays on Sport History and Sport Mythology*, ed. A. Guttman, R. D. Mandell, S. A. Reiss, D. Hardy, and D. G. Kyle. College Station, TX: Texas A&M University Press.

Sammons, Jeffrey T. 1988. *Beyond the Ring: The Role of Boxing in American Society.* Urbana: University of Illinois Press.

Ward, Geoffrey C. 2004. *Unforgivable Blackness: The Rise and Fall of Jack Johnson.* New York: Knopf.

Weiss, Sheila F. 1990. "The Race Hygiene Movement in Germany, 1904–1945." In *The Wellborn Science: Eugenics in Germany, France, Brazil and Russia*, ed. Mark Adams. New York: Oxford University Press.

Wiggins, William H., Jr. 1988. "Boxing's Sambo Twins: Racial Stereotypes of Jack Johnson and Joe Louis Newspaper Cartoons, 1908 to 1938." *Journal of Sports History* 15 (3): 242–254.

Joseph L. Graves Jr.

BRACEROS, REPATRIATION, AND SEASONAL WORKERS

Braceros (in Spanish, "laborer," derived from *brazo*, "arm"), or field workers from Mexico, have long been an important feature of U.S. agriculture, especially in the southwestern United States. Since the early twentieth century, many millions of such workers have left Mexico on a seasonal or permanent basis in search of jobs on U.S. family farms and in corporate "factories in the fields." Some workers have come legally and others illegally, sometimes under contract with employers and sometimes as undocumented "freelancers."

Although economically beneficial to both countries, for generations this cross-border migratory flow has generated significant international conflict, as well as controversy within the United States. The positive aspects of Mexican immigration to the United States have gone largely unrecognized and unappreciated among most Americans, who have stigmatized this group of immigrants and repeatedly turned against them during hard times. Many critics have charged these newcomers with harming the country, both economically and socially. Additional reasons for rejection include racial intolerance, cultural bias, linguistic prejudice, a predominantly negative view of Mexico, and the fact that many immigrants have entered the United States illegally.

THE GREAT DEPRESSION

From the 1920s to the present, intense anti-Mexican sentiments have flared up repeatedly during downturns in the U.S. economy, with attendant demands by the public for wholesale deportation of Mexicans, imposition of legal restrictions on immigration, and stronger enforcement measures at the border. The prime example of this response is the decade of the Great Depression, which began in 1929. The U.S. economic collapse during that time deepened the opposition to immigration and spawned a movement to rid the nation of foreigners. Mexicans became the principal target of the attacks, leading to massive deportations and repatriations. Thus, in the 1930s, from half a million to one million Mexicans departed the United States. Reflecting the overall composition of the Mexican-origin population, most of those who exited hailed from the working classes. But many families of higher social status also left, depleting an already small Mexican/Mexican-American middle class and elite sector.

The trauma unleashed by deportations and repatriations touched Chicano communities everywhere. Sweeps and raids by immigration agents and local policemen heightened U.S. nativism and encouraged private citizens to attack Mexicans directly. Extreme hostility flared up in the workplace in states and cities that passed laws prohibiting the hiring of non-U.S. citizens in publicly financed projects. Although such statutes applied to all aliens, in the Southwest they were clearly directed against Mexican immigrants. Violations of civil and human rights became commonplace, including harassment, intimidation, illegal arrest and imprisonment, separation of families, and expulsion.

U.S. officials escorted deportees and repatriates across the border and turned them over to Mexican officials, who had the responsibility of meeting their immediate needs, arranging for transportation to their places of destination, and beginning the process of reintegration into Mexican society. The Mexican government waived customs regulations and allowed migrants to import personal belongings and occupational tools. Mexico also provided employment assistance and offered land to those who wished to go into farming. From the Mexican government's perspective, many of the returning immigrants could be helpful to the Mexican economy because of skills and experience acquired in the United States. Despite the good intentions, however, the Mexican government could not deliver on many of its promises, and the migrants suffered many hardships in Mexico.

By the mid-1930s the harsh reality of life in an impoverished Mexico began driving desperate repatriates back to the United States. But many, even those born north of the border, encountered difficulties recrossing the border at a time when the U.S. Immigration Service exercised strict control over immigration. The U.S. Catholic Welfare Conference stepped in to help the migrants, with mixed results. Large numbers who could not reenter legally because they lacked birth certificates and other papers simply waded across the Rio Grande or walked through the desert into the United States.

WORLD WAR II AND LATER

Immigration restrictions eased substantially when World War II created serious labor shortages in the United States. Americans now welcomed the returning repatriates as well as first-time entrants. The demand for Mexican workers continued beyond 1945 as the cold war, the Korean conflict, and intervention in Vietnam spawned a steady expansion of the U.S. economy. Consequently, from 1940 to the mid-1960s Mexican immigration in the United States rose substantially; close to 400,000 Mexicans immigrated legally as permanent U.S. residents while an undetermined number crossed the border without documentation.

Mexican men entered the United States in large numbers as part of a landmark guest-worker program that began in 1942, shortly after Americans became involved in World War II. At the time, serious shortages of workers, especially in agriculture, had created a crisis for the national economy. Accordingly, the two countries signed a bilateral agreement known officially as the Mexican Farm Labor Supply Program and informally as the Bracero Program. The U.S. Congress approved the program under Public Law 45.

The U.S. government assumed primary responsibility for recruiting and transporting male workers from Mexico to the United States and back home again when contracts ended. Employers took on the obligation to pay fair wages and provide adequate working and living conditions. The pact excluded women because Mexico feared they would be subjected to unacceptable treatment and abuse at the hands of greedy employers and sundry predators. In some ways the provisions of the Bracero Program resembled those of the first guest-worker program implemented by the United States, the Temporary Admissions Program of 1917, which had also addressed emergency labor shortages during a time of war.

The 1942 agreement continued in force until the end of 1947, when the U.S. Congress allowed the legislation to expire because wartime labor shortages no longer existed. About 220,000 braceros participated in the program during that five-year period. Over the next four years, even though employers who desired braceros had to recruit them with only limited assistance from the two governments, over 200,000 contracted workers entered the United States. More than twice that number, however, crossed the border without documentation. Significantly, the U.S. Immigration Service intermittently facilitated labor recruitment by allowing employers to contract undocumented workers directly from detention centers in the Southwest. The procedure of turning apprehended "wetbacks" into legal braceros became known as the "drying out" process.

When the Korean conflict broke out in 1950 and the United States showed renewed interest in large-scale labor importation, Mexico, wishing its workers to have greater protection abroad, suggested a return to a formal arrangement. In 1951 the two countries enacted the Migratory Labor Agreement. This new Bracero Program functioned until 1964, facilitating the signing of almost 3.5 million bracero contracts.

The Bracero Program in its various incarnations stirred controversy in both countries for more than two decades. Labor unions in the United States charged bitterly that braceros displaced U.S. workers and depressed wages and working conditions. South of the border, many activists complained about the discrimination and exploitation suffered by braceros in the United States, while agricultural interests blasted the government in Mexico City for helping foreign employers take away their laborers. The strongest promoters of the Bracero Program were U.S. growers, its primary beneficiaries. They contended that the United States needed braceros because Americans would not perform hard agricultural work for modest wages. Support for the program in Mexico rested primarily with ordinary people in need of employment and the government, which saw the remittances sent back home by braceros as an important source of foreign-exchange earnings for the nation.

Although most braceros worked in the Southwest, significant numbers went to the Northwest, the Great Plains, and the Midwest. Between 1943 and 1947, most of the nearly 47,000 braceros in Idaho, Oregon, and Washington performed farm work, but some were recruited for other tasks, including assisting the National Forest Service to put out forest fires. During the same period, over 28,000 braceros worked in agriculture, railroad maintenance, and industry in Ohio, Indiana, Illinois, Michigan, Wisconsin, Minnesota, Iowa, Missouri, Nebraska, and Kansas. Chicago became a major recruitment and distribution point for braceros during two crucial war years, from 1943 to 1945.

In his classic book *Merchants of Labor* (1964), Ernesto Galarza details many abuses suffered by braceros during their work stints in the United States. Complaints registered by workers included unsatisfactory wages, poor working conditions, job hazards, crowded living quarters, inadequate food, inflated prices for necessities, and even

Braceros Crossing the Border, 1956. *The Bracero Program brought many workers into the United States, but the program became notorious for its abuses of the workers, who were often not paid what they were promised and forced to work in difficult and unsafe conditions* © LEONARD NADEL/NATIONAL MUSEUM OF AMERICAN HISTORY/HANDOUT/REUTERS/CORBIS.

physical abuse. Employers and compliance officers routinely ignored the complaints or failed to follow up with concrete solutions, prompting individuals and groups of braceros to engage in work stoppages and even to desert their contracts. In addition to mistreatment in the workplace, braceros had to contend with discrimination in the communities where they worked. Many establishments posted "No Mexicans, White Trade Only" signs in an effort to keep braceros away. Many Mexicans reported verbal abuses, false arrests, and physical attacks.

In the case of Texas, deeply rooted anti-Mexican racism and grower disdain for official wage and working guidelines prompted the Mexican government to exclude that state from participation in the Bracero Program from 1942 to 1947. The ban forced employers to find alternative sources of cheap labor, and they resorted to recruiting undocumented workers without much difficulty.

The Temporary Admissions Program of 1917 and the various Bracero Programs that functioned between 1942 and 1964 illustrate the long tradition in the United States of working with Mexico to implement guest-worker programs when the need for labor arises north of the border. Such arrangements, of course, have consequences beyond the economic benefits to both countries. Inevitably, such programs stimulate greater cross-border migration and permanent settlement of many braceros and their families in the United States. These migratory flows have played an important role in expanding the Mexican-origin population, which as of 2007 numbered about 27 million.

BIBLIOGRAPHY

Balderrama, Francisco E., and Raymond Rodríguez. 2006. *Decade of Betrayal: Mexican Repatriation in the 1930s*, rev. ed. Albuquerque: University of New Mexico Press.

Conover, Ted. 1987. *Coyotes: A Journey through the Secret World of America's Illegal Aliens*. New York: Vintage.

Galarza, Ernesto. 1964. *Merchants of Labor: The Mexican Bracero Story*. San Jose, CA: Rosicrucian Press.

García, Juan Ramon. 1980. *Operation Wetback: The Mass Deportation of Mexican Undocumented Workers in 1954*. Westport, CT: Greenwood Press.

González, Gilbert G. 2006. *Guest Workers or Colonized Labor?: Mexican Labor Migration to the United States*. Boulder, CO: Paradigm.

Guerin-Gonzáles, Camille. 1994. *Mexican Workers and American Dreams: Immigration, Repatriation, and California Farm Labor, 1900–1939*. New Brunswick, NJ: Rutgers University Press.

Oscar J. Martínez

BRAZILIAN RACIAL FORMATIONS

Brazil has the largest nonwhite population of any country outside the African continent. The 2000 Brazilian census found that 45 percent of Brazilians, out of a population of some 185 million, identified themselves as "people of color." In Brazil, this term implies a range of skin tones from very dark to the many shades usually included under the English rubric "Mulatto." The term is widely used in Brazil because it is among the most racially heterogeneous nations on earth. This is a result of the long tradition of race mixture and a consequence of violent sexual relations, as well as formal and informal unions between Portuguese men and African and indigenous women.

This tradition is evident from a 2000 DNA study of the Brazilian population. Even among the self-reported "white" population in Brazil, the study found that of those Brazilians who consider themselves "white," fully 97 percent do, indeed, have paternal parentage from Europe. However, only 39 percent have maternal parentage from Europe, while 33 percent have indigenous parentage on the maternal side and 28 percent have African parentage on the maternal side. In short, fully 61 percent of Brazilians who consider themselves "white" also have African or Indian ancestry, a result of the nation's history of miscegenation.

A NATION OF MANY COLORS

The term "people of color" is key to the most important feature of race relations and racial classification in Brazil: the absence of sharply defined racial groupings. In Brazil there is no distinct "black" group or distinct "white" group, as there is in the United States. There are, of course, individuals with distinctly Negroid and Caucasoid physical features, as well as intermediate types, but whites, Mulattoes, and blacks in Brazil do not belong to separate, identifiable social segments. Because well-defined social groups based on racial characteristics are absent, segregation and discrimination based on discrete social units are impossible.

The best way to describe racial classification in Brazil is to contrast it with that of the United States. In Brazil there is no "one-drop rule", the U.S. custom that defines anyone with any known or suspected African ancestry as "black." Because of the one-drop rule (also known as the rule of hypodescent), all people with any known African ancestry in the United States are said to be "black," whatever their personal appearance. Hence, millions of people are called "black" or "African American," even though their racial ancestry is decidedly mixed. The one-drop rules simply avoids the ambiguity of an intermediate identity.

The Brazilian system of racial classification is far more complex. In Brazil, people are assigned to racial groups based on what they look like—their skin color, hair type, and facial features—regardless of their ancestry. As such, individuals may be assigned to different racial groups than their parents, siblings or other relatives. Moreover, how individuals are classified racially does not depend solely on their physical appearance. Social class, education, and manner of dress all come into play in assigning someone to a racial category. As Brazilians put it, "money whitens," so the higher the social class, the lighter the racial category to which an individual belongs. A well-to-do, well-educated woman with dark skin and Negroid features might be referred to as a *moreno* (roughly, "brunette"), while an illiterate sharecropper with fair skin might be assigned to a darker racial category than his physical appearance alone would warrant.

Because of this system of racial classification, Brazilians necessarily recognize and have terms for a wide variety of racial types. There are perhaps twelve principal categories based on varying combinations of physical features, with dozens of racial terms in daily use. Moreover, many of these terms are ambiguous, in that there is no wide agreement on their abstract meaning or on to whom they should be applied. As a result, the same individual may be called by different racial terms at different times and by different people. Because there is no rule of descent, people can actually change their racial identity by becoming better educated and moving up the social ladder.

RACIAL CLASSIFICATION IN BRAZIL

A system of racial classification developed in Brazil that blurred racial distinctions, a result of the absence of the one-drop rule. Why did this occur? One must look to Brazilian history for an answer. First, emigration from Portugal to Brazil during the first two centuries of colonization was small scale and largely male. As such, once the importation of black slaves got under way, the people of African origin going to Brazil vastly outnumbered those from Europe. The forced passage of more than 3 million Africans to Brazil in the seventeenth and eighteenth centuries was ten times the number of slaves who were brought to North America. Most slaves worked on sugar plantations in northeast Brazil, and later in mining gold in the southeast and on coffee plantations in the south. Even with the increase in migration from Portugal to Brazil spurred by the discovery of gold in the state of Minas Gerais in the eighteenth century, by the time of independence from Portugal, in 1822, well over two-thirds of Brazil's population of 4 million was of African or mixed heritage.

Not all blacks and people of mixed race were slaves, however. A sizeable but unknown percentage were free people of color, descendants of unions between Portuguese, Africans, and Brazil's indigenous population. What is key here is the large number of free people of color in relation to the number of whites. This contrasts with the situation in the United States, where 80 percent of the population was white. Even in the American South, no state had a majority population of African origin.

Why the difference? Compared to the flow of people from the British Isles to the North American colonies, emigration from Portugal to Brazil was relatively sparse. There were simply too few Portuguese to provide the labor for the myriad economic and military functions that slaves themselves could not perform. White slave owners needed plantation foremen and hands to guard their property and hunt for runaway slaves. Labor was also required to staff the ranches that provided the oxen and horses so necessary to the sugar industry. There was also a growing demand for artisans in the colony's towns and cities, and for farmers who could help feed the burgeoning slave population. With relatively few people of European origin, most of these positions were filled by the growing population of free blacks and Mulattoes. In the United States, however, the influx of African slaves occurred only after a large intermediate class of whites had been established, so there was nowhere for the freed slave, whether Mulatto or black, to go.

Hence, in the United States, the one-drop rule became a way of segregating all nonwhites—of whatever shade—into a singular, undifferentiated "black" category. Because of prejudice and discrimination, those in this category could not compete with the white majority. But no one would have gained from such a rule in Brazil, for the large black and Mulatto component of the population rarely competed directly with the nation's relatively small white segment.

BRAZIL: A RACIAL PARADISE?

It has been claimed that Brazilians lack racial prejudice because of the absence of the one-drop rule and the myriad of racial terms in daily use. It is undeniable that many Brazilians do believe that their land is a "racial democracy," one without prejudice towards its darker-skinned citizens. They compare race relations in their homeland favorably with those in the United States, highlighting their nation's racial harmony. This harmonious multiracial heritage thesis is mirrored in the widely cited view of Gilberto Freyre, one of Brazil's preeminent twentieth-century scholars, who wrote that "with respect to race relations the Brazilian situation is probably the nearest approach to paradise to be found anywhere in the world" (Freyre 1963, p. 9). In the 1930s, Freyre was instrumental in recasting discussions of Brazil's multiracial legacy, making it a source of pride rather than shame, as it had been throughout most of the nineteenth and early twentieth centuries. He asserted that because of its unique blending of African, European, and Amerindian elements, Brazil is a tolerant racial democracy, entirely lacking in harsh racism. This prideful representation has become part of national discourse.

It has been said that this ideology shapes the contours of interracial behavior in Brazil, smoothing its edges. And, it is, indeed, the case that there is quite widespread miscegenation and intermarriage among Brazil's diverse racial groups, and that Brazil has never had an organized system of segregation based solely on race as existed in the American south. Moreover, the notion of a continuum of shades of color plays into the racial democracy ideal because such slight phenotypical variations make it difficult or impossible to discriminate against individuals solely based on their physical appearance.

Nonetheless, this rather rosy picture of race relations in Brazil has been strongly contested. Some scholars suggest, for example, that there has been an over-emphasis on color gradations, and they have questioned the degree to which such blurred linguistic distinctions have concrete consequences for an individual's well-being. Others claim that, despite the wide variety of color terms in use in Brazil, there is still a great divide between whites and nonwhites. It has long been known that prejudice and negative stereotypes against dark skin and Negroid features are widespread in the country. In short, scholars have begun to challenge this national myth, attempting to show that race relations are characterized by exclusion, not inclusion, and that fair-skinned Brazilians continue to be privileged and hold a disproportionate share of the nation's power and wealth.

RACE AND SOCIAL CLASS

Social scientists have long argued that discrimination in Brazil is more a matter of social class than of race, that one's life chances as a poor person in Brazil are bleak, regardless of one's color. While whites and nonwhites do not have equal social standing in Brazil, and while dark-skinned people are more likely to be poor than light skinned people, scholars have posited that all members of the national lower class are equally lacking in opportunities—regardless of race—because social class largely determines where one lives, attends school, works, and socializes. In Brazil, it is suggested, racial discrimination is relatively mild, while discrimination in terms of social class is sharp and pervasive. Finally, it has long been said that in Brazil membership in the lower class, and the disabilities that go along with it, are akin to those of belonging to a racial minority in the United States.

Researchers are questioning this "class over racism" thesis, however, because it has been shown that even when they hold markers of social class such as income and education as constants, people of color fare worse than whites in certain aspects of life, including rates of infant mortality and average life expectancy. While it is true that the color gap in life expectancy and child mortality diminished during the last decades of the twentieth century, whites continue to have longer life expectancies than nonwhites. Research also suggests that even when socioeconomic factors are held constant, the race of the mother continues to have a strong effect on infant mortality, and that this is likely due to differences in health care and housing.

Additional studies have shown the presence of discrimination in other areas, including educational and occupational opportunities and wages. Children of color enter school later and leave school earlier than white children, and they have a lower probability of being in school at any given age. People of color are also disproportionately employed in the lowest-paying occupations in Brazil, a fact likely linked to the deficit in education. One study found that—when matched for education and

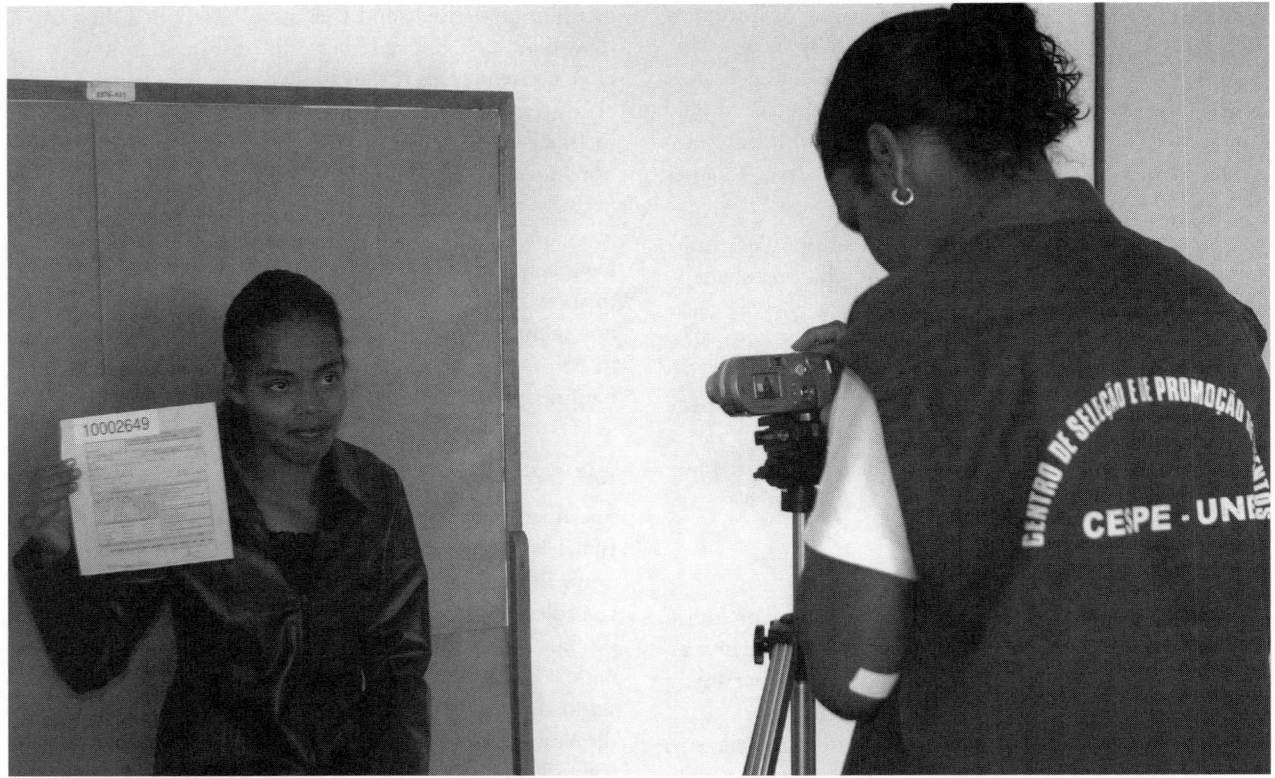

Brazilian Quota Program. *A young woman is photographed in April 2004 to establish that she is black, in order to be eligible for a quota program at the University of Brasilia.* © JAMIL BITTAR/REUTERS/CORBIS.

job experience—nonwhites, both male and female, have lower wages than whites of either sex. This new research suggests that racial discrimination, independent of social class, explains such findings.

Are these different views of race relations in Brazil irreconcilable? Perhaps it is just that their levels of analysis are different. Followers of the Freyre school emphasize horizontal relations between the races, stressing their easygoing interactions and relaxed sociability. But those who question the racial democracy ideal underscore vertical relations between the races, pointing to the widespread disparities in life opportunities, as evidenced in the studies cited.

These two views have been interpreted as a generational divide. In the years following World War II, Brazilian and North American scholars almost invariably viewed the Brazilian paradigm as a far kinder and gentler model than that of the United States, with its ugly history of blatant racism and segregation. But since the 1970s, a new generation of scholars has questioned what they see as an idealistic interpretation of the racial situation in Brazil. They have sought, through their research, to unmask the profound racial inequalities in that nation.

GROWING RACIAL CONSCIOUSNESS IN BRAZIL

The discourse on Brazil as a racial paradise long served to dampen Afro-Brazilian social and political movements. Moreover, because of the absence of the one-drop rule, racial consciousness has always been more muted in Brazil than in the United States, making it more difficult to organize on the basis of race. Then, too, until recent years, the traditional claim that Brazil had harmonious race relations compared with the United States led the Brazilian government to do almost nothing to address the issue of racial discrimination, other than passing a largely ignored law criminalizing it.

Still, some evidence does suggest that Brazil has been moving toward a system of racial classification similar to that of the United States. The multitude of racial terms commonly used by Brazilians may be giving way to a bifurcate system of *negro* and *blanco* (black and white). On the other hand, the more inclusive term *Afro-brasileiro* (Afro-Brazilian) has gained popularity, particularly among political activists, and more groups celebrating Brazil's African heritage have emerged.

Nevertheless, it was not until the late 1990s that Fernando Henrique Cardoso, the president of Brazil, officially acknowledged the existence of racial discrimination in

Brazil. He followed this up by appointing a national commission to propose remedies. In 2003 an affirmative action program (called *discriminação positiva* or "positive discrimination") was instituted for university admissions. This was a quota system intended to enhance the educational opportunities for nonwhites (who then made up only 2 percent of university students) and close the socioeconomic gap between the races. A number of Brazilian universities began reserving roughly 20 percent of their places for nonwhite and public school students. The next president of Brazil, Luiz Inácio "Lula" Da Silva, expanded these initiatives by creating the Special Ministry to Promote Racial Equality and initiating additional legislation.

Brazil's embrace of affirmative action generated a backlash, however, particularly among some elements of the white elite, who argued that racial preferences were unconstitutional and that affirmative action was an "imported" ideology foreign to Brazil. The prestigious State University of Rio de Janeiro, which led the way by instituting reserved places for students of color in 2002, faces legal challenges from hundreds of private school graduates who claim they were unfairly denied admission under the new policy.

Ironically, in trying to take advantage of university affirmative action programs, some white middle-class Brazilians have initiated the one-drop rule by claiming to have a black ancestor. Said one university administrator of the practice: "It's disappointing because that means the program is not always benefiting poor or underprivileged kids. But at the same time, what can you do? We have no idea really who is black and who is not. This is Brazil."

SEE ALSO *Affirmative Action; Blackness in Latin America; HIV and AIDS; Latin American Racial Transformations; Multiracial Identities; Racial Formations; Social Welfare States.*

BIBLIOGRAPHY

Brown, Walton L. 1997. *Democracy and Race in Brazil, Britain, and the United States.* Lewiston, NY: Edwin Mellen Press.

Degler, Carl N. 1971. *Neither Black nor White: Slavery and Race Relations in Brazil and the United States.* New York: Macmillan.

Freyre, Gilberto. 1933 (1986). *The Masters and the Slaves: A Study in the Development of Brazilian Society.* Translated by Samuel Putnam. Berkeley: University of California Press.

———. 1959. *New World in the Tropics: The Culture of Modern Brazil.* New York: Knopf.

Goldstein, Donna. 2003. *Laughter Out of Place: Race, Class, Violence, and Sexuality in a Rio Shantytown.* Berkeley: University of California Press.

Harris, Marvin. 1964. *Patterns of Race in the Americas.* New York: Walker.

Lovell, Peggy, and Charles H. Wood. 1998. "Skin Color, Racial Identity, and Life Chances in Brazil." *Latin American Perspectives* 25 (3): 90–109.

Sheriff, Robin E. 2001. *Dreaming Equality: Color, Race and Racism in Urban Brazil.* New Brunswick, NJ: Rutgers University Press.

Skidmore, Thomas. 1974. *Black into White: Race and Nationality in Brazilian Thought.* New York: Oxford University Press.

———. 2003. "Racial Mixture and Affirmative Action: The Cases of Brazil and the United States." *American Historical Review* 108 (5): 1391–1396.

Telles, Edward E. 2004. *Race in Another America: The Significance of Skin Color in Brazil.* Princeton, NJ: Princeton University Press.

Twine, France Winddance. 1998. *Racism in a Racial Democracy: The Maintenance of White Supremacy in Brazil.* New Brunswick, NJ: Rutgers University Press.

Wood, Charles H., and José Alberto Magno de Carvalho. 1988. *The Demography of Inequality in Brazil.* Cambridge, U.K.: Cambridge University Press.

Maxine L. Margolis

BROWN, JOHN
1800–1859

John Brown was born on May 9, 1800, in Torrington, Connecticut, and he died on the scaffold in Charlestown, Virginia, on December 2, 1859. He was the only white abolitionist who repeatedly took up arms against slavery before the Civil War. Convinced that the standard tactics of persuasion and politics had done nothing to dislodge the South's "peculiar institution," the deeply religious Brown became the self-appointed leader of a personal holy war against slavery. His violent forays against slavery in Kansas and later at Harpers Ferry, Virginia, helped intensify the sectional animosities that led to the Civil War.

The second son of Owen Brown (1771–1856) and Ruth Mills (1772–1808), John Brown inherited his parents' hatred of slavery and devotion to Calvinistic Christianity, and he was taught to respect people of all races. When he was three, the family moved from Connecticut to Hudson, Ohio, where his father ran a tannery. At the age of twelve, young John witnessed a slave boy being beaten and driven outdoors to sleep in the cold. He later claimed that this cruel incident "in the end made him a most *determined Abolitionist*," leading him to swear "*Eternal war* with Slavery."

When he was sixteen, Brown briefly attended schools in New England, with the aim of training for the Congregational ministry. However, financial difficulties and eye troubles forced him to return to Ohio, where he started his own tannery. In 1820 he was married to Dianthe Lusk; the couple eventually had seven children. In 1825 he moved to New Richmond, Pennsylvania, where, for ten years, he ran a highly successful tannery with fifteen employees. His property was also a haven for fugitive slaves.

Dianthe died in 1832, and within a year Brown married Mary Ann Day, with whom he had thirteen children over the next two decades. Of his twenty children, only eight would outlive him. Among the remainder, two died shortly after being born, six were victims of childhood illnesses, one was scalded to death in a kitchen accident, and three others—Frederick, Oliver, and Watson—died while accompanying their father in his war against slavery.

In 1836 Brown moved to Kent, Ohio, where he took up real estate speculation. He was battered by the depression of 1837–1842, however. He tried to stay afloat by trading livestock and surveying, but in 1842 he declared bankruptcy. He entered into partnership with the Ohio businessman Simon Perkins in a wool distribution company based in Springfield, Massachusetts. Serving as a middleman between western wool growers and eastern manufacturers, Brown proved to be an energetic but maladroit businessman. With the business faltering, Brown tried to salvage it in 1849 by going to England to find foreign buyers for American wool. That effort failed, and his partnership with Perkins soon dissolved.

At this point, Brown had long been active in the Underground Railroad. In the late 1830s, enraged by the murder of the Illinois antislavery editor Elijah Lovejoy, he began to plot a military response to slavery. At a service in memory of Lovejoy, he rose, lifted his right hand, and said, "Here, before God, in the presence of these witnesses, from this time, I consecrate my life to the destruction of slavery!"

In early 1851 in Springfield, Brown founded a cadre of blacks, called the League of Gileadites, aimed at encouraging armed resistance to the recently passed Fugitive Slave Act. He took his family to upstate New York to live in North Elba, where a colony of blacks occupied land purchased for them by the antislavery philanthropist Gerrit Smith. Brown started a farm and tried to help his black neighbors establish an agricultural community. He worked with them, surveyed their lands, and socialized with them. North Elba was his principal base for his remaining years, and it is the place where he chose to be buried.

In 1855 Brown joined five of his sons in the Kansas Territory, the scene of a fierce struggle between proslavery and antislavery forces. Brown raised a small band and engaged in several pitched battles against proslavery militants. On May 24, 1856, in Pottawatomie, Kansas, he led a party of eight armed men on a nighttime raid, during which they hauled five proslavery settlers out of their cabins and slaughtered them with broadswords. In late December 1858, he invaded the neighboring slave state of Missouri with twenty followers. The men liberated eleven slaves and traveled with them for eighty-two days and more than 1,100 miles to Detroit, where the blacks took a ferry to Windsor, Canada.

Brown's most influential act was his October 16, 1859, raid on Harpers Ferry, Virginia. He had with him a band of twenty-one men, including five blacks and two of his sons. He intended to take over the arsenal at Harpers Ferry, forcibly liberate slaves in the region, and then escape with the freed blacks to the nearby Appalachian Mountains. He hoped to use mountain hideaways to evade capture as he moved southward, making periodic raids on plantations in order to free additional slaves who would become part of his growing army of liberation. His ultimate goal was to initiate a political process that would lead to slavery's demise. He ignored warnings, however, by Frederick Douglass, among others, of the futility of his plans. In the end, Brown stalled too long at Harpers Ferry and, after a bloody battle, was taken captive by federal troops under Colonel Robert E. Lee. He was found guilty of murder, treason, and inciting a slave revolt. By the time of his execution on December 2, he had become a sharply divisive figure on the national scene, increasingly admired in the North and vilified in the South.

Brown has remained controversial since his death. His reputation peaked during Reconstruction, when he was honored as an antislavery martyr, but it plummeted during the period of Jim Crow, when he was widely regarded as a murderer, fanatic, and madman. The civil rights movement of the 1950s and 1960s brought increased sympathy for his racial agenda and his uncompromising stance on slavery. Having been close to blacks, including such abolitionist leaders as Frederick Douglass and Harriet Tubman, Brown has been long revered by African Americans. W. E. B. Du Bois hailed him as "the man who of all Americans has perhaps come nearest to touching the real souls of black folk."

BIBLIOGRAPHY

DeCaro, Louis A., Jr. 2002. *"Fire from the Midst of You": A Religious Life of John Brown.* New York: New York University Press.

Oates, Stephen B. 1970. *To Purge This Land with Blood: A Biography of John Brown.* New York: Harper & Row.

Reynolds, David S. 2005. *John Brown, Abolitionist: The Man Who Killed Slavery, Sparked the Civil War, and Seeded Civil Rights.* New York: Alfred A. Knopf.

Villard, Oswald Garrison. 1910. *John Brown, 1800-1859: A Biography Fifty Years After.* Boston: Houghton Mifflin.

David S. Reynolds

BROWN V. BOARD OF EDUCATION

The Supreme Court's historic school desegregation decision, *Brown v. Board of Education of Topeka*, was one of the most significant events of the twentieth century. The 1954 ruling outlawed racial segregation in public schools and led to the dismantling of a legal regime that had relegated African Americans to a subordinated position in American society. *Brown* was the culmination of a carefully orchestrated litigation campaign by the National Association for the Advancement of Colored People (NAACP), which had challenged segregation in a series of lawsuits spanning two decades.

The events that led to *Brown* commenced more than a half-century earlier, when the Reconstruction era ended and southern states began to enact laws that established a system of racial segregation. In 1892, a test case was organized in New Orleans, Louisiana, that challenged an ordinance requiring segregation on public transportation. Acting on a prearranged plan, Homer Plessy was arrested after refusing to leave a railroad car reserved for white passengers. Plessy's lawyers were confident that the law violated the Fourteenth and Thirteenth Amendments of the U.S. Constitution because it treated African Americans differently and less favorably than white passengers. In 1896, however, the Supreme Court ruled in *Plessy v. Ferguson* that, "the enforced separation of the races . . . neither abridges the privileges or immunities of the colored man, deprives him of this property without due process of law, nor denies him equal protection of the law, within the meaning of the Fourteenth Amendment."

Plessy endorsed segregation and established the "separate but equal" doctrine. The Court held that segregation laws did not violate the Fourteenth Amendment if the facilities provided for blacks were equal to those reserved for whites. Reflecting the racial sentiments of the time, the Court concluded that "[i]f one race be inferior to the other socially, the Constitution of the United States cannot put them on the same plane." After *Plessy*, the Fourteenth and Fifteenth Amendments were essentially nullified in the South. African Americans were disenfranchised, confined to substandard housing in segregated neighborhoods, and excluded from all but the lowest-paying, least desirable occupations.

THE NAACP'S LEGAL CAMPAIGN AGAINST SEGREGATION

In 1909, the NAACP was established to promote the equality rights of African Americans. After years of unsuccessful lobbying and protest efforts, however the organization shifted its focus. In 1935 the organization hired Charles H. Houston, a brilliant, Harvard-trained visionary, to lead a campaign that would challenge segregation in the courts. Houston was the dean of the Howard University School of Law, where he inspired the generation of African-American lawyers who waged the legal battle against segregation. Houston was the architect of the NAACP's legal strategy, and Howard University was his laboratory.

By the early 1930s the separate but equal doctrine was firmly entrenched in the law. Given the conservative legal climate of the time, Houston did not want to risk a reaffirmation of *Plessy*. Instead, he devised an indirect approach: the "equalization strategy." When the plan was implemented, cases would be filed arguing that states operating segregated schools were in violation of the Fourteenth Amendment based on the substandard and demonstrably unequal facilities maintained for black students. Houston calculated that if the equality aspect of *Plessy*'s "separate but equal" doctrine were enforced, states would be compelled to make black schools physically and otherwise equal to white institutions. Local school districts, however, would not be able to bear the resulting economic burden. Under the pressure of litigation, segregation would eventually collapse under its own weight.

The litigation campaign focused on graduate and professional schools, where the southern states were most vulnerable. Several publicly funded black colleges had been established in the South, but virtually none of them provided graduate or professional training. The first "equalization" case, *Pearson v. Murray*, involved the efforts of Donald Murray, a black student, to be admitted to the University of Maryland Law School. Houston and a young lawyer named Thurgood Marshall represented the student. They argued that the university violated the Fourteenth Amendment because it had failed to establish a law school for black students. At the trial's conclusion, the judge ordered the university to admit Murray to the entering class the following semester. A similar case, *Missouri ex rel. Gaines v. Canada*, was filed in Missouri, with the same arguments being made. When that case reached the Supreme Court, it ordered the black student's admission to the University of Missouri's Law School.

Murray and *Gaines* were decided in the late 1930s. With the outbreak of World War II in 1941, the NAACP's attention was diverted to other matters. When the war ended in 1945, conditions were very different from the conservative legal climate of the 1930s. There were many factors that directly and indirectly influenced civil rights efforts. Significantly, the United States and its European Allies had prevailed against a Nazi regime that was premised on racial supremacy. Having fought Nazism abroad, African -American veterans were determined to fight racism at home.

Elite attitudes toward racial injustice also showed evidence of change. President Harry Truman commissioned a study that resulted in a 1947 report, *To Secure These Rights*, which took a strong, pro–civil rights position. In 1948 Truman issued an executive order requiring the desegregation of the armed forces. In addition, the "scientific" racism of previous decades was on the wane. One of the era's most influential publications was *An American Dilemma* (1944), a two-volume study prepared by a team of researchers led by the Swedish economist, Gunner Myrdal. It explored, in considerable detail, the adverse effects of discrimination and segregation on black and white Americans, and it urged the repeal of segregation laws.

Moreover, the United States and the Soviet Union were competing for influence with the postcolonial democracies that were emerging in Africa and Asia. America's mistreatment of its black citizens undermined its claim as "the land of the free" and provided an easy target for anti-American propaganda. In "*Brown* as a Cold War Case" (2004), Professor Mary Dudziak argues persuasively that the Supreme Court justices who decided *Brown* were probably influenced by the political realities of the cold war. These changing circumstances were the context in which the final school desegregation cases were decided.

In 1946 the NAACP filed a suit against the University of Oklahoma. The Supreme Court held, in *Sipuel v. Board of Regents*, that the university was obligated to provide legal instruction to black students. A similar case, *Sweatt v. Painter*, was filed in Texas and another, *McLaurin v. Board of Regents*, was also brought in Oklahoma. The Supreme Court issued decisions in both of these cases on the same day in 1950. In opinions that acknowledged the stigmatic and other intangible injuries that segregation caused, the Court ruled in the NAACP's favor, but it stopped short of reversing *Plessy*.

After the rulings in *Sweatt* and *McLaurin*, the NAACP lawyers decided that an adequate foundation for a direct challenge to *Plessy* had been established. Eventually, six cases were filed in five jurisdictions by Thurgood Marshall and other NAACP lawyers: *Brown v. Board of Education of Topeka* arose in Kansas; *Briggs v. Elliott* involved schools in South Carolina; *Davis v. County School Board of Prince Edward County* was brought in Virginia; and there was a District of Columbia proceeding, *Bolling v. Sharpe*. The two other cases, *Belton v. Gebhart* and *Bulah v. Gebhart*, took place in Delaware.

The cases were consolidated and argued in the Supreme Court in December 1952, but they were held over and re-argued in December 1953. The decision in *Brown v. Board of Education* was announced on May 17, 1954. Chief Justice Earl Warren read the unanimous opinion to a packed courtroom. It concluded that, under the Equal Protection Clause of the Fourteenth Amendment, "separate educational facilities are inherently unequal." The decision represented the beginning of the end of segregation.

THE ERA OF MASSIVE RESISTANCE

The Supreme Court's 1954 decision did not address a remedy for school segregation. It was not until 1955, in *Brown v. Board of Education II*, that the Supreme Court remanded the cases and ordered the school boards to develop plans in which desegregation would proceed with "all deliberate speed" under the supervision of the local federal courts. While the *Brown* decision has been praised as the decisive blow to American Jim Crow, *Brown II* has been criticized as a weak decision that set no real timetable for desegregation and emboldened southern racists. Immediately after *Brown II*, white southern politicians and community leaders, determined to fight desegregation by any means necessary, embraced a strategy known as "massive resistance." State legislatures passed laws to impede implementation of the *Brown* decision, school boards sought to evade compliance by closing schools, opening state funded "segregation academies" and, where necessary, embracing token desegregation; politicians such as Governor George Wallace of Alabama and Governor Orval Faubus of Arkansas exploited and encouraged mass public opposition to integration; and acts of violence and intimidation were carried out against black communities and activists.

Civil Rights Victory, 1954. *The winning attorneys in the* Brown v. Board of Education *case pose outside the U.S. Supreme Court building after the landmark case was decided. Standing left to right are George E.C. Hayes, Thurgood Marshall, and James Nabri.* © BETTMANN/CORBIS.

The decision in *Brown,* and white resistance to it, helped to spark the era of civil rights activism. Mass marches, "sit ins," and other forms of nonviolent protest activities were organized in localities across the South as grassroots activists sought to expand the desegregation principle from education to other areas of civic life. Martin Luther King Jr., A. Phillip Randolph, Dorothy Height, Bayard Rustin, Ella Baker, and others emerged as leaders of the movement. Yet despite the unprecedented levels of demonstrations and other protest activities during the 1950s and 1960s, very little progress was made toward school desegregation. In 1961 there were no black students attending white schools in Alabama, Mississippi, South Carolina, Florida, and Georgia.

In the late 1960s the Supreme Court finally took steps to end to the South's "massive resistance." *Griffin v. County School Board of Prince Edward County* dealt with a school district involved in the original *Brown* cases that had closed all of its schools to avoid desegregation. In 1964, Prince Edward County was ordered to reopen its schools. In the 1969 case *Alexander v. Holmes County Board of Education,* the Supreme Court ruled that the "continued operation of segregated schools under a standard allowing 'all deliberate speed' for desegregation is no longer constitutionally permissible... the obligation of every school district is to terminate dual school systems at once and operate now and hereafter only unitary schools." In *Green v. County School Board of New Kent County* (1968), the Court held that states that operated segregated schools had an affirmative duty to eradicate all vestiges of the segregated system "root and branch." In *Swann v. Charlotte-Mecklenburg Board of Education,* decided in 1971, the Court endorsed busing as a means of achieving racial balance in individual schools.

School desegregation efforts took place against a backdrop of residential segregation. In the 1940s and 1950s, white families were rapidly moving to suburban communities. This demographic shift was facilitated by a prosperous postwar economy, and by subsidy programs such as mortgages guaranteed by the Veterans Administration and Federal Housing Administration. Yet black families with the resources to purchase homes in suburban neighborhoods were excluded by discriminatory policies, many of which were imposed by the federal government.

The effect of racially segregated housing patterns on school desegregation efforts was the focus of *Milliken v. Bradley,* a 1974 case involving schools in Detroit, Michigan. As a consequence of "white flight" to suburban communities, the schools in Detroit were rapidly shifting to predominately black enrollments. The lawyers in *Milliken* argued that racial balance could not be achieved without including the suburban districts in the desegregation plan.

The Supreme Court held that suburban districts could not be required to participate in court-ordered desegregation plans unless it could be proven that their actions contributed to segregation in the jurisdiction in which the case arose. This meant that there could be no court-ordered busing across district lines without a showing of an interdistrict violation. In most localities, therefore, suburban districts were effectively insulated from the desegregation process.

THE RESEGREGATION DECISIONS

Court-supervised school desegregation proceeded slowly for several years after *Milliken,* relying heavily on intra-district busing to achieve racial balance in schools. In the early 1990s, the Supreme Court revised its approach with a number of "resegregation" decisions: *Board of Education of Oklahoma City v. Dowell*; *Freeman v. Pitts*; and *Missouri v. Jenkins.* In *Dowell,* the Supreme Court modified the standard for determining "unitary status"—the point at which the desegregation obligation has been satisfied and court supervision is no longer necessary. The Court ruled in *Dowell* that the test for determining unitary status was whether the school board "had complied in good faith with the [original] desegregation decree," and whether all "vestiges of past discrimination had been eliminated to the extent practicable." In *Freeman v. Pitts,* a case involving a school district adjacent to Atlanta, Georgia, the Court found that when segregated schools persist because of changes in the racial composition of neighborhoods or other "external" factors, school districts could not be held responsible unless those conditions were caused by actions taken by school officials.

Dowell and *Freeman* eviscerated the *Green* standard, which established an obligation to eliminate all vestiges of segregation "root and branch." Under the Court's relaxed formula, school districts were obligated to eradicate vestiges of segregation only to "the extent practicable." This was affirmed in *Jenkins,* where the majority ruled that the test for determining unitary status was not a determination that all vestiges of the formerly segregated system had been eliminated "root and branch," but whether school districts complied in good faith with the desegregation decrees, and whether the remnants of past discrimination had been eliminated to the "extent practicable." The Court also found that segregated housing patterns, which affected the racial composition of schools, would not preclude a unitary status finding unless they could be directly attributed to the actions of school officials.

The assumption underlying the resegregation decisions is that schools only have to desegregate to the extent that it is possible to do so. Any segregation that continues is caused by housing patterns that reflect what the Supreme Court characterized as the "private choices" of individual families. This is a debatable premise, because black and Latino families do not have the range of housing choices that are available to whites with comparable incomes and credit histories. Studies regularly produced by the U.S. Department of Housing and Urban Development and other organizations demonstrate that the choices of these groups are constrained by discriminatory practices that perpetuate segregated neighborhoods.

The Supreme Court's redefinition of unitary status requires lower courts to hold that the desegregation obligation has been satisfied, even when school enrollments reflect the segregated housing patterns of the neighborhoods in which they are located. This has led to unitary status findings in school districts across the nation. As high levels of residential segregation persist in most urban neighborhoods, public schools in those communities have been resegregating since the mid-1990s.

CRITICISMS OF THE *BROWN* DECISION

Critics of the *Brown* decision fall into two categories: those that argue that *Brown* went too far, and those that argue that it did not go far enough. Some critics, such as Michael Klarman, have argued that *Brown* unnecessarily radicalized the social and political climate in the South. These critics claim that, without *Brown,* segregation would have ended in a more gradual manner with broader support among southern whites. Other critics, including Derrick Bell, assert *Brown* put too great a focus on desegregation at the expense of educational quality, and point out that one consequence of *Brown* has been the loss of black institutional control of some schools, to the detriment of black students. In Bell's view, competent and caring instruction in an all-black environment would have been preferable to the obstacles encountered by many black students in the years following the *Brown* decision. A third group of critics argue that, notwithstanding *Brown*'s holding, a failure of enforcement has made the decision impotent. Gary Orfield and James Patterson have each identified a trend toward resegregation in Brown's aftermath, a persistent black-white achievement gap, and a mood of pessimism at *Brown*'s uncertain legacy.

Brown v. Board of Education was among the most important and far-reaching Supreme Court decisions of the twentieth century, and its imprint extended well beyond public school desegregation. The decision sparked the civil rights movement of the 1950s and 1960s and ultimately led to the nullification of a network of state and local laws that enforced discrimination and segregation. Those in a position to do so took advantage of the educational, employment, and other opportunities that were not available to African Americans during the first half of the twentieth century. For this segment of the African-American population, the civil rights movement created unprecedented avenues for advancement.

However, the benefits that flowed from the *Brown* decision have not been evenly distributed across the urban landscape. For the one-fourth of the African-American population that have low incomes and reside in the nation's inner cities, the *Brown* decision has had little tangible affect. Families that reside in those communities endure conditions that are, in many ways, as distressed as those their forbears endured during the depths of the segregation era. They suffer from high levels of unemployment, substandard educational opportunities, and unsafe communities.

SEE ALSO *Houston, Charles Hamilton; Marshall, Thurgood; NAACP; NAACP: Legal Actions, 1935-1955; Plessy v. Ferguson.*

BIBLIOGRAPHY

PRINT RESOURCES

Cottrol, Robert J., Raymond T. Diamond, and Leland B. Ware. 2003. *Brown v. Board of Education: Caste, Culture, and the Constitution.* Lawrence: University Press of Kansas.

Dudziak, Mary. 2004. "Brown as a Cold War Case." *Journal of American History* 91 (1): 32.

Friedman, Leon, ed. 1983. *Argument: The Oral Argument before the Supreme Court in Brown vs. Board of Education of Topeka, 1952–55.* New York: Chelsea House.

Greenberg, Jack. 1994. *Crusaders in the Courts: How a Dedicated Band of Lawyers Fought for the Civil Rights Revolution.* New York: Basic Books.

Irons, Peter H. 2002. *Jim Crow's Children: The Broken Promise of the Brown Decision.* New York: Viking.

Kluger, Richard. 1975. *Simple Justice: The History of Brown v. Board of Education and Black America's Struggle for Equality.* New York: Knopf.

Lewis, David Levering. 1994. *W.E.B. Du Bois: Biography of a Race, 1868–1919.* New York: Henry Holt.

Martin, Waldo E. 1998. *Brown v. Board of Education: A Brief History with Documents.* Boston: St. Martin's.

Massey, Douglas S., and Nancy A. Denton. 1993. *American Apartheid: Segregation and the Making of the Underclass.* Cambridge, MA: Harvard University Press.

McNeil, Genna Rae. 1983. *Groundwork: Charles Hamilton Houston and the Struggle for Civil Rights.* Philadelphia: University of Pennsylvania Press.

Motley, Constance Baker. 1998. *Equal Justice Under Law: An Autobiography.* New York: Farrar, Straus, and Giroux.

Orfield, Gary, and Susan E. Eaton. 1996. *Dismantling Desegregation: The Quiet Reversal of Brown v. Board of Education.* New York: New Press.

Patterson, James T. 2001. *Brown v. Board of Education: A Civil Rights Milestone and Its Troubled Legacy.* New York: Oxford University Press.

Tushnet, Mark V. 1994. *Making Civil Rights Law: Thurgood Marshall and the Supreme Court, 1936–1961.* New York: Oxford University Press.

Williams, Juan. 1998. *Thurgood Marshall: American Revolutionary.* New York: Times Books.

COURT CASES

Alexander v. Holmes County Board of Education, 396 U.S. 19 (1969).

Board of Education of Oklahoma City v. Dowell, 498 U.S. 237 (1991).

Brown v. Board of Education, 347 U.S. 483 (1954).

Fisher v. Hurst, 333 U.S. 147 (1948).

Freeman v. Pitts, 503 U.S. 467 (1992).

Green v. County School Board of New Kent County, Virginia, 391 U.S. 430 (1968).

Griffin v. County School Board of Prince Edward County, 377 US 218 (1964).

McLaurin v. Okla. State Regents for Higher Educ., 339 U.S. 637 (1950).

Milliken v. Bradley, 418 US 717 (1974).

Missouri v. Jenkins, 515 U.S. 70 (1994).

Missouri ex rel. Gaines v. Canada, 305 U.S. 337 (1938).

Plessy v. Ferguson, 163 U.S. 537 (1896).

Sipuel v. Bd. of Regents, 332 U.S. 631 (1948).

Swann v. Charlotte-Mecklenburg Board of Education, 402 US 1 (1971).

Sweatt v. Painter, 339 U.S. 629 (1950).

Leland Ware

BUFFALO SOLDIERS

The black soldiers known as "Buffalo Soldiers" played a crucial role in the fight for black equality in the armed forces. They were created and served in the United States military during perhaps the most volatile period in the history of America, the post–Civil War era. Often the victims of racial discrimination, the Buffalo Soldiers conducted themselves with dignity and honor. Their efforts during peacetime, as well as during conflicts such as the Indian Wars and the Spanish American War, clearly established that blacks were capable soldiers, and thus aided in the desegregation of the armed forces.

While blacks fought in both the Revolutionary War and the War of 1812, it was their participation in the Civil War that led to the creation of organized black regiments. Because a policy established in 1820 barred blacks from serving in the regular army, many of them fought for the Union Army in volunteer regiments such as the Seventy-third Regiment of U.S. Colored Troops, Hunter's Regiment, the First Kansas Colored, and the Fifty-fourth and Fifty-fifth Regiments of Massachusetts. In *The Forgotten Heroes: The Story of the Buffalo Soldiers*, Clinton Cox notes that by the end of the Civil War, in excess of 180,000 black men had fought for the Union Army, and that more than 38,000 of these soldiers died in the war.

The bravery that blacks exemplified during the Civil War led Congress to consider the formation of black divisions in 1866. Opinions varied on this idea. Some objected, claiming that blacks could not perform military duties as well as whites, that they were unwanted in the North, and that in the South they would be a nagging reminder of the Union's victory over the Confederacy.

In spite of the opposition, Congress voted to enlist six black regiments for two reasons. First, given their strong record of participation in the Civil War, several members of Congress voted to create the black regiments out of a sense of fairness. Second, Congress realized that blacks were less likely than whites to desert, because they had fewer opportunities in civilian life. Therefore, on July 28, 1866, Congress passed an act establishing the Ninth and Tenth Cavalries and the Thirty-eighth, Thirty-ninth, Fortieth and Forty-first Infantry Divisions, which were later reorganized into the Twenty-fourth and Twenty-fifth Infantry Regiments.

Scores of blacks rushed to enlist for five-year terms at thirteen dollars per month. The men came from several states, including Louisiana, Georgia, Alabama, Kentucky, Tennessee, and Virginia. Their ages ranged from eighteen to thirty-four, and many of them were former slaves. According to Cox, a typical group of 100 recruits in the Ninth Cavalry had worked as soldiers, laborers, farmers, painters, and cooks prior to enlisting.

A group of 100 enlistees in the Tenth Cavalry had held similar positions, but they were from more diverse geographic locations, such as Missouri, New York, Massachusetts, Pennsylvania, New Jersey, and Halifax, Nova Scotia. In contrast to the men of the Ninth Calvary, the majority of these men had not been slaves. However, their societal position was made clear when they arrived for service and found that blacks had been deemed unfit to lead, and that all of the black regiments had white commanding officers.

THE INDIAN WARS

Ironically, the black regiments were primarily used during the Indian Wars (1775–1890), which pitted them against fellow people of color who were also being oppressed by the U.S. government. Native Americans had inhabited the land long before white settlers arrived, but the U.S. government viewed them as inferior and waged a campaign to remove them from the plains and onto reservations. In *Buffalo Soldiers*, Catherine Reef notes that the U.S. government's primary objective in the conflict had been clear since the early 1800s, when President Andrew Jackson declared that "the American people had a duty to bring a dense and civilized population to a land where only a few savage hunters lived" (1993, p. 21)

Despite the difficult nature of the conflict, the all-black regiments served with pride and distinction. They initially began patrolling the Great Plains in April 1867. Their main duties included removing tribes considered to be dangerous and mapping the unsettled western frontier for white settlers seeking land. Additionally, the soldiers helped to remove settlers from unassigned land and protect law-abiding citizens from Native Americans attempting to either reclaim or remain on the land that the federal government had taken away from them.

Although the all-black regiments' main duties did not involve fighting, there were many instances when they engaged the enemy. A notable battle occurred on August 1, 1867, when the Tenth Cavalry became involved in a skirmish with the Cheyennes after a panic-stricken railroad worker rode into their post near Fort Leavenworth, Kansas. He explained that Cheyenne warriors had attacked the workers' camp and killed seven men.

Under the command of Captain George Armes, thirty-four black soldiers mounted their horses and raced toward the camp. While riding, the troops found themselves surrounded by Cheyenne braves and a gunfight broke out. The Cheyennes had superior position and the soldiers were trapped. After approximately six hours of fighting the soldiers were low on ammunition. Realizing that they needed to escape in order to survive, Captain Armes gave the command and the soldiers broke through the circle, fleeing with nearly three hundred Cheyenne warriors in pursuit. The men rode hard for fifteen miles before they were met by reinforcements who assisted them in driving the Cheyennes away.

While the Tenth Cavalry survived the battle, thirteen soldiers were wounded and two were killed. Sergeant William Christy of Mercersburg, Pennsylvania, and Private Thomas Smith of South Carolina became the first black casualties of the Indian Wars.

While the Tenth Cavalry lost two men, they gained something significant from the battle—the nickname "buffalo soldiers." There are two popular theories explaining why the Cheyennes referred to the black troops as buffalo soldiers. One flattering theory contends that the Native Americans, who honored the buffalo because it fought ferociously when cornered, were impressed with the bravery and skills that the black soldiers exemplified while surrounded. Thus, the Cheyenne warriors likened them to the buffalo. A second theory posits that the Cheyennes referred to them as "buffalo soldiers" because they wore thick buffalo skins to stay warm during the harsh plains winters. When wrapped in the hides, their dark skin and curly hair reminded the Native Americans of the animal.

Regardless of which theory is true, Native Americans used it as a term of respect and the Tenth Cavalry embraced the name. Significantly, they included a buffalo as the primary symbol in the crest when they designed their regimental flag. While the name was initially given to the Tenth Cavalry, it was later used to refer to all of the black divisions.

The Buffalo Soldiers distinguished themselves as valiant troops during the Indian Wars. The service of Sergeant Emanuel Stance shows the manner in which they fought. On May 20 and 21, 1870, Stance and nine fellow members of Company F of the Ninth Cavalry engaged a band of Apaches while on patrol near their post at Fort McKavett, Texas. At the time, an Apache band was moving toward the Texas panhandle with a herd of horses and two white children that they had taken captive. Stance and the other soldiers charged the Native Americans, who abandoned their horses and fled toward the mountains. A warrior sharing a horse with one of the kidnapped children pushed him off into the brush to make his escape. The buffalo soldiers captured all nine of the horses that the Apaches left behind and the child eventually made his way to safety at the fort. The child's older brother remained with the Apaches before later being reunited with his parents.

The following morning, overloaded by the extra horses, Stance and his detail decided to return the animals to the fort. As they traveled back, they witnessed a group of approximately twenty Native Americans en route to attack a group of soldiers guarding a small herd of government horses. Stance again ordered his detail to charge and the Native Americans retaliated, but to no avail. They soon fled leaving behind five horses, which Stance and his men captured. As they continued their journey to Fort McKavett, the Native Americans followed them and launched a final attack. Again, Stance and his men successfully drove them away, eventually returning to the fort with fifteen captured horses and all of his men uninjured.

Stance's bravery did not go unnoticed. The skirmishes that he fought on May 20 and 21 marked his fourth and fifth encounters with Native Americans and, as in the previous battles, he demonstrated courage under fire. He distinguished himself so well that his commanding officer, Captain Henry Carroll, praised his performance. On June 20, 1870, based on Carroll's recommendation, Stance became the first black soldier in the U.S. Regular Army to receive the Congressional Medal of Honor.

FACING RACISM

Despite demonstrating loyalty to the U.S. government, the Buffalo Soldiers endured a great deal of racial discrimination while participating in the Indian Wars. Ironically, the white settlers that they were charged to protect were repeatedly hostile toward them. Their hatred of blacks often manifested itself in the form of violence. Events that occurred at San Angelo, a town adjacent to the Tenth Cavalry's post at Fort Concho, Texas, serve as a prime example of the kind of hostility that the Buffalo Soldiers had to endure.

Cox notes in *The Forgotten Heroes* that San Angelo was home to many seedy cowboys, ex-Confederate soldiers, and pimps and prostitutes. Unfortunately, the disreputable inhabitants demonstrated their intolerance of blacks on several occasions. In one instance, Private Hiram Pinder of the Ninth Cavalry was shot and killed by a white gambler in a saloon. The townspeople helped the killer escape and he was never captured. Twelve days after Pinder's death, Private William Watkins was singing and dancing for drinks in another saloon. He tired of performing and decided to quit for the evening, but a rancher named Tom McCarthy insisted that he continue. When Watkins refused, McCarthy shot and killed him. McCarthy then fled, but he was captured by soldiers who turned him over to the sheriff. Instead of jailing McCarthy, however, the sheriff allowed him to remain free because killing a

Buffalo Soldiers, circa 1895. *Members of a famed "Buffalo Soldier" cavalry regiment stand next to their horses. After the Civil War, the U.S. Congress authorized the formation of black regiments in the U.S. Army. These soldiers fought during the Indian Wars, the Spanish-American War, and other conflicts through World War II.* © UNDERWOOD AND UNDERWOOD/CORBIS.

black person was only considered a minor crime. When he was finally tried for the murder of Private Watkins, an all-white jury found him not guilty.

In addition to facing discrimination from civilians, the Buffalo Soldiers also encountered systemic prejudice within the military. For instance, black soldiers were always second to their white counterparts when equipment was distributed. White soldiers selected the most pristine weapons and best horses, leaving the Buffalo Soldiers with old rifles and worn-out mares. Furthermore, they were often forced to live in substandard housing infested with bugs and rodents.

Acts of discrimination against the Buffalo Soldiers extended beyond weapons and living quarters. They were constantly reminded of their place in society because high-ranking officers continually denigrated them or shunned them altogether. For example, Gerald Astor notes in *The Right to Fight: A History of African Americans in the Military* that when the Tenth Cavalry, commanded by Colonel William Grierson, initially arrived in Fort Leavenworth, Kansas, the post commander assigned the troops a campsite in a swamp, but he later criticized them for having muddy tents and uniforms. Furthermore, the post commander also informed the Buffalo Soldiers that they were not allowed within fifteen feet of white soldiers. Additionally, General George Custer refused to accept assignments leading black soldiers, while Captain Ambrose Hooker, commander of the Ninth Cavalry's Company E, referred to the Buffalo Soldiers as "baboons" and regularly used racial epithets toward them. Although the soldiers' complained about Hooker's behavior, no action was taken against him.

Lieutenant Henry O. Flipper serves as another notable example of how the Buffalo Soldiers were mistreated. In 1877 Flipper became the first black graduate of West Point, and he later became the first black commanding officer in the history of the U.S. Regular Army. After receiving his diploma, he passed on several military assignments before choosing to serve at Fort Sill, Oklahoma, with the Tenth Cavalry. Even though he was an officer, Flipper never saw any significant combat and was instead relegated to performing menial tasks such as supervising the erection of poles for telegraph lines and maintaining law and order on the frontier.

Flipper's military career ended prematurely after he was reassigned to Fort Davis, Texas, where he began a friendship with a white woman. The relationship generated resentment among several of the white officers, and the animosity toward Flipper heightened. His primary duty while stationed at Fort Davis was running the commissary and in July 1881, he was arrested after a discrepancy was discovered in his accounts. He was charged with embezzlement and conduct unbecoming an officer. During the ensuing court-martial, Flipper and his lawyers charged that disgruntled white officers had framed him by stealing the missing funds. Although the money was eventually returned and another prime suspect emerged, Flipper was still tried and found guilty of both charges. As a result, he received a dishonorable discharge from the army on June 30, 1882. (Flipper was finally pardoned, by President William Jefferson Clinton, on February 19, 1999.)

Although they were met with hostility, the Buffalo Soldiers exhibited valor, both on and off the battlefield, throughout the duration of the Indian Wars. By the end of the conflict they had helped settle the Western frontier, for they strung hundreds of miles of telegraph lines and built frontier outposts where towns were soon built. In combat, the Buffalo Soldiers rode more miles and took more prisoners than any other regiment while assisting in the defeat of powerful Native American leaders such as Black Kettle, Victorio, and Geronimo. Furthermore, some of the Buffalo Soldiers, such as Corporal Clinton Greaves, Sergeants William McBryar and Henry Johnson, Sergeant Major Brent Woods, and Private Augustus Walley, were awarded the Congressional Medal of Honor.

THE SPANISH-AMERICAN WAR

While the Buffalo Soldiers are most well known for their service during the Indian Wars, they also participated in the Spanish-American War, which was fought between the United States and Spain in 1898. The sinking of the USS *Maine*, which had been stationed in Havana harbor as a statement of support for the Cuban revolution against Spain, was a major catalyst for the conflict. Specifically, on February 15, 1898, the ship exploded, killing 260 sailors, and while there was no evidence that a Spanish mine led to the detonation, the incident increased tensions between the United States and Spain. When Spain ended diplomatic talks, the United States responded with a declaration of war on April 20, 1898.

Prior to joining the effort in Cuba, the Buffalo Soldiers once again found themselves the victims of racial discrimination on the home front. All military soldiers were sent to southern states for deployment to Cuba. Upon arriving in the South, the Buffalo Soldiers were greeted with hatred by white soldiers and civilians alike. Kai Wright, the author of *Soldiers of Freedom,* notes, "Local militias refused to accommodate the black units sent from predominately northern and midwestern states. And local police aggressively enforced Jim Crow laws in public places, violently harassing black troops" (2002, p. 111).

Despite enduring southern racism, all four Buffalo Soldier regiments fought with dignity and honor after arriving in Cuba. On June 24, 1898, the Ninth and Tenth Cavalries fought alongside the First Volunteer Cavalry, which is better known as Theodore Roosevelt's Rough Riders, in a key battle in the village of Las Guasimas. The Rough Riders stormed the village but were pinned downed by Spanish gunfire. The Tenth Cavalry fought its way through the jungle, rescued the Rough Riders, and helped force the Spanish soldiers away.

After the battle at Las Guasimas, the Twenty-fourth and Twenty-fifth Infantry Regiments joined the Rough Riders and the Tenth Cavalry. Together they fought significant battles at San Juan Hill and Kettle Hill. Casualties were high, and the Tenth Cavalry lost 20 percent of its men. At one point, the Twenty-fourth regiment suffered massive losses when they charged past several white regiments that were reluctant to move forward. Frank Knox, a Rough Rider and future Secretary of the Navy, later remarked about the Buffalo Soldiers, "I must say that I never saw braver men anywhere" (Wright 2002, p. 114). At the conclusion of the battles at San Juan Hill and Kettle Hill, the U.S. troops were firmly in control of the war. Unfortunately, the Buffalo Soldiers' role in winning the conflict is rarely documented. Instead, the Rough Riders are often glorified as the lone heroes of the war.

THE DEMISE OF THE BUFFALO SOLDIERS

After the Spanish American War, the Buffalo Soldiers took part in the Philippine-American War (1899–1902) and the Punitive Expedition in New Mexico (1916–1917), which marked their last considerable combat action. Incidents of racial violence involving the Buffalo Soldiers in Brownsville, Texas, in 1906, and Houston, Texas, in 1916 served as rallying points for whites calling for an end to black military service. Therefore, at the onset of World War I, the Buffalo Soldiers were not called upon to serve, while other blacks were relegated to menial positions. When Congress finally expanded the military draft to include black combat troops, the War

Department opted to create the all-black Ninety-second and Ninety-third Divisions in October and December 1917, respectively. These divisions were reactivated during World War II, but the Buffalo Soldiers were formally recreated when the War Department expanded the Ninety-third Division to include the Twenty-fourth and Twenty-fifth Infantry Regiments. In 1941 the War Department activated the Second Cavalry Division, into which it put the old Ninth and Tenth Cavalries. Unfortunately, the three units saw limited combat during the conflict.

After World War II, black soldiers returned home with a renewed sense of hope. They believed that because the American people recognized that Hitler's persecution of the Jews was wrong, they would also realize that treating blacks as second-class citizens was unfair. While it took many years for the United States to fulfill black America's desire for equality, President Truman took an important step toward making it a reality. On July 28, 1948, the president signed Executive Order 9981, which permanently ended racial segregation in the military. The process of full integration took several years to complete, but by the time of the Korean War (1950–1953), the Twenty-fourth Regiment was the last remaining unit of the Buffalo Soldiers. The Twenty-fourth Regiment was used sparingly in Korea and was officially deactivated on October 1, 1951.

The Buffalo Soldiers played an integral role in paving the way for blacks seeking to enlist in the military. They endured racism and served in harsh conditions, making it possible for blacks to be accepted as equals. While they were scarcely used late in their tenure, their skill, bravery, and valor led to the establishment of other successful black units, such as the Fifty-first Defense Battalion, the 761st Tank Battalion and the Tuskegee Airmen. They also paved the way for the desegregation of the military. Although largely missing from history books, the Buffalo Soldiers have been commemorated with statues and museums in places such as Fort Riley, Kansas; Fort Leavenworth, Kansas; Fort Bliss, Texas; Junction City, Kansas; Tucson, Arizona; and Washington, D.C.

SEE ALSO *Black Civil War Soldiers.*

BIBLIOGRAPHY

Arnold, Thomas St. John. 1990. *Buffalo Soldiers: The 92nd Division and Reinforcement in World War II, 1942–1945.* Manhattan, KS: Sunflower University Press.

Astor, Gerald. 1998. *The Right to Fight: A History of African Americans in the Military.* Novato, CA: Presidio.

Carlson, Paul Howard. 2003. *The Buffalo Soldier Tragedy of 1877.* College Station: Texas A&M University Press.

Cox, Clinton. 1993. *The Forgotten Heroes: The Story of the Buffalo Soldiers.* New York: Scholastic.

Downey, Fairfax. 1969. *The Buffalo Soldiers in the Indian Wars.* New York: McGraw-Hill.

Leckie, William H. 1967. *The Buffalo Soldiers: A Narrative of the Negro Cavalry in the West.* Norman: University of Oklahoma Press.

Reef, Catherine. 1993. *The Buffalo Soldiers.* New York: Twenty-First Century Books.

Schubert, Frank N. 1997. *Black Valor: Buffalo Soldiers and the Medal of Honor, 1870–1898.* Wilmington, DE: SR Books.

———. 2003. *Voices of the Buffalo Soldier: Records, Reports, and Recollections of Military Life and Service in the West.* Albuquerque: University of New Mexico Press.

Stovall, TaRessa. 1997. *The Buffalo Soldiers.* Philadelphia, PA: Chelsea House.

Tucker, Phillip Thomas. 2002. *Cathy Williams: From Slave to Female Buffalo Soldier.* Mechanicsburg, PA: Stackpole Books.

Wright, Kai. 2002. *Soldiers of Freedom: An Illustrated History of African Americans in the Armed Forces.* New York: Black Dog & Leventhal.

Novotny Lawrence

BURAKUMIN

In James Clavell's celebrated 1975 novel, *Shogun*, the following description appears:

> Jan Roper interrupted, "Wait a minute, Vinck!"
>
> "What's wrong, Pilot."
>
> "What about eters?"
>
> "It is just that the Japanese think of them as different. They are the executioners, and work the hides and handle corpses." (p. 870)

Elsewhere in the book the term *eta* (*eters*) appears, yet a fuller explanation of these people is never provided. *Eta*, meaning "much filth" in Japanese, is a derisive term, still used in the early twenty-first century, for the *burakumin.*

Burakumin (literally meaning "village people"; although there are alternative terms, *burakumin* and *buraku* will be used herein) refers to a group of ethnic Japanese, numbering approximately three million, that is discriminated against by the majority Japanese population. (The number three million may be high but is the number routinely provided by the various *buraku* liberation organizations. While debate continues on the actual number, if this number is at least approximately correct, then, as Herman Ooms [1996] notes, it makes the *buraku* people the largest Japanese minority.)

Although some in the majority Japanese population continue to believe that the *buraku* people are racially distinct from the majority of the Japanese people, the prevailing scholarly opinion is that the *buraku* people are racially indistinct from the majority Japanese and are oppressed because of specific historic occupational lineages. Therefore, the discrimination against the *buraku* people is more similar to that of the Dalits in India rather than to the discrimination shown in Japan toward the Japanese Ainu.

Several scholars argue that the term *racism* is appropriate to use in regard to *buraku* discrimination as they "comprise a 'race' in the sociological sense of Western racism, but an 'invisible' (i.e., not genetic or phenotypic) one" (Ooms 1996, pp. 245–246). Emiko Ohnuki-Tierney (1987) states that the *buraku* people are "invisible" because there are no physical characteristics that distinguish them from other Japanese. A continuing issue for the *buraku* liberation movement is the question of what constitutes *buraku* identity, with some residents of designated *buraku* areas claiming ancestral lineages and others socially defined as *buraku* people simply by the fact of residing in such areas. Perhaps the most inclusive definition for those termed *burakumin* in modern Japan is that offered by Tomohiko Harada (1981): "those people who were born, brought up and living in [*b*]*uraku*, those who were not from [*b*]*urakumin* family but came to live in [*b*]*uraku* in the recent past and those who are living outside the [*b*]*uraku* but have blood relationship with [*b*]*urakumin*—all these are considered the [*b*]*urakumin* minority by the majority Japanese" (quoted in Reber 1999, p. 5).

To accentuate the complexity of identifying the *burakumin*, some estimates hold that more than 50 percent of the population in *buraku* areas are non-*buraku*. Additionally, even those that come from *burakumin* families likely have little blood connection to the original medieval families from which the lineage of discrimination is sourced. Invisibility is hard to quantify.

HISTORICAL ROOTS OF DISCRIMINATION

There is a scholarly debate as to the historical origin of *buraku* discrimination. During the Heian period (794–1185), the lowest in society (*senmin*, as opposed to the *ryomin*, the good) often crafted leather saddles, harnesses, "armor," and ceremonial drums in support of warlords (*daimyo*), and for their contribution they were generally provided with some tax relief and poor land. They were also given "unclean" tasks such as those of jailer and executioner as well as expected to be the first line of defense in case of attack.

Some scholars conjecture that this social segmentation was the beginning of what came to be the *buraku* designation; it was distinctly in the Tokugawa period (1603–1867), however, when the discriminatory policies and structure were established in a stratified social order (samurai, farmer, artisan, and merchant) that excluded the *kawata* ("leather worker," which was a self-referential term). The majority Japanese during this period referred to *kawata* as *eta-hinin* (*hinin* translating as "nonhuman), and this compound term was used as a social designation at the time. These terms, but particularly *eta*, are still used in Japan to pejoratively refer to the *buraku* people. The use of the Japanese number *yottsu* (four), often accompanied by holding up four fingers, is used to refer to a *buraku* person as an animal (having four legs).

During the Tokugawa period, prohibitions against the group included forbidding intermarriage; designating allowable places to live, often on undesirable plots of land; specifying clothing; and restricting the *kawata* from engaging the other classes in an equal way, including forbidding them from entering non-*buraku* houses, temples, and shrines (Meerman 2003). Anti-*buraku* discrimination thus originated in traditional occupations that were deemed "unclean" or "polluted" by the majority Japanese, such as butchery, tanning, and leatherwork. Other forms of *kawata* work included roadwork, stone cutting, bamboo manufactures, sweeping, subsistence farming, fish mongering, night soil and garbage disposal, cremation, and burial (Meerman 2003). In modern Japan, however, while descent from earlier groups is an operative factor, the primary determinant of *buraku* identity is location, as many *buraku* people live in designated, government-supported housing and support areas.

In 1871 the Emancipation Edict (*Eta Kaihō Rei*) abolished discrimination against this subgroup, but the edict had little effect on conditions for the *buraku* people. The edict identified *burakumin* with a label meaning "new common people," which the general public understood as referring to the same stigmatized group. The more positive appellation still segregated the group from the majority Japanese, and the *burakumin* were as easy to discover in lists as previously.

In March 1922, the National Levelers Association (*Zenkoku Suiheisha*) was founded as an organized effort to address the persistent discrimination against the *buraku* people. After being outlawed in 1937 in militarist Japan, the movement reinstituted itself in 1946 as the National Committee for Buraku Liberation (becoming the Buraku Liberation League [BLL] in 1955). The BLL has been the predominant voice for the betterment of the *buraku mondai* (problem) since its formation.

In 1969, through sustained political activism by the *buraku* organizations and their supporters, the Japanese government enacted special legislation that dramatically bettered conditions for the *buraku* people by greatly multiplying the amount of government funds for improving *buraku* housing and roads, providing scholarships, reducing taxes for *buraku* businesses, subsidizing rents, and other improvements. Local bodies, influenced by the BLL, often decided how this government funding was spent. The funding ended in 2003.

THE "POLLUTED" ASPECT OF *BURAKU* DISCRIMINATION

Japan has a long tradition of emphasizing cleanliness and purity. The philosophical basis of this tradition can be traced to the indigenous tradition of Shinto as well as Buddhism, which was imported into Japan in the mid-sixth century CE. Buddhism is often associated with purity/impurity in its opprobrium against killing and eating meat. This negative attitude was extrapolated to the handling of dead animals and their by-products.

Both Shinto and Japanese Buddhism supported the "polluted" determination of the historic *buraku* occupations. Shinto, with its strong emphasis on ritual pollution and taboo, helped shape the majority Japanese view that anyone who handled dead bodies, animals, or animal by-products was unclean. The distinction with the *buraku* people is that they could not be made clean again from this "pollution" through purification rituals.

The Japanese Buddhists also contributed to the system of discrimination through their association with the death rituals of the Japanese. In Japan, for many centuries, Buddhism has functioned as the religion of death rituals. Traditionally, a Buddhist priest gives the deceased a death name (*kaimyo*) that the person is to carry into the next world. As William Bodiford (1996) contends, there is strong evidence of the use of prejudicial *kaimyo* in temple necrologies (death registries) and "off-registers" as well as on corresponding grave markers (*haka*).

The use of registries is critically important to understanding the history of oppression against the *burakumin*. If one were a handler of meat or dead bodies, or engaged in other polluting activities, then one would be ritually impure for a period of time. After this period, the impurity could be expunged or would no longer be operative. Yet, with the use of registries, such as the temple necrologies, the incidence of pollution associated with certain families and occupations became stigmatizing and permanent. Not only was an individual deemed as inalterably impure because of his or her actions, but so too was the family name extending across generations, even if the polluting occupation was no longer followed by the person's heirs. Discriminatory passages in Buddhist texts may have been used to provide "doctrinal cover" for abusing the *burakumin*. To the credit of Japanese Buddhism, it has acknowledged this troubled past and has sought through its own offices and in cooperation with the BLL to change its views of and practices concerning the *burakumin*. In addition, other religious movements, such as Christianity and Tenrikyo, have reached out to the *buraku* community with some success.

MODERN FORMS OF DISCRIMINATION

In 1963 Kazuo Ishikawa was convicted of killing a young girl and sentenced to death. The body was discovered near a *buraku* area, and Ishikawa is a member of the *buraku* community. This case has become a cause célèbre for the *buraku* liberation movement in Japan, and it has become known across Asia among similar liberation groups as the Sayama case (Sayama is the town where Ishikawa lived). The belief is that Ishikawa was falsely accused because of his being a *buraku* person. After thirty-one years in prison, Ishikawa was released on probation in 1994, and three appeals (as of 2006) have been filed to clear his name. This case has become a rallying point for change in the criminal justice system in Japan and crystallized the *buraku* liberation movement in its fight against discrimination.

Since World War II, discrimination against the *buraku* people has often manifested itself, compared to the mainstream Japanese, in higher illness rates; illiteracy challenges; higher unemployment; hiring for menial, dangerous jobs; lower wages for the same jobs; illegal lists that corporations buy and use to avoid hiring *buraku* people; marriage discrimination; and the historic biases of some Japanese religious bodies. Moreover, from the 1990s into the early twenty-first century, the Internet has been used to post defamatory statements against this group as well as, purportedly, to distribute lists of the location and residents of *buraku* areas—information that could be used to discriminate in such areas as employment and marriage. There is no national law against the use of these lists for background checks, although access to them has been officially restricted.

Physical conditions have improved for those living in *buraku* areas, as the Japanese government through its Special Measures Law of 1969 has improved housing and hygiene conditions, and constructed community support centers, even though the older population of *buraku* people continue to struggle with health problems, some of which were cause by earlier deprivations. As the older generation of *buraku* people often did not advance past middle school, literacy among this group has been a challenge, and community centers often offer reading and writing classes for this group. Struggling with illiteracy in a country such as Japan, which claims essentially universal literacy, is particularly burdensome. The problems of the modern *buraku* communities are compounded by higher percentages of unemployment than the majority, lower-paying occupations in small to medium-sized businesses, and discrimination by the larger corporations.

There has also been an improvement in higher *buraku* graduation rates from secondary schools, more *buraku* persons matriculating to college, and a notable increase in marriage to non-*burakumin* mates. All the critical indicators, based on the data collected and published by the Buraku Liberation and Human Rights Research Institute, point to a closing of the gap between the majority Japanese population and the *buraku* population at the end of the twentieth century and continuing into the twenty-first century, though a gap nevertheless endures. The use of lists of *buraku* persons and areas persists, and Shinto and Buddhist authorities continue to work to expose and address discriminatory practices in their arenas.

It is with the growth of intermarriage that the *buraku* situation may change most radically in the future, particularly as the younger generation of Japanese does not seem to adhere as rigidly to the stigma against marrying someone of *buraku* descent. Even in the recent past, there were many stories printed of marriages called off when one of the partners was discovered to be of *buraku* origin. (The parents often conducted a private investigation to see if such a background existed prior to their son or daughter marrying.) Furthermore, even when the marriages were allowed, discrimination persisted, as in one published case, in which the wife of *buraku* origin was not allowed to enter her in-laws' house, register her children in her in-laws' family register, or attend her husband's family observances during their marriage.

CONTEMPORARY DEVELOPMENTS

As *buraku* discrimination persists into the twenty-first century, the efforts to address the changing face of prejudice will require new approaches. The primary continuing issue for the *buraku* people is how the end of government funding in 2003 will continue to affect their community and the notable advances they have made.

One of the controversial tactics the BLL has employed in its attempt to publicize discriminatory acts perpetuated against the *buraku* community is the use of denunciation (*kyūdan*). Denunciation entails isolating the one guilty of a discriminatory act and then bringing this party to a meeting where he or she is publicly denounced and forced to repent the act and pledge to change his or her ways. This activity has been justified as necessary in the face of government inaction or the lack of a legal remedy, but it has also spawned questions of its legality and ethical fairness.

Attempting to broaden the movement's efforts in the wake of the government funding cutoff, the Buraku Liberation and Human Rights Research Institute has focused its attention on human rights legislation inside Japan that calls for the systematic identification and enforcement of antidiscrimination laws not only as they would affect *buraku* people but also foreign residents, the physically and mentally handicapped, and others. The movement has also closely aligned itself with human rights initiatives from the United Nations and other international bodies. Similarly, there continues to be an effort to align kindred liberation groups across Asia, including such countries as India, Korea, Nepal, and Bangladesh.

This movement may result in less direct attention to education efforts specifically on the *buraku* situation and instead evolve into a national movement to better educate all Japanese, particularly through the school system, on human rights. The content of Japanese textbooks, which have typically either omitted *burakumin* or included discriminatory language against them, has provoked controversy in Japan (and East Asia) for many decades. As the *buraku* movement has declared, it is time for Japan to defy the axiom to not wake the sleeping baby and to stir the baby awake toward positive, sustainable change.

Certainly, the major ongoing issue for the *buraku* liberation effort, as with many similar human rights efforts across the globe, is how to sustain the energy and communal effort to improve the attitude of mainstream Japan toward the *buraku* people into the next generation, while external living conditions improve and intermarriage continues to increase.

BIBLIOGRAPHY

Bodiford, William. 1996. "Zen and the Art of Religious Prejudice: Efforts to Reform a Tradition of Social Discrimination." *Japanese Journal of Religious Studies* 23 (1–2): 1–27.

"Buraku Liberation News." Buraku Liberation and Human Rights Research Institute. Available from http://www.blhrri.org/blhrri_e/news/news.htm.

Clavell, James. 1975. *Shogun*. New York: Atheneum.

Kitaguchi, Suehiro. 1999. *An Introduction to the Buraku Issue: Questions and Answers*. Translated by Alastair McLauchlan. Richmond, Surrey, U.K.: Japan Library.

McLauchlan, Alastair. 2003. *Prejudice and Discrimination in Japan: The Buraku Issue*. Lewiston, NY: Edwin Mellen Press.

Meerman, Jacob. 2003. "The Mobility of Japan's Burakumin: Militant Advocacy and Government Response." In *Boundaries of Clan and Color: Transnational Comparisons of Inter-group Disparity*, edited by William Darity Jr. and Ashwini Deshpande, 130–151. London: Routledge.

Neary, Ian. 2003. "*Burakumin* at the End of History." *Social Research* 70 (1): 269–294.

Ohnuki-Tierney, Emiko. 1987. *The Monkey as Mirror: Symbolic Transformations in Japanese History and Ritual*. Princeton, NJ: Princeton University Press.

Ooms, Herman. 1996. *Tokugawa Village Practice: Class, Status, Power, Law*. Berkeley: University of California Press.

Reber, Emily A. Su-lan. 1999. "*Buraku Mondai* in Japan: Historical and Modern Perspectives and Directions for the Future." *Harvard Human Rights Journal* 12: 297–359.

Leslie D. Alldritt

C

CAGOTS

The Cagots, or Agotes, were an ethnic minority that inhabited parts of the Pyrenees Mountains, which form a natural border between France and Spain. Spurned by the local populations until the early twentieth century, they lived a nomadic life as outcasts, principally in the Spanish and French Basque provinces, including Béarn and Gascony, parts of the Languedoc, and as far north as Brittany. Also known as Ghézitains, Gahets, Gafos, Canards ("ducks") and Chrestians (or Chrestias), the name Cagot is believed to derive from the Vulgate *Canis Gothi*, or "Dog of a Goth."

Although their origins remain shrouded in mystery, many believe that the Cagots were a group of Visigoths who refused to abandon Arianism when Reccared, the king of the Visigoths, renounced Arian Christianity and converted to Catholicism in 587. Although fantastic descriptions of Cagots go back to the Carolingian period (c. 751–987), at the height of the thirteenth century repression of the Albigensian heresy in southern France they were referred to as *Chrestians*, one of the names the Albigensian Cathars used for themselves. Perhaps for this reason, a group of Cagots identified themselves as the last descendants of the Albigenses in a petition to Pope Leo X in 1517, in which they requested absolution for the heresy of their forefathers. The Pontiff responded in a bull that they should be treated fairly.

Partly because of this history, the Cagots were subjected to hate-filled discrimination for nearly seven hundred years. Shunned as lepers, pagans, and even cannibals, they were forced to live in ghettoes called *cagoteries* where they were only permitted the occupations of carpenter, butcher, or executioner. Similar to the fate of their fellow pariahs, the Hindu Dalit, or "Untouchables," the Cagots were not allowed to go barefoot because of the alleged overwhelming stench of their feet. When they were permitted entrance to a Church (in many cases they were refused admittance), they were segregated from the rest of the congregation, and the Eucharist was handed to them at the end of a long stick. They were compelled to wear the sign of a duck or goose foot in red (hence the name "canards"), and because it was believed that they were carriers of leprosy, they were obliged to carry a bell to warn all others of their approach.

The Cagots were treated as an inferior race, and legend attributed various bizarre physical features to them. They are often described in medieval archives as being completely bald, with webbed hands and feet and missing ears or ear lobes. Various nineteenth century authors, however, attributed typical Germanic traits (such as blond hair and blue eyes) to them. The Basque author Pio Baroja (1872–1956) described the Cagots in his memoir *Las horas solitarias* as "a central European type or a Northerner. There are elderly in Bozate (a Navarran locality) that look like they stepped out of a portrait by Dürer, with a Germanic look. There are also others, with long faces and darker complexions, who remind me of gypsies."

Despite various attempts to improve their standing over the centuries, substantial progress came only after the French Revolution and the establishment of the First Empire. In 1818, the Navarran Cortes (legislature) in Pamplona voted to abrogate the discriminatory laws that had been in effect since the Middle Ages. Nonetheless, racial prejudice against the Cagots lasted well into the twentieth century. By the end of that century, thanks to intermarriage, they had melded into the local populations, finally ending a seven-hundred-year-old history of repression and discrimination.

BIBLIOGRAPHY

Aguirre Delclaux, and Maria del Carmen. 2006. *Los Agotes, el final de una maldicion*. Madrid: Silex Ediciones.

Baroja, Pio. 1918. *Las horas solitarias, notas de un aprendiz psicologo*. Madrid: R. Caro Raggio.

Descazeaux, René. 2002. *Les Cagots, histoire d'un secret*. Monein, France: PyréMonde.

Christopher Jones

CALHOUN, JOHN C.
1782–1850

John Caldwell Calhoun was a South Carolina politician who served in several state and federal offices from 1808 until his death in 1850. He was a candidate for the presidency of the United States several times without ascending to the post, but he nevertheless became one of the most powerful figures in the pre–Civil War United States. Calhoun used his considerable influence and political acumen to defend the right of states to control their own destiny—specifically the ability of the southern states to retain the institution of slavery.

EARLY LIFE

Calhoun was born on March 18, 1782, to Patrick Calhoun and Martha Caldwell, both of Scotch-Irish descent, in the northwestern region of South Carolina called Abbeville. Calhoun's early childhood was spent on his father's plantation, which was cultivated by thirty-one enslaved Africans. There was little formal schooling available for the young Calhoun, and he did not attend school regularly in his adolescent years. At the age of eighteen he entered an academy founded by Moses Waddell, a young Presbyterian minister who had married Calhoun's older sister. Calhoun read voraciously at Waddell's academy and entered Yale College (present-day Yale University) in 1802. He then attended Litchfield Law School, and after completing apprenticeships in Litchfield, Connecticut, and Charleston, South Carolina, he began his own law practice in Abbeville.

In 1807, after a British frigate attacked an American vessel, Calhoun led the public outcry over the transgression. At a town hall meeting, he gave a speech advocating aggressive retaliation and his popularity soared. He was elected to the South Carolina legislature as a representative from the Abbeville district in 1808. He would serve in this post for two years.

PROMINENT POLITICIAN

Calhoun began his national political career when he was elected to the Twelfth Congress as the representative from the Sixth Congressional District of South Carolina. In these early years Calhoun quickly gained a reputation for favoring aggressive national action. Along with Henry Clay and other politicians dubbed the "War Hawks," Calhoun helped convince President James Madison to declare war on Britain, sparking the War of 1812. Calhoun would serve in Congress from 1811 to 1817. Among his career highlights during this period were arguing in favor of increasing government power through consolidation of the banking system and increasing the federal government's ability to levy taxes.

In 1817 Calhoun left the House of Representatives to serve as secretary of war in James Monroe's cabinet. In this post, which he held until 1825, Calhoun continued to advocate nationalist legislation. He strengthened national defense by centralizing the military administration in Washington and increasing funding for military infrastructure and troop necessities. Calhoun made a brief run for the presidency in 1824, before accepting the post of vice president under John Quincy Adams. He served as vice president to John Quincy Adams in 1824 and again under Andrew Jackson in 1828, making him the only person in U.S. history to serve as vice president for two different administrations.

Calhoun's two tenures as vice president marked a turning point in his career. The Tariff of 1828 (called the Tariff of Abominations) called for a tax on British goods imported into the United States. This tariff benefited northern manufacturing interests at the expense of southern raw material exporters. The South Carolina legislature passed a nullification bill in retaliation, revoking the federal tariff. The U.S. government passed the Force Bill in return, which authorized the use of the military to enforce federal tariffs. This standoff, called the Nullification Crisis, marked the turning point in Calhoun's political thinking. Calhoun changed his political ideology from pro-federal government to pro-states rights, and sided with the state of South Carolina.

Calhoun resigned as vice president in 1832 to return to the Senate. He would take one other cabinet post in his lifetime, as secretary of state in John Tyler's cabinet from 1844 to 1845—but it was as a senator (1832–1843, and 1845–1850) that he made his most indelible mark on the American political landscape.

RACE AND SLAVERY

Calhoun spent most of his life on a 900-acre plantation in Fort Hill, South Carolina. He owned approximately eighty slaves. Calhoun defended the institution of slavery vigorously up until his death, notoriously calling it a "positive good" for slave and master alike. In 1836 he blocked the reading of petitions against slavery on the Senate floor, arguing that because the Fifth Amendment declared that no person be deprived of property without due process of law, and since slaves were property, the discussion of the petitions was a moot point. Congress finally rejected Calhoun's position, with many of its members declaring that the "gag rule" violated the right to petition. That same year, when abolitionists wanted to send mail into the southern states, he supported the suppression of such mail, including the vigilante search of the interstate mails in Charleston. He cited the First Amendment, arguing that it was the right of the states to control mail if they chose to, and that the federal government had no say in the matter.

Calhoun's views had racial as well as economic justifications. He repeatedly asserted that the African was innately inferior to the European, and he viewed slavery as a positive good that afforded the inferior blacks an opportunity to advance faster than any other civilization. Economically, Calhoun argued that in every civilization, one portion of society always depended on the labor of another. The South had a unique economy that allowed the laboring class—the black slaves—to be always well fed and have their children and elderly cared for. He contrasted the slave labor of the South with the degraded conditions of the working class in Britain, arguing that the southern blacks had a far more favorable existence.

Calhoun's beliefs in European racial superiority were applied to other groups as well. In his arguments against a potential war and colonization of Mexico, he asserted that mixing Indian blood and culture with that of Americans would lead to degradation and destroy the cultural institutions of the United States.

CALHOUN'S LEGACY

John C. Calhoun will always be remembered as one of America's most able politicians. His proslavery arguments were at times unassailable, however. Yet despite his staunch defense of states rights and slavery, his writings do not reveal a support for a southern secession or war. A man of ascetic behavior who rarely lost his temper and had no documented instances of lascivious behavior, Calhoun appears to have garnered the respect of both friend and foe.

BIBLIOGRAPHY

Meigs, William M. 1970 (1917). *The Life of John Caldwell Calhoun*. 2 Vols. New York: De Capo Press.

Niven, John. 1988. *John C. Calhoun and the Price of Union: A Biography*. Baton Rouge: Louisiana State University Press.

Peterson, Merrill D. 1987. *The Great Triumvirate: Webster, Clay, and Calhoun*. New York: Oxford University Press.

Spain, August O. 1951. *The Political Theory of John C. Calhoun*. New York: Bookman Associates.

Roderick Graham

CANADIAN RACIAL FORMATIONS

The phrase "Canadian racial formation" refers to the historical and social process by which groups of people in Canada came to be known as racially differentiated. Categories such as "charter groups," "Native Indians," and "visible minorities" are socially constructed and have been produced over time through social relations and, at times, through state intervention.

CHARTER GROUPS

In Canada, "charter groups" refers to the British and the French, the founding members of the Canadian Confederation formed in 1867. From the beginning of the seventeenth century to the beginning of the nineteenth century, the fur trade influenced the development of New France and British North America (colonies of France and Britain, respectively) and shaped the competitive relationships between the British and the French. After the British conquest of New France in 1760, the British influence continued to increase. The British North America Act of 1867, passed in the British parliament to create a confederation of Canada, was a political compromise between the British and the French to unify Upper Canada (now Ontario) and Lower Canada (now Quebec), along with Nova Scotia and New Brunswick.

Throughout the history of Canada, the political and numerical dominance of the charter groups has been unequivocal. The 1871 Census of Canada shows that 61 percent of Canada's three-and-a-half million people were of British origin, 31 percent of French origin, and 7 percent of European origin other than British and French. Less than 1 percent were Native Indians, the original people of the land. This demographic configuration persisted, with only minor deviations, throughout the nineteenth century and the first half of the twentieth century.

Among the charter groups, the French assumed a minority status relative to the British because of the prevailing cultural and linguistic influence of the British and their political dominance. In 1971, Pierre Vallières used the title *White Niggers of America* to describe the oppression and plight of French Canadians. Throughout the 1960s, rising political aspirations of Francophones (those speaking French as a first language) in Quebec were seen by the federal government as a potential threat. In 1969, at the recommendation of the Royal Commission of Bilingualism and Biculturalism, Canada adopted the Official Languages Act, which recognized both English and French as official languages of Canada. However, discontent continued in Quebec, where most Francophones resided, culminating in what became known as the October Crisis of 1970, when some Quebecois engaged in public bombing and political kidnapping as a protest against British dominance. The federal government invoked the War Measures Act to mobilize the army, which brought civil order back to Quebec but alienated the city's Francophones. In 1976, Quebec elected Parti Québécois, a separatist provincial party, to power, openly challenging federalism and promoting independence. But a 1980 province-wide referendum failed to obtain support for the sovereignty of Quebec. The tension between the British and the French was further increased when the federal government moved to repatriate the constitution of Canada from Britain in 1982, with the support of all the provinces except Quebec. Attempts to bring Quebec back to the constitutional fold through the Meech Lake Accord in 1987 and the Charlottetown Accord in 1990 failed. Thus, the charter groups in Canada continued to develop through historical antagonism, continuous struggle, occasional compromise, and frequent tensions.

Native Peoples Land Claim. *A group from the Six Nations of the Grand River occupies a piece of land near Caledonia, Ontario, Canada, in April 2006. Since the 1960s, aboriginal peoples have intensified their political and economic demands based on aboriginal rights.* AP IMAGES.

NATIVE INDIANS

Native Indians can be understood as another racial formation in Canada. In *The Canadian Indian* (1971), E. Palmer Patterson divides the history of relations between Canadian Indians and Europeans since the sixteenth century into four phases. The first was the initial contact between Native peoples and Europeans, leading to a period of prosperity as the two groups exchanged technology and goods. In the second phase, from the seventeenth to the eighteenth century, Indians were increasingly drawn into the economy of white people as they became more involved in fur trading, and less reliant on their traditional livelihood, resulting in a weakening of political autonomy. The third phase began with the creation of reserves for Native peoples in order to clear the way for the agricultural settlements of whites. With the passage of the Indian Act in 1876, the colonial status of Native peoples was legally confirmed, because the act placed Indians under the legislative and administrative control of the federal government. The last phase began in the period after World War II, as more Native peoples became aware of their plight and demanded control of their future.

Since the 1960s, aboriginal peoples have intensified their political and economic demands based on aboriginal rights. The process of bringing the constitution from England to Canada in 1982 gave the Native peoples an opportunity to assert their special aboriginal status. Aboriginal rights encompass two main categories: the rights that derive from aboriginal title over land and resources, and the rights of self-determination. Two types of claims have been pursued by Native groups in Canada. The first type–comprehensive claims–is based on aboriginal title. These are land claims over areas still in use by Native peoples, but not covered in treaties. The second type–specific claims–refers to clauses in treaties and claims by Indian bands over the loss of reserve land or the misappropriation of the government trusteeship. These two types of claims represent the two strategies pursued by aboriginal peoples and Native organizations.

Comprehensive claims are premised on the interpretation of the *Royal Proclamation* of October 7, 1763. In this view, those parts of the Dominion or territories not ceded to or purchased by the Crown remain reserved for

Indians. The basis of specific claims is that Native peoples have lost lands and financial assets that are protected by treaties between the Indian Nations and the Government of Canada. From the 1870s until 1921, eleven numbered treaties were signed between Native Indians and various provincial and territorial jurisdictions. James Frideres, in *Aboriginal Peoples in Canada* (2004), notes that the success rate of Native claims has been low.

VISIBLE MINORITIES

Nonwhites in Canada make up another racial formation. Throughout the latter part of the nineteenth century, Canada used Asian workers extensively in the development of western Canada, but it did not consider them worthy citizens. More than ten thousand Chinese workers were brought to Canada to work on the construction of the Canadian Pacific Railway in 1881 and 1882. When the railroad was completed in 1885, the federal government passed the Chinese Immigration Act, which imposed a head tax on Chinese arrivals. From 1923 until 1947, Chinese were barred from entering Canada, and those already in the country were denied many political, economic, and mobility rights that other Canadians took for granted. Japanese Canadians represent another racial formation that Canada treated harshly in the past, especially during World War II when they were removed from their homes, confined in camps, and had their properties confiscated because they were branded as enemy aliens.

Canada adopted a multiculturalism policy in 1971 and passed the Multiculturalism Act in 1988. In 1986 the Employment Equity Act addressed the employment conditions of disadvantaged groups; it included nonwhites—referred to officially as "visible minorities"—among the four target groups. However, the notion of collective rights for the visible minority remains vague in the statutes of Canada.

Since the 1970s, the single most important factor contributing to the growth of the visible minority in Canada has been immigration. Nonwhites made up 6 percent of Canada's population in 1986, 9 percent in 1991, and 13 percent in 2001. Census data indicate that most visible-minority members are first-generation immigrants born outside of Canada, in contrast to most European Canadians, who, because of a historical immigration policy favoring their admission, tend to be Canada-born. Studies of racial inequality suggest that race remains an enduring feature in Canadian society, and that the life chances of visible minorities are often affected by superficial physical features and perceived cultural idiosyncrasies. The laws in Canada do not permit blatant racial discrimination, nor do they condone racism. However, Frances Henry and colleagues (2006) have shown that racism in Canada is articulated in a subtle and benign fashion in arts, the media, and social institutions in a mode they call "democratic racism."

OTHER FACTORS

Contemporary racial formations in Canada shape the country in three specific areas. First, despite official bilingualism, some Francophones in Quebec continue to feel alienated from Canada's federation, and they rally their support behind separatist political forces dedicated to Quebec sovereignty. The threat of Quebec separating is a continuing political challenge in Canada. Second, the aboriginal population in Canada continues to fall behind other groups in education, occupational status, health status, and quality of life. Demographic shifts resulting from fertility and rural to urban migration have exacerbated problems of Native youth unemployment, health care, and other related issues. Aboriginal peoples are also overrepresented in the criminal justice system, and many complain about mistreatments by law enforcement agencies. Some aboriginal organizations continue to press for legal and political settlements with the government on issues of land claims, aboriginal entitlements, and self-governance.

Third, as Canada accepts increasingly more immigrants from non-European countries, many urban centers—such as Toronto, Vancouver, Montreal, and Calgary—are experiencing a shift toward a more racial diverse population. Canada has not faced the same type of backlash toward immigration as some European countries and the United States have, in part because the stocks of immigrants are different. But issues related to diversity and national identity, religious freedom and fundamentalist values, and globalization and border security have entered the political and public discourse, and these issues are becoming more racialized.

SEE ALSO *Racial Formations; Social Welfare States; White Settler Society.*

BIBLIOGRAPHY

Frideres, James S., and René R. Gadacz. 2005. *Aboriginal Peoples in Canada: Contemporary Conflicts*, 7th ed. Toronto: Pearson Education.

Henry, Frances, and Carol Tator, with Winston Mattis and Tim Rees. 2006. *The Colour of Democracy: Racism in Canadian Society*, 3rd ed. Toronto: Thomson Nelson.

Li, Peter S. 1998. *The Chinese in Canada*, 2nd ed. Toronto: Oxford University Press.

Patterson E. Palmer. 1971. *The Canadian Indian: A History since 1500.* Don Mills, ON: Collier-Macmillan Canada.

Porter, John. 1965. *The Vertical Mosaic: An Analysis of Social Class and Power in Canada.* Toronto: University of Toronto Press.

Peter S. Li

CAPITALISM

Capitalism, as a way of organizing economic and social relations, has always depended on assertions about human inequality and valorization (including racism) that have been enforced through localities, states, and empires. It has not been the only economic system in human history to do so, but capitalism's very definition and possibility relies on the exploitation of one or more groups by others, as Karl Marx pointed out during the rise of global, free-market capitalism in concert with European colonialism and imperialism. Marx, as a journalist, was a thorough chronicler of capitalism in nineteenth-century Europe, and his analysis in *Das Kapital*, completed in collaboration with Friedrich Engels, remains key to understanding the logic of capitalism.

Marx and Engels argued that capitalist relations necessitate the alienation of workers from the products they make, so that both the workers' labor and what they produce become commodities circulating in an expanding market. Once laborers are seen as interchangeable workers (rather than artisans connected inextricably to what they make), it is in the interest of capitalists (those who invest in everything necessary to produce a product, including labor) to have low-wage or non-wage workers. In that way, capitalists can create surplus money from their initial investments as the commodities they have invested in circulate in the market. This surplus can be reinvested in the production of more commodities, with the capitalists (rarely the workers) making the decisions about what commodities—ranging from goods to services—to sell and how to convince consumers they need to exchange money for the commodities.

While capitalism seems to have begun in the fields, markets, and farm-related factories of England, it was a system that thrived through investment ventures such as the English East India Company and the Dutch East India Company, which linked commodities new to Europeans with low-wage labor and sources of raw material extracted with the backing of colonial guns and legislation. As Sydney Mintz documents in *Sweetness and Power* (1986), underpaid workers in England, urged by factory managers into the consumption of new commodities such as tea and sugar, were more tied than they knew to underpaid workers on the tea and sugar plantations in the Caribbean and South Asia, whose labor made empire-building possible. The commodity most vital to the success of early capitalism was human beings. For example, enslaved workers were shipped between colonial locations to facilitate monocropping on large plantations and to provide labor for constructing colonial cities like New York. As St. Clair Drake put it, "Commerce in black bodies rapidly became big business" (Drake 1990, p. 275).

Eric Williams, who was prime minister of Trinidad and Tobago from 1962 to 1981, pointed out the diversity of sources of enslaved labor across the colonial landscape. He noted, "Slavery was not born of racism: rather, racism was the consequence of slavery. Unfree labor in the New World was brown, white, black, and yellow; Catholic, Protestant and pagan." (Williams 1994 [1944], p. 7) His terms are not those one would choose in the early twenty-first century, but his point is a significant one: Capitalists in the colonial era relied not on a single strategy for securing indentured and enslaved labor, but rather on a complex and global strategy. The overwhelming similarity, though, was the ability to view humans as commodities whose value floated with other commodities on the whimsical seas of the market. They were not seen as individuals with agency who had been ripped from their social networks. In his book *Capitalism and Slavery,* Williams argued that capitalists supported or renounced slavery according to its economic viability more often than in answer to a moral compass. Morality has certainly been important to the development of capitalism. As Max Weber documented in 1926, Protestant Christianity, and particularly Calvinism, was well suited to the managerial ideology of capitalists, because the predestination doctrine of Calvinists necessitated the worldly performance of good stewardship of resources.

From the outset, capitalists—or those investing in commodities and benefiting from surpluses by reinvesting them to become richer—have tended to be from the global North, white, and in control of the social apparatuses necessary to secure further profits—particularly states, militaries, and colonial authorities. While the low-wage or non-wage workers making capitalism possible have been more diverse, there has been an ideology, (described by theorists beginning with Marx and continuing actively in the early 2000s) or logic, facilitating capitalism that naturalizes the inequitable position between capitalists and the workers from whose labor they profit. This can be thought of as "strategic alterity," or the "practice of shifting between strategic assertions of inclusion and exclusion (or the marking and unmarking of 'selves' and 'others') to both devalue a set of people and to mask that very process of strategic devalorization" (Kingsolver 2001, p. 110).

The labor forces on which capitalist arrangements have rested have been diverse, as Williams pointed out, but they have always been marked as different from the capitalists, and naturalized as inferior to them, meriting lower earnings in a polarized economy. Capitalism—in all its many forms and relationships—always ensures that polarization. The naturalization of differently valued actors in a capitalist economy most often happens through the lens of racism, but it also occurs through related distinctions, including sexism, nativism, ageism, and ethnic prejudice. One of the things that makes capitalism so flexible and enduring is that the lens can shift, but the justification remains, in capitalist logic, for what Étienne

Balibar calls "class racism," or "the institutionalized racialization of manual labor" (Balibar 1999, p. 327). In an article titled "Global Capitalism: What's Race Got to Do with It?", Karen Brodkin examines the shifting lenses used in exploitation. She concludes that "race in the United States has historically been a key relationship to the means of capitalist production, and gender constructions are what has made race corporeal, material, and visible" (Brodkin 2000, p. 239). Various kinds of institutionalized inequality—such as sexist, racist, and anti-immigrant legislation and social practice—have served capitalist formations by facilitating the rationalization and naturalization of non- and low-wage labor.

Colonized peoples were not passive in accepting the imposition of capitalism, whether it was in the shifting of massive numbers of people around the globe against their will to provide capitalist labor, or in the uncompensated extraction of raw materials that fueled the Industrial Revolution in Europe (and that, as Andre Gunder Frank has pointed out, resulted in ongoing North-South economic inequalities). The social and infrastructural damage done to colonized nations through colonial and capitalist extraction was foreseen and resisted by colonized peoples, in examples as wide-ranging as the Haitian Revolution in the 1790s and the Gandhian protests at the salt mines in India in 1930. These movements were fundamentally threatening to both colonialism and capitalism, which is why colonizing nations that were otherwise competitors in the global capitalist market closed ranks to blockade Haiti after its independence in 1804. Agency to resist the imposition of capitalist structures and their accompanying violent inequalities was diverse in its expressions across colonized nations. Kathryn Ward, for example, describes the Igbo Women's War of 1929 in Nigeria as resistance to "incorporation into the capitalist world system." Igbo women's demands, as they occupied the British government buildings, were: "women should occupy one-half of the administrative units, and all white men should return from whence they came" (Ward 1988, p. 121–122).

Just as racism is intertwined with paternalism (constructing colonized people and low-wage workers as childlike), colonialism and neocolonialism have been intertwined with the creation and enforcement of economic and social dependence of nations of the South on nations of the North, with some exceptions. The colonial strategy of monocropping, as many have pointed out, made it impossible for a single colony to support itself, thus reinforcing dependence on the colonial trade system for basic commodities. Scientific-racist stories about inferior merit, evidenced by inferior performance in schools, workplaces, and markets, have been paralleled by just-so stories about Third World poverty. Critiques of both specious arguments have been based on close examinations of structural violence (see Harrison 1997) and the ways that, over time, racism and the infrastructural inequalities persisting from colonialism (referred to as "neocolonial relations") have assaulted the possibilities of individuals and groups to thrive in the same ways as those who have consistently benefited from capitalist social and economic organization. While class relations, North-South relations, and racialized relations are compounded and confounded in myriad individual ways, they are nonetheless powerfully persistent and may be seen as responsible for a continually widening gap between rich and poor.

The partnership between capitalism and colonialism did not end with the widespread independence movements of the nineteenth and twentieth centuries. Those in globalized Northern countries have often, though not always, maintained neocolonial control of resources, markets, and infrastructure (e.g., transportation and educational systems) through ongoing control of debt relations. The post–World War II transnational economic organizations, including the International Monetary Fund (IMF), the World Bank, and the World Trade Organization (WTO), have allowed the United States and some European countries (the dominant voices in those bodies) to continue controlling the infrastructure of nations of the South through dictating the terms of loans. In the film *Life and Debt* (2001), for example, Michael Manley, the former prime minister of Jamaica, describes the difficulties faced by his country (particularly the local farmers and garment workers) when structural adjustment policies were imposed externally as part of a loan repayment plan, along with the enforced importation of U.S. agricultural goods and workers from other countries in the foreign trade zones.

With new forms of capitalism come new forms of racism, as Carter A. Wilson pointed out in *Racism: From Slavery to Advanced Capitalism* (1996). Workers in various countries are concerned about job restructuring and employers moving jobs to other regions or employing transnational migrant workforces. Unemployment-related anxieties can lead to xenophobic expressions, as documented in 1997 by Patricia Zavella in California, and new forms of racism that serve to rationalize both symbolic and physical violence. As Manning Marable notes in *How Capitalism Underdeveloped Black America* (1983), violence in current forms of capitalism is not only anti-immigrant, it is recurrently aimed at racialized minorities within states. The forced migration associated with colonialism, which was both impelled by and led to racist economic inequalities, was the antecedent to the persistent global North-South economic inequalities of the early twenty-first century. South-North migration has often been met with waves of racist, anti-immigrant sentiment, rather than any acknowledgment of the dependence of the North on the material and labor contributions of the South for its

Antiglobalization Protest. *A Korean activist takes part in a protest during the World Social Forum in Porto Alegre, Brazil, on January 31, 2005. The large banner behind him reads "Our World is Not for Sale." The annual World Social Forum began in 2001 as a protest against globalization and in opposition to the World Economic Forum, held annually in Davos, Switzerland.* JEFFERSON BERNARDES/AFP/GETTY IMAGES.

"developed" status, long noted by Andre Gunder Frank and others.

These causal connections have been exposed clearly in the coalitions that are often labeled "antiglobalization," but that are discussed in venues such as the World Social Forum, the complex relationship between racialized, gender, and other forms of social inequity and the organization and local expressions of global capitalism. One of the strategies within capitalist logic has been to divide class-based, antiracist, gender-based, and other forms of organizing by framing them as unrelated. Widespread coalitions critical of the current rapidly increasing polarization (and often white control) of wealth are forming analyses that view the bases of inequality—and the possibilities for economic equality—in a single, though still complex, frame (Alvarez, Dagnino, and Escobar 1997). One of the most promising avenues for addressing the intertwined inequalities resulting from capitalism, colonialism, and racism is global South-South networking, which can create an economic infrastructure free of colonial and neocolonial Northern control of financial investment, transportation, and markets. At the fifth Pan-African congress in 1945, alternatives to capitalism and imperialism—and associated racist oppression—were discussed. Proposals for a New International Economic Order—as raised in the United Nations Conference on Trade and Development and strengthened at the South-South dialogue convened in New Delhi in 1982—have led, decades later, to South-South trade agreements that use forms of capitalist strategies (combined with more democratic decision making than in the WTO) to try to address North-South with inequities resulting from capitalist practices reflecting paternalism and racism.

SEE ALSO *African Economic Development.*

BIBLIOGRAPHY

Alvarez, Sonia E., Evelina Dagnino, and Arturo Escobar, eds. 1997. *Cultures of Politics/Politics of Cultures: Re-visioning Latin American Social Movements.* Boulder, CO: Westview Press.

Balibar, Étienne. 1999. "Class Racism." In *Race, Identity, and Citizenship: A Reader*, edited by Rodolfo D. Torres, Louis F. Mirón, and Jonathan Xavier Inda, 322–333. Oxford: Blackwell Publishers.

Black, Stephanie. 2001. *Life and Debt*. Produced and directed by Stephanie Black. Narration written by Jamaica Kincaid. Tuff Gong Productions.

Brodkin, Karen. 2000. "Global Capitalism: What's Race Got to Do with It?" *American Ethnologist* 27 (2): 237–256.

Drake, St. Clair. 1990. *Black Folk Here and There: An Essay in History and Anthropology*. Vol. 2. Los Angeles, CA: Center for Afro-American Studies, University of California.

Frank, Andre Gunder. 1978. *World Accumulation, 1492–1789*. New York: Algora Publishing.

Harrison, Faye V. 1997. "The Gendered Politics and Violence of Structural Adjustment: A View from Jamaica. In *Situated Lives: Gender and Culture in Everyday Life*, edited by Louise Lamphere, Helena Ragoné, and Patricia Zavella, 451–468. New York: Routledge.

Jha, Lakshmi K. 1982. *North South Debate*. Delhi: Chanakya Publications.

Kingsolver, Ann E. 2001. *NAFTA Stories: Fears and Hopes in Mexico and the United States*. Boulder, CO: Lynne Rienner Publishers.

Marable, Manning. 1983. *How Capitalism Underdeveloped Black America: Problems in Race, Political Economy and Society*. Boston: South End Press.

Mintz, Sidney W. 1986. *Sweetness and Power: The Place of Sugar in Modern History*. New York: Viking.

Ward, Kathryn B. 1988. "Female Resistance to Marginalization: The Igbo Women's War of 1929." In *Racism, Sexism, and the World-System*, edited by Joan Smith, Jane Collins, Terence K. Hopkins, and Akbar Muhammad, 121–135. New York: Greenwood Press.

Weber, Max. 2001 (1926). *The Protestant Ethic and the Spirit of Capitalism*. London: Routledge.

Williams, Eric. 1994 (1944). *Capitalism and Slavery*. Chapel Hill: The University of North Carolina Press.

Wilson, Carter A. 1996. *Racism: From Slavery to Advanced Capitalism*. Thousand Oaks, CA: Sage Publications.

Zavella, Patricia. 1997. "The Tables are Turned: Immigration, Poverty, and Social Conflict in California Communities." In *Immigrants Out! The New Nativism and the Anti-immigrant Impulse in the United States*, edited by Juan F. Perea, 136–161. New York: New York University Press.

Ann Kingsolver

CARIBBEAN IMMIGRATION

Immigration from the Caribbean can take a number of forms, including refugees fleeing political turmoil in Cuba, Haiti, and the Dominican Republic; economic migrants from Jamaica, Trinidad and Tobago, Guyana, the Dominican Republic, Haiti, and Puerto Rico; and others who migrate for family reunification purposes. Caribbean immigration to the United States significantly increased after World War II due to the repeal of Jim Crow laws and the slow dismantling of the institutional architecture of racial discrimination. This immigration peaked in the post–civil rights era, as more people sought to emigrate because of employment opportunities, political upheaval at home, and for family reunification. Due to their nonwhite ethnicity (e.g., African, Hispanic, East Indian, Chinese, Jewish, Lebanese), when Caribbean immigrants were incorporated into the U.S. social system, they were typically ascribed minority status, in line with the color code in American society. The concept of "race at the gate," referring to U.S. immigration officials who decided whether or not to let people in depending on the racial group they belonged to, influenced the trajectory of these immigrants' journeys through the American social and political landscape.

First-generation immigrants from the Caribbean often experience a shift in racial ideology, because the continuum of "black-mulatto-white" they were accustomed to is condensed in the United States into a "black-white" spectrum. Thus, some Caribbean immigrants find their racial identity and status changed from somewhere between black and white into the subaltern African-American group, which often views them with suspicion and ambivalence. The Caribbean immigrant population in the United States is estimated by observers and activists to be approximately ten to fifteen million people, with strong concentrations on the East Coast—including the New York and Miami metropolitan areas—and with vibrant enclaves in Jersey City, Boston, Atlanta, Philadelphia, Chicago, Washington D.C., and Los Angeles.

Some of these Caribbean immigrants have distinguished themselves with their lasting contributions to American society through the arts, politics, education, sports, and other professions and institutions. In the process, many have become household names, including Harry Belafonte, Stokely Carmichael, Shirley Chisholm, Kenneth Clark, Celia Cruz, Rep. Lincoln Diaz-Balart (R), Rep. Mario Diaz-Balart (R), St. Clair Drake, Marcus Garvey, Alexander Hamilton, Rep. Luis V. Gutierrez (D), Leroi Jones, June Jordan, Elizabeth Lange, Jose Marti, Sen. Mel Martinez (R), Rep. Robert Menendez (D), Homer Plessy, Sydney Poitier, Colin Powell, Arthur Schomberg, Rep. Jose Serrano (D), Sammy Sosa, Cicely Tyson, Jean Baptiste Point Du Sable, Rep. Ileana Ros-Lehtinen (R), Rep. Nydia M. Velazquez (D), and Malcolm X.

IDEOLOGICAL AND ECONOMIC MOTIVATIONS FOR CARIBBEAN IMMIGRATION

Historically, social conditions that led to Caribbean emigration to the United States have differed from island to island. The early waves of Haitian migration between 1791 and 1809 were a result of the Haitian Revolution. After World War II, a mass migration of Puerto Ricans occurred. They came to the East Coast cities not as foreigners, but as U.S. citizens, and therefore were simply engaged in internal migration as they relocated to the mainland to improve their economic conditions. As U.S. citizens, they did not experience the hurdles that other groups of Caribbean immigrants had to confront, and deportation was not an option they needed to fear. Cubans immigrated under special conditions, because they were offered legal status upon arriving in the United States. They came to escape a Communist regime, and the first wave of immigrants mostly comprised of former members of the Cuban political and commercial elite (often characterized as "whites, Jews, and Chinese"). The dictatorship of François "Papa Doc" Duvalier from 1957 to 1971, which transformed Haiti into a terrorist state, was the primary initial cause for the second wave of Haitian emigration to the United States. Later, the continuously poor performance of the Haitian economy led many people to seek asylum or refugee status in the United States. Migration from the Anglophone Islands has been caused not so much by political instability but by a desire to improve one's economic condition. This movement gained strength after Jamaica achieved its independence in 1962.

While immigration has provided a safety valve for the surplus population and a source of revenues for Caribbean economies (because of the remittances from abroad), it has concurrently contributed to the political and social dysfunction of some of these states. This occurs because of the departure of educated citizens, which negatively impacts the functioning of the school system, public administration, and the democratic political system.

The mass migration of the middle class to the United States was accompanied in many cases by a migration of the rural population to urban areas, and particularly to the capital cities. This severely impacted the Caribbean agricultural sector, and some of the states have been forced to import basic food staples, such as rice and beans, that they were once able to produce for domestic consumption. It also created overcrowding and the transformation of capital cities into large slums, which has generated a rise in street violence that undermines the ability of the police to maintain law and order.

RACIAL DISCRIMINATION

Caribbean immigrants have had different experiences of racial discrimination in the United States, depending on their racial background. Historically, white immigrants received better treatment by immigration authorities than their black counterparts. By approximately 1800, laws were passed in some states, such as Maryland, to prevent black refugees from Saint Domingue (Haiti) from coming to the United States. From 1960 to 1990, white Cubans and black Haitians arriving at the port of Miami were treated differently: The former, in general, were welcome to stay, while the latter were incarcerated and deported. This clearly illustrates the racialization and double standards of U.S. immigration policies and practices.

Although discrimination in the United States was more brutal in the South than in the North, in both places West Indian immigrants reacted vigorously to protect their civil rights. For example, a group of Haitians in New Orleans were the complainants in the historic 1896 Supreme Court case *Plessy v. Ferguson*, which led to the creation of the "separate, but equal" doctrine. In the North, after the Jamaican leader Marcus Garvey established his Universal Negro Improvement Association in 1916, he and members of his organization were the targets of countless forms of harassment by the local New York authorities, and he was eventually thrown in jail and deported to his homeland.

While these were public cases that appeared in the press, they are representative of the discrimination of West Indians from every walk of life faced on a daily basis. The most blatant form was housing discrimination, which forced them to live in Harlem or other segregated areas in Brooklyn. Puerto Ricans had no other choice but to develop their *barrio*, or enclave, within the physical borders of a black ghetto. One such barrio in New York City became known as Spanish Harlem.

Racial discrimination involves a system of practices that must be deconstructed to understand the aspects of its deployment and crude impact. It manifests itself not simply in housing, employment and physical interactions, but also in laws and institutions. For example, *country discrimination* refers to the technological mechanisms used to infuse race into the process of admission to a country, and by which individuals from some countries are made less welcome than others. *Statistical discrimination* refers to the decisions and policies of the federal government that pertain to the racial balance of the U.S. population. What are the percentages of non-Europeans allowed to immigrate (often hidden in the per-country quota system for the Western and Eastern Hemispheres) in order to maintain the viability of the racial state?

Certificatory discrimination refers to the ability to get one's professional qualification approved by the receiving state, so that a person can seek equivalent employment. Certification is not simply based on expertise and experience; it is a value judgment based on whether or not the receiving country recognizes the validity of the institution that grants a diploma or provides training. *Classificatory discrimination* refers to the situation whereby one is identified with a subaltern racial group irrespective of one's previous racial status. In interacting with American

Haitians Protest U.S. Immigration Policy. *On May 19, 2000, a group of Haitians gathered in Miami's "Little Haiti" district to protest the policy that allows Cubans who reach U.S. soil to stay but generally sends Haitians back to their homeland.* © COLIN BRALEY/ REUTERS/CORBIS.

institutions such as schools, hospitals, or government offices, Caribbean immigrants are identified simply as African Americans, rather than as Trinidadian, Dominican, or Guyanese American (in reference to the country of origin), as some may prefer.

RELATIONS WITH AFRICAN AMERICANS

Historically, relations between African Americans and Caribbean immigrants have often been strained. Prior to the civil rights movement, there were two main reasons for the ethnic tension between African Americans and Caribbean residents in New York. First, most Caribbean immigrants learned about African Americans through the white press (newspapers and books) and Hollywood (films depicting black characters). By and large, these images and descriptions were negative (e.g., black riots, black maids, segregated housing). As a result of this exposure, civil rights–era Caribbean immigrants developed an ambiguous, if not critical, conception of African Americans. The second aspect of these encounters reflected differences between the two groups of newly arrived migrants—one of which was from the Deep South, the other from the Caribbean islands. The first was a lower-class group striving for better economic conditions and an improved quality of life; the second was an educated middle class intent on maintaining its standing. This encounter did not occur in the upper echelons of a firm or on a university campus. Rather, it happened in the lower echelons of the employment ladder or in a segregated housing complex, with its attendant problems of juvenile delinquency, crime, and vagrancy. Such early encounters were tension-filled because they involved people of different class backgrounds, aspirations, educational attainment, and professional skills. Up until the civil rights era, because of socialization and cultural differences, Caribbean immigrants tended to look down on African Americans.

The civil rights movement was a catalyst that changed the social context of the interaction between African

Americans and Caribbean islanders. Collaboration, cooperation, and, at times, competition became strong features of the relationships between the two groups. Relatively speaking, Caribbean immigrants have succeeded in their economic pursuits, with Jamaicans and Cubans generally being more successful than others, such as Puerto Ricans and Dominicans. Many Caribbean businessmen, because of discrimination barriers, have opened their own shops, and Caribbean economic enclaves have become thriving business centers that provide an infrastructure capable of sustaining Caribbean-American communities.

Between the two groups, "coalition" has become the name of the game within the political arena. Caribbean political candidates may depend on African American votes, and vice versa, to be elected to public office. For example, in Brooklyn it is unlikely that a Caribbean or African American could be elected to public office, particularly at the state or national level, without the support of the other group. The strategy developed by Caribbean immigrants is to seek the cooperation of African Americans for certain activities. For other activities, such as the Caribbean Carnival in Brooklyn, they seek the cooperation of all the Caribbean groups, whereas for still other activities they seek only people from their country of origin, especially if they are concerned about events occurring in their homeland.

SEE ALSO *Caribbean Racial Formations; Civil Rights Movement; Immigration Reform and Control Act of 1986 (IRCA); Immigration to the United States.*

BIBLIOGRAPHY

Duany, Jorge. 2002. *The Puerto Rican Nation on the Move: Identities on the Island and in the United States.* Chapel Hill: University of North Carolina Press.

Hernández, Ramona. 2002. *The Mobility of Workers Under Advance Capitalism: Dominican Migration to the United States.* New York: Columbia University Press.

Kasinitz, Philip. 1992. *Caribbean New York: Black Immigrants and the Politics of Race.* Ithaca, NY: Cornell University Press.

Laguerre, Michel S. 1984. *American Odyssey: Haitians in New York City.* Ithaca: Cornell University Press.

Palmer, Ransford W. 1995. *Pilgrims from the Sun: West Indian Migration to America.* New York: Twayne Publishers.

Pedraza-Bailey, Silvia. 1985. *Political and Economic Migrants in America: Cubans and Mexicans.* Austin: University of Texas Press.

Michel S. Laguerre

CARIBBEAN RACIAL FORMATIONS

Although the concept of "racial formation" originated and developed principally from the experience of continental America, it still has relevance to Caribbean conditions and contexts. Briefly defined, the concept refers to a particular political system in which racial considerations are given privileged positions in policy matters and human relationships. In this racially structured political system, a privileged racial section (regarded as superior) governs over subordinate but numerically significant racial sections (regarded as inferior). Within this system the state becomes a racial state that distributes resources unequally along racial lines, and always to the benefit of the dominant racial section. Some theorists, such as Michael Omi and Howard Winant (1994), regard this race-biased inequality in resource distribution as the principal project of the state within the particular racial formation.

The Caribbean resembles the United States in some crucial respects, but it also differs from it in other fundamental ways. The resemblances entail: (1) A similar history of slavery and European colonization, (2) the prevalence of racial or color criteria in influencing who gets economic and political power, (3) the slow evolution of political freedoms, including full democratic participation involving all groups within the system, and (4) periodic political struggles for racial and social equality on the part of significant minority groups. The differences tend to be equally significant. For example, while the Caribbean comprises several separate and diverse ministates involving many language groups (English, French, Spanish, Dutch), the United States is a federation of large, culturally similar states. Also, while the Caribbean middle classes in the early twenty-first century can boast of attaining hegemonic status (the highest positions of political and cultural leadership) there is a comparative lack of such power on the part of the American middle classes.

EVOLUTION OF PLANTATION SOCIETY

From the sixteenth to the nineteenth centuries, slavery set the stage for the evolution of a political and social system in the Caribbean that was structured principally along race and class lines. However, the racial and class considerations coincided so closely with each other that something closely approximating a caste system developed in early Caribbean history. In this system an exclusive white owner-planter class dominated over darker-skinned races or classes—with the mixed (Mulatto) population just below the whites, and the majority black population (both freed and slaves) occupying the lowest rungs of the racial formation. This was the plantation system, which the Caribbean scholar George Beckford (1972) claimed was a peculiar institution that totally controlled all of economic, political, and social life within it and throughout the region.

The Haitian Revolution, 1791-1804. *In August 1791, Haitian slaves rose up against their French masters. Plantations were burned and French slave owners and soldiers were executed.* **MANUSCRIPTS, ARCHIVES, AND RARE BOOKS DIVISION, SCHOMBURG CENTER FOR RESEARCH IN BLACK CULTURE, THE NEW YORK PUBLIC LIBRARY, ASTOR, LENOX AND TILDEN FOUNDATIONS.**

Except for Haiti, whose black slave population won its independence from France through a revolutionary uprising (1791–1804), emancipation came earliest to the British Caribbean slaves (in 1834). The post-emancipation period introduced added complexities to the Caribbean racial and class social structures, which significantly altered cultural perspectives and social relationships. During this era, immigrant indentured labor was imported from as far away as Portuguese-controlled Madeira, China, and India, to replace black ex-slaves as manual labor on the plantations. The result was a historical shift from the typical white-black racial confrontation patterns to a persistent conflict situation between ethnicities: from black-Portuguese and black-Chinese confrontations in the late nineteenth and early twentieth centuries to an almost pervasive black-East Indian ethnic conflict situation throughout a wide variety of Caribbean territories, including Guyana, Trinidad and Tobago, Surinam, and Jamaica, in the late twentieth and early twenty-first centuries.

It was also during this post-emancipation, indentured immigration period that the Caribbean middle classes rose to greater prominence. The original light-colored basis of their privileged classification shifted to include less rigid criteria, such as educational, occupational, and economic status. The bankruptcy of many white-owned plantations following the post-emancipation labor crises in the region led to a significant return migration of members of the dominant white classes back to Europe, paving the way for the upward mobility of a mixed group of largely colored and minimally black middle-class elements into the newly vacated seats of political power. By the latter part of the twentieth century, these middle classes (mostly the black and brown educated and professional elite) controlled the leadership positions of political parties and states throughout the region.

But the evolution of the middle-class elite into national leadership positions did not come about without constant, serious, and often deadly struggles, largely characterized by confrontations with the traditional white power structures. Struggles from below for greater democratic participation within a system that was closed to a majority black population, and towards political independence from European colonial control (objectives that were eventually realized only during the latter part of the twentieth century), were only some of the projects necessary to confront or modify the racial and class structures of domination in the Caribbean. But the realization of political power and independence by the national black and brown elite did not necessarily shatter the foundations of white domination throughout the region. Economic power was still in the hands of the expatriate white ownership classes even after political independence was won in the 1960s, and the Caribbean racial formations spawned by slavery and colonialism are still intact.

What makes the racial factor so pervasive and dominating despite persistent popular struggles (including violent revolution) directed against it throughout Caribbean history? The answer would seem to lie in the peculiar configurations of Caribbean social structure and political culture, and in the contradictions involved in the hegemonic power of middle-class political control.

CARIBBEAN SOCIAL STRUCTURE

During the slavery period, Caribbean social structure was basically a hierarchical one in which Amerindians, blacks, and browns were subordinated to white control. While the lighter-skinned (Mulatto) classes were generally spared the more onerous plantation work, the system routinely dehumanized Amerindian and black labor through a regime of constant brutality to ensure absolute obedience. Levels of brutality meted out to disobedient or rebellious slaves were extreme, and often public, in order to set an example for the rest. Such ruling-class violence defined the very nature of plantation life, for it was thought to be necessary for the very survival of the system as a whole. Few Amerindians survived plantation enslavement, and those that did (principally in the mainland territories such as Guyana) were eventually restricted behind institutionalized and remote reservations.

The distribution of resources within Caribbean plantation society was definitely along racial and, later, ethnic lines. Black slaves were regarded as cheap labor necessary to replace an earlier white indentured labor, which had proved to be unreliable. Such cheap labor policies influenced the maintenance of low wages, which continued with the immigration of indentured servants after emancipation. Unlike the lighter-skinned indentured servants, the black ex-slaves were denied credits and loans to go into more lucrative self-employment and business ventures. Compared to blacks, lighter-skinned ethnicities were given more favors and facilities by the colonial office to succeed in wealth creation, while every opportunity was taken by the planter classes to force blacks back into plantation labor. To this end, planters destroyed fruit trees and provision grounds, diverted water supplies from black living areas, and prosecuted former slaves from venturing into plantation areas if they were not plantation workers. In addition, the colonial authorities instituted a tax on land. These measures were meant to keep blacks from living independently of the plantations (Williams 1971; Knight 1994).

This unequal type of resource distribution in early plantation society in the Caribbean has left a legacy of stark poverty, which is reflected in the living conditions of those at the bottom of the social pyramid. In the more multiethnic Caribbean territories, such as Guyana, Trinidad and Tobago, and Suriname, most of the East Indian and Amerindian populations share with most of the black population the same depressed and impoverished space on the social pyramid.

A second legacy of Caribbean plantation society is the way in which both race and ethnicity become more sharply defined by the conflicts between groups. These sometimes deadly conflicts are themselves spawned by the inequalities of plantation social structures, and by the long term impact of colonial "divide and rule" policies. This divisive colonial legacy could be observed, for example, in the almost life and death conflicts for political power since the 1960s between the two highly politicized ethnicities in Guyana (blacks represented by the People's National Congress [PNC] Party, and East Indians by the People's Progressive Party [PPP]), a conflict situation that still persists in the early twenty-first century. Similar deadly ethnic or color-based political conflict and violence are routinely observed in Trinidad and Tobago, Jamaica and Suriname.

Yet the inequalities in Caribbean social structure breed continual resistance from below. The major examples of this resistance are the Haitian Revolution of 1791–1804; the establishment of what are called Maroon societies of defiant runaway slaves in the larger territories such as Jamaica and Suriname throughout the slavery period; post-emancipation rebellions for greater democracy, such as the Morant Bay Rebellion in Jamaica in 1865; the rise of the leftist movements in the 1940s and 1950s towards independence and in the 1960s and 1970s towards socialism; and the emergence of Rastafarian and Black Power struggles towards greater black consciousness and empowerment (Campbell 1987).

CARIBBEAN POLITICAL CULTURE

The racial subordination of blacks in the plantation hierarchy was usually justified by theories professing the universal superiority of whites. In 1854, for example, The Comte de Gobineau developed his "scientific" classification of races, with the whites at the top and blacks at the far bottom of the totem pole. One of Gobineau's disciples, Thomas Carlyle, a renowned British historian and scholar suggested a similar hierarchy with what he termed "the wisest man" at the top and "the Demerara nigger at the bottom" (Williams 1971, p. 398).

Established religion also played a role in cultivating racial attitudes and belief in the inferiority of blacks. The influence and complicity of the Catholic Church in the outlawing of Africanist religions such as Vodou in Haiti, and Obeah in the British Caribbean, which were regarded as devil worship, is one example of the church's role in associating blackness with evil. However, it is also fair to say that some of the Christian churches—particularly the non-established Presbyterians and Congregationalists—played an admirable role in helping to free the slaves, sometimes at the costs of the lives of some of their priests. At the same time, some Africanist religions, particularly Haitian Vodou and Jamaican Rastafarianism, have played a significant role historically in the liberation and creativity of the black masses throughout the region. The lyrics and songs of the famous Rastafarian reggae artist Bob Marley bear ample testimony to this liberating and creative spirit of Africanist ways of life in the region.

Like the established churches, public schools have often become ideological institutions by consistently reinforcing European centrality and domination in the Caribbean. This was experienced more sharply during the colonial period, when the curriculum of public schools emphasized the study of the histories and languages of the various European states, to the exclusion of Caribbean history and native languages. The reading books for elementary schools were not only biased in this ideological direction, but they tended to de-emphasize the development of critical thinking and insights by concentrating on what the "Mighty Sparrow," a Trinidad calypso singer, called "too much a' stupid ness" in his famous calypso song "Dan is the Man in the Van." Sparrow concluded the song with the ironic note that if during his time at school "his head was bright" (meaning if he had studied or internalized the books too well) he would have ended up becoming "a damn fool."

Caribbean activist intellectuals have also offered major challenges to the racial structures inherited from colonialism. The most notable of these have been Marcus Garvey from Jamaica in the 1920s and 1930s, C.L.R. James from Trinidad in the 1940s and 1950s, Aimé Césaire and Frantz Fanon from Martinique during the 1960s, and Walter Rodney from Guyana during the 1970s. Their challenges to the system involved an anticolonialism coupled with a message of black consciousness and empowerment. Some, like James and Rodney, have gone as far as challenging the capitalist system itself, while others, like Fanon, have advocated extreme responses, such as collective violence against the system.

MIDDLE-CLASS HEGEMONY

The Caribbean middle classes, because of their diverse characteristics, play a rather complex and controversial role in the maintenance and survival of the existing structures and culture of Caribbean racial formations. For example, while the tendency of some sections of the middle classes (particularly the business section) is to champion the privileges derived from the race and class inequalities in the system, a smaller but significant section of that class (particularly the intellectuals) often challenges the discrepancies and seeks appropriate and often radical changes in that system. These conflicting conjunctures often assume ideological forms, dividing Left from Right in the contest for political power. Bitter contests over the issues of colonialism and nationalism during the 1950s, followed by cold war struggles for and against socialism of the 1970s, eventually led to the violent destabilization and defeat of the Left by powerful international forces (mainly the United States) during the 1980s. It was the dual and seemingly contradictory character of Caribbean middle-class politics that led C.L.R. James to discern what he regarded as their "inherent instability" (James 1962).

The hegemony, or political and cultural dominance, of these classes depends upon their maintaining the support of powerful economic and political forces in the international system. The Caribbean middle classes, through their commercial linkages with international and global capitalism, benefit from the persistence of international economic inequalities along racial lines in the international system. From their inception during the slavery period, the Caribbean middle classes (originating from the Mulatto sections of the population) reinforced the white racial order by championing their own derived or assumed superiority over the black populations (free and slave), based on their own snobbish order of degrees of lightness of skin color. Eric Williams, who was prime minister of Trinidad and Tobago from 1962 to 1981, suggested that there were at least ten different hierarchical degrees of skin color gradations, ranging from "mixed bloods" and "octoroons" closest to white at the top, to the "griffe," "sacatra," and other darker-skinned Mulattoes closest to black at the bottom of the color pyramid (Williams 1971, pp. 187–188).

In the early 2000s, the middle classes benefit from the rather incomplete system of democracy that Caribbean states inherited from the European colonial powers. The qualifications for voting moved very gradually from ownership of slaves and high-priced property in the eighteenth and nineteenth centuries to income, literacy, and finally "age" (universal suffrage) during the twentieth century. This late development of democracy favors the upper classes in the Caribbean racial order. In addition, the better access of the middle classes to economic power and wealth, coupled with the high cost of qualifications to run for office, obviously give these classes an edge over the darker-skinned masses in the control of political power.

Meanwhile, there is a great deal of authoritarianism (or dictatorship) within Caribbean democracy, as reflected in the usually skewed system of representation between rulers and ruled. Such dictatorial control by the lighter skinned over the darker races is most starkly exemplified in the cases of the French- and Spanish-speaking territories with significantly large black populations, such as Haiti and the Dominican Republic, respectively. The case of Haiti is most noteworthy for the frequent derailment of democratic participation of the overwhelming black masses by a few rich middle-class families and businessmen (working mostly behind the scenes). A stark example of this is the overthrow of the democratically elected president, Jean Bertrand Aristide, and his overwhelmingly black Lavallas party, both in 1991 and in 2004.

That race significantly contributes to the structuring of Caribbean society, economy, and political culture does not necessarily mean that the racial factor is always obvious. In fact, the racial formations in the Caribbean would seem to represent what Michael Omi and Howard Winant (1994) regard as essentially unconscious rules of classification within a sociohistorical process. Thus, race is often realized in both theory and practice in the Caribbean sociohistorical experience. What essentially defines the Caribbean racial formation is the continual experience by the Caribbean people of a social process in which race—directly or indirectly, and consciously or unconsciously—plays a significant, although not exclusive, role in people's activities and relationships.

The racial/class hierarchical structure inherited from colonialism in the Caribbean, with white and light-colored representations at the top and the masses of the darker-skinned races and ethnicities at the bottom, keeps reinforcing itself by the following means: (1) Continuing white control of pivotal economic resources at the international level, coupled with skewed or unequal distribution of those resources along hierarchical racial lines at the domestic levels; (2) the cultivation of middle-class historical dominance of the political system, coupled with their comprador (or service) status with regard to international capitalism, and a traditional color-based snobbery with regard to the darker-skinned races and ethnic groups; and (3) a flawed or incomplete democratic system in the region, which marginalizes or excludes the lower classes by putting a relatively high economic price on electoral competition and access to political power.

SEE ALSO *Children, Racial Disparities and Status of; Cuban Racial Formations; Haitian Racial Formations; HIV and AIDS; Racial Formations; Social Welfare States.*

BIBLIOGRAPHY

Beckford, George. 1972. *Persistent Poverty: Underdevelopment in Plantation Economies of the Third World.* London: Oxford University Press.

Campbell, Horace. 1987. *Rasta and Resistance: From Marcus Garvey to Walter Rodney.* Trenton, NJ: Africa World Press.

Césaire, Aimé. 2000 (1972). *Discourse on Colonialism.* New York: Monthly Review Press, 2000.

Fanon, Frantz. 1967. *The Wretched of the Earth.* Translated by Constance Farrington. Middlesex, U.K.: Penguin Books.

James, C.L.R. 1989 (1938). *The Black Jacobins.* New York: Vintage.

———. 1962. *Party Politics in the West Indies.* San Juan, Trinidad, West Indies: Vedic Enterprises.

Knight, Franklyn. 1990. *The Caribbean: The Genesis of a Fragmented Nationalism,* 2nd ed. New York: Oxford University Press.

Omi, Michael, and Howard Winant. 1994. *Racial Formation in the United States: From the 1960s to the 1990s,* 2nd ed. New York: Routledge.

Rodney, Walter. 1969. *Groundings with My Brothers.* London: Bogle/L'Overture.

Sunshine, Catharine. 1985. *The Caribbean: Survival, Struggle, and Sovereignty.* Washington, DC: EPICA.

Waters, Anita. 1985. *Race, Class, and Political Symbols: Rastafari and Reggae in Jamaican Politics.* New Brunswick, NJ: Transaction Books.

Williams, Eric. 1970. *From Columbus to Castro:* The History of the Caribbean, 1492–1969. London: Andre Deutsch.

Perry Mars

CENTRAL AMERICANS

Central America is a diverse and complex region, and Central Americans living in the United States reflect this heterogeneity. Unlike Mexican immigrants, who have dominated U.S.-bound Latin American migration, Central Americans are socioculturally and economically diverse, and they have been received by the U.S. government in different ways. As Nestor Rodriguez and Jacqueline Hagan (1999) observe, the Latin American population in the United States includes both well-educated and unskilled immigrants, political refugees, wealthy landowners, and peasants. Central Americans also have diverse linguistic traditions. For example, Guatemalans who are of Mayan descent may speak one or more Mayan languages (and not Spanish). Hondurans who come from the Caribbean coast of their country (and some Belizeans) may speak Garifuna. Garifuna and Nicaraguans who come from the Atlantic coast of Nicaragua may speak English or Mesquito at home instead of Spanish.

CENTRAL AMERICAN MIGRATION PATTERNS

There has been a noticeable presence of Central Americans in the United States since the early twentieth century. In the early 1900s, Salvadoran and Nicaraguan coffee growers traveled to and from the United States for business and pleasure. The commercial ships that transported bananas from Honduras to the United States brought news of new opportunities, and Hondurans traveled north in the search of them. But the growth of the largest Central American groups in the United States (Guatemalans, Hondurans, Salvadorans, Nicaraguans) began in the late 1970s, when a political and economic crisis destabilized several countries in the region and forced many of their citizens to abandon their homes. Many (mostly Guatemalans, Nicaraguans and Salvadorans) relocated to adjacent Central American countries, while others (mostly Guatemalan Maya) settled in refugee camps in southern Mexico. Many of these refugees have since returned to their homeland, but others have made their way further north to the United States and Canada, where they have established vibrant communities. Central Americans, as a whole, now constitute one of the fastest-growing Latino groups in the United States. For instance, the number of Salvadorans (the largest group of Central Americans) in the United States stood at 34,000 in 1970. This number increased to 94,447 in 1980; to 565,081 in 1990; and to 823,832 in 2000, according to the U.S. Census Bureau. Thus, whereas in 1980 El Salvador was not among the top 25 immigrant sending countries to the United States, by 1990 it was in eleventh place and by 2000 it had moved to eighth place.

MEDIA IMAGES OF CENTRAL AMERICANS

Despite a long immigration history and the strong influence of the United States in the Central American countries, Central Americans were relatively unknown to the U.S. public before the 1980s. Up until then, they had remained relatively invisible, often "passing" for white or being mistaken for Mexicans. This changed around 1980, when the media began portraying Central Americans in a negative fashion—sometimes as renegade army men murdering Catholic nuns, and sometimes as guerrillas confiscating homes and businesses. The notion of Central Americans as thugs (perhaps even as terrorists) began to be implanted in the minds of the U.S. public. These negative stereotypical portrayals have been sustained both on the big screen and in the media. For instance, in *A Beautiful Mind*, the film biography of the mathematician John Nash, the Salvadoran nationality of Nash's highly intelligent wife is not mentioned. Housekeepers and nannies, however, are often portrayed as Salvadorans or Guatemalans in films. Furthermore, when media portrayals of Salvadoran and other Central American gang members appear in the media, their nationalities are almost always noted in these media accounts. Thus, racialized negative images of Central Americans did not stop with the images of war in the 1980s. On the contrary, they have continued to define this group.

MILITARY CONFLICT AND IMMIGRATION

Two major, interrelated events occurred in 1979 that helped focus attention on Central American immigrants. The first was the beginning of a long and tumultuous civil conflict in El Salvador and Nicaragua, in which the United States was deeply involved. The second was the resultant flow of U.S.-bound refugees from both countries. A similar conflict had been raging in Guatemala since 1970, and this struggle also began to attract attention. Images of suffering Mayan women, men, and children began to appear in the U.S. media.

Although the migratory flows that the political upheaval in El Salvador, Guatemala, and Nicaragua generated might fit the classic profile of refugees, the U.S. administrations of Ronald Reagan, George Bush, and Bill Clinton refused to grant blanket refugee status to Salvadorans and Guatemalans. The reception given to Nicaraguans varied depending on the political climate in Central America (particularly the dynamics of the Contra war) and the level of support they received from the Cuban community in Miami, where many settled. The major problem with Central Americans was that the U.S. government could not legally recognize refugees generated by a conflict the U.S. government itself was financially and militarily supporting.

As a result, many of these refugees were considered undocumented or illegal immigrants, even though their situation mirrored the profile of people from other countries who were formally designated as refugees. This meant that Salvadorans, Guatemalans, and Nicaraguans (to a certain extent) were ineligible for government assistance for their resettlement. They were denied the "structure of refuge," as Rubén Rumbaut calls the government resettlement aid available to officially recognized refugees. They were left on their own to cope with the economic, social, and cultural consequences of their flight. Many Central Americans crossed several international borders to reach their families and friends already in the United States. These ties had been forged throughout the course of U.S. political, military, economic, and cultural involvement in Central America. Thus, when the conditions in that region deteriorated to the point where many sought refuge elsewhere, the United States emerged as the preferred choice of destination (Menjívar 2000).

THE CONTEXT OF EXIT AND RECEPTION

The circumstances of their departure and the context of arrival are of particular importance for Central Americans because these experiences have shaped their lives in the United States. Many have brought with them traumatic memories of political upheaval in their countries during the past three decades. The thirty-six-year Guatemalan civil conflict that ended in December 1996, the twelve-year Salvadoran civil war that ended in December 1991, and the decade-long "Contra" war in Nicaragua that ended in 1990 all left profound levels of devastation, especially in the countryside. The Guatemalan army's scorched-earth campaigns and brutal repression left 440 Mayan villages destroyed (by the army's own account), decimating an entire generation of community leaders and youth (Alvarez and Loucky 1992). Moreover, between half a million and one million Guatemalans were displaced (Manz 1988). Massacres in El Salvador and similar state terror tactics against popular social movements calling for social, political, and economic justice left approximately 75,000 dead or disappeared. In 1979, after a mass insurrection, the Sandinista National Liberation Front (FSLN) toppled the Nicaraguan government of Anastasio Somoza Debayle. The FSLN proclaimed the creation of a "mixed economy" to correct the social and economic injustices of the past, as

The Guatemalan Civil War, 1960–1996. *A man and his relatives carry the coffin of Maria Chel, killed by the Guatemalan Army in 1983, during her burial in Tzalbal, Guatemala, on October 6, 2004. The decades of civil war had a devastating effect on the people of Guatemala.* **AP IMAGES.**

well as an independent and "nonaligned" foreign policy to terminate the country's historical dependence on the United States. In response, the Reagan administration launched a multifaceted assault against the Sandinista government that included a trade embargo and funds for the training, equipping, and directing of a counterrevolutionary army (the "Contras"). The Sandinista government countered this attack, using up to 50 percent of the national budget, which brought to a halt the social programs instigated by the revolution. This combination of factors unleashed a profound economic crisis from which the Sandinistas never recovered; their government only lasted a decade. Although there were no overt political upheavals in Honduras, this nation was involved in the regional conflicts by proxy, as it served as a base for the Nicaraguan Contras and other military operations in the region. A U.S. base was opened there during the 1980s.

Many Central American refugees fled to neighboring areas (mainly southern Mexico), but a significant number made their way to the United States. Some had lost family members to the violence, others had received death threats, and others were economic refugees dislocated by the crisis. By and large, the United States did not consider Central Americans as deserving of protection, even though the U.S. State Department had noted on several occasions the disastrous human rights record of the Guatemalan and Salvadoran governments and the severity of the political conflict in the region. As with other refugee populations in the United States, the Central Americans' legal status has been shaped by the intersection of immigration and refugee policy with foreign policy. Thus, these were *de facto* refugees who lacked *de jure* recognition. Once on U.S. soil, Central Americans could apply for political asylum, but throughout the 1980s less than 3 percent of Salvadoran and Guatemalan applicants were granted such status.

In the case of the Nicaraguans, who were fleeing a country whose government the United States was intent on overthrowing, the U.S. government could have granted them refugee status as a symbolic gesture, as it had done with various groups fleeing Communist regimes. However, the U.S. government needed Nicaraguans disenchanted with the revolution to be as close to Nicaragua as possible, not in the United States (Portes and Stepick 1993). Granting these Nicaraguans refugee status, and thus giving them a place to settle and the aid to do so, would have dissuaded them from pressuring for a regime change in their native land. Thus, throughout the conflict years, Nicaraguans' success rate in asylum applications oscillated, but it was never high. Hondurans were only given Temporary Protected Status (TPS), a designation created in 1990 to deal with victims of political conflicts and natural disasters (this status was also given to Salvadorans, but not to Guatemalans) after Hurricane Mitch in 1998.

Thus, U.S. immigration law has been applied unevenly to Central Americans, which reflects upon the discrepancies in U.S. foreign policy toward their countries of origin. The case of Central Americans makes evident that defining a particular group of immigrants as refugees is not based solely upon unsafe conditions in the country of origin or human rights considerations, but rather on the extent to which the United States recognizes them as deserving asylum and assistance (Zolberg, Suhrke, and Aguayo 1989). The case of Central Americans highlights the enduring power of the state in creating immigration laws that shape the everyday lives of immigrants.

RACIAL, ETHNIC, AND PAN-ETHNIC IDENTITIES

Despite the increased presence of Central Americans in the United States, they have remained relatively invisible. As the Guatemalan writer and scholar Arturo Arias observes, Central Americans are hidden "within the imaginary confines of what constitutes the multicultural landscape of the United States" (Arias 2003, p. 170). Only in prominent destination areas of Central American immigration—notably Los Angeles, San Francisco, Washington, D.C., and Miami—are they recognized as distinct from the major Latino groups. Within the racial landscape of the United States, they are often a minority within a minority, a situation that Arias (2003) links to a colonial history in which Central America was considered inferior to Mexico.

This invisibility also has homogenized Central Americans, and they have been simply labeled as "other Latinos," "other Hispanics" or, at best, "Central Americans." This has occurred in spite of the wide variety of languages, ethnicities, histories, and cultures present in this group, and despite the fact that not all Central Americans identify themselves in the same racial terms. For instance, 36 percent of Salvadorans living in the United States identified themselves as white in the 2000 U.S. Census, compared to 38 percent of Guatemalans, 43 percent of Hondurans, and 54 percent of Nicaraguans. Whereas 5 percent of Hondurans and 2 percent of Nicaraguans identified themselves as black, less than 1 percent of Salvadorans and 1 percent of Guatemalans chose this category. Even though an estimated half of Guatemalans are of Mayan descent, only 1.5 percent identified themselves as American Indian. However, this self-identification might be due to a bureaucratic misunderstanding rather than an absence of American Indians among Central Americans. In addition, more than half of Salvadorans and Guatemalans, 42 percent of Hondurans, and 36 percent of Nicaraguans identified themselves as "other race," and between 7 and 8 percent of the people in each group marked some combination of two or more races. Central Americans are, therefore, increasing in their visibility and contributing to the complexity of Latinos within the U.S. ethnic and racial landscape.

The racial self-identification of a person from any one group is not simply an individual decision; it also reflects the social construction of race and ethnicity within the specific country. In addition, racial-ethnic identity differs by generation and subgroup (e.g., a minority within a minority). In the case of Central Americans this identification or classification is very much linked to how the U.S. government has received them, for this reception has shaped many aspects of life among the various groups. Such identifications affect intragroup relations as well, particularly between groups that have little linguistic and cultural common ground, and they shape whether and how Central Americans carve out spaces within the larger Latino mosaic.

Even those Central Americans who share a racial identification with U.S. minority groups, or even with other immigrant groups, do not automatically follow the racial politics or paths of those groups. For instance, Jason DeFay (2005) found that Central American Garifuna immigrants (who likely identified themselves as black in the U.S. Census) have an acculturation pattern that is distinctly different from that of blacks identified as Jamaican, Haitian, or Belizean. He argues that the formation of intergenerational voluntary organizations and the politics of racial and national identity in the United States have permitted Garifuna immigrants to carve out a niche distinct from the larger minority groups. Thus, one should not expect that simply identifying with other Latino (or non-Latino) groups will place Central Americans on similar paths. Furthermore, as Arias observes, Central Americans constitute a population that "has not yet earned the hyphen to mark its recognition, its level of assimilation and integration, within the multi-cultural landscape of the United States" (Arias 2003, p. 171).

It is important, however, to note that intragroup relations among the different Central American groups, as well as between them and the larger Latino groups, have included many instances of collaboration, particularly in campaigns to work on issues of social justice. Interestingly, the categorization of the newer Central American groups within larger pan-ethnic categories (e.g., Mexicans, Latino, Hispanic) has had important consequences for political mobilization and empowerment. A recognition by Central Americans and larger Latino groups of a common ground and ancestry (e.g., indigenous descent or black heritage) and the use of a broader racial-ethnic label have contributed to the development of political agendas focused on common interests and conditions. This recognition has been spurred, in part, by the history of political mobilization among Latino domestic minorities, particularly Chicanos in the western United States and Puerto Ricans on the East Coast, as well as a recognition of their own history among Central Americans themselves. Time will tell if these intragroup dynamics translate into more political power for Latinos.

SEE ALSO *Immigration to the United States; Latin American Racial Transformations; Latinos; Mayan Genocide in Guatemala; Puerto Ricans.*

BIBLIOGRAPHY

Alvarez, Lynn, and James Loucky. 1992. "Inquiry and Advocacy: Attorney-Expert Collaboration in the Political Asylum Process." *NAPA Bulletin* 11: 43–52.

Arias, Arturo. 2003. "Central American Americans: Invisibility, Power and Representation in the US Latino World." *Latino Studies* 1 (1): 168–187.

DeFay, Jason Bradley. 2005. *Identity Matters: Immigration and the Social Construction of Identity in Garifuna Los Angeles.* Ph.D. diss., University of California, San Diego.

Manz, Beatriz. 1988. *Refugees of a Hidden War: The Aftermath of Counterinsurgency.* Albany: State University of New York Press.

Menjívar, Cecilia. 1999. "Salvadorans and Nicaraguans: Refugees become Workers." In *Illegal Immigration in America: A Reference Handbook*, edited by David Haines and Karen E. Rosenblum, 232–253. Westport, CT: Greenwood Press.

———. 2000. *Fragmented Ties: Salvadoran Immigrant Networks in America.* Berkeley: University of California Press.

———. 2002. "Living in Two Worlds?: Guatemalan-Origin Children in the United States and Emerging Transnationalism." *Journal of Ethnic and Migration Studies* 28 (3): 531–552.

———. 2006. "Liminal Legality: Salvadoran and Guatemalan Immigrant Lives in the United States." *American Journal of Sociology* 111 (4): 999–1037.

Mountz, Allison, Richard Wright, Ines Miyares, and Adrian J. Bailey. 2002. "Lives in Limbo: Temporary Protected Status and Immigrant Identities." *Global Networks* 2 (4): 335–356.

Portes, Alejandro, and Alex Stepick. 1993. *City on the Edge: The Transformation of Miami*. Berkeley: University of California Press.

Rodriguez, Ana Patricia. 2005. "'Departamento 15': Cultural Narratives of Salvadoran Transnational Migration." *Latino Studies* 3 (1): 19–41.

Rodriguez, Nestor P., and Jacqueline Hagan. 1999. "Central Americans in the United States." In *The Minority Report: An Introduction to Racial, Ethnic, and Gender Relations*, 3rd ed., edited by Anthony Gary Dworkin and Rosalind J. Dworkin, 278–296. Fort Worth, TX: Harcourt Brace College Publishers.

Rumbaut, Rubén G. 1989. "The Structure of Refuge: Southeast Asian Refugees in the U.S., 1975–85." *International Review of Comparative Public Policy* 1 (1): 97–129.

Zolberg, Aristide, Astri Suhrke, and Sergio Aguayo. 1989. *Escape from Violence: Conflict and the Refugee Crisis in the Developing World*. New York: Oxford University Press.

Cecilia Menjívar

CHAIN GANGS

Nearly half a century after the Civil War, the southern states' prison systems, with a largely black population, comprised two models of outdoor convict labor: The prison farm and the road chain gang. The chain gang started in Georgia in 1908 and was envisioned as a progressive penal reform movement, the direct consequence of the ending of the convict lease system, as well as public demand for improved transportation. Chain gangs flourished throughout the South and by the 1920s and 1930s chained prisoners, mostly black, became a common sight along southern roadways. Georgia grasped the economic and social benefits of the chain gang, which soon developed into the "good roads movement." "Bad boys," a Georgia folk saying went, "make good roads." Hired labor and even conscription had proved unreliable in the past, as free men were not disposed to work the roads if they could help it. Advocates for the good roads movement considered it advantageous to the state if convicts were made to serve their time building roads without creating unfair competition with labor. On a "humanitarian" level, proponents claimed that it would take the convict out of his cramped cell and provide him with work in the fresh air and sunshine. The federal government under, the auspices of the United States Department of Agriculture's Office of Public Roads, joined in and spearheaded the movement as a way to modernize the South's economy.

Magazine editorials applauded Georgia for having abolished the convict lease program, and for building more good roads than any other Southern state, encouraging other states to follow its lead. The race factor, for the most part, enhanced the enthusiasm for the chain gang as there was overwhelming white support for the good roads movement. The tragic plight of the black lawbreaker, however, was not diminished by the shift from the lease system to county chain gangs. To a southern black prisoner there was little difference between his situation as a slave on the plantation, as a leased convict forced to toil in the coal mine, or as a chained prison worker on the roads. The chained southern black man on the southern county road had been transformed from the plantation owner's chattel into a "slave of the state."

Georgia's reform efforts merely shifted the atrocities from the private to the public sector. For southern whites the chain gang had much of the attraction of the legacy of slavery. The state now became the actual master responsible for the welfare of a growing pool of forced black labor. Black prisoners labored and even slept together, with chains fastened through their feet and around their ankles. Their rations were infested with maggots. With an armed white overseer, the black convict slaved from sunup to sundown. Brutalities, corporal punishments (beatings with a leather strap, thumpings with rifle butts and clubs) and outright torture, were commonplace. Major atrocities, such as the staking treatment (chaining an inmate between stakes and pouring molasses over his body while flies, bees and other insects crawled all over him); the sweat box treatment (locking a prisoner for days into a wooden box that was neither high enough to stand nor deep enough to sit, while temperatures exceeded one hundred degrees); and the Georgia rack (stretching the inmate between two hooks with a cable and a turn crank) were all meted out for the most trivial disobedience.

Chain gangs had a brief existence, as economic forces played a central role in their demise. During the Great Depression, as jobs became scarce, criticism was heard that convict chain gangs took work that rightfully belonged to free labor. The government stopped providing federal funds to finance roads built using convict labor. Enthusiasm for chain gangs also decreased as the number of white convicts on the roads increased. By the 1940s, chain gangs had almost vanished. The last few chained prisoners were pulled off the roads when Georgia finally eliminated the practice in the early 1960s.

The media contributed significantly to the practice's demise. Films ranging from Meryn LeRoy's graphic expose, *I Am a Fugitive from a Chain Gang* (1932) to Stuart Rosenberg's *Cool Hand Luke* (1967) showed the atrocities of the system. As shameful as the abuses chronicled in the movies were, they could not capture the raw vivid details of

The Return of the Rock Pile. *On August 21, 1995, the Limestone Correctional Facility in Gadsden, Alabama, reinstituted the practice of putting convicts to work on a chain gang. This form of punishment had been abandoned half a century earlier, but it was brought back as a way to "get tough on criminals."* AP IMAGES.

everyday life suffered by black convicts on the chain gang. Prisoners were restrained at all times with heavy chains that were riveted around their ankles and were only removed (by a chisel) when the convict was released. At night another long chain was run between his legs, so that every man was connected to every other man, and no one was able to go to the toilet (a hole in the floor) without waking everybody on the chain gang. In the movies, the protagonists were mostly white, while in reality, the racial composition of the chain gangs were disproportionately African American. It took white actors, however, to generate a national scandal and shame a mostly Caucasian audience.

Half a century after their disappearance, convicts working in shackles once again became a sight on southern roads. The practice was reinitiated in 1995, when four hundred convicts, predominately black, were marshaled into a chain gang, at the Limestone Correctional Facility in Alabama. The reemergence of the chain gang began when Ron Jones, a prison warden, recommended it to gubernatorial candidate Forrest "Fob" James as a "get tough on crime" measure. Once elected, Governor James, with overwhelming white support, established chain gangs, alleging that it was an effective crime deterrent that made Alabama a safer place for the law-abiding citizen. The governor added that he reintroduced chain gangs because some convicts found prison life much too easy, and that they ought to be out working hard rather than cuddled by lifting weights and watching cable TV. Arizona, Florida, Massachusetts, Iowa and Wisconsin shortly joined Alabama. In Arizona, women inmates also began to work on a chain gang, burying dead indigent bodies. Juvenile chain gangs shortly became yet another manifestation of the practice.

Commentators have urged that the chain gang's historical connection to slavery is indisputable, and that the practice offends human dignity and should be condemned as a form of cruel and unusual punishment under the mandate of the Eighth Amendment. Other critics have pointed to the Thirteenth Amendment, although its constitutional prohibition on involuntary servitude specifically provides an exception for those convicted of crime. Although the Supreme Court has prohibited many forms of prison abuse, it has not specifically addressed the constitutionality of chain gangs. The Court has, however, condemned Alabama's "hitching post practice" (chaining convicts to a hitching post for over a seven-hour period where they were exposed to the heat of the sun, deprived of bathroom breaks, and subjected to prolonged thirst and taunting) as gratuitous infliction of wanton and unnecessary pain in violation of the Eighth Amendment. Additionally, in response to a civil action by the Southern Poverty Law Center, the state of Alabama reluctantly, without admitting that chain gangs violated the Eighth Amendment's "cruel and unusual punishment" clause, agreed to end the practice of shackling convict work crews together.

The spectacle of black prisoners in chains is powerfully linked to the images of slavery serving as a forceful reminder of their heritage of racial oppression in America. It brings to mind southern slave auctions where black families, linked by leg irons and iron collars, were sold and transported to the plantations. After the Civil War when slavery was abolished, southern states passed Jim Crow laws to hinder migration and control freed blacks. Blacks found guilty of these laws were forced to work as convict contract workers, and on the prison farms and southern roads in chains. The iron chains were the emblem of degradation and humiliation. The states that have revived and continue to use chain gangs (a practice embedded into the cultural history of oppression of an entire race) undermine the moral legitimacy of their criminal justice system.

SEE ALSO *Black Codes; Criminal Justice System; Criminality, Race and Social Factors; United States Constitution.*

BIBLIOGRAPHY

"Chain Gangs Arrive in Massachusetts." 1999. *Florida Today.* June 17.

Commonwealth v. Baldi, 106 A.2d 777, 781–782 (Pa. 1954) (Musmanno, J., dissenting), *cert. denied*, 348 U.S. 977 (1955).

Cook, Rhonda. 1995. "Around the South Back to Hard Labor." *Atlanta Journal and Constitution*, August 20.

Cool Hand Luke. 1967. Directed by Stuart Rosenberg. Warner Bros., DVD edition: Warner Home Video, 1997.

Garvey, Stephen P. 1998. "Freeing Prisoners' Labor." *Stanford Law Review* 50: 339–398.

Gorman, Tessa M. 1997. "Back on the Chain Gang: Why the Eighth Amendment and the History of Slavery Proscribe the Resurgence of Chain Gangs." *California Law Review* 85: 441.

Gutterman, Melvin. 2002. "'A Failure to Communicate': The Reel Prison Experience." *SMU Law Review* 55: 1515.

Hope v. Pelzer, 536 U.S. 730, 122 S.Ct. 2508, 153 L. Ed.2d 666 (2002).

I am a Fugitive from a Chain Gang. 1995 (1932). Directed by Mervyn LeRoy. Warner Bros. DVD edition: Warner Home Video.

James, Fob, Jr. 1995. "Prison is for Punishment." Editorial, *USA Today*, Aug. 28: 14A.

Lichtenstein, Alex. 1993. "Good Roads and Chain Gangs in the Progressive South: 'The Negro Convict Is a Slave.'" *Journal of Southern History* 59: 85.

———. 1996. *Twice the Work of Free Labor: The Political Economy of Convict Labor in the New South*. London: Verso.

Mancini, Matthew J. 1996. *One Dies, Get Another: Convict Leasing in the American South, 1866–1928*. Columbia: University of South Carolina Press.

Montgomery Advertiser. 1996. "Alabama Agrees to Abolish Chain Gang Shackles." June 21.

Whitin, E. Stagg. 1912. "The Spirit of Convict Road-Building." *Southern Good Roads* VI (December 1912): 12–13.

Zimmerman, Jane. 1951. "The Penal Reform Movement in the South during the Progressive Era, 1890–1917." *Journal of Southern History* 17: 462–463.

Mel Gutterman

CHAMBERLAIN, HOUSTON STEWART
1855–1927

Houston Stewart Chamberlain, who was born into a family of English military officers on September 9, 1855, became a widely recognized advocate of race inequality and Aryan superiority in his adopted country of Germany. In his writings he built his enthusiasm for German cultural and intellectual achievements into an eclectic theory of the superiority of the "Teutonic" race, a category that he used synonymously with "Aryan" and "Germanic." After initial university studies in the biological sciences, he developed a career as an independent author of widely disseminated essays and biographical treatises on German cultural, philosophical, historical, political, and religious themes. In the latter half of his life, Chamberlain developed a close association with family members and admirers of the anti-Semitic opera composer Richard Wagner (1813–1883). Chamberlain's writings were widely admired in conservative German political circles, and he became an early supporter of Adolf Hitler and the Nazis. Indeed, he is often considered an important intellectual and ideological precursor of the Nazi movement.

Chamberlain's education had two elements that developed into the primary themes of his writings. Because he suffered from poor health and abhorred the regimentation of English schools, his early education took place largely under private tutors. Long tours of continental Europe provided the first of his major themes: a deep admiration for the artistic and musical achievements associated with Italy and Germany. The other major theme of his writing developed out of his university training at the University of Geneva (1879–1884), where he studied the biological sciences (botany, zoology, and physiology). His professors included Carl Vogt, an outspoken proponent both of Darwinism and of the intellectual inferiority of women and non-European races. Chamberlain never completed the requirements for his doctorate in botany. Nonetheless, he pursued his biological research further, and in 1897 he published a treatise on sap flow in plants that he had written under the supervision of the botanist Julius Wiesner in Vienna, where he resided from 1889 to 1908.

These two themes of cultural glory and scientific investigation combined to form the structure of his arguments about race. He knew the work of other theorists of Aryan superiority, such as Arthur de Gobineau (1816–1882) and Ernest Renan (1823–1892), but he developed his own views independently. He never began his arguments with a simple assertion of the superiority of the Germanic race. Instead, he claimed to reach that conclusion based on what appeared to be the evidence provided by broad-ranging references to earlier texts, documents, and cultural objects. He supported his racial theories with a loose definition of the privileged Germanic, Teutonic, or Aryan groups. Italians, for example, could sometimes count as Teutonic because of the influence of Germanic tribes and aristocrats in Italy over many centuries.

The most significant personal and intellectual encounter of Chamberlain's life and career was with the operas and writings of Wagner, who was himself an anti-Semite. His single personal meeting with the composer, at the Bayreuth Festival in 1882, led to a correspondence with Wagner's widow, Cosima. In 1892 he published a short study of Wagner's operas. On the basis of that work, and on Cosima's recommendation, the Munich publisher Friedrich Bruckmann commissioned him to write a full-scale biographical study of Wagner, which was published in 1896. He took Wagner's daughter Eva as his second wife in 1908, the same year that he took up residence in the Wagner household.

Bruckmann was pleased with the success of the biography of Wagner, and he contracted Chamberlain to write a comprehensive study of the culture of the nineteenth century intended for a broad audience. The resulting book, *Foundations of the Nineteenth Century*, was published to wide notice in 1899. More than 100,000 copies were sold by 1915. A massive brief for "racial purity," this book undergirded the messages of such works as Charles Carroll's *The Negro a Beast* (1900), and Thomas Dixon's *The Leopard's Spots* (1902) and *The Clansman* (1905). Chamberlain argued that the creative forces of the Aryan-Teutonic race allowed German culture to triumph over the European "racial chaos" that followed the fall of the Roman Empire. He thus saw Germans as the true defenders of Christianity and a counterweight to the invidious, "alien" influence of the Jews. He believed that Germans always displayed an intuitive, 'regenerative' creativity that justified their cultural and racial superiority. He defended this claim in further biographical studies of major German figures, including the philosopher Immanuel Kant (1905) and the writer Johann Wolfgang von Goethe (1912).

Throughout his wide-ranging writings, Chamberlain pursued a concept for which he drew support both from the arts and from the biological sciences: the *Gestalt*. In Chamberlain's mind, both living organisms in their environments and broadly conceived systems of creative ideas (e.g., Wagner's operas, Goethe's literature, Kant's philosophy, or German Protestant Christianity) all carried the wholeness of *Gestalt*, or an integrated formal order within a dynamic system. For Chamberlain, no boundary existed between the methods and insights of the natural sciences and those of the arts and humanities. These opinions also made him ambivalent about Darwinism, which he considered destructive of the necessary religious order.

During his later career, Chamberlain polemically supported Germany in its political and military conflicts. During World War I, for example, he wrote vigorous pro-German propaganda. In the final years of his life, which he spent in poor health at the Wagner household in Bayreuth, his work inspired the admiration of several important Nazi figures, including the party propagandist Alfred Rosenberg and Adolf Hitler himself. He died on January 9, 1927, and Hitler attended his funeral.

SEE ALSO *Wagnerian Music.*

BIBLIOGRAPHY

Allen, Roger. 2005. "*Die Weihe des Hauses* (The Consecration of the House): Houston Stewart Chamberlain and the Early Reception of *Parsifal*." In *A Companion to Wagner's Parsifal*, edited by William Kinderman and Katherine R. Syer. Rochester, NY: Camden House.

Biddiss, Michael. 2004. "Chamberlain, Houston Stewart." *Oxford Dictionary of National Biography*. Vol. 10. Oxford: Oxford University Press.

Field, Geoffrey. 1981. *Evangelist of Race: The Germanic Vision of Houston Stewart Chamberlain*. New York: Columbia University Press.

Harrington, Anne. 1996. *Reenchanted Science: Holism in German Culture from Wilhelm II to Hitler*. Princeton, NJ: Princeton University Press.

Kevin S. Amidon

CHÁVEZ, CÉSAR ESTRADA
1927–1993

César Estrada Chávez was born on March 31, 1927 in Yuma, Arizona. He was a civil rights activist, community organizer, and founder of the United Farm Workers of America (UFWA), the first union to successfully organize agricultural workers in the United States. A self-educated follower of Gandhi's nonviolent protest strategy and Catholic theories of penance, he began his organizing career in 1952 with the Community Service Organization (CSO), a leading civil rights organization advocating on behalf of urban Mexican Americans in California. He became the executive director of the CSO in 1958.

In 1962 Chávez founded the National Farm Workers Association, the predecessor of the UFWA. In August 1966, he became director of the United Farm Workers Organizing Committee (UFWOC), a merger of the NFWA and the Agricultural Workers Organizing Committee (AWOC/AFL-CIO), which he led until his death. His major contribution was applying a nonviolent protest strategy to the challenge of organizing farm workers, a group that suffered intense discrimination, little community cohesion, and high levels of poverty, even as they labored in the most profitable sector of American agribusiness. In 1994, Chávez was posthumously recognized with the Medal of Freedom, the U.S.'s highest civilian honor, for his work on behalf of Mexican-American civil rights and the rights of farm workers to organize, and in 2003 a U.S. commemorative postal stamp was issued in his honor.

Chávez was born on a small family farm outside of Yuma, Arizona, to Juana and Librado Chávez. In 1937 his family lost their farm and migrated to central California to work in the fields. Over the next decade, Chávez attended more than thirty schools, eventually dropping out in the eighth grade when his father was no longer able to work. In 1952 he joined the CSO as an organizer in San Jose, California, working with Fred Ross, who had been trained by the famed radical and activist Saul Alinsky (1909–1972). Chávez worked on Mexican-American civil rights issues, including racial discrimination in the schools and public facilities (including "whites only" restrictions in theaters and restaurants). He also conducted language and citizenship classes and voter registration drives. A key tactic was the "house meeting," in which volunteers used their personal networks to recruit others. Frustrated that the CSO was unwilling to organize farm workers, Chávez resigned in March 1962 and moved to Delano, California, to found the NFWA.

The NFWA focused on cooperative shopping, burial insurance, and a credit union. By 1965 there were several thousand members in the Delano area. In the summer of 1965, Chávez recruited student volunteers who had been involved in the southern civil rights movement and several clergy to organize rent strikes and school discrimination protests. Like Chávez, they were paid five dollars per week plus room and board. In September 1965, Filipino members of the AWOC called a strike in the Delano table-grape harvest. The NFWA joined the strike, with strong support among the workers, but the growers refused to negotiate, hiring immigrant workers as replacements. Chávez called for a boycott against Schenley Industries, a liquor conglomerate with a small grape ranch, and he organized a 340-mile march on the state capital to publicize the boycott. Media coverage of the boycott led Schenley to sign the first agricultural union contract. The next target was DiGiorgio Corporation, an agribusiness giant with vulnerable grocery trade labels, which agreed to a union recognition election that the union won. The NFWA and AWOC then merged to form the UFWOC (AFL-CIO).

The UFWOC next organized a table-grape strike, which received broad support, but was broken by immigrant workers, many of whom were undocumented. In fact, in the grape harvest, well over half of the labor force was undocumented. Mounting a three-year grape boycott energized by Chávez' twenty-five-day fast, farm workers picketed grocery stores across the country. This cut national grape sales by more than a third and closed off foreign exports, leading to an industry-wide contract in August 1970. Strikes and a boycott against iceberg lettuce, however, failed to produce contracts. Lettuce was harder to target. Growers confused the issue by signing "sweetheart" contracts with the Teamsters, and they intimidated workers with violence. Chávez decided to support state collective-bargaining legislation to allow workers to be able to vote for their union of choice, leading to the Agricultural Labor Relations Act (ALRA) of 1975, which created secret ballot elections and negotiations in the state of California. The UFWA won most of the elections, and by 1980 it had more than 45,000 members. In 1983 Governor George Deukemejian closed down the ALRA Board, and subsequent legislation weakened its authority, undermining many of the UFWA contracts. In 1986 Chávez kicked off a third grape boycott, focusing this time on the issue of pesticide use, which was a major health hazard to workers as well as to consumers of grapes. After Chávez's death in 1993, the UFWA signed new contracts under more favorable political conditions.

Chávez' tactical brilliance and commitment to *La Causa* (the cause) were extraordinary. Recognizing the organizational and political difficulties in agricultural strikes, he focused on boycotts and protests, including hunger strikes that enlisted broader community support. Countering frustrations that might lead to strike violence and recurrent violent attacks against strikers, he conducted three major fasts all framed in terms of religious penance and claims for worker dignity. In addition to appealing to the moral identity between workers and growers, his fasts called for personal sacrifice and discipline, which energized workers and garnered broader community support. Chávez died on April 23, 1993, in San Luis, Arizona.

SEE ALSO *Day Laborers, Latino; Farmworkers; Immigrant Domestic Workers; Undocumented Workers; United Farm Workers Union.*

BIBLIOGRAPHY

César Chávez Foundation. Available from http://www.cesarechavezfoundation.org.

Ganz, Marshall. 2000. "The Paradox of Powerlessness: Leadership, Organization and Strategy in the Unionization of California Agriculture, 1959–1977." *American Journal of Sociology* 105: 1003–1062.

Jenkins, J. Craig. 1985. *The Politics of Insurgency: The Farm Worker Movement in the 1960s.* New York: Columbia University Press.

Levy, Jacques. 1975. *César Chávez: Autobiography of La Causa.* New York: W. W. Norton.

Taylor, Ronald. 1975. *Chavez and the Farm Workers.* Boston: Beacon Press.

United Farm Workers of America. Available from http://www.ufw.org.

J. Craig Jenkins

CHEAP LABOR

SEE *Labor, Cheap.*

CHICANA FEMINISM

Chicana feminism emerged in the 1960s out of the gender inequalities Chicanas experienced during their active participation in the Chicano civil rights movement. Although women supported the struggle for racial and class equality, Chicana feminists challenged the existing patterns of male-domination within the Chicano movement, as well as its ideology of cultural nationalism. An ideology of cultural nationalism among racial and ethnic groups, such as Chicano activists during this historical period, extolled an exaggerated sense of cultural pride as a source of political mobilization and exclusionary collective identity. They demanded, therefore, that Chicanos integrate a gender analysis into their political ideology. Such demands resulted in serious internal political turmoil within the movement and spurred the rise of a generation of Chicana activists, whose writings, organizations, and protest activities remain a testament to feminist struggles.

CHICANA FEMINIST WRITINGS

Beginning in the early 1960s and through the 1980s, the writings by Adelaida Del Castillo, Marta Cotera, Francisca Flores, Dorinda Moreno, Anna Nieto Gomez, Bernice Rincon, Enriqueta Longeaux y Vasquez, and others reveal the tensions and contradictions that they were experiencing as women of color participating in both a nationalist movement and the larger American society. Chicana feminists struggled to gain social equality and put an end to sexist and racist oppression. Like black and Asian-American feminists, Chicana feminists struggled to gain equal status in a male-dominated movement. Their writings addressed a variety of specific concerns, including educational inequalities, occupational segregation, poverty, lack of adequate child care, welfare rights, prison reform, health care, and reforms in the legal system. They also supported the right of women to control their own bodies and mobilized around the struggle for reproductive rights. Chicanas believed that feminism involved more than an analysis of gender because, as women of color, they were affected by both race and class in their everyday lives. Chicana feminism, as a social movement to improve the position of Chicanas in American society, represented a struggle that was both nationalist and feminist.

Chicana feminists engaged in a wide range of activities that stand as landmarks in the development of their movement. Throughout the Southwest, Chicanas developed their own feminist publication outlets. Founded in the early 1970s by Francisca Flores, the journal *Regeneracion* (Regeneration) became one of the most influential Chicana publications during the late 1960s and through the 1970s. It contained essays, editorials, poetry, short stories, and feature stories written about and by Chicanas. In 1971, students at California State University at Long Beach started a newspaper. With Anna Nieto Gomez and Adelaida Del Castillo serving as the founding editors, *Hijas de Cuauhtemoc* (Daughters of Cuauhtemoc), provided additional forums for Chicanas to discuss their experiences with male domination, racism, and classism. Although the newspaper only ran a few issues, its coverage of the social and economic marginalization of Chicanas in American society, and of the perpetuation of historical and contemporary stereotypes of Chicanas, provide critical documents of this period. In 1973 the newspaper developed into the feminist journal *Encuentro Femenil* (Women's Encounter) but stopped publication within two years.

Enriqueta Longeaux y Vasquez and Elizabeth Martinez, both from New Mexico, edited the newspaper *El Grito del Norte* (The Cry of the North) from 1968 to 1973. It published many articles, some written by the editors, that shaped the course of Chicana feminism. In 1973 Dorinda Moreno edited *La Mujer en Pie de Lucha* (Women Ready for Struggle), an anthology of Chicana feminist writings. She also founded the San Francisco newspaper *La Razón Mestiza* (The Mestiza Cause) in 1974. In 1977 Marta Cotera, a Chicana feminist from Texas, published her very influential *Chicana Feminist*, a collection of her political essays and speeches.

Chicana artists depicted their feminist ideology in literature, poetry, art, and theater. The creative writings of Gloria Anzaldúa, Ana Castillo, Lorna Dee Cervantes, Sandra Cisneros, Pat Mora, Cherrie Moraga, Bernice Zamora, and others portray various aspects of Chicana feminism. Yolanda López's art symbolizes the struggles of Chicanas and the development of a feminist consciousness.

By the late 1970s a small group of Chicanas entered the academy in a variety of disciplines and continued a Chicana feminist discourse within academic publishing outlets. Melville's *Twice a Minority* (1980) and Magdalena Mora's and Adelaida R. Del Castillo's *Mexican Women in the United States* (1980) remain classic anthologies that document the struggles of Chicanas. Chicana feminist writings contain common threads. They called for a critique of Chicano cultural nationalism, an examination of patriarchal relations, an end to sexist stereotypes of Chicanas, and the need for Chicanas to engage in consciousness-raising activities and collective political mobilization.

ORGANIZING THE MOVEMENT

Chicana feminists established autonomous woman-centered organizations that would facilitate their protest activities. In 1969, a group of Chicana university students started *Las Hijas de Cuauhtemoc* (Daughters of Cuauhtemoc), which served as a consciousness-raising organization, a clearinghouse of resources for Chicana students, and a basis for other feminist activities. The group started their own newspaper two years later and named the newspaper after their group. The *Comision Femenil Mexicana Nacional* (CFMN, or National Mexican Women's Commission) was founded in 1970 as a result of a resolution written by a group of Chicanas at the National Chicano Issues Conference. They founded an organization, run by and for Chicanas, that addressed their concerns. The CFMN set up the Chicana Service Action Center, a Los Angeles–based community social services center that focused on job training. Dorinda Moreno formed *Concilio Mujeres* (Women's Council), a women's support group based at San Francisco State University.

Chicana feminists mobilized their efforts by organizing local, regional, and national conferences to address their concerns. Having experienced marginalization and direct antifeminist attacks at many Chicano conferences, Chicana feminists adopted the strategy of organizing their own autonomous conferences. Organized in the early 1970s were the Chicana Regional Conference in Los Angeles, the First National Chicana Conference in Houston, the UCLA Chicana Curriculum Workshop and the Chicana Identity Conference at the University of Houston. These gatherings mobilized Chicanas and deepened their feminism.

At the academic level, an increasing number of Chicana feminists focused their collective effort on continuing the feminist legacy inherited from the early 1970s. In June 1982 a group of Chicana academics in Northern California organized a national feminist organization called *Mujeres Actives en Letras y Cambio Social* (MALCS, or Women Activists in Letters and Social Change) in order to build a support network for Chicana professors, undergraduates, graduate students, and community activists. The organization's major goal was to fight against the race, class, and gender oppression facing Chicanas in institutions of higher education. In addition, MALCS aimed to bridge the gap between academic work and the Chicano community.

During the 1982 conference of the National Association for Chicano Studies (NACS), a panel organized by *Mujeres en Marcha* (Women on the Move), a feminist group from the University of California at Berkeley, discussed the legitimacy of a Chicana feminist movement and the need to struggle against patriarchy. In 1983 Chicanas in NACS formed a Chicana Caucus, whose first political demand was that the organizers for the 1984 conference adopt the theme, "*Voces de la Mujer*," (Voices of Women). The conference plenary session featured Chicana feminists who addressed sexism in the organization and the community. Their presentations were collected in one of the key anthologies of Chicana feminism: *Chicana Voices: Intersections of Class, Race, and Gender* (1984).

DISSENT IN THE CHICANO MOVEMENT

Not all women who participated in the Chicano movement supported Chicana feminism. Some saw themselves as "loyalists" who believed that the Chicano movement did not have to deal with sexual inequities because both Chicano men and Chicano women experienced racial oppression. A common view among loyalists was that if men oppressed women, it was not the men's fault but rather that of the larger society. Even if gender oppression existed, the loyalists maintained that this type of inequality would best be resolved internally within the movement. They denounced the formation of a separate Chicana feminist movement on the grounds that it was politically divisive and would undermine the unity of the Chicano movement. Loyalists viewed racism as the most important issue within the Chicano movement. In a political climate that already viewed feminist ideology with suspicion, Chicana feminist lesbians came under even more attacks than other feminists. A cultural nationalist ideology that perpetuated stereotypical images of Chicanas as "good wives and good mothers" found it difficult to accept a Chicana feminist lesbian movement advocated by writers and activists such as Cherrie Moraga and Gloria Anzaldúa.

JOINING WITH OTHERS

Chicana feminists considered the possibility of forming coalitions with white feminists after their attempts to work within the Chicano movement were suppressed. Because white feminists were themselves struggling against sexism, building coalitions with them was seen as an alternative strategy for Chicana feminists. Several issues made such coalition building difficult, however. Chicana feminists criticized white feminists for only addressing gender oppression in explaining the life circumstances of women. Chicana feminists believed that the white feminist movement overlooked the effects of racial and class oppression experienced by Chicanas and other women of color. They criticized white feminists who believed that a general women's movement would be able to overcome racial and class differences among women, interpreting this as a failure to deal with the issues of racism and classism. Without the incorporation of an analysis of racial and class oppression to explain their experiences, Chicana feminists believed that such a coalition would be problematic. Chicana feminists also viewed the white feminist movement as a middle-class movement, while they viewed their struggle as a working-class movement.

Chicana feminism went beyond the limits of an exclusively racial theory of oppression embedded in Chicano cultural nationalism. Through their political mobilization, writings, conferences, and organizations, Chicanas built an autonomous feminist movement. Since its early beginnings in the 1960s, Chicana feminism has followed a trajectory that has combined political activism and academic research, usually rejecting the separation of the two. While the militant politics of protest have ended, Chicana feminism continues in the early twenty-first century, using different venues and strategies to struggle against race, gender, class, and sexual-orientation inequalities.

SEE ALSO *African Feminisms; Black Feminism in Brazil; Black Feminism in the United Kingdom; Black Feminism in the United States; Feminism and Race.*

BIBLIOGRAPHY

Anzaldúa, Gloria. 1987 *Borderlands: La Frontera.* San Francisco: Aunt Lute Books.

Cordova, Teresa. 1994. "Roots and Resistance: The Emergent Writings of Twenty Years of Chicana Feminist Struggle." In *Handbook of Hispanic Cultures in the United States: Sociology,* edited by Feliz Padilla, Nicolas Kanellos, and Claudio Esteva-Fabregat, 175–200. Houston, TX: Arte Publico Press.

———, et al. 1986. *Chicana Voices: Intersection of Class, Race, and Gender.* Austin: Center for Mexican American Studies, University of Texas.

Garcia, Alma M. 1997. *Chicana Feminist Thought: The Basic Historical Writings.* New York: Routledge.

———. 1989. "The Development of Chicana Feminist Discourse, 1970–1980." *Gender & Society* 3 (2): 217–238.

Melville, Margarita B, ed. 1980. *Twice a Minority: Mexican American Women.* St. Louis, MO: Mosby.

Mora, Magdalena, and Adelaida R. Del Castillo. 1980. *Mexican Women in the United States: Struggles Past and Present.* Los Angeles: UCLA Chicano Studies Research Center Publications.

Roth, Benita. 2004. *Separate Roads to Feminism: Black, Chicana, and White Feminists Movements in America's Second Wave.* Cambridge, UK: Cambridge University Press.

Alma M. Garcia

CHICANO MOVEMENT

The Chicano movement of the 1960s and 1970s provides a window into the construction of race in the United States. Never a unified entity, the Chicano insurgency was instead a series of events and actions waged by organizations that used cultural nationalism and Marxist-Leninist ideas to press their demands. Among these organizations were the Brown Berets, the National Chicano Moratorium Committee, the Crusade for Justice, the Movimiento Estudiantíl Chicano de Aztlán (MEChA), La Raza Unida Party (LRUP), and the Centro de Acción Social Autónomo (Autonomous Center for Social Action, commonly known as CASA). The all used the common anti-American political language of Chicanismo, which gave them the semblance of a mutual identity and experience. Another notion that the groups shared was the idea that Chicanos were an internal colony of the United States.

Perhaps the most celebrated of the Chicano movement organizations was the Brown Berets, a paramilitary group similar in outlook and style to the Black Panthers. The group was founded in 1966 under the leadership of David Sánchez, a high school student in Los Angeles. The Berets espoused a militant outlook, if not substantively at least symbolically, and they soon captured the imagination of Chicano youth throughout Los Angeles and the Southwest. For the next six years the Berets would be present at, and take an active role in, demonstrations and protests in the Los Angeles area, including the 1968 high school "blowouts," in which Chicano students walked out of school to protest unequal conditions. Their struggle also incorporated the protests against the Vietnam War and police brutality staged by the Chicano Moratorium Committee from 1969 through 1971. These actions proved short-lived, but they ensured that the Brown Berets would become a sensation in the ethnic Mexican community. Before their demise in 1973, they established the East Los Angeles Free Clinic, which still exists. Ultimately, the Brown Berets were more concerned with symbolic gestures to bring to light Chicanos' unequal living and working conditions. Nevertheless they inspired the ethnic Mexican community to fight for empowerment and strive to change the status quo.

The fight for empowerment and the quest to change the status quo were also undertaken by the Crusade for Justice, a Denver-based organization founded by a former boxer turned community activist, Rodolfo "Corky" Gonzales, in 1965. Unlike the Berets, the Crusade for Justice believed in substantive change, and they imagined a community that would be guided by a strong adherence to Mexican culture, which would manifest itself through the building of institutions. To that end, the Crusade operated a school named Tlatelolco: La Plaza de las Tres Culturas. At its height, Tlatelolco had 200 preschool to college-age students. The Crusade also ran a curio shop, a bookstore, and a social center.

Like the Brown Berets, the Crusade protested police brutality and was concerned with young ethnic Mexicans, as was evident when it sponsored the 1969 National Chicano Youth Liberation Conference, which is notable for issuing El Plan Espiritual de Aztlán (The Spiritual Plan of Aztlán), which called for Chicano separatism in the face of white oppression. This became the blueprint for Chicano student activism in the years to come. The plan also called for the establishment of a nationwide Mexican-American student movement based in high schools and college campuses, which would be spearheaded by local chapters of the Movimiento Estudiantíl Chicano de Aztlán (MEChA). In addition, the conference issued calls for a Mexican-American anti–Vietnam War effort and

Los Angeles Mayor Antonio Villaraigosa. *On May 17, 2005, Villaraigosa, a leader for Chicano rights during his college days at UCLA, unseated Mayor James Hahn to become the city's first Hispanic mayor in over a century. He is seen here celebrating his victory with his wife, Corina, and his son, Antonio Jr.* AP IMAGES.

pressed for a Chicano political party to lead electoral efforts.

The plan's anti–Vietnam War call was taken up by the National Chicano Moratorium Committee. Founded in September 1969 by Los Angeles-based activists Ramses Noriega and Rosalio Muñoz, the organization's impetus came from the disclosure of the disproportionate numbers of Mexican American youths dying in Southeast Asia (a three to one ratio, compared to whites). In order to bring greater awareness to this issue, and to the squalid living conditions and unequal educational opportunities that both pushed Chicano young men to enlist and guaranteed that they would be drafted into the military, the Moratorium Committee staged five demonstrations against the war in the Los Angeles area. The largest took place on August 29, 1970, and attracted 20,000 protesters. This march and rally ended in violence initiated by the Los Angeles County Sheriff's Department and resulted in three deaths, most notably that of that journalist Ruben Salazar. The tragic events of that day changed the direction of the organization, and from then on the Chicano Moratorium Committee focused primarily on combating police brutality, with the war protest being put on the back burner. This resulted in the loss of wider support and eventually led to the organization's demise in August 1971.

As opposed to the marches and demonstrations staged by the Chicano Moratorium Committee, La Raza Unida Party (LRUP) founded in 1969 by Crystal City, Texas, residents José Angel Gutiérrez and Luz Gutiérrez, among others, sought to empower Chicanos by using the ballot box. Of all the Chicano movement organizations, history of the LRUP sheds light on the fractured nature of the ethnic Mexican community in the United States. Never a national organization, but rather a series of local chapters that had the common goal of voting Chicanos into office, the LRUP sprang up throughout the Southwest, most prominently in Texas, Colorado, and California. However, because each state had different statutes governing ballot qualifications, and thus for attaining official party status, the LRUP was never able to succeed in establishing a strong voter base. The party's 1972 national convention in El Paso, Texas, symbolized the organization's potential to unify its various cells, but ultimately led to its undoing as one contingent supported Colorado's Corky Gonzales for chairman, while another delegation backed José Angel Gutiérrez, who was from Texas. In the end, Gutiérrez emerged as the leader, causing the LRUP to splinter into factions, and thus it was never able to forge a nationwide entity.

In contrast to La Raza Unida Party, which ultimately believed in the American system, the Centro de Acción Social Autónomo (CASA) merged nationalism with a Marxist-Leninist philosophy. It was founded in 1969 by Bert Corona and Soledad Alatorre as a mutual aid organization that offered services to Mexican immigrant workers. In 1975, CASA merged with the Committee to Free Los Tres, which fought for the release of three young men accused of selling drugs in a Los Angeles barrio. The Committee to Free Los Tres was composed primarily of college students and young professionals, and they transformed CASA into a Communist "pre-party" organization that would be guided not only by Marxism-Leninism, but also by Mexican proto-nationalist ideas. Given this lodestar, CASA rejected the label "Chicano" and instead insisted that there was no difference between ethnic Mexicans in the United States and those in Mexico.

According to CASA, capitalism had made ethnic Mexicans into workers, regardless of nationality, and organizers should therefore disregard the international boundary between the two countries. This notion of "sin fronteras" (without borders) would become CASA's guiding principle. To that end, over the course of its three-year existence as a pre-party organization, CASA worked with other groups to defeat the anti-immigrant Rodino Bill. It also joined in the struggle to influence the U.S. Supreme Court to maintain affirmative action, which it ultimately did in the 1978 Bakke case. Yet CASA was never able to bring greater numbers into its fold. Eventually, internal fighting broke out over how best to make an impact in the ethnic Mexican community, and over the inherent contradictions of merging nationalist and internationalist ideas, and the group disbanded.

The Chicano movement was never a unified entity, but during its short-lived existence it sought to empower Mexican Americans in a more militant and sensational manner than had been done before. Ultimately, it was a moment of political experimentation that imagined community in a myriad of ways, and in the process brought to the forefront the dynamic and multifaceted nature of the ethnic Mexican community in the United States. Thus, understanding the Chicano movement allows for greater insight into the construction of race and racism in America.

SEE ALSO *Affirmative Action; Aztlán; Corona, Bert; El Plan de Santa Barbara; Immigration Reform and Control Act of 1986 (IRCA); Immigration to the United States; Indigenismo in Mexico; Mexicans.*

BIBLIOGRAPHY

Acuña, Rodolfo. 2004. *Occupied America: A History of Chicanos*, 5th ed. New York: Pearson Longman.

Chávez, Ernesto. 2002. *"¡Mi Raza Primero!" (My People First!): Nationalism, Identity, and Insurgency in the Chicano Movement in Los Angeles, 1966–1978*. Berkeley: University of California Press.

Muñoz, Carlos, Jr. 1989. *Youth, Identity, Power: The Chicano Movement*. London: Verso Press.

Oropeza, Lorena. 2005. *Raza Si! Guerra No!: Chicano Protest and Patriotism during the Viet Nam War Era*. Berkeley: University of California Press.

Ernesto Chávez

CHILDREN, RACIAL DISPARITIES AND STATUS OF

The U.S. Census Bureau has released data that reveals racial disparities in areas that impact upon the fortunes of children in diverse racial/ethnic groups in America (Table 1). These data reveal that Hispanics are least likely to hold a high school diploma or a bachelor's degree compared with all groups. Even though African Americans have a high rate of securing a high school diploma, they have a low economic return on that level of educational attainment. That is, they have the lowest median household income and home ownership rate, and highest poverty rate, of all groups.

Racial disparities in poverty rate affect children and their future. Children are poor because they live in poor families. Arloc Sherman (1997) has pointed out that poverty matters in a number of significant child outcomes related to health and education. In the area of health, poor children are at a higher risk of suffering death in infancy, premature birth (under 37 weeks), and low birth weight. They are also more likely than non-poor children to have no regular source of health care, and to receive inadequate prenatal care. In education, children who are poor have a risk, at ages seven to eight, of math scores that are five test points lower and reading scores that are four test points lower. Poor children are twice as likely to repeat a grade; are 3.4 times more likely to be expelled from school; are 3.5 times as likely to be a dropout at ages sixteen to twenty-four; and are half as likely to finish a four-year college (Sherman 1997, p. 1).

The Children's Defense Fund (CDF) compared poverty between African American children under eighteen

Racial Disparities in Education, Income, Home Ownership, and Poverty Rate, 2005

	African American	White	Hispanic	Asian
High School Diploma	80%	89%	60%	86%
Bachelor's Degree	17%	30%	12%	49%
Median Household Income	$30,939	$50,622	$36,278	$60,637
Home Ownership Rate	46%	75%	48%	59%
Poverty Rate	24.9%	8.3%	21.8%	11.1%

SOURCE: Complied from data from the U.S. Census Bureau.

Table 1.

years of age and children of all other races (CDF 2003). They found that 4.0 percent of children among all races live in extreme poverty, whereas 8.4 percent of African American children live in extreme poverty. CDF describes a deepening of the severity of poverty for already-poor children in the wake of the 1996 welfare law. More than eight in ten black children on Aid for Dependent Children (AFDC) were already poor in 1995, the year before the law was signed. Even though there was no change in the official poverty rates, nearly one million black children were found to live in "extreme poverty" with after-tax income of less than half of the poverty line. The percentage of black children in extreme poverty in 2001 was at a near record high, the highest level in twenty-three years. Also, fewer and fewer extremely poor children of all races receive cash public assistance.

HEALTH DISPARITIES IN THE UNITED STATES

The Children's Defense Fund (2003) has identified disparities in health for poor and minority children, especially black and Latino children. They continue to lag behind white and affluent children in almost every health indicator. Most of the current research is focused upon eliminating health disparities in health care for adults. Research on children indicates "that disparities persist in the areas of infant mortality, immunizations, asthma, dental care, lead poisoning, and obesity, to name a few of the conditions that affect children" (p. 2). These conditions can affect children's development and functioning before birth, in adolescence, and over the course of a lifetime.

Socioeconomic status is a strong determinant of health outcomes because it affects access to insurance and health services. The population groups with the worst health status are those with the highest poverty rates and the least education. As pointed out earlier, racial minorities do not compare well with whites on a variety of socioeconomic indicators that are the strongest predictors of health. In addition to the aforementioned indicators, minorities have fewer employment opportunities. Black and Hispanic unemployment rates are much higher (sometimes over two times higher than whites) (CDF 2003, p. 3). As a result, minorities are less likely to have employer-sponsored health insurance and are more likely to be uninsured. The health coverage a person has governs how quickly the person will get health care and whether it is the best care available. Blacks are almost twice as likely and Latinos almost three times as likely to be uninsured as whites. A 2005 study (Lillie-Blanton and Hoffman) shows that these disparities would be significantly reduced if black and Latinos were insured at levels comparable to those of whites.

According to CDF (2003), there is a growing body of published research that indicates that racial and ethnic minority patients receive a lesser amount of care and a lower quality of care for the same illness, even when they are at the same income level and insurance coverage level as white patients.

Infant Mortality and Prenatal Care. One of the most important indicators of children's health is infant mortality and birth weight rates in different populations. Although overall infant mortality rates dropped as of 2002, the gap between the white and black infant mortality rate has not narrowed. According to Matthews, et al. (2004), in 2002 there were more than 28,000 infant deaths in the United States, more than all the deaths among children between the ages of one and nineteen. Black infants were more than twice as likely to die as white infants.

Low birth weight is the leading cause of infant mortality among all races. It is the greatest cause of death for black infants. According to Martin, et al. (2003), non-Latino black infants were almost twice as likely to be born at low birth weight as were non-Latino white infants (13.4% versus 6.9%).

The most critical component of reducing the incidence of infant mortality and low birth weight is prenatal care for pregnant women. The level and timing of such care is used as a proxy for access to care and birth outcomes. There are racial and ethnic differences in the timeliness of prenatal care. In 2002, 75.2 percent of non-Latino black and 76.7 percent of Latino women received prenatal care in the first trimester, compared to 85.4 percent of non-Latino white women (Martin, et al. 2003). Non-Latino black and Latino women were more than twice as likely as non-Latino white women to have late or no prenatal care (6.2% and 5.5% respectively, versus 3.1%).

Hunger. The U.S. Department of Agriculture (USDA) defines "food security" as having access to enough food for active healthy living (Nord, Andrews, and Carlson 2003). Families without enough food are often referred to as "food insecure" households. Most food insecure households avoid hunger by limiting the types of food they buy and relying on public assistance food programs. However, in about one-third of food insecure households, one or more household members are hungry at some time.

Children who are hungry and food insecure are at greater risk for deficits in cognitive development and academic achievement. According to the USDA, in 2003, 28.5 percent of African American and 28.1 percent of Hispanic households with children experienced food insecurity, compared with 11.3 percent of white households.

VIOLENCE

According to the U.S. Centers for Disease Control and Prevention, 2,827 children and teens in the United States died from gunfire in 2003. There were 1,822 who were homicide victims; 810 committed suicide; and 195 died in accidental or undetermined circumstances. Of this number, 2,502 were boys and 325 were girls (CDF 2006).

Of the children and teens who were victims of violence, 1,554 were white; 1,172 were black; 51 were Asian or Pacific Islander, and 50 were American Indian or Alaska Native. Additionally, 553 of the children and teens across all of the races were identified as Latino. The age breakdown for the victims was: 378 under age fifteen; 119 under age ten, and 56 under age five; the remainder were fifteen to nineteen. In addition to the death toll, four to five times as many children and teens suffered non-fatal bullet wounds.

The Children's Defense Fund (2006) has pointed out that black children and teens are more likely to be victims of firearm homicide, whereas white children and teens are more likely to commit suicide. They also note that children are more likely to be killed by adults than by other children. They state further that "The rate of firearm deaths among children under age fifteen is far higher in the United States than in twenty-five other industrialized countries combined" (p. 2).

TRENDS IN REFUGEE STATUS

Refugees escaping war often move in large groups and flee the same conditions within the same time frame. Those persons are often accorded refugee status on a group prima facie basis. According to the United Nations High Commissioner for Refugees (UNHCR), ten asylum countries reported the arrival of more than 1,000 prima facie refugees during 2005, including Chad (32,400), Benin (25,500), Uganda (24,000), Ghana (13,600), and Yemen (13,200) (UNHCR, 2006). The article reported data on 28 industrialized countries with available data. The major receiving countries were the United Kingdom, Austria, Switzerland, the Netherlands, Germany, and Norway. Together these five asylum countries accounted for 73 percent of all claims lodged by unaccompanied and separated children. There were six countries of origin that produced more than 10,000 prima facie refugees in 2005: Togo (39,100), Sudan (34,500), the Democratic Republic of the Congo (15,600), Somalia (13,600), the Central African Republic (11,500), and Iraq (10,500).

Data has been collected by UNHCR (2004) on the status of "unaccompanied" and separated children seeking asylum in industrialized countries. They define unaccompanied children as "persons under eighteen years of age who have been separated from both parents and are not being cared for by an adult who by law or custom is responsible to do so" (p. 2). UNHCR advocates the usage of the term "separated" children as a more precise international definition for this phenomenon. There are children who are being cared for on some level by extended family members, so they are not "unaccompanied" in the true sense of the word. They do, however, face risks in that they are separated from their parents.

UNHCR (2004) reports that, "Asylum flows to most countries in Central and Western Europe have been dominated by children from Asia (Afghanistan, Iraq). Some countries in Western Europe have reported important inflows of children from Africa" (pp. 5–6). According to UNHCR (2004), Africa is overrepresented in the numbers of unaccompanied and separated children seeking asylum, but the reverse is true for children from Asia, Europe, Latin America, and the Caribbean. Of the 39,900 unaccompanied and separated children seeking asylum between 2001 and 2003, only 13 percent originated from Europe (while 24 percent of all asylum seekers were from Europe).

Gene B. Sperling (2005) has pointed out that orphaned children are less likely to be enrolled in school than their peers who live with at least one parent. He states further that "Only 6 percent of children in refugee camps are enrolled in secondary education, and opportunities for internally displaced children are even more limited" (p. 1).

SCHOOLING

Preschool Education. An important descriptor of the educational fortunes of children is participation in preschool education. Center-based early childhood education

Learning Amid Poverty in America. *Principal Ora Cummings helps first-grade students read at Uniontown Elementary School in Alabama. The school is in Perry County, which has a mostly black population and the largest percentage of children living below the poverty level in the state.* AP IMAGES.

programs include day care centers, Head Start programs, preschool, nursery school, and pre-kindergarten. According to the National Center for Education Statistics (NCES), a greater percentage of non-poor children ages three to five participated in center-based programs than poor children in the United States. In addition, a greater percentage of black and white children than Hispanic children participated in center based programs (NCES 2006). "In 2005, 66 percent of Black children and 59 percent of White children participated in such programs, compared with 43 percent of Hispanic children" (Indicator 2, NCES 2006a). White and Hispanic children who were not poor were more likely than their poor counterparts to participate in center-based programs in 2005. There was no difference found between poor and non-poor black children.

Latin America and the Caribbean lead the developing world in the provision of preschool education, according to UNESCO (2006). They report that half of the world's countries have no early childhood care and education policy for children under age three. "Participation in preschool ranges from 62 percent in Latin America and the Caribbean compared to only 35 percent in the developing countries of East Asia and the Pacific, 32 percent in South and West Asia to 15 percent in the Arab States and 12 percent in Sub-Saharan Africa" (p. 1).

UNESCO (2006) reports further that there is universal preschool in most Western European countries. There was an enrollment decline in transition countries after the break up of the Soviet Union, but they are now recovering.

Primary and Secondary School. Just about every child of primary school age starts school in countries of the Organization of American States (OAS), however, far fewer actually complete their primary education. According to a UNESCO report (2005), Barbados and Chile are the only two countries out of twenty-seven with available data where more than 95 percent of enrolled children reach the final grade of primary school. The rate of completion of Mexico and Uruguay is about 90 percent. Less than 75 percent of primary school-aged children are expected to complete primary school by 2010 in Guatemala, Honduras, and Nicaragua. There are a large number of children who are starting school late and repeating grades.

According to the "Education for All Global Monitoring Report" (UNESCO 2005b), an average of 1.7 percent of primary students repeat a grade in the world's richest countries; in the poorest, the average is 7.7 percent. In sub-Saharan Africa, the rate is nearly 20 percent. The report has not found any significant gender disparities at the primary level of education. At the secondary level they have found that boys and young men are disadvantaged with the exceptions of Bolivia, Guatemala, and Peru. Female enrollment rates are one-fifth higher than that of males in Dominican Republic, Saint Lucia, and Suriname.

There are eleven countries that have 75 percent of the appropriate age group enrolled in secondary education. Six additional countries—Belize, Bolivia, Peru, Trinidad, Tobago, and Uruguay—are close to achieving this level. However, secondary education enrollment dips below 65 percent in thirteen of the OAS countries, according to UNESCO Institute for Statistics (UIS) data (UNESCO 2006b).

In one out of four African countries, half of the children enrolled at the end of primary school do not continue their education in secondary school in the following year. According to the UIS (UNESCO 2006b), 85 percent of primary pupils make the transition in most countries of Europe, Asia, North and South America. According to the latest figures, Africa has the lowest primary school completion ratios in the world. Almost all of the countries in Europe have ratios exceeding 90 percent. Only eight (out of forty-five) African countries reach this level: Algeria, Botswana, Cape Verde, Egypt, Mauritius, Seychelles, South Africa, and Tunisia. In nineteen African countries, the ratios are 50 percent or lower. This means that at least every second child does not finish primary school.

According to the UIS, in one out of four African countries, half of the children who complete primary school do not transition to secondary school the following year (UNESCO, 2006b). Basically, few families can afford to continue sending their children to school. Girls are affected more severely than boys. In some countries, there are simply not enough spaces to accommodate eligible children, so the children are screened by public examinations and other methods.

A more accurate picture of the racial disparities in education internationally is given by an examination of the extent to which children are enrolled in upper as compared to lower secondary education. In some countries, lower secondary education (ages ten to fifteen) takes place in primary school and is treated as a part of basic education. Upper secondary education is more of a bridge to higher education and provides a curriculum that facilitates entry into the labor market.

The UIS (2005) documents that the lowest participation rates in upper secondary education are found in Africa, where the gross enrollment ratio is 45 percent. In half of the countries in Africa, the enrollment ratios are below 40 percent. This is compared with enrollment ratios reaching 100 percent in Europe; between 70 percent and 80 percent in the Americas; 40 percent in West Asia; and 48 percent in East Asia. In Africa, less than one-third of children (29%) are enrolled in upper secondary education.

Gender Disparities. According to Sperling (2005), an estimated 110 million children—60 percent of them girls—between the ages of six and eleven will not attend school this year. Another 150 million are likely to drop out before completing elementary school. He points out further that more than half of all girls in sub-Saharan Africa do not complete primary school. Only 17 percent are enrolled in secondary school. For girls in rural areas, taking Niger as an example, 12 percent were enrolled in primary school compared with 83 percent of girls living in the capital city.

Sperling notes that extremely impoverished parents often feel they need their girls' labor for extra income or just to help with grueling chores, such as the long hours spent collecting water and firewood or caring for younger children. He calls for policies that reduce the costs and increase the benefits of sending girls to school so that parents will choose a better future for their children. He points out the need to "develop and widely implement policies that work to align the temporary interests of parents with the long term well-being of their girls and their societies" (p. 2).

High School Dropout Rate and Exit Exams. The high school dropout rate represents the percentage of sixteen-through twenty-four-year-olds who were out of school without a high school credential. According to NCES (2006b), 10 percent of young people fell into this category in 2004 in the United States. There was also a difference by race/ethnicity. The status dropout rate was lowest for whites and highest for Hispanics. They point out that "the gaps between the rates of Blacks and Whites and between Hispanics and Whites both decreased from 1972 to 2004, but there was no measurable change in the Hispanic-Black gap over this period" (Indicator 26, NCES 2006b).

The CDF (2004) points out that by the year 2009, half of all U.S. states will use a single standardized test as the sole means of determining whether a student will graduate. It has been well documented (Center for Education Policy 2004) that standardized testing has led to negative outcomes, particularly for low-income and minority students. By 2009, eight out of ten minority public school students (compared to seven out of ten public students in general) will be denied a high school diploma because they did not pass a high school exit exam. CDF advocates for using multiple indicators of achievement for making important decisions about child educational progress.

Misidentification of Minority Youth in Special Education. In the United States, the disproportionate assignment of minority children to special education services is a significant impediment in their journey through school. There is a significant correlation between assignment to special education and dropout, drug addiction, incarceration, and unemployment of children from particular racial/ethnic groups.

According to David Osher, Darren Woodruff, and Anthony E. Sims (2002), in twenty-nine states black students are twice as likely as white students to be labeled with an emotional or behavior disorder. Black students are more than twice as likely to be labeled as mentally retarded in thirty-nine states. Native American children are more than twice as likely to be labeled as mentally retarded in ten states.

James Conroy and Edward Fierros (2002) point out that once labeled as disabled, minority students are disproportionately excluded from regular education classrooms. Among students classified with disabilities, black students are twice as likely as whites to be educated in a separate setting where 60 percent of the day is spent out of school. black and Latino children are significantly less likely than white children to receive special education services as mainstreamed students in an "inclusive" classroom.

There is considerable evidence that minority students classified with disabilities receive harsher discipline than their white peers. Black students with disabilities were more than three times as likely as whites to be given short-term suspensions (Osher, et al. 2002). They were also nearly three times more likely than white students to be suspended for more than ten days. Black, Latino, and Native American youths with disabilities were 67 percent more likely than white children to be removed from the school on grounds of dangerousness. Once removed from the classroom, black and Latino youths with disabilities were between two and four times more likely to be educated in correctional facilities than white youths who were similarly removed. Additionally, studies show that the designation of racialized special education categories results in minority children in special education receiving unequal services.

Jean Crockett and James Kaufman (1999) document the harmfulness of this treatment on minority youths. Twice as many black students categorized as having emotional and behavioral disorders drop out of school (58.2%) compared to those who graduate from high school (27.5%). Further, they find that 75 percent of black youths with disabilities, compared to 47 percent of white youths with disabilities, are not employed two years out of school. They point out finally that 40 percent of black students with disabilities are arrested after leaving high school, compared to 27 percent of white youths with disabilities.

This entry highlighted racial disparities and the status of children from an international perspective. A profile of disparities related to race are described in the areas of socioeconomic status, health, infant mortality, prenatal care, hunger, violence, trends in refugee status, schooling and gender comparisons. The data reveals that in every category, children of color within the United States experience the worst child outcomes. Only Hispanic children exceed African Americans in school dropout rate. Likewise, the data suggests that the fortunes of children from Africa suffer in comparison to children on all other continents.

SEE ALSO *Brazilian Racial Formations; Canadian Racial Formations; Caribbean Racial Formations; Cuban Racial Formations; Haitian Racial Formations; Social Problems; South African Racial Formations; Transnationalism; United Kingdom Racial Formations.*

BIBLIOGRAPHY

Center on Education Policy. 2004. *State High School Exit Exams: A Maturing Reform.* Washington, DC: U.S. Government Printing Office.

Children's Defense Fund. 2003. "Analysis: Number of Black Children in Extreme Poverty Hits Record High." Available from http://www.childrensdefense.org.

———. 2004. "High School Exit Exams: Quick Facts." Available from http://www.childrensdefense.org.

———. 2006. "Protect Children Not Guns." Available from http://www.childrensdefense.org.

Conroy, James W., and Edward G. Fierros. 2002. "Double Jeopardy: An Exploration of Restrictiveness and Race in Special Education." In *Racial Inequity in Special Education,* edited by Daniel J. Losen and Gary Orfield. Cambridge, MA: Harvard Education Press.

Crockett, Jean B., and James M. Kauffman. 1999. *The Least Restrictive Environment: Its Origins and Interpretations in Special Education.* Mahwah, NJ: Erlbaum.

Lillie-Blanton, Marsha, and Catherine Hoffman. 2005. "The Role of Health Insurance Coverage in Reducing Racial/Ethnic Disparities in Health Care." *Health Affairs* 24 (2): 298–408.

Martin, Joyce A., Brady E. Hamilton, Paul D. Sutton, et al. 2003. "Births: Final Data for 2002." *National Vital Statistics Reports* 52 (10): 1–116.

Matthews, T. J., Fay Menacker, and Marian F. MacDorman. 2004. "Infant Mortality Statistics from the 2002 Period Linked Birth/Infant Death Data Set." *National Vital Statistics Reports* 53 (10): 1–32.

Nord, Mark, Margaret Andrews, and Steven Carlson. 2003. "Household Food Security in the United States, 2003." *Food Assistance and Nutrition Report* FANRR42. Available from http://www.ers.usda.gov/publications/fanrr42/.

Osher, David, Darren Woodruff, and Anthony E. Sims. 2002. "Schools Make a Difference: The Overrepresentation of African-American Youth in Special Education and the Juvenile Justice System." In *Racial Inequity in Special Education*, edited by Daniel J. Losen and Gary Orfield. Cambridge, MA: Harvard Education Press.

"Racial Division Still Permeates Key Areas of Life in U.S.: Census." 2006. *Jet Magazine* 110 (22): 22.

Sherman, Arloc. 1997. *Poverty Matters: The Cost of Child Poverty in America.* Washington, DC: Children's Defense Fund.

Sperling, Gene B. 2005. "The Case for Universal Basic Education for the World's Poorest Boys and Girls." *Phi Delta Kappan*, November. Available from http://www.cfr.org.

UNESCO. 2005a. "Educational Panorama 2005: Progressing Toward the Goals." Available from http://www.uis.unesco.org.

———. 2005b. "Education for All Global Monitoring Report: The Quality Imperative." Available from http://www.uis.unesco.org.

———. 2006a. "Early Childhood Care and Education the Forgotten Link." Available from http://www.uis.unesco.org.

———. 2006b. "How Many Children in Africa Reach Secondary Education?" Available from http://www.uis.unesco.org.

UNESCO Institute for Statistics (UIS). 2005. *The Global Education Digest.* Available from http://www.uis.unesco.org.

United Nations High Commissioner for Refugees (UNHCR). 2004. "Trends in Unaccompanied and Separated Children

Seeking Asylum in Industrialized Countries, 2001–2003." Available from http://www.unhcr.org.

———. 2006. "2005 Global Refugee Trends: Statistical Overview of Populations of Refugees, Asylum-Seekers, Internally Displaced Persons, Stateless Persons, and Other Persons of Concern to UNHR." Available from http://www.unhcr.org.

United States Department of Education, National Center for Education Statistics. 2006a. "The Condition of Education 2006, Indicator 2" (NCES 2006–071). Available from http://nces.ed.gov.

———. 2006b. "The Condition of Education 2006, Indicator 26" (NCES 2006–071). Available from http://nces.ed.gov.

U.S. Department of Health and Human Services, Centers for Disease Control and Prevention, National Center for Injury Control and Prevention. "Web-based Injury Statistics Query and Reporting System (WISQARS)." Available at http://www.cdc.gov/ncipc/wisqars.

Janice E. Hale

CHINA-U.S. RELATIONS AND CHINESE AMERICANS

When Chinese immigrants encountered racial oppression and exclusion in the United States in the late nineteenth and early twentieth centuries, they immediately equated their mistreatment with China's weakness and the Chinese government's inability to protect their rights and welfare through diplomacy, as the U.S. government did for U.S. citizens in China. They concluded that the only way to protect their rights was to help modernize and strengthen China. So in their own ways—through remittance; investments in modern utilities, transportation, and manufacturing industries; and participation in various educational, economic, and political reform movements in China (such as the Yangwu Yundong, the political reform led by Kang Youwei, and the revolutionary movement led by Sun Yat-sen), they expressed their nationalistic sentiment and tried to make China strong. Thus, modern Chinese nationalism was born among the oppressed Chinese abroad and then exported to China.

Unfortunately, the Chinese government regarded any attempt to modernize China to be an act of disloyalty and a threat to the homeland government. China therefore established policies and institutions designed to keep the Chinese diaspora under surveillance and control. Through its diplomatic missions, the government began to monitor the Chinese-American community. Various coercive measures were used to ensure the loyalty of Chinese Americans toward Chinese culture, hometowns, and, above all, the homeland government. Those who criticized the government and advocated change within America's Chinatowns or in their hometowns in China were punished. In so doing, the Chinese government violated the sovereignty of the United States and the rights of Chinese Americans to speak freely and freely associate.

The U.S. government, motivated by racism toward the Chinese-American community, viewed such flagrant extraterritorial interference with indifference or silent consent. Indeed, the U.S. government thought it was best for the Chinese immigrant population to be under control, even if this control was carried out by an alien government. As long as this interference did not harm the interests and welfare of mainstream America, the government chose to look the other way. Among the examples of this interference was the effort by Ambassador Wu Ting-fang to stop the reformer Liang Qi-chao from arriving in Honolulu in 1900. When that failed, he met with the Chinese Six Companies (officially, the Chinese Consolidated Benevolent Association) and instigated a death-threat letter sent to Liang. Similarly, Sun Yat-sen was kidnapped by Chinese diplomats in London during his visit there on October 11, 1896, with the intent to bring him back to China, where he faced certain death. Fortunately, his unlawful detention was discovered by a friend and he was rescued.

Thus, Chinese in the United States were subjected to a highly institutionalized structure of dual domination. On the one hand, they were targets of racial exclusion and oppression from white society in the United States, and on the other hand, they were vulnerable to the extraterritorial, and at times repressive, domination of their homeland government. These two dynamic forces converged in exerting an extraordinary influence on Chinese-American lives and communities across the United States, and they were themselves shaped, respectively, by ever-changing U.S. racial politics and by bilateral diplomacy between China and the United States. Chinese-American interactions and negotiations with, and resistance to, these two forces were what constituted the substance of their experience in the United States. In this sense, the Chinese-American encounter with racism in American democracy has historically been unlike that of other immigrant groups and racial minorities in the United States.

RACIALIZATION OF NATIONAL SECURITY AND ASSIMILATION

World War II realigned global geopolitics and gave rise to new forms of racism and accommodation for Chinese America. China and the United States became allies in the war against German Nazism and Japanese militarism and fascism. At the end of the war, the United States emerged as the unchallenged global power and the leader of the Western world against the Communist world, led by the Soviet Union. In China, the corrupt, U.S.-backed Guomindang (or Kuomintang) regime, led by Chiang Kai-shek, was quickly driven out of Mainland China in 1949 by the Communist leader Mao Zedong. Chiang and his forces fled to China's offshore province, Taiwan, under U.S. military protection. By then, the world had entered a new period of cold war. The United States became the global defender against communism at home and abroad. Building U.S. global military superiority and achieving a domestic ideological consensus was the vision of successive U.S. presidents in the 1950s and 1960s. Communist China was declared "Enemy No. 1," and the U.S. policy of containment of China by military, political, and economic means became a bipartisan consensus until President Richard Nixon inaugurated a new policy of détente and engagement with China in 1972.

World War II brought mixed blessings to Chinese Americans. With China as a wartime ally of the United States, the public perception of Chinese in the United States turned positive, and Chinese Americans were actively recruited to enlist in the U.S. Armed Forces and work in war-related industries. Chinese Americans saw a decline in racial hostility and an opportunity to become assimilated. At the same time, Japan saw an opportunity to exploit America's Chinese exclusion laws (initiated in 1882 with the Chinese Exclusion Act) and racial discrimination against Chinese Americans. Through leafleting and radio broadcasts, Japan urged China and its people not to fight for racist America and instead join Japan in liberating China and the rest of Asia from American and European imperialism and colonialism.

To counter Japanese propaganda, President Franklin D. Roosevelt pushed the U.S. Congress in 1943 to repeal the Chinese exclusion laws as a necessary military strategy to bolster the morale of Chinese resistance and win the war. Congress, however, resisted the proposal, fearing that the repeal would bring a huge influx of unwanted and unassimilable Chinese immigrants. In a compromise, the exclusion laws were repealed and, in their place, a new exclusion formula was substituted that severely limited the admissible number of Chinese immigrants to an annual quota of 105.

THE COLD WAR ERA

The repeal, therefore, did little to advance Chinese-American rights, and exclusion and discrimination against Chinese Americans persisted after World War II. In fact, the cold war quickly inaugurated a new type of racism and exclusion that Chinese Americans had never before encountered: the racialization of national security and a subtle form of racism that, in early twenty-first century language, is known as "racial profiling." Because China was declared Enemy No. 1, being Chinese American became synonymous with treason and espionage. From the point of view of J. Edgar Hoover, the director of the FBI, Chinese in the United States were part of China's fifth column, intent on subverting America. Overnight, all federal law enforcement agencies (the CIA, FBI, IRS, INS, etc.) were mobilized to keep Chinese Americans under surveillance.

The good will garnered during World War II, when China was an ally, disappeared overnight when China turned Communist. Political recriminations began over who was responsible for "the loss of China," and McCarthyism turned the nation paranoid and repressive. In place of good will were suspicion, racial hostility, and discrimination against Chinese Americans. Instead of confronting this new form of racism, the leadership of Chinese America in the 1950s and 1960s chose not only to condone political repression based on race, but also to assist the Nationalist government in Taiwan and U.S. law enforcement agencies in red-baiting and suppressing any Chinese Americans critical of the dictatorship and corruption of the Guomindang regime. Many Chinese Americans were harassed and intimidated, while others were denaturalized or threatened with deportation. Some committed suicide, others emigrated. Still others became targets of suspicion and were excluded from jobs and research projects connected to national security. Under the pretext of fighting communism, Chinese Americans were presumed to be untrustworthy, if not treasonous, and they were frequently discriminated against in housing, employment, and education. The constitutional rights of thousands of Chinese Americans were effectively suspended under the repressive atmosphere.

No organization, except the Chinese Hand Laundry Alliance (CHLA) and the *Chinese Daily News* (both in New York) openly protested such blatant violations of Chinese-American civil rights. In the face of such overpowering political repression, many Chinese Americans tried to prove their loyalty to the United States by forming anticommunist groups and denouncing China. Most chose to remain silent and tried to become accepted by becoming thoroughly Americanized or assimilated. Political repression and assimilation became two sides of the same coin. It was without doubt the darkest years of Chinese America and a shameful chapter in U.S. history.

GLOBALIZATION AND THE RISE OF CHINA

If the cold war injected a new dimension into race relations for Chinese Americans, the racialization of national security, the acceleration of globalization after the cold war, and the rise of China added both complexity and complications to the racism facing Chinese Americans. Globalization, of course, antedated the end of the cold war. In fact, the arrival of transnational Chinese capital from Taiwan, Hong Kong, and Southeast Asian countries began in the early 1970s when President Richard Nixon abandoned the containment of China policy in favor of a new policy of détente and engagement. The new policy promptly sent shock waves across East and Southeast Asia and precipitated an unprecedented geopolitical realignment in the region. Up until then, the dictatorial governments of the region had relied exclusively on U.S. political, economic, and military support and protection. Now, the peoples of the region began to demand human rights, democratic reform, and national liberation.

The ensuing political instability led to the flight of wealthy business owners and investors, a new type of immigrant, and, after 1975, refugees from Vietnam, Laos, and Cambodia, many of whom were, in fact, members of ethnic Chinese minority groups. The impact of globalization was not limited to historic Chinatowns, suburbs, and regional economies around major U.S. cities: It also changed the patterns of Chinese-American participation in electoral politics. By the 1990s both the Republican National Committee (RNC) and Democratic National Committee (DNC) discovered not so much the votes, but the money, in Chinese America. They began a concerted effort to identify and solicit political donations from wealthy Chinese immigrants.

At the same time, the new immigrants realized that business success in America depended to a large extent on political connection and access. The Chinese had the wherewithal, but they lacked the knowledge and know-how to play the game of American plutocracy. This was where they stumbled, and they were caught in the cross-fire between the Republicans and the Democrats. Race and political corruption were linked in the political fight. In the process, Asian fundraisers and big donors became the national focus of one of the fiercest partisan power struggles in the history of the United States.

The great 1996 campaign finance scandal, dubbed variously in the media and by the RNC as "Donorgate," "The Asian Finance Scandal," or "Chinagate," began when the immigrant John Huang, a well-connected Chinese-American banker associated with the Lippo Group, one of the largest conglomerates in Indonesia, was hired by the DNC to undertake a new fundraising strategy among rich Asian-American donors. President Bill Clinton was up for re-election, and so were many congressional seats, and the political future of Vice President Al Gore was at stake.

By well-established party standards, the amount of money Huang and a few of his associates ultimately raised for Clinton and the DNC was insignificant, amounting to only 5 million dollars out of some 1.4 billion dollars raised and spent by both parties in the 1996 federal elections. How Huang raised the money, and who gave it, were the sources of partisan contestation, and this became the focus of the Republican attack and a media feeding frenzy from September 1996, two months before the presidential election, to the indictment of the Chinese-American nuclear scientist Wen Ho Lee in December 1999.

Several congressional committees under the Republican-controlled Congress held high-profile hearings to highlight the seriousness of the scandal, criticize Clinton for selling out U.S. interests in return for China-connected political donations to the DNC, and accuse China of trying to subvert American democracy through its illegal political contributions. There was no evidence for most of these allegations, however. Instead of focusing on fixing the broken and corrupt system of campaign financing, the Republican leaders chose to racialize the scandal, brand small-time Chinese-American wrongdoers as launderers of "Chinese Communist" money, and accuse President Clinton, Vice President Gore, and the DNC of being greedy and unscrupulous. In response, the DNC quickly launched its own investigation into only the Chinese and Asians who contributed to the party. In other words, the DNC joined the RNC in racializing the scandal. By scapegoating Chinese donors and racializing the scandal, both the RNC and DNC succeeded in diverting public attention from the corrupt campaign finance system practiced by both parties.

Most of the Chinese Americans involved in these events either pleaded to lesser charges or had their cases dismissed due to insufficient evidence. All the major foreign donors escaped prosecution, except for James Riady, the head of the Lippo Group of Indonesia, who pleaded guilty to laundering his donations to the DNC, for which he was fined several million dollars and not permitted to enter the United States for two years.

The scandal severely damaged the reputation of the Democrats. It also created sleazy public images of Chinese Americans. Yet in spite of several sensational investigations launched by Republican-controlled congressional committees, no conclusion was reached and no legislative remedy proposed. (The heavily compromised McCain-Feingold reform bill did not pass the U.S. Congress until 2001.) The racialized scandal did open a door for Republicans, however, who linked it to the alleged "threat of China." In May 1998, House Speaker Newt Gingrich appointed a special committee, popularly known as the Cox Committee, to investigate this link, thus planting a seed for a renewed partisan political brawl in 1999 and 2000. The committee determined that China had stolen design information about advanced U.S. thermonuclear weapons. It was the Cox Report, leaked to the media in

December 1998, that prompted the sensational persecution and prosecution of an alleged China spy, Dr. Wen Ho Lee of the Los Alamos National Laboratory (LANL). The report also influenced George W. Bush's new policy of strategic ambiguity and competition with China during his 2000 presidential campaign, as well as his belligerent policy toward China before September 11, 2001, which marked a significant departure from the bipartisan China policy consensus that had existed since Nixon's historic trip to China in 1972.

Behind the Chinese campaign finance scandal and the persecution of Wen Ho Lee were partisan power struggles for the control of both the White House and the Congress. These incidents also reflected the question of how the United States should deal with the inevitable rise of China since the late 1980s and the presumed threat it poses to U.S. global hegemony and national security. Both cases show how Chinese-American rights and interests are intricately linked to how the United States perceives China and how the two countries deal with each other diplomatically in a changing world. In this context, reports on the rise of China and the political discourse accompanying them are of great concern to Chinese Americans. Exactly how this discourse will evolve, and how Chinese Americans will be seen and treated, remains to be seen.

BIBLIOGRAPHY

Chang, Gordon, ed. 2001. *Asian Americans and Politics: Perspectives, Experiences, Prospects.* Washington, DC: Woodrow Wilson Center Press.

Koen, Ross Y. 1974 (1960). *The China Lobby in American Politics.* New York: Harper & Row.

Sandmeyer, Elmer Clarence. 1991. *The Anti-Chinese Movement in California*, 2nd ed. Urbana: University of Illinois Press.

Sutter, Robert G. 1998. *U.S. Policy toward China: An Introduction to the Role of Interest Groups.* Lanham, MD: Rowman and Littlefield.

Tsai, Shih-shan Henry. 1983. *China and the Overseas Chinese in the United States, 1868–1911.* Fayetteville: University of Arkansas Press.

L. Ling-chi Wang

CHINESE AMERICANS AFTER WORLD WAR II

In the 1950s and 1960s, social progress and the African-American civil rights movement opened some doors for Chinese Americans in employment, education, and housing. As a result, there was a steady exodus of Chinese out of America's Chinatowns. The postwar economic boom, an expansion of higher education, and rapid suburbanization created unprecedented job opportunities in selective sectors of the labor market for women and minorities in the suburbs. College-educated Chinese Americans began to enter traditionally white workplaces and schools, neighborhoods and suburbs, and professional and civic organizations. In particular, the rapid growth of the defense industry, especially in the electronic, telecommunication, and aerospace sectors, provided a rare opportunity for Chinese Americans trained in science and technology. In addition, changes in immigration law in 1965 brought a new wave of Chinese immigrants from both ends of the economic spectrum.

ASSIMILATION AND DISCRIMINATION

The exodus to the suburbs proved to be bumpy and at times painful. The Chinese-American arrival in these areas was seen as a transgression into historically white space, and those who chose to move there were frequently greeted with resistance and more subtle forms of discrimination. Chinese-American men were deemed competent technical workers, excelling in mathematics, accounting, science, and technology, and Chinese American women were regarded as compliant and reliable clerical workers. Nevertheless, Chinese Americans found that these racial stereotypes severely limited their occupational choices and upward mobility. This kind of benevolent but selective assimilation gave rise to a Chinese-American concentration in certain types of occupations and residential settlements in neighborhoods and suburbs outside of Chinatowns in major cities, such as the Richmond District of San Francisco and Flushing in New York City. Clusters of Chinese-American populations grew in select suburbs, such Daly City, Fremont, Cupertino, Mountain View, Monterey Park, and Alhambra in California. Even in the midst of some integrated workplace and residential spaces, Chinese Americans remained, by and large, socially segregated.

In 1965 the U.S. Congress enacted amendments to the Immigration and Nationality Act of 1952 that abolished the insulting limitations on immigration from the "Asia-Pacific Triangle" and phased out the discriminatory national origins quotas over a three-year period. The number of Chinese immigrants in the next few years jumped to 25,000 to 30,000 per year, contributing to a sharp increase in the Chinese-American population in the United States. (This population numbered 217,000 in 1960, 433,000 in 1970, 805,000 in 1980, 1.6 million in 1990, and 2.4 million in 2000). In signing the Voting Rights Act on Aug. 6, 1965, President Lyndon B. Johnson declared, "I pledge we will not delay or we will not hesitate, or will not turn aside until Americans of every race and color and origin in this country have the same rights as all others in the progress of democracy." That pledge turned out to be too late and a promise unfulfilled. By the late 1960s, Chinatown populations and socioeconomic problems were bursting at the seams and racial discrimination against Chinese Americans was no longer confined to Chinatown. Traditional social organizations, such as the *huiguan* (district associations) and *gongsuo* (family associations), were too Chinatown-bound, paralyzed, and ill-prepared, having only dealt with issues and problems within the geographic confines of traditional Chinatowns. Among middle-class Chinese Americans in the suburbs, the drive toward assimilation and the obsession with gaining acceptance by Euro-Americans stifled the founding of new Chinese-American civil rights, professional, and political organizations that could speak out effectively for the new Chinese America.

MODEL MINORITY AND NEGLECTED MINORITY

In spite of steady middle- and lower-middle class exodus of Chinese Americans from Chinatowns into white working-class neighborhoods and suburbs after World War II, Chinatowns did not disappear from America's urban landscape, as predicted by the Chinese-American sociologist Rose Hum Lee. What emerged in the early decades after the war was the fragmentation, or more accurately, the bifurcation, of Chinese America. On the one hand, upwardly mobile, well-educated Chinese Americans were settling into middle-class occupations and residential areas in the suburbs. On the other hand, non–English-speaking, poor, new immigrants, especially those who came after 1965, were saturating the already over-crowded, dilapidated Chinatowns by the late 1960s, precipitating an explosive crisis in housing, employment, health, youth, and education, as well as a dire situation for the elderly population. This class divide was further aggravated by the diverse geographic and linguistic origins of the post-1965 Chinese immigrants.

Whereas middle-class Chinese Americans struggled to blend and assimilate themselves into their new neighborhoods, the historic Chinatown came under mounting pressures from both within and outside. From the outside came new spatial contestations: urban renewal versus preservation, and downtown corporate interests versus community and human interests. For example, the encroachment of downtown San Francisco into the historic Chinatown-Manilatown district succeeded in wiping out virtually the entire Manilatown, located next to Chinatown. The protracted high-profile struggle over the I-Hotel, the last building standing between renewal and Chinatown, is a textbook example of the stress and strain a typical Chinatown came under as America's urban downtowns sought both renewal and expansion into minority neighborhoods. It was also a fight that pitted old, poor, vulnerable Chinatown against the interests of both city hall and big business.

Similar patterns can be seen in other Chinatowns across the United States. By the 1990s the gentrification of Chinatowns was occurring in lower Manhattan, Seattle, Portland, Sacramento, Oakland, Los Angeles, San Diego, and Houston. The new Tufts Medical Center in Boston, the freeway approach to the Benjamin Franklin Bridge in Philadelphia, and the MCI Stadium in Washington, D.C., all demolished and replaced as much as half of these cities' Chinatowns.

Chinatown leadership was clearly not prepared to deal with a crisis of this magnitude and intensity. Chinatowns may not have exploded into full-scale urban riots—such as America witnessed on TV in cities such as Los Angeles, Detroit, Newark, Chicago, Philadelphia, Washington, D.C., and Baltimore in late 1960s—but high rates of juvenile delinquency, school dropouts, gang violence, suicide, mental illness, and sweatshop working conditions made local and national headlines. Yet the Chinatown establishments, for face-saving reasons, generally chose to pretend that these problems did not exist. When they did acknowledge them, they insisted the problems were nothing the Chinese themselves could not resolve.

On the other front, those from the Chinese-American middle-class who had left America's Chinatowns and moved into new city neighborhoods and suburbs were joined by newly arrived, highly educated, middle- and upper-class Chinese immigrants, creating both a new class structure never before seen in the history of Chinese America and a class division that frequently undermined the racial solidarity among Chinese Americans in the struggle for civil rights. Moreover, many of the new immigrants became highly accomplished, widely publicized scientists and engineers in research universities, government-run laboratories, and corporate research facilities.

Beginning in the mid-1960s, during the height of the black civil rights protests, the middle- and upper-class Chinese were celebrated as the "model minority" by politicians, social scientists, and the national media. Suddenly, the despised Chinese Americans became successful and revered scientists in the national media, in stark contrast to other racial minorities. Based largely on the theory of assimilation, social scientists generated a substantial body of literature on the so-called success of the Chinese American middle-class in the United States. Using criteria such as achievements in education, occupation, income, language, religion, lifestyle, personality, residential location, and intermarriage, they showed how Chinese Americans had succeeded in unloading or eliminating their Chineseness and in absorbing the dominant white outlook and acquiring Euro-American social and cultural values. In fact, by the same criteria, Chinese Americans had become more successful than some Euro-Americans. This assessment, however, failed to mention the other half of Chinese America, which was desperately in need of public assistance.

Unfortunately, Chinese American "success" was an exercise of self-denial and self-deprecation. Furthermore, the government and the media were using their "success" ideologically, both to celebrate the United States as a land of generosity and unlimited opportunity for all willing to pull themselves up by their own bootstraps, regardless of race, and to denigrate other minorities, most notably militant African Americans, for demanding civil and welfare rights. In the process, the success story was also used in 1970s and 1980s by the government to justify cutbacks in social spending and erode civil rights gains in minority communities across the nation, including Chinatowns. A historically unassimilable racial minority was now more assimilated than even Euro-Americans. It was an incredible transformation in the ideological and political use of the notion of assimilation. The subtext of this new narrative nonetheless remained racist, because it mentioned nothing of the ordeals of assimilation and pitted Chinese Americans against African Americans.

It was within this intensely unsettling environment that the Chinese American postwar baby-boom generation arrived on the campuses of American colleges and universities and injected a new counter-narrative to the assimilationist one. Under the influence of the Black Power movement, they discovered the bifurcated Chinese America, the myth of assimilation, pervasive institutional racism, and the meaning of being poor, disenfranchised, and powerless. They quickly joined other minorities, creating the Asian American movement and the Third World Liberation Front in the fight for a new Asian-American identity, Asian-American Studies programs, and a civil rights agenda on campus and in the communities. They also chose to return to the problem-plagued Chinatowns abandoned by their assimilation-obsessed parents, identifying themselves with the historic Chinatowns and their ongoing struggles against urban renewal and neglect. Along with many young Chinese-American professionals, these students and activists effectively assumed the leadership role in defining what constituted Chinese-American civil rights and what strategies to pursue to achieve their goals for Chinese America. They effectively ushered in a new era of Chinese and Asian-American identity and self-determination.

ANOTHER WAVE OF CHINESE IMMIGRATION

President Richard Nixon's policy of détente with China, political instability in Southeast Asia, and the transfer of Hong Kong from British to Chinese sovereignty were landmarks in a political and economic realignment that brought a new wave of immigrants of Chinese descent to the United States. Middle- and upper-class arrivals with substantial resources joined the push for urban renewal in and around historic Chinatowns.

From New York to San Francisco and from Miami to Chicago, real estate, banking, the high-tech industry, upscale Chinese restaurants, supermarkets, and shopping malls in Chinatowns and in Chinese-concentrated suburbs were among the favorites of transnational capital from Southeast Asia, Taiwan, and Hong Kong. Their investments have profoundly changed the landscape and class structure not only of Chinatowns, but also of those middle-class suburbs with a strong Chinese presence. Nowhere is the change more dramatic and visible than in the string of suburbs along Interstate 10 heading east from downtown Los Angeles. Chinese businesses and shopping malls dominate Monterey Park, Alhambra, Rosemead, San Gabriel, El Monte, Hacienda Heights, Covina, Walnut, Diamond Bar, Roland Heights, and Pomona. Cities such as New York, San Francisco, and Toronto have several Chinatowns, while cities such as Houston, Dallas, Las Vegas, Atlanta, and Miami have Chinese shopping malls here and there. The middle-class suburbs along the two highways—101 and 880—leading to the famed Silicon Valley south of San Francisco and Oakland have the highest concentration of Chinese-American scientists and engineers in the country. The presence of a high percentage of Chinese-American faculty, staff, and students at Stanford University, the University of California, Berkeley, and the University of California, San Francisco also add to the disproportional presence of Chinese-American scientists and engineers in the entire San Francisco Bay area.

A BRAIN TRUST, YET NOT TRUSTED

The original intent of the 1965 immigration law was to promote family reunion and attract brainpower and skillful personnel needed by the U.S. health care, science, and technology industries. Because the exclusion laws had kept Chinese-American families separated by the Pacific Ocean, the new law immediately allowed tens of thousands of family members of prewar immigrants to reunite with their loved ones. Most of them were non–English-speaking and of working-class background. They moved into historic Chinatowns, worked in service and garment industries, and joined their predecessors in pursuing the elusive American dream. The same law also enabled the government, universities, and corporations to massively recruit well-educated and highly skilled Chinese to meet the demand for skilled personnel in science and technology, the most important growth sector of the U.S. labor market in the second half of the twentieth century.

Before 1965, most highly trained Chinese immigrants had to circumvent the exclusion laws by entering the United States as refugees and foreign students pursuing advanced degrees. Most of these students eventually received Ph.D. degrees in science and technology and were absorbed, some legally and others illegally, by industry and academia. Thousands of well-prepared and highly motivated Chinese from Taiwan, Hong Kong, and Southeast Asian countries entered the United States in this way before 1965. The new law not only allowed the pre-1965 students who had completed their advanced degrees to become permanent residents, it also extended preferential treatment to foreign-trained specialists of this type to seek permanent status, as long as their skills were needed and they had company sponsors. From 1950 to 1985, at least 200,000 of "the best and the brightest" Chinese immigrants were admitted, providing needed skills in science and engineering in the high-tech sector of the economy. A disproportionate number of Chinese-American college graduates also selected science and engineering as their career, because they correctly perceived it to be a high-growth sector and less racially discriminatory.

Overall, this represented one of the largest concentrated and timely infusions of scientific talent in U.S. history. Like their counterparts in the second half of the nineteenth century, who provided the indispensable labor needed during the economic development of the West, Chinese-American scientific professionals formed the backbone and brainpower of postwar U.S. scientific and technological development. Most did basic research and performed technical services, but many also became distinguished scientists in virtually every scientific discipline. Quite a number of them would become Nobel laureates, members of the National Academy of Sciences, and leaders in various professional organizations. This was the group of high-profile achievers that contributed to the stereotype of the "model minority" in the 1960s and 1970s. There is no doubt about their contributions to postwar U.S. superiority in science and technology. But the failure of the media and the government to pay attention and do something for the poor and disadvantaged Chinese Americans, and to those racially discriminated against on both sides of the class divide, was a disservice to all Chinese Americans.

Indeed, even accomplished Chinese Americans faced persistent inequality and racial discrimination. Whether they were research scientists in corporate research centers, in government research facilities, or in research universities, they encountered three basic problems: employment discrimination, social isolation, and racial profiling. Selective studies showed subtle but pervasive workplace discrimination against Chinese Americans in several areas, including recruitment, professional training and development, promotional and research opportunity, and salary disparity. Chinese Americans also found themselves socially isolated both in the workplace and outside it, sometimes due to cultural differences, communication barriers, or racial stereotypes, such as a belief that Chinese Americans preferred to be alone or disliked organized games and parties.

Finally, because the war-related industries were the areas where the Pentagon invested the most in research and development, and because much of the biological, chemical, and nuclear research in both public and private sectors had military applications, Chinese Americans found working on jobs in these areas particularly difficult. First, many of the jobs in these areas required security clearances over which they had no control, and they had no way of knowing that a denial of security clearance was based on race or racial profiling. Second, once on the job, they found themselves vulnerable to suspicion of espionage, if not outright accusation of espionage by their colleagues or supervisors, again on account of racial profiling. Lastly, they found their well-being to be dependent on the ups and downs of U.S.-China relations. If the relations were good, they enjoyed the normal treatment that all employees received. But if the relations turned sour or tense, they found themselves in an isolated, if not hostile, work environment.

Even though no Chinese-American scientists have been convicted of treason or a serious breach of national security, many Chinese Americans have been wrongly accused and falsely imprisoned. Among those who have faced such treatment are the rocket scientist and aeronautic engineer Qian Xuesen, the founding director of the Jet Propulsion Laboratory, and the nuclear engineer Wen Ho Lee, who worked at the Los Alamos National Laboratory. Qian was falsely accused of being a member of the Chinese Communist Party in 1955. He summarily lost his rocket research contracts with all three branches of the armed forces, was placed under house arrest for five years, and eventually exchanged for some American POWs from the Korean War. To date, there is no evidence to support the allegations against him.

Likewise, Wen Ho Lee was named as the man responsible for stealing American nuclear secrets for China by the *New York Times* in March 1999, following a deliberate, anonymous government leak. He was summarily fired the next day from the lab for which he had worked for twenty years, in violation of the lab's personnel policies and procedures. For nine months, he and his family, his colleagues, and his friends were subjected to intensive investigation by two hundred FBI agents and eighty computer specialists. The investigation turned up not a shred of evidence, yet he was indicted for the improper handling of classified information in the lab. He was promptly arrested, chained from the waist down, and put in solitary confinement for nine months without a trial or a conviction. He was finally allowed to plead guilty to one count of mishandling classified data and freed by the presiding federal judge, James Parker, with a profound apology from the bench and a strongly worded attack on the government for misleading him and embarrassing the United States in the eyes of the world. In other words, the only reason Lee was prosecuted and persecuted was on account of his race, as the chief of counterintelligence at the Los Alamos National Laboratory testified in congressional hearings in 2000, when Lee was in solitary confinement.

Clearly, the cold war legacy of racially profiling Chinese Americans remains alive and well. In the meantime, the U.S.-China relationship has become even more important, and also more volatile, in the wake of the September 11, 2001, attack on New York's World Trade Center. As long as Chinese Americans continue to be seen as foreigners, the fate of Chinese Americans, especially those in science, will be determined not by specific crimes they commit but by the fluctuation of U.S.-China relations and the racial prejudice deeply imbedded and institutionalized in the law enforcement agencies of the United States. Chinese-American brainpower and talent will remain critical, but Chinese Americans will be distrusted solely on account of their race.

BIBLIOGRAPHY

Chang, Gordon, ed. 2000. *Asian Americans and Politics: Perspectives, Experiences, Prospects.* Washington, DC: Woodrow Wilson Center Press.

Chen, Yong. 1997. "The First Suburban Chinatown: The Remaking of Monterey Park, California." *Oral History Review* (Summer): 126–130.

Lee, Rose Hum. 1960. *The Chinese in the United States of America.* Hong Kong: Hong Kong University Press.

United States Commission on Civil Rights. 1992. *Civil Rights Issues Facing Asian Americans in the 1990s.* Washington, DC: U.S. Commission on Civil Rights.

Wong, Bernard P. 1982. *Chinatown: Economic Adaptation and Ethnic Identity of the Chinese.* New York: Holt, Rinehart and Winston.

Zhou, Min, and James V. Gatewood, eds. 2007. *Contemporary Asian America: A Multidisciplinary Reader*, 2nd ed. New York: New York University Press.

L. Ling-chi Wang

CHINESE DIASPORA

The terms *Chinese diaspora* and *overseas Chinese* refer to people of Chinese descent living outside of China. According to a 2003 estimate (MA 2003), the "Chinese living overseas" include migrants from mainland China and Taiwan and consist of about 33 million people living in 107 countries worldwide. Of this total, the largest populations live in Southeast Asia (76 %), North America (11 %), and Europe (6 %), followed by decreasing numbers in South America, Central America, and the Caribbean; East Asia outside China; Oceania; and Africa. The majority of Chinese who have left China to go overseas have gone as laborers or traders.

DISCOURSES AND PRACTICES REIFYING ESSENTIAL HUMAN DIFFERENCE

It would be surprising if a society such as China—with more than 2,000 years of imperial dynastic history and characterized by several centuries of geographic expansion—did not have a political-ideological order that established a fundamental distinction between those who were loyal and orthodox subjects and those who were not. Indeed, differential moral valuations of groups were based on this distinction between "people of culture" and "barbarians" (called *fan* in Chinese). This distinction was erected around perceived differences that indexed the presence or absence of political loyalty, as measured by obeisance to the emperor, acceptance of imperial administration and law, payment of taxes, residence in lowland sedentary settlements, and worship of the gods of the Buddhist-Daoist-Confucian pantheon, including one's ancestors. To show these attributes was to be, by definition, a member of the Han, China's largest ethnic group. Whether such perceived traits were strictly cultural or were associated with physical traits within imperial discourse is unclear. Still, the explicit criteria could be fulfilled by anyone, and in this sense "barbarian" status need not be inherited. To the Han Chinese, peoples living within the empire but not belonging to the Han were associated with color—sometimes skin color, and sometimes colors associated with occupations or dyes used in clothing. Moreover, some groups enslaved by the Han in the twelfth century were called "devil slaves" and identified by skin, lip, and teeth color, and by their inability to eat cooked foods or to speak Chinese (Dikotter 1992). These distinctions were those made by Chinese elites (officials, scholars, and merchants), and it is unclear whether such distinctions were employed by non-elites in everyday life.

During the premodern and early modern periods, the distinction between people of culture and barbarians was employed to distinguish subjects of the emperor from those living within the territories of the empire whose traits indicated they were disloyal or suspect, as well as those living beyond the empire with whom Chinese came into contact. The extension of the Asia-wide Chinese tribute system until the seventeenth century, however, meant that peoples whose rulers swore loyalty to the emperor might themselves be, if not Chinese, not barbarians either. Within this group were Koreans, Ryuku Islanders, Vietnamese, and Siamese. The Chinese viewed those within Asia but not encompassed by the tribute system (with its administered trade) as barbarians, as were all peoples beyond the reach of the tribute system.

Beginning in the early sixteenth century, Portuguese, Spanish, Dutch, and English merchants, sailors, soldiers, and explorers ventured into the seas within the Chinese maritime tribute system, which extended throughout the insular East and Southeast Asia. Chinese merchants and imperial officials who came into contact with these foreigners classified them as barbarians, as inferior people without learning or culture.

CHINESE CONFRONT EUROPEAN COLONIALISM IN SOUTHEAST ASIA

The Han Chinese whose descendants make up the vast majority of the Chinese diaspora in the early twenty-first century came from the coastal regions of southern and southeastern China, and particularly from southern and eastern Guangdong Province, southern Fujian Province, and Hainan Island. One stream of emigration began in the late eighteenth century and crested in the 1880s through 1930s and was associated with the European colonization of Southeast Asia. Most emigrants came from Han subethnic groups, or "speech groups," living in regions of coastal southern Fujian; inland Fujian, Jiangxi, and Guangdong; eastern coastal Guangdong; and southern Guangdong and Hainan. Chinese from these regions had widely varying customs and spoke mutually incomprehensible Chinese languages. Among Chinese immigrants to Southeast Asia, these speech-group affiliations were overriding, and most viewed people belonging to other speech groups as essentially different from and inferior to their own—as indeed they had within China itself.

The British, Dutch, and French who came to actively colonize Southeast Asia in the nineteenth century faced an enormous deficit in labor, which they needed to "open" the lands they had conquered to administration and exploitation. Laborers were in demand to build roads, railways, harbors, and government buildings, and to clear land for urban settlement, plantations, and mines. This work would supply raw materials for the Industrial Revolution and its new consumers in Europe and North America. Prior experiences of Amoy, Guangzhou, and Shantou merchants in the maritime trade accompanying the tribute system provided the vessels and shipping connections linking the port cities of southern and southeast China to Southeast Asia. Beginning in the 1840s, overpopulation, social disorder, and violence in southern China led large numbers of young Chinese men to flee the hinterlands for these cities, from which they would seek their livelihood and fortune on to the "Southern Seas." The result was the "pig trade," in which Chinese shippers and labor brokers based in these coastal ports transported hundreds of thousands of impoverished laborers to Singapore, Penang, Batavia (now Jakarta), Bangkok, and elsewhere in Southeast Asia. Early in the years of the pig trade, hostilities and even outright violence were frequent between hierarchically organized speech groups of migrants struggling over control of territory and markets in the colonies.

European colonial rule of immigrant Chinese relied on a combination of indirect rule via Chinese leaders ("Kapitans"), on coercion through the police and army, and on a unique form of subjugation via the colonial state's provision of opium, to which many Chinese laborers became addicted. However, from the 1890s onward—as increasing numbers of Chinese migrants became successful "middlemen" merchants, planters, miners, and labor bosses within the colonial economies—the Chinese came to pose a major competitive threat to European commerce and industry. The early 1900s were marked by two features: (1) the implementation by colonial states of laws that limited the economic opportunities of Chinese (e.g., prohibiting their owning land or conducting business, on the ethnocentric grounds that Chinese methods were "primitive" or "backward"), and (2) the creation of the institutions of the colonial color bar (e.g., racially exclusive clubs, schools, railroad cars, and services limited to Europeans) specifically targeting the Chinese immigrants. Although the effects of the former were more encompassing over time, the latter were more personally felt by many Chinese. These laws and institutions continued through the end of the colonial era in the 1950s. Rivalries between speech groups abated, but animosities between Chinese and indigenes (whom they viewed as barbarians but with whom they traded) increased due to the harshness of colonial arrangements for extracting surplus from those ruled.

CHINESE, RACE, AND RACISM IN THE "NEW EUROPES"

A second stream of emigration from China was associated with the rise of new European settlements in North America, Australia, New Zealand, and the islands of Polynesia. This period began in the 1840s and ended by the 1890s. Most of these Chinese migrants were from the Pearl River delta region near Guangzhou and Hong Kong. Chinese migration to the Anglophone "New Europes" dates from the late 1840s and 1850s, when gold was discovered in California, Australia, British Columbia in Canada, and New Zealand. This situation led large numbers of Chinese emigrants to leave Hong Kong to seek their fortunes in the gold fields. Others migrated to Hawaii and Tahiti as plantation laborers. By the 1860s, declining yields in the gold fields led migrants to seek work elsewhere as manual laborers, and they played major roles in the inland development of western North America and the building of transcontinental railroads in the United States and Canada. Chinese immigrants also became small retailers and commercial farmers in Australia, the United States, Hawaii, Canada, and New Zealand.

From the 1860s to 1900, racially motivated animosities against the Chinese by insecure members of the European diasporic working classes, who saw themselves as "white" for the first time, emerged in most of the European-ruled settlement colonies. From the 1860s through the 1880s, racially motivated strikes against Chinese, some organized by labor unions, occurred in the United States and Australia; head taxes and loss of the vote were imposed on Chinese in British Columbia; and the first of many national exclusion acts prohibiting entry to Chinese immigrants were passed in the United States (1882), Canada (1923), Australia (1901), and New Zealand (1881) in the name of racially pure "white" nations. The period from the early 1900s until the 1960s was one of continued legal restrictions on Chinese immigration and voting rights, as well as low-level extralegal violence and anti-Chinese discrimination in these countries.

CHINESE AND POSTCOLONIAL RACIAL FORMATIONS IN SOUTHEAST ASIA

With the exception of Thailand, which was never colonized, postcolonial independence from the European powers took place in Southeast Asia from the 1940s through the 1960s by way of active nationalist struggles in Malaya, Indochina, Indonesia and Burma. These struggles were protracted, at times violent, and pitted indigenous majorities against the European colonizers.

In most Southeast Asian nations, the leaders of the independence movements succeeded Europeans as rulers of the new postcolonial states. In Thailand, leaders from the largest ethnic group, the Thai, continued to govern. The new rulers saw themselves and their followers, who were the majority of the population, as indigenous and having the legitimate right to define who did and did not belong to the nation-state. An ideal citizen of the nation showed loyalty to indigenous rule, a certain religious identity (e.g., Muslim), spoke a certain language (e.g., Malay), and adhered to indigenous custom. Indigenist ideologies placed Chinese citizens outside the nation, for they were considered politically disloyal, immoral, and exploitative toward indigenes in their business practices—despite the fact that many Chinese were not in business or had only petty roles in it. For instance, Indonesian indigenist ideology applied the term *pribumi* (of the earth) to the members of all ethnic groups descending from ancestors who lived in the distant past on islands of the Indonesian archipelago—with the exception of Chinese.

Thus, from the 1950s onward, as indigenist regimes came to power in Malaysia, Indonesia, Thailand, Cambodia, the Philippines, Vietnam, and Burma, they implemented policies that discriminated against Chinese in business, employment, land ownership, university entrance, cultural expression (e.g., Chinese-language schooling and the Chinese-language press), place of residence, and access to religious facilities. During periods of economic and political crisis, Chinese were particularly subject to state expropriation and extralegal indigenist violence, as in the May 13, 1969, riots against the Chinese in Kuala Lumpur, the exiling of Chinese (Hoa) from socialist Vietnam in 1978, and the horrific violence against Chinese lives and property (including rapes of several hundred Chinese women) in Jakarta on May 13–14, 1998.

Hearkening back to earlier categories of race in China, but also in response to discrimination and state-sponsored racist violence, Chinese in Southeast Asia have at times expressed racist discourse and practiced discrimination against indigenes in these countries. In Malaysia, for instance, one derogatory word used by Hokkien speakers to refer to Malays was *huana* (barbarian), or *huan* (*fan* in Mandarin) with diminutive "-a" added. Some spoke of Malay "consciousness" as "backward," and Chinese merchants at times discriminated intentionally against Malay customers and business people.

CHINESE AS ECONOMIC MIGRANTS AND MODEL MINORITIES

Since the 1960s, globalization, multiculturalist policies, and public awareness of the rise of the economies of Asia to world prominence have, compared to the past, led to more positive images and treatment by majorities of both local-born Chinese and new migrants from China, Taiwan, and Southeast Asia to the United States, Canada, Australia, and New Zealand. Many citizens of Chinese descent born in these countries have become economically wealthy and socially prominent, and some occupy prestigious positions in academia and corporate life. New migrants have been attracted to the social stability, economic opportunities, and high levels of education, research, and technological development in these countries. Both groups have benefited from reforms stemming from the civil rights movement in the United States, and from avowedly multicultural policies vis-à-vis immigrants in Canada, Australia, and New Zealand.

Part of globalization has been the advent of neoliberalism, or market fundamentalism, as a prevailing logic of governance in the governments of these countries. As interpreted in immigration policy, neoliberalism has promoted the idea that "economic migrants" bring globally scarce capital, business skills, and technological knowledge into a country and help advance its "comparative advantage" in the "global competition" for resources for economic growth. Within the circles of political elites in these countries, ethnic Chinese migrants with capital, business skills, and scientific education have come to be seen as particularly attractive "economic migrants." Following on prior legislation in the 1960s and 1970s (which repealed the exclusionary laws passed between 1880 and 1910 and allowed for family reunification for Chinese migrants), immigration laws since the 1980s have not focused specifically on Chinese as a group, but rather on this category of economic migrants. Taking advantage of these provisions, wealthy Chinese from Taiwan and Southeast Asia have readily attained permanent residency status in the United States, Canada, and Australia. From the perspectives of the non-Chinese majorities, given that many of the recent migrants are also highly educated, they have melded with populations of citizens of Chinese descent (some of whom have lived in these countries for several generations) to form new "model minorities."

Since the 1980s, in contrast to wealthy and highly educated economic migrants, other Chinese have migrated illegally from China to the United States, Canada, and Australia. These migrants have either been smuggled in or illegally overstayed their visitors' visas. Indentured to transnational labor brokers working in both China and these countries, they have been forced to find work in the new sweatshops of Los Angeles and New York (where they are highly exploited), or they have sought "off-the-books" jobs as cabbies, factory operatives, and dishwashers in Sydney and Toronto, in order to pay off loans made to them for their passage from China.

Does the advent of the discourse of economic migrant and model minority mean the disappearance of racial discourse and racist discrimination against Chinese in these countries? This is unlikely. Now that past racist discourses of political elites have been transformed into the new language of market performance, which sorts out the winners from the losers in the new global economy, what is more likely is that the growing xenophobic resentment felt by the majority of "losers" against the new Asian "winners" will lead to new social tensions and racist violence in the years to come.

SEE ALSO *Racism, China.*

BIBLIOGRAPHY

Arrighi, Giovanni, Takeshi Hamashita, and Mark Selden. 2003. *The Resurgence of East Asia: 500, 150, and 50 Year Perspectives.* London: Routledge.

Dikötter, Frank. 1992. *The Discourse of Race in Modern China.* Stanford, CA: Stanford University Press.

Kwong, Peter. 1997. *Forbidden Workers: Illegal Chinese Immigrants and American Labor.* New York: New Press.

Litzinger, Ralph. 1995. "Review of Frank Dikotter: The Discourse of Race in Modern China." *H-World, H-Net Reviews in the Humanities and Social Sciences.* Available from http://www.h-net.org/reviews/.

Ma, Laurence J. C. 2003. "Space, Place, and Transnationalism in the Chinese Diaspora." In *The Chinese Diaspora: Space, Place, Mobility, and Identity,* edited by Laurence J. C. Ma and Carolyn Cartier, 1–50. Lanham, MD: Rowman & Littlefield.

McKeown, Adam. 2004. "Chinese Diaspora." In *Encyclopedia of Diasporas,* edited by Melvin Ember, Carol Ember, and Ian Skoggard, 65–76. New York: Springer.

Nonini, Donald M. 2004. "Spheres of Speculation and Middling Transnational Migrants: Chinese Indonesians in the Asia Pacific." In *State/Nation/Transnation: Perspectives on Transnationalism in the Asia-Pacific,* edited by Brenda S.A. Yeoh and Katie Willis, 37–66. London: Routledge.

Ong, Aihwa. 1999. *Flexible Citizenship: The Cultural Logics of Transnationality.* Durham, NC: Duke University Press.

Pan, Lynn, ed. 1999. *The Encyclopedia of the Chinese Overseas.* Cambridge, MA: Harvard University Press.

Skinner, G. William. 1957. *Chinese Society in Thailand: An Analytical History.* Ithaca, NY: Cornell University Press.

Donald M. Nonini

CHINESE IMMIGRATION AND EXCLUSION (U.S.), NINETEENTH CENTURY

Significant Chinese immigration to the United States began during the frenzied California Gold Rush, and it continued afterward because Chinese labor was deemed indispensable for West Coast economic development and integration into the national economy. However, Chinese immigrants arrived in significant numbers only in 1852, the year that labor-intensive surface mining of gold by self-employed Euro-American prospectors effectively ended and gold production shifted mostly to capital-intensive company mining. Tens of thousands of gold prospectors went bankrupt, became displaced, or found themselves unemployed, and the California economy experienced its first recession. That same year, the non-Indian population of California was 224,435, a sharp increase from only 15,000 in 1848. Of these, about 9 percent were Chinese, an overwhelming majority of whom had just arrived that year. In other words, Chinese entered California at a politically explosive and volatile time, a time when displaced Euro-American prospectors were unprepared and unwilling to accept relatively low-paying jobs in gold-mining companies. Eager to work, Chinese immigrants entered the gold-mining region by working for these companies, prospecting in nonyielding claims abandoned by Euro-American prospectors, or taking on jobs deemed noncompetitive or below the dignity of Euro-American males, such as cleaning, cooking, and sewing.

With their hopes and dreams dashed, the frustrated Euro-American miners promptly directed their anger and hostility at the arriving Chinese. Incited by demagogic politicians, the Euro-American majority blamed the Chinese "foreigners" for their plight and demanded their ouster from their land. Governor John Bigler of California declared the Chinese to be "non-assimilable" people who must not only be excluded but expelled from California. Being non-Christian and nonwhite, poor Chinese immigrants were also considered heathens, incapable of enjoying Euro-American freedom and democracy. To Euro-Americans, assimilability was the primary criterion and exclusion was the sole remedy, and it was to be accomplished through democratic processes and institutions. In other words, Chinese exclusion was to be carried out through the enactment of explicitly anti-Chinese laws at the local, state, and national levels.

In the mid-nineteenth century, exclusion by racial violence and legislative means were the only viable options. The United States already had well-established policies toward Native Americans, African Americans, and Mexican Americans, the three major nonwhite groups. For the indigenous Indians, the policy was extermination or removal and relocation by force. Africans were brought into the country and kept in chain as slaves in the South. Mexican Americans in the Southwest were defeated, colonized, and suppressed. Because the newly arrived Chinese were not indigenous people, nor slaves, nor colonized people, exclusion and expulsion by democratic process became the chosen strategy and policy.

Faced with mounting anti-Chinese sentiment and organized protests among ex-miners and unemployed workers, including frequent mob violence and the burning of Chinatowns, local jurisdictions, most notably San Francisco and towns from Eureka to San Diego, passed ordinances to restrict Chinese residence, business, and employment. The California state legislature enacted a series of "anti-" laws, such as an alien passenger tax in 1852, the monthly Foreign Miner's License Tax in 1853, a head tax of fifty dollars on the importation of Chinese in 1855, a Chinese exclusion law in 1858, a fishing tax in 1860, and a police tax for Chinese not engaged in mining in 1862. It also repeatedly petitioned the U.S. Congress to stop Chinese immigration. In 1879 California voters succeeded in amending the state constitution to prohibit the hiring of Chinese by corporations, contractors, and government agencies. Many of these laws were subsequently declared unconstitutional or in violation of U.S.-China treaty obligations, but many also stood as laws.

As early as 1854, the judicial branch of the state government also joined the anti-Chinese assault. In a landmark decision, the California Supreme Court ruled that testimonies against whites by Chinese were inadmissible in courts of law. "If we would admit them to testify," Chief Justice Hugh C. Murray warned, we "would admit them to all the equal rights of citizenship, and we might soon see them at the polls, in the jury box, upon the bench, and in our legislative halls." As a result, crimes against Chinese persons and property were carried out by Euro-Americans with impunity throughout the West, giving rise to a popular saying, "Not a Chinaman's Chance."

Finally, in 1882, after thirty years of relentless violence and agitation, the U.S. Congress enacted the Chinese Exclusion Act, the first national immigration law specifically targeting Chinese for exclusion. The intent of the law was to stop the threat of Chinese immigration to the U.S. and end the "Yellow Peril." When it became law, there were about 105,000 Chinese out of a total U.S. population of 50.2 million, or a mere one-fifth of one percent.

It took thirty years to accomplish the task of exclusion because of the unique role Chinese immigrant labor played in the economic development of the West, and because of U.S. interests in and obligations to China. In the mid-nineteenth century, the political agenda for the visionaries in the political class of Washington, D.C., and West Coast developers was already in place. The economic development and integration of the western states was deemed a national priority. This included rapid annexation and settlement, access to the rich natural resources, and the shortest route for U.S. trade and Christian mission in China. Unfortunately, this agenda was severely stifled by both the absence of infrastructure and cheap labor and the steadfast white working-class opposition to the presence of Chinese. European immigrants entering the United States were absorbed quickly by ascending mining and manufacturing industries in the East, and the cheap labor in the southern states was still enslaved on the plantations. The only hope for carrying out the agenda was the use of Chinese labor through immigration. But there was still another obstacle: A Chinese law prohibited Chinese emigration, even though the government was incapable of enforcing it. The law, nevertheless, inhibited large-scale labor recruitment.

CHINESE LABOR ON WESTERN RAILROADS

Nothing symbolizes this challenge more clearly than the need to build the western portion of the transcontinental railroad in 1860s. For six frustrating years the Central Pacific Railway Company could not find the labor necessary to lay the track over the cold and rugged Sierra Nevada in California and the scorching deserts in Nevada and Utah. When western builders such as Charles Crocker, Leland Stanford, Mark Hopkins, and Collis P. Huntington discovered the ability, willingness, and reliability of Chinese workers, they began a massive recruitment in China. To guarantee a steady supply of cheap Chinese labor, Secretary of State William H. Seward and Ambassador Anson Burlingame engineered the Burlingame Treaty of 1868 that committed China to legalize the recruitment of Chinese immigrants and the United States to extend federal protection to Chinese workers under violent, political, legislative, and judicial assaults in the western states. The treaty explicitly recognized "the inherent and inalienable right of man to change his home and allegiance, and also the mutual advantage of the free immigration and emigration of their citizens and subjects respectively from one country to the other, for purposes of curiosity, of trade, or as permanent residents."

The Martyrdom of St. Crispin ***by Thomas Nast (1870).*** *St. Crispin was a third-century shoemaker who was martyred for his Christian faith. This political cartoon portrays the Chinese as the saint's slayers, representing the threat of cheap Chinese labor to American business.* **PICTURE COLLECTION, THE BRANCH LIBRARIES, THE NEW YORK PUBLIC LIBRARY, ASTOR, LENOX AND TILDEN FOUNDATIONS.**

In all, 15,000 Chinese participated in the project, which was completed in 1869. More were recruited to build both the northern and southern routes across the nation, as well as the Canadian transcontinental railroad. Beyond railroad construction, Chinese were also recruited to extract minerals throughout the western states, build a vast network of canals and dikes in California, and work in California's nascent agricultural, manufacturing, and fishing industries. After the Civil War, the plantation owners of the southern states also recruited Chinese in anticipation of the massive desertion of emancipated black slaves. Eastern factory owners used them to break strikes. In short, Chinese were indispensable, even if unwelcome and discriminated against because of their race.

Throughout this period and in subsequent periods, Chinese waged uphill struggles against racial violence, institutional racism, and efforts to deny their rights, dignity, and humanity. For example, Norman Asing, a Chinese-American restaurant owner, forcefully refuted California governor John Bigler's anti-Chinese rhetoric in an 1852 letter published in the *Daily Alta California*; thousands of Chinese transcontinental railroad workers walked off their jobs to protest low and unequal pay in 1867; Wong Chin Foo organized militant protests against both the 1882 and 1892 Chinese exclusion laws through his Chinese Equal Rights League in New York; two Chinese children, Mamie Tape of San Francisco (in 1884) and Gong Lum of Rosedale, Mississippi (in 1924), challenged school exclusion and segregation; Yick Wo, a laundryman in Modesto, California, stood in defiance of one of several unjust anti-Chinese laundry ordinances in 1885; and nationwide civil disobedience was carried out by virtually all Chinese in the United States in a protest against the Chinese exclusion law of 1892. In the end, not even the combined forces of China interests in the East, Chinese diplomatic intervention, developers in the West, and Chinese resistance could prevent the passage of the Chinese Exclusion Act of 1882.

EXCLUSION OR EXTERMINATION

Diplomacy was used to guarantee a steady supply of Chinese labor in the crucial decades of western development. When their labor was no longer needed, Americans turned again to diplomacy and democracy to terminate and exclude Chinese immigration. Up until 1882, the United States had an open door immigration policy. Only convicts, prostitutes, morons, and lepers were on the list of persons to be excluded. In 1880, under mounting political pressure, President Rutherford

B. Hayes appointed a commission to negotiate with China for a new treaty that would allow the United States to unilaterally modify or abrogate the Burlingame Treaty and enact Chinese exclusion laws. The commission succeeded in extracting a new treaty, under which the United States could maintain its interests in China through an open door trade policy but also enact laws to close its door to Chinese immigrants.

By adding Chinese to the list of those to be excluded, the 1882 law effectively terminated the legal immigration of Chinese and denied the right of naturalization for Chinese immigrants already in the country. Race was the sole basis for this exclusion and denial of citizenship. The law did allow teachers, students, merchants, diplomats, preachers, and tourists to visit the country, but not as immigrants. In short, the exclusion law institutionalized Chinese exclusion and anti-Chinese prejudice and rendered all Chinese in the United States perpetual and undesirable aliens, stigmatizing them, if not criminalizing them, by race.

Not surprisingly, anti-Chinese riots broke out and Chinatowns burned down in many towns and cities across the western United States in the decade immediately following the passage of the exclusion law. Among the most violent outbursts were the massacre of twenty-eight Chinese miners and the forceful eviction of several hundred Chinese in Rock Springs, Wyoming, in 1885, and the cold-blooded murder of several Chinese gold miners near the Snake River in Oregon, in 1887. As racial violence spread across the western states, Chinese were forced to flee from rural areas and find refuge either in segregated Chinatowns in cities such as San Francisco, Los Angeles, Marysville, Sacramento, Seattle, Portland, and San Diego, or in new Chinatowns in cities in eastern and midwestern states, such as Chicago, Cleveland, Pittsburgh, New York, Boston, Philadelphia, and Washington, D.C. The 1882 law thus amounted to state-sanctioned racial violence.

In the ensuing three decades, several more restrictive exclusion laws were enacted by the U.S. Congress in an effort to plug up various loopholes and strengthen the discretionary power of immigration enforcement agents. The Border Patrol, for example, was established to enforce the exclusion laws. Many of these laws were upheld by judicial decisions, including the sweeping U.S. Supreme Court decision in the *Fong Yue Ting v. United States* (1893), which upheld the constitutionality of the Geary Act of 1892 and denied the right of due process in summarily deporting aliens "deemed inconsistent with the public welfare." In effect, the decision denied the guarantees of the Bill of Rights to the Chinese in the United States and granted discretionary power to the executive branch of the government. By the time of the Theodore Roosevelt administration, even those exempt from exclusion became the frequent targets of arbitrary denial of admission and physical abuse and molestation, in violation of U.S. laws and international treaties. Terence V. Powderly, appointed by Roosevelt to head the Bureau of Immigration, was determined to keep all Chinese out of the country and expel as many as possible of those residing and working in the United States. Writing in 1909, the Stanford social scientist Mary R. Coolidge characterized the Roosevelt administration as "a sort of reign of terror." It was in response to this strategy of expulsion and exclusion that the people of China, at the behest of the Chinese in the United States, launched a popular boycott of imported American goods in 1905, sending a powerful message to Washington, D.C., that the disenfranchised and oppressed Chinese minority could not send themselves.

In short, the exclusion of Chinese was so thoroughly institutionalized by democratic means that all three branches of the government joined hands in denying the rights, privileges, and sanctuary of Chinese immigrants in Euro-American society. As a result, the Chinese population in the United States, contrary to the experiences of immigrants from throughout the world, declined rapidly—from 127,000 in 1890 to 86,000 in 1920. Indeed, the situation facing the repressed and declining Chinese population was nothing short of ethnic cleansing.

SEE ALSO *Chinese Diaspora; Racism, China.*

BIBLIOGRAPHY

Barth, Gunther. 1964. *Bitter Strength: A History of the Chinese in the United States, 1850–1870.* Cambridge, MA: Harvard University Press.

Hansen, Lawrence Douglas Taylor. 2006. "The Chinese Six Companies of San Francisco and the Smuggling of Chinese Immigrants across the U.S.-Mexico Border, 1892–1930." *Journal of the Southwest* (Spring): 37–62.

McClain, Charles. 1994. *In Search of Equality: The Chinese Struggle against Discrimination in Nineteenth Century America.* Berkeley: University of California Press.

McClain, Lawrence Wu. 2003. "From Victims to Victors; A Chinese Contribution to American Law: Yick Wo versus Hopkins." *Chinese America: History and Perspectives* (January) 53–64.

Saxton, Alexander. 1971. *The Indispensable Enemy: Labor and the Anti-Chinese Movement in California.* Berkeley: University of California Press.

Wong, K. Scott, and Sucheng Chang, eds. 1998. *Claiming America: Constructing Chinese American Identities during the Exclusion Era.* Philadelphia: Temple University Press.

L. Ling-chi Wang

CHISHOLM, SHIRLEY
1924–2005

Shirley Anita St. Hill Chisholm bequeathed a political legacy to the United States that has yet to be fully utilized. She was born in Brooklyn, New York, on November 30, 1924, and credited her father—who was born in Guyana and was a union man, a Garveyite, and a Roosevelt supporter—with fostering her political consciousness. Her mother, a native of Barbados, provided her with a strong work ethic and a desire for education. These attributes served her well as she defined her place in an environment that sought to ignore and silence her because of her race, class, and gender.

Although Chisholm did not want to be remembered as the first black woman in the United States Congress, or the first black person to run for the United States presidency, these distinctions clung to her. They did not define her, however. Chisholm's political spirit was born out of the American dream, but its promises were withheld from her. Her family joined immigrants from the South and Europe in Bedford-Stuyvesant, a racially mixed, multicultural Brooklyn neighborhood, in the 1930s. It was there that Chisholm experienced racism, urban poverty, and survival strategies. It was there, too, that she glimpsed the pathways to political power.

Politics surrounded Chisholm all her life, from her father's free-flowing discussions with friends in their home to her involvement in the National Association for the Advancement of Colored People (NAACP) and the Urban League. She honed her political skills with her involvement in racially segregated political clubs, the Democratic League, the Bedford-Stuyvesant Political League (BSPL, an organization to increase black political representation), and local grassroots organizations.

After earning a B.A. from Brooklyn College in 1946 (she would also earn a master's degree in early childhood education at Columbia University in 1952), Chisholm continued her work in politics in the traditional role for women of fund-raising. At that time, blacks had only token representation at the local political level, and women had none. After assessing the experiences of women in her community, she fought against the limited political roles available to women. In 1958 she challenged her political mentor, Wesley McD. Holder, for the presidency of the BSPL, and although she lost, she learned valuable lessons. In1964 she decided to run for a State Assembly seat. Despite sexist challenges to her running, she won. She served in the New York Assembly until 1968, during which time she sponsored fifty bills, eight of which passed. These bills reflected her concerns for education, disadvantaged youth, women, and the poor, all of which were generally absent from the white male political agenda.

In 1968 Chisholm made history when she defeated the Republican candidate James Farmer's well-funded, anti-female campaign and became the first black woman in the U.S. Congress, representing New York's 12th Congressional District. By her own account, some of her colleagues resented a black woman earning the same salary that they earned. As a politician, however, she did not "play by the rules." For example, she refused her first congressional assignment, to the House Forestry Committee, because she felt it was ill-suited to her skills and her constituents' needs.

Chisholm was one of the founding members of the Congressional Black Caucus (originally called the Democratic Select Committee) in 1969, and of the National Women's Political Caucus in 1971. Yet she did not always fit well in either caucus. As a black, she was marginalized by women who did not want to address the issues that blacks felt were important; as a woman, she discovered that blacks were not interested in women's issues. In essence, she was a "womanist" long before the term was coined, working for the benefit of both men and women.

In 1972 Chisholm again made history when she entered the race for the Democratic nomination for the presidency of the United States. Although her campaign suffered from inexperience and insufficient campaign funds, her grassroots political organizing attracted diverse constituencies, especially women and other minorities. She gave a voice to political issues that rarely made the agenda of the major political candidates, such as unemployment, poverty, the Head Start program, and the Vietnam War. During the campaign, she routinely received hate mail, and she was threatened with attempts on her life.

Race was an ever-present campaign issue. When endorsed by the Black Panther Party in California, she refused to reject them despite the political fallout such an association might bring, but instead welcomed them back into electoral politics. However, the Congressional Black Caucus steered clear of her. She was virtually isolated by its members, as they made political deals driven by expediency. Only Congressman Ron Dellums of California solidly supported her candidacy, but in the eleventh hour, even he made the political decision to support George McGovern. Chisholm nevertheless garnered 151.95 delegate votes at the Democratic Convention.

Chisholm conceded that, of the limitations placed on her, gender was a more formidable obstacle than race. In 1984 she became a cofounder, and the first president, of the National Political Congress of Black Women (NPCBW). The NPCBW was founded on the premise that black women needed a political voice that spoke to their particular concerns. Chisholm stated: "I sincerely believe that the reason so many persons become visibly concerned about the potential emergence of the black woman as a political force is because historically they know that we are resilient, we are strong, we have the stamina, the audacity, the courage, the perseverance to change this country" (Staff of *Southern Changes* 1985, p. 9).

After retiring from Congress in 1983, Chisholm remained active. She held the Purington Chair at Mount Holyoke College, teaching politics and sociology until 1987, and she advised Jesse Jackson during both of his campaigns for the presidency. Her impact on women, blacks, and other minorities was substantial, and one of her campaign workers, Barbara Lee, went on to become a member of Congress. But her political legacy must also be gauged by the inspiration that she instilled in others. Following her example, many individuals realized that this was indeed their country and that they had a right to participate in United States politics at every level, regardless of race, class, or gender.

In Shola Lynch's 2004 film about the 1972 campaign, *Chisholm '72: Unbought & Unbossed*, Chisholm describes her presidential bid as paving the way for other candidates who were ignored by the white male-dominated political machine. She wanted to be remembered as a woman who fought for change in the twentieth century. Shirley Chisholm died on January 1, 2005.

SEE ALSO *Black Feminism in Brazil.*

BIBLIOGRAPHY

Chisholm, Shirley. 1970. *Unbought and Unbossed*. Boston: Houghton Mifflin.

———. 1973. *The Good Fight*. New York: Harper & Row.

Chisholm '72: Unbought & Unbossed. 2004. Documentary movie directed by Shola Lynch. Produced in part by the National Black Programming Consortium.

Staff of *Southern Changes*. 1985. "Organizing for Empowerment: The National Political Congress of Black Women." *Southern Changes: The Journal of the Southern Regional Council* 7 (3): 5–9.

Barbara A. Moss

CHRISTIAN IDENTITY

The religious belief system known as Christian Identity (or just "Identity") serves as a faith foundation for innumerable white supremacists worldwide, with as many as 50,000 adherents in the United States alone (as of mid-2005). It is a complex amalgamation of pseudo-Christian ideas, virulent anti-Semitism, historical revisionism, occultism, apocalyptic fantasies, conspiratorial paranoia, and classic notions of racial superiority. This blend of religion and racism has not only led to some of the most heinous hate crimes in America, but has also given rise to an extensive network of independent churches and organizations that cater to the social, political, and theological needs of racists, ranging from neo-Nazis to Klansmen. Identity's doctrinal paradigm, however, has no centralized authority structure, individual founder, core group of recognized leaders, or standard creed. Consequently, it cannot be classed as either a sect or a "cult." And it certainly is not a mainstream Christian denomination. Identity, therefore, might best be described as an amorphous movement of self-styled leaders and affiliates that reflect racist religious beliefs and sociopolitical ideals.

Although the views expressed by Identity adherents may differ on peripheral issues—such as whether Hitler should be idolized; the best "solution" for ridding America of nonwhites (exportation vs. extermination); Jewish history; the significance of occult concepts (e.g., pyramidology); and the efficacy of violence over political activism—most followers of the faith agree on six tenets:

1. Adam and Eve were not the first humans; they were the first white people (Aryans).
2. Old Testament Israelites were Aryans and their descendants are today's Caucasians.
3. Non-Aryans represent a different species than "whites."
4. Jews are descended from either Satan or the Khazars (an Asiatic tribe).
5. Jesus was a white man, and not a Jew.
6. Armageddon, which will be a race war between whites and nonwhites, is imminent.

These doctrines encompass a total worldview, complete with an alternate historical framework stretching back to the dawn of time, as described in Genesis. But unlike mainstream Christians, Identity believers put a racist twist on the classic Adam and Eve story.

OLD TESTAMENT MYTHOLOGY

Identity teaches that Caucasians were created after God had already brought forth a host of other "races" (commonly called "mud people" or "beasts of the field"). This doctrine was noted in Bertrand Comparet's *The Cain-Satanic Seed Line*. Richard Butler, the founder of the Aryan Nations, likewise taught that Adam was "the father of the White Race only" (*Who, What, Why, When, Where: Aryan Nations*, p. 3). The divine plan was for Adam and his wife, Eve, to populate the world with a new race of superior humans created in God's image. But Satan (i.e., the "serpent") greatly hindered the plan by launching a series of attacks against the Lord's chosen people. These attacks started when the Devil literally seduced Eve.

The unholy union (i.e., original sin) produced Cain, who murdered his half-brother Abel—the son of Adam and Eve. Cain subsequently left the Garden of Eden and during his wanderings he supposedly fathered the Jewish race (the "Seed Line" of Lucifer) through the pre-Adamite "mud people." All Jews, therefore, are Satan's spawn. As page 6 of the *Doctrinal Statement of Beliefs* for Kingdom Identity Ministries says, "We believe in an existing being known as the Devil . . . who has literal 'seed' or posterity in earth (Gen. 3:15) commonly called Jews." As for Adam and Eve, they subsequently sired other children, who in turn propagated the white race. This race, contrary to the standard view of historians and theologians, became the "Israelites" of the Old Testament, represented by the twelve tribes of Israel's northern and southern kingdoms.

Here the mystery surrounding the legendary Ten Tribes (or "Lost Tribes") of Israel's northern kingdom becomes relevant. Historians assume that these tribes (Asher, Dan, Gad, Issachar, Joseph, Levi, Naphtali, Reuben, Simeon, Zebulun), after being led into captivity by the Assyrians (c. 722–721 BCE), were assimilated into the populace of surrounding nations. But Identity asserts that the tribes remained a distinct people who wandered the earth, and in so doing scattered their white "seed" throughout the world. This theory, initially called "British-Israelism," first gained acceptance in Victorian England (1837–1901) as Protestants began embracing the notion that they were descendants of Old Testament Israelites.

FROM ENGLAND TO AMERICA

Early proponents of British-Israelism included Richard Brothers (1757–1824), John Wilson (d. 1871), and Edward Hine (1825–1891). Their writings helped spread British-Israelism not only in England, but also America. By the late 1870s, in fact, their concepts were firmly established on U.S. soil. Throughout America, however, a far broader belief took root—that *all* Anglo-Saxons were Israelites. This position was labeled "Anglo-Israelism."

Interestingly, during its formative years, British/Anglo-Israelism was neither racist nor anti-Semitic. Followers considered "Jews" to be fellow kinsmen descended from the two tribes of Israel's southern kingdom (Judah and Benjamin). But such benign views started changing as America moved into the twentieth century, especially during the 1920s, as a nationwide revival of the Klan injected radical anti-Semitism into British/Anglo-Israelism.

The most notable figure of this era to advance anti-Semitism was William J. Cameron, the editor of Henry Ford's *Dearborn Independent* (1919–1927). Cameron authored *The International Jew*, a four-volume series that included anti-Semitic material from more than ninety issues (1920–1922) of Ford's newspaper. Cameron's series were also based in part on information taken from *The Protocols of the Elders of Zion*, the now infamous forgery of minutes reportedly transcribed during a meeting of Jewish leaders plotting world domination.

In 1923 Cameron added two more *Dearborn Independent* stories to his anti-Semitic writings: "Are the Jews 'God's Chosen People'?" and "'Was Jesus Christ a Jew?'—An Inquiry." These latter works planted serious doubts in the minds of British/Anglo-Israelites about whether or not "Jews" were indeed separated brethren. According to the articles, "Jews" were actually evil descendants of the Khazars, an Asiatic race from the Black Sea region. This theory initiated the transition of British/Anglo-Israelism from a decidedly European belief system into a distinctly American hybrid of mythology, historical revisionism, and hate.

IDENTITY MATURES

From the 1920s through the 1940s, America's newest religion was coalescing as British/Anglo-Israel leaders found common political and theological ground. Many notable figures emerged to shape not only Identity doctrines, but also the network of racist churches and organizations that would become Identity's framework. These leaders included the Klansman Reuben H. Sawyer (1866–1962), Howard B. Rand (1889–1991), and Wesley Swift (1913–1970), who was perhaps the first true "Identity" preacher. Swift's potent brand of anti-Semitism literally blazed the trail of hatred eventually taken by those who would form the backbone of Identity. Important successors of these men include Bertrand Comparet (1901–1983), William Potter Gale (1917–1988), and Gerald L. K. Smith (1898–1976).

Despite the voluminous amount of literature produced by these Identity proponents and their protégés, it was not until the late 1970s to early 1980s that Identity reached full stature. By that time, Identity believers had incorporated into their faith the idea that Jesus was a white man who came to save only whites. Moreover, so-called "race-mixing" had become a paramount abomination to Identity followers, primarily in response to social and cultural changes in post-1960s America.

Identity's hatred of interracial childbearing is rooted in white supremacist fears that their race will be obliterated via dilution of the "white" gene pool. This is seen as being part of an alleged Jewish conspiracy to destroy God's people. It is the same conspiracy that supposedly inspired America's civil rights movement and subsequent attempts to foster multiculturalism. As the Identity preacher Charles Wiesman noted in 1991:

> "Jews are the ones promoting multi-racial immigration and multi-culturalism. . . . [Jews want to] destroy God's order of things by getting the white race to ignore the natural barriers of distinction between races. The Jew thus runs to the aid and cause of the Negro and colored races to elevate them while lowering the status of the white man. . . . Jews, who are mongrels, desire the entire world to be mongrelized, especially the white race" (*Who Is Esau-Edom?*, pp. 108–109).

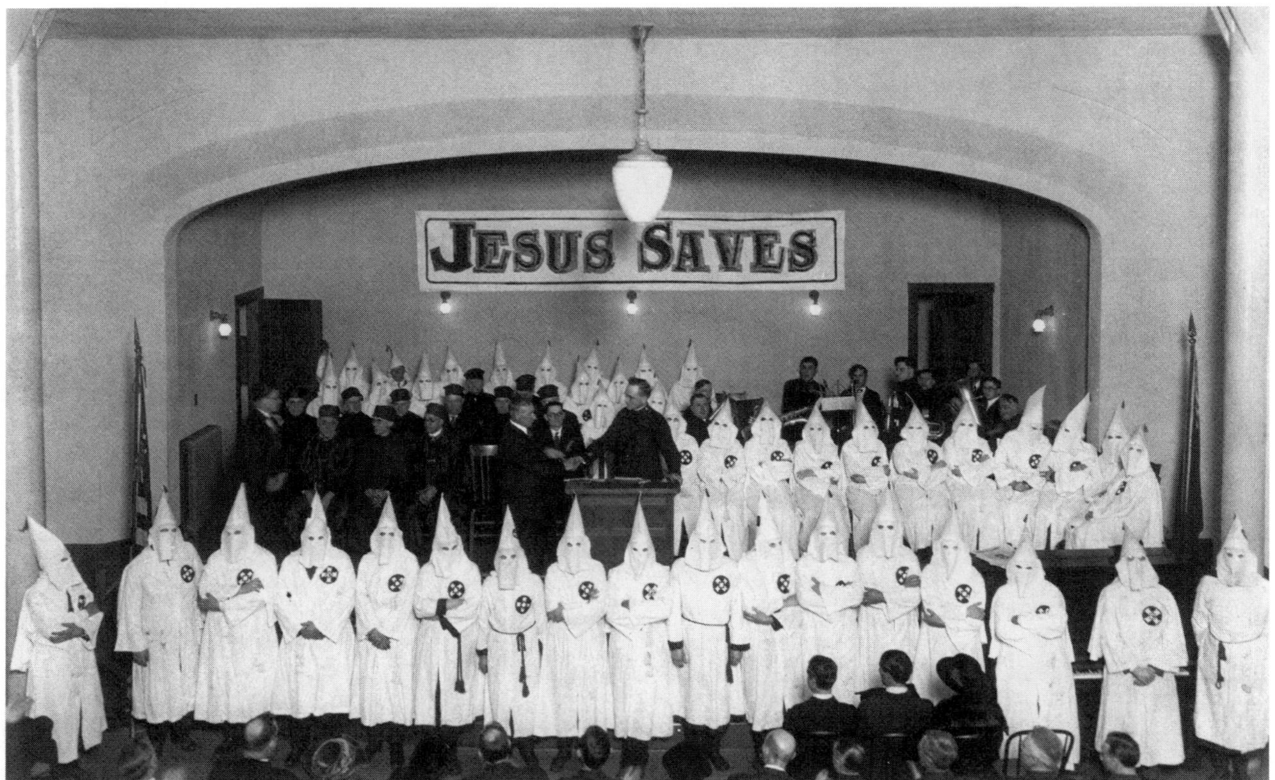

Religion and Racism. *Ku Klux Klan members share a stage, possibly in Portland, Oregon, with members of the Royal Riders of the Red Robe, a Klan auxiliary for foreign-born white Protestants, circa 1922. Protestantism played a strong role in the KKK philosophy of "100 percent American."* **OREGON HISTORICAL SOCIETY, #ORHI 51017.**

Contempt for "race-mixing" also plays a significant role in the apocalyptic visions of Identity adherents, who believe that the United States is teetering on the brink of a catastrophic race war (i.e., Armageddon) that will mark a new beginning for America (the New Jerusalem), which God created for whites only. This war will cleanse the Promised Land of all nonwhites in a manner perhaps not too different from the storyline of *The Turner Diaries*, a horrifically violent screed by William Pierce. In this way, the United States will be delivered from its Zionist Occupational Government (ZOG) and transformed into God's "Heavenly Reich" on earth.

Such a scenario has led some Identity believers to not only adopt the battle cry RAHOWA (i.e., RAcial HOly WAr), but also to manifest violence toward Jews and people of color. The most notorious example of such conduct involved The Order (or *Bruder Schweigen*—the "Silent Brotherhood"), which went on a nationwide rampage in 1984 that included multiple robberies and the murder of Jewish radio talk show host Alan Berg. Other Identity-linked crimes include Timothy McVeigh's 1995 bombing of the Alfred P. Murrah Building, the 1996 Centennial Olympic Park bombing by Eric Rudolph; and the 1998 shootings by Buford Furrow at a Los Angeles Jewish community center.

Mainstream Christians have responded to Identity by arguing that neither racism nor anti-Semitism represents historic Christianity. The Bible declares that there is "neither Jew nor Greek, there is neither slave nor free man, there is neither male nor female; for you are all one in Christ" (Galatians 3:28). The unity of humankind is also exalted in the New Testament, where it is explained that God made from Adam "every" nation of men (Acts 17:26).

Interestingly, many Identity believers have come to reject the "Identity" label because it has become too closely associated with racism and violence. As the Identity pastor Pete Peters put it, "Identity" has been "transformed into an evil icon in the minds of the populace."

SEE ALSO *Swift, Wesley.*

BIBLIOGRAPHY

Abanes, Richard. 1996. *American Militias: Rebellion, Racism, and Religion*. Downers Grove, IL: InterVarsity Press.

Barkun, Michael. 1994. *Religion and the Racist Right: The Origins of the Christian Identity Movement*. Chapel Hill: University of North Carolina Press.

Butler, Richard. "Who, What, Where, Why, When: Aryan Nations." Hayden Lake, ID: Aryan Nations.

Comparet, Bertrand. 1976. *The Cain-Satanic Seed Line.* Hayden Lake, ID: Aryan Nations.

Ezekiel, Raphael S. 1995. *The Racist Mind: Portraits of American Neo-Nazis and Klansmen.* New York: Viking Press.

Ford, Henry. 1921. *The International Jew.* Dearborn, MI: The Dearborn Publishing Co.

George, John, and Laird Wilcox. 1996. *American Extremists: Militias, Supremacists, Klansmen, Communists, and Others.* Amherst, NY: Prometheus Books.

Nilus, Sergei. 1921 (1897). *The Protocols of the Elders of Zion.* Translated by Victor E. Marsden. London: The Britons Publishing Society.

Pierce, William. 1996. *The Turner Diaries*, 2nd ed. New York: Barricade Books.

Quarles, Chester. 2004. *Christian Identity: The Aryan American Bloodline Religion.* Jefferson, NC: Chester L. McFarland.

Ridgeway, James. 1995. *Blood in the Face: The Ku Klux Klan, Aryan Nations, Nazi Skinheads, and the Rise of a New White Culture,* 2nd ed. New York: Thunder's Mouth Press.

Roberts, Charles H. 2003. *Race over Grace: The Racialist Religion of the Christian Identity Movement.* Lincoln, NE: iUniverse.

Singerman, Robert. June 21, 2004. "Contemporary Racist and Judeophobic Ideology Discovers the Khazars, or, Who Really Are the Jews?" Rosaline and Meyer Feinstein Lecture, sponsored by the National Foundation for Jewish Culture, Brooklyn, New York. Available from http://www.jewishculture.org.

Richard J. Abanes

CITIZENSHIP AND RACE

Generally speaking, *citizenship* defines the relationship between the nation-state and those individuals who are considered to be a part of the national polity. Citizenship involves complex notions of rights, obligations, and identity and is a contested social category. Citizenship is a malleable term, which is easily conflated with geopolitical identity. Citizenship can refer to birthplace and national allegiance, but birthplace alone does not define a citizen. Most scholars define citizenship in reference to at least three categories: rights, political activity, and identity. Yet, the most complete definition of citizenship is membership. Citizenship can best be defined by membership in a political community (nation or state) that provides the benefit of political rights of participation, including a right to vote, own property, and participate in governance. Citizenship also involves burdens and duties, including supporting the general will of the nation-state, and participating in activities that benefit the broader community, including paying taxes, subordinating personal interests for the general welfare, and deferring to the broad police powers of the state. In the United States, racial lines and categories demarcated citizenship: whites were citizens, and blacks were, at best, "others."

A review of legislative history before the U.S. Civil War (1861–1865) reveals significant ambiguity as to what the citizenship concerns were or what the term fully meant to legislators or crafters of the U.S. Constitution. However, one issue was clear: wealth and race were determinate factors in one's ability to claim full inclusion and the rights associated with citizenship in the United States. The racial dimension of citizenship can be seen in the way that race determined rights and membership in colonial America, the centrality of race in determining who could become a citizen through the naturalization process, and the use of race to demarcate first- and second-class citizenship from the time of independence until the 1960s.

Immigration and subsequent naturalization petitions served a vital function in the early forming of the United States. Free, white Europeans were needed to pioneer and participate in westward expansion. Their arrival served a vital function in the eighteenth century to help claim territory from indigenous populations and create a new definition of citizenship in the West. The geopolitical taking of land and casting out indigenous populations energized a new identity category, *whiteness,* which defined citizenship at the time and continued to tug at the nation's conception of citizenship through the Civil War, Reconstruction, the civil rights movement, and even post-9/11.

After the Civil War, amendments to the constitution addressed citizenship more clearly and directly by explicitly implementing language using the term *citizenship,* in the Fourteenth Amendment for example. Despite this inclusion, the scope of this term remains disputed largely because (as many people believe and legal cases confirm) citizens have at times been treated differently based on race, gender, sexual orientation, health, and religious status.

RACE AND CITIZENSHIP IN THE COLONIAL ERA

Although Africans were present at the very beginning of viable European settlement of North America, it was clear that they were in no means considered "citizens" of those colonies. A review of the history of black settlement in Jamestown, Virginia, and St. Augustine, Florida, reveals a two-tiered society where Africans were commonly denied the ordinary privileges of local white citizens, including the ability to litigate disputes, own property, and vote. Africans were not considered members of the newly established colonies. In fact, the early colonies permitted slavery and enforced brutal practices to keep slaves in check and enforce the authority of slave owners.

The colonial era came to define future notions of citizenship as well as delineate the proper roles between persons of different social origins. Crucial to the creation of citizenship for whites and denying the same to black people, particularly black women, were the development of anti-miscegenation legislation and the denial of inheritance through the paternal bloodlines, as had been an essential part of English common law tradition. Jack M. Balkin argues, "obviously, a system of subordination cannot be stable if it is too easy to exit from the criteria of subordination status. That is why biological traits can be such useful markers of cultural differentiation. The advantage of immutability lies in its guarantee of stability—it helps ensure that social hierarchy can be reproduced effectively" (1997, p. 2313). (See, for example, Act XII: Negro Women's Children to Serve According to the Condition of The Mother, Virginia 1662; see also Franke 1999.)

Paul Finkelman provides a reminder that in early Virginia comparatively fewer white women settled, therefore white men engaging in sexual relationships often did so with enslaved blacks (1997). These contacts were by no means legally uncomplicated as they were often nonconsensual, produced children, and yet the African women who bore these children were legally on par with animals. Despite tens of thousands of blacks being born to white fathers—who were often connected to plantations (owners, overseers, or their relatives)—they were cast as illegitimate and inherited (non)-citizenship according to their mothers' enslaved status (Finkelman 1997).

In 1662 Virginia led the slave states in differentiating the citizenship of future sons and daughters of the United States. The Act provided (all sic):

> Wheras some doubts have arrisen whether children got by any Englishman upon a negro women should be slave or ffree, Be it therfore enacted and declared by this present grand assembly, that all children borne in this country shalbe held bond or free only according to the condition of the mother, And that if any christian shall committ ffornication with a negro man or women, hee or shee soe offending shall pay double the ffines imposed by the former act. (Act XII, Negro Women's Children to Serve According to the Condition of the Mother, Virginia, 1662).

Law scholar Cheryl Harris explains that this act and similar others were designed to "guarantee that the property in whiteness remained pure and inviolate," but more importantly that the slaveholders would not suffer economic losses through their sexual misadventures with black slave women (quoted in Painter 1996, p. 333–335). Citizenship was naturally coveted as it conferred rights, privileges, and social legitimacy, which became critically important in the "new world." Without citizenship even the black children of white fathers were relegated to what Derrick Bell refers to as the "bottom of the well" (1992).

The founding of American citizenship implicitly relied upon the denial of citizenship to those of African descent. This was most expediently achieved through the collective negative imaging of blacks. Historians comment that blacks were perceived as too immature, unsophisticated, and intellectually inferior to properly exercise the rights granted to citizens, including the right to vote, receive fair wages, contract, and express individual autonomy (Du Bois 1903, Bennett 1999, Painter 1996, Wade 1964).

William H. Harris, in his 1982 work *The Harder We Run: Black Workers since the Civil War,* comments on the economic rights associated with fair wages and labor. Harris observes that the need for black labor was apparent, but that blacks were pacified with diminutive wages, treating them not as respected, adult laborers. Harris also comments that when blacks were inclined to strike in protest of their punitive treatment, whites were known to respond with violence. They were considered an "inferior class of beings" who had to be "subjugated by the dominant race," holding no rights except those the government might choose to give them (from majority decision of *Dred Scott v. Sandford,* 60 U.S. 393,1856).

Dred Scott v. Sanford (1856) is, by all measures, the defining antebellum case on citizenship status. In the *Dred Scott* case, the U.S. Supreme Court determined that persons of African descent were not and could not become citizens of the United States. The Court held that "it is too clear for dispute, that the enslaved African race were not intended to be included, and formed no part of the people who framed and adopted" the Constitution.

Frederick Law Olmsted, an esteemed abolitionist, commented on the superficial, "childlike" relationship between blacks and whites, accepting this notion as a sad reality (1860). Essential to the sanctioning and political health of slavery and the protection of white propertied landowners' interests were the denial of black citizenship and other exclusions (Fox 1999). Thus, although laboring and living in America, slaves were without placement and political identity in the United States. Blacks' lack of political identity and recognition had both psychological as well as economic implications for both blacks and whites. For example, Nell Painter in *Sojourner Truth: A Life, A Symbol* (1996) describes with incredibly rich detail the psychological characteristics of slavery and the affects of subordination and "its characteristics—a lack of self-confidence, personal autonomy, and independent thought ..." (p. 17). Winthrop D. Jordon, in his 1974 work *The White Man's Burden: Historical Origins of Racism in The United States,* provides an excellent exposition on the perceived economic necessities of slavery and the psychological ramifications of reliance on unpaid black labor (see also Johnson 1999, Randall 2001). The psychological dimensions of antebellum period imagery continue to haunt and complicate race relations in America.

The economic empowerment and growth of the United States depended upon unpaid labor of African slaves, and as slavery was "an essential part of the original constitution," blacks were relegated to the status of chattel or property (see also Blassingame 1972). Slavery became the source for economic power and growth for the United States; as Charles Johnson and Patricia Smith observed, "in 1795, the first year of the cotton gin's operation, American planters produced 8 million pounds of cotton. By 1800, production increased more than 400 percent, fueling the demand for additional [slave] labor" (1998, p. 267). David Brion Davis noted that slavery was a "far stronger institution in 1880 than in 1770—largely because of the invention of the cotton gin" (2001, p. 1); Yuval Taylor asserted that "the cotton the slaves produced had become not only the United States' leading export but exceeded in value all other exports combined" (quoted in Robinson 2000). Not only through sales in cotton, tobacco, sugar, hemp (for rope making), and other agricultural crops in the south, slavery also had presence in the American North: "black bondage had long been legal in all 13 colonies when the American Revolution began" (Davis 2001, p. 1). Slaves were bought, sold, used for collateral, and listed as assets in bankruptcy petitions (Weisenburger 1998).

Slavery itself was more easily justifiable if blacks, in the popular cultural imagination and legal texts, possessed infantile and unsavory attributes. Thomas Jefferson referred to slaves in terms of chattel and animals, suggesting that they possessed dull imaginations, were tasteless, and foul in odor (1954). As slaves, lacking voting power, credit power, and access to education, blacks did not possess the legal or social means to move themselves beyond servitude (Harris 1996). By contrast, poor whites, experiencing certainly a compromised status in America, were nonetheless able to benefit economically—even if marginally—from the absolute subjugation of blacks (Bell 1990). Moreover, they were not considered chattel within the law or society. As suggested by W.E.B. Du Bois, this quagmire was not wholly unintentional, as the concept of racial superiority would psychologically compensate poor whites by providing "public and psychological wage," thereby diametrically positioning black inferiority in counterbalance to collective white dominance and citizenship (1935, p. 700). Whiteness is a stock, which needs no investment from whites, but provides economic, political, and social returns for their particular group. Buttressed against that was the unshakably distorted image of blackness; if whiteness is property and citizenship, blackness was an "alien" status.

NATURALIZATION RACE AND CITIZENSHIP

Naturalization, or the process of becoming a citizen when born elsewhere, was significantly determined by race. In the United States, whiteness was the *sine qua non* of becoming a citizen.

The first law setting forth citizenship requirements was the Naturalization Act of 1790. It established the first rules governing the granting of national citizenship in the United States. Citizenship at that time was limited to "free white persons," excluding slaves and indentured servants. Under the Act, Native Americans, Asians, and other non-Europeans did not meet the legal definition of "white" for purposes of naturalization and citizenship. The law also limited citizenship to men, who in turn were free to vote. The naturalization process usually required two years of residency in the United States and one year of residency in a

FRANK LESLIE'S ILLUSTRATED NEWSPAPER

NEW YORK, SATURDAY, JUNE 27, 1857.

The Dred Scott Decision. *The June 27, 1857, edition of* Frank Leslie's Illustrated Newspaper *featured a front page story on the Supreme Court's anti-abolitionist* Dred Scott *decision, including illustrations of the Scott family. The Court had decided that no black person could ever be a citizen of the United States.* THE LIBRARY OF CONGRESS.

state. Upon meeting such requirements, individuals were usually allowed to file a petition for naturalization with common law courts.

In 1790 Congress affirmatively acted to reserve naturalization exclusively for "white persons" (Act of March 26, 1790, Ch. 3, 1 Stat. 103). Because Congress defined naturalization as "[t]he conferring, by any means, of citizenship upon a person after birth," it was clear that even petitions for citizenship would be denied to those who were not white by birth (United States Citizenship and Immigration Services). The racialization of naturalization endured until 1952, long after the abolition of slavery (Immigration and Nationality Act Section 101[a][23], 8 U.S.C. Section 1101[a][23][1952]). It was only then, in 1952, that naturalization was not preconditioned on race (Akram and Johnson 2002). The Immigration and Nationality Act (INA) of 1952 (also known as the McCarran-Walter Act) restricted immigration to the United States, but is also known for organizing a disparate body of statutes and regulations regarding immigration and naturalizing and solidifying U.S. policy under one legislative act.

For more than a century after the passage of the 1790 law, "Congress legislated separately regarding immigration and nationality" (Smith 2002). Marion Smith, a senior historian for the United States Immigration and Naturalization Services, explains that "one congressional committee drafted nationality law, defining U.S. citizenship and how it might be lost or gained. Another committee addressed immigration issues and only began serious attempts to govern or regulate immigration as the nineteenth century came to a close" (2002). Only later, and only for the purpose of excluding Chinese persons from naturalizing in 1882, did the two laws converge.

It was the Fourteenth Amendment, ratified on July 9, 1868, that granted citizenship to all children born of former slaves in the United States. A bold step forward for the country, it sought to protect the status of former slaves by guaranteeing equal treatment under the law as well as the protection of property and liberties typically granted white citizens. The Amendment was significant because it closed the federal and state social policy gap. It made clear that states could not abridge federally conferred rights of citizenship, effectively overturning *Dred Scott v. Sanford*. The Amendment provides:

> All persons born or naturalized in the United States and subject to the jurisdiction thereof, are citizens of the United States and of the State wherein they reside. No State shall make or enforce any law which shall abridge the privileges or immunities of citizens of the United States; nor shall any State deprive any person of life, liberty, or property without due process of law; nor deny to any person within its jurisdiction the equal protection of the laws (United States Constitution, Amendment XIV, Section 1, 1868).

The Fifteenth Amendment, ratified in 1870, recognized as granting citizens the right to vote, essentially extended this right only to black men; white women and black women were yet to be fully incorporated as voting members of the U.S. citizenry. In relevant part, the Amendment protects the right to vote against state or federal acts of discrimination. It gives power to the Congress to enforce the legislation, although the meaningful muscle of this Amendment would come nearly a century later with the Voting Rights Act of 1965.

NATURALIZATION ACT OF 1870

Now that the children of former slaves were automatically granted citizenship status in the United States, an important question remained unanswered: What about their parents and other immigrants? Following the passage of the Thirteenth Amendment (1865), which abolished slavery, the Fourteenth Amendment conferred citizenship on the formerly enslaved. Congress passed the Naturalization Act of 1870; while the 1870 Act ushered in a right for blacks to naturalize, overall the Act held only limited promise of equality in the United States; it provided only for the naturalization of whites and persons of "African descent" and continued to exclude Asians and Native Americans from citizenship. Moreover, the law became symbolic for blacks as their claims to legal citizenship were seemingly trumped by social and political subordination and physical backlash.

In 1882, Congress addressed Asian citizenship directly in the Chinese Exclusion Act. The anti-Asian legislation is considered one of the most significant laws restricting immigration into the United States on the basis of race. Chinese workers were the targets of significant racial animus from working class whites in Western states. Despite the fact that the Chinese comprised less than 1 percent of the U.S. population, Congress intervened to assuage racial fears that Asians were "stealing" jobs from white Americans.

The Exclusion Act, which was renewed in 1892 and in 1902, sought to restrict Chinese immigration and naturalization. The Act formed the basis for other race-based exclusion measures, including successful efforts to deny naturalization to Hindus, Japanese, Middle Easterners, and East Indians. Chinese persons, including Chinese Americans, were ineligible to apply for citizenship until 1943, when the Exclusion Act was effectively nullified.

Citizenship rights for Native Americans were dealt with in the case of *Elk v. Wilkins* (1884), which denied John Elk the right to vote in Nebraska. The Court held that citizenship was established by the federal government and that Native Americans were not included in the guarantees of citizenship, nor extended the right to vote by the Fifteenth Amendment. The Court emphasized that Congress did not intend for such rights to be established for Native persons. That precedent would stand until 1887, when Congress enacted the Dawes General Allotment Act, which granted citizenship to Native Americans who disavowed tribal affiliations and allegiance. Finally, in 1890, twenty years after blacks were granted the right to naturalize, Native Americans were extended the same right with the Indian Naturalization Act of 1890.

WHITENESS AND RACIAL PREREQUISITE CASES

Whiteness was a valuable commodity in the United States; it was unquestionably the most significant feature of citizenship requirements according to Justice Roger B. Taney's infamous holding in the *Dred Scott* decision. Whereas the 1870 Naturalization Act provided citizenship to whites and blacks, for other ethnic, nonwhite populations, efforts to naturalize were met with unyielding legislative and judicial opposition. Color became the measuring stick by which to evaluate citizenship and naturalization in the United States. In a rather ironic twist, throughout the early twentieth century members of Asian and other ethnic groups petitioned courts claiming whiteness in order to gain citizenship.

Chinese Exclusion Act of 1882. *An illustration by Bernhard Gillam shows a group of politicians beating a Chinese man. The Chinese Exclusion Act outlawed Chinese immigration to the United States for 10 years, and the law was renewed until its repeal in 1943.* **PICTURE COLLECTION, THE BRANCH LIBRARIES, THE NEW YORK PUBLIC LIBRARY, ASTOR, LENOX AND TILDEN FOUNDATIONS.**

Petitions for naturalization based on whiteness almost always failed for Asians and other ethnic minorities. Historians have yet to capture the full meaning of such efforts. For example, might some ethnic groups have been more successful applying for citizenship if they had cast themselves as black instead of white? Why was whiteness the natural or preferred avenue to citizenship given that blackness afforded—in naturalization cases—an equal opportunity for citizenship? Whiteness, just as blackness, however, was a social construction enforced by law, built on very unsteady ground. In other words whiteness was an arbitrary physiological distinction, but which courts claimed was clear by "common knowledge."

Whiteness, however, also exposed the fault lines inherent in creating racial hierarchies. Clear distinctions were erected to define the quality of citizenship between whites and nonwhites. Nevertheless, all whites were not treated equally; the English, Irish, French, Scandinavians, Germans, and others found unity in whiteness buttressed against blackness in the competition for jobs, services, public accommodations, and quality schools, but divisiveness based on religion, national origin, or geographical affiliation and minor phenotype distinctions plagued that tenuous coalition throughout the second half of the nineteenth century. Public forms of discrimination against the Irish, including signs posted in windows that read "No Irish Need Apply," evidenced the tension. While the Irish hoped to ascend into politics and assimilate in the United States, southern Europeans, such as the Italians, preferred to build in small communities and often hoped to return to their homelands.

SECOND-CLASS CITIZENSHIP AND RACE

Is citizenship any less meaningful if members of a group enjoy legal entitlements, but experience social, political, and sometimes violent obstacles in obtaining or exercising those rights? The Jim Crow era in the United States (from Reconstruction through the 1960s) signified a return to the tyranny of second-class citizenship for Americans of African descent. The constitutional rights obtained during Reconstruction and later amendments to naturalization policies stood as hollow promises while blacks were subjected to mob violence for attempting to vote, denied equitable public education, and were the victims of heinous lynchings, sexual violence, and systemic brutality.

The tyranny of the Jim Crow era in American life is given stark definition by the murders (too often with the complicity of local law enforcement) of teenagers and young adults attempting to assist blacks in voting during the 1950s and 1960s, and the horrific lynching and castration of Emmett Till, a fourteen-year-old boy murdered in 1955 for allegedly whistling at a white storekeeper's wife. When considering what citizenship meant during Jim Crow, it is clear that there were two tiers of social and political empowerment in society. Those tiers were vertical and not horizontal as the Supreme Court led the nation to believe by its ruling in *Plessy v. Ferguson* (1896).

Plessy v. Ferguson was central in recasting hierarchical differences in citizenship in the United States. In that case, the United States Supreme Court ruled that blacks enjoyed the same rights as whites, but those rights were to be accommodated in separate, but equal, spaces. The ramifications of this case traveled far beyond its original context (a biracial passenger on a train being removed from an all-white car), to justify housing discrimination; segregated schooling, and obstacles in blacks being admitted to universities, medical schools, and law schools; and discrimination in accommodations on trains, buses, and trolleys, and in pharmacies, restaurants, stores, and the voting booth. The reality of *Plessy* was a return to the state of affairs referred to by Taney in the *Dred Scott* decision when he iterated for the nation that those of African descent had no rights that whites were obligated to respect. Despite the U.S. Supreme Court's ruling in *Brown v. Board of Education* (1954), overturning *Plessy* as a matter of law, the legacy of the *Dred Scott* and *Plessy* decisions lives on.

Citizenship is about membership and sociopolitical belonging. The test of one's citizenship in a society may take place at the ballot box, but it also occurs during one's daily routine of going to school, work, shopping, accessing accommodations, worshipping, and returning home. It is in these spheres where the quality of citizenship is often revealed, and it continues to be in these domains where immigrants, those of African descent, and others continue to encounter challenges to their status as U.S. citizens. Racial profiling, the denial of services, and hate crimes evidence that full incorporation of citizenship is not exclusively a legal function, but also a process with social, cultural, and political meaning.

SEE ALSO *Civil Rights Acts; Dred Scott v. Sandford; United States Constitution.*

BIBLIOGRAPHY

Akram, Susan M., and Kevin Johnson. 2002. "Migration Regulation Goes Local: The Role of States in U.S. Immigration Policy: Race, Civil Rights, and Immigration Law after September 11, 2001: The Targeting of Arabs and Muslims." *New York University Annual Survey of American Law* 58: 295.

Balkin, Jack M. 1997. "Group Conflict and the Constitution: Race, Sexuality, and Religion." *Yale Law Journal* 106: 2313, 2324.

Bell, Derrick. 1990. "After We're Gone: Prudent Speculations on America in a Post-Racial Epoch." *St. Louis University Law Journal* 34: 393.

———. 1992. *Faces at The Bottom of The Well: The Permanence of Racism.* New York: Basic Books.

Bennett, Lerone, Jr. 1999. *Forced into Glory: Abraham Lincoln's White Dream.* Chicago: Johnson.

Blassingame, John W. 1972. *The Slave Community: Plantation Life in The Antebellum South.* New York: Oxford University Press.

Davis, David Brion. 2001. "Free At Last: The Enduring Legacy of the South's Civil War Victory." *New York Times,* August 26: 1.

Dred Scott v. *Sandford,* 60 U.S. 393 (1856).

Du Bois, W. E. B. 1903. *The Souls of Black Folk.* Chicago: A.C. McClurg.

———. 1935. *Black Reconstruction in America, 1860–1880.* New York: Atheneum.

Finkleman, Paul. 1997. "Crimes of Love, Misdemeanors of Passion: The Regulation of Race and Sex in the Colonial South." In *The Devil's Lane: Sex and Race in the Early South,* edited by Catherine Clinton and Michele Gillespie. New York: Oxford University Press.

Fox, James W., Jr. 1999. "Citizenship, Poverty, and Federalism: 1787–1882." *University of Pittsburgh Law Review* 60: 421, 479–577.

Franke, Katherine M. 1999. "Becoming a Citizen: Reconstruction Era Regulation of African American Marriages." *Yale Journal of Law and the Humanities* 11(2): 251–309.

Harris, Cheryl I. 1993. "Whiteness as Property." *Harvard Law Review* 106: 1709–1791.

———. 1996. "Finding Sojourner's Truth: Race, Gender and The Institution of Property." *Cardozo Law Review* 18 (2): 309–409.

Harris, William H. 1982. *The Harder We Run: Black Workers since the Civil War.* New York: Oxford University Press.

Hickman, Christine B. 1997. "The Devil and the One Drop Rule: Racial Categories, African Americans and the U.S. Census." *Michigan Law Review* 95: 1161–1265.

Immigration and Nationality Act. 1952. Section 101(a)(23), 8 U.S.C. Section 1101(a)(23).

Jefferson, Thomas. 1954 (1784). *Notes on the State of Virginia,* edited by William Peden. Chapel Hill, NC: Institute of Early American History and Culture.

Johnson, Charles, and Patricia Smith. 1998. *Africans in America: America's Journey through Slavery.* New York: Harcourt Brace.

Johnson, Walter. 1999. *Soul by Soul: Life Inside the Antebellum Slave Market.* Cambridge, MA: Harvard University Press.

Jones, Trina. 2000. "Shades of Brown: The Law of Skin Color." *Duke Law Journal* 49: 1487.

Jordon, Winthrop D. 1974. *The White Man's Burden: Historical Origins of Racism in the United States.* New York: Oxford University Press. Provides an excellent exposition on the perceived economic necessities of slavery and the psychological ramifications of reliance on unpaid black labor.

Olmsted, Frederick Law. 1860. *A Journey in the Back Country.* New York: Mason Brothers. Details the paternalism and violence associated with slavery in southern cities.

Painter, Nell Irvin. 1996. *Sojourner Truth: A Life, A Symbol.* New York: Norton.

Plessy v. *Ferguson,* 163 U.S. 537 (1896).

Randall, Alice. 2001. *The Wind Done Gone.* Boston: Houghton Mifflin.

Robinson, Randall. 2000. *The Debt: What America Owes to Blacks.* New York: Dutton.

Smith, Marion. 2002. "Race, Nationality, and Reality: INS Administration of Racial Provisions in U.S. Immigration and Nationality Law since 1898, Part 1." *Prologue Magazine* 34 (2). Available from http://www.archives.gov.

United States Citizenship and Immigration Services. Available from http://www.uscis.gov.

United States Constitution, Amendment XIV, Section 1 (1868).

Wade, Richard C. 1964. *Slavery in the Cities: The South, 1820–1860.* New York: Oxford University Press.

Weisenburger, Steven. 1998. *Modern Medea: A Family Story of Slavery and Child-Murder from the Old South.* New York: Hill and Wang.

Michele Goodwin

CITIZENSHIP AND "THE BORDER"

In the wake of the events of September 11, 2001 (9/11), and the spurious linkages made between this tragedy and the immigration issue, the United States has witnessed an overwhelming amount of attention to "securing our borders." Of course, this was not the first time national security and immigration were linked to one another. In the early 1990s policy advisers and academics suggested that international migration was a critical concern for peace and stability in the post–cold war era (Doty 1998). However, the attacks of 9/11 did intensify this connection in the minds of many. This attention has taken the form of rhetoric on the part of citizen border patrol groups, immigration "reform" organizations, the news media, and public officials. This attention has also resulted in practices aimed at fortifying entry points, monitoring day labor sites, and increased arrests and deportations of the undocumented. Both the discourse and the practices are based on a simplified view of the extremely complex, multifaceted, and contested nature of "the border." They presume that the border is simply a national, territorial boundary that—given sufficient money and troops, high enough walls, sophisticated enough technology, and the political will—can be fortified, secured, and thus forever ensure the safety and sanctity of "the citizen." However, the border is multifaceted and the territorial border is only one aspect of a much larger phenomenon of border that divides human beings from one another, creates a "self" and "other," a subject who belongs and one who does not, a subject who is deserving and one who is not, a subject who can be called "citizen" and one whose existence can be deemed "illegal." In every sense of the word and in all of its manifestations, "the border" is a site of resistance, which itself takes many forms. The very fact that the border elicits so much attention is an indication of its contested nature. The numerous practices of resistance revolving around the border also attest to this.

The most obvious form of resistance is the physical act of crossing national territorial borders without the proper documents. It is a form of resistance that the label *illegal* erases. *Illegal* conveys a black and white world in which those who cross without documents are deemed criminals regardless of the circumstances. Among Hispanic immigrants, the terms "with papers" or "without papers" are used (*con papeles* or *sin papeles*), which softens the boundary between "legals" and "illegals." The use of the term *illegal immigrant* is not limited to anti-immigrant, nativist groups, but is a rather common designation for migrants without legal documents. This concept is itself implicated in the production of a border that divides the many people who live, work, and contribute to a society. In contrast, if one conceptualizes the very act of crossing the border without documents as a statement about the limitations of *citizen* as a legal concept attached to a national territory, one comes away with a much more complex understanding of the tension between life on the ground, so to speak, and the conceptual apparatus by which one seeks to understand it.

Citizen as a concept struggles to survive in the face of globalization and its own inherent limitations. One can pose the question as to whether the current manifestation of the concept of citizen in political and legal practices that function to exclude and deny rights to those who are not citizens can ultimately survive, or whether one needs to rethink the meaning of this concept in light of the reality of the contemporary world. The human beings who contribute to society but live in fear because of their undocumented status make a silent statement about the limitations of current understandings of the *citizen.* This contestation took a more visible and openly articulated form in the immigrant rights' demonstrations that took place throughout the United States in the spring of 2005.

Perhaps the ultimate and most tragic form of border contestation is exercised by those who pay with their lives in the dangerous crossing locations of the southwestern United States. Their bodies lay scattered across a harsh landscape, sometimes identified by name, often simply labeled *no identificado* (unidentified). The existence of these bodies and the memories of the lives that once surged through them is a form of resistance that disrupts the border between citizen and human being (Doty 2005). They call attention to what we all *are* ultimately, when the trappings of a nationalist identity are stripped away by the heat, the sun, a rattlesnake, lack of water. The desert knows none of these markers of identity, nor do the waters in the Strait of Gibraltar.

Contestation and resistance often result in counter-practices. Several contemporary happenings serve to illustrate practices that seek to reinforce borders and thus the presumed identity of the citizen. One of these is the militarization of the border, which dates back to the 1990s with the beginnings of the "prevention through deterrence" policies of the U.S. Border Patrol. These policies began with Operation Hold the Line in El Paso, Texas, and continued with Operation Gatekeeper in San Diego and a series of other border operations that functioned to seal off major crossing points on the Arizona/Mexico and New Mexico/Mexico borders. The stated purpose of these policies was to deter migrants from crossing in the more populated urban areas. In one sense they were symbolic, a "border game" (Andreas 2000). In actuality they resulted in skyrocketing numbers of deaths of border crossers who were pushed into harsher terrains. In addition, they created another border: a border between those whose lives were deemed dispensable, whose deaths would be the price to show that the United States was serious in trying to secure its borders. In the twenty-first century, the militarization continues: both unofficial, as in civilian border groups such as the Minutemen, and official, as with the National Guard Troops deployed on the U.S.-Mexico border.

Another, perhaps less publicized practice that seeks to reinforce a different kind of border is the effort in the United States to deny "birthright citizenship" to babies born to undocumented parents. Almost every anti-immigrant organization and a number of civilian border groups, as well as some policy makers, favor revoking this long-standing right guaranteed in the Fourteenth Amendment to the U.S. Constitution. House Bill 698, which was sponsored by forty-nine members of the U.S. House of Representatives in 2006, would have eliminated this right. It ran aground in December 2006, but it will likely resurface (Crary 2006). The bill would create a border that divides human beings at the very moment of their birth.

The issues of race and culture inevitably arise within the struggle to reinforce borders that arguably always have been extremely porous. It is extremely difficult to pinpoint precisely how these two complex concepts become intertwined. After biological notions of race have been thoroughly debunked, how does one begin to think of the impact of borders on race and ethnicity? One way is to consider the notion of "cultural racism," or what some have referred to as "neo-racism" (Barker 1981; Balibar 1991; Doty 2003; Taguieff 1990). Neo-racism suggests that it is natural for antagonisms to develop between members of a bounded community—that is, a nation and its "outsiders." "But feelings of antagonism will be aroused if outsiders are admitted" (Barker 1991, p. 21). In the decade around the turn of the twenty-first century, there was a virtual proliferation of books that argue that immigrants threaten the cultural integrity of the United States. Such books include Peter Brimlow's *Alien Nation*, published in 1995, and Samuel Huntington's *Clash of Civilizations and the Remaking of World Order* (1996) and his 2004 work *Who Are We?: The Challenges to America's National Identity*, and Pat Buchanan's *State of Emergency: The Third World Invasion and Conquest of America* (2006); all assert that Mexican immigrants pose dangers to the United States. These are all examples of what the term *neo-racism* is meant to capture. They create the notion of unassimilable "others" who threaten "our" very existence. In contrast to earlier forms of racism, neo-racism professes an ideology of equality while it shuns the mixing of cultures and peoples. Etienne Balibar has suggested that neo-racism is a racism of the reversal of population movement, that is, movements from Third World countries to the rich industrialized countries (Balibar 1991). This way of thinking about peoples and cultures and borders provides a simplified and dangerous way of interpreting the consequences of the movement of human beings all over the world. It creates a border that hinders addressing real issues associated with population movements in a humane way. Theorist Edward Said best posed the question that arises with borders, citizenship, and difference: "Can one divide human reality, as indeed human reality seems to be genuinely divided, into clearly different cultures, histories, traditions, societies, even races, and survive the consequences humanly?" (Said 1979, p. 45).

SEE ALSO *Border Crossings and Human Rights; Border Patrol.*

BIBLIOGRAPHY

Andreas, Peter. 2000. *Border Games: Policing the U.S.-Mexico Divide.* Ithaca, NY: Cornell University Press.

Balibar, Etienne. 1991. "Is There a Neo-Racism?" In *Race, Nation, Class: Ambiguous Identities*, edited by Etienne Balibar and Immanuel Wallerstein. London: Verso.

Barker, Martin. 1981. *The New Racism: Conservatives and the Ideology of the Tribe*. London: Routledge & Kegan Paul.

Crary, David. 2005. "Bitter Debate Over 'Birthright Citizenship.'" *Newsday*, December 6.

Doty, Roxanne Lynn. 1998. "Immigration and the Politics of Security." *Security Studies* 8 (2): 71–93.

———. 2003. *Anti-Immigrationism in Western Democracies-Statecraft, Desire, and the Politics of Exclusion*. London: Routledge.

———. 2006. "Crossroads of Death." In *The Logics of Biopower and the War on Terror: Living, Dying, Surviving*, edited by Elizabeth Dauphinee and Cristina Masters. New York: Palgrave-Macmillan.

Said, Edward. 1978. *Orientalism*. New York: Pantheon.

Taguieff, Pierre-Andre. 1990. "The New Cultural Racism in France." *Telos* 83: 109–122.

Roxanne Lynn Doty

CIVIL RIGHTS ACTS

A civil right is a guarantee by the government, generally in the form of a statute or constitutional provision, that a certain freedom (or freedoms) will be protected through the machinery of the judicial system. If a civil right is interfered with by another person or persons, legal action can be taken against the perpetrators. Some of the most well-known civil rights guarantees include the right to be free from involuntary servitude, the right to vote, and the right to be free from employment discrimination.

THE ORIGINS OF CIVIL RIGHTS LEGISLATION

In the United States, civil rights have their origins in the efforts of the U.S. Congress to free enslaved Africans and, later, to protect them from discrimination because of their previous condition of servitude. Generally, only blacks experienced chattel slavery. Thus, civil rights are associated with efforts by the federal government to protect blacks. Historically, such federal intervention was primarily directed against the overt actions of state officials acting "under color of law." With less effectiveness, federal actions were also tested against nominally private individuals, such as members of the Ku Klux Klan, who took advantage of the postbellum inertia of state officials and threatened the rights of former slaves.

The modern trend has been to universalize notions of equality, and civil rights laws have been expanded in their scope of coverage. As a result, women, Hispanics, and the "differently abled" now have significant protection against discrimination. Civil rights protections also include protection from unreasonable search and seizure, freedom of speech, and other rights that protect all individuals. However, the focus here will be on the particular struggle to establish protections for minorities and people of color, for it is this history that forms the background for all civil rights enforcement.

The history of civil rights has included steps forward and backward over time, leading one author to describe it as "an unsteady march" to equality (Klinkner and Smith 1999). There are at least three important periods in the development of civil rights: the Reconstruction Period; the Period of Segregation, or "Jim Crow"; and the Modern Era, which has been referred to as "the Second Reconstruction."

THE RECONSTRUCTION ERA

The original Constitution protected slavery through several circumlocutory clauses, including the fugitive slave clause, which prohibited northern states from interfering with the recapture of fugitives, and the infamous three-fifths clause, which implicitly recognized slavery and counted all slaves as three-fifths of a person for purposes of congressional apportionment. Under this original constitutional framework, the federal government was conceived as a great danger to liberty. Indeed, in this antebellum context, "liberty" included the right to own slaves as "property" or "chattel." Thus, the first ten amendments to the Constitution limited the power of the federal government. This framework was associated with a notion of "state's rights"—which could have been read as southern state's rights. This meant that individual rights were protected only by the states, if they were protected at all. But the law was merely a rationalization of racial attitudes, and slavery rested ultimately on a "philosophy" of black inferiority. Immediately after the Civil War, the North, dominated by the Republican Party, sought to reintegrate the South back into the Union and address the needs of formerly enslaved African Americans. During this period, known as Reconstruction, Congress passed three constitutional amendments and five civil rights statutes to establish civil rights for the freedmen.

The Thirteenth Amendment, which abolished slavery, was ratified on December 18, 1865. It provides that "neither slavery nor involuntary servitude, except as a punishment for crime whereof the party shall have been duly convicted, shall exist within the United States, or any place subject to their jurisdiction." Congress reserved the right to enforce the amendment through appropriate legislation. This assertion of the supremacy of the federal government over the states was a revolutionary concept at the time.

The new amendment did nothing to overcome traditional beliefs, however, and many southern states enacted laws known as "Black Codes." As Jacobs Tenbroek has written, by virtue of these codes blacks were "socially outcast, industrially a serf, legally a separate and oppressed class" (Tenbroek 1952). Blacks were thus reduced to slavery in all but name. The Black Codes compelled Congress to pass further legislation, namely the Civil Rights Act of 1866. A precursor to the equal protection clause of the Fourteenth Amendment, the act granted citizenship to "all persons born or naturalized in the United States." It thus reversed the Supreme Court decision in *Dred Scott v. Sandford* that held that blacks could not be citizens. It also provided that, among other things, blacks would have the same rights under the law as whites, including the right to sue and be sued, the right to make contracts, and the right to own property. It also made it a crime to deprive any person of his or her civil rights.

Associated with the Civil Rights Act of 1866 was the Anti-Peonage Act of 1867. This law "resulted from the practices found to prevail in the Territory of New Mexico and inherited from the days of Spanish rule" (Gressman 1952). But the law went beyond the specific evil that gave it birth and prohibited involuntary servitude anywhere in the United States. Taken together, the Civil Rights Act of 1866 and the Anti-Peonage Act prohibited forced labor through the institution of slavery as well as through more indirect methods.

When the Black Codes were outlawed by the Civil Rights Act of 1866, hostilities broke out, including a race riot that erupted in Memphis in May 1866. In the backlash that followed, both blacks and the whites that supported civil rights became "victims of terrorism in the South" (Flack 1908).

Yet during this period, opponents of equal rights for blacks avoided public rhetoric on racism. Instead, they based their criticism of the Civil Rights Act on claims of "state's rights." More specifically, the opponents of the bill argued that the Thirteenth Amendment merely abolished slavery and gave Congress no power to require what would later be called "equal protection of the laws." Abolitionists, on the other hand, had long sought to make the federal government the primary protector of individual rights. In the southern view, this legislation was a radical device that wrote the abolitionist perspective into law.

Seeking to place both the issue of black equality and the central role of the federal government beyond the reach of succeeding Congresses, the reigning northern Republicans sought to make civil rights protections a permanent feature of the U.S. Constitution. Thus, the Fourteenth Amendment was born. Tracking the language of the earlier Civil Rights Act, the amendment declared:

> All persons born or naturalized in the United States and subject to the jurisdiction thereof are citizens of the United States and the State wherein they reside. No State shall make or enforce any law, which shall abridge the privileges and immunities of citizens of the United States; nor shall any State deprive any person of life, liberty, or property, without due process of law; nor deny to any person within its jurisdiction the equal protection of the law.

To solidify the supremacy of the federal government over the states in enforcing these civil rights, Section 5 of the Fourteenth Amendment explicitly gave Congress the power to enforce this legislation by appropriate additional legislation. The Fourteenth Amendment was ratified on July 28, 1868. Shortly thereafter, on February 2, 1870, Congress ratified the Fifteenth Amendment, guaranteeing that "the right of citizens of the United States to vote shall not be abridged by the United States or by any state on account of race, color, or previous condition of servitude." Then, on May 31, 1870, Congress reenacted the Civil Rights Act of 1866, which provided for criminal penalties for those violating the Fifteenth Amendment, using the newly minted Fourteenth Amendment as a source of congressional power. This was an attempt to silence those who criticized Congress for legislating equality under an amendment that merely prohibited slavery.

As late as 1871, the terrorism that blacks experienced had not subsided. It was clear that state officials in the South had the power to intervene, but they refused to act to protect the freed slaves. In response, Congress passed what came to be known as the Ku Klux Klan Act on April 20, 1871. Best known in the early twenty-first century is the portion of the statute (now codified as 42 U.S.C. 1983) that prohibited state officials from denying rights to blacks:

> Every person who, under color of any statute, ordinance, regulation, custom, or usage, of any State or Territory, subjects, or causes to be subjected, any citizen of the United States or other person within the jurisdiction thereof to the deprivation of any rights, privileges, or immunities secured by the Constitution and laws, shall be liable to the party injured in an action at law, suit in equity, or other proper proceeding for redress.

At the time, however, the heart of the statute consisted of the sections that prohibited private parties from acting together to deny rights to blacks. Section 2 made it a crime for two or more persons to "conspire together, or go in disguise upon the public highway or upon premises of another for the purpose . . . of depriving any person or any class of persons of the equal protection of the laws."

The high watermark of reconstruction legislation was the Civil Rights Act of 1875, enacted on March 1, 1875. Section 1 of the law required all inns, public conveyances, theaters, and other places of public amusement to open their accommodations and privileges to "all persons within the jurisdiction of the United States . . . regardless of any previous condition of servitude." Section 2 made the violation of the law a criminal offense and gave the injured party a right to recover $500.00 in damages. The law was designed to make blacks full-fledged citizens, and to integrate them into the public life of the states in which they lived. Taken together, the civil rights legislation enacted during Reconstruction represented a constitutional revolution. But it was a revolution that was too swiftly abandoned.

THE EMERGENCE OF JIM CROW

Following the disputed presidential election of 1876, the Democratic supporters of Samuel J. Tilden and the Republican supporters of Rutherford B. Hayes reached an agreement that historians call the Hayes-Tilden Compromise. The "compromise" stipulated that Hayes would get the presidency, but that he would then have to name at least one southerner to his cabinet and remove the troops that had enforced the civil rights laws in the old Confederacy. Hayes thus strode upon the stage of American history as the nineteenth president of the United States, but, as agreed, he withdrew the federal troops from the South, thus bringing down the curtain on Reconstruction.

The force of civil rights legislation was further eroded by the U.S. Supreme Court. In what has been called a judicial *coup d'etat,* the Court held that many of the Reconstruction-era civil rights laws were unconstitutional. They affirmed the autonomy of the states and held again and again that the federal government overstepped its bounds by attempting to assert its authority to protect individual rights.

In the *Slaughterhouse Cases* of 1873, the Supreme Court held that national citizenship conferred few "privileges and immunities." In 1875, the Supreme Court held in *U.S. v. Cruikshank* that the federal government had no jurisdiction over private individuals who deprived blacks of civil rights. Instead, the Court stated, "blacks should look to state officials for protection." Of course, state officials in the South were the very people Congress had sought to protect blacks from. In the ironically named *Civil Rights Cases* of 1883, the Court went on to hold that Congress lacked the power to punish private individuals for denying blacks access to places of public accommodation. The Court held that without state action, no constitutional violation could occur under the Fourteenth Amendment.

Finally, in *Plessy v. Ferguson* (1896) the Supreme Court placed the imprimatur of constitutional approval on state-sponsored segregation. Here, the state of Louisiana had passed a law that required blacks and whites to sit in separate railroad cars. The Court upheld the law on the grounds that blacks had no right to social equality, but only political equality, under the Fourteenth Amendment. With *Plessy,* the Court ushered in the era of segregation. Once the Supreme Court had legitimized it, many states, including but not limited to most southern states, passed laws requiring or permitting segregation. A web of interlocking segregationist laws and customs sprang up, creating the regime of "Jim Crow."

THE SECOND RECONSTRUCTION: THE MODERN ERA OF CIVIL RIGHTS

After seven decades of Jim Crow, the modern civil rights era began with sit-ins and boycotts in the 1950s. In the 1960s Congress passed a series of civil rights acts, including the Civil Rights Acts of 1960, 1964, and 1968.

The impetus for this legislation began as early as 1941 with House Resolution (H.R.) 3994, entitled, "A Bill to Prohibit Discrimination by Any Agency Supported in Whole or in Part with Funds Appropriated by the Congress of the United States." The bill, introduced by Vito Marcantonio from New York, died unceremoniously in committee, as would hundreds like it. President Roosevelt, however, by executive order, prohibited discrimination by defense contractors and created the Fair Employment Practices Commission (FEPC).

Momentum began to build after the racially motivated beating, maiming or lynching of several black men following World War II. In response to the outcry that followed, President Truman set up the President's Committee on Civil Rights, which issued a report, *To Secure These Rights*, in 1947 recommending additional civil rights legislation and a permanent Civil Rights Commission. Subsequently, in 1948, Truman issued an Executive Order calling for desegregation of the armed forces.

Antidiscrimination laws gained further momentum with the enactment, during the Eisenhower years, of the Civil Rights Act of 1957, which created the U.S. Commission on Civil Rights. The reports of this commission spotlighted the glaring inequalities faced by blacks. On May 6, 1960, Eisenhower signed into law the Civil Rights Act of 1960, which established federal inspections of local voter registration polls and introduced penalties for anyone who obstructed a person's attempt to register to vote.

Civil Rights March on Washington, 1963. *A crowd of marchers at Union Station prepares for the March on Washington on August 28, 1963. Martin Luther King's famous "I Have a Dream" speech would make this march one of the most important demonstrations in the nation's history.* © FLIP SCHULKE/CORBIS.

President John F. Kennedy continued the march forward. On March 6, 1961, President Kennedy signed into law an Executive Order establishing the President's Committee on Equal Employment Opportunity and requiring all government contractors to pursue affirmative action policies in the hiring of minorities.

PRELUDE TO 1964

The stage was then set for the Civil Rights Act of 1964. First, H.R. 405 entitled "A Bill to Prohibit Discrimination in Employment in Certain Cases Because of Race, Religion, Color, National Origin, Ancestry or Age" was introduced on January 9, 1963. Setting the tone for the legislation to come, Kennedy, in his message to the 88th Congress in February 1963, advocated "the democratic principle that no man should be denied employment commensurate with his abilities because of his race or creed or ancestry." Originally the bill focused on race, but it was amended by its opponents to include women. These individuals theorized that the possibility of women being given equal rights would doom the bill to failure.

After the longest debate in congressional history, an equal opportunity bill passed the house in February 1963. This launched a tremendous struggle in the Senate. In particular, Title VII of the act threatened to change longstanding baselines of employment law that held that the employer could hire or fire his employee for a good reason, a bad reason, or no reason at all. But more importantly, the bill threatened segregation as a way of life. Southern opponents appealed not to race, however, but to notions of private property. They argued that it was wrong to tell employers whom they had to hire, and that owners of businesses, such as barber shops, had a right to decide with which customers they would associate. Thus, both the ideals of liberty and anticommunism were deployed by the opponents of equal opportunity.

Despite this opposition, the Civil Rights Act of 1964 was signed into law on July 2, 1964. It prohibited discrimination on account of race, sex, color, religion, and national origin. The enforcement machinery was weak in the original formulation, however. Many entities were exempt, and the Equal Employment Opportunity Commission (EEOC), which was created by Title VII of the act, had a limited role in enforcing employment discrimination. Yet, in many respects, the Civil Rights Act of 1964 was the most important legislation of the twentieth century.

Major Amendments. Many members of Congress believed that the "failure to grant the EEOC meaningful enforcement powers has proven to be a major flaw in the operation of Title VII" of the Civil Rights Act of 1964. Therefore, the act was amended in 1972 to include local governments and educational institutions within its coverage and to give the EEOC litigation authority.

However, continuing the political tango of the first Reconstruction, the Supreme Court wrote decisions in the late 1980s that created particularly difficult burdens of proof for Title VII litigants. Perceiving this as a step backward, Congress enacted the Civil Rights Act of 1991, which "overruled" some the most onerous aspects of these decisions. In addition, it provided a right to a jury trial and the right of plaintiffs to not only recover back pay, but also to receive additional financial damages up to a certain ceiling.

Interpretating Title VII. Formally, the courts have interpreted Title VII of the Voting Rights Act to "proscribe not only overt discrimination but also practices that are fair in form, but discriminatory in operation" (*Griggs v. Duke Power* 1971). Thus, as a broad rule, not only is intentional discrimination prohibited, but so is any action that disproportionately excludes minorities in employment. However, the court has limited this theory by creating strict "intent" requirements. For example, an employer can build a factory in Harlem, a predominantly black area, but can then locate his employment office in Beverly Hills. The result may be a factory in Harlem with no black employees. Minorities would have little recourse in such a situation, unless they could prove this was done with an intent to discriminate.

VOTING RIGHTS

The most basic right in a democracy is the right to vote. The Civil Rights Act of 1964 led directly to the Voting Rights Act of 1965, which prohibits any "voting qualification ... which results in a denial ...of the right ... to vote on account of race or color." Enacted pursuant to the Fifteenth Amendment, it has been described as "the most successful piece of federal civil rights legislation ever enacted" (Days 1992).

The Voting Rights Act has two principal provisions. Section 2 forbids the imposition or application of any "voting qualification or prerequisite to voting, or standard, practice, or procedure ... which results in a denial or abridgement of the right of an citizen of the United States to vote on account of race or color." Section 5 requires federal approval of changes in voting procedures in areas with a history of discrimination. Yet despite this legislation, many blacks feel that they still face discriminatory barriers in the voting process.

FAIR HOUSING LEGISLATION

Modern housing segregation dates back to the Great Migration in the early twentieth century. Between 1910 and 1920, approximately 300,000 African Americans migrated from the South to the North. This number increased to 1.3 million between 1920 and 1930; to 1.5 million between 1930 and 1940; and to 2.5 million between 1930 and 1950 (see Bennett 1982). As blacks moved to northern cities from the largely rural South, they confronted both legal and illegal means to restrict their residential choices. These included racial zoning ordinances, racially restrictive covenants, organized realtor practices, and racial violence. The effect of these practices was to create stark patterns of segregation, which still continue in the twenty-first century.

Fair housing laws began as an executive order passed by President Kennedy in 1962. Ignited by Kennedy's leadership and a burgeoning civil rights movement, a substantial movement toward fair housing began. While there was strong resistance, the assassination of Martin Luther King Jr. and the riots that followed served as a catalyst for new legislation. The Fair Housing Act became law on April 11, 1968.

The new law did three things: It prohibited most owners and renters from engaging in discriminatory practices involving their property, it prohibited institutional actors such as banks and real-estate brokers from discriminating, and it called upon the federal government to promote fair housing and establish enforcement mechanisms. In its original form the act prohibited discrimination on the basis of race, sex, national origin, and religion.

Civil Rights Acts

Act (date passed)	Key provisions
Thirteenth Amendment (December 18, 1865)	Abolished slavery
Civil Rights Act of 1866 (April 9, 1866; reenacted May 31, 1870)	Granted citizenship to all persons born or naturalized in the United States; granted rights to sue, make contracts, and own property; made deprivation of civil rights a crime
Fourteenth Amendment (July 28, 1868)	Curbed states' rights claims; made federal government the protector of equal protection under the law
Fifteenth Amendment (February 2, 1870)	Guaranteed the right to vote regardless of race, color, or previous condition of servitude
Civil Rights Act of 1875 (March 1, 1875)	Required inns, transportation services, and places of amusement to be open to all regardless of previous condition of servitude
Civil Rights Act of 1957 (September 9, 1957)	Created U.S. Commission on Civil Rights
Civil Rights Act of 1960 (May 6, 1960)	Established federal inspection of voter registration rolls
Executive Order (May 6, 1961)	Established President's Commission on Equal Employment Opportunity
Civil Rights Act of 1964 (July 2, 1964)	Prohibited discrimination based on race, sex, color, national origin, or religion; also addressed voting rights, segregated schools and facilities, employment
Voting Rights Act of 1965 (August 6, 1965)	Prohibited any voting qualification that results in denial on account of race or color
Civil Rights Act of 1968 (April 11, 1968)	Prohibited discrimination based on race, sex, national origin, or religion in property rental, sales, or financing; protects rights of American Indians
Civil Rights Restoration Act of 1987 (March 22, 1988)	Outlawed discriminatory practices based upon race, religion, color, national origin, gender, age, or disability in any part of any institution that receives federal financial assistance
Civil Rights Act of 1991 (November 21, 1991)	Lightened burden of proof for Title VII equal employment opportunity litigants; provides for jury trial and monetary damages beyond back pay

Civil Rights Acts.

The Fair Housing Act was amended in 1988, when its coverage was extended to two statuses that had not been included in the original Act: handicapped status and familial status. The revised act also gave the Department of Housing and Urban Development (HUD) greater power to investigate and enforce complaints of housing discrimination, while giving administrative judges the power to impose fines on violators.

THE IMPACT OF CIVIL RIGHTS LEGISLATION

Since the passage of Title VII and other legislation, all Americans are heirs to a legacy of equal opportunity and equal justice under law. However, whereas the legal structure in place provides some semblance of formal equality in the early twenty-first century, significant obstacles remain in society that continue to limit the availability of civil rights to all. First, discrimination and prejudice continue to operate against disfavored and disadvantaged groups. Secondly, although one may be a victim of discrimination, access to the resources and evidence to prove it in court, or an administrative hearing, may be another matter.

Finally, the objective value of civil rights has been questioned in the absence of economic and social equality. While the law is explicitly on the side of equal justice, a gulf remains. In the early twenty-first century, minorities are still the victims of racial profiling. Minorities are legally protected from discrimination, but there is still debate about the contours of that concept.

SEE ALSO *Black Codes; Dred Scott v. Sandford; Voting Rights Act of 1965.*

BIBLIOGRAPHY

Bell, Abraham, and Gideon Parchomovsky. 2000. "The Integration Game." *Columbia Law Review* 100 (8): 1965–2029.

Bennett, Lerone, Jr. 2003. *Before the Mayflower: A History of Black America*, 7th ed. Chicago: Johnson.

Days, Drew S., III. 1992. "Section 5 and the Role of the Justice Department." In *Controversies in Minority Voting: The Voting Rights Act in Perspective*, edited by Bernard Grofman and Chandler Davidson. Washington, DC: Brookings Institution.

Finkelman, Paul. 1999. "Affirmative Action for the Master Class: The Creation of the Proslavery Constitution." *Akron Law Review* 32.

Gressman, Eugene. 1952. "The Unhappy History of Civil Rights Legislation." *Michigan Law Review* 50 (8): 1323–1358.

Hench, Virginia E. 1998. "The Death of Voting Rights: The Legal Disenfranchisement of Minority Voters." *Case Western Reserve Law Review* 48 (4): 727–798.

Jones, D. Marvin. 1994. "No Time for Trumpets: Title VII, Equality and the Fin de Siecle." *Michigan Law Review* 92 (8): 2311–2369.

Klinkner, Philip A., and Roger M. Smith. 1999. *The Unsteady March: The Rise and Decline of Racial Equality in America.* Chicago: University of Chicago Press.

Tenbroek, Jacobus. 1952. "The Antislavery Origins of the Fourteenth Amendment." *American Historical Review* 57 (3): 697–698.

Whalen, Charles, and Barbara Whalen. 1985. *The Longest Debate: A Legislative History of the 1964 Civil Rights Act.* Washington, DC: Seven Locks Press.

D. Marvin Jones

CIVIL RIGHTS MOVEMENT

Although America engaged in World War II (1939–1945) supposedly to make the world safe for democracy, in 1945 most of the limitations imposed upon African Americans by racial segregation remained intact in the United States. Major changes affecting the potential for black insurgency had built up within the black community decades before the war, but the war accelerated them. A review of some of these changes is necessary for understanding the later civil rights movement of the 1950–1960 period. Known for generations as Jim Crow, the practice of segregation and discrimination against blacks stamped a badge of inferiority, stigmatizing them as a group. Unapologetic racists disfranchised black voters across the South, having removed African Americans in overwhelming numbers from the political process since the 1890s. Jim Crow also perpetuated the subjugation of blacks economically in domestic service, agricultural, and entry-level industrial occupations.

THE WORLD WAR II ERA

World War II and immediate postwar sociopolitical developments primed the black community for renewed struggles against deeply rooted racism. In response to the suffocating effects of Jim Crow, African Americans by the hundreds of thousands fled the South for greater freedom and dignity and for economic and educational opportunities in urban regions of the North and West. But the Second Great Migration of the 1950s uncovered the realities of racial hostilities in locales outside the South. Northern de facto Jim Crow met the migrants with urban ghettos and widespread employment discrimination, which diluted the promise of economic opportunities. However, the migrants were no longer obsequiously dependent on agriculture or domestic service for livelihood, nor were their lives and limbs endangered because of political agitation. They were free to support racial uplift organizations and programs.

The hallmark of black protest during the World War II era and its immediate aftermath was best signified in the "Double V" campaign: victory at home and victory abroad. Promoted via black media outlets, the "Double V" campaigners insisted that as America fought to secure a victory over fascism abroad, the nation must also secure a victory over racism within its borders. The "Double V" campaign, supported by organizations such as the National Association for the Advancement of Colored People (NAACP) and the Urban League and supported by the black media, achieved some successes helping to drive the civil rights agenda well into the late 1940s. During the war itself, this campaign yielded some positive changes, at least in official governmental employment policies.

A. Philip Randolph, the outspoken labor radical and leader of the Brotherhood of Sleeping Car Porters, an all-black union, led the charge for racial equality during the early 1940s. His March on Washington Movement (MOWM) pressed the federal government to end race discrimination in employment, particularly in defense industries and the military. In 1941 Randolph, Walter F. White of the NAACP, and other leaders threatened to convene 100,000 black marchers in Washington, D.C., if President Franklin D. Roosevelt and the federal government failed to respond to their demands.

Randolph sought a federal measure that would have forbade companies holding federal government contracts to practice racial discrimination. His desired bill called for the eradication of Jim Crow in defense-industry training and urged the total abolition of segregation in the armed forces. In addition, Randolph pushed for a law that would punish unions that refused membership and full union benefits to black workers.

Statistics suggest that by the time the United States entered the war, blacks made up only 5 percent of defense workers and less than 3 percent of the skilled work force in the construction industry. At the start of World War II the percentage of African Americans in industrial occupations was at a thirty-year low. In many respects, when the defense industry began its rapid expansion, African American workers remained marginalized from the upward mobility opportunities stemming from that growth.

In response to Randolph's threat to protest on the lawns of the nation's capital, President Roosevelt issued Executive Order 8802, which created the Federal Employment Practices Commission (FEPC), requiring the federal government to address the problems of employment discrimination affecting black workers. The FEPC was a five-person understaffed and underfunded commission that, lacking strong enforcement powers, could only receive and investigate complaints, draft policy, hold public hearings, and rely on moral suasion and negotiations to stem job discrimination. Nevertheless, the FEPC, Executive Order 8802, and subsequent federal measures did offer some hope that the federal government would react broadly and continuously to persistent demands for African American employment equality. While the basic challenges to employment fairness remained, the exigencies of war and the expansion of the economy increased African American job opportunities. Blacks could be found in entry-level positions in most wartime industries, and they had slowly gained access to some limited benefits associated with membership within organized labor.

In November 1942, Randolph indicated that the MOWM had an agenda called the Program of the March on Washington Movement, which included a series of broader demands, the most comprehensive being "the end of Jim Crow in education, in housing, in transportation and in every other social, economic and political privilege." Among the other demands were the elimination of the segregated military establishment, the enforcement of the due process provisions of the U.S. Constitution, and inclusion of blacks in all governmental policy agencies, including those "which will be sent to the peace conference so that the interests of all peoples everywhere may be fully recognized and justly provided for in the post-war settlement" (quoted in Aptheker 1973).

Randolph's threat to assemble black workers in Washington in his relentless efforts to uproot economic discrimination before, during, and after World II marked the beginning of black mass protest that was to characterize the civil rights movement in later years. Along with attempts aimed at garnering voting rights, desegregated education, and an end to residential segregation, the civil rights community added employment equality to the list of issues as part of its collective platform. These developments emerging from the World War II era set the stage for more dramatic challenges to the racial status quo in future decades during the civil rights movement.

THE POST–WORLD WAR II ERA

Developments during the war invigorated the idea of equality in the consciousness of black veterans who returned having to contest racial inequality in housing and employment. World War II had increased income levels and thus standards of living, particularly for returning black soldiers in the South. When Congress passed the GI Bill of Rights, black veterans looked to benefit as a result of their having laid their lives on the line for the United States.

The Servicemen's Readjustment Act of 1944, known as the GI Bill, emerged out of Congress as a broad reform measure designed to provide veterans with generous education benefits, guaranteed home mortgage loans, and income adjustment allowances during their transition back to civilian life. Black veterans made the most of the measure, taking particular advantage of its education and mortgage benefits. Large numbers of black veterans were able to find employment opportunities either within federal employment circles or in nonagricultural pursuits. Although many benefited from the bill, the legislation represented yet another federal measure marred by the shortcomings of racial bias in its administration, a situation that helped prime ex-soldiers for civic action on the homefront. Scores of black servicemen attended college as a result of the bill, but these veterans were barred on account of race from attending the more prestigious white universities in the Deep South. The Veterans Administration (VA) joined with white universities in funneling black veterans into historically black colleges and universities and even encouraged black veterans to receive training in agricultural and technical trades, further emphasizing beliefs in black mental inferiority and in the relegation of blacks to menial, substandard jobs.

In the area of housing, whereas small numbers of black veterans were able to purchase homes under the GI Bill, most experienced discriminatory practices from banks, lending institutions, and mortgage agencies. The suburbanization of American housing for white veterans virtually excluded blacks, with real estate developers such as William Levitt and Sons seeking "white only" tenants in New York, New Jersey, and Pennsylvania. Residential restrictive covenants confined most African Americans to the growing numbers of racially identifiable overcrowded and often deteriorating urban ghettos. Although the GI bill guaranteed unemployment benefits to veterans, the VA regularly denied benefits to black workers who refused employment at the exploitatively low wages typical of the Jim Crow era. Low wages caused many veterans to seek ever cheaper used housing that had been left behind by whites fleeing their presence.

In response to the effects of discrimination in the immediate post–World War II era, however, African American assaults on the racial practices of the United States actually were continuations of significant prewar influences such as the First Great Migration of World War I, the Garvey movement, the efforts of the NAACP, and the sociocultural activism of the Harlem Renaissance/New Negro Movement. Blacks were becoming less rural and more urban and aggressive. The social energies that fueled postwar activism had been built virtually out of sight of mainstream America. Understanding this earlier evolution of the black community helps one realize that it was not simply World War II exigencies that emboldened blacks to demand major changes in race relations.

In acts of individual resistance and as a means of obtaining better lives for their families, many southern blacks continued the trend of migrating to urban centers of the Northeast, Midwest, and West coast during the World War II era and beyond. This movement of blacks out of the South mirrored the earlier migration of the 1910s and 1920s. The Second Great Migration of black southerners, lasting from 1930 to 1950, was no small exodus. Black populations in the Northeast and Midwest nearly doubled during the twenty-year period, spurred largely by World War II industrial employment opportunities. Southern California and the San Francisco Bay area witnessed dramatic increases in their black urban populations because of job opportunities in the aircraft industry. As was the case during earlier migration years, once blacks arrived in these cities, racial tensions flared sporadically. By the 1950s sections of cities such as Chicago, Detroit, New York, and Los Angeles increasingly became defined as ghettos populated by working-class blacks.

In response to this dramatic influx of black newcomers, white urbanites steadily fled cities to neighboring suburbs. Because of racially engineered residential segregation, blacks were typically locked into urban spaces while millions of whites sought refuge from blacks in burgeoning suburban areas on the margins of these cities. As early as the 1940s, the initial stages of white flight and white economic withdrawal had begun to affect the economies of urban spaces. White flight and residential segregation were fortified through agreements between insurance agencies and real estate agencies, and through policies stemming from the federal government. For example, the Federal Housing Administration (FHA), in conjunction with real estate brokers and lenders, published documents that graded neighborhoods to determine how qualified their respective residents were for loans and mortgages; the higher the score, the greater likelihood of residents winning financial approval. Neighborhoods with even insignificant numbers of black residents were typically given lower scores.

Nonetheless, efforts to limit black opportunity continued to generate upsurges in the budding civil rights community. By 1945, the NAACP could brag of having an impressive 450,000 members, up from only 50,000 in 1941. Even the association's southern chapters could boast of having an official membership of 150,000 across the region, with potentially greater numbers if unofficial membership had been tallied. For decades the NAACP worked to dismantle the legal underpinnings to Jim Crow through the efforts of its Legal Defense and Education Fund (LDF), and in the immediate aftermath of World War II, such legal activism gained momentum.

THE ROLE OF THE COURTS

The successes of the NAACP Legal Defense Fund, incorporated in 1940, are owed to the leadership of Charles Hamilton Houston, then later to his young protégé Thurgood Marshall. For decades the LDF engineered essential U.S. Supreme Court victories that weakened the precedence set by the infamous *Plessy v. Ferguson* (1896) decision and its "separate-but-equal" doctrine. While LDF was a new component within the NAACP in 1940, Houston and Marshall had been the association's legal brain trust for more than a decade. In addition, the organization had already accrued a great deal of experience in the realm of civil rights legal activism. As early as 1915 the NAACP had won its first significant victory in the landmark decision *Guinn v. U.S.* in which the Supreme Court found electoral grandfather clauses unconstitutional. Thus, by 1954 LDF staffers were veterans of legal battles who had earned significant Supreme Court victories over legally mandated racism. With Marshall at the helm, the LDF won the most historic decision of the twentieth century in *Brown v. Board of Education* (1954), in which racial discrimination in public education was ruled unconstitutional.

The LDF began its tactical assault on segregated education in the years prior to World War II, earning precedence-shaping victories on the road to *Brown*. In the following cases, LDF convinced federal courts to compel states to equalize their graduate and professional programs or be forced to admit qualified black applicants. The cases included: *Missouri ex rel. Gaines v. Canada* (1938), *Sipuel v. Oklahoma State Regents* (1948), *McLaurin v. Oklahoma State Regents* (1950), and *Sweatt v. Painter* (1950). Thus, by the 1954 *Brown* decision, much of the legal support for segregated education had already been found unconstitutional by the nation's highest tribunal as a result of the LDF's school desegregation campaign.

LDF also earned noteworthy victories in areas still defined by the legality of Jim Crow but outside the realm of education. In the wartime decision *Smith v. Allwright* (1944), the LDF convinced the Supreme Court to declare unconstitutional the politically exclusive all-white primary election practices of the South. This victory aided in the slow march back to electoral and political participation on the part of African Americans. In *Shelley v. Kraemer* (1948), the LDF showed that racial restrictive covenants indeed violated the equal protection clause of the Fourteenth Amendment.

While the NAACP and the LDF won important victories in the decades of legal struggles leading up to the civil rights movement, these cases did little to change the routine denial of full equality to African Americans. But these victories did suggest that the law might eventually evolve to protect black people's civil rights. The decade prior to the civil rights movement, which included these successes in the courtroom and enduring legacies from the World War II era, paved the way to the turbulent 1960s and the many social changes that followed.

To complement the efforts of leaders such as Randolph and organizations such as the NAACP in battling racism, James Farmer, Bernice Fisher, and Bayard Rustin formed the Congress of Racial Equality (CORE) in 1942, injecting a healthy dose of radical action into the civil rights community. CORE patterned its principles of nonviolent, direct action after Gandhian theories of civil disobedience. These theories and practices ultimately shaped much of the larger civil rights movement's ideology and many of the movement's protest tactics. CORE's Freedom Rides of 1947 were precursors to the types of demonstrations the organization would help engineer during the 1960s. With the emergence of CORE and the growth of the NAACP, the civil rights movement had its two central organizations in place to effectively fight segregation, setting the stage for the nation's second racial reconstruction.

CIVIL RIGHTS AND POPULAR CULTURE

Social, economic and legal demands for racial equality were not the sole expressions of resistance emerging out of black America in the immediate postwar era. Black writers, as extensions of the Harlem Renaissance, produced unabashed literary critiques of race and racism in the United States. This era of literary realism witnessed works by black writers such as Richard Wright (*Native Son,* 1940), Chester Himes (*If He Hollers Let Him Go,* 1945), Ann Petry (*The Street,* 1946), Ralph Ellison (*Invisible Man,* 1952), James Baldwin (*Go Tell It on the Mountain,* 1953), and Lorraine Hansberry (*A Raisin in the Sun,* 1959), and in 1945 *Ebony* magazine began circulation, appealing to a wide array of blacks across the nation.

In other entertainment venues African Americans made similar demands for equality. As late as the 1940s media depictions of African Americans remained openly negative. Black filmmakers and actors responded to these and other racial stereotypes by creating more positive images of African Americans beyond the standard Sambos, coons, and mammies. With Gregory Peck's *Gentleman's Agreement* (1947) on anti-Semitism, Hollywood paved the way for what has been called "social problem" movies. With black audiences larger and more urban than ever, the problem/theme movies appealed to more assertive black communities who rejected the images of black clowns, happy servants, or token entertainers. Among the movies showing blacks as individuals beyond stereotypes were *Home of the Brave* (1949) with James Edwards, *No*

Way Out (1950) with Sidney Poitier, *Member of the Wedding* (1952) with Ethel Waters, *Carmen Jones* (1954) starring Dorothy Dandridge, and *Blackboard Jungle* (1955) with Sidney Poitier, the new and dignified black actor of the era. For African audiences on the verge of the renewed civil rights movement, complacent mammies and lackadaisical handyman servants were literally *Gone with the Wind* (1939).

Racially polarized popular entertainment was not exempt from the mushrooming rebellion against racism. In professional sports African Americans met racial hurdles with momentous achievements. Of these achievements, none was more important than Jackie Robinson integrating the fiercely segregated Major League Baseball. Robinson, a former All-American running back at the university of California, Los Angeles (UCLA) and member of the historic Kansas City Monarchs of the Negro League, was the first African American to break the racial barrier to the hallowed, all-white, male-dominated institution of professional baseball when he was signed by the Brooklyn Dodgers in 1946. One year later, legendary Negro League homerun hitter Larry Doby joined the Cleveland Indians, opening the floodgates for black ballplayers to join major league teams. Ultimately, however, these developments signaled the end of the historic Negro Baseball Leagues. In boxing, Joe Louis reigned as heavyweight champion from 1937 to 1949, winning decisive victories over a multitude of white challengers for blacks to applaud. The accomplishments of these athletes and the many that followed offered African Americans brief respites from the frustrations associated with the norms and practices of Jim Crow America.

THE 1950s AND 1960s

As the cold war entered the political consciousness of the nation, outspoken critics of the United States and especially those with Communist ties were victimized by a congressionally supported witch hunt to expel such subversive elements from the country. Scholar-activist W. E. B. Du Bois and artist-activist Paul Robeson were two of the more prominent African Americans targeted by the House Un-American Activities Committee (HUAC) during the era of McCarthyism. Whereas Du Bois avoided penalties because claims against him were dismissed, Robeson refused to yield in his scathing criticisms of racial practices in America, nor did he denounce his Communist Party affiliations. With little support from civil rights leaders because of fears of being targeted themselves, Robeson, at the mercy of Senator Eugene McCarthy's vicious assaults, was eventually deported. Paul Robeson is widely recognized as one of the most tragic fatalities of McCarthyism and anticommunist aggression in the United States.

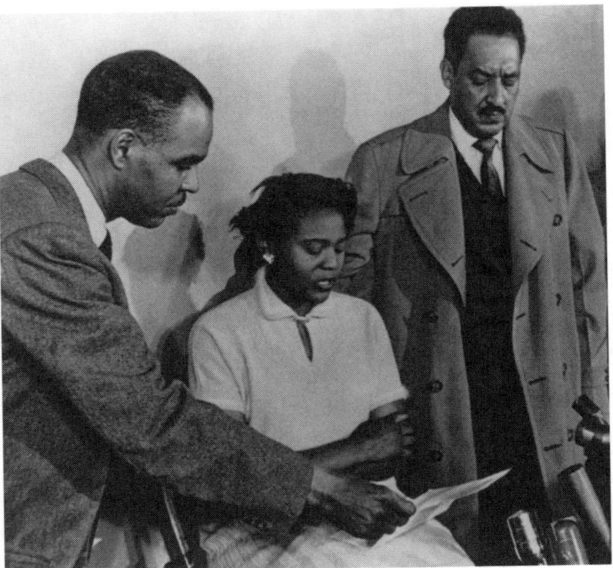

Autherine Lucy at Press Conference, March 2, 1956. *Lucy was accepted as a student at the University of Alabama in 1952, but when university officials realized she was black they rescinded her acceptance. After years of court battles, the Supreme Court decided she had the right to attend.* THE LIBRARY OF CONGRESS.

By the middle of the 1950s, racial realities in the United States still thrived to block black equality and progress. However, developments from the post–World War II era propelled civil rights activism and coordination. With the 1954 victory in *Brown* and the encouraging success of the Montgomery bus boycott of 1955, led by members of the NAACP and CORE, the modern civil rights era was ignited. Jim Crow—America's version of racial apartheid—would soon meet its death knell as well-coordinated protest movements pushed the civil rights agenda, ultimately engendering the consciousness of America.

In February 1960, the student protest movement began when four students at North Carolina A&T walked into a Woolworth store in Greensboro, North Carolina, and sat down, refusing to move until served. Only days later, students across the South were leading numerous sit-in movements against establishments clinging to the practices of Jim Crow. Within a month of the initiation of the sit-ins, hundreds of young radicals convened at Shaw University in Raleigh, North Carolina, and created the Student Non-Violent Coordinating Committee (SNCC). SNCC radicals, black and white, infused a high degree of militancy into the civil rights movement, adding direct, confrontational action to the already successful legal movements and economic boycotts.

Alongside CORE, SNCC continued its direct-action, civil disobedience campaigns, exposing the lengths to which white southerners would go to preserve segregation, even in the face of laws proscribing such practices. CORE reinvigorated its 1947 Freedom Rides by teaming with members of SNCC in 1961 and leading an interracial group of riders through the South, challenging Jim Crow in interstate travel. The Freedom Riders were met with violence in Rock Hill, South Carolina, and in Anniston and Birmingham, Alabama. However, no stop along their ride through the South proved more dangerous than Montgomery, Alabama. In Montgomery, the protesters were met by more than 1,000 whites, with the police nowhere to be found. All the riders and a presidential aide assigned to monitor the crisis were injured by the mob and had to be hospitalized.

Under the coordination of the Southern Christian Leadership Council (SCLC), led by Dr. Martin Luther King Jr., protest movements in Albany, Georgia (1961), and Birmingham, Alabama (1963), propelled the civil rights agenda as young and old joined forces to battle racism in the Deep South. In August 1963, the civil rights movement momentum peaked as nearly 250,000 marchers of many colors and faiths assembled in the nation's capital for the famed March on Washington, where they heard King delivered his famous "I Have a Dream Speech." However, soon after the march concluded, white racists bombed the 16th Street Baptist Church in Birmingham, Alabama, killing four young black girls. Such violent responses were emblematic of the resentment and contempt whites held against blacks challenging racial norms.

Church bombings were only part of the violence directed at African American freedom fighters during the civil rights era. During Mississippi Freedom Summer of 1964, white terror surfaced against volunteers leading voter registration drives in the South's most resistant communities. A collection of young, racially mixed activists from CORE, SNCC, SCLC, and the NAACP joined forces under the Council of Federated Organizations (COFO) in an effort to restore and enhance political participation among blacks in Mississippi. Soon after Freedom Summer began, three volunteers disappeared. Two white volunteers in their early twenties—Michael Schwerner and Andrew Goodman—and James Chaney, a twenty-one-year-old black Mississippi native, were killed near Philadelphia, Mississippi. The efforts of COFO and Freedom Summer ultimately led to the highest political mobilization of blacks across the state since Reconstruction.

One year later, in 1965, SCLC organized a march from Selma to Montgomery to highlight the continued disfranchisement of African American voters in Alabama. As King and the marchers reached the Edmund Pettus Bridge, police officers met them with tear gas and proceeded to beat them before a national television audience. What became known as "Bloody Sunday" spurred Congress and President Lyndon Johnson to pass the Voting Rights Act of 1965, also named the Civil Rights Act of 1965, which outlawed mechanisms whites had used to disqualify black voters for nearly a century. Congress had also passed the Civil Rights Act of 1964, which brought an end to Jim Crow in public accommodations and employment and reaffirmed the congressional commitment to school desegregation.

In a roughly twenty-five year period after World War II, barely one generation, the civil rights community had effectively done away with Jim Crow. With much sacrifice, skillful protest, and charismatic leadership, legally sanctioned second-class citizenship, disfranchisement, and employment injustice reached a formal end.

SEE ALSO *Baker, Ella; Baseball; Du Bois, W. E. B.; NAACP.*

BIBLIOGRAPHY

BOOKS

Andrews, William L., Frances Smith Foster, and Trudier Harris. 1997. *The Oxford Companion to African American Literature.* New York: Oxford University Press.

Aptheker, Herbert, ed. 1973. *A Documentary History of the Negro People of the United States.* Vol. 2. New York: Citadel.

Fairclough, Adam. 2001. *Better Day Coming: Blacks and Equality, 1890–2000.* New York: Viking.

Franklin, John Hope, and Alfred A. Moss Jr. 2000. *From Slavery to Freedom: A History of African Americans,* 8th ed. Boston: McGraw-Hill.

Goldfield, David. 1990. *Black, White, and Southern: Race Relations and Southern Culture, 1940 to the Present.* Baton Rouge: Louisiana State University Press.

Hanchett, Thomas W. 1998. *Sorting Out the New South City: Race, Class and Urban Development in Charlotte, 1875–1975.* Chapel Hill: University of North Carolina Press.

Herbold, Hilary. 1994–1995. "Never a Playing Field: Blacks and the GI Bill." *Journal of Blacks in Higher Education* 6: 104–108.

Hill, Herbert. 1985. *Black Labor and the American Legal System: Race, Work, and the Law.* Madison: University of Wisconsin Press.

Hine, Darlene Clark, William C. Hine, and Stanley Harrold. 2004. *African Americans: A Concise History,* 2nd ed. Upper Saddle River, NJ: Prentice Hall.

Jones, James. 1976. "The Transformation of Fair Employment Practices Policies." In *Federal Policies and Worker Status since the 1930s,* edited by J. P. Goldberg, E. Ahern, W. Haber, and R. A. Oswald. Madison, WI: Industrial Relations Research Institute.

Kelley, Robin D. G. 1990. *Hammer and Hoe: Alabama Communists during the Great Depression.* Chapel Hill: University of North Carolina Press.

Kluger, Richard. 1975. *Simple Justice: The History of* Brown *v.* Board of Education *and Black America's Struggle for Equality.* New York: Knopf.

Nieman, Donald G. 1991. *Promises to Keep: African Americans and the Constitutional Order, 1776 to the Present.* New York: Oxford University Press.

Polenberg, Richard D. 2000. *The Era of Franklin D. Roosevelt, 1933–1945: A Brief History with Documents.* New York: Bedford/St. Martin's Press.

Sugrue, Thomas. 1996. *The Origins of the Urban Crisis: Race and Inequality in Postwar Detroit.* Princeton, NJ: Princeton University Press.

Tushnet, Mark. 1987. *The NAACP's Legal Strategy against Segregated Education, 1925–1950.* Chapel Hill: The University of North Carolina Press.

CASES

Brown v. Board of Education, 347 U.S. 483 (1954).

Guinn v. United States, 238 U.S. 347 (1915).

McLaurin v. Oklahoma State Regents, 339 U.S. 637 (1950).

Missouri ex rel. Gaines v. Canada, 305 U.S. 337 (1938).

Plessy v. Ferguson, 163 U.S. 537 (1896).

Shelley v. Kraemer, 334 U.S. 1 (1948).

Sipuel v. Oklahoma State Regents, 332 U.S. 661 (1948).

Smith v. Allwright, 321 U.S. 649 (1944).

Sweatt v. Painter, 339 U.S. 629 (1950).

Robert Samuel Smith

CIVIL WAR POLITICS AND RACISM

Many historians consider the American Civil War (1861–1865) to be the completion of the American Revolution (1776–1781). The Civil War ended American subservience to England, signaled its emergence as a world-class industrial power, put the Northern industrialists and bankers in charge of the political life of the nation, and ended chattel slavery. The issue of slavery had dominated America's political life throughout the nation's history. For example, the slave-holding states produced thirteen of the first sixteen American presidents, even though they had smaller voting populations than the Northern states.

The political domination of the "slavocracy" can be partially explained by slavery's impact on wealth production in the nation. In the early eighteenth century, tobacco was the dominant cash crop in the South. However, after the invention of the cotton gin in 1810, cotton took over, and by 1859 cotton made up 61 percent of all American exports. The cotton industry depended on slave labor, and the institution of slavery helped create a small class of wealthy landed gentry in the South. This group of Southern elites wielded political influence over American life far in excess of its numbers.

The cotton production system relied on a rigid system of class, which was based upon the concept of race. The vast majority of Southern labor was accomplished using slaves, including the limited amount of manufacturing in the South. This meant that all other occupations in the South revolved around the slave system. For free whites, the choices included being slave overseers, slave catchers, or farming marginal land in the hopes of earning enough to someday be a slave owner. This state of affairs explains, in part, the irrational support of slavery among the majority of Southern whites, most of whom did not own slaves.

African Americans resisted slavery by every means possible, including work slowdowns, sabotage, arson, mass flight, and rebellion. Slave masters feared for their lives, and not without reason, for domestic slaves often poisoned their masters. The South was always on guard against slave rebellion, such as those of Denmark Vessey in 1822, Nat Turner in 1831, and John Brown in 1859. Slaves burned down Dallas, Texas, in 1860. This resistance explained, in part, why slavery was such an inefficient economic system.

However, by the 1830s, national sentiment was beginning to turn against slavery. In the Northern states, the abolition movement, the National Negro Convention, and Free-Soil movements had grown rapidly. Harriet Beecher Stowe's novel, *Uncle Tom's Cabin,* played an important role in publicizing the abuses of slavery by selling 300,000 copies between 1852 and 1853. Stowe had been an organizer for the underground railway in Cincinnati. The book was translated into several languages and sold throughout Europe. Upon meeting Stowe in

Catching Fugitive Slaves. *The vast majority of labor in the South was done by slaves. For free whites, occupation choices included being slave overseers, slave catchers, or farming marginal land.* **PICTURE COLLECTION, THE BRANCH LIBRARIES, THE NEW YORK PUBLIC LIBRARY, ASTOR, LENOX AND TILDEN FOUNDATIONS.**

1862, Abraham Lincoln quipped: "So you're the little lady who wrote the book that started this great war!"

COMPROMISES, WAR IN KANSAS, AND JOHN BROWN

The "Missouri Compromise," passed by the U.S. Congress in 1820, was an attempt to appease both the proslavery and antislavery factions. Under this law slavery was forbidden north of the 36° 30' parallel, Missouri would be a slave state, and Maine would be a free state. The intent, however, was to allow voters to determine, under the principle of "popular sovereignty," whether any new state or territory would allow slavery. Abolitionists saw the "Compromise" as a capitulation to slaveholding interests.

The idea of popular sovereignty was further strengthened by the Compromise of 1850, which allowed California to become a new free state but also allowed New Mexico to decide its own status. This compromise included the infamous Fugitive Slave Law, which required U.S. citizens to assist in capturing runaway slaves. These actions, along with the Kansas-Nebraska Act of 1854 and the Dred Scott Decision of 1857, signaled that abolitionist forces were in retreat and that slaveholders were becoming more assertive in maintaining their "property rights" by violent means.

The Kansas-Nebraska Act opened up Kansas for settlement and repealed the Missouri Compromise. The issue of slavery was to be decided in this territory by popular sovereignty. Proslavery societies tried to subvert this process by organizing an immigration movement into Kansas and seizing the premier land. They also moved in with organized armed bands that included artillery. Northern Free-Soilers, meanwhile, organized emigrant aid societies. Despite Jim Crow laws that forbade them to take up government land, Frederick Douglass agitated for the emigration of free African Americans into Kansas. By March 1855, 10,000 settlers had migrated to Kansas.

Both proslavery and Free-Soil forces attempted to form state governments for federal recognition during 1856. On May 21, 1856, proslavery forces attacked Lawrence, Kansas, reputedly to serve a warrant against a wanted fugitive. They used an artillery piece to blow up the Lawrence jail. Four days later, on May 25, 1856, John Brown and his five sons retaliated by wiping out several proslavery settlers at Dutch Henry's Crossing. The war in Kansas continued, with bands from both sides burning, robbing, and pillaging. The American Civil War had begun, though no one realized it yet. By 1859, Free-Soilers had become the majority in Kansas and elected a legislature and executive branch.

In 1857 John Brown decided to strike a blow directly at slave power by starting an insurrection in Virginia. He chose to attack the federal arsenal at Harpers Ferry hoping to seize the 100,000 to 200,000 rifles stored there. Brown was so convinced of the justice of his actions that he made the plan semi-public in the North (it was even given to the secretary of war).

On Sunday, October 16, 1859, Brown's contingent of twenty-two men, including five African Americans, moved on Harpers Ferry. Unfortunately, the slaves did not flock to John Brown's banner, for he had done little preparation and Harpers Ferry had few field slaves. Brown's forces were quickly overwhelmed by federal forces and he was severely wounded in the battle. Within a week of the battle his trial began. Judge Richard Parker, in Charleston, Virginia, sentenced him and the survivors to death on November 2, 1859. John Brown's final statement to the court was prophetic: "I, John Brown am now quite certain that the crimes of this guilty land will never be purged away but with blood. I had, as I now think, vainly flattered myself that without very much bloodshed it might be done."

THE ELECTION OF 1860 AND SECESSION

Throughout his political career, Abraham Lincoln was opposed to slavery, arguing that it was incompatible with American democracy. "When the white man governs himself," he said, "that is self-government; but when he governs himself, and also governs another man—that is despotism. If the Negro is a man, why then my ancient faith teaches me that 'all men are created equal,' and that there can be no moral right in connection with one man's making a slave of another" (Lincoln 1854). Yet Lincoln was clear to state that while he was opposed to slavery, he did not believe that the Northern states had the right to interfere with slavery where it currently existed. He also carefully distanced himself from what he considered to be violent abolitionism, such as that carried out by John Brown and his supporters. In May 1860 the Republican National Convention met in Chicago, and only Lincoln was an acceptable candidate to all factions of the party. The Democrats held their convention in Charleston, South Carolina. The party was deeply split into Northern and Southern factions over the slavery question. The convention nominated Stephen Douglas for president, but Southern delegates later held a separate convention and nominated John C. Breckinridge of Kentucky (Breckinridge was vice president to the incumbent president, James Buchanan).

The 1860 campaign was one of the most bitterly fought in the history of the United States. When the votes were tallied, Lincoln received 180 electoral votes, a majority. John Breckinridge, who carried the entire Deep South, was second with 72; John Bell, a Tennessean (of the Constitutional Union Party) received 39, and Douglas won only 12.

Lincoln failed to win a single electoral vote in ten Southern states. Thus, despite the results of the Electoral College, Lincoln won only 40 percent of the popular vote.

Even before election day, Southern militants had threatened to secede from the Union if Lincoln was elected. In December, after Lincoln's victory was final, South Carolina seceded. By February, Mississippi, Florida, Alabama, Georgia, Louisiana, and Texas had followed. These states joined together to form the Confederate States of America, or the Confederacy.

President Buchanan did nothing to stop the secessionist movement, and President-elect Lincoln was powerless to intercede. Lincoln remained silent on the issue, hoping that Union sentiment might reassert itself in the South. On March 4, 1861, Lincoln was sworn in as the sixteenth president of the United States. Lincoln attempted to allay Southern fears in his inaugural address. Opening the address he stated: "I have no purpose, directly or indirectly, to interfere with the institution of slavery in the states where it exists. I believe I have no lawful right to do so, and I have no inclination to do so." However, he flatly rejected the right of any state to secede from the Union. He announced that he would "hold, occupy, and possess the property and places belonging to the government." The rebellious states had already seized federal forts, arsenals, and customhouses within their boundaries. Lincoln feared that taking direct action against the Confederacy would lead to the secession of Virginia, North Carolina, Tennessee, and Arkansas.

FORT SUMTER

The Confederate seizure of Fort Sumter forced Lincoln to act. The fort was located at the entrance to Charleston Harbor. The Confederates demanded the evacuation of the fort because it was in their territory. Early in April, Lincoln decided to resupply the fort by sea. He informed Francis Pickens, the governor of South Carolina, of his intention, and Pickens notified the Confederate president, Jefferson Davis. Davis and his cabinet instructed Confederate General Pierre G.T. Beauregard to demand the fort's surrender. The fort's commander, Major Robert Anderson, refused this ultimatum, and at 4:30 AM on April 12, 1861, Beauregard's guns opened fire on Fort Sumter. Lincoln's relief party was unable to land supplies, and two days later Anderson surrendered the fort. Lincoln reacted promptly. He asked the loyal states to provide 75,000 militia for three months' service and he ordered a special session of Congress to convene on July 4. The Civil War had now officially begun.

THE FAILURE OF UNION STRATEGY

On the surface, the Civil War should have never lasted as long as it did or caused as many casualties as it did. The North had vastly superior war potential on every level. There were twenty-three states in the Union but only eleven in the Confederacy. The Union contained 23 million people, while the Confederacy had only 9 million. In addition, 4 million of the South's residents were African-American slaves, most of whom were actively hostile to the Confederate "cause." The Northern army was able to muster 2,898,000 men against 1,300,000 for the Confederacy. The North also had the Union Navy, which could have effectively blockaded the Southern ports and cut off support from Great Britain. Finally, the North had three-quarters of the nation's banking and industrial capital, along with 85 percent of the manufacturing capacity.

The only factor working in favor of the South was it had a better military officer corps at the start of the war. For example, Robert E. Lee was initially offered the command of the Union Army. Even the enlisted men were better trained, due to the fact that the South was essentially an armed state, under constant threat of slave rebellion. Another factor working against the Union was the fact that it was forced to adopt an offensive war strategy. The military tactics employed by both armies at the beginning of the war dated to the Napoleonic era. These tactics required that a massed group of men stand across from each other in open fields firing muskets at each other. The muskets and artillery in use in the Napoleonic period (1800–1812) were very inaccurate. However, by the 1860s, single-shot muzzle-loading muskets were accurate up to 500 yards. Artillery pieces were also more powerful, and explosive shells had been developed. Thus, the tactic of marching men across open fields guaranteed the slaughter of those troops. The Confederates had the advantage of taking defensive positions behind fences and stone walls, as well as fighting on their own terrain. The combination of inept military leadership, inappropriate tactics, and imprecise political strategy meant that the years 1861 and 1862 were a succession of Union military disasters.

The Union failure to win quickly resulted from its failure to comprehend exactly what the overall purposes of the war were for each side. Lincoln's goal was to preserve the Union at any cost. He did not realize that the nation had already split over the issue of slavery. Thus, victory would have been achieved more quickly if slavery had been abolished from the outset. In addition, Lincoln needed to raise African-American regiments, because no other constituency had more to gain by preserving the Union and ending slavery. Indeed, the senior officer corps of the Union was torn by their own friendships and familial relations to the senior officer corps of the Confederacy. Most of those in the Union command were not abolitionists, and many were white supremacists (including Lincoln himself). Some of the

Union Military Disasters of 1861 – 1862

Battle	Result	Casualties*	Commanders	Military Failure
First Bull Run, Manassas Creek, VA	Army of Potomac routed	North 2,896 (460; 1,124; 1,312) South 1,982 (387; 1,582, 13)	McDowell v. Johnston/ Beauregard	Union takes too long to flank Confederate position; Jackson rallied Confederate Center.
Shiloh, Pittsburg Landing, TN	Draw	North > 10,000 South > 10,000	Grant v. Johnston	Johnston surprises Grant, Union pushed back. Grant counter attacks on 2nd day reclaims lost ground.
Seven Pines, VA Seven Days, VA	Union defeat		McClellan v. Johnston/Lee McClellan v. Lee	Union attempt to capture Richmond via peninsula approach. McClellan retreats safely to James River.
Second Bull Run	Union defeat	North 14,500 v. South 9,200	McClellan/ Pope v. Lee/Jackson/ Longstreet	Pope flanked and almost cut off at Manassas Junction.
Antietam	Union victory	North 12,000 v. South 12,700	McClellan v. Lee	McClellan turns back Lee's invasion of Maryland.
Fredericksburg	Union defeat	North 1284, 9600, 1769 v. South 595, 4061, 653.	Burnside v. Lee	Forced frontal attack across pontoon bridge, South held fortified heights above the city.

Note: (killed, wounded, captured/missing)

SOURCE: Adapted from MacDonald, J. (1988). *Great Battles of the Civil War*, New York: Macmillan.

Table 1.

Union commanders also had pro-Southern sympathies (these individuals were called "Copperheads").

From the onset of the conflict, African-American leaders agitated for ending slavery and raising African-American units. Frederick Douglass wrote, "What upon earth is the matter with the American Government and people? Do they really covet the world's ridicule as well as their own social and political ruin? What are they thinking about, or don't they condescend to think at all?" (Douglass 1861). Karl Marx and Friedrich Engels, working as European correspondents, wrote in the *New York Herald Tribune* that ending slavery and the raising of African-American units were necessary to win the war. Marx commented, "A single Negro regiment would have a remarkable effect on Southern nerves." Marx also said that General George McClellan, the union commander, had "incontrovertibly proved that he is a military incompetent," and that he waged war "not to defeat the foe, but rather not to be defeated by the foe."

AFRICAN-AMERICAN MILITARY PARTICIPATION

Lincoln announced the Emancipation Proclamation on January 1, 1863, because the North was on the verge of a military defeat just after the Battle of Antietam. In the following years, African Americans made several significant contributions to the war. For example, Harriet Tubman was a scout, nurse, and military leader for the Union, and she organized a sophisticated spy network among field and house slaves throughout the Confederacy. She was the first woman to ever lead and come under fire on a military raid in U.S. history when she joined Colonel James Montgomery's forces and led a raid up the Combahee River in South Carolina (an event misrepresented in the 1989 film *Glory*).

Frederick Douglass's influence with Governor John Andrew of Massachusetts allowed the 54th Massachusetts Infantry to be organized, one of the first African-American units in the war. Initially, all of the senior officers of the 54th were European-Americans. Colonel Robert Gould Shaw, the son of abolitionists, was commissioned to lead the regiment. Although Shaw was not immune to the white supremacist notions of this time, he counted the African American poet and scholar Charlotte Forten as a personal friend.

The heroism of the 54th Massachusetts at James Island and Fort Wagner is also misrepresented in the popular film *Glory*. For example, the majority of the soldiers who made up this unit were freedmen who could read and write, and many of them gave up farms and businesses to join the unit. The number of freedmen in this unit becomes more significant when one understands that the Confederate Congress drafted legislation calling for the execution of any African American in a federal uniform bearing arms against the Confederacy. The legislation also allowed for the execution of any European-American officer captured in command of African-American troops. Thus, the officers and men of the "colored troops" bore an additional risk in combat not experienced by the rest of the Union Army.

In addition, to add insult to injury, the U.S. Congress paid African-American troops less than European-American troops. In response, the 54th Massachusetts Infantry refused payment for their service.

Eventually, about 185,000 African Americans served in the Union Army and Navy. Twenty-one of these men earned the Congressional Medal of Honor for their

The Massacre at Fort Pillow. *During the Battle of Fort Pillow, which took place on April 12, 1864, in Tennessee, Confederate troops killed a number of black Union troops that had surrendered and thrown down their arms. This account was disputed by the Confederate commander and others, however, though it is generally agreed to be true.* © CORBIS.

heroism during the conflict. By the end of the war, 37,635 African-American troops had been killed (mostly from disease), a mortality rate of 25 percent. This was 35 percent higher than the mortality rate of Euro-American troops of the Union. This is indicative of the way African-American troops were mistreated, especially considering that they did not enter the war until eighteen months after the fighting began. Two egregious examples of the misuse of African-American troops occurred in 1864 at Fort Pillow, Confederate troops were accused of killing African-American troops after they had surrendered, and the Battle of the Crater, in which thousands of black troops were killed after being ordered to charge into a crater where thousands of Union soldiers had already been killed.

DRAFT RIOTS IN NEW YORK

During the same month as the historic charge on Fort Wagner and Battle of Gettysburg (which changed the tide of the war), draft riots broke out in New York City. The riots were carried out mainly by Irish Catholics who had been convinced by Northern Copperheads that the war was a crusade to benefit African Americans. Irish Americans were themselves suffering from oppression at the hands of Northern Protestants (who were mainly of English ancestry). In addition, the proslavery Democratic Party in New York had been agitating among the Irish and German immigrants, saying that ending slavery would cause a flood of former slaves into New York, and that this would threaten the jobs of the immigrants. Democratic Party newspapers had been agitating against the draft for the entire month preceding the July draft lottery. Compounding this racist agitation was the fact that, as a community, the Irish had already suffered a great number of casualties due to the ineptitude of the Union command. Probably the single greatest factor fueling Irish rage over the draft was the provision that allowed wealthy persons to buy themselves out of the draft for a fee of 300 dollars, or else to hire a "substitute" to fight for them.

On July 13th, the riots began as mobs of mostly Irish men attacked the draft office and other federal offices. However, they soon turned their vengeance against any African Americans they came across. African Americans were indiscriminately lynched and beaten. The Colored Orphan Asylum was burned to the ground, although the children had already fled. Protestant churches were also attacked, as well as the offices of Horace Greeley's *New York Tribune* (a pro-Lincoln newspaper). The rioting lasted four days, and local police could not control it. It was eventually put down by federal troops that had been fighting for their lives at Gettysburg only two weeks earlier.

THE CULMINATION AND AFTERMATH OF THE WAR

The Emancipation Proclamation, the raising of African-American regiments, and Lincoln's decision to put the conduct of the war in the hands of competent generals (namely, Ulysses Grant and William Tecumseh Sherman) brought about the end of the war. Grant realized that his numerical and technical superiority could only be realized if he maintained the offensive. His plan was to destroy the Army of Northern Virginia by using a series of rightward flanking movements directed toward Richmond. In the West, Sherman set about to divide the Confederacy in half. Sherman's plan was to destroy the ability of the Confederate Army to supply itself by moving eastward from the Mississippi River toward Atlanta, thus cutting Confederate supply lines.

Lee surrendered the Army of Northern Virginia on April 9, 1865, at Appomattox Courthouse. In the succeeding months the remainder of the Confederate forces surrendered. The Civil War was by far the most costly the United States has ever fought with regard to human life. A total of 360,222 Union troops and 258,000 Confederate troops were killed, out of a total population that numbered 32,300,000. This can be compared to World War II, in which the total American losses were 407,316 out of a population of 133,400,000. From a financial point of view, the war cost the Confederacy $4 billion and the Union laid out $16 billion. The final years of war left the Confederate cities in shambles. When Lincoln entered Richmond in triumph on April 3, 1865, few buildings remained standing.

THE ACCOMPLISHMENTS OF THE WAR

The American Civil War brought about an end to chattel slavery. This broke the control that England had over Southern agricultural production, while simultaneously opening the American South for industrial growth. The settling of the slavery question also prepared America for a westward expansion. The American Indian nations would be brutally defeated by American expansionism by the end of the 1870s. The war freed four million slaves, who now would require resources and education so that they could be prepared for their new life.

The Union victory also created new political and social dynamics. The Northern bankers and industrialists were now the dominant economic and political bloc in the United States. Their political power over the nation was wielded through the Republican Party, which had control of the Union army of occupation in the South and the anti-Indian forces in the West.

The war did not settle the race question in America, however. If anything, it simply recast it in new forms. Many African Americans had fought for the Union, and some for the Confederacy, and their heroism caused some European Americans to change their views about blacks. Abraham Lincoln's own personal views merit attention in this regard. At the beginning of the war, he saw no place for African Americans in the fight to preserve the Union, but as the war dragged on he grudgingly accepted the need for African-American troops, and later he hailed their selfless contributions. Even Robert E. Lee felt that the Confederates should have armed Negroes, and he said he would have welcomed them into the ranks of the Army of Northern Virginia—if they had been willing to serve. Lincoln supported the idea of African-American soldiers receiving the vote after the war. Unfortunately, Lincoln never lived to see any of his plans for Reconstruction realized. Most consider him the "last casualty of the war." He was assassinated by the Southern racist John Wilkes Booth on April 14, 1865, while attending a play at the Ford's Theater in Washington, D.C.

SEE ALSO *Antebellum Black Ethnology; Black Civil War Soldiers; Douglass, Frederick; Emancipation Proclamation.*

BIBLIOGRAPHY

Aptheker, Herbert. 1948. *To Be Free: Studies in American Negro History*. New York: International Publishers.

Burchard, Peter. 1965. *One Gallant Rush: Robert Gould Shaw and His Brave Black Regiment*. New York: St. Martin's Press.

Castel, Albert. 1958. "The Fort Pillow Massacre: A Fresh Examination of the Evidence." *Civil War History* 4 (1): 44–45.

Douglass, Frederick. 1861. "Fighting Rebels with Only One Hand." *Douglass Monthly* (September 1861). Reprinted in *The Life and Writings of Frederick Douglass*, edited by Philip S. Foner. New York: International Publishers, 1975.

Du Bois, W. E. B. 1962. *John Brown*, Centennial ed. New York: International Publishers.

Glathaar, Joseph T. 1990. *Forged in Battle: The Civil War Alliance of Black Soldiers and White Officers*. New York: Meridian Books.

Harris, Leslie M. 2003. *In the Shadow of Slavery: African Americans in New York City, 1626-1863*. Chicago: University of Chicago Press.

Jordan, Ervin L., Jr. 1995. *Black Confederates and Afro-Yankees in Civil War Virginia*. Charlottesville: University of Virginia Press.

Lincoln, Abraham. Speech at Peoria, Illinois, in reply to Senator Douglas, October 16, 1854. In Project Gutenberg E-text of *The Writings of Abraham Lincoln*, Vol. 2 of 7. Available from www.gutenberg.org/files/2654/old/2linc10.txt.

MacDonald, John. 1988. *Great Battles of the Civil War*. New York: Macmillan.

Marx, Karl, and Frederick Engels. 1964 (1861). *The Civil War in the United States*. In *Marx/Engels Collected Works*. Moscow: Progress Publishers.

McPherson, James M. 1988. *Battle Cry of Freedom: The Civil War Era*. New York: Oxford University Press.

Pierce, Edward L. (correspondent for the *New York Tribune*). 1863. Letter to Governor John A. Andrew, July 22.

Redkey, Edwin S. 1992. *A Grand Army of Black Men: Letters from African American Soldiers in the Union Army: 1861–1865*. New York: Cambridge University Press.

Reynolds, David S. 2005. *John Brown, Abolitionist: The Man Who Killed Slavery, Sparked the Civil War, and Seeded Civil Rights*. New York: Alfred A. Knopf.

U.S. Congress Joint Committee Report on the Conduct of the War. "Fort Pillow Massacre." House Report No. 65, 38th Congress, 1st Session.

Ward, Andrew. 2005. *River Run Red: The Fort Pillow Massacre in the American Civil War*. New York: Viking.

Joseph L. Graves Jr.

CLINES

In 1938 the English biologist Julian Huxley proposed using the Greek-derived word *cline* to represent the gradual change of a single biological trait (e.g., skin color) in a given species over a geographical area. The gradient in the expression of any such trait represents a response to the graded change in the intensity of the selective force affecting the manifestation of the trait in question. Many human traits are clinally distributed, but they often require laboratory testing to discover their various manifestations. The most easily perceived trait that has a clinal distribution is skin color. Long-term residents of the tropics have a maximum amount of pigmentation in the skin, while long-term residents of arctic locations have the least amount of pigment in the skin. The transition of pigmentation from the tropics to northern parts of the globe follows an unbroken gradation, making the distribution of skin color a true cline.

The substance that accounts for pigment in the skin is called melanin. The more particles of melanin, the darker the skin. In areas of intense sunlight, such as the tropics, the penetration of ultraviolet B rays in the human skin can lead to cancer. Skin with a lot of melanin particles will block the penetration of ultraviolet rays and protect the person in question against the possibility of contracting skin cancer. In addition, melanin prevents ultraviolet radiation from breaking down folic acid in the body, thus helping to prevent neural tube defects in newborns (Jablonski 2004).

"Neutral theory" notes that where there is no selection maintaining a given trait, random genetic changes will not be selected against. Most such random changes interfere with the development of the structure coded by the genes that control its development. If there is no selection maintaining that structure, random mutations will decrease its manifestation through time—hence the reduction of pigmentation in northern populations.

Visual acuity and color perception are also clinally distributed, but the cline does not have the same distribution as the cline for skin color. As Richard H. Post documented in 1962, those populations that depended on hunting longer than others retained a degree of visual acuity that decreased in proportion to the length of time the other people in question had been practicing farming for their subsistence. Sub-Saharan African populations, for example, have fewer individuals in each population who show extremes of near-sightedness and far-sightedness, color blindness, and astigmatism than European populations. Among the latter, however, the inhabitants of the northwestern edge of Europe have fewer visual defects than people in the Middle East, where farming has been a way of life for longer than anywhere else in the world. In line with this picture, Hugh R. Taylor (1981) has shown that the greatest amount of visual acuity is found among Australian Aborigines, who were hunters up until a century or two ago.

Human tooth size is also clinally distributed, with those who depended on cooking for the longest having the smallest teeth in the world (Brace 2005). The people who inhabited Europe during the last glaciation were dependent on hunting for their subsistence, but they could hardly eat a whole Pleistocene cow at a single sitting. A day or so later it would have frozen solid. The pieces could be cooked, however, and that not only thawed the meat but reduced the amount of chewing necessary to get it to a swallowable consistency. The descendants of these people have the smallest teeth in the world. Sub-Saharan Africans did not have to thaw their food, but eventually they discovered that cooking counteracted the effects of decay. African teeth have been reducing in size, but not for as long as the teeth of the people further north. Cooking was introduced in Australia late in the eighteenth century after first contact with Europeans (later than in other places), and it spread slowly southward from the northern edge of the continent. There is a cline for tooth size in Australia that ranges from African-sized teeth in the north to larger teeth in the south, where the indigenous inhabitants have the biggest teeth in the world, being fully Neanderthal-sized. This is completely the reverse of the skin-color cline in Australia, which ranges from equatorial degrees of darkness in the north to a kind of medium brown in the south (where there is also a visible amount of juvenile blondism).

The ABO blood group genes also have clinal distributions, but it is not certain what the relevant selective forces were that produced those distributions. What is clear, however, is that the distributions have no relationship at all to the distributions of skin color, tooth size, or any other traits that have clinal distributions. The distribution of hemoglobin S, however, is well understood (Brace 2005, pp. 10-11). Hemoglobin is a protein molecule with 574 amino acid residues arranged in two alpha and two beta chains. Hemoglobin S differs from hemoglobin A by having avaline instead of a glutamate at position 6 of the beta chain.

An individual with two genes for hemoglobin S will have sickle-cell anemia and a shorter life expectancy, while an individual with normal hemoglobin (AA) is susceptible to a particular kind of malaria. The person with hemoglobin AS will not suffer from anemia under most circumstances and has the advantage that many of the infecting malaria parasites are removed from the bloodstream before they can reproduce. Where falciparum malaria is prevalent, the possession of a single S gene gives a person a survival edge over the person who only has A at that locus.

The completely independent and unrelated distribution of human traits that are adaptively advantageous is what led the anthropologist Frank Livingstone to declare, "There are no races, there are only clines" (Livingstone 1962, p. 279). This is true, however, only for traits that are under selective-force control, though not all traits under selective-force control are clinally distributed. Members of all human populations have to be able to learn their languages and have the wits to survive, and they all need hearts, kidneys, livers, and other organs that will last a normal lifetime. As a result, there is no demonstrable gradient in any population in either intellectual ability or in the functional capabilities of the internal organs. Many traits—such as eye shape, ear shape, and cheekbone shape—show recognizable regional similarities. Anything that clusters in regional fashion does so because of genealogical relationship and not as the result of natural selection. The regional clustering of such non-adaptive features has been referred to as "family resemblance writ large" (Brace 2005, p. 16).

SEE ALSO *Clines and Continuous Variation; Clusters; Gene Pool; Genes and Genealogies; Heritability; Skin Color.*

BIBLIOGRAPHY

Brace, C. Loring. 2005. *"Race" Is a Four-Letter Word: The Genesis of the Concept.* New York: Oxford University Press.

Jablonski, Nina G. 2004. "The Evolution of Human Skin and Skin Color." *Annual Review of Anthropology* 33: 585–623.

Livingstone, Frank B. 1962. "On the Non-Existence of Human Races." *Current Anthropology* 3 (3): 279.

Post, Richard H. 1962. "Population Differences in Vision Acuity: A Review, with Speculative Notes on Selection Relaxation." *Eugenics Quarterly* 9 (4): 189–212.

Taylor, Hugh R. 1981. "Racial Variations in Vision." *American Journal of Epidemiology* 113 (1): 62–80.

C. Loring Brace

CLINES AND CONTINUOUS VARIATION

Frank Livingstone, a specialist in genetic anthropology, has written that "there are no races, only clines" (Livingstone 1962, p. 279). For centuries, both everyday folk beliefs and the sciences presumed that "races" were separated by genetic boundaries, with a high degree of biological similarity among the members of each group. This was based on thinking in terms of a discrete distribution of traits. It was believed, for example, that all sub-Saharan Africans had black skin, all Europeans were white, and all Asians were yellow. Thinking in terms of homogeneous populations with discrete traits and boundary lines was supported by the selective perception that certain external physical traits fit stereotypical traditions. In the twentieth century, however, thinking in terms of *continuous variation*, also called *clines*, came to provide a more useful and precise way to analyze human variation, making the concept of "race" obsolete. Traits that were assumed to be unique to each race are in fact distributed continuously. For example, skin color, based mostly on the frequency of pigment (melanin), is darker near the equator and becomes lighter as one moves in a northern direction, reaching its lowest frequency in northern latitudes among populations that have resided in those areas for thousands of years.

THE CLINE CONCEPT

The concept of cline was first proposed by the British biologist Julian Huxley in 1938. He derived the name from Greek word *klinein*, meaning "to lean." He defined cline as a "gradation in measurable characters" (Huxley 1938, p. 219). A cline can be based on either directly observable external biological traits, also called *phenotypes* (e.g., hair color, skin pigmentation, stature), or it can be derived from genes (e.g., ABO blood type, sickle-cell hemoglobin) and referred to as a *genotype*. Clines may be continuous and vary gradually over a region, or they may vary abruptly. There may be steep clines or gradual clines as well as sudden mid-cline reversals. Clinal maps of England show areas where 15

The Distribution of the Blood-Group (and gene) B

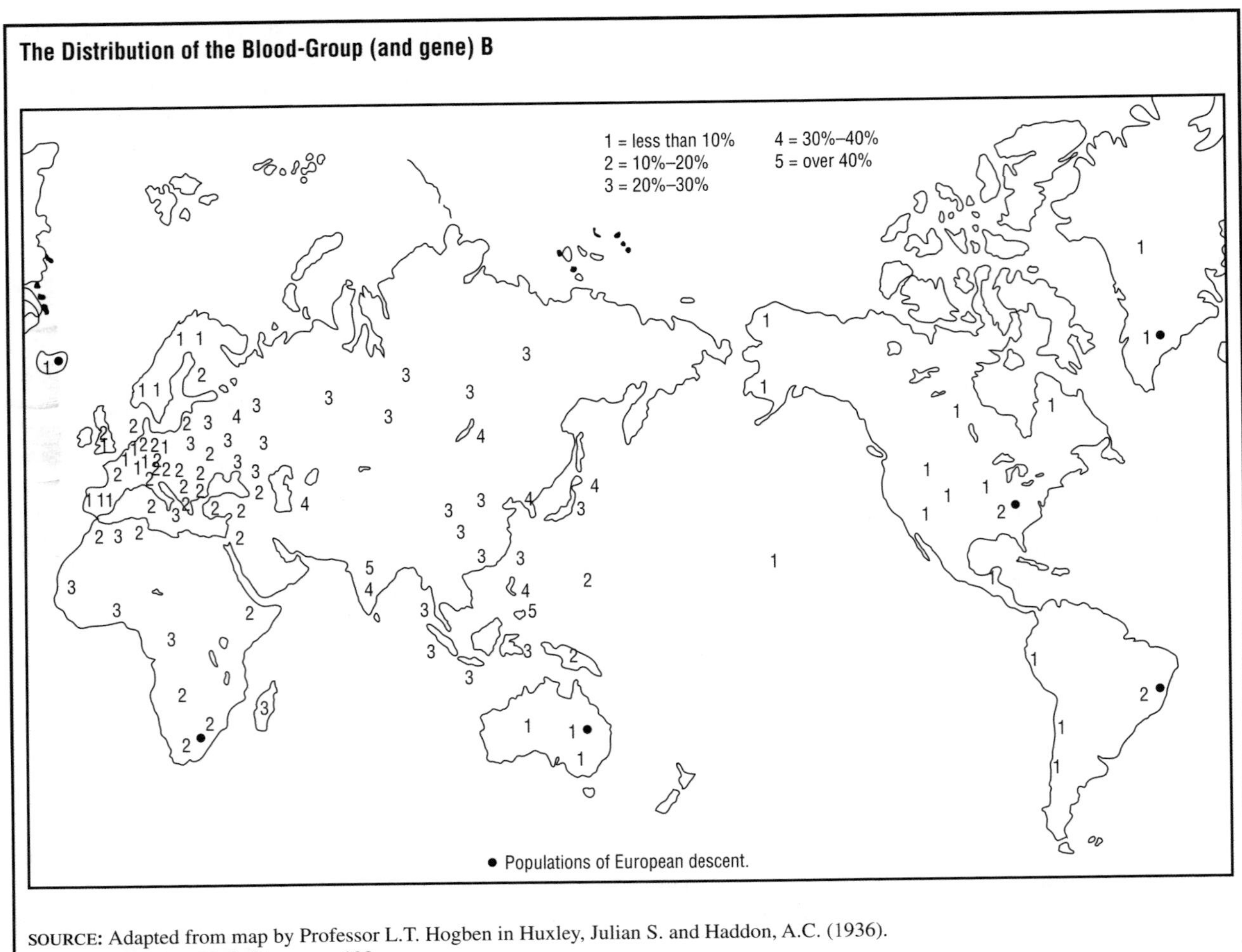

SOURCE: Adapted from map by Professor L.T. Hogben in Huxley, Julian S. and Haddon, A.C. (1936). *We Europeans*. New York: Harper, p. 130.

Figure 1.

percent of the population have red hair adjacent to areas where less than 5 percent have red hair. Variation may not be due to absolute barriers, but may instead be influenced by partly passable mountain ranges, deserts, and bodies of water. Even before the time of Columbus, clines were created or disrupted by the movement of peoples, a trend that intensified after 1492 with the enslavement and forced emigration of millions of Africans and the migration of Europeans into North and South America. The result resembles a weather map on which lines separate temperature variations. On a biological cline map, the lines separating phenotypical traits are called *isophenes*. Lines referring to genotype frequencies are *isogenes*. Similar illustrations of gradients are seen in maps of elevations of land contours above sea level, in this sense the word cline is related to incline and decline in altitude.

Together with his coauthor A. C. Haddon, Huxley presented the evidence for clines in 1936 in a pioneering map (see Figure 1) that showed the decrease of B-type hemoglobin in Europe and its increase into western Asia. Haddon and Huxley concluded that the evidence of clines invalidated the race concept's assertions of racial homogeneity and boundary lines making for discrete races. Later, computers would make possible the analysis of more complete data into interval maps showing other clinal patterns. The exact numerical value varies, but any cline can be represented by a set of intervals. In this sense, a cline refers to both the concept of continual variation and a method of measuring and depicting variation in the frequency of any physical feature or gene frequency over a geographic area.

SICKLE-CELL ANEMIA AND MALARIA

The pioneering efforts of Huxley and Haddon did not receive immediate acceptance. The idea of "race" was too strongly established in Western folk beliefs and scientific tradition. But newer research studies would provide a catalyst for change. Among the first was Livingstone's 1958 study of sickle-cell anemia, which showed that it was more frequent in malarial areas. Prior to this it was believed by some that genes for sickle-cell anemia were a discrete racial trait of black Africans. Livingstone was able to show that the alleles for sickling (Hb^s) are most frequent in populations in West Africa but decline in frequency in areas to the north and east, and are still less frequent around the Mediterranean and throughout South Asia. This is because another mutation, for hemoglobin E, also resists malaria in areas where the intensity of agriculture affects the frequency of mosquitoes.

Malaria continues to kill millions of people, mostly children, each year. Inheriting an allele for sickling from each parent leads to extreme anemia, severely reducing the number of offspring and the percent of sickling alleles in the population. Those inheriting normal hemoglobin—that is, without any sickling blood—contract malaria and have a significant death rate and a reduced number of offspring. Yet inheriting one such allele confers a resistance to the symptoms of malaria. Frequency of survival and reproduction with one sickle-cell allele is relatively greatest in areas where there is more agriculture being practiced, for the clearing of the land produces standing water where mosquitoes can breed. Therefore, the continuous variation over geographic regions is not due to biological race but is produced by human cultural practices in malarial climates.

CLINAL MAPS

Livingstone's data was reported in a list, but a map developed later depicts a graphic clinal pattern (Johnston 1982, Figure 2). It is clearly a clinal pattern distributed through malarial regions of Africa, Europe, and Asia. Livingstone's data demonstrated that continuous clinal variation occurs

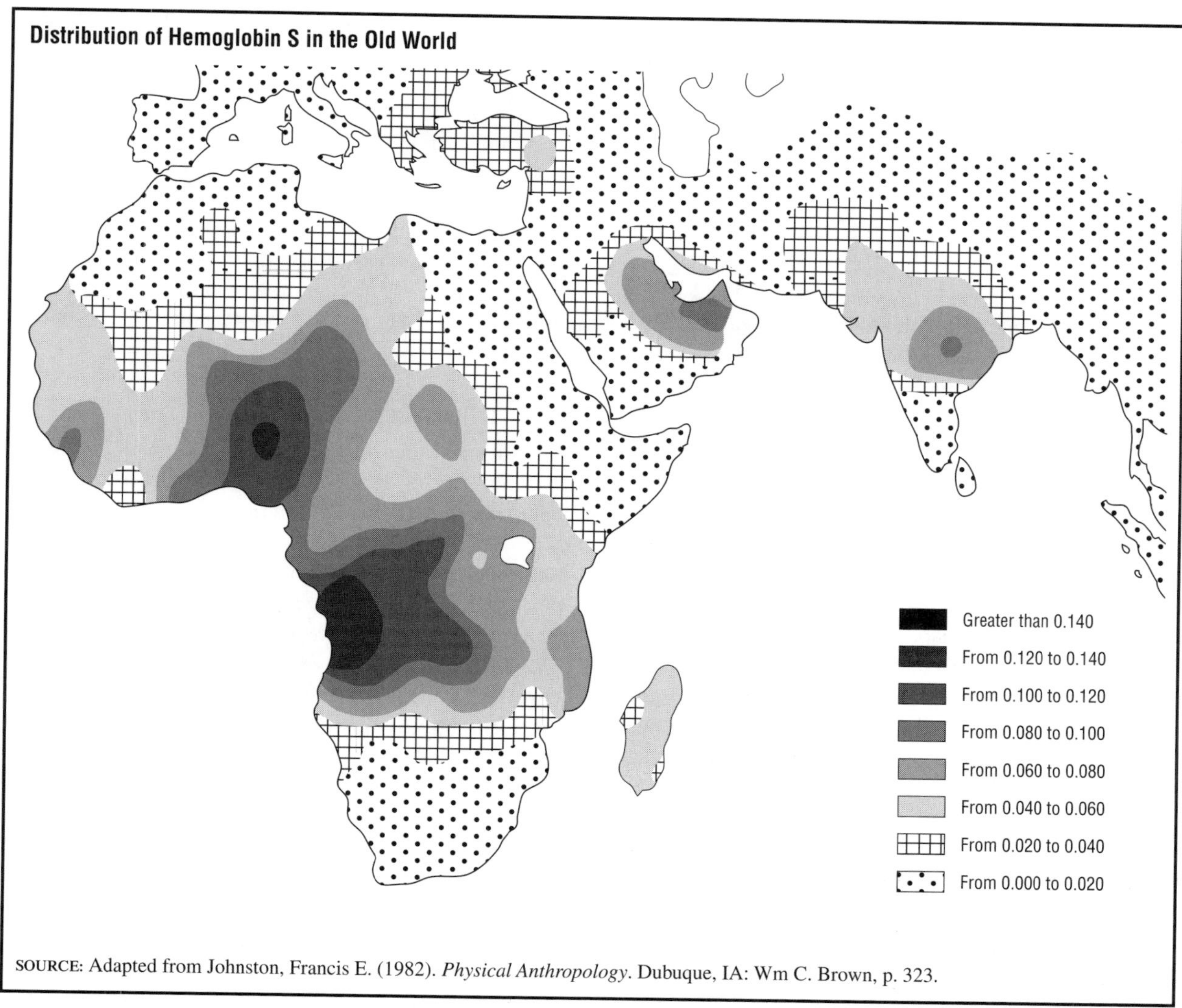

Figure 2.

within populations and across their boundaries, in clear disproof of the validity of the idea of race.

Another influence on the cline concept was presented by C. Loring Brace in "A Nonracial Approach Towards the Understanding of Human Diversity" in *The Concept of Race* (1964). Brace's nonracial approach was the use of clines, and he illustrated it with four clinal maps (derived from Biasutti 1941), covering skin color, hair form, facial form based on relative tooth size, and nose form. All of these are traditional observable physical features (phenotypes) that had been used to construct racial stereotypes. Each clinal pattern can be studied, and Brace showed that evolutionary hypotheses could be developed and tested regarding their origin and distribution. When the four clinal patterns are overlaid on each other, it clearly demonstrates that racial boundaries do not exist, because the clinal patterns are not congruent and do not covary. Instead, they are discordant; that is, their distribution does not correspond with racial boundary lines. Brace declared that it was "extremely difficult to say where one population ends and another begins" (Brace 1964, p. 104). Thinking in terms of clines in this way clarified that racial boundaries are arbitrary cultural errors. The discordance of clines was further presented to biologists by Paul Ehrlich and Richard W. Holm (1964). The biologists Edward O. Wilson and W. L. Brown (1953) used clinal data as a basis for rejecting the concept of "subspecies," in the sense of race.

Beginning in 1938–1939, and again in 1952–1954, genetic anthropologist Joseph B. Birdsell measured Australian Aborigines for a number of traits. Using this data, Birdsell constructed numerous clinal maps. He viewed the data in the context of the concept of race up to the early 1970s, but in 1975 he wrote, in *Human Evolution,* that "The use of the term race has been discontinued because it is scientifically undefinable and carries social implications that are harmful and disruptive" (p. 505). In 1993 he published *Microevolutionary Patterns in Aboriginal Australia, A Gradient Analysis of Clines*. It contains a large number of clinal maps showing lack of covariation, contrary to the Western image of there being one stereotypical image of Australian Aborigines. In 1994, the geneticists L. Luca Cavalli-Sforza, Paola Menozzi, and Alberto Piazza published a worldwide analysis using a database of 76,676 gene frequencies from aboriginal ethnic groups that were believed to be in the same location at the time of the study as they were at the end of the fifteenth century, although the gene pool and ethnic identity of each group had likely altered. They published more than 500 clinal maps, which were condensed into worldwide summary maps using 128 gene variants (alleles). The result did not correspond to racial boundary lines; and the coauthors rejected the race concept as a scientific failure and race classification as a futile exercise.

RESISTANCE TO CLINES

Acceptance of clines as a basis for rejecting the race concept was resisted by some anthropologists, especially by forensic anthropologists who asserted that they could identify an individual's race by examining his or her skull. In doing so they ignored the fact that while crania might have some feature attributed to a person of one race, a particular skull could be that of a very light-skinned person who could be identified either as black or white. In addition, cranial features vary clinally within populations and change over time. Outspoken in defense of race was the forensic anthropologist Alice Brues in *People and Races* (1977). Brues wrote that clines were sometimes the appropriate concept to use, while at other times race was both a necessary and valid concept. Brues pointed out the apparent differences between races with a scenario of flying from a Scandinavian city and landing in Nairobi, Kenya. Brace replied that walking or bicycling between these two areas and progressing southward along the Nile, one would view a gradual change in physical features.

Acceptance of the new clinal concept and data on continuous variation became widespread beginning in the 1970s in anthropology, although the concept was less often explicitly stated than was the underlying and crucial fact of continuous variation. There continues to be reluctance among some scientists to relinquish race as the traditional and convenient way of extending to human populations the classification system of the Swedish botanist Carolus Linnaeus (1707–1778).

EXPLAINING CLINES

Thinking that uses the race concept assumes a high degree of uniformity of each trait, as well as the association of these traits within a population. Brace pointed out that this association "obscures the factors influencing the occurrence and distribution of any single trait. *The most important thing for the analyses of human variation is the appreciation of the selective pressures which have operated to influence the expression of each trait separately*" (Brace 1964, p. 107; italics in original). One example, as described above, is Livingstone's explanation of the cline for sickle-cell allele in relation to the frequency of malaria, which in turn is affected by the intensity of agriculture. Brace proposed explanations for clinal distribution of nose form, hair form, skin color, and relative tooth size affecting face profile. Skin pigment is a protective response to ultraviolet radiation, which causes skin cancer. However, there is some uncertainty about the frequency of skin cancer as an influence on natural selection (through differential fertility), because the cancer develops after the years when reproduction is most likely. A stronger explanation for increased melanin is found in the effect of ultraviolet rays in reducing folic acid (folate) in the body. Low levels of folic acid result in a defect in the neural tube (spina bifida) of the developing fetus, and they may also affect the production of sperm (Jablonski 2004). The clinal pattern in melanin arises as the intensity of ultraviolet exposure decreased away from the equator. The presence of populations with lesser amounts of melanin as one proceeds north occurs because the reduced degree of ultraviolet intensity allows for the persistence of adequate folic acid, coupled with the need to generate more vitamin D for normal bone growth and the possibility of resistance of lighter skin to frostbite.

The covariation of hair form and skin color are an exception to the pattern of clinal discordance. Hair on the head varies, and for a biological reason—spiral and wooly hair insulates the head from ultraviolet radiation. Clinal patterns tend toward smaller teeth in areas with longer histories of food production from agriculture, while larger teeth occur in areas of hunting and gathering. Dental reduction began in the northern latitudes when cooking and the use of pottery for more liquid foods began, reaching equatorial areas later. As food became more tender, natural selection did not require large teeth and mutations for smaller teeth could accumulate. Stature, meanwhile, varied in response to climate. In cold climates, body temperature is conserved by stocky bodies and short arms and legs. In hot, dry areas, a more linear body with long arms and legs dissipates heat more efficiently. The small stature of pygmies is an exception to the linear pattern, but they live in a hot, moist rainforest, along with other species that are smaller than closely related species living in the open savannas.

Particular genetic conditions, such as Tay-Sachs disease or sickle-cell anemia, have mistakenly been viewed as identifying particular races. Tay-Sachs is a condition in which inheriting two recessive genes is lethal. It has been attributed to Jews and explained by the possibility that the presence of one gene conferred a resistance to tuberculosis among the Ashkenazic Jews of eastern Europe who lived in crowded ghettos. The condition is also found in other populations but at a lower frequency, and a slightly different mutation also causes Tay-Sachs among French Canadians of Quebec. Racial stereotypes attribute other features to one or another particular race, such as uniform epicanthic folds over the eyes, prominent cheekbones, or thick lips. However, these vary by degree in a clinal pattern. Explanations for them as advantageous adaptations have not been established. They may have originated in one small population of related families and dispersed with population expansion, becoming more varied due to mating with members of other populations. Clinal variations in physical features are most commonly explained as advantageous for survival in different and sometimes extreme geographic locations. These biological features, mislabeled in the past as racial markers, did not necessarily make migration into those areas possible, but they may have evolved in gradations after movement into those areas. The spread of humans throughout the globe occurred because humans had the potential to live in many different areas, from the Arctic Circle to the semi-arid, near deserts of southwestern Africa. It has been suggested that races varied in their achievements because of their hereditary intelligence, but no proven method of measurement free of the cultural variation in IQ tests has been devised. Genes relating to intelligence have not been found, although many different negative mutations may reduce the functioning intelligence of an individual. The kind of achievements of various populations is best viewed not as the result of biological differences, but rather as a result of human flexibility for problem solving expressed in diverse cultures.

The availability of clinal data was necessary to bring about thinking without the idea of biological races, and an awareness of continuous variation has made racist stereotypes more difficult to use. Clinal thinking has become standard among anthropologists, and it is increasing among biologists.

SEE ALSO *Clines; Genetic Variation Among Populations; Nonconcordant Variation; Racial Formations.*

BIBLIOGRAPHY

Biasutti, Renato. 1941. *Le razzi e i popoli della terra*, 3rd ed. Vol. 1. Turin, Italy: Unione Tipographico-Editrice.

Birdsell, Joseph B. 1975. *Human Evolution: An Introduction to the New Physical Anthropology*, 2nd ed. Chicago: Rand McNally.

———. 1993. *Microevolutionary Patterns in Aboriginal Australia: A Gradient Analysis of Clines*. New York: Oxford University Press.

Brace, C. Loring. 1964. "A Nonracial Approach towards the Understanding of Human Diversity." In *The Concept of Race*, edited by Ashley Montagu, 103–152. New York: Free Press.

Brues, Alice. 1977. *People and Race*. New York: Macmillan.

Cavalli-Sforza, L. Luca, Paolo Menozzi, and Albert Piazza. 1994. *The History and Geography of Human Genes*. Princeton, NJ: Princeton University Press.

Ehrlich, Paul, and Richard Holm. 1964. "A Biological View of Races." In *The Concept of Race*, edited by Ashley Montagu, 153–179. New York: Free Press.

Huxley, Julian, and A. C. Haddon. 1936. *We Europeans: A Survey of "Racial" Problems*. New York: Harper.

———. 1938. "Clines: An Auxiliary Taxonomic Principle." *Nature* 142: 219–220.

Jablonski, Nina G. 2004. "The Evolution of Human Skin and Skin Color." *Annual Review of Anthropology* 33: 585–623.

Johnston, Francis E. 1982. *Physical Anthropology*. Dubuque, IA: Wm. C. Brown.

Livingstone, Frank B. 1958. "Anthropological Implication of Sickle Cell Gene Distributions in West Africa." *American Anthropologist* 60 (3): 533–562.

———. 1962. "On the Non-Existence of Human Races." *Current Anthropology* 3: 279–281.

Moore, John. 1994. "Ethnogenetic Theory." *National Geographic Research and Exploration* 10 (1): 10–37.

———. 1995. "Putting Anthropology Back Together Again: The Ethnogenetic Critique of Cladistic Theory." *American Anthropologist* 96 (4): 925–948.

Wilson, Edward O., and William Brown, Jr. 1953. "The Subspecies Concept and Its Taxonomic Application." *Systematic Zoology* 2 (3): 97–111.

Leonard Lieberman

CLUSTERS

When adaptive traits are considered, the aphorism coined by Frank Livingstone more than forty-five years ago still holds true: "There are no races, there are only clines" (1962, p. 279). Each such trait is distributed as a gradient controlled by the distribution of the selective force that controls the intensity of its expression, and no two such selective forces have the same distribution. In order to make biological sense out of trait distributions, each has to be analyzed separately. The pattern made by the intersection of such traits has no meaning in and of itself. However, people in a given part of the world cluster together and look more like each other than they look like people in other parts of the world. What is being expressed in this is simply local relatedness—"family resemblance writ large"—and such regional groupings based on the sharing of similar traits can be called "clusters" (Brace 1996, p.136; 2005, p. 16).

The features that demonstrate the visible relatedness of local or larger regional clusters of people almost certainly have no particular adaptive value. Where a set of traits operates to show the relatedness of people in a particular region, it can be taken as a given that those traits are unimportant for the survival of the people in question. Whether the shape of the eye sockets is round or oblong, whether their lateral edges are on the same plane as the root of the nose or swept backwards, whether the outline of the whole skull viewed from the top is round or oval, whether the skull viewed from the rear has an unbroken oval contour or displays vertical sides that abruptly change directions at a boss as the flat sides of the roof angle up to the midline—but none of these have any influence on the differential ability to survive.

Such features are clearly different between one population and another and warrant recognition. The problem is in finding an appropriate designation for obvious clusters. The common use of the word "Mongoloid" to refer to the people of Asia runs into the problem that, when craniofacial features are analyzed, the Mongols themselves tend to share the fewest features with the rest of the inhabitants of Asia. If the features of the inhabitants of the Caucasus between Russia and Iran are used to describe "Caucasians," then the Norwegians and the English do not qualify for this designation. "Negro" is based on skin color, an adaptive trait, and it thus lumps together long-time residents of the tropics all the way from New Guinea to southern India and equatorial Africa, even though they may have been separated for the better part of the Pleistocene.

The best thing to do when identifying clusters is to indicate geographic area. One can speak of the inhabitants of Asia, and, when needed, specify whether Northeast Asia, Southeast Asia, South Asia, or West Asia is meant. The same approach can be used for any of the geographic entities of the world. Specifying a locale of long-term residence basically solves the problem of naming human clusters.

SEE ALSO *Clines; Folk Classification; Gene Pool; Genes and Genealogies; Genetic Distance; Genetic Marker; Genetics, History of; Heritability.*

BIBLIOGRAPHY

Brace, C. Loring. 1996. "A Four-Letter Word Called 'Race'." In *Race and Other Misadventures: Essays in Honor of Ashley Montagu in His Ninetieth Year,* edited by Larry T. Reynolds and Leonard Lieberman. Dix Hills, NY: General Hall.

———. 2005. *"Race" Is a Four-Letter Word.* New York: Oxford University Press.

Livingstone, Frank B. 1962. "On the Non-Existence of Human Races." *Current Anthropology* 3 (3): 279.

C. Loring Brace

COLONIALISM, INTERNAL

The concept of "internal colonialism" has become so widely used and applied that almost every minority group in the world has been viewed as an internal colony. The discussion here, therefore, will be limited to the United States, where the "colonial analogy" emerged in the 1960s.

By 1962, when the social commentator and writer Harold Cruse first suggested that black-white relations were a form of "domestic colonialism," the colonial liberation movements throughout the world, and above all in Africa, had become a source of inspiration for African Americans. These overseas developments contributed to the increasing militancy of the civil rights movement, which provided the larger context from which the idea of internal colonialism arose. The new perspective filled a vacuum, for the prevailing theories of race relations did a poor job of helping scholars understand the urban insurrections in Watts and Detroit, as well as the shift in civil rights strategy from an ideal of integration to the more militant "Black Power" and black nationalism. At a time when race relations theory "expected" black Americans to assimilate into the larger society, as various white ethnic groups had done, they were instead calling for the building of their own culture and autonomous institutions. Further, when the big news in America was racial oppression and antiracist movements, sociologists still tended to view racial realities through the prism of class analysis.

In addition to Cruse, internal colonialism theory was pioneered by such black scholars and activists as Kenneth Clark, the author of *Youth in the Ghetto* (1964), and Stokely Carmichael and Charles Hamilton, the authors of *Black Power* (1967). By the late 1960s, the Black Panther Party had adopted the concept of internal colonialism, and even the liberal aspirant for the Democratic Party nomination, Eugene McCarthy, routinely referred to blacks as a colonized people in his 1968 campaign.

A product of 1960s and 1970s militancy, internal colonialism fell out of favor in the United States during the more conservative 1980s, just at the point when it was being used to analyze race relations in other societies. However, when incidents of racism flared up in almost epidemic proportions in the United States in 1987 and 1988, American sociologists got interested in the concept again.

Although the internal colonialism perspective now has a secure position in the panoply of theories of ethnic and racial relations, many social scientists still do not find it convincing, especially when applied to the United States. The eminent anthropologist Margaret Mead once said that she found the differences between America's race relations and the colonial societies she had worked in to be much more compelling than the similarities, and the position that the consequences of these differences are more salient for creating social theory is certainly a reasonable one.

Colonialism traditionally refers to the establishment of domination over a geographically external political unit, most often inhabited by people of a different "race" and culture. This domination is both political and economic, and the colony is subordinated to and dependent upon the "mother country." Typically, the colonizers exploit the land, the raw materials, the labor, and other resources of the colonized nation; formal recognition is given to the difference in power, autonomy, and political status between indigenous and colonial institutions; and various agencies are set up to maintain this subordination.

Seemingly, this model must be stretched beyond utility if the American case is to be included within it, for any discussion of U.S. minorities must be about group relations within a society. The geographical separation between mother country and colony is therefore absent in this case. Although whites certainly colonized the territory of the original Americans, the "colonization" of African Americans did not involve the settlement of whites in a land that was unequivocally black. Unlike the classical situation, there have been no formal recognitions of differences in power since slavery was abolished. In addition, traditional colonialism involves the control and exploitation of the majority of a nation by a minority of outsiders, whereas in America the oppressed black population is a numerical minority and was, originally, the "outside" group.

Both classical overseas colonialism and the internal variety share common features that justify the use of the concept of internal colonialism, however. For both forms of colonialisms—with the British conquest of their colonies in Africa and the Indian subcontinent and slavery in the New World being good examples—developed out of the same historical situation and reflected a common world economic and power stratification. In addition to sharing a historical context, both colonialisms shared critical dimensions that made up a "colonization complex." Five such common features may be spelled out.

The first, and most critical, for it affects all the others, is that colonized groups do not enter a new society voluntarily, as do immigrant groups for the most part. Instead, they become a part of the society through force and violence. Second, they are forced into labor that is either unfree or extremely undesirable, and that typically restricts the group's physical and social mobility as well as its political participation. In the United States, people of color were concentrated in the most unskilled jobs, the least advanced sectors of the economy, and the most industrially backward regions of the country. Third, the cultures of the colonized are not permitted free expression but are constrained, exploited, and often destroyed. The experience of Native Americans is an especially tragic example of this. Fourth, the communities and institutions of colonized groups lack the autonomy that immigrants generally enjoy. Instead, their lives are controlled and administered by government bureaucracies, police forces, and other outsiders. Finally, colonized groups suffer racism, which is qualitatively different than ethnic prejudice and much more damaging to individual selves and group culture.

The perspective of internal colonialism served as an important corrective to previous theories of race and ethnicity in the United States. It provided a hard-hitting analysis that was able to make more sense of the militant racial movements of the 1960s and 1970s than earlier frameworks, which emphasized assimilation and class analysis. It also provided a historical perspective that was too often lacking in other approaches. Its emphasis on race as an "independent variable" was also important, though as the pendulum shifts to a racial analysis, there is always the danger of neglecting class, especially class differences within minority groups.

The British sociologist Ernest Cashmore has provided another important criticism: the distinction between voluntary and involuntary entry, as stated above, is often ambiguous. Groups such as Puerto Ricans, Chinese Americans, and Filipinos entered the United States through processes that involved both voluntary and involuntary aspects. And because the framework of internal colonialism was originally an analogy, it perhaps lends itself to applications that are too often overschematic, rather than being based on fresh approaches that emphasize historical concreteness and complexity.

A final problem with the perspective is that for America's internal colonies there is no "functional equivalent" to colonial liberation. Marxists believe that social contradictions contain within them the seeds of their resolution. Capitalism produced a proletariat that was supposed to end the exploitation of labor and bring down the system. Colonialism produced "natives" who organized into movements to send the colonists back to their mother countries. But in America, even if blacks were to control the politics and economics of their communities (and the Indians their reservations), their autonomy would be quite limited. They would still not control the social and economic forces in the larger society, which would continue to impinge on them.

SEE ALSO *Exploitation; Fourth World; Racial Hierarchy.*

BIBLIOGRAPHY

Carmichael, Stokely [Kwame Ture]. *Stokely Speaks: From Black Power to Pan-Africanism.* Foreword by Mumia Abu-Jamal. Chicago: Lawrence Hill Books, 2007. New foreword and preface to original 1971 edition.

Cashmore, Ernest. 1990. *Introduction to Race Relations.* London and New York: Falmer Press.

Clark, Kenneth. 1964. *Youth in the Ghetto: A Study of the Consequences of Powerlessness and a Blueprint for Change.* New York: Haryou, 1964.

———. 1987. *A Class Divided: Then and Now.* New Haven, CT: Yale University Press.

Giacomo, S. M. D. 1999. "The New Internal Colonialism." *International Journal of Qualitative Studies in Education* 12, no. 3 (July): 263–268.

Oliver, Christopher. 1996. "The Internal Colonialism Model: What the Model Has Done to the Education of Native Americans." ERIC document ED396883. 24 pp. Available from http://eric.ed.gov/ERICDocs/data/ericdocs2/content_storage_01/0000000b/80/26/dc/3d.pdf

Bob Blauner

COLOR-BLIND RACISM

Polls on racial attitudes in the United States consistently find that whites are more racially tolerant than ever. Respondents indicate they do not care if minorities live in their neighborhoods or if people marry across the color line, and they express support for the principles of integration. However, the same polls also find that whites object to government policies developed to ameliorate the effects of discrimination, such as affirmative action and busing. Furthermore, the data also shows that whites believe racism is no longer a major problem in the United States and that existing racial inequality is the product of the culture and behavior of minorities. The sociologist Eduardo Bonilla-Silva has argued that all this means is that the nature of racial discourse has changed and that there is a new way of expressing prejudicial attitudes, which he calls "color-blind racism." Color-blind racism is the dominant racial ideology in post–civil rights America, and unlike its predecessor (Jim Crow racism), it is subtle, apparently nonracial, and avoids traditional racist discourse.

WHITE RACIAL ATTITUDES IN THE POST–CIVIL RIGHTS ERA

Scholars differ in their interpretation and analysis of whites' racial attitudes in the post–civil rights era. Their explanations can be grouped into four categories: (1) racial optimism, (2) racial pesoptimism, (3) symbolic racism, and (4) group position. *Racial optimists,* such as Seymour Lipset and Paul Sniderman, believe whites have, in fact, become more racially tolerant, and that their objections to programs such as affirmative action are not racially motivated. Although the views of these scholars are no longer dominant in academia, they are popular among the masses because they resonate with whites' racial common sense. *Racial pesoptimists,* best represented by the work of Howard Schuman and his colleagues, believe that the change in whites' racial attitudes is best understood as a combination of progress and resistance. Although scholars in this tradition acknowledge the resistance of whites to racial change, they are still wedded to the old perspective elaborated by Gunnar Myrdal in his *An American Dilemma* (1944). Myrdal put forward the idea that whites will overcome their prejudice as soon as they reconcile the facts and realize that discrimination has no place in a truly democratic society.

Symbolic racism scholars, such as David Sears and Donald Kinder, argue instead that whites are still prejudiced, but in a new way that combines a moralistic discourse with antiblack affect. For example, these scholars interpret whites' opposition to programs such as affirmative action as a symbolic expression of their prejudice. Lastly, scholars advocating the idea of *group position,* such as Lawrence Bobo and James Kluegel, believe whites' prejudice is a way to defend white privilege. The defense of group status is done nowadays, according to Bobo, through a "laissez-faire racism" that blames minorities for their inability to improve their economic and social standing. All these approaches, however, share three limitations: (1) They are all fundamentally anchored in the prejudice *problematique*, (2) they derive their data from surveys and thus cannot fully capture contemporary white discourse, and (3) they are ultimately bounded by their methodological individualism (i.e., their unit of analysis is the individual). *Problemátique* is a French structuralist term that refers to the limits or boundaries of a concept. Analysts trapped in the "prejudice *problematique*," for example, cannot "see" or accept the structural nature of racial dynamics.

An explanation of whites' apparently paradoxical attitudes that has gained support is that developed by Eduardo Bonilla-Silva. He argues that whites' racial views in the post–civil rights era represent a new racial ideology: color-blind racism. Unlike Jim Crow racism, color-blind racism articulates whites' defense of the racial order in a subtle, apparently nonracial way. It provides tools to talk about race without appearing to be "racist"—a very important matter, given that the normative climate that has crystallized in the United States since the 1960s disavows the open expression of racial views.

A COLOR-BLIND IDEOLOGY

Bonilla-Silva argues that whites' views constitute an ideology rather than mere prejudice. This means that whites' views should be understood within the context of how power relations between whites and nonwhites are maintained in the racial arena. Thus, because the civil rights movement forced changes in the way racial inequality is reproduced in the United States, new explanations, accounts, and vocabulary emerged to justify the racial status quo.

For analytical purposes, racial ideology can be conceived as comprising the following three elements: frames, styles, and racial stories. The central frames or themes of this ideology are set paths for interpreting information. There are four principal frames: (1) abstract liberalism, (2) naturalization of race-related matters, (3) cultural racism, and (4) minimization of racism. The style element refers to the linguistic strategies used to convey the components of this ideology, which have become slippery, subtle, and indirect. Finally, racial stories are the narratives whites use to articulate and bolster their racial accounts. They take the form of story lines (generic stories without much personal content) and testimonies (stories that are seemingly personal).

The frame of *abstract liberalism* uses ideas typically associated with liberalism, such as "equal opportunity," "meritocracy," and "individual effort," in an abstract and decontextualized way to account for inequality. For example, a young, white, female college student stated the following when asked about whether minorities should be afforded unique opportunities to attend college:

> I don't think they should be provided with unique opportunities. I think that they should have the same opportunities as everyone else … I don't think that just because they're a minority that they should, you know, not meet the requirements, you know. (Bonilla-Silva 2003)

This student's response ignores the effects of past and contemporary discrimination on the social, economic, and educational status of minorities. Therefore, by saying "they should have the same opportunities as everyone else," this student is defending racial inequality in the educational realm while maintaining her non-racist image.

The *naturalization* frame explains racial matters, such as residential segregation or whites' preferences for whites as partners and friends, as natural outcomes. Although this frame does not employ a "color-blind" logic to explain racial differences, it is part of the larger ideology because it reinforces the myth of nonracialism. An example of how whites use this frame is a middle-age, male manufacturing manager who stated:

> I don't think it's anybody's fault. Because people tend to group with their own people. Whether it's white or black or upper-middle class or lower class or, you know, upper class, you know, Asians. People tend to group with their own. … You know, people group together for lots of different reasons: social, religious. You can't force that. (Bonilla-Silva 2003)

By suggesting that segregation is natural, this respondent ignores the legacy of legalized Jim Crow segregation and the structural dynamics that exist in the early twenty-first century to keep racial groups apart. His account also betrays a profound belief in differences between racial groups, for he likens the segregation between whites and nonwhites to the separate lives of two different species.

The *cultural racism* frame relies on arguments based on culture to explain the position of racial groups in society. In essence, whites "blame the victim" by suggesting that the position of minorities is due to their family disorganization, lack of effort, or laziness. A young female college student, for instance, in response to a question that explained the overall situation of blacks in this country as the result of them lacking motivation, having a deficient work ethic, or because they are lazy, stated:

> If they worked hard, they could make it just as high as anyone else could. (Bonilla-Silva 2003)

Believing that blacks live in the projects because they do not work hard, as this student suggests, shows whites' amnesia about past and contemporary discrimination in the labor and housing markets.

The *minimization of racism* frame suggests discrimination is no longer a real problem because civil rights legislation eradicated all racial ills and people are now "beyond race." For example, in response to a question trying to assess the significance of discrimination, a female retail salesperson in her early forties stated the following:

> I think sometimes it's an excuse because people felt they deserved a job, whatever! I think if things didn't go their way I know a lot of people have tendency to use prejudice or racism as whatever, as an excuse. (Bonilla-Silva 2003)

By minimizing the significance of discrimination, whites can deflect minorities' claims of discrimination and bounce them back to them as "excuses," or as playing the infamous "race card."

THE STYLE OF COLOR-BLINDNESS

The "style" of a racial ideology refers to its particular linguistic manners and rhetorical strategies. These are the tools that allow users to articulate the frames and stories of an ideology. Because overt racist talk in public venues is no longer tolerated, contemporary racial discussions must be done in code or with shields that allow actors to express their views in a way that preserve their image of race neutrality. Color-blind racism has five components: avoidance of racist speech, semantic moves, projection, diminutives, and rhetorical incoherence.

Semantic moves, or *strategically managed propositions*, are phrases that are interjected into speech when an actor is about to state a position that is seemingly racist. Two classic examples of semantic moves are "I'm not prejudiced, but" and "Some of my best friends are black." A woman in her sixties used the former move in her explanation of why blacks are worse off than whites in the United States:

> Well, I'm gonna be, you understand, I'm not prejudice or racial or whatever. They're always given the smut jobs because they would do it. Then they stopped, they stopped doing [them]. The welfare system got to be very, very easy. Why work if the government's gonna take care of you? (Bonilla-Silva 2003)

This is a classic example of how these moves are used. After the respondent stated "I'm not prejudice or racial or whatever," she proceeded to state her belief that blacks are lazy and welfare-dependent. The ideological value of the disclaimer is clear, as it allowed this respondent to justify racial inequality in a nasty way without opening herself to the charge of racism.

Another stylistic element of color-blind racism is *projection*. Whites project racism or racial motivations onto blacks and other minorities as a way of avoiding responsibility for racial inequalities and feeling good about themselves. A female college student, discussing the so-called problem of self-segregation, stated the following about African Americans:

> I think they segregate themselves. Or, I mean, I don't know how everybody else is, but I would have no problem talking with or being friends with a black person or any other type of minority. I think they've just got into their heads that they are different and, as a result, they're pulling themselves away. (Bonilla-Silva 2003)

By claiming that segregation in college campuses is a black problem, this student can ignore white tables, white fraternities, white friendship networks, and white bars. More significantly, this projection allows the student to cover the fact that white students dominate the social scene in historically white colleges, and are thus the ones who have the onus of working hard to integrate people of color.

Yet, another stylistic tool whites can use in speech is *diminutives*, which are used to soften racial blows. For instance, if a person wishes to say something that is racially problematic (such as their outright opposition to interracial marriages or affirmative action), the person can use diminutives to cushion the statement. An example of this is a young male college student who used diminutives to express his "concerns" about interracial dating:

> I would say I have a little bit of the same concern about the children just because it's more, I mean more difficult on them. But, I mean, I definitely [*nervous laugh*] have no problem with any form of interracial marriage. That's just an extra hurdle that they would have to over, overcome with the children, but I—(it) wouldn't be a detriment to the kids, I don't think. That just makes it a little more difficult for them. (Bonilla-Silva 2003)

By using diminutives twice ("I have a little bit of the same concern" and "That just makes it a little more difficult to them"), this respondent was able to voice his concerns about interracial marriage in a safe way.

Lastly, when whites discuss racially sensitive matters, they use *rhetorical incoherence*, which means they often become incomprehensible. Although not properly a stylistic tool of color blindness, rhetorical incoherence is included under this rubric because it is part and parcel of contemporary race talk. An example of this is Ray, a very articulate student who could hardly finish his sentences when discussing whether he has ever been attracted to women of color:

> Um, so to answer that question, no. But I would not, I mean, I would not ever preclude a black woman from being my girlfriend on the basis that she was black. It just seems to me like I'm not as attracted

> to black women as I am to white women . . . for whatever reason. It's not about prejudice, it's just sort of like, ya' know, whatever. Just sort of the way, way like I see white women as compared to black women, ya' know? (Bonilla-Silva 2003)

THE RACIAL STORIES OF COLOR-BLIND RACISM

The racial stories associated with color-blind racism assist whites in making sense of their world in ways that reinforce the racial order. Racial storytelling is ideological because the stories are collectively produced and circulated, and they are told as if there is only one way of telling them, or only one way of understanding what is happening in the world. Racial stories are, therefore, extremely powerful tools because they seem to lie in the realm of the matter-of-fact world.

There are two types of racial stories: story lines and testimonies. *Story lines* are socially shared tales that are fable-like and incorporate a common scheme or wording. They are fable-like because they are often based on impersonal, generic arguments with little narrative or personal knowledge of the facts in the story. The dominant story lines of the post–civil rights era are "The past is the past," "I didn't own any slaves," "I did not get a job, or was not admitted to college, because of a minority," and "If Jews, Irish, and Italians made it, how come blacks have not?" Roland, an electrical engineer in his forties, used the first two story lines when expressing his extreme displeasure about the idea of reparations:

> I can't help what happened in the 1400s, the 1500s, or the 1600s, when the blacks were brought over here and put into slavery. I mean, I had no control over that, neither did you, so I don't think we should do anything as far as reparations are concerned. (Bonilla-Silva 2003)

Roland, like most whites, assumes that discrimination means slavery, and that it is thus something in America's remote past. By missing 150 years of racial history, Roland can voice anger over the idea of reparations.

Racial testimonies are also powerful ideological tools that whites use to justify their racial beliefs. Testimonies are accounts in which the narrator is a central participant in the story or is close to the characters in the story. Thus, the aura of authenticity help narrators gain sympathy from listeners. These testimonies can be categorized into three groups: (1) stories of interactions with blacks (negative and positive), (2) stories of disclosure of knowledge of someone close who is racist, and (3) a residual category of *sui generis* testimonies.

A young, female college student who claimed to have liberal values regarding multiculturalism stated the following about the consequences of "busing" black kids to white schools:

California Proposition 209. *State Senator Diane Watson speaks at a Los Angeles Urban League rally in support of Proposition 209 on November 1, 1996. The proposition to ban race or gender preferences in public hiring, contracting, and education was approved by California voters.* AP IMAGES.

> When I was in the P.E. locker room and I set my bag down just to go to the bathroom and . . . I was gone maybe a minute and I come back and I see a really big woman [with other black students] stealing money out of my bag. (Bonilla-Silva 2003)

This student's negative experience with a few blacks allowed her to generalize bad behavior to all blacks, and this justifies her opposition to busing. Personal negative experiences can thus provide a convenient rationale for stereotyping minorities and justifying white privilege.

Testimonies about positive experiences with blacks allow whites to protect their color-blind sense of self. Often, a once-in-a-lifetime encounter with a black person is used as evidence of racial purity on the part of the narrator. For example, a female college student, after attesting that her family is racist, attempted to signify that she was not with the following testimony:

> My floor actually, the year I had a black roommate, happened to be predominantly African American and so those became some of my best friends, the people I was around. And we would actually sit around and talk about stereotypes and prejudices and I learned so much just about the hair texture, you know? (Bonilla-Silva 2003)

Although this respondent speaks highly of her interaction with African-American women, she uses the term "those" and claims she "learned" from this interaction, but she then points out superficial things such as hair texture and does not even mention the name of her "best friends," with whom she does not have currently a meaningful relationship.

COLOR-BLIND RACISM IN TWENTY-FIRST CENTURY AMERICA

Color-blind racism has crystallized as the dominant racial ideology of the United States. Whites no longer need to utter the ugly racial epithets of the past, claim God made whites superior, or argue that minorities are inferior biological beings in order to keep them in a subordinated position. Instead, whites chastise minorities in a color-blind way and, by default, defend their racial privilege in a "now you see it, now you don't fashion." Color-blind racism is thus a formidable weapon to maintain white privilege.

Will color-blind racism increase in significance in the twenty-first century, or will Americans realize the continuing impact of racial stratification in their country? The trends, unfortunately, suggest that, if anything, color-blind racism is bound to become even more salient. For one thing, the Supreme Court may eliminate all forms of race-based policies (e.g., Affirmative Action, busing) as "discriminatory in reverse." Such an outcome will underscore whites' "we are beyond race" racial common sense. In addition, Congress may stop gathering racial statistics, because gathering them presumably racializes Americans. This will make it all but impossible to document racial gaps in income, education, occupations, and other areas. This would only eliminate racial inequality artificially. Finally, the United States is developing a plural racial order, a development that will further diffuse the salience of race. In the emerging racial order, a middle group of "honorary whites" will buffer racial conflict and become arduous defenders of color-blindness.

Hence, the United States may be on its way to becoming a land of racism without racists, where people formerly known as blacks, Latinos, and Asians will still lag well behind the people formerly known as whites. Yet this inequality, formerly known as racial, will no longer be interpreted as such because Americans will believe, like the character Pangloss in Voltaire's novel *Candide*, that they live in the best of all possible worlds.

SEE ALSO *Affirmative Action; Aversive Racism; Cultural Racism; Everyday Racism; Implicit Racism; Symbolic and Modern Racism; White Racial Identity.*

BIBLIOGRAPHY

Althusser, Louis, and Etienne Balibar. 1970. *Reading Capital.* Translated by Ben Brewster. London: NLB.

Bonilla-Silva, Eduardo. 2001. *White Supremacy and Racism in the Post-Civil Rights Era.* Boulder, CO: Lynne Rienner.

———. 2003. *Racism without Racists: Color-Blind Racism and the Persistence of Racial Inequality in the United States.* Lanham, MD: Rowan & Littlefield.

———. 2004. "From Bi-Racial to Tri-Racial: Towards a New System of Racial Stratification in the USA." *Ethnic and Racial Studies* 27 (6): 931–950.

Eduardo Bonilla-Silva
Michelle Christian

CONTINUOUS VARIATION

SEE *Clines and Continuous Variation.*

"CONVERTING THE SAVAGE"

SEE *Missionaries among American Indians.*

CORONA, BERT
1918–2001

Bert Corona was one of the great leaders in the Chicano struggle against racism, ethnic and cultural discrimination, and class exploitation. Although less well known than his contemporary César Chávez, Corona is equally as important in Chicano and U.S. history. Both leaders did what no one else had ever done before: Chávez successfully organized farm workers, while Corona successfully organized undocumented immigrant workers. Corona's life spanned the major periods of twentieth-century Chicano history. But he not only observed history, he made history.

Corona's parents were part of the Mexican Revolution of 1910. His father, Noe Corona, was a follower of Pancho Villa and a member of Villa's elite fighting unit, "Los Dorados." He was assassinated in 1921 while attempting to resurrect the Villa movement. Corona never knew his father, but the memories of his father as a fighter for social justice would instill in him the same values. In addition, his mother and his grandmother always socialized Corona and his siblings to care for the poor and the oppressed. These principles would become the center of his life.

Corona was born in El Paso, Texas, on May 29, 1918. After graduating from high school, he migrated to Los Angeles and got work at a downtown warehouse in the late 1930s, when the militant Longshoremen's Union affiliated with the CIO was organizing that industry. Corona joined the union and quickly became one of its major leaders, helping to organize the unskilled and largely immigrant workforce of various ethnic backgrounds.

It was in the union movement that Corona cut his teeth as an organizer. Here he would learn the importance of building coalitions among different ethnic groups and constructing organizations from the grass roots to include not only workers but also their families. Corona also immersed himself in Mexican-American community affairs. He was involved with the Mexican American Movement (MAM), which lasted from late 1937 to 1945 and encouraged Chicano students to stay in school and to consider going to college, and he was part of the Spanish-Speaking Congress (1939–1945), which focused on civil rights and organizing Chicano workers into the CIO unions. After serving in World War II, Corona returned to Los Angeles to resume his community work. In the late 1940s, he became one of the principal organizers for the Community Service Organization (CSO) in California. He traveled the state for the CSO, registering Mexican-American voters. This work led to the successful election of Edward Roybal to the Los Angles City Council in 1949. Roybal was the first Mexican American elected to that body since the late nineteenth century, and he went on to win a seat in the U.S. Congress in 1962.

In the 1950s, Corona also became a key organizer for ANMA (*Associación Nacional México-Americana*). ANMA was an offshoot of the progressive Mine, Mill and Smelter Workers Union, which was very influential among Mexican-American workers in the Southwest. In California, Corona assisted in the unionization of Latino workers and provided civil rights support. Part of this work consisted of supporting the strikes organized by braceros, the contract workers from Mexico being imported to the United States at that time.

In 1960 Corona, along with Roybal and others, started the Mexican American Political Association (MAPA), which became the principal Latino political and electoral group in the country. It spearheaded civil rights issues for Mexican Americans concerning education, housing, jobs, health, and police brutality. At the same time, MAPA became the first national Latino electoral organization to actively participate in presidential politics. Corona, for example, was one of the key organizers for the campaign of President Lyndon Johnson in California in 1964. Four years later, he was a national codirector of the Robert Kennedy presidential campaign, which ended in tragedy with the assassination of Kennedy following his victory in the June primary in California.

The death of Robert Kennedy, whom Corona was very close to, shifted Corona's attention away from electoral politics and back toward community organizing. He joined and soon led the *Hermandad Mexicana Nacional*, which became the largest self-help organization for undocumented immigrant workers in the United States. For more than thirty years, Corona served as its executive director, organizing thousands of Latino undocumented workers and their families in the struggle to protect themselves against repressive anti-immigrant legislation and movements such as California's anti-immigrant Proposition 187 in 1994. As part of this effort, he also organized CASA (*Centro de Acción Social Autónomo*) as the Hermandad's political wing.

Through his values and his work, Corona inspired and educated numerous Latinos who have gone on to become labor, community, and political leaders in their own right. Even in the months before his death on January 15, 2001, while confined to a wheelchair, Corona lobbied for immigrant rights. When he entered a room, he became the center of attention due to the respect he commanded. When asked when he might retire, he said, "No, I can't, because we still have so many struggles ahead of us." Bert Corona died as he would have wanted, working for social justice and against racism, and trying to make this country live up to its ideals, especially for its most marginalized people.

SEE ALSO *Chicano Movement; Latino Social Movements.*

BIBLIOGRAPHY

García, Mario T. 1989. *Mexican Americans: Leadership, Ideology, and Identity, 1930–1960.* New Haven, CT: Yale University Press.

———. 1994. *Memories of Chicano History: The Life and Narrative of Bert Corona.* Berkeley: University of California Press.

Mario T. Garcia

CRANIAL INDEX

The cranial index is the ratio of the maximum breadth of the skull to its maximum length. In craniometric terms, the maximum breadth of a human skull is measured across the broadest points of its parietal bones. The maximum length is measured from the point furthest forward on the brow, called the glabella, to the point on the occipital bone furthest from this point. This ratio is often expressed as a percentage, by multiplying the ratio by 100.

The cranial index is closely related to the *cephalic index*, which is the ratio of the length and breadth of the head, taken externally by calipers on a living person. The cephalic index was originated by Swedish anatomist Anders Retzius as an instrument to compare the cranial dimensions of living peoples of Europe with ancient skulls. Hence, both indices have been closely interlinked as instruments of comparison. The cranial and cephalic indices differ because the latter includes the soft tissue external to the skull, and the former includes the shrinkage of the skull as it dries. Older authorities often used "cephalic index" to apply to both indices, treated the two as synonyms, or converted the cranial into the cephalic index by the addition of some constant (often 8 millimeters) to the cranial length and breadth dimensions.

Almost all human crania are longer than broad, and therefore the cranial index is nearly always less than 1. Various systems to divide crania into long-headed (dolichocephalic), medium-headed (mesocephalic), and round-headed (brachycephalic) were once used. The boundaries between these categories were somewhat arbitrary and sometimes involved as many as eight grades of shape (Crawfurd 1868). In later years, the most widespread system of categorization classified a skull with a cranial index greater than 80 percent as brachycephalic, less than 75 percent as dolichocephalic, and between 75 and 80 percent as mesocephalic (Hooton 1946, p. 488).

The cranial and cephalic indices gained much of their initial importance from their variation across Europe in living and archaeological populations. This variation became attributed to the migration of ancient races with different head shapes, and anthropological research was directed toward finding the origins of living European peoples among these ancient races. William Ripley (1899) divided Europeans into three races: long-headed "Teutonics" in the north, round-headed "Alpines" in the center, and long-headed "Mediterraneans" in the south (Alexander 1962). At its apex, this craniological enterprise linked the expansion and contraction of cephalic races not only to the movements of ancient peoples but also to the wars of the nineteenth and twentieth centuries (e.g., Grant 1916), and the relations of these races to other peoples of the world were examined.

This view has since been discredited. Not long after the definition of the cephalic index, it was observed that variation in the cranial or cephalic index within populations is more extensive than variation between them. In particular, the categorization of crania into discrete categories of "dolichocephalic" and "brachycephalic" made it easy to point out that these categories could be found in all human races, and even within individual families (Crawfurd 1868). The lack of correspondence between the cephalic index and "race" was employed by Giuseppe Sergi (e.g., 1901) to criticize its application, although some suggested that even more complex categorizations of cranial shape might provide greater accuracy of classification.

The plasticity of the cranial index has been an important element of craniological research. Early investigators observed that artificial deformation of the skull by indigenous peoples could affect the cranial index. Franz Boas (1899) noted that the cranial index was inversely correlated with cranial length, and further that it is correlated with stature and facial dimensions. In a study of immigrants to the United States and their U.S.-born children, Boas (1912) found that the cephalic indices of offspring differed slightly from those of their parents, interpreting this change as the product of their new environment. These results were recently reexamined in two separate studies, which found a strong genetic effect on the cephalic index but confirmed a slight environmental plasticity (Sparks and Jantz 2002; Gravlee, Bernard, and Leonard 2003).

A fully satisfactory theory to account for the ontogeny and evolution of the cranial index has not yet been developed (Holloway 2002). Arthur Thomson (1903) considered that the cranial base was more constrained in development than the vault, so that the cranial index emerged from the interaction of the cartilaginous developing cranial base and growing brain. This hypothesis is consistent with recent research, but the details of the interaction remain unclear. The cranial index remains important to the diagnosis of certain developmental disorders of the skull, such as craniosynostosis (premature fusion of the cranial bones), hydrocephalus (rapid head growth resulting from cerebrospinal fluid blockage), and positional deformation (as may occur from a preferred sleeping position in infants). In terms of evolution, Kenneth Beals, Courtland Smith, and Stephen Dodd (1983) interpreted the cranial index as a thermoregulatory adaptation to ancient climates. In contrast, Maciej Henneberg (1983) suggested that a recent evolutionary trend toward broader skulls was a consequence of structural reduction affecting the length of the skull. Makiko Kouchi (2000) finds that the cranial index has changed in Japan as a consequence of increases in breadth, correlated with larger body sizes. In truth, the mechanisms of the evolution of the cranial index may be diverse in different regions of the world, and they remain poorly characterized.

SEE ALSO *Forensic Anthropology and Race.*

BIBLIOGRAPHY

Alexander, Charles C. 1962. "Prophet of American Racism: Madison Grant and the Nordic Myth." *Phylon* 23 (1): 73–90.

Beals, Kenneth L., Courtland Smith, and Stephen Dodd. 1983. "Climate and the Evolution of Brachycephalization." *American Journal of Physical Anthropology* 62 (4): 425–437.

Boas, Franz. 1899. "The Cephalic Index." *American Anthropology* 1 (3): 448–461.

———. 1912. "Changes in the Bodily Form of Descendants of Immigrants." *American Anthropology* 14 (3): 530–562.

Crawfurd, John. 1868. "On the Classification of the Races of Man According to the Form of the Skull." *Transactions of the Ethnological Society of London* 6: 127–134.

Grant, Madison. 1916. *The Passing of the Great Race*. New York: Scribner's.

Gravlee, Clarence C., H. Russell Bernard, and William R. Leonard. 2003. "Heredity, Environment, and Cranial Form: A Reanalysis of Boas's Immigrant Data." *American Anthropology* 105 (1): 125–138.

Henneberg, Maciej. 1983. "Structural Reduction in *Homo sapiens* Microevolution: Jaws, Gracilization, Brachycephalization." *Przeglad Antropologiczny* 49: 57–76.

Holloway, Ralph L. 2002. "Head to Head with Boas: Did He Err on the Plasticity of Head Form?" *Proceedings of the National Academy of Sciences* 99: 14622–14623.

Hooton, Earnest A. 1946. *Up from the Ape*, 2nd ed. New York: Macmillan.

Kouchi, Makiko. 2000. "Brachycephalization in Japan Has Ceased." *American Journal of Physical Anthropology* 112: 339–347.

Ripley, William Z. 1899. *The Races of Europe*. New York: Appleton.

Sergi, Giuseppe. 1901. *The Mediterranean Race: A Study of the Origin of European Peoples*. London: Scribner's.

Sparks, Corey S., and Richard L. Jantz. 2002. "A Reassessment of Human Cranial Plasticity: Boas Revisited." *Proceedings of the National Academy of Sciences* 99 (23): 14636–14639.

Thomson, Arthur. 1903. "A Consideration of Some of the More Important Factors Concerned in the Production of Man's Cranial Form." *Journal of the Royal Anthropological Institute of Great Britain and Ireland* 33: 135–166.

John Hawks

CRIME AND AMERICAN INDIANS

The racial concept of American Indians, extending back some 500 years, has always included labels of the "alien Other" or the "hostile enemy," as well as a general criminalization of any resistance to conquest, cultural domination, or the discriminatory systems put into place to maintain their subordination in segregated, oppressed areas called "reservations." These exclusionary and discriminatory policies criminalized the cultural and social practices of Native nations and turned the reservations into internal colonies, while also causing high levels of violence, poverty, and crime on most Indian reservations. Luanna Ross, who has studied the "social construction of Native American criminality," calls this process "inventing the savage."

HISTORICAL CONSTRUCTIONS

Violence accompanied the initial expansion of Europeans into the Americas. The indigenous population, given the racial designation of "Indians," or "*los Indios*," was at times sold as slaves for the Western nation-states advancing into the Caribbean. The invasion was called "discovery" by the Europeans, and it was supported by great military might and technological superiority. Early notions of race and "savagery" branded "Indian" peoples as the "Enemy," and thereby criminal, for their resistance to land-takings. The Native population was excluded as the "Other," as distinct from the settlers, colonizers, or civilized citizens of newly created nations, including colonial forebears that became nations such as Mexico, Canada, and Cuba. This treatment was evident in the genocidal conquest of Hispaniola (later called Haiti), and in the destruction of the peoples of Mexico by Spanish conquistadors. Skin-tone visibility, compounded by vast cultural differences, allowed the dominating groups permanent recognition of status through "race" stratification. Racial hierarchies would continue to be used for three centuries by the Spanish, until they became essentially unmanageable. However, the effect on native peoples in the "New World" was always the same: outright genocidal destruction or racial subordination with a loss of culture, and a more powerful loss of sovereignty, freedom, and society.

The English colonies in North America imported their institutionalization of the Irish, designating Indians as "savage" and the Other in their own lands, and subsequently barring Native peoples by religion and "national" (cultural) origin from any real participation in colonial development preceding the United States, including at Jamestown or Plymouth. Both of these colonies, critically important to Anglo-Saxon laws that were inherited by the United States, treated Indians as aliens in their own lands, as either a potential enemy or an inferior Other. Thus began the legal underpinnings of treating Indians as "Hostiles." Both Virginia and Massachusetts slipped into genocidal warfare against Native nations, blurring any distinction between the "criminal" and the alienated enemy resisting further invasion and land-takings. This also became a legacy of United States law, enshrined in the Constitution as "Indians not taxed" (and therefore not citizens) and in U.S. congressional rights to make (and break) treaties with Indian Nations. Indians thereby existed outside the legal protections of citizens of the new republic, yet they retained the dangerous, demonic labels of Enemy, Other, Alien, and Hostile.

CITIZENSHIP

United States law enforcement, and its attendant influence over violence and crime among and against

American Indians, is reliant on historical relations between the nation-state and Native nations or tribes. In addition to wars, treaties, land-takings, the development of the Indian Reservation system, and legal restrictions, the key issue in respect to crime has been the nature of citizenship for Indian people. The U.S. Constitution criminalized the American Indian in ways remarkably similar to modern designations of "enemy combatant" under military law. Relations between the Native peoples and the United States can be divided into four basic historical periods of about a half century each. The first extended from the original era of treaty making through completion of the Indian Removal policies. The second period began with the Civil War and lasted until the killings at Wounded Knee and the end of the "frontier" around 1890. The third period covers the first half of the twentieth century, whereas the fourth, modern, period comprises the rising of social movements and U.S. policies that determine issues of sovereignty. Each period is marked by changing laws, enforcement, violence, and criminology relating to the changing legal position of American Indians, Native nations, and indigenous peoples.

The first two periods, from the founding of the United States (with its acceptance of colonial notions of race and racism) to the last genocidal acts of violence by U.S. military and militia forces, were marked by massive land-takings and a slippage into genocide and culturicide whenever outright theft or dishonest treaty-making could not accomplish the alienation of Indian lands. This included extending colonial claims of sovereign domination through two "legal" principles: the "Right to Conquest" and the "Doctrine of Discovery" (see Deloria and Lytle 1984). These amounted to little more than legal cover for conducting war, eliminating Indian resistance, and taking Native lands that stood in the way of U.S. westward expansion. The overall effect of these policies was to place American Indian people outside the citizenship rights of the new nation-state but provide little recognition of any indigenous rights.

Exemplifying these changing systems of criminality, including the use of genocidal policies arising to the level of war crimes, was the practice of "Indian Removal," especially regarding the "Five Civilized Tribes" (the Cherokees, Chickasaws, Choctaws, Creeks, and Seminoles). Local states, especially the Carolinas and Georgia, took umbrage at Indian resistance and began taking Cherokee land by force and unilateral declaration, leading to new rounds of official relationships between the United States, its own "states," and Indian Nations. Individual Indians had a Faustian choice of remaining in the United States, with little to no protection, or to being forcibly removed to new lands, with a minimum of rights and the certainty of future struggles. The Cherokees took legal action to resist continued state encroachment into their lands, leading to a set of U.S. Supreme Court decisions on this issue. The first was *Johnson v. McIntosh* (1823), in which the court acknowledged a limited "sovereignty" but sided with individual states. Following this was the moot *Cherokee Nation v. Georgia* (1831), in which the Court called the Cherokees "domestic dependent nations," further attempting to define the status of Native American tribes.

Finally, in *Worcester v. Georgia* (1832), the Court ruled against Georgia and, in a limited way, for Indian Nations. However, President Andrew Jackson broke with constitutional law and began removing Indian peoples from the southeastern states, cajoling Congress into passing the Indian Removal Act of 1830. This act led to the forced removal of the Cherokees to Oklahoma in 1838. About 4,000 Cherokees died on the forced march during the brutal winter months, a journey now memorialized as the "Trail of Tears." Jackson based his actions primarily on essentialist notions of the "race" of American Indians, and he essentially eliminated indigenous legal rights. The "Indian" was functionally criminalized as either an enemy or an alien. They were thus criminals on their own lands, and Native nations were targeted for elimination.

The U.S. rejection of its own treaties and laws continued until the 1871 Treaties Statute prohibited the nation from entering into treaties with Indian tribes. The 1868 treaty clearly gave certain rights to the Lakota and Indian peoples, as well as recognition of nations and treaty boundaries, and was thus unexceptable to the U.S. congressional elimination of these rights. This marked the end of a dialogue between nations and the beginning of relations between a dominant nation-state and its internally colonized Indian peoples. U.S. policies shifted from a focus on treaties to one on individual laws, including the Indian Offenses Act of 1883, and the recognition of "tribal" courts with tribal jurisdiction. This was formalized under the Major Crimes Act of 1885, which made U.S. law dominant over tribal law in seven major criminal offenses (expanded to fourteen crimes in 1888).

These policies outlawed many cultural practices, even traditional religious and educational practices, with the ostensible purpose of assimilating Native peoples into mainstream, dominant, "white" American society, albeit without citizenship or other polity rights. The Sun Dance, a peaceful spiritual gathering, was specifically made illegal, further criminalizing Lakota indigenous religious practices. Coercive assimilation against group property and kinship holdings, which was finally ended by the land allotments required by the 1887 Dawes Act, was in fact a form of cultural genocide. The Dawes Act

Crime in Indian Country. *A table holds weapons seized during a methamphetamine investigation near the Pine Ridge Indian Reservation in 2003. American Indians are the most likely racial group to be victims of violent crime.* AP IMAGES.

broke up collective land rights and allowed simple patent fee "rights" causing individually held land to be sold to non-Indians.

Variations on the criminalization and exploitation of American Indians existed in other parts of the country as well, notably in California, where an extensive set of local militias were systematically destroying the native population. Vagrancy laws legitimated indentured servitude under state law, which kept surviving Indian peoples under constant duress, just as the Fugitive Slave Act kept blacks in a state of duress in the pre–Civil War United States. The shortage of white women exacerbated the sexual exploitation of many Native women during this period, creating legitimized violence across California.

This period ended in 1890 with the quasi-genocidal killings at Wounded Knee, aptly described by Dee Brown in his book *Bury My Heart at Wounded Knee*. Brown's title refers to the imprimatur of Euro-American domination and the end of the "frontier," or the world of Indian peoples. Essentially, the aforesaid cultural and religious practices of resisting tribes, such as the Lakota in the Dakotas, were made illegal and were being repressed when a vast social revitalization movement, dubbed the Ghost Dance, spread across the western and northern regions of the United States. The U.S. Indian Commissions asked for and received military assistance to "put down" the Ghost Dance in Lakota country, and it was made illegal as an extension of the Indian Offenses. Indian agents gave lists of names to the government of those to be arrested, leading to the killing of Sitting Bull and some of his supporters on the Standing Rock Reservation. The survivors fled southward and surrendered, along with many Lakota from Cheyenne River, as they entered the Pine Ridge Reservation. Near the end of the disarmament the soldiers opened fire and butchered more than 300 people, signaling the end of American Indian freedom and independence. Civilian and military authorities in the U.S. predicted that Indian nations and tribes would disappear forever in the twentieth century (see Cadwalader and Deloria 1984). However, such reports of the demise of Indian nations were both premature and untrue. Of course, there is not a single case in which a "white man" was brought to justice for killing Indians, although many certainly did, while any violence toward non-Indians were prosecuted to the fullest extent of the law, or by vigilantes.

TWENTIETH-CENTURY LAWS, CRIME, AND VIOLENCE

Military violence subsided as the United States, having centralized federal sovereignty, maintained effective control over the social institutions within the purview of the states, especially through taxation, the judicial system, public education, transportation, and many economic enterprises. This meant that in any conflict (or act of cooperation) between federally recognized Indian nations tribes, the Indians were dealing with two sovereign entities, and were in fact acting as sovereigns themselves (not fully recognized for another fifty-plus years). Among the most contested relationships in twentieth-century America was that between the tribal sovereignty and individual state sovereignty. The general public, meanwhile, continued to racially identify indigenous peoples as "Indians." Confusion over racial, political, and ethno-national identities persist in the twenty-first century, with ambiguous and changing laws applied to American Indians as individuals and as members of tribes or nations.

Finally, in 1924, the U.S. government passed citizenship laws that included Native Americans, perhaps as a last attempt to dissolve tribal sovereignty. In the twentieth century, two distinct forms of struggle over sovereignty began to emerge: sociopolitical sovereignty, related to Supreme Court decisions and jurisdictional relationships, and "cultural" sovereignty, expressed as the ability of a people to speak their own languages, practice their spirituality, and raise their families with "traditional" values. Arising after the civil rights movement and the urbanization of Indian families in the United States, Native social movements converged in the form of the American Indian Movement (AIM). By 1975 there were arrests, false imprisonment, selective assassinations, and a virtual prison industry against American Indian activists across the nation, finally coming to a head on Pine Ridge, when two FBI agents were killed in a conflict with AIM members. Suppression increased as the sovereignty movements of the 1980s became strong. Yet Native activism stayed alive, along with cultural retention struggles.

Complex governmental policies reflect the development of various forms of internal colonization, with laws unequally applied in and around Anglo communities near Indian reservations, very violent environments for Native people, and separate laws constructed for Indian nations. As the United States moved out of the third general time period, following World War II, American Indians began to protest the highly discriminatory systems they found in and around the reservation system and in large urban areas. At the same time, forms of crime that were not common in previous periods became more frequent, including the rise of domestic violence and assault. One example is instructive here. On the Standing Rock Reservation, which has a high rate of violent crime, death, and suicide, internalized and fratricidal violent assault increased in the second half of the twentieth century. Yet domestic abuse was relatively rare in traditional Native society, because a woman's family would be present in living situations and the entire community would be responsible for the welfare of children. As forced assimilation confined Native peoples to the nuclear family structure, private property, and personal accumulation, internal struggles and assaults increased.

Complex criminal law further complicated law enforcement on most Indian reservations. After the Major Crimes Act, and the ensuing federal court decisions, most criminal cases involving Indians were prosecuted under federal guidelines. Jurisdictional issues had to determine whether it was Indian-on-Indian crime. Further, if non-Indians were involved, it had to be determined whether state laws applied. These "inter-racial" cases were often settled without considering Indian law or tribal codes, at least until relatively recently. The Navajo Nation developed a Peacemaker Court system that relies on traditional justice systems, and some other indigenous civil codes have evolved. Tribal court systems arose on most of the larger reservations, with Indian police enforcing laws for Indian peoples, though with mixed results for non-Indians: Questions arise over jurisdiction of tribal police over non-Indians and resulting prosecution and civil laws. "Code of Federal Regulations" (CFR) courts oversee tribal courts. One policy arising from the earlier termination era, that of designated Public Law 280 states, was meant to cause states to provide law enforcement and other services where Indian peoples could not, often because of size or lack of institutional development. However, many, if not most, states interpreted this policy as giving them jurisdiction, and this interpretation often created "lawless" areas for non-Indians. Because tribal law would apply, under federal guidelines non-Indians were not subject to tribal law or police, and local or state police were often not patrolling or enforcing these areas, thus creating lawlessness (see Goldberg 1999).

VIOLENT CRIME AMONG NATIVE AMERICANS

As noted earlier, violent crime rates among Native populations rose during the last decades of the twentieth century, both internal to the reservation system and in towns and cities near reservations. When the U.S. Department of Justice finally studied these rates, they were surprised to learn that American Indians were the most likely racial group to be victims of violent crime, with a crime rate of two and a half times the national average, and many rates are even higher on reservations (see Table 1). Further, Indians were found to be the only victims of violent crime to have the perpetrators come primarily from another racial group, Anglo-Americans. Indeed, about seven out of ten violent victimizations of American Indians involve an offender described by the

Annual Average Rate of Rape and Sexual Assault, Robbery, and Assault, by Race of Victim, 1992-96

	Number of victimizations per 1,000 persons age 12 or older in each racial group			
	American Indian	White	Black	Asian
Rape/sexual assault	7	2	3	1
Robbery	12	5	13	7
Aggravated assault	35	10	16	6
Simple assault	70	32	30	15

SOURCE: Reprinted from Greenfield, Lawrence A. and Smith, Steven K. "American Indians and Crime." U.S. Department of Justice, Bureau of Justice Statistics, Washington D.C. Released February 1999.

Table 1. *About 7 in 10 violent victimizations of American Indians involved an offender who was described by the victim as someone of a different race—a substantially higher rate of interracial violence than experienced by white or black victims.*

victim as someone of a different race; this is a substantially higher rate of interracial violence than experienced by white or black victims (see Greenfield and Smith 1999, Perry 2004). More alarming is the finding that more than one-third of all Native American women will be raped at least once in their lifetime, and nearly two-thirds will be victims of violent assault. Yet, with few exceptions, tribal law enforcement cannot pursue and prosecute non-Indians, who are the most likely perpetrators of this violence (see Eid 2007).

All forms of crime have increased on most Indian reservations, with the notable exception of more well-off tribes with casino wealth. Violent crime is consistently high in communities near larger reservations, with much of the crime perpetuated by non-Indians on Indian victims. There is substantial hate crime as well. Drug use and alcoholism are very problematic and accompanied by the attendant criminal activity, with a shocking 25 percent of federal drug and alcohol prosecutions emanating from "Indian Country" (ironically, this term came into use during U.S. military invasions). Methamphetamine use and production has also posed particular issues for rural Native communities. Law enforcement systems have been underfunded and misdirected, and there are ongoing misunderstandings (and sometimes conflicts) between local and state police jurisdiction over American Indians on sovereign Native territory.

Overall, one can trace four hundred years of violent domination and changing criminal justice systems in the United States, including the limited and coerced assimilation of most American Indian tribes. Traditional justice systems have been suppressed and often eliminated, with only limited inclusion into the dominant social system, and this inclusion has usually proven to be discriminatory. Tribal law enforcement systems have become stronger since the 1970s, as Indian law has developed over a wide range of crime and social control. This may point to a future increase in cross-national justice that respects the sovereignty and cultures of indigenous peoples and Native nations.

SEE ALSO *American Indian Movement (AIM).*

BIBLIOGRAPHY

Berkey, Curtis G. 1992. "United States–Indian Relations: The Constitutional Basis." In *Exiled in the Land of the Free: Democracy, Indian Nations, and the U.S. Constitution*, edited by Oren Lyons and John Mohawk. Santa Fe, NM: Clear Light Publishers.

Berkhofer, Robert, Jr. 1978. *The White Man's Indian: Images of the American Indian from Columbus to the Present.* New York: Random House.

Cadwalader, Sandra D., and Vine Deloria Jr., eds. 1984. *The Aggressions of Civilization: Federal Indian Policy since the 1880s.* Philadelphia: Temple University Press.

Champagne, Duane. 1992. "Organizational Change and Conflict: A Case Study of the Bureau of Indian Affairs." In *Native Americans and Public Policy*, edited by Fremont Lyden and Lyan Legters. Pittsburgh, PA: University of Pittsburgh Press.

Coffey, Wallace, and Rebecca Tsosie. 2001. "Rethinking the Tribal Sovereignty Doctrine: Cultural Sovereignty and the Collective Future of Indian Nations." *Stanford Law & Policy Review* 12, no. 2: 191–221.

Deloria, Vine, Jr., and Clifford Lytle. 1984. *The Nations Within: The Past and Future of American Indian Sovereignty.* New York: Pantheon Books.

Deloria, Vine, Jr., and David E. Wilkins. 1999. *Tribes, Treaties, and Constitutional Tribulations.* Austin: University of Texas Press.

Dippie, Brian W. 1982. *The Vanishing American: White Attitudes and U.S. Indian Policy.* Middletown, CT: Wesleyan University Press.

Dunbar-Ortiz, Roxanne. 1984. *Indians of the Americas, Human Rights and Self-Determination.* London: Zed Books.

Eid, Troy. 2007. "Criminal Justice in Native America." *Indian Country Today,* June 7. Available from http://www.indiancountry.com.

Fenelon, James V. 2002. "Dual Sovereignty of Native Nations, the United States, and Traditionalists." *Humboldt Journal of Social Relations* 27 (1): 106–145.

———. 1998. *Culturicide, Resistance, and Survival of the Lakota (Sioux Nation).* New York: Garland.

Goldberg, Carol. 1999. "Public Law 280 and the Problem of 'Lawlessness' in California Indian Country." In *Contemporary Native American Political Issues*, edited by Troy Johnson. Walnut Creek, CA: AltaMira Press.

Greenfield, Lawrence, and Stephen Smith. 1999. *American Indians and Crime.* Washington, DC: U.S. Department of Justice, Bureau of Justice Statistics. Available from http://www.ojp.usdoj.gov/bjs/pub/pdf/aic.pdf.

Johnston-Dodds, Kimberly. 2002. "Early California Laws and Policies Related to California Indians." Sacramento: California Research Bureau, California State Library. Available from http://www.library.ca.gov/crb/02/14/02-014.pdf.

Lazarus, Edward. 1991. *Black Hills, White Justice: The Sioux Nation versus the United States, 1775 to the Present.* New York: Harper Collins.

Perry, Stephen W. 2004. "American Indians and Crime: A BJS Statistical Profile, 1992-2002." Washington, DC: U.S. Department of Justice, Bureau of Justice Statistics. Available from http://www.ojp.usdoj.gov/bjs/abstract/aic02.htm.

Ross, Luanna. 1998. *Inventing the Savage: The Social Construction of Native American Criminality.* Austin: University of Texas Press.

Smedley, Audrey. 1999. *Race in North America: Origins and Evolution of Worldview*, 2nd ed. Boulder, CO: Westview Press.

Trafzer, Clifford E., and Joel R. Hyer, eds. 1999. *Exterminate Them: Written Accounts of the Murder, Rape and Slavery of the Native Americans during the California Gold Rush, 1848–1868.* East Lansing: Michigan State University Press.

Wallace, Anthony F. C. 1993. *The Long, Bitter Trail: Andrew Jackson and the Indians.* Philadelphia: Hill and Wang.

Wilkins, David E., and K. Tsianina Lomawaima. 2002. *Uneven Ground: American Indian Sovereignty and Federal Law.* Norman: University of Oklahoma Press.

Wright, Ronald. 1992. *Stolen Continents: The Americas through Indian Eyes since 1492.* Boston: Houghton Mifflin.

James V. Fenelon

CRIMINAL JUSTICE SYSTEM

One of the most troubling features of the American criminal justice system is the disproportionate involvement of members of minority groups at every stage of the justice process. Long-standing debate centers on whether this over-representation results from higher rates of criminal acts committed by minority group members (i.e., biological race) or is a consequence of racism in case processing within the criminal justice system. Some scholars suggest that racial disproportion is contextual, depending on the particular circumstances of a case, the race of the defendant and victim, or geographic location. These explanations suggest that racism flows from systemic racism through discriminatory actions by individual judges, court-appointed lawyers, police officers, "three strikes and you're out" laws, composition of juries, and correctional systems.

The background for this problem is a long-standing pattern of historical intolerance and cultural depictions of members of minority groups as deviant or criminal. African-American and Hispanic men in particular have been viewed as suspicious, violent, and dangerous. Such portrayals have contributed to assumptions that they are more likely to be involved in criminal activity, a belief that consequently leads to increased surveillance of their activities and harsher punishments once they come into contact with the criminal justice system.

HISTORICAL TREATMENT

Historically, the criminal justice system has functioned as an instrument of racism and oppression through legislation and the practices of the police, court, and correctional systems. For example, during slavery police were used for patrols to catch runaway slaves and return them to their owners, and in the late 1800s in the western United States, Chinese immigrants faced laws restricting their opportunities to own land and businesses (Mann 1993). The lynching of black men suspected of crimes, particularly rape of white women, was a widespread practice in southern states in the late nineteenth and early twentieth centuries. Such violence occurred with either the explicit consent and participation of criminal justice actors, or a willingness to ignore mob violence against people of color. There has also been a historical pattern of discriminatory treatment of minorities who are victims of crimes.

MEDIA DEPICTIONS

In addition to legislation and decision-making that treated racial and ethnic minorities as inferior, media and popular culture have depicted minorities as deviant and criminal, with differences between the depiction of men (as violent) and women (as irresponsible). In print and television news, and entertainment media such as music and movies, African-American men in particular have been presented as violent and dangerous. These portrayals encourage fear and suspicion of people of color. In contrast, the so-called war on drugs, a movement to give harsh penalties to individuals involved in drug crimes, formulated images of crime and deviance in which women were represented as crack cocaine addicts who neglected and endangered their children. Images of "crack babies" led to legislative efforts to criminalize drug use during pregnancy and imprison women whose babies were born with drugs in their systems. In retrospect, scholars have analyzed the period as a moral panic with little empirical evidence that the scope and magnitude of the problem were accurately presented. Whether these views led to discriminatory processing within the criminal justice system is a central question.

Such media and popular cultural myths and stereotypes perpetuate ideas that people of color are criminal and dangerous or irresponsible and reckless, and therefore should receive harsher treatment and penalties in the criminal justice system (Mann and Zatz 2006).

RACIAL DIFFERENCES IN JUSTICE INVOLVEMENT

The disparity of involvement within the criminal justice system exists at all stages of the process. In 2002, while African Americans comprised 12 percent of the U.S. population, they were 27 percent of people arrested and 37 percent of felony offenders convicted in state courts. The disparities are even greater in rates of incarceration. In 2004, 41 percent of state and federal prison inmates were African American and 19 percent Hispanic. The lifetime likelihood of criminal justice system involvement is also much higher for African Americans. By some estimates, as many as one in three African-American men will be on probation, parole, or in prison in their lifetime. In 2004, 8.4 percent of all black males aged twenty-five to twenty-nine were incarcerated (Pastore and Maguire).

Death Row Exercise Yard, San Quentin, 2003. *Death Row inmates play basketball in the crowded exercise yard at San Quentin State Prison in California. Research on the death penalty indicates that after controlling for legally relevant factors such as offense and defendant's prior record, a death sentence is more likely when the victim is white.* AP IMAGES.

DISPARITY VERSUS DISCRIMINATION

While members of minority groups are disproportionately involved with the criminal justice system, the explanations for this are a source of debate. Samuel Walker, Cassia Spohn, and Miriam DeLone (2007) point out the distinction between disparity and discrimination. A disparity does not necessarily result from racism. For example, when considering legal factors such as offense seriousness or offender's prior record, members of minority groups are more likely to be sentenced to prison because of their greater criminal histories. This may represent a disparity in outcome, but one that is legitimately based on non-racial factors relevant to sentencing.

Yet disparity may result from the use of extralegal factors, such as the defendant's or victim's race, ethnicity, gender, or marital or employment status—and these may operate as indirect causes of discrimination. For example, marital and employment status are related to race, and when criminal-justice decision makers take factors such as these into account, they put members of minority groups at a systematic disadvantage because of race-based differences in background characteristics.

To better understand the differences between disparity and discrimination, Walker, Spohn, and DeLone created a discrimination–disparity continuum regarding processing in the criminal justice system. The five elements on the spectrum, ranging from the highest levels of discrimination to no discrimination at all, are: systematic discrimination, institutionalized discrimination, contextual discrimination, individual acts of discrimination, and pure justice.

At one end of the spectrum, *pure justice*, there is no racism in the system, and longer sentences and higher rates of incarceration for members of minority groups result purely from higher rates of criminal involvement. At the other end, *systematic discrimination* suggests that decisions are made according to racist assumptions and that members of minority groups are always discriminated against at every stage of the process. The intermediate points on the spectrum represent varying levels of discriminatory individuals making unfair decisions and institutional arrangements that work to the disadvantage of minorities.

BIOLOGICAL RACE

There is little credible research proposing that minority involvement in the criminal justice system is attributed to biological inferiority, deviance, or propensity toward violence. There have been periods in history when such ideas were embraced, and promoted for political purposes (Mann 1993). There is a long history of research examining structural factors in crime (unemployment, poverty, neighborhood of residence) that are highly correlated with race (Walker, Spohn, and DeLone 1996).

INDIRECT AND CONTEXTUAL RACISM

Indirect and contextual racism may be the best explanations for why people of color are overrepresented in the criminal justice system. For example, prosecutors and judges look at the offense seriousness and prior record of the offender when they make charging and sentencing decisions. These are the legal factors that legitimately influence decisions if racism was not involved in those prior sentences. Some studies of racial bias in sentencing have found that when these variables are controlled for, evidence of racial discrimination disappears.

There are characteristics of the racial and economic structure in the United States that systematically put people of color at a disadvantage, and some of these disadvantages carry over to the criminal justice system. Minority defendants are more likely to be poor and therefore less likely to be represented by private attorneys or be released before trial. In addition, when law enforcement resources are focused on street crime, white-collar crimes are less likely to be detected, and perpetrators of such crimes go unpunished.

Contextual factors may be important for certain types of crimes, or when a defendant is a person of color and a victim is white. Research on the death penalty, for example, indicates that after controlling for legally relevant factors such as offense and defendant's prior record, a death sentence is more likely when the victim is white (Baldus, Woodworth, and Pulaski 1990).

CONSEQUENCES OF OVERREPRESENTATION

Increasingly, research is focusing on the devastating consequences for communities of color from overrepresentation in the criminal justice system. More than half of the states deny voting rights to individuals under correctional supervision, and fifteen states deny rights to those in prison. It is estimated that 13 percent of black men are permanently banned from voting (Human Rights Watch 1998). Moreover, justice involvement, particularly imprisonment, is geographically concentrated, leading to disparate impact on members of minority groups. The removal and return of large numbers of young men because of incarceration has a destabilizing effect that may reverberate through many aspects of community life.

New approaches to crime and justice issues are attempting to overcome the history and legacy of racist and discriminatory treatment in the criminal justice system. Community-based programs, including policing and court models, revolve around problem solving that may prevent criminal justice involvement and make criminal justice actors more responsive to the needs of specific communities. In addition, there is a growing sentiment that the criminal justice system should be involved in building neighborhoods' capacity to provide safe environments, particularly in the communities that have suffered from systematic racism and discrimination in the United States (Clear and Karp 1999).

SEE ALSO *Criminality, Race and Social Factors; Hoaxing.*

BIBLIOGRAPHY

Baldus, David C., George Woodworth, and Charles A. Pulaski Jr. 1990. *Equal Justice and the Death Penalty: A Legal and Empirical Analysis.* Boston: Northeastern University Press.

Clear, Todd R., and David R. Karp. 1999. *The Community Justice Ideal: Preventing Crime and Achieving Justice.* Boulder, CO: Westview Press.

Human Rights Watch and The Sentencing Project. 1998. "Losing the Vote: The Impact of Felony Disenfranchisement Laws in the United States." Washington, DC: The Sentencing Project and New York: Human Rights Watch.

Mann, Coramae Richey. 1993. *Unequal Justice: A Question of Color.* Bloomington: Indiana University Press.

Mann, Coramae Richey, and Marjorie S. Zatz, eds. 2006. *Images of Color, Images of Crime: Readings*, 3rd ed. Los Angeles: Roxbury Publishing.

Pastore, Ann L., and Kathleen Maguire, eds. *Sourcebook of Criminal Justice Statistics.* Available from http://www.albany .edu/sourcebook/.

Walker, Samuel, Cassia Spohn, and Miriam DeLone. 2007. *The Color of Justice: Race, Ethnicity, and Crime in America*, 4th ed. Belmont, CA: Wadsworth.

Johnna Christian
Todd Clear

CRIMINALITY, RACE AND SOCIAL FACTORS

In 1918 the Bureau of the Census reported that blacks, who made up only 11 percent of the U.S. population, accounted for 22 percent of the inmates of prisons, jails, and reform schools (U.S. Department of Commerce 1918, p. 438). The authors of the report acknowledged that these figures "will probably be generally accepted as indicating that there is more criminality and lawbreaking among Negroes than among whites," and they stated that this conclusion "is probably justified by the facts." The authors then posed a question that would spark debate and generate controversy for years to come. They asked whether the difference "may not be to some extent the result of discrimination in the treatment of white and Negro offenders on the part of the community and the courts."

This question is still being asked in the twenty-first century. As the proportion of the jail and prison population that is African American approaches 50 percent (Bureau of Justice Statistics 2005), social scientists and legal scholars continue to ask whether, and to what extent, racial discrimination infects the criminal justice system. Although most scholars believe that the overrepresentation of African Americans in arrest and incarceration statistics results primarily from the disproportionate involvement of African Americans in serious crime, most also acknowledge that discrimination plays an important role. Michael Tonry, a professor in criminal law at the University of Minnesota Law School, contends that the war on crime, and particularly the war on drugs, "has caused the ever harsher treatment of blacks by the criminal justice system" (Tonry 1995, p. 52). Like Tonry, most scholars concede that the overrepresentation of African Americans in the criminal justice system results "to some extent" from discrimination against racial minorities and the poor.

RACE AND INVOLVEMENT IN CRIME

For many people, the word *crime* evokes an image of a young, African American male who carries a weapon and murders, rapes, robs, or assaults someone of another race. These perceptions, which are fueled by the attention the media, politicians, and criminal justice policymakers give to street crimes such as murder and rape, are inaccurate. The typical crime is in fact not a violent crime; the typical criminal offender—that is, the offender who appears most often in arrest statistics—is not African American; and most crimes are intraracial rather than interracial. According to the Federal Bureau of Investigation's Uniform Crime Reports, in 2004 there were ten times as many property crimes as violent crimes reported to the police. In addition, whites made up 61 percent of those arrested for violent crimes (murder, rape, robbery, and aggravated assault), 69 percent of those arrested for property crimes (burglary, larceny-theft, auto theft, and arson), and 66 percent of those arrested for drug abuse violations. Although data on the race of the offender and the race of the victim are more difficult to come by, the Bureau of Justice Statistics has reported that from 1976 to 2002, 86 percent of white homicide victims were killed by whites, while 94 percent of African-American homicide victims were killed by African Americans.

Using the term *typical offender* in discussing race and crime is somewhat misleading. First, African Americans make up more than half of all arrests for two particular violent crimes—murder (including nonnegligent manslaughter) and robbery. For these offenses, in other words, the typical offender is African American. Second, although it is true that most of those arrested in the United States are white, the percentage of African Americans arrested for most crimes is disproportionate to their percentage in the population. In 2004, African Americans made up approximately 13 percent of the U.S. population, but they accounted for 54 percent of those arrested for robbery, 53 percent of those arrested for murder and manslaughter, 37 percent of those arrested for rape, and 36 percent of those arrested for aggravated assault. For these violent crimes, African Americans were overrepresented (and whites were underrepresented) in arrest statistics. African Americans also were overrepresented in arrests for property crimes (29.4% of all arrests) and drug abuse violations (36.5% of all arrests). In fact, the only crimes for which whites were overrepresented in arrest statistics were driving under the influence (88% of all arrests), liquor law violations (84.8% of all arrests), and drunkenness (83.3% of all arrests). These racial differences are found for both juveniles and adults.

Criminologists have conducted dozens of studies designed to explain the overrepresentation of African Americans in crime statistics. Although many scholars contend that at least some of this overrepresentation can be attributed to racial profiling (that is, the tendency of police and other criminal justice officials to use race as an indicator of an increased likelihood of involvement in crime) and discrimination in the decision to arrest or not, most acknowledge that racial disparities in arrest statistics do reflect racial differences in criminal involvement.

Explanations for the relationship between race and crime generally focus on the effects of economic inequality, community social disorganization, residential segregation, individual- and family-level risk factors, weakened family attachments, weak bonds to school and work, and involvement with delinquent peers and gangs. According to these interrelated perspectives, the higher rates of crime—and particularly the higher rates of violent crime (that is, the number arrested per 1,000 population)—for

African Americans than for whites reflect the fact that African Americans are more likely than whites to be poor, to be unemployed or underemployed, and to live in drug- and gang-ridden communities with high rates of family disruption and social disorganization. African Americans, in other words, have higher rates of crime than whites because of the very different economic, social, and cultural situations in which they often live. As Robert Sampson and William Julius Wilson put it, "the most important determinant of the relationship between race and crime is the differential distribution of blacks in communities characterized by (1) structural social disorganization and (2) cultural social isolation, both of which stem from the concentration of poverty, family disruption, and residential instability" (Sampson and Wilson 2005, p. 182).

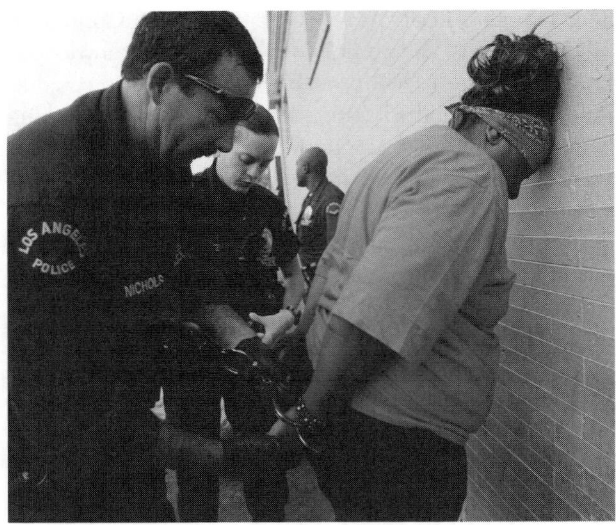

Arrest on Skid Row. *Los Angeles police officers arrest a homeless woman near downtown Los Angeles on October 10, 2006. The percentage of African Americans arrested for most crimes is disproportionate to their percentage in the population.* AP IMAGES.

THE IMPRISONMENT OF AFRICAN AMERICANS

There is irrefutable evidence that racial minorities comprise a disproportionate share of the U.S. prison population. At the end of 2004, there were 1.3 million persons incarcerated in state and federal prisons; 41 percent of these inmates were African American, 34 percent were white, and 19 percent were Hispanic (Bureau of Justice Statistics 2005). The disparities are even more dramatic for males, and particularly for males in their twenties and thirties. The incarceration rates for African-American males in these age groups are seven to eight times higher than the rates for white males, and two-and-a-half to three times higher than the rates for Hispanic males. When these rates are expressed as percentages, they reveal that 8.4 percent of all African-American males age twenty-five to twenty-nine were in prison in 2004, compared to 2.5 percent of Hispanic males and 1.2 percent of white males in this age group. Although the absolute numbers are much smaller, the pattern for females is similar. The incarceration rate for African-American females was more than twice the rate for Hispanic females and four times the rate for white females.

Other statistics confirm that racial minorities face a disproportionately high risk of incarceration. In 2000, substantially more African Americans were under some form of correctional supervision (jail, prison, probation, and parole) than were enrolled in college. Among whites, the situation was just the opposite. In fact, there were more than twice as many whites in college as there were under correctional supervision (Walker, Spohn, and DeLone 2004, p. 297). There also are significant racial and ethnic differences in the lifetime likelihood of imprisonment. According to the Bureau of Justice Statistics (2003), an African-American boy born in 2001 faced a 32 percent chance of being imprisoned at some point in his life, compared to a 17 percent likelihood for a Hispanic boy and a 6 percent likelihood for a white boy.

The crimes for which racial minorities and whites are imprisoned also differ. Although the proportions held in state prisons in 2002 for violent offenses were similar, African Americans and Hispanics were much more likely than whites to be imprisoned for drug offenses. Twenty-seven percent of the Hispanics and 25 percent of the African Americans were imprisoned for drug offenses, compared to only 15 percent of the whites (Bureau of Justice Statistics 2005). Drug offenses also constituted a larger share of the growth in state prison inmates for racial minorities than for whites. From 1990 to 1998, increases in drug offenders accounted for 25 percent of the total growth among African-American inmates, 18 percent of the growth among Hispanic inmates, and 12 percent of the growth among white inmates (Bureau of Justice Statistics 2000).

As all of these statistics indicate, African Americans and Hispanics (particularly African-American and Hispanic males) are substantially more likely than whites to be locked up in U.S. prisons. These statistics suggest that state and federal judges sentence a disproportionately high number of racial minorities to prison, or that racial minorities are sentenced to serve longer terms than whites (or both). The question, of course, is why this occurs.

EXPLANATIONS FOR DISPROPORTIONATE IMPRISONMENT OF RACIAL MINORITIES

Researchers have used a variety of strategies to determine whether, and to what extent, the disparities in imprisonment reflect differential involvement in crime or differential treatment by the criminal justice system. The most frequently cited work compares the racial disparity in arrest rates for serious crimes to the racial disparity in incarceration rates for these crimes. According to Alfred Blumstein, a professor of public policy at Carnegie-Mellon University, if there is no discrimination following arrest, then "one would expect to find the racial distribution of prisoners who were sentenced for any particular crime type to be the same as the racial distribution of persons arrested for that crime" (1982, p. 1264). If, for example, 60 percent of those arrested for robbery are black and 60 percent of those incarcerated for robbery are black, one could conclude (assuming no bias in the decision to arrest or not) that the disproportionate number of blacks imprisoned for robbery reflected differential involvement in robbery by blacks.

To determine the overall portion of the racial disproportionality in prison populations that could be attributed to differential involvement in crime, Blumstein calculated the proportion of the prison population that, based on arrest rates, was expected to be black for twelve separate violent, property, and drug offenses. He then compared these expected rates to the actual rates of incarceration for blacks. Using 1979 data, he found that 80 percent of the racial disproportionality in incarceration rates could be attributed to racial differences in arrest rates. He reached a similar conclusion when he replicated the analysis using 1991 data, finding that 76 percent of the racial disproportionality in incarceration rates was accounted for by racial differences in arrest rates. Blumstein stresses that these results do not mean that racial discrimination does not exist. He notes that "there are too many anecdotal reports of such discrimination to dismiss that possibility." Rather, his findings imply that "the bulk of the racial disproportionality in prison is attributable to differential involvement in arrest, and probably in crime, in those most serious offenses that tend to lead to imprisonment" (1993, pp. 750–751).

THE IMPACT OF THE WAR ON DRUGS

Blumstein's conclusion that from 76 to 80 percent of the racial disproportionality in imprisonment can be explained by racial differences in arrest rates does not apply to each of the crimes he examined. There was a fairly close fit between the percentage of African Americans in prison and the percentage of African Americans arrested for homicide, robbery, and (to a lesser extent) burglary. For drug offenses, however, African Americans were overrepresented in prison by nearly 50 percent. This figure probably exaggerates the degree to which racial differences in imprisonment for drug offenses reflect racial differences in involvement in drug crimes. This is because arrests for drug offenses are not a particularly good proxy for offending. If, as critics suggest, police target African-American neighborhoods where drug dealing is more visible, and where it is therefore easier to make arrests, statistics on the race of those arrested for drug offenses will overestimate offending rates for African Americans. Coupled with the fact that drug offenders make up an increasingly large share of the prison population, this means that a declining proportion of the overall racial disparity in imprisonment can be explained by higher rates of arrests for African Americans.

SEE ALSO *Criminal Justice System; Hoaxing.*

BIBLIOGRAPHY

Blumstein, Alfred. 1982. "On the Racial Disproportionality of United States' Prison Populations." *Journal of Criminal Law and Criminology* 73: 1259–1281.

Bureau of Justice Statistics. 2003. *Prevalence of Imprisonment in the U.S. Population, 1974–2001.* Washington, DC: U.S. Department of Justice. Available from http://www.ojp.usdoj.gov/bjs/abstract/piusp01.htm.

———. 2005. *Prisoners in 2004.* Washington, DC: U.S. Department of Justice. Available from http://www.ojp.usdoj.gov/bjs/.

Mauer, Marc. 1999. *Race to Incarcerate.* New York: The New Press.

Miller, Jerome G. 1996. *Search and Destroy: African-American Males in the Criminal Justice System.* New York: Cambridge University Press.

Sampson, Robert J., and William Julius Wilson. 2005. "Toward a Theory of Race, Crime, and Urban Inequality." In *Race, Crime, and Justice,* edited by Shaun L. Gabbidon and Helen Taylor Greene. New York: Routledge.

Tonry, Michael. 1995. *Malign Neglect: Race, Crime, and Punishment in America.* New York: Oxford University Press.

United States Department of Commerce, Bureau of the Census. 1918. *Negro Population: 1790–1915.* Washington, DC: Government Printing Office.

Walker, Samuel, Cassia Spohn, and Miriam DeLone. 2004. *The Color of Justice: Race, Ethnicity, and Crime in America*, 3rd ed. Belmont, CA: Wadsworth/Thomson.

Cassia Spohn

CRITICAL RACE THEORY

Critical race theory (CRT) is a scholarly and politically committed movement that takes as its starting point the centrality of race in American history and social life. CRT scholars focus on contemporary economic and political arrangements as well as the historic distribution of public and private resources. CRT began as an attempt to identify the ways in which race had either been ignored or minimized in the study of law and legal institutions, and to point out the consequences of that ignorance.

Fundamental to the scholarly inquiries that animate CRT is the idea that race is a socially constructed category that is deeply implicated in the use and circulation of power in society. Thus its two principal objects of analysis are race and power. CRT represents a body of work created primarily, but not exclusively, by legal scholars of color. It has generated related inquiries in the social sciences and humanities, especially history, sociology, anthropology, and education. Because it takes reflective engagement as a fundamental feature of its methodology, CRT sees the knowledge generated by community-based practices as an essential source for the questions that scholars need to ask. Methodologically, this has produced a narrative form of scholarship that uses "storytelling" as a concrete expression of the commitment to reflective engagement. The importance of storytelling is located in its narrative methodology for construing reality, making sense of that reality, and then translating that meaning, through the use of stories to invoke the voices of an excluded community.

SCHOLARSHIP IN THE FIELD

Composing the canon of essential works in critical race theory is difficult because of the heterogeneous nature of the scholars working in the field. Nonetheless, several important early works stand out. Robert M. Cover, in *Justice Accused: Antislavery and the Judicial Process* (1975), A. Leon Higginbotham Jr., *In the Matter of Color: Race and The American Legal Process* (1978), Derrick Bell, in "Serving Two Masters" (1976), and Alan D. Freeman, in "Legitimizing Racial Discrimination through Antidiscrimination Law: A Critical Review of Supreme Court Doctrine" (1978), produced some of the works that presaged the blossoming of the CRT critique. Two things bind these works together and to the scholarship that has followed. The first is the shift in perspective that locates the scholarly inquiry as an effort to understand the impact of law from the viewpoint of the objects of the law. The second important link is an analysis that recognizes the contingent nature of many conventional legal assumptions. These early works challenge many of those things that are taken as given, raising questions about the political meaning and consequences of the doctrinal structure of the law. Finally, these early works, among others, began to sketch out the structural nature of racial exclusion. This is a focus that has continued to animate CRT scholarship.

These practical and intellectual commitments produced a critique of liberal pluralism (the theory that begins from the premise that politics is properly understood as the aggregation of individual preferences or interests) that grew out of the more general critique of liberal legalism. (Liberal legalism is premised on the idea that all fundamental social problems are capable of being understood and resolved by access to the courts through reliance on individual rights.) The critique of rights is most commonly associated with Professor Duncan Kennedy and the critical legal studies (CLS) movement that had its home at the Harvard Law School. Although CLS challenged the neutrality of legal principles, it failed to confront the interaction of race and law; nor did it acknowledge the symbolic power of legal rights to energize and sustain social movements, especially the civil rights movement of the mid-twentieth century. These gaps in the CLS scholarship helped crystallize the CRT critique.

In contrast to the dominant idea that racial discrimination is an individual problem and the product of bad people, CRT took the position that racism is both an individual problem in its concrete expression (that is, a problem for the object of racism) and a social problem in its generation. Whereas there may be individual ill will, the effects of racism embedded in American history can continue to produce racist effects with no individual ill will at all. This methodological stance led to an inquiry into the ways in which law and its institutions have continued to obscure rather than highlight the systemic effects of the system of racial management that characterized the civil rights jurisprudence in the early days of the civil rights movement (usually understood as the era of Martin Luther King Jr. culminating in the passage of the Civil Rights Act of 1964 and the Voting Rights Act of 1965). Once the cases involving southern systems of racial subordination worked their way through the courts and through legislation, the legal, economic, and political elite of the day assumed that most of the heavy lifting was over. Yet because the transformation of legally acceptable race-related conduct and institutional practices was crucial for the alteration of acceptable social behavior, the ideology of individual-rights-based liberal reform was insufficient.

Early CRT scholarship hailed the liberal commitment to rights, noting the inspirational power and civic significance of "civil rights" for those who struggled just to belong. But CRT soon saw the mainstream civil rights jurisprudence largely as a technique to manage racial unrest and to tame the goals and the practices of the civil rights movement. Especially threatening to legal liberals was the idea that group interests, and thus group conflict, were at stake. As CRT matured, its practitioners began to see law being used to take the politics out of the struggle for racial justice. By restricting the claims of subordinate groups to "interests," political engagement was limited to the expression of justice through the protection of group rights as outlined by the courts. But the legal system reduced rights claims to individual claims (sometime aggregated, but at root an individual grievance) predicated on the intentional bad deeds of identifiable individual people. The law demanded formal neutrality as to interests. One response, the cultural nationalism that emerged toward the end of the resurgent mass civil rights movement, was an attempt to construct an oppositional cultural foundation that would facilitate the assertion of claims by those whose interests were first given voice within the legal context of "civil rights."

CONTRIBUTIONS OF CRT

Building on these elements, critical race theorists focused on the role of law in changing the meaning of social action. This transformation was viewed as central to the project of material transformation and, perhaps more importantly, to the possibility of imagining the social innovation that would be necessary to finally confront the ways in which race continues to affect the way American social institutions function and how that stunts the life chances of people of color. The focus on both law and culture was in the service of understanding the ways that power was expressed in support of the existing distribution of social and material goods. Thus, while CRT was engaged in a thoroughgoing critique of legal doctrine, it was also engaged in a critique of the ways in which the ideology contained in that doctrine was expressed through social life.

Another important contribution was CRT's engagement with feminism. By adopting a consciousness-raising methodology and reflective practice from the feminist movement, CRT integrated storytelling into the process of understanding the community that drives the movement. This commitment to understanding the lived experience of communities of color meant that CRT imagined itself speaking to many audiences. The rootedness of the narrative methodology was not just an analytic technique but also an intellectual expression of a political commitment. Perhaps just as importantly it introduced a critique and sustained debate about the nature and content of essentialism (the idea that there are fixed and irreducible traits that define individual members of a social group) as a limiting factor in social analysis. While CRT had introduced a critique of essentialism in the attack on both nationalism and color blindness, the engagement with feminism was an important moment in the evolution of CRT scholarship and produced the idea of using strategic essentialism as a potentially politically expedient stance. Simultaneously, CRT scholars challenged the essentialism of a feminist discourse that uncritically assumed the category "women" was white and middle class. This critique led to the development within the law of intersectional analysis, an approach most closely associated with the work of Kimberlé Williams Crenshaw. Intersectional analysis is premised on the claim that forms of social oppression do not act independently of one another, but must be understood from the points at which they modify one another. The social effect of these compounded oppressions require a critical rethinking of any particular one. Intersectionality necessarily implies, for example, that sexism is modified and has different expressions depending upon the race, class position, or sexual orientation of the women or men to whom that analysis is applied.

CRT also launched a sustained critique of black/white dichotomy in the understanding of race in modern American life. By incorporating intersectional analysis in its engagement with feminism, CRT went further by suggesting that the crosscutting impact of race required a thick understanding of local expression of racial hierarchies. While the legal doctrine took as its cardinal example the experience of African Americans, Latino and Asian participants in CRT demonstrated the partiality of a black-dominated analysis. Yet, to confront the disaggregating of communities of color as a strategy for weakening the critique of racism, CRT reformulated the division not along a white/nonwhite axis, but along a black/nonblack axis in order to put the political nature of racial categories in stark relief and to suggest the oppositional nature of the CRT project.

The latest and perhaps most vital expression of the CRT project is found in the emergence of LatCrit (Latina/o critical theory). LatCrit is a self-conscious amalgam that has come to be called "outsider jurisprudence" or an outsider theory of law. LatCrit has taken the activist bent of CRT and created a space for critical legal studies, feminist legal theory, critical race theory, critical race feminism, Asian-American legal scholarship, and queer theory to engage with one another.

SEE ALSO *Color-Blind Racism; Everyday Racism; Institutional Racism; Orientalism; Racial Formations; Scientific Racism, History of.*

BIBLIOGRAPHY

Bell, Derrick. 1976. "Serving Two Masters: Integration Ideals and Client Interests in School Desegregation Litigation." *Yale Law Journal* 85 (4): 470–516.

———. 1987. *And We Are Not Saved: The Elusive Quest for Racial Justice.* New York: Basic.

———. 1992. *Faces at the Bottom of the Well: The Permanence of Racism.* New York: Basic.

———. 2004. *Race, Racism and American Law,* 5th ed. New York: Aspen Publishers.

———. 2004. *Silent Covenants: Brown* v. *Board of Education and the Unfulfilled Hopes for Racial Reform.* Oxford: Oxford University Press.

Cover, Robert M. 1975. *Justice Accused: Antislavery and the Judicial Process.* New Haven, CT: Yale University Press.

Crenshaw, Kimberlé Williams. 1988. "Race, Reform, and Retrenchment: Transformation and Legitimation in Antidiscrimination Law." *Harvard Law Review* 101 (7): 1,331–1,387.

———, Neil Gotanda, Gary Peller, and Kendall Thomas, eds. 1995. *Critical Race Theory: The Key Writings That Formed the Movement*. New York: New Press.

Delgado, Richard. 1989. "Storytelling for Oppositionists and Others: A Plea for Narrative." *Michigan Law Review* 87 (8): 2,411–2,441.

———, and Jean Stefancic, eds. 2000. *Critical Race Theory: The Cutting Edge*, 2nd ed. Philadelphia: Temple University Press.

Freeman, Alan D. 1978. "Legitimizing Racial Discrimination through Antidiscrimination Law: A Critical Review of Supreme Court Doctrine." *Minnesota Law Review* 62 (6): 1,049–1,119.

Gotanda, Neil. 1991. "A Critique of 'Our Constitution Is Color-Blind.'" *Stanford Law Review* 44 (1): 1–68.

Guinier, Lani. 1994. *The Tyranny of the Majority: Fundamental Fairness in Representative Democracy*. New York: Free Press.

———, and Gerald Torres. 2002. *The Miner's Canary: Enlisting Race, Resisting Power, Transforming Democracy*. Cambridge, MA: Harvard University Press.

Guinier, Lani, Michelle Fine, and Jane Balin. 1997. *Becoming Gentlemen: Women, Law School, and Institutional Change*. Boston: Beacon Press.

Higginbotham, A. Leon, Jr. 1978. *In the Matter of Color: Race and the American Legal Process*. New York: Oxford University Press.

Lawrence, Charles R., III. 1987. "The Id, the Ego, and Equal Protection: Reckoning with Unconscious Racism." *Stanford Law Review* 39 (2): 317–388.

Matsuda, Mari J. 1989. "When the First Quail Calls: Multiple Consciousness as Jurisprudential Method." *Women's Right Law Reporter* 11 (1): 7–10.

———, Charles R. Lawrence III, Richard Delgado, and Kimberlé Williams Crenshaw. 1993. *Words That Wound: Critical Race Theory, Assaultive Speech, and the First Amendment*. Boulder, CO: Westview Press.

Torres, Gerald, and Kathryn Milun. 1990. "Translating *Yonnondio* by Precedent and Evidence: The Mashpee Indian Case." *Duke Law Journal*, 1990 (4): 625–659.

Williams, Patricia J. 1991. *Alchemy of Race and Rights*. Cambridge, MA: Harvard University Press.

———. 1995. *The Rooster's Egg*. Cambridge, MA: Harvard University Press.

Gerald Torres

CUBAN RACIAL FORMATIONS

Racial formations in Cuba can be traced to the conquest of Cuba's original inhabitants, the Guanahatabetes, Ciboneys and Taino. The historian Juan Perez de la Riva estimates that after the first Spanish landing, the indigenous population declined from between 100,000 and 200,000 to only about 4,000. Further, the conquest of Cuba's indigenous population set the stage for Cuba's incorporation into the growing Atlantic slave economy.

CUBA'S INDIGENOUS POPULATION

Bartolomé de Las Casas (1484–1566), a Spanish Dominican friar, documented the atrocities committed against Cuba's indigenous peoples. He recorded the story of Hatuey, the best-known indigenous rebel-hero, who is now celebrated for his resistance and martyrdom at the hands of the Spanish, who eventually burned him at the stake. When indigenous people were subjected to servitude, many fled to the mountains or hung themselves in despair. According to Perez de la Riva, "after 1550, when the indigenous population had been reduced to some five or six thousand, *mestizaje* surely became the main cause of extinction of the indigenous 'race'" (Chomsky et al. 2003, p. 24). Thus, Perez de la Riva argues, *mestizaje*, or race mixing, rapidly absorbed Indo-Cubans into the white population.

The Cuban-born historian Jose Barreiro refutes the widely held notion put forth by Perez de la Riva and Cuba's best-known early twentieth-century intellectual, Fernando Ortiz, that Cuba's indigenous population was eliminated in the 1500s. Barreiro studied isolated eastern Cuban populations in the 1980s and 1990s, and he found an estimated 1,000 to 3,000 people who could be identified as indigenous. Hence, Barreiro argues that Indo-Cuban communities must be considered part of Cuba's hybrid nature of ethnicity. Even though Ortiz ignored the existence of the Indo-Cuban population and indigenous identity, he introduced the word *transculturation* to describe the diverse origins and nature of Cuba's population. Barreiro suggests that Ortiz's concept of transculturation be broadened by incorporating the Indo-Cuban population along with Cuba's European (primarily Spanish), African, and Asian communities.

SLAVERY IN CUBA

During the nineteenth century, Cuba's demography was transformed by the implementation of a slave economy. The production of sugar shaped African slavery in Cuba. The Cuban historian Hortensia Pichardo notes that whites were a minority between 1841 and 1861 (1973, p. 367). By 1869 the Cuban population had grown to 763,176 whites, 238,297 free people of color, 34,420 Asians, and 363,286 African slaves. There are a few significant accounts that document the resistance deployed by African peoples subjected to slavery. According to Louis Pérez Jr., slave uprisings occurred throughout the early colonial period. The large-scale plantation revolts that took place from 1825 to 1845 in the province of Matanzas were so frequent that

Spanish authorities referred to them as "La Escalera" ("the escalation," or "the ladder to revolt"). Government officials responded by arresting, torturing, and executing thousands of slaves and free people of color.

A notable document, published in 1964, is Miguel Barnet's oral history of Esteban Montejo (1860–1973), who escaped plantation life and survived alone in the mountains of Cuba until the end of the nineteenth century. He was among a number of slaves who escaped on their own and survived in nearby caves and mountains. Others, along with indigenous peoples, formed runaway-slave communities called *palenques* in areas outside of Spanish control. According to Aviva Chomsky and colleagues, "For over three hundred years, the *palenque* was a form of resistance to the slave economy and European culture. Africans of different ethnicities, cultures, and languages joined together under the ideal of freedom" (Chomsky et al. 2003, p. 65).

Prior to the late nineteenth century, the sugar plantation system was based mainly in western Cuba. The eastern part of the island had a smaller, but much more heterogeneous population that consisted of free Mulattoes and free blacks, primarily from war-torn Haiti. The expansion of the sugar economy and slave labor into eastern Cuba, along with black migrants from other parts of Cuba and the Caribbean, contributed to a stronger Afro-Caribbean identity than existed in western sectors of the island. Many slaves who worked in urban settings and escaped did not flee to *palenques,* but instead passed as free persons inside the city. Those who escaped were urban slaves who had carried out tasks in the city. This explains why they remained in the city, for they were familiar with it, while the countryside was an environment completely foreign to them.

Caribbean sugar planters sought new sources of cheap labor after the demise of African slavery. It is estimated that between 60 and 200 Chinese indentured laborers were brought to Cuba during the mid-nineteenth century. Perez de la Riva cites harsh conditions that led to a suicide rate of about 500 per 100,000 among Chinese "coolies." In general, Chinese laborers were granted freedom after eight years of working for the extremely low salary of 4 pesos per month. Given that the trade in Chinese laborers was not regulated, it is highly possible that many lived their lives in servitude, or what Evelyn Hu-Dehart calls "neoslavery," because "the coolie system resembled plantation slavery" (1994, p. 48).

Hu-Dehart also notes that the inclusion of Chinese people into Cuban slave society disrupted the Creole ideological code of dividing society into black and white, or slave and free. During the coolie period, official censuses considered free Chinese to be white, thus distinguishing them from both free blacks and black slaves. In some cases, when Chinese married free Cuban women, they were registered as white in the matrimonial registry. Regarding the Chinese population as white perpetuated racial hierarchies in which Afro-Cubans were considered inferior to Chinese.

STRUGGLE FOR INDEPENDENCE

The Ten Years' War, a separatist uprising led by Cuban-born Creole elite of eastern Cuba, lasted from 1868 to 1878. The leaders of this uprising, including Carlos Manuel de Cespedes, were considered reformist rather than revolutionary, though they sought an end to slavery and Spanish colonial rule. Cuba's elite, however, chose Spanish colonial rule over social equality, thus prolonging Afro-Cuban slavery. The American historian Philip Foner has argued that racism contributed to the failure of the Ten Years' War to bring independence to Cuba and end slavery. However, "The Cry of Yara" eventually led to the demise of slavery in the late 1880s and made "pro-independence the dominant political ideology" (Brock 1994, p. 17).

In 1895, Cuban nationalists defined a "nation" as a society where black and whites had to live together in order to avoid replicating the independence struggles in Haiti and the United States. Jose Marti (1853–1895) is recognized for defining Cuba's nationalism by acknowledging and celebrating the country's multicultural heritage. Considered the "father of the Cuban nation," he wrote ideologies of an antiracist and anti-imperialist nationalism while exiled in the United States. Marti's essay "Our America," published in 1891, became one of the most influential documents for Latin American intellectuals and popular movements, helping to create an identity recognized for its differences from that of Europe and the United States.

During this time period, growing U.S. involvement and investment in Cuba's sugar industry impacted Cuba's conceptualizations of and struggles for independence. The Spanish-American War (1898) may have freed Cuba from Spanish colonial rule, but Cuba became a U.S. colony in 1898 rather than an independent nation. Cultural images of Cuba constructed by U.S. media sources reveal the imperialist pretensions of the United States following the defeat of Spain in 1898. According to John J. Johnson, "Cubans were portrayed as black caricatures of infants, carefree children, or rowdy, undisciplined youths, requiring constant guidance from the United States" (quoted in Chomsky, et al., 2003, p. 135). The struggle for Afro-Cuban equality and self-determination could not be successfully waged under the auspices of U.S. imperialism.

THE REPUBLIC OF CUBA

On May 20, 1902, the Republic of Cuba was inaugurated under the presidency of Tomás Estrada Palma. However, Cuba's independence was unstable due to a series of U.S. military and political interventions and occupations from 1902 to 1934, economic dependency on the United States, and treaties such as the Reciprocity Treaty, which was signed in 1903 and constrained economic initiatives by consolidating Cuba's sugar monoculture. In addition, the Platt Amendment, which was appended by the U.S. Congress to appropriations bill in 1901, painted Cuba as a fragile state and served as a constant reminder of U.S. self-declared authority to play a role in Cuban affairs. Article 7 of the Platt Amendment allowed for the establishment of a U.S. naval base at Guantanamo Bay. (In the early twenty-first century, this base remains in place as a reminder of Cuba's neocolonial past.) Such political agreements between the United States and the Cuban elite only ensured privilege, wealth, and social inequalities.

The Cuban nationalist motto of "With All and for the Good of All" did not resolve the problems of national independence and racial inequality. Afro- and Euro-Cubans held very different interpretations of Marti's antiracism, particularly of his association of Cuban nationalism with the eradication of racial discrimination. Euro-Cuban and Afro-Cuban elites considered race-based organizing a threat to national security, while the *El Partido Independiente de Color* (PIC, the Independent Party of Color), founded in 1908 by Evaristo Estenoz, associated racism with colonialism and insisted on the association of independence with racial equality. In 1912 government troops and white militias massacred the PIC leadership, including thousands of Afro-Cubans. The massacre was ordered by President José Miguel Gómez and led by José de Jesus Monteagudo.

Anti-imperialist agendas grew throughout Latin America as a response to U.S. interventions in Central America and the Caribbean during the 1910s. During the 1920s Cuban intellectuals such as Julio Antonio Mella developed a critique of the country's social and economic conditions that focused on an anti-U.S. imperialist ideology. This ideology was strongly associated with the emergence of *Afrocubanismo*, a movement among white Cuban intellectuals who "discovered" Afro-Cuban culture and developed an analysis that placed this culture at the center of Cuban identity.

CUBAN FEMINISM

The decade of the 1930s was marked by the first wave of feminism, a reformist movement of resistance. The goals and ideology of the Cuban feminist movement were shaped by Cuban culture, history, and the class position of the women who led the movement. Cuban feminists based their claim to political and social rights on their roles as mothers. According to K. Lynn Stoner, they advocated that "a feminism centered on motherhood, cooperative with patriarchy, and respectful of class ordering" could humanize traditional male spheres (Stoner 1991, p. 183). As a means of differentiating Cuban feminism from U.S. feminism, the socialist-feminist activist Ofelia Dominguez Navarro stressed that Cuban feminists emphasized their patriotism and commitment to complementary, rather than equal, roles for women and men.

As elite white Cuban women dedicated themselves to social change, many Afro-Cuban women were employed as domestics, others were unemployed, and a substantial number were prostitutes. Much of Havana's prostitution surged with the inception of North American tourism and an investment in real estate during the 1920s. Cuban propaganda portrayed Havana as the "Paris of the Western Hemisphere." Following World War II, Cuba was promoted as a strange, exotic, tropical island filled with African-inspired rhythms and sexually uninhibited "mulattas." Havana's reputation as the "brothel of the Caribbean" attracted foreign tourists as well as Cubans, and tens of thousands of women were employed as prostitutes. Thus, Afro-Cuban women's sexuality was commodified and racialized, transforming the tourist industry and contributing to an essentialized identity based on sexual and racial stereotypes.

THE REVOLUTION

Resistance to neocolonialism imposed its strongest stance in 1953 under the leadership of a young student named Fidel Castro. In 1952 General Fulgencio Batista had staged a coup and became the country's president. Opposed to this regime, Castro led a daring, but unsuccessful, assault on the Moncada Barracks of the Cuban Army in Santiago de Cuba on July 26, 1953. The cadres of the 26th of July Movement eventually undermined the Batista regime by practicing armed resistance, engaging in sabotage in the urban centers, and distributing propaganda. In the Sierra Maestra, guerrilla-controlled zones were established with the help of country people and sugar workers in northern Oriente Province. Women such as Vilma Espine, Celia Sanchez, and Haydee Santa Maria were prominent revolutionary participants. In the early morning of January 1, 1959, Batista fled Cuba for exile in the Dominican Republic. Rebel forces led by Che Guevarra and Camilo Cienfuegos occupied Havana, while Fidel Castro led a victory march from Santiago to Havana.

The Cuban Revolution of 1959 was committed to a new anti-imperialist, antiracist ideology that grew throughout a newly defined Latin America. Cuba's growing economic reliance on the Soviet Union through the late 1960s and

1970s shaped the path of the revolution politically and socially, thus solidifying the revolution while limiting its possibilities. Culturally the Soviet Union had little impact on Cuba, as U.S. culture attracted Cubans of all ages. Ernesto "Che" Guevara remains a very important revolutionary leader, martyr, and myth in Cuba. Guevara emphasized promoting economic change via the radicalization of peoples' consciousness. His idea of "the new man," however, glorified traditional male values, thus failing to engage critical analyses of patriarchy, including sexuality and gender roles. Hence, previous dialogues in associating the eradication of racism with nationalism were subsumed under the newly defined Marxist-Socialist state. The plight of Cuba's citizens was couched in a socialist ideology, which regarded them primarily as workers without critically engaging the complexities of their lives, particularly the way the nation was divided by race, class, gender, and sexuality.

According to Louis Pérez Jr., "The subject of race in twentieth century Cuba is an elusive theme. . . . Therefore, the psychic, psychological, and cultural baggage that has historically accompanied institutional racism was never challenged. Race became the classic 'non-topic' in Cuban scholarship" (Pérez 1992, p. 59). Others, such as Alejandro de la Fuente, suggests there are at least three conceptual issues that make race and racism a complicated debate in contemporary Cuba. First, Fuente argues, issues of race and racism are highly politicized. Supporters of the revolution argue that there has been improvement in the area of race relations, whereas opponents highlight examples of racism and racial inequality. Second, race and racism must be understood within the Cuban context, rather than applying categories and ideas from a U.S. perspective. Third, structural, ideological, and cultural changes are not always complementary.

One of the most widely published critiques of race relations is Carlos Moore's *Castro, the Blacks, and Africa* (1988). Moore claims that Castro's public discourse on race relations has focused on two features: "a commitment to an integrationist stance steeped in white liberal paternalism and a system where Blacks are not allowed to define the content of their own oppression or ethnic emancipation" (Moore 1988, pp.15–16). Lisa Brock and Otis Cunningham criticize Moore, however, for using a "narrow racialisation framework," thus ignoring how class, nation, and international political economy shape the lives of Afro-Cubans (Brock and Cunningham 1991, p. 171). Brock further argues in a 1994 article that the issue of race has been overlooked due to three notable achievements associated with the triumph of the Cuban Revolution: (1) the overall quality of life for blacks was drastically improved, (2) Cubans openly admitted and appreciated their African heritage, and (3) the Cuban government supported African liberation movements.

The Cuban Revolution has been extraordinarily successful in eliminating the legal mechanisms that upheld racial discrimination by implementing comprehensive health care, free and universal education, social security, and subsidized housing. Even though Afro-Cubans benefited greatly from the economic and social policies adopted after 1959, the persistence of a racist mentality toward Afro-Cubans in cultural and social realms remained a challenge. The Cuban scholar Gisela Arandia Covarrubias has suggested that Cubans develop national unity by investigating the contributions of Afro-Cubans to revolutionary culture and identity, and that they move toward demystifying the "colonial residue of racist sensibilities" rather than transcending or ignoring critical discourse on race and racism (quoted in James 1994, p. 5).

The Soviet Union's intention of installing missiles in Cuba, combined with U.S. concerns about a newly defined socialist country just ninety miles from its borders, led President John F. Kennedy to impose a U.S. blockade and embargo of the island in October 1962. During the Cuban Missile Crisis the blockade consisted of a number of provisions, which have the following prohibitions: 1) exportation of all U.S. goods to Cuba, including medicines and foodstuffs; 2) importation of any Cuban goods into the United States, including food and medicines; 3) all other types of commercial activity between the two countries; 4) importation of third country products that contain Cuban materials; 5) restrictions on travel to Cuba for U.S. citizens except for official, journalistic, special professional or family purposes; 6) a restriction on third country ships visiting Cuba from docking in U.S. ports; and 7) a restriction on open trade between Cuba and U.S. subsidiaries. The embargo still holds to the seven restrictions. However, in October 2000, the U.S. Congress voted to allow direct food and medicine sales to Cuba, using third-country banks to finance the transactions. In addition, the U.S. Senate is discussing a Freedom to Travel bill calling to remove all restrictions for all Americans traveling Cuba.

The U.S. embargo toward Cuba is regarded as a blockade by many Cubans, who feel that their lives are being constantly threatened by U.S. attempts to derail the Cuban Revolution. As of 2000, the U.S. government had invested $70 billion (including the estimated loss of monetary profit by direct trade) to enforce the embargo. Despite the overall harsh and inhumane impact of these measures on the Cuban people, the extent to which this policy has been sensible or constructive is still being debated in Washington, D.C.

In 1989 the Cuban Revolution was seriously jeopardized by the demise of the Soviet Union. In particular, Cuba lost nearly 80 percent of its import capacity from the Soviet bloc. Cuba responded to the crisis by declaring a "Special Period in Time of Peace." This was, in essence, a wartime economy, and it involved a considerable rationing of daily survival necessities. The government also responded by investing in tourism for foreigners. This investment was financed by American dollars, however, because the Cuban government needed dollars to participate in the global, capitalist economy. The tourism industry established "dollar stores" for the convenience of foreigners, and restaurants, transportation, and cultural sites were only available to foreigners, for Cubans did not have access to the currency that would allow them to participate in the newly defined tourist industry. Thus, a form of "tourist apartheid" developed, marked by a two-tiered economy: Tourism was operated with dollars, whereas Cuban citizens were dependent on the peso for their daily survival in a society with very scarce resources but an abundance of material goods for foreigners or those who had access to dollars. In the mid-1990s, those who had relatives in Miami were allowed $1,200 per year in remittances. Thus, race relations were affected by remittance dollars from the United States, as the majority of those receiving money were white Cubans, creating a new privileged group in Cuba. Those who had little or no access to dollars sought ways to work in the tourist industry, mainly at hotels, restaurants, and nightclubs or as taxi drivers. Drawing from the work of McGarrity and Cardenas (1995), Lusane notes, "black Cubans appear to be excluded to a great degree from the tourist industry where access to foreign currency is critical for survival" (2000, p. 95). Consequently, many black Cubans are excluded from the lucrative tips in foreign currencies. Hence, many Afro-Cuban women, and eventually both white and Afro-Cuban men, engaged in sex work. Afro-Cuban women's sexuality and racial-ethnic identity were once again colonized and commodified within the tourist industry, providing a stark mirror of pre-revolutionary Cuba.

The contradictions and complexities of the revolution's stance on racism became most transparent during the special period with the inception of capitalist oriented enterprises, namely tourism. In order to better understand racism and race relations in contemporary Cuba, the revolution's general policy on racism merits attention. The revolutionary discourse on racism argues that with the possible exception of individual racial prejudice, evident primarily among the elderly population, Cuban socialism eliminated the material basis for the reproduction of racism and that racism was eliminated within the first post-revolution generation (Lusane 2000). The Cuban Revolution eradicated institutional racism, but racial prejudice and individual discrimination continue to occur. On the flip side of Cuba's policy in eliminating institutional racism, any expressed racial group consciousness, from black as well as white Cubans, is considered racist, a counter-revolutionary act, therefore no specific program of racial affirmative action similar to the programs and efforts to integrate women, youth, and the rural population into the new society was implemented (Lusane 2000).

In general, the Cuban people do not self-identify as either "black" or "white" Cubans, but identify in a nationalist context as "Cuban." It is not uncommon, however, for the term "black Cuban" to be used as a descriptive by all Cubans. In recent years, among a small but increasingly race-conscious cohort of primarily exiled black Cubans, the term "Afro-Cuban" has (re)emerged. The development of a self-classification from black Cuban to Afro-Cuban indicates race consciousness. As noted earlier, race consciousness has generally been considered counter-revolutionary. If the revolution maintains a myopic view of race, there is a great potential that it could become so.

Assessing the nature and contours of race relation in Cuba is further complicated by the challenge of identifying who belongs in what racial category and the government conscious decision not to gather racially-oriented data. Consequently, it is difficult to gauge racial inequality by social indicators such as occupation, age, gender, etc. Economic inequalities that have a disproportionate racial consequences are likely to remain static or even become worse during the special period. It appears that the special period will continue for some time. The United States shows little promise of softening its position of antagonism toward Cuba and the global economy is atrocious. No doubt Cuba's current and future economic transformations will impact race relations. How the Cuban government will respond depends on how strongly the Cuban leadership maintains that racism has been eliminated in Cuba.

Despite continuing U.S. efforts to "democratize" Cuba or penetrate neo-imperialism into a country of color that has survived nearly fifty years of economic and psychological warfare (not to mention the changing economic world order of global capitalism), Cuba has reinvented itself under severe economic and political conditions. In general, the quality of life for all Cubans has improved since the mid-1990s, and the most notable achievements of the revolution, free health care and universal education, have not been compromised. It would be unrealistic to state that Cuba does not continue to struggle with limited resources in food, transportation, medical and educational supplies, and housing. Additionally, the issue of sex workers, primarily among Afro-Cuban women and a growing number of men, calls for critical analyses of international and national discourses on gender, sexuality, racism and patriarchy. Furthermore, Fidel Castro was forced to step down in July 2006 after intestinal surgery leaving the island's fate in the hands of his brother Raul Castro, who has kept Cuba's Communist system intact, avoiding the collapse many Castro detractors have predicted for decades. Raul Castro tends to embrace limited free enterprise and has expressed interest in China's model of capitalist reform with one-party political control. Cuba's revolutionary history is still being written, however, as Cubans continue to compassionately debate and mold their future.

SEE ALSO *Caribbean Racial Formations; Children, Racial Disparities and Status of; HIV and AIDS; Latin American Racial Transformations; Poverty; Racial Formations; Social Welfare States.*

BIBLIOGRAPHY

Barriero, Jose. 2003. "Survival Stories." In *The Cuba Reader*, edited by Aviva Chomsky, Barry Carr, and Pamela Maria Smorkaloff. Durham, NC: Duke University Press.

Brock, Lisa. 1994. "Back to the Future: African-Americans and Cuba in the Time(s) of Race." *Journal of African and Afro-American Studies* 12: 9–32.

———, and Otis Cunningham. 1991. "Race and the Cuban Revolution: A Critique of Carlos Moore's 'Castro, the Blacks, and Africa.'" *Cuban Studies* 21. Available from http://afrocubaweb.com/brock2.htm.

Chomsky, Aviva, Barry Carr, and Pamela M. Smorkaloff, eds. 2003. *The Cuba Reader*. Durham, NC: Duke University Press.

Covarrubias, Gisela Arandia. 1994. "Strengthening Nationality: Blacks in Cuba." *Journal of African and Afro-American Studies* 12: 62–69.

De la Fuente, Alejandro. 1995. "Race and Inequality in Cuba, 1899–1981." *Journal of Contemporary History* 30: 135.

Foner, Philip. 1962. *A History of Cuba and Its Relations with the United States*. New York: International Publishers, 214-228.

Hu-DeHart, Evelyn. 1994. "Chinese Coolie Labor in China in the Nineteenth Century: Free Labor or Neoslavery?" *Journal of African and Afro-American Studies* 12: 38–61.

James, Joy. 1994. "Introduction: Expanding North American and Cuban Dialogues." *Journal of African and Afro-American Studies* 12: 4–7.

Lusane, Clarence. 2000. "From Black Cuba to Afro-Cuban: Issues and Problems Researching Race Consciousness and Identity in Cuban Race Relations." In *Cuban Transitions at the Millennium*, edited by Eloise Linger and John Cotman, 85–101. Largo, MD: International Development Options.

McGarrity, Gayle, and Osvaldo Cardenas. 1995. "Cuba." In *No Longer Invisible: Afro-Latin Americans Today*, edited by Minority Rights Groups. London: Minority Rights Publications.

Moore, Carlos. 1988. *Castro, the Blacks, and Africa*. Los Angeles: Center for Afro-American Studies, University of California.

Pichardo, Hortensia. 1973. *Documentos para la historia de Cuba*, 4 Vols. Havana: Editorial de Ciencias Sociales, 1973. Vol. 4, p. 367, cited from Carlos de Sedano y Cruzart, "Cuba Desde 1850 a 1873," 152–153.

Perez de la Riva, Juan. 2003. "A World Destroyed." In *The Cuba Reader*, edited by Aviva Chomsky, Barry Carr, and Pamela M. Smorkaloff. Durham, NC: Duke University Press.

Pérez, Louis, Jr. 1992. "History, Historiography, and Cuban Studies: Thirty Years Later." In *Cuban Studies Since the Revolution,* edited by Damián J. Fernández. Gainesville: University Press of Florida.

Stoner, K. Lynn. 1991. *From the House to the Streets: The Cuban Women's Movement for Legal Reform, 1989–1940*. Durham, NC: Duke University Press.

Elisa Facio

CUFFE, PAUL

1759–1817

Paul Cuffe was a humanitarian, civil rights advocate, Quaker, businessman, sailor, merchant, and colonizer. He was born on the Massachusetts island of Chuttyhunk in 1759, the son of Cuffe Slocum, a former slave of Asante heritage, and a Native American named Ruth Moses. Refusing to use the name of his father's former owner, a "Mr. Slocum," young Paul chose the first name of his father as his own surname. *Cuffe* was the English version of the Asante word *kofi,* meaning "born on Friday." The family moved to Westport, Massachusetts, where young Cuffe grew up, and in 1773, at the age of fourteen, he went to sea as a whaler. He was bright and energetic, and the earnings from his maritime merchant activities enabled him to marry Alice Pequitis, a Native American. The couple would have seven children.

In 1797, Cuffe decided to purchase farmland near Westport. The price tag of the farmland was about $3,500.00, a rather large sum in those days. Taxes on this property would lead to his active concern about the citizenship status of Massachusetts' free blacks. Cuffe's material status and his interest in the education of his children led him to urge the people of Westport to build a school for the children of the town. He presented his case at a town meeting, but the predominately white group opposed Cuffe's suggestion for several reasons. While some opposed the idea because they believed that their informal school was more efficient than the suggested one, others opposed it because of its potential expense. Still others disliked Cuffe's proposal because it was initiated by a member of a race that they consciously or unconsciously viewed as inferior to their own. Finally, Westport's whites opposed the proposal because they did not want an integrated school in the town.

After his suggestion was rejected, Cuffe used his own money to build a school on his newly acquired farmland. He asked Westport's whites to attend his school, with a teacher paid by him, a request that was well received. This school, built in 1797, would continue to serve as a school for all of Westport's children for many years before it was taken over by public officials of the town.

Despite his generosity and upright personal conduct, Cuffe—along with other blacks in Westport and other Massachusetts towns—was continually discriminated against. For example, although he was a man of significant material status and paid his required property taxes, Cuffe was not allowed to vote or hold public office. Indeed, because of their race, no blacks in Massachusetts were allowed these privileges. Against this backdrop, Cuffe and his brother John Slocum, together with other blacks, decided to send a petition to the General Court of Massachusetts, appealing to that body to spare them from paying property taxes and poll dues. The petition was dismissed. As a protest of the dismissal of the petition, Cuffe and his brother chose not to pay their taxes for the years 1778, 1779, and 1780. This action would lead to their arrest and imprisonment in the jail in Taunton, Massachusetts.

Even though they were later freed, Cuffe continued to fight for the civil rights of blacks. This was reinforced reciprocally by the rise of racism in America, on one hand, and his desire to promote commerce, Western civilization, and Christianity in Africa on the other. Like other African Americans, such as Lott Carey, Daniel Coker, Joseph Jenkins Roberts, and John Brown Russwurm, Cuffe supported colonization. The American Colonization Society, which was founded a year prior to Cuffe's death, promoted Christianity, Western civilization, and commerce through the Liberian colony that the group established on the West African coast in 1822 as a refuge for free American blacks, including former slaves. Cuffe had previously established links, for similar reasons, with Sierra Leone, a colony that had been established by British humanitarians and businessmen in 1787 for their poor blacks and the blacks who sided with the British against the Americans during the American Revolutionary War.

Cuffe's commercial venture in Sierra Leone, unlike his commercial links with Europe and the West Indies, was not solely determined by his material wants; it was also influenced by his desire to promote Western civilization in Africa. He and other Westernized blacks believed that this would help to redeem the continent from its backwardness. Just before his voyage to Sierra Leone on his own vessel, *Traveler*, on January 2, 1811, Cuffe maintained that among the goals of his trip was to explore the possibility of having some black Americans of high moral and religious standards settle among the indigenous Africans in Sierra Leone, where they could promote Western values. These values would, in turn, help to spiritually and socially liberate Africa.

Cuffe's second trip to Sierra Leone, which had been delayed by the War of 1812, began in December 1815, when he and some thirty-eight other black Americans sailed from Boston on board the *Traveler* for West Africa. Also on the vessel were trade items such as tobacco, soap, candles, flour, and iron.

Although they were welcomed unenthusiastically by British colonial officials—obviously because of racism and what they perceived as Cuffe's potential threat to their leadership—the thirty-eight expatriates were allowed to stay in the colony to promote the civilization Cuffe envisioned.

Cuffe's interest in Sierra Leone was reinforced after he returned to America in April 1816. The insults he experienced from whites during his trip from Washington, D.C. to Baltimore played a decisive role in this. That he was refused service in a café in Baltimore because he was black only strengthened his beliefs and goals. He concluded that America was too racist to treat blacks as full Americans. He therefore became a strong advocate of the colonization of black Americans in West Africa just before his death on September 7, 1817.

SEE ALSO *American Colonization Society and the Founding of Liberia; Garvey, Marcus.*

BIBLIOGRAPHY

Beyan, Amos J. 2005. *African American Settlements in West Africa: John Brown Russwurm and the American Civilizing Efforts.* New York: Palgrave Macmillan.

Foner, Philip, S. 1975. *History of Black Americans: From Africa to the Emergence of the Cotton Kingdom.* Westport, CT: Greenwood Press.

Harris, Sheldon, H. 1972. *Paul Cuffe: Black America and the African Return.* New York: Simon & Schuster.

Horton, James O., and Lois E. Horton. 1997. *In Hope of Liberty: Culture, Community, and Protest among Northern Free Blacks, 1700–1860.* New York: Oxford University Press.

Miller, Floyd J. 1975. *The Search for a Black Nationality: Black Emigration and Colonization, 1787–1863.* Urbana: Illinois University Press.

Quarles, Benjamin. 1964. *The Negro in the Making of America.* New York: Collier.

Ruchames, Louis, ed. 1969. *Racial Thought in America: A Documentary History*, Vol. 1: *From the Puritans to Abraham Lincoln.* Amherst: University of Massachusetts Press.

Amos J. Beyan

CULTURAL DEFICIENCY

Cultural deficiency refers to a theoretical argument that the cultural attributes or practices often associated with historically disenfranchised racial/ethnic groups (specifically, blacks and Latinos) have prevented them from assimilating and attaining social mobility within U.S. society. Examples of cultural deficiencies include limited outlooks and attitudes toward the future, a failure to internalize the work ethic, instant gratification behavior, a lack of parent involvement in schools, low intellectual abilities, an emphasis on masculinity and honor, and an aversion to honest work. Other so-called deficiencies, as identified by Stanley Eitzen and Maxine Baca Zinn (2006), may include early initiation to sex among children, female-headed households, a fatalistic attitude toward life, and a limited interest in education. The cultural deficiency argument also posits a causal linkage between certain cultural attributes and upward socioeconomic mobility. It identifies the attributes of economically and socially successful middle-class whites as the mechanisms that enable success (e.g., emphasis on achievement, education, and independence) vis-à-vis legal or institutional structures and social ideologies.

The manner in which cultural characteristics operate forms another significant component of cultural deficiency. Culturally deficient groups are viewed as developing certain cultural qualities so as to adapt to poverty, particularly over time. Such characteristics are passed on from one generation to another, making it difficult for individuals to escape poverty. Thus the identified deficiencies have a cyclical impact; moreover, even with the elimination of many legal barriers to social mobility, these qualities are seen as having created new impediments.

Cultural deficiency has been used since the mid-1900s in academic discourse and in various fields, at times referred to as the "culture of poverty" or "culture of deprivation." Some sociologists have applied the discourse of cultural deficiency to analyses of limited social mobility. Education specialists have used cultural deficiency arguments to explain why differences in academic performance exist and persist among racial/ethnic minority groups. The following is an overview of the operation of cultural deficiency within the discourse of race and ethnicity and that of education.

CULTURAL DEFICIENCY AND RACE/ETHNICITY

The term emerged during the 1930s and gained currency over the next three decades among sociologists who proposed that pre-1930s arguments of race as a biological construct were theoretically limited. Instead, sociologists argued that ethnicity was the prevailing construct of groups, their development, and their persistence. Within this ethnicity discourse, cultural deficiency emerged as an explanation for the differences in the ways blacks and Latinos on the one hand and European immigrants on the other became incorporated into U.S. society.

Much of the research on race during the early 1900s argued that certain attributes, such as attitudes, intelligence, and sexual prowess, were racial characteristics—that is, a construct of biology. During the 1920s, sociologists from the Chicago school of economics challenged this assertion by presenting race as a social category of ethnicity: Ethnicity was a construct of culture, rather than biology, with *culture* understood to represent language, religion, nationality, and other customs of groups. The ethnicity discourse presented group features as involving varying attributes, with race a subset of ethnicity. However, this discourse developed different strands of research: Those following the effects of *assimilation* and *cultural pluralism* asked certain questions about what happens to culture over time. For example, do certain ethnic groups maintain their ethnicity, and if so, what are the factors supporting maintenance? If not, what are the factors preventing maintenance? Although the assimilation and cultural pluralism arguments offered differing explanations of what happens to ethnic groups over time, they both posited that an "Anglo-conformity" majority culture exists within U.S. society.

Assimilation theorists argued that European immigrants, blacks, and Latinos undergo a natural, evolutionary process in which, over time, they adopt the dominant cultural patterns of white Americans. In 1971 Nathan Glazer predicted that, although ethnic minorities, such as blacks, have endured centuries of legalized discrimination and oppression, their migration to the north and experience with wealth and employment opportunity would result, in due time, in their integration into and adoption of dominant cultural patterns. Milton Gordon in 1961 elaborated on this notion of assimilation by arguing that there are two forms of assimilation, behavioral and structural. Behavioral assimilation refers to "absorption of the cultural behavior patterns of the 'host' society" (Gordon 1961, p. 279). Later scholars called this process acculturation. Structural assimilation is defined as the "entrance of the immigrants and their descendants into the social cliques, organizations, institutional activities, and general civic life of the receiving society" (Gordon 1961, p. 279). Such assimilation, Gordon argues, prevents the continued salience of an ethnic identification to an immigrant group and the acceptance of an American identity and value system. The lack of incorporation of blacks and Latinos into American society, however, posed a challenge to the applicability of this model, which was based on the experiences of European immigrants. Gunnar Myrdal's 1944 study, which distilled the elements of American society that black Americans were not experiencing, argued that "pathological" elements of black culture were preventing blacks from following the linear path outlined in the assimilation model. These pathological elements, or cultural deficiencies, represent the values or norms of groups, specifically blacks and Latinos. The 1965 Moynihan Report, a famous study by Sen. Daniel Patrick Moynihan of New York, argued that the main causes of poverty in the black community were female-headed households, low marriage and high divorce rates, and a lack of goal orientation and emphasis on education.

Cultural pluralists, on the other hand, argued that assimilation is not an inevitable or necessarily desirable process; groups can maintain remnants of their racial/ethnic identity while supporting a white or American identity. Cultural pluralism emphasized the significance of groups' maintaining their cultural heritage or identity—whether European immigrant groups, blacks, Mexicans, or Puerto Ricans—while simultaneously assimilating into U.S. society. However, this discourse of identity continued to link cultural deficiencies with the minimizing of mobility. Andrew Greeley (1974) cited third- and fourth-generation European immigrants who had intermarried but maintained an ethnic identification with their original immigrant group. Stanley Lieberson (1963) observed that the persistence of cultural heritage was mainly observed in European immigrants from the second migration wave (post–1865 to 1924), who experienced economic and social conditions different from those experienced by the first wave of European immigrants (the initial immigrants from Europe). Lieberson concluded that the behaviors of later generations of the second wave (e.g., maintenance of a hyphenated American identity, barter systems, civic community) were attributable to the economic and social conditions they faced early in their adaptation process. Their maintenance of cultural identity did not limit their social mobility, whereas the opposite was true of blacks and Latinos. Thus for these minority groups identity as a remnant of ethnicity became a culturally deficient attribute: The persistent use of a non-American identity was not in keeping with American social norms, which include uniformity in cultural affiliation.

CULTURAL DEFICIENCY AND EDUCATION

In the field of education, cultural deficiency was used to explain the differences among racial or ethnic groups in academic achievement. Before the 1960s, it was also used as a justification for separate schools. For example, as Carlos Blanton notes in a 2003 article, from the 1920s to 1940s Mexican-American students were tested for intellectual abilities as a basis for separate classrooms. Many theorists employing the cultural deficiency argument maintained that the low academic performance of Latinos was a consequence of their deficient cultural practices. In this view, familial and community practices suppress the development of low-income, minority children in terms of the linguistic, cognitive, and affective skills necessary for successful school functioning. For example, in 1966 Celia Heller asserted that Mexican-American upbringing "creates stumbling blocks to future advancement by stressing values that hinder mobility—family ties, honor, masculinity, and living in the present—and by neglecting the values that are conducive to it—achievement, independence, and deferred gratification" (pp. 34–35).

Other theorists of cultural deficiency pointed to the perpetuation of patterns of cultural socialization from one generation to the next. Oscar Lewis (1961) argued that low-income Mexicans and Puerto Ricans self-perpetuated a culture of poverty that included violence, an inability to defer gratification, and political apathy. These cultural practices, according to Lewis, became embedded in the behavior of low-income Mexicans and Puerto Ricans by the age of six or seven and continued even if the economic status of the community improved.

POLICY IMPLICATIONS

Cultural deficiency arguments within academia have had significant staying power. Policy makers have taken up the arguments and applied them to many policy agendas, one of the most significant being the War on Poverty campaign of President Lyndon B. Johnson during the 1960s. The campaign was institutionalized with the Economic Opportunity Act of 1964, which led to the creation of the Office of Economic Opportunity (OEO). Programs such as VISTA, Job CORPS, and Head Start emerged from this campaign. The premise of many such programs was to end the cyclical nature of poverty by altering the attributes of low-income minority groups. The emergence of such a policy initiative testifies to the far-reaching significance of cultural deficiency as a theoretical explanation.

The term maintains some academic and policy significance. Although much of the research on cultural deficiency emerged during the mid-1900s, there continue to be significant discussions as to whether identifiable cultural attributes among low-income black and Latino groups explain their persistent underperformance in schools and minimal social mobility. In addition, welfare policy continues to rely on elements of the cultural deficiency argument to explain why some low-income, ethnic minority groups are unable to move out of the cycle of poverty.

SEE ALSO *Colonialism, Internal; Cultural Racism; Education, Racial Disparities; Motherhood, Deficiency in; Underemployment.*

BIBLIOGRAPHY

Blanton, Carlos K. 2003. "From Intellectual Deficiency to Cultural Deficiency: Mexican Americans, Testing, and Public School Policy in the American Southwest, 1920–1940." *Pacific Historical Review* 72 (1): 39–62.

Blauner, Robert. 1969. "Internal Colonialism and Ghetto Revolt." *Social Problems* 16 (4): 393–408.

Eitzen, D. Stanley, and Maxine Baca Zinn. 2006. *Social Problems*, 10th ed. Boston: Pearson/Allyn and Bacon.

Gordon, Milton. 1961. "Assimilation in America: Theory and Reality." *Daedalus* 90 (2): 263–285.

Greeley, Andrew M. 1974. *Ethnicity in the United States: A Preliminary Reconnaissance.* New York: Wiley.

Heller, Celia. 1966. *Mexican American Youth: Forgotten Youth at the Crossroads.* New York: Random House.

Isaacs, Harold. 1975. "Basic Group Identity: Idols of the Tribe." In *Ethnicity: Theory and Experience*, edited by Nathan Glazer and Daniel P. Moynihan. Cambridge, MA: Harvard University Press.

Jensen, A. R. 1969. "How Much Can We Boost IQ and Scholastic Achievement?" *Harvard Educational Review* 39: 1–23.

Kallen, H. 1942. "The National Being and the Jewish Community." In *The American Jew: A Composite Portrait,* edited by Oscar I. Janowsky. New York: Harper and Brothers.

Lieberson, Stanley. 1980. *A Piece of the Pie: Blacks and White Immigrants Since 1880.* Berkeley: University of California Press.

Moynihan, Daniel Patrick. 1965. *The Case for National Action: The Negro Family.* Washington, DC: U.S. Department of Labor, Office of Planning and Research.

Park, Robert E. 1914. "Racial Assimilation in Secondary Groups with Particular Reference to the Negro." *American Journal of Sociology* 19 (5): 606–623.

Edward Fergus

CULTURAL RACISM

Cultural racism is one of several terms that scholars have coined to describe and explain new racial ideologies and practices that have emerged since World War II. The postwar era has seen the demise of overt forms of racism in Europe, North America, Australia, and the global postcolonial world. Reeling from the horrors of Nazism, Europe and other Western nations formally rejected racist values and established antiracism legislation. The world community, through the 1966 United Nations International Convention on the Elimination of All Forms of Racial Discrimination, put itself on record as opposing racism.

The post–World War II era also witnessed the success of anticolonial movements; the dismantling of old colonial, racist structures; and the emergence of newly independent nations, such as India, with strong commitments to equality and social justice. In the United States, the civil rights movement succeeded in eradicating most formal, legal, and other institutionalized forms of racism, from segregated schools, jobs, housing, and public facilities to antimiscegenation laws which forbade interracial sex or marriage.

By the beginning of the 1970s, most overt forms of racism had disappeared in Western countries, colonialism was virtually dead, and with the striking exception of South Africa, majority rule had replaced European minority rule. Yet racial inequality persisted, and in some cases had worsened, judging by standard socioeconomic indicators. This was true on a global scale, when "First World" and "Third World" nations were compared, as well as in western European nations, Australia, Canada, and the United States.

Scholars have struggled to understand the apparent stubborn persistence of racial inequality (Harrison 1995; Mullings 2005). They have tried to identify the more covert forms racism has taken since the 1970s, including its varied permutations in different historical, national, and local settings. They have also tried to explain the processes that foster racial inequality without "overtly targeting its victims" (Mullings 2005, p. 679).

There is general agreement that these new forms are both complex and subtle, and that they operate in ways that do not require the formal assistance of educational, legal, and other institutions. Several terms have emerged to characterize what is sometimes called "the new racism" (or, perhaps, racisms. These include "laissez-faire racism," "cultural fundamentalism," "unmarked racisms," "neoracism," "color-blind racism," and "cultural racism."

"Cultural racism" is not yet a standard label in the race and racism literature, especially in the United States. It is virtually absent in the anthropological literature and has only recently appeared in the U.S. sociological literature (Bonilla-Silva 2003). It is more common in the European literature (Modood 2005) and among U.S. scholars familiar with European debates on race (Wylie 2001). Yet even when scholars use the term "cultural racism," they do not necessarily employ it in the same way.

Yet if one worries less about labels and focuses on recurring themes that emerge in the literature on the "new racism," there is widespread agreement on a set of processes occurring that can be labeled "cultural racism." At its core, cultural racism is a form of racism (that is, a structurally unequal practice) that relies on cultural differences rather than on biological markers of racial superiority or inferiority. The cultural differences can be real, imagined, or constructed. Culture, rather than biology, has become a popular, political, and scientific explanatory framework for understanding and rationalizing the unequal status and treatment of various racial groups. Racialized groups are not burdened or blessed by their genetic traits but by their cultural traits.

Cultural racism manifests itself in different ways. At least three forms of cultural racism are discussed in the literature: (1) cultural-difference explanations and solutions for inequality, (2) a continuing rationale for modern imperialism, and (3) race discourse and political rhetoric.

CULTURAL-DIFFERENCE EXPLANATIONS AND SOLUTIONS FOR RACIAL INEQUALITY

The emergence of cultural racism partially reflects the discrediting of old biological explanations for racial inequality. Arguments of cultural differences in the United States were originally employed as an alternative to biological explanations for racial inequality, often by liberals committed to racial justice. Since the 1960s, anthropologists and other scientists have amassed evidence showing that biological races do not exist, that racial categories are cultural inventions rather than scientifically valid partitions of the human species, and that race is not a useful, accurate, or meaningful description of human biological variation (Mukhopadhyay and Henze 2003; Mukhopadhyay, Henze, and Moses 2007). In short, they have argued that race as biology is fiction and that racial classifications are historical and culturally specific ideologies invented to justify slavery and other forms of systematic, institutionalized inequality.

In the absence of biological explanations for racial differences and racial inequality, researchers turned to culture—exploring, for example, the role of cultural or linguistic factors in the educational achievement of minority groups or the role of family structure in reproducing poverty across generations. For liberals and anthropologists, culture (unlike biology) was never a barrier to achieving racial equality. All humans have the same capacity for culture, and all cultures are learned. Moreover, cultures are dynamic, flexible, creative human adaptations, changing over time and in different circumstances. If, as some argued, the culture of African Americans or Puerto Rican migrants differed from the dominant U.S. culture, that "problem" could be solved. New cultural ways could be learned, either by abandoning old ways or by acquiring a second cultural repertoire, much like a second language. Cultural differences, while recognized, were not viewed as insurmountable obstacles to racial equality. Culture was instead the explanatory paradigm for racial inequality, and cultural assimilation was the solution.

Cultural-difference arguments have come under scrutiny, however, and many scholars have come to consider them examples of cultural racism. Critics have pointed out that, historically, cultural differences between Europeans (or Euro-Americans) and non-Europeans have always been framed in terms of superiority and inferiority. In the United States, Africans and other racial groups were deemed culturally inferior to "whites" (meaning those from northwestern Europe). Nineteenth-century evolutionary science attempted to rank racial groups from "primitive" to "advanced." They did not simply use biology, but also what would come to be called culture. For example, British marriage and kinship forms (monogamy and nuclear families) were considered more "advanced" than other cultural forms (e.g., polygamy or multigenerational, extended families).

During the twentieth century, arguments for the superiority of Anglo (Christian) culture grew more strident as U.S. anti-immigration legislation restricted the entry of "lower ranked" European subraces (such as "Semitic" or "Alpine"). Dominant groups feared cultural pollution from "inferior" cultures, and immigrants were expected to assimilate to the "superior" culture. The only question was whether all races and subraces, such as southern and eastern Europeans or the Irish, were capable of assimilating to the dominant Anglo (Protestant) culture.

With the rejection of race as biology in the post–World War I, post–civil rights era, cultural difference as cultural deficit, or what is now called "cultural racism," was the reigning paradigm. During the 1960s, for example, African American school children were considered linguistically impoverished, possessing linguistic forms fundamentally inferior to the standard American English taught in schools. African American families, with a core matrifocal unit and extended kinship ties, were described as not only inferior but pathological ("dysfunctional") relative to the European American nuclear family.

Oscar Lewis's theory of a "culture of poverty," initially based on fieldwork in Mexico and Puerto Rico, focused on cultural adaptations to the circumstances of poverty. Yet some interpreted his findings within what might be called a "poverty of culture" framework, seeing other cultures as clearly inferior and deficient compared to middle-class U.S. American or Western culture, and as the primary barrier to upward mobility. When applied to racial and ethnic minority groups in the United States, the culture of poverty approach, or more often, the poverty of culture approach, became the explanation for why families remained poor or children did poorly in school. Culture, in short, rather than any larger system of inequality, produced racialized poverty or educational underachievement. In the educational jargon of the late 1960s and early 1970s, minority children were "culturally deprived." Implicitly, for those who wished to see it that way, poor people had only their culture (and hence themselves) to blame. Many scholars now characterize this literature as an example of cultural racism.

During the 1970s and 1980s, largely because of the activism of racial minorities, the U.S. and some European nations, including Britain, began to accept and even celebrate the cultural differences of racial groups. Racial minorities, including indigenous and immigrant groups, embraced their cultural roots, rejecting the prevailing philosophy that assimilation was essential for social advancement. Cultural relativism prevailed, at least in theory. All cultures became valued equally. In this sense, society had become "color-

Kwanzaa in the United States. *A couple celebrates Kwanzaa, an African-American and Pan-African holiday, in December 2005. Racial minorities have begun embracing their cultural roots, rejecting the philosophy that assimilation was essential for social advancement.* AP IMAGES.

blind." That is, "color" was irrelevant. Or rather, all colors were relevant.

From the perspective of many racial minorities, the goal was mutual respect and an institutionalized recognition of cultural diversity as legitimate. The era of "multiculturalism" took various forms. In Britain, it included having Imams as chaplains in prison and setting up separate public schools for Muslim children. In the United States, it ranged from recognizing alternative cultural celebrations such as Kwanzaa, to creating "cultural" (ethnic) clubs on campuses, establishing ethnic studies departments, pursuing Afrocentric curriculum, and broadening affirmative action goals to include cultural diversity.

Old "culturally deprived" terminology was replaced with cultural diversity, cultural competence, and other language that conveyed respect for multiple and equally valid cultural forms. In the educational context, teacher education programs emphasized diverse learning styles, expressive forms, and other educationally relevant cultural resources that children from varied racial backgrounds bring to school. Many well-intentioned educators committed themselves to teaching to the child, rather than forcing the child to assimilate to the culture of the school.

Nevertheless, despite success at institutionalizing multiculturalism, racial inequality persists. Educational underachievement remains a major problem for most indigenous and racial minorities. In a 2006 editorial in the *New York Times*, Orlando Patterson put forward the idea that "cultural" arguments have been totally rejected, and that only structural explanations (the "system") are currently acceptable explanations for underachievement. Yet cultural "differences," while now positively valued, continue as a predominant explanatory framework for variations in the educational achievement of racial groups. Researchers continue to explore more complex, but nevertheless cultural, processes that depress educational achievement, such as cultures of "opposition" among some U.S. racial groups. These school peer cultures consciously "oppose," it is argued, the perceived emphasis of the racially dominant culture on academic excellence.

While culture has become the new explanation for racial inequality, cultural racism employs a concept of culture that is, from an anthropological perspective, enormously simplistic, static, rigid, overly homogeneous, deterministic, ahistoric, and without context. Culture is depicted as so deeply embedded, so tradition-bound, that it is nearly "intrinsic" or "natural" to a group. In short, culture is "naturalized" and "essentialized," making it nearly as immutable as biology. The line between cultural essentialism and biological determinism is sometimes indistinguishable. Culture thus becomes an explanation for racial inequality that offers little hope for change. Cultural racism depicts culture as an insurmountable obstacle for racial minorities or an insurmountable advantage for dominant racial groups.

Minority groups, of course, can also employ essentialized, naturalized images of cultures and ignore underlying structural factors. Sometimes this is a conscious political strategy, such as when it is used by Native Americans (as culturally superior "stewards of the land") to maintain control over their lands. Nevertheless, such examples would not be considered "cultural racism" because of the power relations involved. That is, they are not the dominant groups' characterization of a subordinate group.

Cultural-difference explanations for racial inequality are coming under increasing attack, partially for the reasons just cited. But critics go farther. Focusing on culture, they argue, ignores the larger national, global, economic, and political forces that contribute to social inequality, whether racial or nonracial. Thus, complex, multifactorial, multileveled, and nuanced analysis is needed to understand the processes that contribute, on different levels, to persistent racial inequality.

CULTURAL RACISM AS A CONTINUING RATIONALE FOR MODERN IMPERIALISM

Many scholars argue that social inequality has been racialized, even though its roots are not racial. Cultural racism, from their perspective, is simply a new ideological device for masking more fundamental processes of global capitalism that are responsible for contemporary inequality and stratification. Cultural racism is the latest "discourse" of the powerful to justify domination, a discourse that some say has its roots in the colonial era.

These scholars are examining the relationship between cultural racism and the pursuit of imperialism and capitalist developmental goals. They note how ideas of cultural superiority and inferiority among nations serve to justify the political and economic subjugation of the seemingly economically "backward" Third World countries. With the decline of biological explanations of racial disparities, cultural racism emerges as an updated explanation of continual, yet seemingly hidden, transformations in a postcolonial and globalizing era. Analysts view cultural racism as a widespread manifestation of (and response to) such transformations as global labor competition, powerful multinational corporations, and increasingly concentrated wealth, although these are expressed differently in local contexts.

Studies of colonial and postcolonial migrant labor, particularly within the western European context, trace the emergence of an ideology of cultural racism to industrial and postindustrial capitalism. In the British context, the sociologist Robert Miles (1982) describes the nineteenth-century racialization of Irish migrant laborers, the negative depictions of the Irish, and the use of these culturally racist images to justify the exploitation and mistreatment of Irish. More significant, cultural racism operated to mask the more substantive class relations underlying Irish-British relations. Studies continue to show how racial ideologies, such as cultural racism, are integral to class formations and capitalist development.

Third World social ills are not interpreted as rooted in institutions, in power relations between nations and governments. Rather, proponents of cultural explanations highlight the cultural inferiority of subordinate groups and the cultural superiority of dominant groups. Third World cultures are "mired" in insurmountably "traditional," "static" values and practices—in contrast to purportedly flexible, pragmatic, and "scientific" First World practices. Third World nations can only "benefit" from their inclusion in the global polity and economy. But to do so, Third World countries must undertake significant self-sacrifices and take "individual" responsibility to overcome their traditional "backward" cultural practices.

Frantz Fanon was one of the first to explore the role of cultural racism as a new legitimizing ideology for imperialism. In his 1956 speech "Racism and Culture," the Martinique-born and French-trained psychiatrist used the term "cultural racism" to emphasize the impact of western European cultures on the minds of its colonized and newly independent populous. Fanon referred to it as an "enslavement" doctrine that targets the psyche, destroying cultural values and the ways of life of colonized people and producing alienation. The colonized, in contrast, never question the intrinsic "superiority" of their culture. Fanon viewed this doctrine as the ideological content necessary for the "systematized oppression of a people."

Others have built on Fanon's work, showing how cultural racism reinforces dominant-subordinate relations between former colonies and colonizers, whether between "First" and "Third" World nations or among racial groups within newly independent states, such as South Africa and Zimbabwe. Cultural racism has shaped the social psyche of varying groups and complicates efforts to create "culturally authentic" national institutions in postindependence contexts. For instance, colonial structures of cultural domination often created both western-trained elites and revolutionary fighters, each offering a different cultural version of postindependence, nationalist redemption.

Scholars such as Arun Sivanandan offer reminders that Fanon's notion of cultural racism persists under postcolonial forms of imperialism, as political and economic refugees flow from Third to First World nations. One legacy of cultural racism, he argues, is the continuing appeal of the colonial culture, prompting some former colonials to migrate to Europe. Once there, they encounter, even more pervasively, the colonial legacy, including its assumption of cultural superiority and its erosive effects on the psyche of the formerly colonized. This legacy is visible in all institutions, and it exists subliminally in "the food you eat, the clothes you wear, the music you hear, the television you watch, the newspaper you read" (Sivanandan 1989, p. 12).

Some analysts focus on how cultural racism has been linked since the 1980s to what are called "neoliberal" economic practices. These practices seek to privatize government activities (e.g., public health, education, and prisons), dismantle government laws regulating corporations and protecting labor and the environment, and eliminate restrictions on trade between countries. Institutions such as the World Bank, the International Monetary Fund, and the World Trade Organization argue that neoliberal policies and structural adjustment will help "develop" and "modernize" Third World economies, alleviate poverty, and curtail what they describe as cultural deficiencies such as political corruption, social welfare dependency, and insularity (i.e., economic protectionism).

Critics observe how neoliberalism, through the discourses of government officials, development agencies, and powerful media, implicitly employs cultural-racist explanations for inequality. Third World nations are consistently, if subtly, depicted as culturally incompetent, culturally ignorant, and culturally incapable of managing their own affairs. They are seen as being responsible for their own poverty, health problems, agricultural degradation, educational underachievement, and lack of equal participation in civil society. Cultural deficiencies, therefore, provide a rationale and explanation for persistent economic inequalities, legitimizing neoliberal capitalism as a redemptive solution.

Cultural racism, in its neoliberal guise, appears to be enlightened, seemingly promoting global racial equality through eliminating Third World poverty and including "developing nations" in the "world" economy and culture. Yet it ignores history, the impact of colonialism, and prevailing power relations, thus delegitimizing Third World struggles to achieve global justice. It can also be used to legitimize the seizure of communal land, extraction of material resources, and exploitation of human labor (Wylie 2001).

CULTURAL RACISM AS A RHETORICAL STRATEGY FOR POLITICAL GOALS

Some scholars have studied another form of cultural racism, one embedded in popular and political discourses about race. While the specifics differ across nations, these rhetorical strategies and framing devices share common features that have allowed social institutions and individuals alike to deny the continual significance of racial meanings, identities, and politics. Race, in these discourses, has become irrelevant—if institutions have become color-blind, then policies should reflect this change.

The Color Blind Society. By the late 1970s, the United States and other Western (and non-Western) nations had enacted equal opportunity and affirmative action policies designed to remedy the pervasive institutional racial discrimination of the past. These actions resulted from decades of political mobilization by racial minorities. Antiracism was initially framed in terms of empowerment and equal participation in all levels of society. Subsequently, this call for institutional integration was reframed to include respect and preservation of race-based cultural distinctiveness, but in the context of social equality.

Since the 1980s, scholars have studied how policymakers, mass media, and prominent political figures have strategically employed cultural racism (and other liberal rhetoric) to justify changes in public policies affecting racial groups, particularly as outright expressions of racism have declined. Eduardo Bonilla-Silva (2003) asserts that cultural racism in the United States operates through the recurring notion of color-blindness, reflected in particular rhetorical devices that deny the continuing significance of race, racial identities, meanings, and practices. As a framing device, this produces color-blind and cultural-racism narratives that declare race irrelevant and argue—seemingly logically—for the dismantling of earlier affirmative action and other race-sensitive programs, which are seen as being no longer "needed," and indeed as "discriminatory." Color-blindness is put forth as the most appropriate form of antiracist strategy because it is fair, equitable, and legally provides for equal opportunities for all individuals.

Conservative politicians, in particular, employ rhetorical elements from the civil rights movements (e.g., "equal opportunity," "antidiscrimination," a "color-blind" society) to rationalize continuing racial inequality while simultaneously dismantling affirmative action and other legal remedies for past institutional discrimination.

Affirmative action becomes "reverse discrimination," an "unfair advantage" to those hired, and an "injustice" (though only to those of the dominant racial group). The language of "justice" is used to ignore the continuing legacy of historically rooted injustice.

Color-blind rhetoric also appropriates multiculturalism, including the celebration of racial diversity and cultural pride initially advocated by racial minorities, to "essentialize" culture as immutable cultural practices that, even if voluntary, "prevent" racial minorities from getting ahead in this now color-blind society. Speaking "Ebonics" or "Spanish" is rhetorically placed in opposition to becoming proficient in standard English, rather than as a viable strategy of multilingualism. Multilingualism is equated with educational underachievement, despite evidence from Europe and other countries that academic success and fluency in multiple languages go together. Similarly, in this rhetoric, self-segregation, not covert discrimination, produces racially segregated neighborhoods, workplaces, and social networks.

Political rhetoric also infuses traditional U.S. notions of "individualism," "hard work," "meritocracy," "freedom of choice," "autonomy" and the "the self-made man" into arguments against attempts to eliminate de facto school segregation (e.g., through "forced busing"), discrimination in hiring ("forced government quotas"), or to diversify other institutions. Code words that are substituted for racial terms (e.g., "welfare queen") are partially rooted in cultural (and gender) stereotypes, such as long-standing sexual stereotypes about African Americans. Cultural attributes of "model minorities" (e.g., some Asians) are highlighted, with a presumed emphasis on "education," "family" (nuclear family) life, and "hard work."

Such rhetoric erases the collective cultural memory of past discrimination, ignores its continuing effects, and portrays racial minorities as unjustly demanding "special privileges." Instead, it emphasizes unbounded opportunities and implicitly attributes inequality to individual inadequacies or collective but selective cultural traits (e.g., "rap music," the "drug culture").

"Law and Order" and Preserving the Nation. Scholars have also observed how cultural racism is employed in framing "law and order" as a social problem, a rhetorical device that does not explicitly mention racial groups yet deliberately utilizes markers that associate criminality and cultural differences with particular racial groups. In *Policing the Crisis* (1978), Stuart Hall and his associates focused on the rhetoric of mugging "scares," and on how the British mass media and politicians managed to draw upon and distort cultural traits of young black (especially Caribbean) men in order to portray them as criminals.

While official crime statistics revealed no clear waves of street crimes, British governments from Prime Minister Harold Wilson to Margaret Thatcher managed to frame them as a national crisis and use them to enact a series of strict law-and-order policies. The enforcement rationale portrayed black communities as sites of crime, unemployment, and underground activities that had to be "cleansed" of young men in order to re-establish law and order in Britain. This form of cultural racism was not explicitly racist, but instead utilized notions of criminality and public safety in ways that had clear racial impacts.

Immigration, multiculturalism, and perceived threats to the "nation" (or, more accurately, to national culture) have also been significant frames in the rhetoric of cultural racism. Nativist rhetoric in France, Great Britain, and other countries employs notions of cultural homogeneity, assimilation, and national patriotism. While officially promoting social inclusion, they nonetheless increasingly use cultural criteria, and hence cultural differences, to exclude and to argue for immutable cultural barriers to citizenship. An assumed monolithic national culture underlies rhetoric about "French culture" or the "British character." This allows anti-immigrant groups to portray themselves as supporting racial equality and opposing racial discrimination.

Yet the cultural criteria for full national "citizenship" have differential racial impacts. Cultural criteria are employed to justify increased immigration restrictions, control, and regulation on "cultural" grounds, such as religion, family structure, and marriage practices. This, in effect, limits political rights, economic resources, and social inclusion on racial grounds, creating permanent cultural outsiders of some migrants, refugees, guest workers, and descendants of the formerly colonized.

Some scholars emphasize how the xenophobic and patriotic rhetoric masks and conflates racial grouping, cultural distinctions, and national boundaries. They suggest that "Islamophobic" responses to the Salman Rushdie affair involving the novel *The Satanic Verses* (1988), the headscarf ban instituted in French schools in 2004, and the *Jyllands-Posten* Muhammad cartoons controversy of 2005 are not simply individual forms of racial prejudice, but rather an expression of cultural superiority that intertwines religion, culture, and national differences.

Feminist scholars have shown how groups that promote cultural racism also rely on cultural ideas of femininity, motherhood, and women as the nation's caretaker to justify the persistence of cultural differences and racial inequalities globally. In these images, conflicting gendered and sexualized notions of aesthetics, purity, responsibility, and submission are deployed to maintain national, regional, and familial traditions conceived as culture.

These ideas are embodied in migration laws, which often contain provisions that are both culturally specific and gendered. For example, software engineers (primarily males) usually receive priority over "domestic" workers (primarily females). Family unification laws privilege spouses over parent-child and sibling relations. Policies that admit "guest" workers often do not allow their accompanying spouses to work, implicitly encouraging male immigrants and the nuclear family with a "stay-at-home wife."

This subtle form of cultural racism also has a greater impact on countries in the Americas and Asia who are sending relatively low-skilled, low-wage, workers to Western nations, or on families who need both spouses to be employed (or culturally assume that they will be). Consequently, such laws foster racial inequalities without explicitly targeting particular racial groups.

Cultural racism, at its most basic level, rationalizes and perpetuates racial inequality through an ideology of cultural superiority and inferiority. Subordinate groups are culturally deficient even when the vocabulary is less judgmental. Dominant culture forms, or their presumed superiority, are rarely questioned. Cultural superiority is the rationale for cultural dominance, not racism, as though racial groups had no culture.

Cultural racism, when combined with the rhetoric of individualism and meritocracy, makes social inequality, even when extreme and harsh, seem normal, natural, logical, reasonable, and, in many cases, just. It produces racism without racists. By denying racism but covertly racializing inequality, cultural racism masks other fundamental sources of inequality or sources of change that threaten all racial groups and all people, except powerful and wealthy elites. By attributing current inequality to culture, a meritocracy is asserted, consistent with liberal ideals.

Simultaneously, the history of racism and the struggles of subordinated populations against racism is rendered invisible. There is no past, no history, no prior condition, and no legacy that is carried forward to the present. The erasure of the past subtly erases legitimate claims for special treatment (for reparations) and for affirmative action, creating a supposed level playing field.

SEE ALSO *Affirmative Action; Color-Blind Racism; Language.*

BIBLIOGRAPHY

Anthias, Floya, and Nira Yuval-Davis. 1992. *Racialized Boundaries: Race, Nation, Gender, Colour, and Class and the Anti-Racist Struggle*. London: Routledge.

Baker, Houston A., Jr., Manthia Diawara, and Ruth H. Lineborg. 1996. *Black British Cultural Studies: A Reader*. Chicago: University of Chicago Press.

Balibar, Etienne. 1991. "Is There a 'Neo-Racism'?" In *Race, Nation, Class: Ambiguous Identities*, edited by Etienne Balibar and Immanuel Wallerstein, 17–28. London: Verso.

Bhavnani, Kum-Kum. 1993. "Towards a Multicultural Europe?: 'Race,' Nation, and Identity in 1992 and Beyond." *Feminist Review* 45: 30–45.

———, ed. 2001. *Feminism and "Race."* Oxford: Oxford University Press.

Bonilla-Silva, Eduardo. 2003. *Racism without Racists: Color-Blind Racism and the Persistence of Racial Inequality in the United States*. Lanham, MA: Rowman & Littlefield.

Crenshaw, Kimberlé, Neil Gotanda, Gary Peller, and Kendal Thomas, eds. 1995. *Critical Race Theory: The Key Writings That Formed the Movement*. New York: The New Press.

da Silva, Denise Ferreira. 2001. "Voicing 'Resistance': Race and Nation in the Global Space." In *Identity, Culture, and Globalization*, edited by Eliezer Ben-Rafael with Yitzak Sternberg, 427–440. Leiden, the Netherlands: Brill.

Fanon, Franz. 1967 (1956). "Racism and Culture." In *Towards the African Revolution*, translated by Haakon Chevalier, 29–44. New York: Grove Press.

Gilroy, Paul. 1987. *There Ain't No Black in the Union Jack: The Cultural Politics of Race and Nation*. Chicago: University of Chicago Press.

Hall, Stuart, Chas Critcher, Tony Jefferson, et al. 1978. *Policing the Crisis: Mugging, the State, and Law and Order*. New York: Holmes & Meier.

Harrison, Faye V. 1995. "The Persistent Power of 'Race' in the Cultural and Political Economy of Racism." *Annual Review of Anthropology* 24: 47–74.

Miles, Robert. 1982. *Racism and Migrant Labour*. London: Routledge.

Modood, Tariq. 2005. *Multicultural Politics: Racism, Ethnicity, and Muslims in Britain*. Minneapolis: University of Minnesota Press.

Mukhopadhyay, Carol C., and Rosemary C. Henze. 2003. "How Real Is Race? Using Anthropology to Make Sense of Human Diversity." *Phi Delta Kappan* 84 (9): 669–678. Available from http://www.pdkintl.org/kappan/k0305muk.htm.

———, and Yolanda T. Moses. 2007. *How Real Is Race:? A Sourcebook on Race, Culture, and Biology*. Lanham, MD: Rowman & Littlefield Education.

Mullings, Leigh. 2005. "Interrogating Racism: Toward an Antiracist Anthropology." *Annual Review of Anthropology* 34: 667–693.

Omi, Michael, and Howard Winant. 1994. *Racial Formation in the United States*, 2nd ed. New York: Routledge.

Patterson, Orlando. 2006. "A Poverty of the Mind." Editorial, *New York Times*, March 26.

Sivanandan, Arun. 1989. "New Circuits of Imperialism." *Race and Class* 30 (4): 1–19.

Smith, Anna Marie. 1994. *New Right Discourse on Race and Sexuality in Britain, 1968–1990*. Cambridge, U.K.: Cambridge University Press.

Wylie, Diana. 2001. *Starving on a Full Stomach*. Charlottesville: University Press of Virginia.

Yuval-Davis, Nira. 1997. *Gender and Nation*. London: Sage.

Carol C. Mukhopadhyay
Peter Chua

D

DALITS

Dalit is the word most commonly used for India's untouchables in the early twenty-first century. Its basic meaning is "broken, ground down," but "oppressed" is the best translation for its current use. It is a self-chosen word, made popular by the Dalit Panthers in Bombay (now Mumbai) in the 1970s. It replaces *ex-untouchable* (used because the constitution of independent India made the practice of untouchability illegal) and *Harijan* (children of God), Mahatma Gandhi's kind but patronizing term. *Scheduled castes* is an official governmental designation created in 1935 when a list or schedule was created for castes that qualified for special representation or governmental benefits. *Scheduled tribes* refers to tribes that merit special treatment. The term *Dalit* often includes both castes and tribes and may be used by any group that feels itself oppressed.

The untouchables or scheduled castes comprise one-sixth of the population of India, approximately 160 million people, and there are some four hundred castes considered "untouchable." The phenomenon of a group of outsiders has given English two words: outcaste and pariah. The untouchables, however, are in castes of their own, and pariah literally refers to a drum. One duty of the actual pariah caste was ritual drumming for higher castes.

THE CASTE SYSTEM

The English word *caste* is used for two very different forms of the caste system: *varna* and *jati*. The classic categories of *varna*, depicted in the tenth and last book of the Rig Veda (Sanskrit texts created from 1500 to 900 BCE), describe the gods' sacrifice of primeval man: From his mouth were made the Brahmans, the priests; from his shoulders the Kshatriyas, the warriors and rulers; from his thighs the Vaishyas, farmers (later changing to indicate merchants and traders); and from his feet the Shudras, servants of all, a category that became inclusive of all who worked with their hands, from musicians to farmers. The first three categories could study the Vedas and receive the sacred thread; the fourth category could not. Untouchables, below Shudras, do not appear in the four oldest texts of the Vedas and later came to be known as *avarna*, without *varna*.

The reality of the caste system rests on the *jatis*, endogamous groups that eat together, often work in one occupation, and consider themselves to have a common history and culture. There are probably more than three thousand *jatis* in India. Many can be fitted into the *varna* system, but in Maharashtra and the South there are only two *varnas*: Brahmans and Shudras. There are, of course, merchants and soldiers and rulers in the South, but few call themselves Kshatriya or Vaishya or Shudra, and the *varna* category does not seem to matter except for Brahmans (and untouchables). The system allowed groups coming into India to find a place in the social structure, depending upon their political power and economic skills.

In the modern period, organizations on the basis of *jatis* were formed to cooperate in economic, educational, and even political matters. This, as well as the British census begun in 1872, which gave *jati* and *varna* status to all groups, seems to have strengthened and solidified the caste system.

PURITY AND POLLUTION

Behind the caste system is a strong belief in purity and pollution. Some occupations are polluting, but some castes with no polluting occupation are also polluted by birth. The purity of the upper castes must be preserved, it is believed, and this results in quite literally groups that may not be touched. The classic rationale for the creation of untouchables is twofold: wrongful marriage, that is, the offspring of a male Shudra and a Brahman woman, or karma, misdeeds in this life will result in a low birth in the next life. Few untouchable castes accept either theory, although individuals sometimes attribute their status to a previous birth. Most castes have an elaborate theory whereby some unfortunate and misguided good deed resulted in untouchability.

Three occupations are considered polluting throughout India—the handling of leather or a dead cow, the removal of human waste, and work on the cremation ground. The prohibition against touching a dead cow seems to have extended to the playing of a cowhide drum, hence the pariah caste. In the North, leather workers are known as Chamars (now many call themselves Ravidasis, the name of an untouchable Chamar saint of medieval times). Traditionally the scavenging caste was known as Bhangi but now they prefer to be called Valmikis, after the legendary author of the epic Ramayana. (200 BCE–200 CE.) Other occupations such as washerman and toddy tapper connote untouchability in some areas and not in others. Untouchability by birth is determined in the village setting and is marked by denial of temple entry and the village well, by occupying living quarters outside the village, and usually by having the duty of performing agricultural labor on higher castes' fields.

Although the concept of purity and pollution goes back to the Upanishads (700–500 BCE), the despised "Chandala" in those texts does not seem to indicate a separate caste by birth. The general consensus is that by the fourth century CE, the status and occupational duties of certain groups indicates the formation of a "caste system," with untouchables recognized as such.

THE ORIGIN OF UNTOUCHABILITY

There is no agreement on the origin of untouchable castes. The scholar and political leader Bhimrao Ramji Ambedkar (1891–1956) traced a "broken men" theory and a related previous Buddhist theory to the increasing Hinduization of India in pre-Muslim times. Ambedkar, however, rejected a race theory, holding to the idea of Indians as one race with even the Aryans, thought by most as northern invaders who developed Sanskrit and classical literature in India, as originating in India. There is current controversy about Dalits and race. Most scholars and Dalits prefer the term *discrimination by descent* to a racial category. There is a new move to claim "original inhabitant" status, which is akin to race. There are also traditions of "sons of the soil" and "lords of the earth" in many untouchable traditions, which suggest a non-Aryan background. Early-twentieth-century movements often used the word *Adi* or *Ad* as in Ad Dharm or Adi Dravida, the first or original religion or, in the South, the first Dravidians, as opposed to Brahmanical culture. The current usage is *mulnivashi*, meaning the inhabitants in India before the Aryan invasion who possessed a non-Brahmanical but complete culture.

The government of India, when faced with Dalit demands such as those presented at the World Conference against Racism held in Durban, South Africa, in 2001, and more recently before a United Nations commission, denied that "discrimination by descent" was akin to race and maintained that India must deal with its own peoples without international interference. The practice of untouchability was "abolished" in the constitution of independent India (articles 15 and 17), and the Untouchability (Offenses) Act of 1955 makes such discriminatory practices punishable by law. Article 46 provides the Indian version of affirmative action, specifically the promotion of educational and economic benefits for the "weaker sections" of the society. The Scheduled Castes and Scheduled Tribes (Prevention of Atrocities) Act of 1989 prescribes stringent penalties for violence against these groups. The government of India claims this eliminates the need for Dalits to approach Amnesty International, the United Nations, or Human Rights Watch about their concerns, but Dalits take every opportunity to point out the discrimination and violence that continues. The British House of Lords is the latest group outside of India to take up the issue of violence against Dalits.

ANTI-CASTE MOVEMENTS

Buddhism, founded in the sixth century BCE, held that status should be determined by action, not birth. The only people who were Brahmans were those who fulfilled the specific role of Brahmins. All castes were admitted into the Buddhist *sangha*, the order of monks or *bhikhus*. Although Buddhism was the most consistently egalitarian, there are suggestions of reform in the Siddhas, the Nath cult and the Mahanubhav religion, as well as others.

The *bhakti* movement, which held that devotion to God was the key to salvation and happiness, not any sort of ritual or orthodoxy, began in the South in about the eighth century and moved slowly North, covering most of India by the eighteenth century. From Tamil Nadu, the *bhakti* idea moved to Karnataka where Basavanna (1134–1196) became the most radical of religious leaders. From total equality to intercaste marriage, Basavanna preached a new way, but his followers, the Lingayats, soon became a caste themselves. In the Marathi area, in the fourteenth century, Cokhamela and his family, wife, sister, sister's husband, and son, all wrote songs of both bliss and humiliation, over four hundred of which are now credited to them. In the North, Ravidas, a Chamar of the fifteenth century, is still very influential as model, source of pride, and symbol of identity.

The general consensus is that the *bhakti* movement was spiritually egalitarian, but had little social effect. Nevertheless, all the untouchable saints are remembered—their legends told, their songs sung, and their places secured by proof of creativity and piety.

The reform institutions of the nineteenth century, the Brahmo Samaj based in Bengal, the Prarthana Samaj of Bombay province, and the Arya Samaj of Punjab, the United Provinces, and to some degree throughout India, had various sorts of effects. The Brahmo instituted schools for the so-called depressed classes. The Prarthana Samaj admitted a few untouchables into its group, and the Arya Samaj instituted purification rites that theoretically removed untouchables from any polluting category. All had some effect on the Indian mind, but none had any large effect on the depressed classes. A very radical group, the Satyashodhak Samaj (truth-seeking society) of the non-Brahman Jotirao Phule, flourished in the late nineteenth century and was influential in the area that became Maharashtra.

POLITICAL ACTIVITY

Political activity on the part of Dalits began as early as the 1890s with the attempt to create a petition for reenlistment of Mahars and other untouchable castes into the army. The participation of untouchables in the army had been important in the eighteenth and most of the nineteenth centuries, but the late-nineteenth-century British emphasis on "martial castes" barred untouchables from the army. Gopalnak Baba (Vittalnak) Walankar, a retired Havaldar (native officer in the British army) in Bombay province, created a long petition with the help of Hindu caste reformers, but the ex-army men were too timid to sign it. In the early twentieth century, Dalits from all over the country petitioned the various British commissions for rights and privileges, including the Minto-Morley tour for the 1909 reforms and the Southborough (Franchise) Commission in 1919.

In the testimony before the Southborough Commission, a new and different voice was heard. Ambedkar had returned from his study at Columbia University in New York and had not yet departed for his study at the London School of Economics and Gray's Inn. In long and sophisticated testimony, Ambedkar asked for a very low franchise for untouchables, few of whom were educated or land owning, and representation in such numbers as would "enable them to claim redress." But the government allowed two nominated seats for untouchables in the Madras Legislative Council, and one each in the provinces of Bombay (a few years later increased to two), United Provinces, Bengal, Bihar, and the Central provinces. M. C. Rajah of Madras, who had served on the Madras Legislative Council and had written the first book on untouchables from within the group itself, was nominated to the central Legislative Council. With this unpromising start, the effort of Dalits to serve on legislative bodies and to create new laws was set in ever-increasing motion.

Both Ambedkar and an untouchable from Madras, Rattamalle Srinivasan, were nominated to attend the Round Table Conferences of 1930 to 1932, which were to determine the nature of representation in India. In London, as Sikhs and Muslims pled for separate electorates, that is, electorates in which Muslims would vote for Muslim representatives, Sikhs for Sikh, and so on, Ambedkar also began to think that untouchable representatives in legislative bodies should be elected by their fellow untouchables. This view appealed to the British, and the Communal Award of 1932 gave such representation to the depressed classes. Mahatma Gandhi, however, who was in the Yeravda prison near Pune for civil disobedience, was so opposed to separate electorates for untouchables that he declared a fast unto death. Ambedkar gave in, striking the best bargain he could: enhanced numbers of depressed classes representatives.

GANDHI AND AMBEDKAR

Ambedkar had supported Gandhi as one of the few caste Hindus trying to change the untouchables' situation with his Vaikom Satyagraha movement in the South. Ambedkar became quite critical of the lack of commitment to untouchables' rights on the part of the Indian National Congress, however, and the outcome of the so-called Poona Pact of 1932 made him an implacable critic. Dalits continue to feel that Gandhi betrayed them with his denial of the right of separate electorates, which for them meant genuine political power. In 1933 Gandhi began to use the term *Harijan* (children of God) for untouchables, and until Dalit came to be widely used Harijan was the universal designation for untouchables, in spite of the objection of some.

Gandhi was a caste Hindu, a Vaishya. Ambedkar was a Mahar and knew discrimination firsthand. Gandhi never repudiated the *varna* theory of four major groups, although he fought against the idea of a group below the *varnas* and he held all *varnas* to be equal. Ambedkar repudiated the entire caste hierarchy, dismissing what was a current effort among untouchables to "sanskritize," that is, adopt upper-class customs in order to raise their status. Gandhi did not believe in political battles for untouchables' rights or approve their attempts to enter temples unless the temple authorities agreed. Ambedkar felt political power was part of the solution to untouchability. Basically, Gandhi's faith was in change of heart; Ambedkar's trust was in law, political power, and education. Ambedkar went on to become the best-known voice of the untouchables, and also a powerful representative, serving both the government of India before independence and as law minister in independent India's first cabinet. In the latter capacity he chaired the committee charged with drafting a constitution for India.

POLITICAL PARTIES

Ambedkar began the Independent Labour Party in 1936 and was successful in gaining eleven of the fifteen seats reserved for scheduled castes, plus seats for three Hindu caste legislators. The party was not successful, however, in gaining *rights* for Dalits and for workers. An effort to reintroduce the idea of separate electorates brought about the Scheduled Castes Party in 1942. Ambedkar's Republican Party was the next try but did not come into being until after his death in 1956. Lacking a central figure, it was soon divided into various leaders' components. But Dalits are politically very aware, and the lack of party success resulted in the Dalit Panther movement in Bombay, which was combined with a Dalit literary movement in the 1970s. After a strong initial impact, the Panthers split, and now constitute only minor parties in Tamil Nadu and some cities of Uttar Pradesh. The literary movement, however, has spread to almost all the language areas of India.

The political momentum has been taken over by the Bahujan (majority) Samaj Party (BSP) founded in 1984 by Kanshi Ram, a Punjabi. In the North and to a smaller degree in Maharashtra it has considerable strength. Ram had established two earlier organizations, BAMCEF (All India Backward and Minority Communities Employees Federation) and a political party. BAMCEF claimed 200,000 members, including university-educated Dalits and Bahujans. Both these organizations gave way to the BSP, which has made real inroads into the politics of Uttar Pradesh. Its base is the Chamar community, and although Ram refused to talk about caste, he probably was from the Ramdasi Sikh community, recruited from the Chamars. In 1985 Mayawati Kumari, a single woman commonly called simply Mayawati, emerged as an effective and powerful leader, and she has led the party single-handedly since Kanshi Ram's death in 2006. An early partnership with the Socialist Party of Mulayam Singh Yadav, which promised enormous power, soon broke apart, and Mayawati has ruled Uttar Pradesh as chief minister three times within other alliances. Links with the Brahmanical party of the Bharatiya Janata Party (BJP) have been held suspect by some Dalits but welcomed by others. In the 2007 elections Mayawati's BSP party in combination with Brahmans won a clear majority, and she is now chief minister in Uttar Pradesh.

AFFIRMATIVE ACTION

India and the United States have the most comprehensive affirmative action systems of all the nations in the world. India, however, favors a quota system, which America

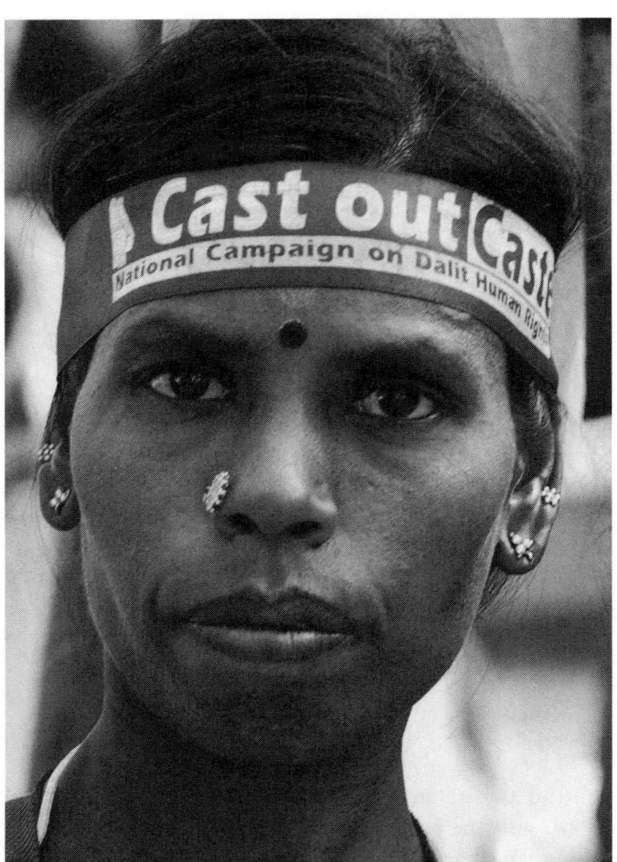

Dalits Reject the Caste System. *At the World Social Forum, held in Bombay in 2004, an Indian Dalit marches against the caste system. Activists demanded that the world pay more attention to the poor, highlighting in particular the plight of the Dalits.* INDRANIL MUKHERJEE/AFP/GETTY IMAGES.

refuses to use. All government positions have quotas for scheduled castes, scheduled tribes, and backward classes, and the system has produced a somewhat effective middle class of educated Dalits. However, the first-class government servant category is rarely filled. Any educational institution that receives government funding must also include the Dalit categories, but the increasing numbers of private educational institutions have no such requirement. Medical schools have seen much protest of reserved places for scheduled castes and tribes and other backward classes. There is considerable pressure to force private businesses to hire scheduled castes and tribes, and many envy the U.S. commitment to affirmative action.

VIOLENCE

Much of the discrimination against untouchables in the cities, in terms of personal insults, has lessened. In the villages especially, however, there is actually increasing violence over such matters as a Dalit marrying into a higher caste, a quarrel over land, or a Dalit assuming a privilege that is not traditional. Rape, arson, physical violence, and boycotts are familiar weapons against Dalits claiming equality. The National Commission for Scheduled Castes records the atrocities that are reported to it, and these vary from 25,000 to 30,000 per year. The statistics vary from state to state, and many violent encounters are not brought to the attention of the police or the courts.

BUDDHISM

Ambedkar rejected Hinduism as early as 1935, but he did not convert until shortly before his death in 1956. He had learned about Buddhism as a boy, read about Buddhism from then on, studied Pali, and compiled *The Buddha and His Dhamma*, based on Theravada texts but adding his own rational and humanitarian views. The fiftieth anniversary of his conversion was celebrated in October 2006. Conversions continue in many parts of India, especially in Delhi. Many use "Navayana," the new vehicle, as a name for Ambedkar Buddhism.

SEE ALSO *Affirmative Action.*

BIBLIOGRAPHY

Ambedkar, Bhimrao Ramji. 1979–2005. *Dr. Babasaheb Ambedkar: Writings and Speeches*. 20 vols. Bombay (later Mumbai): Government of Maharashtra.

Dangle, Arjun, ed. 1992. *Poisoned Bread: Translations from Modern Marathi Dalit Literature*. Bombay: Orient Longman.

Deliège, Robert. 1999. *The Untouchables of India*. Translated by Nora Scott. Oxford, U.K.: Berg.

Kshirsagar, R. K. 1994. *Dalit Movement in India and Its Leaders, 1857–1956*. New Delhi: M.D. Publications.

Kumar, Vivek. 2006. *India's Roaring Revolution: Dalit Assertion and New Horizons*. Delhi: Gangadeep Publications.

Mendelsohn, Oliver, and Marika Vicziany. 1998. *The Untouchables: Subordination, Poverty, and the State in Modern India*. Cambridge, U.K.: Cambridge University Press.

Rodrigues, Valerian, ed. 2002. *The Essential Writings of B. R. Ambedkar*. New Delhi: Oxford University Press.

Singh, K. S., ed. 1993. *The Scheduled Castes*. Delhi: Oxford University Press.

Thorat, Sukhadeo, and Umakant, eds. 2004. *Caste, Race, and Discrimination: Discourses in International Context*. New Delhi: Rawat.

Yagati, Chinna Rao. 2003. *Dalit Studies: A Bibliographical Handbook*. New Delhi: Kanishka Publishers.

Zelliot, Eleanor. 2001. *From Untouchable to Dalit: Essays on the Ambedkar Movement*, 3rd ed. New Delhi: Manohar.

———. 2004. *Dr. Babasaheb Ambedkar and the Untouchable Movement*. New Delhi: Blumoon Books.

Eleanor Zelliot

DANCE

Dance has long provided a key means of expression for the movement of racialized bodies, and it has intersected with notions of race in a number of ways. In particular, dance has been a literal stage upon which ideas about racial superiority and inferiority have played out. It has also been a means for promoting social mobility.

Practiced by nearly every human society in all eras and locations throughout the world, dance enacts the ways in which people relate to each other; it defines the terms of representation for bodies and behavior; it expresses spirituality and sexuality in terms of the body in motion; and it provides a way to physically resist political structures. Dance in all idioms represents an idealized combination of physicality, aesthetic and spiritual possibility, and social occasion. Dance is widely—and wrongly—assumed to be a "universal language" that can be understood easily by any who witness its movements. In truth, dance exists only in relationship to recognizable human interaction, and it is structured according to local beliefs and ideologies. Because dance encompasses so many powerful possibilities, it has always been tinged with material implications for racist ideologies. Thus, racist practices and racialized representations of cultural formations abound in the historical record of dance performance.

RACIALIZED DANCE IN THE UNITED STATES

In the United States, difficult race relations have allowed for an extensive permeation of racist ideologies through dance. Persistent stereotypes of ethnic action abound: Latino dances are "sensual" or "hot"; African Americans are "natural dancers" who specialize in "lascivious" and "grotesque" social dances; Native Americans are "spiritual" dancers who "passively" celebrate their ancestors and the land; and Asian dance forms are "delicate" and "mysterious" to their gathered audiences.

Each of these stereotypes deserves scrutiny. As a whole, Latino dances do indeed value accurate rhythmic meter. They stress fast-paced physical isolation of feet, torso, neck, hips, and arms, and they promote social interaction between partners or groups of people. Variations of group dances, including rumba and samba, are featured at festival events and carnival celebrations, while partnered social dances, including salsa and tango, bring couples into close physical proximity to explore movement possibilities as a single unit. For Latino dancers, these forms enhance social interaction, including group solidarity (in festival dances) and communication skills (in partnered dances).

During the European colonization of the Americas, Native American dances were considered to hold such power as tools of spiritual and social organization that white officials routinely banned them. For example, the Ghost Dance, performed by intercultural groups of Plains Indians from 1888 to 1890, emerged as part of a prophetic religion developed in the face of the hostile white takeover of North America. The dance, which lasted four days at a time, called for a costume that included absolutely nothing made by the white man. In 1890, infamous massacres at Wounded Knee involved the interruption of Ghost Dances by U.S. Army troops. Even before this, Native dancers had been consigned to become secular performers in popular entertainments such as Buffalo Bill's Wild West stage shows of the late nineteenth century.

Asian dance forms practiced in the United States, which range from Indian Bharata Natyam through Javanese Kecak, often rely on symbolic gestures to narrate stories based on legend, mythology, and historical events. Because the term "Asian" encompasses hundreds of ethnicities, it lumps together diverse populations—including Indonesian, Japanese, Chinese, and Korean people—and their vibrant contemporary dance traditions. The broad variety of these cultures and their dance forms, combined with the important and coded gestural significations of each, perpetuates the impression of inscrutability for many Americans unversed in the particularities of any of these forms.

EARLY AFRICAN-AMERICAN DANCES

African-American social dances convey the most consistent ideologies of race in the United States. Black social dances have been banned by city councils and considered lewd and inappropriate for performance in public spaces. They purportedly signaled the breakdown of moral standards and society itself, thus effectively demonstrating the potential for social disorder. Significantly, African-American social dances have effectively defined each historical era of the twentieth century, as with the Charleston of the 1920s, the lindy hop of the 1930s, the twist of the 1960s, and breakdancing idioms in the 1980s.

The cakewalk offers a particular example of race in dance. Created by African Americans, this partnered social and performance dance derived from activities at cornhusking festivals in the early nineteenth century. The cakewalk emerged as a sly parody of the quadrille, a French-derived set dance popular among slaveholders in the South. African-American dancers made fun of the "genteel manners" of the quadrille, adapting its erect posture and precision patterns to include complex rhythmic walking steps, sequences of bowing low, waving canes, tipping hats, and a fast-paced, high-kicking grand promenade. In its competitive form, the cakewalk involved acrobatic stunts performed by duos who strove to maintain an upright stance even as they kicked higher and higher in tandem. Those determined to possess the most precision, grace, ease, and the highest kicks won a highly decorated cake prepared for the occasion.

Surprisingly, whites who witnessed the dance failed to notice its derisive origins, and they clamored to learn it. The form transferred easily into blackface minstrel shows and early Broadway offerings as it spread as a popular pastime. The highly successful African-American minstrel team of Williams and Walker (Egbert Austin Williams and George Walker) became the most famous practitioners of the dance. Walker and his wife, Aida Reed Overton, a noteworthy dancer and choreographer in her own right, brought the cakewalk to the height of its international popularity when they danced a Command Performance at Buckingham Palace in 1897. Thus, the cakewalk, which began as a racialized parody of white manners, offered social mobility to its African-American performers who became professional entertainers to the very people that their dance mocked.

The Cakewalk. *An African-American dancer performs the cakewalk, an early jazz dance, in 1903. The dance originated among slaves as a parody of European ballroom dances.* HULTON ARCHIVE/GETTY IMAGES.

RACE AND THEATRICAL DANCE

As a realm, dance includes theatrical dance and social dance, its two most prevalent idioms in the West. Theatrical dance contains histories of racist exclusion for artists and audiences in the United States, as in the routine barring of black children from ballet classes populated by whites, and the strict segregation of black and white audiences in many theater spaces until the mid-twentieth century. These exclusionary practices held profound significance in the formation of dance performance. For Americans, ballet has stood for the pinnacle of classical achievement in dance, inevitably tied to a winsome white femininity stereotypically considered to be antithetical to African-American womanhood.

The largest ballet schools have resisted efforts to integrate their student bodies in significant numbers, and ballerinas of color have yet to achieve international celebrity in any part of the world, except, perhaps, Chinese ballerinas who tour to Europe and the United States. Because ballet in Europe grew to reflect European ideologies of grace, precision, and physical achievement, many felt that it could not translate to other cultures or geographic locations beyond Europe and the former Soviet Union. But ballet has emerged with vigor in the United States, South Africa, Australia, the Caribbean, and China. Cuba, in particular, holds a place of importance as a training ground for exceptionally trained classical dancers of color who break the mold of "white only" participation in the form. Not surprisingly, Cuban ballet dancers in the United States, some of whom identify as white rather than as people of color, are typically described in terms of their "fiery Latin temperament" while Chinese dancers are often noted for their "shy reticence" and "doll-like stature."

The founding of Dance Theatre of Harlem (DTH) in 1969 by Arthur Mitchell and Karel Shook triumphantly confirmed an African-American presence in classical ballet. In sharp rebuke to racists who contended that their "joints" and "weak feet" rendered African Americans unsuited to ballet, DTH achieved international acclaim at the height of its popularity in the 1990s, drawing on a repertory of some seventy-five ballets danced by a predominantly African-diaspora company of forty-nine dancers.

Mitchell, who had begun his career in 1955 as the only African-American dancer with the New York City Ballet (NYCB), was one of many individual artists who trained in ballet only to find limited possibilities for employment due to race. In Chicago in the 1920s, Katherine Dunham studied ballet with Ludmilla Speranzeva before creating her own Dunham dance technique. The Jones-Haywood School of Ballet, founded in Washington, D.C., in 1940, trained several significant African-American personalities including Sylvester Campbell and Louis Johnson. Philadelphia's Judimar School of Dance, created in 1948, offered ballet classes led by Essie Marie Dorsey that produced several outstanding ballet artists of the 1950s and 1960s including Delores Brown, Tamara Guillebeaux, John Jones, and Billy Wilson. After the civil rights era and the founding of DTH, several individual dancers, many of whom had affiliations of some sort with DTH or its school, rose to the ranks of principal dancer in white-majority companies. In the twenty-first century, important African-diaspora classical artists include Alonzo King, who directs the Lines Ballet based in San Francisco, and the dancers of Atlanta's Ballethnic, who tether classical technique to modern dance and neo-African forms.

At times, some ballet companies presented works that explored racial identity or offered racialized representations to audiences. In 1911, Serge Diaghilev's Ballets Russes, the premiere company of modern ballet of its era, presented *Petrushka*, danced to an original score by Igor Stravinsky. This fantasy ballet tells the story of a lover's triangle between a female doll, the clown Petrushka, and the blackface Moor character, who brutishly slays the clown in a jealous rage. The Swedish-based Ballets Suedois premiered *Sculpture Négre* in 1920 with costumes that imitated African statuettes.

During the civil rights era, representations of black people gained in humanity on ballet stages in works such as *Trinity* by Gerald Arpino (Joffrey Ballet 1970), which featured the Trinidadian-born dancer Christian Holder leading a cast of youthful optimists who imagine a color-blind utopia of dance, and the NYCB choreographer George Balanchine's *Requiem Canticles* (1968), set to music by Stravinsky, which honored the memory of the recently slain civil rights leader Martin Luther King Jr. Balanchine continually expressed an interest in African American–derived jazz rhythms and movement sensibilities, often adopting a propulsive attack in his choreography that suggested the melding of neoclassical and social dance styles. Balanchine allowed black children to train at the School of American Ballet that fed his company, and in 1955 he hired Arthur Mitchell, who became the first principal African-American dancer with a major ballet company. Balanchine featured Mitchell in several original works including the plotless 1957 masterpiece *Agon*. Set to a commissioned score by Stravinsky, the work traded in a precise modernism and, in its central pas de deux, explored the color dynamics of the black and white skin tones of Mitchell and the white ballerina Diana Adams. Balanchine often lobbied for racial integration in ballet, and he refused to accept television engagements that would not allow black and white dancers to partner each other. Still, the ranks of ballet dancers continue to be largely segregated well into the twenty-first century.

MODERN DANCE

Modern dance forms offered a more hospitable climate for black dancers in the United States. The racial division of Americans led to the formation of several separatist,

The Joffrey Ballet in Rehearsal. *Christian Holder rehearses the part of one of the ugly stepsisters for The Joffrey Ballet's production of* Cinderella, *in September 2006. For Americans, ballet has stood for the pinnacle of classical achievement in dance.* AP IMAGES.

all-black dance companies, which have offered performing opportunities for growing numbers of classically trained dancers. Hemsley Winfield's New Negro Art Theater Dance Group brought concert dance to the New York Roxy Theater in 1932, effectively proving that black dancers would be accepted by largely white audiences. John Martin of the *New York Times* noted the dancers' refusal to be "darkskinned reproductions of famous white prototypes," and termed the concert "an effort well worth the making" (Martin 1932, p. X11). Winfield's company performed with the Hall Johnson Choir in dances of his own making.

Modern dance that explores African-American life has tended to valorize religious practice, particularly in myriad versions of dances set to Negro Spirituals. Alvin Ailey's masterpiece *Revelations* (1960) set a standard of exquisite choreographic imagination in telling the story of the African-American progression from slavery to freedom. The work includes scenes that depict profound social resilience in an abstract group prayer, an enactment of an Afro-Caribbean-derived riverside baptism, scenes of solitary penitence, and a gospel-inflected service in a rural southern sanctuary. This work, which suggests a vibrant and closed hegemonic universe of African-American perseverance, has been seen by more audiences than any other modern dance work. Among contemporary artists, the dance company of Bill T. Jones and Arnie Zane, founded in 1982, stands apart in its willingness to confront uncomfortable racial perceptions in large-scale works. Jones, an African American, and his Italian-American partner Zane offered audiences a study in physical contrasts in several duets. As their company's acclaim grew, Jones continued to work as a soloist, and his powerful performances sometimes included improvised movement layered with freely associated autobiographical text. In 1981, he danced an untitled solo built upon spoken oppositional statements such as "I love women; I hate women" and "I love white people; I hate white people."

Jones and Zane were both diagnosed as HIV positive in 1986, and Zane succumbed to AIDS in 1988. After Zane's death, Jones continued to make large-scaled works that addressed themes of racial identity, sexuality, and cultural memory, as in the epic *Last Supper at Uncle Tom's Cabin/The Promised Land* (1990). This four-part, three-hour fantasia is loosely based on the Harriet Beecher Stowe novel and included an intergenerational cast, rap poetry, and scores of nude dancers in its final utopian vision. At the premiere of *Reading, Mercy and the Artificial Nigger* (2003), Jones and actor Susan Sarandon read aloud as the multiracial company shifted in and out of the various characters detailed in Flannery O'Connor's short story *The Artificial Nigger*, underscoring the mutability of race in theatrical dance. O'Connor's story of a bigoted white southern farmer and his grandson's journey to the big city provided the narrative background for a charged exploration of race, gender, and theatrical representation.

Several contemporary dance companies resist racist presumptions surrounding dance technique, including Complexions Dance, founded by two former Ailey dancers, Dwight Rhoden and Desmond Richardson. Based in New York, Complexions features a multiracial ensemble of ballet-trained dancers who work in sleek accord performing Rhoden's abstract choreography.

Dance on the Broadway stage has always embraced transformed African-American social dance forms as the preferred idiom of movement. Jazz dance, acknowledged as the foundational technique of contemporary Broadway-style dance, is built on the codification of eccentric African-American dance movements culled during the early part of the twentieth century. At intervals, segregated, "all black" companies of performers have been assembled to perform energetic or titillating fare on Broadway, from the Charleston dances of *Runnin' Wild* (1923) to the disco-inspired bump choreography of *The Wiz* (1975). Those shows reinforced the truism that African-American social dance forms, best embodied by African-American dancers, could easily entertain audiences of cultural outsiders. Some musicals attempted to confront race: The 1957 hit *West Side Story* pitted an Italian street gang against a Puerto Rican one in a series of danced battles inflected by ballet; while in 1992 George C. Wolfe's *Jelly's Last Jam* (1992) used tap dance and blackface to underscore a ironic narrative of racial jealousy among African Americans of different pigmentation.

By 2005, tap dance, like its footwork and rhythm-based kin flamenco and Bhartya Natyam, had become respected as a classical form in the United States. This shift in attitude must be related to expanding information regarding the artistic nuances of the form for all American audiences. The elevation in status, reflected in a shift of venues from variety stages and community centers to concert halls, mirrors a rise in middle-class patrons of color able to support various art forms.

Another change in racist ideologies surrounding dance derived from its increased media representations. In film, from *Birth of a Nation* (1915) to *You Got Served* (2005), African-American dance has offered audiences an outrageously odd array of physical sociability. Many films of the 1930s and 1940s featured dance to enliven otherwise dull proceedings, as in the flamboyant maneuvers of Whitey's Lindy Hoppers in the 1941 feature *Hellzapoppin*. Another popular narrative strain offers black social dance forms as a passageway to individual salvation, as in *Flashdance* (1983), *Footloose* (1984), or *Save the Last Dance* (2001), in which white teenagers find their mature social voices through their mastery of African-American dances.

Television programs, including *American Bandstand* and *Soul Train*, also introduced black social dances into the living rooms of whites and others who would never have seen them otherwise. More recent television shows include culturally diverse casts of dancers, such as *Dancing to the Hits* (1980s), Debbie Allen's several award show choreographies (1990s), and the syndicated competition show *Dance 360* (2000s), in which dancers of every ethnicity try to imitate each other in African-American–derived social dance forms.

The discipline of dance studies, which came into focus only after the civil rights and women's liberation movements, contributed to an expanded humanitarian sensibility of dance documentation in terms of race. The 1993 video series *Dancing*, created by Rhoda Grauer for PBS and accompanied by an oversized book written by Gerald Jonas, offered an essential, cross-cultural assessment of dance as a realm across geographies and cultural traditions. The video series includes many examples of rarely seen dance cultures, such as Yoruban egungun dances, that might have served as exotic spectacle for earlier generations. Documentary films about African-American dance cultures, including *Paris is Burning* (1991) and *Rize* (2005), have introduced wide audiences to specific scenes of racialized lives deeply invested in dance practice. These films highlight the difficulties of everyday life for young people of color, as well as the ways in which dance mediates some of those struggles.

As the scholarly study of dance has grown, so have the variety of its representations. A vibrant literature that complicates assessments of race in dance has emerged in journals, books, and Internet sites. Outstanding offerings from dance historians such as Lynne Fauley Emery, Richard Long, and John Perpener have detailed African-American dance practice; while the performance theorist Brenda Dixon Gottschild routinely writes about the role of race as a lens that clouds perceptions of dance among African-diaspora people. A cohort of other authors and artists continues to address the persistence of particular cultural practices in dance framed by racial stereotyping.

More recently, queer and feminist activists and scholars have worked to enlarge perceptions surrounding identity in dance, as in the work of feminist choreographer Chandralekha, from India, and the group ethic of the U.S.-based Urban Bush Women, led by Jawole Willa Jo Zollar. Still, even as dance moves beyond its obvious boundaries of performance and social practice to become a valued agent of aesthetic and social change, race becomes a guiding trope that defines its appreciation. "Classical" forms of dance, recognized as the highest forms of physical expression, are often regulated to whites, while dancers of color are often thought to be experts only at "lower-value," social dance forms. It seems that race, alongside sexuality and gender, constructs difficult barriers for artists and audiences to surmount as they approach the realm of dance.

SEE ALSO *African Diaspora; Black Popular Culture.*

BIBLIOGRAPHY

Abrahams, Roger D. 1992. *Singing the Master: The Emergence of African American Culture in the Plantation South*. New York: Pantheon Books.

Browning, Barbara. 1995. *Samba: Resistance in Motion.* Bloomington: Indiana University Press.

Chatterjea, Ananya. 2004. *Butting Out: Reading Resistive Choreographies through Works by Jawole Willa Jo Zollar and Chandralekha*. Middletown, CT: Wesleyan University Press.

Cohen, Selma Jeanne, ed. *International Encyclopedia of Dance*. 6 vols. New York: Oxford University Press, 1998.

Daniel, Yvonne. 1995. *Rumba: Dance and Social Change in Contemporary Cuba*. Bloomington: Indiana University Press.

DeFrantz, Thomas F. 1995. "Ballet." In *Encyclopedia of African-American Culture and History*, edited by Colin Palmer, 236–242. New York: Macmillan.

———. 1996. "The Black Body in Question: Scarce on Ballet Stages, African Americans Nevertheless Pace American Dance." *Village Voice* 23 (April): 9–32.

———. 2004. *Dancing Revelations: Alvin Ailey's Embodiment of African American Culture*. New York: Oxford University Press.

Desmond, Jane. 2001. *Dancing Desires: Choreographing Sexualities On and Off the Stage*. Madison: University of Wisconsin Press.

Emery, Lynn. 1980. *Black Dance in the United States from 1619 to 1970*. New York: Books for Libraries.

Garafola, Lynn. 1989. *Diaghilev's Ballets Russes*. New York: Oxford University Press.

Gottschild, Brenda Dixon. 2003. *The Black Dancing Body: A Geography from Coon to Cool*. New York: Palgrave Macmillan.

Greskovic, Robert. 1998. *Ballet 101: A Complete Guide to Learning and Loving the Ballet*. New York: Hyperion.

Manning, Susan. 2004. *Modern Dance, Negro Dance: Race in Motion*. Minneapolis: University of Minnesota Press.

Martin, John. 1932. "The Dance: A Negro Art Group." *New York Times*, February 14, p. X11.

Murphy, Jacqueline Shea. 2000. "Lessons in Dance (as) History: Aboriginal Land Claims and Aboriginal Dance, Circa. 1999." In *Dancing Bodies, Living Histories: New Writings about Dance and Culture*, edited by Lisa Doolittle and Anne Flynn Banff, 130–167. Banff, AB, Canada: Banff Centre Press, 2000.

Perpener, John. 2001. *African-American Concert Dance: The Harlem Renaissance and Beyond.* Urbana: University of Illinois Press.

Reynolds, Nancy, and Malcolm McCormick. 2003. *No Fixed Points: Dance in the Twentieth Century*. New Haven, CT: Yale University Press.

Thomas F. DeFrantz

DAVIS, ANGELA
1944–

Angela Y. Davis was born on January 26, 1944, in Birmingham, Alabama. An activist and scholar, Davis was appointed a professor in the History of Consciousness Program at the University of California, Santa Cruz, in 1991. She is one of the main architects of a global movement to abolish what she has called the "prison-industrial complex" in the United States and elsewhere in the world. Davis has campaigned against all forms of racism since the mid-1960s, publishing numerous articles and essays in both the popular media and scholarly journals, as well as a half dozen books. A sensational trial in which she was charged by the state of California with murder and kidnapping because of her prominence in a movement for prisoners' rights resulted in her acquittal on all charges in June 1972. As a result of the movement to "Free Angela Davis," she became an icon of revolutionary movements and national liberation struggles worldwide.

The oldest of four children, Davis's mother was Sallye B. Davis, an elementary school teacher, and her father, B. Frank Davis, was the owner of a local service station in Birmingham. At the age of four, her family moved to an all-white section of town, which became known as Dynamite Hill because of the number of racist-inspired bombings undertaken to drive out African-American families. Her family however, persevered. Davis went on to attend Elizabeth Irwin High School in New York City, and she graduated from Brandeis University in 1965 with a degree in French literature. After two years studying abroad, Davis returned to the United States and resumed her graduate studies at the University of California, San Diego, under the tutelage of the Marxist philosopher Herbert Marcuse. She joined the U.S. Communist Party and worked closely with the Black Panther Party in the late 1960s, while also writing her dissertation and teaching in the Philosophy Department at the University of California, Los Angeles.

Her academic career was interrupted by her imprisonment and trial. Davis was charged with first-degree murder, kidnapping, and conspiracy to commit both following an attempted escape by prisoners from San Quentin on August 7, 1970. The escape attempt was organized by Jonathan Jackson, the 17-year old brother of George Jackson, one of the Soledad Brothers. Davis knew Jonathan and was involved in the Soledad Brothers Defense Committee. In the attempted escape Jonathan and two prisoners were killed by San Quentin guards, and a judge was also killed. Another prisoner, Ruchell Magee, was badly wounded, and so was a woman juror. Davis was placed on the FBI's Ten Most Wanted list and was eventually arrested in New York City. She was then extradited to California to stand trial. Her case galvanized a global movement for her freedom, and catapulted her into international fame. Whereas the President of the United States, Richard Nixon, branded her "a terrorist," the "Free Angela" movement insisted upon her innocence and showed the ways in which a racist criminal justice system was deployed to seek to silence Davis for her radical activism. Her trial began on February 28, 1972, in San Jose, California, and ended in an acquittal on all counts on June 4, 1972. Following her acquittal, she resumed her scholarly work and helped to launch the National Alliance against Racist and Political Repression. After some thirty years campaigning to free individual prisoners, Davis helped to initiate a conference at the University of California, Berkeley, in September 2002. This conference launched a new movement called Critical Resistance, which was directed against the prison system itself. In her book *Are Prisons Obsolete?* (2004), Davis argued that prisons are part of a racist criminal justice system, and she showed how the prison-industrial complex was shaped by slavery and its aftermath.

Angela Davis has been pivotal in developing an antiracist feminist scholarship. She has been especially attentive to myriad forms of violence against women of color. While in prison she wrote "Reflections on the Black Woman's Role in the Community of Slaves," originally published in *The Black Scholar* in December 1971. This article helped to initiate the field of black women's studies. A second, very long essay, also written in prison, "Women and Capitalism: Dialectics of Oppression and Liberation," was prepared for a Symposium of the Philosophical Study of Dialectical Materialism in December 1971. (It was subsequently reprinted in the *Angela Y. Davis Reader*). This work is a detailed theoretical and political critique of the writings of white feminists in the women's liberation movement of the 1960s. In addition, Davis published an important collection of essays titled *Women, Race, and Class* in 1981. In 1998 she wrote *Blues Legacies and Black Feminism: Gertrude "Ma" Rainey, Bessie Smith, and Billie Holiday*, a detailed analysis of the feminist consciousness of working-class black women in the 1920s and 1930s. The book includes the lyrics to all the songs of the three singers.

As scholar, teacher, and activist Davis has inspired generations of students, colleagues, and community activists for more than forty years.

SEE ALSO *Black Feminism in the United States.*

BIBLIOGRAPHY

Davis, Angela Y. 1981. *Women, Race, and Class*. New York: Random House.

———. 1988. *An Autobiography*. New York: International Publishers. Originally published as *With My Mind on Freedom: An Autobiography* (New York: Random House, 1974).

———. 1998. *Blues Legacies and Black Feminism: Gertrude "Ma" Rainey, Bessie Smith, and Billie Holiday*. New York: Random House.

———. 2003. *Are Prisons Obsolete?* New York: Seven Stories Press.

James, Joy, ed. 1998. *The Angela Y. Davis Reader*. Malden, MA: Blackwell Publishers.

Bettina Aptheker

DAY LABORERS, LATINO

No formal definition of *day labor* exists, although the term is mostly used to convey a type of temporary employment that is distinguished by impermanency of employment, hazards in or undesirability of the work, the absence of fringe and other typical workplace benefits (e.g., breaks, safety equipment), and the daily search for employment. More specifically, day labor involves a group of men (and some women) who congregate on street corners, empty lots, or parking lots of home improvement stores, rental truck outlets, and paint stores to solicit temporary daily work. This type of work is growing and increasingly visible in those cities throughout the United States that have large concentrations of the working poor and Latino immigrants. Day labor is unstable and poorly paid, with most workers obtaining only one or two days of work per week, with wages clustering between eight and ten dollars per hour. The work that day laborers perform is often dangerous and dirty, and it is mostly in the fields of construction, landscaping, moving, demolition, and painting. With the exception of a few studies, little is known about this labor market because the workers move in and out freely; federal agencies inadequately define day labor, and thus do not count the participants accurately; and a large proportion of these workers are foreign-born, unauthorized, and Latino, making them difficult to study.

THE HISTORICAL CONTEXT OF DAY LABOR

The practice of men and women gathering in public settings in search of work dates back to at least medieval times, when the feudal city was originally a place of trade. In England during the 1100s, workers assembled at daily or weekly markets to be hired. Statutes regulated the opening of public markets in merchant towns and required agricultural workers (foremen, plowmen, carters, shepherds, swineherds, dairymen, and mowers) to appear with tools to be hired in a "commonplace and not privately" (Mund 1948, p. 96). In the United States during the early to mid-1800s, day laborers recruited from construction crews worked as track repairmen for railroad companies. Casual laborers (often out of work from construction jobs) worked in a variety of unskilled positions (e.g., brakemen, track repairmen, stevedores at depots, emergency firemen, snow clearers, or mechanic's assistants). Some of these workers were recent immigrants, particularly Chinese and Mexicans in the West and Germans and Irish in the East (Mohl 1971). Between 1788 and 1830, hundreds of day laborers (or "stand-ups," as they were known then) worked along the waterfront. More than half of New York City's male Irish workers were day laborers. In 1834, a "place was set aside on city streets in New York where those seeking work could meet with those who wanted workers" (Moore 1965). This exchange worked for both men and women, with employment for women (primarily African Americans) concentrated in the domestic labor market sector.

Since at least the mid-1800s, "shape-up" sites in New York and other Northeast ports provided a system of hiring dockworkers for the day or half-day (a minimum of four hours) by a seemingly arbitrary selection from a gathering of men. Under this casual labor system, longshoremen seeking work were forced to gather on the docks every morning to await the shape-up call from a hiring foreman signaling for the men to gather around him, usually in the shape of a circle or horseshoe, to be selected for work for the day or a four-hour shift. The number of men seeking work typically outnumbered the available jobs (Larrowe 1955).

Contemporary day labor in the United States (since at least the early 1970s) is not much different than it was in the past. Most of the participants are men, most are recent arrivals in the country, and most of their work is primarily in the construction industry. To the extent that women participate in day labor, their work is still primarily in domestic help. The growth and development of day labor in the United States and elsewhere has very real implications for thousands of workers and their employers. In its simplest form, day labor provides a distinct service to employers who wish to forego traditional forms of hiring workers and prefer not to undertake the time-consuming and costly activities associated with "regular" employment. The gains from hiring day laborers are clear: Day laborers are plentiful, easy to find, and relatively inexpensive to hire, and employers are spared liability and bureaucratic paper work. A subcontractor needing help to finish a project can easily hire a day laborer for several hours or several days to tidy up, remove debris, clean the site for inspection, or for other types of unskilled and skilled tasks. A job or project that would normally entail paying a regular worker at a higher rate is easily circumvented via this market. Similarly, a homeowner wishing to move from one home to another or uproot a tree in his or her backyard need not hire an expensive contractor for such seemingly simple but labor-intensive jobs. Day laborers also find some benefit from this type of labor market, particularly if they would not otherwise be employed. In addition, day laborers get paid in cash (usually untaxed), they can walk away from a job if dangerous or particularly dirty, and they can negotiate a wage for a day of work. Finally, for some day laborers, this occupation provides a level of flexibility that a regularly scheduled job does not, autonomy from a difficult employer, and the opportunity to learn different skills.

DAY LABOR IN THE UNITED STATES

Based on a national survey of day laborers conducted by Abel Valenzuela and colleagues in 2006, some key facts about the men (and the few women) who undertake this line of work are available. For example, on any given day, approximately 117,600 workers are either looking for day-labor jobs or employed as day laborers. Most day laborers congregate at informal hiring sites that have formed in front of home improvement stores and gas stations, along busy thoroughfares and near expressway on-ramps, or in parks and other public spaces. Because there are a small number (64 nationally in 2006) of officially sanctioned "worker centers," a minority of workers seek work at these formalized hiring halls, where day laborers and employers arrange the terms of employment for the day. The day-labor hiring site is a dynamic labor market whose size and dimensions change by the season, week, day, and even hour. The daily flow of workers through a site can vary dramatically as workers leave the site once they receive a job assignment and new job seekers are drawn to the site in their search for employment.

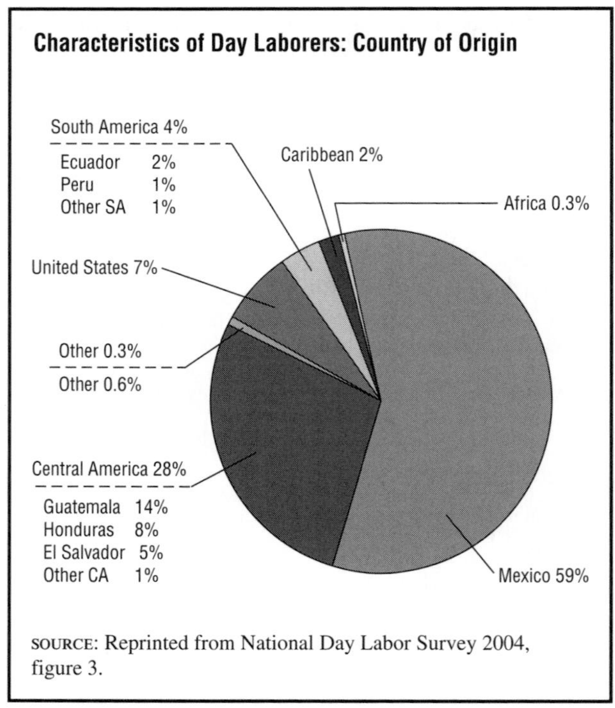

SOURCE: Reprinted from National Day Labor Survey 2004, figure 3.

Figure 1.

Day Laborers, September 2000. *Immigrants from Mexico wait on the street for work opportunities in Farmville, Long Island, New York. The work that day laborers perform is often dangerous and dirty and is mostly in construction, landscaping, moving, demolition, and painting.* © ERIK FREELAND/CORBIS SABA.

The largest concentration of hiring sites and day laborers is in the West, while the Midwest is the region with the fewest number of sites and workers. The day-labor workforce in the United States is predominantly male (just 2% are female) and largely comprised of migrants from Mexico and Central America (see Figure 1). More than half (59%) of day laborers surveyed were born in Mexico, 14 percent were born in Guatemala, and 8 percent were born in Honduras. U.S.-born workers comprise 7 percent of the day-labor workforce, though in the southern region of the country almost one in five day laborers were born in the United States. Three-quarters of the day-labor workforce were undocumented migrants. However, about 11 percent of the undocumented day-labor workforce had a pending application for an adjustment of their immigration status. It has not been possible to determine how many of these workers may indeed be eligible for temporary or permanent immigration relief.

Overall, day laborers tend to be relatively recent immigrants. Almost one in five (19%) migrated to the United States less than one year before they were interviewed at a day-labor hiring site, while 40 percent have resided in the United States for one to five years. Less than one-third of day laborers (29%) have resided in the United States for between six and 20 years, and 11 percent have resided in the United States for more than two decades.

Day laborers experience a high incidence of workplace injury. One in five day laborers suffered an injury while on the job. Rates of work-related injury are highest in the Midwest, where one-third of the day laborers have been hurt on the job. Most day laborers are aware that their work is dangerous, but the pressing need for employment finds them returning to this market to search for work. About three-quarters of day laborers nationwide find their occupations to be dangerous, while in the Midwest, where roofing jobs are undertaken at significantly higher rates than in the other regions, an astounding 92 percent find their work to be dangerous.

Employer violations of day laborers' rights and violations of basic labor standards are an all too common occurrence in the day-labor market. Wage theft is the most typical abuse experienced by day laborers. Nearly half of all day laborers (49%) have been completely denied payment by an employer for work they completed in the two months prior to being surveyed. Similarly, 48 percent have been underpaid by employers during the same time period.

DAY-LABOR WORKER CENTERS

In addition to the hundreds of informal hiring sites that have proliferated across the United States, 64 day-labor worker centers, or formal hiring sites, have been established by community organizations, municipal governments, faith-based organizations, and other local stakeholders. The goal of these centers is to curtail wage theft, abuse, and hazardous working conditions. The creation of day-labor worker centers is a relatively recent phenomenon, with most having been established since 2000. Worker centers are typically located near informal day-labor hiring sites, offering both workers and contractors an alternative to the unregulated sites found on street corners and in parking lots. Indeed, location can be a crucial determinant of a center's success, and these hiring sites are frequently established in areas where both workers and employers have ready access.

Most day-labor worker centers provide fairly basic accommodations to workers and employers. All operate as hiring halls where employers and day laborers can arrange work for the day. Available amenities and services typically include restrooms, drinking water, places to sit, telephones, classrooms, outreach to employers, and parking facilities. But even such simple provisions are a marked improvement over informal hiring sites. Moreover, they serve to establish a worker center's presence in the day-labor market. The primary purpose of day-labor worker centers is to regulate the day-labor market by intervening in the market and establishing rules governing the search for work and the hiring of laborers. Through these core activities, worker centers are able to place a "safety floor" under conditions in the day-labor market and curtail abuses and workplace injuries.

SEE ALSO *Braceros, Repatriation, and Seasonal Workers; Farmworkers; Immigrant Domestic Workers; Immigration to the United States; Undocumented Workers; Workfare and Welfare.*

BIBLIOGRAPHY

Larrowe, Charles P. 1955. *Shape-up and Hiring Hall: A Comparison of Hiring Methods and Labor Relations on the New York and Seattle Waterfronts.* Berkeley: University of California Press.

Mohl, Raymond A. 1971. *Poverty in New York, 1783-1825.* New York: Oxford University Press.

Moore, Mack A. 1965. "The Temporary Help Service Industry: Historical Development, Operation, and Scope." *Industrial and Labor Relations Review* 18 (4): 554–569.

Mund, Vernon A. 1948. *Open Markets: An Essential of Free Enterprise.* New York: Harper Brothers.

Valenzuela, Abel, Jr. 2001. "Day Laborers as Entrepreneurs?" *Journal of Ethnic and Migration Studies* 27 (2): 335–352.

———. 2002. "Working on the Margins in Metropolitan Los Angeles: Immigrants in Day Labor Work." *Migraciones Internacionales* 1 (2): 5–28.

———. 2003. "Day-Labor Work." *Annual Review of Sociology* 29 (1): 307–333.

———, Janette A. Kawachi, and Matthew D. Marr. 2002. "Seeking Work Daily: Supply, Demand, and Spatial Dimensions of Day Labor in Two Global Cities." *International Journal of Comparative Sociology* 43 (2): 192–219.

———, Nik Theodore, Edwin Melendez, and Ana Luz Gonzalez. 2006. "On the Corner: Day Labor in the United States." Technical Report, UCLA Center for the Study of Urban Poverty. Available from http://www.sscnet.ucla.edu/issr/csup/index.php.

Abel Valenzuela Jr.

DEME

Deme (pronounced "deem," from the Greek for "people" and originally referring to a political division within ancient Greece) has been used in biology since the 1930s as a term for a local interbreeding population within a species. As such, the recognition of demes can be confused with, and can appear to provide justification for, the existence of biological races or subspecies.

The rationale for naming population units below the species level comes from the simple fact that members of a species are seldom, if ever, evenly distributed throughout the species' geographical range. Uneven distribution can result in clusters of individuals partially isolated from other such clusters—that is, with more interbreeding within the clusters than between them—simply because of proximity. It is to such clusters that the term *deme* is usually applied. Thus, the green frogs in an isolated pond, a town of prairie dogs, or a field of wild sunflowers might be examples of demes.

If demes inhabit different local environments, natural selection can operate in different directions in these populations with the result that there may be genetic and even physical variation in the characteristics of individual demes. Other processes of evolution, such as mutation and other forms of genetic change, can also enhance these differences, depending upon the extent of demic isolation.

The problem with the concept of the deme is that there is no definitive set of criteria for recognizing demes within species. Normally, some spatial separation or other obvious impediment to genetic exchange is a clue, with genetic or physical distinctions as an expected result. Demes, however, are populations within species, and by definition, exchange genes with other demes of the same species either directly, in the case of adjacent demes, or by a series of steps, in the case of widely separated demes.

Demes are also transitory. According to Stephen Jay Gould in *The Structure of Evolutionary Theory,* demes have "porous borders," they do not function as a "discrete [evolutionary] entities," and are "defined only by the transient and clumpy nature of . . . habitats" (p. 647). Richard Dawkins, in *The Selfish Gene,* likened demes to "clouds in the sky or dust storms in the desert . . . temporary aggregations" (p. 36). Moreover, even if demes are spatially distinct clusters, their phenotypic features might still grade into one another in response to environmental gradients, thus making the boundaries between the demes even less distinct. This is known as a clinal distribution.

Given the accepted general definition, it can certainly be said that demes exist within the human species, where they are identified as semi-isolated endogamous (literally, "marriage within") populations. The isolation may be spatial, as in any of a number of societies inhabiting separate and secluded valleys in the New Guinea Highlands, or cultural, as in the religiously based isolation of groups such as the Hutterites, Mennonites, and Amish.

All human populations consist of members of a single species. Thus, by definition, they exchange genes with other populations, directly or indirectly. More specifically, even the most isolated human population has experienced gene flow with adjacent populations at some point in time. Outsiders have always married into the Hutterites, for example, and Hutterites have married out. Over time, human demes are as ephemeral as those of any other species, and probably more so, given the human proclivities for mobility and genetic exchange.

The question becomes, then, what is the relationship between the concept of the deme and that of the biological race or subspecies? Both are proposed populations below the species level. Traditionally, a biological race was considered to be a group of related demes inhabiting the same general region and sharing genetic and/or physical characteristics (Savage 1977; Mettler et al. 1988).

The limitations noted for the deme concept, however, provide a lesson for considering such larger groups as races or subspecies because those limitations become more pronounced with larger populations. Larger populations within a species contain more genetic and physical variation, and thus stand even less chance of having specific biological characteristics. Because there is more gene flow between large populations, the boundaries between such populations are further blurred and have less real biological meaning and utility. At best, as Lawrence Mettler et al. note, defining and naming subspecific groups is "purely subjective" and a "matter of convenience" for the purpose of "intelligible communication" (1988, p. 48).

SEE ALSO *Clusters; Gene Pool; Subspecies.*

BIBLIOGRAPHY

Dawkins, Richard. 1976. *The Selfish Gene.* Oxford: Oxford University Press.

Gould, Stephen Jay. 2002. *The Structure of Evolutionary Theory.* Cambridge, MA: Belknap.

Mettler, Lawrence E., Thomas G. Gregg, and Henry E. Schaffer. 1988. *Population Genetics and Evolution,* 2nd ed. Englewood Cliffs, NJ: Prentice Hall.

Savage, Jay M. 1977. *Evolution,* 3rd ed. New York: Holt, Rinehart and Winston.

Michael Alan Park

DEMOGRAPHICS AND RACE

The United States Census has collected information about race ever since the first census was taken in 1790. Indeed, the Census and the collection of information about race were originally mandated in the U.S. Constitution. In Article One, Section Two, the founders of the United States set forth the language for collecting information about race in the decennial census:

> Representatives and direct Taxes shall be apportioned among the several States which may be included within this Union, according to their respective Numbers, which shall be determined by adding to the whole Number of free Persons, including those bound to Service for a Term of Years, and excluding Indians not taxed, three fifths of all other Persons. The actual Enumeration shall be made within three Years after the first Meeting of the Congress of the United States, and within every subsequent Term of ten Years, in such Manner as they shall by Law direct.

This language acknowledges several racial designations. In almost all circumstances "free persons" and persons "bound to service for a term of years" meant European immigrants and their descendants. Very clearly, American Indians who resided outside the jurisdiction of Anglo-American communities were excluded, insofar as they could not be taxed. The notorious "three-fifths compromise" was an obvious allusion to African slaves and their descendants, who were born into slavery for the duration of their lives.

Despite the obvious racial overtones of this language, it is important to understand that the Constitution was a product of Enlightenment philosophy. The Enlightenment had an enormous influence on the framing of the U.S. government, but, ironically, this intellectual tradition offered little insight into the nature of race and racial distinctions. As a result, the incorporation of race into the Constitution was shaped more by considerations of conquest and oppression than by abstract philosophical principles. Race, for the founders of the United States, was mostly a matter of civil status.

THE HISTORY OF MODERN RACE CONSCIOUSNESS

The articulation of racial thinking that would justify the collection of information about race awaited the emergence of biology as a full-fledged body of scientific knowledge in the late eighteenth century. The Swedish biologist Carl Linnaeus deserves credit for devising the first racial classification for *Homo sapiens*, published in 1735. This classification consisted of four groups—*Americanus, Africanus, Asiaticus*, and *Europeanus*—and each was associated with race-specific behavioral characteristics. In 1775 the German scientist Johann Blumenbach elaborated Linnaeus's scheme and introduced a vocabulary for describing race that still more or less remains in use. His categories were Caucasian, Malayan, Mongolian, Negro, and American. Blumenbach also assigned particular behavioral traits to each of these groups. The work of Linnaeus, Blumenbach, and the French biologist Jean-Baptiste Lamarck had a profound influence on scientific thinking about race in the United States, and on the way racial data were collected in nineteenth-century censuses.

From 1790 to 1810, there were few changes in the U.S. Census. Households were enumerated according to the number of persons, both free and slave, and most American Indians were excluded from the count. The first significant modification of the census with respect to race occurred in the 1820 enumeration, in which a distinction was made for "colored" persons, free or slave. At the very least, this signified that there were sufficient numbers of free colored persons to merit enumeration, as well as a tacit acknowledgement that race was a physical quality in addition to being a condition of civil status.

The distinction between free and slave colored persons remained in the next several censuses, but the 1840 census was particularly noteworthy; it was the first to precipitate a controversy over the accuracy of racial data. In particular, the 1840 enumeration resulted in an unusually large number of "colored insane" living in northern states. This, of course, became fodder in the slavery debates, with the proponents of slavery using this finding to argue for the deleterious consequences of emancipation (Anderson 1988).

The debates over the accuracy of the 1840 census proved to be long lasting and especially bitter. They also set the stage for a larger role for scientific opinion in the 1850 census. Congress appointed a special Census Board consisting of the secretaries of state and commerce and the Postmaster General. This board received considerable authority to conduct the census, and it appointed Joseph C. G. Kennedy as the superintendent of the census. Kennedy proved to be a highly effective leader and an especially important superintendent because he actively sought scientific advice about how to conduct the census. He sought, for the first time, the advice of leaders in the American Statistical Association and the American Geographical and Statistical Society, as well as leading European statisticians such as Charles Babbage.

The 1850 census was taken in an era when the country was not yet at war, but the sectional conflict over slavery was growing in intensity. It was also a period when eugenics and ethnology were reaching a pinnacle of influence within the scientific community. Among the innovations introduced by Kennedy for the 1850 census was a special schedule for the enumeration of slaves—they were identified by a number along with the name of their owner. The 1850 census also admonished enumerators to carefully record the racial heritage of household members. One noteworthy innovation in this census was the introduction of the term "Mulatto." It was the first tacit acknowledgement that sexual relations transcended racial barriers and that the offspring of these unions existed in sufficient numbers to merit enumeration.

POST-CIVIL WAR CENSUSES

In the decades following the Civil War, the race question was modified in ways that reflected the social and political concerns of the era. The preoccupations of scientific racism played a very large role in the development of the census. The enumerator instructions in the 1870 census epitomized the obsession with racial purity that characterized this period. These instructions admonished enumerators to "Be particularly careful in reporting the class Mulatto. ... Important scientific results depend on the correct determination of this class" (Snipp 2003, p. 567).

The 1890 census did not stress the scientific importance of its racial classification or the gravity of accurately assessing racial heritage. However, it was significant because it introduced an even finer classification for persons with African heritage by identifying persons as Octoroons, Quadroons, or Mulattos. It took careful stock of the racial composition of the American Indian population, particularly the numbers of mixed-race persons. Another significant innovation reflected the racist and nativist concerns about immigration from China and Japan. Earlier censuses had enumerated the presence of Chinese and Japanese immigrants in California. Their numbers had grown sufficiently large in other parts of the country causing an outpouring of alarm that culminated in the 1882 Chinese Exclusion Act. The 1890 census was the first effort to monitor the spread of Chinese and Japanese immigrants to locations outside California.

At the dawn of the twentieth century, ideas about race that first appeared in the early and mid-nineteenth century were still influential. Jim Crow racism institutionalized these ideas and made them the scientific underpinnings for laws and public policy governing race relations in the early twentieth century. For example, the so-called one-drop rule stipulated that even the smallest amount of African heritage was sufficient to be designated as black. Consequently, for the 1900 census, efforts to divide the black population into subgroups such as Octoroon were abandoned. By 1920, at the peak of Jim Crow, even the category of Mulatto was jettisoned.

Changing patterns of immigration and continuing anti-Asian public sentiment led to the addition of several new categories in the 1930 census. Specifically, the government added categories for Mexican, Filipino, Hindu, and Korean. With the exception of "Mexican," these categories were retained in a virtually identical format for the 1940 census. In response to lobbying by the Mexican government, the Census Bureau deleted "Mexican" as a separate designation and counted Mexican Americans as "White." One other change connected with the 1940 census was that data for ethnic minorities ceased to be published as part of the decennial reports for states and localities. Instead, a special subject report was issued titled *Characteristics of the Nonwhite Population by Race.*

Racial measurement in post–World War II America became an urgent matter for at least two reasons. First, a significant undercount of black men was discovered to exist in the 1940 census, and a similar undercount was documented after the 1950 census. Second, and more important, the civil rights movement gathered momentum and the census, as the principal tool for allocating political power and resources, became recognized as essential for ensuring the enfranchisement of blacks and other minorities. Given the unmatched importance of the census for obtaining fair political representation, any undercount of racial or ethnic minorities was simply unacceptable.

SELF-IDENTIFICATION

In every census since World War II, the U.S. government, particularly the U.S. Census Bureau, has struggled to minimize the undercount of racial and ethnic minorities while also confronting other challenges, such as containing the costs of the census. One cost-cutting measure that proved to have profound consequences for the way the census measures race was introduced in the 1960 census. Prior to 1960, the decennial census was taken by enumerators conducting door-to-door interviews. Race was a characteristic that was visually determined and recorded by the interviewer. To save the expense of hiring thousands of enumerators for the 1960 census, the Census Bureau mailed census forms to households and allowed individuals to self-identify their race. This led to a subtle, though fundamentally profound, shift in the measurement of race in the census. The race that individuals reported in the census was determined less by the phenotypical cues that might influence an enumerator's judgment, and more by the personal beliefs, feelings, and attitudes that shape the racial identity of individuals. Race was no longer a matter of observable physical traits; it was now a matter of personal subjectivity.

The shift to self-identification had little or no effect on the enumeration of some groups, such as blacks or whites. However, for one group—American Indians and Alaskan Natives—the effect was profoundly significant. The shift to self-identification resulted in a significant increase in the number of American Indians, rising from 357,000 in 1950 to 524,000 in 1960—an increase of 47 percent. This increase was followed by similar or even larger increases in subsequent decades. Some of this increase was due to an excess of births over deaths. However, an even larger amount was due to the fact that many persons who had once been identified as white or black chose to report their heritage as American Indian.

The Census Bureau continued to use the same question format for obtaining information about race in 1970, 1980, and 1990, albeit with small modifications. The 1990 census proved to be a pivotal event that triggered a storm of protests because it instructed respondents to choose only one race for their heritage. Even more infuriating was the fact that if respondents chose to mark more than one race for their background, the Census Bureau had a complex procedure in place for assigning one and only one race to each individual for whom more than one race was reported. The groups who objected most strongly to this measure were mixed-race couples that were expected to choose one over another in designating a race for their children. Why, they demanded, should a child with a black mother and a white father be forced to choose one race or another, when in fact they were genuinely multiracial?

A MULTIRACIAL POPULATION

These complaints eventually led Congress and the Office of Management and Budget to undertake a thorough review of the procedures the federal government uses for the collection of information about race. In October 1997 the U.S. government issued new guidelines for collecting this information. These guidelines were mandatory for all federal agencies, their contractors, and their grantees, effective January 2003. The new guidelines made two significant changes. One was the creation of a new category: "Native Hawaiians and other Pacific Islanders." Formerly, people in this population had been counted among "Asians and Pacific Islanders." The second and most profound change was a mandate that whenever the federal government (or its contractors or grantees) collects information about race, the instruction to "mark one or more" or "choose one or more" must appear on the questionnaire.

The Census Bureau was the first government agency to adopt this language. Thus, the 2000 census included language on the race question that instructed respondents to "Mark one or more races to indicate what this person considers himself/herself to be." In response to this question, 6.8 million persons were identified as having more than one race—about 2.4 percent of the total U.S. population. Relatively little is known about this population except that it is an extraordinarily diverse group. For example, persons of black and American Indian heritage are very different from persons of white and Asian descent in terms of where and how they live. Another notable quality is that about 22 percent of the multiracial population is composed of Hispanic persons who identify themselves as "White" and "Some Other Race." Studies conducted by the U.S. Census Bureau indicate that multiracial persons frequently change the way they identify their race, perhaps in ways to meet the social expectations of other persons around them (Bentley et al. 2003).

The racial data produced by the 2000 census is an extraordinarily complex body of information, but in many respects it mirrors the racial complexity of American society. Once it seemed possible to frame race and ethnicity in American society entirely as a matter of black and white. The changing nature of American society, however, now demands an approach that allows for myriad forms of racial identification, and data will undoubtedly be even more complex in the future.

BIBLIOGRAPHY

Anderson, Margo. 1988. *The American Census: A Social History.* New Haven, CT: Yale University Press.

Bentley, Michael, Tracy Mattingly, Christine Hough, and Claudette Bennett. 2003. *Census Quality Survey to Evaluate Responses to the Census 2000 Question on Race: An Introduction to the Data.* Washington, DC: U.S. Bureau of the Census. Available from http://www2.census.gov/census_2000/datasets/CQS/B.3.pdf.

Fredrickson, George M. 2002. *Racism: A Short History.* Princeton, NJ: Princeton University Press.

Snipp, C. Matthew. 1989. *American Indians: The First of This Land.* New York: Russell Sage Foundation.

———. 2003. "Racial Measurement in the American Census: Past Practices and Implications for the Future." *Annual Review of Sociology* 29: 563–588.

Woodward, C. Vann. 1974. *The Strange Career of Jim Crow,* 3rd ed. New York: Oxford University Press.

C. Matthew Snipp

DEW, THOMAS RODERICK
1802–1846

In the wake of the Nat Turner rebellion of 1831, which took the lives of fifty-seven whites in Southampton County, Virginia, and startled slaveholders throughout the South, the Virginia House of Delegates conducted an intense debate in 1832 over the institution of slavery itself throughout the South. Although the numbers of whites and blacks directly involved was small, with about seventy slave rebels in Turner's band, the census of 1830 showed that Virginia contained 694,306 whites to 462,031 blacks, including 47,348 free blacks. As a direct result of the insurrection, more than 200 potential slave insurgents were executed; throughout the South, tighter rules were enacted for controlling blacks, free and unfree. Racial membership was seen literally as a matter of life and death.

The idea that any white person could lose his or her life in a slave uprising raised new fundamental issues about the institution of slavery, issues related to justice, safety, property rights, governance, economic value, moral effects, racial status, emancipation, colonization, and the "good" society. The members of the Virginia assembly were aware of the abolition of slavery in Mexico in 1829, as well as the decision of the British government to terminate slavery in the English-speaking West Indies. In January and February 1832 the legislators intensely debated the pros and cons of these issues. When the debates ended with the legality of slavery unchanged but the state seriously divided between its western sections, with few slaves, and the rest of the state, with the nation's largest proportion of blacks, Governor John Floyd requested Thomas R. Dew to write a document to temper the effects of the debates. Dew, a thirty-year-old professor at the College of William and Mary, responded with *Review of the Debate in the Virginia Legislature of 1831 and 1832.*

Born into an affluent family in King and Queen County in Virginia on December 5, 1802, Thomas Roderick Dew studied history, metaphysics, political economy, law, and government at William and Mary College in Virginia. Following his graduation in 1820 at the early age of eighteen, he toured Europe and studied philosophy in Germany before returning to the United States. In 1826 his alma mater hired him to teach history and political economy, and subsequently appointed him in 1836 to serve as its thirteenth president, a position he held to his death of pneumonia in Paris in 1846.

What follows is a summary of the primary points made in Dew's *Review of the Debate in the Virginia Legislature of 1831 and 1832.*

Dew held that, overall, slavery was good for the South and the enslaved blacks. He noted that slavery had not only been part of human history since antiquity, but the Bible also sanctioned it. He chastised—as inexperienced youthful males who were swayed by the enchantments of ill-advised so-called humanitarians—the Virginian lawmakers who supported an aspect of Thomas Jefferson's idea. (Although he accepted Jefferson's racist views about blacks, Dew strongly opposed the black colonization vision that the former had stressed in his book *Notes on the State of Virginia*).

Dew supported slavery and used racist, religious, and moral sentiments, among others, to justify the perpetuation of slavery, precisely because he felt that Virginia and the rest of America would not survive economically or materially without slavery. He hypothesized that southern states would suffer from permanent famine if slavery were immediately abolished. He added that such a famine would be so severe that resources from other states in the Union would not eradicate it.

Perhaps referencing the chaos brought by the abolition of slavery in Haiti and other Caribbean islands in the 1790s and 1830, Dew echoed his opposition to immediate abolition of slavery when he implied that the replacement of enslaved labor with free labor in society would only bring social disruptions and calamities to such a society. To morally validate the continuation of slavery, Dew noted that any immediate abolition of slavery would only bring devastation to both former masters and slaves.

In line with his racist view, Dew noted that slavery changed the slaves from indolent and childlike Africans to a proficient workforce that cultivated crops, such as rice, sugar cane, tobacco, and cotton, and that helped to enrich America and other countries. He further noted that slavery, together with the racism used to justify slavery, was good in another sense because it was obviously helping to alleviate the tension that existed between the privileged and poor white classes in the antebellum South.

Dew's statement that most slave-masters were good to their slaves was apparently intended to provide a further justification for the perpetuation of slavery, because the view implied that slavery was beneficial to the slaves as well as to the masters, and therefore there was no moral justification for its abolition.

Dew's implication was that most slaves showed sincere affection for their masters, because according to him, they received paternal, benevolent treatment from them. Another example of Dew's use of racism to rationalize the continuation of slavery is his view that the enslaved blacks would become the most insignificant and lazy of all Americans if slavery were abolished.

As noted, Dew not only attacked the supporters of abolition of slavery, but he also strongly rebuffed the American Colonization Society's (ACS) attempt to colonize blacks on the coast of West Africa. To turn Southern planters against the ACS, Dew inconsistently envisaged that any regular expatriation of blacks from America would simply increase the cost of slaves, hearten slave procreation, increase the population of blacks in America, and overall would bring about irredeemable economic ruin to the antebellum South. He reminded Southerners as well as Northerners that there was nothing as risky as the attempt on the part of the ACS to tamper with the population of blacks. He added that such a move would increase the population of black people so dramatically that ACS would be unable to accommodate it. Dew declared that the colonization scheme was nothing but madness. He cautioned that if the scheme were to be carried out, it would destroy a large portion of Virginia's wealth, together with its proud history and material achievements.

Thomas Dew's publication was widely distributed and became the pro-slavery guidebook in the Deep South, giving much aid and comfort to those who may have once felt that something was not right in the buying and selling of human beings.

BIBLIOGRAPHY

Beyan, Amos J. 1995. "The Transatlantic Trade and Coastal Area of Pre-Liberia." *The Historian* 57 (3): 757–768.

———. 2005. *African American Settlements in West Africa: John Brown Russwurm and the American Civilizing Efforts*. New York: Palgrave Macmillan.

Clegg, Claude A, III. 2004. *The Price of Liberty: African Americans and the Making of Liberia*. Chapel Hill: University Press of North Carolina.

Dew, Thomas Roderick. 1832. *Review of the Debate in the Virginia Legislature of 1831 and 1832*. Richmond, VA: T.W. White.

Rodney, Walter. 1974. *How Europe Underdeveloped Africa*. Washington, DC: Howard University Press.

Ruchames, Louis, ed. 1961. *Racial Thought in America: From the Puritans to Abraham, A Documentary History*. Amherst: University of Massachusetts Press.

Smith, John S. 1985. *An Old Creed for the New South: Proslavery Ideology and Historiography, 1865–1918*. Westport, CT: Greenwood Press.

Staudenraus, P.J. 1961. *African Colonization Movement, 1816–1865*. New York: Columbia University Press.

Tise, Larry E. 1990. *Proslavery: A History of Defense of Slavery in America, 1701–1840*. Athens: University of Georgia Press.

Tuttle, William M., ed. 1973. *W. E. B. Du Bois*. Englewood Cliffs, NJ: Prentice-Hall.

Williams, Eric. 1994. *Capitalism and Slavery*. Chapel Hill: University of North Carolina Press.

Amos J. Beyan

DIABETES

Starting in the second half of the twentieth century, the prevalence of non-insulin-dependent (type 2) diabetes increased substantially in many populations and ethnic groups, including African Americans, Native Americans, Mexicans Americans, and Pacific Islanders. Diabetes is a metabolic disorder characterized by an inability to regulate blood sugar. The increase in this disease is clearly related to shifts in diet and lifestyle. While some researchers have proposed that it is related to genetic factors, other researchers point to stressful and challenging life conditions resulting from poverty and social inequality.

THE EPIDEMIOLOGY OF TYPE 2 DIABETES MELLITUS

More than 90 percent of all diabetics have type 2 diabetes. Unlike the more rare form of the disease, type 1 diabetes, people with type 2 diabetes produce insulin and therefore seldom need therapeutic insulin at the initial onset of the disease. Type 2 diabetes is considered a late-onset chronic disease and is associated with risk factors such as increased obesity, dietary fat intake, smoking, and low physical activity. Racism, stress, and socioeconomic status have also been implicated in the development of diabetes. Diabetes is diagnosed by measuring the percentage of red blood cells that are bound with glucose. There is no cure for diabetes, but the traditional treatment includes alterations in diet, exercise, and drug therapies to control glucose metabolism.

Prevalence rates follow a strikingly similar pattern in varied populations. For First Nations Canadian men and women, age-adjusted prevalence rates are 3.6 and 5.5 times higher, respectively, than among the general Canadian population. Among Indigenous Australians, the prevalence rates are almost four times higher than the rate for the non-Indigenous population. Researchers comparing age-adjusted prevalence rates for Nigerians and people of African origin living elsewhere found diabetes rates were 2.5 to 5 times higher for those living in the Caribbean and United Kingdom. In the United States, the National Institute of Diabetes and Digestive and Kidney Diseases (NIDDK) estimates that at least 8 to 10 percent of all Latinos, African Americans, and Native Americans aged twenty years or older have diabetes. The comparable prevalence rates for non-Hispanic whites is 4.8 percent.

According to the U.S. Centers for Disease Control and Prevention (CDC), diabetes is the seventh leading cause of death in the United States. The World Health Organization (WHO) has called diabetes an emerging epidemic, with more than 16 million people affected in the United States and millions more in the rapidly urbanizing Southern Hemisphere and China. According to the WHO, approximately 366 million people worldwide will have diabetes by 2025. The very similar epidemiological patterns that exist for U.S. minorities, First Nations Canadians, Indigenous Australians, peoples of the African diaspora, and peoples of the Pacific Islands strongly indicate that diabetes disproportionately affects subordinated groups around the world.

COMPETING ETIOLOGICAL HYPOTHESES: NURTURE VERSUS NATURE

Type 2 diabetes (hereafter referred to simply as diabetes), like heart disease, hypertension, and asthma, is a complex disease because its putative risks lay in both environmental and biological domains. That is, diabetes is caused by an as yet unknown combination of factors such as lifestyle, diet, physical activity, and an array of physiological triggers. The relative overburden of diabetes on people whose social histories contain violent and radical disruptions of their lifeways has not resulted in any real agreement about its cause. Rather, diabetes has engendered competing etiological hypotheses. For simplicity, these three competing theories will be named the social conditions, the fetal origins, and the thrifty genotype hypothesis respectively.

Research into the social conditions that impact diabetogenesis has generated considerable evidence for the link between stress and glucose metabolic impairment. Life conditions such as experiences of racism, poverty, and job insecurity have all been associated with measured levels of elevated blood glucose. These findings clearly suggest that the epidemiological patterns of diabetes reflect sociocultural conditions in nonrandom ways. For example, the increased prevalence of diabetes within Native American, Latino, and African-American groups can be attributed to the differential experiences of social inequality these groups endure compared to nonwhite Hispanics. Similarly, the increasing rates of diabetes in geographic areas where human populations are rapidly moving to urban areas suggests that the disease may be an index of the stressors of rural-to-urban migration and lifeways disruptions resulting from the profound political and economic dislocations required for flexible labor markets.

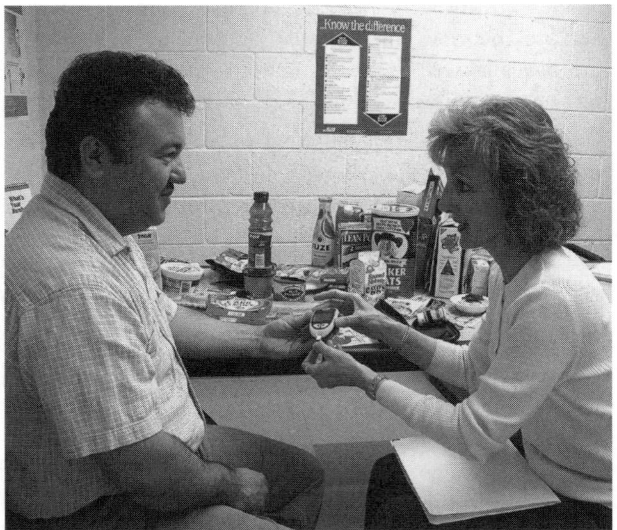

Controlling Diabetes. *A diabetic receives information from a dietician on the use of a blood sugar monitor. In the United States, the National Institute of Diabetes and Digestive and Kidney Diseases (NIDDK) estimates that at least 8 to 10 percent of all Latinos, African Americans, and Native Americans twenty years old or older have diabetes.* AP IMAGES.

Researchers looking for physiological causes of diabetes investigate conditions during fetal development as primarily responsible for the disease. This hypothesis, also called the thrifty phenotype hypothesis, the developmental hypothesis, or the fetal origins hypothesis, proposes that poor fetal conditions, such as those that cause low birth weight, impair the in-utero development of the glucose-insulin physiological systems. Research in a number of populations and animal studies suggests that the fetus adapts itself to its developmental environment as a preparatory response to postnatal life conditions. Because low birth weight is also associated with the deprivations often linked to social inequality, the fetal origins hypothesis implicates historical and contemporary systems of social stratification as causally linked to disease outcomes in groups with these experiences. Fetal origins research offers physiological evidence that social and environmental conditions related to social inequality can impact developmental gene expression and lead to impaired health in adult life.

The other dominant theory for the pronounced differences in the prevalence of diabetes, and perhaps the oldest, is the thrifty genotype hypothesis. Research into this hypothesis attempts to explain disparities in disease patterns between human groups as a function of evolutionary pressures. One of the oldest gene-based theories of chronic disease causation, the thrifty genotype hypothesis postulates the existence of an evolutionarily and advantageous genetic predisposition to the efficient metabolic storage and utilization of caloric energy—a predisposition rendered "maladaptive" by the contemporary widespread overabundance of food. The thrifty genotype hypothesis has enjoyed more than four decades of concerted research attention, coinciding with, and in many respects developing alongside, the molecular revolution.

In this model, disparities in diabetes between various ethnoracial groups are often attributed to the genetic triggering of the "thrifty genes" that are presumed to result from the transition to urban, sedentary lifestyles. The original proponent of the thrifty genotype hypothesis, geneticist James Neel (1915–2000), considered diabetes a condition of environmental origins. In his final statement on diabetes, Neel found "no support to the notion that high frequency of NIDDM [non-insulin-dependent diabetes mellitus] in reservation Amerindians might be due simply to an ethnic predisposition—rather, it must predominantly reflect lifestyle changes" (Neel 1999, p. S3). Still, the thrifty genotype model has widespread allegiance and fuels millions of dollars in research activity.

RACIALIZATION: SOCIAL DESCRIPTIONS VERSUS BIOLOGICAL ATTRIBUTIONS

The technical, methodological, and conceptual premises of the gene-based hypothesis have engendered considerable ethical debates surrounding the use of socially labeled populations for studies of complex diseases like diabetes. Underlying these current debates are laudable goals of disease prevention and harm reduction for all persons, especially descendants of the formerly enslaved or colonized. Yet the persistence of these concerns, in and out of academe, signals a fundamentally sociocultural phenomenon that will not be resolved by attention to analytical considerations alone and will involve complex sociological and cultural factors.

First, owing to advances in genomic biology, genetics-based models of diabetes causation now have considerable advantages in competition for research attention. Researchers claim that finding genetic contributions to complex diseases is the first step to understanding physiology and subsequent drug interventions. In nations where public health infrastructures are already suffering from neglect, the policy impulse to advance a gene-based research that promises drug therapies for the most costly diseases is understandable. Yet while public health interventions to prevent tobacco use, require seat belts, provide prenatal care, and make vaccinations widely available have been proven to be cost effective, no such proof exists for gene-based research into complex diseases such as diabetes. Thus, there is reason to dispute the high investment in capital and human talent for scientific hypotheses that have little translatable application toward disease prevention and treatment.

Second, the use of genetic variation hypotheses to explain ethnoracial differences in complex diseases is a particular form of racialization, which is "a dialectical process by which meaning is attributed to particular biological features of human beings, as a result of which individuals may be assigned to a general category of persons that reproduces itself biologically" (Miles and Brown 2003, p. 102). In other words, racialization is the attribution of innate fixed biological differences between human groups labeled with ethnic, cultural, national, political, or geographical taxonomies. It does not refer to descriptive taxonomic structures, which are the labels humans use to identify themselves or others. Rather, racialization occurs when these descriptions are used in a manner that ascribes a somatic innate and fixed difference between the labeled groups. In the descriptive mode, the labels black, African American, Latino, Mexicano, or white are labels used as identifiers. Yet these identifiers have been shown time and again to be historically and situationally determined, unreliable, and invalid proxies for biological human differences.

Socially derived group labels, at best, work like pronouns, always requiring specification and never defining the person or thing to which the pronoun refers. In the attributive mode, these labels are used to ascribe fixed, innate attributes to the bodies of human groups. This occurs, for example, when geneticists studying diabetes use "Mexicano" as a label and attach to it the meanings of biological features that differentiate Mexicanos from other human groups. When inequalities of morbidity and mortality of a disease such as diabetes are explained or hypothesized as a condition of innate and fixed biological differences among groups, the existence of sociopolitical inequalities between human groups are effectively overlooked, and the related embodied health outcomes are, by default, attributed to biological differences.

Racialization must be distinguished from the descriptions of humans used in studies that measure different health outcomes not attributed to evolution or to the discovery of biogenetic characteristics of one human group. These studies use ethnoracial labels to describe the social histories of health phenomena, the social epidemiology of disease, and the health consequences of sociopolitical phenomena—or to simply socially identify those human groups most impacted by a disease. A non-racialized understanding of disease patterns avoids the biological determinism that is inherent in racialization.

DIABETES AS A BIOCULTURAL DISEASE

As a racializing practice, gene-based approaches to diabetes advance the myth that biology can explain social phenomena. In fact, considerable evidence suggests that biology and social phenomena are co-produced, that biological and social phenomena develop in mutually interdependent ways. In its most crude form, this is evident when genetic researchers use social labels to describe human groups, which renders their findings both biological and social in origin. Similarly, researchers using evolutionary models for complex diseases require genetic samples of the populations most impacted by diabetes. They are thus investigating the physiological impact of social stratification and the radical lifestyle transformation required of advanced capitalism.

Viewing complex disease through a genetic lens is a long-established sociocultural phenomenon, one that has been applied to diseases such as sickle-cell anemia, hypertension, and diabetes. For diabetes, the alleged metabolic adaptation within the thrifty genotype hypothesis presumes that hunter-gatherers experienced severe episodes of feast and famine. Selective evolutionary pressures would therefore favor those whose metabolism would best convert glucose to fat for use during periods of food scarcity. Contemporary human groups impacted by diabetes are viewed as genetically predisposed to the disease by virtue of their current similarity to the lifeways of earlier humans. However, both the extent of the feast-and-famine cycles of hunter-gatherers and the association of contemporary human groups with early human lifeways are unsubstantiated premises, relying on presumed rather than empirically supported benefits of modernity. The widespread adherence to the evolutionary hypothesis of diabetes (and the considerable resources directed toward such studies) is another iteration of a race theory that advances the cultural notion that diabetes affects human groups differently because of innate genetic differences.

Examining diabetes as an evolutionary trait denies the impact of the social dislocation, dispossession, colonization, slavery, racism, and other sociohistorical impact on those groups affected by diabetes. For example, the groups most disproportionately impacted by diabetes, Native Americans, experienced extreme deprivations during the violent dispossession of their lands and subsequent attempts by white settlers to eradicate them. It is the children and grandchildren of those born during this period who now suffer disproportionately from diabetes. These conditions support the fetal origins hypotheses and do not require the logical leap that such recent experiences could have evolutionary significance, and thus result in genotypic human variation. Thus, the widespread adherence to the genetic predisposition thesis for diabetes reflects a dominant cultural way of making sense of relations between groups impacted by the disease.

In order to understand the causes of diabetes, its evolutionary hypothesis must be seen as fitting not the natural history of the disease, but rather the ideological premise of a subordinating majority whose scientists refuse to seriously account for the social history of those peoples most impacted by the disease. Researchers seriously interested in preventing diabetes would greatly benefit by approaching the disease in ethnoracial groups as a biocultural phenomenon. To avoid merely reproducing another unprovable evolutionary genetic predisposition claim, researchers must carefully investigate diabetes as the biological impact of economic and sociocultural changes for human life. This requires uncommon multidisciplinary methods spanning the biological and social sciences and humanities. More importantly, researchers must actively counter the racialized hypothesis of genetic predisposition, especially in research into health inequalities among minority and emerging majority groups in parts of the world with high levels of ethnoracial stratification and an unequal distribution of resources. In short, researchers must recognize the link between diabetes and institutional racism.

SEE ALSO *Diseases, Racial.*

BIBLIOGRAPHY

Australian Bureau of Statistics. 2002. *National Health Survey: Aboriginal and Torres Strait Islander Results, Australia, 2001.* Canberra: Australian Bureau of Statistics. Available from http://www.abs.gov.au.

Barker, David. J. 2005. "The Developmental Origins of Insulin Resistance." *Hormone Research* 64 (Suppl. 3): 2–7. Available from http://content.karger.com.

Benyshek, Daniel C., John F. Martin, and Carol S. Johnston. 2001. "A Reconsideration of the Origins of the Type 2 Diabetes Epidemic among Native Americans and the Implications for Intervention Policy." *Medical Anthropology* 20 (1): 25–44.

Cooper, Richard S., et al. 1997. "Prevalence of NIDDM among Populations of the African Diaspora." *Diabetes Care* 20 (3): 343–348.

Foliaki, Sunai, and Neil Pearce. 2003. "Prevention and Control of Diabetes in Pacific People." *British Medical Journal* 327: 437–439.

Goodman, Alan H., and Thomas L. Leatherman, eds. 1998. *Building a New Biocultural Synthesis: Political-Economic Perspectives on Human Biology*. Ann Arbor: University of Michigan Press.

Hales, C. Nicholas, and David J. Barker. 2001. "The Thrifty Phenotype Hypothesis." *British Medical Bulletin* 60 (1): 5–20.

Karlsen, Saffron, and James Y. Nazroo. 2002. "Relation between Racial Discrimination, Social Class, and Health among Ethnic Minority Groups." *American Journal of Public Health* 92 (4): 624–631.

Kaufman, Jay, and Richard Cooper. 2001. "Commentary: Considerations for Use of Racial/Ethnic Classification in Etiologic Research." *American Journal of Epidemiology* 154 (4): 291–298.

Krieger, Nancy, ed. 2005. *Embodying Inequality: Epidemiologic Perspectives*. Amityville, NY: Baywood.

Maty, S. M., et al. 2002. "Interaction between Childhood Socioeconomic Position, Adult Body Mass Index and 34-year Incidence of Type 2 Diabetes Mellitus." *Annals of Epidemiology* 12 (7): 501–502.

Miles, Robert, and Malcolm Brown. 2003. *Racism*. New York: Routledge.

Neel, James V. 1962. "Diabetes Mellitus: A 'Thrifty' Genotype Rendered Detrimental by Progress?" *American Journal of Human Genetics* 14: 353–362.

———. 1999. "The 'Thrifty Genotype' in 1998." *Nutrition Reviews* 57 (5): S2-S9.

Quinn, Laurie. 2003. "Behavior and Biology: The Prevention of Type 2 Diabetes." *Journal of Cardiovascular Nursing* 18 (1): 62–68.

Sahlins, Marshal. 1972. *Stone Age Economics*. Chicago: Aldine.

Szathmary, Emoke, and R. E. Ferrel. 1990. "Glucose Level, Acculturation, and Glycosylated Hemoglobin: An Example of Biocultural Interaction." *Medical Anthropological Quarterly* 4 (3): 315–341.

Young, T. Kue, Jeff Reading, Brenda Elias, and John D. O'Neil. 2000. "Type 2 Diabetes Mellitus in Canada's First Nations: Status of an Epidemic in Progress." *Canadian Medical Association Journal* 163 (5): 561–566.

Michael J. Montoya

DIE BROEDERBOND

SEE *Afrikaner Broederbond.*

DISCRIMINATION

SEE *Social Psychology of Racism.*

DISEASES, RACIAL

A historical discussion about diseases defined along racial lines is an important part of examining the origins of concepts and ideologies of race. First, the association of particular diseases with certain racial groups was a central part of the project of identifying the so-called immutable differences between blacks and whites, particularly in the United States. Comparative anatomy and morbidity and mortality statistics are only some of the ways in which differences between whites and blacks were usefully delineated. Second, the notion of racial disease factored heavily into initiatives to prevent racial mixing. Therefore, an examination of racial disease is important in understanding how the threat of miscegenation was historically understood and articulated. Third, racial diseases are an ideal site for exploring the constantly shifting meanings and definitions of race, as the association of diseases with certain races often required the shifting of boundaries within and between racial groups. Finally, an examination of racial diseases is helpful in identifying how gender bears on the construction of racial difference. While African Americans were generally targeted as a source of disease in the United States, the bodies of men and women were differentially involved in the construction of racial difference, not to mention differentially affected by these constructions.

The discussion that follows centers on notions of racial disease primarily developed in the United States during the nineteenth and early twentieth centuries. This is an ideal period of focus because information is readily available and notions of race were crystallized and demonstrated in a variety of ways during this time.

MEDICAL SCIENCE AND RACIAL THINKING

Medical language and research played an important role in constructing and reinforcing racial difference. Attributing certain diseases to particular racial groups helped to create and reinforce existing social beliefs in racial difference and in the immutable fixity among races. In addition to diagnostic methods, the linking of certain diseases to certain racial groups by medical scientists was accomplished through the use of analogy and metaphor. Nancy Leys Stepan, in *Race and Medicine: The Role of Analogy in Science* (1993), states that analogies were used to create relationships between previously unrelated elements. In the case of racial disease, a naturalized association between blackness and certain illnesses was constructed. Metaphors were used for the same purpose, allowing for the explanation of cultural elements in biological terms. It is important to note that these are the same methods social authorities use to promote these ideas. This underscores the point that scientific practices and knowledge reflected existing social and political ideas.

The metaphor most central to this project was that of blood. Anthropological research such as that conducted by Audrey Smedley in *Race in North America: Origin and Evolution of a Worldview* (1999) indicates that since the sixteenth century, blood was central to the belief in the heredity of social status. While not yet associated with physical traits or a "racial" type, this notion of blood suggested a fixity of difference in social qualities believed to be transmitted biologically. Arguably, this implication contributed to blood becoming a fundamental element of kin, character, *and* biological identity beginning in the eighteenth century. Therefore, when racial and physical traits became prominent in scientific and social thinking, the physical, cultural, and social differences between racial groups were also tied to differences in blood. The differences between whites and blacks in terms of physical, intellectual, and cultural characteristics reflected a difference in blood as well. This logic was useful in reinforcing notions of biological difference beyond physiognomy, which helped to lay the groundwork for the numerous publications, research projects, and public discussions that began in the nineteenth century about Negroes' susceptibility to and propensity for certain diseases. As a result, certain diseases came to be labeled as "Negro diseases."

THE "NEGRO PROBLEM"

It is important to note that the discourse around Negro diseases developed concurrently with discussions about the place of the formerly enslaved in U.S. society. This is because it was feared that blacks, without being properly confined within the institution of slavery, would fall into a state of poor health and behavior that would have a negative effect on the existing social order and threaten the safety of the white population. Scientists and physicians were called upon to explain and resolve this "Negro problem."

In keeping with existing studies that typed the Negro as the lowest in the hierarchy of humankind on the basis of physical traits, it was generally accepted that the health of African Americans was better in bondage than in freedom. Historians such as Tara Hunter, in *To 'Joy My Freedom: Southern Black Women's Lives and Labors After the Civil War* (1997), note that many physicians studied the effects of emancipation on Negro health and found that after the Civil War, blacks showed a susceptibility to insanity, typhoid, syphilis, alcoholism, idiocy, and tuberculosis. Therefore, freedom caused blacks' mental, moral, and physical deterioration, and many believed it would lead to the extinction of African Americans. In large part, this argument was substantiated by results of comparative morbidity and mortality studies.

Frederick Hoffman, a nineteenth-century statistician for the Prudential Insurance Company, reviewed the results of censuses and doctors' and army surveys to put forth his extinction hypothesis in "Race Traits and Tendencies of the American Negro," published in 1896. Hoffman's statistical evidence suggested that the Negro was susceptible to many illnesses and constitutionally unfit for survival, and thus was destined to die out. Specifically, he argued that emancipation had allowed blacks to fall into immoral living habits resulting in a decline in their vital capacity and corresponding increase in their susceptibility to disease, especially tuberculosis and other respiratory diseases. He further argued that misguided efforts such as the educational work of philanthropists played a key role in their demise. According to Hoffman, these efforts were misdirected because Negro mortality is an indication of racial traits: "It is not in the conditions of life, but in the race traits and tendencies that we find the causes of excessive mortality" (p. 95).

Responses to Hoffman's extinction hypothesis were mixed. Many of the refutations, some from white researchers, were based on the fact that his primary data sources were incomplete and included inadequate information on African Americans. African American scholar Kelly Miller pointed out these shortcomings in his "Review of Hoffman's Race Traits and Tendencies of the American Negro" (1897). In addition, he argued that Hoffman did not give enough weight to environmental conditions as an influence on Negro health and mortality. W. E. B. Du Bois also refuted Hoffman's conclusions on these grounds in a 1906 paper titled "The Health and Physique of the Negro American." Du Bois stressed the difficulty of racial classification and accepting a monolithic image of the race. Regardless of the agreement or disagreement with Hoffman's extinction hypothesis, labeling diseases in terms of race was generally accepted during this period, almost always involving the exaggeration or misinterpretation of statistics.

The following discussion provides examples of three diseases labeled as "Negro diseases" in the nineteenth and early twentieth centuries. Each highlights the utility of examining racial diseases.

Syphilis. Siobhan Somerville, in *Queering the Color Line: Race and the Invention of Homosexuality in American Culture* (2000), notes that beginning in the nineteenth century, sexuality was used as a primary means for establishing racial difference and the hierarchy between whites and blacks. Negroes were thought to possess an excessive sexual desire that was seen as a threat to white society. As such, blacks were especially prone to venereal disease. As with other diseases, the high incidence of syphilis was attributed in part to emancipation. Some doctors, such as H. L. McNeil in "Syphilis in the Southern American

Negro" (1915), determined that while virtually free of disease as slaves, over 50 percent of all free Negroes were prone to venereal disease. This in turn caused the high numbers of stillbirths that caused the population to dwindle, as well as increased criminal behavior and insanity. These exaggerations aided in the demonization of blacks as a threat to white society and in predictions of their extinction.

There are two important gender dimensions to the construction of syphilis as a "Negro disease." One particular feature of blacks' hypersexuality doctors noted was black males' desire for white women, something thought to be specific to the Negro racial character. Neither syphilis nor the hypersexuality of black men was seen as a threat to black women because they were also characterized as hypersexual. While black males were the focus of discussions regarding syphilis, the examination of black female bodies provided the historical basis for establishing sexual differences that reflected racial differences. Specifically, Cuvier's nineteenth-century anatomical study of Sarah Baartman, outlined in "Account of a Dissection of a Bushwoman" by Flower and Murie (1867), also known as the "Hottentot Venus," initiated the practice of locating the boundaries of race through the bodies of African women. African women's (and later African American women's) bodies were characterized in terms of excess, especially the sexual organs, which supposedly placed her body outside the boundaries of normalcy. Her anatomy was explained by her characteristically unladylike hypersexuality. Therefore, black women were also marked as sexually deviant and diseased in their "natural" state.

While the Tuskeegee experiment is a well-known demonstration of these beliefs, medical research on the prevalence of syphilis among blacks conducted beforehand during the 1920s and 1930s contested these ideas. A study funded by the Julius Rosenwald fund in 1929 actually illustrated the success of mass treatment for syphilis among blacks in Macon County, Alabama, but the results were ignored. Rather, the high prevalence of syphilis in the county was interpreted as "an unusual opportunity" to conduct a natural study of the disease. This perspective reflects the generally accepted idea that blacks, in their "natural state," were diseased. In addition, this logic contributed to the lack of consideration for socioeconomic factors when examining black health. The biological basis of the Negro had to be accepted as unchangeable. Not surprisingly, the exaggeration of statistics was central to the construction of this naturalized state. U.S. Public Health Service physicians at the helm of the Tuskegee experiment argued that "lust and immoralities, unstable families, reversion to barbaric tendencies" made blacks especially prone to venereal diseases. Allan Brandt, in "Racism and Research: The Case of the Tuskegee Syphilis Study" (2000), states that some doctors "estimated" that over 50 percent of blacks over the age of twenty-five were syphilitic. In reality, the rates of syphilis fell way below expectations. Therefore, research revealed more about the pathology of racism than the pathology of syphilis.

Tuberculosis. The high incidence of tuberculosis was also attributed to both the freedom and hypersexuality of blacks and was seen as a harbinger of their eventual extinction. However, during the antebellum period, tuberculosis was thought of as a white disease. Susan Craddock, in *City of Plagues: Disease, Poverty and Deviance in San Francisco* (1997), states that specifically it was a disease of standing, associated with the upper and artistic classes. Tuberculosis was transformed into a black disease only after the "quarantine effect" of slavery was removed.

In the segregated South, black female domestic workers were targeted in particular as disease vectors for tuberculosis. It was generally accepted that they infected whites (in most cases their employers) as a result of their daily movement between black and white worlds. Black women were targeted not only because of their mobility in and out of white households but also because of the stereotypes about black female hypersexuality. Whites considered black women as "naturally promiscuous" and depicted them as seducers of "innocent white boys." Their bodies were receptacles for dangerous germs, including venereal diseases and tuberculosis. As such, they were considered a threat to white society.

Throughout the nineteenth and early twentieth centuries, medical research was constantly focused on determining whether tuberculosis assumed a unique form in the Negro. During the 1830s, U.S. physicians such as Louis Yandell (1831) published articles in medical journals about "Negro consumption," "struma Africana," and "Negro poisoning." As indicated by the terms, doctors argued that this form of consumption was specific to blacks and was a more acute type than that found among whites. During the Civil War, black Union Army soldiers were subjected to batteries of tests and measurements to the end of identifying disease susceptibilities. The results of this study indicated that Negroes had an inferior lung capacity to whites. According to Hunt (1869), the Negro had a smaller "tropical lung" that could not function adequately in temperate climates. Although initial comparative research on Negro and white lungs was inconclusive, the inferior lung theory persisted into the twentieth century.

Researchers were also preoccupied with the possibility of isolating characteristics of susceptibility in the population. In keeping with the exploration of the "Negro problem," these inquiries were made to the end of identifying how Negroes, now uncomfortably situated within U.S. society, were beings different from whites. The issues of Negro increase or decline in the population and the prospects of race mixing were also in the forefront of the minds of scientists. Whites were worried about the proximity of a race considered to be a vector for disease.

Research on tuberculosis gained renewed fervor in the wake of emancipation, as rates among Negroes increased. Marion Torchia, in "Tuberculosis Among Negroes: Medical Research on a Racial Disease, 1830–1950" (1977), states that the statistics on Negro mortality from tuberculosis factored heavily in the prediction of Negro extinction. As with discussions of syphilis, emancipation allowed blacks to fall into immoral living habits resulting in a decline in their vital capacity and an increase in their susceptibility. However, some scholars (e.g., Holmes 1937) countered this logic by emphasizing consideration of socioeconomic factors in the prevalence of the disease. Others pointed out the misinterpretation of mortality statistics, arguing that results showed that Negro deaths from consumption fluctuated according to population density.

Research on Negro susceptibility to tuberculosis fell out of popularity in the late 1930s. By the 1950s, racial studies of tuberculosis were deemed particularly suspect in light of racial integration initiatives and the role that antibiotics played in nearly eradicating the disease.

Sickle Cell Anemia. Sickle cell anemia was first discovered in 1910. The disease was recognized as a Mendelian dominant disorder specific to African Americans. Therefore, it could be spread by an individual parent who carried the trait to her or his offspring. As with the other diseases discussed, this perception of heredity and the nature of the disease reflected concerns about race mixing and the general dangers of associating with Negroes brought about by emancipation. By 1925, cases of sickle cell in whites were being reported in medical journals. Rather than leading to a broader conceptualization of the disease as affecting multiple races, these cases confirmed that the disease could be spread through miscegenation: "Its occurrence depends entirely on the presence of Negro blood, even in extremely small amounts it appears that the sine qua non for the occurrence of sickle cell anemia is the presence of a strain, even remote, of Negro blood" ("Sickle Cell Anemia" 1947, p. 33).

Keith Wailoo, in "Genetic Marker of Segregation: Sickle Cell Anemia, Thalassemia and Racial Ideology in American Medical Writing, 1920–1950" (1996), states that in the 1910s and 1920s, the development of methods to identify individuals with blood that had the potential or tendency to sickle led to statistically tying sickling to race. Physicians became heavily engaged in research to confirm that sickle cell anemia was specific to the Negro. This included sampling the blood of hundreds of individuals as well as studies of individual families. Again, because of the detection of sickling among whites, attention turned to investigating this particular problem.

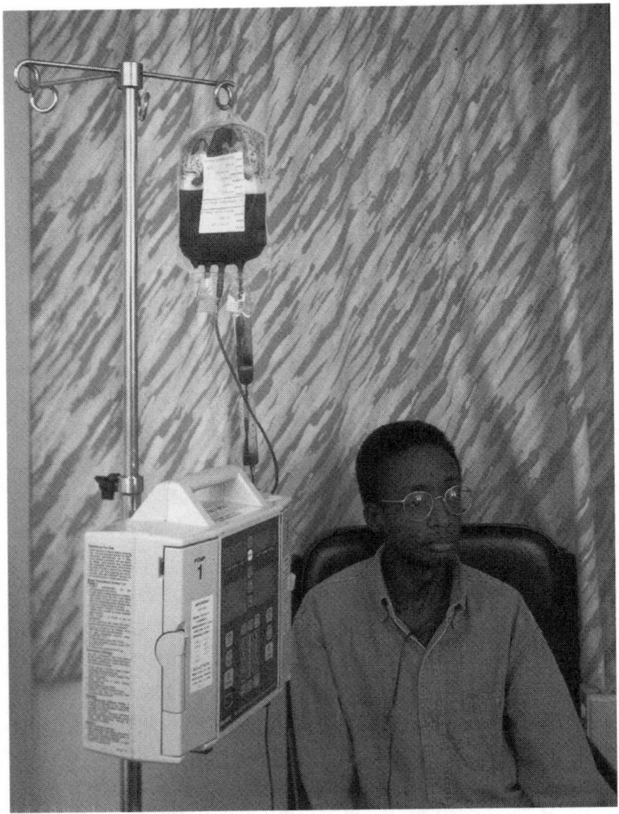

Sickle-Cell Anemia Patient. *An African-American patient suffering from sickle-cell anemia recieves a blood transfusion. This hereditary disorder mostly affects people of African ancestry, and about 70,000 Americans suffer from the disease.* **CUSTOM MEDICAL STOCK PHOTO.**

Such diagnostic techniques reproduced and reflected the dominant ideology, as scientists took for granted the distinction between black and white bodies. Research was used to confine sickle cell anemia to the black body and to represent the distinctiveness between black and white bodies as a product of indisputable scientific evidence. Therefore, sickle cell was employed as a test to specify who was black and white, as well as an instrument for policing the boundaries between these groups.

Diagnosing sickling in a person presumed to be white called the true racial identity of the person into question. During the 1940s, literature on individuals who could not easily be identified as black increased. In most cases, the articles made clear that the identification of sickle cells led to a closer examination of family background. Specifically, physiognomy, geography, and genealogy were relied on to clarify the picture. Faces were examined for evidence of admixture, and genealogies were examined for places of family origin where "significant crossbreeding" between blacks and whites took place. As such, the medical practice of revealing black ancestry in apparently white individuals became commonplace. This information was used to explain sickling among whites as the result of association with blacks in the remote past. Justifying the presence of sickle cell in white populations was achieved through means such as noting the geographical proximity of a country to Africa or identifying "Negro strains" in seemingly isolated populations because of historical events, such as Hannibal's invasion of Spain.

Ironically, at the same time that this logic reinforced racial boundaries between blacks and whites, it also led to the creation of new criteria for defining and identifying true whiteness. A new set of lines was essentially drawn around the white body rather than accepting the occurrence of sickling in the population. In other words, medical authorities used the emergence of these cases to reveal black ancestry in people who only appeared to be white, thus refining the technique of determining who was and was not "racially pure." As noted by Melbourne Tapper (1995), this line of thinking destabilized the notion of whiteness being solely identifiable by skin color and other physical features at the same time that it reinforced the notion of racial fixity. The necessity for shifting racial boundaries to maintain racial fixity is one of the many reasons that race was rarely defined in the literature pertaining to research on racial diseases.

CONTINUED CLASSIFICATION

Each of the three diseases discussed here reveals different elements of the historical construction of racial disease. Misconceptions about syphilis reflected the way in which racial difference was constructed through an association with abnormal sexuality. Discussions about the etiology of tuberculosis indicate, among other things, the reliance upon differential physiology in delineating racial difference. The dilemma raised in the case of sickle cell speaks to the important role that disease played in creating meaning around the concept of racial purity, as well as identifying it. All three cases illustrate how maintaining racial boundaries was privileged over disease treatment and prevention. They also underscore the fact that race, be it in the past or present, is not solely articulated on the visible surface of the body.

Arguably, this practice of seeking and finding racial difference "below the skin" factors heavily into understanding what became of racial diseases. A vast amount of research in the biological sciences over the past 35 years confirms that human diversity cannot be genetically organized into racial categories. However, the rise of genetic technologies has fostered explanations of disease associated with "inherited predisposition." As with racial diseases, the notion of "genetic disease" is at odds with epidemiological evidence that health disparities can be attributed to social and historical factors. In addition, summaries of genetics research result in the scientific and popular press often including the use of racial groups to delineate the "increased risk" that some individuals have to certain diseases. These summaries wrongfully imply that race is both a genetic reality and useful category for understanding differences in disease frequencies between human groups (Braun 2002).

SEE ALSO *Hottentot Venus; Medical Racism; Mental Health and Racism; Sexuality; Sickle Cell Anemia.*

BIBLIOGRAPHY

Brandt, Allan. 2000. "Racism and Research: The Case of the Tuskegee Syphilis Study." In *Tuskegee's Truths: Rethinking the Tuskegee Syphilis Study*, ed. Susan Reverby, 15–33. Chapel Hill: University of North Carolina Press.

Braun, Lundy. 2002. "Race, Ethnicity, and Health: Can Genetics Explain Health Disparities?" *Perspectives in Biology and Medicine* 45 (2): 159–174.

Craddock, Susan. 1997. *City of Plagues: Disease, Poverty and Deviance in San Francisco*. Minneapolis: University of Minnesota Press.

Du Bois, W. E. B. 1906. "The Health and Physique of the Negro American." *American Journal of Public Health* 93 (2): 272–276.

Flower, W., and J. Murie. 1867. "Account of a Dissection of a Bushwoman." *Journal of Anatomy and Physiology* 1: 208.

Hoffman, Frederick. 1896. "Race Traits and Tendencies of the American Negro." *Publications of the American Economic Association* 11 (1–3): 1–329.

Holmes, S. 1937. "The Principal Causes of Death Among Negroes: A General Comparative Statement." *Journal of Negro Education* 6 (3): 289–302.

Hunt, S. 1869. "The Negro as Soldier." *Anthropological Review* 7: 40–54.

Hunter, Tara. 1997. *To 'Joy My Freedom: Southern Black Women's Lives and Labors After the Civil War*. Cambridge, MA: Harvard University Press.

Leys Stepan, Nancy. 1993. "Race and Gender: The Role of Analogy in Science." In *The Racial Economy of Science: Toward a Democratic Future*, ed. Sandra Harding, 359–376. Bloomington: University of Indiana Press.

McNeil, H. L. 1915. "Syphilis in the Southern American Negro." *Journal of the American Medical Association* 67: 1001–1004.

Miller, Kelly. 1897. "A Review of Hoffman's Race Traits and Tendencies of the American Negro." The American Negro Academy. Occasional Papers, No. 1. Washington, DC.

"Sickle Cell Anemia, a Race Specific Disease." 1947. *Journal of the American Medical Association* 133: 33–34.

Smedley, Audrey. 1999. *Race in North America: Origin and Evolution of a Worldview*, 2nd ed. Boulder, CO: Westview Press.

Somerville, Siobhan. 2000. *Queering the Color Line: Race and the Invention of Homosexuality in American Culture*. Durham, NC: Duke University Press.

Tapper, Melbourne. 1995. "Interrogating Bodies: Medico-Racial Knowledge, Politics and the Study of a Disease." *Comparative Studies in Society and History* 37 (1): 76–93.

Torchia, Marion. 1977. "Tuberculosis among Negroes: Medical Research on a Racial Disease, 1830–1950." *Journal of the History of Medicine and Allied Sciences* 32: 252–279.

Wailoo, Keith. 1996. "Genetic Marker of Segregation: Sickle Cell Anemia, Thalassemia, and Racial Ideology in American Medical Writing, 1920–1950." *History and Philosophy of Life Sciences* 18 (3): 305–320.

Yandell, Louis. 1831. "Remarks on Struma Africana, or the Disease Usually Called Negro Consumption." *Transylvania Journal of Medicine* 4: 83–103.

Rachel J. Watkins

DIXON, THOMAS, JR.
1864–1946

Thomas Dixon Jr. was born January 11, 1864, in Shelby, North Carolina. He is best known for his racist novel *The Clansman* (1905), which served as the basis for D. W. Griffith's infamous film *The Birth of a Nation* (1915). Throughout his long artistic career as a lecturer, playwright, filmmaker, and novelist, Dixon railed about the horrors of Reconstruction, the inferiority of African Americans, and the dangers of miscegenation. Whereas he was popular in his day, especially in the South, his strident views on race have left his name tainted in history.

EARLY YEARS

Dixon was born the son of Thomas Dixon Sr., a Baptist minister, and Amanda Evira McAfee, the daughter of a wealthy plantation owner. Growing up in the rural South in the midst of Reconstruction left an indelible mark on the young Dixon. He would always characterize this era as one of history's greatest tragedies, a time when good southerners suffered at the hands of corrupt northerners and freed slaves. It was also during this period that Dixon became acquainted with the Ku Klux Klan. His most direct influence came from his uncle, Leroy McAfee, who later in life became a leader of the original Ku Klux Klan in Cleveland County, North Carolina. Dixon would go on to justify the original Klan's actions in his writings, his plays, and his lectures as a harsh but necessary response to a desperate situation. For him, black freedom meant disaster in mainstream public life and miscegenation in private life.

From 1879 to 1883 Dixon attended Wake Forest College, and upon graduation he enrolled at Johns Hopkins University. Dixon was an excellent student, but he soon realized that theater was his true love. He decided to drop out and attend Frobisher's School of Drama in New York City. Unfortunately, the tall, lanky Dixon was awkward on stage, and his dream of becoming an actor ended quickly. After returning home to Shelby, North Carolina, in 1885, he served a term as a state legislator, earned his law degree, and married Harriet Bussey in 1886.

Dixon soon found a new audience as an ordained Baptist minister. Beginning in 1887, Dixon would go on to hold several ministerial posts over the next decade, including with the Dudley Street Church in Boston and the Twenty-third Street Baptist Church in New York City. As one biographer has noted, Dixon was a "flamboyant and sensationalist preacher," whose mastery of oratory skills and penchant for showmanship gained him a popular following (Slide 2004, p. 20). His sermons from the pulpit were joined by lucrative lecture tours that, by 1897, made him a very wealthy man. He was known for appealing to the emotions of the crowd, and his favorite topics included the plight of the working man and, especially in the South, the evils of Reconstruction.

WORKS

Dixon's first novel, *The Leopard's Spots* (1902), was written as a satirical sequel to Harriet Beecher Stowe's *Uncle Tom's Cabin*, which he condemned for its gross misrepresentation and mistreatment of southerners (Cook 1968, p. 51). Appropriating a number of Stowe's characters, including Simon Legree and George Harrison, Dixon wrote an emotionally charged, melodramatic novel of white southern victimization by vengeful former slaves and scheming carpetbaggers. *The Leopard's Spots* was the first part of Dixon's best-selling "Trilogy of Reconstruction," which also included his most famous novel, *The Clansman* (1905), and *The Traitor* (1907).

Most notable in these works is Dixon's treatment of race. His African-American characters are racist stereotypes. He portrayed black men as highly sexualized, brutish beings driven by their desire to violate white southern women. Dixon felt that African Americans were a threat to white purity, and he railed in his trilogy against the perils of miscegenation. In Dixon's novels, the horrors of Reconstruction only end with the emergence of the Klan and the reestablishment of white rule in the South through the use of lynching, Jim Crow laws, and the disenfranchisement of African Americans. This theme is most fully developed in *The Clansman*, in which Dixon presents the robed and hooded horsemen as modern day medieval knights out to protect the white southern population from harm. While Dixon claimed to have opposed slavery and argued that he had no sympathy for the modern Ku Klux Klan, he was a committed segregationist, believing that miscegenation and racial integration would destroy white American civilization in the South.

Dixon's other notable novels include another trilogy, comprising *The One Woman* (1903), *Comrades* (1909), and *The Root of Evil* (1911). These books focus on the evils of socialism and communism. Over his lifetime, Dixon wrote twenty-two novels, a number of plays, numerous sermons, and other works of nonfiction.

Dixon was well aware of the theatrical potential of his novels, and he labored diligently to bring his works to the stage. He wrote the script for the play version of *The Clansman*, which opened in Norfolk, Virginia, on September 22, 1905. Like his novels, the production was a melodramatic spectacle, complete with live horses carrying hooded Klansmen on stage. Dixon would go on to adapt several of his novels for the stage, including *The One Woman* (1903), *The Traitor* (1907), and *The Sins of the Father* (1912).

An early admirer of motion pictures, Dixon sought to get his play *The Clansman* onto the movie screen as early as 1910. After two attempts at producing the film failed, the project was taken over by D. W. Griffith, whose adaptation, *The Birth of a Nation*, opened in 1915. Whereas Dixon's storyline was the basis for the movie, Griffith was, by all accounts, the real creative force behind *The Birth of a Nation*. Dixon increased his wealth as the holder of a quarter interest in the film, which earned millions. Both Dixon and Griffith denied any responsibility for the inspiration the film provided to the creation of the modern Ku Klux Klan in the early twentieth century. Dixon went on to write a total of sixteen movie screenplays, including *The Fall of a Nation* (1916), *The Foolish Virgin* (1924), and *Nation Aflame* (1937).

LATER YEARS

Dixon's fame and fortune declined greatly in his later years. He lost nearly all of his money in the stock market crash of 1929, and by the 1930s he was no longer a popular author. In 1937 he gained modest employment as a court clerk in Raleigh, North Carolina. After suffering a cerebral hemorrhage in 1939, he was cared for by his second wife, Madelyn Donovan. Dixon died on April 3, 1946.

SEE ALSO *Birth of a Nation, The.*

BIBLIOGRAPHY

Cook, Raymond A. 1974. *Thomas Dixon*. New York: Twayne Publications.

Gillespie, Michele K., and Randal L. Hall. 2006 *Thomas Dixon Jr. and the Birth of Modern America*. Baton Rouge: Louisiana State University Press.

Slide, Anthony. 2004. *American Racist: The Life and Films of Thomas Dixon*. Lexington: University Press of Kentucky.

Kevin Hicks

DOUGLASS, FREDERICK
1818–1895

Frederick Douglass was the black face of antislavery and civil rights in the United States from the mid-1840s until his death in 1895. As a speaker, writer, newspaper editor and publisher, he influenced public opinion and perspectives about African Americans. His autobiography became a classic American literary masterpiece. A world-renowned orator, he battled slavery and racial segregation, and also championed women's rights. The masthead of his signature *North Star* newspaper carried the motto, "Right is of no sex—Truth is of no color—God is the Father of us all, and we are all Brethren."

Douglass was born on Maryland's Eastern Shore in February 1818. His mother was a slave named Harriet Bailey. Speculation held that his father was probably Aaron Anthony, his mother's white owner. Douglass stole himself from slavery on September 3, 1838, assisted by Anna Murray (1813–1882), a free black Baltimore resident whose savings supplemented his expenses. Forged seaman's protection papers got him from Baltimore to Philadelphia, and then to New York City, where he and Anna reunited and wed. The couple soon moved on to New Bedford, Massachusetts. Jettisoning parts of his birth name of Frederick Augustus Washington Bailey, he took his last name from the heroic character in *The Lady of the Lake*, a popular 1810 novel by the Scottish novelist and poet Sir Walter Scott. His renaming was both a break from the past and a disguise for the future.

In New Bedford, a haven for fugitive slaves, Frederick and Anna had three sons and two daughters in ten years. In August 1841 the radical American Anti-Slavery Society leader William Lloyd Garrison invited Douglass to speak against slavery to an audience of whites in Nantucket, Massachusetts. The precision and eloquence of his speaking ability stirred the audience, and Douglass soon became something of a living antislavery exhibit, recounting his experiences as a slave. He attacked American hypocrisy about freedom and he challenged the Christian pronouncements of U.S. churches. He mixed moral fervor with a vision of enlightenment democracy that challenged America to shun the prejudices and practices of white supremacy and embrace the egalitarianism of universal human rights.

Written to convince skeptics he had indeed been a bondsman, the first version of Douglass's autobiography, *The Narrative of the Life of Frederick Douglass, an American Slave* (1845), made him a national and international celebrity. However, as a fugitive slave, he stood liable under U.S. law to be captured and returned in chains to his legal owner, Thomas Auld. Reacting in part to the prospect of capture, and also to many invitations to speak abroad, Douglass sailed to Great Britain in 1845. He was lionized during a near two-year stay in England, Ireland, and Scotland, and the British bought his freedom for about seven hundred dollars.

Returning to the United States as a legally free man, Douglass struck out on his own, though his growing

Frederick Douglass. *This portrait of Douglass appeared on the frontispiece of his 1845 autobiography,* Narrative of the Life of Frederick Douglass. SPECIAL COLLECTIONS LIBRARY, UNIVERSITY OF MICHIGAN.

independence caused a breach with Garrison. With $2,174 from his British admirers, Douglass launched his *North Star* newspaper in December 1847. To imitators, he retitled the publication *Frederick Douglass' Paper* (1851–1860) and also produced *Douglass' Monthly* (1859–1863). He subsidized his publications with some $12,000 of earnings from his public appearances.

On the editorial pages of the *North Star,* Douglass rejected Garrison's belief that moral suasion, rather than political action, was the best way to abolish slavery, and that the U.S. Constitution was primarily a proslavery document. He held instead that the Constitution's basic principles supported freedom. Responding in May 1857 to the U.S. Supreme Court's infamous *Dred Scott* decision which classified blacks as noncitizens, Douglass declared, "I base my sense of the certain overthrow of slavery, in part, upon the nature of the American Government, the Constitution, the tendencies of the age, and the character of the American people."

U.S. law was not inherently racist, Douglass argued. The law that elevated concepts of race and racism could also reduce and erase them. He persisted in this view even after the backlash of postwar Reconstruction reversed the nation's apparent progress, as reflected in the Thirteenth, Fourteenth, and Fifteenth Amendments to the U.S. Constitution. Douglass persisted in his quest to have the United States honor universal individual liberty, fully recognizing that the end to slavery had not ushered in equal rights.

While editing the *New National Era* newspaper in Washington, D.C., from 1870 to 1874, Douglass continued to speak and write for expanding civil rights. Yet the racially conservative politics of postbellum America increasingly shunted him from the national stage. Aligned with the Republican Party of Abraham Lincoln, and with the Constitutional amendments ending slavery and bestowing citizenship upon blacks, Douglass was increasingly dismissed as a mere partisan. Apparently unable to fully recognize the distinct differences of economic condition that beset the mass of blacks after slavery's end, Douglass's later voice oversimplified the efficacy of civil rights, middle-class uplift, and simple self-reliance amid violent white reaction and rising industrial capitalism's oppression.

Douglass's marriage to the white feminist Helen Pitts (1838–1903) in 1884, two years after Anna Murray's death, symbolized his commitment to racial integration and his sense that racism in America would end only when race in America was no longer visible. Prior to their marriage, Pitts worked for Douglass, and she later led the preservation work on their home on Cedar Hill in Washington, D.C. In the early twenty-first century the house is a national historic site visited by tens of thousands of tourists. Douglass died at home of a heart attack on Wednesday, February 20, 1895, just after appearing nearby at a meeting of the National Council of Women.

SEE ALSO *American Anti-Slavery Society.*

BIBLIOGRAPHY

Blassingame, John W., ed. 1979. *The Frederick Douglass Papers.* New Haven, CT: Yale University Press.

Blight, David W. 1989. *Frederick Douglass' Civil War: Keeping Faith in Jubilee.* Baton Rouge: Louisiana State University Press.

Douglass, Frederick. 1845. *The Narrative of the Life of an American Slave.* Boston: Anti-Slavery Office.

———. 1855. *My Bondage and My Freedom.* New York: Miller, Orton and Mulligan.

———. 1892. *The Life and Times of Frederick Douglass.* New rev. ed. Boston: De Wolfe, Fiske.

Foner, Philip S., ed. 1950. *The Life and Writings of Frederick Douglass,* 5 vols. New York: International Publishers.

Lampe, Gregory P. 1999. *Frederick Douglass: Freedom's Voice, 1818–1845.* East Lansing: Michigan State University Press.

Martin, Waldo E., Jr. 1984. *The Mind of Frederick Douglass.* Chapel Hill: University of North Carolina Press.

Preston, Dickson J. 1980. *Young Frederick Douglass: The Maryland Years.* Baltimore, MD: Johns Hopkins University Press.

Stauffer, John. 2002. *The Black Hearts of Men: Radical Abolitionists and the Transformation of Race*. Cambridge, MA: Harvard University Press.

Thomas J. Davis

DRED SCOTT V. SANDFORD

Dred Scott v. Sandford is probably the most important Supreme Court case involving race and African Americans decided before the Civil War. The facts of the case are complicated, as is the lengthy opinion of the court, written by Chief Justice Roger B. Taney. But the implications for blacks and American race relations were profound.

DRED SCOTT'S LIFE AND SUIT FOR FREEDOM

Dred Scott was born a slave in Virginia sometime between 1795 and 1800. In 1830 his owner, Peter Blow, moved to St. Louis, taking Scott with him. After Blow's death, Scott was sold to Dr. John Emerson, a U.S. Army surgeon. Emerson took Scott to Fort Armstrong in Illinois, and then to Fort Snelling in what was then the Wisconsin Territory and eventually became part of Minnesota. Illinois was a free state, while the Missouri Compromise of 1820 Congress had prohibited slavery in the Wisconsin Territory. While living at Fort Snelling, Scott married Harriet Robinson, a slave owned by Major Lawrence Taliaferro, the Indian Agent stationed near Fort Snelling. Taliaferro was also a justice of the peace, and in that capacity he performed a formal wedding ceremony for his slave and her new husband. This was extraordinary and significant. Under the laws of the slave states, no slave could actually participate in a legal marriage. Slaves might be married by their masters or by a clergyman, but because a marriage is a legal contract, these ceremonies were always informal. This formal marriage by the local justice of the peace may be an indication that after living in nonslave jurisdictions for more than two years, people at Fort Snelling presumed Scott to be free.

Scott did not gain his freedom at this time, however, and he remained Emerson's slave until the physician died in 1843. Scott then asked Emerson's widow, Irene Sanford Emerson, to allow him to purchase his own freedom. When she refused, Scott sued for freedom based on his residences in Illinois and the Wisconsin Territory. His case was delayed for a variety of reasons, but in 1850 a jury of twelve white men in St. Louis declared Scott, his wife, and their two daughters to be free. This decision was supported by nearly thirty years of Missouri precedents, which held that a slave became free when allowed to live in a free jurisdiction. Irene Emerson then appealed to the Missouri Supreme Court, which in 1852 overturned the jury's decision and held that Scott was not free. The Court explicitly rejected its long-held position that if a slave resided or worked in a free state because of the voluntary act of a master, the slave became free. In a frankly political decision, Justice William Scott explained:

> Times are not now as they were when the former decisions on this subject were made. Since then, not only individuals but States have been possessed with a dark and fell spirit in relation to slavery, whose gratification is sought in the pursuit of measures, whose inevitable consequence must be the overthrow and destruction of our Government. Under such circumstances, it does not behoove the State of Missouri to show the least countenance to any measure which might gratify this spirit.

The case should have ended at this point. Scott's status had been determined by the highest court of his state, and he had no appeal to the U.S. Supreme Court. At this time, the U.S. Constitution did not generally protect the liberties or rights of individuals, and personal status was generally determined by the states.

At about the time Scott won his jury trial, his owner, Irene Emerson moved to Springfield, Massachusetts, where she married a Massachusetts physician named Calvin Chafee. Irene Emerson Chafee's brother, John F.A. Sanford, now looked after her interests. By 1854, Sanford, who had assumed ownership of Scott, had moved to New York. This set the circumstances for Scott to make one more attempt to gain his freedom. (The Supreme Court would misspell Sanford's name as "Sandford," and thus the case would be argued as *Dred Scott v. Sandford.*)

THE MOVE TO FEDERAL COURT

In 1854 Scott's lawyers initiated a suit against Sanford in the U.S. Circuit Court in St. Louis. Scott could not directly sue for his freedom, but he could use the federal courts to test his freedom indirectly. The U.S Constitution allows a citizen of one state to sue a citizen of another under what is called "diversity jurisdiction." This phrase simply means that citizens of different states can sue each other in federal courts. As long as Irene Emerson lived in Missouri, Scott could not claim a diversity of citizenship because he also lived in Missouri. But when Sanford, his new owner, moved to New York, a diversity of residence was clearly created: Scott lived in Missouri; Sanford lived in New York.

The problem for Scott—and this would become a key to the decision by the U.S. Supreme Court—was what constitutes citizenship. Scott was a resident of Missouri, but was he a citizen of Missouri? Scott's new

Dred Scott. *Dred Scott sued for his freedom in the landmark Supreme Court case* Dred Scott v. Sandford. **THE LIBRARY OF CONGRESS.**

lawyer, Roswell Field, made a complicated argument in federal court. Field argued that Scott was free on the basis of his residence at Fort Snelling, and that if he was free he must be a citizen for the purpose of diversity jurisdiction. He did not argue that Scott had all the rights of a citizen; instead, he argued that if Scott was not a slave he must be able to sue as citizen of Missouri. On this basis, Field brought suit against Sanford for false imprisonment and battery against Scott, his wife, and their two daughters. These claims were really a subterfuge for gaining a hearing before the Court to test Scott's freedom.

Scott assumed that Sanford would argue that Scott was a slave, and that he therefore had a right to imprison or beat him. Scott's answer would be that he was free, and that Sanford was not, therefore, entitled to imprison or beat him. This would set the stage for a trial on Scott's freedom. If the Court decided he was free, then Sanford would lose and pay minimal damages, and Scott would go free. Sanford would, in fact, make these arguments, but only after he made a more important one.

Sanford's first answer to Scott's suit was not about ownership, but about race. Sanford argued that, as a black man, Scott could never be a citizen, and thus could never sue in federal court. Sanford did not say that Scott could not sue because he was a slave. Rather, he argued that even if Scott were free, he could not vindicate that freedom in federal court because blacks could never be considered citizens under the Constitution, and thus could never sue in diversity. In making this argument, Sanford's lawyers filed a "plea in abatement," asking the Judge to abate, or end, the case immediately because a black could not be a plaintiff in a diversity suit in federal court.

U.S. District Judge Robert W. Wells rejected Sanford's claim in the plea in abatement. Judge Wells held that if Scott was free, then he was entitled to sue in federal court. However, after hearing the evidence in the case, Judge Wells ruled that Scott's status as a slave or a free person could only be decided by Missouri law, and the Missouri Supreme Court had already ruled that Scott was still a slave. In reaching this decision, Wells ignored the force of the Missouri Compromise and did not consider whether the Missouri Supreme Court had the power to overrule, or ignored the federal law that made slavery illegal in the federal territory north of Missouri.

THE SUPREME COURT

This set the stage for Dred Scott to take his case to the U.S. Supreme Court. What had begun as a relatively simple claim by a slave to be free had now turned into an extremely important case involving race, citizenship, federal law, the power of Congress, and national politics. The Supreme Court heard arguments on the case in the spring of 1856, but it did not decide the case then; instead, it ordered a reargument for December 1856. In the intervening months the nation went through a presidential campaign in which the recently created Republican Party promised to prevent the spread of slavery into the western territories and to prevent any more slave states from entering the Union. The party carried eleven free states, sending a shudder through the South. Had the Republican candidate, John C. Fremont, carried just a few more states, he would have become president. Instead, a proslavery Democrat, James Buchanan, won the election.

In March 1857, two days after Buchanan's inauguration, Chief Justice Taney announced the decision in the Dred Scott case. In his "Opinion of the Court," Taney declared that no black person could ever be a citizen of the United States, and that Dred Scott, even if free, could therefore not sue Sanford in federal court. On the basis of this part of the decision, Taney might have declared that he had no jurisdiction to hear the case at all. Critics of the decision argued he should have done this. However, Taney did not stop with this pronouncement. He also addressed the effect of the Missouri Compromise on the status of slaves brought into territories made free by federal law. He concluded that Congress did not have the power to prohibit slavery in the federal territories, and he thus held that the Missouri

Compromise of 1820 was unconstitutional, as were all other restrictions on slavery in the territories. These two dramatic and controversial rulings placed the decision at the center of American politics and law for the next decade-and-a-half.

Thus, Taney argued that framers of the Constitution did not intend to include blacks as citizens and that they could not now be considered citizens. He wrote:

> The question is simply this: Can a negro, whose ancestors were imported into this country, and sold as slaves, become a member of the political community formed and brought into existence by the Constitution of the United States, and as such become entitled to all the rights, and privileges, and immunities, guarantied by that instrument to the citizen? One of which rights is the privilege of suing in a court of the United States in the cases specified in the Constitution.

The very nature of this question led Taney to conclude that blacks had no such rights. This analysis conflicted with both the history of the nation's founding and with current practice. At the time of the founding, blacks voted in a number of states and even held office in some of them. In most of the northern states and at least one southern state (North Carolina), free blacks voted in the elections to choose delegates to attend the state conventions to ratify the Constitution. These voters were certainly considered citizens when the nation ratified the Constitution. Furthermore, at the time that Taney wrote his opinion, free blacks could vote in a number of states, and in some states free blacks had held public office since the American Revolution. But he argued that even free blacks living in those states could never be citizens of the United States and have standing to sue in federal courts. Thus, Taney set up the novel concept of dual citizenship. He argued that being a citizen of a state did not necessarily make one a citizen of the United States.

Taney based this novel argument entirely on race. He offered a slanted and one-sided view of American history that ignored the fact that free blacks had voted in a number of states at the time of the ratification of the Constitution. Ignoring this, the Chief Justice nevertheless argued that at the founding of the nation blacks were either all slaves or, if free, without any political or legal rights. He declared that blacks:

> Are not included, and were not intended to be included, under the word "citizens" in the Constitution, and can therefore claim none of the rights and privileges which that instrument provides and secures to citizens of the United States. On the contrary, they were at that time [1787] considered as a subordinate and inferior class of beings, who had been subjugated by the dominant race, and, whether emancipated or not, yet remained subject to their authority, and had no rights or privileges but such as those who held the power and government might choose to grant them.

According to Taney, blacks "had for more than a century before been regarded as beings of an inferior order, and altogether unfit to associate with the white race, either in social or political relations; and so far inferior, that they had no rights which the white man was bound to respect; and that the negro might justly and lawfully be reduced to slavery." Thus, he concluded that blacks could never be citizens of the United States, even if they were born in the country and considered to be citizens of the states in which they lived.

This dual citizenship meant that Massachusetts, where blacks were full and equal citizens, could not force its notions of citizenship on the slave states. It also meant that Southern states did not have to grant privileges and immunities, or any other rights, to the free black citizens of Massachusetts and other Northern states.

Taney's opinion horrified not only free blacks, but also many Northern whites.

The antebellum North was hardly a bastion of racial equality, but many northerners who would never have advocated social equality or political rights for blacks nevertheless believed that blacks had minimal rights of citizenship.

The vast majority of Northern whites were even more shocked by Taney's conclusion that Congress could never ban slavery from the federal territories. Taney reached this conclusion through two routes. First, he asserted that the Territory Clause of Article IV of the Constitution did not apply to territories acquired after 1787. This argument was weak and unpersuasive, and may not even have had a majority of the court supporting it. More persuasive, and more ominous for Northerners, was Taney's assertion that the Fifth Amendment prevented Congress from ever freeing slaves because slaves were property that was specifically protected by the Constitution.

The message of *Dred Scott* was profoundly depressing for African Americans and their white allies in antebellum America. Taney's statement about the rights of blacks—that they were "so far inferior, that they had no rights which the white man was bound to respect"— may have been a statement of Taney's vision of history, but in fact most Americans understood that this is what the Chief Justice of the United States believed should be the legal and social condition of African Americans. "They had no rights" was the lesson of *Dred Scott.*

The impact of the decision, however, was hardly what Taney expected. In the North, there was an uproar of protest and a rededication of purpose for Republicans. In Illinois, Abraham Lincoln, a relatively obscure railroad lawyer and one-term Congressman, re-entered politics to denounce the decision. In 1862 and 1863—less than six years after Taney announced his decision—Lincoln, by this time the President of the United States, would sign legislation ending slavery in the District of Columbia and the federal territories, and he would then issue the Emancipation Proclamation ending slavery in most of the South. By 1865, the Thirteenth Amendment would end slavery throughout the nation. In 1866, Congress would declare that all people born in the United States—including all former slaves—were citizens of the United States. In 1868, the nation as a whole would reaffirm this position by ratifying the Fourteenth Amendment, which permanently reversed *Dred Scott.* At that point, blacks would have the same Constitutional rights as whites, even if it would take another century to insure that the laws throughout the nation were applied equally to all people.

SEE ALSO *Slavery and Race; United States Constitution.*

BIBLIOGRAPHY

Allen, Austin. 2006. *Origins of the Dred Scott Case: Jacksonian Jurisprudence and the Supreme Court, 1837–1857.* Athens: University of Georgia Press.

Fehrenbacher, Don E. 1978. *The Dred Scott Case: Its Significance in American Law and Politics.* New York: Oxford University Press.

Finkelman, Paul. 1997. *Dred Scott v. Sandford: A Brief History With Documents.* Boston: Bedford Books.

———. 2006. "*Dred Scott v. Sandford.*" In *The Public Debate over Controversial Supreme Court Decisions,* edited by Melvin I. Urofsky, 24–33. Washington, DC: CQ Press.

Paul Finkelman

DU BOIS, W. E. B.
1868–1963

William Edward Burghardt Du Bois's life spanned the two great reconstructions of democracy in the United States. He was born in Great Barrington, Massachusetts, on February 23, 1868, as the former slaves were entering political life in the South, and he died in Accra, Ghana, on August 27, 1963, on the eve of the March on Washington that marked a high point in the modern civil rights movement. In his ninety-five years, Du Bois not only bore eloquent witness to his country's advances toward and retreats from interracial democracy but, as a scholar, activist, and artist, he actively participated in the cause of racial justice in the United States and around the world. He also contributed to the understanding of the nature of race and the causes of racism, offering a powerful refutation of scientific conceptions of race and insisting on the distinctive cultural, political, and economic contributions of Africans and African Americans.

Du Bois often observed that he spent his childhood in New England largely detached from African American life and unaware of the power of racial hierarchies. It was as a college student at Fisk University in Nashville, Tennessee, that he encountered both the privations of Jim Crow segregation and the richness and variety of African American culture. During this period, Du Bois's work as a schoolteacher in rural Tennessee also impressed on him the ongoing after effects of slavery. Leaving Fisk in 1888, Du Bois went on to study philosophy, history, and economics at Harvard and the University of Berlin. In 1895, he became the first African American to receive a doctorate from Harvard, and his first book, based on a dissertation on Americans' erratic efforts to withdraw from the international slave trade, heralded the entry of a remarkable scholar.

In the first phase of his scholarly career, Du Bois pursued the conviction that ignorance was the root of racial prejudice and that collecting and disseminating knowledge about black life was crucial to obtaining full citizenship for African Americans. To that end, he published a groundbreaking sociological study of the African American community in Philadelphia, and as a professor at Atlanta University, produced sixteen studies of African American life. Over time, Du Bois came to believe that knowledge alone would not eliminate racial injustice, and his writing increasingly focused on the importance of unconscious racism and economic self-interest in sustaining racial hierarchies. Among his greatest achievements, *Black Reconstruction in America: 1860–1880* (1935) rewrote the history of Reconstruction by highlighting the central role of the slaves in securing the Union's victory and by countering the prevailing view that the experiment in interracial democracy was a disaster. *Black Reconstruction* also explored the links between capitalism and white supremacy, revealing the growing influence of Marx's ideas on Du Bois's thought.

Persistent violence against African Americans convinced Du Bois to trade academic life for full-time activism in 1910. He had already come to public attention when he published an essay in *The Souls of Black Folk* (1903) that criticized the leadership of Booker T. Washington and when he established the Niagara Movement in 1905 to demand civil and political rights for African Americans. He was one of the founding members of the National Association for the Advancement of Colored People (NAACP), its only original African American board member, and the founder-editor of its journal, *The Crisis.* Over the next twenty-four years, Du Bois used this platform to advocate for anti-lynching legislation, black political and civil rights, women's suffrage, international peace, and a host of other social justice issues.

Du Bois never confined the fight against racism to the United States. Even his early writings indicate an awareness of connections between racial hierarchies at home and European colonialism in Africa and Asia. When he first prophesied that "the problem of the Twentieth Century is the problem of the color-line" in his 1900 "Address to the Nations of the World," Du Bois insisted that the color line encompassed the globe. After World War I he organized a series of Pan-African Congresses to encourage cooperation among people of African descent; and after World War II he continued to work with transnational networks of activists, fighting for human rights at home and abroad, for the independence of colonized nations, and for the cause of world peace.

Art was, for Du Bois, an essential element of the struggle against racism. "All art is propaganda and ever must be," he declared in his 1926 essay, "The Criteria of Negro Art." Du Bois never meant that beauty should be sacrificed to politics. Rather, he insisted that beauty was intimately connected to truth telling, particularly to conveying the truth of African American humanity. He understood, furthermore, that poetic expression could change people's perspectives where a mere recitation of facts might fail. To that end, Du Bois wrote constantly and in a variety of genres; he published essays, novels, poetry, autobiographies, and a wide range of occasional pieces; he staged elaborate pageants that displayed the glories of black civilization; and he served as a conduit for other writers and artists as editor of *The Crisis*. The best known of his books, *The Souls of Black Folk*, exemplifies Du Bois's ability to blend historical and sociological detail with profoundly moving passages about the impact of race on his own life and that of his fellow citizens.

Although Du Bois's final years have received relatively less scholarly attention, he remained active until his death. He continued to write prolifically, and after an unsuccessful bid for the U.S. Senate as an American Labor Party candidate in 1950, he dedicated much of his energy to the peace movement. A victim of cold war politics, Du Bois was indicted in 1951 on charges of operating as an agent for foreign interests. Despite his acquittal, he was denied a passport in 1952 and was not allowed to travel abroad until 1958. In 1961, he joined the Communist Party and left the United States for Ghana, where, upon his death, he was buried as a hero. Fittingly, at his death, Du Bois was at work on the *Encyclopedia Africana*, a comprehensive study of black life and history.

SEE ALSO *Niagara Movement; Pan-Africanism; Racial Hierarchy.*

BIBLIOGRAPHY

PRIMARY WORKS

1997 (1903). *The Souls of Black Folk*. Edited by David W. Blight and Robert Gooding-Williams. Boston: Bedford Books.

1998 (1935). *Black Reconstruction in America, 1860–1880*. New York: Free Press.

1984 (1940). *Dusk of Dawn: An Essay Toward an Autobiography of a Race Concept*. New Brunswick, NJ: Transaction Publishers.

1995. *W. E. B. Du Bois: A Reader*. Edited by David Levering Lewis. New York: Henry Holt.

SECONDARY WORKS

Lewis, David Levering. 1993. *W. E. B. Du Bois: Biography of a Race, 1868-1919*. New York: Henry Holt.

———. 2000. *W. E. B. Du Bois: The Fight for Equality and the American Century: 1919–1963*. New York: Henry Holt

Marable, Manning. 1986. *W. E. B. Du Bois: Black Radical Democrat*. Boston: Twayne.

Rampersad, Arnold. 1976. *The Art and Imagination of W. E. B. Du Bois*. New York: Schocken.

Lawrie Balfour

DUKE, DAVID

1950–

David Duke was born in Louisiana in 1950 and is perhaps America's most well-known racist. While attending Louisiana State University, Duke founded the White Youth Alliance, a youth organization affiliated with the National Socialist White People's Party. Upon graduation in 1974, he founded the Knights of the Ku Klux Klan (KKK), which remains one of the largest and most influential Klan groups in the country.

Duke realized early in his career that violent racism was no longer acceptable to the majority of the American middle class, and he altered his message in order to gain wider support. He changed the title of Klan leader from Grand Wizard to National Director. He stopped "burning crosses" and began holding "cross lighting" ceremonies, and he used "coded racism." For example, he quit speaking in public about the danger of racial and ethnic minorities, referring instead to the "lawless underclass" and "perpetual welfare recipient."

In order to gain even broader middle-class support and to build a political career, Duke left the KKK in 1980 and founded the more acceptable-sounding National Association for the Advancement of White People, which retained the Klan's membership roster and mailing list, and in fact operated out of the same office.

In 1989 Duke ran successfully for the Louisiana legislature and served as a member of the state House of Representatives. He then ran unsuccessfully for the U.S. Senate in 1990, the Louisiana Governor's office in 1991, the U.S. Presidency in 1992, the U.S. Senate again in 1996, and the U.S. House in 1998. However, he did receive the majority of votes from white voters in both the 1990 and 1991 races.

In 2000, Duke retired from politics and founded yet another new white supremacist organization, the National

Organization For European American Rights, or NOFEAR. Since founding NOFEAR, Duke has traveled throughout Europe and to Russia in particular, gathering supporters. His anti-Semitic essays have been translated into Arabic and republished throughout the Middle East. He has also authored two significant books: *My Awakening: A Path to Racial Understanding* in 1998, and *Jewish Supremacism: My Awakening on the Jewish Question* in 2002.

In March 2003 Duke was convicted in federal court on charges of mail fraud and tax evasion, charges related to funds raised during his political campaigns. He spent thirteen months in federal prison and was released in May 2004.

SEE ALSO *Ku Klux Klan.*

BIBLIOGRAPHY

Bridges, Tyler. 1995. *The Rise of David Duke.* Jackson: University Press of Mississippi.

Bullock, Charles S., et al. 1995. *David Duke and the Politics of Race in the South.* Nashville, TN: Vanderbilt University Press.

Rose, Douglas, ed. 1992. *The Emergence of David Duke and the Politics of Race.* Chapel Hill: University of North Carolina Press.

J. Keith Akins

E

EDUCATION, DISCRIMINATION IN HIGHER

Colleges and universities play an important role in advancing equity through their efforts to recruit and retain students, faculty, and staff of color. Despite the great improvement in educational equity since the 1950s, racial discrimination in institutions of higher education continues to exist in the early twenty-first century. To overcome the barriers to advancement in higher education for racialized people, institutions of higher education must make real commitments to greater racial equity on campus. Such commitments do not come in the form of proclamations, but rather in the form of bodies, time, and monetary and community resources. Educational institutions must closely examine the racial climate on campus and work toward ideological shifts that will remove any existing barriers for racial/ethnic groups. Such commitments result in the sort of institutional transformation that is necessary in order to see a meaningful reduction in racial discrimination at colleges and universities. There are a number of basic ideas that institutions can implement in order to both address issues of discrimination and attempt to retain faculty of color.

STUDENT ISSUES

Colleges and universities have not traditionally provided equitable educational opportunities to students of color, and in the early 2000s, students of color are not represented in higher education at proportions that reflect their numbers in the population as a whole. Table 1 demonstrates this point by examining the number of students earning doctorates in 2002.

This table indicates that the number of earned doctorates is well below any reasonable expectations for any racialized groups, except for whites and Asian Americans. According to the 2000 census, 12.5 percent of the U.S. population identifies as Latino/Latina, 12.3 percent identify as African American, 3.7 percent identify as Asian American, .9 percent identify as American Indian/Alaska Native, .1 percent identify as Pacific Islander, and 69.1 percent identify as white. One might reasonably expect the student population receiving doctorates to be more closely aligned with these numbers. This is not to say that the ratios should be exactly the same, but the discrepancies indicate a lack of access to and retention in institutions of higher education. Clearly, there are barriers for some racialized groups to institutions of higher learning.

One strategy for improving admissions, retention, and hiring in institutions of higher education is through affirmative action programs. Race-based affirmative action programs in higher education have been advocated by a number of scholars, and they are often supported by traditionally marginalized students. Yet attacks on these programs have been fierce, and the discontinued use of affirmative action in some states has resulted in significantly fewer students of color applying to and attending institutions of higher education. Although arguments abound in support of need-based rather than race-based affirmative action programs, a number of scholars have expressed the view that institutions of higher education have a moral obligation to repay communities of color for past injustices, and that need-based programs are likely to divert more resources to white men (see Feinberg 1996, Heller 2002, St. John 2004).

Earned Doctorates for Racial Groups in the United States, 2005

Racial and ethnic group of U.S. citizens	
American Indian and Alaska Native	0.5%
Asian	5.3%
Black	6.6%
Latinas[1]	4.9%
White	81.0%
Other	1.7%

[1]In this entry, we use the term Latinas to indicate both Latinos and Latinas. U.S., state, and local governments often use the term "Hispanic" to denote this group.

SOURCE: Reproduced by permission of *The Chronicle of Higher Education. Chronicle of Higher Education: The Almanac, 2005.* Volume 52, Number 1, p. 19.

Table 1.

Once students are on campus, the racial climate of the institution is crucial in determining whether students persist in their studies and graduate. Campus climate is an important issue because even if institutions of higher education are able to recruit more diverse student bodies, students are less likely to persist and graduate if they experience a hostile environment on campus. Evaluating campus racial climate has been the topic of much research since the 1980s. A 1991 survey by the American Council on Education found that 36 percent of all institutions (and 74 percent of research institutions) reported incidents of intolerance involving race, gender, or sexual orientation. Further, despite current efforts, many students—including many minority students, white women, gay and lesbian students, and disabled students—still find the campus climate unresponsive to their needs, past experiences, and educational expectations (see Humphreys 1998). In their book *The Agony of Education* (1996), Joe Feagin, Hernan Vera, and Nikitah Imani argue that when researchers examine campus racial climate and racism in institutions of higher education, they need to consider not just overt racial incidents, but also patterns of human recognition of racialized students and how social spaces are racially marked. Critical-race scholars have focused on the microaggressions experienced by students of color on college campuses across the nation. In 1998, for example, David Solorzano analyzed the microagressions experienced by Chicana and Chicano students who were Ford Foundation Minority Fellows, and his findings led him to challenge the colorblind meritocracy ideology that tries to pass these microagressions off as "oversensitivity." Researchers have also documented how students of color experience greater emotional stress due to prejudice, and that racial tensions are more likely to be perceived by students of color (see Hurtado 1992, Johnson-Durgans 1994). These experiences of hostile racial climates also impact the academic success of students of color such that they are less likely to do well in college. Walter Allen, a professor of higher education at University of California, Los Angeles, has documented that black students at historically black institutions have better completion rates and report closer connections to their universities than black students at predominantly white institutions. Ana Alemán, an associate professor at Boston College, reported in 2000 that the dominant culture of predominantly white universities makes friendships with racially matched peers even more important for the success of racialized students. Clearly, then, access to institutions of higher education is not enough to ensure equity within these institutions, because the campus climate experienced by students of color is often extremely hostile and stands as a barrier to these students' academic achievement.

FACULTY ISSUES

The proportion of people of color in faculty positions continues to lag behind that of whites and closely mirrors the rate of those people earning doctorates. Table 2 illuminates the disparities in faculty positions at all levels.

The low proportion of doctorates being awarded to people of color is often blamed for the dismal increase in faculty of color since the mid-1990s. However, there is more to the problem of low numbers of faculty of color than the "pipeline" argument. Octavio Villalpando and Dolores Delgado-Bernal argue that faculty of color face "institutional barriers at most stages of their academic careers" (2002, p. 244). Reflecting on the framework for diversity outlined by Sylvia Hurtado, Jeffrey F. Milem, Alma Clayton-Pedersen, and Walter R. Allen in 1998 provides a reminder that problems in achieving structural diversity are related to issues of psychological and behavioral diversity, and to the historical legacies of individual institutions and the broader institution of higher education. In the following examination of literature regarding faculty diversity in higher education, the focus is on available research, most of which examines the experiences of faculty of color and the barriers they face.

Biases against people of color "contribute to unwelcoming and unsupportive work environments for faculty of color" (Turner, Myers, and Creswell 1999, p. 28). Overt and covert racial barriers include: tokenism, isolation, racial and ethnic bias in recruiting and hiring, barriers found in tenure and promotion practices, the devaluation of "minority research," and isolation and lack of mentoring. Tokenism is a problem common to environments where structural diversity is low. Relatedly, researchers have pointed out that faculty of color feel alone and often invisible when they are the only scholar of color in departments or colleges (see

Number of Full-Time Faculty Members by Rank and Racial and Ethnic Group during Fall, 2003

American Indian and Alaska Native		
Professor	507	0.3%
Associate Professor	529	0.4%
Assistant professor	661	0.5%
TOTAL	1,697	0.4%
Asian American		
Professor	10,202	6.2%
Associate Professor	9,183	7.1%
Assistant Professor	13,216	9.3%
TOTAL	32,601	7.5%
Black		
Professor	5,343	3.2%
Associate Professor	7,204	5.5%
Assistant Professor	9,464	6.7%
TOTAL	22,011	5.0%
Latinas[1]		
Professor	3,429	2.1%
Associate Professor	3,861	3.0%
Assistant professor	5,321	3.8%
TOTAL	12,611	2.9%
White		
Professor	144,924	88.2%
Associate Professor	109,313	84.0%
Assistant professor	112,920	79.8%
TOTAL	367,157	84.2%
TOTAL OVERALL PROFESSOR	164,405	
TOTAL OVERALL ASSOCIATE PROFESSOR	130,090	
TOTAL OVERALL ASSISTANT PROFESSOR	141,582	
TOTAL OF ALL	436,077	

[1]In this entry, we use the term Latinas to indicate both Latinos and Latinas. U.S., state, and local governments often use the term "Hispanic" to denote this group.

SOURCE: Reproduced by permission of *The Chronicle of Higher Education. Chronicle of Higher Education: The Almanac, 2005.* Volume 52, Number 1, p. 26.

Table 2.

Essien 2003). Biases in recruiting and hiring can reflect the racism of individuals, but they also mirror an institution's lack of attention to its own legacy of exclusion. The mechanism of tenure and promotion in higher education is an institution itself, and it is rife with barriers to faculty of color, including the devaluation of the extraordinary service responsibilities of faculty of color and the lack of legitimacy granted to research agendas that fall outside of the mainstream. In a 1994 article in *Educational Researcher*, Amado M. Padilla discussed the concept of "cultural taxation" to illuminate the fact that many underrepresented faculty are expected to cover minority affairs, in addition to completing a rigorous agenda in research, teaching, and institutional service.

In addition to questions regarding their research agendas, faculty of color find their legitimacy questioned by those who challenge their place in the institution due to the role of affirmative action in the hiring process. Linda Johnsrud and Kathlee Sadao found in 1998 that such ethnocentrist behaviors and attitudes are rampant in college and university faculty. In a 2000 survey by the American Council on Education, Geoffrey Maruyama and colleagues found that the faculty in their survey who had more experience working with diverse groups of students had more positive attitudes towards institutional and departmental values about diversity and the importance of having a diverse population. As with students, it appears that faculty exposure to and interaction with diverse groups and individuals leads to an increased acceptance of diversity.

Another challenge to faculty of color is the amount of institutional service they are asked or required to perform. Indeed, they "often complain about overwhelming counseling responsibilities" (Allen et al. 2002, p. 192). Faculty of color serve on a myriad of institutional committees and are expected to represent the "minority voice." Additionally, these faculty become mentors and counselors to students of color in their departments. Departments may have only one or two people of color on staff and they are often expected to serve larger numbers of students of color. While time spent on these activities is important, and faculty gladly undertake it, it does detract from research responsibilities, which are more highly valued in the promotion and tenure process. In this way, institutional service expectations for faculty of color actually represent barriers to their professional progress. Increasing structural diversity will add more faculty of color to share the responsibilities of institutional service. However, it is important to also examine institutional histories and the psychological climate on campuses, and to assess their impact on differential service expectations for faculty of color and white faculty. Working towards diversity in these areas will create better institutional environments in which faculty of color can focus on performing excellent research, teaching, and service to further institutional missions, including diversity initiatives.

TRANSFORMING INSTITUTIONS OF HIGHER EDUCATION

Institutions are transformed by increased diversity through positive changes in campus climate. Some researchers have argued that these changes are evident in the increase in the acceptance and value of diversity that they bring. Further, Hurtado and colleagues (1998) suggest that a recognition of historical legacies of inclusion and exclusion and a desire to make the campus more inclusive of all people and groups are ways institutions can increase diversity. This mirrors the argument that as students are exposed to different groups and individuals they become more committed to the concept of diversity. Devon Williams argues that university teachers can improve intergroup relations by employing "jigsaw" groupings in their classrooms (forming groups and then switching members to new groups) in order to force students to cooperate and interact with their peers. Finally, diversity courses often challenge students to think in more complex ways about identity and history and to avoid cultural stereotyping. Diversity in the curriculum has a positive impact on attitudes toward racial issues, on opportunities to interact in deeper ways with those who are different, and on overall satisfaction with the university. These benefits are particularly powerful for white students who have had less opportunity for such engagement (see Humphreys 1998).

Institutional transformation can be evident in more tangible ways as well. For instance, changes in institutional mission are indications of institutional transformation. Roxane Harvey Gudeman, a psychology professor at Macalester College in Saint Paul, Minnesota, has found that such adjustments in mission statements reflected the institutional value of diversity. Mission statements are often criticized as having purely symbolic value, but once adjusted to reflect changing attitudes toward diversity, they do contribute to improving the climate for people of color at all levels of the institutions. It can be argued that this kind of transformation accompanies an institution's examination of its historical legacies of exclusion and inclusion. However, mission statements alone do not reflect historical context or change psychological climate. They are, as with all other steps towards increasing diversity, only factors in a larger approach to a continuing problem.

Institutional transformation can also be assessed in terms of policies that either do or do not advance greater equity. Research that has examined university policies as they relate to diversity and equity generally shows that institutions still have much to do. The shift to distance education and a greater reliance on Internet technology may open doors to students in rural areas, but, as Rachel Moran argues in "Diversity, Distance, and the Delivery of Higher Education" (1998), it actually further stratifies higher education because those without access to the technology are largely people of color and those from low-income backgrounds. When colleges and universities fail to implement ethnic fraud policies, they are "allowing a charade to continue" and thus fail to advance more equitable hiring, admissions, and financial aid practices (Pewewardy 2004). Angelina Castagno and Stacey Lee point out in a 2007 article that universities that continue to embrace Native American mascots contribute to the perpetuation of racism and stereotypes against Indigenous peoples, whereas Delgado Bernal noted in 2002 that admissions criteria largely exclude students of color because of the Eurocentric epistemologies that shape and guide them. In general, the thrust of this work is that universities have a significant responsibility to work toward greater equity in their policies and practices, and that many institutions are currently failing in this regard.

Focusing on institutional transformation in relation to discrimination and the benefits of diversity contributes to the effort to move the emphasis away from the idea that students of color come to college with deficits. A spotlight on the institution, rather than the individual, allows for a recognition of the role institutional strategies and policies play in the culture of exclusion on many higher education campuses.

BIBLIOGRAPHY

Alfred, Mary V. 2001. "Reconceptualizing Marginality from the Margins: Perspectives of African American Tenured Female Faculty at a White Research University." *Western Journal of Black Studies* 25 (1): 1–11.

Allen, Walter R. 1992. "The Color of Success: African-American College Student Outcomes at Predominantly White and Historically Black Public Colleges and Universities." *Harvard Educational Review* 62 (1): 26–44.

———, et al. 2002. "Outsiders Within: Race, Gender, and Faculty Status in U.S. Higher Education." In *The Racial Crisis in American Higher Education: Continuing Challenges for the Twenty-First Century*, rev. ed., edited by William A. Smith, Philip G. Altbach, and Kofi Lomotey, 189–220. Albany: State University of New York Press.

Alemán, Ana. M. M. (2000). "Race Talks: Undergraduate Women of Color and Female Friendship." *Review of Higher Education* 23 (2): 133–152.

Banks, Cherry A., and James A. Banks. 1995. "Equity Pedagogy: An Essential Component of Multicultural Education." *Theory into Practice* 34 (3): 152–158.

Bernal, Delgado. 2002. "Critical Race Theory, Latino Critical Theory, and Critical Raced-Gendered Epistemologies: Recognizing Students of Color as Holders and Creators of Knowledge." *Qualitative Inquiry* 8 (1): 105–126.

Blackburn, Robert T., Stacy Wenzel, and Jeffrey P. Bieber. 1994. "Minority vs. Majority Faculty Publication Performance: A Research Note." *Review of Higher Education* 17 (3): 217–282.

Castagno, Angelina E., and Stacey J. Lee. 2007. "Native Mascots and Ethnic Fraud in Higher Education: Using Tribal Critical Race Theory and the Interest Convergence Principle as an Analytic Tool." *Equity and Excellence in Education* 40 (1): 3–13.

Essien, Victor. 2003. "Visible and Invisible Barriers to the Incorporation of Faculty of Color in Predominantly White Law Schools." *Journal of Black Studies* 34 (1): 63–71.

Feagin, Joe R., Hernan Vera, and Nikitah Imani. 1996. *The Agony of Education: Black Students at White Colleges and Universities.* New York: Routledge.

Feinberg, Walter. 1996. "Affirmative Action and Beyond: A Case for a Backward-Looking Gender- and Race-Based Policy." *Teachers College Record* 97 (3): 362–399.

Fenelon, James. 2003. "Race, Research, and Tenure: Institutional Credibility and the Incorporation of African, Latino, and American Indian Faculty." *Journal of Black Studies* 34 (1): 87–100.

Gudeman, Roxanne Harvey. 2001. "Faculty Experience with Diversity: A Case Study of Macalester College." In *Diversity Challenged: Evidence on the Impact of Affirmative Action*, edited by Gary Orfield and Michal Kurlaender. Cambridge, MA: Harvard Education Publishing Group.

Heller, Donald E. 2002. "State Merit Scholarship Programs: An Overview." In *State and Merit Scholarship Programs and Racial Inequality*, edited by Donald E. Heller and Patricia Marin, 15–22. Boston: The Harvard Civil Rights Project.

Humphreys, Debra. 1998. *Higher Education, Race and Diversity: Views from the Field.* Washington, DC: Association of American Colleges and Universities.

Hurtado, Sylvia. 1992. "The Campus Racial Climate: Contexts of Conflict." *Journal of Higher Education* 63 (5): 539–569.

———, Jeffrey F. Milem, Alma Clayton-Pedersen, and Walter R. Allen. 1998. "Enhancing Campus Climates for Racial/Ethnic Diversity through Educational Policy and Practice." *Review of Higher Education* 21 (3): 279–302.

Johnson-Durgans, Vanessa D. 1994. "Perceptions of Racial Climates in Residence Halls between African-American and Euroamerican College Students." *Journal of College Student Development* 35 (4): 267–274.

Johnsrud, Linda K., and Kathleen C. Sadao. 1998. "The Common Experience of 'Otherness': Ethnic and Racial Minority Faculty." *Review of Higher Education* 21 (4): 315–342.

Maruyama, Geoffrey, et al. 2000. *Does Diversity Make a Difference? Three Research Studies on Diversity in College Classrooms.* Washington DC: American Council on Education.

Moran, Rachel F. 1998. "Diversity, Distance, and the Delivery of Higher Education." *Ohio State Law Journal* 59: 775–792.

Padilla, Amado M. 1994. "Ethnic Minority Scholars, Research, and Mentoring: Current and Future Issues." *Educational Researcher* 23 (4): 24–27.

Pewewardy, Cornel. 2004. "So You Think You Hired an 'Indian' Faculty Member? The Ethnic Fraud Paradox in Higher Education." In *Indigenizing the Academy: Transforming Scholarship and Empowering Communities*, edited by Devon Mihesuah and Angela Wilson, 200–217. Lincoln: University of Nebraska Press.

Richardson, Richard C., Jr., and Elizabeth Fisk Skinner. 1990. "Adapting to Diversity: Organizational Influences on Student Achievement." *Journal of Higher Education* 61 (5): 485–511.

Solmon, Lewis C., Matthew S. Solmon, and Tamara W. Schiff. 2002. "The Changing Demographics: Problems and Opportunities." In *The Racial Crisis in American Higher Education: Continuing Challenges for the Twenty-First Century*, edited by William A. Smith, Philip G. Altbach, and Kofi Lomotey, 43–75. Albany: State University of New York Press.

Solorzano, David G. 1998. "Critical Race Theory, Race, and Gender Microaggressions and the Experiences of Chicana and Chicano Scholars." *Qualitative Studies in Education* 11 (1): 121–136.

St. John, Edward P., et al. 2004. *Diversity and Persistence in Indiana Higher Education: The Impact of Preparation, Major Choices, and Student Aid.* IPAS Research Report #04–01. Bloomington: Indiana Project on Academic Success: Smith Center for Research in Education.

Turner, Caroline S.V., Samuel L. Myers, and John W. Creswell. 1999. "Exploring Underrepresentation: The Case of Faculty of Color in the Midwest." *Journal of Higher Education* 70 (1): 27–59.

Villalpando, Octavio, and Dolores Delgado-Bernal. 2002. "A Critical Race Theory Analysis of Barriers That Impede the Success of Faculty of Color." In *The Racial Crisis in American Higher Education: Continuing Challenges for the Twenty-First Century*, edited by William A. Smith, Philip G. Altbach, and Kofi Lomotey, 243–269. Albany: State University of New York Press.

Williams, Devon. 2004. "Improving Race Relations in Higher Education: The Jigsaw Classroom as a Missing Piece to the Puzzle." *Urban Education* 39: 316–344.

Bryan McKinley Jones Brayboy
Angelina E. Castagno
Kristi Ryujin

EDUCATION, RACIAL DISPARITIES

The Universal Declaration of Human Rights, the Declaration on the Rights of the Child, and other international agreements make plain that education is a fundamental and universal human right. To achieve this right for all people, the United Nations Educational, Scientific, and Cultural Organization (UNESCO) has affirmed the principles of nondiscrimination, equality of opportunity and treatment, universal access to education, and solidarity. Further, UNESCO considers it the responsibility of states to advance and implement these principles, and disparities in educational opportunities and outcomes along ethnic or racial lines is considered to be a violation of this fundamental right to education. Nevertheless, such disparities are widespread in the United States and elsewhere. This entry will explain why these disparities continue to exist despite the fact that most nations profess a commitment to racial and ethnic equality.

In many cases, racial and ethnic inequities are a consequence of the legacies of colonialism and slavery. In the North American colonies, for example, slavery created a racial order with whites at the top and nonwhites at the bottom of the hierarchy. Poor whites were encouraged to find common cause not with their class allies across racial lines, but with the ruling whites. As Howard Zinn points out in *A People's History of the United States* (2003), when and if blacks and whites did join together to rebel, these rebellions were met with very harsh punishment for both parties.

Under slavery, Africans and their descendants were forbidden to receive any sort of education. After emancipation, the doctrine of "separate but equal" ensured that the education of blacks continued to be inferior to that of whites. It was not until 1954, in the *Brown v. Board of Education* decision, that the U.S. Supreme Court declared that school segregation was unconstitutional. Nevertheless, while this was an important step towards equality in educational opportunity in the United States, it left much to be desired. Moreover, a 2003 study conducted by Jaekyung Lee reported that some of the gains made in the 1970s in terms of diminishing the achievement gap between blacks and whites were lost as the gap widened again in the early 1990s.

The United States gained its independence from Great Britain following the American Revolution, but most Latin American countries had to wait until the early nineteenth century to achieve their independence, and many African countries remained European colonies up until the twentieth century. However, many of these former colonies won their independence from Europe only to become dependent on the United States or the Soviet Union for survival during the Cold War. The dismantling of the Soviet Union and the consequent abandonment of client states after the Cold War led to economic crises and ethnic strife in a number of African and East European countries. This had, among other things, negative repercussions for access to education for ethnic minorities.

The 2001 UN Report on the World Social Situation reported that in sub-Saharan Africa teacher's salaries had decreased since the 1980s, and that the civil war in Rwanda resulted in more than 60 percent of its teachers either being killed or fleeing the country. The aftermath of the Cold War also wreaked havoc on the educational system in the former Yugoslavia. The withdrawal of autonomy in the province of Kosovo resulted in 300,000 children of Albanian origin being removed from school. In Bosnia and Herzegovina, at least one-third of the school buildings were destroyed during the war. In addition, Gladys Mutangandura, Vicki Lamb, and Judith Blau reported in 2002 that structural adjustment programs in Africa and Latin America negatively affected schooling because countries were required to curtail educational programs to comply with International Monetary Foundation mandates. In each of these cases, large-scale crises ended up causing the most harm to the most vulnerable populations—the poor, women, children, and ethnic and religious minorities.

While many experts predicted that globalization and the spread of capitalism would be beneficial across social classes and for rich and poor alike, it is hard to ignore the figures that demonstrate that inequality has increased since the 1980s, both within countries and between countries. The 2001 UN Report on the World Social Situation declared that, in many developing countries, this has meant that children are obligated to work and forego their education. Roughly 250 million children worked in 2001, and many of them did not attend school. One report found that more than 30 percent of fifteen to eighteen year olds in Bolivia, Chile, El Salvador, and Venezuela who were not in school reported that it was their need to work that kept them out of school. A 1998 Inter-American Development Bank report found that in El Salvador, 50 percent of fifteen-year olds in the poorest 30 percent of the population were not enrolled in school, while 50 percent of the richest 10 percent were still in school at age twenty-one. In addition, the top 10 percent of Salvadorans completes an average of six more years of schooling than the poorest 30 percent. In many countries, children are not able to attend school because their families cannot afford the direct costs associated with school attendance. In Indonesia, for example, direct costs for attending a primary school, such as school fees, uniforms, and books, are 38 percent of the per capita income of the poorest 20 percent of Indonesians. In Georgia, in the former Soviet Union, a set of new books for a student entering the seventh grade costs twice as much as the average worker makes in a month. Worldwide, children that are from ethnic, religious, racial, or linguistic minorities are often more likely to be poor, and thus less likely to be able to attend school for these reasons.

Racial and ethnic inequalities exist around the world, despite the fact that most governments profess agreement with international conventions that decry discrimination and advance universal education as a human right. Leaders of countries utilize distinct discourses to talk about the racial and ethnic discrimination and inequality that exist in their respective countries. Joe Feagin argues in his book *Racist America* (2000) that, in the United States, representatives of the government are willing to recognize that racial inequality exists, but that they are frequently not willing to admit that racial disparities are the result of past or present racial discrimination. In Brazil, on the contrary, the government not only attests a commitment to racial democracy, but also claims to have achieved it, thereby curtailing any possibility of discussions of eliminating disparities. This has begun to change, however, and the top Brazilian state universities have begun to implement affirmative action programs.

Many Brazilians uphold this ideal of a racial democracy, although studies show that most recognize that this is an ideal, not a reality (Bailey 2004). Robin Sheriff's 2000 ethnographic study of a *favela* in Rio de Janeiro demonstrates that the prevalence of this myth makes Brazil a candidate for achieving racial equality insofar as most Brazilians do see this as a desirable goal. In her book, *Racism in a Racial Democracy* (1998), France Twine argues that the lack of an antiracist curriculum in schools in Brazil inhibits Brazilian children from developing an understanding of racism and leads them to believe that a racial democracy does indeed exist.

Michael Omi and Howard Winant have described the distinction between the United States and Brazil as the difference between a racial dictatorship and racial hegemony. Similarly, Anthony Marx has argued that apartheid

Brazilian Students Wait for School Buses. *Poorer people do not have the same educational opportunities as their wealthier counterparts. Here Brazilian students wait for buses to go to school at the Vila Estrutural slum as part of a program in which the government provides poor families with money if they send their children to school.* AP IMAGES.

and legal segregation in South Africa and the United States encouraged black solidarity and opposition, while the ideology of racial democracy in Brazil elicited more muted racial identity and mobilization. In the United States, black solidarity brought about the civil rights movement, while Brazil has not witnessed a movement of such strength. When legal apartheid existed in the United States and South Africa, Brazilians could compare themselves to these two countries and claim that their government at least did not endorse apartheid. In a similar fashion, Joe Feagin points out that U.S. government officials have argued that now that racial discrimination is no longer legal, it is not the responsibility of the leaders of this country to ensure that racial equality is achieved.

Capitalism generates inequalities, and these inequalities are superimposed on racial and ethnic divisions. In the United States, despite legal measures taken to ensure equality of opportunity across ethnic and racial lines, nonwhites continue to be disadvantaged in the educational system. In her book, *Bad Boys* (2000), Ann Ferguson demonstrates how institutions such as elementary schools devalue black culture, and thus black children. She explains how teachers and administrators interpret black children's behavior with a different lens than that used for white children, which leads to black boys getting into much more trouble, and thus getting behind in school. In *Race in the Schools* (2003), Judith Blau discusses how schools racialize opportunities and the educational process, to the advantage of white children.

In Brazil, Peru, and the United States, illiteracy and low literacy are more prevalent among nonwhite populations. Weiss et al. (1995) reported that about 10 percent of the adult population in the United States lacks basic reading skills. Further, ethnic and racial minorities and inner-city residents are overrepresented both in terms of illiteracy and low literacy in the United States. In Brazil, one quarter of African-descended people have no schooling at all. Overall, they have about two-thirds of the level of education of whites. In addition, Patricia Justino and Arnab Acharya (2003) report that Afro-Brazilians who do graduate from high school are only about half as likely as white Brazilians to go on to university. In Peru, the overall illiteracy rate is about 13 percent. However, 33 percent of the indigenous population is illiterate, and 44 percent of indigenous women in Peru are illiterate.

Anthropologist Marisol De la Cadena describes how Peruvian educational reforms of the 1950s were designed to culturally whiten indigenous Peruvians by teaching them to no longer wear braids or traditional dress and to speak only Spanish, and that the curricula devalued indigenous customs and values (De la Cadena 2005). These sorts of assaults on indigenous cultural forms contribute to educational inequality, because by devaluing indigenous culture the schools deprecate indigenous people, making them less inclined to complete their schooling. Sociologist Tanya Golash-Boza has described how the globalization of capitalism and the end of protectionism for internal markets in Peru have led to extreme poverty in indigenous and Afro-Peruvian farming communities. In these isolated communities, the availability of qualified teachers, up-to-date textbooks, and even school supplies is much more limited than in the larger cities where whites are concentrated.

Another factor working against minority youngsters is the digital divide. Modern technology brings great opportunities for expanding educational materials, even to those not attending school. Many children in developing countries are unable to do well in school because they cannot afford textbooks, while textbooks have become somewhat obsolete for children with access to the Internet. The sort of basic information held in textbooks could easily be made available over the Internet, but unfortunately the children who most need textbooks are also the ones with the least access to the World Wide Web. This problem is not restricted to the developing world. In the United States, Mexican Americans and African Americans are only about half as likely as white Americans to have a computer or Internet access in the home (Fairlie 2004).

A world in which racial equality of opportunity and of outcomes in education exists is still a long way off, despite the fact that most countries not only profess a commitment to education, but also invest in it. The poorest and very poor countries spend about the same percentage of their country's total Gross National Product (GNP) on education as do the rich countries, roughly 5 percent. The staggering obstacle worldwide is poverty. Poor people in rich and poor countries simply do not share the same educational opportunities as their richer counterparts.

A world where pluralism prevails and where universal human rights take precedence over ethnic and racial interests is far from being achieved. Basic human rights are not met in many parts of the world, much less social, cultural, and collective rights. In line with the Universal Declaration of Human Rights, it is the responsibility of international organizations as well as individual states to ensure universal access to quality education, regardless of gender or racial, ethnic, national, or religious background.

SEE ALSO *Brown v. Board of Education; Capitalism; Education, Discrimination in Higher; Social Problems.*

BIBLIOGRAPHY

Bailey, Stanley R. 2004. "Group Dominance and the Myth of Racial Democracy: Antiracism Attitudes in Brazil." *American Sociological Review* 69 (5): 728–747.

Blau, Judith. 2003. *Race in the Schools: Perpetuating White Dominance?* Boulder, CO: Lynne Rienner.

De la Cadena, Marisol. 2005. "Are *Mestizos* Hybrids? The Conceptual Politics of Andean Identities." *Journal of Latin American Studies* 37: 259–284.

Fairlie, Robert W. 2004. "Race and the Digital Divide." *Contributions to Economic Analysis & Policy* 3 (1), Article 15: 1–38.

Feagin, Joe. 2000. *Racist America: Roots, Current Realities, and Future Reparations.* New York: Routledge.

Ferguson, Ann Arnett. 2000. *Bad Boys: Public School in the Making of Black Masculinity.* Ann Arbor: University of Michigan Press.

Golash-Boza, Tanya. 2004. "Sociologists without Borders." Available at http://www.sociologistswithoutborders.org/contributions/golash-boza_peru_Feb.02.04.pdf.

Inter-American Development Bank. 1998. "Facing up to Inequality in Latin America: Report on Economic and Social Progress in Latin America, 1998-1999." Available at http://www.iadb.org/exr/english/PRESS_PUBS/ipintr.htm.

Justino, Patricia and Arnab Acharya. 2003. "Inequality in Latin America: Processes and Inputs." PRUS Working Paper No. 22. Brighton, U.K.: Poverty Research Unit, University of Sussex.

Lee, Jaekyung. 2002. "Racial and Ethnic Achievement Gap Trends: Reversing the Progress toward Equity?" *Educational Researcher.* 31 (1): 3–12.

Marx, Anthony W. 1998. *Making Race and Nation: A Comparison of South Africa, the United States, and Brazil.* New York: Cambridge University Press.

Mutangandura, Gladys B., Vicki Lamb, and Judith Blau. 2002. "External Debt and Secondary Education in Sub-Saharan Africa." *Journal of African Policy Studies* 8: 1–16.

Omi, Michael, and Howard Winant. 1994. *Racial Formation in the United States: From the 1960s to the 1990s,* 2nd ed. New York: Routledge.

Sherriff, Robin E. 2001. *Dreaming Equality: Color, Race, and Racism in Urban Brazil.* New Brunswick, NJ: Rutgers University Press.

Twine, France. 1998. *Racism in a Racial Democracy.* New Brunswick, NJ: Rutgers University Press.

United Nations Economic and Social Council. "2001 UN Report on the World Social Situation." Available from http://www.un.org/esa/socdev/rwss/Intro&overview.pdf.

Weiss B. D., R. L. Reed, and E. W. Kligman. 1995. "Literacy Skills and Communication Methods of Low-Income Older Persons." *Patient Educational Counseling* 25 (2): 109–119.

Zinn, Howard. 2003 (1980). *A People's History of the United States.* New York: Harper Collins.

Tanya Golash-Boza

EL MESTIZAJE

In many Latin American nations, October 12, Columbus Day, is known (or has been known) as *el día de la raza,* "the day of the race". On this day in 1492, Christopher Columbus made landfall on one of the islands of the Bahamas, in what was to be called the Caribbean Sea. The very next day he described the natives as a *generación* (generation, connoting ancestry and descent), writing that they "are of the color of the Canarians, neither black nor white." He carefully noted that they should be good and intelligent servants. On the way back to Spain with his indigenous chattel, the name *indios* (feminine *indias*) emerged, because Cristobal Colón, the Admiral of the Ocean Sea, insisted that he had reached India, the gateway to Asia, wherein dwelled the Great Kahn and his kingdom of riches.

On his second voyage in 1493, Columbus carried black slaves, called *negros,* as well as sugar cane and cattle to the territory he named Española (now Hispañola, which includes Haiti and the Dominican Republic), and though he and his fellow explorers, conquerors, and administrators named islands and territories everywhere (ignoring the native Taíno names), he and others routinely used *indio* as a designation for the diverse populations that could be "profitable" (*provechoso* is the word used by Columbus) for the Europeans. As the geographical constructions became diversified the cultural constructions of profitable labor became condensed to *indio* (Indian) and *negro* (black). In spite of the cultural construction of Españoles (and later

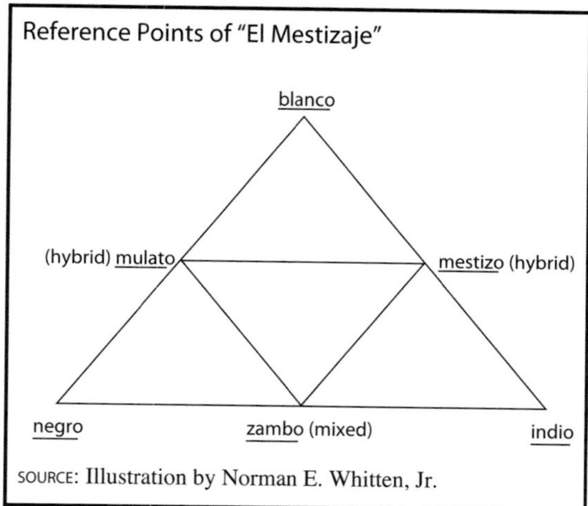

SOURCE: Illustration by Norman E. Whitten, Jr.

Figure 1. *Reference points of* El Mestizaje.

blanco [white]) at the top of an economic pyramid, with African Americans and Indigenous Americans on the bottom, the flow of genes among those of European, African, and Native American descent created phenotypic diversity and a system of multiculture, known in colonial times as *las castas* (breeds).

RACE, *MESTIZAJE*, AND THE *CASTAS*

By 1500 the concept of *raza* (race) replaced that of *generación* in the Americas, and the phenomenon of *el mestizaje*, a category that already existed under various names along the West African coast, emerged in the crucible of European hybridity that stressed the blending of civilization with savagery. *El mestizaje* means "the blending," or "the mixing" of "races" and the mixing of "cultures." But more than that, *el mestizaje* means "hybrid," the breeding of the domesticated with the wild to improve the stock, or the "race." Hybridity, and hence colonial *mestizaje*, exists where the civilized mixes with the savage or barbarian. Synonyms given in Spanish-English dictionaries for this phenomenon of culturally constructed miscegenation are "half-breed, "crossbreed," and "half caste." *Mestizos*, the result of the hybrid mixing of Spanish or other Europeans with Africans and Native Americans, may derive from the medieval Spanish word *mesta*, which referred to an association of cattle breeders. What is clear is that concepts of culture and the powerful social construction of race emerge in the idea of *el mestizaje*.

People in the *castas* were subdivided again and again into imputed "blood mixtures" according to how they appeared to others. Examples included dark people who were only one part white or light people who were three parts white. Other categories proliferated in Spanish including names such as "wolf," "throwback," "near Spanish," and even "there you are" or "where are you?" The types were so far from a person's genetic make-up that a couple's six children might each be categorized as being in a different *casta*. It was the label of *mestizo* that encompassed them, that set them off from elite Spanish or whites, as well as from those classed as black and Indian.

As the socially constructed race of *mestizos* grew and grew, it remained separate from whites on the top of the economic, social, and political pyramid, and from those classed as *indios* and *negros* on the bottom. To paraphrase slightly the words of Ronald Stutzman, writing about the twentieth-century education system in Ecuador, *el mestizaje* became an all inclusive doctrine of exclusion. Two subdivisions of *el mestizaje* endured, and a third emerged to confound the entire notion of the tripartite pyramid of white, black, and Indian. One of these was the cultural construction of "hybridity" between white and Indian to produce *mestizo*. This is the prototype of *el mestizaje* in many Spanish-speaking nations, especially Mexico. In Guatemala, just to the south of Mexico, such people are known as *ladinos*. On the other side of the triangle is the cultural construction of "hybridity" between white and black to produce the *mulato*. This word is more complex and more explicitly racist than *mestizo*. It comes directly from horse and donkey breeding, wherein the cross between the two produces a sterile mule, from whence derives *mul-ata* (muled). What confounded all of this is the fact that indigenous people and people of African descent also interbred, shared cultural systems, and intermarried. Beginning about 1502, the very first African runaways on the Caribbean Island of Hispañola escaped to the forested hills of the interior, which were occupied by Taíno indigenous people, who called these refuge zones *haití*, from which derives the contemporary Republic of Haiti. Indigenous people also fled oppression to areas secured by runaway Africans or black people from Spain, who were also enslaved in the Americas as the cultural concept *negro* (black) fused with *esclavo* (slave). The mixture without hybridity of indigenous people and African-descended people became known in many places as *zambo* or *zambaigo*. They soon came to constitute a confrontation with the European-American notions of hybridity because their socially constructed appearances and cultures owed nothing to the conquerors or colonials. The Spanish crown rejected this category and sought to convert it to *mulato*.

The liberator of northern South American from colonial rule, the Venezuelan Simón Bolívar (1783–1830), drew explicitly on this inverted triangle within a pyramidal triangle to create an ideology of continental unity against Spain (but not against whiteness), throughout South America. Together with the call for a liberation of enslaved peoples to serve the cause of an Americas revolution against colonial rule, he also championed a racial unity bound to common hybridity of the people of the continent. This ideology of hybridity, perhaps ironically, contributed directly to both the commemoration of Columbus Day as the *día de la raza* and the nationalist and continent-wide concept of *el mestizaje*. But following the revolutions, the idea of oneness shattered in the face of the exclusions of indigenous people, on the one side, and the African-descended people, on the other. Another ideological force was necessary to forge unity within the diversity created by the Conquest and the 300 year-old colonial regimes.

THE COSMIC RACE

In *The Rise and Fall of the Cosmic Race* (2004), Marilyn Grace Miller introduces the hubris of the Mexican educator, philosopher, and politician José Vasconcelos (1882–1959), who coined the figure of speech *la raza cósmica* (the cosmic race) to refer to the hybridized and whitening peoples of Latin America.

> Although celebrated figures such as Simón Bolívar and José Martí had already posited equations between mixed race and Latin American identity, the 1925 publication of Mexican educator and politician José Vasconcelos' *La raza cósmica: Misión de la raza iberoamericana* (The Cosmic Race: Mission of the Ibero-American Race) marked the inception of a fully developed ideology of *mestizaje* that tied political and aesthetic self-definition and assertion to a racial discourse at both the national and the regional levels (p. 27).

Vasconcelos specifically contrasted ideologies of Latin America, as epitomized by the homogenizing vision of Simón Bolívar, with those of North America (the United States), as characterized by James Monroe. The former saw beauty and spiritual redemption in the concept of *mestizaje*, in its power of lightening or improving races, while the latter saw the darkening menace of miscegenation and sought to conquer those of darker skin living in Latin America and the Caribbean through what is, to Latin Americans, the infamous Monroe Doctrine. Vasconcelos spelled this out in his book *Bolivarismo y Monroísmo: Temas iberoamericanos* (Bolivarism and Monroism) in 1937. His first edition of *La raza cósmica* was published in Paris in 1925, then in Mexico in 1948, and again there in 1966, a span of some forty years, during which period the doctrine of *mestizaje*, and its accompanying, if often implicit, insistence on *blanqueamiento*, (whitening—in racial and cultural terms) and "improving the race and culture," became an undergirding theme of Latin American developmentalism, permeating every area of life.

According to Miller, the slogan "*Por mi raza hablará el espíritu*" (the spirit will speak through my race) was to replace the fractured unities drawn together in revolution by warlords, heroes, and political bosses, and thus restore the Mexican people to a new homogeneity. Along the way, a united continent of Latin Americans opposed to the missions of the imperial north was to emerge. The tragic flaw in this "cosmic race" notion as hubris for national identity or for a continent-wide movement of self-identity was the issue of *blanqueamiento*, and of its corollary concept *mejor la raza* (improve the race). Those classed as *mestizo* were stigmatized for their hybridity with Indian "blood," or (less frequently in most countries) with African-descended phenotypes, both often referred to as *la mancha*, or "the stain" (of race).

The Puerto Rican poet and social critic Fortunato Vizcarrondo, in his satirical and ironical writings (published in his book of poems *Dinga y Mandinga*), summarized this stigmatizing affect of ancestry with the poem "*¿ y tu agüela, a'onde ejtá?*" The Spanish is folk Puerto Rican for *¿ y tu abuelo, adonde está?* (where is your grandfather from?, or figuratively, "where are you hiding your ancestors?") meaning "you may be lightening but we know you descend from blackness." The latter is signaled by the concepts of "Dinga" and "Mandinga," representing different African peoples well known by Iberians until the term *negro* came to subsume them. In some parts of Latin America the very concept of *mestizo* refers to the darkening of racial features, not lightening. This is the colonial notion of "throw back." In fact, the figure of speech (common in both Puerto Rico and Cuba) "*lo que no tiene de dinga tiene de mandinga*" (what you don't have of the Dinga you have of the Mandinga) denies "whiteness" to the majority of people. Hybridity, in other words, cuts both ways: People who are lightening may be said to be upwardly mobile toward desired phenotypic and cultural features, or they may be backsliding into their darker indigenous- or African-descended roots.

ENDURING RACISM: MESTIZAJE AS A POLARIZING SYMBOL

In the Andes of Ecuador and Peru, where the indigenous people far outnumber those of African descent, this phrase becomes "*lo que no tiene del inga tiene de mandinga*" (what you don't have of the Inca you have of the Mandinga). To move from the "racial" to the "cultural" stigma, one may say or write, "*quien no toca la flauta, toca el tambor*" (who doesn't play the flute [*indio*] plays the drum [*negro*]). These ditties stigmatize those classed as *mestizo* as either indigenous- or African-descended, or as a mixture of both. A very prominent liberal intellectual, Osvaldo Hurtado (1939–), the one-time president of Ecuador and one-time head of the Leftist Democratic political party in Ecuador, also favors the phrase in his often reprinted and updated book *Political Power in Ecuador* (1980, p. 325). He explicates the phrase by stating that it refers to that which is "in the blood," which can be overcome only by cultural whitening. When he was president of Ecuador, Hurtado coined the phrase *indomestizaje* to refer to the populace of the country, but not to those of his upper-class position.

By doing so, he consciously omitted all traces of African-descended peoples from the nation's cultural make-up.

It should be clear by now that the doctrine, or ideology, or hubris of *el mestizaje* is best regarded as a polarizing symbol. From the standpoint or perspective of elites and those who are upwardly mobile with aspirations to adopt elite values, *mestizos* are those in the middle to lower rungs of a social ladder who have shed indigenous or African descended cultural orientations, values, dress, speech, or physical features. For those in the middle, however, who choose to move upward, *blanqueamiento* is their aspiration and *mestizaje* is their stigma. To those self-identifying as indigenous or black, *mestizos* are those who have shed their cultural orientation for a position to which they aspire, but which they cannot attain. This is the living dilemma of those whom many sociologists and journalists call the *clase mestiza*.

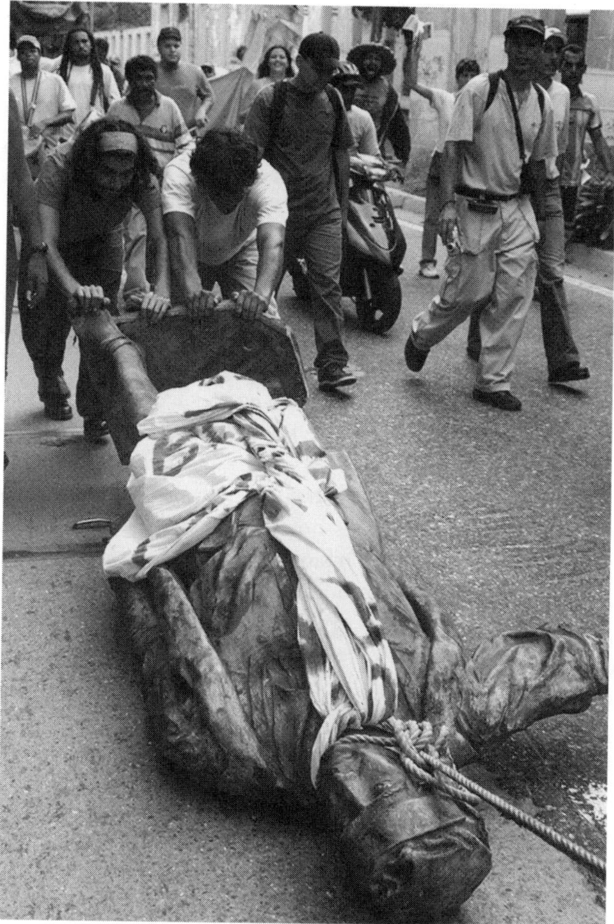

Venezuelans Protest Columbus Day. *Protestors push a statue of Christopher Columbus through the street after pulling it down from a plaza in Caracas, Venezuela. In 2001, Venezuelan president Hugo Chávez declared Columbus Day as* el día de la resistencia indígena *(the day of indigenous resistance).* **AP IMAGES.**

COUNTERFORCES TO "WHITENING" IDEOLOGY

There are many forces that work contrary to the doctrine of *el mestizaje* in Latin American nations. According to David M. Guss, in his book about Venezuela titled *The Festival State* (2000), *mestizaje* constitutes what many call the myth of racial democracy, the false nationalist premise promulgated by essentially white people (*los blancos*, or *blanquitos*) that Venezuelans do not have a perspective of "race": "the language of *mestizaje* masks unequal social relations between blacks and whites wherein *blanqueamiento* or 'whitening' is the unstated physical and cultural goal" (p. 61). Not only have blacks been subject to exclusion on the basis of *mestizaje* ideology in Venezuela, so too have its approximately 50,000 indigenous people. The fiery and controversial president of Venezuela, Hugo Chávez, changed the October 12 (Columbus Day) celebratory figure of speech from the *día de la raza* to *el día de la resistencia indígena* (the day of indigenous resistance) in 2002. By doing so, President Chávez was seeking to conjoin those against elitism and classism, against "whitening" as a key to upward mobility, as "indigenous." Thus far, those so categorized seem to accept this imagery and constitute a formidable political base.

Chávez prides himself in being of mixed heritage—black and indigenous—and he does not promulgate a doctrine of *mestizaje*. Rather, he regards himself as *pardo*, here meaning the mixing of Afro-descended people and indigenous-descended people. He proudly informs his followers, most of whom (if not all) are from lower classes and who are noticeably darker complexioned than those in upper socio-economic brackets, that his father was mixed Indian and black and that his grandmother was a Pumé Indian. This is a significant change in Latin American perspectives on "self" and "other," particularly for someone at the pinnacle of executive power and privilege. It marks the first time in Venezuelan history that a president has proclaimed himself to be *pardo* and to identify with those who have been and are *pardo*.

Chávez hails from the southern plains, or *llanos*, of Venezuela, an area long known for its black and indigenous mixtures, and for its spirit of rebellion. The liberator Simón Bolívar marched through these *llanos negros* (black plains, as they are known by some in Colombia) with an army of Haitian black soldiers, collecting another army of *pardo* warriors who swept through the Colombian *llanos* to their west. This turned into a successful campaign to free what is now Venezuela, Colombia, and Ecuador from the yoke of colonial rule. But, in the end, Bolívar promulgated a doctrine of *mestizaje*, fearing the force of the indigenous and black people upon whom he depended during the revolution. Slaves were freed, but they were neither socially nor culturally liberated.

By bringing the power of the rebellious mixed-race *pardo* into the national scene, Chávez is spearheading a cultural-ethnic revolution, based on the actions of Simón Bolívar but divorced from the ideology of *mestizaje*. This is the cultural dimension of his *revolución bolivariano* (Bolivarian Revolution) that complements his goal of a populist-classist-socialist revolution. Other social movements resonate with that of Venezuela. For example, in Ecuador and Bolivia, indigenous people are forcefully seeking to exorcise the image of the whitening *mestizo* from their lexicon of self-liberation, and they are striving to change the national celebration of the Day of the Race to "*500 años de resistencia*" (500 years of resistance). The polarization of the two perspectives on the Day or the Race, which also constitutes the polarized perspectives on the celebration of *mestizaje*, places in strong relief a major cultural tension permeating many Latin American countries during the late twentieth and early twenty-first centuries.

INTERCULTURALITY AND NORTH AMERICAN *MESTIZAJE*

Perhaps ironically, as the ideology of *el mestizaje* gives way to an ethos of *interculturalidad* (interculturality) in nations undergoing transformations to respect for the plurality represented by, especially, those of indigenous and African descent, the early to mid-twentieth century forces of cultural blending are making inroads in the United States. Near the end of her book on this subject, Miller writes:

> "*Mestizaje* has repeatedly proven to be a flawed doctrine of Latin American identity that nonetheless continues to distinguish Latin Americans from their Northern neighbors. At the same time, it is newly mobilized and empowered through electronic diffusion that renders it ever more ubiquitous, so that its ideology is now pervasively felt in the United States, that same national and cultural power it was fashioned to repel" (Miller 2004, p. 142).

The transformation of *mestizaje* to interculturality in many Latin American nations, and its transformative manifestation among Chicano and Latina movements in the United States, suggests that the phenomena of Latin American interculturality and North American *mestizaje* stem from the same roots and have merged to become the same overall phenomenon. In Latin American nations, interculturality stresses a movement from one cultural system to another, whereas social and cultural pluralism and hybridity stress the institutional separation forced by the *blanco* (white) elite on diverse peoples. The latter is national, regional, and static; the former is local, regional, global, and dynamic. Latin American *mestizaje* emanates from the top of social hierarchies and stifles creativity and the celebration of difference within a nation state. But in North America, the semantics change, for the ethos—probably born in the Mexican Revolution—is a bottom-up appreciation of the multiple experiences shared by peoples of other Latin American nations within the United States.

SEE ALSO *Blackness in Latin America; Blood Quantum; La Malinche; Latin American Racial Transformations; Multiculturalism; Multiracial Identities.*

BIBLIOGRAPHY

Columbus, Christopher. 1989. *The Diario of Christopher Columbus's First Voyage to America, 1492–94*. Transcribed and Translated into English with Notes by Oliver Dunn and James E. Kelley, Jr. Norman: University of Oklahoma Press.

Forbes, Jack D. 1993. *Africans and Native Americans: The Language of Race and the Evolution of Red-Black Peoples*, 2nd ed. Urbana: University of Illinois Press.

Fuentes, Carlos. 1992. *The Buried Mirror: Reflections on Spain and the New World*. Boston: Houghton Mifflin Company.

Guss, David M. 2000. *The Festive State: Race, Ethnicity, and Nationalism as Cultural Performance*. Berkeley: University of California Press.

Hurtado, Osvaldo. 1980. *Political Power in Ecuador*. Translated by Nick D. Mills, Jr. Albuquerque: University of New Mexico Press.

Miller, Marilyn Grace. 2004. *Rise and Fall of the Cosmic Race: The Cult of Mestizaje in Latin America*. Austin: University of Texas Press.

Mörner, Magnus. 1967. *Race Mixture in the History of Latin America*. Boston: Little, Brown.

Stephens, Thomas M. 1999. *Dictionary of Latin American Racial and Ethnic Terminology*, 2nd ed. Gainesville: University Press of Florida.

Stutzman, Ronald. 1981. "El Mestizaje: An All Inclusive Ideology of Exclusion." In *Cultural Transformations and Ethnicity in Modern Ecuador*, edited by Norman E. Whitten Jr. Urbana: University of Illinois Press.

Vasconcelos, José. 1925. *La raza cósmica, misión de la raza iberoamericana*. Paris: Agencia Mundial de Librería.

Weismantel, Mary J. 2001. Cholas *and* Pishtacos*: Stories of Race and Sex in the Andes*. Chicago: University of Chicago Press.

Whitten, Norman E., Jr., editor. 2003. *Millennial Ecuador: Critical Essays on Cultural Transformations and Social Dynamics*. Iowa City: University of Iowa Press.

Norman E. Whitten Jr.

EL PLAN DE SANTA BARBARA

During the heyday of the civil rights movement, in April 1969, the Coordinating Council on Higher Education, a network of Chicano students and professors, sponsored a meeting at the University of California, Santa Barbara. This event became one of the most crucial episodes in the history of Chicanos in California. Out of the conference came *El Plan de Santa Barbara* (The Santa Barbara Plan), a schemata calling for the implementation of Chicano studies programs throughout the California university system. Many of the participants at Santa Barbara had attended the National Chicano Liberation Youth Conference at the Crusade for Justice (CFJ) Center in Denver, Colorado, organized by the CFJ's founder, Rodolfo "Corky" Gonzales, just one month earlier. More than 1,000 young people, most from California, participated in the Denver conference, engaging in the most intense celebration of Chicanismo (Chicano political ideological activity) to date. The most enduring concept that came out of this meeting was *El Plan Espiritual de Aztlán* (The Spiritual Plan of Aztlán), which proposed Chicano cultural separatism, if not a separate geo-political state, a position justified, according to the framers, by the "brutal 'gringo' invasion of our territories." The separate Chicano region in the southwest would be given the name "Aztlán."

This ideological experience inspired the Chicano student community in California to implement a higher education plan that would go beyond previous pronouncements. A major objective was to create a college curriculum that was relevant and useful in redressing social and economic inequality in Chicano communities. Higher education, the students reasoned, was a publicly funded infrastructure that enhanced the business community and other white bastions of power, while very little was spent on the needs of the tax-paying Chicano community. The Chicano students' plan of action centered on supporting a unified student movement called *El Movimiento Estudiantil Chicano de Aztlán* (MEChA, or the Aztlán Student Movement). The Santa Barbara activists claimed the term "Chicano" after this meeting vis-à-vis Mexican American, and the label became associated with community activism among the emerging young Mexican-origin intelligentsia. Activists elevated the word "Chicano" from its use in the 1920s to denote lower class Mexican immigrants, and from the slang of the 1940s and 1950s when it substituted for Mexicano, to symbolize the realization of a new found and unique identity. Because of its working class connotation, the term appeared more appropriate for a movement claiming grass roots membership; "Mexican American," according to this line of thinking, denoted individual upward mobility and class separation.

The most tangible and important accomplishment of the conference was the formulation of *El Plan de Santa Barbara*. The plan articulated the most resounding rejection of Mexican-American assimilationist ideology to date. Young Chicano activists insisted that older leaders of the "Mexican American Generation," active from the 1930s to the 1950s, had followed a strategy to gain civil rights objectives through litigation, electoral power, and diplomatic appeals (and sometimes by claiming to be white), and that these approaches had not been successful. The framers of the plan advocated "Chicanismo," or a Chicano-centered ideology. According to the plan:

> Chicanismo involves a crucial distinction in political consciousness between a Mexican American and a Chicano mentality. The Mexican American is a person who lacks respect for his culture and ethnic heritage. Unsure of himself, he seeks assimilation as a way out of his "degraded" social status. Consequently, he remains politically ineffective. In contrast, Chicanismo reflects self-respect and pride in one's ethnic and cultural background.... The Chicano acts with confidence and with a range of alternatives in the political world.

The curriculum envisioned by the Santa Barbara Plan would train a vanguard of future Chicano leaders, providing them with intimate knowledge of how American capitalism and racism had colonized their people. Each of these future leaders would know that "The liberation of his people from prejudice and oppression is in his hand and this responsibility is greater than personal achievement and more meaningful than degrees, especially if they are earned at the expense of this identity and cultural integrity."

The plan did specify a commitment to physical action, such as unionizing or to striving for a separate country. It also encouraged students to enroll in higher education. The Mexican American emphasis on getting a good education remained integral to the Chicano movement, but not at the expense of assimilating into Anglo society and forgetting their roots in the community. According to the plan, students should share control with the faculty in administrating Chicano studies programs, including participating in the hiring and firing of professors in accordance with criteria established by Chicanos, not by the university administration.

After the meeting at Santa Barbara, Chicano studies departments, programs, and research centers became instituted—many, if not most, through student militancy. Most of the California state colleges and universities instituted such centers and teaching programs, as did numerous institutions of higher education in the Southwest, Michigan, Wisconsin, and New York. An enduring legacy of the *El Plan de Santa Barbara* is the "ownership" many college students articulate and insist on within these academic departments and research centers. Any tension this creates is resolved in different ways across different settings, but ultimately the goal of the plan to support civic engagement in the university is a vibrant intellectual and political force in higher education.

SEE ALSO *Aztlán*.

BIBLIOGRAPHY

Coordinating Council on Higher Education. 1969. *El Plan de Santa Barbara.* Oakland, CA: La Causa Publications. Available from http://www.panam.edu/orgs.

Muñoz, Carlos, Jr. 2003. *Youth, Identity, Power: The Chicano Movement.* London: Verso.

Rosales, F. Arturo. 1996. *Chicano! A History of the Mexican American Civil Rights Movement.* Houston: Arte Público Press.

F. Arturo Rosales

EMANCIPATION PROCLAMATION

The Emancipation Proclamation was issued by President Abraham Lincoln on January 1, 1863. It declared that "all persons held as slaves" in the rebellious jurisdictions of the Confederate States "are, and henceforward shall be free." With this executive proclamation, which Lincoln justified as a matter of "military necessity," approximately 3.5 million African Americans in the Confederacy were emancipated from the bonds of slavery.

The Emancipation Proclamation was part of a lengthy process by which Lincoln, the first avowed antislavery president to be elected, moved the United States toward eliminating the enslavement of Africans. Lincoln had long harbored a distaste and opposition to slavery. However, he did not believe the federal Constitution allowed the federal government to abolish slavery unilaterally. Moreover, he believed slavery was a regressive institution that would eventually die out on its own. Lincoln's inactivity disappeared after the passage of the Kansas-Nebraska Act of 1854, which appeared to open the western territories of the United States to slave expansion. Lincoln stood for the U.S. Senate in 1855 as an opponent of the Kansas-Nebraska Act, and again in 1858 as a candidate of the new anti-antislavery Republican Party. He was elected president in 1860.

Lincoln attempted to calm dissension in the slave states, chiefly by agreeing to enforce the Fugitive Slave Act, but it was feared in these states that Lincoln would use the discretionary powers of the presidency to subvert slavery all the same. In fact, within six months of his inauguration, Lincoln composed a federal buyout plan that used offers of federal bonds to induce slave state legislatures to emancipate their slaves. By the spring of 1861, eleven slave states severed their ties to the federal Union and organized their own rival slave republic.

Lincoln interpreted the secession of the states as an "insurrection," and he invoked the president's war powers under the Constitution. Many antislavery advocates urged him to use the insurrection as the occasion to

Emancipation Proclamation. *This illustration by J. W. Watts depicts an African American slave family gathered to hear about the Emancipation Proclamation.*

emancipate the enslaved through a war powers proclamation. Lincoln, however, was aware that the legal status of his war powers was ambiguous and he was unwilling to risk an emancipation proclamation that the federal courts might strike down. Furthermore, Lincoln was wary of alienating the four slave states (Delaware, Missouri, Kentucky, and Maryland) that had remained loyal to the Union. By 1862 Lincoln became convinced that a presidential proclamation was the only remaining option. The war had gone badly for the North, Lincoln's caution on the slavery issue had failed to break the cohesion of the South, and the Confiscation Acts of 1861 and 1862, which freed slaves used in the Confederate war effort, had limited effect.

The Confiscation Acts provided only for the "confiscation" of rebel property, including slaves, but did not guarantee change of title; hence, slaves "confiscated" under the federal government legally remained slaves but were now in the custody of the federal government. Lincoln believed that the Acts, as *in rem* proceedings and as punishments for treason, violated the Constitution's ban on bills of attainder, and in fact, very little enforcement of the Acts was undertaken. Even the Acts' chief architect, Lyman Trumbull, admitted that the Confiscation Acts were mostly designed for political effect and would result in freedom for very few slaves. On July 22, 1862, Lincoln read a first draft of an emancipation proclamation to his cabinet; on their advice, he waited until after a Union victory in battle to issue the proclamation in preliminary form, which was done on September 22, 1862. He signed it into law on January 1, 1863.

The proclamation was not, in many respects, a radical document. It freed slaves, but did not abolish slavery as an institution, and it limited the extent of emancipation only to the geographical areas of the Confederacy still in actual rebellion and out of Union control so that the slaves in the loyal slave states and the occupied districts of the confederacy remained in slavery. These limitations, however, represent Lincoln's interest in heading off federal court challenges. In other respects, the proclamation was radical indeed: All of the slaves remaining within the Confederacy were declared permanently free, and "the armed service of the United States" was now opened to freed slaves who would enlist to fight against their former masters. Moreover, once issued, Lincoln refused any suggestion that he use the proclamation as a bargaining chip with the Confederate authorities.

Lincoln nevertheless remained anxious about possible court challenges after the war's close, and in 1864 he urged Congress to pass a Thirteenth Amendment to the Constitution and completely abolish slavery as an institution. He also remained unsure about the civil status of the freed slaves, at one point underwriting an experiment in colonizing freed slaves out of the United States to the Caribbean. By 1864 it was clear that the freed slaves had no desire to leave the United States, and Lincoln turned to a variety of initiatives for granting citizenship and equal civil rights to the freed men and women.

Black enthusiasm for Lincoln and the proclamation was, in the generation following emancipation, almost reverential. Modern African-American interpretation has been more inclined to fault Lincoln for the proclamation's limitations. But a total presidential abolition may have incurred precisely the judicial retaliation Lincoln feared. In the end, the Proclamation and the Thirteenth Amendment together pointed the nation in the direction of the Fourteenth and Fifteenth Amendments and full civil equality for African Americans.

SEE ALSO *Abolition Movement; Black Civil War Soldiers; Civil War Politics and Racism; Slavery, Racial; United States Constitution.*

BIBLIOGRAPHY

Berlin, Ira, et al. 1992. *Slaves No More: Three Essays on Emancipation and the Civil War.* New York: Cambridge University Press.

Foner, Eric. 1983. *Nothing but Freedom: Emancipation and Its Legacy.* Baton Rouge: Louisiana State University Press.

Franklin, John Hope. 1963. *The Emancipation Proclamation.* Garden City, NJ: Doubleday.

Allen Carl Guelzo

ENGLISH SKINHEADS

"Skinheads" have become the most recognizable group within the white supremacist movement in America and Europe. Their unique haircuts and modes of dress set them apart from nonracist youth, and their propensity for violence distinguishes them from their more staid racist colleagues. The skinhead movement has spread throughout most Western nations and has evolved far beyond its simple beginnings in 1960s London.

The earliest British Skinheads appeared in the late 1960s as an outgrowth of the "mod" movement. They were sons of the working class and began dressing in what was essentially a caricature of the working man's uniform: short denim jeans, T-shirts, suspenders, and black Doc Marten boots. They clustered in nightclubs featuring reggae bands in the early 1970s, and music remains central to the subculture, though the preferred musical genre has evolved from reggae to punk to Oi! (a blend of "street punk," various forms of rock, and football cheers) and to White Power rock-and-roll.

In the early twenty-first century, there are essentially two conflicting skinhead cultures, both remarkably similar yet in violent opposition to each other. On one side of the divide are nonracist skinheads, led by organizations such as Skinheads Against Racial Prejudice (SHARP) and Anti-Racist Action (ARA), and on the other side are the racist skinheads. They dress in a similar manner, they listen to similar music, and they spend time in the same clubs, but they fight over which side represents the true skinheads—the white supremacists or the antiracists.

Skinheads in Britain generally eschew large, organized groups, preferring to spend their time in tight-knit, geographically determined packs. The groups, or gangs, are overwhelmingly male, and the rare female is generally treated as a sexual object, unless she is in her thirties or older, when she may be treated as a mother to a local gang. Skinhead violence occurs over issues of turf, class-based ideology, and ethnicity. The violence is often brutal, and it typically involves mass assaults against individuals or smaller groups. The preferred method of violence is a stomping party, in which a group gathers around a downed victim and stomps him with their Doc Marten boots. Such assaults usually result in death or severe injury.

SEE ALSO *Gangs and Youth Violence; Neo-Nazis; White Racial Identity.*

BIBLIOGRAPHY

Christensen, Loren. 1994. *Skinhead Street Gangs.* Boulder, CO: Paladin Press.

Knight, Nick. 1982. *Skinhead.* London: Omnibus Press.

Marshall, George. 1996. *Skinhead Nation.* Glasgow, Scotland: S.T. Publishing.

J. Keith Akins

ETHNIC CLEANSING

Cultural diversity within the same state or society has often led to problems of accommodation in sharing space and designing an acceptable form of governance. With few exceptions, nearly all of the 187 countries of the world are polyethnic, with about 40 percent comprising five or more ethno-national communities. This proliferation of ethno-national groups within states has resulted in numerous internal struggles, which in turn have generated costly humanitarian crises and created millions of refugees. Among the more nefarious tactics for coping with ethno-cultural diversity, apart from genocide and partition, has been the policy called "ethnic cleansing." This peculiar practice involves a deliberate and often planned program of forcible removal and expulsion of an ethno-cultural community from its homeland and territory. The term itself is derived from the Serbian-Croatian phrase *etnico ciscenje*. It emerged in the early 1990s during the Bosnian-Yugoslav war, and it has since become generalized and popularized for any similar practice by any perpetrator, not only in relation to contemporary ethnic conflicts but for all structurally similar conflicts throughout history.

Episodes of ethnic cleansing have generally been marked by violence and egregious human rights violations and atrocities. The "cleansed" community is compelled to leave, usually on very short notice, and they are transported to inhospitable regions, with many dying along the way. The intent, however, is not to physically eliminate the community, as in genocide, but to remove it from a territory. The brutal methods employed, however, often border on the genocidal. The context of a security threat or war, either before or after the event, usually offers the cover for the cruel and callous mass removal of the victims to inhospitable or dangerous destinations. Often implicated as ethno-cultural factors are ethno-racial motives and patterns.

DEFINING ETHNIC CLEANSING

In ethnic cleansing, the target may be a group that is perceived as possessing a distinctive way of life, or it may simply be an ethnic or ethno-cultural community. Ethnicity can be defined as a collective group consciousness that imparts a sense of belonging and is derived from membership in a community putatively bound by common descent and culture. The ethnic group is thus a cultural community, an intimately interactive society of shared symbols and meanings, and, as Walker Connor notes, it is "the largest group that can be aroused, stimulated to action, by appeals to common ancestors and to a blood-bond" (Connor 2004, p.23). Generally, ethno-cultural communities in polyethnic states tend to stake their claims to a distinctive identity by attributing to themselves in their narratives of origin not only cultural and historical differences, but also racial myths of superiority over rival groups.

The term *race*, as used here, refers to socially constructed categories assigned to putative physical and biological human differences, which tend to establish structures of inequality and political hegemony (UNESCO 1951). In many cases, racial claims in the construction of cultural identities tend to be quite explicit, as in apartheid in South Africa. In many other cases, however, the racial aspect is less evident and intermixed with other factors. It is also frequently denied altogether. Some communities that are deemed "ethno-racial" are actually recent inventions, as in the case of Rwanda. In the nineteenth century, colonial conquest, accompanied by European theories of scientific racism, led to the creation of many "racial" categories among colonial peoples.

JUSTIFYING AND EXPLAINING ETHNIC CLEANSING

Many economic, strategic, religious, and other justifications have been advanced by perpetrators of ethnic cleansing. Outright racial reasons have also been used. Under the apartheid system in South Africa, for example, this involved the uprooting of African peoples and the setting up of segregated residential townships and "homelands." In nineteenth-century Europe, the development of so-called scientific theories of racial differentiation and hierarchy served to justify the forcible displacement and expulsion of indigenous and colonized Third World peoples from their homelands. In 1797 the British expelled the indigenous Caribs from St. Vincent Island in the Caribbean because they offered sanctuary to escaped slaves. The people of St. Vincent were removed to Roatan Island off the coast of Honduras. The larger context for this action was a concept of racial categorization in which a militarily superior European group could displace a black community deemed to be inferior.

Similar racial categorizations allowed the indigenous peoples of North America to be pushed into the interior hinterland and finally consigned to reservations. While mainly executed under the Indian Removal Act of 1830, there were numerous cases of Native Americans being forcibly uprooted and relocated. The practice of expelling native peoples from their land to peripheral areas was also enacted in conjunction with the establishment of white settler colonies in Africa, South America, and Australia. In Tasmania, systematic displacement eventually led to the virtual liquidization of an entire aboriginal community.

Many theories have been advanced to explain the phenomenon of ethnic cleansing, ranging from internal psychological drives to materialistic and rationalistic economic propositions. Perhaps the best known of these theories focuses on the idea of "ancient hatreds" to account for the periodic resurgence of ethnic strife in certain regions, such as the Balkans. Ethnic cleansing is thus linked to deeply embedded animosities. Implicit in this explanation is the idea of descent, or blood, suggesting an inherent feature inscribed in the rituals, historical narratives, and cultural symbolism of these communities, and implying a natural and recurrent trajectory of revenge and retaliation. Yet in an empirical investigation on the recurrence of ethnic cleansing worldwide, John Fearon and David Laitin found that in sub-Saharan Africa, where all states are multiethnic, "there are only a few cases of murderous ethnic cleansing" (Fearon and Laitin 1996, p. 21).

THE ROLE OF NATIONALISM

Another notable explanation of ethnic cleansing identifies nationalism as the key factor. In this proposition, the idea of "territory" has become connected with the cultural and linguistic uniformity of the state. Nationalism thereby becomes a homogenizing element, with national identity as the acid test of belonging. Each of the major European states, although populated by several minorities, has a dominant ethnic core so that the imperatives of nationalism, in sanctioning the demand of each ethno-cultural people for its own state, create a justification for mass expulsion, genocide, and ethnic cleansing. Hence, since the inception of the nation-state, there have been waves of ethno-nationalist movements accompanied by mass expulsions and ethnic cleansing.

After World War I, with the dissolution of the multiethnic Austro-Hungarian, Ottoman, and Russian empires, the principle of ethno-national self-determination guided the creation of several new states that required the transfer of several minority groups. Under the Treaty of Lausanne of 1923, compulsory population transfers between Greece and Turkey occurred, involving 1.5 million Greeks and 400,000 Turks. Under the Neuilly Treaty of 1919, some 100,000 Bulgarians and 35,000 Greeks were exchanged between Greece and Bulgaria. Under the Potsdam Protocol of 1945, German minorities in certain European nations were forced to migrate back to German soil. This movement of some 12 to 16 million persons expelled from Poland and Czechoslovakia remains the largest mass expulsion in history. Finally, after the collapse of Yugoslavia in the early 1990s, some three million persons were displaced as Croats, Serbs, and Muslims took turns—each often using mutually dehumanizing racio-cultural slurs and categories—cleansing claimed territory of their communal adversaries. It was from these campaigns of terror and inhumane brutality that the Croat-Serbian term *ethnic cleansing* was coined.

In implicating the state as a main culprit of violence against minorities, especially through ethnic cleansing, not only have nationalism and industrial technology been implicated, but so has the principle of democracy. According to this view, majoritarian democracy, combined with the statist ideology of nationalism, offers a potent justification for the expulsion and repression of minorities. Michael Mann has argued that in the making of contemporary liberal democratic states in the West, especially settler democracies like the United States, "murderous ethnic cleansing" was pervasive. "The countries inhabited by Europeans are now safely democratic, but most have been ethnically cleansed" (Mann 2005, pp. 4–5).

Ethnic Albanian Regufees, 1999. *An ethnic Albanian woman and her baby are part of a group of refugees driven from their village near Pristina, Kosovo, by violent clashes betweeen ethnic Albanian rebels and Serbian security forces.* AP IMAGES.

THE ROLE OF RELIGION

Many theorists of ethnic cleansing have singled out the ethno-religious factor as paramount. Andrew Bell-Fialkoff argues that in ancient times religious diversity and tolerance were the norm, and that population cleansing was mainly motivated by economic gain and political power. Following this period, with the emergence of Christianity and Islam as universalizing faiths linked to the state and the territory of empires, religion became politicized and the main marker of identity and belonging. As a result, religious fervor and intolerance became widespread, compelling conversion, expulsion, and even massacres. Hence, the First Crusade (1096–1099) left wide swaths of territory cleansed of Muslims and Jews. The expulsion of Jews from various parts of Europe, including expulsions from Spain in 1492 and from Portugal in 1497, is a well-known example of ethno-religious cleansing. After the *Reconquista* in Spain, expulsions of Muslims and Jews occurred from the eighth through the fifteenth centuries. When the Christian Church suffered its major schismatic division following the Reformation, religious wars between Catholic and Protestant forces, especially in France and Germany, led to numerous massacres and expulsions. Noteworthy is the St. Bartholomew's Day Massacre of Protestants in France in 1572, as well as the dispersal of French Protestants after the Revocation of the Edict of Nantes in 1685.

Other notable cases of European ethno-religious cleansing refer to the expulsion of the Catholic Irish from Ulster between 1609 and 1641, when their land was taken over by Scottish and English settlers. Religion also played a pivotal role in the Balkan Wars in the 1880s, when the pushing back of the borders of Ottoman Empire saw the wholesale expulsion of Muslims. In the collapse of the Ottoman Empire following World War I, widespread ethno-religious expulsion and exchanges occurred, including the large-scale movement of Armenians and Greeks from Anatolia and other areas. In the twentieth century, the partition of India to create two separate states, India and Pakistan, led to extensive ethnic cleansing as millions of Hindus and Muslims were removed from their old communities. Following the collapse of Yugoslavia in 1991, the civil wars in Bosnia-Herzegovina, Kosovo, Serbia, and Croatia saw widespread ethnic cleansing with a religious motive. In Kosovo, both Albanians and Serbs took turns forcibly removing one another. In the twenty-first century, religious differences between Muslims and Christians have played a pivotal role in the murder and cleansing that has occurred in Darfur, Sudan. Hence, while the religious variable is rarely the sole motivator, it often offers a justification for economic and political greed.

Quite frequently, religion is combined with other factors to justify the mass expulsion of a group. For instance, religion and economic interests have featured in European colonization projects that included the displacement of indigenous peoples in the Americas, Australia, and Africa. These settlers saw the acquisition of the land of native peoples as divinely ordained, while it simultaneously served economic interests and provided land for settlement.

ECONOMIC FACTORS

Economic motivations for ethnic cleansing, including the expropriation and looting of property of the victims, have accounted for the forcible displacement of ethno-cultural communities. Among the most frequent claims by perpetrators of ethnic cleansing is a demand for equity and rectification in the face of exploitation and unjust gain by the other group. In culturally plural societies, this proposition relates to the perception of comparative collective shares and benefits that the communal groups enjoy relative to each other. Any perceived incidence of inequality assumes a particularly piquant and penetrating quality that can awaken images and stereotypes of rival ethno-cultural communities in the same state. Many of the claims of an aggrieved community, which could be the majority ethno-cultural group against a relatively more prosperous minority group marked off by religion and culture, seem to be elucidated by this dynamic. Both the Chinese in Indonesia and the Asian Indians in Uganda were deemed economic exploiters and expelled. In part, the displacement of the Armenians and Greeks by the Turks after World War I was driven by jealousy because these groups were relatively more prosperous and industrious than the majority Muslim population.

POLITICAL FACTORS

Political and strategic explanations have often taken center stage in elucidating ethnic cleansing. Included in this category are security and power perspectives. Essentially, as a political act of power, ethnic cleansing incorporates multiple motives of a military and strategic nature, as well as political acquisition and consolidation, economic aggrandizement, land settlement, cultural domination, racial discrimination, greed, and jealousy. In the Ottoman Empire, which was ethnically diverse, Armenians and Greek communities located in frontier or strategically significant regions were removed. Stalin's uprooting of the Chechen-Ingush peoples in the Caucasus during World War II was similarly motivated. Among the most prominent of the ingredients that enter into the calculus for territorial cleansing, apart from military-strategic interests, is the creation of a culturally homogenous state.

State creation that seeks congruence between territorial claims and cultural uniformity has already been discussed under the rubric of nationalism. Population transfers became part of the process of establishing more homogenous states with cruel expulsions and uprooting being part of the process, especially after the collapse of the Ottoman, Hapsburg, and Russian empires after World War I and with the defeat of the Axis powers after World War II. With the growth of industrial technology in the well-organized centralized states, ethnic cleansing became more complete and bordered on genocide. The twentieth century witnessed the worst cases of large-scale ethnic cleansing culminating in the 1990s when the Soviet Union collapsed leaving some 25 million ethnic Russians living outside of their homeland. Many of these Russians, though they had resided in these other countries of the Soviet Union for many years—even generations—were subject to overt and covert pressures by the liberated states such as Estonia, Latvia, and Lithuania, and forced to leave. Likewise, when the Yugoslav state disintegrated there was a massive displacement of peoples. In the twenty-first century, ethnic cleansing continued in Darfur, Sudan, as well as in Iraq, where Sunnis and Shias expelled each other from their regions and neighborhoods.

QUESTIONS AND AMBIGUITIES

Overall, several controversies and areas of ambiguity surround the use of the term *ethnic cleansing*. Are instances of the phenomenon always violent and swift? As a deliberate and planned policy of population transfer, can it not also be gradual and nonviolent? Among the nonviolent methods that can be applied, a state can deploy discriminatory policies and sanction unofficial abusive tactics to pressure an ethno-cultural community to migrate voluntarily. In Fiji, for example, after the military coup of 1987, the new regime—claiming to be guided by Christian principles—resorted to religiously discriminatory policies and terrorist tactics aimed at reducing, if not eliminating, the Asian Indian community, the members of which were mainly Hindus and Muslims. Over the course of a few years, with procedures simplified for their departure, Indians went from being the majority population in Fiji to being only 35 to 37 percent of the population.

Another question is whether the removal of an ethno-cultural community has to be officially planned and executed to qualify as ethnic cleansing. The use of terrorist tactics by thugs and paramilitaries can be condoned with impunity, for example, while a complicit governing regime denies any involvement.

In practice, it is not always clear that ethnic cleansing is a distinct category. It often seems to shade into other related practices, such as genocide and pressured migration. The term *genocide* was first coined in 1944 by Raphael Lemkin, a Russian lawyer of Polish-Jewish descent. It is defined by the United Nations as a criminal act aimed at destroying, in whole or part, an ethnic, religious, or national group. What distinguishes it from ethnic cleansing is the intent of genocidal acts to exterminate a community rather than transport them to another area. Periodically, however, during the frenzy to uproot and remove an ethno-cultural community, as in the cases of the expulsion of Germans after World War II and the Armenians and Greeks during World War I in Turkey, methods may quickly degenerate from nonviolent pressure to open massacres suggestive of genocide. It thus seems to fit in a continuum of methods ranging from the most indirect and subtle, such as policies of multiculturalism and assimilation, to the most brutal, such as physical extermination. Likewise, the intent of the perpetrators can alternate between displacement and genocide. Given the wartime context and aura under which most programs of ethnic cleansing tend to occur, the role of old prejudices and the settling of scores can be concealed from view, as can greed for the easy acquisition of the property and wealth of the victims. Official strategic justifications can thus obscure the true intent of perpetrators.

Generally, the racial aspect of ethnic cleansing raises fundamental issues in the general scholarship pertaining to race, culture, and biology. The biological perspective, in which genetic heredity and phenotype are paramount, is often embedded in a culturalist idiom. This means that many of the ethno-cultural conflicts in which the expulsion of minorities occurs should be categorized as ethno-racial as well. All of this suggests that race, as an idiomatic expression of culture, is a much more pervasive feature of social relations and constitutes a silent subtext in many conflicts, including ethnic strife in the industrial countries of the West. In effect, in many ethnic conflicts that are not manifestly focused around racial categorization, the claims and identities created by ethnic groups have a subtext that includes a belief in some sort of common descent. In the contemporary international context of widespread media exposure it is difficult to conceal ethnic cleansing, but the true intent of perpetrators remains, such that many brutal acts of murder and mayhem seem to border on genocide. The case of Darfur in the Sudan is such an example.

SEE ALSO *Apartheid; Genocide; Genocide and Ethnocide; Genocide in Rwanda; Genocide in Sudan; Holocaust; Mayan Genocide in Guatemala; Social Problems.*

BIBLIOGRAPHY

Appiah, K. Anthony, and Amy Gutmann. 1996. *Color Conscious: The Political Morality of Race*. Princeton, NJ: Princeton University Press.

Bell-Fialkoff, Andrew. 1996. *Ethnic Cleansing*. New York: St. Martin's Press.

Bulmer, Martin, and John Solomon, eds. 2004. London: Routledge.

Connor, Walker. 2004. "A Few Cautionary Notes on the History and Future of Ethnonational Conflicts." In *Facing Ethnic Conflicts: Toward a New Realism*, ed. Andreas Wimmer, et al. Lanham, MD: Rowman & Littlefield.

Fearon, John D., and David D. Laitin. 1996. "Explaining Interethnic Cooperation." *American Political Science Review* 90 (4)715–735.

Mann, Michael. 2005. *The Dark Side of Democracy: Explaining Ethnic Cleansing*. Cambridge, U.K.: Cambridge University Press.

Naimark, Nornam M. 2001. *Fires of Hatred: Ethnic Cleansing in Twentieth-Century Europe*. Cambridge, MA: Harvard University Press.

Premdas, Ralph. 2004. "Belize: Identity and Ethnicity in a Multi-Ethnic State." *Canadian Review of Studies in Nationalism* 31 (1-2): 1–21.

———. 1997. *Ethnic Conflict and Development: The Case of Fiji.* Aldershot, U.K.: Avebury Press.

UNESCO. 1961. *The Race Question in Modern Science: Race and Science.* New York: Columbia University Press.

Várdy, Steven Béla, and T. Hunt Tooley, eds. 2003. *Ethnic Cleansing in Twentieth-Century Europe.* New York: Columbia University Press.

Ralph R. Premdas

ETHNOCENTRISM

Ethnocentric persons believe that the principles and practices of their own tribe, nation, or ethnic group are not just different from other groups, but superior in some sense, perhaps because they are more sacred, or perhaps more reasonable, or more practical. At the highest intellectual level, some cultures regard their own religious beliefs and systems of morality as representing the wishes of the only true God, while they assert that the beliefs of others are derived from a false god, or have been misinterpreted by false prophets. Even among religions that represent "people of the book"—Jews, Christians, and Muslims—some denominations maintain that they are the only people who "got it right," while other denominations and religions are wallowing in sin and ignorance. Ironically, congregations and denominations are oftentimes most critical of those who, by any objective measure, are most similar to themselves—Shia and Sunni Muslims, Protestant and Catholic Christians, Theravada and Mahayana Buddhists.

Disagreements among religionists at an apparently theological level frequently have social and political consequences for their respective adherents. Mahayana Buddhism, for example, is more ecumenical than Theravada Buddhism. The role of women is frequently at issue among religionists, as well as the proper structure of a family and attitudes toward other "races" and nations. In many cases, these social beliefs are part of a formal cosmology, frequently incorporating a creation story that delineates and rationalizes proper roles in society. For people of the book, the cosmology/creation story that they share is included in the Book of Genesis, with its narratives of the stories of Adam and Eve, Cain and Abel, and the flood, which have been variously interpreted by theologians of the three faiths. All three religions have added supplemental sacred texts—such as the Jewish Mishnah, the Christian New Testament, and the Islamic Koran—which address the cultural differences among the three groups—concerning such social and political issues as pacifism, polygyny, diet, government, and even business practices such as the sanctity of contracts and charging interest for loans.

While large-scale, literate religious groups such as those above have most often accepted each other as "civilized," in some sense, the same courtesy has not been extended historically to the practitioners of "primitive" religion. The most famous of the early comparative religious scholars, Sir James Frazer, contrasted civilized with "primitive" religions as a matter of real religion versus "magic." In a classically ethnocentric manner, he managed to define *magic* in a way that made tribal religions seem to be magical while the "great religions" were not, being characterized as monotheistic and abstract instead of superstitious and magical. Critics soon challenged Frazer's definitions, pointing out, for example, that Christian beliefs in transubstantiation or the power of prayer clearly constituted "magic" by Frazer's own definition.

The acknowledged founder of modern anthropology, Sir Edward Burnett Tylor, wrote easily and ethnocentrically about "primitive" beliefs in his book, *Primitive Culture* (1871). Like other cultural evolutionists of his day, he placed existing "primitive" societies on a historical scale leading from savagery to civilization, with different tribal societies of his day representing extinct societies that were the antecedents of "civilized" peoples. At that time, the word *savage* was also used to describe people known in the twenty-first century as *tribal* or *pre-literate,* an even more derogatory term than *primitive.* Franz Boas, the usually progressive founder of anthropology in the United States, used the milder term in his 1911 book, *The Mind of Primitive Man,* but his contemporary Bronislaw Malinowski wrote of *The Sexual Life of Savages* in 1929, and a 1966 book by Claude Levi-Strauss was entitled *The Savage Mind,* although the term *sauvage* is considered less offensive in his original French than in English.

For a time in the seventeenth and eighteenth centuries, the languages of tribal peoples were likewise regarded as "primitive." European traders and travelers often reported that the native peoples of Africa and Indonesia spoke languages that were "guttural," consisting of mere grunts and noises. Of course, the people who made these observations did not speak the languages in question, and so these comments are more an expression of European ignorance than of the "primitive" condition of native languages. In the twentieth century, textbooks in general linguistics made a serious effort to dispel these misunderstandings about language, pointing out that some languages had more sounds than others, and some had grammars that were more complicated than others, but there were no general criteria that could be used to categorize certain languages as "primitive." A language might be simple in some respects, such as number of sounds, but very complicated in other respects, such as grammar. Also, they pointed out, it is ethnocentric to describe one language as intrinsically easy to learn and another as difficult. Whether it is easy or difficult depends on what language one speaks already. From the standpoint of English, Chinese is a difficult language. But to one who already speaks a Tibetan language, Chinese is easy. And to a speaker of Chippewa Indian language, Pequot is easy. And to those who speak English, German is easy.

The complexities of cultures maintained by supposedly "primitive" peoples are also apparent in their religious beliefs and ceremonies. The Cheyenne Indians of North America, for example, envision a universe of two poles, male spirituality at the zenith and female materiality at the nadir. The cardinal directions represent philosophical contrasts between such entities as life and death, fertility and sterility, sickness and health, energy and nothingness, good luck and bad, symbolized by various colors, animals, and astronomical features. In their ceremonies, which have been well described, they celebrate good and beneficial plants and animals, and each supporting pole of the sacred ceremonial lodge represents a human virtue. Descriptions of many other religious and ceremonial complexes of tribal peoples on every continent were published in the twentieth century, for example, descriptions of the Tukano Indians of South America, the Kachin of Burma, and the Ndembu of Africa (Reichel-Dolmatoff 1971, Leach 1970, Turner 1967). As with languages, the observation that tribal religions were in any sense "primitive" says more about the ethnocentric and often racist and intolerant attitudes of the European observers than about the condition of tribal religions.

Although anthropologists were responsible for drawing attention to the notion of *primitive* in the nineteenth century, with its ethnocentric connotations of cultural and racial inferiority, they also developed ideas of *psychic unity* and *cultural relativity*, which are opposite to the notion of ethnocentrism. The German scientist Adolf Bastian is generally credited with inventing the idea of psychic unity, which states that the brain power and sensitivities of all human beings are essentially the same, no matter where they live or who they are. He offered this idea in his 1860 book *Der Mensch in der Geschichte* (People in history). Cultural relativism is a similar idea but with many authors, gaining widespread acceptance among social scientists in the twentieth century. The earliest antecedent for these ideas is probably Charles de Montesquieu, who wrote in *The Spirit of the Laws* in 1748 that whereas Islamic laws worked very well for Arabs in North Africa, Christian laws worked just as well for European societies, because the two cultures were generally different from one another. One culture was not superior to the other, they were merely different. This idea was picked up by twentieth century scholars and elaborated as structural functionalism, making the point that each legal code, like everything else, had to be understood in its social and historical context. All cultures had component parts that fit together to make an integrated whole.

BIBLIOGRAPHY

Leach, Edmund. 1970. *Political Systems of Highland Burma.* London: Athlone Press.

Levi-Strauss, Claude. 1966. *The Savage Mind.* Chicago: University of Chicago Press.

Malinowski, Bronislaw. 1929. *The Sexual Life of Savages in North-Western Melanesia.* New York: Eugenics Publishing Co.

Montesquieu, Charles. 1989 (1748). *The Spirit of the Laws,* translated and edited by Anne M. Cohler, Basia Carolyn Miller, and Samuel Stone. Cambridge, U.K.: Cambridge University Press.

Powell, Peter. 1969. *Sweet Medicine,* 2 vols. Norman: University of Oklahoma Press.

Reichel-Dolmatoff, Gerardo. 1971. *Amazonian Cosmos.* Chicago: University of Chicago Press.

Turner, Victor. 1967. *The Forest of Symbols.* Ithaca, NY: Cornell University Press.

John H. Moore

ETHNOCIDE

SEE *Genocide and Ethnocide.*

EUGENICS, HISTORY OF

Eugenics, or the selective breeding of humans with the aim of improving their hereditary quality, has been entangled with ideas about race since the modern eugenics movement was founded by the British explorer, cartographer, and statistician Francis Galton (1822–1911) in the second half of the nineteenth century. Although Galton was primarily concerned with inherited individual differences, he also provided a scientific gloss on the standard racial views of his time, place, and social class. Thus, Galton thought he had shown scientifically that not just individuals, but also nations and races (defined as broadly as blacks and whites and as narrowly as Bohemians, Prussians, Bantus, Irish Celts, and Lowland Scots) differed in their inborn mental, moral, and temperamental as well as physical characteristics. (In the nineteenth century, the categories of race and nationality were often conflated.)

Among the "races" existing in his own time, Galton ranked Australian Aborigines at the bottom and Anglo-Saxons and Teutons at the top. Not all eugenicists, in Galton's day or later, were as biased as he was, however, and some were concerned only with the future of the "human race" as a whole. On occasion, especially in Latin countries, race mixing was even viewed as desirable. But eugenicists generally favored maintaining racial purity, and their concerns about foreign admixture played an important role in shaping eugenic attitudes and programs in many countries, most notably in the United States, Canada, Australia, and Germany.

THE IMPACT OF EVOLUTIONARY THEORY

Although the concept of eugenics extends back at least to Plato, the idea that human breeding should be consciously controlled remained largely theoretical until the late nineteenth century. An important factor in converting an abstract idea into a social movement was the newfound anxiety associated with the prospect of biological degeneration, which was prompted by the new theory of evolution by natural selection. In 1859, Galton's cousin, Charles Darwin (1809–1882), published his revolutionary treatise *On the Origin of Species*. Darwin argued that evolution occurred and that its main mechanism, natural selection, involved a fierce struggle for existence in which the fittest organisms survive to reproduce their kind, while the less fit leave few if any progeny. Both Darwin and his readers (unlike most modern biologists) conceived of natural selection as a progressive process that led inexorably to the improvement of plants and animals. Although Darwin cautiously avoided any discussion of his own species in the *Origin*, questions immediately arose about whether humans had also evolved (and if so, were they evolving still?).

Darwin himself believed that humans were indeed products of natural selection, but that this process had been largely halted in "civilized societies," where medical care and public and private charity salvaged many of those who would in previous times or in less advanced societies have succumbed to cold, hunger, or disease. Although troubled by the implications of this relaxation of selection, Darwin kept his worries largely to himself at that point. Others were much less reticent, however. Among the first to explore the meaning of Darwin's theory for human social arrangements was Galton. In his 1869 book *Hereditary Genius*, Galton argued for intervention in human breeding based on the assumption that natural selection was no longer effective at culling the weak in mind and body, and that hereditary paupers, imbeciles, and criminals were reproducing at a dangerously rapid rate. At the same time, meanwhile, the most capable members of society married late and had few children. Thus, Galton argued, only a program of artificial selection could reverse the resulting degeneration. In 1883 he named this program *eugenics*, from the Greek word for "well-born," and described its two dimensions: "negative eugenics" would aim at discouraging the inferior members of society from having children, and "positive eugenics" would encourage the most capable to reproduce early and often.

Sir Francis Galton. *British scientist Sir Francis Galton is credited as the founder of eugenics.* © BETTMANN/CORBIS.

DEBATING INNATENESS

Galton's argument rested on the assumption that mental, moral, and temperamental traits were innate and largely fixed at birth, and that when people succeeded in life it was because they had inherited the requisite traits. Likewise, when people failed it was because they lacked the requisite traits. The inferior social condition of women, the poor, Irish, Africans, and others was explained by their inborn traits. Because bad heredity was to blame for pauperism and vice, selective breeding was the only effective response.

The idea that individuals and groups differed by nature was not new, nor was its use in rationalizing social inequalities. Since the Enlightenment and the associated rise of "scientific racism," innate differences had been invoked to explain why some people possessed social, political, and economic power while others did not. Indeed, at the time Galton wrote, the question of the relative influence of "innate character" and "institutional arrangements" in explaining human differences, especially in respect to gender, nation, and race, was being bitterly debated in Britain.

In this controversy, the philosopher and economist John Stuart Mill became the chief standard-bearer for the view that human nature is not fixed and that institutions shape character. Thus, in his influential *Principles of Political Economy* (1848), Mill wrote: "Of all the vulgar modes of escaping from the consideration of the social and moral influences on the human mind, the most vulgar is that of attributing the diversities of conduct and character to inherent natural differences" (p. 319). Indeed, Mill thought that the chief barrier to social reform was the belief that differences among individuals and groups were largely innate and fixed rather than the product of circumstances.

IRELAND AND JAMAICA

During the Irish famine of the 1840s, Mill published a series of newspaper articles on conditions in Ireland. His portrait of the Irish was not flattering, for he viewed them as lazy and brutish. But unlike many other commentators, Mill did not attribute their degraded condition to innate racial characteristics. On the contrary, he argued that it resulted from patterns of land tenure, and he proposed that the government drain uncultivated wastelands and divide them into small farms in order to create a class of independent peasants. Mill argued that peasant proprietorship would be morally transformative, and that if peasants came to feel that they counted for something, they would not choose to live in squalor.

Many others considered the Irish to be a distinct inferior race whose condition resulted from their nature and was unalterable. For example, in his 1869 "Realities of Irish Life," the essayist William Greg wrote:

> "Make them peasant-proprietors," says Mr. Mill. But Mr. Mill forgets that, til you change the character of the Irish cottier [landless agricultural laborers who sublet tiny patches of potato ground], peasant-proprietorship would work no miracles. He would fall behind the installments of his purchase-money, and would be called up to surrender his farm. He would often neglect it in idleness, ignorance, jollity and drink, get into debt, and have to sell his property to the newest owner of a great estate. . . . Mr. Mill never deigns to consider that an Irishman is an Irishman, and not an average human being. (p. 78)

The question of innate character was also central to the debate over the status of black labor in Jamaica, where 13,000 whites ruled 420,000 impoverished blacks. In his 1849 essay "Occasional Discourse on the Negro Question," the historian and essayist Thomas Carlyle (1795–1881) proposed that Jamaican blacks be returned to compulsory servitude. He argued that the emancipation of slaves in the West Indies had been a terrible failure, with the islands reduced to a "Black Ireland." He saw the "pumpkin people" of the Caribbean as counterparts to the "potato people" of Ireland. In his view, both the Irish and blacks were naturally idle and would not work unless compelled to do so.

In response, Mill noted that Carlyle was apparently not bothered by the idleness of the white proprietors, and he suggested that what Carlyle really wanted was access to cheap spices. In this context he wrote: "But the great ethical doctrine of the discourse, that which a doctrine more damnable, I should think, never was propounded by a professed moral reformer, is, that one kind of human beings are born servants to another kind," and he charged Carlyle with "the vulgar error of imputing every difference which he finds among human beings to an original difference of nature" (Mill 1850, p. 93).

These are only two of numerous nineteenth-century voices involved in the debate about the inherited nature of human differences, but they are perhaps enough to demonstrate the importance of the colonial context for thinking about such differences, and to indicate that Galton did not initiate the "nature-nurture" debate (although, as with *eugenics*, he did name it). But Galton's intervention was nevertheless a crucial one, for he was the first to invoke *science* in support of the hereditarian position.

GALTON'S PROJECT

To prove what others had only assumed, Galton consulted the biographical reference works of his day, such as *Dictionary of Men of the Time*. From these sources he was able to show that high achievement runs in families. He argued that scientists, statesmen, military commanders, literary figures, judges, musicians, artists, and divines who were prominent enough to be listed in such works were more likely than members of the public at large to have near male relatives who were also prominent enough to be listed. Galton was aware that this fact alone might not convince doubters that the traits important for success were inherited. After all, the training, experience, and associations of the children of poets or scientists would also differ from that of persons chosen at random. Galton dismissed the idea that social circumstances could explain achievement, at least in the fields he considered meritocracies such as science, literature, and the law. In his view, those born with natural ability would succeed no matter how unfavorable their environment, while those who lacked it would fail, however auspicious their start in life or powerful their social connections.

What was true of individuals applied equally to larger groups. In *Hereditary Genius*, Galton devoted a chapter to analyzing the comparative worth of different races. According to his calculations, which relied on estimating the proportion of eminent men in each race, black Africans, on average, ranked at least two grades below whites in natural ability, while Australian Aborigines were three grades below whites. Galton also found considerable variation among whites, with the Lowland Scots and the North-Country English representing a higher standard than individuals from other parts of Great Britain. He thought it obvious that the ablest race in history was the ancient Greeks, especially the subrace of Athenians, who stood as far above his compatriots in their achievements, and thus in their innate abilities—just as whites stood above blacks. But he also found that the most accomplished Athenian women often failed to marry and bear children, while emigration and immigration sapped the purity of the race. Thus, to humanity's great misfortune, the "high Athenian breed decayed and disappeared" (Galton 1892, p. 331).

As historian Nancy Stepan notes in *The Idea of Race in Science* (1982), Galton did not consider African blacks, Australian Aborigines, or other "savages" a threat to the Anglo-Saxon and other "civilized" races. Rather, he believed that the stronger races would inexorably eliminate the inferior in a natural process that was already well underway. His concerns were thus focused inward, on the problematic condition of his own Anglo-Saxon race. Galton feared that even races that were superior in a global perspective would be unable to meet the mental demands of an increasingly complex modern society. As in the case of ancient Greece, degeneration would be the inevitable result of failing to breed from the best. Among his proposals to address the problem was an 1890 scheme to encourage the early marriage of female Cambridge University students who were especially superior in physique and intellect. These women would be given 50 pounds if they married before age twenty-six, and 25 pounds on the birth of each child.

DARWIN'S *DESCENT*

Galton had originally been inspired by Darwin to investigate the inheritance of talent and character, and Darwin's view of human evolution would in turn be shaped by Galton's studies. After reading the first fifty or so pages of *Hereditary Genius*, Darwin wrote that whereas he had previously been inclined to attribute differences among individuals mostly to enthusiasm and hard work, he had been largely converted to his cousin's viewpoint. Galton's influence is explicitly acknowledged in Darwin's book on human evolution, *The Descent of Man*, and in his *Autobiography* (Barlow 1958), where Darwin notes: "I am inclined to agree with Francis Galton in believing that education and environment produce only a small effect on the mind of any one, and that most of our qualities are innate" (Darwin 1879, p. 43). Of course, to agree with Galton was to dissent from Mill. Although Darwin greatly admired Mill, he thought he had a blindspot when it came to inherited mental and moral differences. In *The Descent*, Darwin specifically criticized Mill's belief that moral feelings are not innate, and in the second edition he added: "The ignoring of all transmitted mental qualities will, as it seems to me, be hereafter judged as a most serious blemish in the works of Mr. Mill" (Darwin 2004 [1879], p. 121).

In the chapter of *The Descent* dealing with the social implications of the theory of natural selection, Darwin expressed the view that civilized societies are continually displacing savage ones in a process that is sometimes distressingly brutal but also inevitable. Thus, like Galton and many other contemporary figures, Darwin was not worried about competition from barbarous nations. Being inferior, they would eventually succumb in the struggle for existence anyway. The situation at home was more worrying, however. There, the process of natural selection had largely been checked. Vaccinations against smallpox, the establishment of asylums for the sick and insane, poor laws to support the unemployed, and other medical and charitable measures all counteracted the beneficial effect of natural selection by keeping the mentally and physically weak alive. Because their traits were inherited, the stupidity, insanity, and tendencies to laziness, intemperance, sexual promiscuity, and so forth responsible for their condition would be passed to their offspring. Darwin complained that "excepting in the case of man himself, hardly any one is so ignorant as to allow his worst animals to breed" (Darwin 2004 [1879], p. 159).

Darwin himself had mixed feelings about whether humans should inhibit breeding. After all, the social and sympathetic impulses that lead people to help others are also the products of natural selection. There were also countervailing forces—such as high mortality among the urban poor, suicides of the insane, emigration of the restless, and sterility among the sexually profligate—that limited the scope of the problem. Thus, although Darwin worried aloud about the harmful effects of relaxing selection, he did not propose any specific measures to counter the process. His book certainly reinforced the anxieties felt by many of his contemporaries. Like Galton's work, it also reinforced prevailing racial views, giving them a new scientific authority.

Darwin himself was vehemently opposed to slavery, and in 1865, when a riot in Jamaica was brutally suppressed by the island's British governor, Darwin subscribed to the committee (headed by Mill) that unsuccessfully pressed to have the governor condemned for murder and the victims compensated. He also assumed that virtually all aboriginal peoples were inferior, by nature, to Europeans. The real threat to England, however, came from a European source: the Irish. Darwin quoted Greg in support of his claim that the reckless and degraded members of society tend to increase their number at a faster rate than their prudent compatriots: "The careless, squalid, unaspiring Irishman multiplies like rabbits: the frugal, forseeing, self-respecting, ambitious Scot ... passes his best years in struggle and celibacy, marries late, and leaves few behind him." Thus, at home, Darwin believed, it was the inferior race that was prevailing in the struggle for existence (Darwin 2004 [1879], p. 143).

EUGENICS IN COMPARATIVE PERSPECTIVE

Galton's work received a mixed reception when it originally appeared, but by the end of his life his ideas had become quite popular, at least among middle-class citizens of predominantly Protestant nations. In the first decade of the twentieth century, eugenics societies were established in many countries, and by the 1920s the goal of improving heredity found numerous adherents, not only in the Anglo-American countries and much of Europe, but also in Latin America, Russia, China, and Japan. (In some Asian countries eugenics remains quite respectable today). Of course there also were skeptics and opponents, including the Catholic Church, which held that reproduction was not a matter for human tampering; immigrants and others who were the targets of eugenic policies; and those who continued to believe, along with Mill, that human differences were largely due to differences in education and training.

There were also important national variations because religious, scientific, political, and cultural traditions influenced the ways that eugenics was taken up in any particular setting. Latin countries were not only religiously Catholic, but scientifically they leaned toward a "neo-Lamarckian" view of heredity. From this standpoint, heredity was malleable rather than fixed, so there was no sharp distinction between nature and nurture. Social problems might be due to bad heredity, but if heredity improved with improved environments, the solution could be better nutrition and schools and other social reforms. Thus, what it meant to subscribe to eugenics tended to have a different meaning in Brazil or Mexico, for example, where many eugenicists endorsed race mixing and even a "cult of the mestizo," than it did in the United States or Germany, where race mixing was more often feared. In France and some other Latin countries, eugenics tended to be not only less racist than elsewhere, but it also implied a commitment to maternal and infant care rather than harsh policies of selection. Different perspectives existed within, as well as among, countries, with eugenicists heatedly debating such issues as whether immigration was desirable (and if so what kind), whether the distribution of birth-control information and devices would promote or retard eugenical aims, and what methods to prevent mental and moral defectives from breeding were effective and moral.

In Britain, where the Labour Party was hostile to eugenics and workers were not fractured by religious and ethnic/racial differences, eugenics was largely restricted to propaganda. Indeed, even a campaign to legalize voluntary sterilization was unsuccessful. In the United States and many European countries, especially Germany, eugenics would take a harsher turn. In 1907, Indiana became the first state to authorize compulsory sterilization of confirmed "criminals, idiots, rapists, and imbeciles." (Sterilization was accomplished through vasectomy in men and tying of the Fallopian tubes in women.) The movement gained ground after the 1927 Supreme Court decision in *Buck v. Bell*, which upheld the Virginia sterilization statute. Speaking for the Court, Justice Oliver Wendell Holmes famously wrote: "It is better for all the world if, instead of waiting to execute degenerate offspring for crime, or to let them starve for their imbecility, society can prevent those who are manifestly unfit from continuing their kind. ... Three generations of imbeciles is enough." With the worldwide economic depression that soon followed, support for such laws increased because of the large expense required to provide institutional care for the feebleminded, insane, and delinquent. By 1940, involuntary sterilization had been legalized in thirty-three American states, two Canadian provinces, and many countries, including Germany, all of Scandinavia, Australia, and Japan.

RACIAL EUGENICS

A number of countries, including the United States, adopted legislation to restrict immigration. That effort was not motivated solely or even principally by eugenic concerns, however. In the United States, immigrants from Asia and southern and eastern Europe were thought to be culturally unassimilable, and it was believed that they would drag down wages. Fears of biological degeneration were part of the mix. In the United States, which in the 1880s began to experience a large increase in the number of immigrants from Russia, Poland, Hungary, Greece, and Italy, race theorists such as Edward Ross and Madison Grant warned that the country was committing "race suicide," meaning that biologically inferior immigrants were flooding the country and, once there, multiplying their numbers.

Ross was an intellectual mentor to Theodore Roosevelt, who, both as vice president and president, did much to popularize the views of the race theorists. Claiming that Americans of Anglo-Saxon stock were engaged in a desperate "warfare of the cradle" with lesser races, Roosevelt warned both of the need to curb immigration from southern and eastern Europe (immigration from China and Japan having already been halted) and to increase the reproductive rates of old-stock families. Concern with the apparent high fertility of recent immigrants and the prospect that they would interbreed with older Americans, resulting in racial decline, was a factor in the success of the effort to restrict immigration and make it more selective. That effort culminated in passage of the Immigration Restriction Act (or Johnson-Reed Act) of 1924, which greatly reduced the number of allowable entrants to the United States and applied a national-origins quota system that ensured that few of those allowed would come from southern and eastern Europe.

Racialist policies reached their zenith in Germany, where eugenic measures of all types were taken to their ultimate extremes. These policies were aimed at Jews, Gypsies, the offspring of German women and black French soldiers, and others. About 400,000 Germans were sterilized (compared to about 62,000 in the much larger United States) under the Law for the Prevention of Genetically Diseased Progeny enacted shortly after the National Socialists came to power in 1933. The Nazis also instituted a program to rid the country of mental patients and the physically disabled through starvation, gassing, and lethal injection. Other legal and extra-legal measures had explicit racial motivations, as in the *Lebensborn* program that operated in both Germany and occupied countries and allowed unmarried women who were considered "racially valuable" to give birth in special maternity homes run by the Schutzstaffel (SS). In addition, the Nuremberg Laws of 1935 stripped Jews of German citizenship and forbade their marriage with "Germans." Ultimately, the campaign against the Jews led to the program of mass extermination called the Holocaust. The outcome of eugenics in Germany cast a shadow over the field of human genetics. Thus, the question of whether and in what ways developments in that field constitute a "new eugenics" still carries an emotional charge.

According to some scholars and journalists (e.g., Duster 1990), reproductive genetic services that involve the selection of gametes, fetuses, or embryos—including the use of ultrasound for sex selection, amniocentesis and embryo screening to detect abnormalities, and the procurement of eggs and sperm from carefully chosen "donors"—are a form of back-door or private eugenics. In their view, the term is appropriately applied not only to state policies such as involuntary sterilization that were clearly coercive, but also to activities that may be freely adopted or even demanded by prospective parents. Other commentators disagree, arguing that the latter practices, which are not only voluntary but based on sound science and largely devoid of race and class bias, differ so greatly from those that gave past eugenics its bad name that they should not be tagged with the same label. A few scholars concede that contemporary reprogenetics constitutes eugenics but believe that there is a need to sharply distinguish the bad eugenics of the past from the benign eugenics practiced by private individuals for their own reasons in the early twenty-first century. Whether these writers believe that contemporary practices are eugenics of a good kind or bad or are not rightly considered eugenics at all, there is close to a consensus that race has not been an important factor in their development or use.

The racial concerns that animated much past eugenics do remain evident in studies that argue for the genetic inferiority of blacks and sometimes other minorities and warn that "dysgenic" public policies discourage breeding by the intellectual elite while encouraging those of inferior ability and character to reproduce. The Pioneer Fund, a rather secretive organization founded by the eugenicist and textile magnate Wickliffe Draper in 1937, has been an important sponsor of such work. Historically, the Fund pursued an aggressively antiblack and anti-Semitic agenda, including support for a proposal to repatriate blacks to Africa and opposition to the Supreme Court decision in *Brown v. Board of Education* as well as civil rights legislation more generally (Kenny 2002; Tucker 2002). More recently, it has promoted research and publication in the field of behavior genetics that emphasizes the contribution of genes to both individual and group differences. *The Bell Curve* (1994) by psychologist Richard Herrnstein and political scientist Charles Murray, which argued that the gap in black-white IQ scores reflects real and for all practical purposes unalterable differences in innate ability, drew heavily on Pioneer-supported research by Arthur Jensen, Richard Lynn, and J. Philippe Rushton (the last was appointed president of the Fund in 2002). Despite its length and often dense technical content, *The Bell Curve* received many initially favorable reviews and became a best-seller. Subsequently, Rushton and Jensen published a lengthy article confirming Jensen's original claim of a substantial genetic component to the black-white IQ score difference (Jensen 1969; Rushton and Jensen 2005; for a contrasting view see Dickens and Flynn 2006). Thus it seems that the racial views and associated policy concerns that motivated many eugenicists continue to inform at least some strands of behavior genetics research.

SEE ALSO *Galton, Francis; Genetics, History of; Holocaust; Human and Primate Evolution; Human Genetics.*

BIBLIOGRAPHY

Anderson, Warwick. 2002. *The Cultivation of Whiteness: Science, Health, and Racial Destiny in Australia.* Melbourne, Australia: Melbourne University Press.

Barlow, Norma, ed. 1958. *The Autobiography of Charles Darwin, 1809–1882.* New York: Harcourt Brace.

Broberg, Gunnar, and Nils Roll-Hansen, eds. 2005. *Eugenics and the Welfare State: Sterilization Policy in Denmark, Sweden, Norway, and Finland,* rev. ed. East Lansing: Michigan State University Press.

Carlyle, Thomas. 1849. "Occasional Discourse on the Negro Question." *Fraser's Magazine* 40: 670–679.

Darwin, Charles. 2004 (1879). *The Descent of Man, and Selection in Relation to Sex,* 2nd ed. Introduction by James Moore and Adrian Desmond. London: Penguin.

Dickens, William T,. and James R. Flynn. 2006. "Black Americans Reduce the Racial IQ Gap." *Psychological Science* 17: 913–920.

Duster, Troy. 1990. *Backdoor to Eugenics.* New York: Routledge, 1990.

Galton, Francis. 1892. *Hereditary Genius: An Inquiry into its Laws and Consequences,* 2nd ed. London: Macmillan.

Greg, William R. 1869. "Realities of Irish Life." *Quarterly Review* 126: 61–80.

Herrnstein, Richard, and Charles Murray. 1994. *The Bell Curve.* NY: Free Press.

Jensen, Arthur R. 1969. "How Much Can We Boost IQ and Scholastic Achievement?" *Harvard Educational Review* 39: 1–123.

Kenny, Michael G. 2002. "Toward a Racial Abyss: Eugenics, Wickliffe Draper, and the Origins of the Pioneer Fund." *Journal of History of the Behavioral Sciences* 38: 259–283.

Kevles, Daniel J. 1995. *In the Name of Eugenics: Genetics and the Uses of Human Heredity.* New York: Knopf.

McClaren, Angus. 1990. *Our Own Master Race: Eugenics in Canada, 1885–1945.* Toronto: McClelland and Stewart.

Mill, John Stuart. 1965 [1871; 1st ed. 1848]. *Principles of Political Economy, with Some of their Applications to Social Philosophy.* In *Collected Works of John Stuart Mill.* Books I-II. Edited by J. M. Robson, with an introduction by V.W. Bladen. Toronto: University of Toronto Press.

———. 1850. "The Negro Question," *Fraser's Magazine* 41: 25–31.

Paul, Diane B. 1995. *Controlling Human Heredity: 1865 to the Present.* Amherst, NY: Prometheus.

———. 2003. "Darwin, Social Darwinism, and Eugenics." In *The Cambridge Companion to Darwin*, edited by Jonathan Hodge and Gregory Radick. Cambridge, U.K.: Cambridge University Press.

Peart, Sandra, and David Levy. 2005. *The "Vanity of the Philosopher": From Equality to Hierarchy in Post-Classical Economic Thought.* Ann Arbor: University of Michigan Press.

Rushton, J. Philippe, and Arthur R. Jensen. 2005. "Thirty Years of Research on Race Differences in Cognitive Ability." *Psychology, Public Policy and Law* 11: 235–394.

Stepan, Nancy. 1982. *The Idea of Race in Science: Great Britain 1800–1960.* Hamden, CT: Archon Books.

———. 1991. *The Hour of Eugenics: Race, Gender, and Nation in Latin America.* Ithaca, NY: Cornell University Press.

Stern, Alexandra Minna. 2003. "From Mestizophilia to Biotypology: Racialization and Science in Mexico, 1920–1960." In *Race and Nation in Modern Latin America,* edited by Nancy P. Applebaum, et al. Chapel Hill: University of North Carolina Press.

Stone, Dan. 2002. *Breeding Superman: Nietzsche, Race and Eugenics in Edwardian and Interwar Britain.* Liverpool, U.K.: Liverpool University Press.

Tucker, William H. 2002. *The Funding of Scientific Racism: Wickliffe Draper and the Pioneer Fund.* Urbana: University of Illinois Press.

Diane B. Paul

EVERYDAY RACISM

The concept of "everyday racism" emerged in the United States in the 1980s and was meant to identify as theoretically relevant the lived experience of racial oppression. Everyday racism is not about racists, but about racist practice, meaning racism as common societal behavior. Racial inequality perseveres even when the dominant ideology mutes reference to color, as witnessed in the United States following the successes of the civil rights movement. Some use the term "color-blind racism" to account for racist systems without legally sanctioned race-supremacy ideology.

Racism is easily recognized in its extreme forms (e.g., white youth beating up and killing dark-skinned people), or in its overt forms (e.g., throwing bananas at black players on European soccer fields). Everyday racism can be more coded (a white teacher saying to an African-American student: "How come you write so well?"); ingrained in institutional practice (appointing friends of friends for a position, as a result of which the workplace remains white); and not consciously intended (when lunch tables in a canteen or cafeteria are informally racially segregated and the white manager "naturally" joins the table with the white workers where only they will benefit from casually shared, relevant information and networking).

Everyday racism is a process of smaller and bigger day-to-day violations of the civil rights of ethnic minorities—and of their humanity and their dignity. Sometimes the meaning of the event remains contestable: Is it or is it not racial discrimination? It may take circumstantial evidence or inference from other experiences to understand the possible racial connotations. The outcome of an event is often more telling than the reported motive. Take the following example:

> A 747 aircraft to Amsterdam has a business class section in the front, separated from economy class by a blue curtain with the sign "business class only." Various passengers sneak behind the curtain to use the business class lavatories right behind the divide. They happen to be white men. But when a young woman of color does the same thing, a flight attendant blocks her way, kindly explaining that she has to use the economy-class facilities. The entrance then gets sealed off with a food trolley.

Discrimination often operates through rules being applied differently or more strictly to people of color. But does this also apply to this particular case? Imagine the reply of the flight attendant: "We treat everybody equally." When told that others did the same thing, the response is: "Oh really, I did not notice." Did the young woman get caught because her brown skin color stands out? Did the white men get through because they blend in more easily in the predominantly white (male) business class, indicative of global institutionalized racial (and gender) inequality? This surely must have happened on other flights, and whites too must have been sent back at times. Was the limit reached when a person of color started to take the same liberties? It could be shortsighted to quickly downplay the racial dimension of put-downs and other demotions with seemingly race-neutral arguments such as "it could have happened to anyone."

The fact of the matter is that in this particular situation the woman of color was the only one to be put in her place. Perceiving the event as racially significant in its implications reveals how one event, where the person of color is the only one to receive less favorable treatment, links to both historical and contemporary patterns of racial discrimination. Any situation with random options between better or worse treatment can be a vehicle for racial discrimination, whether it occurs in or outside institutions, in schools, at work, through the media, at a shopping mall, or in the neighborhood.

At work, the accumulation of seemingly petty experiences of disrespect, humiliations, rejections, blocked opportunities, and hostilities symbolically signifies the "glass ceiling" or "concrete wall," where color is a determining factor for upward mobility or for moving sideways, to the center of an organization. Because human beings communicate mostly through images and words, everyday racism is often expressed visually and discursively in what is being said or portrayed and how it is being said. In addition, facial expressions or avoidance of contact can "say" a lot too. Such behavior may even feel trivial or normal.

Everyday racism means that members of the dominant racial/ethnic group automatically favor members of their own group, not simply because they want to be with those they feel are their own, but because they believe, deep down, that white lives count more, that they are more human, that theirs is a superior culture and a higher form of civilization than others. Yet it would be incorrect to see everyday racism simply as a black-versus-white phenomenon. When dominated groups internalize the belief that European-derived cultures are superior, they may themselves become agents of everyday racism.

Everyday racism may cause ethnic minorities to anticipate racism in their contacts with members of the dominant group regardless of whether they are actually discriminated against on each occasion. This is a strategy of self-protection. Counter to the common-sense belief that people of color are overly sensitive to discrimination, research has indicated that most people of color are reluctant to label a given situation as racism before carefully considering all other possible explanations to account for unfair treatment. On the contrary, the common-sense belief that racism is a problem of the past makes members of the dominant group insensitive in recognizing when and how racism permeates everyday life.

Everyday racism adapts to the culture, norms, and values of a society as it operates through the prevalent structures of power in society. The more status or authority involved, the greater the damage resulting from common-sense prejudiced statements and discriminatory behavior. When members of a parliament or legislature make discriminatory statements or sanction discriminatory policies in the course of their normal everyday duties, the safety and civil rights of ethnic minorities and refugees are at stake. When teachers underestimate, discourage, or ignore ethnic-minority children, the futures of ethnic-minority generations are at stake. When employers discriminate against people of color, jobs, incomes, and career mobility are at stake.

Everyday racism is not a singular act in itself, but the accumulation of small inequities. Expressions of racism in one particular situation are related to all other racist practices and can be reduced to three strands of everyday racism, which interlock as a triangle of mutually dependent processes: (1) The *marginalization* of those identified as racially or ethnically different; (2) the *problematization* of other cultures and identities; and (3) symbolic or physical *repression* of (potential) resistance through humiliation or violence. Accusations of oversensitivity about discrimination, continuous ethnic jokes, ridicule in front of others, patronizing behavior, rudeness, and other attempts to humiliate and intimidate can all have the effect of discouraging action against discrimination.

Although the term *everyday racism* has such an informal ring that it may sound as if it concerns relatively harmless and unproblematic events, it has been shown that the psychological distress due to racism on a day-to-day basis can have chronic adverse effects on mental and physical health. The anticipation that discrimination can happen becomes in itself a source of stress. The same holds true for fretting over how to respond, whether the response has been effective, and whether victimization will follow. Studies have demonstrated a link between exposure to everyday racism and blood pressure. This is not to say that targets of racism are only victims, powerless or passive against the forces of exclusion. Throughout history, active community resistance against racial discrimination has emerged from anger about the indignities of everyday life.

Legal battles against racial discrimination are a mixed bag, even with progressive laws in place. The European Equal Treatment Law, for instance, follows the principle of a shared burden of proof. If the party who feels discriminated against provides "facts" that give reason to believe that racial discrimination may have occurred, it is the other party's responsibility to prove that the accusation is not true. But what the "facts" are is a tricky issue. The accused party is likely to deny that anything happened and witnesses may refuse to cooperate out of fear of retaliation. As a result, ethnic minorities often refrain from filing complaints, feeling their stories will not be believed anyway, or because they have doubts about the gains to be made. Studies have shown that testimonies and stories can provide relevant and detailed information about *what* happens and *how* racial injustices happen. The more these stories are voiced and circulated, the more sensitivity people develop for recognizing these everyday violations as forms of everyday racism.

SEE ALSO *Color-Blind Racism; Critical Race Theory; Institutional Racism; Orientalism; Racial Formations; Scientific Racism, History of.*

BIBLIOGRAPHY

Bell, Ella L. J., and Stella M. Nkomo. 2001. *Our Separate Ways: Black and White Women and the Struggle for Professional Identity.* Boston, MA: Harvard Business School Press.

Bonilla-Silva, Eduardo. 2004. *Racism without Racists: Color-Blind Racism and the Persistence of Racial Inequality in the United States.* Lanham, MD: Rowman & Littlefield.

Das Gupta, Tania. 1996. *Racism and Paid Work.* Toronto: Garamond Press.

Essed, Philomena. 1990. *Everyday Racism: Reports from Women of Two Cultures.* Translated by Cynthia Jaffé. Claremont, CA: Hunter House.

———. 1991. *Understanding Everyday Racism: An Interdisciplinary Theory.* Newbury Park, CA: Sage.

St. Jean, Yanick, and Joe R. Feagin. 1998. *Double Burden: Black Women and Everyday Racism.* Armonk, NY: M.E. Sharpe.

Philomena Essed

EXPLOITATION

In the social sciences, the term *exploitation* is generally used to refer to economic relations of production or exchange in which a dominant social class or group benefits by using the labor or resources of a subordinate social class or group. The term has been used in analyses of social class, of colonialism and imperialism, and of racial and ethnic relations within nation-states.

In *Capital,* (1967 [1867]) Karl Marx defined exploitation as characterizing relations of production in which nonproducers control the access of direct producers to essential means of production (e.g., land, tools, or raw materials), thus allowing the systematic appropriation of a surplus of goods from direct producers by nonproducers. For Marx, exploitation is a feature of all class societies, and it can be measured by the difference between necessary labor (that performed to produce the laborers' own subsistence or its equivalent value) and surplus labor (that which produces the surplus appropriated by the nonproducers). Necessary labor is not defined as a minimum subsistence level required for survival. Rather, the ratio between necessary and surplus labor, as well as the form of surplus appropriation, depends on the historically developed relations of production. The appropriation of surplus constitutes the basis for renewed exploitation because it reinforces the control of the exploiters and the dependence of the exploited.

Although Marxists have analyzed exploitation in a variety of class societies (e.g., slavery, feudalism), the concept is most fully developed in the analysis of capitalist relations of production. In capitalist societies, relations of production take on the appearance of relations of exchange. Labor power thus becomes a market commodity. Unlike other commodities, however, it has the ability to produce more value than is embodied in it. This is the surplus value appropriated by the capitalists.

The literature on colonialism and imperialism uses the concept of exploitation to define the relationships between the imperial nations (the core) and the colonized regions (the periphery). The spread of capitalist relations of production from the core to the periphery required the separation of farmers and artisans in the periphery from direct access to the means of production, thereby creating a class of laborers who must sell their labor power to survive. In *Unequal Development* (1976) Samir Amin coined the term "superexploitation" to describe how the low wages of the periphery have allowed transnational capitalists to extract a larger surplus than is possible in the core nations. A similar conception is contained in the works of Andre Gunder Frank (e.g., *Lumpenbourgeoisie, Lumpendevelopment* 1972), who saw colonial class structures as permitting "ultra-exploitation."

The role of racial or ethnic discrimination in imperialism has been explicitly addressed by several authors. Marx came to view anti-Irish sentiment as a major obstacle to working-class solidarity in England. In an 1870 letter he wrote:

> The ordinary English worker hates the Irish worker as a competitor who lowers his standard of life. In relation to the Irish worker he regards himself as a member of the ruling nations and consequently he becomes a tool of the English aristocrats and capitalists against Ireland, thus strengthening their domination over himself. He cherishes religious, social, and national prejudices against the Irish worker (*Selected Correspondence* 1975).

W. E. B. Du Bois embraced a Marxist analysis of imperialism in *The World and Africa* (1947), in which he argued that the British system of colonialism, which he saw as even more murderous than slavery, was based on the exploitation of native labor in their colonized homelands. Eric Williams also addressed exploitation in *Capitalism and Slavery* (1944), arguing that many of the largest fortunes of English capitalists had their origins in the exploitation of African slave labor in the American colonies.

In *The Political Economy of Race and Class in South Africa* (1979), Bernard Magubane shows how underdevelopment and racial inequalities developed together in South Africa. The ideology of racism was born out of the socioeconomic relations of capitalist imperialism, and it resulted in the ordering of exploitative relations of production along racial lines. "The essence of modern capitalism is the ruthless transfer of wealth from the colonized to the colonizer, from black to white, from worker to capitalist" (Magubane 1979, p. 4).

In "Internal Colonialism and Ghetto Revolt" (1969), Robert Blauner compares the situation of African Americans in the United States to that of colonized peoples. In this formulation, racism is fundamental to maintaining a higher rate of exploitation for black labor than for white labor. Internal colonialism is facilitated not only by ideologies of racism, but by historical and continuing structures (such as de jure and de facto segregation) that favor white workers over nonwhites. A similar approach is taken by Mario Barrera in *Race and Class in the Southwest* (1979), in which he analyzes structures of inequality affecting people of Mexican origin in the southwestern United States.

SEE ALSO *Capitalism; Colonialism, Internal.*

BIBLIOGRAPHY

Amin, Samir. 1976. *Unequal Development: An Essay on the Social Formations of Peripheral Capitalism.* Translated by Brian Pearce. New York: Monthly Review Press.

Barrera, Mario. 1979. *Race and Class in the Southwest.* South Bend, IN: University of Notre Dame Press.

Blauner, Robert. 1969. "Internal Colonialism and Ghetto Revolt." *Social Problems* 16 (4): 393–408.

Du Bois, W. E. B. 1947. *The World and Africa.* New York: Viking Press.

Frank, Andre Gunder. 1972. *Lumpenbourgeoisie, Lumpendevelopment.* NY: Monthly Review Press.

Magubane, Bernard. 1979. *The Political Economy of Race and Class in South Africa.* New York: Monthly Review Press.

Marx, Karl. 1967 (1867). *Capital,* Vol. 1. New York: International Publishers.

Williams, Eric. 1944. *Capitalism and Slavery.* Chapel Hill: University of North Carolina Press.

Alice Littlefield

EYSENCK, HANS JURGEN

1916–1997

Hans Jurgen Eysenck was an influential British psychologist who became the scion of twentieth-century psychometry. Eysenck believed that intelligence was highly inheritable and that racial differences in IQ were mainly due to genetic

Hans J. Eysenck. *British psychologist Hans J. Eysenck, seen here operating a machine that measures eye blinks, studied the relationship between heredity and intelligence.* CHRIS WARE/ KEYSTONE/GETTY IMAGES.

differences among races. He formulated racial arguments that would stimulate the careers of his two most famous students, Arthur Jensen and J. Philippe Rushton. Eysenck was born in Berlin, Germany, on March 4, 1916. Ironically, he left the country in 1934 in protest of the Nazi movement. His professional education occurred at London University, where he earned a Ph.D. in psychology under Cyril Burt in 1940. During World War II he was chief psychologist at the Mill Hill Emergency Hospital. After the war he founded the Psychology Department at the University of London's Institute of Psychiatry, where he worked as a professor until 1983.

Eysenck's academic and professional achievements were legion. He founded the first clinical psychology program in England, published more than 1,000 professional journal articles by the time of his death, introduced statistical analysis to a wide range of psychological data, popularized psychology by writing books for the general public, and advocated for the genetic basis of intelligence and the role of genetics in determining racial differences in IQ.

Eysenck suggested that there was an essential distinction between three classes of phenomena associated with cognitive performance. He defined *Intelligence A* as the biological substrate of mental ability resulting from the brain's neuroanatomy and physiology. *Intelligence B* is the manifestation of intelligence A and of those things that influence its expression in real life behavior. *Intelligence C* is the level of performance on psychometric tests of cognitive ability. Eysenck recognized that both genetic and environmental influences contributed to all three attributes of intelligence, but he asserted that the heritability (genetic component) of these was high (80%). In this way, he never broke with the views of his mentor Cyril Burt, who had previously asserted the overwhelming influence of genes on IQ. His lifelong views on this subject are set out in *The Intelligence Controversy*, a debate with Leo Kamin published in 1981, and in *Intelligence: A New Look*, published in 1998, after his death. He was also a signatory of "The Mainstream Science on Intelligence," a manifesto published in the *Wall Street Journal* on December 13, 1994. The document was drafted in response to criticism of Richard Herrnstein and Charles Murray's *The Bell Curve,* which had been published earlier that year. *The Bell Curve* stated that general intelligence was the main factor determining one's position in society. Thus the concentration of African Americans in the lowest social positions in society was not due to historical and ongoing discrimination, it was due to their lower mean IQ. Criticisms of the book entailed its non-professional use of statistical inference and its classification of humans into discrete racial groups, matching the social conceptions of race used in America. The mainstream statement was meant to weaken these criticisms by lending the authority of the psychometricians to the core claims of *The Bell Curve.*

Eysenck's views on race, genetics, and IQ were published in *The IQ Argument: Race, Intelligence, and Education* (1971). He based his supposition that genetics is responsible for racial differences in IQ on the long-standing 15-point IQ differential between whites and blacks in America. He further noted that there was greater variability in white IQ scores than in black IQ scores. This suggested that there would be a greater percentage of whites in both the lowest and the highest IQ categories. Blacks were said to perform better on aspects of the IQ test that resulted from education as opposed to innate ability. These results, Eysenck claimed, were supported by studies of blacks around the world, including in Uganda, Jamaica, Tanzania, South Africa, and Ghana (average IQ scores between 70 and 80.) Furthermore he argued that the fact that Japanese and Chinese performed better than whites did on IQ tests that measured innate ability, as opposed to learned abilities, was evidence of the genetic superiority of these groups with regard to intelligence. Finally, he suggested that Jews were the most genetically gifted population, with a 300 percent greater proportion of Nobel Prize winners than non-Jews.

Eysenck's career and contributions may be best understood in the context of a researcher that overstated one aspect of his problem (genetics) in response to what seemed to him an irrational denial of its role in human cognition. Modern genetic analyses have conclusively demonstrated that intelligence, broadly defined, is inherited to some extent. However, most estimates of the heritability of intelligence, however defined, range between 30 and 50 percent, as opposed to Eysenck's 80 percent. Yet it is important to understand that conceding the heritability of intelligence does not mean that it plays the roles ascribed to it by the psychometrician research program as outlined by Galton, Burt, Eysenck, Herrnstein, and Rushton. In other words, there is little evidence that intelligence determines social structure, as opposed to one's social position determining one's manifested intelligence. Furthermore, the case for genetic determination of racial IQ differentials is always weakened by the absence of shared environmental conditions between the racially oppressed and the racially dominant. Genomic research that examines quantitative trait loci is underway. This work will eventually identify loci that contribute to an individual's cognitive function and will most likely identify hundreds of loci whose influences are profoundly influenced by multiple and complex environmental influences. Such a result will demonstrate that the main point of the psychometricists is correct, that genes do influence cognitive function, but it will also demonstrate that these effects are far more complicated than they suggest.

SEE ALSO *Heritability; IQ and Testing; Jensen, Arthur.*

BIBLIOGRAPHY

Colman, Andrew M., ed. 1994. *Companion Encyclopedia of Psychology*, Vol. 1. New York: Routledge.

Eysenck, Hans J. 1971. *The IQ Argument: Race, Intelligence, and Education.* New York: Library Press.

———. 1998. *Intelligence: A New Look.* New Brunswick, NJ: Transaction Publishers.

———. Official Web Site. Available from http://freespace.virgin.net/darrin.evans/.

Eysenck, Hans J., and Leon Kamin. 1981. *The Intelligence Controversy.* New York: John Wiley.

Fancher, Raymond E., ed. 1984. *The Intelligence Men: Makers of the IQ controversy.* New York: W. W. Norton.

Lewis, Ricki. 2001. *Human Genetics: Concepts and Applications*, 4th ed. Boston: McGraw Hill.

Joseph L. Graves Jr.

F

FACIAL ANGLE

In the eighteenth century, the increasing involvement of European nations with colonies in the tropics brought Europeans into contact not only with tropical human populations but also with tropical nonhuman animals. A major attempt to classify the creatures of the world on the basis of assumed relationships was one of the consequences of this expanded European consciousness, and the major system of classification drawn up by the Swedish naturalist Carolus Linnaeus (1707–1778) was one of the results. His *Systema Naturae* was first published in 1735, with a definitive tenth edition appearing in 1758. Linnaeus assigned human beings, whom he defined in binomial fashion as *Homo sapiens*, to the order he called "Primates," which also includes monkeys and apes.

Later in the eighteenth century, the Dutch anatomist Petrus Camper (1722–1789), suggested a quantitative way to assess the relationships of some of the members of the order Primates. Camper developed his method in 1760 and presented it for public discussion in 1770, but it was not formally published until 1791, two years after his death. Camper took as his horizontal orientation a line on the face drawn from the ear opening to the base of the nose. Then, to generate his "facial line," he drew a line from the forehead to the junction between the upper and the lower lips. The angle made by the horizontal line with the facial line was his "facial angle." As he viewed it, the normal human condition was represented by facial angles between 70 and 80 degrees. Everything above 80 degrees he declared belonged to the realm of art, and everything below 70 degrees belonged to the animal kingdom.

With monkeys and apes included in the same zoological order as humans, Camper constructed a diagram displaying the facial angle of a monkey, an ape, and a number of human examples. The monkey has not been identified as to species, but the ape is a young orangutan. The orangutans, of course, were native to those parts of Indonesia and Borneo under Dutch control, so a Dutch anatomist would have had access to such specimens. The orang he depicted was a very immature individual, prior to the eruption of any of its permanent dentition. The first human shown was a young Negro bordering on adolescence, and the next was someone from Central Asia, although a number of observers have noted that the individual depicted is markedly different from other examples from this region. The other individuals are Europeans who display nearly vertical faces, for they lack the forward projecting dentitions that contribute to a reduction in the facial angle.

This points up the problem with the facial angle. The size of the brain case and the size of the teeth are under separate and completely unrelated selective force constraints. A single figure, then, cannot reveal anything of much biological significance concerning these two separate features. An increase in the facial angle can be produced by an increase in brain and skull size while face and tooth size remain constant, or by a decrease in tooth and face size while brain and skull size remain constant. The single figure of the facial angle cannot indicate which of these processes has produced that change in the facial angle. The difference in Camper's illustration between monkey and ape and human being is almost certainly due solely to a relative increase in brain size, while the difference between recent human groups is almost certainly because of the relative differences in tooth size between populations.

SEE ALSO *Great Chain of Being.*

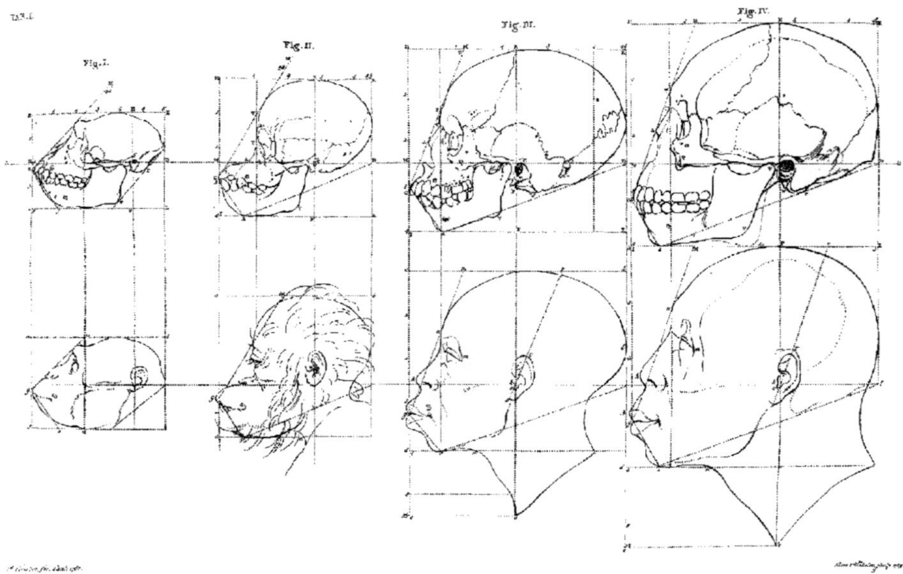

Figure 1. *Petrus Camper's representation of an unkown Old World monkey, a juvenile orangutan, a young male African, and a male Calmuck from Central Asia.* FROM BRACE, C.L. 2005. *"RACE" IS A FOUR-LETTER WORD.* OXFORD UNIVERSITY PRESS. ORIGINALLY TAB. I IN *DISSERTATION PHYSIQUE* BY P. CAMPER (B. WILD AND J. ALTHEER, AUTRECHT, 1791).

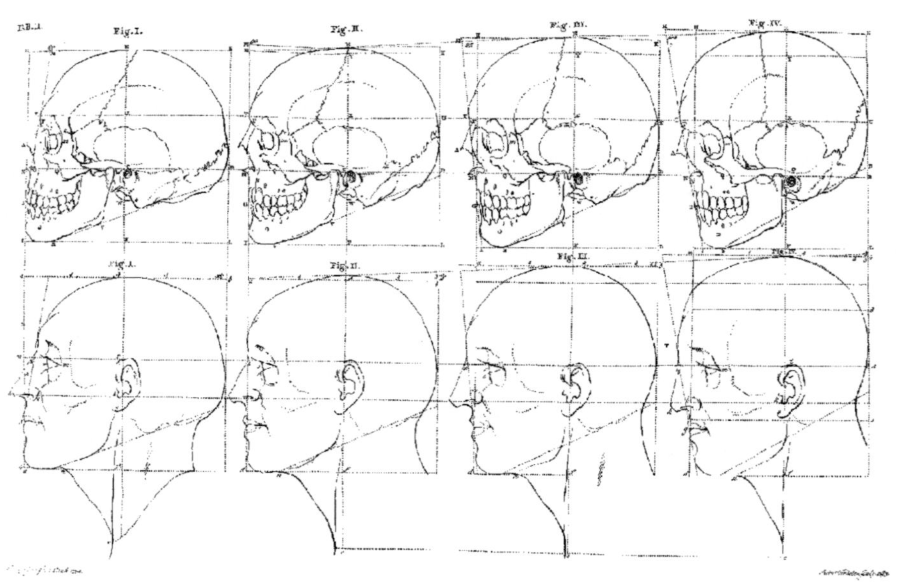

Figure 2. *Camper's representation of four European males.* FROM BRACE, C.L. 2005. *"RACE" IS A FOUR-LETTER WORD.* OXFORD UNIVERSITY PRESS. ORIGINALLY TAB. II IN *DISSERTATION PHYSIQUE* BY P. CAMPER (B. WILD AND J. ALTHEER, AUTRECHT, 1791).

BIBLIOGRAPHY

Brace, C. Loring. 2005. *"Race" Is a Four-Letter Word.* Oxford: Oxford University Press.

Camper, Pierre. 1791. *Dissertation Physique de Mr. Pierre Camper Sur les Différences Réelles que Présentent les Traits du Visage Chez les Hommes de Différents Pays et de Différents*

Âges; Sur le Beau qui Caractèrise les Statues Antiques et les Pierres Gravées. Published after the death of the author by his son Adrien Gilles Camper, translated from the Dutch by Denis Quatremere D'Isjonval. Autrecht: B. Wild & J. Altheer.

Linné, Caroli a. 1788–1793. *Systema Naturae: Per Regna Tria Naturae, Secundum Classes, Ordines, Genera, Species, cum Characteribus, Differemtiis, Synonimis, Locis,* 13th ed. 3 Vols. Lipsiae: Georg. Emanuel Beer.

C. Loring Brace

FAMILIES

This essay focuses on the implications of race and racism for family functioning and family formation. Rather than attempting the impossible task of examining all aspects of race and racism as they apply to all racial-ethnic groups, the discussion here is limited to black families. Given both the historical significance of inequality for African Americans and the importance of research on the African American experience for the development of theory and concepts about race and racism, the focus on black families is easily justified.

The Negro Family (1965), often referred to as the Moynihan Report, is a foundational, if controversial, study in the modern literature on black families. The report, which emphasized high rates of teenage pregnancy, absent fathers, welfare dependency, and crime in the black community, concluded that the black family structure was weak due in large part to the disproportionate number of female-headed households, or a "matriarchal" family structure. This conclusion, not surprisingly, has stimulated an extensive body of critical research into the conditions of the black family. Two broad themes can be identified in this literature. First, without necessarily taking issue with some of the basic findings, many scholars argue that this conclusion ignores the impact of racism, classism, and segregation. That is, the black family is more fractured and less stable than the nonblack family for reasons linked to endemic structural and cultural conditions that disadvantage the black family. Second, others more directly attack the conclusion that the black family is somehow dysfunctional, and instead point to the *strength* of the black family structure, as evidenced, for example, by strong kinship networks.

This entry provides a brief historical overview of perspectives on the black family, then a brief discussion of the contemporary black family, with a special emphasis on motherhood and fatherhood. The final section focuses on differences and diversity within and among black families.

BLACK FAMILIES IN HISTORICAL CONTEXT

A major misconception in the early literature on slavery and black families, as written by white scholars, was that slave owners understood the economic benefits of a strong nuclear black family and therefore tried to preserve the family structure of slaves. Researchers later "discovered" what the descendants of slaves already knew, that about one out of every three slave marriages ended because of partners being sold. This discovery questioned the validity of the idea that slave owners cared about the well-being of slave families and, more importantly, provides an example of how research can be seriously flawed if it is informed by racism and a worldview fostered by privilege. More recent scholarship demonstrates that slave owners often used specific strategies (i.e., labor migration, interference in marriage, and sexual exploitation) to endanger the well-being of African American families.

It is now known that some of the characteristics of the black family that have been both criticized and praised have their roots in slavery. Predominantly female-headed households were the norm during slavery primarily due to the forced migration of male slaves but also to gender-segregated slave quarters. This forced black families to rely on extended kinship and/or community networks for support. Despite these difficulties, enslaved families demonstrated remarkable resilience and worked hard to maintain a strong family unit.

Although emancipation freed slaves from bondage in a formal sense after the Civil War, it was a hollow freedom for many. Political leaders were more concerned with repairing the fractured relations with the white South than fulfilling their promises to the ex-slaves (e.g., ten acres and a mule) and making it possible for black families to thrive in freedom. Only a small portion of ex-slaves managed to reunite with their families, and conditions were such that many new families had to endure long periods of separation due to economic troubles, military service, or the demands of work.

THE CONTEMPORARY BLACK FAMILY

A traditional Eurocentric view of the family assumes that parenting takes place in a nuclear family where the mother is responsible for child rearing and the care of the home and the father is responsible for the economic well-being of the family. This is not a representative picture of the African American family, neither historically nor contemporaneously. And it is precisely because it is measured against the normative and idealized white nuclear family that the black family has so often been designated as dysfunctional. However, the structure of the black family not only has different historical roots but also has been persistently impacted by racism, whether overtly in policies against miscegenation or more covertly in color-blind institutional practices. As a result, the notions of motherhood and fatherhood have developed somewhat differently in the African American community than in a Euro-American context.

Motherhood. Mothers have long been praised and respected in the African American community. However, the idea that in order to be classified as "good mothers" women must make child rearing their full-time responsibility is traditionally much less pervasive in African American families. That is, in contrast to white women, black women's standing as mothers is not threatened by their participation in the labor market. Moreover, strong women-centered networks have fostered an expansion of the notion of motherhood in the black community to include women who help care for the well-being of children outside the nuclear family, and others in the community as well. These networks make women less dependent upon, and concerned with, male participation, and hence strengthen their position within the family and in the community at large. Thus, the historical evolution of the black family, combining internal cultural developments with severe external constraints, has contributed to the much higher proportion of female-headed households among black families and the continued respect that women receive as mothers.

From the perspective of the white majority community, however, the strong woman who is celebrated in the African American community has often been turned into a threat. Historical images of the mammy and the matriarch and, more recently, the welfare mother are designed to oppress and control black women. Negative stereotypes such as the welfare queen are held up as examples of what is wrong with society and hence can be used as political weapons against the movement to achieve equality and eradicate racism. Moreover, because the image of the "welfare queen" designates a single mother without a husband, it can also be used to control men. That is, the continued reliance on explanations for the fractured black family that emphasize female-headed households and the absence of fathers and husbands implicates not only fathers but also black manhood.

Fatherhood. The celebration of motherhood does not necessarily de-emphasize fatherhood in the black community. The consistent absence of black fathers has been a major issue since slavery. More recently, high incarceration rates, the difficulties undereducated black men face in the job market, and various regulations in the welfare system that discourages marriage are among the issues

An Ecological Model of the Intersectionality of Gender, Race and Class

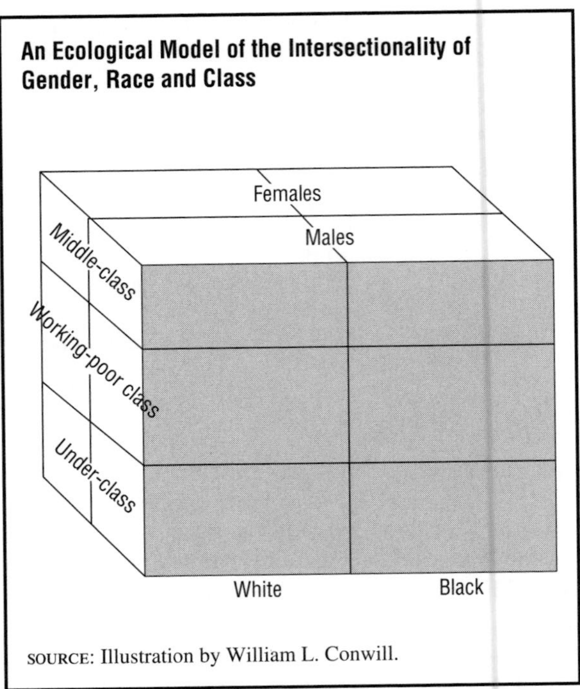

SOURCE: Illustration by William L. Conwill.

Figure 1.

debated both inside and outside the academy. For some observers, this picture constitutes a crisis in the black family, especially since absent or distant fathers are ineffective role models for African American boys and young men. The reintroduction of black fathers into the family, from this perspective, will foster a healthy and stable environment for black children.

Others suggest that although it may be unfortunate that black men play a more marginal role in family life than their white counterparts, the tradition of strong women makes the presence of husbands and fathers less critical for the stability of black families than for white families. The lesser reliance on men for economic support, however, does not necessarily mean an absence of men in the black family. On the contrary, the tradition of extended family networks makes each individual family less isolated than the ideal-typical nuclear family and hence facilitates the development of other male familial roles, such as brother, grandfather, cousin, and uncle.

FAMILY DIVERSITY

Following the lead of E. Franklin Frazier and, later, Daniel Patrick Moynihan, much of the twentieth-century research literature has focused on the conditions that impacted the black family uniquely and pushed it in different directions than the majority white family. More recently, however, researchers have started to pay attention to family diversity within the African American community, which requires taking into consideration the interlocking systems of oppression that impact the lives of all African Americans, albeit in different ways. Gay families, interracial families, and young families represent a growing number of families within the black community, and these new family constellations raise novel issues and bring new challenges for family members and scholars alike.

Teenage Parenthood. While there is a fairly extensive literature on teenage pregnancy, generally speaking this is not a literature grounded in family studies; rather, teenage parenthood is typically approached as a form of youth deviance, not as a legitimate family form. This is the case especially regarding African American teenagers, who get pregnant and have children at significantly higher rates than their white counterparts. It is this particular family form that is so often referred to as a major cause of the vicious cycle of absent fathers and economic instability. Although there can be no doubt that parenthood brings hardship to many teenagers and that, generally speaking, children who live in two-parent households do better in many ways, the placing of the explanatory focus on the family form itself—a teenage mother with children—can easily distort a deeper understanding of the social forces that privilege some family forms and bring disadvantages to others.

Moreover, the pervasive assumption that teenage childbearing is essentially accidental and a result of poor planning, lack of information, inability to negotiate sexual encounters, and any number of other unfortunate circumstances has preempted research on teenage families in their own terms. At least some evidence suggests that black teenagers do not always view having a baby as stifling and/or debilitating; instead, they view it as a "rite of passage." Moreover, rather than viewing a pregnancy as an unfortunate accident, some teenage girls are actively looking to replace something that is missing in their lives, whether a connection to a missing father or the prospect of a successful future.

Black LGBT Families. Much of the literature on black families has ignored the implication of sexual orientation on the structure of the family. Feminist scholars are currently working to remove the heterosexual bias that pervades the family literature. The use of the traditional nuclear family as a model for family research contributes to the marginalization and discrimination that LGBT (lesbian, gay, bisexual, transgendered) families experience in social life, especially for black families. Not only are black LGBT families stigmatized in the white community, alongside their white counterparts, they are also stigmatized in the black community. Generally speaking, social institutions are structured to benefit those who conform to the nuclear family structure, which means that LGBT families have difficulties accessing those benefits. In addition, the traditional linkage of strong black femininity with motherhood, in conjunction with fragile but sexualized black masculinity, has placed black same-sex families in a particularly uneasy position in the African American community. And yet, while scholarship is still fairly limited, at least some evidence suggests that same-sex families are neither less functional nor weaker, despite the multiple systems of oppression they face.

Interracial Marriage. In the United States, interracial marriage was illegal in more than twenty states until 1967. The removal of the legal barriers against interracial families did not automatically eradicate social disapproval of such unions, however. Although the number of interracial couples has increased dramatically over the last few decades, the proportion of interracial families is still very small. People opposed to interracial marriage in the black community typically look at the union from the standpoint of the historical evolution of race and racism and conclude that interracial marriage is detrimental to the existence of the black community. In contrast, white unease with interracial unions is currently framed more in cultural rather than racial terms, even though traces of racial superiority are clearly evident. Moreover, both black and white unease is linked to concern for the children that might result from interracial unions.

Neither perceptions nor practices of interracial unions are gender neutral, which is not surprising considering the violent history of such unions (lynching for black men and forced sexual subordination of black women). Couples in which the man is black and the woman white are much more prevalent than unions with white men and black women. This is so for several different reasons. Marrying outside the race is a form of betrayal to many black women, whereas black men have more freedom in this regard. Moreover, the intersection of race and gender lessens the status differential between black men and white women, but increases it for white men and black women.

SEE ALSO *Black-White Intermarriage; Motherhood.*

BIBLIOGRAPHY

Billingsley, Andrew. 1992. *Climbing Jacob's Ladder: The Enduring Legacy of African American Families.* New York: Simon & Schuster.

Clayton, Obie, Ronald D. Mincy, and David Blankenhorn, eds. 2003. *Black Fathers in Contemporary American Society: Strengths, Weaknesses, and Strategies for Change.* New York: Russell Sage Foundation.

Collins, Patricia Hill. 2000. *Black Feminist Thought: Knowledge, Consciousness, and the Politics of Empowerment*, rev. ed. New York: Routledge.

Davis, Richard A. 1993. *The Black Family in a Changing Black Community.* New York: Garland.

Dunaway, Wilma A. 2003. *The African-American Family in Slavery and Emancipation.* New York: Maison des sciences de l'homme and Cambridge University Press.

Feldstein, Ruth. 2000. *Motherhood in Black and White: Race and Sex in American Liberalism, 1930–1965.* Ithaca, NY: Cornell University Press.

Frazier, Edward Franklin. 1939. *The Negro Family in the United States.* Chicago: University of Chicago Press.

Hill, Robert Bernard. 1999. *The Strengths of African American Families: Twenty-Five Years Later.* Lanham, MD: University Press of America.

McAdoo, Harriette Pipes. 2007. *Black Families.* Thousand Oaks, CA: Sage Publications.

Moynihan, Daniel P. 1965. *The Negro Family: The Case for National Action.* Office of Planning and Research, United States Department of Labor. Washington, DC: U.S. Government Printing Office.

Stevenson, Brenda. 1996. *Life in Black and White: Family and Community in the Slave South.* New York: Oxford University Press.

Willie, Charles Vert, and Richard J. Reddick. 2003. *A New Look at Black Families,* 5th ed. Walnut Creek, CA: Altamira Press.

Tamika Corinne Odum

FARMWORKERS

The history of farmworkers in the United States, as well as their current situation and their future prospects, reflects the complex ways in which labor-force dynamics interact with social classification systems to shape the intertwined and often-confused concepts of "race," "ethnicity," and "national origin." In a global context, transnational migrants are almost always on the lowest tier of the economic ladder. In the United States, most farmworkers have historically been economically and politically disadvantaged, not so often as a consequence of their being racial minorities, but more because of their status as unauthorized immigrants. However, the high association between farm work and certain racial-ethnic minorities has reinforced negative racial views of these groups and often supported stereotypes about their abilities and employment preferences.

The relationship between farm-labor market dynamics and the farmworkers' quasi-racial identity as the lowest-ranking occupational group in U.S. society is systematic, paradoxical, and in no sense accidental. Agribusiness representatives argue that immigrants are "naturally" more motivated or more productive than native-born workers. But the most recently arrived transnational migrant farmworkers are, in fact, remarkably unproductive, primarily because they have had no prior experience in contemporary labor-intensive large-scale agriculture. They are simply more easily exploitable because they will accept wages and working conditions that workers with other options will not consider. Mexican immigrants' experience in using extended family and social networks to secure employment in a highly unstable labor market allows them to navigate in an environment that is daunting to native-born Americans accustomed to more formal processes for securing and keeping a job.

THE LEGAL CONTEXT OF FARMWORKERS' EMPLOYMENT

While the ethnic composition of the U.S. farmworker population is always changing, an unchanging reality is that the agricultural workplace is largely exempt from the framework of labor laws that protect mainstream workers. Farmworkers were initially excluded from the protection of the Fair Labor Standards Act when it was passed in 1938. Subsequent legislative "fixes" intended to bring the "rule of law" to the agricultural workplace have been undermined by an immigration policy crafted to allow continued influxes of unauthorized Mexican and Guatemalan migrant farmworkers while simultaneously effectively stripping these workers of human and labor rights.

While immigration status constrains the ability of farmworkers to organize to demand improvements in wages or working conditions, progress has been made in some cases. In 2005, for example, a national campaign by a Florida farmworker group resulted in an increase of a penny per pound in piece-rate wages for harvesting tomatoes. This was a 70 percent increase over their former earnings of 50 cents per 35-pound bucket.

The heavy reliance on farm labor contractors for recruiting, supervising, and serving as the employer of record for at least one out of every five farmworkers also distances agricultural producers from accountability for substandard working conditions and the irregular supervision of their workforce. Farmworkers employed by labor contractors have lower earnings and worse working conditions than any other subgroup in the agricultural labor market.

Although most farm labor contractors are themselves former farmworkers, they reject traditional Mexican norms of mutual reciprocity and consistently emphasize the rules of a market economy in order to justify a variety of exploitative practices, including overcharging workers for food, lodging, and drink, and in extreme cases employing a form of indentured servitude to assure that immigrants are unable to pay their debts to the *coyotes* or *raiteros* (immigrant smugglers) who helped them cross the border and find employment.

THE AGRICULTURAL PRODUCTION SYSTEM CONTEXT

The rapid increase in the size of the farm labor force is closely linked to the evolution of the U.S. food production and distribution system and the twentieth-century transformation of a rural economy of small family farms into increasingly larger agribusiness enterprises. As farm production unit size increased and as food distribution systems evolved, more and more farms turned to the fruit, vegetable, and horticultural production, which characteristically has sharp spikes in labor demand. Employers' labor recruitment strategy has always rested on attracting a surplus pool of underemployed migrant and seasonal workers. Although there have been significant technology-driven decreases in labor demand, these have been offset by rapidly increasing market demand for fresh fruit and vegetables, as well as increases in nursery and horticultural production.

SUCCESSIVE ETHNIC WAVES OF MIGRANTS

In his classic study *Factories in the Fields* (1939), the social historian Carey McWilliams detailed the successive waves of different ethnic groups of farmworkers who worked in California fields from the late nineteenth century up until World War II, including Chinese, Indian, Filipino, and Japanese workers. Because California accounts for almost half of the nation's labor-intensive agriculture, this pattern has helped shape the composition of the entire U.S. farm labor force, though there are regional variations. In the East and the Midwest, for example, there was heavy reliance on eastern European immigrants as farm laborers, while African-American workers predominated in the Southeast. The famous Farm Security Administration photographic documentation of migrant workers in the 1940s include, in addition to Dust Bowl migrants from Oklahoma, African-American sugar cane harvesters in south Florida, Polish carrot harvesters in New Jersey, Greek farmworkers in California, and Mexicans in South Texas.

In more recent years, there have been brief influxes of refugees from other areas of the world, including Haitians who came to work in south Florida in the early 1980s. Likewise, Russian "Old Believers," who initially settled in China and Brazil, migrated to Oregon's Willamette Valley in the 1970s and 1980s. But these workers rapidly moved on to other types of employment. Mayan refugees from the genocidal civil war in Guatemala during the 1970s and early 1980s are one of the important ethnic groups who entered the U.S. farm labor force as the result of civil unrest, and many of them have continued to work in farm work. They are now an important part of the "Eastern Migrant Stream" of labor-intensive agricultural production stretching from Florida up to the Delmarva Peninsula.

MEXICAN MIGRANTS' ENTRY INTO THE U.S. FARM LABOR MARKET

Although U.S. agriculture has always relied on immigrant workers of diverse ethnicities, Mexican immigrant workers have, at least since the 1950s, been the most important single ethnic group in the farm labor force. As early as 1935, the famous DiGiorgio farms in southern California relied heavily on workers recruited in Mexico (although by the late 1930s there were also Yemenis, U.S.-born Dust Bowl migrants ["Okies"], and Filipinos).

In the lower Rio Grande Valley of Texas, immigrant workers from northeastern Mexico were crucial to the establishment of a huge citrus production industry. While south Texas's history as a racially diverse "borderlands" region stems from the beginning of the twentieth century, the history of racism and farmworkers is, in Texas (and elsewhere), linked to the development of large-scale agribusiness. By the 1950s, Mexican migrant farmworker crews from "the Valley" had joined the local African-American farmworkers in the labor-intensive Florida citrus harvest. The era of the long-haul Texas-based migrant crews of family workers began to draw to a close in the early 1960s, when the mechanization of cotton and sugar-beet harvesting created gaps in their follow-the-crop itinerary.

The influx of Mexican migrants into U.S. farm work was fueled by the Bracero Program, which was instituted in 1942 as a means to counter labor shortages resulting from World War II. Although the program had justified the enlistment of farm hands, and the movement of some into war production industries such as shipbuilding (which drew large numbers of African-American workers out of field work), the actual recruitment of Mexican farmworkers peaked in 1956 with 445,000 guest workers. The Bracero Program did a great deal to institutionalize Mexico-U.S. migration, especially from the "core migrant-sending region" of Jalisco, Michoacan, and Guanajuato.

Large numbers of Mexican indigenous migrants from Oaxaca, first recruited to work in labor-intensive tomato and cotton production in northwestern Mexico and Baja, California, began working in California and Oregon in the early 1980s. Most of this new wave of indigenous migrant farmworkers are of Mixtec origin, but the farmworker population has become increasingly diverse. Other important ethnic groups from the Oaxacan village migration networks working in U.S. agriculture in the early twenty-first century include Triquis, Zapotecs, Amuzgos, and Chatinos. The U.S. farmworker population also includes Purepecha from central Michoacan, Otomi from the states of Hidalgo and San Luis Potosi, and Nahuas from the state of Guerrero.

The increasing ethnic diversity of the U.S. farmworker population, and the reliance on Spanish as the lingua franca in the workplace and rural agricultural communities (set against a background of "racial" discrimination against *indios* in Mexico and Guatemala), has led to an emerging sense of pan-indigenous identity in the context of U.S.

Farmworkers Harvest Strawberries in California, 2006. *Going back to at least the 1950s, Mexican immigrant workers have been the single most important ethnic group in the farm labor force.* SANDY HUFFAKER/GETTY IMAGES.

farmworker life. This shift has increased. Traditionally, in their home villages, indigenous-origin migrants felt closely bound to members of their own family, extended family, their spouse's family, and fellow villagers. These bonding ties obligated them to help each other even when they, themselves, were in difficult straits, and facilitated collective action within their own social network. Commonalities of migration experiences have come to outweigh years of historical conflict among indigenous villages, creating "bridging" social capital, which cuts across home country networks based on a newly defined identity as indigenous peoples. Consequently, even some ethnic groups that were at odds in their home country are closely allied in the United States, and some may even think of themselves as *paisanos*.

THE CURRENT U.S. FARMWORKER POPULATION (2001-2002)

There are currently about 2.5 million farmworkers in the U.S. (including fruit, nut, and vegetable processing and packing but excluding meat packing and forestry workers) and perhaps 1.0 to 1.5 million non-working family members in farmworker households. The National Agricultural Worker Survey (NAWS) provides long-term trend data on the changing demographic composition of the farmworker population. The most recent tabulations are from 2001–2002. According to NAWS, two-thirds of U.S. farmworkers are Mexican or Central American immigrants (62% from Mexico and 4% from Central America [mostly Guatemala]). The majority are limited in English, with 30 percent speaking no English and 29 percent speaking it only "a little." Most have worked in the U.S. for less than ten years.

The average farmworker is seriously underemployed, only managing to find thirty-two weeks of agricultural employment and earning about $10,000 annually. Less than one-quarter (24%) have health insurance, and only about one-third (36%) believe they would be eligible for unemployment insurance.

Since the mid-1990s, less than one-quarter of the farm labor force have been women, but since 2001 the proportion of women working in farm work has begun to increase again as the number of family workers has grown and the proportion of young, solo, "shuttle migrant" workers has decreased, probably as a result of payments to *coyotes* for border crossing increasing to about 20 percent of a typical farmworkers' average annual earnings. The lives of women working in farm work are difficult, as most bear primary responsibility for childrearing and housekeeping, in addition to farm work. Complaints of sexual harassment are also common, and finding adequate (or any) childcare is a constant problem. Living conditions are typically very crowded and housing is substandard. While farmers used to provide migrants with free, on-farm housing, in the early twenty-first century only 22 percent receive this benefit.

SEE ALSO *Braceros, Repatriation, and Seasonal Workers; Day Laborers, Latino; United Farm Workers Union.*

BIBLIOGRAPHY

Aguirre International. 2005. "National Agricultural Workers Study: Frequencies for Public Access 1989–2002." Available from http://aguirreinternational.com/naws/downloads/National_report_2002.pdf.

Commission on Agricultural Workers. 1993. *Report of the Commission on Agricultural Workers*. Washington, DC: U.S. Government Printing Office.

Fox, Jonathan, and Gaspar Rivera-Salgado, eds. 2004. *Indigenous Mexican Migrants in the United States*. Boulder, CO: Lynne Rienner.

Gabbard, Susan, Richard Mines, and Beatriz Boccalandro. 1994. *Migrant Farmworkers: Pursuing Security in an Unstable Labor Market*. Research Report No. 5. Washington, DC: U.S. Department of Labor.

Galarza, Ernesto. 1964. *Merchants of Labor: The Mexican Bracero Story*. Charlotte, NC: McNally and Loftin.

Griffith, David, and Ed Kissam. 1995. *Working Poor: Farmworkers in the United States*. Philadelphia, PA: Temple University Press.

McWilliams, Carey. 1939. *Factories in the Field*. Boston: Little, Brown.

Rubel, Arthur. 1966. *Across the Tracks: Mexican-Americans in a Texas City*. Austin: University of Texas Press.

Edward Kissam

FEDERAL RECOGNITION: WHAT IS AN INDIAN?

Three different perspectives are most common for considering the question, What is an Indian? The first perspective is from the viewpoint of Native peoples themselves, who can offer as many diverse answers to this question as there are tribal nations in the Americas—more than 1,000 cultural entities. The second perspective is from university scholars, who over the last 400 years have created a rather unified and consistent "outsider" view of Native American culture and history, presented mostly in published books and articles. Last is the perspective, in the United States and Canada, of the governments of the dominant Anglo societies—a perspective consisting largely of ethnocentric and self-serving fabrications, and full of legal myths about native peoples and their relations with colonial powers and with the Euro-American governments that succeeded them.

Perhaps no colonized group in the world has been so mislabeled by European colonists as the "American Indians." The historians of Alexander the Great more than 2,000 years ago began the problem in nomenclature by referring to the peoples of the Indus River region of the South Asian subcontinent, conquered by Alexander and comprising most of modern Pakistan, as *Indians,* a term that later came to mean any peoples south of China and east of Africa. In ancient and medieval times, the entire South Asian subcontinent became known as "India" and the large islands of present-day Indonesia were labeled "the Indies." It was the value of trade goods from this area, procured at first by lengthy and exhaustive coastal and overland transport, that led Columbus and others to seek a direct westerly route across the Atlantic to the Indies in the fifteenth century.

After explorers and mapmakers had determined in the sixteenth century that the Caribbean islands they had found were not part of Indonesia, they differentiated the two by calling the Pacific location the "East Indies" and the Caribbean location the "West Indies," even though they were about 10,000 miles apart. To differentiate between the respective native peoples, the inhabitants of the Caribbean islands and subsequently the adjacent continents were first referred to as "West Indians" and then simply "Indians." After mapmaker Amerigo Vespucci formalized the nomenclature and immodestly named the two continents after himself in 1502, the inhabitants became known as "American Indians." In Britain, to differentiate South Asian Indians from American Indians, both of whom had a place in British culture and history, the racial term "Red Indians" was used for the Americans, a term picked up by scientific racists in the nineteenth century when they characterized the skin colors of the world as fourfold—black, white, yellow, and red, making a complete chromatic set. This was perhaps aesthetically pleasing but biologically gibberish, because all human beings occur simply in various shades of brown. So the native peoples of the Americas were forced to live with a three-layered insult—named after a river in Asia they had never seen, bearing the personal name of a European who had barely set foot in "America," and characterized as contrasting with Europeans by being "red" in color.

NATIVE PERSPECTIVES

A standing complaint among Native Americans is being asked by tourists to "speak Indian," as if all native people spoke the same language, presumably the abbreviated Pamunkey trade language spoken in Virginia in colonial times, used by James Fenimore Cooper in writing his *Leatherstocking Tales* and made more famous by Tonto, the Lone Ranger's television sidekick. But in fact, the linguistic situation in aboriginal America was and is much richer and more complex than that of Europe. In all of Europe, only three language families are represented. A language family is defined as a group of languages that are historically related—all derived from a single parent language spoken perhaps thousands of years ago, but which historical linguists can reconstruct. Most Europeans speak an Indo-European language, such as those of the Romance group derived from Latin, or the Germanic languages, including English. Hungarians and Finns each speak a Finno-Ugric language, and the Basques (or more properly, Euzkadis) of Spain and France speak an "isolated" language, perhaps representing languages spoken in Europe before the Roman expansion.

But in the Americas, there are altogether about nineteen language families comprising nearly a thousand separate and mutually unintelligible languages, some of which are as different in their phonetic and grammatical structure as English and Chinese, or Bantu and Samoan. In North America alone, there are about ten language families and 216 separate languages (scholars differ in their estimates and classifications; see Ruhlen 1986, and Goddard 1996).

Native Americans are as diverse in their culture, religious beliefs, and traditional histories as they are in their languages, although tribal nations with related languages often share certain beliefs about creation and cosmology. Many of the traditionalist Native peoples of eastern North America, for example, have shared the cosmological view that the earth rests on the back of a turtle, and that the firmament was created from mud brought to the surface of the ocean by a crawfish. A few, but not all, of these groups have the traditional belief that at the time of creation humans were surrounded by a dense fog, and organized themselves with other non-human creatures as clans. They did not realize that they had become the comrades of certain non-human animals, plants, and other phenomena until the Master of Breath blew away the fog. The people of the Kiowa Nation of the Great Plains believe traditionally that they were uniquely created and placed on earth through the agency of a sacred hollow log situated in the Wichita Mountains. Their neighbors the Cheyenne believe that they too are unique, born with a layer of waxy yellow vernix from the high God, Maheo, as a symbol of their special status among humans. Similarly, some Nakota groups believe that their children uniquely bear a dark spot on their lower back, which biologists call the "Mongoloid Spot," a characterization that the Nakota forcefully reject. Height, body build, beards, and skin color have also been used as indices of humanness among Native American peoples, as well as between natives and colonists. In addition, Native people invoke the physical characteristics of freckles and moles, body hair, pattern baldness, and eye color to differentiate themselves racially from "Whites" and from "Mixed Bloods."

In their diverse beliefs, Native Americans have been sometimes more and sometimes less generous in bestowing human status on their neighbors, depending on history and circumstance. At the extreme, some nations did not bestow completely human status on traditional enemies, using words equivalent to *savage* or *primitive* to describe them, or insulting their enemies as cannibals, carrion-eaters, or incestuous persons. European colonists exploited this racism and chauvinism to enact a "divide and conquer" strategy against Native peoples in the New England and Virginia colonies. Later, to get the cooperation of Native people such as the Yamasees of Georgia in recovering escaped slaves, they imparted their own notions of African inferiority as well.

Soon after the European invasion, Native Americans recognized that they must eschew previous hostilities among themselves, and the accompanying racism and chauvinism, to present a united front against the European invaders. The Iroquois Indians were precocious in this regard, confronting the Europeans with the League of the Hodenosaunee or Iroquois, a confederacy of nations who spoke several different languages within the same Iroquoian language family. They invented political protocols emphasizing the political power of women that overcame parochial divisions, allowing the Iroquois League to dominate frontier politics in the eastern Great Lakes area during the eighteenth century.

Farther south, the Mvskoke Creeks went even farther in creating a pan-Indian, international confederacy, inviting the remnants and refugees of disintegrating coastal groups to join them by town as full citizens of their confederacy, which was called the Etelaketa. At first the Confederacy included only Yuchis, Hitchitis, Apalachees, and a few Cherokees and Natchez, but later it comprised larger populations of Shawnee, Alabama, and Koasati towns, representing altogether four language families and twelve distinct languages. In addition, as escaped indentured servants of European ancestry began to arrive in Creek territory in the late seventeenth century, they were assigned to three new towns, if they were not married into existing towns. A bit later, escaped African slaves were welcomed, forming five of their own towns, mostly as clients to Indian towns. An even broader confederacy was planned by the legendary Tecumseh toward the end of the eighteenth century, who proposed a grand alliance of all tribes south of the Great Lakes and north of the Ohio River. He failed, but the remainder of his movement went south to join the Seminoles in Florida at the end of the eighteenth century, forming a society that created a formal equality among its citizens of African, European, and Native American ancestry, a feat not accomplished in the American colonies or the United States until the twentieth century.

Pan-Indianism began to supercede nativism among Native Americans in North America with the emergence of the so-called Ghost Dance religion after the Civil War. Founded by the Paiute prophet Wovoka, the movement—in which nearly all Plains Indians participated—anticipated the creation of a new Earth west of the horizon, over which Jesus was sovereign, and which in the form of a hemispherical shell would move east over the globe, soon covering over a despoiled earth and the white people and their destructive and sinful ways. The buffalo would return to the new earth, dead ancestors would be resurrected, and Native people would be well fed and happy. The movement was notable not only for its Christian elements, but also its pan-Indian character. It was emphatically not a tribal religion. The Peyote religion, or Native American Church, is similar in being explicitly Christian and pan-

Indian, although it is not a mass movement but is organized into small local groups. At the turn of the twentieth century, organized pow-wows and ubiquitous sweat lodges in the Unites States and Canada also gained recognition as pan-Indian institutions. Intellectually, the twentieth century saw the development of pan-Indian literature and poetry, and pan-Indian political ideas from native writers such as Vine Deloria and Ward Churchill, and pan-Indian groups such as the National Congress of American Indians and the Native American Rights Fund.

THE SCHOLARLY PERSPECTIVE

If Native American intellectuals have historically been skeptical of Anglo-American scholarship concerning Indian origins and identity, they have good reasons. The first wave of Europeans, including Anglican priests, Puritan ministers, and French Jesuits, believed that Native Americans were worshippers of Satan, if they were not indeed the actual children of the Devil. English explorer Martin Frobisher, later hero of the battle with the Spanish Armada, previously served the Crown as explorer of the North American continent. While coasting Labrador and Baffin Island in 1560 looking for a Northwest Passage to the East Indies, he took the opportunity to go ashore, seize an Indian woman and hike up her skirts to see if she had cloven hooves instead of feet, thereby marking her as one of the Devil's brood. Such early observers as John Smith and Jonathan Edwards, after questioning native people of New England and Virginia, confirmed to their British readers that they were all worshippers of the Devil (see Sayre 1997). An alternative view was that they had no religion at all, and the consensus was that they were savages who lived in "promiscuous hordes" in the forests, as described by philosopher Thomas Hobbes, thereby justifying the theft of their land.

In Central and South America, among the first philosophical and theological questions the Spanish and Portuguese colonists formally faced were whether Indians constituted any kind of human at all, and if they had souls. If they were defined as animals, then they could be killed at will, worked to death in the mines, and did not have to be converted to Christianity (the "colonialist" position). If they were humans, then they had to be converted, could not be murdered legally, and could share communion in the Church (the "indigenist" position). In an historic debate in Valladolid, Spain in 1550–1551, Juan Genés de Sepúlveda defended the colonialist position, while Bartolomé de las Casas defended the human status of Native Americans. After lengthy deliberations, the judges in the case could not reach a decision, but the indigenist position ultimately prevailed by means of a series of royal decrees leading to the Basic Law of 1573 (Hanke 1959).

Having determined in the colonial period that Indians were something less than human, or at least something less than civilized, Western scholars then had to account for the rise of the civilizations of the Aztecs and Incas, and for the magnificent mounds and pyramids that were found when colonists penetrated the interior of North America. Having already demonized, literally, the "savage" occupants of North America, they could only hypothesize that somebody else must have built these impressive monuments. The hypothesized builders included well-known figures from Classical European history and mythology—refugees from the lost continent of Atlantis, Ancient Egyptians or Phoenicians, and the lost tribes of Israel. Isolated from Spanish sources by their ignorance of the language, British prehistorians did not concern themselves very much with Latin America, but parallel theories grew in Mexico and South America that the Aztec culture was inspired by immigrants from the African medieval empires, and that the Incas were inspired by Chinese or Japanese cultures. In 1968, Erich von Daniken, in his book *Chariots of the Gods,* even hypothesized that the pyramids and other structures had been built or at least designed by space travelers from another solar system. All such theories have served to denigrate the intellect of Native Americans, while ignoring the continuity of 10,000 years of archeological evidence indicating a slow and steady development, not a sudden appearance of high cultures in the Americas.

Among the pioneers in careful description of Native American culture—scientific ethnography—are John Smith of Jamestown, who despite his racism and religious bigotry provided accurate descriptions of Pamunkey economics and politics, while John White made accompanying sketches illustrating native life in North Carolina and Virginia. Father Joseph François Lafitau, who unlike most of his Jesuit confreres understood the complex structures of Indian kinship and politics, published a two volume description of Indian cultures in 1724 criticizing the views of his ethnocentric brethren, entitled *Customs of the American Indians Compared with the Customs of Primitive Times.* The best of these early ethnographers, however, was Lewis Henry Morgan, who in the next century helped to found the science of comparative kinship, or ethnology, was adopted by the Iroquois, and visited Native peoples up and down the Missouri River from 1859 to 1862, taking notes of differences in language and culture. His 1851 book *League of the Hodenosaunee or Iroquois* was perhaps the first full ethnography of any tribal society, anywhere. His magnum opus, *Systems of Consanguinity and Affinity of the Human Family* (1871), is still consulted by ethnologists. Morgan's Iroquois friend and sponsor, Ely S. Parker, was Ulysses S. Grant's adjutant during the Civil War, and was the first Indian person appointed as head of the U.S. Bureau of Indian Affairs (BIA), beginning his term in 1869.

In the nineteenth century, scholarly studies of Native American culture and societies were largely generated by government agencies, beginning with the publications of Henry Rowe Schoolcraft, an Indian Agent for the Chippewas (or Ojibwas), who received Congressional support to publish the six volumes of his *Historical and Statistical Information Respecting the Indian Tribes of the United States*, from 1851 to 1857. Following the Civil War, the government organized its own research institution for studying Indians, the Bureau of American Ethnology (BAE), under the premise that Indian culture, and Indian people themselves, had to be studied immediately because they would soon disappear, killed by diseases and their inability to adapt to a new situation. The BAE was merged with the Smithsonian Institution in 1965. The Smithsonian preserves its special status as providing the official scholarly perspective on Indians in its new edition of the *Handbook of North American Indians*, projected to comprise twenty volumes. The authors' guide for scholars writing articles for the *Handbook* recognizes the original premise of the BAE by requiring authors to refer to Indians and their cultural activities in the past tense.

THE GOVERNMENT PERSPECTIVE

In the British part of colonial North America, settlement had originally proceeded on the basis of charters issued to companies or groups of settlers to enter a particular area for purposes stated in their charter. It was up to the colonists to entreat with aboriginal residents and set boundaries and terms of interaction. Later in the seventeenth century, however, the Crown began to recognize the dangers of this arrangement, and forbade colonies from signing treaties with Indian polities on their own, and insisted that all treaties must be ratified by the Crown. The form of the treaties with Indians was the same as protocols followed by the Crown with other European governments or those of Africa or the Middle East. That is, the individual Native American groups were each treated as a sovereign nation. When the Treaty of Paris was signed in 1783, ending the American Revolution, the United States promised to honor all treaties written between former British colonies and Indian nations, which had mostly been ratified by the Crown. The reservations of land made for Indians under these treaties became known as "state reservations," comprising such entities as the Mohegans, Pequot, Pamunkey, and Catawba tribes in the eastern United States. The Iroquois groups also had treaties and titles for large tracts in upstate New York.

As the American frontier moved west of the Appalachian Mountains after independence, the former method of treaty-making was maintained. Typically, a meeting was called between U.S. and Native leaders, an agreement was worked out concerning such matters as land, boundaries, trade, and travel, then signed and ratified by both groups *inter pares*, "between equals." As the frontier reached the Mississippi River, however, federal policy changed dramatically. Land was becoming scarce in the east, and so a policy of Indian Removal was implemented in 1828, stating that all Indians east of the Mississippi had to move to reservations in the far west, across the Mississippi. The Cherokees, with a large educated elite and many friends in Washington, refused to move and sued, so that the case, *Cherokee Nation* v. *Georgia*, was ultimately heard in the U.S. Supreme Court. The Cherokees were confident of victory. If the Court decided that they were citizens of the United States, then they could go to court and defend their rights like any other citizen. If the Court decided that they were a sovereign nation, then the United States had to respect their treaties. Either way, they figured, they had the legal power to maintain control of their lands in Tennessee, Georgia, and North Carolina. But they were wrong.

In an unprecedented and self-contradictory ruling in 1831, Chief Justice John Marshall invented the concept of the "domestic dependent nation." Even though, up to then, the word *nation* legally and semantically meant that the group was sovereign or free and independent of any other government, Marshall redefined it to mean the opposite in the case of American Indians. He rewrote the dictionary. Indians east of the Mississippi were ordered to go west, and populist President Andrew Jackson was very willing to start them moving to please his constituency. Some Indian people on state reservations pleaded exception to the decision, because they had treaties that antedated the formation of the United States, and some of them won their cases. The Iroquois pleaded a special exception—their treaty with the United States was approved in that interim period after U.S. independence but before there was a Constitution, which was not completed until 1787. Therefore, they argued, the constitutionality of their treaty was irrelevant. Caught in a legal contradiction, the U.S. side capitulated and the Iroquois stayed in New York. Elsewhere, the Indian Removal Act was enforced unevenly, depending on local situations. In one odd case, the Catholic Potawatomies of Indiana were removed to Indian Territory, while the Methodist Potawatomies were allowed to stay, reflecting the anti-Catholic sentiments of the day. Perhaps in retribution, the Catholic Potawatomies sold their land to the Catholic Church, which promptly distributed it to Irish immigrants and built Notre Dame University on the site of the former reservation.

The U.S. government continued to write treaties in the same mode as before, first with nations of the Northwest Territory, and increasingly with Plains Indians and those in California and Oregon Territory. They neglected to tell the Indian signers about the Marshall decision, which had determined that even in signing a treaty recognizing them as a sovereign nation, the government had reduced their status to that of a *dependent* nation. These treaties were meaningless, because they could be overridden by Congress or even by an executive order of the president. Between 1831 and 1871, when treaty writing was abandoned entirely by act of Congress, Indian nations were moved around and their reservation boundaries and memberships revised and redetermined at the whim of the federal government.

FEDERAL ACKNOWLEDGEMENT

As Indians were pacified, missionized, and sent to prisons and boarding schools intensively after 1890, the federal government had time to organize them and their reservations as it liked. They either did not realize or did not care that their perspective on Indians was quite different from the perspectives of scholars or the Native peoples themselves, in many ways. First of all, there was the question of what to call these entities they had collected onto bounded, exclusive reservations. The government was careful to use the term *tribe* for these people, because that implied a lesser political status than *nation*. Native leaders were just as careful to use the word *nation* in their discourse with government officials, constantly reminding them of their claims to sovereignty. Then there was the question of the proper and polite names for the different "tribes." Some of the official names selected over the years were at least informal or colloquial, some were incorrect, and some downright insulting. The "Sioux," for example, had been given the name used by the Chippewas to degrade them as "snakes," *Nadouessioux*. They called themselves Dakota, Nakota, or Lakota, depending on their language, history, and location. The "Delawares," a conglomeration of Algonquian-speaking tribes living around Chesapeake Bay, had been named after an English nobleman, Thomas West, Lord de la Warr, without their knowledge or consent. They called themselves Lenape (Original people). The "Gros Ventres" (Big bellies) were burdened with a nickname bestowed by French traders; they called themselves A'ananin. In the same spirit, the Nimi'ipuu (Real People) had been labeled the Nez Percé (Pierced Noses), another French traders' nickname. Yet another group, which will not be identified, bears a native version of the name "Those Who Drink Our Urine," bestowed by a hostile neighboring group and transcribed by some trader or bureaucrat who did not speak the language. There are many other examples of misnaming, which are in the process of correction as traditional groups become more forceful in asserting their identity and naming themselves. They are also overcoming the objections of Anglo administrators that their names are difficult to spell or to pronounce. And so the Papago have officially become the Tohono O'odham, and the Sarcee of Canada have become the Tsuu T'ina.

Next there is the issue of whether an official tribal label applied by the government to a bounded reservation group accurately reflects the membership of the group. The Mvskoke Creeks, the officially recognized confederacy mentioned above, who were enrolled as one "tribe," notably includes several towns of Yuchis, whose language and history are distinct from the Mvskokes. The modern Creeks of Oklahoma also include a community of Shawnees, living at the edge of their Oklahoma reservation near the official Shawnees. Other unofficial Shawnees live with the Cherokees, and others are divided between the Shawnees proper, who were present at a treaty signing, and the Absentee Shawnees, who were assigned that name because they boycotted the treaty meeting. Some Delawares reside with the Cherokees, whereas others are with the Caddoes, from Texas. Some entire ethnic Cherokee communities are enrolled as Creeks in eastern Oklahoma, and some Creek communities as Cherokees, occupying part of the Cherokee Reservation. In the last several decades, such immersed tribes have been denied the right to organize themselves as separate entities because, according to the BIA, they already have an identity. In fact, one of the present rules of federal recognition is that a group cannot be separately recognized if the members are already members of a recognized group. So the Yuchis are destined by Anglo law and policy to remain Creeks, no matter what their cultural and linguistic differences might be, and no matter what their desires might be.

The Seminoles are another striking example of the differences between a native perspective, a scholarly perspective, and the perspective of a national government. Originally, the Seminoles were a group of Hitchitis, members of the Mvskoke Creek Confederacy, who moved from Georgia into north Florida to avoid hostilities with Anglo settlers. They were soon joined by the militants of Tecumseh's time and moved farther into Florida, accompanied by Black Seminoles, who formed their own towns. Other Hitchitis went to Indian Territory with the Creeks between 1830 and 1835. The Seminole Hitchitis began to call themselves Mikasukis. So there were and remain two groups of Seminoles in Florida, the Hitchiti-speakers in the Everglades, and the Mvskoke-speakers near Lake Okeechobee. The so-called Creeks of Indian Territory have comprised a multitude of language and cultural groupings—Mvskokes, Hitchitis, Shawnees, Alabamas, Koasatis, Cherokees, Yuchis, and Natchez—as well as comprising three towns descended from white indentured servants and five more comprising the descendants of escaped black slaves. As in other venues, the BIA has continued to use ethnic and "racial" differences to promote dissension and thus control tribal politics, especially between people characterized in racial terms as red, white, and black, the title of an influential book on the subject by Gary B. Nash (2000). Oddly, in view of its policy with its own citizens, the federal government did not discriminate legally among different kinds of Indians. Whether red, white, or black, they were all enrolled as Indians and given a tribal label.

In sum, the BIA created its "standard brands" of Indians by ignoring the real social, cultural, historical, and even "racial" differences among them, which were well known to scholars and of course to Indian people themselves. The existence of these standard brands was reinforced by treaties, confinement to reservations, enrollment procedures, and the organization of "tribal" governments after the passage of the Indian Reorganization Act in 1934. But during the twentieth century, demographic forces were developing that would make the BIA's job of accounting for Indians much more difficult. First of all, the process of tribal intermarriage continued apace despite the segregation of Indians on reservations and their removal to isolated places, as attested by data collected by anthropologist Franz Boas from the 1900 U.S. Census (see Moore and Campbell 1995). Roughly 15 percent of tribal members were found to be marrying outside their ethnic group every generation. Secondly, as the different entities intermarried, their portion of blood in their natal tribe constantly diminished, confounding the racist system of "blood quantum" invented by the BIA. In this system, Indian people could apply for enrollment as a tribal member only by submitting documents to an enrollment office that certified their extent of "Indian blood" by tribe. If their documents were approved, they were issued a Certificate of Degree of Indian Blood (CDIB), which allowed them to enroll in a tribe if they had the required fraction of ancestry there. People with CDIBs fulfill one requirement of being a "legal Indian."

Intermarriage among Indians progressed until, by 1980, some people with ancestry in several tribes found that they did not have enough blood quantum in any one tribe to be accepted for enrollment. Even some "full blood" Indians could not enroll anywhere. The system was further confounded by the practice within many tribes of considering ancestry to be only through the male line or the female line. Therefore, if one had a father from a matrilineal tribe and a mother from a patrilineal tribe, one could not enroll in either tribe. Scholars since the days of Lafitau and Morgan had recognized this situation, as of course had Indians since time immemorial, but the Bureau had made no accommodation to this cultural convention. In the 1880s, the BIA did not expect that there would be any Indians at all by 1980, and they frequently said so. But when it appeared by 1928 that Indians were here to stay, and in fact increasing in population, the BIA accommodated some of their own rules of citizenship in tribal nations under the Indian Reorganization Act.

A new problem in recognizing Indians and placing them in a tribe occurred with the reappearance in the twentieth century of tribes that had been neglected, or who were thought to be extinct. As early as colonial times, some Indian people had fled to the hinterlands to escape the genocidal attacks of the whites; William Christie McLeod (1928) and Helen Hunt Jackson (1881) catalogued some of these cases. To avoid hostilities, some groups denied their Indianness and called themselves names like "Portuguese Colored" or "Jackson Whites." When Indian Removal was enacted in the 1830s, large numbers of Cherokees and Choctaws especially, but also other smaller tribes, found refuge in mountain valleys, swamps, or on land that whites did not covet, while their brethren were being forcibly marched to Indian Territory. Some Indian people, even whole communities, had "opted out" of being official Indians, and diffused into their home communities among whites and blacks, and made their own way. Prominent among these were the Lumbees of North and South Carolina and the Keetowah Cherokees. Others used their own resources to emigrate independently to Indian Territory, refusing to be enrolled as Indians, and refusing to take land when it was offered under allotment in severalty, most notably some Cherokees, as well as some groups of Choctaws, Delawares, and Mvskoke Creeks.

By the 1970s, the political climate had changed to the extent that many submerged groups wanted to come out of hiding. Spurred by the example of Black Power among African Americans, Indian people began talking about Red Power. This was the period when the American Indian Movement (AIM), the International Indian Treaty Council, and many similar groups were founded. In the 1970s and 1980s, many previously little-known or unknown Indian communities began to identify themselves and seek some kind of recognition as Native people. They were encouraged in these efforts by a series of federal judicial decisions that emphasized that as the federal government had encroached on Indian lands and resources through the assignment of people to reservations and allotment in severalty in 1888, they had thereby accumulated an increasing fiduciary responsibility to uphold the interests of these tribes. In fact, the federal government was forced to take the Indian side in disputes concerning state reservations.

More importantly, it became clear that the federal government had to create a mechanism to officially recognize newly emerging groupings of Indian people. Many of them merely wanted to be admitted as a group to an existing tribe, some wanted federal recognition for tribes recognized only by states, perhaps living on state reservations, while others wanted an entirely new reservation established for them by federal authority. The most dramatic of these groups was a band of Shoshones who had somehow been overlooked in their homeland in the Great Basin of Utah and Nevada. Never enrolled, they wandered into Las Vegas during a drought in the 1960s, asking for help. To accommodate such demands, the U.S. Congress, through the BIA, established a new procedure for recognizing previously unrecognized groups in 1978. The criteria for recognition changed over the following three decades, but the criteria in the early twenty-first century emphasize the documentation of continuity of a petitioning group with an historically known Indian entity, the continued existence of the group as a community, and the genealogical connections and Indian blood quanta of the petitioners. In 2007 more than 300 petitioning groups were at some stage in the process of petitioning for federal recognition. The criteria are available at the website of the Federal Register and the BIA, as well as several other locations as 25 CFR Part 83, Procedures for Establishing that an American Indian Group Exists as an Indian Tribe.

The criteria for federal recognition of a tribe are distinct from the criteria used for recognition as an individual Indian. For personal recognition, as opposed to group recognition, several levels of Indian identity have been defined. In the last several decades of the twentieth century, softer or looser criteria were developed for the private sector as well as government institutions, to fulfill the requirements of affirmative action. Currently, many different standards are applied to determine "what is an Indian?" At the bottom of the identity hierarchy are self-identified Indians. They rank among other levels of identity as follows, from least rigid to most rigid:

1. Self-Identified Indian. This is merely a person who claims to have Indian ancestry.
2. Documented Indian. Someone who has documents tracing ancestry to someone noted in government records as an Indian, for example on a U.S. Decennial Census.
3. Legal Indian. Someone who has submitted documents resulting in the award of a Certificate of Degree of Indian Blood, issued by the federal government.
4. Enrolled Indian. Someone with a CDIB who has been accepted for membership by a federally recognized "tribe."

Only enrolled Indians can receive federal services provided through tribes. For some purposes, for example for federal employment and education benefits, some preference is shown for legal Indians, even if they are not enrolled in a tribe, but the federal government has been tightening up these benefits for unenrolled Indians as more and more Indian groups have been granted federal recognition.

Because of these differences in status and location, the total number of "Indians" in the United States is difficult to determine. Most do not live on reservations, and many do not bother to enroll unless they are resident on a reservation or if some special situation arises, such as a special election or the settlement of an outstanding legal claim. But according to the BIA and the Bureau of the Census, on their respective Web sites, there are about five million self-identified Indians on current U.S. censuses, about half of whom are affiliated in some manner with a particular reservation or tribal nation. There are many people of Indian ancestry who are qualified to receive a CDIB or to enroll with a tribe, who for various reasons, including their disgust at the process, have failed to do so. Those who have struggled over the years to collect documents to receive a CDIB, to be enrolled in an existing tribe, or to participate in a federal recognition petition, often become very angry and frustrated at the process. One often hears the complaint: "White people don't have to carry an ID card proving that they're white, so why do I have to carry a card proving that I'm an Indian?" A very good question.

The relations between the First Nations of Canada and their federal government are somewhat different from the United States. In the historically British or Anglophone area of Canada, from Ontario and the Great Lakes westward, the historical pattern of treaty writing and the establishment of reservations was similar to that of the United States, except that the areas set aside for Indians are called Reserves, and the occupants called Bands, further demoting native groups from the status of nation. In Quebec and other areas formerly under French control until the 1763 French-British treaty ended the Seven Years War, Indian claims to land and status have been complicated by the existence of prior French-Indian treaties, and British-French agreements. These treaties had provisions for Native people with consequences for Canadian law. Also, the status of some lands historically awarded by the French government to missionaries and traders seemed ambiguous under British law.

Between 1871 and 1922, the Canadian government undertook to write a series of numbered treaties (1–11) with tribal nations in the Canadian West, which was still sparsely populated and where the government could claim no "right of conquest" over native groups. In many cases, because of the complications of intermarriage and ethnic identity, people of Indian ancestry were given the choice of becoming a member of a band, a "status" or legal Indian, or a regular citizen of Canada, with consequences that are still being worked out in Canadian courts. In addition to comprising about two million Indians, Canada is also the home of about 300,000 Metis, of mixed Indian-French ancestry, many of whom speak their own original mixed language, Michif. The Canadian government regards them as an aboriginal people. In the same spirit, the United States regards native Hawaiians as Native Americans, but not as

Indians. In Latin America, relations between Indians and Europeans have been extremely complicated and have varied dramatically from country to country. Ethnogenesis has generated hundreds of hybrid and mixed populations who have different political and cultural statuses in different countries (Hill 1996).

SEE ALSO *Blood Quantum.*

BIBLIOGRAPHY

Asch, Michael, ed. 1997. *Aboriginal and Treaty Rights in Canada.* Vancouver: UBC Press.

Brown, Dee. 1970. *Bury My Heart at Wounded Knee.* New York: Holt, Rinehart and Winston.

Churchill, Ward. 2003. *Perversions of Justice: Indigenous Peoples and Angloamerican Law.* San Francisco: City Lights.

Deloria, Vine, Jr. 1969. *Custer Died for Your Sins.* New York: Macmillan.

Goddard, Ives, ed. 1996. *Handbook of North American Indians,* Vol. 17: *Languages.* Washington, DC: Smithsonian Institution.

Hanke, Lewis. 1959. *Aristotle and the American Indians.* Chicago: Henry Regnery.

Hill, Jonathan D. 1996. *History, Power, and Identity: Ethnogenesis in the Americas.* Iowa City: University of Iowa Press.

Jackson, Helen Hunt. 1881. *A Century of Dishonor.* New York: Harper and Brothers.

Macklem, Patrick. 2001. *Indigenous Difference and the Constitution of Canada.* Toronto: University of Toronto Press.

McLeod, William Christie. 1928. *The American Indian Frontier.* New York: Knopf.

Moore, John, and Janis Campbell. 1995. "Blood Quantum and Ethnic Intermarriage in the Boas Data Set." *Human Biology* 67 (3): 499–516. Special issue edited by Richard Jantz.

Nash, Gary B. 2000. *Red, White, and Black,* 4th ed. Upper Saddle River, NJ: Prentice Hall.

Ruhlen, Merritt. 1987. *A Guide to the World's Languages.* Stanford, CA: Stanford University Press.

Sayre, Gordon M. 1997. *Les Sauvages Américains.* Chapel Hill: University of North Carolina Press.

Schmeckebier, Laurence F. 1927. *The Office of Indian Affairs.* Baltimore, MD: Johns Hopkins University Press.

John H. Moore

FELONY DISENFRANCHISEMENT

The term *felony disenfranchisement* (or, more specifically, *felony voting disenfranchisement*) refers to the denial of the right to vote to incarcerated persons and released ex-offenders who were convicted of certain classified crimes, though not necessarily felonies. Since the adoption of the practice in colonial America, felony disenfranchisement has become a common practice within the United States. This practice has been particularly harmful to racial minorities, who have had the ability to exercise their political clout compromised.

CURRENT PRACTICE

In the late first decade of the twenty-first century, nearly 5 million Americans—or one in forty-three adults—are currently without voting rights as a result of a felony conviction. Forty-eight states and Washington, D.C., deny the right to vote to felony offenders. Only Maine and Vermont do not impose felony disenfranchisement. Although there is variety in felony disenfranchisement legislative schemes, such legislation may generally be classified under three categories: permanent, modified permanent, or restorative disenfranchisement.

In a permanent disenfranchisement jurisdiction, a felony offender is denied the right to vote for life. Three states—Florida, Kentucky, and Virginia—deny the right to vote to all ex-offenders, and can thus be classified as permanent disenfranchisement jurisdictions. In these jurisdictions, the restoration of voting rights is still possible, but only through a pardon by the governor or by the action of the probation or parole board. Twelve states are modified permanent jurisdictions. Here, permanent disability is imposed only on certain classes of ex-offenders, and restoration may be subject to a waiting period.

In a restorative felony disenfranchisement jurisdiction, restoration is either automatic after incarceration, probation, or parole, or it is available after the ex-offender completes a designated process following incarceration, probation, or parole. The restorative process varies from jurisdiction to jurisdiction, and it is often too cumbersome, and sometimes too expensive, for most ex-offenders to successfully complete.

RACE AND DISENFRANCHISEMENT

Racial minorities are disproportionately denied the right to vote by felony disenfranchisement legislation. More than a third of those disenfranchised are African-American men. It is estimated that 1,400,000 African-American men (or about 13% of African-American men) have been denied the right to vote by felony disenfranchisement legislation. The rate of disenfranchisement of African-American men is seven times that of the national average. In at least six states, one in four African-American men is permanently disenfranchised. Further, it is projected that if current disparities in incarceration continue, 30 percent of the next generation of African-American men will be disenfranchised over the course of their lives, and that in some states nearly 40 percent of African-American men will be permanently denied the right to vote.

The disparate disenfranchisement of African Americans is the result of both intent and effect. Felony disenfranchisement was specifically and consciously co-opted during the post-Reconstruction era as a tool—along with the poll tax and literacy requirements—to prevent blacks from availing themselves of the political clout that the Thirteenth, Fourteenth, and Fifteenth Amendments of the U.S. Constitution promised. White legislators of this era boldly asserted their racist desire and expectation that disenfranchisement would diminish the ability of African Americans to secure political power. Thus, southern states required the disenfranchisement of defendants convicted of crimes that the legislature associated with African Americans, although some of these crimes were not, in fact, felonies. These legislatures often refused to require the disenfranchisement of those crimes believed to be primarily committed by whites, such as murder, even though these crimes were much more severe than the offenses associated with African Americans, such as theft. The racially influenced categorization of offenses subject to disenfranchisement remained in place until the mid-1980s, when the U.S. Supreme Court struck down Alabama's disenfranchisement scheme, which disenfranchised people for reasons of "moral turpitude."

In the early twenty-first century, legislatures perpetuated and tolerated the predictable racial disparities produced by felony disenfranchisement. The disparate disenfranchisement rates were the product of the racial disparities produced by the criminal justice system. As a result of the targeting of minorities through various efforts waged in the name of the war on drugs and various wars on crime, minorities were disparately prosecuted, convicted, and incarcerated for felonies.

Promoting Felon Voting. *Artist and ex-felon Steve Nighthawk, holding his niece, stands underneath a billboard he designed as part of a Nevada campaign to encourage voter registration among ex-felons.* AP IMAGES.

POLITICAL IMPACT

Felony disenfranchisement has had a political impact. It is generally believed that this demographic tends to lean more to the left than to the right politically. Several critical elections, including the 2000 presidential election, are believed to have been effected by the exclusion of ex-offenders from the electoral process. In each of these circumstances, it is alleged that if liberal-leaning ex-offenders had been permitted to vote, then the more conservative candidate would have lost the election. Instead, in each of these critical races, the more conservative candidate prevailed.

THE RATIONALE

Proponents of felony disenfranchisement justify the practice by pointing to tradition, conventional rationales for criminal punishment, and crime prevention. In medieval England, felony disenfranchisement existed as part of the panoply of disabilities imposed on convicted felons. Felons typically suffered both physical death (incarceration until the imposition of capital punishment) and civil death (the inability to perform civil functions, including the right to vote). Some U.S. states appear to continue felony disenfranchisement merely as a historic practice, although disenfranchisement in early England was of little consequence because most felons were subject to the death penalty. In the United States, however, only murder and treason are subject to the death penalty.

Other proponents of felony disenfranchisement argue that, independent of the legislation's lineage, disenfranchisement is a justified form of punishment based on either a utilitarian or retributive theory of punishment. Thus, proponents argue that disenfranchisement will deter future criminality and represents the felon's just deserts for the breach of societal norms. Finally, felony disenfranchisement is supported as a means to protect "ballot purity." Proponents argue that felony disenfranchisement prevents felons from promoting corrupt agendas through the vote, and that it limits the threat of voter fraud.

CRITICISM

Critics of felony disenfranchisement complain that the practice violates traditional penological objectives and the democratic ideal. They maintain that it violates the goals of rehabilitation and the reintegration of ex-offenders into the community and the body politic. In addition, disenfranchisement schemes are not proportional, thereby violating another goal of criminal sentencing schemes. Critics also question whether felony disenfranchisement can be reconciled with the goals of widespread democratic participation and a commitment to universal suffrage.

INTERNATIONAL COMPARISON AND REFORM

The breadth and extent of felony disenfranchisement legislation in the United States is out of step with the practices of other civilized countries and international law. Most civilized countries have limited or abolished voting restrictions imposed on ex-offenders. Moreover, international human rights organizations argue that disenfranchisement policies within the United States violate international law. In particular, they insist that the imposition of permanent disability and blanket disability on all incarcerated persons violates Article 25 of the International Covenant of Civil and Political Rights, which requires that restrictions on the right to vote be based on grounds that are "objective and reasonable." These organizations argue that disenfranchisement within the United States—which denies all incarcerated persons the right to vote, regardless of offense, and denies to some the right to vote for life—is neither objective nor reasonable.

These organizations also urge that disenfranchisement legislation in the United States violates the International Convention on the Elimination of All Forms of Racial Discrimination (CERD), which has been ratified by the United States. They insist that the scope and the increasing racial impact of this legislation violates CERD's command that states eliminate legislation that restricts the right to vote in a racially disparate manner, regardless of the intention of the legislature.

Legal challenges to disenfranchisement legislation premised on race have generally not been successful. Students of the legislation, therefore, advocate the abandonment of such approaches and the adoption of strategies that target legislative action rather than seek judicial invalidation.

SEE ALSO *Black Reconstruction; Criminal Justice System; Voting Rights Act of 1965.*

BIBLIOGRAPHY

Demleitner, Nora V. 2000. "Continuing Payment on One's Debt to Society: The German Model of Felon Disenfranchisement as an Alternative." *Minnesota Law Review* 84 (4): 753–804.

Gottlieb, Michael J. 2002. "One Person, No Vote: The Laws of Felon Disenfranchisement." *Harvard Law Review* 115 (7): 1939–1963.

Human Rights Watch, and the Sentencing Project. 1998. "Losing the Vote: The Impact of Felony Disenfranchisement Law in the United States." Available from http://www.hrw.org/reports98/vote/.

Lippke, Richard. 2001. "The Disenfranchisement of Felons." *Law and Philosophy* 20 (6): 553–580.

Magee, Robin K. 1994. "Myth of the Good Cop and the Inadequacy of Fourth Amendment Remedies for Black Men." *Capital University Law Review* 23 (1): 151–219.

Preuhs, Robert R. 2001. "State Felon Disenfranchisement Policy." *Social Science Quarterly* 82 (4): 733–748.

Sentencing Project. "Felony Disenfranchisement: A Review of Scholarly Literature." Available from http://www.sentencingproject.org/pdfs/fvrlitreview.pdf.

Robin K. Magee

FEMINISM AND RACE

The term *feminism* means advocacy for the well-being of women in both theoretical and practical ways. In the United States, feminist scholarship and practice in the nineteenth century was dominated by white middle- and upper-class heterosexual Anglo-American women, and the same was true in the twentieth century up until the 1960s. But from about 1970 onward, the concerns of women of color, poor women, and lesbians have become more prominent in feminist discourse, and they have also been explicitly recognized by traditional white feminists, both in the academy and in mainstream organizations such as the National Organization for Women (NOW). Among the women at the forefront of this movement, bell hooks has insisted on a distinct identity for black women, Patricia Hill Collins has argued that black women need to bring their own life knowledge into the field of sociology, and Paula Gunn Allen has shown that women were respected leaders in many indigenous societies before European contact.

Still, at the turn of the twenty-first century, establishment American feminism continued to be mostly white and middle class, although not exclusively heterosexual. However, lesbian feminism has certainly grown as a field of inquiry, particularly through the work of Adrienne Rich, Audre Lorde, Marilyn Frye, Mary Daly, Sheila Jeffreys, and Monique Wittig. Also, some academic feminist scholars during the late twentieth century took up the postmodern theories of French feminists, such as Julia Kristeva and Luce

Irigaray, who provided literary critiques of male-dominated Western culture by criticizing its canonical texts. As Cynthia Willett indicates in *The Soul of Justice* (2001), however, addressing women's problems via such criticism is usually restricted to privileged educated women.

At the same time, women's studies scholars have increased their recognition of feminism and women's problems and social movements in Europe, Latin America, Africa, and Asia. The twenty-first century challenge for feminism is to include all women's voices, and to support and generate social movements that do not divide women by race. When feminism, in both theory and practice, does not include the concerns of women of color, then women of color may view feminism itself as one of the causes of their social disadvantages.

THE HISTORY OF FEMINISM AND RACE

American feminists often refer to their history as comprising three "waves." The first wave occurred between 1790 and 1920. During this period, feminism overtly excluded women of color and was, at times, explicitly racist. The second wave took place between 1950 and 1980, and it began to address social divisions among women based on race. Unfortunately, these attempts at inclusion resulted in a fragmentation of feminism itself. The third wave began after 1980, and it will need to be inclusive across race if feminism is to remain credible as a movement for all women, even though scholarly work by feminists has historically supported a diversity of feminisms.

The first wave began with Mary Wollstonecraft's 1790 publication in England of *Vindication of the Rights of Women*. Wollstonecraft was inspired by the promise of universal human equality in the philosophies that motivated the French Revolution. She argued for the education of girls and the entry of wives and mothers into public life, with full rights as citizens. The philosopher and English political activist John Stuart Mill published *The Subjection of Women* in 1869. Both Wollstonecraft and Mill argued for child custody rights for divorced women, independent property ownership for married women, and suffrage for all women, precisely so that they could better serve their families and contribute to society as wives and mothers. However, those advocating for such rights were focused solely on white middle-class women, who had become overly domesticated and confined to their households after the Industrial Revolution. Wollstonecraft and Mills did not apply their arguments to poor women or women of color, who had always worked outside their homes in fields or factories, or in the homes of white women. For most of these women, such work was necessary to help support their families.

Women did achieve the right to vote in both the United States and Great Britain by 1920. According to the historian Eleanor Flexner, in *Century of Struggle* (1974), as a social and political movement, the achievement of suffrage developed by fits and starts, in ways that were closely related to the abolitionist movement to free the American slaves. Elizabeth Cady Stanton and Lucretia Mott emerged as the leaders of the suffrage movement after the 1848 Seneca Falls Convention in upstate New York. Susan B. Anthony was the great organizer of this movement, while Stanton supplied much of its rhetoric. The Seneca Falls Convention had occurred, at least in part, because female abolitionists were frustrated at not being able to speak publicly against slavery. (Public speaking was generally a privilege reserved for men.) The suffragists were bitterly disappointed that the rights of women were not recognized when slavery was abolished, and some veered toward racist comparisons between themselves and uneducated blacks after blacks were granted suffrage.

As the first wave grew on a state by state basis in the second half of the nineteenth century, a strong women's club movement took shape, especially when temperance, or the outlaw of alcoholic beverages, became a women's issue (many women saw men's drunkenness as a problem for their families). These clubs were mainly restricted to white women. African American women formed their own clubs and civic organizations to secure education in their communities, protest against lynching, and create social standards for new generations (see Hine 1993).

Despite the racism within the first wave of the women's movement, the second wave, as a political movement that brought American women into the workforce and secured entry into higher education, was inspired and assisted by the civil rights movements of the 1960s. The Civil Rights Act of 1964, for example, outlawed discrimination "because of race, color, religion, sex, or national origin." On the theoretical and ideological side, the second wave was inaugurated in the early 1950s through the publications of Betty Friedan's *The Feminine Mystique* and Simone de Beauvoir's *The Second Sex*. Friedan proclaimed that the domestic lives of middle class women obstructed human fulfillment and de Beauvoir argued that women's social differences from men, which were based on ideas about their biological differences, resulted in a second-class status compared to men.

THEORETICAL ISSUES IN FEMINISM AFTER 1970

Throughout the second wave, American women gained unprecedented access to employment and higher education. Colleges and universities supported programs in women's studies, ethnic studies, and Afro-American studies. As a result, feminism developed a theoretical foundation across the humanities, with a strong focus on issues of racial and cultural difference. Supporting such diversity in feminism was an implicit and explicit realization that the capabilities of women and the social roles they occupied were not determined by their female biology, but by historical events, cultural circumstances, and male rule. Indeed, it was on the issue of patriarchy that women of color began to protest that the concerns of white women did not mirror their own. They argued that for women of color, racism was as much or more of a problem than sexism. The questioning of the ability of white feminists to speak for women of color raised wider questions about whether there was one essence that all women shared, which made them *women*. Elizabeth Spelman, in her 1988 book *Inessential Woman*, brought the question of women's commonality to the forefront of feminist theory. However, as Linda Alcoff pointed out in 1989, both the lack of a biological essence and the emphasis on culture could also lead to new oppressive assumptions that the lives of women of color were completely defined and shaped by their cultures. From the perspective of women of color, a new branch of feminism, known as *intersectionality*, developed. Proponents of intersectionality—such as Kimberle Crenshaw, in legal studies, and Irene Browne and Joya Misra, writing about labor markets in 2003—have held that women's "genders," or their social and economic roles and experiences, are a result of both racism and economic factors. Out of this perspective came the well-known equation, "race + class = gender." This means that women of color have different "genders" than white women. Insofar as theorists such as Judith Butler have viewed biological sex as an effect of social factors and beliefs, or as a social construction, feminism itself has become very divided according to racial divisions. It would likely be further divided according to class, except that poor women rarely have a direct voice in theoretical discourse.

FEMINISM AND WOMEN'S PROBLEMS IN THE TWENTY-FIRST CENTURY

At the beginning of the twenty-first century, there was wide recognition among U.S. feminists that the women's movement is global, and that much can be learned from feminisms in less affluent and more traditional cultures, and from those societies that are more proactive about women's rights and concerns. Women's groups in India, Latin America and Russia, for example, have often gained political support, not through advocacy of equality between women and men, but through demands for governmental and social support for women as wives and mothers. Throughout Africa and Southeast Asia, the practice of microfinance (usually taking the form of loans to women of several hundred dollars or less) and outright gifts of domestic animals have been important contributions to the family well-being of poor women responsible for providing food to their children and relatives. In Latin America and Russia, mothers' groups have effectively prevailed on government and military authorities to furnish information about missing husbands, sons, and brothers who have died or suffered in military service. In Norway after the 1970s, it became a legal requirement that 40 percent of all members of parliament be female, with the understanding among political elites that women in government have stronger interests in family welfare and social well-being issues than do men. Moreover, Norway's "Credo on Difference" recognizes that the political inclusion of "women's issues," such as education, pensions, and welfare, on the top tier of the national agenda benefits all members of society, and not just women.

As Gayle Rubin has pointed out, and as feminist followers of Karl Marx have stressed, women perform work in agricultural and industrial societies, which enables male heads of household to do their paid labor. Mothers are still not paid for child rearing, housework, social tasks, and other parts of "women's work," so that many women who work outside of their homes must also perform a "second shift" without compensation. While women have secured the vote, child custody rights after divorce, and reproductive autonomy, they are still not fully the political equals of men, in even the most affluent Western countries. Those women who do participate in political leadership, even women of color (e.g., Condoleezza Rice, who became the U.S. secretary of state in 2005), often do so without special attention to the concerns of women or people of color.

Intersectionality and the "second shift" problem present a challenge to feminism: Is it possible for feminism to be both a system of belief and a source of change in the world that furthers the interests of all women? For this to occur, it is necessary to recognize the historical disadvantages of women and their future potential, and to acknowledge both what women have in common and the ways in which they are different. One way that feminist theorists could do this would be to abandon attempts to posit a common essence in all women, and instead view women as human beings who have been assigned to, or identify with, a group that makes up at least half of humankind. To be assigned to this group or identify with it would not mean that one had to be a mother, a man's heterosexual choice, or a female at birth, but only that this was one's social identity. Surely it is as mothers, men's heterosexual choices, and human females that women have suffered the problems that first led to feminism and women's movements in many different social, national, cultural, and racial/ethnic contexts. Such a common basis for women's social identity would not negate the real-life differences, demands, and expectations of justice experienced by women on account of their racial diversity. It would allow women to come together across their racial differences to address common problems, such as the second shift, while they continue to think about and act against specific race-based problems.

SEE ALSO *Antiracist Social Movements; Asian-American Feminism; Black Feminism in Brazil; Black Feminism in the United Kingdom; Black Feminism in the United States; Chicana Feminism; Sexism.*

BIBLIOGRAPHY

Afshar, Haleh, ed. 1996. *Women and Politics in the Third World.* London: Routledge.

Alcoff, Linda M. 1989. "Cultural Feminism versus Post-Structuralism: The Identity Crisis in Feminist Theory." In *Feminist Theory in Practice and Process*, edited by Micheline R. Malson, Jean F. O'Barr, Sarah Westphal-Whil, and Mary Wyer, 295–326. Chicago: University of Chicago Press.

Allen, Paula Gunn. 1986. *The Sacred Hoop: Recovering the Feminine in American Indian Traditions.* Boston: Beacon Press.

Browne, Irene, and Joya Misra. 2003. "The Intersection of Gender and Race in the Labor Market." *Annual Review of Sociology* 29: 487–513.

Collins, Patricia Hill. 1990. *Black Feminist Thought: Knowledge, Consciousness, and the Politics of Empowerment.* Boston: Unwin Hyman.

Flexner, Eleanor. 1972. *Century of Struggle: The Woman's Rights Movement in the United States.* New York: Atheneum.

Hine, Darlene Clark, ed. *Black Women in America: An Historical Encyclopedia,* 2 Vols. Brooklyn, NY: Carlson, 1993.

hooks, bell. 1981. *Ain't I A Woman: Black Women and Feminism.* Boston: South End Press.

Moi, Toril. 1985. *Sexual/Textual Politics: Feminist Literary Theory.* London: Methuen.

Nicholson, Linda J., ed. 1997. *The Second Wave: A Reader in Feminist Theory.* New York: Routledge.

Rubin, Gayle. 1997. "The Traffic in Women: Notes on the 'Political Economy' of Sex." In *The Second Wave: A Reader in Feminist Theory*, edited by Linda J. Nicholson, 27–62. New York: Routledge.

Skjeie, Hege. 1998. "Credo on Difference: Women in Parliament in Norway." In *Women in Parliament: Beyond Numbers.* Stockholm, Sweden: International Institute for Democracy and Electoral Assistance. Available from http://www.idea.int/publications/wip/upload/CS_Norway.pdf.

Spelman, Elizabeth V. 1988. *Inessential Woman: Problems of Exclusion in Feminist Thought.* Boston: Beacon Press.

Willett, Cynthia. 2001. *The Soul of Justice: Social Bonds and Racial Hubris.* Ithaca, NY: Cornell University Press.

Zack, Naomi. 2005. *Inclusive Feminism: A Third Wave Theory of Women's Commonality.* Lanham, MD: Rowman & Littlefield.

Naomi Zack

FILM

SEE *Filmography* in the Appendix at the end of Volume 3.

FILM AND ASIAN AMERICANS

Cinema representations of Asians and Asian Americans are rooted in the history of Euro-American colonial occupation and military struggles with China, the Philippines, Korea, Japan, and Vietnam. Euro-American, or "white," racial identity was used as a form of ideological control that helped to sustain the political subordination of colonial subjects. Asian Americans are the heirs of these images, which take on additional colorations when extended to the U.S. setting, because of the supposed competitive threat Asian Americans pose to white power and native-born nonwhites, African Americans in particular. Further, Asians and Asian Americans often function as totems that help forge and maintain white racial identity. Michael Rogin (1998) has observed that the immigrant Jews (and Greeks) who commercialized the movie industry staked their claim to white racial membership by producing films that reinforced the social subordination of native peoples, Latinos, Blacks, and Asian Americans.

EARLY MOTION PICTURES

The stock characterizations of Asians and Asian Americans (predominantly Chinese) found in early cinema are a legacy of a vital and robust vaudeville tradition, through which ideas on race-power, ethnic politics, and white racial nationalism were articulated on stage. Through music, song, and dance, vaudeville served as a key institution in the formation of white racial identity among mid- to late nineteenth-century European immigrant groups such as the Irish, who won white racial privilege by lampooning Negroes and Orientals, especially the Chinese (Roediger 1999). By the 1880s, leading into the age of cinema, Chinese and Chinese Americans had been racialized in vaudeville performance in a manner that clearly marked them as socially subordinate to white people of all social classes (Moon 2005).

The exterminationist military campaigns against Native Americans, known as the "Indian Wars"; the holocaust of African slavery; the annexation of what was once northern Mexico in 1848; and the exploitation and subsequent ban in 1882 on Chinese "coolie" labor all occurred before the commercial motion picture began to take form during the last decade of the nineteenth century. It is no coincidence that Edison kinetoscopes dating from the mid- to late-1890s featured Indian performers in Buffalo Bill's Wild West Show, the black male dancers of Lucy Daly's Pickaninnies, knife-dueling and lasso-throwing Mexicans, and genre scenes of Chinese laundries (Musser 1991). Whether immigrant, native-born working class, or bourgeois, the diverse white audience could share equally in celebrating the consolidation of the U.S. racial republic via the moving image.

THE CINEMA OF RACE-WAR

In the same way that the nascent art of early motion pictures assisted in the ideological strengthening of white privilege and power, the industry was put to the service of the state by glorifying the bloody military campaigns of early

Charlie Chan. *A scene from* Charlie Chan in Panama. *The Charlie Chan films were an extremely popular series in the 1930s and 1940s that featured a non-Asian actor starring as a Chinese private detective* © JOHN SPRINGER COLLECTION/CORBIS.

imperial America. Victorious in the Spanish-American War (1898), the United States ceded the Philippines by the tottering empire that had once controlled much of the New World. When Filipino nationalists during the Philippine-American War (1899-1902) resisted the colonial ambitions of the United States, the Kinetograph Department of the Edison Manufacturing Company helped feed American jingoist fervor by staging re-enactments of military clashes between the contending armies, offering such titles as *Advance of Kansas Volunteers at Caloocan* (1899) and *Filipinos Retreat from Trenches* (1899). Thus began one hundred years of documentary and narrative race-war movies pitting the United States against the Asian enemy of the moment. Anti-Asian American racism within the U.S. homeland, simmering since the mid-nineteenth century, could rapidly be brought to a boil against foreign enemies during times of war. It was through the Philippine-American War that the term *gook* entered the American lexicon, courtesy of U.S. military personnel who used the epithet to disparage the natives. The "mere gook rule," whereby the life of an Asian was worth substantially less than that of a white American, was subsequently applied to a succession of militarist movies, including countless World War II patriotic epics, Korean War action films such as *Fixed Bayonets* (1951) and *Pork Chop Hill* (1957), and post–Vietnam War victory fantasies such as *Missing in Action* (1984) and *Rambo: First Blood, Part II* (1985) (Hamamoto 1994).

At the midpoint of the Vietnam War, films such as *55 Days at Peking* (1963) and *The Sand Pebbles* (1966)—both set in China as it was being carved up by the Western imperial powers—gave dramatic legitimacy to the history of U.S. military intervention in Asia. Only during the latter stages of the Vietnam War did select movies begin to diverge from the propagandistic function of earlier features such as John Wayne's celebratory *The Green Berets* (1968). Although set in the Korean War, *M*A*S*H* (1970) stood as a perversely comedic gloss on the U.S. military presence in Vietnam. Despite the liberal humanism conveyed in antiwar narrative films, they persisted in placing white Americans in the foreground while relegating Asians to roles that functioned primarily as local color. Although overtly antimilitarist in its burlesque of the Vietnam War, even *Full Metal Jacket* (1987) failed to rise above predictable scenes such as that featuring an exchange between a Vietnamese streetwalker ("Me so horny. Me love you long time.") and two white servicemen. As an American colonel expresses it in this classic Stanley Kubrick film, "We are here to help the Vietnamese, because inside every gook, there is an American trying to get out."

In the cinema of empire, Asian racial identity serves only a totemic function for the white American protagonist struggling to think through existential dilemmas. The bedrock reality of white-dominant race-power, however, goes unquestioned even in seemingly "progressive" antiwar movies such as *The Killing Fields* (1984), based on the real-life experiences of the American journalist Sydney Shanberg and the Cambodian photojournalist Dith Pran.

NATIONALISM AND ECONOMIC CRISIS

During the post-Vietnam War period, the historically rooted battle against Asians moved from jungle warfare to open competition in the economic arena. East Asian nations such as Japan and South Korea benefited from the erosion of U.S. economic dominance, which was partly due to the enormous fiscal resources expended in maintaining its global military presence. As crises began to mount among an American public being squeezed by mass job loss attended by fundamental economic restructuring, Asians and Asian Americans once more were put into service as racial scapegoats by the corporate moviemaking industry. In *Rising Sun* (1993)—adapted from the best-seller by Michael Crichton—police detective Capt. John Connor (Sean Connery) teamed with Lt. Web Smith (Wesley Snipes) to unravel a murder mystery involving a Japanese corporation. The film is noteworthy for its enlisting of African Americans by the white power structure to fight a common Asian enemy.

The social drama *Falling Down* (1993) captured the mounting anxieties of the violently reactionary "angry white male" in the character of William "D-Fens" Foster (Michael Douglas). An early scene has D-Fens brutalizing a Korean American shopkeeper whom he berates for speaking nonstandard English in "his" country. He angrily asks, "You have any idea how much money *my* country has given *your* country?" before trashing the store with a sawed-off baseball bat.

INTERRACIAL TENSIONS

Through the 1990s and into the early years of the 2000s, the further contraction of the U.S. economy, the massive export of jobs overseas, record levels of immigration, and the economic challenge represented by East Asian nations led to an intensification of racial conflict. Spike Lee's *Do the Right Thing* (1989), anticipating the Los Angeles Riot of 1991, dramatized the tensions that had developed among blacks, Latinos, and Asian Americans during the post–civil rights era, as each group contended for diminishing economic resources. Predating the Spike Lee film by several years, the futuristic *Blade Runner* (1982) offered the spectacle of Latinos, Asians, and Blacks slithering among each other in a dark, dystopian vision of the future.

Through the 1990s, African Americans were deployed more directly against Asians and Asian Americans. In *Lethal Weapon 4* (1998), blacks, white ethnics, and a white feminist are aligned with white power (as personified by Mel Gibson) against the yellow enemy, personified by the character Wah Sing Ku (played by respected *Wushu* master and international film star Jet Li). In *The Art of War* (2000), Neil Shaw (Wesley Snipes) is an operative with a covert diplomacy program sponsored unofficially by the United Nations. Here, a black man, wielding appropriated martial arts skills, vanquishes a slew of Asian villains and ends up with the prized yellow woman (Julia Fang, played by Marie Matiko) thus recapitulating the history of African Americans being recruited by white power to fight the Asian enemy.

Rush Hour (1998) featured Jackie Chan and Chris Tucker in a yellow-black buddy film, while *Romeo Must Die* (2000) paired Jet Li with the pop singer Aaliyah. The conflicts driving these movies were rooted in tense interracial relations caused by jobs lost to low-wage Asian nations and the perceived threat posed by the rapid rise in Asian immigration to the United States. The comedy *Next Friday* (2000) offered a parable of post–Los Angeles Riot race relations, bringing together a troublesome Latino household, a Korean-American woman, and an African-American family, all of whom have fled the central city for the relative security of the suburban cul-de-sac they share.

ALTERNATIVES

The recruitment by Hollywood of successful Asian directors such as John Woo might appear to present opportunities for bringing about more equitable representations of Asian Americans in cinema. Such hopes are misplaced, however, because the net effect of U.S.-based companies in hiring foreign-born directors has been to stave-off competition from overseas film production, while also raising the quality of domestic product through the innovations of artists such as Woo (Miller et al. 2005). In any case, Woo himself seems content to put his stylistic imprint on conventional U.S. action movies featuring white actors (Fang 2004). The Taiwan-born director Ang Lee fared well in documenting the rich lives of transnational Asian Americans in his earlier films, such as

Pushing Hands (1992) and *The Wedding Banquet* (1993). But once having established his credentials, Lee was enlisted to direct a succession of films with the white world as their focus. Even the glorious *wuxia* pastiche *Crouching Tiger, Hidden Dragon* (2000) was primarily intended for a non-Asian mainstream audience. Lee's winning of the Academy Award for Best Director in 2006 for *Brokeback Mountain* (2005) caps his passage into the white cinema establishment.

Better Luck Tomorrow (2002), directed by Justin Lin, features an all–Asian American cast and explores dark themes that go far beyond those of most of the other narrative films coming out of the vital Asian-American independent media movement that began during the late 1960s (Hamamoto and Liu 2000). Despite the critical acclaim enjoyed by this distinctively Asian-American film, Lin was lured by Hollywood to direct *Annapolis* (2006) and *The Fast and the Furious: Tokyo Drift* (2006), and will be remaking a Korean drama, with white people occupying the central roles. As talented Asian and Asian-American filmmakers are brought into the corporate moviemaking fold, there is little expectation that Asian Americans themselves will benefit substantively from having a co-ethnic in the director's chair. Rather, the primary challenge to white dominance in commercial filmmaking will continue to spring from the Asian-American independent media arts movement.

BIBLIOGRAPHY

Fang, Karen. 2004. *John Woo's* A Better Tomorrow. Hong Kong: Hong Kong University Press.

Hamamoto, Darrell. 1994. *Monitored Peril: Asian Americans and the Politics of TV Representation.* Minneapolis: University of Minnesota Press.

———, and Sandra Liu, eds. 2000. *Countervisions: Asian American Independent Film Criticism.* Philadelphia, PA: Temple University Press.

Library of Congress. "The Spanish-American War in Motion Pictures." Available from http://memory.loc.gov/ammem.

Miller, Toby, et al. 2005. *Global Hollywood 2.* London: British Film Institute.

Moon, Krystyn R. 2005. *Yellowface: Creating the Chinese in American Popular Music and Performance, 1850s–1920s.* New Brunswick, NJ: Rutgers University Press.

Musser, Charles. 1991. *Before the Nickelodeon: Edwin S. Porter and the Edison Manufacturing Company.* Berkeley: University of California Press.

Roediger, David R. 1991. *The Wages of Whiteness: Race and the Making of the American Working Class,* rev. ed. New York: Verso.

Rogin, Michael. 1996. *Blackface, White Noise: Jewish Immigrants in the Hollywood Melting Pot.* Berkeley: University of California Press.

Darrell Y. Hamamoto

FIRMIN, ANTÉNOR
1850–1911

Anténor Firmin was the author of a pioneering work in race and anthropology, *De l'égalité des races humaines: Anthropologie positive* (1885). He was perhaps the first anthropologist of African descent. Firmin was born into a working class family on October 18, 1850, in Cap-Haitien in northern Haiti. His formal education was entirely in Haiti and included the study of the classics and exposure to the anthropological writings of European scholars. After studying law in Haiti, he became a successful advocate in Cap-Haitien; he later became a diplomat.

Firmin was a product of the third generation of post-independence Haitians who took justified pride in the heroic achievement of the world's first black republic (Haiti became independent on January 1, 1804). While serving as a diplomat in Paris from 1884 to 1888, he was admitted to the Paris Anthropological Society, where he was one of three Haitians to observe their proceedings (though he was not encouraged to participate). In those years the Anthropology Society of Paris was dedicated primarily to racialist anthropometry and craniometry, and to racist interpretations of human physical data. In the preface to his book, Firmin wrote that he considered requesting a debate within the society on the issue of the division of the human species into superior and inferior races, "but I risked being perceived as an intruder and, being ill-disposed against me, my colleagues might have rejected my request without further thought. Common sense told me I was right to hesitate so it was then that I conceived the idea of writing this book" (2000, p. liv).

Anténor Firmin's *De l'égalité des races humaines* was a general response to European racialist and racist thought in the nineteenth century. However, the title suggests that his scientific rebuttal was especially directed at the work of Arthur de Gobineau, whose four-volume work *Essai sur l'inégalité des races humaines* (Essay on the inequality of the human race) (1853–1855) asserted a hierarchical ranking of races from white to yellow to Negro, as well as the racial superiority of Aryan peoples. Now available in English, *The Equality of the Human Races* (2000) can be studied by a wider audience as a remarkable yet obscure work of anthropology and early critical-race thinking. This nineteenth-century work anticipated the eventual scope and breadth of anthropology beyond the narrow, racialist physical "science" that it critiqued.

Contrary to de Gobineau's ideas of racial hierarchy and Negro inferiority, Firmin's work affirmed the opposite, that "All men are endowed with the same qualities and the same faults, without distinction of color or anatomical form. The races are equal" (2000, p. 450). As Ashley Montagu noted, "It is a fact worth remarking that throughout the nineteenth century hardly more than a handful of scientific voices were raised against the notion of a hierarchy of races" (1997, p. 80). Subtitled *Anthropologie Positive,* Firmin was a committed positivist, and he argued that the empirical study of humanity would disprove speculative theories about the inequality of races.

De l'égalité des races humaines contained 662 pages of text with twenty chapter headings, some of which are "Anthropology as a Discipline"; "Monogenism and Polygenism"; "Criteria for Classifying the Human Races"; "Artificial Ranking of the Human Races"; "Comparison of the Human Races Based on their Physical Constitution"; "*Métissage* and Equality of the Races"; "Egypt and Civilization"; "The Hindus and the Arya"; "European Solidarity"; "The Role of the Black Race in the History of Civilization"; "Religious Myths and Words of the Ancients"; and "Theories and their Logical Consequences."

Firmin criticized the prevailing polygenist use of craniology and anthropometry espoused by Paul Broca and others (which came to be referred to as "scientific racism"). In fact, he used the craniometric tables devised by these scholars as a basis for their refutation. He critiqued their numeric tables of differential measures of cranial capacity, brain weight, nasal index, and stature, and he showed that the claims of European superiority based on these measures were arbitrary and lacking in logical consistency and scientific rigor. With his attack on the scientific misuse of racial craniometry, Firmin challenged anthropometry, which was the hallmark of nineteenth-century anthropology.

Firmin's introductory chapter "Anthropology as a Discipline" may be one of the earliest statements outlining the new comprehensive science of anthropology, which he defined as "the study of Man in his physical, intellectual, and moral dimensions as he is found in any of the different races which constitute the human species" (2000, p. 10). He thus envisioned anthropology as an integrated study of humanity.

Although the concept of race had already shaped nineteenth-century scholarship, Firmin questioned the underlying biological premise of race. He critiqued the racial mythology of his day, and he was one of only a few black scholars addressing the subject. "Observing that human beings have always interbred whenever they have come in contact with one another," he maintained, "the very notion of pure races becomes questionable" (p. 64). Firmin noted that classification by race led to theories of difference that ultimately led science away from the unitary view of the human species and spawned ideas of separate evolution and development of the races. Firmin was among the first to insist that racial typologies are not only flawed as individual isolates—Ethiopian/black or Caucasian/white—but that these "inclusive" types fail to acknowledge or account for the vigor and achievements of New World hybrid populations. The failure of the racial classifiers to include in their typologies the mixed races (*métis*)—not only in the New World, but in other parts of the globe as well—made him even more skeptical about any "science" of racial types.

Firmin stressed the scientific basis for the constitutional unity of the human species arguing that all groups retain the primordial constitutional imprint of the species, bearing the same intellectual and moral traits inscribed in the original common human blueprint. He discussed the multiple factors of climate and geography that affect skin color (as well as physical form), and he was among the first scholars to state the scientific basis for skin pigmentation—the substance melanin in the epithelial cells of the dermis. Responding to the claim of the French naturalist Jean Louis Armand de Quatrefages that black people sweat less than whites, Firmin responded with the voice of authority of a black man: "I am Black and nothing distinguishes me anatomically from the purest Sudanese. However, I transpire abundantly enough to be able to have some idea of the facts. My congeners are not beyond the laws of nature" (2000, p. 60). Firmin also dismissed the racist myth about black odor: "I shall not bother to discuss the issue of a putative *sui generis* odor that is supposedly a particular characteristic of the Negro race. The idea is more comical than scientific" (p. 62–63).

As a student of African antiquity, Firmin read and cited the leading Egyptologists of the day, including the Egyptologist Jean-Francois Champollion, from whom he took the Egyptian hieroglyphic word *Retous,* meaning "real humans," which he adopted as a general term for the original African people. He recognized the historical ties in the Nile Valley between Nubia and Egypt as distinctive African civilizations. He saluted African history in the Nile Valley from "Memphis to Meroë," thus including the Sudanese civilizations of Kush-Meroë, referred to as "Ethiopia" in Greek texts. This stands in sharp contrast to Samuel Morton's "Caucasoid Egyptians" and the "Hamitic Myth," which denied the ability of black Africans to create civilizations. His analysis of the nonracist images of blacks in the classical European civilizations of Greece and Rome presaged comparable findings in the latter half of the twentieth century. His critique about skin color and myth—including the biblical myth of the "Curse of Ham"; the plethora of associations of blackness with evil and the devil in Europe; and Shakespeare's choice of a dark Moor for Othello—all have a thoroughly modern resonance with postcolonial literary criticism.

Among the early writers to view Egyptian civilization as the fountainhead from which sprang the Greek and Roman cultures, he saw the development of their culture as resting upon an African foundation. Not only was the ancient past an affirmation of the equality of the black race, but the modern example of Haiti proved the essential thesis once again. As a symbol of black regeneration, it was not surprising that Haitians would play a role in the Pan-African movement that began in the closing years of the nineteenth century. Firmin attended the First Pan-African Conference in London in 1900, along with W.E.B. Du Bois of the United States, Henry Sylvester Williams of Trinidad, and delegates from Abssyinia, Liberia, South Africa, Sierre Leone, Gold Coast, and Canada.

While critical of race classifications and racial hierarchies, Firmin did not reject the concept of race. Too much was vested in the concept by late nineteenth-century scholars for him to dismiss race, and he made liberal use of the proclamation of black racial pride. Pan-Africanism and the link between Haiti, black people in the diaspora, and the greatness of African antiquity depended upon the race concept, as is still largely true in the early twenty-first century.

Firmin believed that positivist science would lead to an acceptance of the doctrine of the equality of the human races. But he was also a humanist. He believed this doctrine to be a regenerative force for the harmonious development of humankind. The last words of his 1885 tome invoke Victor Hugo's famous quote—"Every man is man"—and implore every human simply to "Love one another" (2000, p. 451).

SEE ALSO *Anthropometry; Haitian Racial Formations; Racial Hierarchy; Scientific Racism, History of.*

BIBLIOGRAPHY

Firmin, Anténor. 2000 (1885). *The Equality of the Human Races: Positivist Anthropology.* Translated by Asselin Charles; with an introduction by Carolyn Fluehr-Lobban. New York: Garland. Paperback edition, University of Illinois Press, 2002.

Fluehr-Lobban, Carolyn. 2000. "Anténor Firmin: Haitian Pioneer of Anthropology." *American Anthropologist* 102 (3): 449–466.

———. "Anténor Firmin and Haiti's Contribution to Anthropology." *Gradhiva, revue d'anthropologie et de muséologie*, No. 1 nouvelle série, Paris.

Montagu, Ashley. 1997 (1942). *Man's Most Dangerous Myth: The Fallacy of Race.* Walnut Creek, CA: AltaMira Press.

Price-Mars, Jean. 1964. *Joseph Anténor Firmin.* Port-au-Prince, Haiti: Imprint Séminaire.

Carolyn Fluehr-Lobban

FOLK CLASSIFICATION

Scientists believe that folk classifications of human groups, or "races," are distinct from, and must have preceded, those the scientific community began devising in the eighteenth century. Such classifications (usually ethnocentric) were part of the written record centuries before the birth of Christ. Early travelers distinguished foreign groups according to their obvious physical traits, such as skin color or hair form, but more subtle distinctions were made at home, between "Ourselves" and those "Others" who lived nearby. Folk taxonomies categorized "Us," with flattering and exaggerated claims of superior intelligence, greater sexual prowess, or cleanliness (e.g., "'We' understand at a much deeper level than other societies the way God meant the world to operate"), "Them," with their inferior understandings of human civility, failure to observe incest prohibitions or food taboos (e.g., "'They' are cannibals, fond of rude practices and marrying their sisters").

A fifth-century BCE example comes from the writings of Aristotle, who characterized his northern (European) neighbors as hotheaded and difficult, while his southern (Eastern Mediterranean) neighbors were lazy and careless. In between, his own people (those now called Greeks) were blessed with what Aristotle believed was just the right mixture of intelligence and industry. A more recent example from anthropological investigations: often the tribal name given to one's own group meant "human beings," while the name for a neighboring group, e.g., Navajo, meant something like "those sub-human thieves over there." The Navajo call themselves *Dinee*, which in their language means "humans."

The ethnocentric biases that accompanied Us-Them distinctions were carried over into what were considered "scientific" studies of human differences. In 1735 Carl Linnaeus published the first edition of his *Systema Natura*, in which he included humans as one species, undivided into races (a designation contemporary biologists would agree with). In subsequent editions, however, Linnaeus included four human "varieties," mainly based on geography: Asian, African, European, and North American. These included physical characteristics such as skin color as well as "temperamental" or psychological characteristics. Europeans were characterized as "light and lively," while Africans were "choleric" and lazy, Asians were "crafty," and North Americans were "impotent." These fanciful imputations were to increase greatly in later classificatory schemes, such as that of the German anthropologist Johann Friedrich Blumenbach (1752–1840). Scientific racism, or the linking of learned or cultural traits to real or imagined physical characteristics, may have been born in Linnaeus's writings, but its subsequent growth and development owed more to Blumenbach and his colleagues, who never hesitated to include traits from highly biased folk classifications in their scientific categories.

Definitional debates about what constituted a human "race" continued over the next centuries, and by the 1940s as many as two hundred "races" had been defined. In the minds of many social scientists, the question of whether human races even existed was moot by the time most of these discussions ceased, soon after the extent of Hitler's atrocities in the name of "racial purity" became known. In the 1930s, Hitler had declared that although he did not believe in it, the idea of race was one that served his purposes: "I know perfectly well that in a scientific sense there is no such thing as race . . . but I as a politician need a conception which enables the order which has hitherto existed on historic bases to be abolished and an entirely new and antihistoric order enforced and given an intellectual basis. . . . And for this purpose the conception of races serves me well" (quoted in Shanklin 1994, p. 10).

Since the 1940s, there has been a debate in anthropology about the wisdom or necessity of discarding the term "race," and an increasing number of pro-race debaters have come to concede the point (Lieberman and Jackson 1995). Thus, as a scientific concept, race has lost its salience, despite occasional misplaced attempts at rekindling stereotypes, as in the insouciant use of the term by Richard Herrnstein and Charles Murray in their book *The Bell Curve* (1994), or misguided usages, such as those retained in forensic anthropology and displayed at length in the unfortunate debate over Kennewick Man's "status" as Caucasian (Brace 1995a and 1995b). Once race was discarded as a biological concept in the late twentieth century, scientists adopted and continue to use evolutionary systematics to distinguish species, especially cladistics, which distinguishes features of common descent from those that are derived.

There is hope in this change in the discourse of both social and biological sciences, though it should not be taken as evidence that "racial" categories arising from folk classifications of hereditary and learned characteristics have lost their venomous power. The scientific rejection of the idea of human "races" has not resolved the problems of the persistence of racism, prejudice, stereotyping, and ethnocentrism. To the extent that this kind of discriminatory thinking has its origins in the human socialization process and in folk classifications biased in favor of membership in a particular in-group, it remains for social scientists to find ways of countering the biases against "others" that may have been part of the socialization process since time immemorial.

SEE ALSO *Human and Primate Evolution; Kennewick Man.*

BIBLIOGRAPHY

Brace, C. Loring. 1995a. "Biocultural Interaction and The Mechanism of Mosaic Evolution in the Emergence of 'Modern' Morphology." *American Anthropologist* 97 (4): 711–721.

———. 1995b. "Region Does Not Mean Race: Reality vs. Convention in Forensic Identification." *Journal of Forensic Sciences* 40 (2): 171–175.

Lieberman, Leonard, and Fatimah Linda C. Jackson. 1995. "Race and Three Models of Human Origin." *American Anthropologist* 97 (2): 231–242.

Shanklin, Eugenia. 1994. *Anthropology and Race.* Belmont CA: Wadsworth.

Eugenia Shanklin

FOOTBALL (U.S.)

Institutional racism and individual racism have been fundamental components of sports in America. The playing fields of America were slowly integrated in the twentieth century, and in the twenty-first century the struggle has shifted to equity in off-the-field opportunities.

EARLY ORGANIZED SPORTS

The growth of the American sporting scene began during the mid-nineteenth century and then accelerated after the Civil War, primarily as a result of urbanization and industrialization. Sadly, participation in this growing sporting experience was greatly affected by race and racism. As America embraced formal legal segregation toward the end of the century, the eviction of African Americans from many professional sports was already underway. African Americans were involved in all of the major popular sports of the late nineteenth and early twentieth centuries, ranging from horse racing, baseball, and bicycling to boxing and football. Black athletes were systematically removed from all professional sports with the creation of formal color barriers by the early twentieth century. Professional football was one of the last sports to force black athletes out of its ranks by the 1930s, but one of the first to reintegrate beginning in 1946.

The sport of football has intersected with notions of race in a number of ways. It has been a stage on which ideas about racial superiority and inferiority have played out, and it has been a means for promoting social mobility. In exploring the social history of race and football, one sees the development of "racial" integration, racial separateness by position, the rise of black coaches, racial epithets about football players, and finally the internationalization of the sport.

THE BEGINNING OF ORGANIZED FOOTBALL

The National Football League (NFL) included black players from its inception in 1920, but a color barrier was created after the 1933 season; there was then a reintegration of pro football beginning in 1946. Professional football evolved from local athletic clubs, and these clubs traced their beginnings to college football. In 1869

Princeton and Rutgers played the first intercollegiate football game in the United States. By the 1880s and 1890s football was a central feature of all college social life, including that of African Americans. In 1892 Biddle College (now Johnson C. Smith College in Charlotte, NC) took on and defeated Livingstone College, 4-0, in Salisbury, North Carolina, marking the first intercollegiate football game between historically black schools.

The first black player to play at a white college was William Henry Lewis, who played center for both Amherst College and Harvard beginning in 1888. Lewis also became the first black player to be selected as an All-American when he was placed on Walter Camp's prestigious 1892 and 1893 teams. Several other black players followed Lewis: William Tecumseh Sherman Jackson was a halfback and teammate of Lewis at Amherst in 1890; George Jewett was a punter, field-goal kicker, and halfback at the University of Michigan in 1890. William Arthur Johnson played halfback at the Massachusetts Institute of Technology that same year; George A. Flippin starred at halfback from 1892 to 1894 at the University of Nebraska; and William Lee Washington lettered at Oberlin as a halfback from 1895 to 1897.

More than fifty black players played on white college teams from 1889 through 1920. However, there were seldom more than two blacks on one team, and most white schools had no black players at all. Likewise, professional football was not about to embrace African-American athletes during this golden age of legal segregation, and, as in college football, only a few opportunities were extended to black players, beginning with the first black professional, Charles Follis. In 1904 the Shelby Athletic Club signed Follis to a contract to play halfback. Follis's professional career only lasted three seasons, because white players went out of their way to hurt him. Leg and shoulder injuries eventually forced him from the game. While helping the Shelby team to several wins with his dazzling runs, Follis was the frequent victim of opposing players' knuckles and knees, and fans subjected him to constant taunts and racial epithets. Nevertheless, he laid the foundation for other black players to follow during this period of limited integration.

Following in the shadow of Follis were three other black professionals who played prior to the 1920 formation of the American Professional Football Association, which changed its name to the National Football League in 1922. In 1906 Charles "Doc" Baker played halfback for the Akron Indians. He was followed by Henry McDonald, a running back for the Oxford (NY) Pros in 1911 and the Rochester Jeffersons in 1912. The last African American to play during this pre-NFL era was Gideon E. Smith, who played for the Canton Bulldogs in 1915. Smith played only once during the 1915 season, at tackle, making him the last black to play professional football before the formation of the APFA. During its first three decades of existence, the newly formed NFL desperately competed with college football for attention. Ivy League teams and college teams in the Midwest and on the West Coast drew fans in numbers that NFL owners could only envy. But this did allow several black stars from the college ranks to be extended opportunities in hopes of drawing fans. The Akron Pros brought on Fritz Pollard from Brown University in 1919 and one year later Akron signed the Rutgers player Paul Robeson, who would later achieve fame as a singer, actor, and civil rights activist. Joe Lillard left Oregon and played for the Chicago Cardinals during the 1932 and 1933 seasons.

It appears that by this time black players had fulfilled their roles as curiosity objects for white fans, and that the NFL had established itself as a legitimate sport. The black player, therefore, was no longer needed to help in this process. No black players played on NFL teams after the 1933 season, until Kenny Washington and Woody Strode were added to roster of the Los Angeles Rams during the 1946 season. Bill Willis and Marion Motley played with the Cleveland Browns during the 1946 season as well, in the newly formed All-American Football Conference.

FOOTBALL AFTER WORLD WAR II

Arguably, sports was the first arena in American society to undergo postwar integration, and football led the way. One full year before Jackie Robinson took the field with the Brooklyn Dodgers in 1947, Washington, Strode, Willis, and Motley were playing a contact sport with white players. These four pioneers laid the foundation for the reintegration of pro football, which was finally completed during the 1962 season when the Washington Redskins desegregated by adding Bobby Mitchell, Leroy Jackson, John Nisby, and Ron Hatcher. The Redskins were led by a stubborn owner, George Preston Marshall, who finally relented under pressure from the Kennedy administration. Marshall portrayed the Redskins as a team of the South, with southern traditions such as playing "Dixie" at games, which facilitated "rebel" yells from fans.

Postwar College Football. Without question, southern college teams put up the greatest resistance to black participation. Several African Americans were members of squads that played against white teams in the south. In 1951 Johnny Bright, running back for Drake University in Iowa, played in a game against Oklahoma A&M, during which he was intentionally punched in the face and subsequently suffered a broken jaw. In 1955 Marvin Griffin, the governor of Georgia, banned Georgia Tech from playing in the Sugar Bowl against the University of

Pittsburgh, which had a black player, Bobby Grier. Interestingly, students from Georgia Tech marched on the Capital and forced the governor to relent. Grier thus became the first African American to play in the Sugar Bowl. Two years later in 1958, Prentiss Gault became the first black player at a major southern white school when he signed to play at the University of Oklahoma. Gault led the way for other black players at white universities; among those who followed Gault was Jerry LeVias, who played with Southern Methodist University in 1966 as a receiver and was the first African American in the Southwest Athletic Conference (SAC).

In the Atlantic Coast Conference (ACC), Freddie Summers became the first African-American player in 1967 when he played quarterback for Wake Forest University. Two African-American players integrated the Southeastern Conference (SEC) when the University of Kentucky signed Nat Northington and Greg Page in 1966. However, only Northington is credited with breaking the color barrier, for he played against the University of Mississippi as a receiver in 1967. Page had been injured the day before during a drill and was paralyzed; he died from his injuries thirty-eight days later. Northington appeared in three more games before leaving the team.

Kentucky may have initiated the integration of college football in the Deep South, but a game played by the University of Alabama made it acceptable. On September 12, 1970, the University of Southern California, led by Sam "Bam" Cunningham, defeated Alabama in Birmingham, 42 to 21 in a much anticipated matchup that forced many white fans to reevaluate the merits of the black player. Although Alabama coach Paul "Bear" Bryant had a signed black player (who was sitting in the stands), Cunningham's performance validated extending opportunities to African Americans all over the South.

INTEGRATION, POSITION BY POSITION

While the process of integrating both college and professional teams was slow and arduous, black players also faced similar resistance integrating various positions. The unwritten policy of "stacking," or confining black players to specific positions, was embraced by many white coaches, particularly at the professional level. In 1957, when Jim Brown entered the NFL as a running back with the Cleveland Browns, he noticed that black players tended to play running back, receiver, corner back, and on the defensive line. Brown also felt that teams typically carried an even number of black players to avoid having a black player possibly room with a white player on the road. The policy of stacking arguably existed in the NFL until the late 1960s and early 1970s, when positions such as middle linebacker, offensive lineman, and safety began to be integrated.

Ernie Davis, a halfback from Syracuse University was the first African American to be selected first overall in the 1962 NFL draft. The Washington Redskins picked him then traded his rights to the Cleveland Browns for Bobby Mitchell and Leroy Jackson.

The position of quarterback was the last opened to black players. Fritz Pollard, Joe Lillard, and George Taliaferro, an otherwise outstanding halfback, had played quarterback during games only out of necessity. In 1953 the Chicago Bears drafted the black quarterback Willie Thrower out of Michigan State, but they released him before the season ended without giving him any legitimate playing time. In 1955 the Green Bay Packers drafted Charlie Brackins out of Prairie View A&M, but he only played in one game before being released. The first black quarterback to play regularly was Marlin Briscoe, who set records at the University of Omaha before he joined the Denver Broncos of the American Football League in 1968. James Harris, who played at Grambling College, had a twelve-year career, from 1969 to 1981, and played for the Buffalo Bills, Los Angeles Rams, and San Diego Chargers. Arguably, Doug Williams, who played for Grambling before turning professional, helped change forever the perception of the black quarterback in the NFL. In 1987 Williams became the first African American to lead his team (the Washington Redskins) to the Super Bowl. His dominating performance led the Redskins to victory over the Denver Broncos, and Williams shattered the myths of intellectual and athletic shortcomings that had been used to keep black players out of the most important position on the field.

In 2001 Michael Vick became the first African American to be selected as the number one overall draft pick as a quarterback when he was chosen by the Atlanta Falcons. In some ways this represented the crowning achievement for black players in their struggle to integrate football fields across America. It also caused many to change the focus to challenges that African Americans faced off the field.

INTEGRATION OFF THE FIELD

The integration of coaching ranks and administrative positions, both in college and the NFL, has been an ongoing process. In 1981 Dennis Green became the first black college football coach at a predominantly white school when he was hired by Northwestern University. Fritz Pollard co-coached the Akron Pros in the APFA, thus making him the first black coach in professional football. Art Shell was hired by the Oakland Raiders in 1989, which made him the first black coach in the NFL's modern era. In 2007 there were six black head coaches among the thirty-two NFL teams: Marvin Lewis of the Cincinnati Bengals,

Colts Coach Tony Dungy. *Indianapolis Colts head coach Tony Dungy confers with players during their training camp in 2006. Dungy, along with Chicago Bears head coach Lovie Smith, made history in 2007 as the first two black coaches to lead their teams to the Super Bowl.* AP IMAGES.

Herman Edwards of the Kansas City Chiefs, Tony Dungy of the Indianapolis Colts, Romeo Crennel of the Cleveland Browns, Lovie Smith of the Chicago Bears, and Mike Tomlin of the Pittsburgh Steelers. Tony Dungy and Lovie Smith made history in February 2007 as the first two black coaches to face each other in the Super Bowl, which was won by Dungy's Colts, 29 to 17.

In 2007 there were three African Americans serving as general managers in the NFL: Ozzie Newsome of the Baltimore Ravens, Rick Smith of the Houston Texans, and Jerry Reese of the New York Giants. But there are no African-American majority owners in the NFL, where black players constitute 67 percent of the league. Clearly, more opportunities must be extended off the field by a league that is largely reliant on the physical skills of black players. The same is virtually true in college football, though the number of off-the-field opportunities are far fewer. In 2007 there were only six African American head coaches of the 119 Division I schools: Randy Shannon of the University of Miami, Sylvester Croom of Mississippi State University, Karl Dorrell of UCLA, Turner Gill of the University of Buffalo, Ron Prince of Kansas State, and Tyrone Willingham of the University of Washington. Interestingly, there were twelve African-American athletic directors at the Division I level at this time. Black players, meanwhile, made up 50 percent of the student athletes in Division I college football in 2007. The NFL has attempted to open its ranks to African-American head coaches by requiring teams to include a minority in the respective pools of candidates during their hiring process. The National Collegiate Athletic Association (NCAA) has not instituted such a policy, however, and indeed it has been openly resistant to such a policy.

The lack of opportunities beyond the football field is a by-product of institutional racism. Many NFL owners, college athletic directors, and university presidents apparently do not think African Americans deserve the same chance as whites to be head coaches. In January of 1988 Jimmy "the Greek" Snyder, who provided betting odds for NFL games, was fired by CBS after comments made to a reporter that indicated he felt blacks were "naturally superior athletes" because of slavery. Synder's remarks followed those of Al Campanis, a former baseball player who had played with Jackie Robinson. One year earlier, during a live television interview, Campanis addressed the issue of why there were few black managers and no black general managers in Major League Baseball. He stated that he felt African Americans "may not have some of the necessities to be, let's say, a field manager, or, perhaps, a general manager." Many characterized the comments of Synder and Campanis as individual, isolated views that were not indicative of the larger culture in which they worked.

The reality of the NFL and college football being fueled by the labor of a black majority but not coached by one is, at the very least, extremely contradictory. The NFL has been gradually attempting to broaden its fan base internationally, while at the same time allowing teams to develop players with potential. Many of the players who participate in what is now called NFL Europa are African American. Founded in 1991 as the World League of American Football, the current league has six teams and has been very successful in generating fan enthusiasm and support. The opening weekend of the 2007 season witnessed a record attendance of 89,367 fans. Black players are instrumental to the success of this league, but of the six teams only one has an African-American head coach—the Frankfurt Galaxy, coached by Mike Jones. The international marketability of pro football has made it one of the most supported and economically viable sports in the world. Close to one billion people watched the Super Bowl on February 4, 2007, with about nineteen television and radio stations from fourteen countries broadcasting from Miami's Dolphin Stadium. The game was televised in 232 countries and territories in thirty-four languages.

Both the NFL and college football have experienced unprecedented financial success, and increases in average attendance, the building of new stadiums, the expansion of existing stadiums, the rise in coaching salaries, and increases in the cost of television contracts are all testaments to this success. Black players are certainly responsible for at least part of the financial windfall that this sport is experiencing. In Division I sports, college football is the leading revenue-generating sport on most campuses, whereas most other sports on major college campuses do not turn a profit. Without college football, many institutions would not be able to comply with the U.S. law known as Title IX, which requires equal opportunity for female athletic participation. Sports such as women's swimming, rowing, gymnastics, volleyball, rifle, and softball, which are overwhelmingly white, could not exist without the funds generated by football.

The salaries of head coaches have reached new zeniths in college football, led by the 2007 contract signed between Nick Saban and the University of Alabama for 32 million dollars over eight years. The top twenty highest-paid coaches in college football are all white, and the only African American in the top twenty-five is Tyrone Willingham at the University of Washington. These coaches lead teams that perennially play in bowl games, which generate added income for the coach, conference, and team. But when the black player's eligibility is up, his chances of becoming a part of the coaching fraternity is very limited. To many observers, this situation in untenable and needs to change.

BIBLIOGRAPHY

Ashe, Arthur R., Jr. 1988. *A Hard Road to Glory:* A *History of the African-American Athlete.* New York: Warner.

Brown, Jim. 1989. *Out of Bounds.* New York: Kensington.

Lapchick, Richard. 2006. "The 2005 Racial and Gender Report Card: National Football League." Orlando: De Vos Sport Business Management Program, University of Central Florida. Available from http://www.bus.ucf.edu/sport/public/.

———. 2007. "Decisions from the Top: Diversity among Campus, Conference Leaders at Division IA Institutions: All-Time High Diversity among Athletic Directors." Orlando: De Vos Sport Business Management Program, University of Central Florida. Available from http://www.bus.ucf.edu/sport/public/.

Meggyesy, David. 1970. *Out of Their League.* Berkeley, CA: Ramparts Press.

Ross, Charles K. 1999. *Outside the Lines: African Americans and the Integration of the National Football League.* New York: New York University Press.

Charles K. Ross

FORCED STERILIZATION

Historically, the practice of forced sterilization has varied according to time and place. Nevertheless, in every case, the practice has been implemented to serve the interests of the ruling elite. Right into the early twenty-first century, the forces of colonialism, capitalism, and patriarchy have kept the practice alive in order to diminish the power of those deemed "inferior" or "unfit." In particular, poor women of color have borne the brunt of this practice.

EUGENICS IDEOLOGY

In the latter part of the nineteenth century, Sir Francis Galton (1822–1911), a proponent of eugenics theory, argued that eugenics should be used to ensure the survival of the fittest. The pseudoscience of eugenics is based on the belief that "defects" in the species are passed on from generation to generation through defective genes. Just as the quality of the species can be improved in animal and plant species by selective breeding, it was thought by some that similar principles could be applied to maintain the quality of the human species. Thus, drawing upon the principals of social Darwinism, hereditary factors were privileged while environmental factors were ignored. It was believed that the "unfit" were reproducing at a faster rate than the fit, and that this would lead to a degeneration of racial stock. Some believed that intellectual imbecility would have the consequence of contaminating the race, and that if those with mental defects are allowed to reproduce it would lower the quality of the racial stock. In addition to mental defectiveness, it was believed that "moral" imbecility would lead to a similar outcome.

Eugenics laws were in force in several Western and North American countries in the early part of the twentieth century. These laws gave governments the authority to prevent those deemed "unfit" from reproducing, and eugenics boards were set up to determine who would be deemed unfit. Experts in the field of eugenics, as well as those considered to be the custodians of moral standards in society, served as members of these boards. Eugenics was taught in almost all of the prominent institutions of higher learning during this period, thereby establishing its professional credibility. Those who got degrees in medicine, social work, and law, among other fields, were taught courses on this subject, and universities took an active part in nominating professionals to sit on the eugenics boards. These experts exuded a stance of objectivity and value neutrality in the true tradition of scientific positivism. The boards passed judgment on the fitness of individuals to reproduce, based on their judgment as to whether or not the individuals concerned were intellectual or moral imbeciles. The media gave ample exposure to the tenets of the "science," making it popular among the public.

Eugenics was well received at a time when the conviction that the "white race" is superior to all other races was accepted without question. Emerging from an era of successful colonization, the belief in the divine mission of white people in saving humanity through their superior accomplishments was taken for granted. The fear that white race is in danger of being polluted and marginalized by nonwhite races was one of the major motivating factors that made this theory popular at the time. These fears were intensified by studies showing that the unfit were somehow more fecund than the fit. It was believed that, unless one stemmed the tide by preventing the unfit from reproducing, there was a real danger of a degeneration of white racial stock. Professionals in medicine and social work lent their expertise to implement this project, with the firm conviction that they were contributing to the establishment of a qualitatively superior society.

Racism, sexism, and classism intersected to produce the kinds of eugenics laws that were enacted and implemented at this time. Eugenics discourse was so popular that those who participated in the enactment of these laws and the implementation of policies derived from these laws acted with the conviction that it was a necessary and desirable project, fully justified on moral grounds. Many progressive thinkers, including well-known feminists, participated enthusiastically in the implementation of this project.

FORCED STERILIZATION IN NORTH AMERICA

Thirty states in the United States passed eugenics laws between 1907 and 1931, and these laws were upheld by the U.S. Supreme Court in 1916 and 1927. By the end of the World War II, it was estimated that 40,000 sterilizations had taken place, mostly on poor white women. Because of racial segregation, it was not deemed necessary to sterilize black people at this time. This situation was to change, however. Between 1949 and 1960, for example, of the 104 surgical sterilizations performed in South Carolina mental hospitals, all but two were performed on blacks. All these sterilizations were done on women. Cox (1997) writes that these federally funded practices were prevalent in Alabama and North Carolina also in the 1970s.

The Native American population has also been subjected to forced sterilization. From 1973 to 1976, for example, 3,406 American Indian women were sterilized, many of whom were under twenty-one years old. For many decades, disdain towards American Indians as a people was pervasive among health professionals and social workers, and the eugenics boards were quick to characterize women of Indian origin as mentally defective, and therefore as unfit to reproduce. The Native American Women's Health Education Resource Center, which reports abuses by the Indian Health Services (IHS), reports that sterilization abuse is found to be still going on as late as the 1990s and Depo-Provera and Norplant are routinely used as birth control methods. Paternalistic policies toward American Indians allow the federal government to make decisions on their behalf without their full consent or participation. Sterilization abuse has been going on for quite some time but they were investigated only since the 1970s. Carpio (2004) writes that even though some reforms have taken place with regard to conditions of sterilization, imposition of mainstream social standards and the inability of women to challenge professional health workers from the mainstream who have stereotyped beliefs about American Indians leads to continuation of these practices. Grekul et al. (2004) state that in Alberta, Canada, aboriginal people

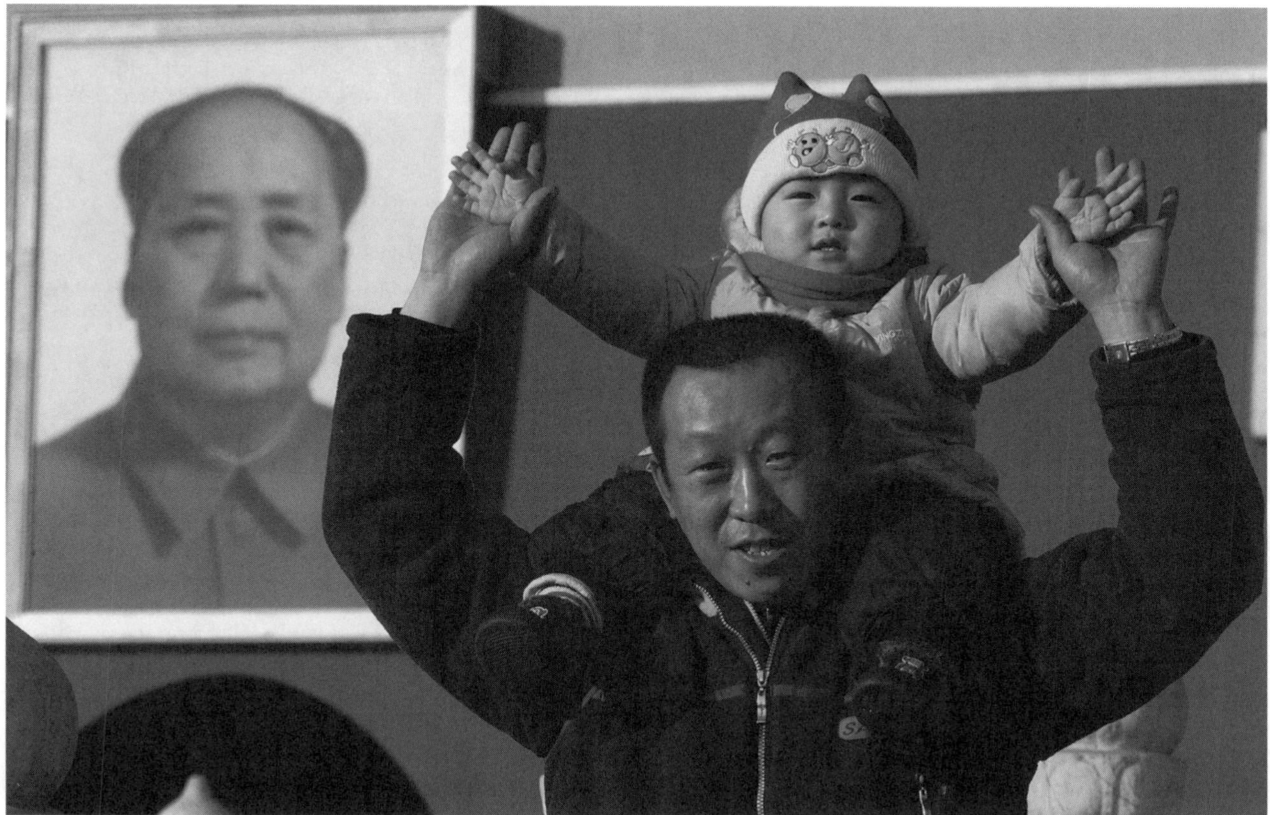

One-Child Policy. *A Chinese man lifts his child onto his shoulders in front of a portait of Mao Zedong in Beijing, China, 2005. In 1979, China adopted a one-child-per-family policy. Since then, sterilization and abortion have been routinely used.* AP IMAGES.

were the main targets of Eugenic boards in the years 1929 to 1972. They were overrepresented among the cases presented for sterilization and overrepresented among those who were sterilized without consent. In the latter part of the twentieth century some of these women in Alberta sued the provincial government for damages and were compensated for this injustice.

In the neoliberal environment of the late twentieth century poor people have often been denied access to government and social support. They have been persuaded to undergo sterilization because they cannot afford to support large families. In the United States, individuals are expected to be self-reliant and to not expect social support, even when social conditions are not conducive for them to be self-reliant. Social assistance is available for sterilization purposes, however. Under these circumstances, those who suffer from poverty and destitution may be forced to "choose" sterilization to control their reproduction. People in this situation, who are mostly women of color, have been denied economic support but encouraged to use government subsidies to use sterilization or pharmaceutical methods such as Norplant for birth control. Writing in 1996, Broomfield stated that the bundle of so-called welfare reform measures with their family caps and Norplant provisions in place in the United States are essentially punitive. Instead of helping those in need to become able to take care of their children with provisions of education and skills training, they blame the victims and punish them. She argued that one theory behind the reform package is based on eugenic premise that certain people in society do not deserve to procreate. The often incorrect public perception of welfare recipient is based on stereotypes grounded in racism, sexism, and classism.

FORCED STERILIZATION AND POPULATION CONTROL

Forced sterilization as a method of population control is evident in the neoliberal climate of the late twentieth and early twenty-first centuries. In China, in the context of the "one-child policy," sterilization and abortion are routinely used to slow population growth. Neo-Malthusian arguments are used to justify these policies. Linking economic development and population control in the so-called Third World has also become common practice. Very often, foreign aid is contingent upon the implementation of population-control policies, either through sterilization or the use of pharmaceuticals provided by Western corporations. United Nations agencies for population control have been closely involved with these projects. In these discourses on overpopulation, one often finds that it is not just the numbers that matter, but the kind of people. The targets of these programs are often those marginalized due to poverty or racial background. Poor women from Bangladesh and India and Indian women in Peru are important examples. The International Monetary Fund and World Bank have made population control a part of their structural adjustment policies (SAPs).

Under the presidency of Alberto Fujimori, during the period 1996 to 2000 at least 200,000 sterilizations took place in Peru. Poor and often illiterate women from the Quechua and Aymara indigenous ethnic groups were the majority of the victims (Robbins 2004). *60 Minutes* aired a television program in October 1998 on American medical establishment, showing how Quinacrine, a drug that sterilizes women permanently, was planted in the uteri of more than 100,000 women through the initiative of two U.S. doctors without testing for their side effects. The doctors claimed that they were doing their country a social service by addressing the epidemic of population explosion in the Third World. State intervention for fertility control in India began under the pressure of aid-giving agencies such as the World Bank in the 1970s, which linked economic development to population control. Women were the main targets in the 1970s and 1980s even though vasectomies were performed in the mid- and late-1970s. Women were also the main targets in Bangladesh where food subsidies under the group feeding program (VGF) were given to only those with certificates showing that they had tubectomies (Miles and Shiva 1993).

Fortunately, there is a growing awareness around the world that it is not the overpopulation of the Third World but the unbridled consumerism and misuse of the Earth's resources through poor management in the industrialized nations that are causing serious problems. But there is a long way to go before changes in policies and practices that have a negative impact on marginalized people are reversed.

Thus, racism in biological and cultural forms has led to policies and practices that are detrimental to the health and well-being of marginalized people everywhere. This is particularly true for nonwhite women in the lower echelons of the socioeconomic ladder. And more often than not, it is these marginalized women who are the targets of forced sterilization.

SEE ALSO *Eugenics, History of; Feminism and Race; Forced Sterilization of Native Americans; Galton, Francis; Genocide and Ethnocide; Reproductive Rights.*

BIBLIOGRAPHY

Abrams, Laura S., and Laura Curran. 2004. "Wayward Girls and Virtuous Women: Social Workers and Female Juvenile Delinquency in the Progressive Era." *Affilia* 15 (1): 49–64.

Brady, Susan M. 2001. "Sterilization of Girls and Women with Intellectual Disabilities." *Violence against Women* 7 (4): 432–461.

Broomfield, Michael G. 1996. "Controlling the Reproductive Rights of Impoverished Women: Is This the Way to 'Reform' Welfare?" *Boston College Third World Law Journal* 16 (2): 217–244.

Carpio, Myla Vicenti. 2004. "The Lost Generation: American Indian Women and Sterilization Abuse." *Social Justice* 31 (4): 40–53.

Chossudovsky, Michel. 1997. *The Globalization of Poverty: Impacts of IMF and World Bank Reforms.* London: Zed Books.

Cox, Clinton. 2002. "From Columbus to Hitler and Back Again." *Race & Class* 43 (3).

Dhruvarajan, Vanaja. 2002. "Feminism, Reproduction, and Reproductive Technologies." In *Gender, Race, and Nation: A Global Perspective*, edited by Vanaja Dhruvarajan and Jill Vickers. Toronto: University of Toronto Press.

Diekema, Douglas S. 2003. "Involuntary Sterilization of Persons with Mental Retardation: An Ethical Analysis." *Mental Retardation and Developmental Disabilities Research Reviews* 9 (1): 21–26.

Ekerwald, Hedvig. 2001. "The Modernist Manifesto of Alva and Gunnar Myrdal: Modernization of Sweden in the Thirties and the Question of Sterilization." *International Journal of Politics, Culture, and Society* 14 (3): 539–561.

Grekul, Jana, et al. 2004. "Sterilizing the 'Feeble-minded': Eugenics in Alberta, Canada, 1929-1972." *Journal of Historical Sociology* 17 (4): 358–384.

Larson, Edward J. 1995. *Sex, Race and Science: Eugenics in the Deep South.* Baltimore: Johns Hopkins University Press.

Miles, Maria, and Vandana Shiva. 1993. *Ecofeminism.* London: Zed Books.

Park, Deborah C., and John P. Radford. 1998. "From the Case Files: Reconstructing a History of Involuntary Sterilization." *Disability & Society* 13 (3): 317–342.

Purewal, Navtej K. 2001. "New Roots for Rights: Women's Responses to Population and Development Policies." In *Women Resist Globalization: Mobilizing for Livelihood and Rights*, edited by Sheila Rowbotham and Stephanie Linkogle. London: Zed Books.

Robbins, Richard. H. 2004. *Talking Points on Global Issues: A Reader.* London: Pearson.

Schoen, Johanna. 2001. "Between Choice and Coercion: Women and the Politics of Sterilization in North Carolina, 1929–1975." *Journal of Women's History* 13 (1): 132–156.

Stehlik, Daniela. 2001. "A Brave New World?: Neo-Eugenics and Its Challenge to Difference." *Violence against Women* 7 (4): 370–392.

Vanaja Dhruvarajan

FORCED STERILIZATION OF NATIVE AMERICANS

During the late 1960s and the early 1970s, a policy of involuntary surgical sterilization was imposed upon Native American women in the United States, usually without their knowledge or consent, by the federally funded Indian Health Service (IHS), then run by the Bureau of Indian Affairs (BIA). It is alleged that the existence of the sterilization program was discovered by members of the American Indian Movement (AIM) during its occupation of the BIA headquarters in 1972. A 1974 study by Women of All Red Nations (WARN), concluded that as many as 42 percent of all American Indian women of childbearing age had, by that point, been sterilized without their consent. A subsequent investigation was conducted by the U.S. General Accounting Office (GAO), though it was restricted to only four of the many IHS facilities nationwide and examined only the years 1973 to 1976. The GAO study showed that 3,406 involuntary sterilizations were performed in these four IHS hospitals during this three-year period. Consequently, the IHS was transferred to the Department of Health and Human Services in 1978.

During this and earlier periods, similar involuntary sterilization programs were being performed on other women of color, among them Chicanas of the Los Angeles area (Acuña 2004). It is estimated that by 1966, one-third of the women of childbearing age on the island of Puerto Rico had been sterilized without their "informed consent." In addition, MULANEH (Mujeres Lationoamericanas de New Haven), a mainland Puerto Rican women's organization, discovered that 44 percent of Puertorriqueñas in New Haven, Connecticut, had been sterilized by 1979. In Hartford, Connecticut, the figure stood at 51 percent. Women in Puerto Rico were also part of experimentation studies of the early birth control pill before it was released on the U.S. mainland.

Such sterilization practices are clearly a blatant breach of the United Nations Genocide Convention, which declares it an international crime to impose "measures intended to prevent births within [a national, ethnical, racial or religious] group." Andrea Smith, in her book *Conquest* (2005), connects this use of "sexual violence as a tool of genocide" with early boarding school abuse, medical experimentation in native communities, and "the (U.S.) colonization of Native Women's reproductive health." According to Smith, "communities of color, including Native communities, ... continue to inform the contemporary population control movement." Native women are targeted because their "ability to reproduce continues to stand in the way of the continuing conquest of Native lands" (p. 79). She found that the "Department of Health, Education, and Welfare (HEW) accelerated programs in 1970 that paid for the majority of costs to sterilize Medicaid recipients," and that the HIS "initiated a fully federally funded sterilization campaign in 1970." Dr. Connie Uri, a Cherokee/Choctaw medical doctor, was one of the first to uncover this mass sterilization, after a young Indian woman entered her office in Los Angeles in 1972 to request a "womb transplant" (p. 81).

Eventually, Senator James Abourezk, a Democrat from South Dakota, requested a study of IHS sterilization policies, which resulted in the GAO study. Smith notes, however, that "Native activists have argued that the percentage of Native women sterilized is much higher" than the 5 percent reported by the GAO. "Dr. Uri conducted an investigation of sterilization policies in Claremore, Oklahoma, and charged that the Claremore facility was sterilizing one woman for every seven births" (Smith 2005, p. 82). Smith illustrates how these abuses were carried on through experimentation with birth control methods, such as Depo-Provera and Norplant, which targeted Native American women and other women of color communities (p. 88).

There is also evidence that indigenous peoples of the Americas, and elsewhere, are being targeted for genetic engineering, particularly in the harvesting of their DNA genomes by geneticists who are in collaboration with corporate pharmaceutical interests. The indigenous women targeted are especially coveted human subjects in the genome research of ancient human origins. This is because it is possible to trace *mitochondria DNA* through the matrilineal descendency lines, from mothers to daughters (Jaimes-Guerrero 2003, 2004).

Native women are also finding that by organizing with other women of color communities around these issues they can be more effective. The book *Undivided Rights: Women of Color Organized for Reproductive Justice* (2004) helps to link women from communities that have been targeted for sterilization campaigns and other medical experimentations. The book highlights women-of-color organizations that are making a difference in raising awareness of these issues, particularly in "ethnic minority" communities and populations. All of these organizations are working towards better health conditions for women of color, and they are challenging what they perceive as the racist, sexist, and class structures of U.S. society. U.S. history is viewed by many as being built on a legacy of "patriarchal colonization." This stands in contrast to the traditional "matrilineal kinship" indigenous societies that gave women respect and authority as "clan mothers" in "pre-patriarchal and pre-colonialist times prior to the conquest of the Americas" (Jaimes-Guerero 2004).

The authors of *Undivided Rights* take a strong view on identity politics. They assert:

> Contrary to broadly based critiques, which argue that identity politics fracture movements, we found that women of color organizations, by defining

> themselves through race and ethnicity, created spaces that nurtured their activism. ... Whereas the larger society and the pro-choice movement marginalize women of color perspectives and concerns, these identity-based organizations validated their particular perceptions of reality. ... Through this process, they developed culturally based styles of organizing and communicating and created focal points for action. Though not utopian, these spaces facilitated the imagining of alternative paths to achieve reproductive freedom. (Silliman et al., 1996)

This bridge between theory and activist practice exemplifies what can be called "activist scholarship."

For Native American women and other women of color, the primary question is how one negotiates power on an unequal playing field. In continuing to dismantle the U.S. legacy of "patriarchal colonialism" put upon all women, women-of-color organizations are leading the charge for a bigger piece of the pie. By connecting their histories with the present, they seek a more egalitarian society and greater openness and freedom in the areas of gender-based reproduction, health, and well-being.

SEE ALSO *American Indian Movement (AIM); Forced Sterilization; Genocide and Ethnocide.*

BIBLIOGRAPHY

Acuña, Rudolfo. 2004. *Occupied America: A History of Chicanos,* 5th ed. New York: Pearson Longman.

Jaimes, M. Annette, with Theresa Halsey. 1992. "American Indian Women: At the Center of Indigenous Resistance in North America." In *The State of Native America: Genocide, Colonization, and Resistance,* edited by M. Annette Jaimes, Chapter XI. Cambridge, MA: South End Press.

Jaimes-Guerrero, M. A. 2003. "Global Genocide and Biocolonialism: On the Effect of the Human Genome Diversity Project on Targeted Indigenous Peoples/Ecocultures as 'Isolates of Historic Interest.'" In *Violence and the Body, Race, Gender, and State,* edited by Arturo Aldama. Bloomington: Indiana University Press.

———. 2004. "Biocolonialism and Isolates of Historic Interest." In *Indigenous Intellectual Property Rights: Legal Obstacles and Innovative Solutions,* edited by Mary Riley, Chapter 9. Walnut Creek, CA: AltaMira Press.

———, Anne Waters, and Inez Talamantez, eds. 2004. "Indigenous Women in the Americas." Special issue, *Hypatia: Journal of Feminist Philosophy* 18 (2).

Silliman, Jael, Marlene Gerber Fried, Loretta Ross, and Elena Gutiérrez. 2004. *Undivided Rights: Women of Color Organize for Reproductive Justice.* Cambridge, MA: South End Press.

Smith, Andrea. 2005. *Conquest: Sexual Violence and American Indian Genocide.* Cambridge, MA: South End Press.

Women of All Red Nations. 1975. *Native American Women.* New York: International Indian Treaty Council.

———. 1978. "Women of All Red Nations." Porcupine, SD: WARN, We Will Remember Group.

M. A. Jaimes-Guerrero

FORENSIC ANTHROPOLOGY AND RACE

Forensic anthropology is the application of the scientific study of the human skeleton within the context of medical and legal problems, usually in cases involving personal identification and evidence of foul play. Accountability of the dead involves a legal procedure in the United States that requires investigations by the police, a medical examiner (M.D.) who may perform an autopsy, a coroner who provides the death certificate, and in cases with skeletal remains a forensic anthropologist (usually a biological anthropologist holding a Ph.D. degree).

Training in archaeological field techniques (forensic archaeology) allows the forensic anthropologist to understand better the nature of the environmental context of a buried skeleton, and by visiting the burial deposit he/she will ensure that all bones and teeth are collected. Methods of the forensic anthropologist may be used in studies of the "eminent dead" when there is uncertainty about the true identity of an interred individual and the name on the grave marker, and when information is sought about the manner of death of known deceased persons whose bodies may be exhumed. With archaeologically recovered remains, the forensic goals are also problem oriented. Discoveries of prehistoric skeletons are not considered forensic cases, although some of the same descriptive procedures used in the study of decomposed bodies and skeletal remains reveal aspects of the lifeways of extinct populations that could not be deduced from artifacts, cemeteries, or other aspects of ancient cultural-behavioral patterns.

CATEGORIES OF INVESTIGATION

Determination of ancestral background (race) of a human skeletal or decomposed body is one essential element in the protocol of a forensic anthropologist's laboratory examination. Other categories of investigation are the following:

1. Are the remains human? Bones and teeth of non-human animal species and inorganic materials may be present in a burial deposit.

2. Do the skeletal remains indicate presence of a single individual? More than one skeleton may be encountered in burials, as in cases of mass genocide, battlefield disposal of the dead, common graves for victims of epidemics, and other situations where commingling of human remains is encountered.
3. The sex of the decedent.
4. The individual's age at time of death.
5. The stature of a subject may be estimated if bones of the upper and lower extremities are present and sufficiently complete for measurement and the use of regression formulas appropriate for different human populations.
6. Some diseases leave markers on bones and teeth. If a diagnosis is accurate, this may assist the forensic anthropologist in personal identification.
7. Evidence of past or recent traumatic assaults to the body, such as bullet holes, infliction of blunt- or sharpforce agents and strangulation, may provide some information about the life history of the decedent.
8. Time elapsed since death may be estimated on the basis of degree of body tissue degeneration, microenvironment, and insect activity at a burial deposit.
9. Markers of occupational stress (MOS) are bone or dental modifications resulting from habitual activities continued over relatively long periods of time.
10. DNA analysis is possible if there is no contamination of the tissues being tested. It may reveal degrees of genetic affinities between individuals and populations.
11. Cultural practices, such as capping the front teeth with gold for a more sparkling smile, tooth filing, cranial deformation introduced in childhood, and foot binding, may lead to personal identification. These physical characteristics and customs for disposing of the dead may shed light on the lifeways of the deceased.
12. The manner of death involves determination of evidence of natural causes, accidents, homicides, and suicides, although how the decedent died may be uncertain. Cause of death is determined by a medical examiner.
13. Determination of ancestry (race).

THE CONCEPT OF RACE

With respect to this last focus of an investigation, the present-day forensic anthropologist acknowledges the existence of two very different concepts of human biological diversity: (1) a traditional race theory perpetuated in the United States today in census data, applications to schools and universities, and in media sources where it is assumed that humankind is classifiable into natural entities called "races," for example, blacks, whites, Asians, Native Americans, and so on; (2) recognition that "races," so defined, do not exist in humans or other organisms as classifiable subspecies (or varieties, breeds, stocks). This conviction is held for the reason that those physical and behavioral criteria (traits) that had been used in naming and classifying populations adapted to natural and cultural conditions in geographically separate regions had been arbitrarily selected by systemic biologists, anthropologists, and historians. Phenotypic traits (detectable manifestations of genotypes) are now understood to be gradients that may occur in high frequencies in some populations, less so in others, or even absent. Thus, it is understood today that while human populations may exhibit relatively high or low phenotypic appearances of given physical traits, such as skin pigmentation, hair form, eye color, and cranial shape, they are not naturally divisible into groupings formerly identified as markers of discrete "races." The traditional concept of "race" is not predicated on a biological reality (Kennedy 1976; Livingstone 1962; Molnar 2006).

However, the traditional concept that humans, ancient and modern, are divisible into discrete categories based upon physical and behavioral characters continues today as a popular way of referring to an individual's ancestry. It serves as a social construct of human biological diversity expressed by commonly held images of our species' physical diversity. When the forensic anthropologist submits his/her written examination and research report to a medical examiner or legal representative, the old terminology is conjured up. The point of this inconsistency is that the common "racial" names may assist in giving one's client an understandable label to define the ancestry of an unidentified body or skeleton. (A historical account of the fall of the traditional race concept in science would not be helpful to the work of legal and medical practitioners for example.) If the forensic anthropologist receives a subpoena to appear in court to answer questions about a report, both judge and jury will gain a clearer comprehension of the identity of the decedent when the labels "Caucasian" or "white," "black" or "Negroid," "Mongoloid," "American Indian" and "Malaysian" are used.

Forensic anthropologists are well aware of this contradictory mind-set. Norman Sauer (1992) titled one of his papers "If Races Don't Exist, Why Are We So Good at Identifying Them?," and one of his forensic anthropology colleagues published an article with the title "But Professor, Why Teach Race Identification if Races Don't Exist?" (Kennedy 1995). In short, in the United States, Canada, and most of Western Europe this conflict is recognized by

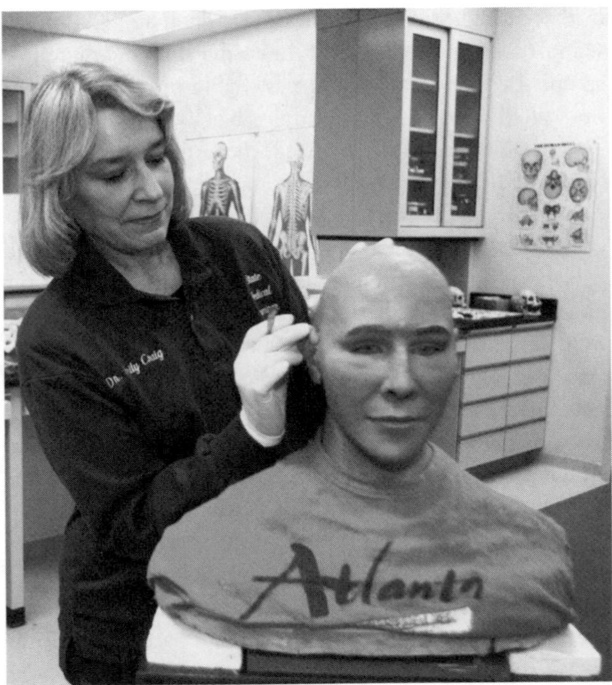

Forensic Anthropology. *In order to identify a murder victim, a forensic anthropologist attemps to recreate his facial features in a three-dimensional model. She will also examine a variety of traits that may help determine the victim's race.* AP IMAGES.

anthropologists: They maintain a social view of human biological diversity, sometimes called "ethnicity," and a scientific perspective that does not support the traditional race concept. The consequences of assuming there is a natural classification of humans into races, as understood in its social context among most North American citizens, is a reasonable reaction of confusion when one is informed by biological science that "races" do not exist. This is because phenotypic diversity in ancient and modern humans is misunderstood as classifiable into natural subspecies or natural entities.

Forensic anthropologists have replaced the earlier appellations assigned to physically and culturally diverse human populations by identifying them by the names of their geographical habitats, for example, peoples of south-central Europe (not "Alpinoids"), northern Europeans including Scandinavians (not "Nordics"), peoples of China (not "Mongoloids"), and so on. An elaborate nomenclature had developed by the early half of the last century, for example, "Indo-Afghans," "Pre-Dravidians," "Melanides," and "Proto-Australoids." These specific "racial divisions" were imagined by anthropologists to be present in a single landmass—the Indian subcontinent. Other terms flourished for prehistoric and living populations of the Asian landmass, Africa, Europe, Oceania, and the Americas.

No single physical or genetic trait provides an answer to the question of ancestry of a skeletalized or decomposed individual. The forensic anthropologist examines a number of bone and dental features known from other research sources to appear in highest frequencies among inhabitants of different geographical regions. Most of the traits are nonconcordant. That is, darkly pigmented skin and black hair, both resulting from a high amount of the substance melanin, may not always appear together in an endogamous population, nor are these variables genetically linked with blood groups. Blood group B of the ABO system appears very often in people of Near Eastern and Asian descent, but B blood is present also in human inhabitants of other continents. Blue eyes are frequent in northern Europe, but they appear as well in people of the Hindu Kush Mountains of northern Pakistan. In short, these and other phenotypic traits of interest to the forensic anthropologist have their separate patterns of geographical distribution within our species because each trait selected for observation has its own independent "history" of diffusion over the earth in space and time. Some traits are subject to the forces of natural selection, but if these have an adaptive value and are therefore an advantage to the reproductive success of a population, then they may endure over many generations. New features appear as a result of genetic mutation and interbreeding of neighboring or foreign peoples, but no individual contains all of the genetic materials in his/her population.

ANCESTRY AND FORENSIC ANTHROPOLOGY

But how does the forensic anthropologist determine ancestry? No single methodological approach provides an answer; rather, several kinds of data acquisition are required. One of these involves the examination of the form and structure of the skeleton as a whole and of each of its bony components and teeth. This is called "morphological analysis." Examples are the configuration of the nasal aperture (is it long and narrow? short and broad?), presence or absence of "shovel-shaped" incisor teeth, straightness or projection of the lower portion of the face, heavy or small brow ridges, degree of curvature of one or more bones of the lower extremities, and literally scores of other physical features.

"Metric analysis" refers to measurement of bones and teeth with precision instruments, such as calipers, head spanners, and osteometric boards for measuring the lengths of bones of the upper and lower extremities. Since the end of the eighteenth century hundreds of different "anthropometric" instruments have been invented and patented with the goal of achieving very accurate size values, and today an instrument employed in dental measurements is graduated to one-tenth of a millimeter. The metric system is used in taking anthropometric measurements. From these numerical data, a ratio of length-breadth measurements is called the "index" (plural "indices" when references are made to multiple ratios). Commonly known indices include the relationship of maximum cranial length to maximum cranial breadth, the so-called "Cranial Index" (with its classifications into "dolichocrany," or long-headedness, and "brachycrany," or broad-headedness). Measuring instruments are set in place on standard "landmarks," which may be anatomical points or regions of bones and teeth.

Metrical data are quantified for statistical analyses that may reveal degrees of biological relationships between modern human populations as well as between prehistoric peoples when their skeletal remains have been preserved. Today a host of multivariate statistical procedures shed light on population affinities. Metric data are added to molecular biological-genetic studies, which are also useful in estimations of the degree to which populations are genetically related. However, molecular biologists would not be able to account for age at the time of death of adult subjects, markers of trauma or MOS, and other aspects of the life history and lifeways of a skeletal subject.

Accurate determination of an individual's ancestry from skeletal remains rests upon the analyses of the data from a forensic anthropological investigation acquired by some of the instruments listed above, comparative studies of skeletons of known ancestry, and the level of training achieved by the forensic anthropologist.

THE PROFESSION

Prior to World War II in the United States, individuals practicing forensic anthropology were men with medical backgrounds and anatomists. An American anthropologist, W. M. Krogman (1939), published his "A Guide to the Identification of Human Skeletal Material" in the FBI *Law Enforcement Bulletin* in 1939. This marks a turning point in the development of the forensic sciences, as skeletal biologists were needed by U.S. military forces for identification of war dead at the end of World War II, the Korean War, and the Vietnam conflict. The Pentagon and FBI were interested in Krogman's description of the kinds of information that could be used for personal identification. By 1972 a new section of the American Academy of Forensic Sciences (AAFS), founded in 1948, was organized. Beginning with fourteen practicing forensic anthropologists, the Section of Physical Anthropology had a 2005 membership of over 275 forensic anthropologists. The latter fall into rankings of fellow, member, associate member, honorary member, trainee affiliate, and student affiliate within a total membership of over 5,152 forensic science experts. The AAFS official organ of publication is the *Journal of Forensic Sciences* to which forensic anthropologists and other members of the association's ten sections may submit research articles for publication. These other sections include Criminalistics, Engineering Sciences, General, Jurisprudence, Odontology, Pathology-Biology, Psychiatry and Behavioral Science, Questioned Documents, and Toxicology.

Independent of the AAFS is the American Board of Forensic Anthropology (ABFA), established five years after the Physical Anthropology Section was formed. At present there are nearly seventy Diplomates. This title (Diplomate of the American Board of Forensic Anthropology, or D.A.B.F.A.) is awarded to practicing forensic anthropologists who take written and practical board examinations for certification. This process offers a credential that guarantees that the title's holders are considered by their peers to be among the finest and most experienced professionals in forensic anthropology. It is an advantageous award for establishing one's qualifications when examined in court as an expert witness.

Forensic anthropologists conduct their research with colleagues in other disciplines. Radiologists can provide X-ray plates that can reveal the nature of a bone fracture or the age of a young individual by the state of dental eruption and the growth and development of cranial and postcranial bones. Molecular biology and DNA analyses may assist in estimating degrees of genetic relationships between individuals and the ancient populations from which their ancestry may be traced. Photography is an essential step in any case because it serves as a visual record of a decedent's subjection to trauma and disease. Forensic odontologists cooperate with anthropologists with respect to comparisons of dental records, recognizing irregularities in enamel development and confirming data about sex and age at time of death.

The forensic sciences in general have gained great popular interest through television programs, novels in which the forensic anthropologist is the key figure, and in magazine and newspaper articles. Unfortunately, few of these media sources accurately represent the real world of any of the forensic sciences. Efficient training in its anthropological side involves an undergraduate background in the biological sciences, mathematics, and anthropology; a graduate program leading to the doctoral degree (Ph.D.) at a college or university where field and laboratory training is available (at present about a dozen institutions of higher education in the United States and Canada); personal attributes that allow for working well with others, facing the challenges of examining decomposed bodies as well as skeletal remains; commitment to assisting the M.D. or professor; and acquiring a sound background in statistics. After a few years of field and laboratory experience, the junior forensic anthropologist begins attendance at AAFS meetings and may study for certification according to the directives of the ABFA.

At present no academic departments in anthropology and the biological sciences in North America are staffed entirely by forensic anthropologists. Rather, the expert in this field is usually hired by a college or university depending upon his/her qualifications as a biological anthropologist capable of teaching courses about human palaeontology and evolution, biological variables of living human populations and genetics, nutritional anthropology, and other specialties within the broad spectrum of anthropology. However, for the applicant who is able to command these subjects and is trained in forensic anthropology, a position may open up at a research institution, college or university, or the offices of the FBI and other government agencies. Certainly all of the forensic sciences are expanding, and anthropologists with research interests in estimating the ancestry of modern and prehistoric humans will discover a vast literature on the subject and opportunities for refinement of present methods in morphology, anthropometry, human genetics, and the history of how the traditional race concept has been modified in the twentieth-first century.

Forensic anthropologists have written several books that go into detail about their cases and provide both overviews of the state of the discipline and depictions of methods for ancestry determination. These resources provide easy-to-read sources for those interested in the subject (Byers 2002; Thomas 1995; Molnar 2006; Rhine 1998; Ubelaker and Scammell 1992).

SEE ALSO *Eugenics, History of; Genetics, History of; Human and Primate Evolution; Human Genetics.*

BIBLIOGRAPHY

Byers, Steven N. 2002. *Introduction to Forensic Anthropology.* Boston: Allyn and Bacon.

Kennedy, Kenneth A. R. 1976. *Human Variation in Space and Time.* Dubuque, IA: W. C. Brown.

———. 1995. "But Professor, Why Teach Race Identification If Races Don't Exist?" *Journal of Forensic Sciences* 40: 797–800.

Krogman, Wilton Marion. 1939. "A Guide to the Identification of Human Skeletal Material." *FBI Law Enforcement Bulletin* 8 (8): 1–29.

Livingstone, Frank B. 1962. "On the Non-existence of Human Races." *Current Anthropology* 3 (3): 279–281.

Molnar, Stephen. 2006. *Human Variation: Races, Types and Ethnic Groups,* 6th ed. Upper Saddle River, NJ: Pearson Prentice Hall.

Rhine, Stanley. 1998. *Bone Voyage: A Journey in Forensic Anthropology.* Albuquerque: University of New Mexico Press.

Sauer, Norman. 1992. "Forensic Anthropology and the Concept of Race: If Races Don't Exist, Why Are Forensic Anthropologists So Good at Identifying Them?" *Social Science and Medicine* 34 (2): 107–111.

Stewart, T. Dale. 1979. *Essentials of Forensic Anthropology: Especially as Developed in the United States.* Springfield, IL: Thomas.

Thomas, Peggy. 1995. *Talking Bones: The Science of Forensic Anthropology.* New York: Facts on File.

Ubelaker, Douglas, and Henry Scammell. 1992. *Bones: A Forensic Detective's Case Book.* New York: HarperCollins.

Kenneth A. R. Kennedy

FORTEN, JAMES
1766–1842

The abolitionist and civil rights advocate James Forten was born in Philadelphia on September 2, 1766, to Thomas and Margaret Forten. James Forten was born free. His father, Thomas Forten, was born also free. James Forten's grandfather was born into slavery and gained his freedom. James Forten's great-grandfather was born in Africa, enslaved, brought to Pennsylvania, and he lived the rest of his life as a slave. Almost nothing is known about his mother. Thomas Forten was a journeyman sail maker in the sail loft of a white craftsman, Robert Bridges. As a child, James learned the rudiments of the sail maker's trade, and he also spent two years at the Quaker-sponsored African School.

The Fortens remained in Philadelphia during the American War for Independence. In 1781 a mix of patriotic fervor and the need for money induced James Forten to join the crew of an American privateer. His ship was captured on its second cruise and he was taken prisoner. While being held on board a British warship, he was assigned to watch over the captain's son. The two youths became friends, and the captain offered to take Forten to England and educate him with his son. Attractive though the offer was, Forten rejected it, insisting he could not desert the cause of independence. He was sent with the rest of the American captives to a British prison ship in New York harbor. After a harrowing seven months of incarceration he was released and returned to Philadelphia. Fighting and suffering alongside white men in the same cause shaped Forten's views about American society. In later years he alluded repeatedly to what he saw as the Revolution's promise of equality without regard to race.

After the war ended, Forten shipped out aboard an American merchant ship bound for London. Once there, he requested to be paid off, and he remained in the British capital for a year, most likely working in a sail loft. When he returned home he was offered an apprenticeship by Robert Bridges. The relationship between Bridges, a white slave-owner, and Forten, a free man of color, proved mutually beneficial. Bridges recognized Forten's ability and promoted him to foreman, a position in which he oversaw a largely white workforce. In return, Bridges gained a conscientious junior partner who helped him expand his business. In 1798 Bridges retired and Forten took over the sail loft.

Race relations in Philadelphia at this time were not as tense as they would later become, and the quality of Forten's work induced many white ship-owners to hire him. He proved a resourceful businessman, investing the profits from his sail-loft in real estate and bank and canal stock. As an employer he insisted on maintaining a racially integrated workforce, and his sail-loft, one of the largest in Philadelphia, was renowned for its harmony and good order.

By the time he was in his early thirties, James Forten had emerged as a vocal champion of African-American rights. In 1799 some seventy black Philadelphians petitioned Congress for action to prevent the kidnapping of free people of color. Congress refused even to consider their petition, however. In his widely reprinted letter of thanks to the lone congressman who had supported the petition, Forten spoke of his fear that the nation was violating its founding principles. He developed this theme in *Letters from a Man of Colour*. Written in 1813 in response to moves in the Pennsylvania Senate to curtail the rights of black citizens, Forten's pamphlet eloquently expressed his belief that all Americans were entitled to equal treatment under the law.

The issue that brought Forten to national prominence was African colonization. He was initially optimistic about prospects in Sierra Leone, believing Britain's West African colony would help stimulate trade in commodities other than human beings, as well as offer a refuge to emancipated slaves from the United States and the Caribbean. He welcomed the formation of the American Colonization Society (ACS) in 1816 and endorsed the idea of an American colony for former slaves in Africa. Others in his community voiced their fear that the ACS's real aim was to deport free blacks. In a matter of months Forten swung from support to outright opposition. The founding of Liberia, the sufferings of the colonists, and the statements of some ACS leaders that their goal was most definitely not to abolish slavery convinced him that the organization was fundamentally proslavery. When prominent ACS members told him it was his duty to lead an exodus of free blacks to Africa, it only intensified his hostility.

Although freeborn, James Forten was a tireless opponent of slavery. He worked in the African-American community to aid the hundreds of fugitives who flocked to Philadelphia each year, and he collaborated with white abolitionists. In 1830, when he was contemplating founding an antislavery newspaper, the white abolitionist William Lloyd Garrison contacted Forten, who responded with money and advice. Garrison's paper, the *Liberator*, gave Forten the chance to reach a wider audience than he could with his speeches and letters, and in his writings for the paper he spoke of the perniciousness of slavery and the evils of racial oppression.

During the last decade of his life, James Forten confronted many challenges. Philadelphia was rocked by repeated outbreaks of racial violence. In an 1834 riot, one of his sons was attacked, and he himself received death threats. He also witnessed a concerted effort to erode the rights of black people. In 1838, Pennsylvania voters ratified a new constitution that disfranchised African Americans. In the face of so much hostility, Forten helped found a new organization, the American Moral Reform Society. The goal of its members was to work for a sweeping restructuring of American society. They rejected racial distinctions and pledged to address the needs of the entire nation. Its critics, however, condemned the AMRS as hopelessly impractical, reasoning that black people were in greater need of aid than the population as a whole. Forten's reply was that all racial divisions were indefensible.

In 1841 deteriorating health forced Forten to relinquish control of his business to his two eldest sons. Even when he became too weak to speak in public, he continued to write in support of the causes he championed. He died on March 4, 1842, at the age of seventy-five. Despite the tense racial climate in Philadelphia, some five thousand citizens, black and white, lined the route of his funeral procession to pay tribute to him.

SEE ALSO *American Colonization Society and the Founding of Liberia; Garrison, William Lloyd.*

BIBLIOGRAPHY

Newman, Richard, Patrick Rael, and Phillip Lapsansky, eds. 2001. *Pamphlets of Protest: An Anthology of Early African American Protest Literature, 1790–1860*. New York and London: Routledge.

Winch, Julie. 2002. *A Gentleman of Color: The Life of James Forten*. New York: Oxford University Press.

Julie Winch

FORTUNE, TIMOTHY THOMAS

1856–1928

Timothy Thomas Fortune is one of the earliest black journalists and civil rights activists whose career was devoted entirely to the advocacy of laws that would grant equal political rights to blacks as equals in the United

States. He was the founder of the first major all-black civil rights organization, the Afro-American League.

Timothy Thomas Fortune was born into a slave family in Marianna, Florida, on October 3, 1856. He was freed from slavery with the Emancipation Proclamation of 1863. He attended a school established by the Freedmen's Bureau after the Civil War and eventually moved to Washington, D.C., where he worked as a compositor for a black newspaper. While in Washington, Fortune attended Howard University from 1876 to 1877. Throughout his life, Fortune was an advocate for the rights of blacks and a fighter against racial discrimination and segregation.

In 1880, he moved to New York City, where he established himself as a leading journalist, editor, and publisher. He was the editor and publisher of the *New York Globe* and the *New York Freeman*, which later became the *New York Age*. Fortune's publications were the most consulted among blacks for information on racial discrimination, lynching, mob violence, and disenfranchisement.

What set Fortune apart from others was his work in the broad area of civil rights for blacks. Fortune dedicated himself to what he called "Problems Peculiar to the Negro" through the National Afro-American League, which he founded. It took three years, from 1887 to 1890, to organize the National Afro-American League. At its first convention in Chicago in 1890, the league outlined a six-point program:

1. securing voting rights;
2. passing legislation to combat lynching;
3. abolishing inequities in state funding of public education for blacks and whites;
4. reforming the southern penitentiary system—particularly its chain gang and convict release practices;
5. combating discrimination in railroad and public-travel conveyances;
6. and eliminating discrimination in public places, hotels, and theaters.

Fortune's organization, established ten years after the period of Reconstruction, focused on issues particular to the South, which at the time was moving swiftly to erode the rights blacks had won through the Fourteenth and Fifteenth Amendments and the Civil Rights Acts of 1866 and 1875. The intent of the southern states was to disenfranchise and completely remove blacks from participation in the region's politics. By 1890, all the southern states had rewritten their constitutions to reestablish white supremacy and legal segregation based on race and color in all facets of life. Not a single point outlined by the league found backing or public support at the local, state, or national level.

Though Fortune was not able to secure support or funding for any of his six points, he found a way to be useful by agitating for the passage of the Blair Education bill, which had been introduced in Congress in 1881. The bill aimed at providing public funding of education for blacks and whites, especially in the South. Fortune's organization joined the fight to pass the measure in 1888, but it was eventually killed in 1890.

The National Afro-American League struggled to establish itself as a legitimate civil rights organization from 1890 to 1908. A part of the problem of the league finding its niche was the coming to prominence of Booker T. Washington in 1895. Washington's speech in Atlanta in 1895 endeared him to influential whites in the North and South. He essentially assured whites that blacks would stay in their places and work on improving themselves rather than agitate for integration and equality.

Through his league, however, Fortune was able to provide a debating platform not only for his ideals but for the views of such notables as W. E. B. Du Bois, William Monroe Trotter, Booker T. Washington, Bishop Alexander Walters, Ida B. Wells, and several others. In 1898, Fortune changed the name of his organization to the Afro-American Council. Whether this had an impact on the work of the organization has never been clearly established.

The task before the Afro-American Council was impossible to achieve. It attempted to forge a consensus among a cadre of black leaders so that they could work together on such issues as funding of public schools for blacks throughout America. The council could not agree on a leadership style, ideology, or a philosophy, nor agree on methods to be used to achieve goals that would benefit blacks. Ultimately, the Afro-American Council failed to achieve its goal of being an organization of blacks, by blacks, and for blacks. The failure of the Afro-American Council was not the failure of Fortune. His efforts exposed the weaknesses of the people he fought for: They were disunited and could not trust each other, put aside their egos, face their fears and insecurities, or contain their anger and follow other blacks in the interests of their community. This experience was an invaluable lesson on black leadership, a critical issue that continues to be a serious problem for black America.

The failure of the Afro-American Council led directly to the founding of the National Association for the Advancement of Colored People (NAACP). It is not lost on astute observers that where an organization composed entirely of blacks was not able to survive, a reformed civil rights organization composed of New York socialites, blacks, and Jews could survive and has continued to do so.

W. E. B. Du Bois was the most prominent member of the Afro-American Council to become a member of the NAACP. For a time, he attempted to have the Blair

Education bill revived, but it was doomed because by the late nineteenth century, northern white liberals and other constituencies had decided to leave blacks to the vagaries of the white South. It is worth noting that the Blair Education bill was aimed as much at illiterate whites as illiterate blacks. In essence, if it meant educating blacks as well, the South refused federal assistance and support for publicly funded education for its own people. It did not matter even if blacks would be educated in separate schools, showing the level of hatred southern whites in charge of the governments in the several states had for blacks.

Fortune remained a firebrand for justice for blacks throughout his life. He never thought it was right to have separate classrooms for blacks and whites. He always thought blacks should enjoy the rights and benefits of full citizenship in American society. When he died in Philadelphia in 1928 at age seventy-two, the words he uttered at the first convention of the National Afro-American League in Chicago in 1890 still had the ring of truth:

> As the agitation, which culminated in the abolition of African slavery in this country, covered a period of fifty years, so may we expect that before the rights conferred upon us by the war amendments are fully conceded, a full century will have passed away. We have undertaken no child's play. We have undertaken a serious work which will tax and exhaust the best intelligence of the race for the next century.

SEE ALSO *Du Bois, W. E. B.; Freedmen's Bureau; NAACP; Washington, Booker T.*

BIBLIOGRAPHY

Crofts, Daniel W. 1971. "The Black Response to the Blair Education Bill." *Journal of Southern History* 37 (1): 41–65.

Cruse, Harold. 1987. *Plural but Equal: A Critical Study of Blacks and Minorities and America's Plural Society.* New York: William Morrow.

Franklin, John Hope. 1947. *From Slavery to Freedom: A History of Negro Americans.* New York: Knopf.

———, and August Meier, eds. 1981. *Black Leaders of the 20th Century.* Chicago: University of Illinois Press.

Russell Mootry Jr.

FOURTH WORLD

The term *Fourth World* traditionally refers to marginalized and oppressed groups such as the indigenous peoples living either in Third World (relatively undeveloped) or First World (developed and capitalist) countries. (The term *Second World* is used to designate developed and predominantly socialist countries.) Specific definitions for these terms are provided by documents and conventions of the United Nations (UN), the International Labour Organization, and the World Bank. According to the Draft United Nations Declaration on the Rights of Indigenous Peoples (adopted without a vote on August 26, 1994, by the Sub-Commission on Prevention of Discrimination and Protection of Minorities) and the International Labour Organization Convention concerning Indigenous and Tribal Peoples in Independent Countries (adopted in 1989; came into force in 1991), the contemporary working definition of *Fourth World* includes cultural groups and their descendants who can claim a historical continuity or association with a given region, or parts of a region. These groups must currently inhabit or have formerly inhabited the region before its subsequent colonization and annexation. Alternatively, they must have inhabited the region alongside other cultural groups during the formation of a nation-state, and yet done so independently or largely isolated from the influence of governance practiced by this state. Furthermore, groups and communities constitutive of the Fourth World are distinguished from other minorities based on having maintained, at least in part, their distinct linguistic, cultural, or sociological characteristics, and in doing so have remained separate from the surrounding populations and the dominant culture. In related debates on the status of indigenous peoples, it is also expected that peoples of the Fourth World are self-identified as indigenous as well as being recognized by others as such.

Other related terms for the Fourth World include *Native Peoples*, *First Peoples*, and *First Nations*. Fourth World has become the preferred term due to its relatively neutral perspective on the history of such minority groups, particularly in contrast to the negative connotations associated with terms such as *aborigines*. However, the term also suffers from historical ambiguities. Indigenous societies cover a wide range of peoples. The Fourth World includes those who have suffered tremendously following colonization by European societies, sometimes to the point of total disappearance (including many native tribes of eastern North America, such as the Beothuk), and those who remain in comparative isolation from external influence, such as those in the Andaman Islands in the Bay of Bengal. Consequently, estimates for the total population of the world's indigenous, or Fourth World, peoples are difficult to determine, both because of the difficulties in the identification of these groups and the lack of available census data. Most nation-states refuse to mark indigenous populations as a separate category, fearing subsequent claims that could be made on land and resources or for the settlement of historical injustices. Taking these factors into account, according to the Office of the United Nations High Commissioner for Human Rights at the United Nations and the International Work Group for Indigenous Affairs (IWGIA), conservative estimates of the population of the peoples of the Fourth World range from 300 million to 370 million persons, including at least 5,000 distinct peoples in more than 72 countries.

Most often, contemporary indigenous communities and societies live amid and among populations that have historically been engaged in practices of grave injustice toward them. Their rights have generally been negotiated as part of the scheme of minority rights to be guaranteed and protected by the state. In select instances such as in Australia and Canada, compensation has also been sought and received for the forcible loss of land and resources and the eradication of cultural livelihood. Despite these developments, the majority of the world's indigenous peoples continue to see a decline in population. It is only in very few cases that indigenous populations are undergoing a recovery or expansion in numbers, such as in Canada's Northern Territories.

The majority of indigenous societies no longer inhabit their traditional lands, owing to migration, relocation, forced resettlement, or having become a minority among other groups that arrived in the territory. As a result, the lands-claim issue constitutes the major bone of contention between the Fourth World and other municipalities, provinces, and national governments. An exemplary case for the examination of these conflicts is Canada. There is a specifically Canadian term of ethnicity referring to the indigenous peoples and their descendants in Canada who are neither Inuit nor Métis: the First Nations. Collectively, First Nations, Inuits, and Métis (the descendants of Indian and French ancestors) are known as Aboriginal Peoples, First Peoples, or Indigenous Peoples. The national representative body of the First Nations in Canada is the Assembly of First Nations. Other terms used in the Canadian context include "Status Indian" and "non-Status Indian," the latter designating a member of an indigenous community who is not entitled to benefits from the Canadian state.

Indigenous peoples are officially recognized by the Government of Canada as a separate group of citizenry. They are entitled to benefits as well as distinct communal legal rights under the Indian Act administered by the Ministry of Indian and Northern Affairs. Created in 1966, the Department of Indian and Northern Affairs Canada (INAC) is a decentralized organization established to respond to the changing needs of culturally, economically, and geographically diverse peoples. The legislation establishing the department, as amended in 1970, made its minister responsible for Indian and Inuit affairs, as well as the residents of the Yukon and Northwest Territories and their resources. The rights exclusive to indigenous peoples defined by the Indian Act are beyond legal challenge and are protected by the Canadian Charter of Rights and Freedoms. Meanwhile, according to international law covenants, *First Nations* or *First Peoples* are terms that have no distinct standing. Thus, what worked for the Canadian society internally does not necessarily find direct translation in other societies with indigenous populations.

At the level of international politics, indigenous peoples were able to represent their interests more directly to a major body of the United Nations following the establishment of the United Nations Permanent Forum on Indigenous Issues in 2002. The UN uses the term indigenous despite its earlier "negative connotations" due to a mixture of institutional clementure and legal precedents in addressing the relevant issues. The aforementioned UN Permanent Forum is an advisory body to the UN Economic and Social Council (ECOSOC), with a mandate to discuss indigenous issues related to economic and social development, culture, the environment, education, health and human rights. In 1982 the UN Working Group on Indigenous Populations (WGIP) of the Sub-Commission on the Promotion and Protection of Human Rights (then called Sub-Commission on Prevention of Discrimination and Protection of Minorities) was established by a decision of the ECOSOC. The Draft Declaration on the Rights of Indigenous Peoples is a result of the work of this UN Working Group between 1985 and 1993. Following the WGIP, the new Permanent Forum reports and makes recommendations to ECOSOC. Its mandate includes raising awareness, promoting the integration and coordination of activities relating to indigenous issues within the UN system, and, preparation and dissemination of information on indigenous issues.

Organizations of indigenous peoples that have consultative status with the ECOSOC include the Aboriginal and Torres Strait Islander Commission, Asociación Kunas Unidos por Nabguana, the Four Directions Council, the Grand Council of the Crees (Quebec), the Indian Council of South America, the Indian Law Resource Center, the Indigenous World Association, the International Indian Treaty Council, the International Organization of Indigenous Resource Development, the Inuit Circumpolar Conference, the National Aboriginal and Islander Legal Services Secretariat, the National Indian Youth Council, the Saami Council, the Sejekto Cultural Association of Costa Rica, Yachay Wasi, and the World Council of Indigenous Peoples.

SEE ALSO *Indigenous.*

BIBLIOGRAPHY

Dean, Bartholomew, and Jerome M. Levi, eds. 2003. *At the Risk of Being Heard: Identity, Indigenous Rights, and Postcolonial States.* Ann Arbor: University of Michigan Press.

International Work Group on Indigenous Affairs (IWGIA). 2007. *Indigenous Rights. The UN Special Rapporteur*

Experiences and Challenges. IWGIA Document No. 118. Copenhagen, Denmark: IWGIA.

Johansen, Bruce E. 2003. *Indigenous Peoples and Environmental Issues: An Encyclopedia*. Westport, CT: Greenwood Press.

Niezen, Ronald. 2003. *The Origins of Indigenism: Human Rights and the Politics of Identity*. Berkeley: University of California Press.

United Nations Working Group on Indigenous Populations. 2001. *Indigenous Peoples and the United Nations System: An Overview*. Geneva: United Nations Office of the High Commissioner for Human Rights. Available from http://www.unhchr.ch/html/racism/indileaflet1.doc.

Nergis Canefe

FREEDMEN'S BUREAU

The U.S. Congress established the Bureau of Refugees, Freedmen, and Abandoned Lands on March 3, 1865, as part of its plans for reconstructing the post-Civil War South. Better known as the Freedmen's Bureau, this temporary federal agency undertook the formidable and unprecedented responsibility of safeguarding the general welfare of both recently liberated slaves and white refugees in the former Confederacy. In all of its activities, the Bureau sought to teach black and white southerners the meaning of freedom and how to negotiate their seemingly incompatible visions of life and labor in the new order.

In overseeing the transition from slavery to freedom, the Freedmen's Bureau became "the principal expression and extension of federal authority in the defeated South" (Cimbala and Miller 1999, p. ix). Despite a short existence, the bureau played a critical role in defining the meaning of freedom for some four million former slaves. Charged with exercising "control of all subjects relating to refugees and freedmen from the rebel states," its activities were myriad. It provided "issues of provisions, clothing and fuel" to refugees, freedmen, "and their wives and children"; it assisted in reuniting black families; it supervised labor agreements between blacks and their former masters; it monitored state and local officials' treatment of the former slaves; it established informal tribunals to settle disputes between whites and blacks and among African Americans themselves; it instituted clinics and hospitals for the former slaves; and it aided efforts to provide freed people education in the Civil War's immediate aftermath (*U.S. Statutes at Large* 13: 507–509).

Major General Oliver Otis Howard was appointed as commissioner of the Bureau in May 1865, and he served as the agency's only commissioner until Congress formally dismantled it in 1872. This thirty-four-year-old "Christian Soldier" from Maine was a former commander of the Army of the Tennessee, and he gave the agency its character and course. A wartime convert to emancipation and a firm believer in the ability of humanitarian assistance to uplift the former slaves, he provided a moral purpose, an ideological framework, and a vision for the bureau. The task ahead of him was formidable. Indeed, upon hearing of his friend's appointment, General William Tecumseh Sherman confided to Howard, "I hardly know whether to congratulate you or not." He cautioned Howard of the inevitable difficulties that lay ahead. "So far as man can do, I believe you will," he told the new commissioner, but "though in the kindness of your heart you would alleviate all the ills of humanity it is not in your power, nor is it in your power to fulfill one tenth of the expectations of those who formed the Bureau." "I fear," Sherman confessed, "you have Hercules' task" (Howard 1907, vol. 2, pp. 209–210).

Howard undertook his new commission with great limitations. Congress initially limited the federal agency's existence to one year following the end of hostilities, and it appropriated no funds for the bureau's efforts in the postwar South. Given a home in the War Department, the bureau was left to survive off of army funds and personnel, in addition to the resources and compassion of various private relief, missionary, and educational associations of the North. The official statute creating the Bureau permitted, although it did not require, the secretary of war to provide the agency personnel for its staff, as well as surplus food, clothing, and fuel to aid former slaves and refugees. It also gave the agency control of abandoned and confiscated lands held by the government. The Bureau had the authority to divide this land into forty-acre plots to be sold or rented to former slaves and loyal refugees. (In September 1865, President Andrew Johnson effectively ended bureau efforts to distribute lands to black southerners by commanding Howard to issue Circular No. 15, which rescinded earlier land circulars and ordered that the land be returned to its former owners, who were pardoned by the president.) Beyond these provisions, the statute provided little guidance to Howard as to his agency's role and powers. Thus, while granting the bureau authority over "all subjects relating to refugees and freedmen," Congress offered little support, direction, or authority for doing so. In 1866, over a presidential veto, and again in 1868, Congress would extend the life and powers of the federal agency. But the bureau was always viewed as a temporary agency, and Congress ended all but its educational activities on January 1, 1869.

In its efforts to reconstruct the South, the Freedmen's Bureau established a multitude of policies to transform the former Confederacy from a slave society into one in which free labor reigned. Stationed in Washington, D.C., Howard provided the shape and direction for these policies. But it was his assistant commissioners at the state

The Freedman's Bureau at Richmond, Virginia (1867). *The Freedman's Bureau was established to safeguard the general welfare of both recently liberated slaves and white refugees in the former Confederacy.* © BETTMANN/CORBIS.

level, and their appointees at the district and county or parish levels, who would be most influential in carrying out the agency's goals. The assistant commissioners exercised considerable authority. These men determined how Howard's orders, general as they were, would be applied in individual states, and they issued additional orders and directives applicable to "freedmen's affairs" there. By 1872, fifty-five men had served the agency as assistant commissioners. Whatever policies and directives were issued, the effectiveness of the bureau rested on some 900 officials who implemented them at the local level. Any achievement of the bureau was measured by the actions of agents in the field. With varying degrees of success and commitment, these men—known in the agency's bureaucratic language as superintendents, assistant superintendents, subcommissioners, or assistant sub-assistant commissioners—endeavored to aid, advise, promote, and protect the freedpeople's general welfare on a day-to-day basis. Upon acceptance of a post in the bureau, Commissioner Howard commented, the local agent became at once "a magistrate with extraordinary judicial power—overseer of the poor of all classes in his district, agent to take charge of abandoned lands, and required to settle, in a few days, [the] most intricate questions with reference to labor, political economy, &c., that have puzzled the world for ages" (*Washington Chronicle*, August 13, 1866). The local agent was, as Eric Foner notes in *Reconstruction*, a "diplomat, marriage counselor, educator, supervisor of labor contracts, sheriff, judge, and jury" (1988, p. 143).

In attending to the daily business of the bureau, local agents faced formidable obstacles. Their caseloads were staggering, and there never seemed to be enough agents. Historians estimate that 2,441 different men served the bureau throughout its lifetime, but at the height of its strength the agency employed only 900 men, with more than 300 of them serving as clerks rather than agents. By 1869 the bureau's manpower withered to a mere 158 men across the entire South. If they were lucky, local field agents had a horse and a clerk to help with the responsibilities of the office. And if they were truly fortunate, Union troops were nearby, willing to enforce their orders and dictates and ready to provide protection. More often, however, local agents found themselves unaided in a hostile environment and responsible for several counties or parishes encompassing hundreds of miles and thousands of people. "My satrapy," complained a South Carolina agent named John William De Forest, "contained two state districts or counties, and eventually three, with a population of about eighty thousand souls and an area at least two thirds as large as the state of Connecticut." "Consider the absurdity of expecting one man," he continued, "to patrol three thousand miles and make personal visitations to thirty thousand Negroes" (De Forest 1948, p. 39).

Both the competence and level of dedication varied greatly among bureau officials, for they came to their positions with diverse motives and disparate ideologies. Seemingly fearless and faithful to the old abolitionist quest, some agents braved the opposition, hostilities, and outright violence of white Southerners in an effort to protect the former slaves from fraud and violence. Some even sacrificed their lives. Others were not so noble, however. Desiring acceptance from white Southerners, and possessing similar racist views about former slaves, some agents blatantly chose to become instruments of the planter class and aid in the effort to restore slavery in all but name. More often, however, agents fell somewhere in between. Many operated with a pragmatism that showed an understanding that the bureau was a fleeting agency. Most simply tried to do a job that presented fierce obstacles. At times they came to the aid of freedmen and women, while at other times they supported the defeated rebels. Declaring that bureau agents "varied all the way from unselfish philanthropists to narrow-minded busybodies and thieves," W.E.B. Du Bois offered a balanced judgment, ultimately concluding that the "average was far better than the worst" (1901, p. 360).

Whatever their level of preparedness or dedication, much was expected of bureau officials. According to Foner, their duties included "introducing a workable system of free labor in the South, establishing schools for freedmen, providing aid to the destitute, aged, ill, and insane, adjudicating disputes among blacks and between the races, and attempting to secure for blacks and white Unionists equal justice from state and local governments" (1988, p. 142). Guiding each of these activities was the desire to "teach" southerners what freedom meant by establishing a free labor society in the South. Thus, enforcing the obligation of contracts was at the heart of all bureau activities. The agency readily supported the cause of free labor and viewed the contract as the governing model for all social relations, including both labor and domestic relations. At every turn, therefore, agency officials underscored the relationship between freedom and contract. "While the freedmen must and will be protected in their rights," Virginia Assistant Commissioner Orlando Brown exhorted in his November 4, 1865, circular, "they must be required to meet these first and most essential conditions of a state of freedom, *a visible means of support, and a fidelity to contracts.*" Commissioner Howard certainly agreed. If the freedpeople recognized the sanctity of the contract—whether a labor agreement or the covenant of marriage—they would benefit from both the responsibilities and the privileges of freedom. Freed from the clutches of slavery, Howard trusted that former slaves would achieve independence by becoming self-reliant men and women who could provide for and protect themselves and their families.

In a time of social and political upheaval however, Southerners, both black and white, encountered profound difficulties providing for themselves. Without question, the administration and disbursement of relief was central to every local agent's job. By August 1865 the bureau was aiding 148,120 people daily. Despite the very real need for relief, Howard nonetheless sought to cut these numbers from his first days in office. His relief policies stressed the importance of labor, self-reliance, and independence, and they provided relief to the "deserving" poor while compelling others to enter the labor market. Met with petitions of every kind, distinguishing between the worthy and unworthy poor was no simple task. Local agents refused assistance only to able-bodied freedmen, however, and continued to support some able-bodied freedwomen and other "deserving" poor, including orphans, the sick and disabled, and the elderly. Due to increasingly restrictive policies and limited resources, the number of people supported by the Bureau shrank to 74,951 in September 1865. Whether viewed as heroic in its compassion and humanity, a movement ahead of its time, or a failure for what it did not accomplish, Bureau relief efforts provided real assistance to Southerners, black and white. By the fall of 1868, the Bureau had furnished more than 20 million rations of food—almost 15 million of which directly aided former slaves—through its "war on dependency" (Foner, p. 152).

With this "war," the Freedmen's Bureau became the mediator between former-slaves-turned-laborers and former-masters-turned-employers as they negotiated a new labor system. In the process, the two contending races encountered, turned to, trusted, challenged, and used the bureau in an effort to control one another. White planters sought to regain power and restore slavery in all but name. Freedpeople wanted economic independence and freedom from white supervision. The bureau desired a free labor system in which blacks freely consented to work and whites granted them the benefits possessed by laborers in the North. In so many ways, as in the case of its relief efforts, the Bureau regarded employment as a cure-all for Southern ills. If sufficient work could be provided to former slaves, officials reasoned, the best interests of blacks themselves, their former owners, the South, and the nation as a whole would be served. To the Bureau, unforced labor promised the return of stability and prosperity to the South. As it undertook the task of laying a foundation for a free labor society, it endorsed labor policies aimed at forming labor contracts between former masters and former slaves.

Bureau labor policies were far from perfect, however. Despite stipulations that blacks were now free to choose their own employers, what developed was a seemingly inherent contradiction—a "compulsory" system of "free" labor. At the heart of this labor program were provisions guarding against vagrancy. Bureau labor policies ordered, first, that all freedpeople be urged to find work and make contracts, and second, that those who rejected labor or violated contracts be considered vagrants who would be fined, imprisoned, and hired out to employers until, as Commissioner Howard insisted, they understood the virtue of "honest toil."

Until Southern courts recognized and protected the rights of freedpeople—most notably, the right to testify in court—informal tribunals operated by the bureau acted as a conduit of justice for Southern blacks. In addition to complaints against employers regarding wages, abuse, and property, freedpeople filed grievances arising from domestic clashes, demands for their children, and violence. The "freedmen's courts," as they soon came to be known, sought to ensure, in Howard's words, "the protection of negroes against small personal persecutions and the hostility of white juries" (Howard 1901, vol. 2, p. 253). Ideally, these courts included three officials—a Bureau agent and two representatives, one chosen by local freedpeople and the other by area whites—and settled only minor cases. The meaning of "minor" varied greatly from state to state and agent to agent, however. More serious offenses, such as felonies or capital crimes, were referred to federal, provost, or—if they assured blacks' rights—state courts. As Donald Nieman notes in *To Set the Law in Motion*, federal authorities "were unwilling to permit individual officers and agents, most of whom had no legal training, to try such serious matters as grand larceny, burglary, arson, rape, assault with intent to kill, and murder" (Nieman 1979, p. 9). In the end, bureau officials believed that ensuring equal justice under the law to Southern blacks would, in turn, allow them to protect themselves from unscrupulous whites, and thus end the need for the Freedmen's Bureau. With or without the bureau's assistance, however, former slave men and women found justice elusive during and after Reconstruction.

Given its emphasis on instructing southerners as to the meaning of freedom, it is not surprising that perhaps the most lasting legacy of the Freedmen's Bureau resulted from its efforts to promote education. Although it did not open schools itself, the Bureau remained dedicated to systematizing and facilitating education for former slaves throughout its brief life. Under the direction of Reverend John W. Alvord, the Bureau's Superintendent of Education, the agency provided rations and transportation for teachers, supplies, buildings, encouragement, and oversight to northern benevolent societies and freedpeople themselves, who provided and paid teachers. By July 1870, more than 3,000 schools, with some 3,300 teachers and 149,581 students, reported to the bureau. Moreover, with bureau support, northern benevolent associations established the first black colleges in the South, including Berea in Kentucky, Fisk in Tennessee, Hampton in Virginia, and Tougaloo in Mississippi. Bureau support for education, as Eric Foner points out, "helped lay the foundation for Southern public education." Indeed, he concludes, it "probably represented the agency's greatest success in the postwar South" (1988, p. 144).

In the end, it cannot be questioned that the Freedmen's Bureau fell short in accomplishing all that it promised. The Bureau and its role in the failure of Reconstruction in the South have generated much debate. Historians, as well as the federal agency's contemporaries, have not been kind, damning the bureau for doing both too little and too much. With the notable exception of W. E. B. Du Bois—who noted more than a century ago that the agency had "accomplished a great deal"—early scholarly works flatly condemned the Bureau. Arguing that the Bureau failed to push hard enough for African Americans, more recent Reconstruction scholarship has denounced the agency for failing to challenge the racial assumptions and racial hostility of the postwar South. The Bureau has also been accused of exercising a racist paternalism that forced former slaves into labor agreements clearly more advantageous to white employers. Since the 1980s, however, historians have offered significant challenges to such interpretations. Presenting a more evenhanded interpretation, these historians view the Freedmen's Bureau as a limited protector, guardian, and even ally of the freedpeople. Recognizing the complicated landscape in which the Bureau operated, their scholarship goes beyond the agency's limitations, weaknesses, and failures to underscore the significant role the agency played in former slaves' lives, particularly at the community level, and what it did for freedpeople. Most historians in the early twenty-first century would agree with Du Bois, who concluded that whatever work the bureau "did not do" was "because it could not" (1901, pp. 364–365).

SEE ALSO *Black Reconstruction.*

BIBLIOGRAPHY

Bentley, George R. 1955. *A History of the Freedmen's Bureau.* Philadelphia: University of Pennsylvania.

Cimbala, Paul A. 1997. *Under the Guardianship of the Nation: The Freedmen's Bureau and the Reconstruction of Georgia, 1865–1870.* Athens: University of Georgia Press.

———. 2005. *The Freedmen's Bureau: Reconstructing the American South after the Civil War.* Malabar, FL: Krieger.

———, and Randall M. Miller, eds. 1999. *The Freedmen's Bureau and Reconstruction: Reconsiderations*. New York: Fordham University Press.

Crouch, Barry A. 1992. *The Freedmen's Bureau and Black Texans*. Austin: University of Texas Press.

De Forest, John William. 1976 (1948). *A Union Officer in the Reconstruction*. Edited by James H. Croushore and David Morris Potter. Baton Rouge: Louisiana State University Press.

Du Bois, W. E. B. 1901. "The Freedmen's Bureau." *Atlantic Monthly* 87: 354–365.

Farmer-Kaiser, Mary. 2004. "'Are They Not in Some Sorts Vagrants?': Gender and the Efforts of the Freedmen's Bureau to Combat Vagrancy in the Reconstruction South." *Georgia Historical Quarterly* 88 (1): 25–49.

Finley, Randy. 1996. *From Slavery to Uncertain Freedom: The Freedmen's Bureau in Arkansas, 1865–1869*. Fayetteville: University of Arkansas Press.

Foner, Eric. 1988. *Reconstruction: America's Unfinished Revolution, 1863–1877*. New York: Harper and Row.

Howard, Oliver Otis. 1907. *Autobiography of Oliver Otis Howard*. 2 vols. New York: Baker and Taylor.

Nieman, Donald G. 1979. *To Set the Law in Motion: The Freedmen's Bureau and the Legal Rights of Blacks, 1865–1868*. Millwood, NY: KTO Press.

Mary Farmer-Kaiser